# Public Interest Profiles

## 1998–1999

Foundation for Public Affairs

Congressional Quarterly Inc.
Washington, D.C.

*Public Interest Profiles, 1998–1999*
Editor: *James J. DeAngelis*
Research Assistants: *Joseph J. Savitsky, Sin Hang Lai*
Contributing Editors: *Talia Greenberg, Chris Karlsten*

The Library of Congress catalogued the first edition of this title as follows:

Public interest profiles, 1988–1989.

Includes indexes.
1. Pressure groups—United States—Directories.
I. Foundation for Public Affairs (Washington, D.C.)
JK1118.P8   1988        322.4′025′73        86-645195
ISBN 0-87187-461-X

ISBN 1-56802-424-X
ISSN 1058-627X

# Contents

Preface                                                                    ix

## BUSINESS/ECONOMIC                                            CHAPTER 1

American Business Conference                                          3
American Council for Capital Formation                               6
Americans for Tax Reform                                            10
The Business Roundtable                                             13
Center for the New West                                             16
Center for the Study of American Business                           19
Center on Budget and Policy Priorities                              22
Citizens for a Sound Economy                                        26
Citizens for Tax Justice                                            31
Committee for a Responsible Federal Budget                          34
Competitive Enterprise Institute                                    36
The Conference Board, Inc.                                          39
Council on Competitiveness                                          44
Families and Work Institute                                         47
National Association of Manufacturers                               50
National Federation of Independent Business                         55
National Taxpayers Union                                            58
U.S. Chamber of Commerce                                            61

## CIVIL/CONSTITUTIONAL RIGHTS                                 CHAPTER 2

American-Arab Anti-Discrimination Committee                         69
American Civil Liberties Union                                      72
Americans United for Separation of Church and State                77
Asian American Legal Defense and Education Fund                     80
Center for Democratic Renewal                                       84
Children's Defense Fund                                             87
Handgun Control, Inc./Center to Prevent Handgun Violence            92
Human Rights Campaign                                               95
Lambda Legal Defense and Education Fund, Inc.                       99
Leadership Conference on Civil Rights, Inc.                        103
League of United Latin American Citizens                           106
Mexican American Legal Defense and Educational Fund                109
NAACP Legal Defense and Educational Fund, Inc.                     111
National Abortion and Reproductive Rights Action League            115
National Association for the Advancement of Colored People         117
National Association of Arab Americans (NAAA, Inc.)                121
National Coalition for the Homeless                                123

National Congress of American Indians 126
National Council of La Raza 128
National Council of Senior Citizens 131
National Council on the Aging, Inc. 134
National Gay and Lesbian Task Force 138
National Organization for Women 142
National Organization on Disability 146
National Partnership for Women & Families 150
National Rifle Association of America 152
National Urban League 156
9to5, National Association of Working Women 160
Operation Rescue National 163
People for the American Way 166
Planned Parenthood Federation of America, Inc. 170
Servicemembers Legal Defense Network 174

## CHAPTER 3  COMMUNITY/GRASSROOTS

American Family Association 179
American Society for the Prevention of Cruelty to Animals 182
Association of Community Organizations
    for Reform Now (ACORN) 185
Center for Community Change 188
Concerned Women for America 191
Eagle Forum 194
Family Research Council 197
Mothers Against Drunk Driving 201
National Center for Neighborhood Enterprise 204
National Coalition Against Domestic Violence 208
National Training and Information Center (NTIC)/
    National People's Action (NPA) 211
U.S. ENGLISH Foundation, Inc. 214
United States Public Interest Research Group 216

## CHAPTER 4  CONSUMER/HEALTH

Action on Smoking and Health 223
Advocates for Highway and Auto Safety 226
AIDS Action Council 230
American Association of Retired Persons 234
American Council on Science and Health 239
American Foundation for AIDS Research (AmFAR) 243
American Public Health Association 247
Center for Auto Safety 251
Center for Science in the Public Interest 254
Center for Study of Responsive Law 258
Consumer Alert 260
Consumer Federation of America 263
Consumers International 269
Consumers Union of the United States, Inc. 272
Co-op America 278
Families USA Foundation 281

Food Research and Action Center                                     285
National Center for Nonprofit Boards                                288
National Center for Tobacco-Free Kids                               291
National Charities Information Bureau                               295
National Consumers League                                           298
Public Voice for Food and Health Policy                             302

## *CORPORATE ACCOUNTABILITY/* *RESPONSIBILITY*                     *CHAPTER 5*

Business for Social Responsibility                                  309
Catalyst                                                            313
Center for Business Ethics                                          317
Coalition for Environmentally Responsible Economies (CERES)         320
Committee for Economic Development                                  322
Council of Institutional Investors                                  325
Council on Economic Priorities                                      328
Council on Foundations                                              331
Ethics Resource Center                                              335
The Foundation Center                                               337
Independent Sector                                                  340
INFACT                                                              344
National Alliance of Business                                       346
National Committee for Responsive Philanthropy                      349

## *ENVIRONMENTAL*                                                 *CHAPTER 6*

American Rivers                                                     355
Center for Marine Conservation                                      359
Center for Health, Environment and Justice                          363
The Conservation Fund                                               366
Conservation International                                          369
Defenders of Wildlife                                               373
Earth First! Journal                                                376
Earth Island Institute                                              379
Environmental and Energy Study Institute                            384
Environmental Defense Fund                                          386
Environmental Law Institute                                         390
Environmental Working Group                                         394
Farm Animal Reform Movement (FARM)                                  398
Foundation on Economic Trends                                       400
Friends of the Earth                                                404
The Fund for Animals                                                407
Greenpeace USA                                                      411
Humane Society of the United States                                 414
In Defense of Animals                                               418
Izaak Walton League of America                                      421
The Keystone Center and Public Policy Program                       425
League of Conservation Voters                                       428
National Audubon Society                                            431
National Coalition Against the Misuse of Pesticides                 435
National Parks and Conservation Association                         438

National Trust for Historic Preservation 441
National Wildlife Federation 446
Natural Resources Defense Council 450
The Nature Conservancy 456
People for the Ethical Treatment of Animals 460
Pesticide Action Network North American
(PANNA) Regional Center 464
Rainforest Action Network 467
Resources for the Future 470
Sea Shepherd Conservation Society 473
Sierra Club 476
The Wilderness Society 481
World Resources Institute 486
World Wildlife Fund 492

## CHAPTER 7    *INTERNATIONAL AFFAIRS*

American Israel Public Affairs Committee (AIPAC) 499
Amnesty International USA 503
The Atlantic Council of the United States 507
Center for Defense Information 509
Center for Strategic and International Studies 513
Council on Foreign Relations 518
DataCenter 522
Federation for American Immigration Reform (FAIR) 524
Human Rights Watch 528
Institute for International Economics 532
Peace Action 537
Physicians for Social Responsiblility 540
TransAfrica 543
Union of Concerned Scientists 546
The Washington Institute for Near East Policy 549
Zero Population Growth 552

## CHAPTER 8    *MEDIA/TECHNOLOGY*

Accuracy in Media, Inc. 557
Center for Democracy and Technology 559
Center for Media and Public Affairs 562
Center for Media Education 565
Electronic Frontier Foundation 569
Electronic Privacy Information Center 572
Fairness & Accuracy in Reporting (FAIR) 574
Media Access Project 577
Media Research Center 580
National Coalition on Television Violence 584

## CHAPTER 9    *POLITICAL/GOVERNMENTAL PROCESS*

Advocacy Institute 589
American Conservative Union 592
American Legislative Exchange Council 595

Americans for Democratic Action, Inc. ........................ 598
Arab American Institute .......................................... 601
Business-Industry Political Action Committee ............... 604
Center for Public Integrity ..................................... 607
Center for Responsive Politics ................................. 611
Citizens' Research Foundation .................................. 615
Common Cause ..................................................... 618
Concord Coalition ................................................ 624
Congressional Management Foundation ........................ 627
Council for Excellence in Government ......................... 631
Council of State Governments .................................. 635
Empower America .................................................. 639
The League of Women Voters of the United States .......... 643
National Conference of State Legislatures ................... 647
National Governors' Association ................................ 652
National League of Cities ....................................... 657
National Women's Political Caucus ............................. 661
OMB Watch ........................................................ 664
Project Vote Smart/Center for National
   Independence in Politics ................................... 667
Public Citizen, Inc. ............................................. 669
U.S. Term Limits ................................................ 673
United States Conference of Mayors ........................... 676
Women's Campaign Fund .......................................... 681

# PUBLIC INTEREST LAW

*CHAPTER 10*

Alliance for Justice ............................................. 685
Atlantic Legal Foundation, Inc. ................................ 688
Institute for Justice ........................................... 690
Landmark Legal Foundation ...................................... 694
Mountain States Legal Foundation .............................. 697
National Legal Center for the Public Interest ............... 700
Pacific Legal Foundation ........................................ 703
Rutherford Institute ............................................ 706
Southern Poverty Law Center .................................... 711
Trial Lawyers for Public Justice ............................... 715
Washington Legal Foundation .................................... 720

# RELIGIOUS

*CHAPTER 11*

American Jewish Committee ....................................... 725
American Jewish Congress ........................................ 729
Anti-Defamation League .......................................... 733
Christian Coalition ............................................. 738
Focus on the Family ............................................. 741
The Interfaith Alliance ......................................... 745
Interfaith Center on Corporate Responsibility ............... 748
National Conference of Catholic Bishops/
   U.S. Catholic Conference ................................... 752
National Council of the Churches of Christ in the USA ...... 756
Traditional Values Coalition .................................... 761

# CHAPTER 12 — THINK TANKS

Alexis de Tocqueville Institution ..... 767
American Enterprise Institute for Public Policy Research ..... 770
The Brookings Institution ..... 774
Capital Research Center ..... 780
Cato Institute ..... 784
Center for National Policy ..... 788
Center for Policy Alternatives ..... 792
Economic Policy Institute ..... 796
Ethics and Public Policy Center ..... 801
Free Congress Foundation ..... 805
The Heritage Foundation ..... 809
Hoover Institution on War, Revolution and Peace ..... 813
Hudson Institute ..... 817
The Independent Institute ..... 822
Institute for American Values ..... 825
Institute for Policy Studies ..... 827
Investor Responsibility Research Center ..... 830
Joint Center for Political and Economic Studies ..... 834
Manhattan Institute for Policy Research ..... 838
Pacific Research Institute for Public Policy ..... 842
Political Economy Research Center ..... 846
Progress & Freedom Foundation ..... 849
Reason Foundation ..... 853
The Rockford Institute ..... 856
The Urban Institute ..... 859
Worldwatch Institute ..... 864

Name Index ..... 869
Subject Index ..... 885

# Preface

*Public Interest Profiles, 1998–1999,* is an in-depth guide to the most influential public affairs groups in the United States. The more than 230 organizations profiled in this directory cover a wide range of views from many political orientations.

The groups are organized into twelve chapters that address nearly every aspect of the national agenda. In addition to providing updated information for organizations in the previous edition, the ninth edition of *Public Interest Profiles* includes a dozen new profiles of organizations that recently have achieved prominence.

This edition has expanded the categories in the "Method of Operations" sections. With ten new categories, readers now can quickly determine whether an organization provides professional development services, offers internships or scholarships to students, or uses e-mail alerts or fax-on-demand services to deliver its message.

## RESEARCH METHOD

In compiling this new edition of *Public Interest Profiles,* Congressional Quarterly editors worked closely with the Foundation for Public Affairs (FPA). The FPA, with its affiliate organization, the Public Affairs Council, maintains a national, nonpartisan clearinghouse of information on public interest groups and corporate public affairs programs.

The organizations included in this book represent a wide range of political points of view, which in many cases reflect the diversity of their members or constituents. By using the term "public interest groups" we do not intend to imply that they represent the interests of the general public. These organizations are more commonly referred to by the media as special interest groups, advocacy groups, pressure groups, and public policy organizations.

### Selection of Organizations

The Foundation for Public Affairs used the following criteria as a basis for selecting groups for inclusion in this edition:

—the extent of the group's influence on national policy;
—the number of inquiries about the group fielded by FPA staff;
—the volume of news coverage about the group; and
—the representative nature of the group in its field of interest and activity.

Research at Congressional Quarterly yielded a few modifications to this list, primarily to reflect the prominence of several newly formed organizations.

### Contact with Organizations

In preparing the profiles, CQ compiled data from questionnaires sent to organizations. Further information was gleaned from annual reports, publications catalogs, lists of current boards of directors, financial statements, and other relevant literature. When information was not available directly from the organizations, researchers relied on other sources. The word "Unavailable" appearing under certain sections in some profiles indicates that the organization either did not respond to the questionnaire or did not provide all of the information requested.

*Balance of Coverage*

It is important to note that *Public Interest Profiles* is not intended to be a rating service. In compiling the sections on the "Effectiveness" and "Political Orientation" of organizations, CQ editors have attempted to provide balance, both in terms of content and sources. However, the appearance of quotations that are critical of an organization in some profiles and their absence in others does not imply an evaluation of any organizations by the Foundation for Public Affairs or Congressional Quarterly.

Some organizations, by their very nature, generate more press coverage than others. Readers should consider the subjective sections of the profiles to be merely a representation of available commentary—nothing more, nothing less. Finally, the length of the profile does not reflect the relative influence of the organization.

## ORGANIZATION OF THE PROFILES

Each profile includes the following components:

**Year of Founding.** The date following the organization's name indicates the year in which the group was founded.

**Address.** When two addresses appear under an organization's name, the first is the organization's headquarters; the second address is the group's Washington office. Internet addresses follow, when available; in most instances these serve an entire organization rather than a specific office or chapter.

**Purpose.** In most cases, the organizations provided the language for this section. In general, the text is a quotation from a group's mission statement.

**Staff.** When available, the number of staff members is subdivided into professional, support, part-time personnel, interns, and volunteers.

**Director.** When available, a brief biography of the executive director is provided.

**Tax Status.** Most of the organizations described in this book are recognized as tax-exempt under section 501(c) of the Internal Revenue Code and fit into one of three categories:

*501(c)(3).* This designation is given to the following types of nonprofit organizations: charitable, religious, scientific, literary, and educational. This designation also includes groups that seek to prevent cruelty to children and animals and test products and services for public safety. Contributions to 501(c)(3) organizations are deductible as charitable donations for federal income purposes. Lobbying may not be a "substantial" part of the activities of a 501(c)(3) organization.

*501(c)(4).* Organizations ruled to be tax-exempt under this section of the Internal Revenue Code are civic leagues, social welfare organizations, and local associations of employees. Contributions to 501(c)(4) organizations may be deductible as a business expense. There are fewer restrictions on lobbying by 501(c)(4) groups than by 501(c)(3) organizations.

*501(c)(6).* Organizations ruled to be tax-exempt under this section of the Internal Revenue Code include business leagues, chambers of commerce, real estate boards, and boards of trade. Contributions to 501(c)(6) organizations are not deductible as charitable donations for federal income tax purposes. If an individual or business supports a 501(c)(6) organization financially, that individual or business can deduct the amount as a business expense "if ordinary and necessary in the conduct of the taxpayer's business."

**Budget.** When available, information on an organization's operating revenue is provided.

**Funding sources.** An analysis of an organization's income is provided.

**Scope.** Details on an organization's membership, locations of branch or chapter offices, and affiliated groups are listed. An organization's Washington office is not included in the total number of branch offices.

**Political Action Committee (PAC).** A political action committee is a legal vehicle for individuals to pool financial contributions to support political candidates. Affiliated PACs are indicated in this section.

**Method of Operation.** Provides a standardized list of general methods of operation from "Advertising" and "Boycotts" to "Training" and "Technical assistance."

**Current Concerns.** Outlines the current interests of an organization.

**Publications.** Lists books, directories, databases, and videos published since 1995.

**Newsletters.** Lists current periodicals published by an organization.

**Conferences.** Provides details on conferences, seminars, and workshops sponsored by a group.

**Board of Directors.** Lists the organization's current governing body.

**Effectiveness.** Provides commentary from third-party sources on a group's efficiency and potency.

**Political Orientation.** Excerpts quotations from third-party sources on the political leanings of a group.

We hope that you will find *Public Interest Profiles,* Ninth Edition, a useful addition to your library. We welcome your comments and suggestions.

James J. DeAngelis
Editor

# Business/
# Economic

## Chapter 1

# American Business Conference (1981)

1730 K Street, NW
Suite 1200
Washington, D.C. 20006
Phone: (202) 822-9300
Fax: (202) 467-4070

"The mission of the American Business Conference (ABC) is the promotion of public policies to encourage growth, job creation, and a higher standard of living for all Americans. ABC executives believe their own business success carries with it a responsibility to help expand economic opportunity throughout the economy." | **PURPOSE**

5 total | **STAFF**

Barry K. Rogstad, president | **DIRECTOR**

501(c)(6) | **TAX STATUS**

1998—Unavailable
Proposed 1999—Unavailable | **BUDGET**

Unavailable | **FUNDING SOURCES**

Members: 100 chief executive officers, chairmen, and presidents of companies
Branches/chapters: N/A
Affiliates: N/A

"To qualify for membership in ABC, a company must have annual revenues of at least $25 million and must be growing in revenues or earnings at a minimum average annual rate of three times the growth rate of the economy plus inflation. Member firms who can no longer maintain the growth criterion leave the organization and are replaced with other qualified companies." | **SCOPE**

None | **PAC**

| | |
|---|---|
| ...OF ...ION | ◆ Coalition forming  ◆ Conferences/seminars  ◆ Legislative/regulatory monitoring (federal)  ◆ Lobbying (federal)  ◆ Participation in regulatory proceedings (federal)  ◆ Polling  ◆ Research |
| ...RENT ...ONCERNS | ◆ Fiscal policy  ◆ Human capital  ◆ International trade and finance |
| PUBLICATIONS | Unavailable |
| NEWSLETTER | None |
| CONFERENCES | Annual American Business Conference (members only)<br>American Business Conference Membership Meeting (members only) |
| BOARD OF DIRECTORS | Unavailable |
| EFFECTIVENESS | "... Analysts have been closely watching whether the economy cooled in October, November and December [1997], after sprinting ahead during the four previous quarters. For one thing, unemployment has sunk to a remarkably low 4.6% of the work force, leading analysts to worry that a rise in inflation is inevitable. Also, they are trying to gauge the effect of the Asian financial crisis on the U.S. economy.... <br><br>"... A survey by the American Business Conference, also released yesterday, showed that chief executives of midsize firms believe the first quarter will be 'strong.' Indeed, 'the very worrying economic disruption we are seeing in Asia has yet to spark so much as a hiccup in the midsize sector,' said Barry Rogstad, president of the group...." (*Wall Street Journal*, January 6, 1998) <br><br>"Personal income and consumption both rose sharply in the first two months of this year [1997].... <br><br>"Spurred by job growth and longer workweeks, income in February jumped 0.9% from January, the biggest one-month increase since June, the Commerce Department said.... <br><br>"Separately, a private survey of rapidly growing midsize companies found that their chief executives expect continued strong growth with low inflation in the coming months. The Washington-based American Business Conference said 80% of its members expect greater sales and shipments in the second quarter than in the first period. <br><br>"At the same time, 43% of the nearly 70 respondents said they expect wider profit margins. The executives hold the rosy profit expectations even though 56% of them expect to be paying higher wages, while only 17% expect to raise prices. |

" 'The business environment is being driven by productivity improvements,' said Barry Rogstad, president of the organization. 'There is no other explanation.' " (*Wall Street Journal*, April 1, 1997)

"Inflation will probably stay in check while the economy continues to advance at a moderate tempo, a series of reports released yesterday [Oct. 1, 1996] predict. . . .

"A separate quarterly survey of midsize, rapidly growing companies also painted a picture of low inflation with sustained growth. Seventy-seven percent of the companies polled by the American Business Conference said they expect greater sales and shipments in the current quarter, down slightly from 80% in the previous quarter. Meanwhile, only 40% of American Business Conference members said they expected to pay higher wages this quarter, compared with 71% that expected wage pressures in the previous quarter. Six percent expect higher costs for materials, down from 7% last quarter, and 11% expect higher investment-capital costs, down from 32% in the last period.

" 'While not quite as bullish as our last survey, these numbers describe an economic engine that is purring along nicely and in no danger of overheating,' Barry Rogstad, president of the conference, said in a statement. 'This is not an environment in which inflation looms large.'. . ." (*Wall Street Journal*, October 2, 1996)

Unavailable

# *POLITICAL ORIENTATION*

# American Council for Capital Formation (1976)

1750 K Street, NW
Suite 400
Washington, D.C. 20006
Phone: (202) 293-5811
Fax: (202) 785-8165
Internet: info@accf.org *or* http://www.accf.org

| | |
|---|---|
| **PURPOSE** | "To help redefine and restructure U.S. tax, regulatory, and environmental policies so that this country [the United States] can increase the pace of economic growth, employment, and competitiveness in world markets." |
| **STAFF** | 9 total—5 professional; 4 support; plus 1 intern |
| **DIRECTOR** | Mark A. Bloomfield, president. He served as secretary of President-elect Reagan's Transition Task Force on Tax Policy for the first Reagan Administration. Bloomfield received a J.D. from the University of Pennsylvania Law School, earned an M.B.A. from the Wharton School, and graduated from Swarthmore College. Bloomfield lectures on politics and economics and testifies periodically before congressional committees. He is a coeditor or contributor to a number of books on tax and economic policy. |
| **TAX STATUS** | 501(c)(6) |
| **BUDGET** | 1997—$1.4 million<br>1998—$1.5 million<br>Proposed 1999—$1.5 million |
| **FUNDING SOURCES** | Corporate donations, 72 percent; associations, 19 percent; individuals, 5 percent; conferences, 3 percent; foundation grants, 1 percent |
| **SCOPE** | Members: 200 corporate, foundation, association, and individual supporters<br>Branches/chapters: N/A<br>Affiliate: ACCF Center for Policy Research, a 501(c)(3) organization |
| **PAC** | None |

♦ Coalition forming ♦ Conferences/seminars ♦ Congressional testimony ♦ Educational foundation ♦ Internet (Web site) ♦ Internships ♦ Legislative/regulatory monitoring (federal) ♦ Lobbying (federal) ♦ Media outreach ♦ Research ♦ Speakers program

♦ Environmental policy ♦ Regulatory policy ♦ Tax policy ♦ Trade policy and sanctions

*Balancing Economic Growth & Environmental Goals*
*Climate Change Policy, Risk Prioritization, and U.S. Economic Growth*
*Economic Effects of the Corporate Alternative Minimum Tax*
*An Economic Perspective on Climate Change Policies*
*Enhancing Environmental Quality Through Economic Growth*
*The Impact of Climate Change Policy on Consumers: Can Tradable Permits Reduce the Cost?*
*The Impact of the U.S. Tax Code on the Competitiveness of Financial Service Firms*
*Strategies for Improving Environmental Quality and Increase Economic Growth*
*Tax Policy for Economic Growth in the 1990s*
*Tools for American Workers: The Role of Machinery and Equipment in Economic Growth*
*U.S. Environmental Policy and Economic Growth: How Do We Fare?*
*U.S. Investment Trends: Impact on Productivity, Competitiveness & Growth*
*U.S. Waste Management Policies: Impact on Economic Growth and Investment Strategies*

Also publishes special reports, congressional testimonies by ACCF staff members, and issue briefs

*Capital Formation* (bimonthly)

ACCF Economic Evenings (monthly)
Capital Formation Forums (monthly)
Symposiums and Briefings (periodic)

Charles E. Walker, chairman; Mark A. Bloomfield, president; Mary Lee Dunn, senior vice president; Margo Thorning, senior vice president and chief economist

Other members:
♦ Lloyd Bentsen ♦ William E. Brock ♦ John J. Byrne ♦ Carroll A. Campbell Jr. ♦ Andrew H. Card Jr. ♦ Red Cavaney ♦ Brian H. Dovey ♦ David J. Drury ♦ Kenneth M. Duberstein ♦ James Ericson ♦ Matthew P. Fink ♦ Robert W. Galvin ♦ James B. Graham ♦ William H. Gray III ♦ James R. Jones ♦ Allen J. Krowe ♦ Marc E. Lackritz ♦ Kenneth L. Lay ♦ Donald L. Lucas ♦ Frederic V. Malek ♦ Edward F. Mitchell ♦ W. Henson Moore ♦ John S. Nolan ♦ M.B. Oglesby Jr. ♦ Richard W. Rahn ♦ Ronald W. Readmond ♦ Jack D. Rehm ♦ James E. Rogers, Jr. ♦

*TVENESS*

"Last Thursday . . . a massive tax bill that would cut the top rate on capital gains from 28 percent to 20 percent, with another 2-point reduction due in 2001, neared congressional approval with President Clinton's signature assured.

"[Mark] Bloomfield, a curious mix of eccentric professor and dapper influence broker, runs one of the city's most durable coalitions, the American Council for Capital Formation. . . .

" 'We have always taken the long-term view' he said with understatement. Congress last cut capital-gains taxes in 1981, just after Ronald Reagan became president. Since then, taxes on investment income have crept upward.

"Through it all, Bloomfield held his coalition together and slogged to Capitol Hill.

"Bloomfield and [his mentor, superlobbyist Charles] Walker kept plugging away, fueled by contributions from brokerage houses, insurance companies, manufacturers, accounting firms, oil companies and conservative foundations.

"Every couple of months, Bloomfield would invite to his home a select group of Congress members to schmooze with business executives and journalists about economic issues." (*Philadelphia Inquirer*, August 3, 1997)

"Bowing to colleagues and small business, Rep. Bill Archer dropped plans to repeal the corporate minimum tax and instead fattened the estate-tax relief in his tax-cut package. The fight pitted heavy industry against the small-business lobby, which relied on its close ties to the House GOP leadership to pressure the Ways and Means Committee chairman to bolster estate-tax relief. . . .

"Yesterday [June 11, 1997], Mr. Archer (R., Texas) dropped a proposal to repeal the 20% minimum tax by Jan. 1, 2006, a plan that was backed by an industrial coalition that included Mobil Corp., AlliedSignal Inc., and Bethlehem Steel Corp. But he retained a plan to phase out, beginning Jan. 1, 1999, provisions of the minimum tax that critics contend crimp business investment.

"The changes freed up about $13 billion over 10 years. About $3 billion will be used to address airlines' concerns about the bill, Mr. Archer said, while the balance will be plowed back into a proposal to raise the exemption on estate taxes to $1 million, from $600,000, backed by small and independent business. . . .

" 'The revised plan, which would phase in the $1 million threshold by 2007 instead of the originally proposed 2014, would cost about $28.8 billion over 10 years.

" 'This tax package is as much a debate about the direction of the Republican Party as it is about tax policy,' said Mark Bloomfield, president of the American Council for Capital Formation, a business-backed group lobbying to scale back the minimum tax. . . ." (*Wall Street Journal*, June 12, 1997)

"Although congressional Republicans are fighting the White House over the specifics of tax cuts in their balanced-budget deal, the next brawl will be among themselves. . . .

"Only by much shaving and finagling can Republicans shoehorn within the limit all the promised cuts: reductions in capital gains and estate taxes; a $500-a-child income-tax credit for many families; expanded breaks for individual retirement accounts; and the president's top priority, $35 billion in five-year tax breaks for post-high school education costs. Both parties also want to add or extend other cuts, including breaks for business-research costs and for hiring welfare recipients and cleaning up hazardous-waste sites. . . .

"Business lobbies and their congressional supporters already are scrambling to promote their favorites. For example, the corporate-supported American Council for Capital Formation, which has pushed capital-gains cuts for years, rushed out a newsletter on the budget deal with a headline, 'Capital Gains Tax Cut Faces Stiff Competition.' It urged recipients to contact their congressmen, and to 'pass this copy to five friends.'

"The effort to accommodate as many special interests as possible will determine such things as the size of a capital-gains rate cut and whether gains could be exempted because of inflation; how much of an estate is exempt from taxes beyond the current $600,000, and which types of estates; whether families can claim teenagers or only younger children for a child-tax credit; and what the income cutoff point should be to be eligible for the credit. 'You won't satisfy all the expectations out there,' said Rep. Ben Cardin (D., Md.), a member of the tax-writing House Ways and Means Committee. 'There will clearly be tradeoffs.'. . ." (*Wall Street Journal*, May 9, 1997)

## POLITICAL ORIENTATION

"Wall Street has been extremely generous to American investors. . . . Now Washington appears to be set to add a nice bonus. Prospects for a big cut in the capital-gains tax seem better this year [1997] than at any time since the federal government increased tax rates a decade ago on profits from selling investments. . . .

". . . Despite reservations by the Treasury Department and White House budget office, President Clinton says he would accept some reductions in a bipartisan budget deal. . . .

"But not all cuts are equal. While a reduction of some sort seems likely if Congress and the White House draft a balanced-budget plan this year, the question of exactly how to reduce capital-gains rates only now is being seriously addressed. . . .

" 'There's no doubt that a cut is doable in 1997,' says Mark A. Bloomfield, a lobbyist known here as 'Mr. Capital Gains' for his two decades of cheerleading. 'But the question is whether what's doable is worth doing.' Mr. Bloomfield represents the Washington-based American Council for Capital Formation, an alliance of trade groups and individuals calling for a reduction. As he wrote to rally his troops, 'political considerations could . . . produce a cut so watered down when it reaches the President's desk that it fails the test of a sensible capital-gains tax. . . . Much hard work is needed on Capitol Hill.' " (*Wall Street Journal*, February 14, 1997)

# Americans for Tax Reform (1985)

1320 18th Street, NW
Suite 200
Washington, D.C. 20008
Phone: (202) 785-0266
Fax: (202) 785-0261
Internet: info@atr.org *or* http://www.atr.org

**PURPOSE**

"To inform Americans of the full costs of taxation, which include not just the actual revenue collected, but also the costs of tax collection, the economic production lost because of disincentives to producers, the damage done by unnecessary bureaucracy, and the costs of supporting the regulatory bureaucracy with tax dollars."

**STAFF**

Unavailable

**DIRECTOR**

Grover G. Norquist, president. Before coming to Americans for Tax Reform, Norquist worked on the 1988 and 1992 Republican Platform Committees, served as an advisor to the 1988 Bush/Quayle campaign, and was an economist and chief speech writer for the U.S. Chamber of Commerce in 1983 and 1984. He is past executive director of both the National Taxpayers' Union and the College Republicans. Norquist writes a monthly column for the *American Spectator* and co-hosts a monthly show on the National Empowerment Television. He holds an M.B.A. and a B.A. in economics, both from Harvard University.

**TAX STATUS**

501(c)(4)

**BUDGET**

1998—Unavailable
Proposed 1999—Unavailable

**FUNDING SOURCES**

Membership contributions

**SCOPE**

Members: Unavailable
Branches/chapters: N/A
Affiliate: Americans for Tax Reform Foundation, a 501(c)(3) organization

None

♦ Advertisements ♦ Coalition forming ♦ Congressional testimony ♦ Grassroots organizing ♦ Information clearinghouse ♦ Initiative/referendum campaigns ♦ International activities ♦ Internet (Web site) ♦ Legislative/regulatory monitoring (federal and state) ♦ Media outreach

♦ Flat tax concept ♦ Regulation initiatives and referenda ♦ Size and scope of government ♦ Social Security ♦ Taxpayer Protection Pledge ♦ Value added tax (VAT)

None

*American Tax Reformer* (quarterly)

None

Unavailable

"By now, mutual-fund savvy Americans have figured out that they are losing money in FDR's ancient Social Security regime. Exactly how much becomes evident only when citizens punch up a new free service available from the tax lobby, Americans for Tax Reform. Tap in 'www.atr.org,' click on the 'social security estimator,' and enter a few numbers. The benefits engine will calculate the approximate Social Security benefit you can expect when you retire, as well as the pay off you could get if your money went to bonds and mutual funds instead." (*Wall Street Journal*, March 19, 1997)

"In a rare move, the outgoing commissioner of the Internal Revenue Service said the agency is willing to give Congress confidential tax-return information in order to challenge 'inaccurate and misleading' news reports about its alleged politically motivated audits of tax-exempt organizations.

"At a hearing before the National Commission on Restructuring the IRS, Commissioner Margaret Richardson released letters she sent to Sen. William Roth (R., Del.), chairman of the Senate Finance Committee, and Rep. William Archer (R., Texas), chairman of the House Ways and Means committee.

" 'Recent media reports have alleged politically targeted examinations of tax-exempt organizations by the Internal Revenue Service,' the commissioner wrote. She went on to 'express our willingness' to provide these committees with such information. . . .

"The disclosure came after Grover Norquist, president of Americans for Tax Reform . . . pressed IRS officials at the hearing to explain how exactly it selects nonprofit groups for audit. A number of conservative nonprofits, including the Heritage Foundation, Citizens Against Government Waste and the National Rifle Association, have recently disclosed that they are being audited." (*Wall Street Journal*, February 27, 1997)

"Think tanks and independent political organizations, meanwhile, are gearing up to supply the propaganda. Americans for Tax Reform leader Grover Norquist plans a media blitz, from op-ed pieces to radio talk shows. 'Forty-five days from now, I want every American to know how much corporate welfare spending there is, and what's included,' he promises." (*Wall Street Journal*, December 18, 1996)

## POLITICAL ORIENTATION

"tax lobby" (*Wall Street Journal*, March 19, 1997)

"a nonprofit group fighting for lower taxes" (*Wall Street Journal*, February 27, 1997)

"antigovernment" (*Wall Street Journal*, January 17, 1997)

# The Business Roundtable (1972)

1615 L Street, NW
Suite 1100
Washington, D.C. 20036
Phone: (202) 872-1260
Fax: (202) 466-3509
Internet: http://www.brtable.org

"The Business Roundtable is an association of chief executive officers who examine public issues that affect the economy and develop positions which seek to reflect sound economic and social principles. Established in 1972, the Roundtable was founded in the belief that business executives should take an increased role in the continuing debates about public policy." | *PURPOSE*

20 total—10 professional; 10 support | *STAFF*

Samuel L. Maury, president. Maury joined the Business Roundtable in 1982 and became executive director in 1983; he was appointed president in 1994. Previously Maury worked as an attorney for U.S. Steel. He has also served in the U.S. Air Force. | *DIRECTOR*

501(c)(6) | *TAX STATUS*

1998—Unavailable
Proposed 1999—Unavailable | *BUDGET*

Membership dues, 100 percent | *FUNDING SOURCES*

Members: approximately 200 corporations represented by their chief executive officers
Branches/chapters: N/A
Affiliates: N/A | *SCOPE*

None | *PAC*

| METHOD OF OPERATION | ♦ Advertisements ♦ Awards program ♦ Coalition forming ♦ Congressional testimony ♦ Internet (Web site) ♦ Internships ♦ Legislative/regulatory monitoring (federal and state) ♦ Lobbying by BRT members (federal and state) ♦ Media outreach ♦ Polling ♦ Research ♦ Task forces |
|---|---|

| CURRENT CONCERNS | ♦ Construction cost effectiveness ♦ Corporate governance ♦ Education reform (K-12) ♦ Environment ♦ Federal budget ♦ Global warming ♦ Health care and retirement income ♦ Human resources ♦ International trade and investment (IMF, sanctions, FastTrack) ♦ Regulatory reform ♦ Taxation ♦ Tort policy |
|---|---|

| PUBLICATIONS | The following is a list of sample publications:<br><br>*A Business Leader's Guide to Setting Academic Standards*<br>*The Business Stake in Effective Project Systems*<br>*Confronting the Skilled Construction Work Force*<br>*Corporate Ethics: A Prime Business Asset*<br>*The Kyoto Protocol: A Gap Analysis*<br>*Moving to the Head of the Class: 50 Simple Things You Can Do*<br>*Quality Health Care is Good Business: A Survey of Health Care Quality Initiatives by Members of The Business Roundtable*<br>*Retirement Income Security Principles*<br>*Rush to Judgment: A Primer on Global Climate Change*<br>*The Spillover Effect: How Quality Improvement Efforts by Large Employers Benefit Health Care in the Community*<br>*Statement on Corporate Governance*<br>*Strengthening Your Child's Academic Future*<br>*Taxing U.S. Corporations in the Global Marketplace*<br>*Toward Smarter Regulation*<br>*Understanding the Corporate Income Tax* |
|---|---|

| NEWSLETTER | None |
|---|---|

| CONFERENCES | None |
|---|---|

| BOARD OF DIRECTORS | Dana G. Mead, chairman; Joseph T. Gorman, Walter V. Shipley, and John F. Smith Jr., co-chairmen; Samuel L. Maury, president; Patricia Hanahan Engman, executive director<br><br>Other members:<br>♦ Lawrence A. Bossidy ♦ M. Anthony Burns ♦ Robert N. Burt ♦ George M.C. Fisher ♦ Donald V. Fites ♦ H. Laurance Fuller ♦ Edward B. Rust ♦ William C. Steere ♦ Thomas J. Usher |
|---|---|

| EFFECTIVENESS | "About two dozen CEOs from the Business Roundtable visited Capitol Hill this week to kick off the effort by a new coalition of seven employer groups. Dozens more business leaders are expected to get involved. The |
|---|---|

coalition will stress to employers, especially midsize and small businesses, the need for high-quality health-care plans for workers. The point of the campaign, which will run for several months: That 'the free market system is the way to improve quality,' says Ryder System Chairman M. Anthony Burns, who is heading the effort." (*Wall Street Journal*, April 3, 1998)

"Early February was a busy time for Donald V. Fites, the chairman and CEO of Caterpillar Inc., a global giant that's worried about fallout from the Asian economic crisis. At the World Economic Forum in Davos, Switzerland, Fites buttonholed House Speaker Newt Gingrich, R-GA., and delivered a blunt message: Congress needs to pass legislation providing $18 billion to replenish the International Monetary Fund (IMF). On February 3, Fites and a handful of other corporate chieftains made a similar appeal to Senate Majority Leader Trent Lott, R-Miss., over dinner on Capitol Hill. And the following day, Fites and several other CEOs pushed the IMF cause in separate meetings with Treasury Secretary Robert E. Rubin and House Republican Conference chairman John Boehner of Ohio. All of these Washington meetings were organized by the powerful Business Roundtable—its members head some 200 of the largest U.S. corporations—which Fites also chairs." (*National Journal*, February 21, 1998)

## POLITICAL ORIENTATION

"Republican leaders are adopting a tough post-election strategy: 'Don't get mad, get even.' And the foe this time isn't the Democrats or organized labor.

"It's Corporate America.

"Annoyed that big business has been hedging its bets by giving lots of money to the Democrats as well as to the Republicans, the GOP says the Business Roundtable, a group of 200 chief executives from the nation's biggest companies, is about to receive an ultimatum: Stop donating so much to the Democrats and become more involved in partisan politics, or be denied access to Republicans in Congress.

"The GOP strategy is a high-risk one. While Business Roundtable companies gave more than $11.04 million to the Democrats during the 1996 election cycle, as of figures from Dec. 2 they gave more than double that amount—$25.76 million—to Republicans, according to the Center for Responsive Politics, a Washington-based public-interest group that monitors campaign spending." (*Wall Street Journal*, January 9, 1997)

# Center for the New West (1989)

600 World Trade Center       3100 Landfall Lane
1625 Broadway                Annapolis, Maryland 21903
Denver, Colorado 80202       Phone: (301) 263-5660
Phone: (303) 572-5457
Fax: (303) 572-5499

Internet: cnwinfo@newwest.org *or* http://www.newwest.org

## PURPOSE

"Explores trends transforming the West and the nation . . . to assist leaders of business, civic, and political institutions respond to and shape forces that affect these changes and the political environment. We focus on the West for a simple reason: The region increasingly defines America's place in the global economy and global consciousness. The West leads the nation in population growth, job creation, political reform movements, new technologies and innovation, educational achievement and institutional reform, leadership by women and minorities and new approaches to workplace management."

## STAFF

27 total—21 professional; 6 support; plus 8 interns and a network of 50 senior fellows

## DIRECTOR

Philip M. Burgess, president. Before founding the Center for the New West in 1989, Burgess spent 19 years as a professor at the Ohio State University, the University of Colorado, and the Colorado School of Mines. He has served as executive director of the Federation of Rocky Mountain States and president of the Western Governors Policy Office. Burgess also was a member of the U.S. Department of State European Advisory Council, the first Privacy Commission, and the Western Interstate Commission on Higher Education. Burgess is the author of several books. He earned his undergraduate degree at Knox College in Illinois and a Ph.D. at American University in Washington, D.C.

## TAX STATUS

501(c)(3)

## BUDGET

1998—$2.3 million
Proposed 1999—$3 million

## FUNDING SOURCES

Membership dues, 54 percent; foundation grants, 24 percent; government research contracts, 16 percent; speakers bureau, 3 percent; conferences and other, 3 percent

Members: 250 corporations, foundations, and civic organizations

Branches/chapters: Environmental Education Research Institute in Tucson, Arizona, and National Affairs office in Washington, D.C.

Affiliates: Center for the New West institutes: Institute for Telemedicine; Institute for Telework; Institute for Information Law and Policy; Institute for the New American Workplace; Western Hemisphere Institute

None

♦ Conferences/seminars ♦ Congressional testimony ♦ International activities ♦ Internet (Web site) ♦ Legislative/regulatory monitoring (federal and state) ♦ Publications ♦ Research ♦ Speakers program ♦ Telecommunications services (mailing lists) ♦ Training and technical assistance

♦ Biotechnology ♦ Environmental education ♦ Free trade ♦ High performance communications ♦ Infrastructure development ♦ Intellectual property rights ♦ Small office/home office movement (SoHo) ♦ Technology and society ♦ Western policy studies

*Great Plains in Transition* (series)
*Points West Advisory* (periodic)
*Points West Lecture Series* (periodic)
*Points West Special Reports* (periodic)
*Points West Review* (periodic publication that provides a lengthy digest of studies and books by Senior Fellows of the Center)
*Profile of Western North America: Indicators of an Emerging Continental Market*

*Points West Chronicle* (quarterly)

Sponsors various seminars, conferences and roundtables on regional and hemispheric trade, energy and economic issues

Solomon D. Trujillo, chairman; Philip M. Burgess, president

Other trustees:
♦ A. Gary Ames ♦ Steve Bartolin ♦ Harry P. Bowes ♦ Averell H. Elliot ♦ William A. Franke ♦ Steven T. Halverson ♦ Kenneth D. Hubbard ♦ Michael Leavitt ♦ Thomas A. Levin ♦ John Naisbitt ♦ Barbara J. Nelson ♦ Kenneth Olsen ♦ Fred Palmer ♦ Bill Post

## EFFECTIVENESS

"Democrats who thought a surge of liberal, environmentally savvy new-comers to the booming West would pump up their power in the region are getting a nasty surprise and should brace themselves for more bad news, a Denver think tank says.

"Far from boosting the Democrats, new arrivals in the West are defying expectations by rejecting Democratic candidates and programs, the Center for the New West said in a report released Monday." (*Associated Press,* May 18, 1998)

"Economists from six Midwest states and three Canadian provinces agree that the region's economy is at its strongest point ever, but they note that all the states face a common problem—not enough workers.

"The overview of the economies of Minnesota, Iowa, the Dakotas, Kansas, Nebraska, Alberta, Manitoba and Saskatchewan came at a conference on the Great Plains Economy sponsored by the Center for the New West, a nonprofit group based in Denver." (*Associated Press,* June 28, 1997)

"In North Dakota, the explosion of the telecommunications industry has been so sudden, with thousands of jobs added in the last two years, that planners say it may be the way to stop a long-running brain drain.

" 'A fundamental shift is occurring,' said Philip M. Burgess, president of the Center for the New West, a policy and research group in Denver. 'For the first time in modern history we have jobs chasing people instead of people chasing jobs. In remote areas like the Dakotas or Montana, you start looking at levels of educational attainment or work ethic, and you find that those states rank among the highest. So companies move out there.' " (*New York Times,* February 3, 1997)

## POLITICAL ORIENTATION

"economic think tank" (*Wall Street Journal,* September 29, 1995)

# Center for the Study of American Business (1975)

Washington University
1 Brookings Drive
Campus Box 1027
St. Louis, Missouri 63130-4899
Phone: (314) 935-5630
Fax: (314) 935-5688
Internet: http://csab.wustl.edu

"To improve public understanding of the private enterprise system in a global context, thereby fostering a policy environment in which the U.S. market economy can prosper."

**PURPOSE**

21 total—11 professional; 10 support

**STAFF**

Virginia V. Weldon, M.D., director. Weldon became the director of the Center for the Study of American Business (CSAB) on July 1, 1998. Prior to her becoming the director of CSAB, she had served as a senior vice president of public policy at the Monsanto Company since 1989. She also held various positions at Washington University, including deputy vice chancellor for medical affairs, professor of pediatrics, and vice president of the Washington University Medical Center. A graduate of Smith College, Weldon received her medical degree from the University of Buffalo Medical School. She also completed her residency at Johns Hopkins University.

**DIRECTOR**

501(c)(3)

**TAX STATUS**

1998—Unavailable
Proposed 1999—Unavailable

**BUDGET**

Corporate donations, 72 percent; foundation grants, 12 percent; individual donations, 15 percent

**FUNDING SOURCES**

Members: N/A
Branches/chapters: N/A
Affiliates: N/A

**SCOPE**

| | |
|---|---|
| *PAC* | None |
| *METHOD OF OPERATION* | ◆ Academic program (research assistanceships, student dissertations, workshops) ◆ Awards program (John M. Olin Prize that recognizes outstanding graduating seniors in economics) ◆ Conferences/seminars ◆ Congressional testimony ◆ Internet (Web site) ◆ Legislative/regulatory monitoring (federal) ◆ Mailing lists ◆ Media outreach ◆ Research |
| *CURRENT CONCERNS* | ◆ Corporate governance ◆ Environmental policy ◆ Government regulation ◆ International competitiveness ◆ Organizational change ◆ Taxation and spending issues |
| *PUBLICATIONS* | The following is a list of sample publications:<br>*Are Storm Clouds Brewing on the Environmental Justice Horizon?*<br>*The Case for America's Role in the Global Marketplace*<br>*The Coming Social Security Crisis: Why It Happened and What We Can Do*<br>*Corporate Governance: When More's at Stake than Meets the Eye*<br>*"Cliffs Notes" for a Midterm Exam on the U.S. Economy*<br>*Economic Navigation in a Period of Great Uncertainty*<br>*Environmental Crossing Guards: International Environmental Treaties and U.S. Foreign Policy*<br>*Frameworks: An Innovative Process for Turning the Challenges of Change into Opportunities for Growth*<br>*Getting Rich in America: A Few Easy Rules to Follow*<br>*Global Deception: The Exaggeration of the Global Warming Threat*<br>*The Growing Pace of Regulation: An Analysis of the Regulatory Programs of the 1999 U.S. Budget*<br>*Leave It to the Market*<br>*Local Sanctions—Global Reactions: States, Cities, and Economic Sanctions*<br>*Recasting the Role of Government to Promote Economic Prosperity*<br>*Time for the Federal Environmental Aristocracy to Relinquish Some Power*<br>*Trade, Feeding the World's People and Sustainability: A Cause for Concern*<br><br>Regularly publishes reports on issues such as economics, environment, global markets, management, and regulation |
| *NEWSLETTER* | *CSAB Update* (2 times a year) |
| *CONFERENCES* | Sponsors industrial organization workshops and seminars on macroeconomic issues at CSAB throughout the year |
| *BOARD OF DIRECTORS* | Murray Weidenbaum, chair; Kenneth Chilton, director; Melinda Warren, associate director, finance; Robert Batterson, communications director; William Toney, associate director, communications and publications; Richard Mahoney, distinguished executive in residence |

"The average small firm with fewer than 20 employees spent nearly twice as much per employee complying with federal regulations in 1992 as firms with 500 or more employees, concludes a study by the Center for the Study of American Business at Washington University in St. Louis. . . ." (*Wall Street Journal*, November 20, 1996)

Unavailable

# Center on Budget and Policy Priorities (1981)

820 First Street, NE
Suite 510
Washington, D.C. 20002
Phone: (202) 408-1080
Fax: (202) 408-1056
Internet: http://www.cbpp.org

| | |
|---|---|
| **PURPOSE** | "To analyze government spending, programs, and public policy issues on both the national and state level that have an impact on low- and moderate-income Americans." |
| **STAFF** | 55 total |
| **DIRECTOR** | Robert Greenstein, director. Before founding the Center on Budget and Policy Priorities (CBPP), Greenstein served as administrator of the Food and Nutrition Service in the U.S. Agriculture Department and as special assistant to the secretary of agriculture. He also worked for the Community Nutrition Institute, a nonprofit food and nutrition advocacy organization. Greenstein has contributed articles to a number of publications and has been a guest on network, cable, and local television and radio programs. He received an undergraduate degree from Harvard University. |
| **TAX STATUS** | 501(c)(3) |
| **BUDGET** | 1998—$4 million<br>Proposed 1999—$4.5 million |
| **FUNDING SOURCES** | Supported primarily by major foundation grants |
| **SCOPE** | Members: N/A<br>Branches/chapters: N/A<br>Affiliate: None |
| **PAC** | None |

♦ Conferences/seminars ♦ Congressional testimony ♦ Internet ♦ Legislative/regulatory monitoring (federal and state) ♦ Library/information clearinghouse (disseminates policy analysis to policymakers, government staff, the media, nonprofit personnel, and the general public) ♦ Media outreach ♦ Research

♦ Federal budget issues ♦ Federal tax policies ♦ Food and nutrition programs ♦ Jobs creation ♦ Minimum wage ♦ Poverty and income ♦ Unemployment insurance ♦ State fiscal policies ♦ State welfare and low-income issues ♦ Welfare issues

The following is a list of sample publications:

*Consequences of Eliminating the EITC for Childless Workers*

*Developing Innovative Child Support Demonstrations for Non-Custodial Parents*

*Don't Let the Tax Foundation Figures Persuade You Otherwise: Taxes on Households in the Middle of the Income Spectrum are Neither Exceptionally High nor Rising*

*Earned Income Tax Credit Outreach Campaign Kit*

*Federal Government Would Continue to Consume Less of Economy Under Administration's Budget*

*Federal Welfare-to-Work Grants: New Opportunities to Create Jobs and Assist Non-Custodial Parents*

*Highway Bill Likely to Cut into Funding for Other Non-Defense Discretionary Programs*

*Housing and Welfare Reform: Some Background Information*

*How Big Is the Federal Government—And Would the Administration's Budget Make it Bigger?*

*In Search of Shelter: The Growing Shortage of Affordable Rental Housing*

*IRS Reform Bill Includes New Salvo of Tax Cuts for Wealthy*

*New Federal Food Stamp Restoration for Legal Immigrants: Implications and Implementation Issues*

*New Findings From Oregon Suggest Minimum Wage Increases Can Boost Wages for Welfare Recipients Moving to Work*

*New Research Findings on the Effects of the Earned Income Tax Credit*

*Proposed Constitutional Amendment Would Impede Deficit Reduction and Protect Special Interest Tax Breaks*

*Proposed House-Senate Compromise on Income Targeting Would Cut Housing Assistance to Poor Families as Much as 63 Percent*

*Regional Opportunity Counseling (ROC): Realizing the Promise of Section 8 Mobility*

*Reinvesting Welfare Savings: Aiding Needy Families and Strengthening State Welfare Reform*

*Roth Amendment Health Insurance Tax Deduction Benefit Higher-Income, Already-Insured Families*

*Setting the Record Straight: A Response to the Tax Foundation's Response*

*Should States Tax Food? Examining the Policy Issues and Options*

*State Earned Income Tax Credits Build on the Strengths of the Federal EITC*

*State Income Tax Burdens on Low-Income Families in 1997: Assessing the Burden and Opportunities for Relief*

*Strengths of the Safety Net: How the EITC, Social Security, and Other Government Programs Affect Poverty*

*Taking the Next Step: State Can Now Expand Health Coverage to Low-Income Working Parents Through Medicaid*

*Tax Foundation Figures Produce Misleading and Inaccurate Impressions of Middle Class Tax Burdens*

*Taxpayers Will Have New Tax Cuts Even If No Additional Reductions Are Enacted*

*Understanding the Financial Status of the Social Security System in Light of the 1998 Trustees' Report*

*Using IRA Tax Break to Fund IRS Reform Leaves Revenue Hole When Baby Boomers Retire*

*Washington State's Community Jobs Initiative*

*Welfare-to-Work Vouchers: Making Welfare Work*

*What Surplus?*

*Would the Proposed National Tobacco Settlement Compensate the Federal Government Adequately for Tobacco-Related Health Care Costs?*

*Would Using the Budget Surplus For Tax Cuts or Entitlement Expansions Affect Long-Term Social Security Solvency?*

---

## NEWSLETTER

WIC Newsletter (9 times a year)

---

## CONFERENCES

Annual state services conference

---

## BOARD OF DIRECTORS

♦ Henry J. Aaron ♦ Barbara Blum ♦ Marian Wright Edelman ♦ David de Ferranti ♦ James O. Gibson ♦ John R. Kramer ♦ Richard P. Nathan ♦ Marion Pines ♦ Sol Price ♦ Robert D. Reischauer ♦ Audrey Rowe ♦ Susan Sechler ♦ Juan Sepulveda Jr. ♦ William Julius Wilson

---

## EFFECTIVENESS

"The millions of American investors who climbed aboard the Starship Dow before its takeoff in the 1990s have watched their net worth soar to dizzying heights. But many more have missed the ride. . . .

" 'The market's rise may be increasing assets of some middle-income families, but the overall effect has got to be widening the already large gaps in wealth and income,' said Robert Greenstein, executive director of the Center on Budget and Policy Priorities. 'Sure, the average middle-class guy with a few shares in a mutual fund is making a little money. But those gains are quite small in relation to very big increases for wealthy families.'. . .

"According to an analysis of Congressional Budget Office data by the Center on Budget and Policy Priorities, between 1977 and 1994 the average after-tax income of the wealthiest 1 percent of Americans rose 72 percent, after adjustment for inflation, while the average income of the highest-earning 20 percent of families rose 25 percent.

By contrast, the average after-tax income of the middle fifth of the population stagnated, while that of the poorest fifth of families shrank 16 percent. . . ." (*Washington Post*, April 7, 1998)

"Debate heats up about how much the typical American family pays in taxes.

"In a report to be issued today [March 11, 1998], the Center on Budget and Policy Priorities, a nonprofit group in Washington, estimates the median-income family pays between 26% and 30% of its income in federal, state and local taxes. The center says this range is before taking into account the 1997 federal tax law, which it says lowers the typical family's effective tax rate. Author Iris J. Lav says the tax burdens of median-income families have been 'relatively stable over the past two decades.

"These views conflict with a 1997 study by the Tax Foundation, another nonprofit research group. It said total taxes claimed 38% of a median-income two-earner family's income, the most since 1981. . . .

" 'There doesn't seem to be a definitive analytical answer, but there seem to be lots of definitive philosophical answers,' says Perry D. Quick, national director of economics at Ernst & Young. . . ." (*Wall Street Journal*, March 11, 1998)

"Like the fabled feud between the Hatfields and the McCoys, the partisan battle over a balanced budget has been going on so long that many Americans have long since forgotten what it means to them. . . .

" 'The simple way to think of it is that, over a period of time, we'd all be richer,' said Martin Baily, who recently left the White House Council of Economic Advisers to join the consulting firm McKinsey & Co.

"Well, not all of us. Because the deal also entails cuts in government spending, a good number of Americans would lose something, particularly lower income Americans who rely disproportionately on government services and income support programs. . . .

" 'The real standard against which a budget should be measured is whether it addresses our long-term fiscal problems and reaches balance in a way that the sacrifices required are equally shared,' said Robert Greenstein, director of the Center on Budget and Policy Priorities. Greenstein argues that the budget deal announced last week disappoints on both counts, noting the package of tax cuts envisioned by the plan skews heavily in favor of upper-income families. . . ." (*Washington Post*, May 4, 1997)

## POLITICAL ORIENTATION

". . . [A] new study from the liberal Center on Budget and Policy Priorities shows that the war on poverty has not been in vain. The center found that, despite years of budget-cutting and a steady decline in wages at the bottom of the income ladder, the government's social safety net remains an effective tool in raising people above the official poverty line. . . . [A]fter taking into account the beneficial effects of current government programs, it would now take only $61 billion more to bring the incomes of all poor Americans up to the poverty line. That's less than 1 percent of the country's total annual output, the gross domestic product. And $61 billion is about what some private analysts now expect the federal budget surplus to be this year or next. . . ." (*Washington Post*, March 12, 1998)

"liberal" (*Wall Street Journal*, July 3, 1997)

# Citizens for a Sound Economy (1984)

1250 H Street, NW
Suite 700
Washington, D.C. 20005
Phone: (202) 783-3870 or (888) JOIN-CSE
Fax: (202) 783-4687
Internet: http://www.cse.org

| | |
|---|---|
| **PURPOSE** | "To promote economic freedom and opportunity for all citizens by mobilizing people who can change public policy." |
| **STAFF** | 65 total—53 professional; 12 support; plus 1 part-time professional; 1 part-time support; 6 interns |
| **DIRECTOR** | Paul Beckner, president. Beckner joined Citizens for a Sound Economy (CSE) in 1987, serving as vice president for membership, director of public policy, and director of development. He previously worked for Bantam Books and the Tribune Company. Beckner received an M.B.A. from the Wharton School and an B.A. from Northwestern University. |
| **TAX STATUS** | 501(c)(4) |
| **BUDGET** | 1997—$9.2 million<br>1998—$6.73 million<br>Proposed 1999—Unavailable |
| **FUNDING SOURCES** | Corporate donations, 68 percent; individuals, 15 percent; trade associations, 12 percent; other, 5 percent |
| **SCOPE** | Members: 250,000 individuals, corporations, and foundations<br>Branches/chapters: State chapters in Alabama, Florida, Illinois, Louisiana, New Jersey, New York, Oklahoma, Texas, and Virginia<br>Affiliate: Citizens for a Sound Economy Educational Foundation, a 501(c)(3) organization |
| **PAC** | None |
| **METHOD OF OPERATION** | ♦ Advertisements ♦ Awards program ♦ Coalition forming ♦ Conferences/seminars ♦ Congressional testimony ♦ Educational foundation ♦ Grassroots organizing ♦ Internet (Web site) ♦ Internships ♦ Lobbying (federal, state, and grassroots) ♦ Media outreach ♦ Polling ♦ Research |

♦ Electricity deregulation ♦ Environment regulation ♦ FDA reform ♦ Health care reform ♦ Insurance reform ♦ International trade ♦ Natural resources ♦ Regulatory reform ♦ Tax and budget reform ♦ Telecommunications reform ♦ Tort reform

*Addicted to Big Government*
*An Analysis of Retail Competition in America's Electric Industry*
*The Case Against OPIC*
*The Clandestine Cost Analysis of The Kyoto Protocol*
*Competition Through Innovation—Not Regulation*
*Competition Will Lower Rates for Reliable Service*
*Congress's $50 Billion Tax Increase*
*Consumers, Credit, and Classification: The NAIC Misses the Mark*
*Do Particulates Matter?*
*Does It Take a Village to Drug Test a Child?*
*"Don't Eat and Drive": The Milkshake Case*
*The EPA's Exaggeration of Health Risk from PM$_{2.5}$*
*The EPA's New Clean Air Standards: A Primer*
*The EPA's Proposed Air Quality Standards: First, Do No Harm*
*EPA Ups Expected Cost of Air Quality Standards to $46 Billion*
*The Era of Surplus Politics*
*The FDA's Party Patrol*
*The FDA's Report Card Shows Another Failing Grade*
*FDA Suppresses Therapies for Kids With Cystic Fibrosis*
*FDA User Fees Have Done Nothing for Patients*
*The Flat Tax Lowers Taxes for America's Families*
*Free Trade: Fast Track to Prosperity*
*Giving Away the Budget Store*
*Global Warming: A Political, Economic and Scientific Backgrounder*
*Global Warming: The Little Engine That Couldn't*
*Gray Skies Ahead Over New Air Quality Standards*
*The Heat Is On*
*Implementing Kyoto Without Senate Ratification: Clinton-Gore's "Think Globally Regulate Locally" Campaign*
*Lawsuit Reform Requires Laws That Make Sense*
*A Look at Joint Liability*
*MediKid: A Republican Congress Hands ClintonCare Its First Victory*
*MediKid: Whose Idea Was This Anyway?*
*PM$_{2.5}$ : A Closer Look at Where It Comes From*
*A Real Patients' Bill of Rights*
*Risky Business: Insurance, Risk Classification and the Consumer*
*Setting the Record Straight: The Consumer Wins with Competition*
*Smoggy Science: The Truth Behind Ozone Transport*
*Stealth March of ClintonCare*
*Superfund: The Good, The Bad, and The Broken*
*Surprising Critics of the New Clean Air Standards: The U.S. Government*
*Telecom Reform, One Year Later*
*Think Globally, Tax Locally: The EPA's Global Warming "Action Plan"*
*Three Simple Steps Toward A Sound Encryption Policy*
*Top Ten Reasons to Reject the Clinton-GOP Budget Deal*
*Universal Service Reform: Benchmarks for Success*

*Why America Should Renew MFN for China*
*Why Congress Must Enact a Moratorium on the EPA's New PM$_{2.5}$ Standards*
*Weird Science: Did CASAC Really Support PM$_{2.5}$*

Also publishes impact statements on trade, the federal budget, and regulation; Capitol comments; economic and regulatory perspectives; fact sheets; and "issues and answers." Most publications are available on CSE's Web site.

## NEWSLETTER

*Citizen Alert* (bimonthly; produced by Citizens for a Sound Economy Foundation)
*Sentinel* (bimonthly)

## CONFERENCES

*Scrap the Code* (a tax debate that tours cities across America)
Also issue-related conferences (not regularly scheduled)

## BOARD OF DIRECTORS

♦ Gordon Cain ♦ David Dewhurst ♦ Joseph G. Fogg ♦ C. Boyden Gray ♦ Deecy Gray ♦ Tom Knudsen ♦ James C. Miller III ♦ Nancy L. Mitchell ♦ David H. Padden ♦ James A. Pope ♦ Richard J. Stephenson ♦ Dirk Van Dongen

## EFFECTIVENESS

"In a five-city tour, House Majority Leader Dick ('The current tax code will be road kill before you know it') Armey is arguing the merits of a single-rate flat tax of 17%. Opposing him is Rep. Billy ('Rip the IRS out by its roots') Tauzin, a Republican from Louisiana who wants to abolish the infernal agency and replace it with a 15% national sales tax. Their show, sponsored by the nonprofit Citizens for a Sound Economy, is called 'Scrap the Code.' Its best crowd so far was 12,500, in Bakersfield, Calif. Its best souvenir is a rubber foam soda cooler labeled 'Can the Code.' Mr. Tauzin (pronounced 'TOE-zan') doesn't speak with the same authority as the majority leader. But he has the backing of House Ways and Means Chairman Bill Archer (R., Texas), who has hinted approximately a thousand times that he too wants a national sales tax. . . ." (*Wall Street Journal*, October 23, 1997)

". . . Deregulating the nation's electric utilities could save consumers and businesses at least $40 billion a year, according to Citizens for a Sound Economy, by opening the industry to competition and allowing users to shop for a power provider the way they currently shop for long-distance telephone service. Today, the Energy Information Administration is scheduled to release a report that provides a more conservative estimate of potential savings than of that estimated by Citizens for a Sound Economy. . . ." (*Wall Street Journal*, August 13, 1997)

"Konrad Norstog's tractor churns up great clouds of gray dust on days when the soil is dry, and even his cows have been known to kick up a clod or two. But the North Dakota farmer never connected dirt with air pollution until he heard an ad on the radio a few weeks ago. . . .

"Score another round for the pro-industry alliance at the center of an extraordinary, multimillion-dollar campaign to turn back EPA regulations for smog and soot that are scheduled to take effect July 19. With provocative messages carefully targeted at farmers, small businesses and other audiences far beyond the Washington Beltway, a coalition of industries and allied political groups has attempted to stir up a groundswell of opposition to the proposals. By many accounts, the strategy is succeeding. . . .

"The 'dust' ads were the latest in a series that predicts lifestyle changes for millions of Americans—and perhaps even a ban on outdoor barbecues—if the EPA standards are approved. Produced by the free-market advocacy group Citizens for a Sound Economy (CSE), they are but one component of what is widely described as an expensive, highly sophisticated campaign that is setting a new standard in the long history of industry attempts to stave off unwanted regulation. . . .

"Citizens for a Sound Economy, with its own $5 million war chest to promote regulatory reform, specialized in ads that sought to characterize the regulations as a government intrusion on personal liberty. The ads predicted that the standards would lead to forced carpooling or bans on outdoor barbecues—claims the EPA dismisses as ridiculous. . . ." (*Washington Post*, June 17, 1997)

"Seven months ago, a little-known Washington think tank, Citizens for a Sound Economy Foundation, issued what seemed like another dull report: an analysis of the nation's electric power industry. In it, two Clemson University economists argue that by removing legal restraints on competition between electricity producers, federal and state governments could expand market share for 'efficient' utilities, shrink less-productive companies and slash the average consumer's electric bill by 43%.

"In a city where most such reports go unread, this one lit quite a few light bulbs. Rep. Dan Schaefer (R., Colo.), chairman of a House Commerce subcommittee, started thinking about a political power play that could make competition happen within an industry long considered a natural monopoly. . . .

"In July, Mr. Schaefer introduced legislation that would give all consumers the ability to choose their own electricity service by Dec. 15, 2000. That thunderbolt squarely hit the tightly regulated, $200 billion-a-year electricity industry, splitting its normal alliances. Now, a potentially enormous legislative battle—one that many had hoped to postpone or avoid—is probably inevitable.

"At least a dozen other bills are in the works. 'The number of economic interests affected by this are simply staggering,' says Ralph Cavanagh, the Natural Resources Defense Council's chief energy expert. 'In terms of combined economic and environmental impact, it may be the most important bill put forward in this decade.' . . ." (*Wall Street Journal*, December 17, 1996)

# POLITICAL ORIENTATION

"a non-partisan free market group that favors lower taxes and less environmental regulation" (*Cox News Service*, April 23, 1998)

"an anti-tax advocacy group" (*Florida Sun-Sentinel*, March 22, 1998)

"conservative" (*USA Today*, October 10, 1997)

"a Washington-based free market advocacy group" (*Wall Street Journal*, August 13, 1997)

# Citizens for Tax Justice (1979)

1311 L Street, NW
Suite 400
Washington, D.C. 20005
Phone: (202) 626-3780
Fax: (202) 638-3486
Internet: http://www.ctj.org

"Works to give middle- and low-income families a greater voice in the development of tax laws at the national, state, and local levels."

**PURPOSE**

7 total—6 professional; 1 support; plus 4 interns

**STAFF**

Robert S. McIntyre, director. McIntyre has been with Citizens for Tax Justice (CTJ) since 1980 and was formerly director of federal tax policy. Prior to joining CTJ, he was director of Public Citizen's Tax Reform Research Group. A graduate of the University of Pennsylvania Law School and Providence College, McIntyre also holds an LL.M. from Georgetown University Law Center.

**DIRECTOR**

501(c)(4)

**TAX STATUS**

1998—Unavailable
Proposed 1999—$400,000

**BUDGET**

Foundation grants, 50 percent; labor unions, 40 percent; membership dues, 10 percent

**FUNDING SOURCES**

Members: 2,200 individuals and 25 organizations
Branches/chapters: N/A
Affiliates: N/A

**SCOPE**

None

**PAC**

♦ Coalition forming ♦ Conferences/seminars ♦ Congressional testimony ♦ Educational foundation ♦ Internet (E-mail alerts, Web site) ♦ Internships ♦ Lobbying (federal) ♦ Local/municipal affairs ♦ Media outreach ♦ Performance ratings ♦ Polling ♦ Research

**METHOD OF OPERATION**

## CURRENT CONCERNS

♦ Opposing flat tax and national sales tax ♦ Opposing further reductions in capital gains tax ♦ Support greater progressivity ♦ Tax fairness

## PUBLICATIONS

*Building a Better Arkansas Tax System: Evaluating the Options*
*CTJ's Guide to Fair State and Local Tax Policy*
*Deep Blues in the Ocean State: Inequity and Rhode Island's Fiscal Crisis*
*Falling Short: Florida's Unfair Tax System*
*Growth and Equity: Tax Policy Challenges for the 90's*
*The Hidden Entitlements*
*How Taxes Affect Elections: The Politics of Paying for Government*
*Inequity: Indiana's Unfair Tax System and How to Fix It*
*Mass Inequity: The Massachusetts Tax System and Prospects for Reform*
*The New Jersey Tax System: It's Broken; Here's How to Fix It*
*Tax Loss Mandates: The Impact of the House-Passed "Contract" Capital Gains and Depreciation Tax Changes on Tax Revenues in the States*
*Tax Strategies for a Strong Minnesota*
*Time for a Better Deal: Fixing Mississippi's Unfair Tax System*
*Who Pays? A Distributional Analysis of the Tax Systems of All 50 States*

Also publishes fact sheets, press releases, and articles by CTJ staff

## NEWSLETTER

*CTJ Update* (9 times per year)

## CONFERENCES

None

## BOARD OF DIRECTORS

Unavailable

## EFFECTIVENESS

"Last August, with Speaker Newt Gingrich at his side, President Clinton signed the Taxpayer Relief Act of 1997, praising it as a milestone that focused most of its benefits on the middle class through a $500 child tax credit, education tax breaks and the new Roth individual retirement accounts.

"But as 174 million Americans struggle to file their 1997 income tax returns before April 15, only 1 in 17 poor and middle-class taxpayers will enjoy any tax relief. . . .

"The cut in the capital gains rate means that the wealthiest 1 percent of taxpayers will enjoy $1,189 of tax benefits in 1997 for each dollar of tax relief enjoyed by the bottom 80 percent of Americans—the 97.6 million tax-paying households that earned less than $59,000 last year, according to a new analysis of Government data by Citizens for Tax Justice, a liberal nonprofit organization in Washington that believes that the tax system favors the affluent.

"The Treasury Department did not dispute these figures. 'Our numbers are similar,' said Dan Israel, a Treasury Department spokesman. . . .

"The analysis by Citizens for Tax Justice found that the top 1 percent, who averaged $666,000 of income last year, saved an average of $7,315 in 1997 because the rates were cut. The bottom 80 percent, those making $59,000 or less, saved an average of $6." (*New York Times*, April 5, 1998)

"For the vast majority of Americans, the alternative minimum tax is much the way soccer was a few years ago—something they might have heard of, but not something they knew or cared much about. . . .

"House Ways and Means Committee Chairman Bill Archer (R-Tex.) recently called the AMT 'a tax hike time bomb,' and urged President Clinton in a letter Friday to include in next year's budget 'a proposal to prevent the alternative minimum tax from applying to an ever-growing number of taxpayers.' . . .

"Those who grasp the situation and still try to do their own taxes will face a daunting situation. The IRS has not yet addressed the question, since most of the new provisions don't take effect until next year. But Robert S. McIntyre of Citizens for Tax Justice here said he has been trying to devise a form for the child credit, and with all the phase-outs and other requirements 'it's 26 lines long and requires you to fill out the AMT' work sheet.

"McIntyre generally favors provisions that prevent well-off taxpayers from greatly reducing their taxes. But he said the AMT situation shows that whenever dollar amounts are used in the tax code, they should be indexed for inflation unless they reflect some deliberate policy, such as slowly squeezing out a deduction or other benefit." (*Washington Post*, September 21, 1997)

"Robert McIntyre of Citizens for Tax Justice, a liberal tax policy research group, argues that the Treasury doesn't go far enough in assessing the effect of tax changes for the well-to-do. He notes that the Treasury doesn't measure the impact of proposed reduction in inheritance taxes on large estates. Those changes would primarily benefit upper-income families. Under current law, estate taxes affect only the richest 2 percent of estates.

"Working with fiscal analysts at the Urban Institute and the Center on Budget and Policy Priorities, Citizens for Tax Justice has attempted to construct a more complete estimate of how tax benefits would be distributed by Republican and Democratic tax plans. The model developed by those three groups takes into account the effect of estate tax provisions, as well as proposed changes in excise taxes on airline tickets and cigarettes and other goods and services. Its conclusion: Households in the top 20 percent of the income scale would reap 87 percent of the benefits under the House tax program, and 47 percent under the Clinton plan." (*Washington Post*, July 21, 1997)

"a liberal tax policy research group" (*Washington Post*, July 21, 1997)

*POLITICAL ORIENTATION*

# Committee for a Responsible Federal Budget (1981)

220½ E Street, NE
Washington, D.C. 20002
Phone: (202) 547-4484
Fax: (202) 547-4476
Internet: crfb@aol.com

| | |
|---|---|
| **PURPOSE** | "To educate the public regarding federal budget process and issues that have significant fiscal policy impact." |
| **STAFF** | 3 total—2 professionals; 1 support |
| **DIRECTOR** | Carol Cox Wait, president. Cox Wait joined the Committee for a Responsible Federal Budget (CRFB) in 1981. Previously she served as legislative director for the Senate Budget Committee. Cox Wait is a graduate of Whittier College. |
| **TAX STATUS** | 501(c)(3) |
| **BUDGET** | 1998—Unavailable<br>Proposed 1999—Unavailable |
| **FUNDING SOURCES** | Primarily through corporate contributions; does not accept government funding |
| **SCOPE** | Members: N/A<br>Branches/chapters: N/A<br>Affiliates: N/A |
| **PAC** | None |
| **METHOD OF OPERATION** | ♦ Conferences/seminars ♦ Congressional testimony ♦ Media outreach ♦ Research ♦ Speakers program ♦ Technical assistance |

♦ Impact of changing long-term economic and demographic conditions on the federal budget ♦ Federal budget process ♦ Preparing for the retirement of the baby boom generation

## CURRENT CONCERNS

*Building a Better Future: The Exercise in Hard Choices* and *Background Booklet* (two booklets)
*Building a Better Future, The Graying of America Project Part I* (booklet)
*Exercise in Hard Choices* (workbook)
*The Graying of America, Part I*
*Health Care Reform Project*

## PUBLICATIONS

*Budget Issue Update* (periodic)

## NEWSLETTER

Annual meeting (January or February, location varies)
Exercise in Hard Choices (periodic in several locations throughout the United States)
Congressional breakfasts (1–2 per year)
Symposia (1–2 per year)

## CONFERENCES

Bill Fremzel and Timothy Perry, cochairmen; Carol Cox Wait, president; Susan Tanaka

Other members:
♦ Roy L. Ash ♦ Thomas L. Ashley ♦ Jim Cooper ♦ Willis Gradison ♦ William H. Gray III ♦ Robert S. Kerr Jr. ♦ James T. Lynn ♦ James I. McIntyre Jr. ♦ W. Henson Moore ♦ Howard Moskof ♦ Marne Obernader Jr. ♦ Rudolph G. Penner ♦ Peter G. Peterson ♦ Leland S. Prussia ♦ Robert Reischauer ♦ John J. Rhodes ♦ Charles Schultze ♦ James Slattery ♦ John W. Snow ♦ Elmer Staats ♦ David A. Stockman ♦ Robert S. Strauss ♦ Paul A. Volcker ♦ Carol Cox Wait ♦ Betty Anderson Wood ♦ Joseph R. Wright Jr.

## BOARD OF DIRECTORS

Unavailable

## EFFECTIVENESS

Unavailable

## POLITICAL ORIENTATION

# Competitive Enterprise Institute (1984)

1001 Connecticut Avenue, NW
Suite 1250
Washington, D.C. 20036
Phone: (202) 331-1010
Fax: (202) 331-0640
Internet: info@CEI.org *or* http://www.cei.org

| | |
|---|---|
| ***PURPOSE*** | "A pro-market, public policy group committed to advancing the principles of free enterprise and limited government." |
| ***STAFF*** | 29 total—17 professional; 12 support; plus 7 interns |
| ***DIRECTOR*** | Fred L. Smith Jr., president. Before founding the Competitive Enterprise Institute (CEI), Smith was a senior policy analyst with the Environmental Protection Agency, senior research economist for the Association of American Railroads, and director of government affairs for the Council for a Competitive Economy. He is a frequent guest on radio and television programs and has written numerous articles for newspapers and magazines. Smith received his undergraduate degree from Tulane University and his graduate training in economics and research at the University of Pennsylvania. |
| ***TAX STATUS*** | 501(c)(3) |
| ***BUDGET*** | Fiscal year ending September 30, 1997—$2.2 million<br>F.Y. 1998—$2.22 million<br>Proposed F.Y. 1999—$3 million |
| ***FUNDING SOURCES*** | Individual donations, 38 percent; corporate contributions, 32 percent; foundation grants, 28 percent; publications, 2 percent |
| ***SCOPE*** | Members: N/A<br>Branches/chapters: N/A<br>Affiliates: N/A |
| ***PAC*** | None |

♦ Advertisements ♦ Coalition forming ♦ Conferences/seminars ♦ Congressional testimony ♦ Congressional voting analysis ♦ Direct action ♦ Fellowships (Warren T. Brookes Fellowships in Environmental Journalism, "yearly appointments granted to journalists to enable them to research, study, and write about private and public approaches to environmental protection") ♦ Films, video, audiotapes ♦ Grassroots organizing ♦ Information clearinghouse ♦ Internet (E-mail alerts, Web site) ♦ Legislative/regulatory monitoring (federal and state) ♦ Litigation ♦ Media outreach ♦ Participation in regulatory proceedings (federal and state) ♦ Polling ♦ Research

♦ Airline deregulation ♦ Antitrust reform ♦ Banking reform ♦ Budget and tax reform ♦ Corporate Average Fuel Economy (CAFE) standards ♦ Deregulation ♦ Environmental policy ♦ Financial services and deposit insurance reform ♦ Gasoline taxes ♦ Global warming and global climate changes ♦ Intellectual property ♦ International trade ♦ Litigation on economic and constitutional issues ♦ Privatization ♦ Risk and insurance

The following is a list of sample publications:

*CAFE's "Smashing Success": The Deadly Effects of Auto Fuel Economy Standards, Current and Proposed*

*Calmer Weather: The Spin on Greenhouse Hurricanes*

*The Costs of Kyoto: Climate Change Policy Its Implications* (book or video)

*Environmental Audits: State Carrots Versus Federal Sticks in Environmental Enforcement*

*Facts, Not Fear: A Parent's Guide to Environmental Education*

*The Free Market Environmental Bibliography (Fourth Edition, 1995–1996)*

*ISO14000: Environmental Regulation by Any Other Name?*

*Michigan's Insurance Industry: New Direction*

*A National Survey: Should the Federal Government Continue to Mandate Air Bags?*

*Privileged Polluters: The Case Against Exempting Municipalities from Superfund*

*Rethinking Insurance Regulation: Volume I—Catastrophic Risks*

*Rethinking Insurance Regulation: Volume II—Perspectives on Insurance*

*Sudden Impact: The Collision Between the Air Bag Mandate and Ethics*

*Superfund XVII: The Pathology of Environmental Policy*

*Swamped: How America Achieved "No Net Loss"*

*Talking About Overregulation* (video)

*Ten Thousand Commandments: A Policymaker's Snapshot of the Federal Regulatory State, 1998 Edition*

*Treatment Delayed, Treatment Denied: Therapeutic Lag and FDA's Performance*

*What Risk? Science, Politics, & Public Health*

*The Yellowstone Affair: Environmental Protection, International Treaties and National Sovereignty*

Also publishes books, videos, testimonies, and statements

## NEWSLETTER

*CEI Update* (monthly)

## CONFERENCES

Warren T. Brookes Memorial Dinner (annual)
Other conferences are held throughout the year

## BOARD OF DIRECTORS

♦ William Dunn ♦ Michael Greve ♦ Leonard Liggio ♦ Thomas G. Moore ♦ Frances Smith ♦ Fred L. Smith Jr.

## EFFECTIVENESS

". . . [T]he Competitive Enterprise Institute . . . issued 'Ten Thousand Commandments: An Annual Policymaker's Snapshot of the Federal Regulatory State.' Its report says regulatory costs hit $688 billion in 1997, or 20 times the $34 billion federal deficit.

"Clyde Wayne Crews Jr., regulatory fellow at the CEI, said the focus is on costs, not benefits, because the parties who pay the cost of complying with rules often are not the parties benefiting from the rule. 'I think it's important to focus on compliance costs. Someone has to pay for it,' Crews said." (*Washington Post*, February 6, 1998)

## POLITICAL ORIENTATION

"a conservative think tank" (*Washington Post*, February 6, 1998)

"a nonpartisan, free-enterprise-oriented think tank" (*Washington Post*, July 20, 1996)

# The Conference Board, Inc. (1916)

845 Third Avenue
New York, New York 10022-6679
Phone: (212) 759-0900
Fax: (212) 980-7014

1755 Massachusetts Avenue, NW
Suite 300
Washington, D.C. 20036
Phone: (202) 483-0580
Fax: (202) 462-4694

Internet: info@conference-board.org *or*
http://www.conference-board.org

| | |
|---|---|
| "To improve the business enterprise system and to enhance the contribution of business to society." | ***PURPOSE*** |
| 222 professional | ***STAFF*** |
| Richard E. Cavanagh, president and chief executive officer. Before joining The Conference Board, Cavanagh was executive dean of the Kennedy School of Government at Harvard University. He was previously director of the White House Office of Management and Budget and a partner at McKinsey and Company, a business consulting firm. Cavanagh is a graduate of Wesleyan University and the Harvard Business School. | ***DIRECTOR*** |
| 501(c)(3) | ***TAX STATUS*** |
| 1998—Unavailable<br>Proposed 1999—Unavailable | ***BUDGET*** |
| Unavailable | ***FUNDING SOURCES*** |
| Members: over 2,900 organizations in more than 60 nations<br>Branches/chapters: regional offices in Chicago; San Francisco; Brussels (The Conference Board Europe); Frederiksberg, Denmark; Freiburg, Germany; London; New Delhi, India; Mexico City; Ottawa (The Conference Board of Canada); Singapore; San Roque, Spain; Warsaw; Zurich<br>Affiliates: N/A | ***SCOPE*** |

## PAC

None

## METHOD OF OPERATION

♦ Conferences/seminars ♦ International activities ♦ Library/information clearinghouse ♦ Local/municipal affairs ♦ Media outreach ♦ Surveys ♦ Research ♦ Speakers program

## CURRENT CONCERNS

♦ Business and the environment ♦ Consumer confidence ♦ Corporate governance and strategy ♦ Economics ♦ Global management ♦ Human resources and organizational effectiveness ♦ Performance excellence

## PUBLICATIONS

The following is a list of sample publications:

*Achieving Environmental Excellence*
*Benchmarking Corporate International Contributions*
*A Business Guide to Support Employee and Family Involvement in Education*
*Case Studies in Strategic Performance Measurement*
*CFO 2000: The CFO as Global Business Partner*
*The Changing Global Role of Marketing*
*The Changing Global Role of the R&D*
*Communicating Corporate Performance: A Delicate Balance*
*Compensation: Present Practices & Future Concerns*
*Computers, Productivity, and Growth: Explaining the Computer Productivity Paradox*
*Consumer Affluence: The Next Wave*
*Corporate Boards: CEO Selection and Evaluation*
*Corporate Contributions in 1996*
*The Corporate Contributions Plan: From Strategy to Budget*
*Corporate Directors' Compensation in 1997*
*Corporate Innovation in EH&S*
*Corporate Practices in Diversity Measurement*
*Corporate Practices in Management Development*
*Corporate Reengineering: Stratetgies for Growth*
*Corporate Response to HIV/AIDS*
*Corporate Volunteerism: How Families Make a Difference*
*Diversity: Business Rationale and Strategies*
*The Dynamics of Continuous Growth*
*Electronic Commerce: The Risks & Rewards*
*Energizing Performance with Communications*
*Environmental Alliances*
*Executive Annual Incentive Plans*
*The European Regional Design*
*The Evolving Role of Ethics in Business*
*Giving Strategies That Add Business Value*
*Global Quality: Competitive Successes & Challenges*
*The Globalization of U.S. Investor Activism*
*Growth: Top Priority for Future Success*
*How CEOs Drive Global Growth*
*Information Technology*
*Innovative Public-Private Partnerships: Environmental Initiatives*
*Investing in Profitable Customer Relationships*
*Leveraging Frontline Capability*

*The Link Between Corporate Governance & Performance*
*Linking Quality to Business Results*
*Making International Strategic Alliances Work*
*Managing Knowledge For Business Success*
*Managing Reputation with Image and Brands*
*Measuring Corporate Community Involvement*
*Meeting the Challenge of Global Logistics*
*Meeting the Demands of Tomorrow's Customers*
*New Corporate Performance Measures*
*The New Deal in Employment Relationships*
*North American Outlook 1997–1998*
*Organizing for Global Competitiveness*
*Partners in Strengthening Urban Communities*
*People Practices in Baldrige Companies*
*Performance Enhancement*
*Perspectives on Environmental Issues*
*Reinventing the Sales Organization*
*Rethinking Human Resources*
*Rewriting the Rules of Human Resources*
*Salary Increase Budgets 1998–1999*
*Strategic Alliances: Institutionalizing Partnering Capabilities*
*Strategic Purchasing: Sourcing for the Bottom Line*
*Strategies for Maximum Global Competitiveness*
*Top Executive Compensation in 1996*
*Top Executive Compensation: US, UK, and Canada*
*Top Executive Pay for Performance*
*Total Top Executive Compensation in 1996*
*The Value of Training in the Era of Intellectual Capital*
*Venturing in India: Opportunities and Challenges*

The Conference Board also issues Global Business White Papers, an Organization Chart Collection for 500 corporations, and periodicals including:

*Across the Board* (10 times a year)
*Business Cycle Indicators* (periodically)
*Composite Index of Leading Indicators* (periodically)
*Consumer Confidence Survey* (monthly)
*Economic Times* (10 times a year)
*HR Executive Review* (periodically)
*International Economic Scoreboard* (quarterly)
*Regional Economies and Markets* (quarterly)
*StraightTalk* (10 times a year)
*Work-Family Roundtable* (quarterly)

---

*Straight Talk* (10 issues per year)

## NEWSLETTER

---

Holds more than 110 conferences annually on topics that include: corporate communications, diversity, environmental concerns, ethics, human resources, marketing, and work and family issues

## CONFERENCES

## BOARD OF DIRECTORS

## EFFECTIVENESS

"The index of leading indicators, reported by the Conference Board, and sales of new homes, reported by the Commerce Department, both were below economists' estimates for December. The reports caused some investors who had been betting on further declines in Treasury prices after Monday's losses to buy back borrowed securities yesterday to limit their losses, causing what is known as a short-cover rally." (*New York Times*, Febuary 4, 1998)

"The Conference Board . . . said its Help Wanted Advertising Index fell in December to 87 from November's 92, but was still higher than 86 in the year-earlier month.

"The company said its survey of 51 newspapers found that help-wanted advertising rose in five regions and fell in four. The biggest declines were in the mid-Atlantic region and what the company calls West South Central. . . . The biggest increase was in the East North Central region, which includes Chicago.

" 'We see a steady, high level of job recruitment efforts,' said Ken Goldstein, a company economist. 'There are no signs it is about to drop off at the national level.'. . ." (*Wall Street Journal*, January 30, 1998)

"The fight over how software or any other product gift is valued, of course, isn't an issue of substance, but of corporate bragging rights. No one is quarreling about the gifts themselves. . . .

"Nevertheless, critics charge that technology companies' virtuous philanthropy is more like virtual philanthropy—giving that looks a lot bigger and better than it actually is. . . .

"But other big donors weren't so pleased. They have been complaining to the Conference Board, the big nonprofit business group in New York whose members are among the nation's largest corporations, that there was a lot less to such product donations than meets the eye. . . .

"Members are arguing whether the Conference Board's contributions council, which tracks corporate giving, should set standards for valuing gifts of products.

" 'Frankly, we don't have a clue what companies are really giving away,' says Curt Weeden, corporate-giving chief for Johnson & Johnson and an influential member of the council. 'Banks, insurance companies and investment firms are really ticked off, saying, 'You guys giving away your own products are beating your chests and making us look like skinflints,' he says." (*Wall Street Journal*, September 9, 1997)

"Technology have-nots are the target of a new partnership program.

"The Conference Board, a business-research group in New York, spearheads the Digital Partnerships Program, a two-year project aimed at enhancing the role of technology companies in community economic development. Funded by the Ford Foundation and others, the project will work with executives and community groups to identify business ventures that will both reduce poverty and enhance business." (*Wall Street Journal*, December 18, 1997)

---

"a business research firm" (*Wall Street Journal*, January 30, 1998)

"nonpartisan" (*National Journal*, September 18, 1993)

## POLITICAL ORIENTATION

# Council on Competitiveness (1986)

1401 H Street, NW
Suite 650
Washington, D.C. 20005
Phone: (202) 682-4292
Fax: (202) 682-5150
Internet: council@compete.org *or* http://www.compete.org

**PURPOSE**

Is "a nonpartisan, nonprofit forum of chief executives from the business, university, and labor communities working together to set a national action agenda for U.S. leadership in global markets, technological innovation, and education training that will raise the standard of living of all Americans."

**STAFF**

15 total—10 professional; 5 support

**DIRECTOR**

John N. Yochelson, president. Prior to becoming president of the council in 1995, Yochelson was senior vice president at the Center for Strategic and International Studies (CSIS), where he was responsible for policy research on international trade, investment, and finance. He created the CSIS program in international business and economics. He also launched the bipartisan Strengthening of America Commission co-chaired by Senators Pete Domenici (R-N.M.) and Sam Nunn (D-Ga.) and managed the CSIS International Councillors under the chairmanship of Henry Kissinger. Yochelson received a bachelor's degree from Yale University and a master's degree from the Woodrow Wilson School of Princeton University. He served in the U.S. Army from 1967–1970.

**TAX STATUS**

501(c)(3)

**BUDGET**

1998—Unavailable
Proposed 1999—Unavailable

**FUNDING SOURCES**

Membership dues, foundations, and other granting institutions

**SCOPE**

Members: More than 150 chief executives from corporations, labor unions, and academia

Branches/chapters: N/A

Affiliates: More than 40 prominent research institutions, professional societies, and trade associations serve as National Affiliates

None

♦ Conferences/seminars ♦ Congressional testimony ♦ Internet (Web site) ♦ Legislative/regulatory monitoring (federal) ♦ Media outreach ♦ Research

*METHOD OF OPERATION*

Human resources and education reform
Role of government, industry, and academia in research and development of technology

*CURRENT CONCERNS*

*Breaking the Barriers to the National Information Infrastructure*
*Capital Choices: Changing the Way America Invests in Industry*
*Competing Through Innovation: A Report of the National Innovation Summit*
*Competition Policy: Unlocking the National Information Infrastructure*
*Competitiveness Index* (annual)
*Critical Technologies Update 1994*
*Economic Security: The Dollar$ and Sense of U.S. Foreign Policy*
*Elevating the Skills of the American Workforce*
*Endless Frontier, Limited Resources: U.S. R&D Policy for Competitiveness*
*Gaining New Ground: Technology Priorities for America's Future*
*Highway to Health: Transforming U.S. Health Care in the Information Age*
*Human Resources Competitiveness Profile*
*Industry as a Customer of the Federal Laboratories*
*Roadmap for Results: Trade Policy, Technology and American Competitiveness*
*Winning the Skills Race*

Also publishes a policy studies series

*PUBLICATIONS*

*Challenges* (bimonthly)

*NEWSLETTER*

Sponsors meetings for members only

*CONFERENCES*

William R. Hambrecht, chairman; Charles M. Vest, university vice chairman; Jack Sheinkman, labor vice chairman; Donald R. Bell and Joseph T. Gorman, co-industry vice chairmen

Other executive committee members:
♦ F. Duane Ackerman ♦ Paul A. Allaire ♦ Richard C. Atkinson ♦ Linda Chavez-Thompson ♦ G. Wayne Clough ♦ Thomas E. Everhart ♦ Sandra Feldman ♦ George M.C. Fisher ♦ Raymond V. Gilmartin ♦ Katharine Graham ♦ Jerry J. Jasinowski ♦ Thomas G. Labrecque ♦ Peter Likins ♦ Richard A. McGinn ♦ Victor E. Millar ♦ Thomas J. Murrin ♦ Richard C. Notebaert ♦ Michael E. Porter ♦ Heinz C. Prechter ♦ Ray Stata ♦ William C. Steere Jr. ♦ Gary L. Tooker ♦ John A. Young

*BOARD OF DIRECTORS*

## EFFECTIVENESS

"For a long while, no one worried seriously about America's ability to innovate. In the 1980s, Japanese rivals were outflanking U.S. companies in industry after industry. Today, America is the envy of the world, in software, in networking technologies, in much of life sciences and in other emerging industries. Even some mature industries have been revitalized. The rise of the Internet is probably the most potent symbol of America's technical renaissance in the 1990s. . . .

"All this might have been the backdrop for yet another round of American chest-thumping, but triumphalism wasn't the prevailing mood the other day at the Massachusetts Institute of Technology, where 150 business, government and educational leaders assembled for a conference on the state of American innovation. They all acknowledged the good fortune of the moment. . . .

"But just how likely is the U.S. to be dislodged from its current perch? That is a tough question. To those with a vested interest in heavy spending for government-sponsored science programs, the glass will probably always be half-empty; alarmism goes with the territory. Moreover, the conference was organized by the Council on Competitiveness, a business-funded nonprofit group that a decade ago won praise for benchmarking U.S. industrial decline in high technology and remains vigilant in looking for chinks in the armor." (*Wall Street Journal*, March 23, 1998)

## POLITICAL ORIENTATION

Unavailable

# Families and Work Institute (1989)

330 Seventh Avenue
14th Floor
New York, New York 10001
Phone: (212) 465-2044
Fax: (212) 465-8637
Internet: http://www.familiesandworkinst.org

| | |
|---|---|
| "A center for policy and worksite research on the changing workforce and changing family/personal lives." | *PURPOSE* |
| 16 full-time; plus 2 part-time; 2 interns; 1 consultant; 1 research fellow | *STAFF* |
| Ellen Galinsky, president. Galinsky was previously on the faculty of Bank Street College of Education. She is a past president of the National Association for the Education of Young Children. Galinsky has served on numerous task forces and advisory committees for the state of New York, the U.S. Health and Human Service Department, and the U.S. Labor Department. She is an author of more than 20 books. She received her B.A. from Vassar College and her M.S. from Bank Street College. | *DIRECTORS* |
| 501(c)(3) | *TAX STATUS* |
| 1998—Unavailable<br>Proposed 1999—Unavailable | *BUDGET* |
| Unavailable | *FUNDING SOURCES* |
| Members: N/A<br>Branches/chapters: N/A<br>Affiliates: N/A | *SCOPE* |
| None | *PAC* |

| | |
|---|---|
| *METHOD OF OPERATION* | ◆ Conferences/seminars ◆ Congressional testimony ◆ Internet (Web site) ◆ Grassroots organizing ◆ Media outreach ◆ Mediation ◆ Performance ratings ◆ Polls and surveys ◆ Research ◆ Speakers program ◆ Technical assistance ◆ Training |
| *CURRENT CONCERNS* | ◆ Early childhood development ◆ Low-income employees and work-family concerns ◆ Quality and availability of child and elder care ◆ Quality of work and its effect on employees ◆ Support for men's involvment in child rearing ◆ Trends in employers' work-life programs, policies, and initiatives ◆ Welfare to work |
| *PUBLICATIONS* | *The 1997 National Study of the Changing Workforce*<br>*The Changing Employer-Employee Contract: The Role of Work-Family Issues*<br>*The Changing Workforce: Highlights from the National Study*<br>*Child Care Aware: A Guide to Promoting Professional Development in Family Child Care*<br>*College and University Guide to Work-Family Programs*<br>*Community Mobilization: Strategies to Support Young Children and Their Families*<br>*Corporate Reference Guide to Work-Family Programs*<br>*An Evaluation of Johnson & Johnson's Balancing Work and Family Program*<br>*An Examination of the Impact of Family-Friendly Policies on the Glass Ceiling*<br>*The Family Child Care Training Study: Highlights of Findings*<br>*The Family-Friendly Employer: Examples from Europe*<br>*The Florida Child Care Quality Improvement Study: 1996 Report*<br>*The Flordia Child Care Quality Improvement Study: Interim Report*<br>*Getting Men Involved: Strategies for Early Childhood Programs*<br>*The Implementation of Flexible Time and Leave Policies: Observations from Employers*<br>*New Expectations: Community Strategies for Responsible Fatherhood*<br>*Parental Leave and Productivity: Current Research*<br>*Rethinking the Brian: New Insights into Early Development*<br>*The Role of Child Care Centers in the Lives of Parents*<br>*The Study of Children in Family Child Care and Relative Care: Highlights of Findings*<br>*Women: The New Providers*<br>*Working Fathers: New Strategies for Balancing Work and Family* |
| *NEWSLETTER* | None |
| *CONFERENCES* | Annual work and family conference (co-sponsored with The Conference Board; offered once on each coast)<br>Other occasional seminars |
| *BOARD OF DIRECTORS* | Unavailable |

"... The National Study of the Changing Workforce, released by the Families and Work Institute this week, reached the same conclusion. The study was compiled from interviews with 2,877 employees over the age of 18 and provides one of the most comprehensive looks at today's workplace culture, experts say. The findings confirm some spreading notions about the nature of workers in the 1990s, while also debunking a few prevalent myths. Additionally, the study offers a historical perspective by comparing its findings to similar studies conducted in 1992 and 1977.

" 'The most incredible thing that the study demonstrates is that having [worker-friendly] programs is really important for profitability,' said Bernie Milano, partner in charge of work-life programs at KPMG Peat Marwick LLP, which was one of the corporate sponsors of the study. 'It takes it out of the realm of human resources programs and moves it to the bottom line.'..." (*Washington Post*, April 19, 1998)

"At a time when policy makers are discussing ways to improve the quality of child care, a new study by the Families and Work Institute has found that children fared better in day care when the teacher-to-child ratios were lowered.

"When each teacher was responsible for fewer children, the study found, the children spent more time in learning activities and engaged in more complex play. They were also more securely attached to their teachers, more proficient in language, and less likely to have behavioral problems like aggression or hyperactivity....

" 'Now there is general agreement that the most important factor is the teacher's relationship with the child, that the teacher must be responsive,' said Ellen Galinsky, president of the institute, a research organization in New York.

"The institute's study, Ms. Galinsky said, was part of a new wave of research, going beyond the examination of the overall impact of child care to assess what difference it makes to children when particular elements of care are changed...." (*New York Times*, March 7, 1998)

"Recent studies by the University of Colorado, the Families and Work Institute of New York, and the National Institute of Child Health and Development, for example, have concluded that more than 80 percent of day care in child-care centers is inadequate and that, for infants, out-of-home care, especially day-care centers, tend to be inferior to parental care...." (*Washington Post*, October 19, 1997)

Unavailable

# National Association of Manufacturers (1895)

1331 Pennsylvania Avenue, NW
Washington, D.C. 20004-1790
Phone: (202) 637-3000
Fax: (202) 637-3182
Internet: http://www.nam.org

## PURPOSE

"To enhance the competitiveness of manufacturers and improve living standards for working Americans by shaping a legislative and regulatory environment conducive to industrial development and economic growth, and to increase understanding among policy-makers, the media, and the general public about the importance of manufacturing to U.S. economic strength."

## STAFF

180 total—90 professional; 90 support; plus interns

## DIRECTOR

Jerry J. Jasinowski, president. Jasinowski became president of the National Association of Manufacturers (NAM) in 1990 after serving as its executive vice president and chief economist. Prior to joining the NAM, Jasinowski served as assistant secretary for policy at the U.S. Commerce Department and was the director of the economic transition group for the Treasury, Commerce, and Labor departments; the Council of Economic Advisors; and the Federal Reserve during the Carter administration. Jasinowski received an A.B. in economics from Indiana University and a master's degree in economics from Columbia University. He is a graduate of Harvard Business School's Advanced Management Program.

## TAX STATUS

501(c)(6)

## BUDGET

1998—Unavailable
Proposed 1999—Unavailable

## FUNDING SOURCES

Membership, 86 percent; meetings, publications, and investments, 14 percent

## SCOPE

Members: 14,000 companies and subsidiaries
Branches/chapters: National Division plus 10 regional offices
Affiliates: Association Council, Employer Association Group, The Manufacturing Institute, National Industrial Council, State Associations Group

None

♦ Advertisements ♦ Awards program ♦ Coalition forming ♦ Conferences/seminars ♦ Congressional testimony ♦ Congressional voting analysis ♦ Educational programs in schools ♦ Films/video/audiotapes ♦ Grassroots organizing ♦ International activities ♦ Internet (electronic bulletin boards, Web site) ♦ Legislative/regulatory monitoring (federal) ♦ Litigation ♦ Lobbying (federal and grassroots) ♦ Media outreach ♦ Participation in regulatory proceedings (federal) ♦ Polling ♦ Product merchandising ♦ Research ♦ Speakers program ♦ Telecommunications services (Hotline: [800] USA-XPORT) ♦ Television and radio production ♦ Voting records

♦ Estate taxes ♦ Exports/international trade ♦ Federal budget policy ♦ Global competitiveness ♦ Health care costs and quality ♦ Immigration reform ♦ Legal system reform ♦ Mandated employee benefits ♦ Regulatory reform ♦ Social Security reform ♦ Tax reform ♦ Workforce training and education

The following is a list of sample publications:

*The 1997 Association Council Directory*
*America's Best: Industry Week's Guide to World-Class Manufacturing Plants*
*Communications and Climate Building in the Union-Free Environment*
*Complying with the ADA: A Small Business Guide to Hiring and Employing the Disabled*
*Corporate Environmental Strategy: The Avalanche of Change Since Bhopal*
*Deskbook on Corporate Criminal Law and Compliance*
*Elimination of the Lobbying Deduction: The NAM Compliance Manual for Corporate and Association Executives*
*Employee Evaluation Reference Guide*
*Employer's Unemployment Compensation Cost Control Handbook*
*Employer's Workers' Compensation Cost Control Handbook*
*Employment-Labor Law Audit, 1998 Edition*
*Ernst & Young Tax Guide 1997*
*Export Sales and Marketing Manual*
*The Facts About Modern Manufacturing*
*Free Money From the Federal Government*
*Highlights of Federal Unemployment Compensation Laws*
*How to Comply With Federal Employee Laws*
*How to Survive Superfund: A 1990s Communications Guide*
*Implementing Activity-Based Management in Daily Operations*
*Making it in America*
*A Manufacturing CEO's Secret Tips for Improving Profit*
*Manufacturing in America: A Legacy of Excellence*
*Manufacturing Trade Associations: Operating Ratio Report*
*Media Relations in Your Spare Time: A Step-by-Step Guide for Anyone in Business*
*New Estimates of the Cost of Legal Services*
*Product Liability in the United States*

*Products Liability Law, Loss Control and Insurance*
*RCRA Contingency Plan: Guidance Manual*
*Self-Defense Finance for Small Business*
*SOS: Navigating the New Corporate Sentencing Guidelines*
*Spill Prevention, Control and Countermeasures Plan*
*Storm Water Pollution Prevention Plan: Guidance Manual*
*Technology on the Factor Floor II: Benchmarking Manufacturing Technology in the United States*
*Union Organizing 101: A Whole New Ballgame*
*The Workforce Challenges of the 21st Century*
*Worldtariff: Custom Tariff Guidebook*

## NEWSLETTER

Unavailable

## CONFERENCES

Sponsors various conferences

## BOARD OF DIRECTORS

Earnest W. Deavenport Jr., chairman; William J. Hudson, vice chairman; Jerry J. Jasinowski, president

Other members:
◆ Ralph H. Anderson ◆ Frank A. Archinaco ◆ Brian R. Baker ◆ Dexter F. Baker ◆ Robert L. Barnett ◆ Warren L. Batts ◆ Roger C. Beach ◆ Donald Bender ◆ Bruce Bennett ◆ Georgia Berner ◆ Robert Black ◆ William H. Blair ◆ Jeffrey L. Bluestein ◆ Harold F. Boardman Jr. ◆ Douglas L. Boles ◆ Richard T. Bourns ◆ John D. Bowlin ◆ James W. Bradford Jr. ◆ Larry D. Brady ◆ Alton J. Brann ◆ Duane E. Brasch ◆ Peter C. Browing ◆ Wendell F. Bueche ◆ William F. Buehler ◆ Ronald D. Bullock ◆ Calvin A. Campbell Jr. ◆ Robert H. Campbell ◆ James R. Carlson ◆ Roger T. Caron ◆ W. Rowell Chase ◆ Kenneth Churchill ◆ Anthony Ciorciari ◆ Robert Cizik ◆ Lawrence W. Clarkson ◆ Arthur D. Collins ◆ John F. Cooke ◆ Jeffrey H. Coors ◆ Robert A. Cornog ◆ John D. Correnti ◆ Steven A. Cossé ◆ Dennis C. Cuneo ◆ Marc S. Czachorski ◆ C. Frederick Dahlberg Jr. ◆ John R. Danzeisen ◆ Donald W. Davis ◆ Robert A. Davis ◆ Earlyn Dean ◆ Earnest W. Deavenport Jr. ◆ Thomas A. Decker ◆ Robert F. Dee ◆ J. Richard Derickson ◆ Vincent G. De Stefano ◆ Richard M. DeVos Jr. ◆ Gary DiCamillo ◆ Robert E. DiCenso ◆ George S. Dibble Jr. ◆ Joe K. Donald ◆ Robert W. Drewes ◆ James M. Dunstan ◆ Edward J. Dwyer ◆ Michael L. Eagle ◆ Thomas A. Ebert ◆ William J. Eisenman ◆ Paul Eisman ◆ Irl F. Engelhardt ◆ Sheldon R. Erikson ◆ Gorton M. Evans ◆ Richard D. Farman ◆ Giannantio Ferrari ◆ John W. Fisher ◆ Donald V. Fites ◆ J. Michael Fitzpatrick ◆ William D. Ford ◆ Fred J. Fowler ◆ David Freeman ◆ Robert P. Gannon ◆ John C. Garrett ◆ Morman E. Garrity ◆ Robert A. Garvey ◆ Donald A. Gaudion ◆ Stanley C. Gault ◆ Murray A. Gerber ◆ Joseph E. Gonzalez Jr. ◆ Jeffery T. Grade ◆ Robert J. Grow ◆ Werner P. Gullander ◆ Leonard A. Hadley ◆ J. Michael Hagan ◆ Ralph F. Hake ◆ Larry Hambly ◆ James D. Hanauer ◆ James S. Haney ◆ Thomas E. Hannah ◆ Roger A. Hannay ◆ James F. Hardymon ◆ Ruth R. Harkin ◆ John T. Harley ◆ Philip M. Hartung ◆ Derek C. Hathaway ◆ Charles A. Hayes Jr. ◆ Mark Hazelwood ◆ William F. Hecht ◆ James B. Henderson ◆

Herbert L. Henkel ♦ Ted M. Henry ♦ Edward H. Herdery ♦ William C. Hilleary ♦ Richard E. Hockert ♦ Joni Hodgson ♦ John R. Hodowal ♦ John R. Horne ♦ Richard F. Hrdlicka ♦ Steven M. Hroneo ♦ S. Michael Hudson ♦ Wendell P. Hurlbut ♦ Phillip W. Hussey Jr. ♦ Collie Hutter ♦ Manuel J. Iraola ♦ J.L. Jackson ♦ Jerry D. Jackson ♦ Robert H. Jenkins ♦ Charles S. Johnson ♦ Gerald E. Johnston ♦ Rudolph G. Johnstone Jr. ♦ Frank Jones ♦ Kathy H. Jones ♦ Joseph J. Kaminski ♦ Richard C. Kautz ♦ Terry Kautz ♦ Peter-Hans Keilbach ♦ Bernard J. Kelley ♦ J. Fredrick Kelly Jr. ♦ J. Peter Kelly ♦ E. Douglas Kenna ♦ James H. Keyes ♦ W. Leo Kiely III ♦ Richard Korpan ♦ Robert E. Koski ♦ John A. Krol ♦ Steven G. Lamb ♦ Stephen K. Lambright ♦ William M. Landuyt ♦ Scot H. Laney ♦ R. Heath Larry ♦ William Laule ♦ Robert Lawless ♦ William B. Lawrence ♦ Ken R. LeSuer ♦ D.L. Lemmon ♦ Gerry Letendre ♦ H. William Litchtenberger ♦ Charles E. Long ♦ John Mdallroy ♦ Sven-Peter Mannsfeld ♦ R.G. McBride ♦ Mike McCarty ♦ Tom J. McDaniel ♦ Daniel P. McGregor ♦ Henry A. McKinnell ♦ Dana G. Mead ♦ Mark A. Medley ♦ James P. Melican ♦ Douglas L. Meyer ♦ James M. Micali ♦ Jack D. Michaels ♦ David A. Miller ♦ Ronald A. Mitsch ♦ Clyde R. Moore ♦ Gary B. Moore ♦ Gerd D. Mueller ♦ James J. Mulva ♦ Robert E. Nason ♦ Erik G. Nelson ♦ Larry Nichols ♦ Mack G. Nichols ♦ J. Tracy O'Rourke ♦ Robert J. O'Toole ♦ Stanley C. Pace ♦ Michael D. Parker ♦ John W. Paxton ♦ D.P. Payne ♦ George A. Peapples ♦ Roger P. Penny ♦ Steven W. Percy ♦ Peter J. Pestillo ♦ Donald K. Peterson ♦ Douglas K. Pinner Jr. ♦ Victor T. Podd ♦ John R. Price Jr. ♦ Robert Pritzker ♦ Anthony F. Raimondo ♦ Donald D. Rainville ♦ Robert J. Ratliff ♦ Burt F. Raynes ♦ Bernard G. Rethore ♦ Robert L. Rich ♦ Lisa A. Rickard ♦ Richard K. Riederer ♦ James M. Ringler ♦ J. Lawrence Robinson ♦ James E. Rogers ♦ Carole Rogin ♦ Henry A. Rosenberg Jr. ♦ Ronald P. Sandmeyer Jr. ♦ Lalit Sarin ♦ Michael E. Shannon ♦ William J. Sharp ♦ Wilfred G. Shedd ♦ George A. Sissel ♦ Jeffrey K. Skilling ♦ Adrian J.R. Smith ♦ Robert M. Spears ♦ Ruth Stafford ♦ Warren Staley ♦ Thomas T. Stallkamp ♦ Gordon L. Stauffer ♦ Albert E. Suter ♦ Mitsunobu Takeuchi ♦ William A. Taylor III ♦ Richard F. Teerlink ♦ Michael Thieneman ♦ C. Stephen Thomas ♦ Ronald L. Thompson ♦ W.R. Timken Jr. ♦ J. Frank Travis ♦ Philip M. Tredway ♦ Alexander B. Trowbridge ♦ Jean-Paul Valles ♦ Gerlad B. Vernon ♦ Michael A. Vokema ♦ Arthur D. Wainwright ♦ Charles B. Walker ♦ Susan Walter ♦ Chet Walthall ♦ Jonathan P. Ward ♦ Maurice J. Wanock ♦ Douglas G. Watson ♦ Kenneth R. Weisshaar ♦ Harry K. Wells ♦ Robert H. West ♦ Bill Williams Jr. ♦ Luke G. Williams ♦ Philip C. Wolf ♦ Stephen R. Wood ♦ Paul A. Yhouse ♦ Larry D. Yost

## EFFECTIVENESS

"No one was more surprised by the latest television ad from the National Association of Manufacturers than Sen. Edward M. Kennedy (D-Mass.).

"The commercial uses footage of John F. Kennedy as it touts the Republican tax cut plan in Congress. In the black-and-white footage from 1963, the late president almost appears to be a pitchman for the GOP proposal, saying, 'I strongly urge you to support this bill for your family's sake and for your country's sake.' The senator rushed out a terse statement, saying, 'There is not a chance in the world that President Kennedy would support the unfair Republican tax cut. NAM is wasting its money.'...

"The NAM campaign comes as the White House and Congress are hashing out competing versions of a $135 billion tax cut, with the Democrats accusing GOP leaders of tilting toward the wealthy. Other Republicans have invoked President Kennedy's support for a 1961 tax cut in making their case for the current legislation, but this is the first time his image and voice have been appropriated.

"[NAM senior vice president Paul] Huard says the commercial, which began in Washington last weekend, will air nationally and in 20 congressional districts in which the AFL-CIO has been running ads attacking the GOP plan." (*Washington Post*, July 20, 1997)

"Business seeks to enlist backyard chefs to fight clean-air rules.

"The National Association of Manufacturers leads a drive to protect the 'little guy and his freedom' against EPA proposals. The NAM's strategy team, including oil company lobbyists, sends small-business owners to Capitol Hill to complain. Its ally, Citizens for a Sound Economy, mounts a media campaign saying the rules might ban outdoor barbecues and July 4th fireworks.

"EPA chief Carol Browner calls the claims false 'scare tactics.' The talk of a fireworks ban seems to be based on an off-hand joke by a researcher. The NAM's internal files show that in meetings with 137 House members, many Democrats were uncertain about joining the fight, but many Republicans earned the group's top rating: 'Fine-coached on media'. . . ." (*Wall Street Journal*, April 4, 1997)

"The U.S. is too quick to impose unilateral economic sanctions against other countries, and most of those sanctions don't work, according to a report from the National Association of Manufacturers.

"The association found that from 1993 to 1996, 61 U.S. laws and executive actions were enacted targeting foreign countries for various grievances, including human-rights abuses and drug-trafficking. Thirty-five countries were specifically targeted. 'In only a handful could an arguable claim be made that the sanctions changed the behavior of the targeted government,' the report said. . . ." (*Wall Street Journal*, March 5, 1997)

"A debate is gathering steam over how fast the economy can grow without accelerating inflation. An increasingly vocal side in the debate is arguing it's time to gamble on faster growth. . . .

"The most vocal of the growth advocates is the NAM. 'Our failure to create adequate demand in the economy is preventing us from even approaching the conventional measure of 2.5% growth,' says NAM President Jerry Jasinowski. He believes the economy's potential growth rate consistent with stable inflation is about 3% or above, not 2.5%.

"Economists derive the potential growth rate by adding the annual rate of labor force growth to the annual productivity rate. The NAM agrees the labor force is growing at about 1.2% annually. But it finds fault with the government's measure of productivity, saying there's higher service-sector productivity. That would mean the economy can grow faster without adding jobs that bring inflation." (*Wall Street Journal*, February 26, 1996)

## POLITICAL ORIENTATION

Unavailable

# National Federation of Independent Business (1943)

53 Century Boulevard
Suite 300
Nashville, Tennessee 37214
Phone: (615) 872-5800
Fax: (615) 872-5899

600 Maryland Avenue, SW
Suite 700
Washington, D.C. 20024
Phone: (202) 554-9000
Fax: (202) 554-0496

Internet: http://www.nfibonline.com *or* comments@nfibonline.com

---

"To influence public policy at the state and federal levels for the benefit of small and independent business in America."

**PURPOSE**

---

1,000 total

**STAFF**

---

Jack Faris, president and chief executive officer. Before becoming president of the National Federation of Independent Business (NFIB), Faris ran his own consulting firm, working primarily with small and independent businesses. He has also worked in the construction and banking industries. Faris was campaign finance director for Tennessee governor Lamar Alexander in 1978 and subsequently served as executive director of the Republican National Finance Committee. He is past president of the Nashville Rotary Club and a national board member for Junior Achievement. Faris is a graduate of David Lipscomb University.

**DIRECTOR**

---

501(c)(6)

**TAX STATUS**

---

1997—$72 million
1998—Unavailable
Proposed 1999—Unavailable

**BUDGET**

---

Membership dues

**FUNDING SOURCES**

---

Members: 600,000 business owners
Branches/chapters: Legislative offices in 50 states
Affiliate: NFIB Education Foundation, a 501(c)(3) organization

**SCOPE**

---

| **PAC** | NFIB Safe Trust Political Action Committee |
| --- | --- |

| **METHOD OF OPERATION** | ◆ Awards programs (Guardian of Small Business Awards—in 1994, NFIB recognized approximately 239 members of Congress "who proved by their voting records that they supported a large majority of NFIB-member positions during the 103rd Congress.") ◆ Campaign contributions ◆ Coalition forming ◆ Conferences/seminars ◆ Congressional testimony ◆ Congressional voting analysis ◆ Educational foundation ◆ Grassroots organizing ◆ International activities ◆ Legislative/regulatory monitoring (federal and state) ◆ Lobbying (federal, state, and grassroots) ◆ Media outreach ◆ Participation in regulatory proceedings (federal and state) ◆ Research |
| --- | --- |

| **CURRENT CONCERNS** | ◆ Balancing the federal budget ◆ Death tax repeal ◆ Government mandates ◆ Health care reform ◆ Legal reform ◆ Regulatory reform ◆ Superfund reform ◆ Tax relief and simplification ◆ Wage reform |
| --- | --- |

| **PUBLICATIONS** | *The Economic Impact of Mandated Family Leave on Small Businesses and Their Employees* (NFIB Foundation)<br>*Editor's Guide to Small Business*<br>*How Congress Voted*<br>*NFIB Small Business Agenda*<br>*Small Business Economic Trends*<br>*Small Business Problems and Priorities* (NFIB Foundation)<br>*Small Business Financial Resource Guide*<br>*Small Business Matters*<br>*Small Business Starts and Stops*<br>*Small Business: The Year 2000 and Beyond* (NFIB Foundation)<br>*The Taxes Small Businesses Pay* (NFIB Foundation) |
| --- | --- |

| **NEWSLETTER** | *Capitol Coverage Newsletter* (6 times a year)<br>*IB Magazine* (6 times a year)<br>*NFIB Mandate Ballot/State Ballot* (issues polling; 6 times a year) |
| --- | --- |

| **CONFERENCES** | National Leadership Conference<br>Congressional Small Business Summit (biennial) |
| --- | --- |

| **BOARD OF DIRECTORS** | Jack Faris, president and chief executive officer; Richard S. Briggs, secretary<br><br>Other members:<br>◆ Susan A. Andrews ◆ Noelle Clark ◆ Joe Greenstreet ◆ James S. Herr ◆ Mary Kelley ◆ Eamonn McGeady ◆ Tom Musser ◆ Richard L. Reinhardt ◆ Sid Small ◆ William G. Thornton, Jr. ◆ Pete Van de Putte ◆ Lu Ann Walker-Maddox |
| --- | --- |

"Rep. Bill Archer's tax package came under attack from both President Clinton and from senior GOP leaders, who are nervous about the Ways and Means chairman's proposed repeal of the corporate minimum tax. . . .

"Meanwhile, opposition grew within the House Republican leadership to key planks of the measure. At a late-afternoon meeting, Rep. John Boehner of Ohio, the House's fourth-ranking Republican, urged that the measure's phaseout of the minimum tax be dropped. The tax was created in 1986 to ensure no profit-making enterprise avoids federal tax liability.

"Backing Mr. Boehner and others is the politically powerful small-business lobby, led by the National Federation of Independent Businesses, which is proposing to take the $17.3 billion that repealing the minimum tax would cost over five years and devote the money to estate-tax cuts.

"Overall, Mr. Archer's bill would cut taxes by $135 billion over five years, while raising $47 billion in new revenue. The Texas Republican will put the measure before the House Ways and Means Committee. . . ." (*Wall Street Journal*, June 11, 1997)

"Advocates for California's working poor have apparently collected enough signatures to get their initiative to sharply raise the minimum wage onto the state's November ballot. The deadline for submitting roughly 500,000 valid signatures isn't until next week, but organizers of a coalition of labor unions and community groups called the Livable Wage Campaign here say they already have collected more than 600,000 signatures. . . .

"Business lobbies in California, which oppose an increase in the state's minimum wage of $4.25 an hour, concede that the measure will make the ballot. They are already bracing themselves for a tough fight against a measure that would raise the minimum wage to $5.75 an hour over two years.

" 'It is indeed an uphill battle to defeat this,' said Martyn B. Hopper, state director for the National Federation of Independent Businesses . . . that says it has 44,000 members in the state. Mr. Hopper predicted that employer interests would have to spend 'at least $10 million to defeat [the initiative], and that's a conservative figure.' " (*Wall Street Journal*, April 10, 1996)

"conservative" (*Wall Street Journal*, April 10, 1996)

# National Taxpayers Union (1969)

108 North Alfred Street
Alexandria, Virginia 22314
Phone: (703) 683-5700
Fax: (703) 683-5722
Internet: ntu@townhall.com *or* http://www.ntu.org

| | |
|---|---|
| **PURPOSE** | "Works for constitutional limits on spending, debt and taxes, lower taxes, less wasteful spending, taxpayer rights, and accountability from elected officials at all levels of government." |
| **STAFF** | 15 total—9 professional; 6 support; 2 part-time; plus volunteers and interns |
| **DIRECTOR** | John E. Berthoud, president and chief executive officer. Berthoud also is an adjunct lecturer at George Washington Universiy. Before taking the position as president of the National Taxpayers Union, Berthoud was vice president of the Alexis de Tocqueville Institution. Prior to that, he was legislative director for Tax and Fiscal Policy at the American Legislative Exchange Council. Berthoud received his Ph.D. from Yale University, M.A. in International Affairs from Columbia University, and B.A. from Georgetown University. |
| **TAX STATUS** | 501(c)(4) |
| **BUDGET** | 1997—$3 million<br>1998—$3.5 million<br>Proposed 1999—$4 million |
| **FUNDING SOURCES** | Membership dues and contributions, 95 percent; dividends, royalties, rental income, and other sources, 5 percent |
| **SCOPE** | Members: 300,000<br>Branches/chapters: NTU works closely with over 900 independent state and local organizations and individuals<br>Affiliate: National Taxpayers Union Foundation, a 501(c)(3) organization |
| **PAC** | National Taxpayers Union Campaign Fund |

♦ Advertisements ♦ Awards program ♦ Campaign contributions ♦ Coalition forming ♦ Conferences/seminars ♦ Congressional testimony ♦ Congressional voting analysis ♦ Demonstrations ♦ Direct action ♦ Electoral politics ♦ Films/video/audiotapes ♦ Grantmaking ♦ Grassroots organizing ♦ Initiative/referendum campaigns ♦ International activities ♦ Internet ♦ Legislative regulatory monitoring (federal and state) ♦ Library/information clearinghouse ♦ Litigation ♦ Lobbying (federal, state, and grassroots) ♦ Media outreach ♦ Performance ratings ♦ Polling ♦ Research ♦ Telecommunications services (databases, electronic bulletin boards, mailing lists) ♦ Training and technical assistance ♦ Voting records

♦ Balanced Budget Amendment ♦ Congressional pay and perks ♦ Deregulation ♦ IRS reform ♦ Internet taxation ♦ Limiting the growth of entitlements ♦ Limiting taxpayer exposure to financial industry bail-out ♦ Line-item veto ♦ Privatization ♦ Spending reform ♦ State and local issues ♦ Tax Limitation Amendment ♦ Term limits

*Amendment to the Constitution*
*The Balanced Budget Amendment*
*A Call for Revolution*
*A Compelling Case for a Constitutional Amendment to Balance the Budget and Limit Taxes*
*Complete NTU Ratings and List of Tax Votes*
*Congressional Spending Study* (annual)
*Entitlements and the Aging of America*
*The Government Racket*
*The Hoax of a "Runaway" Constitutional Convention*
*House Office Expenditure Report*
*How to Fight Property Taxes*
*The Legal Authority of the Treasury to Promulgate a Regulation Providing Indexation of Capital Gains*
*List of Tax Votes*
*Losing Ground: American Social Policy*
*NTU Rating of Congress*
*Save a Fortune*
*Survey on Retirement Confidence*
*The Taxpayer's IRS Survival Manual*
*When You Owe the IRS*
*Why Term Limits? Because They Have it Coming!*
*Why We Need a Separate Constitutional Convention Now*
Also publishes brochures

*Capital Ideas* (bimonthly)
*Dollars & Sense* (bimonthly)
*Tax Savings Report* (published 10 times a year)

National Taxpayers Conference (biennial)

## BOARD OF DIRECTORS

## EFFECTIVENESS

"A national taxpayers group said yesterday that it will help citizen activists in Loudoun County. . . .

"The National Taxpayers Union said it will rally the group's 7,000 members in Virginia and organize rallies, demonstrations and a statewide radio talk show campaign. The Loudoun group . . . says supervisors had no authority to enter into a lease-purchase agreement on the building a year after voters rejected a $35.5 million bond referendum for the project." (*Washington Post*, April 1, 1998)

"The National Taxpayers Union, which has fueled the balanced budget amendment campaign for decades, has vowed to fight on. Noting that previous major plans to eliminate the deficit—such as the Gramm-Rudman-Hollings law of the late 1980s—have failed, the National Taxpayers Union contends there is no reason to assume the latest balanced budget legislation will work any better.

" 'I think the momentum for the balanced budget amendment will still be there,' said Peter J. Sepp, the taxpayers union's press secretary. 'Many members see the balanced budget amendment as the best way to assure that the budget not only is balanced by 2002 but that it stays balanced beyond then.' " (*Washington Post*, June 8, 1997)

## POLITICAL ORIENTATION

"nonpartisan" (*Los Angeles Times*, April 16, 1998)

". . . While coalition members are unanimous in favoring cuts in spending programs for big business, conservative groups like the National Taxpayers Union have strongly opposed attacking business tax breaks or loopholes, arguing that that would be tantamount to raising taxes unless tax rates were dramatically reduced.

"Grover Norquist, leader of the National Taxpayers Union, said conservatives would support the elimination of tax loopholes only 'in the context of tax reform' while 'the guys on the left want more money for the federal government—and we can't agree on that.' (*Washington Post*, January 29, 1997)

"conservative" (*Wall Street Journal*, January 17, 1996)

# U.S. Chamber of Commerce (1912)

1615 H Street, NW
Washington, D.C. 20062
Phone: (202) 659-6000
Fax: (202) 463-5800
Internet: http://www.uschamber.org

| | |
|---|---|
| "To fight for business and to promote small business." | *PURPOSE* |
| 990 total—210 professional; 240 support; 540 sales; plus 20 interns and 50 part-time | *STAFF* |
| Thomas J. Donohue, president and chief executive officer. Prior to assuming his current position in September 1997, Donohue served for 13 years as the president and chief executive officer of the American Trucking Associations (ATA). He also held positions as deputy assistant postmaster general in Washington, D.C., and vice president of Fairfield University. Donohue earned a bachelor's degree from St. John's University and a master's degree in business administration from Adelphi University. | *DIRECTOR* |
| 501(c)(6) | *TAX STATUS* |
| 1998—$72 million<br>Proposed 1999—$72 million | *BUDGET* |
| Membership, 75 percent; periodical and broadcast advertising income, 15 percent; publications sales, conferences, and other, 10 percent | *FUNDING SOURCES* |
| Members: 215,000 businesses; 3,000 state and local chambers of commerce; 1,200 trade and professional associations; 72 American chambers of commerce abroad representing more than 3 million businesses and organizations of every size, sector, and region<br>Branches/chapters: 5 regional offices in San Mateo, California; Alpharetta, Georgia; Oak Brook, Illinois; Rockville, Maryland; and Dallas, Texas<br>Affiliates: National Chamber Foundation, National Chamber Litigation Center, Center for International Private Enterprise, Center for Workforce Preparation, U.S. Chamber Institute for Legal Reform | *SCOPE* |

| PAC | None |

**METHOD OF OPERATION**

♦ Advertisements ♦ Awards program ♦ Coalition forming ♦ Conferences/seminars ♦ Congressional testimony ♦ Congressional voting analysis ♦ Direct action ♦ Electoral politics ♦ Films/video/audiotapes ♦ Grassroots organizing ♦ Initiative/referendum campaigns ♦ International activities ♦ Internet (IBEX [International Business Exchange], computer network, Web site) ♦ Legal assistance ♦ Legislative/regulatory monitoring (federal) ♦ Litigation ♦ Lobbying (federal and grassroots) ♦ Media outreach ♦ Participation in regulatory proceedings (federal) ♦ Polling ♦ Research ♦ Speakers program ♦ Television and radio production (BIZNET satellite network) ♦ Training and technical assistance

**CURRENT CONCERNS**

♦ Alternative minimum tax reform ♦ Balanced Budget Amendment ♦ Clean air quality standards ♦ Clean Water Act ♦ Davis-Bacon Repeal ♦ Fast-Track Trade Negotiating Authority ♦ Health care reform ♦ Home office deduction ♦ Illegal immigration ♦ Individual Retirement Accounts ♦ Labor law reform: National Labor Relations Board (NLRB) ♦ OSHA reform ♦ Privatization ♦ Social Security solvency ♦ Solid and hazardous waste ♦ Superfund ♦ Tax reform ♦ Telecommunications infrastructure ♦ Transportation: ISTEA ♦ Welfare reform

**PUBLICATIONS**

*Analysis of Workers' Compensation Laws*
*Building an Effective Government Affairs Program*
*Congressional Handbook* (annual)
*Congressional Issues* (annual)
*Developing a Chamber of Commerce: Personnel and Procedures Manual*
*Developing a Program of Work*
*Directory of American Chambers of Commerce Abroad*
*Directory of State Chambers of Commerce*
*Employee Benefits*
*Employment Law: A Checklist*
*How They Voted* (annual)
*NAFTA Impact*
*New and Innovative Approaches to Dues and Non-Dues Income*
*Non-Dues Income*
*Organizational Culture in Chambers of Commerce*
*Raising and Managing Money*
*Selecting and Orienting Volunteers: A Key to Strengthening Your Board of Directors*
*Selecting the Staff Executive for Your Chamber*
*Survey of Local Chambers of Commerce*
*Volunteer Development*
*What Business Must Know about the ADA: Compliance Guide*

**NEWSLETTER**

*Association Agenda* (monthly)
*The Business Advocate* (magazine for members only, 10 times a year)
*Chamber to Chamber* (monthly)
*Nation's Business* (monthly magazine)

International Forum (brings together business and professional people with government officials involved in foreign trade)

Policy Insiders (brings together representatives from the business community and trade and professional associations with government officials)

Also sponsors a variety of conferences and meetings annually on national and international legislative issues, many via satellite

## BOARD OF DIRECTORS

William G. Little, chairman; Thomas J. Donohue, president; Will F. Nicholson, vice chairman; Michael S. Starnes, chairman, executive committee; Carol L. Ball, treasurer; William C. Marcil, Dennis W. Sheehan, Edwin A. Lupberger, and Michael S. Starnes, senior council; William E. Bradford, Emmanuel A. Kampouris, Donald E. Moffitt, and Kelly N. Stanley, regional vice chairmen

Other members:
♦ Randolph J. Agley ♦ Wayne Allen ♦ Wayne E. Alter Jr. ♦ Joe M. Anderson Jr. ♦ Phillip F. Anschutz ♦ John W. Bachmann ♦ William J. Bandy Jr. ♦ Galen R. Barnes ♦ Richard S. Barton ♦ Thomas D. Bell Jr. ♦ Michael R. Bloomberg ♦ R. Emmett Boyle ♦ William P. Cahill ♦ Garrey Carruthers ♦ William Cavanaugh III ♦ Philip E. Cline ♦ John T. Cody Jr. ♦ Vance D. Coffman ♦ James E. Copeland Jr. ♦ Bruce D. Cowen ♦ Jeffrey C. Crowe ♦ A. William Dahlberg ♦ John B. Davies ♦ Michael S. Dell ♦ Maura W. Donahue ♦ James R. Donnelley ♦ Donald W. Dorr ♦ H. Michael Dye ♦ Michael D. Flynn ♦ Theodore R. French ♦ Robert Frenzel ♦ Craig L. Fuller ♦ Ronald J. Gidwitz ♦ Paul E. Glaske ♦ David R. Goode ♦ Daniel M. Gottlieb ♦ James L. Hebe ♦ Scott L. Holman ♦ C.G. "Kelly" Holthus ♦ C.A. Howlett ♦ Allan B. Hubbard ♦ J. Clifford Hudson ♦ Robert C. Hunter ♦ James E. S. Hynes ♦ Robert Jensen ♦ Edmund F. Kelly ♦ Paul J. Klaassen ♦ John W. Koeberer ♦ Thomas R. Kuhn ♦ Patricia L. Langiotti ♦ Larry A. Liebenow ♦ Ronald R. Lyons ♦ Toby Malichi ♦ James W. Moore ♦ Richard E. O'Leary ♦ Donn R. Osmon ♦ Carlos Pascual ♦ Lawrence J. Pelka ♦ Carol A. Rae ♦ Richard Ratcliffe ♦ Robert W. Roten ♦ John R. Ruan III ♦ T. William Samuels Jr. ♦ Joseph S. Schuchert ♦ Gerald L. Shaheen ♦ David Shea ♦ Donald J. Shepard ♦ A.J.C. Smith ♦ Hyrum W. Smith ♦ Paul Speranza ♦ Carey I. Stacy ♦ James Stein ♦ Jamie B. Stewart Jr. ♦ Peter Stieb ♦ Edward M. Straw ♦ Gerald A. Sumida ♦ William R. Toller ♦ Harold E. Turner ♦ Michael S. Uffner ♦ Steve Van Andel ♦ Mark Van Stekelenburg ♦ Frank L. VanderSloot ♦ Roland H. Vaughan ♦ Joan Verplanck ♦ Christopher Wass ♦ Jeffrey Weitzen ♦ Victoria A. Wicks ♦ Ronald F. Williamson

## EFFECTIVENESS

". . . [T]he U.S. Chamber of Commerce and other powerful business organizations are mounting a full-court press for a proposed $17.9 billion appropriation for the International Monetary Fund (IMF), to help stabilize the Asian financial crisis and protect American jobs. But social conservatives such as Rep. Christopher H. Smith, R-N.J., have successfully linked the issue to overseas family planning policy, severely undercutting the prospects for the funding. . . .

"Business lobbyists make no secret of their overall disappointment with Congress. 'There is increasing disenchantment in the business community with the tilt to the social conservative side of the agenda, as opposed to the economic conservative side,' said Paul R. Huard, senior vice president of the National Association of Manufacturers. 'Things that are important to the business community and to the nation's economy are getting screwed up, like IMF funding.'. . .

"Any doubts about the weakness of large corporations were put to bed April 23, when the House defeated a Democratic move to instruct conferees on the supplemental spending bill to include $17.9 billion for the IMF. Even though the nation's most venerable business organizations, led by the Chamber of Commerce and The Business Roundtable, spent months lobbying top Republicans for the measure, Majority Leader Dick Armey, R-Texas, took to the floor to curtly dismiss the IMF as a 'blind racehorse'—and sealed the motion's defeat. . . ." (*CQ Weekly Report*, May 30, 1998)

"The U.S. Chamber of Commerce announced yesterday that it is leaving broadcasting for 'cybercasting' in an effort to better inform and rally its members and influence government officials on their behalf.

"The nation's most powerful business lobbying group said it will discontinue 'First Business,' its half hour television news show, which airs weekdays on about 100 stations across the country. . . .

"The Internet will play a key role in this beefed-up advocacy effort, said Carl Grant, a senior vice president of the group. He said the Washington-based group plans to rapidly expand its online programming, or cybercasts. For instance, the group will offer live audio-video broadcasts of a global climate conference next month. . . .

"The organization already has begun offering some online programming, but its capabilities will be greatly enhanced after a technology upgrade, Grant said." (*Washington Post*, April 24, 1998)

"Indeed, for the first time in decades, the forces lobbying against the embargo appear to be as well-financed—if nowhere near as passionate—as those defending it.

"A week before the Pope's visit, the U.S. Chamber of Commerce formed a broad coalition of businessmen, politicians and humanitarian groups to lobby for the food and medicine legislation. Its advisory council ranges from Joan Brown Campbell of the National Council of Churches and film director Oliver Stone to conservative former Sen. Malcolm Wallop, former Federal Reserve Chairman Paul Volcker and Dwayne Andreas, chairman of Archer-Daniels-Midland Co. John Howard, director of international policy at the U.S. Chamber of Commerce, credits the Pope's visit, humanitarian concerns and a 'growing awareness of the folly of unilateral sanctions' for bringing together such a diverse group. 'The fact that we're talking about the embargo's most absurd aspect, restrictions on the sale of food and medicine,' makes the case even more compelling, he says." (*Wall Street Journal*, April 15, 1998)

"The U.S. Chamber of Commerce has asked a federal court to strike down one of the government's most ambitious new workplace-safety initiatives.

"In a lawsuit filed . . . in the U.S. Court of Appeals, the chamber said the Occupational Safety and Health Administration is trying to coerce thousands of employers to join its Cooperative Compliance Program by threatening to inspect them if they don't." (*Wall Street Journal*, January 26, 1998)

"The U.S. Chamber of Commerce is getting ready to launch a multimillion-dollar assault against some longtime foes: the nation's trial lawyers.

"Starting early next year, Washington's largest business lobbying group will ask member corporations to contribute to a full-bore attack on tort and product-liability laws, an attack that could threaten the livelihoods of thousands of plaintiffs' lawyers. Additionally, the chamber for the first time will target employee-bias litigation, a growth area for many of these lawyers. 'We've decided to broaden our traditional approach to include workplace issues,' said Larry Kraus, the Chamber's senior vice president, who will orchestrate the effort. 'Whenever an employee is dismissed these days, they find some reason to sue. A lot of those suits have merit, but many are frivolous, and battling those suits is an enormous expense.' " (*Washington Post*, December 12, 1997)

"The Clinton administration abandoned its legal effort to enforce a presidential order that would have barred companies from getting government contracts if they permanently replaced striking workers.

"The government had until yesterday to petition the Supreme Court to overturn an appeals-court ruling that struck down President Clinton's March 8, 1995, executive order. A U.S. district court judge temporarily blocked the order after a number of business groups, led by the U.S. Chamber of Commerce, challenged it as unconstitutional. A three-judge panel of the U.S. Court of Appeals unanimously overturned the president's order Feb. 2, concluding that the order conflicts with employers' rights under federal labor law. The entire 11-judge court let the panel's ruling stand in May." (*Wall Street Journal*, September 10, 1996)

# POLITICAL ORIENTATION

"Across the country, the U.S. Chamber of Commerce is putting politicians through their paces at 'Candidate Forums,' like the one in Rosemont, and making endorsements for the November elections. For pro-business politicians—most of them Republicans—a chamber endorsement is a ticket that can open the wallets of some of the country's richest corporations." (*Washington Post*, June 26, 1998)

"The Chamber of Commerce chief says that both President Clinton and Congress are out of step with the needs of small business. . . .

"The U.S. Chamber is the nation's largest business federation and Donohue is leading the charge for a renewed organization 'with enthusiasm and a little sting.' He said that means that the Chamber will not shy away from letting lawmakers and other government officials know what obstacles are impeding business growth." (*Providence Journal-Bulletin*, May 13, 1998)

"The nation's most powerful business lobbying group." (*Washington Post*, April 24, 1998)

# Civil/ Constitutional Rights

Chapter 2

# American-Arab Anti-Discrimination Committee (1980)

4201 Connecticut Avenue, NW
Suite 300
Washington, D.C. 20008
Phone: (202) 244-2990
Fax: (202) 244-3196
Internet: adc@adc.org *or* http://www.adc.org

| | |
|---|---|
| "To protect the rights of people of Arab descent, promote and defend the Arab-American heritage, and serve the needs of the Arab-American community." | *PURPOSE* |
| 13 total—11 professional; 2 support; plus 9 to 10 interns | *STAFF* |
| Hala Maksoud, president. Maksoud taught International Relations, the Middle East, and Arab women's issues at Georgetown and George Mason University. She publishes and lectures extensively and sits on the board of several organizations, including the American Committee on Jerusalem, and is a founding member of the Arab Women's Council. She holds a doctorate in political theory, a master's in government from Georgetown, and a master's in mathematics from the American University of Beirut. | *DIRECTOR* |
| Nonprofit organization (not tax-exempt) | *TAX STATUS* |
| 1998—Unavailable<br>Proposed 1999—Unavailable | *BUDGET* |
| Individual contributions | *FUNDING SOURCES* |
| Members: 10,000 individuals<br>Branches/chapters: 70 chapters in North America<br>Affiliate: ADC Research Institute, a 501(c)(3) organization | *SCOPE* |
| None | *PAC* |

| | |
|---|---|
| *METHOD OF OPERATION* | ◆ Awards program ◆ Coalition forming ◆ Conferences/seminars ◆ Congressional testimony ◆ Demonstrations ◆ Films/video/audiotapes ◆ Grassroots organizing ◆ International activities ◆ Internet ◆ Legal assistance ◆ Library/information clearinghouse ◆ Lobbying (grassroots) ◆ Local/municipal affairs ◆ Media outreach ◆ Research ◆ Speakers program ◆ Telecommunications services (databases, mailing lists) |
| *CURRENT CONCERNS* | ◆ Airport profiling ◆ Census data ◆ Civil rights consequences of the Counter-Terrorism Bill ◆ Discrimination ◆ Human rights ◆ Immigration counseling ◆ Promoting Arab heritage ◆ U.S. policy in the Middle East |
| *PUBLICATIONS* | *ABSCAM: Arabiaphobia in America*<br>*Affirming Palestinian Statehood*<br>*American Public Opinion and the Question of Palestine*<br>*Arab Contributions to Civilization*<br>*The Arab Image in American Film and TV*<br>*Celebration of Life: Arab-Americans in Cleveland*<br>*The Children of the Stones*<br>*Cruel and Unusual* (English and Arabic)<br>*Educational Outreach and Action Guide*<br>*The FBI and Civil Rights of Arab Americans*<br>*Harassment in the Holy Land*<br>*The Image of Arabs in American Fiction*<br>*Immigration Law 1997* (English and Arabic)<br>*Influence of the Arab Stereotype on Children*<br>*Iron Fist*<br>*Kahlil Gibran*<br>*Legal Guide* (English and Arabic)<br>*Living by the Sword*<br>*Media Monitoring Guide*<br>*Oral History Guide*<br>*Political Action Guide*<br>*Social and Political Attitudes of Arab-Americans*<br>*Special Report: Conference on Somalia*<br>*Taking Root* (volumes 1 and 2)<br>*Teacher Resources on the Middle East*<br>*Through Different Eyes*<br>*Unholy Alliance* (English and Arabic)<br>*Unmasking Job Discrimination*<br>*The Uprising in Cartoons*<br>*Victims Speak Out*<br>*Wrapping the Grapeleaves* |
| *NEWSLETTER* | *ADC Times* (monthly)<br>*Inter Perspective* (annually) |
| *CONFERENCES* | Annual national convention in Arlington, Virginia |

Naila Asali, chairperson; Hala Maksoud, president

Other members:
◆ Olfet Agrama ◆ Halim Awde ◆ Naim Ayoub ◆ Cheryl Faris ◆ Mazin Irani ◆ A. Carl LeVan ◆ Clovis Maksoud ◆ Chris Mansour ◆ Rania Masri ◆ Khaled Mattawa ◆ Hisham Melhelm ◆ Albert Mokhiber ◆ Adnan Mourany ◆ Safa Rifka ◆ George Saba ◆ George Younan

"As history, the film, 'Path to Paradise,' tracks much of the riveting story as it emerged in the investigations and trials that followed the attack on Feb. 26, 1993. It even uses some of the words of Sheik Omar Abdel Rahman and other conspirators—as they were later proved to be—from secret tape recordings. But it is hardly, as the subtitle claims, an 'untold story.'. . .

" 'Path to Paradise' drew controversy this week with complaints by the American-Arab Anti-Discrimination Committee in Washington that the movie prejudicially portrays Muslims as a menace to American society. The group called every Arab or Muslim character in the movie 'an ugly stereotype' and said that the film would be given the group's 'Intolerance Award.'

"HBO defended the film and said it would broadcast a statement that the movie was not intended to reflect the views of most Muslims and Arabs." (*New York Times,* June 14, 1997)

"A White House commission called for 're-engineering' U.S. aviation safety and security, but its final recommendations don't entail substantial increases in authority or budget for the Federal Aviation Administration. . . .

"Although the recommendations, which won the endorsement of President Clinton, are broad in scope and are intended to anticipate long-term aviation trends and needs, the nuts and bolts of the report were toned down from earlier drafts so they are strong in rhetoric but contain few specific regulatory or funding details. Rather than focusing on tougher enforcement measures, the panel decided to stress closer industry-government cooperation and voluntary compliance efforts by airlines. . . .

"Antiterrorism recommendations urging the FAA and airlines to develop 'profiles' of potentially threatening airline passengers drew fire from some civil-liberties advocates who contend they go too far and could be discriminatory. . . .

". . . the commission included a civil-liberties advisory panel's recommendations that the passenger profiles used in the bag-matching system exclude, among other things, information about race and religion. Still, at least 16 groups, including the American Civil Liberties Union and the American-Arab Anti-Discrimination Committee, sent Mr. Gore a letter yesterday to protest the profiling plan." (*Wall Street Journal,* February 13, 1997)

Unavailable

# American Civil Liberties Union (1920)

125 Broad Street
New York, New York 10004
Phone: (212) 549-2500

122 Maryland Avenue, NE
Washington, D.C. 20002
Phone: (202) 544-1681
Fax: (202) 546-0738

Internet: info@aclu.org *or* http://www.aclu.org

**PURPOSE**

"To preserve, defend and expand application of the constitutional guarantees and freedoms set forth in the Bill of Rights."

**STAFF**

150 total—105 professional; 45 support (not including affiliates)

**DIRECTOR**

Ira Glasser, executive director. Glasser has been executive director of the American Civil Liberties Union (ACLU) since 1978. He spent the previous eleven years with the New York Civil Liberties Union, first as associate director, then as executive director. Glasser was associate editor and editor of *Current* magazine from 1962 to 1967. He served on the faculties of Queens College, Sarah Lawrence College, and the University of Illinois from 1960 to 1965. Glasser has written numerous books and articles. He earned a B.S. in mathematics at Queens College and an M.A. in mathematics at Ohio State University.

**TAX STATUS**

501(c)(4)

**BUDGET**

1997—$35 million
1998—$35 million
Proposed 1999—$37 million

**FUNDING SOURCES**

Private organizations and individuals; no government funding

**SCOPE**

Members: 275,000 individuals

Branches/chapters: 53 affiliate offices, including one in each state; plus local chapters

Affiliate: ACLU Foundation, a 501(c)(3) organization

**PAC**

None

♦ Advertisements ♦ Awards program ♦ Coalition forming ♦ Conferences/seminars ♦ Congressional testimony ♦ Congressional voting analysis ♦ Demonstrations ♦ Films/video/audiotapes ♦ Grassroots organizing ♦ Information clearinghouse ♦ Internet (E-mail alerts, Web site) ♦ Internships ♦ Legal assistance ♦ Legislative/regulatory monitoring (federal and state) ♦ Litigation ♦ Lobbying (federal, state, and grassroots) ♦ Media outreach ♦ Polling ♦ Research

♦ Affirmative action ♦ Civil rights ♦ Gay rights ♦ Reproductive rights ♦ Government regulation of the Internet ♦ Rights to privacy of information

The following is a list of sample publications:
*Crack in America, Demon Drugs, and Social Justice*
*Defending Rights: A Life in Law and Politics*
*In the Shadow of the Poorhouse: A Social History of Welfare in America*
*May It Please the Court/The First Amendment*
*Saving Old Glory*
*Sex and Sensibility: Reflections on Forbidden Mirrors and the Will to Censor*
*Shades of Freedom: Racial Politics and Presumptions of the American Legal Process*
*Through the Keyhole: Privacy in the Workplace—An Endangered Right* (video)
*Us and Them: A History of Intolerance in America*
*What's a Nice Republican Girl Like Me Doing In the ACLU?*
*When Work Disappears: The World of the New Urban Poor*
*Without a Prayer: Religious Expression in Public Schools*

Also publishes briefing papers, handbooks, videos, "Ask Sybil Liberty" briefers for students, calendars, posters, buttons, and T-shirts

*Arts Censorship Newsletter* (quarterly)
*Civil Liberties* (periodic)
*Reproductive Rights Update* (semiannual)

Internet forums: America OnLine keyword: ACLU, ACLU web site at http://www.aclu.org

Nadine Strossen, president

Other members:
♦ Frank Askin ♦ Jeanne Baker ♦ Robert Bastress ♦ Marc O Beem ♦ Alice Bendheim ♦ Judith Bendich ♦ Phil Bereano ♦ Vivian Berger ♦ Karen "Bert" Bertonaschi ♦ Liz Barker Brandt ♦ John Burnett ♦ Isaac Byrd ♦ Candace M. Carroll ♦ Charlie Cerf ♦ Ronald Chen ♦ Kenneth B. Clark ♦ James Crawford ♦ Harlon Dalton ♦ Julie Davis ♦ H. Stewart Dunn Jr. ♦ Marjorie Esman ♦ Milton Estes ♦ Ellen Feingold ♦ Eugene Feingold ♦

James E. Ferguson II ♦ Joyce S. Fiske ♦ Bern Friedelson ♦ Gloria Furman ♦ Mary Ellen Gale ♦ Marcia M. Gallo ♦ Diane Gerachty ♦ Danny Goldberg ♦ Ralph Goldberg ♦ Paul Grant ♦ Kevin A. Gray ♦ Jeremiah Gutman ♦ James Hall Jr. ♦ Susan N. Herman ♦ Art J. Heyderman ♦ William Hinkle ♦ Linda K. Hunt ♦ Marina Hsieh ♦ Woody Kaplan ♦ Stuart Kaplan ♦ Hamid R. Kashani ♦ Vern L. Klingman ♦ Joan Laskowski ♦ Denise LeBoeuf ♦ Micki Levin ♦ M. Calien Lewis ♦ Pamela G. Lichty ♦ Imogene "Gene" Lindsay ♦ Roslyn Litman ♦ Joan Mahoney ♦ Gary Mandinach ♦ Elizabeth M. McGeever ♦ Cyndy McGovern ♦ Michael Meyers ♦ E. Walter Miles ♦ Martha Morgan ♦ Wendy C. Nakamura ♦ Ilene Nelson ♦ Rolland O'Hare ♦ R. Samuel Paz ♦ Susan Poser ♦ Robert B. Remar ♦ William F. Reynard ♦ Turhan E. Robinson ♦ David Rudovsky ♦ Margaret Russell ♦ Phillippa Strum ♦ Frank Susman ♦ Joseph Sweat ♦ John M. Swomley ♦ Gwen Thomas ♦ JoNell Thomas ♦ Randall D.B. Tigue ♦ Leland Ware ♦ David Waxse ♦ Carl Wedekind ♦ Vivian Weisman ♦ Richard Zacks

# EFFECTIVENESS

"The Federal Trade Commission should stem the growing volume of unsolicited electronic mail by cracking down on mailers that use fake return addresses, according to a report that will be issued today by a coalition of industry and advocacy groups working on the issue.

"Allowing consumers to respond directly to these mailers, who often sell sexually oriented material, would go a long way to making them accountable, the report said. The group also recommended that the industry voluntarily create an 'opt-out' system that would let people insist they get no such mail.

"The coalition, created by the FTC last summer to devise policy recommendations, did not agree on tougher approaches, such as banning the mail, which is known colloquially as 'spam' and ranks as one of the most common complaints of Internet users. . . .

"The coalition included groups as diverse as the American Civil Liberties Union and the Direct Marketing Association, as well as companies such as AT&T Corp. and America Online Inc." (*Washington Post*, July 14, 1998)

"The city has agreed to sever ties to Boy Scouts of America programs until the group accepts gays and stops requiring a religious oath.

"The agreement Wednesday settles a federal lawsuit filed against Chicago by the American Civil Liberties Union, which sought to end city sponsorship of 28 Scout programs. The lawsuit alleged the city's involvement violated the separation of church and state principle and that the Scouts' ban on admitting gays is discriminatory. The ACLU called the settlement a victory and urged other cities to 'take a cue from Chicago's action and end their sponsorship of these discriminatory programs.' " (*Washington Post*, February 6, 1998)

"Under threat of a lawsuit from the American Civil Liberties Union, the Miami-Dade County school district has revised its drug-testing program to allow high school students to refuse random checks.

"Tests would begin in March in grades 9 through 12, but only on students whose parents have signed consent forms. If a student refused after his parents signed, the parents would be notified, but the student would face no other punishment.

"The Florida chapter of the A.C.L.U. had threatened a lawsuit if students in the district, the nation's fourth largest, were not given the right to refuse." (*New York Times*, January 16, 1998)

"The decision last week on the county's public library Internet computers seemed to be good news for those wanting to cruise the World Wide Web unimpeded: There would be no software filters installed.

"But residents still might be barred from certain Web sites under new regulations the Prince William County Library Board has asked the library director to draft. The proposed new rules, the director has said, would seek to keep residents from accessing graphically sexual or vulgar material and would allow the library staff to keep people from looking at those sites. . . .

"The American Civil Liberties Union's Virginia chapter said that such action would be a clear violation of First Amendment rights. It's a dangerous precedent, the group says, to allow library staff to determine what is acceptable for patrons to view.

" 'It's unfair for the person using the computer and for the employee who has to apply such a vague policy,' said Kent Willis, director of the ACLU's Virginia chapter, who said material shouldn't be banned just because someone might not like what is on another person's computer screen. 'People's view of what is acceptable and unacceptable vary greatly. If a majority doesn't like a book, we don't allow them to censor that book. The First Amendment is very clear that you have the right to that information.' " (*Washington Post*, January 28, 1998)

"The American Civil Liberties Union has accused Maryland State Police of underreporting the number of black motorists its troopers search for drugs, in violation of court-ordered monitoring of traffic stops by troopers.

"In papers filed in federal court here, the ACLU also said state police maintain 'two sets of books,' one to satisfy monitoring requirements, the other for internal use that appears to contain additional reports about black motorists. 'It raises all kinds of red flags,' said ACLU lawyer William J. Mertens in an interview." (*Washington Post*, December 5, 1997)

"The American Civil Liberties Union and a number of library, publishing and Internet groups sued New York state, alleging its new law imposing restrictions on 'indecent' on-line material is unconstitutional.

"In the suit filed in federal court here, the plaintiffs argue that the law's prohibition on on-line distribution of such material to minors would effectively ban distribution of the same material to adults. The suit seeks a declaration that the New York law is unconstitutional, as well as preliminary and permanent injunctions barring the state from enforcing it. . . ." (*Wall Street Journal*, January 15, 1997)

# POLITICAL ORIENTATION

"The American Civil Liberties Union has stirred many a brouhaha over the years by taking up the cudgel for free speech on behalf of any and all, even neo-Nazis and the Ku Klux Klan.

"But now, tired of being seen as an unfocused bunch of lefties, the group is taking a page from the marketing playbook and trying for a more thoughtful image, with the first sustained advertising campaign in ACLU history.

"This week, as the President Clinton-Monica Lewinsky drama dragged on, the ACLU launched its splashy new ad campaign on the Op-Ed page of the *New York Times*. The ad shows a photo featuring the smiling mouth of a woman talking on the telephone—and then raises a frightening thought. 'How would you feel if all your phone conversations last night were secretly taped and made public today? That's what Linda Tripp did to Monica Lewinsky. . . .'

"The goal here isn't just to provoke debate. The ACLU says it is misunderstood by the public and wants to change its image. Most Americans think of the group as 'liberal left,' Mr. Glasser says. But the ACLU considers itself staunchly in the middle—agreeing with conservatives on some issues, with liberals on others. . . ." (*Wall Street Journal*, February 6, 1998)

# Americans United for Separation of Church and State (1947)

1816 Jefferson Place, NW
Washington, D.C. 20036
Phone: (202) 466-3234
Fax: (202) 466-2587
Internet: americansunited@au.org *or* http://www.au.org

| | |
|---|---|
| "Supports the principle of religious liberty by advocating for separation of church and state. Educates public about the importance of church-state separation." | ***PURPOSE*** |
| 22 total—15 professional; 7 support | ***STAFF*** |
| Barry W. Lynn, executive director. Before joining Americans United, Lynn was legislative counsel for the American Civil Liberties Union and served in a variety of positions with the national offices of the United Church of Christ, including legislative counsel for its Office of Church in Society. An ordained minister, Lynn received his degree in Theology from Boston University School of Theology, his law degree from Georgetown University Law Center, and his bachelor's degree from Dickinson College. | ***DIRECTOR*** |
| 501(c)(3) | ***TAX STATUS*** |
| 1997—$2.7 million<br>1998—$1.8 million<br>Proposed 1999—$1.8 million | ***BUDGET*** |
| Membership support, 100 percent | ***FUNDING SOURCES*** |
| Members: 50,000 individuals<br>Branches/chapters: 40 chapters in 25 states<br>Affiliates: None | ***SCOPE*** |
| None | ***PAC*** |

| | |
|---|---|
| *METHOD OF OPERATION* | ◆ Advertisements ◆ Awards program ◆ Coalition forming ◆ Conferences/seminars ◆ Congressional testimony ◆ Congressional voting analysis ◆ Grassroots organizing ◆ Internet (Web site) ◆ Legal assistance ◆ Legislative/regulatory monitoring (federal and state) ◆ Library/information clearinghouse ◆ Litigation ◆ Media outreach ◆ Speakers program |
| *CURRENT CONCERNS* | ◆ Impact of the religious right ◆ Religious liberty ◆ School prayer ◆ School vouchers |
| *PUBLICATIONS* | None |
| *NEWSLETTER* | *Church and State Magazine* (11 times per year) |
| *CONFERENCES* | National Conference on Church and State (annual) |
| *BOARD OF DIRECTORS* | John W. Webster, president; Betty Evans Boone, treasurer; Albert C. Walker, secretary<br><br>Other trustees include:<br>◆ Robert S. Alley ◆ Charlotte H. Coffelt ◆ Calvin W. Didier ◆ James M. Dunn ◆ Ronald B. Flowers ◆ Cynthia S. Holmes ◆ Elenora Giddings Ivory ◆ Robert McConnell ◆ Nanette M. Roberts ◆ John M. Suarez ◆ Eddie Tabash |
| *EFFECTIVENESS* | "Advocates of publicly financed vouchers for religious schools took heart when the Supreme Court on June 23 reversed one of its own precedents. The court ruled that it does not violate the Constitution to send public school teachers—paid by taxpayers' money—into parochial schools to teach remedial classes to disadvantaged children. . . .<br><br>"With greater education and poverty problems than any other school district in Wisconsin, Milwaukee, starting in 1990, permitted any public school student to attend any nonsectarian school in the city at public expense. . . .<br><br>"Then, in 1995, the state legislature and governor Tommy Thompson expanded the Milwaukee Parental Choice Program to include the use of state vouchers in religious schools. But any pupil can be exempt from a school's religious activity if the parent requests it.<br><br>"Lawsuits were brought challenging the constitutionality of using public funds for sectarian schools. Among the plaintiffs were the American Civil Liberties Union, Americans United for Separation of Church and State, the Milwaukee Teachers' Education Association and the NAACP." (*Washington Post*, July 19, 1997) |

"If you thought the Rev. Jerry Falwell had faded from view, think again.

"So says the national church-state watchdog group, Americans United for Separation of Church and State. The group says Falwell conspired with other Virginia clergy members to use their pulpits during the spring to endorse state Sen. Mark L. Earley (Chesapeake), who won the Republican nomination for attorney general June 10. This month, the group asked the Internal Revenue Service to investigate political activity by Falwell and other pastors that the group said violates IRS codes and jeopardizes the churches' tax-exempt status.

" 'If Falwell and his clergy allies want to play hardball politics in Virginia, they ought to form a political action committee,' Americans United Executive Director Barry W. Lynn said. 'Churches are supposed to be houses of prayer, not dens of political iniquity.'. . .

" 'They have a highly orchestrated campaign here, a major campaign to create a national model in Virginia for political influence of churches all across the United States,' Lynn said." (*Washington Post*, July 17, 1997)

"Televangelist Pat Robertson denounces their leader as 'a bit lower than a child molester.' The North Carolina Republican Party accuses them of shameless 'gutter tactics.' The Rev. Jim Way, whose Texas Baptist church has drawn their censure, says they don't have any 'business, professional or Christian courtesy.'

"They are Americans United for Separation of Church and State. Their mission: a high-profile campaign to get politically active churches audited by the Internal Revenue Service for possible violations of their tax-exempt status. . . .

"Nobody is a more active, organized IRS informant than Mr. Lynn and Americans United. The group was founded—as a tax-exempt organization—in 1947 by some Protestant clergymen opposed to Catholic church lobbying for government aid to parochial schools. Americans United itself lost its charity status in the 1960s for engaging in what the IRS considered excessive grass-roots lobbying. The group regained the IRS's approval in 1980 and hasn't had any problems since, Mr. Lynn says.

"Today, the organization—headquartered in a well-appointed $1.7 million Washington, D.C., townhouse with a framed copy of the Declaration of Independence in its main lobby—has $6.5 million in assets, 22 full-time employees and 50,000 members nationwide. The group gets about $2 million a year in annual membership fees and donations, most for less than $1,000, and foundation grants." (*Wall Street Journal*, March 20, 1997)

## POLITICAL ORIENTATION

"an almost absolutist advocate for keeping religion out of government institutions" (*Wall Street Journal*, March 23, 1998)

". . . To charges of bias, Mr. Lynn notes that four of the churches on his hit list backed Democrats. Two months ago, for example, Americans United told the IRS that the Windsor Village United Methodist Church, an African-American church in Houston, held a service in late 1996 where House Minority leader Richard Gephardt of Missouri asked congregants to re-elect Democratic Rep. Ken Bentsen Jr. Richard Keeton, the church's attorney, says the charge is based on an inaccurate news article. 'Dick Gephardt did not say, "vote for him." The church and pastor did not say 'vote for Ken Bentsen.' "

"Still, nearly two-thirds of the organizations fingered by Americans United backed Republicans or abortion foes. . . ." (*Wall Street Journal*, March 20, 1997)

# Asian American Legal Defense and Education Fund (1974)

99 Hudson Street
12th Floor
New York, New York 10013-2869
Phone: (212) 966-5932
Fax: (212) 966-4303
Internet: aaldef@worldnet.att.net

**PURPOSE**

"To protect the legal rights of Asian Americans through litigation, legal advocacy, and community education."

**STAFF**

10 total—8 professional; 2 support; plus 100 volunteers and 5 interns

**DIRECTOR**

Margaret Fung, executive director. Fung previously held a judicial clerkship in the U.S. Court of Appeals for the Second Circuit. She is a board member of many organizations, including the National Asian Pacific American Legal Consortium, the Committee on Modern Courts, the New York Civil Liberties Union, and the New York Foundation. A graduate of Barnard College and New York University Law School, Fung also studied journalism as a Charles H. Revson Fellow at Columbia University.

**TAX STATUS**

501(c)(3)

**BUDGET**

Fiscal year ending June 30, 1997—$540,200
F.Y. 1998—$825,000
Proposed F.Y. 1999—$645,000

**FUNDING SOURCES**

Foundation grants, 43 percent; special events/projects, 30 percent; corporate donations, 13 percent; individuals and membership, 10 percent; attorney fees and other earned income, 4 percent

**SCOPE**

Members: Unavailable

Branches/chapters: N/A

Affiliates: National Asian Pacific American Legal Consortium, Asian Law Caucus, and Asian Pacific American Legal Center of Southern California—all are 501(c)(3) organizations

**PAC**

None

| | |
|---|---|
| ◆ Awards program ◆ Coalition forming ◆ Congressional testimony ◆ Demonstrations ◆ Direct action ◆ Grassroots organizing ◆ Information clearinghouse ◆ Internet (E-mail alerts) ◆ Internships ◆ Legal assistance ◆ Legislative/regulatory monitoring (federal and state) ◆ Litigation ◆ Lobbying (federal, state, and grassroots) ◆ Local/municipal affairs ◆ Mailing lists ◆ Media outreach ◆ Professional development services ◆ Research ◆ Speakers program ◆ Telecommunications services (mailing lists) ◆ Training and technical assistance ◆ Voter registration ◆ Voter surveys | *METHOD OF OPERATION* |
| ◆ Affirmative action ◆ Elimination of Anti-Asian violence ◆ Economic justice for workers ◆ Immigration and immigrants' rights ◆ Language rights ◆ Voting rights | *CURRENT CONCERNS* |
| *Get Involved* (legal education series)<br><br>Also publishes immigration alerts and legal rights pamphlets in English, Chinese, Korean, Japanese, and Hindi | *PUBLICATIONS* |
| *Outlook* (semiannually)<br>*Righting Wrongs* (monthly) | *NEWSLETTER* |
| None | *CONFERENCES* |
| Michael Shen, president; Vivian Cheng-Khanna, vice president; Harsha Murthy, treasurer; Joan L. Washington, secretary<br><br>Other members:<br>◆ Nicholas V. Chen ◆ Denley Chew ◆ Ira Glasser ◆ Jack Greenberg ◆ Chung Wha Hong ◆ Grace Y. Hwang ◆ Peter D. Lederer ◆ Chanwoo Lee ◆ Donald H. Liu ◆ JoAnn Lum ◆ Phil Tajitsu Nash ◆ Karen Sauvigné ◆ Ko-Yung Tung ◆ Susan Chong Wong ◆ Margaret Y.K. Woo ◆ Gail J. Wright-Sirmans | *BOARD OF DIRECTORS* |
| "The fee for a citizenship application would more than double to $225 as early as Oct. 1 under a proposal by the Immigration and Naturalization Service. . . .<br>   "The expected increase has spurred several immigrants' rights groups in New York to step up citizenship drives. . . .<br>   "During yesterday's three-hour citizenship drive in Chinatown, more than 300 people crowded around two tables where volunteers for the Asian American Legal Defense and Education Fund passed out application forms and fliers that read: 'Beat the fee increase! Become a U.S. citizen!' " (*New York Times*, June 28, 1998)<br><br>"Opening a new front in the fight against conditions in local sweatshops, workers have sued a Sunset Park garment factory and the women's apparel manufacturer who contracts with it. | *EFFECTIVENESS* |

"This is the first case brought on the East Coast that seeks to hold the garment manufacturers who contract with them equally responsible for working conditions. . . .

" 'This lawsuit represents the ability to go after a factory and an owner, but also the manfacturer for the conditions and wages at these places.' said Ken Kimerling of the Asian American Legal Defense and Education Fund, which is representing the workers in the suit. . . ." (*Daily News*, May 5, 1998)

"In a rare move, a federal judge called on the U.S. Marshals Friday to stop a garment factory owner from continuing to move equipment out of her two Lower Manhattan businesses in violation of a court order, according to an advocacy group representing workers there.

"The Asian American Legal Defense and Education Fund filed a suit Wednesday on behalf of 46 workers at MSL Sportswear and Laura and Sarah Sportswear, alleging that the employees and had not been paid more than $200,000 in back wages and were additionally owed overtime, said Ken Kimerling, a staff attorney at the fund." (*Newsday*, November 15, 1997)

"In what Asian-American labor groups are calling a big victory, China-town's largest restaurant has agreed to pay more than $1.1 million to 58 workers who said they had been cheated out of tips and wages, officials said yesterday.

"The Attorney General's office filed a lawsuit in January that charged Jing Fong restaurant with cheating workers out of more than $1.5 million in tips and wages since 1993 by illegally controlling the distribution of tips and withholding some of them. The Asian-American Legal Defense and Education Fund had filed a lawsuit against Jing Fong in Federal District Court seeking $500,000 on behalf of workers who said the restaurant had failed to pay overtime and violated minimum-wage laws. . . ." (*New York Times*, October 30, 1997)

"Flagstar Cos., which operates the Denny's restaurant chain, hasn't won a lot of praise over the years for racial sensitivity, having been slapped with several lawsuits alleging discrimination.

"But now, in an effort to burnish its image—and most important, Flagstar insists, better the lives of its employees—the embattled company is offering English-language proficiency classes aimed at helping Latino workers and others here move up the ladder. . . .

"One critic of the language classes is Elizabeth Ou-Yang, a staff attorney with the Asian American Legal Defense and Education Fund in New York. She is representing 10 Syracuse University students—mostly Asians—who filed suit against Flagstar and Denny's in U.S. District Court in New York just last month, alleging that they had been denied seating and then roughed up by restaurant security guards. (The Onondaga County district attorney has declined to take up the case, contending that the students 'orchestrated' the event.)

" 'You measure a company's principles and ethics by its day-to-day operation of its businesses as opposed to outside endeavors,' Ms. Ou-Yang says. Flagstar 'needs to ensure that their day-to-day delivery of services is done in a nondiscriminatory manner. That's more indicative of their commitment . . . than anything else.' " (*Wall Street Journal*, September 24, 1997)

"Against the stunning backdrop of a glittering Manhattan skyline at dusk, TriStar Pictures Executive Vice President of Production Chris Lee was awarded the 'Justice In Action Award' by the Asian American Legal Defense and Education Fund. At its awards dinner held at Windows on the World, Tony Award winning playwright David Henry Hwang presented his great friend Chris with the award and set the tone for a classy, entertaining and important evening during which some of this country's most distinguished Asian Americans were recognized for their unique contributions to the Asian American cause." (*A. Magazine*, June/July 1997)

Unavailable

# POLITICAL ORIENTATION

# Center for Democratic Renewal (1979)

P.O. Box 50469
Atlanta, Georgia 30302
Phone: (404) 221-0025
Fax: (404) 221-0045
Internet: cdr@ipc.apc.org

## PURPOSE

To "advance the vision of a democratic, diverse and just society, free of racism and bigotry."

## STAFF

6 total—5 professional; 1 support; plus 1 part-time professional; 3 consultants; 2 interns

## DIRECTOR

Beni Ivey, executive director. Before joining the Center for Democratic Renewal (CDR) in 1993, Ivey was special assistant to Coretta Scott King at the Martin Luther King, Jr., Center for Nonviolent Social Change. She was a founder of the Atlanta Black United Fund and currently serves on its board of directors. Ivey is the past chair of the Fund for Southern Communities and the former assistant state coordinator of the Jimmy Carter for President campaign.

## TAX STATUS

501(c)(3)

## BUDGET

1998—$635,000
Proposed 1999—$635,000

## FUNDING SOURCES

Foundation grants, 83 percent; individual donations, sales, special events, and other, 10 percent; membership dues, 7 percent

## SCOPE

Members: 2,000 contributing members; 500 organizational members
Branches/chapters: None
Affiliates: 60 organizations

## PAC

None

## METHOD OF OPERATION

♦ Capacity building ♦ Coalition forming ♦ Conferences/seminars ♦ Congressional testimony ♦ Direct action ♦ Grassroots organizing ♦ International activities ♦ Internet ♦ Legal assistance ♦ Library/information clearinghouse ♦ Research ♦ Training ♦ Technical assistance

♦ Anti-gay violence ♦ Immigration ♦ Minority issues ♦ White supremacy ideologies' effects on mainstream America

*Ballot Box Bigotry: David Duke and the Populist Party*
*Bitter Harvest: Gordon Kahl and the Posse Comitatus—Murder in the Heartland*
*Blacks, Jews, and White Supremacy: Redirecting the Fight*
*Blood in the Face: The KKK, Aryan Nations, Nazi Skinheads and the Rise of a New White Culture*
*The Changing Faces of White Supremacy*
*The Christian Identity Movement*
*The Electronic Connection: White Supremacists and the Information Super-highway*
*Fundraising for Community-Based Groups*
*Hiding Behind Righteousness: Decoding the Language of the Radical Right*
*Lyndon LaRouche & the New American Fascism*
*Memoirs of a Race Traitor*
*Neo-Nazi Skinheads & Youth Information Packets*
*Quarantines and Death: The Far Right's Homophobic Agenda*
*Standing Toe to Toe: Fighting Racism in Georgia*
*They Don't All Wear Sheets: A Chronology of Racists and Far-Right Violence, 1980 to 1986*
*Verbal Violence: Free Speech vs. Hate Speech*
*When Hate Groups Come to Town: A Handbook of Effective Community Responses*
*Women's Watch: Violence in the Anti-Abortion Movement*

*Activist Update*
*The Monitor* (3 times a year)
*The Right Unmasked*

Schedule varies

C. T. Vivian, chairman; Tom Turnipseed, president; Joann Watson, vice president; Joe Agne, secretary; Leah Wise, treasurer

Other members:
♦ Julian Bond ♦ Anne Braden ♦ Marilyn Clement ♦ Ron Daniels ♦ Lois Dauway ♦ Judy Hanenkrat ♦ Martin Luther King III ♦ Ralph Paige ♦ Suzanne Pharr ♦ Othello Poulard ♦ Mab Segrest ♦ Hilary Shelton ♦ Lucius Walker

## EFFECTIVENESS

"The battle flag 'means a great deal emotionally to many whites—and these people are not necessarily racists—who respect their ancestors and the sacrifices they made,' said [Reuben] Greenberg, [Charleston's, S.C., black police chief,] a history buff and Civil War reenactor whose office is decorated with flags from every continent. After a brief truce, the war over the Confederate flag is flaring anew here in the only state where a full-fledged version still flies over the capitol.

"Only a month ago, it looked as if an accord was near when Gov. David M. Beasley (R) proposed a compromise that would have moved the flag from atop the statehouse in Columbia to a Confederate memorial on the capitol grounds.

"But the state House of Representatives, which was expected to follow the governor's lead, balked after heated debate and called for a statewide referendum in November. . . .

"The Confederate flag became a more potent symbol of white heritage after 'the push for multiculturalism' had encouraged African Americans to express their own racial pride, said Dexter Wimbish, a staff attorney with the Center for Democratic Renewal, an organization that tracks hate groups. The center considers the Confederate flag offensive.

"Those expressions, among them Malcolm X caps and T-shirts proclaiming 'It's a Black Thing, You Wouldn't Understand,' were 'polarizing points' for whites, said Wimbish, who is African American. 'Mainstream whites then adopted the flag as representative of their history,' even though 'it invoked a painful time when our forefathers were enslaved.' " (*Washington Post*, February 20, 1997)

## POLITICAL ORIENTATION

Unavailable

# Children's Defense Fund (1973)

25 E Street, NW
Washington, D.C. 20001
Phone: (202) 628-8787
Fax: (202) 662-3530
Internet: http://www.childrensdefense.org

"To provide a strong and effective voice for all the children of America, who cannot vote, lobby, or speak for themselves. . . . Our goal is to educate the nation about the needs of children and to encourage preventive investment in children before they get sick, drop out of school, suffer family breakdown, or get into trouble."

*PURPOSE*

136 total—106 professional; 30 support; plus 3 part-time professionals; approximately 120 interns and volunteers per year

*STAFF*

Marian Wright Edelman, founder and president. Edelman formerly directed the NAACP Legal Defense and Education Fund in Mississippi. In 1968 she founded the Washington Research Project, which became the Children's Defense Fund in 1973. Edelman also has served as the director of Harvard University's Center for Law and Education. A 1960 graduate of Spelman College, Edelman earned her law degree from Yale Law School in 1963.

*DIRECTOR*

501(c)(3)

*TAX STATUS*

1997—$20.6 million
1998—$17 million
Proposed 1999—$17.7 million

*BUDGET*

Foundation grants, 46 percent; individuals, 20 percent; special events/projects, 8 percent; investment income, 5 percent; gifts for endowment, 5 percent; other gifts, 5 percent; publications, 4 percent; corporate donations, 4 percent; other revenue, 3 percent

*FUNDING SOURCES*

Members: N/A
Branches/chapters: 9 state offices
Affiliate: Stand For Children, a tax-exempt organization

*SCOPE*

None

*PAC*

## METHOD OF OPERATION

♦ Advertisements ♦ Awards program ♦ Coalition forming ♦ Conferences/ seminars ♦ Congressional testimony ♦ Congressional voting analysis ♦ Demonstrations ♦ Direct action ♦ Educational foundation ♦ Films, videos, audiotapes ♦ Grassroots organizing ♦ Information clearinghouse ♦ Internet (E-mail alerts, Web site) ♦ Internships ♦ Legislative/regulatory monitoring (federal and state) ♦ Lobbying (federal and grassroots) ♦ Local/municipal affairs ♦ Media outreach ♦ Polling ♦ Research ♦ Telecommunication services (mailing lists) ♦ Training ♦ Voting records

## CURRENT CONCERNS

♦ Child care and after-school programs ♦ Child poverty ♦ Children's health insurance ♦ Early childhood development ♦ Education ♦ Gun violence and children ♦ Maternal and child health ♦ Welfare reform ♦ Youth employment

## PUBLICATIONS

*30 Simple Things Parents Can Do To Help Keep Children Safe From Violence*
*The Adolescent and Young Adult Fact Book*
*An Advocate's Guide to Fund Raising*
*An Advocate's Guide to the Media*
*An Advocate's Guide to the Summer Food Service Program*
*Children in the States 1997*
*CHIP Check-Up: A Healthy Start for Children*
*The Costs of Child Poverty*
*Guide My Feet: Prayers and Mediations on Loving and Working for Children*
*Helping Children by Strengthening Families*
*Helping Parents Work and Children Succeed: A Guide to Child Care and the 1996 Welfare Act*
*Key Facts About Child Care and Early Education: A Briefing Book*
*Lemon-Aid? Making the New Welfare Law Work for Children and Families*
*Locked Doors: States Struggling to Meet the Child Care Needs of Low-Income Working Families*
*Outside the Dream: Child Poverty in America*
*Poverty Matters: The Cost of Child Poverty in America*
*Rekindling the Spirit: A Vision for the New Millennial Movement to Leave No Child Behind*
*Rescuing the American Dream: Halting the Economic Freefall of Today's Young Families with Children*
*Stand for Children: A Parent's Guide to Child Advocacy*
*State Development & Child Care*
*State of America's Children Yearbook* (annual)
*Your Family's Rights Under the New Fair Housing Law: Protecting Families and Children from Discrimination*

Also offers a selection of research papers, posters, sweatshirts, T-shirts, and watches

## NEWSLETTER

*CDF Reports* (monthly)

## CONFERENCES

Annual conference

## BOARD OF DIRECTORS

## EFFECTIVENESS

"Gov. George Pataki made a promise in his State of the State address to provide health coverage to every uninsured child in a low-income family in the state. A generous new Federal program will enable him to do just that and more without spending additional state or local money. Yet oddly, Mr. Pataki seems reluctant to take full advantage of the Federal money. Under the $48 billion, 10-year program created by Congress last year to pay for health care for uninsured children, New York will be getting roughly $255 million a year for the next decade, with future adjustments depending on population changes. . . .

". . . [B]ut Mr. Pataki can afford to do much more. Indeed, under his proposal, some $410 million of Federal money would be left unspent over the next three years. The Children's Defense Fund and a coalition of child and health agencies are pushing for higher subsidies for children in families earning up to 200 percent of the poverty level. They are also asking for more comprehensive benefits, similar to those provided under Medicaid. New Jersey and Connecticut will use their Federal grants to pay for better benefits. . . ." (*New York Times*, February 1, 1998)

"Nearly one in seven children in the United States lacked health insurance in 1995, the Children's Defense Fund reported . . . warning that the nation needs to make expanding health coverage for children a top priority.

"In its annual 'State of America's Children' report, the nonprofit group also found that in the District, 18,654 children—or about one in six—had no insurance. Just over one out of every 10 children in Maryland and Virginia were uninsured the report found: 146,606 in Maryland and 185,006 in Virginia. Marian Wright Edelman, the group's president, said her organization plans to mobilize religious groups, other children's organizations and women's groups to push for legislation to address the problem. . . .

"More than 15 bills addressing children's health coverage are expected to be introduced this session, according to James Weill, the Defense Fund's general counsel.

"The children's advocacy group also announced yesterday that it will hold a series of 'Stand for Children' rallies around the country on June 1. On that date last year, hundreds of thousands gathered at the Lincoln Memorial to support the general goal of putting children first. The organization also plans to host a 'virtual' Stand for Children Day on the Internet. . . ." (*Washington Post*, March 13, 1997)

". . . [Marian Wright Edelman's] increasing fame masks some serious problems facing the organization and movement she created 23 years ago. The Children's Defense Fund is a top-heavy Capitol Hill lobby at a time when more decisions affecting children are being made by state governments. Despite her close White House ties, Ms. Edelman this month heard President Clinton embrace a Wisconsin initiative that abolishes something she has fought for all along: the entitlement to welfare provided by Aid to Families with Dependent Children. Her take-no-prisoners approach has opened rifts with would-be allies, while the CDF suffers internal strain; it recently let seven staff members go and has retained a consultant to decide whether it should recast itself. . . .

"Besides dealing with internal stress, the CDF has been losing credibility. Its once-vaunted policy research is less respected, say congressional and administration staffers, who now favor alternative sources such as the Center on Budget and Policy Priorities. The Republican takeover of Congress in 1994 didn't help the CDF's influence, of course, but the decline began earlier.

" 'The fund's credibility in Washington is sharply reduced,' says Douglas Besharov, of the center-right American Enterprise Institute. Though he considers Ms. Edelman 'one of my heroes,' he thinks the CDF 'has lost sight of the need to be and seem absolutely impartial. They have a traditional 1960s agenda in a world that's much more complicated.' The CDF says that its research hasn't changed, but that public skepticism over statistics has increased.

"Still, Ms. Edelman's group has been remarkably successful at winning mainstream appeal at a time when some other traditionally 'liberal' groups have been on the run. Because it has counted as board members such prominent Clintonites as Health and Human Services Secretary Donna Shalala, Mrs. Clinton (whose chief-of-staff, Maggie Williams, is a former CDF staffer) and Mrs. Clinton's friend Susan Thomases, it has unusually close ties to the administration. Long before the Clintons came to Washington, Ms. Edelman and her group were credited with helping to push through the child-welfare laws, Medicaid expansions and the Child Care and Development Block Grant of the 1980s, and with defending Head Start. 'She's the mother of the modern child-advocacy movement,' says Eve Brooks, president of the National Association of Child Advocates. . . .

"Also impressive is Ms. Edelman's unrivaled access to corporate dollars. Its long list of donors includes AT&T Corp., Anheuser-Busch Cos., Exxon Corp. and Ford Motor Co. Half of its $16 million annual budget is from corporate and foundation money. . . .

"But the CDF's powerful friends, funds and respectability haven't helped it overcome unfavorable trends in government. Policy is steadily shifting from Washington to the grass-roots level. Yet the fund has actually closed offices in Mississippi, Texas and Washington, D.C., and now has fully fledged offices only in Ohio and Minnesota. The National Association of Child Advocates, by contrast, has operations in 42 states. 'They really can't orchestrate things in D.C. the way they once could,' says Bill Treanor, publisher of the newsletter *Youth Today*. The CDF treated state groups as 'country bumpkins,' he says, so now 'there really aren't any grass roots.' " (*Wall Street Journal*, May 28, 1996)

"Last fall, as [Marian Wright] Edelman watched the welfare battle take shape, she privately implored the President not to compromise federal standards. When Clinton nevertheless signaled his support for a Senate bill that would transform federal welfare spending into a system of smaller, block grants to the states—thereby eliminating the safety net of protections that children have, regardless of which state they live in— Edelman spoke out.

"In 'An Open Letter to the President,' which ran last Nov. 3 in the *Washington Post*, Edelman urged Clinton to oppose welfare and Medicaid block grants. She wrote, 'Do you think the Old Testament prophets, Isaiah, Micah and Amos—or Jesus Christ—would support such policies?' If he were to let federal protections go, she warned, 'we may not get them back in our lifetime or our children's.' She concluded: 'What a tragic irony it would be for this regressive attack on children and the poor to occur on your watch. For me, this is a moral litmus test for your presidency.' In the end, Clinton withdrew his support for the bill, perhaps because he was shamed by his old friend, but also because it was good politics to do so. . . .

"The word moral appears seven times in Edelman's letter, and the certitude with which she plunges ahead is both her greatest strength and her greatest flaw. What looks like 'morality' to her is merely discredited 1960s liberalism to others." (*Time*, June 3, 1996)

# Handgun Control, Inc./Center to Prevent Handgun Violence (1974)

1225 Eye Street, NW
Suite 1100
Washington, D.C. 20005
Phone: (202) 898-0792 (HCI); (202) 289-7319 (CPHV)
Fax: (202) 371-9615 (HCI); (202) 408-1851 (CPHV)
Internet: http://www.handguncontrol.org *or*
http://www.cphv.org

| | |
|---|---|
| **PURPOSE** | HCI: "To work for legislation on the federal and state levels to keep guns out of the wrong hands."<br>CPHV: "To reduce gun violence through education, research, and legal advocacy." |
| **STAFF** | HCI: 45 total—32 professional; 13 support; plus 1 intern<br>CPHV: 25 total—18 professional; 7 support; plus 1 intern |
| **DIRECTOR** | Sarah Brady, chair. Before becoming chair of Handgun Control, Inc. (HCI) in 1989, Brady had been active in the gun control movement since the mid-1980s. The "Brady Bill" gun law is named for her husband, Jim, a former White House press secretary who was injured in an assassination attempt on President Reagan. Sarah Brady previously worked for the Republican National Committee, the National Republican Congressional Committee, and two members of Congress. She also has worked as a public school teacher and is a graduate of the College of William and Mary. |
| **TAX STATUS** | HCI: 501(c)(4)<br>CPHV: 501(c)(3) |
| **BUDGET** | 1998—Unavailable<br>Proposed 1999—Unavailable |
| **FUNDING SOURCES** | HCI: Membership, 58 percent; general contributions, 39 percent; other, 3 percent<br>CPVH: General contributions, 95 percent; other, 5 percent |
| **SCOPE** | Members: HCI—360,000<br>Branches/chapters: regional offices for both HCI and CPHV in Los Angeles, San Diego, and Sacramento<br>Affiliates: N/A |

Handgun Control Voter Education Fund

HCI:
♦ Advertisements ♦ Campaign contributions ♦ Coalition forming ♦ Conferences/seminars ♦ Congressional testimony ♦ Congressional voting analysis ♦ Demonstrations ♦ Direct action ♦ Electoral politics ♦ Films/video/audiotapes ♦ Grassroots organizing ♦ Legislative/regulatory monitoring (federal and state) ♦ Lobbying (federal, state, and grassroots) ♦ Local/municipal affairs ♦ Media outreach ♦ Television and radio production ♦ Voting records

CPHV: ♦ Advertisements ♦ Coalition forming ♦ Media outreach ♦ Research ♦ Speakers program

**METHOD OF OPERATION**

Gun control laws

**CURRENT CONCERNS**

None

**PUBLICATIONS**

*HCI Progress Report* (quarterly)
*Law Enforcement Bulletin* (quarterly for the law enforcement community)
*Legal Action Report* (quarterly for legal community)
*Progress Report* (quarterly for HCI and CPHV members)
*Project Lifeline* (quarterly for health care community)

**NEWSLETTER**

Unavailable

**CONFERENCES**

HCI: Sarah Brady, chair; Mark Ingram, treasurer; Byrl Phillips-Taylor, secretary

Other members:
♦ David Birenbaum ♦ Kevin Chavous ♦ Stanley Foster ♦ Mary Lewis Grow ♦ Clarence Harmon ♦ Frank Hartmann ♦ John Hechinger Sr. ♦ Richard Parise ♦ John Phillips ♦ John Rosenthal ♦ Nancy Schoenke ♦ Mimi Sutherland ♦ Jerry terHorst ♦ Jann Wenner

CPHV: Sarah Brady, chair; Mark Ingram, treasurer; Byrl Phillips-Taylor, secretary

Other members:
♦ David Birenbaum ♦ James S. Brady ♦ Nick Brown ♦ Kevin Chavous ♦ Roscoe Dellums ♦ Stanley Foster ♦ Mary Lewis Grow ♦ Frank Hartmann ♦ Maggie Kemp ♦ Victoria Reggie Kennedy ♦ John Phillips ♦ John Rosenthal ♦ Phyllis Segal ♦ Lynne Wasserman ♦ Jann Wenner

**BOARD OF DIRECTORS**

## EFFECTIVENESS

"Advocates of gun control are also bringing legal cases to expand the definition of product liability law. They are seeking to hold gun makers responsible for violent shootings if their products fail to have the latest safety features and are sold in ways that get them to criminals.

"These advocates are not asserting, as in most product liability cases, that the gun industry makes defective goods. Rather, they say that because guns are so lethal, the conduct of gun makers in designing and selling their products creates a legal accountability.

" 'We want to make the gun industry accountable for violence in a way it has never been held accountable before,' said Dennis Henigan, legal director of the Center to Prevent Handgun Violence, a nonprofit organization.

"The $2 billion firearms industry, battered by slumping profits and a poor public image, has already made it clear it does not want to suffer the same fate as the tobacco industry." (*New York Times*, December 18, 1997)

## POLITICAL ORIENTATION

Unavailable

# Human Rights Campaign (1980)

1101 14th Street, NW
Suite 200
Washington, D.C. 20005
Phone: (202) 628-4160
Fax: (202) 347-5323
Internet: hrc@hrc.org *or* http://www.hrc.org

"Lobbies Congress, provides campaign support, and educates the public to ensure that lesbian and gay Americans can be open, honest, and safe at home, work, and in the community."

**PURPOSE**

64 total—56 professional; 8 support; plus 12 interns

**STAFF**

Elizabeth Birch, executive director. Prior to joining the Human Rights Campaign (HRC) as executive director in 1995, Birch was director of litigation and human resources counsel for Apple Computer, Inc. Her background also includes work in private law practice and a clerkship with the California Supreme Court. Birch founded AIDS Legal Services in Northern California and is a former co-chair of the National Gay and Lesbian Task Force. She is a graduate of the Santa Clara University School of Law.

**DIRECTOR**

501(c)(3) and 501(c)(4)

**TAX STATUS**

Fiscal year ending March 31, 1998—$11.1 million
Proposed F.Y. 1999—$13.5 million

**BUDGET**

Membership dues, 70 percent; special events/projects, 22 percent; foundation grants, 1 percent; corporate donations, 1 percent; other, 6 percent

**FUNDING SOURCES**

Members: 250,000 individuals
Branches/chapters: N/A
Affiliates: N/A

**SCOPE**

Human Rights Campaign PAC

**PAC**

## METHOD OF OPERATION

◆ Advertisements ◆ Campaign contributions ◆ Coalition forming ◆ Conferences/seminars ◆ Congressional testimony ◆ Congressional voting analysis ◆ Electoral politics ◆ Grassroots organizing (Field Action Network, Speak Out Action Grams [messages to Congress]) ◆ Initiative/referendum campaigns ◆ Internet (databases, electronic bulletin boards, E-mail alerts, Web site) ◆ Legislative/regulatory monitoring (federal) ◆ Internships ◆ Legislative/regulatory monitoring (federal) ◆ Lobbying (federal) ◆ Media outreach ◆ Polling ◆ Product merchandising ◆ Research ◆ Speakers program ◆ Telecommunications services (mailing lists) ◆ Training and technical assistance ◆ Voter registration ◆ Voting records

## CURRENT CONCERNS

◆ Ending workplace discrimination against gays and lesbians ◆ Equal rights for lesbian and gay people ◆ HIV/AIDS issues ◆ Prevent anti-gay hate crimes ◆ Respond to anti-gay legislative attacks

## PUBLICATIONS

*Equality: A Winning Message—Talking About Lesbian and Gay Issues in Your Campaign*
*Resource Guide to Coming Out*

## NEWSLETTER

*HRC Quarterly*

## CONFERENCES

Outvote (election years)
National Coming Out Project
Youth College for Campaign Training (election years)

## BOARD OF DIRECTORS

◆ Gwen Baba ◆ Terry Bean ◆ Timothy Boggs ◆ Jeanne Branson ◆ Mary Breslauer ◆ Tom Buche ◆ Blake Byrne ◆ Stampp Corbin ◆ Michael T. Duffy ◆ Julia Fitz-Randolph ◆ Mark French ◆ Steve Gunderson ◆ Everett Hamilton ◆ Nancy Hamilton ◆ Stephanie Hart ◆ Fred Hochberg ◆ Chuck Holmes ◆ Barry Karas ◆ Candy Marcum ◆ Rob Morris ◆ Marylouise Oates ◆ Michael Palm ◆ Barbara Roberts ◆ Worth Ross ◆ Abby R. Rubenfeld ◆ Jeffrey Sachse ◆ Jessica Stevens ◆ Andrew Tobias ◆ Richard Turner

## EFFECTIVENESS

"President Clinton signed an executive order yesterday to protect homosexual federal workers from job discrimination. . . .

" 'Since early in President Clinton's first term, most Cabinet-level departments and agencies have added sexual orientation to their equal employment policies, but these policies were not uniformly administered,' said Kim I. Mills, education director for the Human Rights Campaign. 'This executive order will remedy that situation.' " (*Washington Times*, May 29, 1998)

"For the last week and a half, the locally based Human Rights Campaign—a gay and lesbian rights organization that claims 225,000 members nationwide—has been using its Web site and e-mail networks to generate a write-in campaign for the renewal of 'Ellen' by ABC. . . .

"So far the campaign is generating 250 letters a day to ABC Entertainment president Jamie Tarses, Disney chairman Michael Eisner and Disney Network TV president David Newsman, all of whose postal and e-mail addresses are listed on the Web site. . . .

"According to spokesman David Smith, the campaign expects to use its telegram network, usually aimed at members of Congress, to blitz CBS and NBC with appeals to pick up the show should ABC drop it." (*Washington Post*, February 6, 1998)

"Officials of two national gay men's and lesbian organizations announced plans yesterday for a 'millennium march' on Washington in the spring of 2000. Human Rights Campaign spokesman David M. Smith said representatives of his group and the Universal Fellowship of Metropolitan Community Churches have been meeting to plan the event. 'It will be the largest event of its kind,' Smith said. 'We plan to build on our successes of the 1990s and set clear objectives to take us into the next century.' " (*Washington Post*, February 6, 1998)

"The Human Rights Campaign continues to hold the title of the largest and most powerful of the national Gay political organizations. It raised $11.1 million for its budget last year and expects to pull in $12 million in income this year. It also runs the nation's largest Gay political action committee. According to the U.S. Federal Elections Commission, HRC's PAC ranked 19th among 826 similar PAC's in terms of the amount of money ($1.13 million) it disbursed to campaigns for candidates for federal offices in the last cycle.

"With 12 lobbyists, HRC is a recognized force in the halls of Congress. If there was any doubt about HRC's ability to get its foot into the door at the offices of large numbers of lawmakers on Capitol Hill, that came to an end in September 1996, when the Senate voted on the Employment Non-Discrimination Act (ENDA), a Gay civil rights bill. Following a lobbying effort coordinated by HRC, the Senate came within one vote of passing ENDA. The strength of the pro-ENDA vote surprised many political observers, who did not think a Gay civil rights bill could come that close to passing under a Republican-controlled Senate. HRC was not the only group lobbying for ENDA. But its visible role in pushing for the legislation, which includes pro-ENDA television ads, caught the attention of the so-called power brokers in the nation's capital." (*Washington Blade*, December 12, 1997)

". . . President Clinton's decision to attend Saturday's Human Rights Campaign national dinner isn't just unusual.

"It is historic.

"The event here . . . will be the first time a president has spoken at an event sponsored by a gay and lesbian group. . . .

"Clinton will talk about a White House conference on hate crimes being held. . . . The event will focus on groups that target gays as well as those that attack minorities.

"Gay and lesbian activists say Clinton's speech marks a coming of age for a political movement that has become a national force in the past decade. . . ." (*USA Today*, November 7, 1997)

"A year into her job, the 39-year old [Elizabeth] Birch is proving to be a public relations virtuoso. By the end of her first month at the HRC, she has blitzed through 10 cities on a speaking tour. She went on to snag Candace Gingrich, the lesbian half-sister of House Speaker Newt Gingrich, R-Ga., for a splashy get-out-the-vote campaign, and she persuaded six gay relatives of members of Congress to fly to Washington to publicize a gay-rights bill.

"Now she's witnessing the results of her PR juggernaut. HRC membership, which was holding steady at about 80,000 before her arrival, has zoomed to 150,000. The HRC raised $7 million last year, an increase of $1.5 million over 1994. And Birch has big plans for the fall elections. Joining with state and local gay groups, the HRC intends to get involved in more than 150 congressional races this fall. The group has also promised to funnel more than $1 million into individual campaigns through political action committee contributions and independent expenditures. This summer the group has scheduled a three-day political conventions in Chicago, where it hopes to train a thousand volunteers in grass-roots organizing techniques.

"By contrast, she isn't afraid to indulge in boosterism, and she sets unabashedly big goals. 'I want HRC to be the AARP of the gay community.' she said, referring to the American Association of Retired Persons." (*National Journal*, March 23, 1996)

## POLITICAL ORIENTATION

"the largest political lobby on gay issues" (*Washington Post*, April 24, 1997)

# Lambda Legal Defense and Education Fund, Inc. (1973)

120 Wall Street
Suite 1500
New York, New York 10005-3404
Phone: (212) 809-8585
Fax: (212) 809-0055
Internet: http://www.lambdalegal.org

| | |
|---|---|
| "Committed to achieving full recognition of the civil rights of lesbians, gay men and people with HIV/AIDS through impact litigation, education and public policy work." | *PURPOSE* |
| 46 total—22 professional; 24 support; 1 part-time; plus 8 interns and 10 volunteers | *STAFF* |
| Kevin M. Cathcart, executive director. Cathcart has been executive director of Lambda Legal Defense and Education Fund (LLDEF) since 1992. Before joining Lambda, he was executive director of Gay and Lesbian Advocates and Defenders (GLAD) in Boston from 1984 to 1992. While in Boston, Cathcart also served on the board of directors of Gay Community News and as a staff attorney at the North Shore Children's Law Project. He has served on the boards of other state and national organizations. Cathcart was educated at Richard Stockton State College, the Harvard Graduate School of Education, and the Northeastern School of Law. | *DIRECTOR* |
| 501(c)(3) | *TAX STATUS* |
| Fiscal year ending October 31, 1997—$3.09 million<br>F.Y. 1998—$3.7 million<br>Proposed F.Y. 1999—Unavailable | *BUDGET* |
| Individuals, 65 percent; donated legal services and attorney fees, 21 percent; foundations, 7 percent; other, 7 percent | *FUNDING SOURCES* |
| Members: 14,000 individuals<br>Branches/chapters: regional offices in Chicago, Atlanta, and Los Angeles<br>Affiliates: N/A | *SCOPE* |

| | |
|---|---|
| *PAC* | None |
| *METHOD OF OPERATION* | ◆ Coalition forming ◆ Information clearinghouse ◆ Internet (Web site) ◆ Legal assistance ◆ Legislative/regulatory monitoring (federal and state) ◆ Litigation ◆ Media outreach ◆ Research ◆ Speakers program |
| *CURRENT CONCERNS* | ◆ Civil rights of people with HIV/AIDS ◆ Lesbian and gay civil rights |
| *PUBLICATIONS* | *Adoption by Lesbians and Gay Men: An Overview of the Law in the 50 States*<br>*Anti-Gay Initiatives: Pre-Election Challenges and Constitutional Challenges*<br>*Asylum Based on Sexual Orientation: A Resource Guide*<br>*Civil Marriage for Lesbians and Gay Men: Organizing in Communities of Faith*<br>*Health Care Reform: Lessons from the HIV Epidemic*<br>*HIV and Family Law: A Survey*<br>*Lesbians and Gay Men Seeking Custody and Visitation: An Overview of the State of the Law*<br>*Life Planning: Legal Documents for Lesbians and Gay Men*<br>*The Little Black Book: This One Can Keep You Out of Trouble*<br>*Negotiating for Equal Employment Benefits: A Resource Packet*<br>*Sexual Orientation Discrimination in Employment: A Guide to Remedies*<br>*Sexual Orientation, HIV and Immigration Law*<br>*Snapshots from a Civil Rights Movement: Lambda 25*<br>*Stopping the Anti-Gay Abuse of Students in Public Schools: A Legal Perspective* |
| *NEWSLETTER* | *The Lambda Update* (3 times a year) |
| *CONFERENCES* | None |
| *BOARD OF DIRECTORS* | Shedrick O. Davis III and Gale Richards, co-chairs; George D. Tuttle, secretary; Frances J. Goldstein, treasurer<br><br>Other members:<br>◆ Barbara Bailey ◆ Alvin H. Baum Jr. ◆ Daniel H. Bowers ◆ Wayne S. Braveman ◆ Stuart C. Burden ◆ Jerry Simon Chasen ◆ Pedro De Armas ◆ Lisa D. Freeman ◆ Joan P. Garner ◆ Kathryn G. Graham ◆ Cynthia H. Hyndman ◆ R. Edward Ishmael Jr. ◆ John C. Jewett ◆ Jill Kasofsky ◆ Clarice Liu ◆ Donald Millinger ◆ Robert W. Ollis Jr. ◆ Susan Owens ◆ Michael S. Rauschenberg ◆ Gregory G. Simoncini ◆ Martha E. Stark ◆ Jay Swanson ◆ Vivian Todini ◆ Vallerie D. Wagner |
| *EFFECTIVENESS* | "A Federal judge ruled for the second time yesterday that the military's 'don't ask, don't tell' policy violated the Constitution by discriminating against homosexuals for no other reason than to cater to the prejudices of heterosexuals. |

"The ruling, by Judge Eugene H. Nickerson of the Federal District Court in Brooklyn, builds on his similar ruling in the same case. This time, however, he struck down the three-year-old policy in its entirety, including its ban on homosexual activity, becoming the first judge to do so. . . .

" 'We are ecstatic,' said Beatrice Dohrn, legal director of the Lambda Legal Defense and education Fund, which filed the suit on behalf of the plaintiffs in 1994 along with the Lesbian and Gay Rights Project of the American Civil Liberties Union.

" 'It is the most devastating blow that the policy has suffered,' Ms. Dohrn said." (*New York Times*, July 3, 1998)

". . . The New Jersey lawsuit, backed by the Lambda Legal Defense and Education Fund, a civil rights advocacy group, involved a man who had been barred from his position as a Scoutmaster in 1990, when he was a student at Rutgers University and Scout officials learned that he was gay. A divided three-judge court found last week that the Scouts were a public accommodation and had violated a New Jersey law protecting homosexuals from discrimination in such areas.

"But both the wording of the decision and George A. Davidson, the lawyer for the Boy Scouts of America, went on to paint the case in moral terms. Mr. Davidson said that the organization was concerned about the 'moral messages' that children would divine from a welcome mat for gay people. . . .

"Some gay leaders said the fight for access to these institutions bucks up against specific, deep-seated sources of discomfort about homosexuality." (*New York Times*, March 8, 1998)

"Lambda Legal Defense and Education Fund, the oldest of the national Gay groups, in essence is a law firm which specializes in Gay and AIDS-related cases. It doesn't take just any Gay or AIDS case, however, only those which, if successful, can provide a breakthrough ruling that can benefit the greatest number of Gays and people with AIDS.

"In recent years, Lambda has played an active role in challenging anti-Gay ballot measures in several states, including the most famous one, Colorado's Amendment 2. That amendment resulted in a landmark U.S. Supreme Court decision, Romer vs Evans, declaring such measures, targeted at Gay people, as unconstitutional.

"Lambda chalked up another important victory that same year when a federal jury in a case Lambda helped litigate found a Wisconsin school district negligent for failing to protect Gay high school student Jamie Nabozny from anti-Gay harassment and abuse from other students. The jury verdict prompted the school district to agree to a settlement in Nabozny's favor of nearly $1 million. The Nabozny case also played a role in prompting the U.S. Department of Education to issue federal guidelines addressing anti-Gay harassment in schools throughout the country." (*Washington Blade*, December 12, 1997)

"Lambda Legal Defense and Education Fund, the country's largest and oldest legal advocacy group for homosexuals, is taking on some of its toughest opponents on their home turf.

"Lambda plans to open a regional office in Atlanta—its first in the Bible Belt—by June. As the Southeast hub for the New York-based group, the Atlanta office will focus on civil-rights cases and disabilities cases involving AIDS patients. . . .

"Already, Lambda spends some of its $3.2 million annual budget fighting custody cases in the Southeast, including one on behalf of a gay father in North Carolina, says Beatrice Dohrn, Lambda's legal director." (*Wall Street Journal*, February 5, 1997)

"Health and Human Services Secretary, Donna Shalala and New York Gov. George Pataki were given failing grades for their response to the AIDS epidemic in a 'report card' issued today by a major gay legal group.

"In a statement to mark World AIDS Day, the Lambda Legal Defense and Education Fund said Defense Secretary William J. Perry would have received its highest grade for opposing a proposal to discharge HIV-positive service members but was instead given an 'incomplete for his support of the military's ban on lesbian and gay service members. . . .'

"The group said it flunked Shalala because of her refusal to endorse needle-exchange programs, her failure to lift federal restrictions on HIV-positive health care workers and her failure to ensure sufficient reimbursement rates in Medicaid programs that switch to managed-care systems.

"It said it failed Pataki for his proposed welfare plan because it would eliminate some housing assistance for people with the AIDS virus and then eliminate assistance to HIV-positive recipients of Aid to Families with Dependent Children." (*Los Angeles Times*, December 1, 1996)

"A school district in Wisconsin agreed to pay nearly $1 million to settle a federal lawsuit accusing it of violating a gay student's rights.

"The case could force schools nationwide to re-examine their policies set up to protect students from discrimination, experts say.

"The settlement came a day after a federal jury found three Ashland, Wis., school administrators liable for not protecting Jamie Nabozny, now 21, from anti-gay harassment.

" 'This is the first case in the country where school officials were found liable for failing to address anti-gay abuse,' said David Buckel, a lawyer for Lambda Legal Defense and Education Fund, a gay-rights organization that represented Nabozny." (*USA Today*, November 21, 1996)

# POLITICAL ORIENTATION

"At 25, LAMBDA Legal Defense and Education Fund, Inc. has become the oldest and largest lesbian and gay organization in the country.

"Since it waged its first battle to incorporate in 1973, Lambda has fought in court to win honorable discharges for gay and lesbian military personnel; medical coverage for AIDS patients; domestic partnership benefits for gay couples; adoption and visitation rights for gay and lesbian parents; equal rights treatment for gay and lesbian youths at public schools; and protection for gay and lesbian immigrants and political asylum seekers.

"The group, which is celebrating its 25th anniversary with events throughout the year, finds the 21st century looking equally as challenging. 'Some of the issues haven't changed, they have just shifted geographically,' said Kevin Cathcart, Lambda's executive director. Lambda still faces custody, adoption and employment discrimination in many states. . . ." (*New York Law Journal*, July 20, 1998)

# Leadership Conference on Civil Rights, Inc. (1950)

1629 K Street, NW
Suite 1010
Washington, D.C. 20006
Phone: (202) 466-3311
Fax: (202) 466-3435
Internet: http://www.civilrights.org

| | |
|---|---|
| "To advance civil rights through enactment, enforcement, and monitoring of federal legislation." | **PURPOSE** |
| 7 total—4 professional; 3 support | **STAFF** |
| Wade Henderson, executive director. Henderson previously served as the Washington Bureau Director of the NAACP. He is the author of numerous articles on civil rights and public policy. Henderson is a graduate of Howard University and Rutgers University School of Law. | **DIRECTOR** |
| 501(c)(4) | **TAX STATUS** |
| 1997—$350,000<br>1998—$350,000<br>Proposed 1999—$400,000 | **BUDGET** |
| Membership dues and annual fundraiser, the Hubert H. Humphrey Civil Rights Award dinner | **FUNDING SOURCES** |
| Members: 185 national organizations representing minorities, women, persons with disabilities, older Americans, labor, gays and lesbians, and major religious organizations<br>Branches/chapters: N/A<br>Affiliate: Leadership Conference Education Fund, a 501(c)(3) organization | **SCOPE** |
| None | **PAC** |

| **METHOD OF OPERATION** | ◆ Advertisements ◆ Awards program ◆ Coalition forming ◆ Conferences/seminars ◆ Congressional testimony ◆ Congressional voting analysis ◆ Demonstrations ◆ Educational foundation ◆ Grassroots organizing ◆ Information clearinghouse ◆ Internet (E-mail alerts, Web site) ◆ Internships ◆ Legislative/regulatory monitoring (federal and state) ◆ Library/information clearinghouse ◆ Lobbying (federal and grassroots) ◆ Media outreach ◆ Research ◆ Voter registration ◆ Voting records |
|---|---|
| **CURRENT CONCERNS** | ◆ Affirmative action ◆ Employment Non-Discrimination Act ◆ English-only language legislation ◆ Fair housing ◆ Welfare reform |
| **PUBLICATIONS** | Publishes brochures, reports, public service announcements |
| **NEWSLETTER** | *The Civil Rights Monitor* (quarterly) |
| **CONFERENCES** | Hubert H. Humphrey Civil Rights Award Dinner (annual) Holds approximately four other conferences per year |
| **BOARD OF DIRECTORS** | Dorothy I. Height, chairperson; Antonia Hernandez, Judith Lichtman, and William L. Taylor, vice chairpersons; Horace Deets, secretary; Gerald W. McEntee, treasurer; Jane O'Grady, legislative chairperson; Joseph L. Rauh, Jr., counsel emeritus

Other members of the executive committee: ◆ Barbara Arnwine ◆ Elizabeth Birch ◆ Becky Cain ◆ Joan Brown Campbell ◆ Robert Chase ◆ Jackie DeFazio ◆ Anita Perez Ferguson ◆ Matthew Finucane ◆ Marcia Greenberger ◆ Harry Guenther ◆ Patricia Ireland ◆ Rebecca Isaacs ◆ Elaine Jones ◆ Joseph Lowery ◆ Leon Lynch ◆ Kweisi Mfume ◆ Laura Murphy ◆ Hugh Price ◆ David Saperstein ◆ Richard Womack ◆ Patrisha Wright ◆ Stephen P. Yokich ◆ Raul Yzaguirre ◆ Daniel Zingale |
| **EFFECTIVENESS** | "... But a leading civil rights group said the White House initiative would add much-needed muscle to the nation's anti-discrimination effort.
" 'Vigorous enforcement of the nation's civil rights laws is the single most important step the administration can take to achieve the promise of one America for all,' said Wade Henderson, executive director of the Leadership Conference on Civil Rights, a coalition of more than 180 national advocacy groups representing racial and ethnic minorities, the disabled and homosexuals." (*Washington Post*, January 20, 1998) |

". . . But like much of what's left of the liberal coalition, the conference finds itself scrambling to hold ground. After some internal dissent, the conference was defeated when it attempted to oppose the Supreme Court appointment of Clarence Thomas. Now the conference, like the entire civil rights community, is fighting to stave off attacks on affirmative action. [Executive director Wade] Henderson said he also planned to get the group more deeply involved in shaping welfare reform, in immigration issues and in extending civil rights laws to gays and lesbians." (*Washington Post*, May 5, 1996)

"liberal" (*Wall Street Journal*, November 10, 1994)

# League of United Latin American Citizens (LULAC) (1929)

1133 20th Street, NW
Suite 750
Washington, D.C. 20036
Phone: (202) 408-0060
Fax: (202) 408-0064
Internet: lulac@aol.com *or* http://www.lulac.org

| | |
|---|---|
| *PURPOSE* | "To advance the economic condition, educational attainment, political influence, health and civil rights of the Hispanic population of the United States." |
| *STAFF* | 6 total—4 professional; 2 support; plus 1 intern; 40 volunteers |
| *DIRECTOR* | Brent A. Wilkes, national executive director. Wilkes has worked in various capacities for the League of United Latin American Citizens (LULAC) since 1988. He is a graduate of Dartmouth College. |
| *TAX STATUS* | 501(c)(4) |
| *BUDGET* | 1998—Unavailable<br>Proposed 1999—Unavailable |
| *FUNDING SOURCES* | National conference, 40 percent; membership, 20 percent; foundation grants, 15 percent; corporate donations, 15 percent; federal, state, and local grants, 10 percent |
| *SCOPE* | Members: 115,000 individuals<br>Branches/chapters: 650 councils nationwide<br>Affiliates: LULAC Foundation, a 501(c)(3) organization; LULAC Federal Training Institute; LULAC National Education Service Centers; LULAC National Scholarship Fund; SER-JOBS for Progress, Inc. |
| *PAC* | None |

♦ Advertisements ♦ Awards program ♦ Boycotts ♦ Coalition forming ♦ Conferences/seminars ♦ Congressional testimony ♦ Congressional voting analysis ♦ Demonstrations ♦ Direct action ♦ Film/video/audiotapes ♦ Grantmaking ♦ Grassroots organizing ♦ Initiative/referendum campaigns ♦ International activities ♦ Internet (Web site) ♦ Legislative/regulatory monitoring (federal and state) ♦ Library/information clearinghouse ♦ Litigation ♦ Lobbying (federal, state, and grassroots) ♦ Local/municipal affairs ♦ Media outreach ♦ Participations in regulatory proceedings (federal and state) ♦ Performance ratings ♦ Polling ♦ Research ♦ Scholarships ♦ Speakers program ♦ Telecommunications services ♦ Voter registration

## METHOD OF OPERATION

♦ Affirmative action ♦ Census ♦ Citizenship ♦ Civil rights ♦ Economic development ♦ Education ♦ Elderly ♦ Employment and training ♦ Health ♦ Housing ♦ Immigration ♦ Leadership ♦ Voter registration and rights ♦ Women ♦ Youth

## CURRENT CONCERNS

None

## PUBLICATIONS

*LULAC News* (bimonthly)

## NEWSLETTER

National convention (annual)
State conventions (annual)
Civil rights summit
Educational summit

## CONFERENCES

Members of the national executive committee (voting members):
Rick Dovalina, national president; Belen B. Robles, immediate past national president; Jason Arce, national youth president; Carolina Munoz, national treasurer; Ana Estrada, national vice president for women; Juan Carlos Lizardi, national vice president for youth; Damaris Sifuentes, national vice president for young adults; Ursulo Castillo, national vice president for elderly; Hector Flores, national vice president for Southwest; Augustin Sanchez, national vice president for Midwest; Jose R. Pacheco, national vice president for Far West; Carlos Lopez Nieves, national vice president for Southeast; Regla Gonzalez, national vice president for Northeast

Members of the national executive committee (nonvoting members):
Brent A. Wilkes, national executive director; Ray Velarde, legal advisor; Frank Ortiz, chief of staff; Louis Adame, sergeant at arms; Alfonso Maldonado, parliamentarian

## BOARD OF DIRECTORS

## EFFECTIVENESS

"Meet the new Hidalgo County establishment. Like the old guard, its members have master's degrees and country-club memberships. Unlike the old guard, they have Hispanic surnames, and they credit their rise to prosperity to a university that some Texans still call 'Taco Tech,' but is properly known as the University of Texas-Pan American. . . .

"Indeed, while the Anglo elite in McAllen was sending its sons and daughters to the University of Texas at Austin, Southern Methodist University or the Ivy League, the offspring of local Hispanic families were swelling the ranks of Pan Am in nearby Edinburg. And just as New York's City College was once a gateway to the middle class for generations of European immigrants, Pan Am has served as the means to the mainstream for recent generations of this region's long-disadvantaged Hispanic majority. . . .

"Higher education wasn't seen as an option for many Mexican-Americans until the 1960s, when the civil-rights movement and such incentives as Pell Grants and federal student loans encouraged poor youth to go to college. And through the late 1980s, the student body at Pan Am quadrupled in size. Almost all new students came from Hispanic backgrounds, and almost all were first-generation college students.

"Still, it wasn't exactly a premier institution. Established in 1927 as Edinburg College, a two-year community college, it expanded to a four-year university in 1952 but had no professional schools and no doctoral program. It didn't offer its first master's degree—in education—until 1971.

"Then, in 1987, the League of United Latin American Citizens filed a lawsuit on behalf of Hispanic students, alleging that public universities throughout South Texas didn't adequately serve the students' needs. As a result, the Texas Legislature awarded $350 million in new funds for South Texas schools and later incorporated many into either the University of Texas or Texas A&M systems.

"Pan Am has since added five undergraduate degrees, 14 graduate degrees and a full doctoral program in business administration, as well as a shared doctoral program in educational administration with the College of Education at UT-Austin. Other universities in the Rio Grande Valley are flourishing, too." (*Wall Street Journal*, July 16, 1997)

## POLITICAL ORIENTATION

Unavailable

# Mexican American Legal Defense and Educational Fund (1968)

634 South Spring Street
11th Floor
Los Angeles, California 90014
Phone: (213) 629-2512
Fax: (213) 629-8016

1518 K Street, NW
Suite 410
Washington, D.C. 20005
Phone: (202) 628-4074
Fax: (202) 393-4206

Internet: http://www.maldef.org

"To protect and promote the civil rights of the more than 29 million Latinos living in the United States."

**PURPOSE**

75 total—50 professional; 25 support; plus 15 interns

**STAFF**

Antonia Hernandez, president and general counsel. Hernandez was elected president of the Mexican American Legal Defense and Educational Fund (MALDEF) in 1985 and has served the organization in various capacities since 1981. An attorney by training, she was staff counsel to the U.S. Senate Committee on the Judiciary and directing attorney for the Legal Aid Foundation of Los Angeles. Hernandez earned a B.A. degree from the University of Los Angeles and received her law degree from UCLA School of Law.

**DIRECTOR**

501(c)(3)

**TAX STATUS**

1997—$5 million
1998—$4.7 million
Proposed 1999—$5 million

**BUDGET**

Unavailable

**FUNDING SOURCES**

Members: N/A
Branches/chapters: Regional offices in Los Angeles, San Francisco, Chicago, and San Antonio, Texas; satellite office in Sacramento, California; program office in Phoenix
Affiliates: N/A

**SCOPE**

| | |
|---|---|
| *PAC* | None |
| *METHOD OF OPERATION* | ♦ Awards program ♦ Coalition forming ♦ Congressional testimony ♦ Congressional voting analysis ♦ Films/video/audiotapes ♦ Grantmaking ♦ Internet (E-mail alerts, Web site) ♦ Legal assistance ♦ Legislative/regulatory monitoring (federal and state) ♦ Litigation ♦ Media outreach ♦ Scholarships for Latino law and communications students |
| *CURRENT CONCERNS* | ♦ Civil rights ♦ Electoral districts ♦ Education ♦ Immigrants' rights ♦ Protecting equal access measures |
| *PUBLICATIONS* | Annual report |
| *NEWSLETTER* | *MALDEF* (2 times a year)<br>*Leading Hispanics* (2 times a year) |
| *CONFERENCES* | N/A |
| *BOARD OF DIRECTORS* | ♦ Lillian G. Apodaca ♦ Zöe Baird ♦ Joseph Barish ♦ Martin R. Castro ♦ Alex Chaves ♦ Hector J. Cuellar ♦ Bette F. DeGraw ♦ Robert F. Falkner ♦ Herlinda Garcia ♦ Leo Gomez ♦ Al Gurule ♦ Paul Gutierrez ♦ Ana Margarita (Cha) Guzman ♦ Frank Herrera Jr. ♦ Teresa Leger de Fernandez ♦ Gregory Luna ♦ Raymond C. Marshall ♦ Totcho Mindiola Jr. ♦ Gloria Molina ♦ Max Navarro ♦ Donald L. Pierce ♦ Matthew J. Piers ♦ Frank J. Quevedo ♦ Irma Rangel ♦ Thomas B. Reston ♦ Jose R. Ronquillo ♦ Miriam Santos ♦ Joseph Stern ♦ Andrew I. Sun ♦ Robert E. Valdez ♦ Karen Wegmann ♦ Ann Marie Wheelock ♦ Peter D. Zeughauser |
| *EFFECTIVENESS* | Unavailable |
| *POLITICAL ORIENTATION* | Unavailable |

# NAACP Legal Defense and Educational Fund, Inc. (1940)

99 Hudson Street
Suite 1600-10
New York, New York 10013
Phone: (212) 219-1900
Fax: (212) 226-7592
Toll-free: (800) 221-7822

1275 K Street, NW
Suite 301
Washington, D.C. 20005
Phone: (202) 682-1300
Fax: (202) 682-1312

To provide "free legal representation to individuals and classes and groups who are challenging race discrimination in education, employment, housing, voting rights, and the administration of criminal justice."

**PURPOSE**

63 total—32 professional; 31 support

**STAFF**

Elaine R. Jones, president and director-counsel

**DIRECTOR**

501(c)(3)

**TAX STATUS**

1998—$9.2 million
Proposed 1999—$9.2 million

**BUDGET**

Contributions, 37 percent; investment income, 30 percent; special events, 8 percent; court costs/attorney fees awarded, 19 percent; bequests, 2 percent; other, 4 percent

**FUNDING SOURCES**

Members: N/A
Branch/chapter: Los Angeles regional office
Affiliates: N/A
The NAACP Legal Defense and Educational Fund, Inc. (LDF) is not part of the National Association for the Advancement of Colored People (NAACP), although it was founded by the NAACP in 1940. LDF has had a separate board, program, staff, offices, and budget since 1957.

**SCOPE**

None

**PAC**

| | |
|---|---|
| *METHOD OF OPERATION* | ♦ Awards program ♦ Coalition forming ♦ Conferences/seminars ♦ Congressional testimony ♦ Legal assistance ♦ Legislative/regulatory monitoring (federal) ♦ Library/information clearinghouse ♦ Litigation ♦ Scholarships ♦ Training and technical assistance |
| *CURRENT CONCERNS* | ♦ Affirmative action in education and the workplace ♦ Fair employment and welfare reform ♦ Environmental justice ♦ Legislative redistricting ♦ Preserving access to health care ♦ School desegregation |
| *PUBLICATIONS* | Unavailable |
| *NEWSLETTER* | *Equal Justice* (quarterly) |
| *CONFERENCES* | Annual Institute (May, in New York City) Sponsors lawyers' training institutes and seminars on civil rights |
| *BOARD OF DIRECTORS* | William T. Coleman Jr. and Robert H. Preiskel, co-chairs; Daniel L. Rabinowitz, vice chair; James M. Nabrit III, secretary; Eleanor S. Applewhite, treasurer; Elaine R. Jones, president and director-counsel; Theodore M. Shaw, associate director-counsel; Norman J. Chachkin, director of litigation; Edward H. Gordon, director of finance and administration; Patricia A.M. Grayson, director of development

Other members:
♦ Billye Suber Aaron ♦ Clarence Avant ♦ Mary Frances Berry ♦ Julius L. Chambers ♦ Theodore L. Cross ♦ Kenneth C. Edelin ♦ Toni G. Fay ♦ Jack Greenberg ♦ Louis Harris ♦ Quincy Jones ♦ Vernon E. Jordan ♦ David E. Kendall ♦ David S. Lindau ♦ John D. Maguire ♦ Martin D. Payson ♦ C. Carl Randolph ♦ Judith T. Sapers ♦ William H. Scheide ♦ Jay Topkis ♦ John W. Walker ♦ George Wallerstein ♦ Roger W. Wilkins ♦ Karen Hastie Williams ♦ Andrew Young |
| *EFFECTIVENESS* | "In a demonstration of the impact of California's referendum that banned the use of race and ethnicity in college admissions, the state's most competitive public universities today [March 31, 1998] announced steep drops in admissions of black and Hispanic applicants for next fall's freshman class.

"At the University of California at Berkeley, the most selective public university in the country, African-Americans, Hispanic Americans and American Indians together made up 10.4 percent of the admitted freshmen for 1998; in 1997, they made up 23.1 percent. At the University of California at Los Angeles, representation by these groups fell to 12.7 percent, from 19.8 percent last year. . . . |

"The figures are among the first on admissions to California state universities since Proposition 209 was passed in November 1996. The ballot initiative, which for undergraduate admissions went into effect this year, made California the only state to ban the consideration of race, ethnicity and sex in the public sector. . . .

"Across the country, where the California situation is being carefully watched, supporters of affirmative action said they were not surprised by the numbers. They expressed depression and fury.

" 'We are seeing these campuses returning to a race-exclusive status,' said Theodore M. Shaw, associate director-counsel of the NAACP Legal Defense [and Education] Fund. 'This shows that economics will not substitute for race. We know that the great majority of the poor are white. You know, it is pretty depressing when you think that this is 30 years, almost to the day, after the assassination of Martin Luther King and we're still fighting a battle we thought we had moved beyond.' " (*New York Times*, April 1, 1998)

"In one of the nation's first court challenges involving the new wave of higher state education standards, 14 students and their parents have sued a North Carolina school district over its policy automatically denying students promotion unless they pass statewide reading and mathematics tests.

"The lawsuit, filed last week in the Federal District Court in Raleigh, maintains that the Johnston County public schools violated the rights of students by using this single set of tests alone to determine whether they should move on to the next grade. The suit argues that the tests are a measure only of how well schools in North Carolina are teaching the state-mandated curriculum, not of individual performance. . . .

"Lawyers for the suing Johnston County families said the plaintiffs objected not to standardized testing in itself but instead to school officials' relying solely on one set of tests in determining whether to promote students.

" 'The misuse of tests is a widespread phenomenon,' said Norman Chachkin, a lawyer with the NAACP Legal Defense and Educational Fund, one of the groups that brought the suit on the plaintiffs' behalf. 'That misuse is going unchallenged.'

"The policy at issue was adopted last year by the Johnston County Board of Education, whose school system educates 19,000 children in an area of tobacco and sweet-potato farms in eastern North Carolina. The policy required all students from third through eighth grade to achieve a specified score on the state reading and math tests before they could be promoted to the next grade, regardless of their performance in class (although the cases of students with a C average or better can be appealed to the district)." (*New York Times*, August 6, 1997)

". . . Mr. Greenwood told an Army equal employment opportunity counselor about the harassment, and he noted that blacks were almost always relegated to the lowest-paying, most menial jobs. When word got out that Mr. Greenwood had complained, a co-worker threatened to shoot him. One day Mr. Greenwood arrived at work to find that someone had gone into his locker and stuffed human feces into his work boots. He complained about that, too. The harassment continued.

"The final outrage for Mr. Greenwood came in January 1990, when someone broke into his locker and poured battery acid over his clothing. When he reported it, his supervisor suggested the matter be 'kept among ourselves.' Mr. Greenwood contacted a lawyer, a white sole practitioner from Pittsburgh named Caroline Mitchell. Eventually Ms. Mitchell, along with lawyers from the NAACP Legal Defense and Educational Fund and the New York law firm of Christy & Viener, brought a class-action discrimination suit against the Army.

" 'I personally find it hard to believe,' Ms. Mitchell said, 'that in America in the 1990's any human being could treat a fellow worker the way some of these black men were treated on the job by their white co-workers.'. . .

"The Army, after fighting the suit for years, has worked out a settlement, which will be the focus of a Federal court hearing today in Pittsburgh. The black workers will get some money and the Army has agreed to step up its hiring and increase the promotion of blacks in the Pittsburgh district." (*New York Times*, January 24, 1997)

## POLITICAL ORIENTATION

"a liberal civil rights group" (*New York Times*, November 1, 1997)

# National Abortion and Reproductive Rights Action League (1969)

1156 15th Street, NW
Suite 700
Washington, D.C. 20005
Phone: (202) 973-3000
Fax: (202) 973-3096
Internet: http://www.naral.org

"To secure and protect the freedom to choose while promoting policies and programs that reduce the number of unintended pregnancies and thus the need for abortions."

**PURPOSE**

47 total—35 professional; 12 support; plus 10 interns

**STAFF**

Kate Michelman, executive director. Michelman became executive director of the National Abortion and Reproductive Rights Action League (NARAL) in 1985, after serving as executive director of Tri-County Planned Parenthood, Inc., in Harrisburg, Pennsylvania, for five years. Michelman holds master's degrees in both developmental psychology and classical archeology from the University of Michigan. She has also been a fellow at the John F. Kennedy School of Government.

**DIRECTOR**

501(c)(4)

**TAX STATUS**

1998—Unavailable
Proposed 1999—Unavailable

**BUDGET**

Membership donations and individual contributions

**FUNDING SOURCES**

Members: 500,000 individuals
Branches/chapters: 36 state affiliates
Affiliate: The NARAL Foundation, a 501(c)(3) organization

**SCOPE**

NARAL PAC

**PAC**

| METHOD OF OPERATION | ♦ Advertisements ♦ Awards program ♦ Campaign contributions (federal and state) ♦ Coalition forming ♦ Conferences/seminars ♦ Congressional testimony ♦ Congressional voting analysis ♦ Demonstrations ♦ Electoral politics ♦ Films/videos/audiotapes ♦ Grassroots organizing ♦ Internet (E-mail alerts, Web site) ♦ Legislative/regulatory monitoring (federal and state) ♦ Lobbying (federal, state, and grassroots) ♦ Media outreach ♦ Polling ♦ Research ♦ Training ♦ Voting records |
|---|---|
| CURRENT CONCERNS | ♦ Ensuring access to safe abortion services ♦ Ensuring comprehensive sexuality education in schools ♦ Opposing coercive reproductive health policies ♦ Protecting women's reproductive freedoms ♦ Working to prevent unintended pregnancy and make abortion less necessary |
| PUBLICATIONS | *Choices: Women Speak Out About Abortion*<br>*Who Decides? A State-by-State Review of Abortion and Reproductive Rights, 1998* |
| NEWSLETTER | *NARAL News* (biannual) |
| CONFERENCES | None |
| BOARD OF DIRECTORS | Unavailable |
| EFFECTIVENESS | "Abortion right opponents in both chambers are rallying behind legislation that they hope will give Congress another route to curb abortions.<br><br>"Two bills . . . would make it a federal crime to take a minor across state lines to evade state laws requiring parental notification before an abortion can be performed. . . .<br><br>"Proponents of the bills argue that since parents must give permission for their children to receive an aspirin from a school nurse or go on a school field trip, parents surely should give their consent before their daughter has an abortion. . . .<br><br>"But Kate Michelman, president of the National Abortion and Reproductive Rights Action League said the proposals were simply another way for abortion rights opponents to chip away at a woman's legal right to an abortion.<br><br>" 'The reality is that most minors do involve a parent in their decision about abortion,' she said. 'But for the young women who cannot—because of family violence or sexual abuse—this bill would prohibit them from seeking assistance from a trusted adult.' " (*CQ Weekly Report*, May 23, 1998) |
| POLITICAL ORIENTATION | Unavailable |

# National Association for the Advancement of Colored People (1909)

4805 Mount Hope Drive
Baltimore, Maryland 21215
Phone: (410) 358-8900
Fax: (410) 486-9257

1025 Vermont Avenue, NW
Suite 1120
Washington, D.C. 20005
Phone: (202) 638-2269
Fax: (202) 638-5936

Internet: http://www.naacp.org

| | |
|---|---|
| "To insure the political, educational, social and economic equality of minority group citizens; to achieve equality of rights and eliminate race prejudice among citizens of the United States; to remove all barriers of racial and other discrimination through democratic processes." | **PURPOSE** |
| 60 total | **STAFF** |
| Kweisi Mfume, president and chief executive officer. Mfume previously represented Baltimore in the U.S. House of Representatives. He also served as chairman of the Congressional Black Caucus during the 103rd Congress. | **DIRECTOR** |
| 501(c)(3) | **TAX STATUS** |
| 1998—Unavailable<br>Proposed 1999—Unavailable | **BUDGET** |
| Unavailable | **FUNDING SOURCES** |
| Members: 500,000 individuals<br>Branches/chapters: 1,700 chapters<br>Affiliate: NAACP/Special Contribution Fund, a separate 501(c)(3) organization | **SCOPE** |
| None | **PAC** |

## METHOD OF OPERATION

♦ Advertisements ♦ Awards program ♦ Coalition forming ♦ Conferences/seminars ♦ Congressional testimony ♦ Congressional voting analysis ♦ Demonstrations ♦ Grassroots organizing ♦ International activities ♦ Legal assistance ♦ Legislative/regulatory monitoring (federal and state) ♦ Litigation ♦ Lobbying (federal, state, and grassroots) ♦ Local/municipal affairs ♦ Media outreach ♦ Participation in regulatory proceedings (federal) ♦ Research ♦ Scholarships ♦ Television and radio production ♦ Training and technical assistance ♦ Voter registration

## CURRENT CONCERNS

♦ Affirmative action ♦ Environmental racism ♦ Hate crimes ♦ Human rights in Nigeria ♦ School choice initiatives ♦ Supreme Court

## PUBLICATIONS

None

## NEWSLETTER

*Crisis* magazine (10 times a year)

## CONFERENCES

Annual conference

## BOARD OF DIRECTORS

Myrlie Evers-Williams, chairman; Bishop William Graves, vice chairman; Francisco L. Borges, treasurer; Carolyn Q. Coleman, assistant secretary

Other members:
♦ Ophelia Averitt ♦ Ben Andrews Jr. ♦ Fred L. Banks Jr. ♦ Bobby Bivens ♦ Julian Bond ♦ Eric E. Boone ♦ Richard Burton ♦ Ayanna Boykins ♦ Franklin E. Breckenridge ♦ Charles H. Butler ♦ Sally G. Carroll ♦ Larry W. Carter ♦ William E. Cofield ♦ Babette Colouett ♦ Philip R. Cousin ♦ Ernest Coverson ♦ James H. Daniel ♦ Hazel N. Dukes ♦ Anthony Fugett ♦ Erayne N. Gee ♦ James E. Ghee ♦ Evangeline Guidry ♦ Sonya Jackson ♦ Nancy L. Lane ♦ Ernest Lofton ♦ Henry J. Lyons ♦ William Lucy ♦ Chelle Luper ♦ Joseph E. Madison ♦ Annie B. Martin ♦ Roslyn McCallister-Brock ♦ Sandra McGray ♦ Enolia P. McMillan ♦ Korey M. Randolph ♦ Mary Ratliff ♦ Mrs. Rupert Richardson ♦ Franklin Roberts ♦ Alfred J. Rucks ♦ Leon W. Russell ♦ Ronald Sailor Jr. ♦ David Saperstein ♦ Raymond Scott ♦ Morris L. Shearin ♦ Louise A. Simpson

## EFFECTIVENESS

"As his expected presidential bid continues to take form, Vice President Al Gore did a little preaching to the choir . . . telling thousands of NAACP members that too many African Americans are excluded from the benefits of the nation's prosperity.

"Amplifying a theme discussed throughout the NAACP's annual convention here, Gore cited wide disparities in black and white wealth, education and health statistics as causes for concern. He said the gaps can be closed only if government plays an active role in extending opportunities and African Americans are prepared to take advantage of them. . . .

"Here, Gore announced a new Small Business Administration partnership with the NAACP to aid black business. He also garnered applause by announcing President Clinton signed a bill today to build a monument to civil rights leader Martin Luther King, Jr. on the Mall." (*Washington Post*, July 17, 1998)

"Declaring that 'race and skin color' still dominate every aspect of American life, NAACP President Kweisi Mfume said today [July 13, 1998] that protecting the nations embattled affirmative action programs must remain at the top of the civil rights group's agenda.

"Speaking before several thousand NAACP members gathered here for the organization's 89th annual convention, Mfume credited affirmative action with sparking the explosive growth of the black middle class in the last 30 years. Consequently, he said, efforts to eliminate the program amount to an attack on black progress. 'We are not going to let these years of progress be taken away from us without a fight.' Mfume said. . . .

"The NAACP and its allies have been successful in defeating legislative attempts to end affirmative action in 14 states, according to the Southern Regional Council, a civil rights think tank. But affirmative action opponents have had one huge victory: the 1996 passage of Proposition 209, which outlawed most government affirmative action programs in California." (*Washington Post*, July 14, 1998)

"Minorities are few and far between when it comes to managing and owning franchises of hotel companies.

"The NAACP highlighted this problem in a report last year that was highly critical of the nation's largest hotel chains. The group graded more than a dozen hotel companies on how many African Americans worked for the company, owned franchises, or supplied goods or services to its hotels. The highest grade, a C-plus, went to Marriott International Inc. of Bethesda, while another local company, Choice Hotels International Inc. of Silver Spring, received a C-minus. In the nine months since the NAACP report card, many of the hotel chains have taken steps to improve their employment and franchising performance with respect to minorities. Today, Choice Hotels, the nation's second-largest hotel franchiser, will announce it is creating a multi-ethnic advisory council whose mandate is to address issues of concern to minorities in franchising. . . .

"Industry officials said the NAACP study helped motivate some of the companies to change. 'There are a number of hotel companies that are initiating substantive change as opposed to cosmetic ones,' said Valerie Ferguson, chairman of the American Hotel and Motel Association and general manager of the Ritz-Carlton in Atlanta." (*Washington Post*, March 4, 1998)

"Six black Montgomery County [Maryland] residents complained yesterday that county authorities have ignored their reports of mistreatment by 'rogue' police officers, prompting local NAACP officials to renew their demand that Police Chief Carol A. Mehrling resign.

" 'This is a police department out of control,' Leroy Warren, chairman of the national NAACP's criminal justice committee, said during a news conference at which the six residents spoke. 'Decent people are being treated like dogs.' Linda M. Plummer, president of the Montgomery County NAACP, said Mehrling lacked the 'management skills' and 'operational control' to run the police department.

"The news conference marked the latest development in a three-year dispute between the NAACP and Mehrling over allegations of widespread police harassment and abuse of African Americans. NAACP officials said the testimonials were in response to County Executive Douglas M. Duncan's complaints that the group has not offered enough specific examples of police mistreatment." (*Washington Post*, February 10, 1998)

"The NAACP yesterday called for boycotts of 10 of the nation's largest hotel chains, saying they either provided few workplace opportunities for black professionals and contractors or did not respond to an NAACP survey about their business practices.

"The boycotts were announced as part of what the NAACP called the start of an 'unprecedented consumer movement' to help African Americans better leverage their estimated $450 billion in annual buying power. Participating in the boycotts are 55 black professional, fraternal and civil rights organizations representing 9 million members who spend $200 million a year at conventions. 'We will buy your goods and services if you buy our goods and services,' said NAACP President Kweisi Mfume, who added that the NAACP soon plans to target other industries. . . .

"In rating hotel chains, the NAACP called for boycotts of those that received failing grades: ITT Sheraton, Westin, Best Western, Radisson, Renaissance, Holiday Inn, Omni, Doubletree, Promus, which owns Embassy Suites and Hampton Inns, and Choice Hotels International, whose properties include Quality Inn and EconoLodge. Marriott, Hilton, Hyatt, Adam's Mark, Ritz-Carlton and HFS were given passing grades." (*Washington Post*, February 27, 1997)

---

## POLITICAL ORIENTATION

"the oldest and proudest civil rights group in the nation" (*Wall Street Journal*, February 1, 1996)

# National Association of Arab Americans (NAAA, Inc.) (1972)

1212 New York Avenue, NW
Washington, D.C. 20005
Phone: (202) 842-1840
Fax: (202) 842-1614
Internet: http://www.naaa.net

| | |
|---|---|
| To promote "an evenhanded U.S. foreign policy based on justice and peace for all parties in the Middle East." | **PURPOSE** |
| 3 total | **STAFF** |
| Khalil E. Jahshan, president. Jahshan became president of the National Association of Arab Americans (NAAA) in 1990, after serving as associate executive director for public affairs. From 1983 to 1989 he was the assistant director of the Palestine Research and Educational Center. Previously, Jahshan was director of the national office of Arab-American University Graduates and taught Arabic at the University of Chicago Extension and Northwestern University. He earned a B.A. in political science from Harding University and completed graduate coursework at the University of Chicago. Jahshan is a frequent lecturer about the Arab-Israeli conflict, the Palestine problem, Israeli politics, and U.S. foreign policy in the Middle East. He appears frequently on radio and television and has written numerous articles on Middle East issues. | **DIRECTOR** |
| Nonprofit (not tax-exempt) | **TAX STATUS** |
| 1998—Unavailable<br>Proposed 1999—Unavailable | **BUDGET** |
| Unavailable | **FUNDING SOURCES** |
| Members: Unavailable<br>Branches/chapters: Los Angeles and San Francisco chapters<br>Affiliate: NAAA Foundation, a 501(c)(3) organization | **SCOPE** |

| | |
|---|---|
| *PAC* | NAAA PAC |
| *METHOD OF OPERATION* | ♦ Legislative/regulatory monitoring (federal) ♦ Lobbying (federal) |
| *CURRENT CONCERNS* | ♦ Arab-Israeli conflict ♦ Democracy and human rights issues ♦ Jerusalem ♦ Middle East peace negotiations ♦ U.S. foreign aid |
| *PUBLICATIONS* | None |
| *NEWSLETTER* | *Voice* (bimonthly) |
| *CONFERENCES* | None |
| *BOARD OF DIRECTORS* | Unavailable |
| *EFFECTIVENESS* | Unavailable |
| *POLITICAL ORIENTATION* | Unavailable |

# National Coalition for the Homeless (1982)

1012 14th St., NW #600
Washington, D.C. 20005
Phone: (202) 737-6444
Fax: (202) 737-6445
Internet: nch@ari.net *or* http://nch.ari.net

| | |
|---|---|
| "To end homelessness through the promotion of systemic and attitudinal change that will remove the three primary causes of homelessness—lack of livable incomes, lack of affordable, quality housing, and lack of adequate holistic health care." | *PURPOSE* |
| 7 total—6 professional; 1 support; plus 7 interns | *STAFF* |
| Mary Ann Gleason, executive director. Gleason cofounded the Colorado Coalition for the Homeless in 1984 and has worked with many health care and community service organizations. She holds a master's degree from St. Louis University. | *DIRECTOR* |
| 501(c)(3) | *TAX STATUS* |
| Fiscal year ending June 30, 1997—$535,000<br>F.Y. 1998—$500,000<br>Proposed F.Y. 1999—$580,000 | *BUDGET* |
| Individual donations, 51 percent; foundation grants, 20 percent; corporate donations, 12 percent; membership dues, 11 percent; publications, 3 percent; conferences, 3 percent | *FUNDING SOURCES* |
| Members: 600 organizations; 1000 individuals<br>Branches/chapters: N/A<br>Affiliates: N/A | *SCOPE* |
| None | *PAC* |

## METHOD OF OPERATION

♦ Awards program ♦ Coalition forming ♦ Conferences/seminars ♦ Congressional testimony ♦ Congressional voting analysis ♦ Grassroots organizing ♦ Information clearinghouse ♦ Internet (databases, electronic bulletin boards, E-mail alerts, Web site) ♦ Internships ♦ Legislative/regulatory monitoring (federal and state) ♦ Library/information clearinghouse ♦ Lobbying (federal, state, and grassroots) ♦ Media outreach ♦ Research ♦ Scholarships ♦ Telecommunications services (hotline: 202-775-1372, mailing lists) ♦ Training and technical assistance ♦ Voter registration

## CURRENT CONCERNS

♦ Access to holistic health care ♦ Adult education ♦ Affordable, quality housing ♦ Civil rights ♦ Education ♦ Employment ♦ Income maintenance ♦ Livable wages ♦ Mental health policies ♦ Shelter ♦ Training ♦ Welfare reform

## PUBLICATIONS

*The 1997 Empowerment Directory*

*The 1997 Fall Organizing Manual*

*Addiction on the Streets: Homelessness and Substance Abuse in America*

*Addressing Homelessness: Status of Programs under the Stewart B. McKinney Assistance Act and Related Legislation*

*A Bitter Pill, Welfare Reform and the Health of Homeless People*

*Broken Lives: Denial of Education to Homeless Children*

*The Choice is Ours: Housing or Homelessness*

*Closing Door: Economic Causes of Homelessness*

*A Directory of National, State, and Local Homeless & Housing Advocacy Organizations*

*A Directory of North American Street Newspapers*

*The Essential Reference on Homelessness: A Fully Annotated Bibliography*

*Heroes Today, Homeless Tomorrow? Homelessness Among Veterans in the United States*

*A Home in Between: Designing Transitional Housing for Women and Children* (video)

*Homelessness in America: Unabated and Increasing*

*Housing and Homelessness—The Teaching Guide*

*Life and Death on the Streets: Health Care Reform and Homelessness*

*Mourning in America: Health Problems, Mortality and Homelessness*

*Necessary Relief: The Stewart B. McKinney Act*

*Over the Edge: Homeless Families and the Welfare System*

*A Place Called Hopelessness: Shelter Demand in the 90's*

*Rewind: It Could Have Been Me* (animated film)

*Shredding the Safety Net: The Contract With America's Impact on Poor and Homeless People*

*Summary of the Cranston-Gonzalez National Affordable Housing Act*

*'Tis a Gift to be Simple: Homelessness, Health Care Reform, and the Single Payer Plan*

*The Unbalanced Budget: The Impact of the Congressional Budget on Homelessness*

*Unfinished Business: The Stewart B. McKinney Act After Two Years*

Also publishes fact sheets on specific issues

*Safety Network* (semi-monthly)

Conferences on various issues related to homelessness

◆ Barbara Anderson ◆ Martha Are ◆ Anita Beaty ◆ Paul Boden ◆ Christine Byrd ◆ Jim Cain ◆ Katt Clark ◆ Callie Cole ◆ Sheila Crowley ◆ Roosevelt Darby Jr. ◆ Diane Doherty ◆ John Donahue ◆ Robert Erlenbusch ◆ Bill Faith ◆ Robert Ferrell ◆ Theola Fort ◆ Hugh Grogan ◆ Paul Haskell ◆ Kim Hopper ◆ Donna James ◆ Lynn Lewis-Rayo ◆ John Lozier ◆ Rita Markley ◆ Glorin Marti ◆ Bev Merrill ◆ Della Mitchell ◆ Rolando Morales ◆ Robert B. More ◆ Phoebe Nelson ◆ Gordon Packard ◆ Phillip Pappas ◆ John Parvensky ◆ Greg Payne ◆ Sue Watlov Phillips ◆ Terry Scofield ◆ Eirther Shelmonson-Bey ◆ Louisa Stark ◆ Delena Stephens ◆ Richard Troxell ◆ Matias Vega ◆ Donald Whitehead

". . . In the shadow of parade floats, with the sounds of motorcade sirens droning on, advocates for the poor and homeless gathered at a shelter run by the Community for Creative Non-Violence to bemoan a 'culture of silence' that keeps Americans from dealing seriously with the nation's social and economic problems.

" 'Instead of recognizing that we have a flawed system, where 26 percent of Americans who work full time are still in poverty, we continue to bash the poor as irresponsible,' said Mary Ann Gleason, executive director of the National Coalition for the Homeless. 'Economic self-sufficiency is not the same as personal responsibility. The problem is that we simply are not serious about providing equal opportunity in this country.'

"At the counter-inauguration, speakers painted a picture of a nation where millions of Americans struggle and die in poverty each year, many of them lacking affordable housing or jobs that pay decent wages." (*Washington Post*, January 22, 1997)

Unavailable

# National Congress of American Indians (1944)

1301 Connecticut Ave., NW
Suite 200
Washington, D.C. 20036
Phone: (202) 466-7767
Fax: (202) 466-7797

| | |
|---|---|
| **PURPOSE** | "To protect and advance the rights of American Indians and Alaskan Natives to continue to exercise Tribal self-government." |
| **STAFF** | 12 total—9 professional; 3 support; plus 1 part-time professional; 1 part-time support; 1 intern |
| **DIRECTOR** | JoAnn K. Chase, executive director. Chase, a Mandan-Hidatsa Indian, previously worked as a policy analyst for the National Congress of American Indians (NCAI) and as a special assistant to Rep. Barbara Boxer. She also has worked for the U.S. Justice Department and served as deputy director of the National Commission on American Indian, Alaska Native and Native Hawaiian Housing. As a law student Chase served as president of the American Indian Law Students Association. She is a graduate of Boston University and the University of New Mexico School of Law. |
| **TAX STATUS** | 501(c)(3) |
| **BUDGET** | 1997—$1.6 million<br>1998—$2.1 million<br>Proposed 1999—$2.4 million |
| **FUNDING SOURCES** | Conferences, 35 percent; government contracts, 20 percent; tribal donations, 20 percent; corporate donations, 15 percent; membership, 10 percent |
| **SCOPE** | Members: More than 250 tribes and 4,000 individuals<br>Branches/chapters: N/A<br>Affiliates: N/A |
| **PAC** | NCAI Political Action Committee |

| | |
|---|---|
| • Coalition forming • Conferences/seminars • Congressional testimony • Congressional voting analysis • Direct action • Grassroots organizing • International activities • Internet • Legislative/regulatory monitoring (federal and state) • Lobbying (federal) • Media outreach • Participation in regulatory proceedings (federal and state) • Training and technical assistance | *METHOD OF OPERATION* |
| • Defending tribal sovereignty • Welfare reform • Indian child welfare • Transportation • Housing • Gaming • Religious, cultural and human rights • Nuclear waste • Native American mascots • Interior appropriations | *CURRENT CONCERNS* |
| None | *PUBLICATIONS* |
| *NCAI Sentinel* (quarterly) | *NEWSLETTER* |
| Annual convention (fall) Executive Council Session (every February in Washington, D.C.) Mid-Year Conference (summer, usually June) | *CONFERENCES* |
| Executive committee: W. Ron Allen, president; Ernie Stevens Jr., first vice president; Lela Kaskalla, recording secretary; Russell Mason, treasurer | *BOARD OF DIRECTORS* |
| "Indian leaders warned Congress . . . [about] changing the long-standing sovereign immunity of their tribes, saying the result could be calamitous for future generations of Indians.

"A bill introduced by Sen. Slade Gorton (R-Wash.) to restrict their immunity would 'render Indian tribes impotent to protect their lands, resources, cultures and future generations,' said W. Ron Allen, president of the National Congress of American Indians. At a hearing before the Senate Indian Affairs Committee, Indian leaders said the proposal would severely hinder tribal governments, open them to a host of potential lawsuits and sharply limit their economic opportunities. . . .

"But supporters said the bill would make tribal governments more accountable and boost state revenue by allowing stricter tax enforcement of Indian-operated businesses. . . ." (*Washington Post*, March 12, 1998) | *EFFECTIVENESS* |
| Unavailable | *POLITICAL ORIENTATION* |

# National Council of La Raza (1968)

1111 19th Street, NW
Suite 1000
Washington, D.C. 20036
Phone: (202) 785-1670
Fax: (202) 776-1792
Internet: http://www.nclr.org

| | |
|---|---|
| **PURPOSE** | "To reduce poverty and discrimination, and improve life opportunities for Hispanic Americans of all nationality groups in all regions of the country." |
| **STAFF** | 84 total—67 professionals; 17 support; plus 2–10 interns |
| **DIRECTOR** | Raul Yzaguirre, president and chief executive officer. Yzaguirre was elected executive director of the National Council of La Raza (NCLR) in 1974 and was named president and chief executive officer in 1978. Formerly he was executive director of a Hispanic consulting firm, which he cofounded, and a program analyst with the migrant division of the Office of Economic Opportunity. Yzaguirre is chairperson of Independent Sector and President Clinton's Advisory Commission on Educational Excellence for Hispanic Americans, president of the Mexican and American Solidarity Foundation, and a director of many other organizations. He received a B.S. from George Washington University. |
| **TAX STATUS** | 501(c)(3) |
| **BUDGET** | 1998—$17 million<br>Proposed 1999—$17 million |
| **FUNDING SOURCES** | Unavailable |
| **SCOPE** | Members: Serves more than 3 million individuals through 240 affiliates<br>Branches/chapters: 4 field offices in Phoenix, Los Angeles, Chicago, and San Antonio, Texas<br>Affiliates: Approximately 240 nonprofit, community-based organizations |

None

♦ Advertisements ♦ Awards program ♦ Coalition forming ♦ Conferences/seminars ♦ Congressional testimony ♦ Films/video/audiotapes ♦ Grassroots organizing ♦ Legislative/regulatory monitoring (federal) ♦ Lobbying (federal) ♦ Media outreach ♦ Research ♦ Training and technical assistance

## METHOD OF OPERATION

♦ Civil rights enforcement ♦ Education ♦ Employment and training ♦ Health care ♦ Housing and community development ♦ Immigration ♦ Poverty ♦ Trade and foreign policy

## CURRENT CONCERNS

The following is a list of sample publications:

*Burden or Relief? The Impact of Taxes on Hispanic Working Families*
*Childhood Immunization in the Hispanic Community 1997*
*"Don't Blink: Hispanics in Television Entertainment"*
*Issue Brief: Immigration and Welfare Reform Legislation: The Impact on Latinos*
*Locked Out: Hispanic Underrepresentation in Federally-Assisted Housing Programs*

Also publishes fact sheets, policy statements, and congressional testimony on specific issues

## PUBLICATIONS

*Agenda* (quarterly)

## NEWSLETTER

Annual conference (mid-July)
Also holds workshops, luncheons, and special events on current issues facing the Hispanic community

## CONFERENCES

Ramon Murguia, chair; Herminio Martinez, first vice chair; Lillian Cruz, second vice chair; Humberto Fuentes, secretary/treasurer; Irma Flores Gonzales, Arabella Martinez, and Guillermo Linares, executive committee members

Other members:
♦ Mari Carmen Aponte ♦ Zulma X. Barrios ♦ Cordelia Canderlaria ♦ Roger Cazares ♦ Amancio J. Chapa Jr. ♦ Rita DeMartino ♦ Fernando Flores ♦ Mary Gonzalez-Koenig ♦ Linda Leher ♦ Monica C. Lozano ♦ Pedro Narezo ♦ Daniel Ortega Jr. ♦ Angel Luis Ortiz ♦ Cecilia Ortiz ♦ Deborah Ortiz ♦ Verma Pastor ♦ Edward Reilly ♦ Deborah Szekely ♦ Maria Elena Torralva-Alonso ♦ Arturo G. Torres ♦ Yvonne Martinez Vega ♦ Charles E. Vela ♦ Carmen Velasquez ♦ Jose Villarreal

## BOARD OF DIRECTORS

## EFFECTIVENESS

"After a report in August that an American Airlines training manual characterized Latin American passengers as potentially drunk and unruly, Raul Yzaguirre, president of the National Council of La Raza, quickly threatened a boycott.

"As a result, AMR Corp. and the council have signed an eight-point agreement expanding AMR's role in the Hispanic community and reiterating some of its many existing commitments.

"The carrier agreed to improve service to Hispanic customers. It reaffirmed its desire to achieve full employment parity for minority workers and to expand philanthropic efforts, including offering more free tickets to certain Hispanic groups. It will also consider adding a second Hispanic member to its board, which already has two African-Americans." (*Wall Street Journal*, December 3, 1997)

"The increasingly complex economic situation confronting Hispanics was laid out in a report released today by the National Council of La Raza, the nation's largest Hispanic advocacy group. The findings, compiled from an array of government reports and academic studies, are being trumpeted by La Raza leaders at their annual convention here [in Chicago] as both the promise and the challenge posed by the nation's fast-growing Hispanic population. 'We will become an economic powerhouse for the United States if, and only if, this nation begins to reward—instead of punishing or neglecting—the positive economic values and characteristics this community embodies,' said Raul Yzaguirre, the group's president.

"To be sure, Hispanics are becoming an increasingly potent economic force in this country, according to the new NCLR report: The number of Latino-owned businesses has skyrocketed in recent years, the percentage of Hispanic women who hold professional jobs has grown substantially, and the purchasing power of Latinos has increased to $350 billion, a 65 percent rise since 1990. All that has led to a 25 percent increase in the size of the Hispanic middle class in the last decade.

"Despite those impressive gains, Hispanics continue to suffer from stubborn poverty that is closely linked to relatively low education levels that often relegate them to low-wage jobs. In 1995, for example, Latinos were the only ethnic group to experience a drop in median income. Overall, Hispanic income is only two-thirds that of whites and slightly lower than blacks, making them the poorest of the nation's ethnic groups. . . .

"Vice President Gore seemed eager to take up that challenge during a speech to some 2,500 La Raza activists here, saying Hispanics must be allowed to share more fully in the nation's prosperity." (*Washington Post*, July 22, 1997)

## POLITICAL ORIENTATION

"the nation's largest Hispanic advocacy group" (*Washington Post*, July 22, 1997)

# National Council of Senior Citizens
# (1961)

8403 Colesville Road
Suite 1200
Silver Spring, Maryland 20910
Phone: (301) 578-8800
Fax: (301) 578-8999
Internet: http://www. ncscinc.org

"To advocate on behalf of older Americans, with emphasis on federal and state programs designed to improve life for the elderly."

**PURPOSE**

Unavailable

**STAFF**

Steve Protulis, executive director. Protulis was named executive director of the National Council of Senior Citizens (NCSC) in August 1995. Before coming to NCSC, he spent nearly eight years coordinating all senior efforts for the AFL-CIO COPE Department. A longtime auto worker, Protulis became a member of the UAW in 1962. He formerly ran the union's national political arm and served as administrative assistant to UAW president Douglas Foster. In 1976, Protulis was deputy field director for the Jimmy Carter presidential campaign. He is a board member of the Congressional Hispanic Caucus Institute and the National Council on Aging.

**DIRECTOR**

501(c)(4)

**TAX STATUS**

1998—Unavailable
Proposed 1999—Unavailable

**BUDGET**

Unavailable

**FUNDING SOURCES**

Members: more than 500,000
Branches/chapters: 2,000
Affiliates: National Senior Citizens Education and Research Center, a 501(c)(3) organization; NCSC Housing Management Corporation

**SCOPE**

| | |
|---|---|
| *PAC* | None (NCSC Political Action Committee was discontinued) |
| *METHOD OF OPERATION* | ♦ Advertisements ♦ Awards program ♦ Boycotts ♦ Coalition forming ♦ Conferences/seminars ♦ Congressional testimony ♦ Congressional voting analysis ♦ Demonstrations ♦ Direct action ♦ Electoral politics ♦ Films/video/audiotapes ♦ Grassroots organizing ♦ Initiative/referendum campaigns ♦ Legislative/regulatory monitoring (federal) ♦ Library/information clearinghouse ♦ Lobbying (federal, state, and grassroots) ♦ Local/municipal affairs ♦ Media outreach ♦ Member services ♦ Participation in regulatory affairs (federal and state) ♦ Research ♦ Training and technical assistance ♦ Voter registration ♦ Voting records |
| *CURRENT CONCERNS* | ♦ Employment of senior citizens ♦ Improving health care for seniors ♦ Medicaid reform proposals ♦ Preservation of Social Security and Medicare ♦ Reauthorization of Older Americans Act ♦ Securing housing and jobs for low-income seniors |
| *PUBLICATIONS* | Brochures |
| *NEWSLETTER* | *Seniority* (bimonthly) <br> *Pension Plus* (monthly) |
| *CONFERENCES* | Constitutional conventions and legislative conferences held every four years <br> Regional conferences in alternate years |
| *BOARD OF DIRECTORS* | George J. Kourpias, president; John E. Turner, secretary-treasurer; Eugene Glover and Harry Guenther, presidents emeritus; Dorothy Walker, vice president emeritus <br><br> Other governing board members: <br> ♦ John J. Barry ♦ George F. Becker ♦ Elmer E. Blankenship ♦ R. Thomas Buffenbarger ♦ B.L. Cleveland ♦ Barbara J. Easterling ♦ Lily Eskelson ♦ Jane G. Gould ♦ Val Halamandaris ♦ Bill Holayter ♦ Genevieve Johnson ♦ Hani F. Lipp ♦ Eleanor Litwak ♦ Marie Malagreca ♦ John Marvin ♦ Jay Mazur ♦ Mary C. Mulvey ♦ Howard Owens ♦ Matthew Peulen ♦ Steve Protulis ♦ Steve Regenstreif ♦ Dennis Rivera ♦ Cecil E. Roberts ♦ Charles Sanders ♦ Frank Stella ♦ Rosalie Whelan ♦ Charlie Williams ♦ Walter J. Williams ♦ Kenneth L. Worley |
| *EFFECTIVENESS* | "The National Council of Senior Citizens is among the most influential lobbying organizations in Washington, D.C., according to *Fortune* magazine. In its new survey of clout in the nation's capital, *Fortune* ranks NCSC above such groups as the League of Women Voters, American Heart Association, Handgun Control. . . . |

"It appears that even NCSC's enemies also recognize our unique abilities. Pointing out that 'the tactics of the National Council of Senior Citizens are something to behold.' James L. Martin and Donald J. Senese of 60 Plus Association report that 'NCSC's political operations are sophisticated, clever and deceptive. . . . and helped defeat Representatives Randy Tate (R-WA) and Andrea Seastrand (R-CA) in the 1996 elections.' Regular readers of *Seniority* will recognize 60 Plus Association as one of the right-wing conservative groups under investigation for their 'scare tactics' against older Americans." (*Seniority*, April/May 1998)

Unavailable

# *POLITICAL ORIENTATION*

# The National Council on the Aging, Inc. (1950)

409 Third Street, SW
2nd Floor
Washington, D.C. 20024
Phone: (202) 479-1200
Fax: (202) 479-0735
Internet: http://www.ncoa.org

| | |
|---|---|
| **PURPOSE** | "Committed to promoting the dignity, self-determination, well-being, and contributions of older persons and to enhancing the field of aging through leadership and service, education and advocacy." |
| **STAFF** | 90 total |
| **DIRECTOR** | James P. Firman, president. Prior to becoming president of the National Council on the Aging (NCOA), Firman spent ten years as president and CEO of the United Seniors Health Cooperative, an organization that he cofounded. He served as senior program officer at the Robert Wood Johnson Foundation from 1981 to 1984 and was a cofounder of Grantmakers in Aging. More recently, he was a commissioner of the American Bar Association's Commission on Legal Problems of the Elderly and served on the NCOA's Board of Directors. |
| **TAX STATUS** | 501(c)(3) |
| **BUDGET** | 1998—Unavailable<br>Proposed 1999—Unavailable |
| **FUNDING SOURCES** | Government contracts, 93 percent; foundation and corporate grants, 3 percent; memberships, publications sales, and other services, 4 percent |
| **SCOPE** | Members: more than 7,500 individuals and organizations<br>Branches/chapters: N/A<br>Affiliates: Health Promotion Institute, National Association of Older Worker Employment Services, National Adult Day Services Association, National Center on Rural Aging, National Institute of Senior Centers, National Institute of Senior Housing, National Institute on Community-based Long-term Care, National Institute on Financial Issues and Services for Elders, National Interfaith Coalition on Aging |

None

♦ Advertisements ♦ Awards program (Achievement Award, Civic Commitment Award, Community Service Award, Distinguished Achievement Award) ♦ Coalition forming ♦ Congressional testimony ♦ Fellowship program ♦ Films/video/audiotapes ♦ International activities ♦ Internet (electronic bulletin boards, Web site) ♦ Legislative/regulatory monitoring (federal and state) ♦ Library/information clearinghouse ♦ Lobbying (federal) ♦ Media outreach ♦ Research ♦ Telecommunications services (mailing lists) ♦ Training and technical assistance

## METHOD OF OPERATION

♦ Arts and humanities programs for older adults ♦ Employment options for older workers ♦ Equitable access to health care, including long-term services ♦ Housing needs of older Americans ♦ Interdependence of children, youth, families, and the elderly ♦ Literacy ♦ Mid-life and retirement planning ♦ Services for older persons ♦ Social Security income

## CURRENT CONCERNS

None

## PUBLICATIONS

*Abstracts of Social Gerontology: Current Literature on Aging* (quarterly journal of abstracts and related citations)
*Innovations in Aging* (quarterly)
*NCOA Networks* (bimonthly newspaper)

## NEWSLETTER

Annual meeting
Cosponsors a variety of institutes, workshops, and meetings on issues dealing with the elderly
Teleconferences

## CONFERENCES

Thomas E. Brown Jr., chair; W. Andrew Achenbaum, chair elect; James P. Firman, president and chief executive officer; Michael Cooley, secretary; Ronald W. Cavill, treasurer; Reba Schafer, past chair

Other members:
♦ Mark Beers ♦ Josselyn Bennett ♦ Joyce T. Berry ♦ Donald E. Chapman ♦ Elbert Cole ♦ Neal E. Cutler ♦ Barb Dampman ♦ Susan Eisenberg ♦ Nancy Erckenbrack ♦ Charles J. Fahey ♦ Timothy Foley ♦ Paula French ♦ Sandra King ♦ Jean Leonatti ♦ Eileen Lynette ♦ Martha Pelaez ♦ Stephen Protulis ♦ Skip Schlenk ♦ Herbert Shore ♦ Pat Shull ♦ Charles H. Smith ♦ Donald R. Smith ♦ Mark Spradley ♦ Daniel Thursz ♦ Satya Verma ♦ Bonnie Watson ♦ Herbert S. Wilbert ♦ Peter Wyckoff

## BOARD OF DIRECTORS

"Many baby boomers, kept out of their parents' financial affairs for years, are now finding they must untangle Mom and Dad's financial records, take over investment decisions, find professional advisers and often even end up paying the bills. . . .

"With a $750,000 grant from the National Institute on Aging, Prof. Cutler and the National Council on Aging hope to increase awareness. In partnership with Intuit Inc., the Mountain View, Calif., maker of Quicken personal-finance software, they're developing programs to help plan for long-term care. The software may first appeal to those now worried about aging parents, but it's really targeted at the baby boomers whose inevitable aging will soon begin to create its own stresses. 'This set of issues is going to mushroom like every other issue the boomers have had,' says Prof. Cutler. . . ." (*Wall Street Journal*, December 1, 1997)

"In October, the National Council on the Aging, representing 26 advocacy groups, wrote to President Clinton and Congressional leaders urging that the Medicare commission take account of several important complaints of the elderly, including the cost of prescription drugs and the need to care for the chronically ill.

" 'In addition,' the letter said 'the health care peril faced by the pre-Medicare population—those who do not receive or cannot afford private insurance and who do not yet qualify for Medicare—also deserves serious attention if we hope to reduce the ranks of the nation's uninsured.' " (*New York Times*, November 24, 1997)

"A survey released this month by the National Council on the Aging and the Pew Charitable Trusts provides a glimpse of America's fractured society: Nearly 7 million people help care for an older relative or friend who lives at least an hour away. Many seniors are much farther away, and their primary caregivers devote an average of 35 hours a month—equal to nearly one week of work.

"This exacts a physical and emotional toll. More than half of those polled for the survey said their responsibilities interfere with personal or family activities, and one-fourth of caregivers who also are employed indicated they miss at least one day of work each month. The survey predicted significant increases in the number of people affected by such situations, a conclusion that is seconded in a broader report on caregiving to be released today at the American Society on Aging's annual conference. . . .

"The implications are significant for families, the corporate world and social service and health care fields. From the latter has already emerged a new job description, the 'geriatric care manager,' usually social workers or nurses experienced in dealing with the elderly. They may assess whether a person should remain at home or hire a daytime aide or nurse, oversee insurance eligibility, provide counseling or monitor a nursing home placement.

"Families often are caught in a maelstrom of stresses. Children feel guilty over being so far away and not helping more, yet often they are unfamiliar with services in their parents' community. Tensions may erupt between siblings over what to do or who should do it. Discerning over the telephone how ailing relatives truly are managing can be difficult, since they frequently insist they are managing just fine." (*Washington Post*, March 23, 1997)

"The American family has been getting a bad rap on elder care. On top of the old stereotype of adult children as neglectful nomads who move away and abandon their aged parents, the Medicaid funding debate portrays them as trying to dodge responsibility for their parents' nursing-home bills.

"New national elder-care research paints a sharply different picture: The 'fragmented' American family is actually immersed in elder care with an intensity and breadth that belies the stereotype.

"A study of 200 care-givers by the National Council on the Aging, focusing on people who live more than an hour from their elders, suggests even distant family members spend a lot of time and money on elder care. These care-givers commit 35 hours a month, equal to nearly one work week, to providing or arranging housekeeping, meals and other services for their elders. They spend an unexpectedly high $196 a month on their elders and make other financial sacrifices, too, with 15% of employed care-givers taking unpaid leave from work. They have been helping out for a long time, an average 5.1 years, says the study, funded by Pew Charitable Trusts. . . ." (*Wall Street Journal*, March 12, 1997)

Unavailable

*POLITICAL ORIENTATION*

# National Gay and Lesbian Task Force (1973)

2320 17th Street, NW
Washington, D.C. 20009
Phone: (202) 332-6483
Fax: (202) 332-0207
Internet: ngltf@ngltf.org *or* http://www.ngltf.org

| | |
|---|---|
| *PURPOSE* | "To eliminate prejudice, violence and injustice against gay, lesbian, bisexual and transgendered people at the local, state and national level." |
| *STAFF* | 18 total—12 professional; 6 support; plus 30 volunteers; 6 interns |
| *DIRECTOR* | Kerry Lobel, executive director |
| *TAX STATUS* | 501(c)(3) |
| *BUDGET* | 1997—$2.3 million<br>1998—$3.8 million<br>Proposed 1999—$4.1 million |
| *FUNDING SOURCES* | Membership dues, 37 percent; individuals, 24 percent; foundation grants, 15 percent; special events/projects, 14 percent; conferences, 6 percent; honoraria, ads, in-kind donations, 3 percent; corporate gifts, 1 percent |
| *SCOPE* | Members: 40,000 individuals and organizations<br>Branches/chapters: N/A<br>Affiliate: NGLTF Policy Institute, a separate 501(c)(3) organization |
| *PAC* | None |

♦ Advertisements ♦ Awards program ♦ Boycotts ♦ Coalition forming ♦ Conferences/seminars ♦ Congressional testimony ♦ Demonstrations ♦ Direct action ♦ Films/video/audiotapes ♦ Grassroots organizing assistance ♦ Initiative/referendum campaigns ♦ International activities ♦ Internet (databases, electronic bulletin boards, E-mails, Web site) ♦ Legislative/regulatory monitoring (federal and state) ♦ Library/information clearinghouse ♦ Lobbying (federal, state, and grassroots) ♦ Media outreach ♦ Polling ♦ Research ♦ Training and technical assistance

*METHOD OF OPERATION*

♦ Anti-gay legislative and ballot measures ♦ Anti-gay violence ♦ Countering the Right Wing ♦ Discrimination against the gay community ♦ Ex-gay movement ♦ Gay, lesbian, bisexual, and transsexual family issues ♦ Gay, lesbian, bisexual, and transsexual youth issues ♦ Gay rights movement ♦ Government response to HIV ♦ HIV/AIDS crisis ♦ Medicaid reform ♦ Repeal of sodomy laws

*CURRENT CONCERNS*

*Anti-Gay/Lesbian Violence in 1994*
*Beyond the Beltway: State of the States 1995*
*Capital Gains and Losses: Annual State-by-State Review of Gay-Related Legislation*
*Countering Right Wing Rhetoric*
*Fight the Right Action Kit*
*Fortune 1000 Survey*
*From Wrongs to Rights: Public Opinion of Gay and Lesbian Americans Moves Toward Equality*
*Gay and Lesbian Health Recommendations*
*Gay, Lesbian, Bisexual Civil Rights in the U.S.*
*Lesbian Health Roundtable Report*
*Lesbians & Cancer*
*LGBT Campus Organizing: A Comprehensive Manual*
*Persuasive Patterns of Discrimination*
*Report on Lesbian Health*
*To Have & To Hold: Organizing for Our Right to Marry*
*Voters' Attitudes on Gay, Lesbians, and Bisexual Civil Rights*

Also offers a variety of fact packets, organizing tools, position papers, and resource lists

*PUBLICATIONS*

*NGLTF Newsletter* (quarterly)

*NEWSLETTER*

Creating Change Conference (annual, November)

*CONFERENCES*

## BOARD OF DIRECTORS

Jerry Joseph Hall and Rachel Rosen, cochairs; Jerry Clark, treasurer; Russell Roybal, secretary

Other board members:
♦ Clarence Bagby ♦ Leslie Belzberg ♦ Roberta Bennett ♦ Margaret A. Burd ♦ Michael Chapman ♦ Kelvin Lunn Cothren ♦ Don Davis ♦ John R. Dreyer ♦ John Huebler ♦ Pat Hussain ♦ L.J. Irving ♦ Lani Ka'Ahumanu ♦ Arturo Nava ♦ Gordon VeneKlasen ♦ Carla F. Wallace ♦ Michele A. Zavos

## EFFECTIVENESS

"American acceptance of gay men and lesbians has swelled substantially in recent years, as has support for their civil rights, but a majority of the population still disapproves of homosexuality, according to a study released on Friday by the National Gay and Lesbian Task Force. . . .

"The report, commissioned by the group and billed as the most extensive analysis yet of recent trends in public attitudes toward gay men and lesbians, focused on steep rises over the last 20 years in support for equal rights in housing, employment and the military. . . .

"But for all the signs of increased tolerance, the report also represented a half-empty glass for gay men and lesbians: It found that though disapproval of homosexuality had dropped by nearly 20 percentage points since its peak of 75 percent in the late 1980's, it was still 56 percent in 1996, the most recent year examined on that question. . . .

" 'I think the lesson for us out of this data is that the strategy of education and the continued effort we expend on public education is more important than ever,' said Urvashi Vaid, director of the Policy Institute at the National Gay and Lesbian Task Force, the group's think tank. 'To the extent we've seen changes in public opinion over the last 20 years, it's been because we have a community that's come out of the closet.'. . .

"In general, the report highlighted the complexity of Americans' attitudes on gay issues, public opinion analysts said. . . ." (*New York Times*, May 31, 1998)

" 'Anti-gay rhetoric has its consequence in violence,' said Matt Foreman, executive director of the New York City Gay and Lesbian Anti-Violence Project. 'If you're preaching from a pulpit or a political forum, if you're saying that gays and lesbians are immoral, evil pederasts recruiting children, and then don't anticipate and expect violence, then that is absurd. For the younger people, the ones responsible for most of this [violence], the message is clear: We are not fully human.'

"Compiling a record of hate crimes against gays remains a frustratingly sketchy endeavor. In the past, victims so feared exposure that many of these crimes went underreported, but that has begun to change as anger at being targeted replaces such worries. But police often do not categorize anti-gay incidents as hate crimes, and seldom is evidence of intent as clear as in the Mangione slaying. Still, in the past few years, disturbing statistics have emerged.

"According to the National Gay and Lesbian Task Force, based in Washington, there has been nearly a 100 percent increase nationally in anti-gay homicides between 1992, when 30 were confirmed, and 1994, when the number reached 59. During that period, 10 such deaths were documented in Texas, 10 in Colorado, 9 in California, 8 in North Carolina, 17 in the Washington metropolitan area and 28 in New York City alone, according to the Anti-Violence Project. . . .

"Foreman's group also has tracked lesser acts of violence against homosexuals for the past 10 years and, he said, 'the trend has been ever upward.' Last year, in nine U.S. cities surveyed by the group, 2,064 anti-gay incidents were reported." (*Washington Post*, January 31, 1996)

---

"NGLTF's offices, in contrast to HRC's, are located in the heart of the funky ethnic neighborhood of Adams Morgan. The group's lease in the handsomely renovated concrete-and-glass building is up this summer, but [Kerry] Lobel is not worried about a rent increase. Few organizations, she explained, would choose to locate so far from the White House and the Capitol, outside the downtown area's magnetic political field.

"Such a determinedly outsider status is in keeping with Lobel's vision of the group, which has forged a reputation as the most progressive of the national ones. 'Some groups tell you that to be a gay person you have to leave your race, gender, or socioeconomic status behind,' she says. 'We try to represent people who are disadvantaged in a number of ways because they don't always have a voice in politics.' " (*The Advocate*, June 1998)

"an advocacy group based in Washington" (*New York Times*, May 31, 1998)

## POLITICAL ORIENTATION

# National Organization for Women (1966)

1000 16th Street, NW
Suite 700
Washington, D.C. 20036
Phone: (202) 331-0066
Fax: (202) 785-8576
Internet: now@now.org *or* http://www.now.org

| | |
|---|---|
| **PURPOSE** | "To take action to bring women into full participation in the mainstream of American society now, exercising all the privileges and responsibilities thereof in truly equal partnership with men." |
| **STAFF** | 30 total staff; plus 15 interns and 20 volunteers |
| **DIRECTOR** | Patricia Ireland, president. Ireland became president of the National Organization for Women (NOW) in 1991, having served as its executive vice president and treasurer since 1987. Prior to that she was in private law practice in Miami, where she was also legal counsel to Florida and Dade County NOW. Ireland earlier worked as a flight attendant, during which time she became active in NOW. She earned her law degree from the University of Miami. |
| **TAX STATUS** | 501(c)(4) |
| **BUDGET** | 1998—Unavailable<br>Proposed 1999—Unavailable |
| **FUNDING SOURCES** | Membership dues, 74 percent; contributions, 17 percent; sales and royalties, 6 percent; conferences and other, 4 percent |
| **SCOPE** | Members: 260,000 individuals<br>Branches/chapters: 500 local chapters<br>Affiliate: NOW Foundation, Inc., a 501(c)(3) organization |
| **PAC** | National NOW PAC and NOW Equality PAC |

◆ Advertisements ◆ Awards program ◆ Boycotts ◆ Campaign contributions ◆ Coalition forming ◆ Conferences/seminars ◆ Congressional testimony ◆ Demonstrations ◆ Direct action ◆ Electoral politics ◆ Films/video/audiotapes ◆ Grassroots organizing ◆ Initiative/referendum campaigns ◆ International activities ◆ Internet (World Wide Web home page) ◆ Legislative/regulatory monitoring (federal and state) ◆ Litigation ◆ Lobbying (federal, state, and grassroots) ◆ Local/municipal affairs ◆ Media outreach ◆ Participation in regulatory proceedings (federal and state) ◆ Product merchandising ◆ Research ◆ Speakers program ◆ Telecommunications services ◆ Training and technical assistance ◆ Voter registration ◆ Voting records

## METHOD OF OPERATION

◆ Affirmative action ◆ Civil rights ◆ Constitutional equality ◆ Economic empowerment ◆ Equal educational opportunity ◆ Global feminism ◆ Lesbian, gay and bisexual rights ◆ Marriage and family law ◆ Pay equity ◆ Reproductive freedom ◆ Sexual harassment ◆ Violence against women ◆ Welfare rights ◆ Women in the military

## CURRENT CONCERNS

Publishes various books, brochures, videos, and NOW merchandise

## PUBLICATIONS

*National NOW Times* (4 times a year)

## NEWSLETTER

Sponsors an annual national conference, regional and state conferences, and issue conferences as appropriate

## CONFERENCES

Patricia Ireland, president; Kim Gandy, executive vice president; Elizabeth Toledo, vice president-action; Karen Johnson, vice president-membership

NOW's list of national board members was unavailable.

## BOARD OF DIRECTORS

"A United States District Court jury today [April 20, 1998] ruled that three anti-abortion leaders had violated a Federal racketeering law by conducting a nationwide campaign to intimidate abortion providers and patients.

"The jury of two men and four women, who had deliberated since Thursday, found that 21 acts of intimidation, including physical violence outside clinics, amounted to a vast enterprise of extortion under the Racketeer Influenced and Corrupt Organizations law.

"The RICO Act was passed in 1970 as a way to fight organized crime, and some legal scholars have argued that it should not apply to political groups.

"The civil case decided today, which was brought by the National Organization for Women, awarded $85,926 in damages to two abortion clinics that were targets of harassment. Under the terms of the racketeering act, the judge is expected to automatically triple that figure, which the individual defendants must pay.

## EFFECTIVENESS

" 'We cannot tolerate the use of threats and force by one group to impose its views on others,' said Fay Clayton, the lawyer who argued the case for NOW." (*New York Times*, April 21, 1998)

"An 80-member chapter of the National Organization for Women in Fairfax County, Va., has voted unanimously to call for the group's national leadership to resign for its 'hypocrisy' in not speaking out on President Clinton's alleged affair with Monica Lewinsky. . . .

"The Virginia group says it has received support from many NOW members, and there is word that chapters in Texas, Kansas, California and Florida are joining the agitation. The leader of the NOW revolt is Marie-Jose Ragab, a French immigrant, who served as the international director of NOW from 1990 to 1995, working under President Patricia Ireland. She said she was driven into action by the comments of her old boss on ABC's 'This Week' on Feb. 1.

"After days of silence, Ms. Ireland offered a distinction between NOW's stance in the Clarence Thomas and Bob Packwood cases and that of President Clinton. She said that if the allegations are true with Mr. Clinton, 'it appears to be a pattern of consensual sex' and 'that is a distinction that I think people opposed to women's rights are trying to hide.'

"That set Ms. Ragab off. Monica Lewinsky was the only one of 250 interns in her class to land a paying White House job. She was then transferred to a high-security Pentagon job, granted access to the White House 37 times after that and received extraordinary help securing a private-sector job. 'This is exactly the message we don't want to send,' Ms. Ragab says." (*Wall Street Journal*, March 3, 1998)

"Promise Keepers, a Christian men's group whose praying, rejoicing devotees have packed stadiums across the country, said it expects to attract several hundred thousand men to the Mall on Oct. 4 for a spiritual coming together at which participants will recommit themselves to living responsible lives. While leaders of the group describe the event as a rallying of a 'diverse multitude in the name of Jesus,' the National Organization for Women contends that the gathering is meant to encourage men to put women in the 'back seat' of society.

"NOW's national president, Patricia Ireland, this week announced a national 'No Surrender' campaign in which NOW plans to portray Promise Keepers as a conservative political group intent on forcing women into subservient roles.

" 'We want to say, Yes, it's good to take responsibility for your family, but you don't have to do it by treating your wife as a subordinate,' Ireland said in an interview. 'It's very likely that some very well-meaning men who will come to the rally have little or no grasp of the group's political agenda.'

"But Promise Keepers national spokesman Mark DeMoss dismissed NOW's charges, saying there is no evidence that the organization has a political agenda and wants to degrade women. He said politicians will not be among the 40 speakers at the Washington rally." (*Washington Post*, August 27, 1997)

"Jesse L. Jackson's Rainbow/PUSH Coalition and the National Organization for Women said today they had agreed to call off their consumer boycott of Mitsubishi Motor Manufacturing of America Inc. in exchange for the company's commitment to provide more than $200 million in potential business opportunities for minorities and women.

"The boycott began in May when Jackson and NOW President Patricia Ireland urged consumers to spurn Mitsubishi products, particularly automobiles, to protest the company's handling of the allegations of sexual harassment and sex and race discrimination at its auto plant in Normal, Ill. . . .

"Jackson called the agreement he had reached with the company a 'joint covenant' that represents a 'new model' of business cooperation between business and civil rights organizations. Also attending the news conference were Ireland, Mitsubishi executives and former secretary of labor Lynn Martin, who was hired by Mitsubishi after the lawsuits were filed and the boycott launched, to help overhaul the company's employment practices.

"Jackson and Mitsubishi officials said the company had agreed to boost its percentage of minority- and women-owned auto dealerships from 9 percent to 15 percent within five years; create a program to help steer business opportunities, such as purchasing orders, real estate ventures and professional services, to minority and female entrepreneurs; and seek to hire women and minorities to work at Mitsubishi auto dealerships with the goal of helping them develop the business skills to become auto dealers." (*Washington Post*, January 16, 1997)

## POLITICAL ORIENTATION

"NOW President Patricia Ireland said her office was deluged with calls Monday and Tuesday from activists in state and local chaptes, almost all of whom argued against filing a friend-of-the-court brief in the [Paula] Jones lawsuit. That, combined with opposition from the organization's 50 state coordinators and its national board . . . convinced the group not to weigh in on the appeal.

" 'This is a classic of hard cases make bad law,' Ireland said in an interview yesterday. Not only is the case too politically charged, she said, but it is weakened by the trial judge's ruling that Jones had not proved she had been harmed.

" 'We are also disinclined to work with the disreputable right-wing organizations and individuals advancing her cause,' Ireland said, because of their 'long-standing political interest in undermining our movement to strengthen women's rights and weakening the laws that protect those rights.'

"The announcement yesterday was the latest twist in a controversy over whether NOW and other women's groups have, for political reasons, shied from criticizing Clinton for his alleged sexual misconduct in the Jones case. Critics, particularly conservative groups, have said that the silence from these women's organizations was inconsistent given their stance against Supreme Court Justice Clarence Thomas and former senator Bob Packwood (R-Ore.), when they were accused of sexual harassment." (*Washington Post*, April 23, 1998)

# National Organization on Disability (1982)

910 16th Street, NW
Suite 610
Washington, D.C. 20006
Phone: (202) 293-5960
Fax: (202) 293-7999
Internet: http://www.nod.org

**PURPOSE**

Dedicated "to . . . promoting the full and equal participation of people with disabilities."

**STAFF**

12 total—7 professional; 5 support; plus 2 volunteers and 1 intern

**DIRECTOR**

Alan A. Reich, president. Before founding the National Organization on Disability (NOD), Reich served as president of its predecessor, the U.S. Council for the International Year of Disabled Persons (1981). Previously, he was an executive with the Polaroid Corporation and deputy assistant secretary of state for educational and cultural affairs. Reich is past chairman of the People-to-People Committee on Disability and the Paralysis Cure Research Foundation. He is chairman of the World Committee on Disability. He has a B.A. from Dartmouth College, an M.A. from Middlebury College Russian School, and an M.B.A. from Harvard University.

**TAX STATUS**

501(c)(3)

**BUDGET**

1997—$1.4 million
1998—$1.5 million
Proposed 1999—$1.8 million

**FUNDING SOURCES**

Corporate donations, 50 percent; individuals, 29 percent; foundation grants, 20 percent; publications, 1 percent

**SCOPE**

Members: N/A
Branches/chapters: N/A
Affiliates: N/A

**PAC**

None

♦ Awards program (FDR International Disability Award) ♦ Conferences/seminars ♦ Grassroots organizing ♦ International activities ♦ Internet (Web site) ♦ Internships ♦ Media outreach ♦ Polling ♦ Research

## METHOD OF OPERATION

♦ Community accessibility ♦ Employment of people with disabilities ♦ Franklin D. Roosevelt Memorial in Washington, D.C. ♦ Public awareness of disability issues

## CURRENT CONCERNS

*1994 Closing the Gap: A Summary of N.O.D./Harris Survey of Americans with Disabilities*
*1994 N.O.D./Harris Survey of Americans with Disabilities*
*1995 N.O.D./Harris Survey on Employment of People with Disabilities*
*1998 Survey of Americans with Disabilities*
*FDR International Award Booklet*
*From Barriers to Bridges*
*Loving Justice*
*That All May Worship*

## PUBLICATIONS

*Update* (quarterly)
*Disability Agenda* (quarterly)

## NEWSLETTER

Community Partnership Program Statewide Conference (various states during the year)
That All May Worship Conferences (held throughout the year across the nation)

## CONFERENCES

Michael R. Deland, chairman; Christopher Reeve, vice chairman; Alan A. Reich, president; George Bush, honorary chairman

Other members:
♦ Arlene A. Anns ♦ Philip E. Beekman ♦ Henry Betts ♦ Richard Bishop ♦ Bertram S. Brown ♦ J. Harold Chandler ♦ Tony Coelho ♦ Deedee Corradini ♦ Richard M. DeVos ♦ Stephen L. Feinberg ♦ Bruce G. Freeman ♦ George H. Gallup Jr. ♦ Stephen L. Hammerman ♦ William R. Howell ♦ Young Woo Kang ♦ Harold McGraw III ♦ Mercedese M. Miller ♦ James E. Oesterreicher ♦ Mary Jane Owen ♦ John W. Patten ♦ Itzhak Perlman ♦ Robert C. Pew ♦ Russell G. Redenbaugh ♦ Jeffrey P. Reich ♦ Kenneth Roman ♦ Michael T. Rose ♦ E. John Rosenwald Jr. ♦ Alan Rubin ♦ Vincent A. Sarni ♦ Raymond Phillip Shafer ♦ Humphrey Taylor ♦ W. Reid Thompson ♦ Jack Valenti ♦ Harold Wilke

## BOARD OF DIRECTORS

"The National Organization on Disability has announced a campaign that aims to commit 2,000 U.S. religious congregations to welcoming people with disabilities by the year 2000.

## EFFECTIVENESS

"Organizers of the 'Accessible Congregations Campaign' hopes houses of worship will pledge to accept people with disabilities as valued members of congregations and will remove barriers to their full participation and encourage their involvement in worship services and leadership. . . .

"Close to 60 national and regional groups have endorsed the campaign, including the National Council of Churches Committee on Disabilities, Paralyzed Veterans of America and the Council for Jews with Special Needs Inc. . . ." (*Stuart News/Port St. Lucie News*, July 4, 1998)

"Vice President Gore unveils plans today to add a life-size statue of Franklin Delano Roosevelt in his wheelchair to the sprawling memorial that bears his name.

"The announcement officially concludes a long-running controversy over the city's most popular tourist attraction. After a disability-rights group raises $1.5 million to pay for it, construction will begin on a life-size sculpture to be placed in the center of a new display in the 7.5-acre FDR Memorial.

"Showing that he led the nation through the Great Depression and World War II with a crippling disability 'will make Roosevelt even more heroic' to future generations, says National Organization on Disability Chairman Michael Deland, who fought for the new statue and whose group offered to raise the money for the project. . . ." (*USA Today*, July 2, 1998)

"Seven cities, including the City of New York, and three counties are the recipients of cash prizes in the 1998 $30,000 National Organization on Disability/United Parcel Service Community Awards Competition. The competition recognized outstanding local programs and actions that expand the participation of citizens with disabilities.

"Alan A. Reich, President of the National Organization on Disability, stated 'the disability community in New York City worked with police to conduct a Sting Operation which ticketed cab drivers who refused to pick up wheelchair users and persons with assistive dogs. Ideas that come from the grassroots are very often simple and innovative.'. . ." (*New York Able*, February 1998)

". . . Clinton, in a statement released by the White House, responded to a potent campaign by advocacy groups that have made the memorial's design the focus of a poignant debate over the change in the last half-century in national attitudes toward people with disabilities. Those groups had threatened to disrupt the May 2 dedication ceremonies for the memorial—at which Clinton is scheduled to deliver the dedication address—to protest the decision by the FDR Memorial Commission and its artists not to portray Roosevelt's paralysis from polio. They argued that the failure to show him in a wheelchair treated his disability, and other disabilities, as something shameful to be hidden. . . .

" 'Future generations need to know Roosevelt as he was: He was a president who served 12 years in a wheelchair,' said Alan A. Reich, president of the National Organization on Disability, after meeting with White House aides yesterday.

"Reich stopped short of saying the coalition of groups representing the disabled will call off the protest, during which they had promised to disrupt Clinton's speech. But he said that if the White House follows through quickly on a promise to introduce legislation to add another statue, 'we are hopeful we can turn the demonstration into a celebration.'

"Reich's group has offered to pay for the additional statue, which would have to be commissioned, sculpted and placed at the 7.5-acre Tidal Basin memorial after its dedication. . . ." (*Washington Post*, April 24, 1997)

Unavailable

# POLITICAL ORIENTATION

# National Partnership for Women and Families (1971)

(formerly known as Women's Legal Defense Fund)
1875 Connecticut Avenue, NW
Suite 710
Washington, D.C. 20009
Phone: (202) 986-2600
Fax: (202) 986-2539
Internet: http://www.nationalpartnership.org

| | |
|---|---|
| **PURPOSE** | "Dedicated to improving the lives of women and families. Through public education and advocacy the National Partnership promotes fairness in the workplace, quality health care, and policies that help women and men meet the dual demands of work and family." |
| **STAFF** | 25 total—17 professional; 8 support |
| **DIRECTOR** | Judith L. Lichtman, president. Before joining the National Partnership for Women and Families (NPWF) in 1974, Lichtman was a legal adviser to the Commonwealth of Puerto Rico, a consultant and senior attorney with the U.S. Commission on Civil Rights, a staff assistant at the Urban Coalition, and a history and political science instructor at Jackson State College. She earned B.S. and LL.B. degrees at the University of Wisconsin. |
| **TAX STATUS** | 501(c)(3) |
| **BUDGET** | Fiscal year ending March 3, 1997—$2.2 million<br>F.Y. 1998—$2.3 million<br>Proposed F.Y. 1999—$3.1 million |
| **FUNDING SOURCES** | Foundations, 43 percent; individuals, 36 percent; corporate donations, 18 percent; other, 3 percent |
| **SCOPE** | Members: 2,500<br>Branches/chapters: N/A<br>Affiliates: N/A |

| | |
|---|---|
| None | **PAC** |
| • Coalition forming • Conferences/seminars • Congressional testimony • Internet (E-mail alerts, Web site) • Legislative/regulatory monitoring (federal and state) • Library/information clearinghouse • Litigation • Lobbying (federal, state, and grassroots) • Media outreach • Participation in regulatory proceedings (federal) • Research • Speakers program | **METHOD OF OPERATION** |
| • Affirmative action • Equal Employment Opportunity enforcement • Family/medical leave • Health care • Sexual harassment • Welfare reform | **CURRENT CONCERNS** |
| *The Guide to the Family and Medical Leave Act: Questions and Answers* <br> *Guide to HIPAA: What the Health Insurance Reform Law Means for Women and Familes* <br> Also publishes fact sheets on current topics | **PUBLICATIONS** |
| *National Partnership News* (quarterly) | **NEWSLETTER** |
| National Partnership Luncheon (annual luncheon usually held in June, Washington, D.C.) | **CONFERENCES** |
| Ellen Malcolm, chair; Pauline Schneider, vice chair; Judy Langford, secretary; Chris Sale, treasurer; Judith L. Lichtman, president <br><br> Other members: <br> • Nancy L. Buc • Sara-Ann Determan • Linda D. Fienberg • Douglas A. Fraser • Perry Granoff • Nikki Heidepriem • Antonia Hernandez • Lowell Douglass Johnston • Patricia King • Melissa Moss • Sheli Rosenberg • Judith Scott • Cynthia Anne Telles | **BOARD OF DIRECTORS** |
| Unavailable | **EFFECTIVENESS** |
| Unavailable | **POLITICAL ORIENTATION** |

# National Rifle Association of America
## (1871)

11250 Waples Mill Road
Fairfax, Virginia 22030
Phone: (703) 267-1000
Fax: (703) 267-3976
Internet: http://www.nra.org

## PURPOSE

"The purpose and objectives of the NRA are: 1) to protect and defend the Constitution of the United States, especially with reference to the inalienable right of the individual American citizen guaranteed by such Constitution to acquire, possess, transport, carry, transfer ownership of, and enjoy the right to use arms, in order that the people may always be in a position to exercise their legitimate individual rights of self-preservation and defense of family, person, and property, as well as to serve effectively in the appropriate militia for the common defense of the Republic and individual liberty of its citizens; 2) to promote public safety, law and order, and the national defense; 3) to train members of law enforcement agencies, the armed forces, the militia, and people of good repute in marksmanship and in the safe handling and efficient use of small arms; 4) to foster and promote the shooting sports, including the advancement of amateur competitions in marksmanship at the local, state, regional, national, and international levels; and 5) to promote hunter safety, and to promote and defend hunting as a shooting sport and as a viable necessary method of fostering the propagation, growth, conservation, and wise use of our renewable wildlife resources."

## STAFF

Unavailable

## DIRECTOR

Wayne R. LaPierre, Jr., executive vice president. Prior to being named executive vice president of the National Rifle Association (NRA) in 1991, LaPierre was executive director of the NRA Institute for Legislative Action, the NRA's lobbying arm. He served in this position from 1986 to 1991. LaPierre began his career with the NRA in 1978 as a state liaison and was named director of state and local affairs in 1979. In 1980 he became director of federal affairs.

## TAX STATUS

501(c)(4)

## BUDGET

1998—Unavailable
Proposed 1999—Unavailable

| | |
|---|---|
| Contributions, membership dues, publication sales | *FUNDING SOURCES* |
| Members: More than 2.8 million<br>Branches/chapters: None<br>Affiliate: NRA Foundation, a 501(c)(3) organization, and NRA Institute for Legislative Action (NRA-ILA) | *SCOPE* |
| Political Victory Fund | *PAC* |
| ◆ Advertisements ◆ Awards program ◆ Campaign contributions ◆ Coalition forming ◆ Computer services ◆ Conferences/seminars ◆ Congressional testimony ◆ Congressional voting analysis ◆ Demonstrations ◆ Electoral politics ◆ Films/video/audiotapes ◆ Grantmaking ◆ Grassroots organizing ◆ Initiative/referendum campaigns ◆ International activities ◆ Internet (E-mail alerts, Web site) ◆ Legal assistance ◆ Legislative/ regulatory monitoring (federal and state) ◆ Library/information clearinghouse ◆ Litigation ◆ Lobbying (federal, state, and grassroots) ◆ Local/municipal affairs ◆ Media outreach ◆ Participation in regulatory proceedings (federal and state) ◆ Performance rating ◆ Polling ◆ Product merchandising ◆ Research ◆ Scholarships ◆ Shareholder resolutions ◆ Speakers program ◆ Training and technical assistance ◆ Television and radio production ◆ Voter registration | *METHOD OF OPERATION* |
| ◆ Federal, state, and local legislation protecting the rights of law-abiding gun owners ◆ Hunting restrictions ◆ National campaign of firearms safety and training ◆ Sportsmen's issues ◆ Wilderness and park hunting | *CURRENT CONCERNS* |
| None | *PUBLICATIONS* |
| *American Hunter* (magazine)<br>*American Rifleman* (magazine)<br>*The Guardian* (magazine) | *NEWSLETTER* |
| Annual convention and local meetings and training sessions on gun use and safety | *CONFERENCES* |
| Unavailable | *BOARD OF DIRECTORS* |

*National Rifle Association of America* 153

# EFFECTIVENESS

"... Supporters of handgun control lost a big one in Washington state. They put a perfectly reasonable gun safety initiative on the ballot and got buried by a margin of 70-30.

"The problem did not lie with the basic provisions of Initiative 676. It proposed two good things: that every handgun transferred in the state be equipped with a trigger lock and that every handgun owner be licensed. The owner would have had to pass a test or take an eight-hour course on safety. Cost—$5 a year for the license—was not a big deal. Even the gun industry accepts the need for trigger locks. And it's hard to refute the argument that if you need to take a test to drive a car, you ought to take one to own a handgun.

"When the campaign for 676 began, that's how a majority of Washington state's voters saw things: 57 percent backed the initiative at the start, according to Richard Maullin, pollster for the gun control advocates.

"Enter the National Rifle Association with $4 million to $5 million, and probably more. As advocates of 676 told it in a series of interviews, they were buried under NRA money.

"They have a point. Supporters of the initiative raised only about $1 million, one-third of it spent to get the proposal on the ballot. 'We just did not have the resources to prevent our voice from being drowned out,' said Tom Wales, a prosecutor who headed the 676 campaign.

"But the NRA spent its money shrewdly. Its media campaign made voters more afraid of the eight-page proposal than they were of handgun violence. The NRA did not attack 'the concept' of 676 so much as 'nibble away at aspects of the measure,' said Maullin." (*Washington Post*, November 11, 1997)

"The National Rifle Association is campaigning to persuade Virginia Gov. George Allen to veto a bill that would bar guns, knives and other weapons from Fairfax County's recreation centers, an effort that county officials are calling 'ridiculous' and 'senseless.'

"Fairfax officials pushed for the legislation, written to apply only in their county, after several incidents in which people showed up at community centers with guns or knives. Virginia law allows non-felons 18 and older to carry guns in public without a permit as long as the weapons aren't concealed. 'We are trying to provide a safe place for our kids to congregate,' said Board of Supervisors Chairman Katherine K. Hanley (D). Her office has received 70 letters and calls of protest from NRA members. 'For the NRA to take that and turn it into a gun control issue is ridiculous.'

"The NRA posted a warning on the Internet and sent letters to members, urging them to oppose the pending legislation as a dangerous step toward further restrictions on gun owners in the Old Dominion. A second bill opposed by the NRA would bar guns from county police stations. Both would exempt holders of concealed-weapons permits from the restrictions.

" 'There is a long-standing hostility in Fairfax County to the rights of citizens to defend themselves,' said NRA spokesman Jim Manown. 'This is really an attempt to erode the uniform firearms laws in Virginia.' " (*Washington Post*, March 20, 1997)

"In signs of continuing financial trouble, the National Rifle Association has laid off 30 workers and suspended production of its weekly cable-TV program, according to NRA officials. Two NRA board members, who asked not to be named, said the gun lobby has furloughed almost 10% of its roughly 400-employee work force in recent weeks. The group also is relocating staff in its headquarters building in Fairfax, Va., to free up space to rent to other companies in order to generate enough rental revenue to help cover payrolls in coming months, one board member said. . . .

"The NRA's financial woes stem from a multimillion-dollar membership campaign, a plan that backfired amid negative publicity. Last year, as membership reached 3.5 million, former President Bush quit the NRA after a fund-raising letter referred to federal agents as 'jackbooted government thugs.'

"Since then, membership has dropped to about 2.8 million." (*Wall Street Journal*, September 23, 1996)

"The nation's gun lobbies are blazing away at one of President Clinton's new antiterrorist proposals—to put tiny plastic markers called taggants in explosives and gunpowder.

"Taggants are color-coded identifiers that allow authorities to trace explosives back to the retailer, which could ultimately lead to the buyer. Originally developed in the U.S., taggants have been used for 11 years in Switzerland. According to Microtrace Inc. of Minneapolis, Minn., which manufactures them, Swiss police have used the microscopic markers to trace the source of explosives in more than 500 cases of bombing or illegal possession of explosives.

"The gun lobbies, however, consider taggants an invasion of privacy as well as a potential safety hazard. . . .

" 'I don't believe you achieve safety by introducing hazards into the homes of millions of Americans,' argues Tom Wyld, a spokesman for the National Rifle Association, which claims three million members. . . .

"The NRA, one of the strongest and most free-spending lobbies in Congress, wants an independent study of taggants before any commitment is made. Taggants have been under consideration since the late 1970s. . . ." (*Wall Street Journal*, July 31, 1996)

## POLITICAL ORIENTATION

"Even the National Rifle Association, one of the country's biggest and most Republican-leaning PACs, donated almost half its money to Democrats in this year's first quarter, after giving Republicans more than four times as much as their opponents last year. NRA lobbyist Tanya Metaksa says her PAC pays no attention to party labels when contributing, calling the Democrats' increased share of NRA contributions 'a coincidence.' " (*Wall Street Journal*, May 23, 1996)

# National Urban League (1910)

120 Wall Street
New York, New York 10005
Phone: (212) 558-5300
Fax: (212) 344-5332

1111 14th Street, NW
Suite 1001
Washington, D.C. 20005
Phone: (202) 898-1604
Fax: (202) 408-1965

Internet: http://www.nul.org

| | |
|---|---|
| **PURPOSE** | "To assist African Americans in the achievement of social and economic equality." |
| **STAFF** | Unavailable |
| **DIRECTOR** | Hugh B. Price, president and chief executive officer. He has served as a member of the *New York Times* editorial board and the New York City mayor's cabinet and supervised the city's Head Start program and services for youth and senior citizens. Price is a graduate of Yale Law School. |
| **TAX STATUS** | 501(c)(3) |
| **BUDGET** | 1997—$32 million<br>1998—$35 million<br>Proposed 1999—Unavailable |
| **FUNDING SOURCES** | Grants and contracts from government agencies, 56 percent; contributions, 17 percent; donated materials and services, 9 percent; program service fees, 6 percent; affiliate dues, 4 percent; interest, dividends and gain on investments, 3 percent; special events, 2 percent; other, 3 percent |
| **SCOPE** | Members: Approximately 50,000<br>Branches/chapters: N/A<br>Affiliates: 115 local affiliates in 31 states and the District of Columbia |
| **PAC** | None |

♦ Awards program ♦ Coalition forming ♦ Conferences/seminars ♦ Congressional testimony ♦ Internships ♦ Job bank ♦ Legislative/regulatory monitoring (federal) ♦ Research ♦ Scholarships ♦ Support programs ♦ Voter registration

## METHOD OF OPERATION

♦ Education and career development ♦ Employment and job training ♦ Racial inclusion for African Americans ♦ Youth and family development

## CURRENT CONCERNS

*Community Surveys and Reports* (periodic)
*State of Black America* (annual)
*Urban League Review* (semiannual)

## PUBLICATIONS

*BEEP Newsletter* (quarterly)
*Urban League News* (quarterly)

## NEWSLETTER

Annual conference
Black Executive Exchange Program (annual)
"Economic Power: Leveling the Playing Field"
National Urban League Youth Conference
Regional assemblies

## CONFERENCES

Jonathan S. Linen, chairman; Charles M. Collins, senior vice president; Reginald K. Brack Jr. and Kenneth D. Lewis, vice chairmen; Martha M. Mitchell, secretary; William M. Wewis Jr., treasurer; Hugh B. Price, president and chief executive officer

## BOARD OF DIRECTORS

Other trustee members:
♦ Michael B. Alexander ♦ Shawn M. Barney ♦ Stephanie Bell-Rose ♦ Leland C. Brendsel ♦ Glen M. Brooks ♦ Alma Arrington Brown ♦ Thelma Scott Brunson ♦ Ronald W. Burkle ♦ Philip J. Carroll ♦ Barbara Bell Coleman ♦ Leonard S. Coleman Jr. ♦ Michael J. Critelli ♦ Cal Darden ♦ John W. Dean ♦ Danielle V. Eaddy ♦ Elinor J. Ferdon ♦ Samuel Gresham Jr. ♦ Joseph S. Helewicz ♦ Bonnie Guiton Hill ♦ Kevin E. Hooks ♦ Eleanor V. Horne ♦ C. Robert Kidder ♦ Charles E. Kiernan ♦ Jim King ♦ Richard Lovett ♦ Arthur C. Martinez ♦ Carol A. Mason ♦ William G. Mays ♦ James E. Oesterreicher ♦ Jonathan Ogden ♦ Diane Stevens Robinson ♦ Gerald S. Robinson ♦ Benjamin S. Ruffin ♦ Ivan Seidenberg ♦ Candace N. Smith ♦ William J. Stephney ♦ Louisa Strayhorn ♦ Paul Tagliabue ♦ Robert D. Taylor ♦ Israel Tribble Jr. ♦ William Julius Wilson ♦ Carolyn L. Wright-Lewis

"[Hugh G.] Price has pulled together 20 national black organizations, comprising some 25 million members and ranging from fraternities and sororities to the Congress of National Black Churches, to launch a program designed to do two things:

## EFFECTIVENESS

" 'Convince black children and their parents that education matters now as never before.

" 'Create a wave of consumer demand for improving the public schools.

" '[Yale child psychiatrist and education reformer] Jim Comer said the other day that for the first time in history you need a good education to earn a good living,' Price said in an interview. . . .

" 'Employers expect more, even for nonprofessional jobs, and states are imposing higher standards—insisting, for instance, on algebra rather than what they used to call business math.'

" 'That's the first thing. And the second is this. No matter what I feel about affirmative action and special admissions and all that, the fact is that the era of dual standards is over. We have got to get our kids clearly and unquestionably qualified.'

"Price and his coalition plan to do it by changing the very culture in which black youngsters grow up. 'There is a street culture that has taken over that devalues educational achievement. The culture is, I believe, a function of the collapse of the urban economy and the fact that so many children have parents who are disconnected from the economy. They listen to people like us telling them that if they get an education they can have a good life, and they look around them at people who don't seem to have a place in the economy, and they say, Don't believe the hype. Uncle Economy doesn't want you.'. . .

"And, he said, it's necessary to change the schools—the way they teach, the way they hire, the way they relate to the communities they are supposed to serve.

"What Hugh Price and his coalition have in mind is nothing less than a national crusade to save the children—as broad and as powerful as the 1960s crusade for civil rights." (*Washington Post*, December 5, 1997)

"Iris Baez says there was a time when she instinctively trusted the police. But that changed when her son, Anthony, died in a violent confrontation that erupted after his football hit an officer's patrol car.

"Baez and prosecutors said Anthony Baez, 29, was strangled in a police choke-hold. The officer involved in the 1994 incident said Baez's death was a tragic accident triggered by an asthma attack. Last fall, the officer was cleared by a Bronx judge. 'Before this happened, I would have said police don't hurt innocent people because that's illegal,' said Iris Baez, whose son's death remains under federal investigation. 'Now, I know better.'

"The case is among dozens of questionable police-involved deaths that several hundred community and civil rights activists attending a national conference here cite as evidence of a surge in police brutality.

"Civil rights leaders including Hugh Price, president of the National Urban League, and Jesse L. Jackson have urged the White House to take up the issue and have called for congressional hearings into allegations of increases in police brutality." (*Washington Post*, April 27, 1997)

". . . The National Urban League itself faces grave financial and internal problems, a transition to new leadership and the lack of a grass-roots base. It is still not a widely known institution among black Americans. It was never a civil rights organization; instead it serves as the black community's foremost social service agency." (*Wall Street Journal*, October 17, 1996)

"The decision of an organization with the size and influence of the Urban League—114 affiliates in 34 states, serving more than two million people annually—to reassert its efforts in education and economic development is significant. . . .

"Blacks have won the battle for political equality, thanks in no small part to groups like the NAACP and the Urban League. But these groups have neglected what today is clearly black Americans' greatest need: to enter the economic mainstream through entrepreneurship and educational achievement. Mr. Price calls this the new frontier for black America. 'We're getting reacquainted with the rudiments of self-reliance,' he says. 'We have a history of understanding the importance of it.' " (*Wall Street Journal*, August 13, 1997)

# 9to5, National Association of Working Women (1973)

231 West Wisconsin Avenue
Suite 900
Milwaukee, Wisconsin 53203
Phone: (414) 274-0925
Fax: (414) 272-2870

1313 L Street, NW
Washington, D.C. 20005
Phone: (202) 898-3494
Fax: (202) 898-3348

Internet: http://www.members.aol.com/naww925

**PURPOSE**

"To strengthen women's ability to work for economic justice."

**STAFF**

15 total—13 professional; 2 support; plus 2 part-time; 2 intern; many volunteers

**DIRECTOR**

Ellen Bravo, codirector. Since helping to found the Milwaukee chapter of 9to5 in 1982, Bravo has been very active on issues concerning women in the workplace. She was appointed as an observer to the Wisconsin Comparable Worth Task Force in 1984 and the Wisconsin Minimum Wage Advisory Council in 1986. Bravo holds degrees in classical literature from Cornell University and Cambridge University, which she attended on a Fulbright Scholarship.

Gloria Santa Anna, codirector. Santa Anna has worked with 9to5 since 1994. She has shepherded 9to5's long-range planning process, staff development, and internal anti-oppression training. She has managed numerous workshops on diversity issues, labor/management relations, nonprofit management, and program design and evaluation.

**TAX STATUS**

501(c)(5)

**BUDGET**

Fiscal year ending September 30, 1997—$1 million
F.Y. 1998—$850,000
Proposed F.Y. 1999—$900,000

**FUNDING SOURCES**

Grants, donations, contracts, conferences, membership dues, seminars/workshops, publications, and corporate training

| | |
|---|---|
| Members: 15,000 individuals<br>Branches/chapters: 23 chapters nationwide<br>Affiliates: N/A | *SCOPE* |
| None | *PAC* |
| ♦ Awards program ♦ Conferences/seminars ♦ Grassroots organizing ♦ Internet (Web site) ♦ Legal assistance ♦ Lobbying (grassroots) ♦ Media outreach ♦ Speakers program ♦ Training | *METHOD OF OPERATION* |
| ♦ Antidiscrimination (sex, race, and sexual orientation) ♦ Contingent work (temporary and part-time) ♦ Political participation ♦ Sexual harassment ♦ Welfare/Workfare reform ♦ Work/family policies | *CURRENT CONCERNS* |
| *9to5 Guide to Combatting Sexual Harassment*<br>*9to5 Guide to Job/Family Challenge: Not for Women Only*<br>Publishes research reports on various issues | *PUBLICATIONS* |
| *9to5 Newsline* (bimonthly) | *NEWSLETTER* |
| Annual leadership conference (Washington, D.C.) | *CONFERENCES* |
| ♦ Leonie Carter ♦ Kathy Dean ♦ Cathy Deppe ♦ Kathy Gomez ♦ Lillian Morisky ♦ Susan Schiller ♦ Terry Masse ♦ Phyllis Owens ♦ Carmen Perez ♦ Donna Skenadore ♦ Sheryl Woods | *BOARD OF DIRECTORS* |
| | *EFFECTIVENESS* |

"Now that everyone has exchanged gifts and eaten enough turkey and stuffing to feed several small countries, there's only one thing left to do: make resolutions. . . .

"9to5, the National Association of Working Women, a Milwaukee-based group that studies discrimination issues, also made two resolutions.

"One is to work with those affected by welfare reform and try to frame the issue not in terms of reducing welfare rolls but [of] ending poverty. To make the transition to the work world, welfare recipients need family-supporting jobs, training, child care and other help, 9to5 said.

"Employers should resolve to hire women moving from welfare, and to pay attention not just to the flexibility and mentoring they may require, but also to changes in work culture that would benefit everyone, the group said.

"9to5's other priority is making family leave more accessible and affordable.

"Its suggestion for an employer resolution: Have a leave policy at least equivalent to the federal Family and Medical Leave Act, regardless of the size of the firm; and for all employees, regardless of the number of hours worked or the length of employment." (*Washington Post*, December 28, 1997)

". . . Let's face it: On the road to financial security, kids are a major detour. Sure, that bundle of joy is an automatic tax write-off when it arrives. But in the 1997 tax year, that comes to only $2,650—and that's, well, less than the bundle it will cost you to provide housing, food, transportation, clothing, education, health and child care, not to mention all those blocks, Barbies and birthday parties.

"Then there's the career problem. Moms and dads in their late 30s and early 40s have had time to establish careers and climb the corporate ladder. And in many cases it's more punishing financially for them to step off that ladder.

"For one thing, experts and couples both cite the difficulties of getting back onto the job merry-go-round after stepping off—particularly for women. 'There is still a definite bias against women who take time out of the work force,' says Ellen Bravo, executive director of the 9-to-5 National Association of Working Women, based in Milwaukee. She cites an academic study that shows women who took leave before going back full time earned on average 17% less than women who hadn't taken a break.

"And never mind slashed income down the road—there's the immediate loss of a paycheck every week. Career counselors and financial planners say that the higher careers and paychecks rise, the harder it is for couples to swallow a 50% cut in the family income." (*Wall Street Journal*, December 12, 1996)

# POLITICAL ORIENTATION

Unavailable

# Operation Rescue National (1988)

P.O. Box 740066
Dallas, Texas 75374
Phone: (972) 348-8866
Fax: (972) 276-9361
Internet: http://www.orn.org

| | |
|---|---|
| To "take up the cause of preborn children in the name of Jesus Christ. . . . Jesus Christ is the only answer to the abortion holocaust. It is upon our activist repentance at abortion mills, abortionists' homes, churches, and practices that the Gospel is visibly lived out. We become to the church, to our city, and to our nation living parables which rightly represent God's heart toward His helpless children." | **PURPOSE** |
| 10 total | **STAFF** |
| Philip "Flip" Benham, national director. Benham co-founded Operation Rescue in 1988 and has served as its national director since 1994. He earned B.A. degrees in political science and international relations from Florida State University and holds a master of divinity degree from Asbury Theological Seminary. | **DIRECTOR** |
| Nonprofit (not tax-exempt) | **TAX STATUS** |
| 1998—Unavailable<br>Proposed 1999—Unavailable | **BUDGET** |
| Donations | **FUNDING SOURCES** |
| Members: N/A<br>Branches/chapters: Chapters in some states<br>Affiliates: N/A | **SCOPE** |
| None | **PAC** |

| METHOD OF OPERATION | ♦ Boycotts ♦ Demonstrations ♦ Direct action ♦ Films/video/audiotapes ♦ Grassroots organizing ♦ Initiative/referendum campaigns ♦ Litigation ♦ Media outreach |
|---|---|
| CURRENT CONCERNS | ♦ Abortion ♦ Homosexuality ♦ Pornography |
| PUBLICATIONS | *Daily Bible Reading Schedule* *Down the Slippery Slope* *Higher Laws* *No Cheap Solution* |
| NEWSLETTER | Monthly newsletter |
| CONFERENCES | Holds three conferences annually: Holy Week Conference, national conference in January, and a summer conference |
| BOARD OF DIRECTORS | Unavailable |
| EFFECTIVENESS | "A United States District Court jury today [April 20, 1998] ruled that three anti-abortion leaders had violated a Federal racketeering law by conducting a nationwide campaign to intimidate abortion providers and patients. . . .

"The suit named as defendants two militant anti-abortion groups, Operation Rescue and the Pro-Life Action League, and their leaders, Joseph Scheidler, Timothy Murphy and Andrew Scholberg. Randall Terry, the president of Operation Rescue, had earlier agreed to pay damages in a settlement.

"The suit sought damages for two clinics, in Milwaukee and Wilmington, Del., that had been targeted for harassment. . . ." (*New York Times*, April 21, 1998)

". . . The right of free speech and the right of access to abortion clinics clash in a legal dispute between Planned Parenthood of Houston and the antiabortion group Operation Rescue.

"Planned Parenthood and several family-planning clinics filed suit against Operation Rescue and four members after the antiabortion group organized a series of protests to coincide with the 1992 Republican National Convention in Houston.

"In Harris County State District Court, a jury imposed a permanent injunction that barred Operation Rescue protesters from interfering with the clinics and that created 'demonstration-free' buffer zones around clinics and doctors' homes. At the same time, the jury found that the protesters engaged in a civil conspiracy and ordered Operation Rescue to pay the clinics nearly $205,000 in actual damages and more than $1 million in punitive damages. |

"An appeals court upheld the injunction and the monetary damages. Operation Rescue appealed to the Supreme Court, contending the buffer zones infringe on the constitutional right to free speech." (*Wall Street Journal*, September 10, 1997)

"In a rare protest at the doorstep of the Magic Kingdom, about 75 to 100 anti-gay activists caused a minor slowdown for thousands of tourists streaming into Walt Disney World.

"Though Disney officials said the protest had no effect on operations, it was the first of what might be many demonstrations at Disney and elsewhere this year by Operation Rescue National, a Texas-based anti-abortion group that is expanding its mission to target homosexuality. . . .

"Benham [executive director of Operation Rescue National] said one catalyst for targeting Disney was its decision to offer health insurance to the partners of gay employees." (*Washington Post*, December 30, 1997)

"The Food and Drug Administration said that the French abortion pill, RU-486, is safe and effective in ending pregnancies early and that it stands ready to approve the drug, once it gets more information about how it will be manufactured and labeled.

"The FDA decision on the emotionally charged issue drew an immediate denunciation from the antiabortion group Operation Rescue. 'RU-486 has only one purpose: to kill,' the group said in a statement. But supporters of the drug applauded the FDA move, saying it's important to make safe, nonsurgical abortion procedures available for women who wish to end pregnancies." (*Wall Street Journal*, September 19, 1996)

---

"radical group" (*Wall Street Journal*, February 22, 1996)

"militant" (*Newsweek*, August 21, 1995)

## POLITICAL ORIENTATION

# People for the American Way (1980)

2000 M Street, NW
Suite 400
Washington, D.C. 20036
Phone: (202) 467-4999
Fax: (202) 293-2672
Internet: http://www.pfaw.org

**PURPOSE**

"To preserve a climate in which every citizen has the right to believe, worship, think and speak freely."

**STAFF**

65 total—15 professional, 50 support; plus 19 interns and 4 volunteers/part-time staff

**DIRECTOR**

Carole Shields, president. Prior to coming to her current position in 1996, Shields was a board member of People for the American Way/People for the American Way Foundation for six years. During that period, she also was vice chair of the Public Health Trust of Dade County, Florida. She also served on the board of the State of Florida's Health and Rehabilitative Services and the Dade Children's Partnership. Shields also served several philanthropic foundations, including the Kettering Foundation, the Lilly Endowment, and the Davis Foundation. She also has served for three years as panelist for the White House Fellows competition. Shields has an M.B.A. from the University of Miami.

**TAX STATUS**

501(c)(4)

**BUDGET**

1998—$8.2 million
Proposed 1999—$10 million

**FUNDING SOURCES**

Membership contributions, 31 percent; special donors, 31 percent; special events, 20 percent; foundation grants, 12 percent; interest income, 1 percent; in-kind contributions, 1 percent; state operations, 1 percent; sale of books and materials, 1 percent; other, 2 percent

**SCOPE**

Members: 300,000 individuals

Branches/chapters: 3 regional offices in California, Florida, and New York

Affiliate: People for the American Way Action Foundation, a 501(c)(3) organization

None

♦ Advertisements ♦ Citizen action ♦ Coalition forming ♦ Curriculum development ♦ Extremist activities monitoring ♦ Films/video/audiotapes ♦ Grassroots organizing ♦ Internet ♦ Library/information clearinghouse ♦ Litigation ♦ Media outreach ♦ Polling ♦ Research ♦ Speakers program ♦ Televangelist monitoring

♦ Artistic freedom ♦ Censorship ♦ Education ♦ First Amendment rights ♦ Race relations ♦ Regulation of the Internet ♦ Religious expression

*An Activist Guide to Protecting the Freedom to Learn*
*Attacks on the Freedom to Learn*
*Congressional Handbook*
*Democracy's Next Generation: A Study of Youth and Teachers*
*Democracy's Next Generation II: A Study of American Youth on Race*
*Hate in the Ivory Tower: A Survey of Intolerance on College Campuses and
    Academia's Response*
*Hostile Climate: A State-by-State Report on Anti-Gay Activity*
*How to Win: A Practical Guide for Defeating the Radical Right in Your
    Community*
*Invisible Walls: A Study of Racial Division and the Challenge of Building
    Bridges of Understanding*
*The San Diego Model: A Community Battles the Religious Right*
*Teaching Fear: The Religious Right's Campaign Against Sexuality Education*
*Tucson Talks: A Search for Common Ground*
*A Turn to the Right: A Guide to Religious Right Influence in the 103rd/104th
    Congress*
*Twelve Rules for Mixing Religion and Politics*
*Winning Through Reason, Not Fear: Meeting the Challenge of the Religious
    Right*

Videos:
*Censorship in Our Schools: Hawkins County, Tennessee*
*First Vote*
*Redondo Beach: A Stand Against Censorship*
*The Religious Right: In Their Own Words*
*STAR: A New Dialogue About Diversity*

*People for the American Way Activist* (quarterly)
*People for the American Way News* (quarterly)
*Right Wing Watch Online* (monthly)

Sponsors conferences periodically

## BOARD OF DIRECTORS

## EFFECTIVENESS

"In his public high school classroom here, Mark Axford, a history teacher, was gingerly telling his new students what the course would entail. He was being cautious because the subject was the Old Testament, the textbook the Bible, and every word he said was being videotaped for review by lawyers and a Federal judge in a pioneering legal case. . . .

"The class, called Bible History, was begun on Jan. 21 at Riverdale High School, where Mr. Axford teaches, and at six other high schools in Lee County after a contentious two-year battle among parents, religious leaders, community organizations and civil liberties groups.

"With more school districts adding the Bible to literature or history curriculums, Lee County's experience promises to help refine the legal boundaries of such courses, but experts say that the litigation and the videotaping could also have a chilling effect around the country. . . .

"Already, a lawyer for those opponents said that he may have detected enough violations to ask again for an injunction. The lawyer, Thomas R. Julin of Miami, represents seven parents and religious leaders, assisted by the American Civil Liberties Union and the People for the American Way Foundation, who sued the school system in December after the school board in this largely Republican county approved the course. Mr. Julin said that in one class, students were shown a documentary called 'Jerusalem,' in which the narrator says, 'The memory of Jesus and the miracle of His Resurrection live in Jerusalem every day.' This, Mr. Julin said, violates the prohibition against teaching the New Testament." (*New York Times*, February 17, 1998)

"The D.C. Court of Appeals has barred a group called the Coalition for Voluntary Prayer from putting a school prayer initiative on the District's ballot, ruling that the measure is unconstitutional.

"The appellate ruling, issued Tuesday, was another setback for the coalition, which first attempted to put the initiative on the ballot in 1995. A lawsuit filed by the American Civil Liberties Union, People for the American Way and 22 D.C. residents blocked the group from moving forward." (*Washington Post*, January 1, 1998)

"An effort to amend the Virginia Constitution to recognize the 'fundamental right' of parents to control their children's upbringing and education was narrowly killed today by Senate Democrats.

"With opponents arguing that schools could be paralyzed by lawsuits from parents who would have the power to veto everything from the curriculum to the dress code, the parental rights amendment produced 90 minutes of passionate dialogue. Sen. Joseph V. Gartlan Jr. (D-Fairfax) raised the specter of a mother molesting her son, then defending her actions as her right to teach her child about sexuality. Or, he said, a parent could sue a school system because it allowed students to wear only white shirts, not blue ones. . . .

"Christian conservatives have made the amendment one of their key political goals for the last two years. The Christian Coalition is pushing for a national version as part of its 'Contract With the American Family.' The amendment has been introduced in 28 legislatures but has not passed in any of them. . . .

"A liberal group that is fighting the amendment state by state, People for the American Way, contends that the amendment is a sneaky means to reach broader goals by the Christian right.

" 'If we got into a situation where each parent could rewrite the entire curriculum, we've thrown the schools into chaos, and that's what the parental rights amendment is intended to do,' said Mary Jean Collins, the group's national field director." (*Washington Post*, January 29, 1997)

---

"liberal group" (*Washington Post*, January 29, 1997)

## POLITICAL ORIENTATION

". . . While social conservatives were triumphing in California, they went down to defeat in Colorado on a proposal to enshrine the 'inalienable right' of parents into the state constitution. Colorado was a test state for the controversial amendment backed primarily by a conservative Christian organization, Of The People, and opponents feared it could catch on nationally if passed.

"Parental-rights supporters argued that the proposal would protect families and reduce government intrusion into family life and education. But liberal groups, especially People for the American Way, spent about $300,000, arguing that the amendment would restrict the ability to investigate child abuse and set public-school curriculums.

" 'We put together 150 groups from the PTA to police officers to district attorneys, which caused voters to say there could be something wrong' with the initiative, said Michael Hudson, a vice president for People for the American Way. One especially important opponent of the measure was former Colorado Sen. Bill Armstrong, a deeply religious conservative Republican." (*Wall Street Journal*, November 7, 1996)

# Planned Parenthood Federation of America, Inc. (1916)

810 Seventh Avenue
New York, New York 10019
Phone: (212) 541-7800
Fax: (212) 245-1845

1120 Connecticut Avenue, NW
Suite 461
Washington, D.C. 20036
Phone: (202) 785-3351
Fax: (202) 293-4349

Internet: communications@ppfa.org *or*
http://www.plannedparenthood.org

## PURPOSE

"To provide comprehensive reproductive and complementary health care services in settings which preserve and protect the essential privacy and rights of each individual; to advocate public policies which guarantee these rights and ensure access to such services; to provide educational programs which enhance understanding of individual and societal implications of human sexuality; to promote research and the advancement of technology in reproductive health care and encourage understanding of their inherent bioethical, behavioral, and social implications."

## STAFF

Approximately 5,000 full-time; 5,000 part-time; 10,000 volunteers

## DIRECTOR

Gloria Feldt, president. Feldt assumed leadership of Planned Parenthood Federation of America (PPFA) in 1996. Before taking on the national leadership role, she was executive director of Planned Parenthood of Central and Northern Arizona, the largest provider of family planning and reproductive health services in the state. During her tenure in Phoenix, Feldt became a national leader, serving as chair of PPFA's National Executive Director's Council, from which she received its highest honor, the Ruth Green Award. She also is president of the Planned Parenthood Action Fund, the political arm of PPFA.

## TAX STATUS

501(c)(3)

## BUDGET

1997—$495 million
1998—Unavailable
Proposed 1999—Unavailable

## FUNDING SOURCES

Clinic income, 35 percent; government grants, 33 percent; private contributions, 26 percent; Planned Parenthood Action Fund and other, 6 percent

Members: N/A
Branches/chapters: 136 affiliates (with 886 clinic sites)
Affiliate: Planned Parenthood Action Fund, a 501(c)(4) organization

Planned Parenthood Political Action Committee

♦ Advertisements ♦ Awards program ♦ Coalition forming ♦ Conferences/seminars ♦ Congressional testimony ♦ Congressional voting analysis ♦ Electoral politics ♦ Films/video/audiotapes ♦ Grassroots organizing ♦ Health care services ♦ Initiative/referendum campaigns ♦ International activities ♦ Legislative/regulatory monitoring (federal and state) ♦ Litigation ♦ Lobbying (federal, state, and grassroots) ♦ Local/municipal affairs ♦ Media outreach ♦ Medical services via clinics throughout the United States ♦ Polling ♦ Research ♦ Speakers program ♦ Telecommunications services (Hotline: 800-230-PLAN) ♦ Training and technical assistance ♦ Voter registration ♦ Voting records

♦ Contraceptive coverage in health care insurance plans ♦ Emergency contraception ♦ Family planning ♦ Legislation imposing restrictions on abortion ♦ Reproductive health care ♦ Reproductive rights ♦ Restrictions on international family planning programs (i.e., global gag rule on the mention of abortion in family planning programs) ♦ Teen pregnancy ♦ Universal and confidential access to health care (including contraception and abortion) ♦ Violence and harassment aimed at reproductive health care patients and providers

*25th Anniversary Video: The Meaning of Roe*
*All About Birth Control: The Complete Guide*
*All About Sex: A Family Resource on Sex and Sexuality*
*Planned Parenthood Women's Health Encyclopedia*
*Roe v. Wade: 25th Anniversary Plenary Video*
*Talking About Sex: A Guide For Families* (includes a video, activity workbook, and parents' guide)

Also offers a selection of educational booklets, audiotapes, T-shirts, sweatshirts, caps, totebags, buttons, and more

*What's Up?* (weekly)

Annual conference

## BOARD OF DIRECTORS

## EFFECTIVENESS

"The decades-old struggle for gender equity in health care has come down to this question: Why have many insurance companies moved so swiftly to pay for the male sex drug Viagra when they have been far slower to pick up the bill for birth control?

"Less than two months after it exploded onto the market, more than half the prescriptions for the new drug are being subsidized by health plans. That immediate acceptance by the insurance industry is producing howls of frustration from many physicians and women's rights advocates who have been waging a long, arduous campaign—in legislatures and in the court of public opinion—to coax insurers to cover prescription contraceptives that enable women to enjoy sex without worrying about whether they'll become pregnant. Viagra's potential to overcome impotence and enhance male sexual performance has made it the fastest seller of any drug ever introduced. . . .

"But if its effect on sex lives seems revolutionary, women's advocates say, it's worth remembering that other drugs have been just as transformational.

" 'I don't think [Viagra] made any more of a splash than the [birth control] Pill,' said Gloria Feldt, president of the Planned Parenthood Federation of America, which yesterday became the latest group to complain. Yet for many years after the advent of birth control pills in 1960, Feldt said, many insurers did not pay for them. . . .

"Planned Parenthood's protest was made a week after the 39,000-strong organization representing the nation's obstetricians and gynecologists said it believed health plans' reticence to cover contraceptives represented a form of bias against women." (*Washington Post*, May 20, 1998)

"A Federal judge's ruling could allow Planned Parenthood to open an abortion clinic in Bettendorf, Iowa, in the nation's largest metropolitan area without such services.

"The ruling . . . by Judge Charles R. Wolle of United States District Court in Des Moines said that Bettendorf, one of the Quad Cities on the Iowa-Illinois border, was using its zoning ordinances unfairly to prohibit Planned Parenthood from developing the clinic.

"Judge Wolle said the city applied its laws specifically to prevent the clinic from being developed, 'violating the constitutional rights of the women who would be served' in the area, which includes Davenport, Iowa, and Moline and Rock Island, Ill. . . .

"The Quad Cities have a population of 320,000, but the nearest clinic is 50 miles away, in Iowa City. Ms. Cook said Planned Parenthood would continue with its development plans and hoped to break ground for the clinic in May and be in operation by the fall.

"Abortion opponents, however, have vowed to continue fighting the clinic. Launa Stoltenberg, a spokeswoman for the Life and Family Coalition, told The Associated Press, 'My faith says we're not going to see a clinic there.' " (*New York Times*, February 15, 1998)

"bane of the modern GOP" (*Wall Street Journal*, April 4, 1995)

# POLITICAL ORIENTATION

# Servicemembers Legal Defense Network

P.O. Box 65301
Washington, D.C. 20035
Phone: (202) 328-3244
Fax: (202) 797-1635
Internet: http://www.sldn.org

**PURPOSE**

Is "the sole national legal aid and watchdog organization dedicated to providing legal assistance to service members harmed by violations of 'Don't Ask, Don't Tell, Don't Pursue' and monitoring the Department of Defense's implementation of this policy."

**STAFF**

9 total; plus 2 part-time; 250 volunteers; 3 interns

**DIRECTOR**

Michelle M. Benecke, co-executive director. A Harvard-trained lawyer, Benecke received her B.A. from the University of Virginia on an ROTC scholarship. She commanded a battery in a combat arms branch of the Army. She has spoken and written extensively on "Don't Ask, Don't Tell, Don't Pursue" and other military personnel issues.

C. Dixon Osburn, co-executive director. Osburn is a lawyer who received his J.D./M.B.A. degree from Georgetown University and his A.B. from Stanford University. He has been honored by gay lawyers' groups in Washington, D.C., and Boston for his leadership. He has appeared on *Nightline* and written extensively on "Don't Ask, Don't Tell, Don't Pursue."

**TAX STATUS**

501 (c)(3)

**BUDGET**

1997—$796,000
1998—$886,000
Proposed 1999—$900,000

**FUNDING SOURCES**

Individuals, 62 percent; foundation grants, 20 percent; special events/projects, 14 percent; corporate donations, 2 percent; unsolicited donations, 2 percent

**SCOPE**

Members: N/A
Branches: N/A
Affiliates: N/A

None

♦ Advertisements ♦ Conferences/seminars ♦ Congressional testimony ♦ Grassroots organizing ♦ Information clearinghouse ♦ Internet (E-mail alerts, Web site) ♦ Internships ♦ Legal assistance ♦ Litigation ♦ Media outreach ♦ Performance ratings ♦ Research ♦ Speakers program ♦ Training

*METHOD OF OPERATION*

♦ "Don't Ask, Don't Tell, Don't Pursue" policy as it pertains to the Defense Department ♦ Ensure proper implementation of DOD recommendations against anti-gay harassment and intrusive investigations ♦ Stop the selective use of criminal charges to threaten, coerce, and imprison gay service members ♦ Stop witch hunts of service members accused as gay, lesbian, or bisexual ♦ Uphold privacy of conversations between service members and their doctors

*CURRENT CONCERNS*

*Conduct Unbecoming* (annual report)
*Survival Guide: How To Survive Under "Don't Ask, Don't Tell, Don't Pursue"*
*Legal Update*

*PUBLICATIONS*

Annual and quarterly reports (untitled)

*NEWSLETTER*

Service Member Training Seminars (various locations, ongoing)
Cooperating Attorney Training Program (various locations, ongoing)

*CONFERENCES*

Capt. Thomas T. Carpenter and Teresa Verges, cochairs

Other members:
♦ Zoe Dunning ♦ Chad S. Johnson ♦ Paul M. Smith ♦ Dixon Taylor

*BOARD OF DIRECTORS*

"By relentlessly bombarding the news media with evidence of the military's maliciousness, SLDN has repeatedly forced the Pentagon not just to take notice but to change. Defense Secretary William Cohen last year ordered an inquiry into SLDN's charges. The official Pentagon response was released this month.

"Although Pentagon spin doctors played down the abuses they confirmed, their report revealed they know far less than SLDN about how field commanders actually treat people suspected of being gay. But even a superficial understanding of the problem was enough to persuade Pentagon investigators to recommend changes SLDN has long demanded. . . .

"SLDN's righteous war against the gay ban is far from won. But the Pentagon now knows it's being watched. Gay servicemembers have a powerful ally in Washington. And the phone keep on ringing." (*Detroit News*, April 25, 1998)

*EFFECTIVENESS*

"The Servicemembers Legal Defense Network is the newest and perhaps the most specifically focused of the 11 national Gay political organizations examined in its report.

"Modeled to some degree after Lambda Legal Defense and Education fund, SLDN is a litigation group. But its sole purpose is to assist members of the U.S. armed services who are adversely affected by the military's 'don't ask, don't tell' policy on Gays.

"Since its founding, SLDN has amassed a network of over 200 attorneys across the country. These attorneys, along with SLDN's nine-member staff in Washington, D.C., rush to the help of servicemembers in all stages of Gay-related investigations." (*Washington Blade*, December 12, 1997)

". . . Servicesmembers Legal Defense Network . . . reported yesterday that the Pentagon discharged 850 men and women last year under the 'don't ask, don't tell' policy, up from 722 discharges in 1995 and 597 in 1994. The increase since 1994 is about 43 percent. . . .

" 'The armed forces repeatedly excused or ignored prohibitions against asking, witch hunts and harassment,' said Dixon Osburn, the group's co-executive director. 'The relentless pursuit of gay personnel has resulted in gay discharges that have soared.' . . .

"[Co-executive director Michele] Benecke said military commanders receive no training on how to enforce the 'don't ask, don't tell' policy, citing a statement from military officials in one case saying 'further investigation may turn up credible information' of homosexuality. . . .

"Benecke pointed to Bay Area native Nicole Galvan . . . who said she was forced out of West Point last spring after her commander ask her whether she was a lesbian and when she refused to answer, seized her personnal diary and e-mails as evidence. . . .

". . . Galvan said she was allowed an honorable discharge with credits and no requirement to pay for her education after the Servicemembers Legal Defense Network intervened." (*San Francisco Chronicle*, February 27, 1997)

## POLITICAL ORIENTATION

"a nonprofit group that gives assistance to gays in the armed forces" (*San Francisco Chronicle*, February 27, 1997)

# Community/
# Grassroots

## Chapter 3

# American Family Association (1977)

P.O. Drawer 2440
Tupelo, Mississippi 38803
Phone: (601) 844-5036
Fax: (601) 844-9176
Internet: http://www.afa.net

| | |
|---|---|
| "Promoting the Biblical ethic of decency in American society with a primary emphasis on television and other media." | **PURPOSE** |
| Unavailable | **STAFF** |
| Donald E. Wildmon, executive director. Wildmon also was the founder and president of the National Federation for Decency (NFD), the predecessor to the American Family Association (AFA). A graduate of Millsaps College, Wildmon attended the seminary at Emory University in Atlanta. After his return to Mississippi, Wildmon served as a pastor of a small Methodist church for twelve years before founding NFD in 1977. | **DIRECTOR** |
| 501(c)(3) | **TAX STATUS** |
| 1998—Unavailable<br>Proposed 1999—Unavailable | **BUDGET** |
| Individual donations | **FUNDING SOURCES** |
| Members: Approximately 425,000 members<br>Branches/chapters: Over 450 local groups; 22 state directors<br>Affiliate: American Family Association Law Center<br>AFA was formerly known as the National Federation for Decency and changed its name in 1988. | **SCOPE** |
| None | **PAC** |

| METHOD OF OPERATION | ◆ Advertisements ◆ Boycotts ◆ Coalition forming ◆ Direct action ◆ Film/video/audiotapes ◆ Grassroots organizing ◆ Legal assistance ◆ Litigation ◆ Local/municipal affairs ◆ Media outreach ◆ Radio production ◆ Research ◆ Speakers program ◆ Telecommunications (American Family Radio) ◆ Training and technical assistance |
|---|---|
| CURRENT CONCERNS | ◆ Abortion ◆ Anti-Christian bigotry ◆ Christian apathy ◆ Church and society ◆ Homosexual movement ◆ National Endowment for the Arts ◆ Pornography ◆ Television and radio programming (i.e., Disney, Jerry Springer, Howard Stern) ◆ United Methodist controversy |
| PUBLICATIONS | *The Case Against Pornography*<br>*Christianity and Humanism: A Study in Contrasts*<br>*The Fight Back Book*<br>*Guide to What One Person Can Do About Pornography*<br>*Homosexuality: Exposing the Myths*<br>*Pornography: Problems and Solutions*<br>*Pornography: A Report*<br>*Public School Sex Education: A Report*<br><br>Also publishes brochures, educational comic books, and audiotapes |
| NEWSLETTER | *AFA Journal* (11 times a year) |
| CONFERENCES | Annual AFA chapter conference |
| BOARD OF DIRECTORS | Unavailable |
| EFFECTIVENESS | "ABC Entertainment had its best Thursday premiere week in three years last week, but it still finished third behind NBC's night of reruns and the season return of 'Diagnosis Murder' on CBS. . . .<br>" 'Nothing Sacred'—the controversial hour about a Catholic priest who just might have chosen the wrong career—debuted on ABC at 8 to a 7.2 national rating and a 12 percent audience share. As well as an estimated 120 phone calls to the network in New York complaining about it. . . .<br>"The American Family Association of Tupelo, Miss., had called the program 'blasphemous' and 'the latest anti-Catholic offering from the Walt Disney Company.' It had urged people to call sponsors to express their opinions, including Kmart, Procter & Gamble, Unilever and Visa USA. . . ." (*Washington Post*, September 22, 1997)<br><br>"The Southern Baptist Convention yesterday launched a long-threatened boycott of the Walt Disney Co., pitting the largest Protestant denomination in the country against the vast entertainment empire in a test of national values. . . . |

"Antagonism toward Disney has been growing among conservative Christians in recent years, with peaks following the release of the films 'Priest,' about a homosexual Catholic clergyman, and 'Kids,' which presented a neutral, even condoning, view of promiscuous teenage sex.

"In yesterday's debate, Baptists seemed especially offended by the celebration of Ellen DeGeneres' lesbianism on the ABC-TV sitcom 'Ellen,' the annual Gay Days festival at Disney World, and Disney's extension of health benefits to partners of homosexual employees. Disney owns both ABC and the company that produces 'Ellen'. . . .

" 'It doesn't mean people are going to go home and burn their tapes,' said Tim Wildmon, vice president of the American Family Association, which has led the campaign for a Disney boycott for nearly two years. 'It's from this day forward that we're asking people not to go buy "Hunchback of Notre Dame" . . . because that's giving [Disney] money to go produce Ellen.' " (*Washington Post*, June 19, 1997)

"The Fairfax County School Board rejected a request . . . to disavow language in a high school biology textbook that equates creationism with astrology, fad diets and other 'pseudoscience.'

"The board voted 6 to 4 against an appeal by the American Family Association, a conservative Christian organization, to put a label in the ninth-grade textbook 'Biological Science: A Molecular Approach.' The association, acting on behalf of parents of a student at Thomas Jefferson High School for Science and Technology, said that the book demeans the family's belief in the Bible. But the majority of board members, all of them Democrats, turned away arguments from the board's four Republicans that the issue was 'religious bigotry,' not the teaching of the biblical version of creation. . . .

"The American Family Association challenged the book in February. After school officials and system administrators denied the group's request for a disclaimer, the group appealed to the School Board. . . ." (*Washington Post*, May 30, 1997)

---

"conservative Christian organization" (*Washington Post*, May 30, 1997)

"a Christian lobby" (*Wall Street Journal*, March 22, 1996)

## POLITICAL ORIENTATION

# American Society for the Prevention of Cruelty to Animals (1866)

424 East 92nd Street
New York, New York 10128
Phone: (212) 876-7700
Fax: (212) 876-9571

1755 Massachusetts Avenue, NW
Suite 418
Washington, D.C. 20036
Phone: (202) 232-5020
Fax: (202) 797-8947

Internet: http://www.aspca.org

**PURPOSE**

"To alleviate pain, fear and suffering in animals through means such as humane law enforcement, legislative advocacy, education and hands-on animal care."

**STAFF**

Unavailable

**DIRECTOR**

Roger A. Caras, president. Caras was named president of the American Society for the Prevention of Cruelty to Animals (ASPCA) in 1991. He was a news correspondent with ABC News for seventeen years and the only television network news correspondent reporting full-time on animals and the environment. Prior to joining ABC in 1974, Caras was the resident naturalist on NBC's "Today Show" for eight years and reported daily on CBS Radio for eleven years with his "Pet & Wildlife" broadcast. Caras is the author of over seventy books, largely on wild and domestic animals. Prior to joining ABC, he was affiliated with more than twenty-five humane and conservation organizations.

**TAX STATUS**

501(c)(3)

**BUDGET**

1997—$21.39 million
1998—$25.24 million
Proposed 1999—$25 million

**FUNDING SOURCES**

Public support, 75 percent; service fees, 15 percent; investment income, 6 percent; other, 4 percent

**SCOPE**

Members: Approximately 450,000 individuals

Branches/chapters: Offices in Los Angeles; Urbana, Illinois; and Albany, New York

Affiliates: N/A

None

## METHOD OF OPERATION

♦ Advertisements ♦ Animal adoption and placement ♦ Awards program ♦ Coalition forming ♦ Conferences/seminars ♦ Congressional testimony ♦ Direct action ♦ Films/video/audiotapes ♦ Grantmaking ♦ Grassroots organizing ♦ Humane law enforcement ♦ Initiative/referendum campaigns ♦ Internet (Web site) ♦ International activities ♦ Legal assistance ♦ Legislative/regulatory monitoring (federal and state) ♦ Litigation ♦ Lobbying (federal, state, and grassroots) ♦ Local/municipal affairs ♦ Media outreach ♦ Participation in regulatory proceedings (federal and state) ♦ Product merchandising ♦ Research ♦ Television and radio production ♦ Telecommunications services (Hotline: 212-876-7700 [ext. HELP for behavior problems, ext. 4203 for medical problems], National Animal Poison Control Center Hotline: 800-548-2423 [24-hour help] ♦ Mailing lists ♦ Training and technical assistance ♦ Veterinary hospital care ♦ Voting records

## CURRENT CONCERNS

♦ Animal overpopulation ♦ Hands-on animal care and placement ♦ Regulating animal experimentation and the raising of food animals ♦ Regulating pet breeding and selling ♦ Responsible pet care ♦ Strengthening and enforcing anti-cruelty laws ♦ Studying the link between animal abuse and domestic abuse ♦ Wildlife issues, especially hunting and trapping

## PUBLICATIONS

*Extend the Web* (catalogue of materials for teachers)

## NEWSLETTER

*ASPCA Animal Watch* (quarterly magazine)
*A Is For Animal* (quarterly teacher's newsletter)
*Animal Land* (10 issues per year, children's magazine)

## CONFERENCES

Teacher workshops
Animal shelter training

## BOARD OF DIRECTORS

Steven M. Elkman, chairman and treasurer; Tatyana D. Olyphant, vice chairman and secretary; Hoyle C. Jones and Edwin M. Hershey, vice chairman

♦ Alexandra G. Bishop ♦ Reenie Brown ♦ Wendy H. Carhart ♦ George G. Clements Jr. ♦ Charles M. Curry Jr. ♦ Fred Drasner ♦ James Gerard ♦ Alan M. Kelly ♦ Linda Lloyd Lambert ♦ Franklin Maisano ♦ Gurdon H. Metz ♦ John M.B. O'Connor ♦ W. Stewart Pinkerton Jr. ♦ Urling I. Searle ♦ William Secord ♦ Donald C. Smaltz ♦ James F. Stebbins ♦ Frederick W. Wagner III ♦ Jeanne W. Waller

## EFFECTIVENESS

"For cat owners and other feline-friendly people, declawing is among the least pleasant of topics. In fact, the first veterinarian contacted for this column refused to speak about it, 'because it is controversial.' It is also common, despite opposition from such groups as the American Society for the Prevention of Cruelty to Animals; another local vet estimated that up to 50 percent of the cats she sees have been declawed.

"People choose to declaw cats for a number of reasons, to protect furniture, to protect young children. Apartment buildings might require it. With some diseases, such as those that impair the immune system, a cat's scratch can produce a dangerous infection. The claw of a cat is the anatomic counterpart of the last phalanx, or bone, of a human finger or toe. A cat uses its claws to defend itself, to seize prey, to climb, to help balance as it walks and to mark territory. The principal reason for routine scratching is to peel the old sheaths off the nails, said Jacque Schultz of the ASPCA. 'The new nail grows inside the old nail,' she said. Scratching also seems to be a form of exercise, an instinctual feline yoga that stretches and presumably refreshes."(*Washington Post*, March 17, 1998)

"As Congress considers the most sweeping changes for public housing in a generation, it faces a list of thorny issues, from eligibility rules to rent limits to privatization.

"Then there's the topic that really has everyone fighting: dogs.

"It is a pitched battle between housing officials—led by the New York City Housing Authority, by far the largest—and a powerful coalition that includes the nation's largest pet-food companies over whether public housing residents should be given, for the first time, a Federal right to own pets. . . .

" 'It would put a terrible legal burden on us,' said Steven Love, the chief lobbyist for the New York City Housing Authority. 'Anything we do is going to have to be weighed against an absolute Federal right.'

"But the amendments' proponents, who also include the American Society for the Prevention of Cruelty to Animals, the American Psychological Association, the Pet Food Institute and the American Kennel Club, contend that the measures would give cities great latitude to make their own rules.

"They further argue that in a country where more than half of all households have pets (in fact, there are more pets than children in American households), the Federal Government must insure that millions of people are not unnecessarily denied pets solely because they live in low-income apartments." (*New York Times*, February 4, 1998)

## POLITICAL ORIENTATION

Unavailable

# Association of Community Organizations for Reform Now (ACORN) (1970)

1024 Elysian Fields Avenue
New Orleans, Louisiana 70117
Phone: (504) 943-0044

739 Eighth Street, SE
Washington, D.C. 20003
Phone: (202) 547-2500
Fax: (202) 546-2483

Internet: http://www.acorn.org/community

| | |
|---|---|
| "To organize the unorganized, and to advance the interests of low to moderate income families." | **PURPOSE** |
| Unavailable | **STAFF** |
| Steven Kest, executive director. Kest has spent the past 20 years as a community organizer. | **DIRECTOR** |
| Nonprofit (not tax-exempt) | **TAX STATUS** |
| 1998—Unavailable<br>Proposed 1999—Unavailable | **BUDGET** |
| Membership dues, grassroots fundraising, and grants | **FUNDING SOURCES** |
| Members: 120,000 individual/family members<br>Branches/chapters: 500 neighborhood chapters in 30 cities<br>Affiliates: ACORN Housing Corporation and ACORN Community Land Association | **SCOPE** |
| ACORN Political Action Committee | **PAC** |

| | |
|---|---|
| **METHOD OF OPERATION** | ◆ Coalition forming ◆ Congressional testimony ◆ Demonstrations ◆ Direct action ◆ Electoral politics ◆ Grassroots organizing ◆ Initiative/referendum campaigns ◆ Internet (Web site) ◆ Legslative/regulatory monitoring (federal) ◆ Lobbying (federal, state, and grassroots) ◆ Local/municipal affairs ◆ Media outreach ◆ Participation in regulatory proceedings (federal) ◆ Research ◆ Training and technical assistance ◆ Voter registration |
| **CURRENT CONCERNS** | ◆ Community media ◆ Community reinvestment ◆ Health and environmental justice ◆ Housing development ◆ Jobs and living wages ◆ Neighborhood safety ◆ School reform ◆ Voter registration and participation ◆ Union organizing |
| **PUBLICATIONS** | None |
| **NEWSLETTER** | Unavailable |
| **CONFERENCES** | None |
| **BOARD OF DIRECTORS** | Unavailable |
| **EFFECTIVENESS** | "About 250 protesters, complaining that former welfare recipients had not been able to find jobs, stormed the hall where Mr. Huckabee was scheduled to talk, but the Governor left the Southwest Regional Civil Rights Conference rather than speak with them in the room. |
| | "The protest was organized by the Association of Community Organizations for Reform Now. Mr. Huckabee left the hotel as protesters called on him to speak on the welfare issue. |
| | " 'What you saw today was an outrage of poor people being excluded from that conference,' said Mitch Klein, a protest organizer. . . ." (*New York Times*, April 29, 1998) |
| | "Since 1991, Hempstead High School has averaged 194 graduates a year, but typically only 11 have qualified for a Regents diploma, given to students who pass advanced state tests. That is one of many troubling statistics issued by a community group today as it charged that the Hempstead school district was failing. |
| | " 'We're going into the year 2000, and our kids are not going to be ready,' said one parent, Michele Embry. She spoke at a news conference held in Village Hall by the Long Island chapter of the Association of Community Organizations for Reform, a national group. |

"The group called on Hempstead school officials to begin a concerted effort to improve the education of its 6,000 students, especially now that the state is phasing in Regents tests for all graduates. One parent, Burbeth Smikle, said the group is setting high expectations for school officials and students alike. The group's recommendations include adding enrichment and remedial classes, improving training for teachers and administrators, and allowing parents to oversee the changes." (*New York Times*, April 28, 1998)

"Almost one in three African Americans and one in four Latino applicants were rejected for conventional mortgages in 1996, according to ACORN, or the Association of Community Organizations for Reform Now, a community organization that analyzed the lending performances of financial institutions in 15 metropolitan areas—including Washington—in 1995 and 1996. To develop its study, ACORN used data compiled by the government under the Home Mortgage Disclosure Act (HMDA). The HMDA data released early last month showed that home lending overall increased to African Americans at 3.1 percent in 1996 from 1995, but that the number of conventional mortgage loans approved for this group declined by 1.5 percent. Last year represented the first year that there was not double-digit lending growth to African Americans since 1991.

"The number of conventional mortgages to white applicants rose by more than 70,000, to 455,919, in 1996, a 19 percent increase, the ACORN study reported. In the same period, 850 fewer loans were made to African Americans and Latinos. . . .

"ACORN attributed the decline in loans to minorities to new automated underwriting methods and the increased reliance on computerized credit-scoring systems, which the group says has created inflexible measurements of creditworthiness that many minorities can't meet. . . .

" 'We are concerned that credit scoring is too rigid and is being used to trim off some portion of the population that goes in to apply for loans,' said Patrick Woodall, a policy analyst with ACORN.

"Bankers and other industry experts, however, say that the HMDA data don't tell the entire story, and that over the past several years financial institutions have greatly improved lending to minorities by relaxing many underwriting standards. And some argue that the rejection of minority loan applications has risen simply because there are more applicants in the borrowing pool." (*Washington Post*, September 10, 1997)

Unavailable

## POLITICAL ORIENTATION

# Center for Community Change (1968)

1000 Wisconsin Avenue, NW
Washington, D.C. 20007
Phone: (202) 342-0519
Fax: (202) 342-1132
Internet: http://www.communitychange.org

| | |
|---|---|
| **PURPOSE** | "To provide technical assistance and other support to low income constituencies and their community based grassroots organizations." |
| **STAFF** | 58 total—50 professional; 8 support; plus 2 part-time and 3 summer interns |
| **DIRECTOR** | Andy Mott, executive director |
| **TAX STATUS** | 501(c)(3) |
| **BUDGET** | Fiscal year ending September 30, 1997—$6 million<br>F.Y. 1998—$7 million<br>Proposed F.Y. 1999—$7.5 million |
| **FUNDING SOURCES** | Foundations, 64 percent; government grants, 18 percent; endowment, 9 percent; corporations, 7 percent; individuals, 2 percent |
| **SCOPE** | Members: Works on-site with more than 250 community groups a year<br>Branches/chapters: San Francisco office; staff outstationed in Chicago; Hartford, Connecticut; Los Angeles; New Castle, Delaware; Boise, Idaho; Richmond, Virginia; and Toledo, Ohio<br>Affiliates: Member of numerous coalitions |
| **PAC** | None |
| **METHOD OF OPERATION** | ♦ Coalition forming ♦ Conferences/seminars ♦ Grassroots organzing ♦ Internet (Web site) ♦ Internships ♦ Legislative/regulatory monitoring (federal) ♦ Lobbying (federal) ♦ Research ♦ Technical assistance ♦ Training |

◆ Banking and lending ◆ Building capacities of grassroots organizations ◆ Economic development ◆ Employment and training ◆ Federal budget issues ◆ Low-income housing ◆ Philanthropy ◆ Poverty issues ◆ Status of nonprofits ◆ Welfare reform

The following is a list of sample publications:

*America's Third Deficit: Too Little Investment in People and Infrastructure*
*Building Systems of Support for Neighborhood Change*
*CDBG: An Action Guide to the Community Development Block Grant Program*
*Developing a Public Policy Agenda on Jobs*
*Estimating the Economic Impact of a Public Jobs Program*
*A Guide to Developing a Housing Trust Fund*
*How—and Why—to Influence Public Policy: An Action Guide for Community Organization*
*How to Save and Improve Public Housing: An Action Guide*
*How to Tell and Sell Your Story: A Guide to Media for Community Groups and Other Nonprofits*
*HUD's Consolidated Plan: An Action Guide for Involving Low Income Communities*
*Linking Human Services and Economic Development*
*New Avenues into Jobs: Early Lessons from Nonprofit Temp Agencies and Employment Brokers*
*Making Connections: A Study of Employment Linkage Programs*
*A Status Report on Housing Trust Funds in the U.S.*

*Community Change* (3–4 times a year)
*News from the Housing Trust Fund Project* (quarterly)
*Organizing* (6 times a year)

Sponsors periodic conferences and workshops

John Carr, chair; Edwin Booth, Roger A. Clay Jr., Rebecca Doggett, Peter Edelman, Irma Gonzales, Marie Kirkley-Bey, and Mary B. Mountcastle, members, executive committee

Other members:
◆ Harriet Barlow ◆ Jim Boucher ◆ Arthur M. Brazier ◆ Gordon Chin ◆ Denise Padin Collazo ◆ Michael Cortes ◆ Jane E. Fox ◆ Douglas Fraser ◆ Carolyn Garland ◆ Ronald Grzywinski ◆ Wade Henderson ◆ Wendy Johnson ◆ John Lewis ◆ Denise Mitchell ◆ Paulette J. Meyer ◆ Benson F. Roberts ◆ Steve Sands ◆ Ron Shiffman

". . . Although it may sound like a cut of beef, 'subprime' refers to the increasingly common practice by finance companies, banks and their subsidiaries of seeking out borrowers whose credit histories are often less than ideal, or below 'prime.' It is not unusual for interest rates on home equity loans, credit insurance or debt consolidation packages in the subprime category to run much higher than average, according to legal advocates. . . .

"In states where there are no usury caps on loans, some companies charge interest of up to 60 percent a year, said William J. Brennan Jr., an attorney who has directed the Home Defense Program of the Legal Aid Society in Atlanta for 10 years. Brennan has represented scores of homeowners who have been taken in by home improvement scams, home equity loans designed to force foreclosure or other fraudulent practices.

"Brennan said seniors are the target of loan predators because they have a valuable piece of collateral: their home. Some 58 percent of all seniors living below the federal poverty level own their own homes, according to federal housing and U.S. Department of Commerce figures. . . .

"Allen Fishbein, general counsel for the Washington-based Center for Community Change, said that most elderly homeowners—including persons of color—don't realize 'that about 30 to 40 percent of all subprime borrowers would actually qualify for conventional loans' from regular banks at lower interest rates. 'But they don't know it and aren't being referred.'

"Fishbein said his group, a national nonprofit that helps communities monitor banking practices, has recently been fielding 'many more complaints about aggressive loan solicitation tactics.'

"He urged homeowners of every neighborhood, income bracket and race who think they have been taken advantage of, 'to ask questions and to come forward. Don't be embarrassed to admit you are confused or can't pay off a loan.'" (*Washington Post*, April 14, 1998)

---

## POLITICAL ORIENTATION

"a community investment group in Washington" (*Washington Post*, May 1, 1995)

# Concerned Women for America (1979)

1015 15th Street, NW
Suite 1100
Washington, D.C. 20005
Phone: (202) 488-7000
Fax: (202) 488-0806
Internet: http://www.cwfa.org

"To protect and promote Biblical values among all citizens—first through prayer, then education, and finally by influencing our society—thereby reversing the decline in moral values in our nation."

**PURPOSE**

Unavailable

**STAFF**

Carmen Pate, president. Before becoming president of Concerned Women for America (CWA), Pate served as the organization's vice president of communications. Prior to joining CWA, she worked for two years as executive director of End Hunger Network-Houston. Pate also worked for 17 years for Kroger Company in its marketing and public relations departments. Currently, Pate co-hosts a nationally syndicated radio program, "Beverly LaHaye Live."

**DIRECTOR**

501(c)(3)

**TAX STATUS**

1998—Unavailable
Proposed 1999—Unavailable

**BUDGET**

Member donations

**FUNDING SOURCES**

Members: more than 500,000 individuals
Branches/chapters: 1,200 CWA Prayer/Action Chapters
Affiliates: N/A

**SCOPE**

None

**PAC**

| | |
|---|---|
| *METHOD OF OPERATION* | ◆ Boycotts ◆ Coalition forming ◆ Congressional testimony ◆ Congressional voting analysis ◆ Educational outreach ◆ Grassroots organizing ◆ International activities ◆ Legislative/regulatory monitoring (federal and state) ◆ Litigation ◆ Lobbying (federal and state) ◆ Media outreach ◆ Research ◆ Speakers program ◆ Television and radio production |
| *CURRENT CONCERNS* | ◆ Abortion rights ◆ AIDS ◆ Education ◆ Euthanasia ◆ Health care ◆ Homosexuality ◆ Judeo-Christian values ◆ Mandated family and medical leave ◆ Parental involvement laws ◆ Religious freedom ◆ Sex education in schools ◆ Taxes ◆ Welfare reform |
| *PUBLICATIONS* | Offers a variety of brochures, booklets, and manuals |
| *NEWSLETTER* | *Family Voice* (monthly magazine) Publishes monthly updates on Capitol Hill legislation, news from around the country, and action updates |
| *CONFERENCES* | National convention (annual) Regional and state conventions Seminars on abortion and family rights issues |
| *BOARD OF DIRECTORS* | ◆ Kathy Arrington ◆ Peggy Bishop ◆ Paulette Brack ◆ Barbara Fanara ◆ Lee LaHaye ◆ Barrie Lyons ◆ Betty Lou Martin ◆ Carmen Pate ◆ Jan Roberto ◆ Lori Scheck ◆ Norma Seifert ◆ Maxine Sieleman ◆ Patti Stockman ◆ Barbara Towne ◆ Jim Woodall |
| *EFFECTIVENESS* | "On three fronts, the fragile alliance between the Christian right and the establishment wings of the Republican Party threatens to deteriorate into bitter disputes endangering the party's Election Day prospects in 1998 and 2000. . . .<br><br>"At their meeting these 15 conservative leaders, including representatives of Concerned Women for America, the Christian Coalition, the Traditional Values Coalition, the Eagle Forum and Focus on the Family, discussed the possibility that they might abandon the Republican Party altogether if the presidential nominee picked in 2000 did not meet their basic requirements. . . .<br><br>"Party leaders, including House Speaker Newt Gingrich (Ga.) and Senate Majority Leader Trent Lott (Miss.), were dismissed for failing to challenge President Clinton's policies. . . . |

"The disputes are becoming worrisome among rank-and-file Republicans. 'Their [Christian conservatives'] concerns and problems need to be taken very seriously and attended to with an open mind and open ears. . . . But there has to be a realization on their part that splitting from Republicans is basically the equivalent of political cannibalism. The result will be no winners at all,' said Rep. Charles F. Bass (R-N.H.). 'These individuals are very passionate believers, but they are not people who are elected and have to stand before the electorate.'" (*Washington Post*, March 27, 1998)

". . . To conservatives, all of this overshadows a development they consider healthy for the party: the growing political involvement of a different kind of woman, one who has traditional values and may be more inclined to stay at home raising a family. They point to a poll commissioned this year by Concerned Women for America . . . indicating a majority of American women are sympathetic to GOP positions on welfare, gay marriage and abortion.

"Still, there is no disputing the unease of some professional women. On the East Coast, it reached a critical mass in 1992, when they defected from the GOP in droves. On Wall Street, Anita Volz Wien, a Republican who helped elect Gov. Whitman, ended up voting for Bill Clinton four years ago. 'I would like to be able to vote for the GOP presidential candidate,' she says. Like Ms. Manus, Ms. Wien, who runs a financial-consulting firm, prefers the Republican economic agenda, but is uncomfortable with its conservative social agenda, especially the abortion plank. . . ." (*Wall Street Journal*, July 17, 1996)

---

"a group that claims 600,000 members opposed to 'the radical feminist agenda'" (*Washington Post*, February 5, 1998)

"a conservative women's group" (*Wall Street Journal*, July 17, 1996)

## POLITICAL ORIENTATION

# Eagle Forum (1975)

P.O. Box 618
Alton, IL 62002
Phone: (618) 462-5415
Fax: (618) 462-8909

316 Pennsylvania Avenue, SE
Suite 203
Washington, D.C. 20003
Phone: (202) 544-0353
Fax: (202) 547-6996

Internet:eagle@eagleforum.org *or* http://www.eagleforum.org

| | |
|---|---|
| **PURPOSE** | "[T]o enable conservative and pro-family men and women to participate in the process of self-government and public policy making so that America will continue to be a land of individual liberty, respect for family integrity, public and private virtue, and private enterprise." |
| **STAFF** | 11 total—3 professional; 8 support; plus 3 interns and 50 volunteer state leaders |
| **DIRECTOR** | Phyllis Schlafly, president. The founder of Eagle Forum, Schlafly is the author of sixteen books and is a syndicated columnist and radio commentator. She holds a J. D. from Washington University Law School. |
| **TAX STATUS** | 501(c)(4) |
| **BUDGET** | 1998—Unavailable<br>Proposed 1999—Unavailable |
| **FUNDING SOURCES** | Unavailable |
| **SCOPE** | Members: 80,000<br>Branches/chapters: 50 state chapters<br>Affiliate: Eagle Forum Education and Legal Defense Fund (EFELDF), a 501(c)(3) organization headquartered in St. Louis, Missouri |
| **PAC** | Eagle Forum Political Action Committee |

## METHOD OF OPERATION

♦ Award program (EFELDF, Annual Fulltime Homemaker Award, Eagle Awards) ♦ Coalition forming ♦ Conferences/seminars ♦ Congressional testimony ♦ Electoral politics ♦ Films/video/audiotapes ♦ Grassroots organizing ♦ International activities ♦ Internet (E-mail alerts, Web site) ♦ Legislative/regulatory monitoring (federal and state) ♦ Library/information clearinghouse ♦ Lobbying (federal, state, and grassroots) ♦ Local/municipal affairs ♦ Media outreach ♦ Ratings on congressional votes ♦ Research ♦ Speakers program ♦ Special projects for EFELDF (Phonics reading course, Parents Advisory Center) ♦ Television and radio production (EFELDF, "The Phyllis Schlafly Report", "Radio Live with Phyllis Schlafly") ♦ Training and technical assistance

## CURRENT CONCERNS

♦ Anti-abortion ♦ Constitutional convention (opposed) ♦ Health care reform ♦ Parents' rights in education ♦ Tax reduction for families

## PUBLICATIONS

*American Inventors* (video)
*Child Abuse in the Classroom* (paperback/video)
*Crisis in the Classroom* (video)
*Global Governance* (video)
*Eagle Forum Collegians* (video)
*Equal Pay for UNequal Work*
*Illiteracy: Its Consequences and Cure* (video)
*On the Wings of an Eagle: The Phyllis Schlafly Story* (video)
*Pornography's Victims*
*Radical Feminism* (video)
*The Sweetheart of the Silent Majority*
*Who Will Rock the Cradle?*
*We the People* (video)

Also offers cassettes and back issues of its newsletters

## NEWSLETTER

*Education Reporter* (monthly by EFELDF)
*The Phyllis Schlafly Report* (monthly)

## CONFERENCES

Annual leadership conference
The Eagle Forum Education and Legal Defense Fund sponsors and participates in various educational conferences and seminars on child care, school curricula, parental rights, and national defense.

## BOARD OF DIRECTORS

Phyllis Schlafly, president; Eunice Smith, first vice president
The remaining board members were unavailable

## EFFECTIVENESS

"The Senate voted overwhelmingly . . . to join the House in approving a major overhaul of federal job-training programs, striking a rare note of bipartisanship on domestic policy in an election-minded Congress.

"The bill would combine about 70 training, vocational and adult education programs into block grants to state and local governments, continuing the trend toward shifting resources and responsibilities out of Washington but without the acrimony stirred by welfare reform and other more emotionally divisive causes. . . .

"Phyllis Schlafly's Eagle Forum sent out an 'alert' in March describing the bill as 'another attempt at government-managed economic planning,' and forum officials said the group intends to concentrate again on trying to defeat the measure in conference. Another conservative group, the American Policy Center, ran a full-page ad yesterday in the *Washington Times* telling Republican members of the Senate, 'Don't Do It.'

"If enacted, the seven-year Workforce Investment Partnership Act would provide the first comprehensive reorganization of job-related programs since passage of the Job Training Partnership Act in 1982. . . ." (*Washington Post*, May 6, 1998)

". . . longtime antiabortion activist Phyllis Schlafly is none too happy with the GOP front-runner's position on abortion.

"Dole's antiabortion credentials became an issue . . . when he appeared on NBC's 'Meet the Press' and said that 'at one time' he supported a constitutional amendment to ban all abortions, but that 'I would not do it again.' Dole said he supported a ban with exceptions for rape, incest and protection of the life of the mother, but he added that this 'shouldn't be a dominant issue in the Republican nomination or the campaign for president in 1996.'. . .

". . . Schlafly, president of the Eagle Forum and chairman of the Republican National Coalition for Life, has repeated a request to Dole that he sign a pledge committing himself to the GOP platform plank calling for a ban on abortions without exception for rape or incest.

"In a statement, Schlafly suggested the candidate's comments had raised 'serious concerns' about his commitment to the antiabortion cause. . . ." (*Washington Post*, December 24, 1995)

## POLITICAL ORIENTATION

"conservative" (*Washington Post*, March 2, 1998)

# Family Research Council (1980)

801 G Street, NW
Washington, D.C. 20001
Phone: (202) 393-2100
Fax: (202) 393-2134
http://www.frc.org

"To reaffirm and promote nationally, and particularly in Washington, D.C., the traditional family and the Judeo-Christian principles upon which it is built."

**PURPOSE**

96 total

**STAFF**

Gary L. Bauer, president. Before joining the Family Research Council in 1988, Bauer served as assistant to President Reagan for policy development and director of the Office of Policy Development in the White House. Prior to his presidential appointment, Bauer served as undersecretary of the Department of Education. From 1982 to 1985 he was deputy undersecretary for planning, budget, and evaluation in the Department of Education. Bauer chaired President Reagan's Special Working Group on the Family in 1986 and the Citizens Committee to Confirm Clarence Thomas in 1991. He is a graduate of Georgetown College in Georgetown, Kentucky, and of Georgetown Law School in Washington, D.C.

**DIRECTOR**

501(c)(3)

**TAX STATUS**

Fiscal year ending September 30, 1997—$11.5 million
F.Y. 1998—$13.5 million
F.Y. 1999—$14 million

**BUDGET**

Individual contributions, 73 percent; foundation grants, 24 percent; publications, 1 percent; corporate donations, 1 percent; special events, 1 percent

**FUNDING SOURCES**

Members: 450,000
Branch/chapter: Distribution Center in Michigan
Affiliates: N/A

**SCOPE**

None

**PAC**

## METHOD OF OPERATION

♦ Advertisements ♦ Coalition forming ♦ Conferences/seminars ♦ Congressional testimony ♦ Grassroots organizing ♦ Legal assistance ♦ Legislative/regulatory monitoring (federal and state) ♦ Library/information clearinghouse ♦ Media outreach ♦ Participation in regulatory proceedings (federal) ♦ Polling ♦ Research ♦ Speakers program ♦ Telecommunications services (Order line: [800] 225-4008) ♦ Television and radio production ♦ Voting records

## CURRENT CONCERNS

♦ Abortion ♦ Adoption/foster care ♦ Child care ♦ Crime and drugs ♦ Definition of the family ♦ Divorce reform ♦ Educational choice ♦ Foreign affairs ♦ Homosexual culture ♦ Parent-child communication ♦ Parental rights ♦ Tax relief for families with children

## PUBLICATIONS

*A Family Fourth*
*Free to Be Family*
*Let Freedom Ring*

Research papers
—*At the Podium*
—*In Focus*
—*Insight*
—*Issues in Depth*
—*Perspective*

## NEWSLETTER

*Family Policy* (bimonthly)
*Gary Bauer's Monthly Newsletter* (Web)
*Washington Watch* (10 times a year)

## CONFERENCES

Occasional symposia and conferences

## BOARD OF DIRECTORS

Gary L. Bauer, chairman; Chuck Donovan, vice president, public policy; Kimberly Mattingly, vice president, constituent services; Phil Olsen, vice president, resource development; Doug Werk, vice president, administration

Other members include:
♦ Thomas R. Anderson ♦ Ronald Blue ♦ James Dobson ♦ Lee Eaton ♦ Elsa D. Prince ♦ Stephen Reed ♦ Larry Smith

## EFFECTIVENESS

"Intensifying the pressure on President Clinton over his intention to appear in Beijing's Tiananmen Square next month, Family Research Council president Gary Bauer announced that his group's lobbying arm has launched a national ad campaign decrying the appearance.

"American Renewal's 60-second spot 'pays tribute to the hundreds of young Chinese democracy advocates who were massacred by the Beijing regime in 1989,' according to a statement. The ad, the statement said, also expresses concern about China's military buildup and suppression of human rights." (*Washington Post*, May 30, 1998)

"The first piece of Republican bad news this month [March 1998] came from California, where Democrat Lois Capps won a special election for the seat of her late husband, Walter. She defeated a staunch conservative, Assemblyman Tom Bordonaro. Bordonaro's victory over moderate Republican Brooks Firestone in the first round of voting was hailed as a triumph for social conservatives. Gary Bauer, the president of the Family Research Council, whose political action committee ran an expensive independent campaign on Bordonaro's behalf, got much of the credit.

"Establishment Republicans had quietly favored Firestone since they feared that, in a pro-choice district, a strong abortion foe such as Bordonaro would lose large numbers of upper-middle-class social moderates. That's exactly what happened as Capps won over many of Firestone's voters. In Montecito, a wealthy Santa Barbara community that had given Firestone a strong vote, Capps won, something her late husband did not do in 1996. . . .

"A Republican postelection analysis confirmed the importance of the sympathy vote for Capps. But it also found, as one Republican operative put it, that the outside spending by Bauer's group and others 'framed the rest of the debate, and our candidate was not able to overcome them.' That was a polite way of saying that the abortion issue hurt, and so did a general backlash against outside money and negative advertising." (*Washington Post*, March 24, 1998)

"National Republican Congressional Committee Chairman John Linder said yesterday his group will poll local voters to determine what impact conservative outside organizations had in the campaign that saw the national GOP's favored candidate, Brooks Firestone, lose a January primary to Mr. Bordonaro, a firebrand conservative.

"Mr. Linder, who is charged with overseeing the House re-election efforts, warned of dire consequences if the party doesn't reunite around issues they agree upon. 'We need to talk generally about how quickly you can become a minority,' the Georgia Republican said.

". . .'It's not going to deter us,' said Gary Bauer, head of the Family Research Council who used his Coalition for Working Families PAC to run ads highlighting Mr. Bordonaro's opposition to partial-birth abortion. . . .

"Mark Miller, director of the Republican Leadership Council and a voice for some of the party's biggest individual donors, said Mr. Bordonaro's defeat was 'a direct hit on the intolerant viewpoints of Republican activist Gary Bauer.' And John Davies, a strategist for Mr. Firestone, said the GOP 'self-destructed. . . . [They] did it to themselves.'" (*Wall Street Journal*, March 12, 1998)

---

"a politically potent group in GOP circles" (*Washington Post*, April 3, 1998)

# POLITICAL ORIENTATION

"Inside the White House, no one wants to tangle with Drug Czar Barry McCaffrey.

"Unlike many of his predecessors, the former four-star general has mastered the White House's Byzantine structure, finding ways to get things done. The latest example was his successful effort to get President Clinton in the 11th hour to kill a proposal for federal funding of needle-exchange programs for intravenous drug users, upsetting advocates of the plan including Health and Human Services Secretary Donna Shalala. . . .

"The Family Research Council, a group of social conservatives, led the successful fight against Clinton Surgeon General nominee Henry Foster and continues to battle the White House over a range of issues like late-term abortions. But almost daily, Robert Maginnis, the council's senior adviser on drug issues, talks with Mr. McCaffrey or his office, sharing polling data, strategy and other information. In fact, after Mr. McCaffrey's big victory on the needle-exchange issue, the council received one of the letters of thanks that he sent out to those who supported him in the bitter dispute. 'We scratch his back and, to certain extent, he helps us by keeping apprised of the issues,' says Mr. Maginnis, who has known the drug czar for years." (*Wall Street Journal*, May 12, 1998)

"conservative" (*Washington Post*, February 6, 1998)

# Mothers Against Drunk Driving (1980)

511 E. John Carpenter Freeway
Suite 700
Irving, Texas 75062-8187
Phone: (214) 744-6233 (MADD)
Fax: (214) 869-2206
(214) 869-2207

1001 G Street, NW
Suite 400 East
Washington, D.C. 20001
Phone: (202) 638-3735
Fax: (202) 638-3516

Internet: http://www.madd.org

---

"To stop drunk driving and to support victims of this violent crime."

*PURPOSE*

---

Unavailable

*STAFF*

---

H. Dean Wilkerson, executive director. Wilkerson was general counsel of Mothers Against Drunk Driving (MADD) before becoming executive director in 1993. He also has a background in private law practice and in sales management. A graduate of the University of Arkansas, Wilkerson holds a law degree from the University of Texas and an M.B.A. from the University of California at Berkeley.

*DIRECTOR*

---

501(c)(3)

*TAX STATUS*

---

1998—Unavailable
Proposed 1999—Unavailable

*BUDGET*

---

Individuals; federal, corporate, and foundation grants; memberships; interest; and in-kind donations

*FUNDING SOURCES*

---

Members: 3 million members and supporters
Branches/chapters: 500 chapters (including state offices and community action teams)
Affiliates: N/A

*SCOPE*

---

None

*PAC*

| | |
|---|---|
| *METHOD OF OPERATION* | ◆ Advertisements ◆ Awards program ◆ Coalition forming ◆ Conferences/seminars ◆ Congressional testimony ◆ Demonstrations ◆ Films/video/audiotapes ◆ Grassroots organizing ◆ Information clearinghouse ◆ International activities ◆ Internet (Web site) ◆ Legislative/regulatory monitoring (federal and state) ◆ Lobbying (federal, state, and grassroots) ◆ Local/municipal affairs ◆ Media outreach ◆ Product merchandising ◆ Polling ◆ Public awareness and education programs (National Sobriety Checkpoint Week, Operation Prom/Graduation) ◆ Speakers program ◆ Telecommunications services (Hotline: 800-GET-MADD, Mailing lists) ◆ Training |
| *CURRENT CONCERNS* | ◆ .08 blood alcohol content (BAC) nationwide ◆ Expanded use of administrative license revocation ◆ Goal 20X2000 (reduce drug- and alcohol-related traffic facilities) ◆ National enforcement of sobriety checkpoints ◆ Victims' rights |
| *PUBLICATIONS* | *Closed Head Injury*<br>*Don't Call Me Lucky*<br>*Drunk Driving: An Unacknowledged Form of Child Endangerment*<br>*Financial Recovery After A Drunk Driving Crash*<br>*Helping Children Cope with Death* (English and Spanish)<br>*How You Can Help*<br>*Men and Mourning*<br>*Someone You Know Drinks and Drives*<br>*Straight Talk About Death*<br>*Victim Information Pamphlet* (English and Spanish)<br>*We Hurt Too: Guide for Adult Siblings*<br>*Will It Always Feel This Way?* (English and Spanish)<br>*You're Not Alone*<br>*Your Grief: You're Not Going Crazy* (English and Spanish) |
| *NEWSLETTER* | Unavailable |
| *CONFERENCES* | MADD Safe and Sober Workshops<br>National Leadership Conference<br>State organization meetings<br>Victim advocacy trainings |
| *BOARD OF DIRECTORS* | Charles W. Babcock, chairman; Karolyn V. Nunnallee, president; Cheryl M. Burrell, vice president, field issues; Diane Biibe, vice president, public policy; Janey M. Fair, vice president, victim issues; Robert Driegert, treasurer; Karroll Ann Searcy, secretary<br><br>Other board members:<br>◆ W.H. (Bill) Blanchard ◆ Robert B. Boas ◆ Martha Brown ◆ Cheryl Misas-Burley ◆ Patricia Eichhorn ◆ Wendy J. Hamilton ◆ Darryl D. Hansen ◆ Ralph Hingson ◆ Charles A. Hurley ◆ Joseph J. LosSchiavo ◆ Kellie Mattson ◆ Carol H. McNamee ◆ Chris Peters ◆ Shirley L. Smith ◆ Wayne Smith ◆ Jan Blaser-Upchurch ◆ Wayne Vincent ◆ Tony Wells |

"Founded in 1980, Mothers Against Drunk Driving is today among the most respected grass-roots organizations in the country. It is also among the largest, with tens of thousands of volunteers working through 600 chapters and community action teams to combat drunk driving and other forms of alcohol abuse. Based in Irving, Tex., MADD has no office in Washington, making do there with a single part-time lobbyist. 'We're not a bunch of politicians or high-priced lawyers,' said Katherine Prescott, who recently ended a two-year term as president. 'We don't have the money to invest in lobbyists and PAC's.' " (*New York Times Magazine*, March 22, 1998)

"The Senate . . . voted to force states to adopt tough uniform drunk driving standards or suffer the loss of federal highway funds as part of a massive highway reauthorization bill that would dramatically boost spending over the next six years. The highway legislation constitutes one of the largest pots of money Congress will divvy up this year and is tailored to respond to the states' demand for increased spending for highway, bridge and mass transit construction and safety programs at a time of bulging surpluses in the federal highway trust fund.

"The Senate's action imposing tough national drunk driving standards marks an important victory for traffic safety groups including Mothers Against Drunk Driving and the National Safety Council. On Tuesday President Clinton signed an executive order imposing the tougher standards on federal property, including military bases and national parks. . . .

"Although the measure received bipartisan support in the Senate—with 26 Republicans joining with 36 Democrats to approve it, the outlook is dimmer in the House. Transportation and Infrastructure Committee Chairman Bud Shuster (R-Pa.) is opposed, arguing, 'The best way to encourage states to curb drunk driving is by providing incentives, not threats.' House Majority Leader Richard K. Armey (R-Tex.) described the proposal as 'a tough one' to pass." (*Washington Post*, March 5, 1998)

"The number of alcohol-related traffic fatalities in Northern Virginia appears to be increasing dramatically over last year, according to preliminary state statistics scheduled to be released today by the local Mothers Against Drunk Driving.

"The statistics show 28 drunken driving fatalities in the first 10 months of 1997, compared with 18 for the same period last year. The president of the Northern Virginia MADD chapter attributed the rise to complacency by the public and a failure by the criminal justice system to discourage drinking drivers. 'There's not the level of involvement from the community like there once was, and that's our fault,' said David Kelly, of Alexandria. 'The public pressure is no longer there.' " (*Washington Post*, November 20, 1997)

Unavailable

# National Center for Neighborhood Enterprise (1981)

1424 16th Street, NW
Washington, D.C. 20036
Phone: (202) 518-6500
Fax: (202) 588-0314

| | |
|---|---|
| **PURPOSE** | "To help low-income Americans achieve self-sufficiency and to support grassroots initiatives addressing societal problems including substance abuse and addition, youth violence, and family dissolution." |
| **STAFF** | 8 total—6 professional; 2 support; plus 5 part-time |
| **DIRECTOR** | Robert L. Woodson Sr., president. Before founding the National Center for Neighborhood Enterprise (NCNE) in 1981, Woodson was a resident fellow and director of the American Enterprise Institute's Neighborhood Revitalization Project. He previously directed the National Urban League's Administration of Justice Division. He is the author of numerous publications and articles and has lectured in colleges and universities in the United States and Europe. Woodson received a B.S. from Cheyney State College and an M.S.W. from the University of Pennsylvania. |
| **TAX STATUS** | 501(c)(3) |
| **BUDGET** | 1998—$1.8 million<br>Proposed 1999—Unavailable |
| **FUNDING SOURCES** | Primarily foundation support |
| **SCOPE** | Members: N/A<br>Branches/chapters: N/A<br>Affiliates: Grassroots organizations in 38 states nationwide |
| **PAC** | None |

♦ Awards program (Annual National Achievement Against the Odds, Regional "Joseph Awards") ♦ Coalition forming ♦ Conferences/seminars ♦ Congressional testimony ♦ Demonstrations ♦ Documentation of community-based initiatives ♦ Films/video/audiotapes ♦ Grassroots organizing ♦ Internet (Web site) ♦ Media outreach ♦ Participation in regulatory proceedings (federal and state) ♦ Research ♦ Training and technical assistance

## METHOD OF OPERATION

♦ Community-based and faith-based substance abuse programs ♦ Corporate/community partnerships ♦ Economic development and financial self-sufficiency ♦ Strengthening families ♦ Welfare reform ♦ Youth crime and gang activities

## CURRENT CONCERNS

*Applying Market Principles in the Social Economy: An Alternative Giving Strategy*

*Bridging the Gap: Strategies to Promote Self-Sufficiency Among Low-Income Americans*

*Empowering Residents of Public Housing: A Resource Guide for Resident Management*

*Entrepreneurial Enclaves in the African American Experience*

*Outcry from the Alamo: Ending the Hostility Toward Faith-based Drug Treatment*

*Race and Economic Opportunity*

*The Silent Scandal: Management Abuses in Public Housing*

*The Triumphs of Joseph: How Today's Community Healers Are Reviving Our Streets and Neighborhoods*

*Violence-Free Zone Initiatives: Models of Grassroots Youth Crime Intervention Success*

## PUBLICATIONS

*AGENDA Magazine*
*In the News* (periodic)
*FROM THE CENTER* (periodic)

## NEWSLETTER

Achievement Against the Odds Awards Dinner
Policy Conference (Washington, D.C.)

## CONFERENCES

♦ Michael Baroody ♦ Herman Cain ♦ Chloe Coney ♦ Ronald Docksai ♦ Pat Ford ♦ Frank Gardner ♦ Robert Hill ♦ James Lentz ♦ Ronald D. McNeil ♦ Robert Moore ♦ Myron J. Resnick ♦ Juan Rivera ♦ Fred Sacher ♦ Richard P. Wiederhold ♦ Robert L. Woodson Sr.

## BOARD OF DIRECTORS

## EFFECTIVENESS

"The idea that social problems can be best addressed by small community-based neighborhood organizations is no longer, of course, the novel concept it was when [Robert] Woodson first began advocating it in the late 1970s. But what sets Woodson apart is that he has actually, repeatedly, put these ideas into practice through his National Center for Neighborhood Enterprise. Over the years, in 38 cities, the center has worked with individuals whom Woodson identifies as 'grassroots leaders.' Hundreds of these leaders have gone through the management training programs the center conducts. But Woodson sees his primary role as being a broker between, in the metaphor of his book, the Josephs and the pharaohs of American society. He is someone who, in the words of a colleague, can work 'in the streets and in the suites.' Carl Hardrick, who works with gangs in Hartford, Conn., says Woodson functions as the 'ambassador from the 'hood.' " (*Philadelphia Inquirer Magazine*, April 19, 1998)

"In a scene reminiscent of the civil rights movement, rows of marchers—former rivals, mothers, neighbors and peace brokers—linked arms and marched for two blocks, symbolically connecting old turfs of the warring street crews once known as 'the Circle' and 'the Avenue.' There were no dirges, just a declaration of success: 'Peace! Peace! Peace in the streets.'...

"The truce process began one year ago when police declared that a rivalry inside a neighborhood gang called the Simple City Crew had led to the daylight abduction and shooting death of 12-year-old Darryl Dayan Hall as he walked home from school.

"In an effort to prevent retaliation for Darryl's death, the Alliance of Concerned Men, a small grass-roots organization, and the National Center for Neighborhood Enterprise, a nonprofit group that helps low-income communities develop and implement solutions to social and economic problems, mediated a truce between young men affiliated with the Circle and the Avenue crew factions.

"Although they denied any connection to Darryl's shooting, the young men who came to those early sessions agreed something needed to be done to ease tensions. In seeking peace, many have transformed their lives. . . ." (*Washington Post*, January 30, 1998)

## POLITICAL ORIENTATION

"Walking to lunch through the heart of Think Tank Country in Northwest Washington, Bob Woodson is still agitated about the exchange he had the night before on CNN with Bill Gray, the former congressman from Philadelphia who now heads the United Negro College Fund. The question was whether the children of affluent African Americans—such as Woodson's and Gray's—should be beneficiaries of affirmative action in college admissions. Gray contended that, since racism affected all blacks, such assistance was in order for all social classes. To Woodson, that was ludicrous, and he argues that it actually detracted from efforts to help those who really needed it. While the exchange clearly annoyed him, Woodson is also chuckling about it. 'I believe,' he says, 'that I have suffered gladly my last angry, *rich* black man.' " (*Philadelphia Inquirer Magazine*, April 19, 1998)

"Consider the case of Robert Woodson Sr., the president of the National Center for Neighborhood Enterprise. For 20 years, Mr. Woodson has been criticizing the agenda of black liberals, but he has also been helping grass-roots organizations expand economic opportunities in their low-income communities.

"It distresses Mr. Woodson that so little interest in this work is shown by some conservative intellectuals even as they insist that government has no answers and that blacks must help themselves. Indeed, two years ago, Mr. Woodson and I publicly terminated our association with the conservative American Enterprise Institute for its support of Mr. D'Souza, who was a research fellow there.

"Mr. Woodson has also rebuffed conservatives who want him to speak out against affirmative action. He fears that other African-Americans may see him as an instrument of forces hostile to blacks' interests. Mr. Woodson has a valid point, but few conservatives can see it. They think he is hostile to conservative interests—even though his work otherwise embodies the very ideals they uphold!" (*New York Times*, November 30, 1997)

". . . the Washington-based National Center for Neighborhood Enterprise [is] a 16-year-old organization founded on the premise that the most effective solutions to urban ills often come from the communities themselves, rather than government. The center coordinates efforts of groups like the alliance in 38 states and further assists them by raising money and helping find jobs for the young people they are turning away from crime." (*New York Times*, March 10, 1997)

# National Coalition Against Domestic Violence (1978)

P.O. Box 18749
Denver, Colorado 80218
Phone: (303) 839-1852
Fax: (303) 831-9251

119 Constitution Ave., NE
Washington, D.C. 20002
Phone: (202) 544-7358
Fax: (202) 544-7893

Internet: http://www.ncadv.org

**PURPOSE**

"To provide a national network of programs and state coalitions serving battered women and their children."

**STAFF**

4 total; plus 5 interns and 6 part-time and volunteers

**DIRECTOR**

Rita Smith, executive director. Smith has worked with the National Coalition Against Domestic Violence (NCADV) since 1992. She has worked in shelters since 1981, holding positions as a crisis counselor, program supervisor, and director.

**TAX STATUS**

501(c)(3)

**BUDGET**

1997—$350,000
1998—$450,000
Proposed 1999—Unavailable

**FUNDING SOURCES**

Membership, 30 percent; product sales, 22 percent; corporations and foundations, 20 percent; Combined Federal Campaign, 18 percent; contributions and miscellaneous, 10 percent

**SCOPE**

Members: Organizations and individuals
Branches/chapters: None
Affiliates: None

**PAC**

None

◆ Boycotts ◆ Coalition forming ◆ Conferences/seminars ◆ Congressional testimony ◆ Demonstrations ◆ Direct action ◆ Films/video/audiotapes ◆ Grassroots organizing ◆ Initiative/referendum campaigns ◆ International activities ◆ Legislative/regulatory monitoring (federal) ◆ Library/information clearinghouse ◆ Lobbying (federal and grassroots) ◆ Media outreach ◆ Product merchandising ◆ Speakers program ◆ Training and technical assistance

## METHOD OF OPERATION

◆ Domestic violence

## CURRENT CONCERNS

*Current Analysis of Battered Women's Movement*
*National Directory of Programs*
*Rural Resource Packet*

## PUBLICATIONS

*Update* (3 times a year)
*Voice* (quarterly)
*Grassroots Connection* (quarterly)

## NEWSLETTER

National Domestic Violence Conference (biennial)

## CONFERENCES

Kay Mixon, chair; Diane Purvin, secretary; Barbara A. Blunt, treasurer

Other members:
◆ Joyce M. Brown ◆ Darla Hesketh ◆ Bridgett Jackson Fahnbullch ◆ Karlene John ◆ Diana Olvedo Munoz ◆ Maria Delmar St. John ◆ Rita Smith ◆ Pam Willhoite ◆ Joan Zorza

## BOARD OF DIRECTORS

"Last September, Congress passed the domestic offender gun ban, making it illegal for anyone convicted of a domestic violence misdemeanor to carry a gun. . . . The new law recognized that although domestic violence often results in serious injury to the woman, the charges also are frequently reduced through a plea bargain to misdemeanors. Battered women often will forgo the ordeal of a trial in return for financial security for their children and safety. Pamela Coukos, public policy director for the National Coalition Against Domestic Violence, says these crimes are marked by high rates of recidivism and escalations in the level and frequency of attacks, which become especially deadly when the abused spouse, usually a woman, tries to leave. . . . Spouses prosecuting police officers face the additional burden of going against someone well connected within the system. . . .

"After the law was passed, however, out came one of law enforcement's dirty little secrets: Some of its own people had domestic violence misdemeanors on their records. They were looking at losing their jobs or being reassigned to duty where they did not have to carry guns.

## EFFECTIVENESS

"With that information exposed, some law enforcement unions and the NRA now are lobbying to get rid of the ban or restrict it so that only officers convicted of misdemeanor domestic violence offenses since last September would lose their weapons. But that would leave untold numbers of women vulnerable. One thing that is known about batterers is that they carry long grudges and don't reform easily.

"If retroactivity is eliminated, a police officer who had terrorized his wife with firearms and finally pleaded guilty to a misdemeanor gun offense a few years ago would get his gun back, and the woman would have to live with the fear he is once again armed, Coukos says. Coukos cites the case of a woman whose husband attacked her and her children with a shotgun during court-ordered visitation. She lost a leg as a result. She had left him three years earlier. . . ." (*Washington Post*, May 16, 1997)

## POLITICAL ORIENTATION

Unavailable

# National Training and Information Center (NTIC)/National People's Action (NPA) (1972)

810 North Milwaukee Avenue
Chicago, Illinois 60622
Phone: (312) 243-3035 (NTIC)
Phone: (312) 243-3038 (NPA)
Fax: (312) 243-7044
Internet: HN1742@handsnet.org

| | |
|---|---|
| NTIC: "To empower neighborhood people through leadership development so they can influence the decisions that affect them." <br> NPA: "To organize neighborhood groups nationwide into a vocal and powerful people's lobbying and pressure group." | **_PURPOSE_** |
| NTIC: 17 total—15 professional; 2 support; plus 1 intern <br> NPA: volunteers from neighborhood organizations nationwide | **_STAFF_** |
| Gale Cincotta, executive director, National Training and Information Center and chairperson, National People's Action. Cincotta cofounded the National Training and Information Center and has served as its executive director since 1973. She has been the chairperson of National People's Action since 1972. A native of Chicago, Cincotta served on the U.S. Department of Housing and Urban Development's National Commission on Regulatory Barriers to Affordable Housing and the Federal Home Loan Bank of Chicago's Community Investment Advisory Council. | **_DIRECTOR_** |
| NTIC: 501(c)(3) <br> NPA: 501(c)(4) | **_TAX STATUS_** |
| NTIC/NPA: <br> 1998—Unavailable <br> Proposed 1999—Unavailable | **_BUDGET_** |
| NTIC: Corporate contributions, 44 percent; foundation grants, 32.5 percent; government contracts, 21.3 percent; programs, 2.2 percent <br> NPA: Individual donations | **_FUNDING SOURCES_** |
| Members: N/A <br> Branches/chapters: N/A <br> Affiliates: NPA—302 grassroots neighborhood groups in 38 states | **_SCOPE_** |

| | |
|---|---|
| **PAC** | None |
| **METHOD OF OPERATION** | NTIC: ◆ Coalition forming ◆ Conferences/seminars ◆ Grantmaking ◆ Grassroots organizing ◆ Legislative monitoring (federal and state) ◆ Local/municipal affairs ◆ Media outreach ◆ Participation in regulatory proceedings (federal and state) ◆ Research ◆ Training and technical assistance<br><br>NPA: ◆ Coalition forming ◆ Conferences/seminars ◆ Congressional testimony ◆ Demonstrations ◆ Direct action ◆ Grassroots organizing ◆ Lobbying (grassroots) ◆ Negotiations with corporate and elected officials |
| **CURRENT CONCERNS** | ◆ Community development funds ◆ Corporate leveraging of profits for social and neighborhood improvements ◆ CRA legislation ◆ Credit and lending policies ◆ Crime ◆ Drugs in neighborhoods ◆ Environmental racism ◆ Federal budget cuts ◆ FHA policies ◆ Housing ◆ Job development ◆ Private sector involvement in meeting community needs ◆ Rights for people with disabilities ◆ Utility rates |
| **PUBLICATIONS** | Published by NTIC:<br>*Asset Forfeiture: Getting a Piece of the Pie*<br>*Basics of Organizing: You Can't Build a Machine Without Nuts and Bolts*<br>*Blessed Be The Fighters*<br>*A Challenge for Change*<br>*The Community Reinvestment Handbook*<br>*Devils In the Details: Analysis of FHA Default Concentration and Lender Performance in 20 U.S. Cities*<br>*Dynamics of Organizing*<br>*Partnerships for Reinvestment: An Evaluation of the Chicago Neighborhood Lending Programs*<br>*The Silent Bomb: FHA Devastation of Neighborhoods*<br>*Strategies for Developing a Drug Free Zone*<br>*Taking Our Neighborhoods Back!*<br>*Who, Me a Researcher? Yes You!* |
| **NEWSLETTER** | *Disclosure* (NTIC, 6 times a year)<br>*NTIC Reports* (4 times a year to NTIC funders) |
| **CONFERENCES** | NTIC holds numerous workshops and training sessions throughout the year, including two week-long core training sessions in Chicago<br>NPA holds an annual neighborhood conference in Washington, D.C. |
| **BOARD OF DIRECTORS** | NTIC: ◆ Paul Battle ◆ Calvin Bradford ◆ Gale Cincotta ◆ Roger Coughlin ◆ Marilyn Evans ◆ Joseph Fagan ◆ Bruce Gottschall ◆ John McKnight<br><br>NPA: ◆ John Allen ◆ Barbara Busch ◆ Gale Cincotta ◆ Roger Hayes ◆ Craig Taylor |

"With all the upscale housing being built in trendy areas near the lake-front, it's easy to forget that other more prosaic, city neighborhoods are losing more units to demolition than are being added. . . .

"It's an old story, even though the city has fought back over the years with numerous public-private housing subsidy programs to infuse new money into such neighborhoods. There are not, however, enough such subsidies to help all the low- and moderate-income families who need them. Nor will there be given the bipartisan consensus in Congress for balancing the federal budget.

"It is amazing, though, what the private sector can do to close the affordability gap. Already this month there have been three major announcements about large pools of unsubsidized mortgage money to be targeted at Chicago's less-affluent neighborhoods.

"Two were made by First Chicago NBD, beginning with a pledge to loan $4 billion—that's with a 'b'—over the next ten years in Chicago neighborhoods. Under an agreement with the National Training and Information Center, the Chicago-based watchdog group headed by activist Gale Cincotta, the First will be lending $1.2 billion in home mortgages, $130 million in home improvement loans and the balances in loans to small businesses and multifamily developers. . . ." (*Chicago Tribune*, July 24, 1998)

"One factor not much credited for these happy totals is the Federal Housing Administration (FHA) mortgage insurance program. And no wonder, because last year some 71,000 of these government-insured mortgages went bad, triggering $5 billion in claims by lenders and saddling thousands of neighborhoods with empty, loan-defaulted houses.

"Now comes U.S. Housing Secretary Andrew Cuomo with a dubious proposal to raise to $227,150 the amount of money FHA will lend on a single house. He hopes that FHA insurance premiums paid by upscale borrowers (you'd have to make at least $80,000 a year to qualify for such a loan) will help cover the mounting claims caused by defaults at the lower end. . . .

"Little wonder that Gale Cincotta (of NTIC), the neighborhood activist who has led a 30-year fight against FHA abuses, has scheduled a protest at 11 a.m. Monday outside Secretary Cuomo's offices on West Jackson Street. May she be in good voice." (*Chicago Tribune*, January 31, 1998)

"The National Training and Information Center, which advises community groups serving low-income homebuyers, wants the F.H.A. to prevent defaults by providing lower-end borrowers with better counseling and other services. That is wiser than inviting the F.H.A. to reach out to families already served by private mortgage lenders." (*New York Times*, January 23, 1998)

Unavailable

# U.S. ENGLISH Foundation, Inc. (1983)

1747 Pennsyvania Avenue, NW
Suite 1100
Washington, D.C. 20006
Phone: (202) 833-0100
Fax: (202) 833-0108
Toll-free: (800) U.S.ENGLISH (1-800-873-4547)
Internet: info@us-english.org *or* http://www.us-english.org

| | |
|---|---|
| **PURPOSE** | "To make English the official language of the U.S. government, and to promote opportunities for all in America to learn English." |
| **STAFF** | Unavailable |
| **DIRECTOR** | Mauro E. Mujica, chairman. Mujica has been chairman and chief executive officer of U.S. ENGLISH and U.S. ENGLISH Foundation since 1993. An architect and businessman, he is a native of Chile who migrated to the United States in 1965 and became a naturalized citizen in 1970. Mujica holds undergraduate and master's degrees from Columbia University. |
| **TAX STATUS** | 501(c)(3) |
| **BUDGET** | 1998—Unavailable<br>Proposed 1999—Unavailable |
| **FUNDING SOURCES** | Member contributions, 100 percent |
| **SCOPE** | Members: N/A (U.S. ENGLISH membership: 650,000 individuals)<br>Branches/chapters: N/A<br>Affiliate: U.S. ENGLISH, Inc. (not tax-exempt) |
| **PAC** | None |

| | |
|---|---|
| ◆ Advertisements ◆ Coalition forming ◆ Congressional testimony ◆ Congressional voting analysis ◆ Demonstrations ◆ Grantmaking ◆ Grassroots organizing ◆ Initiative/referendum campaigns ◆ Internet (Web Site) ◆ Legislative/regulatory monitoring (federal and state) ◆ Lobbying (federal, state and grassroots) ◆ Media outreach ◆ Polling ◆ Research ◆ Speakers program | *METHOD OF OPERATION* |
| ◆ Bilingual education reform ◆ Multi-lingualism in government | *CURRENT CONCERNS* |
| Publishes a variety of fact sheets and issue briefings | *PUBLICATIONS* |
| *U.S. ENGLISH Update* (quarterly) | *NEWSLETTER* |
| None | *CONFERENCES* |
| Unavailable | *BOARD OF DIRECTORS* |
| Unavailable | *EFFECTIVENESS* |
| Unavailable | *POLITICAL ORIENTATION* |

# United States Public Interest Research Group (1983)

218 D Street, SE
Washington, D.C. 20003
Phone: (202) 546-9707
Fax: (202) 546-2461
Internet: http://www.pirg.org

| | |
|---|---|
| **PURPOSE** | "Researches consumer and environmental issues, monitors corporate and governmental actions, and lobbies for reform at the national level." |
| **STAFF** | 25 total |
| **DIRECTOR** | Gene Karpinski, executive director. Karpinski previously worked for Congress Watch and People for the American Way and served as executive director of the Colorado Public Interest Research Group. He is a graduate of Georgetown Law School. |
| **TAX STATUS** | 501(c)(4) |
| **BUDGET** | 1998—$750,000<br>Proposed 1999—Unavailable |
| **FUNDING SOURCES** | Primarily individual donations |
| **SCOPE** | Members: United States Public Interest Research Group (USPIRG) serves as "the national lobbying office for state Public Interest Research Groups (PIRGs), which are nonprofit . . . statewide research and advocacy organizations." Its membership is the aggregate of the various state PIRGs.<br>Branches/chapters: 20 state groups<br>Affiliates: N/A |
| **PAC** | None |

| | |
|---|---|
| ◆ Coalition forming ◆ Congressional voting analysis ◆ Grassroots organizing ◆ Internet ◆ Legislative/regulatory monitoring (federal) ◆ Lobbying (federal) ◆ Research ◆ Voter registration | *METHOD OF OPERATION* |
| ◆ Defending and enforcing environmental protection laws ◆ Energy: renewable sources, increased efficiency ◆ Government subsidies of polluting industries ◆ Increasing the market for recycled materials ◆ Placing limits on political campaign contributions ◆ Preservation of natural resources ◆ Protecting consumer ◆ Protecting endangered species ◆ Stopping global climate change | *CURRENT CONCERNS* |
| None | *PUBLICATIONS* |
| *Citizen Agenda* (quarterly) | *NEWSLETTER* |
| Twice per year—an eastern and western PIRG organizational conference | *CONFERENCES* |
| Unavailable | *BOARD OF DIRECTORS* |

*EFFECTIVENESS*

"As several dozen protesters marched outside, House Speaker Newt Gingrich signed copies of his new book, 'Lessons Learned the Hard Way,' at the Trover Shop on Capitol Hill. . . .

"The demonstrators from Public Citizen and U.S. Public Interest Research Group were complaining about Gingrich's stance on campaign finance reform. 'Newt's here to sign his book for dollars,' said Public Citizen's Maura Kealey, 'but we think he ought to sign for reform instead,' referring to an effort to force a House vote on a reform measure the groups support. . . ." (*Washington Post*, April 18, 1998)

"Nationally, a survey by the U.S. Public Interest Research Group found the percentage of banks charging fees when a non-customer uses their ATMs rose to 71 percent from 58 percent in 1997. The charge is in addition to the fee that banks charge their customers for using another bank's ATM. Bigger banks charged more often—83 percent, compared with 65 percent for small banks—and the fees were substantially higher, averaging $1.35 per transaction, compared with $1.16 for the smaller banks. . . .

"The consumer group surveyed 470 banks in 28 states and the District. It was the group's third survey since ATM networks such as Cirrus Systems Inc. and Plus in 1996 began to allow financial institutions to charge fees when consumers use their cash machines to conduct transactions. . . .

"The survey results prompted Sen. Alfonse M. D'Amato (R-N.Y.), chairman of the Senate Banking Committee, to vow . . . that legislation would be passed this year to ban ATM surcharges. . . ." (*Washington Post*, April 2, 1998)

"The U.S. Public Interest Research Group found nearly one-third of all consumer credit-bureau reports contain serious errors that could cause unfair denial of a car loan, a mortgage or even a job. Some consumers who are savvy enough to request their reports after being turned down for a loan can't obtain them, the national consumer lobbying group said.

"The report, called 'Mistakes Do Happen,' was written after 88 people, all of them PIRG staff or volunteers, obtained 133 credit reports from the three major credit-reporting companies. An additional 22 participants never received their credit reports, even after repeated calls to request them.

"Ed Mierzwinski, PIRG's consumer program director, said that even after Congress strengthened the law on credit reports, 'I still get complaints, and I still know that credit-bureau errors cause some of the worst problems that consumers face in their financial lives.'. . ." (*Wall Street Journal*, March 13, 1998)

"Celeste Blumenauer, a Rockville mother, thought the 'eyeball ball' looked suspicious. Her 10-month-old son, Joseph, used to sit in his highchair and gnaw on the toy, a rolling eyeball in plastic sphere about the size of a golf ball.

"Blumenauer said. 'It made us nervous so out it went.' The eyeball ball now is sitting atop the Blumenauers' refrigerator, well out of the youngster's reach. It turns out the Blumenauers' instincts were right, according to a new report on dangerous toys by the U.S. Public Interest Research Group (PIRG). This week, the private watchdog group released its annual list of toys that it says pose choking or other safety risks to young children. PIRG has put out the list for 12 years, just before the busy holiday shopping season.

"The eyeball ball was one of 18 toys cited by PIRG this year. The group said the eyeball ball violates the 1994 Child Safety Protection Act, which banned toys with small parts for children younger than 3 and mandates warnings about choking hazards for children ages 3 to 6. The problem with the ball and with many of the toys on the PIRG list is not with the toys themselves but that the toys aren't labeled or marketed in a way that lets parents know they are inappropriate for children younger than 3. . . ." (*Washington Post*, November 28, 1997)

"Until now, efforts by [House Budget Committee Chairman John R.] Kasich and others to scale back corporate subsidies and tax loopholes have made little headway, largely because of resistance from deep-pocketed business interests with strong allies within the Republican-dominated Congress and at the White House. 'We have not always been able to match our actions with our lofty rhetoric,' Kasich conceded. . . .

" 'There is an unrelenting effort and an unstoppable drumbeat to really end welfare as we know it,' Kasich said in announcing formation of the coalition. Consumer advocate Ralph Nader, another coalition member, predicted that 'There are going to be a lot of sparks flying as a result of this effort.'

"The new coalition—called 'Stop Corporate Welfare!'—is a political patchwork of liberal advocacy groups such as U.S. Public Interest Research Group and Public Citizen; environmental advocates including Friends of the Earth; and conservative organizations including the National Taxpayers Union and Americans for Tax Reform. . . ." (*Washington Post*, January 29, 1997)

## POLITICAL ORIENTATION

"The U.S. Public Interest Research Group is the national lobbying office for state PIRGs, a network of nonprofit consumer and environmental groups founded by Ralph Nader." (*Wall Street Journal*, March 13, 1998)

"a nonprofit, nonpartisan consumer advocacy group" (*Washington Post*, June 18, 1997)

# Consumer/
# Health

Chapter 4

# Action on Smoking and Health (1967)

2013 H Street, NW
Washington, D.C. 20006
Phone: (202) 659-4310
Fax: (202) 833-3921
Internet: http://www.ash.org

| | |
|---|---|
| "To act as the legal arm of the nonsmoking majority." | *PURPOSE* |
| 9 total | *STAFF* |
| John F. Banzhaf III, executive director and chief counsel. Banzhaf founded Action on Smoking and Health (ASH) in 1967. He also is a professor of law at the George Washington University's National Law Center. Previously Banzhaf was with the New York law firm of Watson, Leavonworth, Kelton, and Taggart. He has been a spokesman on national news programs and has written for numerous publications worldwide. Banzhaf earned an undergraduate degree in electrical engineering at Massachusetts Institute of Technology and a J.D. at Columbia University. | *DIRECTOR* |
| 501(c)(3) | *TAX STATUS* |
| Unavailable | *BUDGET* |
| Public subscription, 100 percent; "no government aid of any sort" | *FUNDING SOURCES* |
| Members: N/A<br>Branches/chapters: N/A<br>Affiliates: N/A | *SCOPE* |
| None | *PAC* |

| | |
|---|---|
| *METHOD OF OPERATION* | ♦ Advertisements ♦ Awards program ♦ Conferences/seminars ♦ Congressional testimony ♦ Educational materials ♦ Films/video/audiotapes ♦ Grassroots organizing ♦ International activities ♦ Internet (Web site) ♦ Legal assistance ♦ Legislative/regulatory monitoring (federal and state) ♦ Litigation ♦ Lobbying (federal, state, and grassroots) ♦ Media outreach ♦ Participation in regulatory proceedings (federal and state) ♦ Polling ♦ Research |
| *CURRENT CONCERNS* | ♦ Protection of children from tobacco use ♦ Protection of public property from abuse by tobacco advertising ♦ Public education on dangers of environmental tobacco smoke ♦ Restriction of tobacco advertising ♦ Workplace smoking limitations or bans |
| *PUBLICATIONS* | *Custody Information Package* ("information on child custody when one parent smokes and the other does not")<br>*Taking Action to Protect You and Your Family from Tobacco Smoke*<br>*Taking Action to Protect Yourself from Tobacco Smoke in Public Places*<br>*Taking Action to Protect Yourself from Tobacco Smoke in the Workplace*<br><br>ASH also publishes other individual papers and materials on tobacco-related health issues |
| *NEWSLETTER* | *ASH Smoking and Health Review* (bimonthly) |
| *CONFERENCES* | Sponsors conferences on the occasion of landmark events |
| *BOARD OF DIRECTORS* | Martin Adam Jacobs, chairman; Joli Kansil, vice chairman; John F. Banzhaf III, executive director and chief counsel<br><br>Other members of the board of trustees:<br>♦ Margaret A. New ♦ Louis W. Sullivan ♦ Ethel R. Wells |
| *EFFECTIVENESS* | "Citing a new report on cancer risks, an anti-smoking group has petitioned the Federal Trade Commission to require health warnings on cigars.<br>　"Action on Smoking and Health based its request largely on a National Cancer Institute report that concluded cigar smoking can be as deadly as cigarette smoking. Smoking one or two cigars a day doubles the risk of oral and esophageal cancers and increases the risk of larynx cancer more than six-fold, according to the report." (*Wall Street Journal*, April 14, 1998)<br><br>"At least one provision of the landmark tobacco settlement raises unsettling constitutional questions that are almost certain to be fought over in court. |

"Opponents of the pact said that the provision eliminating punitive damages for past industry conduct may violate constitutional safeguards guaranteeing due process of law and the right to a jury trial. And at least one antitobacco organization, Action on Smoking and Health, or ASH, is mobilizing to challenge the agreement if it becomes law. 'I have significant reservations about its constitutionality,' said ASH executive director John Banzhaf." (*Wall Street Journal,* June 23, 1997)

"antitobacco organization" (*Wall Street Journal,* June 23, 1997)

"[John] Banzhaf . . . is optimistic that the new Republican majority on Capitol Hill will not give the tobacco industry its way. 'The antismoking movement has never relied on Congress,' he said." (*National Journal,* December 17, 1994)

# POLITICAL ORIENTATION

# Advocates for Highway and Auto Safety (1989)

750 First Street, NE
Suite 901
Washington, D.C. 20002
Phone: (202) 408-1711
Fax: (202) 408-1699
Internet: http://www.saferoads.org

| | |
|---|---|
| **PURPOSE** | "To promote adoption of effective highway safety legislation, standards, policies and programs at national and state levels." |
| **STAFF** | 9 total—7 professional; 2 support; plus interns |
| **DIRECTOR** | Judith Lee Stone, president. Stone has been with Advocates for Highway and Auto Safety since its inception in 1989. Previously, she served as executive director of the National Association of Governors' Highway Safety Representatives, as director of federal affairs with the National Safety Council, and in the Department of Transportation during the Carter administration. She was appointed to the Federal Motor Carrier Advisory in 1994 and elected to the board of directors of the National Insurance Crime Bureau in 1995. Stone is a graduate of Northwestern University. |
| **TAX STATUS** | 501(c)(4) |
| **BUDGET** | 1997—$1.4 million<br>1998—$1.5 million<br>Proposed 1999—Unavailable |
| **FUNDING SOURCES** | 100 percent private funding (insurance companies) |
| **SCOPE** | Members: 22 organizations ("Equal, shared leadership and membership. For each insurance company funder [dues $100,000 per year] there is a seat on the board for a consumer/safety organization. Each side selects/elects its own representatives. All decisions are by consensus of the group.")<br>Branches/chapters: Chapters in California, Connecticut, New York, and Florida<br>Affiliates: N/A |

None

♦ Advertisements (limited) ♦ Awards program ♦ Coalition forming ♦ Congressional testimony ♦ Grassroots organizing ♦ Internet ♦ Legislative/regulatory monitoring (federal) ♦ Litigation ♦ Lobbying (federal and state) ♦ Media outreach ♦ Participation in regulatory proceedings (federal) ♦ Performance ratings of states ♦ Polling ♦ Research ♦ Television and radio production

## METHOD OF OPERATION

♦ Highway and auto safety laws and regulations (federal and state)

## CURRENT CONCERNS

Publishes informational brochures, fact sheets, research reports, and policy statements

## PUBLICATIONS

None

## NEWSLETTER

None

## CONFERENCES

Richard D. Crabtree and Stephen W. Hargarten, cochairs; Judith Lee Stone, president

Members of consumer and safety organizations:
♦ Stephen Brobeck ♦ Joan Claybrook ♦ Clarence Ditlow ♦ Donald Friedman ♦ Ralf Hotchkiss ♦ Mary Jagim ♦ Richard A. Levinson ♦ Andrew McGuire ♦ Karolyn Nunnallee ♦ Hubert Williams

Members of insurance and agents organizations:
♦ Patricia A. Borowski ♦ Herman Brandau ♦ G. Edward Combs ♦ John Conners ♦ Steve Hasenmiller ♦ Rodger S. Lawson ♦ Gerald Maatman ♦ Thomas G. Myers ♦ David C. Turner ♦ Robert Vagley

## BOARD OF DIRECTORS

"A traffic safety group is asking federal regulators to improve tougher side-impact-protection standards on automakers to better protect occupants of passenger cars in crashes with light trucks.

"The petition—filed Thursday by Advocates for Highway and Auto Safety—is the latest salvo in the ongoing debate over vehicle mismatches fueled by the explosion in sport-utility vehicle sales.

" 'Big, heavy, stiff sport-utility vehicles, full-size vans and large pickups are causing a rising toll of deaths and serious injuries, especially in side impacts with smaller, lighter passenger vehicles,' " said Judith Lee Stone, president of the Washington, D.C.-based group, which lobbies Congress on highway safety issues." (*Detroit News*, July 7, 1998)

## EFFECTIVENESS

"We have global cars, global automakers, and global mergers such as the one proposed between Chrysler Corp. and Germany's Daimler-Benz AG. It's in the natural order of things that global automobile regulation comes next.

"That's what proponents of globalization would say. The new world order calls for one rule book that every car manufacturer could follow, no matter where the vehicle is made or sold. In other words, build a car in Ohio and sell it in Jakarta, the same rules apply. This is what government negotiators from the United States, Japan and the European Union have been working on over the past few years. The idea is to 'harmonize' safety and environmental standards for automobiles, an effort that would eliminate differences in existing rules or develop new rules.

"Working through a United Nations conference called Working Party 29, the negotiators have produced an agreement that would create a process for reviewing more than 100 rules that cover brakes, headlights, mirrors, turn signals and a side-impact crash standard. The United States will sign onto the agreement in June, but implementation could take years. . . .

"Before the United States signs on the dotted line, Advocates for Highway and Auto Safety would like NHTSA to air the whole idea in a formal rulemaking procedure with public comment. 'We want a public hearing on this issue,' said Henry Jasny, general counsel for Advocates. 'We don't want to derail the proceeding, but we want the American public to weigh in on what the government plans to do.'. . .

"Jasny believes that . . . intentions are good but that Geneva, where the negotiating will take place, is awfully far away." (*Washington Post*, May 22, 1998)

"A national drunken-driving mandate has been tossed out of a $200.5 billion six-year transportation bill nearing completion in Congress, and the prospect of Ohio voluntarily adopting the proposed standard seems remote.

"A final bill could be approved by Friday, with Ohio in line for a significant increase over the $625 million in federal highway dollars it received this year.

"Leaders of the House-Senate conference committee negotiating the final bill announced yesterday that the House position against a federal mandate won out over the Senate's desire for a uniform national standard. . . .

"However, Sen. Mike DeWine, R-Ohio, and other proponents of a national limit said they aren't optimistic financial incentives will lure states to adopt the 0.08 standard. Under the Senate proposal, states would have lost up to 10 percent of their highway dollars if they failed to adopt the standard.

"Advocates for Highway Safety, an alliance of consumer and safety groups, called on President Clinton to veto a final transportation bill if it doesn't include the 0.08 standard." (*Columbus Dispatch*, May 19, 1998)

"The moment of truth comes when the car is well into the intersection and the driver realizes, sometimes with a guilty-looking glance through his windshield, that two rapid-fire flashes of a strobe light have just cost him $271 for running a red light.

"Smile, you're on a candid camera! A police camera, to be more precise. And about two weeks later a complimentary photograph arrives in the mail, accompanied by a summons to appear in court or pay a fine. A three-year, federally backed program to put the automatic cameras in busy intersections in 31 cities nationwide has reduced red light crashes by as much as 43 percent in some communities, safety officials say. Since more than 8,000 people die and another million are injured each year in accidents in which someone has run a red light, the program has been hailed as a success in combating what U.S. Transportation Secretary Rodney E. Slater called 'one of the most dangerous acts of aggressive driving.'

"But in California, where six cities have been testing the program and several others want to try it next year, the state legislature has voted to put an end to the use of cameras at intersections with traffic lights amid heated rhetoric about Orwellian 'Big Brother' surveillance by the government. . . .

"A national poll released . . . by the Washington-based Advocates for Highway and Auto Safety suggested American drivers are tired of cars running red lights. The Lou Harris poll showed that 65 percent of drivers favor the use of intersection cameras.

" 'These systems have been in use in Australia and Europe for years. The time for red light cameras in this country has come,' said Judith Lee Stone, president of the advocacy group." (*Washington Post*, May 10, 1998)

". . . Supporters of higher speeds, long chafing under the federal cap, insist there isn't any proof that higher speeds mean more deaths. But with speed-limit increases expected in many states, legions of lobbyists from highway safety groups and the medical profession to the insurance industry—which is worried about a new wave of auto-accident-related claims—are waging new state campaigns in support of safety-oriented 'tradeoff' bills. Advocates for Highway and Auto Safety, a broad coalition based in Washington, is targeting 12 states, such as California and Illinois, as offering the best chances for safety-related results.

"For example, safety lobbyists want to persuade more states to enact 'primary' belt-enforcement laws. These laws, in effect in about 10 states, let police cite motorists just for violating buckle-up laws. In most states, officers can do so only when they stop offenders for other causes." (*Wall Street Journal*, February 21, 1996)

"a partnership of Government agencies and private companies" (*New York Times*, November 19, 1997)

# POLITICAL ORIENTATION

# AIDS Action Council (1984)

1875 Connecticut Avenue, NW
Suite 700
Washington, D.C. 20009
Phone (202) 986-1300
Fax: (202) 986-1345
Internet: aidsaction@aidsaction.org *or* http://www.aidsaction.org

**PURPOSE**

Is a "national voice on AIDS, representing all Americans affected by HIV/AIDS and 3,200 community-based organizations that serve them by ensuring a fair and effective national AIDS policy."

**STAFF**

21 total—19 professional; 2 support; plus 1 intern and 1 part-time professional

**DIRECTOR**

Daniel Zingale, executive director. Prior to joining AIDS Action, Zingale served as political director of the Human Rights Campaign (HRC). Representing the HRC, he became the first member of a gay and lesbian organization to sit on the board of the Leadership Conference on Civil Rights. Zingale also served as managing director of government relations for the American Psychological Association from 1991 to 1993. He earned a bachelor's degree in political science from the University of California–Berkeley and a master's degree in public administration from Harvard University's John F. Kennedy School of Government.

**TAX STATUS**

501(c)(4)

**BUDGET**

1997—$2.03 million
1998—$2.05 million
Proposed 1999—$2.09 million

**FUNDING SOURCES**

Community-based organization membership, 41 percent; program grants, 26 percent; national and community events, 17 percent; individual support, 16 percent

**SCOPE**

Members: 3,200 AIDS service provider organization members and 25,000 individual members
Branches/chapters: N/A
Affiliate: AIDS Action Foundation, a 501(c)(3) organization

**PAC**

None

♦ Advertisements ♦ Awards program ♦ Coalition forming ♦ Conferences/seminars ♦ Congressional testimony ♦ Congressional voting analysis ♦ Direct action ♦ Educational foundation ♦ Fellowships ♦ Grassroots organizing ♦ Internet (databases, E-mail alerts, Web site) ♦ Lobbying (federal and grassroots) ♦ Media outreach ♦ Participation in regulatory proceedings (federal) ♦ Performance ratings ♦ Polling ♦ Product merchandising ♦ Research ♦ Speakers program

## METHOD OF OPERATION

♦ AIDS policy issues ♦ Disability issues ♦ Discrimination ♦ Health care access

## CURRENT CONCERNS

None

## PUBLICATIONS

*AIDS Action Update* (quarterly magazine)
*AIDS Action Hotwire* (weekly fax and e-mail newsletter)

## NEWSLETTER

State of AIDS Forum (annual)
State of AIDS Congressional Breakfast (annual)
Regional events in New York, Los Angeles, Washington, D.C., and Houston (annual)

## CONFERENCES

David Wexler, chair; Larry Kessler, vice chair; Judy Stanfield, treasurer; Craig Thompson, secretary

Other members:
♦ Charles Albrecht ♦ John L. Barnes ♦ Tony Braswell ♦ Errol Chin-Loy
♦ A. Gene Copello ♦ Ravinia Hayes Cozier ♦ David Curtis ♦ Oscar de la O ♦ Shauna Dunn ♦ Luigi Ferrer ♦ Linda Frank ♦ Mike Gifford ♦ John Gile ♦ Jim Graham ♦ Barbara Hughes ♦ John Humphries ♦ Mike Isbell
♦ Ron Johnson ♦ William Kersten ♦ Jeremy G. Landau ♦ Joan Lawrence
♦ Mike McKay ♦ Fred Miller ♦ Thomas Nylund ♦ Mark Robinson ♦ Sue W. Scott ♦ Victoria L. Sharp ♦ Craig Schniderman ♦ Rick Siclari ♦ Gloria Smith ♦ Terry Stone ♦ Lorraine Teel ♦ Steve Townley

## BOARD OF DIRECTORS

"AIDS Action brought together public health officials and AIDS workers yesterday to call for programs that could act as a 'virtual AIDS vaccine,' including:
"—A 25 percent increase in the CDC's $634 million budget for AIDS education and other HIV prevention programs.
"—TV networks that air programs rated 'S' for sexual content to also allow condom ads to air during those programs.
"—[D]octors, clinics and hospitals to begin using a new 10-minute HIV test immediately. An older test takes about a week to get results, and thousands of Americans who get tested each year never return to learn if they're infected.

## EFFECTIVENESS

"—AIDS education to reach more teen-agers by creating an AIDS prevention Web site that links to popular teen Internet sites.

"—CDC to launch a new campaign to persuade more people at risk to get tested." (*Baltimore Sun*, July 21, 1998)

"An Illinois life insurer, in a move further signaling the success of new AIDS treatments, is testing sales of policies to people with the HIV infection.

"The policies are believed to be the first, following years in which people testing positive for HIV were automatically denied insurance.

"Advocacy groups representing those with the infection welcomed the effort by Guarantee Trust Life Insurance Co., a mutually owned insurer based in Glenview, Ill. But they cautioned that a slim number of people may actually benefit. The insurer has some restrictive criteria, and the policies are pricey, they added. . . .

"Among other restrictions, the company will sell only to people who have good track records in treatment spanning at least nine months. The price: about $300 a month for a $50,000 whole-life policy, substantially higher than the $55-a-month paid to Guarantee Trust by a 30-year-old man with lesser health problems.

". . . Javier Salazar, a lobbyist for AIDS Action Council in Washington, D.C., termed a $300-a-month policy 'a definite luxury when many people are having to use all their resources simply to keep themselves alive.'" (*Wall Street Journal*, April 16, 1997)

"Deaths from AIDS in the United States last year fell significantly for the first time since the AIDS epidemic began in the early 1980s, federal health officials reported yesterday.

"The decline in AIDS deaths occurred in all regions of the country and in all racial and ethnic groups. However, the trend was not seen among women or among people infected with the AIDS virus through heterosexual contact—two groups that account for an increasing proportion of the total number of Americans with AIDS. . . .

" 'Like much in recent AIDS news, this news is mixed,' said Christine Lubinski, deputy executive director of the AIDS Action Council, which represents hundreds of AIDS service organizations in the country. 'It's good to see that AIDS deaths declined . . . however the deaths are increasing for women, and the infection rates are increasing for people of color. What we now need to do is to ensure that everyone at risk for HIV, or living with HIV, has access to good prevention and health care.'

"Worldwide, AIDS deaths continue to rise. Last year, more than 1.5 million people died from the disease, which amounted to about 25 percent of all AIDS deaths since the start of the epidemic." (*Washington Post*, February 28, 1997)

"Last year, drug-company officials and conservative think tanks dominated the debate, bashing the agency and demanding major changes. This year, patients' groups are jumping into the fray on both sides, and will have a big influence on the ultimate fate of the FDA.

"The biggest and best organized is the Patients' Coalition, which is made up of more than 50 national nonprofit health groups, including the American Cancer Society, the Arthritis Foundation, the National Hemophilia Foundation and several AIDS organizations, such as AIDS Action Council and Gay Men's Health Crisis. The coalition is rushing to the FDA's defense, urging Congress to reject proposals it says will weaken the FDA and hurt consumers. But some patient groups take an opposing view and are pressing for sweeping changes at the agency. . . .

"The Patients' Coalition was begun last summer after several nonprofit health groups got tired of hearing industry proposals described as good for consumers when they didn't support them. They were particularly irked that a GOP-backed FDA-reform conference last fall, entitled 'Putting the Consumer First,' featured only industry representatives and congressional critics of the FDA. . . .

"Nevertheless, the Patients' Coalition, with its roster of well-known members, is emerging as a major FDA ally. Even its detractors say it represents one of the agency's best hopes for staving off big changes." (*Wall Street Journal*, February 22, 1996)

Unavailable

# POLITICAL ORIENTATION

# American Association of Retired Persons (1958)

601 E Street, NW
Washington, D.C. 20049
Phone: (202) 434-2277
Fax: (202) 434-6484
Toll-free: (800) 424-3410
Internet: http://www.aarp.org

**PURPOSE**

"AARP is a nonprofit membership organization dedicated to addressing the needs and interests of persons 50 and older. We seek through education, advocacy and service to enhance the quality of life for all by promoting independence, dignity and purpose."

**STAFF**

1,824 total—1,099 professional; 725 support

**DIRECTOR**

Horace B. Deets, executive director. Before assuming his present position in 1988, Deets was director of the AARP Executive Staff Office for seven years. He has also held other management positions since joining AARP in 1975. Previously, Deets worked for the Equal Employment Opportunity Commission and was director of outreach at the Washington Hospital Center's project for alcoholism and drug abuse. He serves on a number of board and commissions. Deets received an undergraduate degree from St. Bernard College and a master's degree from Catholic University.

**TAX STATUS**

501(c)(4)

**BUDGET**

1998—Unavailable
Proposed 1999—Unavailable

**FUNDING SOURCES**

Membership dues, 31 percent; group insurance administrative allowances, 24 percent; programs and royalties, 18 percent; investment income, 15 percent; publications, 13 percent

**SCOPE**

Members: 32.5 million individuals
Branches/chapters: 5 regional offices; 25 state offices; 3,700 chapters
Affiliate: National Retired Teachers Association, a tax-exempt organization

**PAC**

None

◆ Advertisements ◆ Awards program ◆ Conferences/seminars ◆ Congressional testimony ◆ Films/video/audiotapes ◆ Grantmaking (AARP Andrus Foundation [provides grants for applied research in gerontology at universities throughout the United States]) ◆ Grassroots organizing ◆ International activities ◆ Internet (electronic bulletin boards, Web site) ◆ Legal assistance ◆ Legislative/regulatory monitoring (federal and state) ◆ Library/information clearinghouse ◆ Lobbying (federal, state, and grassroots) ◆ Media outreach ◆ Member services (AARP Motoring Plan; annuities program; credit card programs; insurance—group health, auto/homeowners, mobile home, and life, investment program—eight mutual funds, purchase privilege program; travel discounts) ◆ Research ◆ Speakers program ◆ Telecommunications services (databases) ◆ Television and radio production (Mature Broadcast News, Mature Focus, Maturity News Service, production and distribution of video news releases) ◆ Training and technical assistance (Experience for Hire promotes use of qualified, experienced professionals to meet changing staffing needs in business; Law Enforcement and Older Persons trains law enforcement officers to help them communicate and deal more effectively with older persons; National Older Workers Information System provides a database for employers; Work Force Training Institute provides training programs and presentations to businesses and organizations on age diversity, intergenerational work teams, employment, and retirement planning) ◆ Volunteer programs (55 Alive/Mature Driving retrains motorists age 50 and older; Grandparent Information Center provides grandparents raising their grandchildren with information and referrals to local support groups and other programs; Health Advocacy Services provides information about health promotion, disease prevention and long-term care, Money After 50 helps lower-income adults develop money management skills; Senior Community Service Employment Program trains economically disadvantaged older persons and helps place them in permanent jobs; Senior Environmental Employment Program places qualified individuals age 55 and older in full-time and part-time paid positions in the Environmental Protection Agency; Tax-Aide uses volunteer tax counselors trained by AARP in cooperation with the Internal Revenue Service; Widowed Persons Service provides organizational and training resources to local groups interested in community-wide programs to serve newly widowed men and women; Women's Financial Information Program gives training in financial decision-making)

## METHOD OF OPERATION

◆ Age discrimination ◆ Consumer protection ◆ Economic security ◆ Health care ◆ Independent living ◆ Long-term health care ◆ Medicare ◆ Social Security pensions ◆ Worker opportunities

## CURRENT CONCERNS

# PUBLICATIONS

The following is a list of sample publications:

*AARP Purchase Privilege Program*

*Age Discrimination on the Job*

*Are You Struggling to Pay for Medicare?: QMB or SLMB Coverage Could Help You Save Over $500 a Year!*

*Checkpoints for Managed Care: How to Choose a Health Plan*

*Choosing Mutual Funds*

*A Consumer's Guide to Homesharing*

*The Do-Able Renewable Home*

*Do You Have a Low Income and Few Resources?*

*Do You Need Help Paying for Your Health Care Bills?*

*Facts about Financial Planners*

*Finding Legal Help: An Older Person's Guide*

*Grandparents Raising Their Grandchildren*

*A Home Away from Home: A Consumer Guide to Board and Care Homes and Assisted Living Facilities*

*Home Conversion Kit*

*Home Made Money*

*How Well Does Your Home Meet Your Needs?*

*Knowing Your Rights: Medicare Protections for Hospital Patients*

*Look Before You Leap: A Guide to Early Retirement Incentive Programs*

*Managed Care: An AARP Guide for Medicare Beneficiaries*

*Nine Ways to Get the Most from Your Managed Health Care Plan*

*Nursing Home Life: A Guide for Residents and Families*

*On Being Alone*

*Resource Guide for Persons Who Are Blind or Visually Impaired*

*Resource Guide for Persons Who Are Deaf or Hard of Hearing*

*Selecting Retirement Housing*

*Senior Employment Program*

*Setting a Policy Agenda: AARP and Its Members*

*The Social Security Book: What Every Woman Absolutely Needs to Know*

*Social Security Q&A—Earnings Limit*

*Social Security Q&A—Windfall Reduction*

*Staying at Home: A Guide to Long-Term Care and Housing*

*Staying in Charge: 25 Tips to Help You Remain Independent in Your Home and Community*

*A Survey of Retirement Planning Software*

*To Serve, Not To Be Served: A Manual of Opportunity and a Challenge*

*When Your Medicare Bill Doesn't Seem Right*

*Woman's Guide to Pension Rights*

*Writing to Your Federal and State Legislators*

*Your 401(k) Plan: Building Toward Your Retirement Security*

*Your Pension Plan: A Guide to Getting Through the Maze*

Also produces many audiovisual programs on a wide range of issues

# NEWSLETTER

*AARP/NRTA Bulletin* (monthly)

*Connections* (for volunteers; monthly)

*Modern Maturity* (bimonthly magazine)

Convention (biennial)
National Retired Teachers Association (biennial)
Sponsors frequent meetings and forums for internal and external audiences

Allan W. Tull, chair; John G. Lione, vice chair; Joseph S. Perkins, president; Esther (Tess) Canja, president elect; Margaret A. Dixon, immediate past president; J. Kenneth Huff Sr., secretary/treasurer

Other board members:
♦ Jane O'Dell Baumgarten ♦ Beatrice S. Braun ♦ Rutherford Jack Brice ♦ C. Keith Campbell ♦ Douglas C. Holbrook ♦ Charles J. Mendoza ♦ Ann Miller ♦ Mrs. Chris Lamberti ♦ Jane K. Pang ♦ James G. Parkel ♦ Otto H. Schultz ♦ Betty J. Severyn ♦ Kenneth B. Smith Sr. ♦ Marie V. Sonderman ♦ Virginia L. Tierney

"Long dismissed as politically unthinkable, the idea of 'privatizing' Social Security is gaining ground, raising the prospect that the Depression-era federal retirement program will be tied, at least in part, to the ups and downs of the stock market.

"... Now Democrats and Republicans are offering competing proposals that would establish personal retirement accounts for seniors and divert some of the billions of dollars collected in Social Security payroll taxes into stocks or other private investments. Any shift toward privatization would be a sharp departure from the federal government's longtime policy of distributing benefits to retirees according to a fixed formula, based on earnings history and family status, and investing the Social Security trust fund solely in risk-free government bonds. ...

"The idea of shifting Social Security funds into the financial market worries champions of the current system, including some Clinton administration officials. ...

"At a Social Security forum in Kansas City, Mo., earlier this month, Clinton rejected the idea of complete privatization. But he surprised many Democrats by signaling his willingness to consider personal retirement accounts and proposals that would shift Social Security money into the stock market. 'Could you construct some system which also made allowance for private accounts?' Clinton asked. 'I think you could, yes.'

"Leaders of the AARP, the powerful seniors' lobby invited by the White House to co-sponsor the Kansas City forum and three others like it later this year, also have held their fire. 'I think the [personal retirement] accounts are important to take a look at,' AARP executive director Horace Deets said in a recent appearance on CBS-TV's 'Face the Nation.'" (*Washington Post*, April 27, 1998)

"... [M]embers of Washington's power elite gather ... at the Hay-Adams Hotel to celebrate their inclusion in *Fortune* magazine's listing of the most powerful interest groups in the nation's capital. ...

"The Cold War is over, and *Fortune* says those crusty old generals and admirals turned lobbyists who gave us those legendary $600 hammers and toilet seats are no longer power players in Washington. The closest any aerospace lobby came was the International Association of Machinists and Aerospace Workers, a union that was ranked No. 63 in power out of 120 groups. Aside from the omission of the aerospace-defense industry, the *Fortune* list contains few surprises. The selection of the 33-million member American Association of Retired Persons (AARP) as No. 1 came 'to no one's surprise,' the magazine said. No. 2 was the American Israel Public Affairs Committee; No. 3, the AFL-CIO; No. 4, the National Federation of Independent Business; and No. 5, the Association of Trial Lawyers of America.

"The rankings were based on returns from a questionnaire mailed to 2,200 individuals including members of Congress, lobbyists, academics and senior White House staff. A smaller panel had selected the 120 groups." (*Washington Post*, November 20, 1997)

## POLITICAL ORIENTATION

"the nation's largest seniors group" (*Washington Post*, March 4, 1998)

"The AARP is so big and diverse that it sometimes remains quiet on major issues or is slow to adopt positions. And when it commits, Republicans complain, it usually aligns with Democrats." (*National Journal*, May 6, 1995)

# American Council on Science and Health (1978)

1995 Broadway
2nd Floor
New York, New York 10023
Phone: (212) 362-7044
Fax: (212) 362-4919
Internet: http://www.acsh.org

---

"To add reason and balance to debates about public health issues and to bring commonsense views to the public."

---

9 total—7 professional; 2 support; plus 1 intern and 2 part-time

---

Elizabeth M. Whelan, president and founder. Whelan has been president of the American Council on Science and Health (ACSH) since its formation. She was previously a research associate at the Harvard School of Public Health. Whelan holds degrees from Connecticut College, Yale School of Medicine, and the Harvard School of Public Health, where she received her doctorate. She also has authored or co-authored more than 20 books.

---

501(c)(3)

---

1998—$1.2 million
Proposed 1999—Unavailable

---

Foundation grants, 52 percent; corporate donations, 42 percent; individual memberships and publications sales, 7 percent

---

Members: 5,000 companies and individuals
Branches/chapters: N/A
Affiliates: N/A

---

None

---

## METHOD OF OPERATION

♦ Advertisements ♦ Awards program ♦ Coalition forming ♦ Conferences/seminars ♦ Congressional relations ♦ Congressional testimony ♦ Editorial fellowship program ♦ Internet (Web site) ♦ Media outreach ♦ Participation in regulatory proceedings (federal) ♦ Performance rating ♦ Public television documentaries ♦ Research ♦ Speakers program

## CURRENT CONCERNS

♦ Alcohol ♦ AIDS ♦ "Alternative" medicine ♦ Alzheimer's disease ♦ Cancer and carcinogens ♦ Chemicals ♦ Heart disease ♦ HMOs ♦ Lifestyle factors and health ♦ Media coverage of health and environmental issues ♦ Nutrition ♦ Osteoporosis ♦ Pesticides ♦ Pharmaceuticals ♦ Radiation ♦ Risk assessment ♦ Tobacco

## PUBLICATIONS

*The ACSH Definitive Report on Smoking*
*The ACSH Holiday Dinner Menu*
*Alcohol: Defining the Parameters of Moderation*
*Asbestos*
*Aspirin and Health*
*Biotechnology and Food*
*Biotechnology: An Introduction*
*Cancer Clusters*
*Chlorine and Health*
*Chronic Fatigue Syndrome*
*Cocaine Facts and Dangers*
*Colorectal Cancer: Myths, Facts, Possibilities*
*Does Nature Know Best?: Natural Carcinogens and Anticarcinogens in America's Food*
*Diet and Cancer*
*Does Moderate Alcohol Consumption Prolong Life?*
*Eating Safety: Avoid Foodborne Illness*
*The Efficacy, Safety and Benefits of Bovine Somatotropin and Porcine Somatotropin*
*Fat Replacers: The Cutting Edge of Cutting Calories*
*Feeding Baby Safely*
*Fluoridation*
*Growing Healthy Kids*
*Hay Fever*
*Health and Safety Tips for Your Summer Vacation*
*HMOs: Are They Right for You?*
*Irradiated Foods*
*The Irreversible Health Effects of Smoking*
*Is There a Cancer Epidemic in the United States?*
*Laboratory Animal Testing*
*Lawn Care Chemicals*
*Lead and Human Health*
*Low-Calorie Sweeteners*
*Lyme Disease*
*Malignant Melanoma*
*Microwave Ovens*
*Modernize the Food Safety Laws*
*Multiple Chemical Sensitivity*

*Of Mice and Mandates: Animal Experiments, Human Cancer Risk, and Regulatory Policies*
*Osteoporosis*
*Pesticides and Food*
*Pesticides: Helpful or Harmful?*
*Priorities in Caring for Your Children: A Primer for Parents*
*Resolve to be Healthy in '98*
*Smoking or Health: It's Your Choice*
*Vegetarianism*
*Vitamins and Minerals: Does the Evidence Justify Supplements?*

Also publishes brochures and special reports

---

*Inside ACSH* (semiannually)
*Media Update* (semiannually)
*PRIORITIES* (quarterly magazine)

## NEWSLETTER

---

Periodic media seminars on various public health issues

## CONFERENCES

---

A. Alan Moghissi, chairman; Elizabeth M. Whelan, president

Other members:
♦ Norman E. Borlaug ♦ Taiwo K. Danmola ♦ F. J. Francis ♦ Raymond Gambino ♦ Jerald L. Hill ♦ Roger P. Maickel ♦ Henry I. Miller ♦ Albert G. Nickel ♦ Kary D. Preston ♦ R. T. Ravenholt ♦ Fredrick J. Stare ♦ Stephen S. Sternberg ♦ Lorraine Thelian ♦ Robert P. Upchurch ♦ Robert J. White

## BOARD OF DIRECTORS

---

"The American Council on Science and Health, which has tracked magazine nutrition reporting for 15 years, has compiled its latest analysis of the best magazines to consult when you're looking for nutrition information.

"The council is a nonprofit consumer education organization in New York City.

"Since the early 1980s, the council said, the accuracy of reporting has improved. The latest survey, 1995 and 1996, found that most magazines (15 out of 21 surveyed) rated excellent or good in accuracy.

" 'These magazines are no longer looking at diet and foods frivolously, as they do . . . clothing fads,' observed one survey judge." (*Atlanta Constitution*, April 16, 1998)

"Its hype machine is calling the book 'the next "Silent Spring," ' and its author, Theo Colborn, a 69-year-old zoologist, the next Rachel Carson. But some industries are already preparing a campaign to prove that neither 'Our Stolen Future' nor Dr. Colborn has the scientific evidence to fill those giant shoes.

## EFFECTIVENESS

" 'It's innuendo on top of hypothesis on top of theory,' says Elizabeth M. Whelan, president of the American Council on Science and Health, which is partially funded by industry groups. Dr. Whelan first heard about the book . . . she procured a galley 'by some mysterious process' and assigned a toxicologist to start pulling it apart. The council has already prepared an 11-page, point-by-point draft refutation of the book.

"Like 'Silent Spring,' the 1962 environmental classic, 'Our Stolen Future' tells an alarming story. Dr. Colborn . . . and two co-authors write that we are threatening the hormones of our progeny with the tiny but constant amounts of toxic chemicals in our bodies.

"The book is getting a nice boost from the environmental establishment: Vice President Al Gore wrote the foreword . . . and Robert Redford provided a pithy quote for the publicity packet. Some of the research done for the book was underwritten by the W. Alton Jones Foundation, a Charlottesville, Va., endowment whose purpose is to 'protect the Earth's life-support systems from environmental harm.' One of the co-authors of the book, John Peterson Myers, is director of the Jones foundation. (The third author, Diane Dumanoski, is an environmental reporter for the *Boston Globe*.) And when Dr. Colborn isn't writing books, she is a scientist for the World Wildlife Fund. . . .

"With so much of the environmental establishment boosting the book, it's no wonder the book's publisher, Dutton, says it has been receiving 'mysterious' phone calls from people who won't identify their 'clients' but who want a copy of the book—representatives of the chemical, plastics or pesticide industries, the publisher suspects. And, indeed, many people in those industries are talking about the book and its possible impact on them." (*Wall Street Journal*, March 7, 1996)

## POLITICAL ORIENTATION

Unavailable

# American Foundation for AIDS Research (AmFAR) (1985)

120 Wall Street
13th Floor
New York, New York 10005
Phone: (212) 806-1600
Fax: (212) 806-1601
Internet: http://www.amfar.org

"Dedicated to the support of AIDS research (both basic biomedical and clinical research), education for AIDS prevention, and sound AIDS-related public policy development."

**PURPOSE**

56 total—44 professional; 12 support; plus 6 part-time; 4 volunteers; 4 interns

**STAFF**

Jerome J. Radwin, executive vice president and chief executive officer. Radwin has spent more than three decades working for nonprofit organizations in the fields of strategic management, volunteer development, fundraising, marketing, and communications. He formerly held positions as director of the March of Dimes' New York unit and executive director of the National Victim Center. Radwin received his B.A. degree in political science from Idaho State University and attended graduate school there until 1966.

**DIRECTOR**

501(c)(3)

**TAX STATUS**

Fiscal year ending June 30, 1997—$14.85 million
F.Y. 1998—$15.7 million
Proposed F.Y. 1999—$16 million

**BUDGET**

Individuals, 34 percent; special events/projects, 22 percent; corporate donations, 14 percent; planned giving, 12 percent; government contracts, 10 percent; other, 1 percent

**FUNDING SOURCES**

Members: N/A
Branch/chapter: Office in Los Angeles, California, and Washington, D.C.
Affiliates: N/A

**SCOPE**

None

**PAC**

## METHOD OF OPERATION

♦ Advertisements ♦ Awards program ♦ Coalition forming ♦ Conferences/seminars ♦ Congressional testimony ♦ Films/video/audiotapes ♦ Gift solicitations ♦ Grantmaking ♦ Initiative/referendum campaigns ♦ Internet (Web site) ♦ Internships ♦ Legislative/regulatory monitoring (federal and state) ♦ Library/information clearinghouse ♦ Lobbying (federal and state) ♦ Local/municipal affairs ♦ Media outreach ♦ Research ♦ Speakers program ♦ Telecommunications services (databases, Hotline: 800-39-AmFAR, mailing lists)

## CURRENT CONCERNS

♦ Basic biomedical and clinical research on HIV disease ♦ Public and professional education on treatment and research issues ♦ Public policy reforms, including needle exchange for IV drug users ♦ Search for and testing of AIDS treatments and preventive measures, including vaccines

## PUBLICATIONS

*AIDS/HIV Treatment Directory* (biannual)
*AIDS in Nepal*
*AIDS: Reflections . . . Responses*
*AIDS/HIV Clinical Trial Handbook* (English and Spanish)
*AmFAR Report* (periodic scientific publication)
*AmFAR Report Special Bulletin*
*Annual Report*
*Partners for the Cure PROFILES* (bi-annual)

Also publishes brochures and bulletins

## NEWSLETTER

*AmFAR Newsletter* (quarterly)
*HIV/AIDS Educator* (3 times a year)
*HIV/AIDS Reporter* (3 times a year)

## CONFERENCES

Conference on Global Strategies for the Prevention of HIV Transmission from Mothers to Infants
Holds various community forums, continuing medical education conferences, and science of AIDS symposia throughout the year

## BOARD OF DIRECTORS

Elizabeth Taylor, founding national chairman; Mathilde Krim, founding cochair and chairman of the board; Wallace Sheft, treasurer; John F. Briglio, secretary

Other members:
♦ Arlen H. Andelson ♦ William M. Apfelbaum ♦ Mouna E. Ayoub ♦ Zev Braun ♦ Robert L. Burkett ♦ Jonathan Canno ♦ Kenneth Cole ♦ Jane B. Eisner ♦ Wafaa El-Sadr ♦ Beatrix Ann Hamburg ♦ Sandra Hernandez ♦ James C. Hormel ♦ Arnold Klein ♦ Michael J. Klingensmith ♦ Sherry Lansing ♦ Jay A. Levy ♦ Kenneth H. Mayer ♦ Michele V. McNeill ♦ Bill Melamed Jr. ♦ Maxine Mesinger ♦ Richard Metzner ♦ Jane F. Nathanson ♦ Randolph Nugent ♦ Leonard Rabinowitz ♦ Allan Rosenfield ♦ Alan D. Schwartz ♦ Michael D. Shriver ♦ Mervyn F. Silverman ♦ Peter R. Staley ♦ William E. Swing ♦ Edward H. Vick

"The doctor's chicken scratch is barely legible, but to Luis Figueroa the scribbles on the little white slips of paper are precious. They are prescriptions for powerful new AIDS medications that once miraculously revived Mr. Figueroa, who was so close to death last year that his parents brought in a priest in case he needed last rites.

"But there is a problem with the prescriptions. Mr. Figueroa cannot afford to fill them, and the government cannot afford to fill them for him.

"The three-drug cocktail costs nearly $12,000 a year—a sum that is beyond the reach of Mr. Figueroa, an unemployed 33-year-old printer who recently moved here from Washington, leaving his health insurance behind. On a recent morning, he went looking for help at a social service agency for people infected with H.I.V., but he found little solace. . . .

"But as H.I.V. continues to spread among the poor, experts say, the main obstacle is increasingly money.

" 'I call it the therapeutic haves and the therapeutic have-nots,' said Dr. Arthur Ammann, president of the American Foundation for AIDS Research. 'Anybody who walks into a pharmacy in a poor neighborhood and looks at the line of people who are trying to negotiate which drugs they can or cannot get understands this.'

"The problem is generating a host of complex public policy issues as well as anxiety for patients like Mr. Figueroa, who is hoping that his doctor will persuade a drug company to give him the medicine free." (*New York Times*, October 14, 1997)

"The number of AIDS cases diagnosed in the United States dropped last year for the first time in the 16-year history of the epidemic, a trend that Federal officials attributed to aggressive new therapies that keep infected patients healthier, as well as the possibility that fewer people are becoming infected in the first place. . . .

"These positive trends do, however, mask a troubling development: cases among women and heterosexuals who do not use drugs, particularly minorities, are on the rise. . . .

" 'We are seeing a substantial decline for the first time in the epidemic, and that's great news,' said Dr. Patricia Fleming, chief of H.I.V.-AIDS reporting at the Centers for Disease Control and Prevention. 'But it is tempered by the fact that we continue to see increases in some populations, specifically minority men and women.' . . .

" 'This announcement is a sober wake-up call to Americans that heterosexual AIDS is not a myth,' said James Loyce, chief executive officer of AIDS Project Los Angeles.

"Dr. Arthur Ammann, head of the American Foundation for AIDS Research, said: 'We've got a very serious situation in the United States. If you look at the problem in developing countries, it's more heterosexual spread, and rapidly increasing among women. We've got a developing-country situation right here in the United States.' " (*New York Times*, September 19, 1997)

"In New Jersey, more than 40,000 residents are living with HIV, the fifth-highest percentage in the country. Of those, two-thirds have contracted the disease through some connection with intravenous drug use—either because they are users themselves, or the children or sex partners of users, according to the State Department of Health.

"Nationally, as well as in New Jersey, the infection rate is rising fastest among the poor, non-whites and females, health experts say, adding that the trend could largely be curtailed by more liberal state and Federal policies allowing addicts easy access to clean needles.

"Studies done after changes in such laws in New York and Connecticut have bolstered these arguments, as have studies of HIV rates in Australia, which allow easy access to needle exchanges. (In that country, where drug laws were liberalized in 1985, intravenous drug use accounted for only 2.5 percent of all new AIDS cases in 1994.)

"A similar lessening of infection rates is being found among participants in New York City's needle exchange programs, which were legalized in 1992. Saliva tests for the virus have shown infection rates among participants to be 2 percent a year, compared with about 6 percent for those not using the exchanges, according to the American Foundation for AIDS Research." (*New York Times*, April 27, 1997)

"The six-word billboard copy was reviewed and debated. Kenneth Cole, the footwear designer and marketer, favored a bold, urgent plea to promote AIDS research. He did not want to give onlookers pause. He wanted to jolt them. So the final slogan read: 'Prayer Won't Cure AIDS. Research Will.'

"The public service advertisement, one of three sponsored by the American Foundation for AIDS Research, was pasted on buses in 19 cities in a campaign to raise public awareness. But the foundation abandoned the effort last week in a clash between old-time religion and attention-getting advertising.

"The message was too bold and struck an uncomfortable chord here and in Fort Worth, said transit officials, who removed all three advertisements from city buses two weeks ago. 'It offended their sense of religion,' a spokesman for Dallas Area Rapid Transit, Morgan Lyons, said. . . .

"The foundation is withdrawing the advertisements in all cities where they ran, including Atlanta, Boston and San Francisco. In the New York area, advertisements on train station platforms and elsewhere are beginning to come down." (*New York Times*, February 24, 1997)

# POLITICAL ORIENTATION

Unavailable

# American Public Health Association
## (1872)

1015 15th Street, NW
Suite 300
Washington, D.C. 20005
Phone: (202) 789-5600
Fax: (202) 789-5661
Internet: http://www.apha.org

Dedicated "to improv[ing] the public's health. It promotes the scientific and professional foundation of public health practice and policies, advocates the conditions for a healthy society, emphasizes prevention, and enhances the ability of members to promote and protect environmental and community health."

**PURPOSE**

65 professional; plus 1 volunteer and 5 interns

**STAFF**

Mohammed N. Akhter, executive director. Prior to becoming the executive director of the American Public Health Association (APHA) on January 2, 1997, Akhter held positions as chief executive officer of the Missouri Patient Care Review Foundation and Commissioner Public Health in Washington, D.C. He also was a Senior Advisor at the U.S. Health and Human Services Department and served as the chairperson of the Health Policy Council. Akhter received his master's in public health degree from Johns Hopkins University and completed his residency in general preventive medicine at Mount Sinai School of Medicine.

**DIRECTOR**

501(c)(3)

**TAX STATUS**

1997—$9.7 million
1998—$10.3 million
Proposed 1999—$10.8 million

**BUDGET**

Membership dues, 34 percent; publications, 33 percent; conferences, 25 percent; investments and grants, 8 percent

**FUNDING SOURCES**

Members: 32,000 individuals
Branches/chapters: N/A
Affiliates: 20,000 state and local affiliates

**SCOPE**

| | |
|---|---|
| **PAC** | None |
| **METHOD OF OPERATION** | ◆ Advertisements ◆ Coalition forming ◆ Conferences/seminars ◆ Congressional testimony ◆ Educational foundation ◆ Films, video, audiotapes ◆ Grassroots organizing ◆ Information clearinghouse ◆ Initiative/referendum campaigns ◆ Internet (Web site) ◆ Internships ◆ Lobbying (federal, state, and grassroots) ◆ Media outreach ◆ Participation in federal regulatory proceedings ◆ Professional development services ◆ Speakers program ◆ Telecommunications services (fax-on-demand number: 703-531-0894, mailing lists) ◆ Technical assistance |
| **CURRENT CONCERNS** | ◆ Children's health ◆ Environment ◆ Patient's Bill of Rights ◆ Public health infrastrucure ◆ Tobacco |
| **PUBLICATIONS** | The following is a sample list of publications: <br> *The APHA: 125 Years Old—And Approaching the Millennium* <br> *Benchmarks of Fairness for Health Care Reform* <br> *Case Studies in Public Health Ethics* <br> *Designing a Modern Microbiological/Biomedical Laboratory* <br> *Ethics And Epidemiology* <br> *The Future of Long-Term Care: Social and Policy Issues* <br> *Health, Economics, and Development: Working Together For Change* <br> *Improving Outcomes in Public Health Practice: Strategy and Methods* <br> *Managing Health Promotion Programs* <br> *Manual para el Control de las Enfermedades Transmisibles* (16th Edition, Spanish) <br> *Maternal and Child Health—Programs, Problems, and Policy in Public Health* <br> *Planning for Community-Oriented Systems* <br> *Principles of Public Health Practice* <br> *Standard Methods for the Examination of Water and Wastewater* (19th Edition Supplement) <br> *War and Public Health* <br><br> Also publishes audiotapes, reports, and APHA apparel |
| **NEWSLETTERS** | *American Journal of Public Health* (monthly) <br> *The Nation's Health* (11 issues per year) |
| **CONFERENCES** | Annual meeting (fall of each year) |

## BOARD OF DIRECTORS

## EFFECTIVENESS

"Anheuser-Busch's popular animal advertising campaign featuring frogs, lizards and other amphibians has placed it in the doghouse with pediatricians and consumer activists.

"The American Academy of Pediatrics and the American Public Health Association have joined a slew of consumer advocates demanding the brewer stop using animated characters in advertising. These critics claim the animation represents an intentional effort to capture the attention of children.

"Activists say they bought a half-page advertisement to appear in the *Washington Post*. . . . The ad shows a series of characters, starting with the 1987 Bud Light dog, Spuds MacKenzie, and ending with this year's ornery lizards, Frank and Louie." (*Wall Street Journal*, April 10, 1998)

"A White House AIDS advisory panel issued a sharply worded rebuke to President Clinton . . . protesting the administration's failure to support needle exchange programs as a means of preventing the spread of HIV and AIDS.

"The 30-member panel, which was appointed by the president three years ago, voted unanimously to express 'no confidence' in the administration's commitment to stop new AIDS infections. It also sent a letter to Health and Human Services Secretary Donna E. Shalala saying, 'We are increasingly dismayed by your almost complete silence and continued inaction' on needle exchange policy. The issue has been a repeated point of contention between the administration and the Presidential Advisory Council on HIV/AIDS. The advisory council wants Shalala to open the door for federal funding to be used by local communities for needle exchange programs, which make clean needles available for intravenous drug users to keep them from using contaminated needles.

"The panel argues that research has shown that such efforts can prevent the spread of the disease and do not encourage drug use. Its members cite support from the American Medical Association, the American Public Health Association and a National Institutes of Health report." (*Washington Post*, March 17, 1998)

"The nation's largest tobacco companies settled Florida's lawsuit against them . . . by agreeing to pay the state $11.3 billion over the next 25 years and to take steps aimed at reducing underage smoking. . . .

"The deal—possibly the largest approved legal settlement in history—is similar to a settlement with Mississippi, and is the latest sign that the industry has shifted away from its historic posture of fiercely battling every legal challenge.

"The agreement could boost the momentum of the proposed national tobacco settlement, which Congress will take up after the summer recess. That proposal calls for the industry to pay $368 billion over the next 25 years and to sharply reduce advertising and promotion of tobacco products in return for protection from some lawsuits. Florida's settlement would be superseded if the national deal goes through. . . .

"The Florida negotiations had stalled in recent weeks. But depositions last week by the heads of Philip Morris and R.J. Reynolds were crucial in getting a settlement, attorneys for the states said. In those depositions, both CEOs admitted—after caveats that they were speaking from personal belief, not stating corporate policy—that tobacco products kill. Lawyers suing the industry claimed that the statements by Geoffrey Bible and Stephen Goldstone showed a new attitude in an industry that allowed Florida—and, eventually perhaps, Congress—to strike a deal. . . .

"Those supporting and opposing the national settlement proposal yesterday claimed that the news out of Florida supported their position. . . .

"Taking a middle ground, Mohammed Akhter, head of the American Public Health Association, said that Florida's deal increases pressure on the White House and Congress to implement a national settlement, but one that is tougher on industry. Because the heads of the two largest tobacco companies made guarded admissions last week that smoking kills, Akhter said, 'Congress will be hard-pressed to confirm their original settlement.'. . ." (*Washington Post*, August 26, 1997)

## POLITICAL ORIENTATION

Unavailable

# Center for Auto Safety (1970)

2001 S Street, NW
Washington, D.C. 20009
Phone: (202) 328-7700
Internet: http://www.autosafety.org

"Dedicated to reducing deaths and injuries from unsafe vehicle design and defects, improving vehicle reliability and quality, reducing the adverse environmental impact of vehicles, and improving fuel efficiency."

**PURPOSE**

10 total; plus 3 interns

**STAFF**

Clarence M. Ditlow III, executive director. Ditlow was formerly with the Public Interest Research Group. He graduated from Georgetown University Law School and received a master's degree in environmental law from Harvard University.

**DIRECTOR**

501(c)(3)

**TAX STATUS**

1998—$750,000
Proposed 1999—$750,000

**BUDGET**

Contributions, 49 percent; publications, 25 percent; foundations, 14 percent; other, 12 percent

**FUNDING SOURCES**

Members: 15,000 individuals
Branches/chapters: None
Affiliates: None

**SCOPE**

None

**PAC**

♦ Coalition forming ♦ Congressional testimony ♦ Grassroots organizing ♦ Legislative/regulatory monitoring (federal and state) ♦ Library/information clearinghouse ♦ Litigation ♦ Media outreach ♦ Participation in regulatory proceedings (federal and state) ♦ Research

**METHOD OF OPERATION**

## CURRENT CONCERNS

♦ Automotive safety ♦ Consumer protection ♦ Government investigations ♦ Lemon laws ♦ Recalls

## PUBLICATIONS

*The Car Book*
*The Lemon Book*
*Little Secrets of the Auto Industry*
*Magnuson-Moss Litigation Manual*
*Mobile Homes: The Low Cost Housing Hoax*
*Recreational Vehicles: Hazardous to Your Health and Pocketbook*
*The Safe Road to Fuel Economy*

Also publishes consumer action guides, short reports, and statements on automobile and highway safety

## NEWSLETTER

*IMPACT* (bimonthly)
*The Lemon Times* (quarterly)

## CONFERENCES

None

## BOARD OF DIRECTORS

♦ Clarence M. Ditlow III ♦ James Fitzpatrick ♦ A. Benjamin Kelley ♦ Katherine A. Meyer ♦ Jon S. Vernick

## EFFECTIVENESS

"Most air bags are designed to inflate instantly in frontal crashes at trigger speeds—crash impact speeds—as low as 9 mph. The speed of deployment varies from 96 mph to 200 mph.

"The high-speed bags recently have been the subject of some controversy, largely because they have been implicated in the deaths of 91 children and adults in low-speed collisions. . . .

"Consumer groups, such as Public Citizen and the Center for Auto Safety, both based in Washington, have petitioned NHTSA to force automakers to provide detailed information on air bags at the dealership or other points of sale. NHTSA has taken the petition under advisement." (*Washington Post*, February 22, 1998)

"A coalition of auto safety and health service groups urged the government yesterday to give consumers information on the kinds of air bags being installed in new cars and trucks.

"The group also asked the government to require that automakers provide the same kind of information to consumers at dealerships or other points of sale. There are many differences in the way air bags are made and installed. Some are folded differently in the steering-wheel or passenger-side dashboard pouches. They are made with different fabrics and use different inflators, deploy at different trigger speeds, and are mounted on dashboards at different angles. . . .

"But the Center for Auto Safety and Public Citizen, two of the other groups signing the petition, have long contended that some air bags are substantially better than others. . . ." (*Washington Post*, February 12, 1998)

"The auto industry and highway safety groups are bracing for a struggle over how best to protect people in cars hit in the side in traffic accidents.

"American and foreign auto makers asked Federal regulators late last month to abandon the American side-impact standard for a new standard being introduced in Europe, where cars are much smaller than in the United States. American adoption of the European standard would make it easier and cheaper for auto makers to design and build cars that are more similar on both sides of the Atlantic.

"The European standard requires cars to protect their occupants when hit in the side in a crash test by an aluminum sled that simulates a sub-compact car weighing one ton. The American standard calls for occupant protection in crash tests using a sled that simulates a midsized sedan weighing a ton and a half.

"But two of the most influential nonprofit safety groups, Public Citizen and the Center for Auto Safety, have decided to oppose the auto makers, arguing that both standards are inadequate because neither is designed to simulate what happens when cars are hit in the side by light trucks. Many light trucks—a category that includes sport utility vehicles, minivans and pickup trucks—weigh two tons, and some of the fastest-selling sport utility vehicles weigh close to three tons.

"The two safety groups have begun drafting a petition that will ask regulators not to adopt the European sled and instead to begin using a larger, heavier sled that would supplement or replace the American sled, which has been used in crash tests since 1996. The petition will also ask that vehicles be required to protect their occupants' heads better in crashes from the side." (*New York Times*, January 17, 1998)

"A General Motors Corp. pickup truck unveiled 25 years ago has killed 1,600 people and remains the deadliest vehicle on the road because of its side-mounted fuel tanks, two auto-safety groups said yesterday.

"Public Citizen and the Center for Auto Safety predicted in a study that 400 more people will die over the next 15 years because GM won't retro-fit its C/K pickup with tanks housed inside the truck frame. The inside-mounted tanks pose less risk of splitting and causing a deadly fire, the study said. More than four million of the vehicles remain in use. . . ." (*Wall Street Journal*, October 15, 1997)

". . . Ford faces a class action lawsuit filed by five consumers, backed by the Washington-based Center for Auto Safety, accusing the automaker of withholding vital information from the federal government in an investigation of allegedly defective ignition systems. The alleged defect in a variety of 1983–85 Ford vehicles could lead to vehicle stalling and ignition system fires, the plaintiffs said in the suit filed in the Superior Court in Alameda County, Calif. Ford denied the allegations, and said the National Highway Traffic Safety Administration has issued several findings in which it said it could find no ignition defect trends in the cited vehicles. Ford said that all documents in the probe had been filed in a timely and complete manner. . . ." (*Washington Post*, September 12, 1997)

Unavailable

# POLITICAL ORIENTATION

# Center for Science in the Public Interest (1971)

1875 Connecticut Avenue, NW
Suite 300
Washington, D.C. 20009
Phone: (202) 332-9110
Fax: (202) 265-4954
Internet: cspi@cspinet.org *or* http://www.cspinet.org

| | |
|---|---|
| **PURPOSE** | "To conduct innovative research and advocacy programs in health and nutrition, and to provide consumers with current, useful information about their health and well-being." |
| **STAFF** | 51 total—38 professional; 13 support; plus 8 part-time; 4 interns |
| **DIRECTOR** | Michael F. Jacobson, executive director. Jacobson helped found the Center for Science in the Public Interest in 1971. He is the author or coauthor of many publications and holds a Ph.D. in microbiology from the Massachusetts Institute of Technology. |
| **TAX STATUS** | 501(c)(3) |
| **BUDGET** | Fiscal year ending June 30, 1998—$16 million<br>Proposal F.Y. 1999—$17 million |
| **FUNDING SOURCES** | Publication sales, 82 percent; individuals, 9 percent; royalties, list rentals, investments, 7 percent; private foundations, 2 percent |
| **SCOPE** | Members: 1 million individuals<br>Branches/chapters: N/A<br>Affiliates: N/A |
| **PAC** | None |
| **METHOD OF OPERATION** | ◆ Coalition forming ◆ Congressional testimony ◆ Films/video/audiotapes ◆ Legislative/regulatory ◆ monitoring (federal) ◆ Litigation ◆ Media outreach ◆ Participate in regulatory proceedings (federal) ◆ Performance ratings ◆ Product merchandising ◆ Research ◆ Telecommunications services (Hotline 202-332-9110) |

♦ Alcohol ♦ Food safety ♦ Nutrition

*Eating Smart Fat Guide*
*Eating Smart Fiber Guide*
*Healthwise Quantity Cookbook*
*Kitchen Fun for Kids* (video)
*New Vegetarian Cuisine*
*Quick and Healthy Low-fat Cooking*
*The Real Scoop About Diet and Exercise* (video)
*Safe Food*

Also offers informational posters

*Nutrition Action Healthletter* (10 times a year)

None

♦ Anne Bancroft ♦ David J. Hensler ♦ Mark A. Ingram ♦ Michael F. Jacobson ♦ Mark Ordan ♦ Kathleen O'Reilly ♦ James Sullivan ♦ Deborah Szekely

"... [T]he advocacy group the Center for Science in the Public Interest asked the Food and Drug Administration to require that foods be labeled with their caffeine content. 'Consumers have a right to know how much caffeine various foods contain,' said Michael Jacobson, executive director of CSPI. 'Knowing the caffeine content is important to many people—especially women who are or might become pregnant, who might want to limit or avoid caffeine.'

"Consumers can find out how much caffeine a particular product contains by calling the manufacturer's 1-800 number listed on the product, according to the National Food Processors Association. ..." (*Washington Post*, August 6, 1997)

"A method used commonly to prepare cattle for slaughter, called 'stunning,' could let 'mad cow disease' eventually enter the U.S. food supply, a consumer health group warned yesterday.

"There is no imminent risk to Americans because no cases of the fatal brain disease, also known as Bovine Spongiform Encephalopathy (BSE), have ever been detected in the United States, said nutritionist David Schardt of the Center for Science in the Public Interest (CSPI). But a mid-1980s outbreak of the disease in British cattle has been linked to the deaths of more than a dozen people, and if BSE were to appear in the United States, stunning could be a route for its spread from cows to humans, Schardt said. He called the practice 'a hole in the fire wall' protecting humans from the disease.

"Many scientists believe that BSE is transmitted by eating central nervous tissues, such as the brain, of infected animals. Meat packing plants take precautions to remove brain and spinal cord from edible meat to avoid the possibility of spreading the disease.

"But stunning might spread those tissues throughout the animal's body before butchering. The decades-old practice, designed to incapacitate cattle while protecting slaughterhouse workers, renders the animal brain-dead by sending a power-driven plunger through its skull. Because stunning is generally considered to be a humane way of preparing cattle for slaughter, some form of the procedure is required by the federal Humane Slaughter Act. . . ." (*Washington Post*, July 25, 1997)

"It has been called everything from competent to alarmist, well written to hyperbolic. Whatever you call it, *Nutrition Action Healthletter* is selling. Big-time.

"This month the 16-page newsletter hits a milestone: 1 million subscribers. That's more than *The New Yorker* has. *Gourmet. Harper's Bazaar.* And it far surpasses the circulations of other health newsletters. All across America, subscribers will read in their June issue that with Green Giant's new frozen Green Bean Casserole 'clogged arteries are as close as your microwave,' courtesy of the publishers of *Nutrition Action*, the Center for Science in the Public Interest, the advocacy group that everyone either loves or loves to hate. Most recently known for its skewering of unhealthful restaurant meals, CSPI is less widely known for its newsletter, started in 1974 to get nutritionists interested in the politics of food. It was rudimentary but free.

"Nowadays, it's four-color and printed on glossy paper, and subscriptions provide more than 70 percent of CSPI's $13 million annual revenue. With its send-this-postcard-to-your-congressman enclosures and its warnings that every substance short of turnip shavings will block your arteries, *Nutrition Action* still acts as a mouthpiece for CSPI causes, but it's no longer just for nutritionists. . . ." (*Washington Post*, June 4, 1997)

"On one side is Procter & Gamble Co., the world's largest advertiser and the maker of the fake fat olestra. P&G has spent 25 years and $300 million on olestra, which is being test-marketed in Cedar Rapids and two smaller cities as the key ingredient in Max fat-free chips, made by Frito-Lay Co.

"Fighting on the other side is the Center for Science in the Public Interest, a self-appointed watchdog of the nation's eating habits. It hopes to persuade the U.S. Food and Drug Administration to ban olestra. The center has 'been terribly successful at picturing Procter and Frito-Lay as bad people,' says Gary Stibel of New England Consulting Group, a marketing consultant.

"Olestra, which mimics the taste of oils in regular chips, is a sugar- and vegetable-oil-based molecule. Because the molecule is too big for the human digestive system to handle, it passes through the body without adding fat. In January the FDA approved it for use in salty snacks as long as the snacks' packaging carries informational labeling about potential gastrointestinal effects, including abdominal cramping. . . .

"The center, which has waged well-publicized attacks on such popular foods as kung pao chicken, fettuccine Alfredo and movie-theater popcorn, went on the offensive early. When P&G opened a bland page about olestra on the Internet's World Wide Web in March, the center followed quickly, billing its site as 'the truth about olestra.'" (*Wall Street Journal*, July 31, 1996)

Unavailable

# *POLITICAL ORIENTATION*

# Center for Study of Responsive Law (1968)

P.O. Box 19367
Washington, D.C. 20036
Phone: (202) 387-8030
Fax: (202) 234-5176
Internet: csrl@csrl.org or http://www.csrl.org *or*
gopher.essential.org/hh/ftp/pub/csrl

| | |
|---|---|
| **PURPOSE** | "Seeks to raise the public's awareness of consumer issues and encourage public and private institutions to be more responsive to the needs of citizens and consumers." |
| **STAFF** | 15 total |
| **DIRECTOR** | John Richard, administrator |
| **TAX STATUS** | 501(c)(3) |
| **BUDGET** | 1998—Unavailable<br>Proposed 1999—Unavailable |
| **FUNDING SOURCES** | Unavailable |
| **SCOPE** | Members: N/A<br>Branches/chapters: None<br>Affiliates: None |
| **PAC** | None |
| **METHOD OF OPERATION** | ♦ Coalition forming ♦ Conferences/seminars ♦ Freedom of Information Clearinghouse ♦ Internet (Web site) ♦ Initiative/referendum campaigns ♦ Grassroots organizing ♦ Legislative/regulatory monitoring (federal and state) ♦ Participation in regulatory proceedings (state) ♦ Research |

| | |
|---|---|
| ◆ Banking regulations ◆ Computerized access to government information ◆ Drug pricing ◆ Political process ◆ Rights of consumers | **CURRENT CONCERNS** |
| *The Frugal Shopper Checklist Book*<br>*Getting the Best from Your Doctor*<br>*It Happened in the Kitchen*<br>*Spices of Life*<br>*Why Women Pay More* | **PUBLICATIONS** |
| *Nader Letter on Banks and Consumers* (monthly) | **NEWSLETTER** |
| None | **CONFERENCES** |
| Unavailable | **BOARD OF DIRECTORS** |
| Unavailable | **EFFECTIVENESS** |
| Unavailable | **POLITICAL ORIENTATION** |

# Consumer Alert (1977)

1001 Connecticut Avenue, NW
Suite 1128
Washington, D.C. 20036
Phone: (202) 467-5809
Fax: (202) 467-5814
Internet: info@consumeralert.org *or*
http://www.consumeralert.org

| | |
|---|---|
| **PURPOSE** | "To educate policy makers, media, and the public about the value of consumer choice, competition, and sound science in advancing consumers' interests." |
| **STAFF** | 4 total—3 professional; 1 support; plus 1 part-time support; 1–3 interns |
| **DIRECTOR** | Frances B. Smith, executive director. Before joining Consumer Alert in 1994, Smith was a senior executive with a financial services trade group, founder of a financial education foundation, and producer of two documentary videos. Smith also was the founder of an award-winning academic journal, the *Journal of Retail Banking*. |
| **TAX STATUS** | 501(c)(3) |
| **BUDGET** | 1997—$225,000<br>1998—$225,000<br>Proposed 1999—$250,000 |
| **FUNDING SOURCES** | Foundations, 40 percent; corporations, 30 percent; individuals and membership dues, 20 percent; publications, 5 percent; royalties and other, 5 percent |
| **SCOPE** | Members: 3,000 individuals<br>Branches/chapters: N/A<br>Affiliate: National Consumer Coalition, which is a coalition of more than 27 public policy organizations with a combined membership of more than 3.9 million |
| **PAC** | None |

## METHOD OF OPERATION

♦ Advertisements ♦ Awards program ♦ Coalition forming ♦ Conferences/seminars ♦ Congressional testimony ♦ Internet (Web sites [http://www.consumeralert.org *or* http://www.globalwarming.org]) ♦ Internships ♦ Legislative/regulatory monitoring (federal) ♦ Litigation ♦ Media outreach ♦ Participate in regulatory proceedings (federal and state) ♦ Research

## CURRENT CONCERNS

♦ Agriculture subsidies ♦ Benefits of new technology on food production and food safety ♦ Biotechnology ♦ Environmental issues ♦ Federal fuel economy standards (CAFE) ♦ International trade ♦ Privacy on the Internet ♦ Regulatory reform ♦ Risk assessment ♦ Taxation

## PUBLICATIONS

Produces monographs and issues briefs

## NEWSLETTER

*Commonsense Consumer* (monthly)
*Consumer Comments* (bimonthly)
*CPSC Monitor* (monthly)
*On the Plate* (monthly)

## CONFERENCES

Various topical seminars

## BOARD OF DIRECTORS

William C. MacLeod, chairman; Barbara Keating-Edh, president ex officio

Other members:
♦ Carol Dawson ♦ Richard H. Collins ♦ Roger Meiners ♦ Terry Neese ♦ Denny Smith ♦ Richard T. Weiss ♦ Frances B. Smith

## EFFECTIVENESS

". . . Northwest Airlines ran an ad in *USA Today* of a child with his head in a bucket—ostensibly searching for a new vacation spot—the airline got a call from Ann Brown, who heads the CPSC.

"Brown called the airline to remind it that 29 children drowned in 1995 in bucket accidents. Bucket manufacturers have agreed to label their products with a warning of drowning hazards to children.

"The airline saw it Brown's way and pulled the ad immediately. Northwest, as part of its mea culpa, agreed to publicize the dangers of 'hidden hazards' in the home with an article in its in-flight magazine this summer. . . .

"Critics of the CPSC, however, said the intervention was inappropriate because the agency has no jurisdiction over advertising.

" 'Should the National Highway Traffic Safety Administration say no more car chasing in movies?' asked Rich Zipperer, policy analyst with Consumer Alert, a conservative public policy group. 'It's not their job to restrict advertising. It's their job to make sure five-gallon buckets are safe.' " (*Washington Post*, May 16, 1997)

"... The drumbeat of provocative Ms.-information gives the Democrats a clear advantage. The more women are rendered insecure, the greater their felt need for programs that Democrats favor and Republicans reject. Two prominent media watchdogs, Consumer Alert and the Media Research Center, released a joint report after the election analyzing the political content of 13 popular women's magazines over a 12 month period. They found that publications like *Working Woman, Glamour* and *Redbook* routinely 'scare women to death' by overstating risks, and they push hard for protective government programs. (In one year, the 13 magazines gave 115 positive portrayals of government activism compared to 18 articles that were critical.) The report calls women's magazines 'a liberal pipeline to Soccer Moms.'

"Republican strategists were clueless about the extent and significance of the ongoing crusade to scare women and persuade them they are victims. Democrats, on the other hand, understood that the message the women's magazines were giving women was political dynamite. Clinton advisor Ann Lewis boasted of the campaign's '*Redbook* strategy.' When *Redbook*'s editor Kate White heard of it, she presciently informed her readers that they were 'the White House's secret weapon.'" (*Washington Post*, January 5, 1997)

---

## POLITICAL ORIENTATION

"a conservative public policy group" (*Washington Post*, May 16, 1997)

"... Consumer Alert is leading a free market consumer campaign that is helping to to redefine the consumer movement." (*Human Events*, September 23, 1994)

# Consumer Federation of America
## (1968)

1424 16th Street, NW
Washington, D.C. 20036
Phone: (202) 387-6121
Fax: (202) 265-7989

"To advance pro-consumer policy on a variety of issues before Congress, regulatory agencies, and the courts; to disseminate information on consumer issues to the public and the media, as well as to policy makers and other public interest advocates; and to provide support to national, state, and local organizations committed to the goals of consumer advocacy and education."

*PURPOSE*

22 total—14 professional; 8 support; plus 2 interns

*STAFF*

Stephen Brobeck, executive director. He serves on the boards of several nonprofits, including Rand Corporation's Institute for Civil Justice, Alliance to Save Energy, Coalition Against Insurance Fraud, Citizens for Tax Justice, and the National Coalition for Consumer Education. Brobeck has taught at Case Western Reserve University and was involved in a number of local consumer efforts in Cleveland during the 1970s. He graduated from Wheaton College and the University of Pennsylvania.

*DIRECTOR*

501(c)(4)

*TAX STATUS*

1998—$2.3 million
1999—Unavailable

*BUDGET*

Membership dues, conferences, and an awards dinner, 40 percent; honoraria, publications sales, and individual contributions, 35 percent; grants and contracts, 25 percent

*FUNDING SOURCES*

Members: 250 organizations
Branches/chapters: N/A
Affiliate: Consumer Research Center, a 501(c)(3) organization

*SCOPE*

Consumer Federation of America Political Action Committee

*PAC*

## METHOD OF OPERATION

♦ Awards program ♦ Coalition forming ♦ Conferences/seminars ♦ Congressional testimony ♦ Congressional voting analysis ♦ Electoral politics ♦ Grassroots organizing ♦ International activities ♦ Legislative/regulatory monitoring (federal and state) ♦ Library/information clearinghouse ♦ Lobbying (federal and grassroots) ♦ Media outreach ♦ Mediation ♦ Participation in regulatory proceedings (federal) ♦ Performance rating ♦ Polling ♦ Research ♦ Speakers program ♦ Training and technical assistance (State and Local Resource Center "exists to strengthen state and local member groups by supplying them with information, technical assistance, and resources")

## CURRENT CONCERNS

♦ Banking issues ♦ Corporate mergers ♦ Electricity service ♦ Energy efficiency ♦ Food safety ♦ Health care ♦ Insurance issues ♦ Investor issues ♦ Indoor air pollution ♦ Liability and victims' rights ♦ Product safety ♦ Telephone service

## PUBLICATIONS

*1996 Congressional Voting Record*
*1997 CFA Policy Resolutions*
*1998 Directory of State and Local Consumer Organizations*
*An Analysis of Cash Value Life Insurance Policies*
*Auto Insurance: Progress Through Reform but More to Be Done*
*Bank Mergers and the Consumer Interest*
*Banks Charge Higher Fees Than Credit Unions*
*Basic Service Rates and Financial Cross-Subsidy of Unregulated Baby Bell Activities*
*Beyond Cash-and-Carry: Financial Savings, Financial Services, and Low Income Households in Two Communities*
*Bulletin for Older Investors*
*Comments to the FCC on Universal Service* (industry proposes to raise phone rates)
*The Consumer Impacts of Expanding Credit Card Debt*
*A Consumer Issue Paper on Electric Utility Restructuring*
*Consumers Overpay on Loans and Underearn on Savings*
*Consumers Waste More Than $6 Billion Annually on Life Insurance Premiums*
*Current Threats to Effective State Regulation of Insurance*
*Economic Concentration and Diversity in the Broadcast Media: Public Policy and Empirical Evidence*
*Encyclopedia of the Consumer Movement*
*Excess Profits and the Impact of Competition on the Baby Bells*
*Federal Policy and Local Telephone and Cable TV Rates: Rate Shock in the 80s and Prospects for the 90s*
*The High Cost of "Banking" at Check Cashers*
*How Big a Problem is the Financial Planner "Name Game"?*
*Investment Advisor Regulation: Deficient Oversight*
*Last Chance for Local Competition: Policies to Open Markets Before Baby Bells Begin to Sell In-Region, Long Distance Service*
*Medical Malpractice Insurance*
*Mergers and Deregulation on the Information Superhighway: The Public Takes a Dim View*
*Most Credit Life Insurance Still a Rip-off*

*A New Paradigm for Consumer Protection in the Transition to Electric Competition*

*Open Skies, Closed Airports: The Impact of the British Airways-American Airlines Merger*

*Pharmaceutical Benefit Managers*

*Planning for the Future: Are Americans Prepared to Meet Their Financial Goals?*

*Playing It Safe: A Third Nationwide Safety Survey of Public Playgrounds*

*Protect Consumers from Managed Care Mega-Mergers*

*Report and Model Law on Public Play Equipment and Areas (2nd Edition)*

*Sixth Annual Report on the Worst Consumer Ripoffs*

*State Legislators and Insurance Conflicts of Interest*

*A Status Report on the Nation's Health and Safety*

*Stonewalling Local Competition: The Baby Bell Strategy to Subvert the Telecommunications Act of 1996*

*The Telecommunications Act of 1996 One Year Later: Time to Deliver the Goods*

*Universal Service: An Historical Perspective and Policies for the 21st Century*

*Used Car Consumer Survey: CFA and 13 State Consumer Groups Look Under the Hood at Used Car Lots*

Also publishes several brochures

---

## NEWSLETTER

*CFAnews* (8 times a year)
*Indoor Air News* (4 times a year)

---

## CONFERENCES

Consumer assembly (annual)
Sponsors a number of single issue conferences yearly

---

## BOARD OF DIRECTORS

Richard McClintock, president; Katrinka Smith Sloan, secretary-treasurer; Virgil Fodness, Paul Hazen, Irene Leech, Kenneth McEldowney, Regene Mitchell, Alan H. Richardson, W. Gary Sauter, and Mark Silbergeld, vice presidents

Other members:
♦ Ann Azari ♦ Larry Blanchard ♦ Bill Borwegen ♦ Diane E. Brown ♦ James L. Brown ♦ Melissa Burkholder ♦ Alfreda Carlton ♦ Fred D. Clark Jr. ♦ Pete Crear ♦ Vernon Dalton ♦ Walter T. Dartland ♦ Ellen DeWind ♦ Janet Domenitz ♦ Evelyn Dubrow ♦ Glenn English ♦ Jeffrey Fiedler ♦ Jon Golinger ♦ Tom Heller ♦ Hubert Hoosman Jr. ♦ William J. Klinefelter ♦ George J. Kourpias ♦ Robert Krughoff ♦ Dan McCurry ♦ Larry M. Mitchell ♦ Florence M. Rice ♦ Kenneth Robinson ♦ Phyllis Rowe ♦ Rosemary Shahan ♦ Charles E. Snyder ♦ William A. Spratley ♦ Leland Swenson ♦ Joseph S. Tuchinsky

---

## EFFECTIVENESS

"American consumers continued to add substantially to their credit card balances this year, incurring annual interest charges that exceed $1,000 for many households and in many cases digging themselves a financial hole they can escape only through bankruptcy, according to a study released yesterday.

"The report, by the Consumer Federation of America, said much of the problem is a result of consumers' lack of self-discipline, but it also accused some banks and other credit card lenders of enticing consumers who are ill-prepared to handle credit responsibly. The report is 'fundamentally bad news,' said Stephen Brobeck, the CFA's executive director. Brobeck said he had expected that rising losses would by now have caused card issuers to curb their marketing and adopt tougher standards. But while some institutions have done that, others have continued to pass out plastic without adequately screening the recipients, he said. . . .

"The CFA study found that total revolving consumer debt rose 6.4 percent, to $529.7 billion, at the end of October, from $498 billion at the end of 1996. After subtracting for non-credit-card debt and so-called convenience use—charges incurred by consumers but then paid off in full at the end of the month—CFA concluded that American families were carrying credit card debt in excess of $450 billion." (*Washington Post*, December 17, 1997)

"Consumer and business groups asked the Federal Communications Commission to renew its push to reduce charges local telephone carriers collect to connect long-distance calls. . . .

" 'If the FCC will follow the wisdom of this filing . . . consumers and business users will save $8 billion to $10 billion in long-distance costs, and local rates will be driven down to cost,' said Gene Kimmelman, co-director of Consumers Union. 'We will finally start seeing the fruits of competition.' The petition was filed by the Consumer Federation of America, the International Communications Association and the National Retail Federation. Consumers Union said it supports the filing." (*Wall Street Journal*, December 10, 1997)

"Last week, the Consumer Federation of America, Public Citizen and Consumers Union, along with states' attorneys general, pushed to derail legislation moving quickly through Congress that would decide how much damage a car must suffer in an accident before it is technically considered salvage—a polite word for junk. In a nutshell, the legislation would encourage states to stamp on the ownership certificates, or titles, of used cars that they are salvage when repairs after an accident account for 80 percent of the car's pre-crash value. Cars more than seven model years old, or worth more than $7,500, would not be covered by the law, regardless of their condition.

"The bill has outraged consumer groups and law enforcement officials who are seeking a much broader definition of salvage vehicles and better disclosure of a vehicle's true condition to warn car owners that they may be driving a rebuilt wreck.

"The Consumer Federation of America said in congressional testimony that the bill is 'an astonishingly bad piece of proposed legislation that would, in effect, actually support the sale of more vehicles with undisclosed salvage damage to unwitting consumers.' They point out that about half of used cars sold are more than six years old and would not be subject to the law. . . .

" 'You have millions of people in rebuilt wrecks who don't know it,' said Bernard Brown, an attorney representing the Consumer Federation of America. 'There is no Mothers Against Wrecked Cars.' " (*Washington Post*, November 14, 1997)

"... Congress and federal regulators decided that the nation's pay phone industry, which has $4 billion in annual revenue, should be deregulated because it now contains many companies competing against each other. But that doesn't necessarily mean consumers can choose between companies when they need a public phone—they're pretty much stuck with whatever phone is nearest.

"Competition in the industry takes the form of pay phone companies vying with each other for the right to place their phones in restaurants, bars, shopping malls, airports and other public places. Whichever firm offers the best commission to the proprietor—ranging from 10 percent to 30 percent of the phone's take—generally wins the contract.

"As a result, competition in the pay phone industry often means higher, not lower rates for consumers.

"'Other companies that have raised prices on pay phones can pay higher commissions to business owners,' Daley said. 'We will not be able to match those commissions unless we raise our coin rates.'

"Says Mark Cooper, research director for the Consumer Federation of America: 'There is no competition at the point of sale. You have this perverse incentive where people bid up the price to get the site owner to put their phone at their location. The general public is not going to be protected by competition in the pay phone market.'" (*Washington Post*, November 13, 1997)


"'Is Snoopy a loan shark?' asks actuary Jim Hunt, referring to one of the Charles Schulz cartoon characters that appear in MetLife ads.

"Hunt, who consults for the Consumer Federation of America in Washington, says MetLife charges people who make monthly payments at an annual percentage rate of 17 percent.

"MetLife customers who make premium payments semiannually pay at an astonishing annual rate of 25 percent or 35 percent a year, Hunt said, depending on when the policy was issued. The CFA calls these interest rates 'confiscatory.'

"Furthermore, these rates aren't disclosed. If you check the policy illustration . . . you can figure out the extra cost in dollars and cents. But most people can't turn that into monthly compounded rate of interest. . . .

"The industry's average annual percentage rate is about 10 percent, Hunt said." (*Washington Post*, November 2, 1997)


"Two big consumer groups are expected to announce today a plan to put pressure on the Federal Communications Commission to lower cable-subscription rates.

"Consumers Union, which publishes *Consumer Reports*, and Consumer Federation of America said they plan a news conference to 'attack the agency charged with overseeing the cable industry for its failure to crack down on cable-industry abuses and skyrocketing rates.'

"While the groups refused to release any details, they said they will unveil data showing the largest-ever price increases in cable-TV rates as well as a 'detailed legal plan of action' aimed at pressuring the FCC. . . .

"The consumer groups' effort faces an uphill battle. Last year's telecommunications law calls for further deregulation of the cable industry; one provision would eliminate regulation of pricing of expanded program packages in 1999. While the FCC could take steps on its own, it is likely to face congressional pressure not to reregulate. There is little sentiment in Congress for reregulation of the industry, and lawmakers could block the FCC from acting." (*Wall Street Journal*, September 23, 1997)

"Two of the nation's leading consumer groups have written a letter urging the Justice Department to challenge Visa USA and MasterCard International over rules barring member banks from issuing American Express cards.

"The letter, which is jointly signed by the Consumer Federation of America and Consumers Union, comes as the Justice Department is wrapping up a nearly eight-month investigation into competition in the credit-card industry. Government lawyers have been preparing an antitrust suit against the two credit-card associations, though a final decision on the matter has been postponed until at least April, according to people familiar with the situation. . . .

"Antitrust attorneys said that while the letter probably doesn't carry much legal weight, it does embarrass the two credit-card associations. 'It certainly may reinforce a feeling that there is some consumer harm from these rules and it's not just a battle between a bunch of big financial powerhouses,' said Seymour Dussman, a recently retired attorney in the Justice Department antitrust division. 'To that extent, it may have some influence.'" (*Wall Street Journal*, March 20, 1997)

## POLITICAL ORIENTATION

"the country's largest consumer organization" (*Washington Post*, March 14, 1998)

"Congress shouldn't toughen federal bankruptcy laws, but should instead force credit-card issuers not to approve credit lines worth more than 20% of consumers' annual income, the Consumer Federation of America said in a report released yesterday.

"The CFA, a nonprofit association of consumer groups, said consumers and creditors alike share responsibility for the rising level of credit-card debt and personal bankruptcies. . . .

"The American Bankers Association, the bank industry's biggest trade group, called the CFA's suggestions 'anticonsumer' and 'anticompetitive.'" (*Wall Street Journal*, February 26, 1997)

# Consumers International (1960)

(formerly International Organization of Consumers Unions)
24 Highbury Crescent
London N5 1AL, United Kingdom
Phone: (44) (171) 226-6663
Fax: (44) (171) 354-0607
Internet: consint@consint.org *or*
http://www.consumersinternational.org

| | |
|---|---|
| To "promote consumer policy internationally and assist with institution building." | **PURPOSE** |
| 70 total | **STAFF** |
| Julian Edwards, director general. Edwards has long acted as a leading figure in the United Kingdom and international consumer movement. | **DIRECTOR** |
| Tax-exempt | **TAX STATUS** |
| 1997—$3.34 million<br>1998—$2.5 million<br>Proposed 1999—$2.75 million | **BUDGET** |
| Foundation grants and government contracts, 50 percent; membership dues, 50 percent; publications, less than 1 percent | **FUNDING SOURCES** |
| Members: 235 consumers unions in more than 106 countries<br>Branches/chapters: Regional offices in Penang, Malaysia; Santiago, Chile; and Harare, Zimbabwe<br>Affiliates: N/A | **SCOPE** |
| None | **PAC** |
| ♦ Coalition forming ♦ Conferences/seminars ♦ International activities ♦ Internet (Web site) ♦ Legislative/regulatory monitoring (international) ♦ Library/information clearinghouse (open to public) ♦ Lobbying (regional and international) ♦ Media outreach ♦ Research ♦ Training and technical assistance | **METHOD OF OPERATION** |

## CURRENT CONCERNS

♦ Consumer legislation ♦ Genetically modified food ♦ Information superhighway ♦ Trade issues

## PUBLICATIONS

The following is a sample list of publications:

*Adverse Effects: Women & the Pharmaceutical Industry*
*Asia Pacific Member's Profile*
*Consumers in the Global Age*
*Consumer Lifelines: A Resource Book For Consumer Journalists*
*Developing Consumer Law in Asia*
*Health & Pharmaceuticals in Developing Countries: Towards Social Justice and Equity*
*Inside the Biorevolution: A Citizens Action Resources Guide on Biotechnology and the Third World Agriculture*
*International Consumer Directory 1997*
*IOCU on Record*
*The Model Law for Africa: Protecting the African Consumer*
*The Pesticide Handbook: Profiles for Action–3rd revised edition*
*Tobacco Control in the Third World: A Resource Atlas*

Also publishes pamphlets, briefing papers, and position papers on specific issues

## NEWSLETTER

*African Consumer* (6 times a year)
*AP Consumer* (6 times a year)
*Consumer 21* (quarterly)
*Consumer Currents* (6 times a year)
*Consumidores y Desarrollo* (6 times a year in Spanish)
*World Consumer* (quarterly)

## CONFERENCES

Triennial World Congress (next scheduled for 2000)

## BOARD OF DIRECTORS

Pamela Chan, president; Louise Sylvan, vice president; Rhoda Karpatkin, honourary secretary; Vo Kyung Song, treasurer; Jayen Chellum, Marilena Lazzarini, Sheila McKechnie, and Dick Westendorp, other executive members

Other council members:
♦ Hamdan bin Hj Adnam ♦ Alexander Auzan ♦ Benedicte Federspiel ♦ Anne Lore Kohne ♦ Breda Kutin ♦ Ana Maria Luro ♦ Mathias Some ♦ N.G. Wagle ♦ Armand deWasch ♦ Erna Witoelar

## EFFECTIVENESS

"Metromail Corp. has built a thriving business by finding out everybody else's business. Baby on the way? Metromail knows, and will sell the information to diaper makers and other merchants for 25 cents a name. Moved to a new house? Metromail will furnish your name to junk mailers and telephone pitchmen for prices beginning at 25 cents a name.

"This month, Metromail, a Lombard, Ill., company, agreed to a buyout offer from Britain's Great Universal Stores PLC, which sells everything from household goods to Burberrys raincoats and already owns one of the world's great information storehouses. Days later, American Business Information Inc., an Omaha, Neb., concern with its own data trove, made an unsolicited offer for Metromail. American Business has filed suit in Delaware Chancery Court in Wilmington to block the Great Universal-Metromail deal. . . .

"The battle over Metromail reflects the escalating value of personal data in a wired age. Needham & Co., a Boston investment firm, counts nearly two dozen acquisitions in the field in the past three years alone. Metromail, whose revenue has doubled to $328 million since 1993, is one of the biggest prizes. . . .

"Many consumer advocates are troubled by a possible combination involving these already-large data companies. Unless carefully controlled and regulated, their ability to gather and sell information about unsuspecting consumers could easily turn into an Orwellian invasion of privacy, the advocates say. And with companies' cross-border operations, the advocates fear consumers could have a hard time figuring out how and where to complain.

" 'It's frightening,' says Lucy Harris, a policy officer at Consumers International, a federation of consumer advocacy groups. 'We often don't know how that information is gathered, and we don't give our consent to how it is used.' " (*Wall Street Journal*, March 30, 1998)

"With the furor over 'mad cow' disease fueling fears about the safety of what people eat, European environmental and consumer groups are poised to step up the debate over genetically engineered food. Danish researchers gave biotech foes new ammunition recently by reporting how a rape plant re-engineered to be resistant to an herbicide actually passed the resistance on to a weed that the herbicide is intended to kill. The experiment called into question key assumptions about the reproductive attributes of 'designer' crops and suggested that tougher regulatory scrutiny—perhaps the inclusion of extensive field trials—may be needed to assess adequately the potential environmental effects of these crops. . . .

". . . [C]onsumer and environmental groups are digging in and demanding tougher regulatory scrutiny. The U.K. chapter of Consumers International, an international federation of consumer groups, recently called for enforcement of international rules for field trials and for post-marketing surveillance of bioengineered crops. Once genetically engineered foods are allowed on the market, CI said, comprehensive labeling should be mandatory so consumers can make informed choices about what they eat." (*Wall Street Journal*, March 29, 1996)

Unavailable

## POLITICAL ORIENTATION

# Consumers Union of United States, Inc. (1936)

101 Truman Avenue
Yonkers, New York 10703
Phone: (914) 378-2000
Fax: (914) 378-2900

1666 Connecticut Avenue, NW
Suite 310
Washington, D.C. 20009
Phone: (202) 462-6262
Fax: (202) 265-9548

Internet: http://www.consunion.org *or*
http://www.ConsumerReports.org

| | |
|---|---|
| **PURPOSE** | "Advances the interests of consumers by providing information and advice about products and services and about issues affecting their welfare, and by advocating a consumer point of view." |
| **STAFF** | 480 total, including Auto Test Center and advocacy offices<br>Headquarters: 378 total; 279 professional; 99 support; plus 15 part-time and 2 interns |
| **DIRECTOR** | Rhoda H. Karpatkin, executive director. Karpatkin served as legal counsel for Consumers Union (CU) prior to becoming executive director. She also is vice president of Consumers International, headquartered in London. Karpatkin presently serves on the board of Helsinki Watch and the Center for Health Care Strategies. She is a graduate of Brooklyn College and Yale Law School. |
| **TAX STATUS** | 501(c)(3) |
| **BUDGET** | Fiscal year ending May 30, 1997—$135 million<br>F.Y. 1998—Unavailable<br>Proposed F.Y. 1999—Unavailable |
| **FUNDING SOURCES** | Publications, 92 percent; individuals, 7 percent; foundation grants, 1 percent |
| **SCOPE** | Members: Approximately 5 million *Consumer Reports* subscribers (*Consumer Reports* subscribers can become members by voting in the annual election for CU's board of directors)<br>Branches/chapters: Offices in Austin, Texas, and San Francisco<br>Affiliates: N/A |

None

## METHOD OF OPERATION

♦ Coalition forming ♦ Conferences/seminars ♦ Congressional testimony ♦ Electronic publishing ♦ Films/video/audiotapes ♦ International activities ♦ Internet (Web sites) ♦ Internships ♦ Legislative/regulatory monitoring (federal and state) ♦ Litigation ♦ Lobbying (federal and state) ♦ Media outreach ("From Consumer Reports" newspaper column) ♦ Product testing/reporting ♦ Participation in regulatory proceedings (federal and state) ♦ Performance ratings ♦ Polling ♦ Product merchandising ♦ Publishing ♦ Research ♦ Speakers program ♦ Telecommunications services (Consumer Reports Books: 800-272-0722, Facts by Fax: 800-896-7788, New Car Price Service: 303-745-1700, Used Car Price Service: 900-446-0500) ♦ Television and radio production ("Report to Consumers" daily radio feature, television specials)

## CURRENT CONCERNS

♦ Banking and credit ♦ Economic discrimination ♦ Environmental issues ♦ Financial services ♦ Food safety ♦ Health care reform ♦ Housing ♦ Insurance ♦ Product safety ♦ Telecommunications

## PUBLICATIONS

*Auto Insurance Price Service*
*Consumer Reports Buying Guide* (annual)
*New Car Price Service* (annual)
*Report to Consumers*
*Used Car Price Service* (annual)

Also produces videos and *Consumer Reports Television*

## NEWSLETTER

*Consumer Reports* (monthly; also available via searchable databases, online services, and on cd-rom)
*Consumer Reports on Health* (monthly)
*Consumer Reports Travel Letter* (monthly)
*Zillions* (bimonthly, for 8- to 14-year-olds)

## CONFERENCES

Annual meeting (October, in Yonkers, New York)

## BOARD OF DIRECTORS

James A. Guest, chair; Jean Ann Fox, vice chair; Sharon L. Nelson, treasurer; Bernard E. Brooks, secretary

Other Members:
♦ Robert S. Adler ♦ Christine A. Bjorklund ♦ Joan L. Chambers ♦ Joan Claybrook ♦ Clarence M. Ditlow ♦ Stephen Gardner ♦ Eileen Hemphill ♦ Elizabeth Jensen ♦ Richard L.D. Morse ♦ Joel J. Nobel ♦ Burnele Venable Powell ♦ Milton M. Presley ♦ Norman I. Silber ♦ Julian A. Waller

## EFFECTIVENESS

"Karpatkin said the values she learned in her early years have profoundly shaped every aspect of her personal and professional life. . . .

"Karpatkin's accomplishments in the consumer movement have long been recognized by her peers.

"Her influence goes far beyond *Consumer Reports*, with more than 4.5 million subscribers and 20 million readers each month. The magazine tests and rates products ranging from washing machines to VCRs and features articles on issues such as long-term care insurance and privacy rights.

"CU's strong advocacy role has also helped to influence state and federal public policies. It has an office in Washington, D.C., and regional offices in California and Texas that focus on issues that are of particular concern to low-income people, like food prices and utility rates.

" 'She is the most important consumer leader in the world,' said Stephen Brobeck, executive director of the Consumer Federation of America. . . ." (*Gannett Newspapers*, June 28, 1998)

"A coalition of consumer groups wants federal regulators to halt funding to wire schools and libraries to the Internet, saying long-distance telephone rates should first be forced downward and no new fees should be added to pay for the $2.25 billion program.

"The Consumer Federation of America, Consumers Union and groups representing business telephone users made the plea in May 21 letters to the Federal Communications Commission. Their letters remove a key source of support for the program, which phone companies and foes of the Clinton administration alike have criticized as too costly. The groups want the FCC, before it begins to fund the program, to cut more than $1 billion annually from 'access charges' that long-distance carriers pay to local phone companies to begin and end long-distance calls. The groups want the savings from access-charge reductions to go toward wiring the schools and lowering long-distance rates.

"The $1 billion is the amount, the groups said, that consumers are now being unfairly charged through unrelated new line-item charges that began appearing on long-distance bills earlier this year. Those charges are part of a larger restructuring of subsidies underway at the FCC." (*Washington Post*, May 26, 1998)

"*Consumer Reports*, the magazine that does testing for Consumers Union in Yonkers, publishes at least one article about automobiles in every issue and for 60 years has produced an annual issue devoted to cars. Yet employees associated with the magazine's special televised report on car safety become impassioned when they discuss it.

"Much of that passion will be seen in the half-hour special 'Staying Alive,' produced by Consumer Reports Television, in association with Connecticut Public Television. . . .

"Narrated by Jason Robards, the film explores automotive controversies. Dr. R. David Pittle, a Consumers Union technical director and former United States Consumer Product Safety Commissioner, said, 'We've raised concerns about the safety of sport utility vehicles, which has culminated in our doing a special on all car safety features that reduce deaths and accidents.'. . .

"Dr. Pittle also believes that sport utility vehicles are 'inherently unstable and more likely to roll over.' He said Consumers Union has petitioned the Government to develop tests for the vehicles that will evaluate their handling in emergency situations and their propensity to roll over. The organization has also asked the Government to make the information available to the public and require manufacturers of sport utility vehicles to meet more stringent standards of fuel consumption, matching the guidelines for passenger cars rather than light trucks. The present regulations, he said, have allowed an army of large tanks that doesn't need good gas mileage.' " (*New York Times*, May 17, 1998)

"Last fall, Consumers Union tested almost 1,000 chickens, purchased in 36 cities over a five-week period, and the results were not heartening. It found that 71 percent of the chickens were contaminated with either of two harmful bacteria: 63 percent with campylobacter and 16 percent with salmonella. Eight percent of the chickens had both. Only 29 percent were free of contamination.

"The chickens tested were Perdue, Tyson, Holly Farms, Foster Farms, Country Pride, Bell & Evans, Green Pastures, Rocky Junior and Wellington Farms Free Range.

"What was worse, the so-called premium chickens—more expensive and free-range—were the most contaminated.

"Public health officials estimated that campylobacter was responsible for 1.1 million to 7 million food-borne illnesses each year and between 110 and 1,000 deaths. Salmonella, they said, was responsible for 700,000 to 4 million illnesses and the deaths of as many as 2,000." (*New York Times*, February 25, 1998)

"Two big consumer groups are expected to announce today a plan to put pressure on the Federal Communications Commission to lower cable-subscription rates.

"Consumers Union, which publishes *Consumer Reports,* and Consumer Federation of America said they plan a news conference to 'attack the agency charged with overseeing the cable industry for its failure to crack down on cable-industry abuses and skyrocketing rates.'. . .

"As recently as last week, Gene Kimmelman, codirector of the Washington office of Consumers Union, testified before a Senate subcommittee that 'cable rates have shot up more than three times faster than inflation' since the passage of the Telecommunications Act of February 1996. Consumers Union said the Telecommunications Act has failed to 'promote competition and protect consumers.' " (*Wall Street Journal*, September 23, 1997)

"Discovering things product designers would have rather learned on their own is the mission of Consumers Union. For the last 61 years its motto—'Test, Inform, Protect'—has inspired testers to drop bowling balls on mattresses to test comfort and durability, tumble luggage around in a giant torture chamber to simulate airline abuse, stretch socks on a machine that looks like the medieval rack, and cleverly stretch, poke, tear, burn or otherwise violate the warranty of virtually every class of products for sale in the U.S.

"In a world of Niketowns, Disney stores, megamalls and other cathedrals to the evangelizing power of marketing, the skeptics and product testers at Consumers Union are capitalism's modern unrepentant heretics. But during six decades of publishing product reviews that celebrate performance over style and value over faddism, Consumers Union and its authoritative magazine *Consumer Reports* have not only avoided being burned at the stake by its critics, it has produced its own army of passionate consumers.

"The 65-year-old head of Consumers Union is Rhoda Karpatkin, who has been running the place for more than 20 years. Under her leadership, the circulation of *Consumer Reports* has more than doubled; moved from a leaky, rat-infested building to a modern $40 million testing facility; and revenues have soared from about $16 million to more than $100 million annually. Today Consumer Union is a nonprofit with a stunning cash engine and a mission Karpatkin says hasn't changed, even though the marketplace barely resembles the Betty Crocker and Geritol era of her youth. 'Our readers are information seekers, not status seekers. I would say that we have always been the consumer's antidote to manipulation.'...

"*Consumer Reports* is one of the few magazines that can make guaranteed national headlines by issuing a product warning. Its tests of pesticides in the sixties and seventies were partly responsible for important safety modifications to aerosol sprayers and for the elimination of some products altogether. 'I've seen pesticides come and go,' says chemist Ed Miller, the most senior worker at Consumers Union with more than 40 years on the job. It was his almost single-handed warning of the dangers of the chemical DDVP that eventually led to the removal of the Shell No-Pest Strip, a hanging indoor insecticide, from the market." (*International Design Magazine*, May 1997)

---

"Consumer Union has set the standard for objective, reliable information for the shopping public.

"True to its role as an independent, nonprofit testing and information organization serving consumers, CU accepts no advertising and allows no use of its ratings for commercial purposes." (*Honolulu Advertiser*, November 9, 1997)

"*Consumer Reports* has become one of the most trusted institutions in America. Its tests, carefully documented in photographs as well as words, offer images that are both sheer technology and rampant surrealism: Man Ray and Thomas Edison getting together to run a lab.

"Consumers Union helped bring into the mainstream a tradition of consumer activism that had grown out of the muckraking years of the beginning of the century, when journalists' exposes led to the establishment of the Food and Drug Administration. The tradition runs deep and steady, from Ida Tarbell and Upton Sinclair to Vance Packard, Jessica Mitford, and 'Sixty Minutes.'...

"Today product testing has become so dominant a feature of life, and the consumer so much more the focus of our economy than the worker, that the heroism of the assembly line has been succeeded by the anti-heroism of product testing...."

## POLITICAL ORIENTATION

"In a litigious society, manufacturers are forced to do more and more testing of their own. To know the limits of a product—its 'performance envelope,' as test pilots say—you must test it to destruction: overload it with sandbags, worry it back and forth until it snaps, or fill it until it bursts. IBM boasts that the new folding keyboard of its Thinkpad laptop computer has been opened and closed 25,000 times. Automakers regularly talk of how many miles of desert or tundra their vehicles have traversed before being judged good enough to sell. And in car commercials, actors and race-car drivers have been forsworn in favor of crash-test dummies.

"Meanwhile, Consumer Union goes on stolidly, testing everything under the sun, remaining the bland, unimpeachable standard of earnest impartiality at the center of our image-hawking, competition-fired consumer universe." (*Audacity*, Spring 1996)

# Co-op America (1982)

1612 K Street, NW
Suite 600
Washington, D.C. 20006
Phone: (202) 872-5307
Fax: (202) 331-8166
Internet: info@coopamerica.org *or* http://www.coopamerica.org

| | |
|---|---|
| **PURPOSE** | "Co-op America collaborates with both businesses and individual consumers in order to promote sustainable and just societies. Every purchase or management decision has impact. . . . [Co-op America] emphasizes economic democracy, worker participation, and cooperation." |
| **STAFF** | 23 professional; plus 4 part-time and 10 interns |
| **DIRECTOR** | Alisa Gravitz, executive director. Gravitz has been involved with environmental issues for more than fifteen years. She serves on the board of several social change organizations, including the Coalition for Environmentally Responsible Economies (CERES), and coauthored the CERES Principles, guidelines for business to protect the environment. Her background includes work in marketing and a position in the U.S. Department of Energy. Gravitz holds a B.A. from Brandeis University and an M.B.A. from Harvard Business School. |
| **TAX STATUS** | 501(c)(3) |
| **BUDGET** | 1998—$2.5 million<br>Proposed 1999—Unavailable |
| **FUNDING SOURCES** | Individual donations, 75 percent; foundation grants, 10 percent; other, 15 percent |
| **SCOPE** | Members: 50,000 individuals; 2,000 businesses<br>Branches/chapters: N/A<br>Affiliates: N/A |
| **PAC** | None |

| | |
|---|---|
| ◆ Advertisements ◆ Boycotts ◆ Coalition forming ◆ Education/information ◆ Grassroots organizing ◆ Internet (Web site) ◆ Library/information clearinghouse ◆ Media outreach ◆ Performance ratings ◆ Research ◆ Shareholder resolutions ◆ Telecommunications services (databases, electronic bulletin boards, mailing lists) | *METHOD OF OPERATION* |
| ◆ Corporate social and environmental responsibility ◆ Energy efficiency ◆ Environmentally and socially responsible purchasing practices ◆ Globalization ◆ Improving quality of life ◆ Pesticide exports to the Third World ◆ Rainforest replenishment ◆ Recycling ◆ Socially responsible investing ◆ Sustainable consumption | *CURRENT CONCERNS* |
| *Action Guide to Finding a Socially Responsible Job* *Financial Planning Handbook* *National Green Pages* *Woodwise Consumer Guide* | *PUBLICATIONS* |
| *The Co-op America Quarterly (CAQ)* (quarterly) *Boycott Action News* (quarterly in *CAQ*) *Co-op America Connections* (quarterly for business members) | *NEWSLETTER* |
| Seminars for small businesses | *CONFERENCES* |
| Diane Keefe, president; Elizabeth Glenshaw, vice president; Denise Hamler, secretary; Alisa Gravitz, executive director; Paul Freundlich, ex officio president<br><br>Other members:<br>◆ Ben Edelman ◆ Elizabeth Elliott McGeveran ◆ Steven Morris ◆ Liz Wessel | *BOARD OF DIRECTORS* |
| "Probably the most comprehensive source for environmentally friendly products and services is the National Green Pages, published by Co-op America, a Washington-based nonprofit. 'There's a direct link between what people are consuming and what's happening to the environment,' says Denise Hamler, project director for the publication. 'It's very, very important that environmentally sensitive consumer products are made widely available.'<br><br>"To help reach that goal, the National Green Pages lists nearly 1,600 businesses and organizations around the country that have met Co-op America's guidelines on environmental and social responsibility. Companies listed in the directory sell everything from recycled-paper envelopes and mailing tubes to chemical-free fertilizers and pest controls. The directory also features architectural firms, bed-and-breakfasts, landscaping companies, public relations agencies and other entities that have made environmental responsibility a key part of their business." (*Washington Post*, April 19, 1996) | *EFFECTIVENESS* |

"Flush with cash, mutual funds are seeing green, but Co-op America, a Washington group that promotes socially conscious investing, contends that they are not investing green.

"The group reported yesterday that 15 of the nation's largest mutual funds, including those offered by Fidelity Investments, the Vanguard Group, Capital Research and Management Company and the Janus organization, owned $30 billion, or an average of $2 billion each, of shares of companies the group regards as environmentally unfriendly. . . .

"Topping Co-op America's list of environmentally unfriendly mutual funds was the $20 billion Vanguard Index Trust 500 Portfolio, which mirrors the Standard & Poor's 500-stock index. The fund had big positions in 81 energy, tobacco, chemical and other companies that Co-op America found objectionable." (*New York Times,* April 13, 1996)

"Many tobacco stocks pop up in the biggest funds. Nine of the 15 biggest funds recently listed tobacco stocks among their 10 largest holdings, according to a study by Co-op America, a consumer group based in Washington, which provides information on the social and economic consequences of investing. The data were based on the most recent complete shareholder reports from each fund at the time, and in some cases are now many months old.

"Together, the nine funds owned 70 million shares worth about $3 billion. The heaviest concentrations were at the Fidelity Growth and Income fund and the Investment Company of America, each of which listed Philip Morris as its biggest holding.

"Six of the 15 biggest funds held no tobacco stocks at the time of the study, including the Fidelity Magellan fund, the nation's largest. . . ." (*New York Times,* March 17, 1996)

# POLITICAL ORIENTATION

Unavailable

# Families USA Foundation (1981)

1334 G Street, NW
Suite 300
Washington, D.C. 20005
Phone: (202) 628-3030
Fax: (202) 347-2417
Internet: info@familiesusa.org *or* http://www.familiesusa.org

---

"To secure high-quality, affordable health care for all Americans."

**PURPOSE**

---

30 total—23 professional; 7 support; plus 6 interns

**STAFF**

---

Ron Pollack, executive director. Pollack has served as director of Families USA Foundation since 1983. Previously, he held positions as dean of the Antioch School of Law and founding president of Food Research and Action Center. He currently serves as a member of the President's Advisory Commission on Consumer Protection and Quality in the Health Care Industry. Pollack received his J.D. degree in 1968.

**DIRECTOR**

---

501(c)(3)

**TAX STATUS**

---

1997—$4.4 million
1998—$4.6 million
Proposed 1999—$4.7 million

**BUDGET**

---

Foundation grants, 67 percent; endowment, 24 percent; individuals, 4 percent; conferences, 4 percent; publications, 1 percent

**FUNDING SOURCES**

---

Members: Approximately 10,000 affiliated activists
Branch/chapter: N/A
Affiliates: N/A

**SCOPE**

---

None

**PAC**

| **METHOD OF OPERATION** | ♦ Awards program ♦ Coalition forming ♦ Conferences/seminars ♦ Congressional testimony ♦ Films, video, audiotapes ♦ Grantmaking ♦ Information clearinghouse ♦ Internet (Web site) ♦ Internships ♦ Legislative/regulatory monitoring (federal and state) ♦ Media outreach ♦ Polling ♦ Research ♦ Telecommunications services ♦ Technical assistance ♦ Training |
|---|---|
| **CURRENT CONCERNS** | ♦ Changes in Medicaid and Medicare ♦ Creation of a Patients' Bill of Rights ♦ Creation of patients' ombudsman programs ♦ Implementation of Children's Health Insurance Program ♦ Incremental improvements in access to health care |
| **PUBLICATIONS** | *Comparing Medicare HMOs: Do They Keep Their Members?*<br>*Consumer Health Action '98 Tool Kit*<br>*Doing Without: Sacrifices Families Make to Provide Home Care Families USA*<br>*A Guide to Access to Providers in Medicaid Managed Care*<br>*A Guide to Complaints, Grievances, and Hearings Under Medicaid Managed Care*<br>*A Guide to Marketing and Enrollment In Medicaid Managed Care*<br>*A Guide to Meeting the Needs of People with Chronic and Disabling Conditions in Medicaid Managed Care*<br>*Health Action '98 Tool Kit*<br>*Health Care Choices for Today's Consumer*<br>*Hit and Miss: State Managed Care Laws*<br>*HMO Consumers at Risk: States to the Rescue*<br>*How Americans Lose Health Insurance*<br>*Making Radio Work For You*<br>*Medicare Managed Care: Securing Beneficiary Protections*<br>*Monitoring Medicare HMOs: A Guide to Collecting and Interpreting Available Data*<br>*One Out of Three: Kids Without Health Insurance, 1995–1996*<br>*A Preliminary Guide to Expansion of Children's Health Coverage*<br>*Premium Pay: Corporate Compensation in America's HMOs*<br>*Shortchanged: Billions Withheld from Medicare Beneficiaries*<br>*State Children's Health Insurance Program: Resources for Advocates*<br><br>Also offers a public service—subscribers automatically receive reports, issue briefs, and other publications |
| **NEWSLETTER** | *asap!* (periodic) |
| **CONFERENCES** | Annual conference (each January in Washington, D.C.) |
| **BOARD OF DIRECTORS** | ♦ Robert Crittenden ♦ Judith Feder ♦ Douglas A. Fraser ♦ Lance E. Lindblom ♦ Velvet G. Miller ♦ Angela Z. Monson ♦ Charlene Rydell ♦ Murray Saltzman ♦ Fernando Torres-Gil ♦ Philippe Villers |

"A Presidential commission that recommended a bill of rights for patients is now deadlocked on the important question of how to enforce those rights.

"With its final meeting just a few days away, the panel cannot agree on whether new Federal laws are needed to protect consumers against abuses by health insurance companies, as President Clinton contends.

"The 34-member commission approved the bill of rights in November, but remains deeply divided over the need for a 'patient protection' law to supplement the voluntary efforts of health plans and employers in securing those rights.

"Moreover, the commission is split over proposals to guarantee compensation for injuries that people suffer when they are improperly denied health care benefits. . . .

"Ronald F. Pollack, executive director of Families USA, a consumer organization, spoke for one group of commission members when he said: 'A right without a remedy is not a right. For us to walk away from this issue and be silent would be unconscionable.'. . .

"The commission includes a wide range of health-care experts. Consumer advocates, doctors and some labor union leaders on the panel favor more Federal regulation of health insurance. . . .

"But panel members from insurance companies, health maintenance organizations and businesses of all sizes have generally opposed new regulation. They say that it would make health benefits more costly, so that employers would cut back coverage, and more people would be uninsured." (*New York Times*, March 9, 1998)

"President Clinton is poised to endorse a broad range of patient protections being developed by an advisory panel charged with improving the quality of managed health care, administration officials said. . . .

"Dubbed the 'Consumer's Bill of Rights,' the recommendations are being hammered out by a subcommittee of the president's advisory panel on consumer protections and quality in the health-care industry. The full 34-member commission, which was appointed in March, is scheduled to debate the recommendations today and may adopt them as early as tomorrow.

"But some consumer representatives, however, worry that the proposed protections might not go far enough and changes still may occur. Ron Pollack, a member of the subcommittee and executive director of Families USA, a health-policy group, said that he will continue to press for more sweeping protections. He contended that while the proposed changes would be a step forward, they are far too limited. 'It's like having the true Bill of Rights without the freedoms of speech or religion,' he said. 'The rest of the rights may be worth adopting, but the document still falls short overall.'" (*Wall Street Journal*, October 21, 1997)

"A political backlash is building against managed care across the country as doctors and patients protest what they see as potentially dangerous penny-pinching by the health-care industry. . . .

"The regulatory movement has been fueled by a steady drumbeat of publicity about alleged failings or shortcomings of managed-care plans. The legislative effort in Texas was energized by a March report in which the state Department of Insurance accused Kaiser Foundation Health Plan of Texas Inc. of 'an unacceptable disregard for quality of care issues.' . . .

"Some of the legislation has the political halo of motherhood itself. By the end of 1996, 28 states and the federal government had set minimum coverage standards for the length of a hospital stay when a woman delivers a baby, according to Families USA Foundation, an advocacy group. The bills were a reaction to 'drive-through deliveries,' in which mothers were being sent home within a day of giving birth. . . .

"According to Families USA, at least 23 states including Maryland and Virginia have mandated that HMOs allow women some measure of guaranteed access to obstetrician/gynecologists instead of leaving that to the discretion of 'gatekeeper' physicians. Last year, New York ordered HMOs to allow specialists to serve as primary doctors for patients with life-threatening, degenerative or disabling conditions. . . .

"Is the wave of state legislation destroying managed care?

" 'We have not reached Armageddon,' said Laudicina of the Blue Cross and Blue Shield Association, whose member health plans have 39.3 million managed-care enrollees. However, 'the effectiveness of managed care has been somewhat limited in those states where multiple anti-managed-care bills have been enacted,' she said." (*Washington Post*, June 30, 1997)

## POLITICAL ORIENTATION

"a liberal advocacy" (*Wall Street Journal*, July 14, 1997)

# Food Research and Action Center
## (1970)

1875 Connecticut Avenue, NW
Suite 540
Washington, D.C. 20009
Phone: (202) 986-2200
Fax: (202) 986-2525
Internet: http://www.frac.org

| | |
|---|---|
| "To improve public policies to eradicate hunger and undernutrition in the United States." | *PURPOSE* |
| 20 total | *STAFF* |
| Jim Weill, president | *DIRECTOR* |
| 501(c)(3) | *TAX STATUS* |
| 1998—Unavailable<br>Proposed 1999—Unavailable | *BUDGET* |
| Unavailable | *FUNDING SOURCES* |
| Members: N/A<br>Branches/chapters: N/A<br>Affiliate: Campaign to End Childhood Hunger | *SCOPE* |
| None | *PAC* |
| ◆ Coalition forming ◆ Conferences/seminars ◆ Congressional testimony ◆ Grassroots organizing ◆ Internet (Web site) ◆ Legal assistance ◆ Legislative/regulatory monitoring (federal and state) ◆ Library/information clearinghouse ◆ Lobbying (federal, state, and grassroots) ◆ Media outreach ◆ Participation in regulatory proceedings (federal) ◆ Research ◆ Training and technical assistance | *METHOD OF OPERATION* |

## CURRENT CONCERNS

Hunger and undernutrition in the United States, with emphasis on childhood hunger

## PUBLICATIONS

*Community Childhood Hunger Identification Project (CCHIP): A Survey of Childhood Hunger in the United States*
*Feeding the Other Half: Mothers and Children Left Out of WIC*
*FRAC's Guide to the Food Stamp Program*
*Fuel for Excellence: FRAC's Guide to School Breakfast Expansion*
*Hunger Doesn't Take a Vacation*
*The Relationship Between Nurtition and Learning*
*School Breakfast Scorecard*
*School's Out, Let's Eat*
*State of the States: A Profile of Food and Nutrition Programs Across the Nation*
*WIC: A Success Story*
*WIC Works: Let's Make It Work for Everyone*

## NEWSLETTER

None

## CONFERENCES

National conference (biennial, in Washington, D.C.)

## BOARD OF DIRECTORS

Carol Tucker Foreman, chair; Matthew E. Melmed, vice chair

Other members:
♦ Elliot Bloom ♦ Dagmar Farr ♦ David I. Greenberg ♦ Hilarie Hoting ♦ Charles Hughes ♦ Jerry Klepner ♦ Clinton Lyons ♦ Daniel Marcus ♦ Marshall L. Matz ♦ John G. Polk ♦ Gerald Sanders ♦ W. Gary Sauter ♦ Marion Standish ♦ Judith H. Whittlesey

## EFFECTIVENESS

"The District's School Breakfast Program has had the second-highest increase in participation in the country, according to a recent report by the Food Research and Action Center and D.C. Hunger Action.

"The study found a 22.3 percent participant increase over the last year. A total of 20,477 low-income students have benefited from the District's program in 1997." (*Washington Post*, November 6, 1997)

"A national anti-hunger group singled out the District . . . saying its efforts to increase the number of local children in a federal summer nutrition program were a model for other urban communities.

"The federal program, administered by the U.S. Department of Agriculture, targets the 14.3 million children nationwide who receive free or reduced-price lunches during the school year. A report released . . . by the Food Research and Action Center said that last summer, the nationwide program reached only one in six children who qualified. But in the District, the average number of children served last summer had more than tripled from previous years and reached 42 percent of eligible children. In 1996, 19,805 children received free lunch daily in the District, compared with 6,827 children the previous summer. . . .

"'We have a federal program that works, but it's not being taken advantage of nearly enough in many parts of the country,' said Mike Haga, a senior field organizer for the center. He attributed the District's success to its ability to create lunch programs within existing recreation centers and other community agencies.

"Haga also credited District officials and anti-hunger groups for launching an advertising campaign on city buses and subways and creating a 24-hour hot line. . . ." (*Washington Post,* July 11, 1997)


"President Clinton's $21.6 billion welfare spending package has finally silenced his critics on the left—at least for today. . . .

"But looking ahead, advocates for the poor fret that the president's willingness to restore aid to legal immigrants and food-stamp recipients, and to help beneficiaries seeking work, could evaporate in expected budget negotiations. 'I'm skeptical he'll stay with it,' says former administration welfare official Wendell Primus, who resigned last year in protest of program cuts. They fear, for example, the president would settle for agreement with Republicans on the welfare-to-work provisions and then back down on the controversial food-stamp and immigrant restorations.

"Their skepticism is driven not only by the president's past record—welfare advocates cite his willingness to sign the bill last year after first opposing it—but the recent departure from the White House of voices sympathetic to their cause, in particular former chief-of-staff Leon Panetta.

"'Without him, we have to make our case from scratch,' says Ed Cooney, vice president of the Food Research and Action Center. His organization, he adds, now turns more frequently to the Agriculture Department. For example, last year Mr. Panetta played a key role in talks with Republicans in softening food-stamp cuts and delaying benefit cutoffs for legal immigrants." (*Wall Street Journal,* February 7, 1997)

Unavailable

*POLITICAL ORIENTATION*

# National Center for Nonprofit Boards (1988)

2000 L Street, NW
Suite 510
Washington, DC 20036
Phone: (202) 452-6262
Fax: (202) 452-6299
Internet: ncnb@ncnb.org *or* http://www.ncnb.org

| | |
|---|---|
| **PURPOSE** | "To improve the effectiveness of nonprofit organizations by strengthening their governing boards." |
| **STAFF** | 30 total—25 professional; 5 support |
| **DIRECTOR** | Judith O'Connor, president. O'Connor became president and chief executive officer in February 1997. Her wide-ranging experience in the nonprofit and public sectors includes service with the American Bar Association, the Council on Foundations, and the U.S. Justice Department. She also serves as a trustee for the National Judicial College and is a member of American Bar Association's Commission on Public Understanding of the Law, Columbia Business School's Institute for Nonprofit Management, and the Independent Sector's Leadership and Management Committee. |
| **TAX STATUS** | 501(c)(3) |
| **BUDGET** | 1997—$3.9 million<br>1998—$4.1 million<br>Proposed 1999—$5 million |
| **FUNDING SOURCES** | Foundation grants, 32 percent; publications, 31 percent; conferences, 14 percent; corporate donations, 11 percent; membership dues, 10 percent; investments, 2 percent |
| **SCOPE** | Members: 10,000 individuals and organizations<br>Branches/chapters: N/A<br>Affiliates: N/A |
| **PAC** | None |

| | |
|---|---|
| ♦ Films, video, audiotapes ♦ Information clearinghouse ♦ Internet (Web site) ♦ Media outreach ♦ Product merchandising ♦ Professional development services ♦ Research ♦ Speakers program ♦ Telecommunications services (Fax-on-demand) ♦ Training | *METHOD OF OPERATION* |
| ♦ Charitable tax exemption ♦ Nonprofit organizations and advocacy ♦ Regulation of nonprofits ♦ Volunteer liability | *CURRENT CONCERNS* |

PUBLICATIONS

The following is a list of recent publications:
*Boards that Make a Difference*
*Doing the Right Thing: A Look at Ethics in the Nonprofit Sector*
*Legal Obligations of Nonprofit Boards: A Guidebook for Board Members*
*Lobbying, Advocacy, and Nonprofit Boards*
*Marketing for Mission*
*Merging Mission and Money: A Board Member's Guide to Social Entrepreneurship*
*Nonprofit Board Answer Book: Practical Guidelines for Board Members and Chief Executives*
*The Nonprofit Board's Guide to Bylaws*
*Nonprofit Governancy Series* (16 booklets)
*Reinventing Your Board*
*Strategic Issues* (Booklet series)
*The Troublesome Board Member*

Also publishes video and audiotapes, booklets, and books

| | |
|---|---|
| *Board Member* (10 issues per year) | *NEWSLETTER* |
| Annual conference<br>National Leadership Forum<br>Also sponsors various workshops and seminars | *CONFERENCES* |
| William M. Cietis, chairman; Edward H. Able Jr., vice chairman and chair-elect; Phyllis J. Campbell, secretary; Ellis F. Bullock Jr., treasurer<br><br>Other members:<br>♦ Jameson Adkins Baxter ♦ James E. Canales Jr. ♦ Robert L. Gale ♦ Geneva B. Johnson ♦ David M. Lascell ♦ Herbert L. Lucas ♦ Jane T. Russell ♦ Lorie A. Slutsky | *BOARD OF DIRECTORS* |
| "The New York State Board of Regents removed 18 of Adelphi University's 19 trustees yesterday, saying they had paid the university's president too much, did not keep track of his compensation and failed to review his job performance. | *EFFECTIVENESS* |

"The Regents, who immediately appointed 18 new trustees, said that two of the ousted board members had improperly profited by doing business with the university and that they had failed to disclose details of their dealings. . . .

"For a year and a half, Adelphi's president, Dr. Peter Diamandopoulos, has been attacked by faculty members and others who criticized what they said were his dictatorial management style; his cutbacks in programs; his salary and benefits package, which reached $523,000 in 1994–95; and his close relationship with the trustees, many of whom he had helped select.

"He was among the trustees who were removed yesterday, but he remains president and had no comment. Under state law, the Regents can remove trustees who misuse their power but can take no action against administrators. . . . 'For the past year and a half,' the university said in a statement, 'Adelphi has been subjected to a well-financed 'corporate campaign' by a small group of dissidents, mainly the directorate of the faculty union, who have long been seeking to gain control of campus policy. Through negative publicity, based on lies, distortion and disinformation, they were able to pressure the Board of Regents to hold public hearings, and then to conduct those hearings in an atmosphere utterly indifferent to both due process and basic fairness.'

"The broader implications of Adelphi's case may be to underscore the cautions that nonprofit organizations should exercise in the oversight of their boards and executives.

"'Individuals serving on any type of nonprofit board can learn several important lessons from this,' said Judith O'Connor, president of the National Center for Nonprofit Boards. 'Executive compensation is a potentially explosive issue. Conflict-of-interest policies are essential, since even the appearance of impropriety can be extremely damaging. And board members should be informed, engaged and not afraid to ask tough questions.'" (*New York Times*, February 11, 1998)

# POLITICAL ORIENTATION

Unavailable

# National Center for Tobacco-Free Kids (1996)

1707 L Street, NW
Suite 800
Washington, D.C. 20036
Phone: (202) 296-5469
Fax: (202) 296-5427
Internet: http://www.tobaccofreekids.org

"To protect kids from tobacco by: raising awareness that tobacco use is a pediatric disease; changing public policies to limit the marketing and sales of tobacco to children; altering the environment in which tobacco use and policy decisions are made; and actively countering the tobacco industry and its special interests."

**PURPOSE**

29 total—20 professional; 9 support; plus 1 part-time professional; 4 interns, and volunteers

**STAFF**

William D. Novelli, president. Previously, Novelli co-founded and served as president of Porter/Novelli, the fourth largest public relations agency in the United States. He later served as executive vice president of CARE. Novelli holds a B.A. and an M.A. from the University of Pennsylvania and pursued doctoral studies at New York University.

**DIRECTOR**

501 (c)(3)

**TAX STATUS**

Fiscal year ending April 30, 1997—$5 million
F.Y. 1998—$9 million
Proposed F.Y. 1999—$10 million

**BUDGET**

Foundation grants, corporate donations, individuals, special events/projects, and grants from other public charities

**FUNDING SOURCES**

Members: N/A
Branches/Chapters: N/A
Affiliates: National Center for Tobacco-Free Kids Action Fund, a 501 (c)(4) organization

**SCOPE**

None

**PAC**

| METHOD OF OPERATION | ♦ Advertisements ♦ Awards program ♦ Coalition forming ♦ Congressional testimony ♦ Demonstrations ♦ Grassroots organizing ♦ International activities ♦ Internet (Web site) ♦ Internships ♦ Legislative/regulatory monitoring (federal and state) ♦ Litigation ♦ Lobbying (federal, state, and grassroots) ♦ Media outreach ♦ Participation in regulatory proceedings ♦ Polling ♦ Research ♦ Telecommunications services ♦ Technical assistance |
|---|---|
| CURRENT CONCERNS | Need for comprehensive policies and programs to protect children from tobacco addiction |
| PUBLICATIONS | *Kick Butts Day Activity Guide*<br>*Tobacco Racing: Tobacco's Vehicle to America's Children*<br><br>Also publishes fact sheets and issue briefs |
| NEWSLETTER | *Kicking Butts: Youth Advocates at Work* (quarterly)<br>*National Action Network Legislative Briefing* (periodic)<br><br>Also publishes others on an ad hoc basis |
| CONFERENCES | None |
| BOARD OF DIRECTORS | ♦ Christopher Conley ♦ Ernest Fleishman ♦ Diane D. Miller ♦ William D. Novelli ♦ John Seffrin ♦ Lonnie Bristow ♦ David R. Smith ♦ Dorothy Wilson ♦ Randolph D. Smoak Jr. |
| EFFECTIVENESS | "An anti-smoking organization plans to file a complaint on Monday with the Federal Election Commission accusing the major tobacco companies of making illegal corporate campaign contributions by promising to run political advertisements on behalf of Republican senators. . . .<br><br>"The complaint, prepared by the Campaign for Tobacco-Free Kids, refers to news media accounts of a comment made by Senator Mitch McConnell of Kentucky to his Republican colleagues at a private meeting on June 17. According to the accounts, Mr. McConnell told his fellow senators that if they voted to kill comprehensive tobacco legislation, the cigarette manufacturers would run television advertisements supporting them. . . .<br><br>"The complaint was written by Matthew L. Myers, executive vice president of the Campaign for Tobacco-Free Kids. . . ." (*New York Times,* June 29, 1998)<br><br>"With the leading tobacco control bill dead, those who wanted to see a legislative action on youth smoking reacted yesterday with anger, disappointment—and optimism, among some. . . . |

" 'I'm a bit disappointed, but not discouraged,' said Michael Moore, the Mississippi attorney general who brought the first state lawsuit against tobacco companies in 1994. 'I think we still have a very good chance of reviving this thing and getting something done.' . . .

"Others were angry at what they described as a great opportunity lost. Matthew L. Myers of the National Center for Tobacco-Free Kids said: 'It's a tragedy for America's kids. The Congress had the opportunity to rise above partisan politics and demonstrate that it could free itself from the addiction to tobacco money—and today, it failed that test.' Myers said that lawmakers would continue to try to append tobacco control legislation to other measures considered by Congress in this session." (*Washington Post*, June 18, 1998)

"The tobacco lobby has pulled off a surprising public relations coup, and won a round on Capitol Hill today, thanks in part to the televised image of a harried, sweaty waitress with earrings the size of onion rings who leans into the camera and sighs: 'I'm no millionaire. I work hard. Why single me out?'. . .

". . . [T]he Campaign for Tobacco-Free Kids is running print advertisements in local papers across the country. One in Kansas says: 'Senators Brownback and Roberts: Big Tobacco or Kids? It's time for them to choose. Tobacco vs. Kids. Where America draws the line.' . . .

"William D. Novelli, the president of the Campaign for Tobacco-Free Kids, said of the industry: 'I don't think they'll lose their pariah status, but they have a couple of points they're scoring with—the tax-and-spend message and the black-market message. They're giving people in Congress cover.'

"Mr. Novelli and others said tobacco legislation was still likely to pass at some point. If so, it will not be with the help of the United States Chamber of Commerce, which sees a dangerous precedent in the Government's singling out an industry from which to demand enormous fees." (*New York Times*, May 22, 1998)

"In a report that afforded President Clinton the perfect opportunity to renew his call for comprehensive tobacco legislation, the Surgeon General, Dr. David Satcher, warned today that increases in smoking by minorities, especially minority teen-agers, threaten to reverse significant declines in the incidence of cancer. . . .

"Dr. Satcher then presented the 332-page tome to the President, who wasted no time in denouncing the tobacco industry for advertising to young people. Nearly three dozen children dressed in bright red T-shirts with the logo of the National Center for Tobacco-Free Kids, a Washington advocacy group, lined up behind Mr. Clinton as he spoke. . . .

"Rarely are Surgeon General's reports issued with such pomp and circumstance. But today's, the 24th in a series on tobacco use that began 34 years ago, in addition to being the first issued by Dr. Satcher, came at a time of political uncertainty over the prospects of tobacco legislation." (*New York Times*, April 28, 1998)

"An increasingly bitter rift between two factions of the nation's public health groups over the proposed national tobacco settlement could be moving toward resolution—and a united and harder stance against cigarette-makers. . . .

"One coalition, which includes the American Cancer Society and leadership of the American Medical Association, has been willing to accept limited liability protection from class-action lawsuits and punitive damages to get the sweeping concessions by the industry to help reduce underage smoking. They banded together under the name ENACT. . . .

"Neither ENACT nor a key member, the National Center for Tobacco-Free Kids, has stated support for immunity, focusing instead on the public health issues. But their silence on the issue has been broadly taken as assent. Matthew L. Myers, executive vice president and general counsel of the National Center for Tobacco-Free Kids, disputed that interpretation, however. He said: 'The campaign opposes any changes in the civil justice system that would weaken the courts' ability to protect the public health, permit the tobacco industry to operate outside the normal boundaries of the law, or escape accountability for its wrongdoing. We welcome Dr. Koop's efforts to try to permit the public health community to enter this crucial year as united as possible.'

"In a press briefing yesterday morning, Myers said that the situation in Congress had 'moved beyond' the original national settlement proposal, and 'it's important that Congress set a high mark and move toward' it, while keeping an eye on 'what's achievable.'" (*Washington Post*, January 22, 1998)

# POLITICAL ORIENTATION

Unavailable

# National Charities Information Bureau (1918)

19 Union Square West
New York, New York 10003
Phone: (212) 929-6300
Fax: (212) 463-7083
Internet: http://www.give.org

"To promote informed giving and strengthen private voluntary philanthropy."

**PURPOSE**

13 total—10 professional; 3 support

**STAFF**

James J. Bausch, president. Before joining the National Charities Information Bureau (NCIB) in 1994, Bausch was an independent advisor to nonprofit organizations. Previously he served as president of Save the Children, as vice president of the Population Council, and as a program officer with the Ford Foundation. Bausch has worked for the Peace Corps as a volunteer and an administrator, and has taught at the university level. He has also been a board member of many nonprofit organizations. Bausch will retire from NCIB in mid-1998.

**DIRECTOR**

501(c)(3)

**TAX STATUS**

1997—$1.15 million
1998—$1.29 million
Proposed 1999—Unavailable

**BUDGET**

Individuals, 50 percent; foundations, 40 percent; corporations, 10 percent

**FUNDING SOURCES**

Members: N/A
Branches/chapters: N/A
Affiliates: N/A

**SCOPE**

None

**PAC**

| | |
|---|---|
| *METHOD OF OPERATION* | ◆ Develops and publicizes standards for charitable organizations ◆ Instigates dialogues with other organizations active in the philanthropy field ◆ Informs the public about ways to assess the performance of charitable organizations ◆ Media outreach ◆ Rates the performance of national charities based on NCIB's nine standards |
| *CURRENT CONCERNS* | Promoting informed giving |
| *PUBLICATIONS* | *NCIB Standards in Philanthropy*<br><br>Also publishes detailed evaluations about national charitable organizations |
| *NEWSLETTER* | *Wise Giving Guide* (4 times a year) |
| *CONFERENCES* | None |
| *BOARD OF DIRECTORS* | George Penick, chair; Hugh C. Burroughs and Deborah C. Foord, vice chairs; David S. Ford, secretary; Daniel Lipsky, treasurer; Lewis A. Helphand, assistant treasurer<br><br>Other members:<br>◆ Alice C. Buhl ◆ Sara L. Engelhardt ◆ Anne V. Farrell ◆ Sheila A. Leahy ◆ Wendy D. Puriefoy ◆ Peirce B. Smith ◆ David L. Wagner ◆ Warren G. Wickersham ◆ Valleau Wilkie Jr. |
| *EFFECTIVENESS* | "Despite Washington's gridlock, Congress soon may approve a bill that would make it 'dramatically easier' for people to collect information about many charities and other tax-exempt groups, says Matthew A. Landy of the National Charities Information Bureau in New York. The bill already has been approved by the House. Senate leaders say the chances of passage are excellent.<br><br>"The provision, part of a taxpayer-protection bill, is designed to make it easier for people to get copies of Form 990, which most groups, other than churches and certain small tax-exempt groups, must file with the IRS each year. That form includes details such as gross income and top officers' pay. The law now requires those returns be available to the public. But critics say procedures for getting them often are cumbersome. Among the proposed changes: If someone makes a written request for a form, a copy must be sent within 30 days. A group wouldn't have to respond if it makes the forms widely available or if the IRS agrees that the requests represent harassment." (*Wall Street Journal*, May 29, 1996) |

"In 1982, the state began allowing income tax payers to check off a box on their returns dedicating $5, $10 or more of their 1981 refund check to the New Jersey Endangered and Non-Game Species Program.

"The endangered species program, begun in 1974 by the Division of Fish, Game and Wildlife using Federal grant money, has received no state tax dollars since the checkoff option appeared. So as costs rose, the check-off money enabled the program to sustain such efforts as restoring the state's bald eagle population. 'We started out with one nest that wasn't producing young,' said Dr. Lawrence Niles, the program's director. 'Now we have 14 nests and last year we produced 15 young, and the year before we produced 22 young.'

"But while the bald eagle population is soaring, check-off contributions have gone into a tailspin as legislators have put other checkoffs on tax returns. Dr. Niles now fears that his program, with eight staff members and a $835,000 budget, will no longer be able to accomplish its mandated tasks, including keeping an updated list of endangered species (there are 65) and guarding their habitats. 'We're in a modified panic,' Dr. Niles said. . . .

"James Bausch, president of the National Charities Information Bureau in New York, believes states should have criteria for deciding which and how many charities get a checkoff box, other than having a strong lobby or an influential legislative backer.

"No doubt hundreds of worthy causes would benefit from checkoffs, said Mr. Bausch, who suggested awarding checkoffs on a rotating basis. 'As you add to the number of causes, you get to a point of diminishing returns.'" (*New York Times*, February 9, 1997)

---

Unavailable

# POLITICAL ORIENTATION

# National Consumers League (1899)

1701 K Street, NW
Suite 1200
Washington, D.C. 20006
Phone: (202) 835-3323
Fax: (202) 835-0747
Internet: http://www.natlconsumersleague.org

**PURPOSE**

"Works to win and maintain health and safety protections and to promote fairness in the marketplace and workplace."

**STAFF**

16 total—10 professional; 6 support; plus 5 part-time; 2 interns

**DIRECTOR**

Linda F. Golodner, president. Before joining the National Consumers League (NCL) in 1983, Golodner was the principal of her own public affairs consulting firm from 1975 to 1985 and served as an aide to a member of Congress from 1960 to 1964. She earned a B.A. at the University of Maryland.

**TAX STATUS**

501(c)(3)

**BUDGET**

1997—$1.4 million
1998—$1.6 million
Proposed 1999—Unavailable

**FUNDING SOURCES**

Programs/grants, 86 percent; fundraising/dues, 11 percent; publications, 1 percent; miscellaneous (including interest income and honoraria), 2 percent

**SCOPE**

Members: 5,000 individuals and organizations
Branches/chapters: N/A
Affiliates: Consumers League of Ohio; New Jersey Consumers League

**PAC**

None

♦ Advertisements ♦ Awards program ♦ Coalition forming (Alliance Against Fraud in Telemarketing, Child Labor Coalition, For a Safer America Coalition) ♦ Conferences/seminars ♦ Congressional testimony ♦ Consumer education ♦ Demonstrations ♦ Direct action ♦ Films/video/audiotapes ♦ Grassroots organizing ♦ Information clearinghouse ♦ International activities ♦ Internet (E-mail alerts, Web site) ♦ Legislative/regulatory monitoring (federal and state) ♦ Media outreach ♦ Polling ♦ Research

## METHOD OF OPERATION

♦ Child labor ♦ Consumer fraud, including telemarketing fraud ♦ Consumer product safety ♦ Direct-to-consumer advertising of pharmaceuticals ♦ Environment and environmental packaging ♦ Fair labor standards ♦ Financial services and credit ♦ Food and drug safety ♦ Health care reform ♦ Internet fraud ♦ Labor standards ♦ Managed care—impact on consumers ♦ Patient information ♦ Privacy ♦ Telecommunications and technology ♦ Truth-in-labeling of consumer products

## CURRENT CONCERNS

## PUBLICATIONS

*1997 Conference Report on National Consumers League Centennial Conference: Focus on Health*

*AIDS: Women at Risk*

*Alcohol: How It All Adds Up*

*Alternative Health Care: New Promise, New Pitfalls*

*Be Cool About Fire Safety* (video)

*A Consumer Guide to Home Health Care*

*A Consumer Guide to Hospice Care*

*A Consumer Guide to Life-Care Communities*

*A Consumer Guide to Safe Drinking Water*

*Consumer Credit Education* (manual and video)

*Consumer Credit Series*

*Consumer Guide to Home Safety: For Consumers Who Are Building or Renovating a Home*

*Debit Cards: Beyond Cash and Credit*

*Food and Drug Interactions*

*From Market to Mealtime: What You Should Know About Meat, Poultry, and Seafood*

*The Garbage Problem: Effective Solutions for Consumers*

*The Green Sheet*

*A Guide to Warning Labels on Nonprescription Medications*

*Here Today . . . Gone Tomorrow* (on renters insurance)

*The Holiday Green Sheet*

*Keep it Clean, Keep it Healthy*

*Making Sense of Your New Communications Choices*

*Oops! New Driver's Guide to Automobile Insurance*

*The Pap Test: Assuring Your Good Health*

*Parents Primer on After-School Jobs*

*Proceedings from the National Consumers League Forum on Drinking Water Safety and Quality*

*Protecting Your Eyes from the Sun*

*Putting the Pieces Together: Solving the Financial Puzzle*

*Questions to Ask: Taking Charge of Your Own Health*

*Swindlers Are Calling*

*Take Care* (series on over-the-counter medications)
*They Can't Hang Up* (on Seniors and Telemarketing Fraud) (brochure, video, report)
*When Medications Don't Mix: Preventing Drug Interactions*
*You Make the Call: A Survival Guide for Choosing Your Telephone Service*

## NEWSLETTER

*Child Labor Monitor* (quarterly)
*Community Credit Link* (quarterly)
*NCL Bulletin* (bimonthly)
*Focus on Fraud* (quarterly)

## CONFERENCES

Annual conference/Centennial Countdown Conference
DTC Roundtable
Focus on Financial Services
Focus on Health Care
Workshop on Direct-to-Consumer Advertising of Pharmaceuticals

## BOARD OF DIRECTORS

Brandolyn T. Clanton Pinkston, chair; Robert R. Nathan, honorary chair; Esther Shapiro and Charlotte Newton, vice chairs; Markley Roberts, treasurer; Don Rounds, secretary; Linda F. Golodner, president; Esther Peterson, honorary president; Jack Blum, counsel

Other members:
◆ Erma Angevine ◆ Dorothy M. Austin ◆ Debra Berlyn ◆ Alan Bosch ◆ Ruth Harmer Carew ◆ Jim Conran ◆ Ellen Craig ◆ Ted Debro ◆ Joe Doss ◆ Evelyn Dubrow ◆ Glenn English ◆ Mary Finger ◆ Carolyn Forrest ◆ Eugene Glover ◆ Pastor Herrerra Jr. ◆ Mary Heslin ◆ Arlene Holt ◆ Ruth Jordan ◆ Jane King ◆ Jorge Lambrinos ◆ Harry Kranz ◆ Odonna Mathews ◆ Rob Mayer ◆ Joyce Miller ◆ Larry Mitchell ◆ Patricia Royer ◆ Bert Seidman ◆ Samuel A. Simon ◆ Caroline Stellmann ◆ Ricki Stochaj ◆ Leland Swenson ◆ Patricia Tyson ◆ Barbara Van Blake ◆ Gladys Gary Vaughn ◆ Clair E. Villano

## EFFECTIVENESS

"... [O]n-line auctions have also become the No. 1 Internet scam, according to statistics recently released by the Internet Fraud Watch unit of the National Consumers League (www.natlconsumersleague.org), a consumer advocacy group based in Washington.

"The group said reports of Internet fraud tripled in 1997, compared with 1996. Since Web auctions are so new, they did not even merit a separate fraud category in 1996, said Susan Grant, a National Consumers League vice president. But last year, auctions were cited in nearly 30 percent of the 1,152 complaints of Internet-related fraud the group received. And Ms. Grant said the numbers probably grossly understated the problem because most consumers did not bother to report such incidents.

"On-line auctions can be a fast, economical way to buy a variety of consumer products. . . . Fortunately for the consumer, the vast majority of on-line auction transactions are completed safely.

"But consumers should proceed with caution because there are various ways to stage a swindle in the world of Web auctions. . . ." (*New York Times*, March 5, 1998)

"Almost everyone who has considered using the Internet for commerce has paused at least momentarily to consider the issue of fraud.

"We're not talking about 'security,' which is another issue entirely. We're talking about old-fashioned country-fair-variety fraud in which the gullible are quickly separated from their wherewithal. . . .

"Susan Grant, testifying before the Senate Committee on Investigations last month, described the range of online scams, including 'bogus investments, empty travel and vacation offers, scholarship search services, loans that require advance fees . . . even services to supposedly help immigrants obtain green cards.'

"[Susan Grant is] the director of the National Consumers League's National Fraud Information Center and Internet Fraud Watch Program.

"Internet Fraud Watch's own Web site, launched independently of the consumer league's in September, is reportedly getting between 70,000 and 90,000 hits and more than 1,300 e-mails a week from consumers around the world." (*Richmond Times-Dispatch*, March 1, 1998)

"A White House task force engaged in a groundbreaking effort to eliminate apparel industry sweatshops will propose an independent workplace monitoring system and international standards to address the problems of child labor and harassment. . . .

"President Clinton is expected to endorse the group's proposals and urge major retail chains and apparel manufacturers to voluntarily adopt the standards for both domestic and foreign operations. The efforts could have a major effect on apparel industry conditions worldwide. . . .

"The task force was formed following a spate of scandals in the apparel industry. . . .

"The controversies have generated public concern about working conditions in the apparel industry, said Linda Golodner, co-chairwoman of the task force and president of the Washington-based National Consumers League.

" 'We get calls and letters from consumers who care about this," she said. "This task force is dedicated to doing something to make the apparel industry a better place to work." (*Los Angeles Times*, February 1, 1997)

Unavailable

## POLITICAL ORIENTATION

# Public Voice for Food and Health Policy (1982)

1012 14th Street, NW
Suite 800
Washington, D.C. 20005
Phone: (202) 347-6200
Fax: (202)347-6261
Internet: pubvoice@aol.com

| | |
|---|---|
| **PURPOSE** | "To promote a safer, healthier and more affordable food supply for all Americans." |
| **STAFF** | 5 total |
| **DIRECTOR** | Arthur Jaeger, executive director |
| **TAX STATUS** | 501(c)(3) |
| **BUDGET** | 1998—$500,000<br>Proposed 1999—$500,000 |
| **FUNDING SOURCES** | Industry and foundation grants, conferences, publication sales, and individual contributions |
| **SCOPE** | Members: N/A<br>Branches/chapters: N/A<br>Affiliates: N/A |
| **PAC** | None |
| **METHOD OF OPERATION** | ♦ Awards program (Golden Carrot Award) ♦ Coalition forming ♦ Conferences/seminars ♦ Congressional testimony ♦ Legislative/regulatory monitoring (federal) ♦ Library/information clearinghouse ♦ Lobbying (federal) ♦ Participation in regulatory proceedings (federal) ♦ Research ♦ Technical assistance |

♦ Agricultural subsidy programs ♦ Food contaminants ♦ Food labeling ♦ Inner-city food access ♦ Meat and poultry inspection standards ♦ Pesticide and chemical residues in food

*Consumer Cost of the Northeast Interstate Dairy Compact*
*Cost of the Northeast Interstate Dairy Compact: An Update*
*Green Cuisine Directory*
*Harvesting Handouts I: The Federal Farm Price Support Scandal*
*Harvesting Handouts II: The Federal Farm Income Subsidy Scandal*
*Hope Meets Reality: School Lunch and the Dietary Guidelines*
*Identifying, Addressing and Overcoming Consumer Concerns: A Roundtable on Food Irradiation*
*"Mad Cow Disease"—Bovine Spongiform Encephalopathy*
*Myths and Facts About Sugar Price Supports*
*No Place to Shop: Challenges and Opportunities Facing the Development of Supermarkets in Urban America*
*No Place to Shop: The Lack of Supermarkets in Low-Income Neighborhoods*
*Outdated Federal Standards and Blocking Consumer Access to Lower-Fat Meat and Poultry*
*Over-Order Milk Pricing and Entry into the Northeast Dairy Compact: The Cost to New York State Consumers*
*The Sugar Program and Consumers: An Update*

*Ag Committee Watch* (quarterly)
*EBT Watch* (quarterly)

Food Policy Conference (annual)—combined with Children and Nutrition Conference/Biotechnology Workshop
Golden Carrot Awards Reception (annual)

John Deardourff, chair

Other members:
♦ Stephen Brobeck ♦ James Eaton ♦ Carol Tucker Foreman ♦ Ellen Haas ♦ John Herrick ♦ Nora Pouillon ♦ Frances Volel-Stech

". . . As hundreds of cash-strapped farmers go out of business each year, environmentalists complain that vast tracts of unused farmland are being overgrown or, worse, are falling into the hands of developers. . . .

"The issue has generated intense debate here, with consumer groups and other critics complaining that the solution farmers are demanding could raise the price of milk. The precise amount of the expected increase fluctuates, but would be approximately 15 cents a gallon if it were put into effect today.

"Why, critics ask, should the state help subsidize dairy farms, particularly small and inefficient ones, at the expense of consumers? They also say that the market, not government, should ultimately decide which farms survive.

" 'It's really internal forces in the dairy industry that are hurting small farms,' said John M. Schnittker, a senior economist with Public Voice for Food and Health Policy, a consumer group. 'The solution should not be to raise prices for consumers. Higher prices for consumers will not help small farms in New York State in the long run.'

"The price of milk is generally set by the Federal Government under a Depression-era system established to insure even distribution and fair pricing for this perishable product. But New York's farmers are calling on state lawmakers to enact legislation to let them join a regional dairy group called the New England Dairy Compact, which is permitted under Federal rules to set higher wholesale milk prices." (*New York Times*, March 15, 1998)

"The Food and Drug Administration . . . proposed tough new rules to protect Americans from 'mad cow' disease. The proposal would ban the practice of feeding cows, sheep and goats mixtures containing ground up carcasses of animals that could be infected with the disease.

"While no cases of 'mad cow' disease have been reported in this country, the incubation period is several years. The new rules, then, are designed to keep any disease that might have reached this country from spreading rapidly through feed products. . . .

"The beef industry supported the agency move. 'We applaud the federal government for its continued efforts to prevent BSE from occurring in the U.S. cattle herd,' the National Cattlemen's Beef Association said in a statement. The organization noted that beef and dairy producers voluntarily removed 'ruminant-derived' proteins from their feed last April, and had used relatively little of the available by-products before that time.

"Consumer advocates hailed the changes as well. A representative of a consumer group that had called for a broad animal-derived feeds ban praised the proposal yesterday. Robert Hahn, director of legal affairs and research for the advocacy group Public Voice for Food and Health Policy, said that the new rules 'sound like what we wanted,' but warned, 'This is only a proposal, and there may be a big fight ahead. . . . The U.S. should not be complacent about this problem,' Hahn said." (*Washington Post*, January 3, 1997)

"A consumer group called . . . for new measures to protect against the possibility of a U.S. outbreak of Britain's 'mad cow disease,' which some scientists believe may cause a fatal brain disease in humans.

"Public Voice for Food and Health Policy called for an immediate ban on using tissue from cattle and sheep in feed for other cattle and sheep, and for additional safeguards to keep tissue from cattle spinal cords out of the human food supply. 'Given the lack of understanding of the disease-causing agent, the difficulties of surveillance and the severity of the disease, the federal government should err on the side of caution,' Public Voice President Mark Epstein said.

"Scientists believe that the use of feed containing rendered cattle bones and other tissues may have been responsible for spreading the disease, known formally as Bovine Spongiform Encephalopathy (BSE), in Britain. The infected cow's brain and spinal cord contain the disease-causing agent, which many researchers believe is a defective form of a protein normally found in nerves and other tissues. . . ."

"The Food and Drug Administration has said it will issue regulations within 18 months banning the practice of using tissue left over from slaughter in animal feed, and the beef industry has called for a voluntary ban. . . ." (*Washington Post*, May 1, 1996)

---

"a liberal Washington research organization" (*Wall Street Journal*, February 6, 1996)

## POLITICAL ORIENTATION

# Corporate Accountability/ Responsibility

Chapter 5

# Business for Social Responsibility
## (1992)

609 Mission Street
2nd Floor
San Francisco, California 94105
Phone: (415) 537-0888
Fax: (415) 537-0889

1612 K Street, NW
Suite 706
Washington, D.C. 20006
Phone: (202) 463-9036
Fax: (202) 463-3954

Internet: bsr-info@bsr.org *or* http://www.bsr.org

"To be the leading global resource providing members with innovative products and services that help companies be commercially successful in ways that demonstrate respect for ethical values, people, communities, and the environment."

**PURPOSE**

45 total

**STAFF**

Robert H. Dunn, president and chief executive officer. Before becoming president of Business for Social Responsibility (BSR), Dunn was vice president of corporate affairs at Levi Strauss and Company and executive vice president of the Levi Strauss Foundation.

**DIRECTOR**

501(c)(6)

**TAX STATUS**

Fiscal year ending June 30, 1997—$3.2 million
F.Y. 1998—$4 million
Proposed F.Y. 1999—$6 million

**BUDGET**

Foundation grants, 47 percent; membership dues, 19 percent; conferences, 11 percent; government contracts, 9 percent; consulting, 8 percent; corporate donations, 3 percent; other, 3 percent

**FUNDING SOURCES**

Members: More than 1,400 members and affiliated member companies that collectively employ nearly 5 million workers

Branches/chapters: 11 regional networks: Arizona, Greater Boston, Colorado, Connecticut River Valley, New England, New Hampshire, Oregon/Washington, San Francisco Bay Area, Southern California, Upper Midwest, and Washington, D.C.

Affiliates: Business for Social Responsibility Education Fund, Business for Social Responsibility Maine, and Business for Social Responsibility Vermont, all 501(c)(3) organizations

**SCOPE**

| | |
|---|---|
| *PAC* | None |
| *METHOD OF OPERATION* | ◆ Conferences/seminars ◆ Educational foundation ◆ Information clearinghouse ◆ International activities ◆ Internet (databases, Web site) ◆ Library (members only) ◆ Media outreach ◆ Research ◆ Training ◆ Technical assistance |
| *CURRENT CONCERNS* | ◆ Audits and accountability ◆ Community involvement ◆ Environment ◆ Ethics ◆ Governance ◆ Human rights and the global economy ◆ Marketplace ◆ Workplace |
| *PUBLICATIONS* | *Beyond the Bottom Line*<br>*Greening Your Company's Bottom Line*<br>*Improving Corporate Profitability and Productivity Through Eco-Efficiency*<br><br>Also develops research publications |
| *NEWSLETTER* | *BSR Update* (bimonthly)<br>*BSR Monitor* (periodic)<br>*BSR News Clips* (weekly) |
| *CONFERENCES* | Annual conference<br>Workshops (ongoing) |
| *BOARD OF DIRECTORS* | Arnold Hiatt, chair; Robert H. Dunn, president<br><br>Other members:<br>◆ Ray Anderson ◆ Emiko Banfield ◆ Christie Boulding ◆ Donna Callejon ◆ Sharon Cohen ◆ Gun Denhart ◆ Elliot Hoffman ◆ Roberta Karp ◆ Bruce Klatsky ◆ Josh Mailman ◆ John Onoda ◆ Cole Peterson ◆ Harry Quadracci ◆ Laura Scher ◆ Erik Sklar ◆ Gail Snowden ◆ Deben Tobias ◆ Ella Williams |
| *EFFECTIVENESS* | "So universal is the respect for [Bob] Dunn, and so sensible and useful are BSR's services, that they have attracted dues-paying members from across the vast terrain of US economic life—from makers of Agent Orange to makers of orange sorbet. General Motors Corp., Wal-Mart Corp., Fannie Mae, the Coca-Cola Co., Nike, The Home Depot, Lotus Development Corp., Monsanto Co., Marriott International Corp., and AT&T are all participating members. So are Ben & Jerry's Homemade Inc., Patagonia, Starbucks Coffee Co., Tom's of Maine, Wild Planet Toys, Burrito Brothers, and a smattering of self-employed entrepreneurs.<br>    "BSR member companies collectively employ more than five million people and have revenues exceeding $800 billion. . . .<br>    " 'BSR brings a solid base of data and a clear intellectual framework to a very scary field,' says Deben Tobias, a BSR board member and chief financial officer for Bolder Heuristics, a software company in Boulder, Colorado. |

" 'The sheer range of their resources is unique,' says Sharon Cohen, another board member who is vice president of public affairs at Reebok International, a founding member. 'Let's say you want information on domestic partner benefits,' Cohen says. 'If you read an article about it in a magazine, you might find two or three examples of companies who are doing it. What you really need would take 30 hours of research by your human resources department. Instead, you get a report [from] BSR. They tell you 20 companies who do it, 18 different ways to do it, how much they cost, the pros and cons of each, and a list of people to call to find out more. And they do this on a hundred different topics. That kind of capacity just doesn't exist anywhere else.'. . .

"More and more are turning to BSR. The group has more than 800 members. In the last three years, BSR's annual budget has soared from $800,000 to $5 million; its staff has jumped from 5 to 40. The group moved into larger offices—energy efficient—this spring. It has just hired a business outreach director to serve small businesses and an executive vice president to do strategic planning. Its Social Responsibility Starter Kit, published in June, list 138 things to do in its table of contents and is flying out the door." (*Stratos*, September/October 1997)

"The International Labor Organization, in a report issued yesterday [November 11, 1996], estimates that 120 million children between the ages of five and 14 are working full time and another 130 million work part time. The organization, a Geneva-based affiliate of the United Nations, attributed the jump in child workers to more accurate survey methods and the inclusion of workers under 10 years old, as well as economic forces that are driving more employers to rely on children.

" 'The problem of child labor has been growing for two decades,' said Gabriele Stoikov, the ILO's top expert on child labor. 'Employers are willing to hire children not only because they are cheaper but because they are more docile.'. . .

"Most observers believe that only rising incomes in developing countries will lead to the elimination of abusive child labor. But that could take many years. Meanwhile, there is no agreement on the best way to reduce child labor. . . .

"As a model tactic, Ms. Stoikov points to a voluntary arrangement between garment makers in Bangladesh, the ILO and Unicef, the U.N.'s child-welfare agency, that aims to rid 2,000 Bangladeshi enterprises of child workers under the age of 14. The manufacturers have agreed not to hire any more children and Unicef is working with local agencies to ensure that children attend school instead of working elsewhere.

" 'No one has the answer yet, but I think there's a very earnest effort under way on the part of many people to find cost-efficient ways' of reducing child labor, said Robert Dunn, president of Business for Social Responsibility, a San Francisco group." (*Wall Street Journal*, November 12, 1996)

"Starbucks Coffee Co. has adopted broad guidelines aimed at improving working conditions at its foreign coffee suppliers. The guidelines are believed to be the first ever by a big U.S. importer involving an agricultural commodity. . . .

"Global human-rights activists applauded the guidelines, saying they substantially widen the possibilities for corporate codes of conduct.

" 'This is going to be a benchmark for a lot of importers of agricultural commodities,' says Robert Dunn, president of Business for Social Responsibility, a trade group. 'Starbucks has drawn a roadmap that will make it easier for other companies to assess whether what they currently do is adequate.'...

"Stricter monitoring of foreign agricultural suppliers may indeed score big points with consumers over the long haul, which is why Mr. Dunn, of Business for Social Responsibility, thinks it is inevitable that importers of other agricultural products, such as bananas, will ultimately follow Starbucks's lead." (*Wall Street Journal*, October 23, 1995)

## POLITICAL ORIENTATION

"a San Francisco-based organization that prods U.S. companies to pay more attention to ethics and environmental issues" (*Washington Post*, May 6, 1996)

# Catalyst (1962)

120 Wall Street
New York, New York 10005
Phone: (212) 514-7600
Fax: (212) 514-8470
Internet: http://www.catalystwomen.org

| | |
|---|---|
| "To enable women to achieve their full professional potential and to help employers capitalize fully on women's talents and abilities." | *PURPOSE* |
| 55 total; plus student interns and volunteers | *STAFF* |
| Sheila W. Wellington, president. Before becoming president of Catalyst in 1993, Wellington was the first woman to hold the office of secretary at Yale University. Wellington also worked for over twenty years in public health and was the chief executive officer of two major mental health facilities. | *DIRECTOR* |
| 501(c)(3) | *TAX STATUS* |
| Fiscal year ending August 31, 1997—$4.3 million<br>F.Y. 1998—$5 million<br>Proposed F.Y. 1999—$5.5 million | *BUDGET* |
| A nationwide consortium of corporations, professional firms, and foundations | *FUNDING SOURCES* |
| Members: 247 corporate members<br>Branches/chapters: N/A<br>Affiliates: N/A | *SCOPE* |
| None | *PAC* |
| ♦ Awards program ♦ Conferences/seminars ♦ Corporate and professional advisory services ♦ Corporate board placement ♦ Information clearinghouse ♦ Library services (members only) ♦ Media outreach ♦ Research ♦ Speakers bureau | *METHOD OF OPERATION* |

## CURRENT CONCERNS

♦ Flexibility in the workplace (child care, part-time work, telecommuting) ♦ Glass ceiling components ♦ "Glass wall": line vs. staff positions ♦ Leadership issues—individual strategies ♦ Managing diversity ♦ Mentoring/networking ♦ Sexual harassment ♦ Specialized industry perspectives ♦ Women business owners ♦ Women on corporate boards ♦ Women's workplace networks ♦ Work/family issues

## PUBLICATIONS

The following is a sample list of publications:

*Catalyst Award: Setting the Standard*
*Census of Women Directors of the Fortune 500* (annual)
*Census of Women Corporate Officers and Top Earners* (annual)
*CEO View: Women on Corporate Boards*
*Child Care Centers: Quality Indicators*
*Child Care in Corporate America: Model Programs*
*Closing the Gap: Women's Advancement in Corp. & Prof. Canada*
*Corporate Guide to Parental Leaves*
*Cracking the Glass Ceiling: Strategies for Success*
*FWA II: Succeeding with Part-Time Options*
*Knowing the Territory: Women in Sales*
*Making Work Flexible: Policy to Practice*
*Mentoring: A Guide to Corporate Programs and Practices*
*A New Approach to Flexibility: Managing the Work/Time Equation*
*On the Line: Women's Career Advancement*
*Two Careers, One Marriage: Making It Work in the Workplace*
*Women Entrepreneurs*
*Women in Corporate Leadership: Progress and Prospects*
*Women in Corporate Management: Model Programs*
*Women in Engineering: An Untapped Resource*
*Women of Color in Corporate Management: A Statistical Picture*
*Women of Color in Corporate Management: Dynamics of Career*
*Women on Corporate Boards: The Challenge of Change*

## NEWSLETTER

*Perspective* (monthly)

## CONFERENCES

Annual awards dinner, conference, and pre-conference luncheon (every March, New York City)

## BOARD OF DIRECTORS

J. Michael Cook, chair; Barbara Paul Robinson, treasurer; Paul Allaire, secretary

Other members:
♦ Herbert Allison ♦ John H. Brown ♦ Diana D. Brooks ♦ Jerry D. Choate ♦ F. Anthony Comper ♦ Thomas J. Engibous ♦ George M.C. Fisher ♦ Ann M. Fudge ♦ H. Laurance Fuller ♦ Ann Dibble Jordan ♦ Marie-Josée Kravis ♦ John A. Krol ♦ Reuben Mark ♦ Ann D. McLaughlin ♦ Joseph Neubauer ♦ Katherine D. Ortega ♦ Norma Pace ♦ Joseph A. Pichler ♦ James E. Preston ♦ Michael R. Quinlan ♦ Linda Johnson Rice ♦ Rozanne L. Ridgway ♦ Judith Rodin ♦ Martha R. Seger ♦ John F. Smith Jr. ♦ Cam Starrett ♦ Susan Tohbe ♦ Gary L. Tooker ♦ Lawrence A. Weinbach ♦ Sheila W. Wellington

"In a survey of 802 dual-career couples released last month by Catalyst Inc., an advocacy group that tracks the progress of women in the work world, 46 percent of respondents said they want their companies to offer spouse relocation assistance. In addition, 13 percent of the workers said they've turned down transfers because of the impact on their spouses.

"'Spouses aren't just looking for a place to get their hair done, they're looking for a job when they have to move to a new town,' [Society of Human Resource Management spokesman Barry] Lawrence said. So companies need to pay more attention to them for recruiting and retention purposes, he said." (*Washington Post,* February 22, 1998)

"The dearth of top female executives and the accompanying solitude and obstacles they face was driven home by a survey released last month by Catalyst Inc. The nonprofit group, which promotes economic and career opportunities for women, reported that its third annual analysis of corporate leadership in America showed that only 3 percent of top executives at Fortune 500 companies are female—51 women, compared with 1,677 men.

"That's a slight increase from last year, when Catalyst reported that 2.4 percent of top executives—defined as chairman, vice chairman, CEO, president, chief operating officer, senior executive vice president and executive vice president—were women. In addition, Catalyst said there are only two female CEOs among the Fortune 500: Jill Barad of toymaker Mattel Inc. and Marion Sandler, co-president and co-chief executive, with her husband, at Golden West Financial Corp." (*Washington Post*, January 18, 1998)

"What working couples—both men and women—want most from their employers these days are flexible hours that allow them to handle doctors' appointments, home repairs, classes and parent-teacher conferences, according to a study conducted by Catalyst, a nonprofit business research organization that focuses on corporate efforts to promote women.

"Catalyst surveyed almost 1,000 full-time workers in dual-career marriages nationwide and found that 87 percent of the women and 82 percent of the men said what they value most in an employer are informal policies that give them the ability to arrive at work late or leave early on occasion to accommodate personal needs. 'It was fascinating how consistent their priorities were,' said Marcia Brumit Kropf, vice president of research and advisory services at New York-based Catalyst. 'It really didn't matter if they were men or women, 25 or 65, entry-level or senior management, or even if they had children under age 4, what they all wanted was informal flexibility. They didn't want rigid work hours.'

"Kropf said many companies already offer more expensive programs that are attractive to dual-career families, such as spouse-relocation assistance, telecommuting, and child and elder care assistance. But Kropf said that providing the flexibility that employees want involves more than just money; businesses also need to change the structure of their workdays." (*Washington Post,* January 25, 1998)

"Asian, Hispanic and African American women account for 10 percent of the total U.S. work force, but they hold only 5.6 percent of management jobs in the private sector, according to the report by Catalyst, a New York research organization that works to advance women in the workplace. This leaves them worse off than white women, who account for about 33 percent of the 7.5 million U.S. managerial positions, Catalyst concluded in its three-year study, which was based on an analysis of U.S. Census Bureau data for 1994–95. The study's definition of 'manager' comes from the Census report, which lets workers characterize their duties. The term includes front-line supervisors and chief executives in companies with 10 to 100,000 employees. . . .

"Sheila Wellington, president of Catalyst, said the findings indicate that minority women face considerable barriers to achieving successful careers. Indeed, while numbers are the focus of the report, it also suggests some reasons for minority women's slow progress in gaining higher wages. . . .

". . . [The] report is the first of three that Catalyst plans to complete. Next year it expects to release studies looking at more qualitative issues of minority women in management, including their workplace experiences and barriers to advancement." (*Washington Post*, October 23, 1997)

"Women's advancement on US corporate boards has slowed to a snail's pace, according to a study released yesterday. The number of women serving as directors at Fortune 500 companies increased just 3 per cent [sic] over the past year, says Catalyst, a New York-based agency that tracks females in senior management positions.

" 'Gains are coming much more slowly now, because a lot of companies have what they consider their one token woman, and they don't see the need to add more,' said Sheila Wellington, president of Catalyst." (*Financial Times*, October 2, 1997)

---

## POLITICAL ORIENTATION

"a nonprofit business research organization that focuses on corporate efforts to promote women" (*Washington Post*, January 25, 1998)

# Center for Business Ethics (1976)

Bentley College
175 Forest Street
Waltham, Massachusetts 02452
Phone: (781) 891-2981
Fax: (781) 891-2988
Internet: http://www.bentley.edu/resource/cbe

"Dedicated to promoting ethical business conduct in contemporary society. . . . The center provides an international forum for benchmarking and research in business ethics. The center helps corporations and other organizations strengthen their ethical cultures through educational programming and consulting."

**PURPOSE**

5 total—4 professional; 1 support; plus 5 part-time support

**STAFF**

W. Michael Hoffman, executive director. Hoffman founded the Center for Business Ethics in 1976. He is also professor of the Department of Philosophy at Bentley College. Hoffman was president of the Society for Business Ethics in 1989. He has written or edited fifteen books and published more than fifty articles. He has consulted on business ethics for many major corporations, government agencies, and universities and has been an expert witness in numerous legal cases.

**DIRECTOR**

501(c)(3)

**TAX STATUS**

1998—Unavailable
Proposed 1999—Unavailable

**BUDGET**

Most of the Center's funding comes from Bentley College, although the Center receives corporate and private foundation contributions.

**FUNDING SOURCES**

Members: 200 associate members
Branches/chapters: N/A
Affiliate: Bentley College; Ethics Officer Association (EOA), an organization of "practicing ethics officers from hundreds of companies," which promotes ethical business practices

**SCOPE**

| | |
|---|---|
| *PAC* | None |
| *METHOD OF OPERATION* | ♦ Conferences/seminars ♦ Films/video/audiotapes ♦ Internet (library databases, Web site) ♦ Library/information clearinghouse ♦ Library services open to the public ♦ Media outreach ♦ Research ♦ Scholarships ♦ Speakers program ♦ Training |
| *CURRENT CONCERNS* | ♦ Business values and social justice ♦ Corporate governance and institutionalizing ethics ♦ Ethics and the multinational enterprise ♦ Ethics in banking and finance ♦ Ethics of the management of computer technology ♦ International perspectives in business ethics ♦ Power and responsibility in American business ♦ Work ethic |
| *PUBLICATIONS* | *Business, Ethics, and the Environment: The Public Policy Debate* (eighth national conference) <br> *Business Values and Social Justice* (first national conference) <br> *Corporate Governance and Institutionalizing Ethics* (fifth national conference) <br> *The Corporation, Ethics and the Environment* (eighth national conference) <br> *Emerging Global Business Ethics* (ninth international conference) <br> *The Ethical Edge: Tales of Organizations That Have Faced Moral Crises* <br> *Ethics and the Management of Computer Technology* (fourth national conference) <br> *Ethics and the Multinational Enterprise* (sixth national conference) <br> *Power and Responsibility in the American Business System* (second national conference) <br> *The Ethics of Organizational Transformation: Mergers, Takeovers and Corporate Restructuring* (seventh national conference) <br> *The Work Ethic in Business* (third national conference) <br> *Trust, Responsibility, and Control: The Ethics of Accounting and Finance* (tenth international conference) <br><br> Also offers videotapes of above conference proceedings <br><br> *Bibliography of Business Ethics and Business Moral Values* <br> *Business, Ethics and the Environment* <br> *Business Ethics Reports* <br> *Collection of Syllabi* (collection of more than 200 business ethics course syllabi from around the country) <br><br> Other bibliographies available |
| *NEWSLETTER* | *Business and Society Review* (quarterly) <br> *Center for Business Ethics News* (twice a year) |
| *CONFERENCES* | Managing Ethics in Organizations (course—twice per year) |

## BOARD OF DIRECTORS

## EFFECTIVENESS

"Brian from the purchasing department and Tom from engineering are finalizing contract specifications for an antilock braking system for General Motors Corp. During a trip to the home office of a possible supplier in St. Louis, the two are invited to a stadium suite to view a Rams football game and mingle with the company's senior officers. Should they accept the invitation?

"Definitely not, according to GM's new ethics policy, which includes this fictional scenario.

"The auto maker's revised policy on 'gifts, entertainment and other gratuities,' which was quietly announced to employees last month, is among the toughest in corporate America. It puts an end to the stadium box seats, steak dinners and weekend golf outings that employees have long enjoyed at the expense of GM's suppliers and vendors. Taking gifts, except for the most nominal trinkets, is now forbidden.

"Throughout corporate America, 'a lot of companies are seriously re-thinking their gift and entertainment policies,' says W. Michael Hoffman, executive director of the Center for Business Ethics at Bentley College in Waltham, Mass." (*Wall Street Journal*, June 5, 1996)

## POLITICAL ORIENTATION

Unavailable

# Coalition for Environmentally Responsible Economies (CERES) (1989)

11 Arlington Street
6th Floor
Boston, Massachusetts 02116
Phone: (617) 247-0700
Fax: (617) 267-5400
Internet: ceres@igc.apc.org *or* http://www.ceres.org

| | |
|---|---|
| *PURPOSE* | "To encourage companies . . . to endorse and practice the CERES Principles. Endorsing the CERES Principles represents a commitment for business to make continuous environmental improvement and to become publicly accountable for the environmental impact of all its activities." |
| *STAFF* | 10 total—8 professional; 2 support |
| *DIRECTOR* | Robert Kinlock Massie, executive director |
| *TAX STATUS* | 501(c)(3) |
| *BUDGET* | 1998—$807,000<br>Proposed 1999—Unavailable |
| *FUNDING SOURCES* | Grant revenue, 47 percent; gifts and bequests, 26 percent; endorser and coalition fees, 22 percent; conference fees and other revenue, 5 percent |
| *SCOPE* | Members: Approximately 90 organizations and 50 endorsing companies<br>Branches/chapters: None<br>Affiliates: None |
| *PAC* | None |
| *METHOD OF OPERATION* | ♦ Coalition forming ♦ Media outreach ♦ Mediation ♦ Publicly disclosed corporate environmental reporting ♦ Research ♦ Shareholder resolutions |

| | |
|---|---|
| ◆ Corporate environmental reporting ◆ Shareholder relations | *CURRENT CONCERNS* |
| *CERES Report*<br>*Guide to the CERES Principles*<br><br>Also publishes an annual report | *PUBLICATIONS* |
| None | *NEWSLETTER* |
| Annual conference | *CONFERENCES* |
| Joan L. Bavaria and Denis Hayes, cochairs; Paul Freundlich, treasurer; Joan L. Bavaria, secretary<br><br>Other members:<br>◆ Norman Dean ◆ Jack Doyle ◆ William M. Eichbaum ◆ Deeohn Ferris ◆ Jeanne Gauna ◆ Alisa Gravitz ◆ Ashok Gupta ◆ Robert Kinloch Massie ◆ Mike McCloskey ◆ Andy Smith ◆ Ken Sylvester ◆ Ralph Taylor ◆ Joe Uehlein ◆ Ariane van Buren ◆ Stephen Viederman | *BOARD OF DIRECTORS* |
| Unavailable | *EFFECTIVENESS* |
| Unavailable | *POLITICAL ORIENTATION* |

# Committee for Economic Development (1942)

477 Madison Avenue
6th Floor
New York, New York 10022
Phone: (212) 688-2063
Fax: (212) 758-9068

2000 L Street, NW
Suite 700
Washington, D.C. 20036
Phone: (202) 296-5860
Fax: (202) 223-0776

Internet: http://www.ced.org

| | |
|---|---|
| **PURPOSE** | "Devoted to policy research and the implementation of its recommendations by the public and private sectors." |
| **STAFF** | 31 total—22 professional; 9 support |
| **DIRECTOR** | Charles E.M. Kolb, president. Kolb became CED's president in 1997. Before joining CED, he was general counsel and secretary of United Way of America. Before joining United Way in 1992, he was deputy assistant to President Bush for domestic policy. In the Reagan and Bush Administrations he also served as assistant general counsel for regulations and legislation and deputy undersecretary for planning, budget, and evaluation at the Education Department. A 1973 Princeton graduate, Kolb holds a master's degree in philosophy, politics, and economics from Oxford University and a law degree from the University of Virginia. |
| **TAX STATUS** | 501(c)(3) |
| **BUDGET** | 1997—$4.1 million<br>1998—$4.27 million<br>Proposed 1999— Unavailable |
| **FUNDING SOURCES** | Foundation grants, 20 percent; corporate donations, 7 percent; special events/projects, 5 percent; other (unspecified), 68 percent |
| **SCOPE** | Members: 250 trustees ("mostly heads of major corporations and university presidents")<br>Branches/chapters: N/A<br>Affiliates: N/A |

| | **PAC** |
|---|---|
| None | |

| | **METHOD OF OPERATION** |
|---|---|
| ◆ Awards program ◆ Coalition forming ◆ Conferences/seminars ◆ Congressional testimony ◆ Internet (Web site) ◆ Internships ◆ Media outreach ◆ Research ◆ Speakers program | |

| | **CURRENT CONCERNS** |
|---|---|
| ◆ Business, welfare reform, and the low-wage market ◆ Campaign finance reform ◆ Changing roles for older workers ◆ Legal reform ◆ Social Security reform | |

| | **PUBLICATIONS** |
|---|---|
| *America's Basic Research: Prosperity Through Discovery*<br>*American Workers and Economic Change*<br>*Connecting Inner-City Youth to the World of Work*<br>*Connecting Students to a Changing World: A Technology Strategy for Improving Mathematics and Science Education*<br>*The Employer's Role in Linking School and Work*<br>*Fixing Social Security*<br>*Growth With Opportunity*<br>*Modernizing Government Regulation*<br>*Rebuilding Inner-City Communities: A New Approach to the Nation's Urban Crisis*<br>*U.S. Economic Policy Toward the Asia-Pacific Region* | |

| | **NEWSLETTER** |
|---|---|
| *CED Newsletter* (twice per year) | |

| | **CONFERENCES** |
|---|---|
| Several conferences per year on various policy issues | |

| | **BOARD OF DIRECTORS** |
|---|---|
| Frank P. Doyle, chairman; Philip J. Carroll, Alfred C. Decrane Jr., Raymound V. Gilmartin, Matina S. Horner, and Henry A. McKinnell, vice chairmen; John B. Cave, treasurer | |

| | **EFFECTIVENESS** |
|---|---|
| " 'Contrary to the traditional view of many companies and conservatives that excessive regulation is a mess created by the executive branch of government, the Committee for Economic Development (CED) said in a report released Wednesday that the problems were created under the Capitol dome and that's where they need to be fixed.<br>" 'Unlike most previous examinations of regulatory reforms, which focus on the drafting of regulations in the executive branch, this statement emphasizes the need to revise the basic statutes governing regulation. The legislative process is the true birth stage of regulation, the point at which we have the greatest opportunity to affect the results of the entire regulatory process,' said the report, called *Modernizing Government Regulation*." (*Washington Post*, April 10, 1998) | |

"Americans save far less for retirement than persons in other highly industrialized nations. The Committee for Economic Development (CED) . . . observed: 'Unlike citizens in many other countries . . . Americans are not setting aside resources adequate for their retirement needs. Indeed, overall saving rates in the United States have fallen to record low levels well below those of other industrial nations.' " (*Seattle Times*, March 27, 1998)

"In fact, 'Fixing Social Security,' a report released today by the corporate-sponsored Committee for Economic Development, adds something important to the embryonic debate: the closest thing we are likely to get to the voice of big business. And while many of the committee's ideas can be found elsewhere, the political whole is greater than the sum of the parts." (*New York Times*, February 20, 1997)

## POLITICAL ORIENTATION

"nonpolitical policy and research organization" (*Seattle Times*, October 2, 1996)

# Council of Institutional Investors
## (1985)

1730 Rhode Island Avenue, NW
Suite 512
Washington, D.C. 20036
Phone: (202) 822-0800
Fax: (202) 822-0801
Internet: http://www.cii.org

| | |
|---|---|
| "To address investment issues that affect the size or security of pension plan assets." | **PURPOSE** |
| 7 total—4 full-time and 3 part-time professionals | **STAFF** |
| Sarah Teslik, executive director | **DIRECTOR** |
| 501(c)(6) | **TAX STATUS** |
| 1998—Unavailable<br>Proposed 1999—Unavailable | **BUDGET** |
| Membership dues, 100 percent | **FUNDING SOURCES** |
| Members: 110 public, union, and corporate pension funds<br>Branches/chapters: N/A<br>Affiliates: N/A | **SCOPE** |
| None | **PAC** |
| ◆ Coalition forming ◆ Conferences/seminars ◆ Direct action ◆ Internet (Web site) ◆ Legislative/regulatory monitoring (federal and state) ◆ Lobbying (federal and state) ◆ Research | **METHOD OF OPERATION** |

| | |
|---|---|
| **CURRENT CONCERNS** | ◆ Corporate governance ◆ Global investments ◆ Investor relations ◆ One-share, one-vote controversy ◆ "Poison pill" rulings ◆ Proxy voting reform ◆ Shareholder Bill of Rights |
| **PUBLICATIONS** | *Does Ownership Add Value?: A Collection of 100 Empirical Studies* |
| **NEWSLETTER** | *The Council Letter* (weekly) *Newsletter* (monthly) |
| **CONFERENCES** | Annual meeting (Washington, D.C.) Semiannual meeting (alternates between New York City, Chicago, Boston, and San Francisco) |
| **BOARD OF DIRECTORS** | Terence Gallagher, Patricia Lipton, and William Lucy, cochairs; Andrew Stern, secretary; Henry Joans, treasurer; Sarah Teslik, executive director |
| **EFFECTIVENESS** | "The New York Stock Exchange is running into more opposition to its revised rule for determining when member companies can delist, this time from Congress. "Congressman Michael Oxley, in a letter to Securities and Exchange Commission Chairman Arthur Levitt, said the Big Board hasn't gone far enough in proposed revisions to its Rule 500 in relaxing delisting conditions. . . . "But a pension-fund association has expressed the opposite view, saying the new rule goes too far in removing shareholders from delisting decisions. . . . ". . . [T]he Council of Institutional Investors, which represents 100 pension funds with more than \$1 trillion in investments, says the revisions to Rule 500 go too far in removing any requirement for a shareholder vote. 'A decision as crucial as the company's listing on the stock exchange should require the approval of a majority of the outstanding shares,' Council executive director Sarah Teslik said in a letter to the SEC. A company may delist to thwart shareholder interests, such as to avoid a Big Board requirement for a shareholder vote, she said. "The council also criticized the SEC for not better disseminating the proposed rule change, and scheduling a 'short comment period.' " (*Wall Street Journal*, January 29, 1998) "ITT Corp., stung by a Nevada judge's ruling on its breakup strategy, abandoned its controversial plan to stagger directors' terms and began plotting new ways to win a proxy fight with Hilton Hotels Corp. "The ruling late Monday by a federal judge in Las Vegas that ITT must seek shareholder approval for its restructuring plan, in which it would split itself into three companies, sent ITT stock soaring and breathed new life into Hilton's eight-month takeover battle. |

"ITT shares closed up $5.25, or 8.4%, at $67.75 in trading on Tuesday. Hilton gained $1.5625, or 4.9%, to $33.6875. . . .

"The Washington-based Council of Institutional Investors on Tuesday sent a letter to Mr. Araskog requesting that he 'select any weekday and any time' from Oct. 13 to the Oct. 24 to meet with council members in New York. 'I am certain you are aware that the council members—with their ownership of more than $1 trillion in assets—control swing votes in proxy contests. You can no longer postpone meeting with council members,' wrote Sarah Teslik, the group's executive director." (*Wall Street Journal*, October 1, 1997)

Unavailable

# POLITICAL ORIENTATION

# Council on Economic Priorities (1969)

30 Irving Place
9th Floor
New York, New York 10003
Phone: (212) 420-1133
Fax: (212) 420-0988
Internet: cep@cepnyc.org *or* http://www.cepnyc.org

| | |
|---|---|
| *PURPOSE* | "To enhance the incentives for superior corporate social and environmental performance and to encourage the transfer of cold war resources to a productive civilian economy." |
| *STAFF* | 15 total—10 professional; 5 support; plus interns |
| *DIRECTOR* | Alice Tepper Marlin, executive director. Before founding the Council on Economic Priorities (CEP) in 1969, Tepper Marlin was a securities analyst with Drexel, Burnham and with the Thomas O'Connell Management and Research Corporation. She also edited a tax journal at the International Bureau of Fiscal Documentation in Holland. Tepper Marlin is a graduate of Wellesley College. |
| *TAX STATUS* | 509(a)(1) |
| *BUDGET* | 1997—$1.08 million<br>1998—$1.51 million<br>Proposed 1999—$1.8 million |
| *FUNDING SOURCES* | Foundation grants, 38 percent; corporate donations, 28 percent; membership, 17 percent; publications, 14 percent; individuals, 3 percent |
| *SCOPE* | Members: Approximately 7,500<br>Branch/chapter: Office in London<br>Affiliate: Council on Economic Priorities Accrediation Agency |
| *PAC* | None |

◆ Awards program (Annual Corporate Conscience Awards) ◆ Conferences/seminars ◆ Internet (Web site) ◆ Library/information clearinghouse ◆ Media outreach ◆ Performance ratings ◆ Research (Campaign for Cleaner Corporations, Institutional Investor Research Service) ◆ Speakers program ◆ Training and technical assistance

## METHOD OF OPERATION

◆ Corporate environmental records ◆ Corporate social responsibility ◆ Day care ◆ Economic implications of changes in eastern Europe ◆ Hiring of minorities and women ◆ National security ◆ Production of nuclear or conventional weapons ◆ South Africa investments ◆ Toxic waste ◆ U.S. and Soviet economic conversion

## CURRENT CONCERNS

*Better World Investment Guide*
*Building a Peace Economy*
*Corporate Report Card*
*Forum on Global Standards*
*Human Rights Briefing*
*International Security Program*
*International Sourcing Report*
*Petroleum Refining Industry Report*
*Students Shopping for a Better World*

## PUBLICATIONS

*CEP Research Report* (monthly)

## NEWSLETTER

Forum on Global Standards

## CONFERENCES

Lee B. Thomas Jr., chair; Arthur H. Rosenfeld, vice chair; Alice Tepper Marlin, president

Other members: ◆ R. Gavin S. Anderson ◆ I. Macallister Booth ◆ Dana Chasin ◆ E. Tyna Coles ◆ John Connor Jr. ◆ Edith B. Everett ◆ Michael Goldstein ◆ Lawrence Otis Graham ◆ Robert Heilbroner ◆ Mary Gardner Jones ◆ Saul Kramer ◆ William C. Samuels ◆ Jack Sheinkman ◆ Beth Smith ◆ Terry Thomas ◆ George Wallerstein

## BOARD OF DIRECTORS

"[The Council on Economic Priorities Accreditation Agency (CEPAA) is] a potential breakthrough not just on sweatshops, but on common labor standards for the global economy as a whole." (*Business Week*, October 20, 1997)

"Investors can do just as well with a portfolio of 'socially responsible' stocks as with other stocks, concludes J. David Diltz, associate professor of finance at the University of Texas at Arlington. Mr. Diltz examined 159 common stocks, primarily of large United States companies.

## EFFECTIVENESS

"All the stocks were rated by the Council on Economic Priorities for their environmental and nuclear policies, diversity and community outreach, among other criteria. . . .

"Mr. Diltz created 14 diversified portfolios, broadly pitting socially responsible companies against others, and found little difference in performance from 1989 through 1991. He concluded that equity markets were sufficiently large, liquid and efficient to make social screening irrelevant to the performance." (*New York Times*, May 14, 1995)

## POLITICAL ORIENTATION

Unavailable

# Council on Foundations (1949)

1828 L Street, NW
Suite 300
Washington, D.C. 20036
Phone: (202) 466-6512
Fax: (202) 785-3926
Internet: http://www.cof.org

| | |
|---|---|
| "To achieve five goals: to secure and maintain supportive public policy for philanthropy; to promote responsible and effective philanthropy; to enhance the understanding of organized philanthropy in the wider society; to increase the growth of organized philanthropy; and to support and enhance cooperation among grantmakers." | *PURPOSE* |
| 83 total | *STAFF* |
| Dorothy Ridings, president and chief executive officer | *DIRECTOR* |
| 501(c)(3) | *TAX STATUS* |
| 1998—$11.5 million<br>Proposed 1999—$11.5 million | *BUDGET* |
| Membership dues, 51 percent; additional member contributions for projects, 20 percent; conference and seminar income, 13 percent; investment and other income, 9 percent; publications sales, 7 percent | *FUNDING SOURCES* |
| Members: More than 1,600 independent, community, operating, and public foundations; corporate grantmakers; and trust companies<br>Branches/chapters: N/A<br>Affiliates: N/A | *SCOPE* |
| None | *PAC* |
| ♦ Awards program ♦ Conferences/seminars ♦ Congressional testimony ♦ Films/video ♦ International activities ♦ International networking ♦ Internet (Web site) ♦ Legislative/regulatory monitoring (federal) ♦ Library/information clearinghouse ♦ Media outreach ♦ Research ♦ Training and technical assistance | *METHOD OF OPERATION* |

## CURRENT CONCERNS

♦ Charitable contributions legislation ♦ Corporate community involvement ♦ Current research on grantmaking ♦ Education and development of foundation trustees ♦ Future of philanthropy ♦ Long-term planning as a tool for grantmakers ♦ Media outreach ♦ Post-grant evaluation ♦ Role of trustees in foundation administration ♦ Strengthening community foundations as a vehicle for local giving

## PUBLICATIONS

The following is a list of sample publications:

*Beyond Our Borders—A Guide to Making Grants Outside the U.S.*

*The Charitable Impulse*

*Community Foundations Around the World: Building Effective Support Systems*

*Company Foundations and the Self-Dealing Rules*

*Consensus Building: Managing Conflict in the Family Foundation*

*The Corporate Contributions Handbook: Devoting Private Means to Public Needs*

*Corporate Giving and the Law—Steering Clear of Trouble*

*The Family Advisor* packet series

*Family Foundations & the Law: What You Need to Know*

*Family Foundations Now—And Forever?—The Question of Intergenerational Succession*

*For the Common Good: Voices of Philanthropy*

*A Founder's Guide to the Family Foundation—How to Use, Govern and Enjoy Your Family Foundation*

*Grantmaking for the Global Village*

*The Handbook on Private Foundations*

*Hands-On Grantmaking: The Story of the Boone Foundation*

*How to Calculate the Public Support Test*

*How to Position the Corporate Grantmaking Program: Strategies that Work*

*In the Honor of Giving: Legal and Administrative Options for Indian Tribal Charitable Activities*

*Include Me! Making the Case for Inclusiveness for Community Foundations*

*Include Me! Making the Case for Inclusiveness for Corporate Grantmakers*

*Include Me! Making the Case for Inclusiveness for Private and Family Foundations*

*The Inclusive Community: A Handbook for Managing Diversity in Community Foundations*

*Measuring the Value of Corporate Citizenship*

*Options and Opportunities in Family Philanthropy: A Guide for the Professional Adviser*

*Philanthropy and the Black Church, Volume II*

*Point of View* series

*Remaking America: How the Benevolent Traditions of Many Cultures Are Transforming Our National Life*

*Use of Fiscal Agents: A Trap for the Unwary*

*The Value of Difference: Enhancing Philanthropy Through Inclusiveness in Governance, Staffing & Grantmaking*

*Widening the Circle: Inclusive Practices and Community Foundations*

## NEWSLETTER

*Council Columns* (biweekly)

*Foundation News and Commentary* (bimonthly)

Annual conference
Fall Conference for Community Foundations
Family Foundations Conference
Corporate Community Involvement Conference
Sponsors other conferences and workshops

EFFECTIVENESS

"National foundations that pump billions into innovative projects throughout the country have long tended to take a wide berth around the District
because of its image as a city with a dysfunctional government. . . .

"A major opportunity arrived this week as the city hosted the 49th annual convention of the Council on Foundations—an umbrella group of
1,600 grantmakers that collectively hold $143.4 billion in assets and last
year gave away $7 billion.

"In speeches, in site visits to nonprofit projects and in a seminar titled
'Washington on the Move,' local grantmakers and service agencies have
been preaching a dual message: Creative nonprofits have been performing
despite bad government, and as for the government, it's a new day. . . .

"Bus loads of conventioneers are being driven to nearly a dozen sites in
the city to see how local nonprofits have built housing, theaters and
parks. Youth in arts programs sang, danced and acted for the visitors. . . .

"No one expects to turn that around in a few days. In fact, the majority
of participants on site visits were from small foundations looking for
good ideas to replicate in their own target areas. But local leaders believe
they have a good start on which to build and are optimistic that conventioneers will help get out the word that change is afoot." (*Washington Post*,
April 29, 1998)

". . . Seeking 15 to 18 percent average annual growth in assets is also unusual in the philanthropy world, where an expected return of 10 percent
is more the norm. But several people who direct or advise other endowments and foundations noted that nothing in the tax code interferes with
his investment plans. . . .

"As for asset mix, the Council on Foundations said that its most recent survey, taken of 702 foundations in 1993, found that they held an average of almost 64 percent of assets in stocks and more than 32 percent in fixed-income investments. But some advisers and lawyers suggested that the average equities holding could well have risen in the years since, as the stock market has boomed." (*New York Times*, April 5, 1998)

"Leaders of some of the nation's top charities protested to government officials in Washington about the incursion of for-profit companies, led by Fidelity Investments, into philanthropy.

"Representatives of the charities and the Council on Foundations, a big charitable association, held two meetings yesterday—one with a Treasury Department official and another with staff of a congressional tax-writing committee—to investigate proposing legislation that would restrict investment managers' ability to establish public charities.

"The exploratory talks are specifically aimed at new ventures such as the hugely successful charity set up by FMR Corp.'s Fidelity Investments, the mutual-fund giant. The outcome of this debate also could affect a host of other new charities recently launched by other banks and investment managers." (*Wall Street Journal*, April 1, 1998)

"The nation's biggest charitable foundations grew 22 percent richer last year as skyrocketing stock prices increased the value of their assets by more than $23 billion. . . .

"While most foundations will increase their largess to meet the 5 percent requirements, some critics are suggesting that boom times on Wall Street should trigger even greater generosity in grant-making.

"Curtis W. Meadows, the former president of the Meadows Foundation in Dallas, called on foundations to give more than the minimum. Meadows, who last year received the highest award given by the Council on Foundations—the umbrella organization for 1,500 foundations and corporations that make charitable grants—said philanthropies should use the tremendous new wealth being generated by the robust economy to create a 'dividend for humanity.'

"By contrast, Dorothy Ridings, president of the Council on Foundations, said she believes the optimum payout amount 'truly does depend on the individual foundation.'

" 'There is a lot of good evidence about the trend lines that shows that the 5 percent is an extremely reasonable rate not only in terms of inflation, but in preserving the value of the portfolio over a long period of time,' she said." (*Washington Post*, February 23, 1998)

## POLITICAL ORIENTATION

Unavailable

# Ethics Resource Center (1977)

1747 Pennsylvania Avenue, NW
Suite 400
Washington, D.C. 20006
Phone: (202) 737-2258
Fax: (202) 737-2227
Internet: ethics@ethics.org *or* http://www.ethics.org

---

| | |
|---|---|
| "To be a leader and a catalyst to foster ethical practices in individuals and institutions." | *PURPOSE* |
| 13 total—8 professional; 5 support; plus 1 part-time and 2 interns | *STAFF* |
| Michael G. Daigneault, president. Daigneault was formerly executive director of the American Inns of Court Foundation and president of Ethics, Inc. His background also includes teaching at the Georgetown University Law Center. Daigneault holds undergraduate and law degrees from Georgetown University. | *DIRECTOR* |
| 501(c)(3) | *TAX STATUS* |
| Fiscal year ending June 30, 1997—$2 million<br>F.Y. 1998—$2 million<br>Proposed F.Y. 1999—$2.2 million | *BUDGET* |
| Fees for service, 35 percent; corporate donations, 30 percent; foundation grants, 20 percent; conferences, 15 percent | *FUNDING SOURCES* |
| Members: N/A<br>Branches/chapters: N/A<br>Affiliates: N/A | *SCOPE* |
| None | *PAC* |
| ♦ Coalition forming ♦ Conferences/seminars ♦ Consulting ♦ Educational foundation ♦ Films/video/audiotapes ♦ Information clearinghouse ♦ International activities ♦ Internet (Web site) ♦ Product merchandising ♦ Professional development services ♦ Research ♦ Speakers program ♦ Training and technical assistance | *METHOD OF OPERATION* |

| | |
|---|---|
| *CURRENT CONCERNS* | ◆ Consulting/training in business, government, and associations toward ethical practices ◆ Educating the general public on the importance of ethics ◆ Education in ethical behavior, K–12 |
| *PUBLICATIONS* | *Creating a Workable Company Code of Ethics*<br>*Desktop Guide to Total Ethics Managment*<br>*Downsizing Effectiveness Questionnaire Kit*<br>*Ethics Education in American Business Schools*<br>*Ethics in American Business: Policies, Programs and Perceptions*<br>*Ethics Inventory Kit*<br>*Eye on Integrity* (interactive CD-ROM)<br><br>Videos:<br>*A Matter of Judgment: Conflicts of Interest in the Workplace*<br>*Beyond Borders: Ethics in International Business*<br>*Buying Trouble: Ethics Issues in Purchasing*<br>*Characters Way*<br>*Ethics at Work*<br>*Ethics in the American Workplace* (for grades 9–12)<br>*It's Up to You: A Management Accountant's Decisions*<br>*Management Ethics: A View from the Top*<br>*Managing and Caring for the Survivors of Downsizing*<br>*Marketing Integrity: Ethics Issues for Government Contractors*<br>*Marketplace Ethics: Issues in Sales and Marketing*<br>*Not For Sale: Ethics in the American Workplace*<br>*Tough Decisions: Ethics Issues in Government Contracting*<br>*What Should You Do?: Deciding What's Right* (for grades 4–6) |
| *NEWSLETTER* | *Ethics Today* (quarterly) |
| *CONFERENCES* | ERC Fellows Program |
| *BOARD OF DIRECTORS* | Irving Widmer Bailey II, chairman; Michael G. Daigneault, president; Norman R. Augustine, chairman, fellows program<br><br>Other members:<br>◆ John R. Castle Jr. ◆ Max Chopnick ◆ Madeline K.B. Condit ◆ Fred F. Fielding ◆ Raymond Gilmartin ◆ Thomas B. Hayward ◆ Shaun F. O'Malley ◆ Norma Pace ◆ Brent Scrowcroft ◆ C.J. Silas ◆ Louis W. Sullivan |
| *EFFECTIVENESS* | Unavailable |
| *POLITICAL ORIENTATION* | Unavailable |

# The Foundation Center (1956)

79 Fifth Avenue
New York, New York 10003
Phone: (212) 620-4230
Fax: (212) 807-3677

1001 Connecticut Avenue, NW
Suite 938
Washington, D.C. 20036
Phone: (202) 331-1400
Fax: (202) 331-1739

Internet: http://www.fdncenter.org

| | |
|---|---|
| "To foster public understanding of the foundation field by collecting, organizing, analyzing, and disseminating information on foundations, corporate giving, and related subjects." | *PURPOSE* |
| Unavailable | *STAFF* |
| Sara L. Engelhardt, president. Before becoming president of the Foundation Center in July 1991, Engelhardt served as executive vice president in 1987. Prior to joining the Center, she was the corporate secretary of the Carnegie Corporation of New York for twelve years. | *DIRECTOR* |
| 501(c)(3) | *TAX STATUS* |
| 1997—$11.6 million<br>1998—Unavailable<br>Proposed 1999—Unavailable | *BUDGET* |
| Publications sales, 50 percent; foundation and corporate grants, 38 percent; other, 16 percent | *FUNDING SOURCES* |
| Members: N/A<br>Branches/chapters: 4<br>Affiliates: Foundation Center-operated libraries are located in New York; Washington, D.C.; Atlanta; Cleveland; and San Francisco | *SCOPE* |
| None | *PAC* |

| **METHOD OF OPERATION** | ♦ Associates program ♦ Educational programs ♦ Internet (Web site) ♦ Library/information clearinghouse ♦ Publications ♦ Research ♦ Seminars ♦ Telecommunications services (databases) ♦ Training and technical assistance |
|---|---|
| **CURRENT CONCERNS** | Facilitating "wide and efficient distribution of the most current information about private foundations and their grantmaking programs to grantseekers, grantmakers, government, journalists, researchers, and the general public." |
| **PUBLICATIONS** | *AIDS Funding*<br>*Best Practices of Effective Nonprofit Organizations*<br>*Directory of Missouri Grantmakers*<br>*FC Search: The Foundation Center's Database on CD-ROM*<br>*The Foundation Directory*<br>*The Foundation Directory Part 2*<br>*The Foundation Directory Supplement*<br>*The Foundation 1000*<br>*Foundation Giving*<br>*The Foundation Grants Index*<br>*The Foundation Grants Index Quarterly*<br>*Foundation Grants to Individuals*<br>*Grant Guide Series* (30 titles)<br>*Guide to U.S. Foundations, Their Trustees, Officers, and Donors*<br>*Guide to Proposal Writing*<br>*Human/Civil Rights Grants*<br>*International Grantmaking: A Report on U.S. Foundation Trends*<br>*National Directory of Corporate Giving*<br>*National Guide to Funding for Children, Youth & Families*<br>*National Guide to Funding for Elementary & Secondary Education*<br>*National Guide to Funding for Information Technology*<br>*National Guide to Funding for Libraries and Information Services*<br>*National Guide to Funding for Women & Girls*<br>*National Guide to Funding in Health*<br>*National Guide to Funding in Religion*<br>*New York State Foundations*<br>*PRI Index*<br>*Program Evaluation Grants*<br>*Who Gets Grants* |
| **NEWSLETTER** | *Associates Program News* (members only)<br>*FC Search Light* (database purchasers)<br>*Philanthropy News Digest* (online) |
| **CONFERENCES** | Sponsors seminars |

## BOARD OF DIRECTORS

Unavailable

## EFFECTIVENESS

Unavailable

## POLITICAL ORIENTATION

# Independent Sector (1980)

1828 L Street, NW
Suite 1200
Washington, D.C. 20036
Phone: (202) 223-8100
Fax: (202) 416-0580 and (202) 457-0609
Internet: http://www.indepsec.org

**PURPOSE**
"To strengthen giving, volunteering and not-for-profit initiatives in America."

**STAFF**
42 total—34 professional; 8 support; plus 1 part-time professional and 5 interns

**DIRECTOR**
Sara E. Meléndez, president. Meléndez was formerly president of the Center for Applied Linguistics, vice provost and acting dean of arts and humanities at the University of Bridgeport, and director of special minority initiatives at the American Council on Education. She serves as a trustee on the boards of CIVICUS: World Alliance for Citizen Participation, the National Puerto Rican Forum, and Richmond College, the American University in London. She received her bachelor's degree in English from Brooklyn College, a master's of science degree from Long Island University, and a doctorate from Harvard University's Graduate School of Education.

**TAX STATUS**
501(c)(3)

**BUDGET**
1997—$6.7 million
1998—$6.6 million
Proposed 1999—$6.5 million

**FUNDING SOURCES**
Foundation grants, 60 percent; membership dues, 35 percent; conference, 3 percent; publications sales, 1 percent; corporate donations, 1 percent

**SCOPE**
Members: More than 700 voluntary organizations, foundations, and corporate giving programs with national interest and impact in philanthropy and voluntary action
Branches/chapters: N/A
Affiliates: N/A

None

◆ Advertisements ◆ Awards program ◆ Coalition forming ◆ Conferences/seminars ◆ Congressional testimony ◆ Internet (electronic bulletin boards, E-mail alerts, Web site) ◆ Internships ◆ Legislative/regulatory monitoring (federal) ◆ Media outreach ◆ Research ◆ Telecommunications services (Fax-on-demand)

*METHOD OF OPERATION*

◆ Communication among nonprofit organizations ◆ Develop leadership to promote the common good ◆ Develop relations with the federal government ◆ Increase public awareness of the nonprofit sector ◆ Increase giving and volunteer service ◆ Research on the nonprofit sector

*CURRENT CONCERNS*

The following is a sample list of publications:

*Academic Centers and Programs Focusing on the Study of Philanthropy, Voluntarism, and Not-for-Profit Activity*
*Aiming High on a Small Budget: Executive Searches and the Nonprofit Sector*
*America's Volunteers*
*Board Overboard*
*Changing Social Contract: Measuring Interaction Between the Independent Sector & Society*
*Compendium of Resources for Teaching About the Nonprofit Sector, Voluntarism, and Philanthropy*
*Evaluation With Power: A New Approach to Effectiveness, Empowerment, & Excellence*
*Giving: Big Bucks, Bare Basics, and Blue Skies*
*Nonprofit Almanac 1996–1997: Dimensions of the Independent Sector*
*Nonprofit News Coverage—A Guide for Journalists*
*Origins, Dimensions and Impact of America's Voluntary Spirit*
*Powered by Coalition: The Story of Independent Sector*
*Profiles of Effective Corporate Giving Programs*
*Resource Raising: The Role of Non-Cash Assistance in Corporate Philanthropy*
*Study of Cause-Related Marketing*
*Youth Service: A Guide for Developing and Operating Effective Programs*

Also offers videos, research papers, and publications on government relations and leadership

*PUBLICATIONS*

*Memo to Members* (monthly)
*Public Policy Update* (periodic)

*NEWSLETTER*

Annual conference and meeting of members
Also sponsors research seminars and legal briefings

*CONFERENCES*

## BOARD OF DIRECTORS

## EFFECTIVENESS

"Private enterprise is booming. Government is downsizing. And nonprofits are caught in the middle. . . .

". . . A new survey of 441 Illinois nonprofits other than hospitals, universities and museums found that half of their total income—more than $20 billion—came from government contracts and grants.

"Last week, the sponsors of that survey—the Illinois Facilities Fund and the Donors Forum of Chicago—launched a public awareness campaign to draw attention to this important sector. In conjunction with the Independent Sector, a Washington-based group that works on behalf of the philanthropic community, the campaign hopes to encourage more charitable giving and volunteering, as well as build support for public policies that favor nonprofits.

"One key piece of their effort is the Charitable Giving Relief Act, sponsored in Congress by Rep. Philip Crane (R-Ill.). The bill would allow taxpayers who do not itemize deductions on their tax returns to deduct 50 percent of their annual charitable contributions in excess of $500. Supporters estimate that the measure . . . would cost the U.S. Treasury $12.1 billion in giving over that time, including $762 million in Illinois. It's a tradeoff that may be worth making." (*Chicago Tribune*, July 1, 1998)

"Independent Sector (IS) has begun distributing a 'message initiative' designed to help nonprofits to communicate their value to the community, the sector, and the nation as a whole.

"Not exactly an advertising campaign, 'Giving Voice to Your Heart' is a package that responds to requests by IS members for assistance in defining the sector's value and describing it in such places as op-ed pieces and speeches, said John Thomas, IS's vice president of communications. 'It has been something over the years nonprofits have felt the need for,' he said, 'something to help to define value to communities.'

"The initiative is intended to stress three basic messages, said Thomas. Nonprofits make a difference in the lives of people, communities, the country and the world. The sector puts shared values into action. And citizen involvement is what makes the sector work." (*Non Profit Times*, May 1998)

"The phrase 'paycheck protection' has become a national rallying cry in the battle between conservatives and unions over campaign politics. Unfortunately, some of America's charities could become inadvertent casualties of the war. . . .

"Consider a California charity that receives funds from employees of several businesses via United Way. Under Prop 226, if the charity planned to spend any part of those funds on support or opposition to a local or state ballot measure, it would need to alert the businesses one year in advance. The employer would then be obligated to have each donating employee sign a 'Request for Political Payroll Deductions' for each such charity.

"The discouraging effects of this procedure are obvious. . . .

"So where is the United Way of America, the leading recipient of payroll deductions for charity? In late April, the policy staff at its headquarters in Alexandria released a stinging four-page analysis of Prop 226, warning that it 'is drafted so broadly that it would cause a variety of adverse consequences for nonprofits.'

"This was consistent with what other analysts from the non-profit sector had concluded. Independent Sector, a Washington-based organization that represents more than 700 major charities, and the National Committee for Responsive Philanthropy, which works with alternative workplace-giving programs, have both come out strongly against the measure." (*Washington Post*, May 31, 1998)

"Apparently there's a ton of work for volunteers to do across the country. According to a survey by the Independent Sector, a coalition of 700 nonprofit organizations that tracks volunteering in the United States, 93 million people age 18 and over volunteer each year an average of four hours a week. This number translates into 49 percent of that population, a percentage that has remained steady since the surveys began 10 years ago. The survey also showed that people are four to five times more likely to volunteer if someone asks them personally to participate. 'What happens during the holidays is that more people are out there asking,' says assistant director of research Aaron Heffron. 'Some call it peer pressure but we like to think of it as feeling that you are part of a community.' " (*Washington Post*, January 23, 1998)

"According to Independent Sector, a nonpartisan group that studies philanthropy, the average U.S. family contributed $696, or 1.7 percent of its income, to charitable causes in 1995, the last year for which figures are available. Households with incomes above $100,000 a year contribute an average of $2,994, or 2.2 percent." (*Washington Post*, April 17, 1998)

# POLITICAL ORIENTATION

# INFACT (1977)

256 Hanover Street
Third Floor
Boston, Massachusetts 02113
Phone: (617) 742-4583
Fax: (617) 367-0191
Internet: http://www.infact.org

| | |
|---|---|
| **PURPOSE** | "To stop life threatening abuses of transnational corporations and increase their accountability to people around the world." |
| **STAFF** | Unavailable |
| **DIRECTOR** | Kathryn Mulvey, director |
| **TAX STATUS** | 501(c)(3) |
| **BUDGET** | 1998—Unavailable<br>Proposed 1999—Unavailable |
| **FUNDING SOURCES** | Unavailable |
| **SCOPE** | Members: 30,000 individuals<br>Branches/chapters: Unavailable<br>Affiliates: Unavailable |
| **PAC** | None |
| **METHOD OF OPERATION** | ♦ Advertisements ♦ Boycotts (Tobacco industry boycott, Kraft and Nabisco boycott) ♦ Coalition forming ♦ Demonstrations ♦ Grassroots organizing ♦ Media outreach ♦ Research |

♦ "Stopping the tobacco industry from marketing its products to children and young people around the world." ♦ INFACT's Hall of Shame documents how corporations have "disregarded public opinion and manipulated our democratic ideals for private gain, with devastating consequences for public health and well-being."

Unavailable

*INFACT Update* (quarterly)

Unavailable

Unavailable

"Columbia/HCA Healthcare Corp.'s chairman, Dr. Thomas F. Frist Jr., predicted an end to the federal investigation of the hospital giant by the first quarter of 1999, and the company added a new board member, former Capital Cities/ABC Chairman Thomas Murphy. Both are signs that Columbia may be turning a corner.

"Dr. Frist, in an interview after yesterday's annual shareholders meeting, said that it 'was a reasonable expectation' that the massive federal Medicare-fraud probe that has dogged Columbia for more than a year, as well as the ambitious corporate restructuring undertaken at his command, could both be completed by early next year. 'That is our best estimate—I am not promising,' he said. . . .

"During the meeting, Dr. Frist was asked about Columbia's past ethical conduct, and he rattled off the changes he had brought about inside Columbia since taking over in July 1997 after a boardroom coup. These ranged from creating a more open culture to bringing in the criminal law firm of Latham & Watkins to perform a far-ranging internal investigation. The lawyers, Dr. Frist said, 'have gone into every nook and cranny' of Columbia to search for signs of wrongdoing. He added that the work was 'substantially completed.'

"Representatives from grass-roots organizations, including Infact, which campaigns for corporate responsibility, and the Episcopal Church, quizzed Dr. Frist on everything from Columbia's policies toward tobacco to its lobbying activities. Dr. Frist seemed troubled when told that Infact had named Columbia to its 'Hall of Shame,' last year, saying, 'I can't tell you how much that hurts.' (Columbia recently sold off more than $5 million of tobacco investments.)" (*Wall Street Journal*, May 15, 1998)

Unavailable

# National Alliance of Business (1968)

1201 New York Avenue, NW
Suite 700
Washington, D.C. 20005
Phone: (202) 289-2888 or (800) 787-2848
Fax: (202) 289-1303
Internet: info@nab.com *or* http://www.nab.com

| | |
|---|---|
| *PURPOSE* | "To build a competitive American workforce by enhancing the skills and knowledge of workers to meet the needs of business, beginning in the classroom and continuing in the workplace." |
| *STAFF* | 95 total |
| *DIRECTOR* | Roberts T. Jones, president and chief executive officer. Before joining National Alliance of Business (NAB) as executive vice president in 1994, Jones served in the federal government for 20 years. He also has been vice president of RJR Nabisco's Policy Institute. Jones is a graduate of the University of Redlands in California and studied public administration at American University. |
| *TAX STATUS* | 501(c)(3) |
| *BUDGET* | 1998—$12.5 million<br>Proposed 1999—$13 million |
| *FUNDING SOURCES* | Federal, state, and local government, 45 percent; private contributions, 40 percent; foundations, 12 percent; publications, 3 percent |
| *SCOPE* | Members: 9,000<br>Branches/chapters: 5 regional offices in Los Angeles, Atlanta, Chicago, Boston, and Dallas<br>Affiliates: N/A |
| *PAC* | None |

| | |
|---|---|
| ◆ Advertisements ◆ Awards program ◆ Coalition forming ◆ Conferences/seminars ◆ Congressional testimony ◆ Database ◆ Films/video/audiotapes ◆ Internet (electronic bulletin boards, databases, Web site) ◆ Legislative/regulatory monitoring (federal and state) ◆ Library/information clearinghouse (open to public) ◆ Media outreach ◆ Polling ◆ Research ◆ Telecommunications services (mailing lists) ◆ Training and technical assistance | **METHOD OF OPERATION** |

| | |
|---|---|
| ◆ Education reform ◆ School-to-work transition ◆ Workforce development systems ◆ Workforce quality | **CURRENT CONCERNS** |

| | |
|---|---|
| The following is a sample list of publications: <br> *The Business of Education Standards* (video) <br> *The Corporate Action* (series) <br> *Help Wanted: Progressive Employers Sought by Talented, Qualified Youth With Disabilities* <br> *Joining the Partnership: Recruiting Employers for School-to-Work* <br> *Our Children's Education* (series) <br> *Standards Mean Business Leadership Kit* <br> *Standards Mean Business* (series) <br><br> Also publishes brochures and executive summaries | **PUBLICATIONS** |

| | |
|---|---|
| *Legislative Update* (monthly) <br> *WorkAmerica* (monthly) <br> *Workforce Economics* (bimonthly) | **NEWSLETTER** |

| | |
|---|---|
| Knowledge Network (annual conference) | **CONFERENCES** |

| | |
|---|---|
| Edward B. Rust Jr., chairman; Roberts T. Jones, president and chief executive officer <br><br> Other members: ◆ Keith E. Bailey ◆ Leo C. Beebe ◆ Kathleen J. Burke ◆ Michael Carey ◆ Bruce Carswell ◆ Michelle Darling ◆ John E. Fesperman ◆ Jerome H. Grossman ◆ Richard S. Gurin ◆ John Hall ◆ Sidney Harman ◆ Albert Hoser ◆ Robert Ingram ◆ Jerry D. Jackson ◆ Glenn R. Jones ◆ Daniel H. Leever ◆ Malcolm R. Lovell Jr. ◆ J. Randall MacDonald ◆ Brian McAuley ◆ Jewell Jackson McCabe ◆ John R. McKernan Jr. ◆ Richard Measelle ◆ James F. Orr III ◆ Timothy F. Price ◆ Thomas E. Richards ◆ Norman E. Rickard Jr. ◆ Judy Bryne Riley ◆ Richard F. Schubert ◆ T. Quinn Spitzer ◆ Roger T. Staubach ◆ A. William Wiggenhorn ◆ Alan L. Wurtzel ◆ Sam Yau ◆ Raul Yzaguirre | **BOARD OF DIRECTORS** |

| | |
|---|---|
| "A low-key but high-powered collaboration between Montgomery County businesses and the public school system is winning praise from two national education groups for helping to reform a central school bureaucracy often criticized as too large and inefficient. | **EFFECTIVENESS** |

"In a conference telecast last week to 475 school districts, chambers of commerce and college campuses across the country, the JCPenney Leadership Institute on School Improvement cited the county collaboration as a model for school reform. The institute is a joint venture of the department store company and the National Alliance of Business, a nonprofit group seeking to improve education at all levels." (*Washington Post*, May 15, 1997)

"Overcoming years of dependency on open-ended entitlement programs is daunting, those who administer welfare-to-work efforts say.

"Employers express satisfaction with new employees who show initiative and a willingness to learn, even when that has required training in rudiments like the proper way to answer phones. . . . Many among those hired, while the most qualified of those screened, have problems that include absenteeism, lack of discipline about work hours, poor reading and communications skills, and open resentment when given direction. And the current programs have not even reached people on welfare who have more serious problems, like alcohol and drug abuse or low intelligence. . . .

"President Clinton challenged 'every business person in America who has ever complained about the failure of the welfare system to try to hire somebody off welfare, and try hard.' Yet some leaders of business groups are blunt in disavowing any suggestion that the private sector should assume responsibility for making welfare reform work.

" 'Business is not in the business of providing jobs for welfare recipients,' Robert T. Jones, president and chief executive officer of the National Alliance of Business, said in a telephone interview before the President's speech, contending that it is up to the states to prepare people for entering the work force.

"Still, some communities—notably places where unemployment is low and unskilled workers are in demand—have already undertaken efforts to move welfare recipients into the work force." (*New York Times*, September 1, 1996)

## POLITICAL ORIENTATION

"a nonprofit, business-led organization dedicated to the advancement of education to improve the quality of the work force" (*Washington Post*, February 24, 1997)

# National Committee for Responsive Philanthropy (1976)

2001 S Street, NW
Suite 620
Washington, D.C. 20009
Phone: (202) 387-9177
Fax: (202) 332-5084
Internet: info@ncrp.org *or* http://www.ncrp.org

| | |
|---|---|
| "Committed to making philanthropy more responsive to socially, economically, and politically disenfranchised people, and to the dynamic needs of increasingly diverse communities nationwide. The National Committee's programs aim to maximize the financial capabilities of organizations which seek justice for low-income people, racial and ethnic minorities, women and others who are targets of discrimination and which seek environmental sanity." | *PURPOSE* |
| 16 total—11 professional; 5 support; plus 2 interns | *STAFF* |
| Robert O. Bothwell, president. Bothwell was previously director of the school finance reform project at the National Urban Coalition and associate director of the veterans education and training service at the National League of Cities and U.S. Conference of Mayors. He also has held various positions in the federal government. | *DIRECTOR* |
| 501(c)(3) and 501(h) | *TAX STATUS* |
| Fiscal year ending September 30, 1997—$1.04 million<br>F.Y. 1998—$1.01 million<br>Proposed F.Y. 1999—$1.01 million | *BUDGET* |
| Foundation grants, 60 percent; individual contributions, 12 percent; membership dues, 11 percent; corporations, 8 percent; church/union grants, 4 percent; publication sales, 2 percent; other, 3 percent | *FUNDING SOURCES* |
| Members: 170 organizations<br>Branches/chapters: Regional offices in Minnesota and New York<br>Affiliates: N/A | *SCOPE* |
| None | *PAC* |

## METHOD OF OPERATION

♦ Coalition forming ♦ Conferences/seminars ♦ Grassroots organizing ♦ International activities ♦ Internet (E-mail alerts, Web site) ♦ Internships ♦ Legal assistance ♦ Legislative/regulatory monitoring (federal and state) ♦ Litigation ♦ Lobbying (federal, state, and grassroots) ♦ Media outreach ♦ Participation in regulatory proceedings (federal, state, and local) ♦ Performance ratings ♦ Research ♦ Training and technical assistance

## CURRENT CONCERNS

♦ Alternative funds to United Way ♦ Foundations and corporate giving programs ♦ Philanthropy and social justice ♦ Democracy and philanthropy

## PUBLICATIONS

*Answering the Call: The Telecommunications Industry's Grantmaking for Racial/Ethnic Communities*
*Burgeoning Conservative Think Tanks*
*Charity in the Workplace, 1994*
*Combined Federal Campaign Technical Assistance Packet*
*Community Foundation Evaluations* (series)
*Community Foundations and Citizen Empowerment*
*Community Foundations and the Disenfranchised*
*Corporate Grantmaking to Racial and Ethnic Populations Series*
*The Effects of Workplace Charity Drive Competition on United Way and Total Giving*
*Exploring Charitable Giving Choices in the Workplace*
*Foundation Funding of Civil Rights*
*Foundations in the Newt Era*
*Moving a Public Policy Agenda: The Strategic Philanthropy of Conservative Foundations*
*The New Age of Nonprofit Accountability*
*United Way's Donor Choice: Who Benefits?*
*Workplace Fund Raising: A Primer*

## NEWSLETTER

*Responsive Philanthropy* (quarterly)

## CONFERENCES

Alternatives to United Way (2 regional conferences)

## BOARD OF DIRECTORS

John Echohawk, chair; Pablo Eisenberg, Angelo Falcon, Margaret Fung, Conrad Martin, William Merritt, vice chairs; Robert O. Bothwell, president; Elisa Maria Sanchez, secretary; Paul S. Castro, treasurer

Other members: ♦ James W. Abernathy Jr. ♦ Jean Anderson ♦ Barbara Bode ♦ JoAnn Chase ♦ Donna Chavis ♦ Lorraine Edmo ♦ Juan A. Figueroa ♦ Margaret Gates ♦ Herb Chao Gunther ♦ Thomas Harvey ♦ Thomas Layton ♦ Norma Lopez ♦ Cindy Marano ♦ Ann Mitchell Sackey ♦ Carol Mollner ♦ Louis Nunez ♦ Terry Odendahl ♦ Gordon A. Raley ♦ Nan Steketee ♦ Sarah Stranahan ♦ Bill Treanor ♦ Greg Truog ♦ Y. Bill Watanabe

"A dozen politically conservative foundations spent $210 million in a three-year period on efforts to reshape national policy debates and push Congress and state legislatures toward the right, according to a study released yesterday.

"The study by the National Committee for Responsive Philanthropy, a watchdog group that serves as an advocate for the poor, said the 12 foundations spent $79.2 million between 1992 and 1994 in think tanks and advocacy groups and $88.9 million to support scholarships and college programs that train conservative thinkers. . . .

". . . [T]he study contends that while most U.S. foundations distribute their money to communities and neighborhood projects, these 12 foundations pursue an agenda aimed at influencing Washington's budget and policy priorities.

" 'Two-thirds of their grants dollars went to organizations and programs pursuing policy agendas based on the privatization of government services, deep reductions in federal anti-poverty spending, industrial deregulation and transfer of responsibility for social welfare to state and local government and the charitable sector,' the study said." (*Washington Post*, July 2, 1997)

Unavailable

# Environmental

## Chapter 6

# American Rivers (1973)

1025 Vermont Avenue, NW
Suite 720
Washington, D.C. 20005
Phone: (202) 347-7550
Fax: (202) 347-9240
Internet: http://www.amrivers.org

---

"To protect and restore America's river systems and to foster a river stewardship ethic."

**PURPOSE**

---

30 total—25 professional; 5 support; plus 2–5 volunteers and 8–10 interns

**STAFF**

---

Rebecca Wodder, president. Before joining American Rivers as president in 1995, Wodder spent nearly fifteen years with The Wilderness Society, where she served as vice president for organizational development and in other positions. In 1988, Wodder helped found Earth Share, a coalition of national environmental groups, and served as its chair from 1990 to 1992. She received B.A. and B.G.S. degrees from the University of Kansas and two M.S. degrees from the University of Wisconsin.

**DIRECTOR**

---

501(c)(3)

**TAX STATUS**

---

Fiscal year ending June 30, 1997—$3.3 million
F.Y. 1998—$3.8 million
F.Y. 1999—$5.2 million

**BUDGET**

---

Foundation grants, 48 percent; individuals, 26 percent; membership dues, 13 percent; corporate donations, 7 percent; government contracts, 1 percent; other, 5 percent

**FUNDING SOURCES**

---

Members: 20,000 individuals
Branches/chapters: Branch offices in Seattle and Phoenix
Affiliates: N/A

**SCOPE**

---

None

**PAC**

| | |
|---|---|
| *METHOD OF OPERATION* | ◆ Coalition forming ◆ Conferences/seminars ◆ Congressional testimony ◆ Grassroots organizing ◆ Initiative/referendum campaigns ◆ Internet (Web site) ◆ Internships ◆ Litigation ◆ Lobbying (federal, state, and grassroots) ◆ Media outreach ◆ Participation in regulatory proceedings (federal and state) |
| *CURRENT CONCERNS* | ◆ Flood control reform ◆ Hydropower policy reform ◆ Imperiled aquatic species ◆ Protection of the wild rivers ◆ Restoration of rivers in urban and rural communities |
| *PUBLICATIONS* | *America's Most Endangered Rivers*<br>*A Casebook for Successful Urban River Projects* (yearly publication)<br>*Relicensing Toolkit: Guidelines for Effective Participation in the FERC Relicensing Process*<br>*River of Promise: The Untapped Potential of Recreation and Tourism on the Missouri River*<br>*River Renewal: Restoring Rivers Through Hydropower Dam Relicensing*<br>*River Restoration and Community Revitalization: A Digest of Select Federal Programs for Rivers* |
| *NEWSLETTER* | *American Rivers* (quarterly)<br>*Mississippi Monitor* (monthly) |
| *CONFERENCES* | Endangered Rivers News Conference (annually in April)<br>Upper Mississippi River Summit<br>Urban Rivers Symposium and Awards<br>Other conferences held occasionally |
| *BOARD OF DIRECTORS* | Anthony P. Grassi, chairman; Whitney Hatch, first vice chair; Richard V. Hopple, second vice chair; I. Michael Greenberger, secretary; Richard S. Freedman, treasurer<br><br>Other members:<br>◆ J. David Allan ◆ George V. Allen Jr. ◆ Stephen E. Ambrose ◆ Albert Andrews Jr. ◆ Donald B. Ayer ◆ Martha C. Brand ◆ Louis Capozzi ◆ Ann Crittenden ◆ Sally Davidson ◆ Polly Dement ◆ Dave Grusin ◆ Elizabeth B. Johns ◆ Michael Douglas Keaton ◆ Dan W. Lufkin ◆ David M. Malcolm ◆ Kate McBride ◆ Maura O'Neill ◆ Barbara L. Phillips ◆ John C. Phillips ◆ Robert Pierpont ◆ John A. Rosenthall ◆ John A. Scully ◆ Peter J. Solomon ◆ Ted Strong ◆ John I. Taylor ◆ Cynthia Wilkerson ◆ R. Glenn Williamson |
| *EFFECTIVENESS* | "American Rivers of Washington, a national environmental organization, has given the Hudson River a 'dishonorable mention' on its 1998 list of the country's 20 most endangered rivers. The designation follows the United States Environmental Protection Agency's announcement last month that it would delay its decision on whether to dredge polychlorinated biphenyls from the bottom of the Hudson. |

" 'The decision by E.P.A. to slow its cleanup of PCB's in the Hudson River is outrageous and reckless,' said Margaret Bowman, director of hydropower programs of American Rivers.

"In 1996 and 1997, American Rivers listed the upper Hudson as one of the 10 most endangered rivers in the United States. Last year, several studies were released confirming the need for fast action to clean up contamination by chemicals suspected as carcinogens. The reports indicated that, despite previous assertions, the PCB's—which were discharged by General Electric at two plants in Hudson Falls during the 1970's—were stirred up by the natural river flow and storms and therefore continued to be re-released into the river and ambient air, contaminating fish and wildlife and posing possible health threats to humans.

"Studies indicated that PCB's do not break down and lose toxicity at a rate sufficient to enable the river to restore itself.

"Although PCB levels in the Hudson have dropped since General Electric's direct discharges were prohibited in 1977, a large part of the contaminants remain in sediment 'hot spots,' the environmental group said. The chemical also continues to leak into the Hudson from the bedrock under the General Electric plant at Hudson Falls." (*New York Times*, April 26, 1998)

"A wild stretch of a Pacific Northwest river long protected from human encroachment by nearby pockets of Cold War-era radioactive contamination today was declared the most endangered river in the country.

"Hanford Reach, the last untouched piece of the Columbia River, is threatened by efforts to use it to irrigate land on its eastern banks that for decades was a buffer to some of the world's most toxic waste from the nuclear weapons program, the American Rivers conservation group said. The group issues an annual assessment of rivers most threatened by development, dams, pollution and other man-made maladies that affect waterways and the ecosystems that depend on them.

"This year the group cited particular concern about large hog and chicken farms and the massive amounts of manure they generate, calling them among 'the fastest growing, most devastating' overall threats to waterways.

"While huge livestock operations pose the most pervasive threat, American Rivers said the Hanford Reach faces a different danger.

"Local interests along the 51-mile stretch of Washington state's Hanford Reach want to use the river to irrigate some 90,000 acres that the Energy Department is poised to cut from the Hanford Reservation because it was not contaminated by the nuclear weapons program.

"Introducing agriculture and irrigation there would destroy the last of the Columbia River system's viable habitats for salmon, and would degrade the 'spectacular landscape of towering cliffs, shifting sand dunes and sweeping vistas across an arid shrub-steppe,' the conservation group said.

"Instead, the group is pushing for the stretch of river to receive federal protection as a 'wild and scenic' river, and for the land to be protected as a wildlife refuge.

"Other waterways on its list included the Pocomoke on Maryland's Eastern Shore, which last summer made headlines with a massive fish kill. The group also listed the Missouri, last year's top-ranked endangered river; California's Kern, where six small hydropower dams are degrading aquatic habitat; Montana's Blackfoot, made famous in the film 'A River Runs Through It' and threatened by a proposed gold mine; the Chattahoochee in the Southeast, cited as a polluted urban river; and the Taku in British Columbia and Alaska, threatened by the proposed reopening of a copper and gold mine." (*Washington Post*, April 6, 1998)

"For the first time in history, the federal government yesterday ordered the destruction of a hydroelectric dam that its owner wanted to continue to operate.

"The Federal Energy Regulatory Commission (FERC), an agency that for much of this century has championed hydroelectric dams large and small, ordered Edwards Dam removed from the Kennebec River in Augusta, Maine, in order to restore the habitat of sea-run fish. The commission ruled that power produced at the dam 'can be easily replaced' and that getting rid of the dam will open up the river for fish and fishermen. 'There will be no environmental or social drawbacks,' said the commission, which also required the company that owns the dam to pay for taking it out. . . .

" 'The Edwards decision reflects a change in the way the federal government looks at dams. FERC has recognized that, just like all other things, dams have a finite life cycle,' said Margaret Bowman, director of hydropower programs for American Rivers, a Washington-based group that lobbies for free-flowing rivers. . . .

" 'It may not be pretty, but for the fish traveling downstream it will be a river,' said Bowman of American Rivers. 'We are realizing that dam removal is often less expensive than leaving a dam in place and building fish passage through it.'

"Edwards Dam is a good example. FERC determined it would cost $10 million to build a fishway into the dam, which it estimated was about 1.7 times the cost of simply tearing the structure down.

"Pressure to remove Edwards Dam began building more than 20 years ago as the Kennebec River was slowly cleaned up under federal and state clean water laws. Until the early 1970s, the river was a multi-purpose toilet, polluted with raw sewage, as well as with industrial waste from pulp and paper mills, including highly toxic heavy metals such as mercury and arsenic. It was barely navigable, choked with logs transported in the river's current. Fishermen stayed away because of frequent fish kills and because the river stank.

"Dramatic improvements in water quality and a 1974 ban on log transport opened up the river. The Kennebec has since become one of the better fishing destinations in Maine, especially for striped bass and brown trout. Pressure from fishermen helped persuade Maine politicians to join forces with national environment groups like American Rivers and Trout Unlimited in lobbying for removal of Edwards Dam." (*Washington Post*, November 26, 1997)

## POLITICAL ORIENTATION

Unavailable

# Center for Marine Conservation (1972)

1725 DeSales Street, NW
Washington, D.C. 20036
Phone: (202) 429-5609
Fax: (202) 872-0619
Internet: http://www.cmc-ocean.org

| | |
|---|---|
| "Dedicated to protecting endangered and threatened species and their marine habitats, and to conserving marine ecosystems and resources." | *PURPOSE* |
| 59 total—47 professional; 12 support; plus 2–3 interns | *STAFF* |
| Roger E. McManus, president. McManus previously served as vice president of programs and as director of the Endangered Species Program at the Center for Marine Conservation (CMC). Before joining CMC in 1981, he served on the staff of the President's Council on Environmental Quality during the Carter and Reagan administrations, and with the U.S. Fish and Wildlife Service. McManus earned a B.S. from Northern Arizona University and an M.S. from the University of Arizona. | *DIRECTOR* |
| 501(c)(3) | *TAX STATUS* |
| 1997—$6.77 million<br>1998—Unavailable<br>Proposed 1999—Unavailable | *BUDGET* |
| Contributions, grants, and bequests, 58 percent; gain on marketable securities, 21 percent; investment revenue, 6 percent; federal financial assistance, 4 percent; other government revenue, 4 percent; program income, 2 percent; list rental income, 2 percent; other, 3 percent | *FUNDING SOURCES* |
| Members: 100,000 individuals<br>Branches/chapters: Regional offices in California, Florida, and Virginia<br>Affiliates: N/A | *SCOPE* |
| None | *PAC* |

## METHOD OF OPERATION

♦ Advertisements ♦ Coalition forming ♦ Conferences/seminars ♦ Congressional testimony ♦ Films/video/audiotapes ♦ Grassroots organizing ♦ International activities ♦ Internet (Web site) ♦ Legislative regulatory monitoring (federal and state) ♦ Litigation ♦ Lobbying (federal, state, and grassroots) ♦ Media outreach ♦ Mediation ♦ Participate in regulatory proceedings (federal and state) ♦ Research ♦ Telecommunications services (Hotline: 202-775-2775, databases, mailing lists) ♦ Training and technical assistance

## CURRENT CONCERNS

♦ Bycatching/incidental take of marine life in fishing gear ♦ Federal and state conservation policies ♦ Habitat loss and degradation ♦ Overfishing ♦ Physical alteration of marine ecosystems ♦ Pollution ♦ Promotion of marine protected areas ♦ Recovery of endangered sea turtle and whale species ♦ Regulation of worldwide whaling ♦ Safeguarding threatened and endangered species

## PUBLICATIONS

*An Agenda for the Oceans*
*Citizen's Guide to Plastics in the Ocean*
*Delay and Denial*
*Fish for the Future: A Citizens' Guide to Federal Marine Fisheries Management*
*The Gulf of Mexico: A Special Place*
*The Gulf of Mexico Shrimp Fishery: Profile of a Valuable National Resource*
*Incidental Take of Marine Mammals in Commercial Fisheries*
*International Coastal Cleanup Results*
*The Last Wild Place*
*Limiting Access to Marine Fisheries*
*A Nation of Oceans*
*Managing Shark Fisheries: Opportunities for International Conservation*
*Manatee Coloring Book*
*New England Groundfish: From Glory to Grief*
*No Place to Hide: Highly Migratory Fish in the Atlantic*
*Proceedings of the Shrimp Trawl Bycatch Workshop*
*Sabra Crossing: An Ecological Adventure in the North Atlantic*
*Sea Turtle Coloring Book*
*Sewage Treatment: America's Pipe Dream*
*Shipping Safety and America's Coasts*
*Status of Kemp's Ridley Sea Turtle*
*USS My School: Curriculum on Marine Debris*
*Victory at Sea: "Zero Discharge" Ship to Shore*
*Why People Catch Too Many Fish*

Also offers posters, slide shows, and fact sheets on sea otters, manatees, whales, dolphins, sea turtles, and coral reefs

## NEWSLETTER

*Coastal Connection* (biannually)
*Marine Conservation News* (quarterly)

## CONFERENCES

None

## BOARD OF DIRECTORS

## EFFECTIVENESS

"In a decision that could undercut the use of trade sanctions to promote global environmental goals, the World Trade Organization ruled today that the United States was wrong to prohibit shrimp imports from countries that fail to protect sea turtles from deadly entrapment in the trawls of shrimping boats.

"The United States requires shrimpers in its waters to equip nets with metal grills that exclude turtles and other large animals, and in 1989 Congress passed a law prohibiting shrimp imports from countries not requiring these devices in their fleets. . . .

"The panel found that even under the provisions of the W.T.O. agreement that allow environmental exceptions, the United States would not be permitted to force other nations to adopt policies to protect an endangered species like the turtle.

"Conservation groups called on the Administration to defy the W.T.O. decision and seek international talks aimed at reshaping how the trade group addresses environmental issues.

" 'It is unthinkable that we should not be allowed to mitigate the impacts of our own shrimp markets on endangered sea turtles,' said Deborah Crouse, senior conservation scientist at the Center for Marine Conservation, a Washington-based advocacy group. . . ." (*New York Times*, April 7, 1998)

"Enviros were in despair in the fall of 1996, when House Resources Committee Chairman Don Young (R-Alaska) put a provision, pushed by Rep. Tillie Fowler (R-Fla.), into a big parks bill that would remove eight pieces of undeveloped islands on both coasts of Florida from the Coastal Barriers Resources System.

"Once removed, flood insurance and other federal subsidies would be available to help developers build condos on the beaches. The enviros bitterly opposed the change, saying the developers would destroy the migratory bird and sea turtle habitats. . . .

". . . But then, shortly after the bill was signed, the Interior Department notified Congress that the required maps of the areas that were supposed to be 'on file with the U.S. Fish and Wildlife Service' when the legislation was enacted were missing.

"Young responded quickly, sending the maps over. But two enviro groups, the Coast Alliance and the Center for Marine Conservation, sued, saying the law was clear that the proper maps had to be 'on file' when the bill passed, not sometime later.

"A D.C. federal judge earlier this month ruled for the enviros. The only remedy, Judge Emmet G. Sullivan said, was for Congress to pass a new law. . . ." (*Washington Post*, March 20, 1998)

"... [LaToya] Varner, 20, was one of about 225 volunteers working ... at nine spots along the Potomac in Virginia and at several areas in the District and Maryland, in a cleanup effort sponsored by the National Park Service and the nonprofit Center for Marine Conservation and Clean Virginia Waterways.

"Armed with gloves, boots, garbage bags and a debris checklist, Varner and others spent the morning removing a year's worth of trash—enough to fill 450 bags—left by fishermen, boaters and others who use the banks of the Potomac just south of National Airport as a dumping ground.

"Each piece of trash will be tabulated and sent to the Center for Marine Conservation, which lobbies for laws to protect national waterways. The group also sponsored intercoastal cleanup efforts at other U.S. sites and in several countries during the weekend.

"At last year's event, 1,399 volunteers removed about 64,000 pounds of trash from Virginia shores. . . ." (*Washington Post*, September 21, 1997)

"One of mankind's largest and least regulated harvests of creatures from the wild is ravaging many of the world's shark species, but nascent international efforts to protect the species are hampered by a deep ignorance, not only about how many are killed but also about how they live and what they need to survive.

" 'Little effort has been made to collect even the most basic kinds of information, such as numbers of sharks caught and discarded, necessary for meeting even minimal standards of management of fisheries affecting sharks,' says a report on the species to be issued ... by the Center for Marine Conservation ...

"The report says little is known about the life history and other characteristics of most shark species, like growth rates, reproductive potential, distribution, movements and interactions with other species. . . .

"The Center for Marine Conservation report says: 'Traditional strategies for managing fisheries are predicated on the reproductive biology of fishes that release large numbers of eggs, few of which need survive to adulthood in order to maintain abundance. Sharks, on the other hand, produce few young, many of which survive to adulthood.' " (*New York Times*, March 11, 1997)

# POLITICAL ORIENTATION

Unavailable

# Center for Health, Environment, and Justice (1981)

(Formerly Citizens Clearinghouse for Hazardous Wastes)
P.O. Box 6806
Falls Church, Virginia 22040
Phone: (703) 237-2249
Fax: (703) 237-8389
Internet: cchw@essential.org *or* http://www.essential.org/cchw *or* http://www.sustain.org/hcwh

| | |
|---|---|
| "To assist grassroots leaders in creating and maintaining local community organizations which fight toxic polluters and environmental hazards." | **PURPOSE** |
| 11 total—4 professional; 7 support | **STAFF** |
| Lois Marie Gibbs, executive director. Gibbs founded the Center for Health, Environment, and Justice (CHEJ), formerly the Citizens Clearinghouse for Hazardous Wastes (CCHW), in 1981. She organized and led her neighbors in gaining compensation and resolution in 1978 from damages caused by the storage and disposal of toxic waste at Love Canal in Niagara Falls, New York. | **DIRECTOR** |
| 501(c)(3) | **TAX STATUS** |
| 1998—$919,000<br>Proposed 1999—Unavailable | **BUDGET** |
| Contributions, church and private foundation grants, 78 percent; members, 10 percent; income from events, 5 percent; sales of materials and publications, 5 percent; interest and miscellaneous income, 2 percent<br>CHEJ does not seek or accept grants from the federal government or corporations | **FUNDING SOURCES** |
| Members: 8,000 grassroots organizations; approximately 24,000 individuals<br>Branches/chapters: N/A<br>Affiliates: N/A | **SCOPE** |
| None | **PAC** |

| METHOD OF OPERATION | ◆ Coalition forming ◆ Conferences/seminars ◆ Demonstrations ◆ Direct action ◆ Electronic bulletin boards ◆ Grantmaking (Community Leadership Training Program provides small grants of $500–$5,000 to grassroots groups for education and training programs) ◆ Grassroots organizing ◆ Library/information clearinghouse (open to public) ◆ Media outreach ◆ Research ◆ Speakers program ◆ Special projects (Citizens Alliance Program, Stop Dioxin Exposure Campaign) ◆ Training and technical assistance |
|---|---|
| CURRENT CONCERNS | ◆ Dioxin exposure ◆ Hazardous waste ◆ Medical waste ◆ Military toxics ◆ Pesticides ◆ Plant emissions and discharges ◆ Solid waste ◆ Waste reduction, toxics prevention, and recycling ◆ Workplace exposure |
| PUBLICATIONS | *Common Questions about Health Effects*<br>*Empowering Ourselves: Women and Toxics Organizing*<br>*Environmental Testing*<br>*Hazardous Waste Incineration: The Burning Issue*<br>*How to Win in Public Hearings*<br>*Land Disposal: The Dinosaur of Disposal Methods*<br>*Love Canal: A Chronology of Events that Shaped a Movement*<br>*Mass Burn Status Report*<br>*Medical Waste: Public Health vs. Private Profit*<br>*The Polluters' Secret Plan and How You Can Mess It Up*<br>*Solid Waste Incineration: The Rush to Burn*<br>*Fact Packs* (short, concise information packets) |
| NEWSLETTER | *Dioxin Digest* (quarterly)<br>*Environmental Health Monthly* (monthly)<br>*Everyone's Backyard* (quarterly) |
| CONFERENCES | CHEJ cosponsors:<br>"CEOs—Continuing Education for Organizers"<br>Leadership Development Conferences |
| BOARD OF DIRECTORS | ◆ Clyde Foster ◆ Vilma Hunt ◆ Luella Kenny ◆ Pame Kingfisher ◆ Murray Levine ◆ Esperanza Maya ◆ Ken Miller ◆ Beverly Paigen ◆ Suzi Ruhl ◆ Alonzo Spencer |
| EFFECTIVENESS | "Wagner's Point. A lowdown dirty scrap of land on the tip of a South Baltimore peninsula. Everywhere you look, massive storage tanks, lumbering fences, the high towers of an oil refinery. Funny, you can't even see the water.<br><br>"But stand here, next to this paved playground, and breathe in. Smell it? Might be the sewage treatment plant, might be the refinery. |

"The neighborhood is about 270 people, six blocks of old, narrow row houses. Silver tanker trucks rumble down the street next to the playground. The place was first populated around the turn of the century by cannery workers. Nowadays residents fear fires and the chemical air. They have experienced a high rate of cancer, which may or may not be linked to the environment.

"Most people want out now, and recently Mayor Kurt L. Schmoke offered to purchase the houses at their appraised value and pay residents relocation costs. The city could then enlarge its sewage treatment plant over the area. But not all residents want to leave, and those who do fear their homes would not be worth much. If the city cannot come to an agreement with the residents, it might acquire Wagner's Point through eminent domain.

"This is the kind of community CHEJ [Center for Health, Environment, and Justice] can help.

" 'Basically everything that we have done was her suggestion,' says community leader Rose Hindla of [Lois] Gibbs. 'She doesn't do it *for* us. It's more of, 'You've gotta help yourself but I can help you as you go.'

"In a narrow row house living room, Gibbs and two of her staff sit with Wagner's Point community leaders to discuss an upcoming meeting with the mayor. They're preparing precisely what to say, as they do each time. Gibbs is a gutsy, rallying force. 'Go and get in his face,' she advises one woman who will be speaking with the mayor. And later: 'You had him flustered at that [last] meeting. . . . That equals power, dear.' " (*Washington Post*, July 29, 1998)

---

". . . A network of grassroots environmental groups." (*Washington Post*, July 29, 1998)

## POLITICAL ORIENTATION

# The Conservation Fund (1985)

1800 North Kent Street
Suite 1120
Arlington, Virginia 22209
Phone: (703) 525-6300
Fax: (703) 525-4610
Internet: http://www.conservationfund.org

**PURPOSE**

"Seeks sustainable conservation solutions for the 21st century, emphasizing the integration of economic and environmental goals. . . . The Fund designs innovative, long-term measures to conserve land and water resources."

**STAFF**

62 total—50 professional and 12 support; plus 23 part-time professional; 4 part-time support/contractual; 5 interns; 60 volunteers

**DIRECTOR**

John F. Turner, president and chief executive officer. Before joining The Conservation Fund in 1993, Turner was director of the U.S. Fish and Wildlife Service. Previously he served in the state legislature of Wyoming. The recipient of numerous awards and author of several publications, Turner is also a partner in a family-operated ranch in Wyoming. A graduate of the University of Notre Dame, he also studied at the University of Utah and holds an M.S. from the University of Michigan.

**TAX STATUS**

501(c)(3)

**BUDGET**

1997—$2.5 million
1998—$2.8 million
Proposed 1999—Unavailable

**FUNDING SOURCES**

Gifts of land and related services, 53 percent; foundation grants, 35 percent; government contracts, 6 percent; corporate donations, 3 percent; individuals, 3 percent

**SCOPE**

Members: N/A
Branches/chapters: Regional offices in Alaska, California, Colorado, Florida, Georgia, Idaho, Illinois, Minnesota, New Mexico, North Carolina, Pennsylvania, Texas, Vermont, and West Virginia
Affiliates: N/A

**PAC**

None

| | |
|---|---|
| ◆ Awards program ◆ Community planning ◆ Conference seminars ◆ Demonstration projects ◆ Grantmaking ◆ Internet (Web site) ◆ Legislative/regulatory monitoring (federal) ◆ Local/municipal affairs ◆ Land purchasing for conservation ◆ Research ◆ Training and technical assistance | *METHOD OF OPERATION* |
| ◆ Developing a curriculum to train conservation leaders ◆ Developing models for sustainable community development through demonstration projects ◆ Expanding partnerships for land and water conservation | *CURRENT CONCERNS* |
| *Balancing Nature and Commerce in Gateway Communities*<br>*The Civil War Battlefield Guide*<br>*Dollar$ and Sense of Battlefield Preservation*<br>*Greenways: A Guide to Planning, Design and Development*<br>*Greenways for America*<br>*Inside the Environmental Movement*<br>*Voices from the Environmental Movement* | *PUBLICATIONS* |
| *Common Ground* (bimonthly) | *NEWSLETTER* |
| None | *CONFERENCES* |
| Patrick F. Noonan, chairman<br><br>Other members:<br>◆ Jessica Hobby Catto ◆ Norman L. Christensen Jr. ◆ Sylvia A. Earle ◆ Gilbert M. Grosvenor ◆ KiKu Hoagland Hanes ◆ Hadlai A. Hull ◆ Charles R. Jordan ◆ Ann Dore McLaughlin ◆ John W. Patten ◆ George A. Ranney Jr. ◆ Nelson A. Rockefeller Jr. ◆ William I. Spencer ◆ John F. Turner ◆ Hubert Vogelmann | *BOARD OF DIRECTORS* |
| "A deal signed in Anchorage on Tuesday placed Kennecott—the famously rich copper mine, then ghost town, now tourist attraction—into Wrangell-St. Elias National Park. . . .<br><br>"The deal was negotiated by The Conservation Fund. The Virginia-based nonprofit group has arranged for the public purchase of historic sites, wildlife habitat and open space in more than 30 states, including several in Alaska.<br><br>"The fund put up $10,000 in earnest money two years ago, giving the government time to come up with the Kennecott purchase price. The deal was complex and difficult, the fund's Alaska representative, Brad Meiklejohn, said. | *EFFECTIVENESS* |

" 'We knew it wouldn't happen without persistence,' he said. The organization accepts acquisition targets picked by government agencies, in this case the Park Service. 'We recognized this as one of the most pressing conservation priorities in Alaska,' he said. 'We saw a lot of opportunities in Alaska. This is one people had the most interest in.' " (*Anchorage Daily News*, June 17, 1998)

"The single largest gift of land to Ohio outdoor enthusiasts will be dedicated today as a wildlife conservation area—all 11,200 acres of it. . . .

"The land that will now be known as the Crown City Wildlife Area was donated by the Richard King Mellon Foundation of Pittsburgh, with assistance from The Conservation Fund, according to ODNR, which received the property in December." (*The Columbus Dispatch*, May 5, 1998)

"In a move hailed as one of the most significant protections of wilderness in the Southern Appalachians in 50 years, South Carolina sealed a $54 million deal Monday to preserve 32,000 acres in the Jocassee Gorges. . . .

"The state has committed $10 million through a bond bill and $1 million from the Department of Natural Resources. The Richard King Mellon Foundation, working through the Conservation Fund, also gave $10 million toward the purchase. The Pittsburgh-based foundation has donated more than $200 million toward natural and historic preservation in the last 20 years, according to a spokesman." (*Greenville, SC News*, November 4, 1997)

## POLITICAL ORIENTATION

Unavailable

# Conservation International (1987)

2501 M Street, NW
Suite 200
Washington, D.C. 20037
Phone: (202) 429-5660
Fax: (202) 887-5188
Internet: newmember@conservation.org *or*
http://www.conservation.org

"To conserve the earth's heritage, our global diversity, and to demonstrate that human societies are able to live harmoniously with nature."

*PURPOSE*

252 total—211 professional and 41 support; plus 2 part-time, 4 volunteers, 30 interns

*STAFF*

Russell A. Mittermeier, president. Before joining Conservation International in 1990, Mittermeier was vice president for science at the World Wildlife Fund (WWF) from 1987 to 1989, and a director of four different WWF programs between 1979 and 1989. He has served as chairman of the Primate Specialist Group of the International Union for Conservation of Nature's Species Survival Commission, as SSC's vice chairman for International Programs, and as chairman of the World Bank's Task Force on Biological Diversity. A prominent primatologist and wildlife conservationist, Mittermeier is the author of six books and over 250 papers and articles. He received his B.A. from Dartmouth and his Ph.D. in biological anthropology from Harvard.

*DIRECTOR*

501(c)(3)

*TAX STATUS*

Fiscal year ending June 30, 1997—$10.7 million
F.Y. 1998—$13 million
Proposed F.Y. 1999—$16 million

*BUDGET*

Government contracts, 45 percent; individuals, 27 percent; corporate donations, 16 percent; foundation grants, 10 percent; membership dues, 2 percent

*FUNDING SOURCES*

Members: 4,000 individuals and corporations
Branches/chapters: 2
Affiliates: N/A

*SCOPE*

| | |
|---|---|
| *PAC* | None |
| *METHOD OF OPERATION* | ♦ Advertisements ♦ Awards program ♦ Conferences/seminars ♦ Direct action ♦ Films/video/audiotapes ♦ Grassroots organizing ♦ International activities ♦ Internet (databases, Web site) ♦ Internships ♦ Media outreach ♦ Product merchandising ♦ Research ♦ Training and technical assistance |
| *CURRENT CONCERNS* | Protecting endangered ecosystems |
| *PUBLICATIONS* | The following is a list of sample publications:<br>*Biodiversity Prospecting in Indonesia*<br>*Biosphere Reserves in Tropical America*<br>*Conserving the World's Biodiversity*<br>*The Economics of Biodiversity Conservation in the Brazilian Atlantic Forest*<br>*Encouraging Private Sector Support for Biodiversity Conservation: The Use of Economic Incentives and Legal Tools*<br>*Environmental Reform at the World Bank: The Role of the U.S. Congress*<br>*Ironwood: An Ecological and Cultural Keystone of the Sonoran Desert*<br>*Kakum Conservation Area Development Guide*<br>*Megadiversity: Earth's Biologically Wealthiest Nations*<br>*Natural Resource Extraction in the Latin American Tropics*<br>*Reinventing the Well: Approaches to Minimizing the Environmental and Social Impact of Oil Development on the Tropics* |
| *NEWSLETTER* | *Members Report* (quarterly)<br>*Orion Magazine* (quarterly magazine)<br>*Tropicus* (quarterly) |
| *CONFERENCES* | None |
| *BOARD OF DIRECTORS* | Peter A. Seligmann, chairman and chief executive officer<br><br>Other members:<br>♦ Henry H. Arnhold ♦ Michel Batisse ♦ Nini De Berger ♦ Skip Brittenham ♦ Meredith Auld Brokaw ♦ Louis W. Cabot ♦ Lewis W. Coleman ♦ Michael D. Eisner ♦ Damaris D. W. Ethridge ♦ Mark L. Feldman ♦ Harrison Ford ♦ William Clay Ford Jr. ♦ Michael H. Glawe ♦ Judson Green ♦ Charles J. Hedlund ♦ Saburo Kawai ♦ William H. Kent ♦ Joel Korn ♦ Oscar M. Lopez ♦ Bernard A. Marden ♦ Gordon E. Moore ♦ John E. McCaw Jr. ♦ Takuya Negami ♦ F. Noel Perry ♦ Nicholas J. Pritzker ♦ Lynda Rae Resnick ♦ Story Clark Resor ♦ Alfonso Romo Garza ♦ Claude Rosenberg Jr. ♦ Julio Mario Santo Domingo ♦ Kenneth F. Siebel, Jr. ♦ Edward O. Wilson ♦ Lorenzo H. Zambrano |

". . . [T]here was a small ray of hope in the announcement last week that a small South American country, Suriname, had decided to give permanent protection to four million acres of untouched tropical forests, about one-tenth of the entire country. Suriname reached its decision at the urging of Conservation International, an American environmental group that has set up a private trust fund to help Suriname manage the area. The group became actively involved in Suriname several years ago, when Asian timber interests—having pretty much stripped their own countries of marketable hardwoods—sought timber rights on 11 million acres of Suriname's forests. Suriname rejected that deal, and has now put four million of these acres out of reach.

"What makes this decision so heartening is that Suriname is a poor country that might normally have jumped at the quick profits promised by foreign logging interests. Far richer nations like Brazil have been unable to resist these blandishments, and Asian timber interests are even now burrowing deeper into the Amazon rain forest. At the other end of the economic scale, Guyana, Surname's destitute neighbor, has opened up two-thirds of its forest mass to foreign companies.

"Suriname chose the long-term economic value of forests over short-term revenues from logging and other resource-depleting activities. It hopes over time to make money from tourism generated by the forest and its spectacular animal life, from non-timber forest products like tannins and resins, and from 'bioprospecting'—the search for medicines among forest plants. The National Institutes of Health and big pharmaceutical companies like Bristol-Myers Squibb are already engaged in this search. This avenue has been left unexplored by most of the world's governments, which own 80 percent of the world's forests and which as a rule cannot see beyond the next truckload of mahogany. The lure of short-term gain is also the main reason various international agreements, including the non-binding 'forest principles' adopted at the 1992 Earth Summit in Rio de Janeiro, have had zero impact.

"The larger point here is that a living forest is worth more than a dead forest, locally and globally. Healthy forests prevent erosion and water pollution. They also act as a natural 'sink' for the carbon-based gases that contribute to global warming, and, perhaps most important, they harbor at least half of all plant and animal species, with enormous untapped benefits for human health.

"More than one-half of the world's original tropical forests have now disappeared, mostly in this century. At present rates of destruction, half of what is left could vanish in the next 50 years. This depressing prospect has not, however, inspired the wealthier nations to act constructively. One of the few tangible products of the 1992 Earth Summit was the Global Environmental Facility, a multilateral body designed to persuade poor countries to hang on to their natural assets, rain forests included. But the United States, which pledged $435 million over five years, is $200 million in arrears.

"The task of saving the forests has thus been left to private conservation groups, whose resources are limited. The very fact that one of these groups and one small country have joined to save four million acres might shame Western governments into broader action." (*New York Times*, June 21, 1998)

"Seventeen of the world's nearly 200 nations are home to at least two-thirds of all known plant and animal species. Conservation efforts by these nations are crucial if we want to preserve the biological health of our planet, according to Conservation International, a private nature-protection group, which has just published a report on megadiversity." (*Washington Post*, December 27, 1997)

"When Royal Dutch/Shell Group first explored this remote area of the Amazon [Camisea, Perú] a decade ago, its crews ripped down trees and left garbage in their wake. This time around, Shell sent in a Cambridge University-trained anthropologist and a team of biologists from the Smithsonian Institution.

"Having faced criticism for their practices in other developing countries, companies such as Shell and Mobil Corp., its minority partner in the $3 billion Camisea natural-gas project, say they want to take better care of the environment, as well as make sure that local villagers directly affected by their operations actually benefit from them. . . .

"Oil companies are under particular pressure because they are working more and more in the rain forest, one of the world's most sensitive environments. Conservation International, a Washington-based environmental group, predicts that, over the next decade, 80% of new oil and gas development will take place in the humid tropics, including those of Peru, Bolivia, Colombia and Venezuela. In Peru alone, land leased out to oil companies has tripled in the last three years to about 8.5 million acres, much of which is in the Amazon." (*Wall Street Journal*, July 17, 1997)

## POLITICAL ORIENTATION

Unavailable

# Defenders of Wildlife (1947)

1101 14th Street, NW
Suite 1400
Washington, D.C. 20005
Phone: (202) 682-9400
Fax: (202) 682-1331
Internet: information@defenders.org *or*
http://www.defenders.org

"Defenders of Wildlife is a national, nonprofit membership organization dedicated to the protection of all native wild animals and plants in their natural communities."

Unavailable

Rodger O. Schlickeisen, president. Schlickeisen joined the Defenders of Wildlife in 1991. Previously he was chief of staff to Sen. Max Baucus (D-Mont.) and chief executive officer of Craver, Mathews, Smith & Company. Schlickeisen was the associate director for economics and administration in the Office of Management and Budget during the Carter administration. He earned an undergraduate degree in economics from the University of Washington, a masters degree in business administration from Harvard University, and a doctorate from George Washington University.

501(c)(3)

1997—$12 million
1998—$12.6 million
Proposed 1999—$13.23 million

Individuals, 48 percent; membership dues, 18 percent; bequests, 18 percent; investment, 8 percent; foundation grants, 4 percent; government contracts, 3 percent; corporate donations, 1 percent

Members: 250,000 members and supporters
Branches/chapters: 7 regional offices in Alaska, Florida, New Mexico, Montana, Oregon, New York, and Washington
Affiliates: N/A

| | |
|---|---|
| *PAC* | None |
| *METHOD OF OPERATION* | ◆ Advertisements ◆ Coalition forming ◆ Congressional testimony ◆ Direct action ◆ Internet (E-mail alerts, Web site) ◆ Internships ◆ Legislative/regulatory monitoring (federal) ◆ Litigation ◆ Lobbying (federal) ◆ Media outreach |
| *CURRENT CONCERNS* | ◆ Arctic National Wildlife Refuge ◆ Biological diversity ◆ Endangered Species Act ◆ Federal lands ◆ Habitat destruction ◆ Protection of environmental laws ◆ Reintroduction of wolves to their former habitat ◆ Wildlife |
| *PUBLICATIONS* | *Saving America's Wildlife*<br>*Saving Nature's Legacy* |
| *NEWSLETTER* | *Defenders* (quarterly magazine)<br>*Florida Bear*<br>*Nature Network*<br>*Oregon Biodiversity*<br>*Wildlife Advocate* (quarterly)<br>*Wolf Action* |
| *CONFERENCES* | None |
| *BOARD OF DIRECTORS* | Alan R. Pilkington, chairman; Winsome Dunn McIntosh, vice chairman; Arthur C. Martinez, treasurer; Ann Franks Boren, secretary<br><br>Other members:<br>◆ Edward Asner ◆ Thomas C. T. Brokaw ◆ Grove T. Burnett ◆ Caroline Gabel ◆ Walter Kuhlmann ◆ Katherine A. Meyer ◆ Ruth S. Musgrove ◆ Bryan G. Norton ◆ Brian B. O'Neill ◆ Wayne Owens ◆ Terry C. Pelster ◆ Steward T.A. Pickett ◆ H. Ronald Pulliam ◆ Rodger O. Schlickeisen ◆ Karin Sheldon ◆ Jeanne Whiteing |
| *EFFECTIVENESS* | "Two environmental groups have appealed a Dec. 12 [1997] ruling by a federal judge who said a controversial federal program to reintroduce wolves to the Rocky Mountain region was illegal.<br><br>"Defenders of Wildlife and the National Wildlife Federation filed an appeal on Monday with the 10th Circuit Court of Appeals in Denver and said they were bracing themselves for what could be a long legal battle about reintroducing wolves to Yellowstone National Park and in central Idaho. U.S. District Judge William Downes earlier this month said that under the U.S. Endangered Species Act, the federal government was wrong to have experimentally introduced the wolves three years ago to an area where the animal already was found, siding with the ranchers who brought the case. . . . |

'No matter what the cost or effort, we stand ready to protect the legal right of all Americans to enjoy the splendor of wolves in our nation's oldest national park,' said Rodger Schlickeisen, president of Defenders of Wildlife. . . ." (*Washington Post*, December 31, 1997)

"Three trumpeter swans, trailing an ultralight plane whose pilot they think is their parent, lifted off at dawn yesterday from a frosty hayfield near Warrenton and headed toward the Eastern Shore in an airborne experiment aimed at restoring North America's largest waterfowl to the Chesapeake Bay. . . .

"The black-beaked white swans, named for their melodious call, have eight-foot wingspans and once lived throughout North America. Hunted nearly to extinction by the 1930s—for food, feathers and powder puffs— they now number some 19,000, mostly in the West, because of legal protections. The hope of the Migratory Bird Project is to bring the species back east, where 200,000 used to winter along the Chesapeake Bay.

" 'It's important to try to restore something,' said Rodger Schlickheisen president of Defenders of Wildlife, which is helping to bankroll the $1 million experiment. 'You can't always be losing something.'

"For decades, environmentalists watched helplessly as the United States' rare birds and other species vanished. Recently, they have tried innovative methods to raise endangered animals in captivity and set them free. Peregrine falcons and California condors are success stories, although the release of wolves in Yellowstone National Park and central Idaho, another Defenders of Wildlife campaign, has been challenged in court by ranchers. . . ." (*Washington Post*, December 19, 1997)

"By Washington standards, the protest outside the Australian Embassy on Valentine's Day was pretty tame. About a dozen protesters walked back and forth on the sidewalk. One woman held a sign reading: 'Honk If You Love Cats.' A man in a cat costume had another: 'Socks Says Spare My Mates.'

"The protest was prompted by a proposal by a member of the Australian Parliament to rid his country of a pest he said was endangering his nation's precious native species. The protest, by a group called Alley Cat Allies, was one small thrust in a long duel of sympathies that has divided people who care about animals, not only Down Under but in the United States as well. . . .

". . . [F]eral cats are defended by an assortment of supporters and volunteers who provide food and medical care and have succeeded over the last decade or two in tilting much public sentiment against the routine euthanasia of the animals.

"Like many conservationists, Bob Ferris of the group Defenders of Wildlife views these cats as exotic pests that kill an intolerable number of birds and other small animals. 'There's a whole phenomenon in ecology called co-adaptation—animals evolve to deal with what they're used to,' he said. 'Throw in something unexpected,' like a nonnative cat, and the native animals make easy prey, including, in some instances, endangered species of birds. . . ." (*Washington Post*, March 24, 1997)

Unavailable

# Earth First! Journal (1980)

P.O. Box 1415
Eugene, Oregon 97440
Phone: (541) 344-8004
Fax: (541) 344-7688
Internet: earthfirst@igc.apc.org *or*
http://www.envirolink.org/orgs/ef

| | |
|---|---|
| **PURPOSE** | "To inform, educate, and inspire citizens to take action in defense of wilderness. The Journal articulates the philosophical basis of biocentrism and provides a forum for analysis, criticism, and debate over strategy, tactics, and goals of environmentalism." |
| **STAFF** | 7 total—4 professional; 3 support; plus 1 intern |
| **DIRECTOR** | Unavailable |
| **TAX STATUS** | 501(c)(4) |
| **BUDGET** | 1998—$90,000<br>Proposed 1999—$92,000 |
| **FUNDING SOURCES** | Publications, 60 percent; merchandising, 25 percent; donations, 15 percent |
| **SCOPE** | Members: N/A<br>Branches/chapters: 250 contact groups<br>Affiliates: Bison Action Group, Cascadia Fire Ecology Education Project, Climate Action Now, Coast Watch, Cold Mountain, Cold Rivers, Direct Action Fund, Earth Liberation Prisoners, End Corporate Dominance, Warrior Poets Society, Zero Extraction for Public Lands |
| **PAC** | None |
| **METHOD OF OPERATION** | ◆ Advertisements ◆ Boycotts ◆ Campaign contributions ◆ Coalition forming ◆ Demonstrations ◆ Direct action ◆ Grassroots organizing ◆ International activities ◆ Legislative/regulatory monitoring (federal and state) ◆ Media outreach ◆ Product merchandising |

| | |
|---|---|
| ♦ Ancient forest destruction ♦ "Carmaggedon" ♦ Commodification of wilderness ♦ Congress ♦ Endangered Species Act ♦ Global warming and climate issues ♦ Industrial collapse ♦ Industrial fishing ♦ Multinational corporate control | **CURRENT CONCERNS** |
| *Earth First! Journal* (8 times a year) | **PUBLICATIONS** |
| None | **NEWSLETTER** |
| Annual conference | **CONFERENCES** |
| None | **BOARD OF DIRECTORS** |
| | **EFFECTIVENESS** |

"Enduring a cold and wet El Niño winter, Julia Hill has lived for three months on a small plywood platform here, perched in an ancient redwood 180 feet above a paint slash marking the tree for logging. . . .

"This protest tradition is not likely to disappear with a recently announced $380 million deal designed to preserve Headwaters Forest, the nation's largest stand of old-growth redwoods in private hands.

"Northern California politicians and newspapers have hailed the agreement, which would save 84 percent of the ancient redwoods owned by the Pacific Lumber Company, or Palco. But many environmental groups are focusing on the 'sacrificed 16 percent.' They say that the agreement allows Palco to cut half a billion board feet of old-growth trees, or those ranging in age from several hundred to several thousand years, including one 'cathedral grove' that spreads over an area larger than New York's Central Park. . . .

"The new deal will not stop protests, vowed Ms. Hill, who is supported by the most active group, Earth First. Since Dec. 10, she has camped in this 1,000-year-old tree, nicknamed Luna.

" 'We have to stop the rape of the forest, we have to stop putting the almighty dollar above the environment,' Ms. Hill said by walkie-talkie as she clambered barefoot along the branches of her tree, 15 stories up. . . .

"Protests have included blockades of lumber trucks, sit-ins at Palco offices and a Bonnie Raitt concert that drew 8,000 people to the Earth First base camp here. In a police response that drew national condemnation, county law enforcement officers broke up two sit-ins last fall by swabbing liquid pepper spray on the eyeballs of protesters. . . ." (*New York Times*, March 28, 1998)

"A state court jury has ordered 12 members of the environmental group Earth First to pay $1.15 million in damages to a contractor for damaged equipment and work delays as the result of protests in the virgin forests of northern Idaho. . . .

"Bernard D. Zahela, a Boise lawyer who represented 11 of the 12 defendants, said he would file a motion for a new trial because the Idaho County jury was too sympathetic to the contractor. Timber is one of the dominant industries in the densely forested county. . . .

"Leslie Hemstreet, 31, co-editor of *The Earth First Journal* in Eugene, Ore., said of the decision: 'The magnitude is so huge I can't even conceive of it. But you can't squeeze blood out of a bee.'

"Most of the defendants do not have jobs and will have trouble making any payments, Ms. Hemstreet said. . . .

"Similar lawsuits have been filed by timber interests against Earth First protesters for damage to equipment or work delays at logging sites in southern Oregon, northern California and British Columbia.

"But [defendant] Ms. [Karen] Pickett said her group's protests in the 78,000-acre Cove-Mallard primitive area in the Nez Perce National Forest in northern Idaho would continue 'as long as they're roading and logging in the wilderness.'. . ." (*New York Times,* November 8, 1996)

"When officials announced a tentative agreement last weekend to protect a 7,500-acre swath of redwoods in Northern California, they hoped it would end a decade long struggle over the fate of the last stand of the old-growth trees in private hands. . . .

"In the days since Federal and state officials outlined the plan, which would give $380 million in cash and land to the Pacific Lumber Company in exchange for the Headwaters and Elk Head forest, advocates of environmental causes have held a series of increasingly angry protests.

"On Monday, dozens of demonstrators from . . . Earth First! stormed the Democratic Party's offices in Eureka, Calif., and spread manure and feathers on the floor. In nearby Scotia, 300 people demonstrated at the headquarters of Pacific Lumber, which is controlled by the corporate financier who owns part of the forest.

"Sit-ins blocking logging roads and 'occupations' of the redwoods, where protesters perch in the trees for days at a time, have led to nearly 100 arrests in the last three days.

"The environmentalists have also gone to court, asking a Federal district judge in Philadelphia on Tuesday to block the logging of dead and dying trees in the Headwaters area. The judge, Louis C. Bechtle, denied the request on Wednesday, but he ordered Pacific Lumber to consult with the Fish and Wildlife Service and the United States Forest Service before cutting any dead trees that are still standing. . . ." (*New York Times,* October 5, 1996)

## POLITICAL ORIENTATION

"militant group" (*Washington Post*, February 1, 1998)

"radical environmental group" (*New York Times*, October 5, 1996)

"the group that defined green extremism in the 80s" (*New York Times*, July 14, 1996)

# Earth Island Institute (1982)

300 Broadway
Suite 28
San Francisco, California 94133
Phone: (415) 788-3666
Fax: (415) 788-7324
Internet: earthisland@earthisland.org *or*
http://www.earthisland.org

| | |
|---|---|
| "Develops and supports projects that counteract threats to the biological and cultural diversity that sustains the environment. Through education and activism, these projects promote the conservation, preservation and restoration of the Earth." | *PURPOSE* |
| 50 professional; plus 10 volunteers | *STAFF* |
| John A. Knox and David Phillips, co-executive directors | *DIRECTOR* |
| 501(c)(3) | *TAX STATUS* |
| 1998—Unavailable<br>Proposed 1999—Unavailable | *BUDGET* |
| Individuals, 61 percent; foundation grants, 33 percent; membership dues, 6 percent | *FUNDING SOURCES* |
| Members: 10,000 individuals, libraries, and organizations<br>Branches/chapters: N/A<br>Affiliates: N/A | *SCOPE* |
| None | *PAC* |

| **METHOD OF OPERATION** | ◆ Advertisements ◆ Boycotts ◆ Coalition forming ◆ Congressional testimony ◆ Demonstrations ◆ Direct action ◆ Films/video/audiotapes ◆ Grantmaking ◆ Grassroots organizing ◆ Initiative/referendum campaigns ◆ International activities ◆ Internet (Web site) ◆ Library/information clearinghouse ◆ Litigation ◆ Lobbying (federal, state, and grassroots) ◆ Local/municipal affairs ◆ Media outreach ◆ Research |
|---|---|
| **CURRENT CONCERNS** | ◆ Alternative paper products ◆ Education ◆ Environmental justice ◆ Habitat preservation ◆ International cooperative efforts ◆ Marine mammals ◆ Sea turtles ◆ Species protection ◆ Water pollution |
| **PUBLICATIONS** | *The Case Against Free Trade*<br>*Clearcut*<br>*Energy Policy and Community Economic Development*<br>*From Rubble to Restoration: Sustainable Habitats Through Urban Agriculture*<br>*From the Good Earth: A Celebration of Growing Food Around the World*<br>*Green for Life* (video)<br>*Leaking Underground Storage Tanks: Abandoned Gas Station Site Reclamation*<br>*Let the Mountains Talk, Let the Rivers Run*<br>*On Good Land*<br>*On the Right Track: A Handbook for Transportation and Land Use Planning, Community Action, and Neighborhood Revitalization*<br>*Principles of Environmental Justice*<br>*Reintegrating the Flatlands: A Regional Framework for Military Base Conversion in the San Francisco Bay Area*<br>*Sustainability and Justice: A Message to the President's Council on Sustainable Development* |
| **NEWSLETTER** | *Earth Island Journal* (quarterly)<br>*Northern Forest Forum* (quarterly) |
| **CONFERENCES** | None |
| **BOARD OF DIRECTORS** | David R. Brower, chairman and founder; Robert Wilkinson, president; John A. Knox, vice president and executive director; David Phillips, vice president and executive director; Maria Moyer-Angus, secretary; Tim Rands, treasurer; Peter Winkler, counsel<br><br>Other members:<br>◆ Carole Kay Combs ◆ Veronica Eady ◆ Lisa Faithorn ◆ Michael Hathaway ◆ Katherine Morgan ◆ Susan Marie Reid |

". . . At Padre Island National Seashore, Donna Shaver, who has fought for the last 18 years to save sea turtles, points out a steel table where a sea turtle awaits a necropsy to determine a cause of death. Then she heads to a pit that holds 10 dead turtles—4 of them Kemp's ridleys, which are believed to be the world's most endangered turtles and one of the most endangered species. . . .

"Conservationists say the turtles die when they get trapped in the nets of shrimp boats and drown. The large number of deaths, along with mutilations that conservationists suspect are intentional, have led three groups to demand that the waters off this national seashore be permanently closed to shrimpers.

"The groups, Earth Island Institute's Sea Turtle Restoration Project, the Humane Society of the United States and Help Endangered Animals-Ridley Turtles want 65 miles of coastline designated as a marine sanctuary.

"But the shrimping industry says that any number of causes, including pollution, are causing the deaths and that more turtles are dying because there are simply more of them out there. Putting the area off limits to shrimpers would cause more than $150 million in economic loss to an industry that employs 15,000 people in the state, said Wilma Anderson, the executive director of the Texas Shrimp Association. It would also endanger the existence of the fishing ports of Brownsville and Port Isabel, among the nation's most lucrative, she said.

"But Ms. Shaver said the turtle deaths were clearly related to shrimping. They drop 90 percent in the two months each summer when Texas bans offshore shrimpers to let shrimps grow, she said. . . ." (*New York Times*, April 19, 1998)

"And a nasty feud has exploded over the health and welfare of Hollywood's most famous flop-finned celebrity, who, these days, occasionally trails an unglamorous tapeworm behind him in his 150-foot-long pool. . .

"Keiko's story begins with a dream, one inspired by the Hollywood tear-jerker. On screen, Willy leaped to freedom. In real life, the star who played him languished in a hot, chlorinated pool in Mexico City, doing cheap tricks for dead fish.

"The Free Willy Keiko Foundation launched a rescue effort, backed by money from the movie's producers, telecommunications billionaire Craig McCaw and orca-lovers worldwide. In January 1996, the 3½-ton celebrity was flown to this seaside town and trucked to fancy new high-tech digs at the aquarium as cars honked, kids cheered and more than 350 journalists reported every flick of his fluke.

"The dream was a collaborative one. Together, the aquarium and foundation would rehabilitate Keiko, would try to set him free in the Icelandic waters where he was captured as a 2-year-old calf. The togetherness crumbled in recent months as accusations of negligence and deception flew between the organizations, and key players in both submitted resignations. 'That poor animal has been exploited beyond belief,' aquarium animal husbandry chief Neil Anderson told the *Oregonian* newspaper before resigning late last month. 'It just sickened me to watch it, and I couldn't do it anymore.'

"Exploitation, of course, is all part of show biz. The movie star's black-and-white face graces the walls, the brochures, jewelry, T-shirts, even six-packs of root beer in this town of 9,000. An economic impact analysis shows tourism linked to Keiko has poured as much as $75 million into the local economy. Several foundation members have publicly called Keiko a 'cash cow' and suggested that many in the community would like to turn his halfway house into a permanent retirement home. 'He has become so valuable to the aquarium and to Newport that issues of if and when he's going to be released are colored by that,' says David Phillips, a foundation board member and executive director of the San Francisco-based Earth Island Institute. . . ." (*Washington Post*, October 20, 1997)

". . . The greatest success for fair trade labeling was scored not by a development organization but by a San Francisco-based conservation group, the Earth Island Institute. Earth Island sued over the slaughter of dolphins by tuna fishermen, and in the process helped sensitize North American and European consumers to the point that more than 90 percent of the canned tuna sold in these countries now carry certifications that the fish was caught in nets that spare the dolphins. . . ." (*New York Times*, December 25, 1996)

". . . The U.S. State Department said . . . that such aquatic products can't be brought into the U.S. unless they are harvested in cold-water environments or fish farms where sea turtles aren't endangered, or by using methods that spare the turtles from accidental drowning.

"Under the guidelines, 44 countries, including Indonesia and Sri Lanka, are excluded from the ban on shrimp imports. But China, India, Pakistan, Bangladesh, Thailand and the Philippines are among shrimping nations affected by the ban, the U.S. Information Service said in a statement. . . .

"Glyn Davies, the State Department's acting spokesman, said the agency is acting on an order by the U.S. Court of International Trade that extends the requirements of a federal conservation law to all shrimping nations and not just to 14 Caribbean nations previously affected by the statute.

"The New York-based court issued the order in December in response to a suit filed by the San Francisco-based Earth Island Institute, a conservation group seeking to protect a number of endangered turtle species. The institute claims that a selective embargo on shrimp imports could save as many as 150,000 sea turtles from perishing in shrimp nets every year. The turtle species that the ban seeks to protect are loggerheads, Kemp's ridleys, green turtles, leatherbacks and hawksbills. . . ." (*Wall Street Journal*, May 6, 1996)

## POLITICAL ORIENTATION

"The environmental community is engaged in a rare and bitter brawl over competing Congressional bills aimed at protecting a beloved environmental symbol—the bottle-nosed dolphin. Each side thinks it has the better scheme to protect dolphins that are incidentally trapped and killed by the giant nets used by tuna fleets. This is a complex, emotional issue and all the disputants are animated by the best of intentions. But the approach contained in a measure sponsored by Representative Wayne Gilchrest, a Maryland Republican, and supported by the Clinton Administration, offers the dolphin a better chance than the alternatives.

"Mr. Gilchrest's bill rubs a lot of people the wrong way because it seems to endorse the very fishing methods that got the dolphin in trouble in the first place. For reasons that are not fully understood by scientists, adult tuna in the rich fishing grounds of the eastern Pacific tend to congregate underneath dolphins. Tuna vessels follow a school of dolphins, cast their mile-long nets and haul in the tuna below. Until a few years ago, thousands of dolphins routinely drowned in the nets or were crushed when the boats winched them in. . . .

"The Gilchrest measure has the support of Greenpeace, the Environmental Defense Fund and several other advocacy groups. It is opposed by the Sierra Club and the Defenders of Wildlife, and by the Earth Island Institute in San Francisco, which has done more than any other group to call attention to dolphin mortality. Earth Island's champion in the Senate is Barbara Boxer, the California Democrat, whose bill would continue to ban all tuna caught by the encirclement method. . . ." (*New York Times*, July 7, 1996)

# Environmental and Energy Study Institute (1984)

122 C Street, NW
Suite 700
Washington, D.C. 20001
Phone: (202) 628-1400
Fax: (202) 628-1825
Internet: eesi@eesi.org *or* http://www.eesi.org

| | |
|---|---|
| **PURPOSE** | "To produce a better-informed Congressional debate and generate a credible, innovative policy for environmentally sustainable development." |
| **STAFF** | 18 total; plus 2 interns |
| **DIRECTOR** | Carol Werner, executive director |
| **TAX STATUS** | 501(c)(3) |
| **BUDGET** | 1998—Unavailable<br>Proposed 1999—Unavailable |
| **FUNDING SOURCES** | Foundation grants; publications; corporate donations |
| **SCOPE** | Members: N/A<br>Branches/chapters: N/A<br>Affiliates: N/A |
| **PAC** | None |
| **METHOD OF OPERATION** | ♦ Conferences/seminars ♦ Congressional testimony ♦ Information clearinghouse ♦ Internet (E-mail updates, Web site) ♦ Internships ♦ Legislative/regulatory monitoring (federal) ♦ Lobbying (federal) ♦ Media outreach ♦ Participation in regulatory proceedings (federal) ♦ Telecommunications services |

◆ Agriculture and climate ◆ Alternative energy sources ◆ Alternative vehicle technologies ◆ Climate change ◆ Environmentally sustainable community development ◆ "Green taxes" and tax shifting ◆ Land use ◆ Water issues

*CFC Phaseout: An Environmental Balancing Sheet*
*Changing the Clean Water Act: Congress Kicks off the Debate*
*Clean Water Act Reauthorization*
*Debt in Developing Countries: Obstacle to Sustainable Development*
*Energy and Water Development Appropriations for Fiscal 1995*
*Energy Crops: The Potential of a Growing Resource*
*Fuel Cell Fact Sheet*
*Groundwater: A Missing Part of the Clean Water Solution*
*The Health Costs of Drinking Water Contamination*
*Identifying Threats to Water Quality*
*Interior and Related Agencies Appropriations for Fiscal 1995*
*Briefing Book on Environmental and Energy Legislation* (annual)
*Wrap-up Report: Environment, Energy and Natural Resources Legislation* (annual)
*The 104th Congress: Assessing the Impact of the Republican Majority on Environment and Energy*
*An Ounce of Prevention: Groundwater Protection Proves Cost Effective*
*President Clinton's Fiscal 1994 Budget Proposal*
*The Route to Cleaner Cars: Curves Ahead*
*Safe Drinking Water Act Amendments of 1994*
*Senate Loads up Safe Drinking Water Bill*

*CMAQ Update*
*EESI Weekly Bulletin* (weekly when Congress is in session)
*Pulse* (biweekly)

Conferences on various environmental issues often regarding pending legislation (1–2 per month on Capitol Hill)

◆ Lester R. Brown ◆ Carol E. Dinkins ◆ John E. Echohawk ◆ Richard L. Ottinger ◆ Ruth Patrick ◆ William K. Reilly ◆ John F. Seiberling ◆ John J. Sheehan ◆ Victoria Tschinkel ◆ Donna W. Wise

Unavailable

Unavailable

# Environmental Defense Fund (1967)

257 Park Avenue South
New York, New York 10010
Phone: (212) 505-2100
Fax: (212) 505-2375

1875 Connecticut Avenue, NW
Washington, D.C. 20009
Phone: (202) 387-3500
Fax: (202) 234-6049

Internet: http://www.edf.org

| | |
|---|---|
| **PURPOSE** | "Committed to a multidisciplinary approach to environmental problems, combining the efforts of scientists, economists and attorneys to devise practical, economically sustainable solutions to these problems." |
| **STAFF** | 155 total—134 professional; 21 support; plus 10 part-time and 36 interns |
| **DIRECTOR** | Fred Krupp, executive director. Before joining the Environmental Defense Fund (EDF) in 1984, Krupp was general counsel to the Connecticut Fund for the Environment, a state-level group he helped found. A graduate of the University of Michigan Law School, he has taught environmental law at the University of Michigan and Yale University and worked in private practice. |
| **TAX STATUS** | 501(c)(3) |
| **BUDGET** | Fiscal year ending September 30, 1997—$24.9 million<br>F.Y 1998—$28.3 million<br>Proposed F.Y. 1999—$30.6 million |
| **FUNDING SOURCES** | Membership dues, 32 percent; foundation grants, 31 percent; individuals, 18 percent; special events/projects, 15 percent; government contracts, 4 percent |
| **SCOPE** | Members: More than 300,000 individuals<br>Branches/chapters: N/A<br>Affiliates: N/A |
| **PAC** | None |

| | |
|---|---|
| ◆ Coalition forming ◆ Congressional testimony ◆ Fellowships ◆ Initiative/refendum campaigns ◆ Internet (databases: http://www.scorecard.org, E-mail alerts, Web site) ◆ Internships ◆ Legislative/regulatory monitoring (federal and state) ◆ Media outreach | *METHOD OF OPERATION* |

| | |
|---|---|
| ◆ Defense and restoration of biodiversity ◆ Protection of human health from toxic chemicals and pollution ◆ Rivers and watershed ◆ Safeguarding of oceans from pollution and overfishing ◆ Stabilization of climates | *CURRENT CONCERNS* |

| | |
|---|---|
| The following is a list of major publications:<br><br>*EDF-McDonald's Waste Reduction Task Force Final Report*<br>*Recycling and Incineration: Evaluating the Choices*<br>*Developing Markets for Recycling Multiple Grades of Residential Paper*<br>*Ranking Refineries: What Do We Know About Oil Refinery Pollution From Right to Know Data?*<br>*Global Warming: Understanding the Forecast*<br>*Dead Heat: The Race Against the Greenhouse Effect*<br>*Polluted Coastal Waters: The Role of Acid Rain*<br>*Habitat Restoration in Aquatic Ecosystems*<br>*The Hidrovia Paraguay-Paraná Navigation Project: Report of an Independent Review*<br>*How Wet is a Wetland? The Impacts of the Proposed Revisions to the Federal Wetlands Delineation Manual*<br><br>Also publishes reports, action guides, and brochures | *PUBLICATIONS* |

| | |
|---|---|
| *EDF Letter* (bimonthly) | *NEWSLETTER* |

| | |
|---|---|
| None | *CONFERENCES* |

| | |
|---|---|
| John H.T. Wilson, chairman; Gretchen Long Glickman, Teresa Heinz, and Frank E. Loy, vice chairpersons; Charles J. Hamilton Jr., treasurer; Arthur P. Cooley, secretary<br><br>Other members of the board of trustees:<br>◆ Nancy O. Alderman ◆ Karen M. Barnes ◆ Rod A. Beckstrom ◆ Wendy W. Benchley ◆ James W.B. Benkard ◆ Sally G. Bingham ◆ Jessica Catto ◆ Mimi Cecil ◆ Christopher J. Elliman ◆ John W. Firor ◆ Robert E. Grady ◆ Norbert S. Hill Jr. ◆ Lewis B. Kaden ◆ Gene E. Likens ◆ Jane Lubchenco ◆ George G. Montgomery Jr. ◆ Harold A. Mooney ◆ Robert W. Musser ◆ William A. Newsom ◆ Paul H. Nitze ◆ David P. Rall ◆ Lewis S. Ranieri ◆ E. John Rosenwald Jr. ◆ John McAllen Scanlan ◆ David H. Smith ◆ Frank E. Taplin Jr. ◆ W. Richard West Jr. ◆ Robert W. Wilson ◆ Wren W. Wirth ◆ Paul Junger Witt ◆ Charles F. Wurster | *BOARD OF DIRECTORS* |

## EFFECTIVENESS

"In one of the most far-reaching marriages of computer technology and environmental activism yet, a Web site unveiled Wednesday allows anyone in the United States with Internet access to locate polluting industries in their neighborhood, research the amount of chemicals being released and learn the risk with a few clicks of a mouse.

"The new site was assembled by the Oakland offices of the non-profit Environmental Defense Fund at a cost of more than $1 million and a year of work. . . .

" 'The environmental movement has to get more creative with our approaches,' said Fred Krupp, executive director of the Environmental Defense Fund, based in New York City. 'We're trying to harness the information revolution and empower citizens.'

"If the first day of the Web site's operation is any indication, there is great interest in the pollution data. During its first five hours online, the site received 300,000 hits—causing a temporary overload to the server." (*San Jose Mercury News*, April 16, 1998)

"Now that their quest to protect the environment has evolved from a batty sideshow into a mainstream issue for governments and big business, environmentalists have smartened up their act. Gone are the woolly jumpers and sandals. In their place are smart suits and ties. . . .

"The 1990s transformation of the environmentalist movement had its origins in the US with the Environmental Defense Fund. The group's founding motto in 1967 was 'sue the bastards,' a reference to its goal of forcing companies to improve their behaviour through lawsuits." (Leyla Boulton, *Financial Times*, December 30, 1997)

"Between now and December, when the industrialized nations will meet in Kyoto, Japan, to negotiate a treaty controlling emissions of carbon dioxide and other greenhouse gases, Mr. Clinton must devise a specific American proposal. . . .

"There is one other element to his strategy that he has not talked about, but which may well be his ace in the hole in Kyoto as he tries to draw developing countries into the mix while providing flexibility for American industries. Devised by the Environmental Defense Fund, this is an emissions-trading scheme in which rich nations that cannot meet their assigned targets without crippling taxes or investments would be able to 'buy' pollution permits from poorer countries whose economies are so inefficient that even the tiniest adjustments can achieve big reductions in greenhouse emissions. That money, in turn, would help developing countries invest in cleaner technologies." (Robert B. Semple Jr., *New York Times*, October 6, 1997)

"The single most powerful symbol in the debate over Texas water policy is the 'right of capture' as applied to groundwater. This concept holds that the landowner with the biggest straw gets to draw as much water as desired, when desired.

"But . . . the fear of groundwater overuse grips state water experts. Still, the right of capture is so deeply cherished by rural interests that the Legislature is not yet prepared to end it.

"One promising reform includes market incentives. As Pete Emerson of the Austin office of the Environmental Defense Fund notes, water market mechanisms—including graduated price hikes—can signal consumers to use less water. Large-scale water consumers can be encouraged to buy, sell or trade water rights. The environment and the economy can benefit simultaneously." (*Dallas Morning News*, April 27, 1997)

"... But Fred Krupp, executive director of the Environmental Defense Fund, which has been an ally of the White House in the Kyoto process, credited Gore with initiating a 'diplomatic thaw' that greatly improved chances for a treaty. 'In my view, the deadlock has been broken,' he said." (*Washington Post*, December 9, 1997)

# POLITICAL ORIENTATION

# Environmental Law Institute (1969)

1616 P Street, NW
Suite 200
Washington, D.C. 20036
Phone: (202) 939-3800
Fax: (202) 939-3868
Internet: law@eli.org *or* http://www.eli.org

**PURPOSE**

"Advances environmental protection by improving law, management, and policy. ELI researches pressing problems, educates professionals and citizens about the nature of these issues, and convenes all sectors to develop solutions."

**STAFF**

54 total—54 full-time; plus 2 part-time; 3 interns

**DIRECTOR**

J. William Futrell, president. Before joining the Environmental Law Institute (ELI), Futrell was professor of law at the University of Georgia and the University of Alabama, worked as an attorney in private practice, and served as president of the Sierra Club.

**TAX STATUS**

501(c)(3)

**BUDGET**

1997—$5.3 million
1998—$5.9 million
Proposed 1999—$6 million

**FUNDING SOURCES**

Foundation grants and contracts, 55 percent; publications, 15 percent; associates, 14 percent; royalties, 6 percent; other, 10 percent

**SCOPE**

Members: 3,592
Branches/chapters: N/A
Affiliates: ELI's Wetlands Program, Center for State Environmental Programs, Global Policy Research Center, Center for East European Environmental Programs, Inter-American Environmental Policy Center

**PAC**

None

◆ Awards program ◆ Conferences/seminars ◆ International activities ◆ Internet (Web site) ◆ Internships ◆ Legislative/regulatory monitoring (federal and state) ◆ Library/information clearinghouse ◆ Local/ municipal affairs ◆ Mailing list ◆ Media outreach ◆ Research ◆ Speakers program ◆ Training and technical assistance

◆ Advanced planning for environmental protection ◆ Biodiversity ◆ Efficient land use ◆ Energy efficiency ◆ Environmental auditing and other regulatory reforms ◆ Environmental enforcement and negotiation training ◆ Integration of federal environmental law ◆ Market-based incentives ◆ Medical wastes tracking ◆ Risk management and assessment ◆ Solid waste ◆ Superfund cleanup actions and costs ◆ Surface coal mining ◆ Toxic and oxidant air pollution ◆ Toxic substances and hazardous wastes ◆ Toxic torts and victim compensation ◆ Transboundary air pollution ◆ Wetlands protection and sensitive lands regulation

*Clean Air Deskbook*
*Clean Water Deskbook*
*Development and Environment: Rethinking the Relationship*
*Environmental Crimes Deskbook*
*Environmental Law and Practice*
*Environmental Law Reporter Deskbooks* (series)
*Environmental Regulation of Coal Mining*
*European Community Deskbook*
*Fundamentals of Negotiation: A Guide for Environmental Professionals*
*Hard Rock Mining: State Approaches to Environmental Protection*
*Law of Environmental Protection*
*Measuring the Benefits of Federal Wetland Programs*
*NEPA Deskbook*
*New Uses for Old Tools: Protecting Biodiversity and Preventing Pollution Under Existing Laws*
*Oil Pollution Deskbook*
*Our National Wetland Heritage: A Protection Guide*
*Practical Guide to Environmental Management*
*Protecting the Gulf of Aqaba*
*RCRA Deskbook*
*Reauthorizing Superfund: Lessons from the States*
*Reorienting Risk Assessment*
*Superfund Deskbook*
*Sustainable Environmental Law*
*Toxic Substances and Pesticides Regulation Deskbook*
*The Transition to Sustainable Development Law*
*Wetlands Deskbook*
*Wetlands Protection: The Role of Economics*

Also publishes monographs and research briefs

*The Environmental Forum* (bimonthly)
*Environmental Law Reporter* (monthly)
*The National Wetlands Newsletter* (bimonthly)

## CONFERENCES

ELI Associates Seminars
ELI/EPA Economic Benefits Seminars
ELI National Courses
—Air and Water Pollution Control Law
—Environmental Law Conference (annual)
—Corporate Environmental Management Dialogue
—Cost Recovery for Leaking Underground Storage Tanks
—Environmental Regulation in the 1990s
—Fourth Annual Conference on Wetlands Law and Regulation
—Groundwater Enforcement
—Hazardous Waste, Superfund, and Toxic Substances
—Health & Safety Training for Medical Waste Inspectors
—International Symposium: Wetlands and River Corridor Management
—Medical Waste Roundtable
—National Environmental Moot Court Competition/Litigation Workshop
—Negotiation Skills Workshop
—Professional Education
—RCRA Administrative Process Training
—Waste Crimes
—Water Quality and Agriculture: An International Perspective on Policies Symposium
—Wetlands Enforcement Workshop

## BOARD OF DIRECTORS

Turner Smith Jr., chairman; J. William Futrell, president; Robert Percival, secretary/treasurer

Other members:
◆ Braden Allenby ◆ Wayne Balta ◆ Dorothy Bowers ◆ Francoise Burhenne-Guilmin ◆ Leslie Carothers ◆ Norman Dean ◆ Lynne Edgerton ◆ Mary Gade ◆ James Gilliland ◆ F. Henry Habicht II ◆ Ridgway Hall Jr. ◆ I. Michael Heyman ◆ Elliott Levitas ◆ Thomas Milch ◆ James Moore ◆ Eleanor Holmes Norton ◆ Ann Powers ◆ Kathy Prosser ◆ Stephen Ramsey ◆ Suzi Ruhl ◆ Karin Sheldon ◆ Donald Stever ◆ Margaret Strand ◆ Gerald Torres ◆ Thomas Udall ◆ Gregory Wetstone ◆ Jess Womack ◆ Grover Wrenn

## EFFECTIVENESS

" 'If the federal government were to pull out of new Superfund activity, there would be an incredible demand on the state of Texas,' says the conservation commission's Mr. McBee. 'So we might have to factor that possibility into negotiations on the state program.'

Texas isn't alone. Every state (except Nebraska, which has no Superfund) has struggled financially with its program in recent years, says John Pendergrass, an analyst with the Environmental Law Institute in Washington, D.C.

"For example, Mr. Pendergrass says, New York sold $1.2 billion of bonds in 1986 to clean up its contaminated sites. But the state has already spent half the money, and is expected to look for another source of revenue in coming years, as it cleans up more than 900 contaminated sites. Other states, such as Massachusetts, have borrowed their limit for cleanups, and have had to levy new fees or taxes to keep their programs going, Mr. Pendergrass says." (*Wall Street Journal*, May 8, 1996)

". . . There is a widespread complaint from both the right and left that the 1996 campaign has done little to prepare the country for those challenges. Missing from the dialogue between President Clinton and Robert J. Dole are issues ranging from the possible 'implosion' of North Korea to the explosive problem of urban unemployment and welfare's diminishing safety net. . . .

"Other domestic concerns also pop up with some frequency among the policy brokers. Regulatory issues on electric power, transportation and the environment 'aren't getting much attention,' said Fred L. Smith Jr. of the Competitive Enterprise Institute. 'The whole question of priority-setting and devolution will come up whoever is president.'

"J. William Futrell of the Environmental Law Institute said global and domestic issues, including the unratified biodiversity treaty, are pending. 'The regulatory system we have requires a lot of expertise from business,' he said, 'and this Congress raised legitimate questions about how small business can deal with this challenge. We ought to be discussing that—as well as the public lands and endangered species issues on which there is no consensus.' " (*Washington Post*, October 6, 1996)

Unavailable

# POLITICAL ORIENTATION

# Environmental Working Group (1993)

1718 Connecticut Avenue, NW
Suite 600
Washington, D.C. 20009
Phone: (202) 667-6982
Fax: (202) 232-2592
Internet: info@ewg.org *or* http://www.ewg.org

| | |
|---|---|
| **PURPOSE** | "To improve the environmental performance of the U.S. economy through reform of public policy." |
| **STAFF** | 18 total |
| **DIRECTOR** | Ken A. Cook, president |
| **TAX STATUS** | 501(c)(3) |
| **BUDGET** | 1998—Unavailable<br>Proposed 1999—Unavailable |
| **FUNDING SOURCES** | Foundation grants and private individuals, 100 percent |
| **SCOPE** | Members: N/A<br>Branch/chapter: An office in San Francisco<br>Affiliate: "The Environmental Working Group is a project of the Tides Foundation" |
| **PAC** | None |
| **METHOD OF OPERATION** | ♦ Internet ♦ Legislative/regulatory monitoring (federal) ♦ Library/information clearinghouse (Clearinghouse on Environmental Advocacy and Research [CLEAR]) ♦ Media outreach ♦ Research ♦ Telecommunications services (databases) |

♦ Agricultural subsidies ♦ Environmental implications of federal budget and appropriations policy ♦ Pesticides in food and drinking water ♦ State and local environmental issues

*CURRENT CONCERNS*

*Billboards Report*
*The Cash Croppers*
*Catching the Limit*
*City Slickers*
*Clearing the Air*
*Deal Breaker*
*Dumping Sewage Sludge On Organic Farms?*
*EPA's Air Rule Would Help CA Kids*
*EWG Air Monitoring Finds Toxic Pesticide Drifting Into Mobile Home Park*
*EWG Air Monitoring Results in Castroville, CA*
*EWG Comments*
*Factory Farming: Toxic Fertilizer in the United States 1990–1995*
*Faking Takings*
*First Do No Harm*
*Forbidden Fruit: Illegal Pesticides in the U.S. Food Supply*
*Fox in the Henhouse*
*How Do You Spell Relief? "P-A-C C-A-S-H"*
*In The Drink*
*Last Gasp*
*Mean Streets*
*Methyl Bromide Health Standards Flawed*
*Methyl Bromide Use Near California Schools 1995*
*New Clean Air Standards Are No Sweat in Florida*
*The Other Clean Air Rule: Particle Pollution and Sudden Infant Death Syndrome in the United States*
*Overexposed: Organophosphate Insecticides in Children's Food*
*People of Color in California Breathe the Most Heavily Polluted Air*
*Pesticide Industry Propaganda*
*Pesticides in Baby Food*
*Phase out Cyanazine*
*Potholes and Politics*
*Protecting California's Wetlands?*
*Same As It Ever Was . . .*
*Setting the Record Straight*
*Share the Road*
*Shopper's Guide to Pesticides in Produce*
*Smokestacks and Smoke Screens*
*Something's In The Air*
*State's Internal Study Showed Dangers of Drifting Methyl Bromide*
*Take More Money . . . And Run*
*Tough to Swallow: How Pesticide Companies Profit from Poisoning America's Tap Water*
*Weed Killers by the Glass*

None

## CONFERENCES

None

## BOARD OF DIRECTORS

None

## EFFECTIVENESS

"Vice President Al Gore, trying to mollify an anxious agriculture industry, is ordering the Environmental Protection Agency to revamp the process it uses to decide whether pesticides are dangerous to children.

"His directive follows an escalating lobbying campaign by the agriculture and chemical industries and their allies in Congress, who have complained that the agency is too zealous in carrying out a food safety law that Congress passed unanimously in 1996. . . .

"But the White House's intervention has raised concerns among some environmental advocates, who warned that it might slow down the E.P.A. while it faces an August 1999 deadline for reviewing hundreds of pesticides. . . .

" 'I have a hard time concluding that it is a major sellout, or even any kind of sellout,' said Ken Cook, president of the Environmental Working Group, a leading advocacy group working for stricter pesticide regulations. 'It is a bone that is being thrown to the agriculture interests, it seems to me, that really anticipates tough decisions.'. . ." (*New York Times*, April 8, 1998)

"A report by two nonprofit groups released yesterday says that 71 percent of urban highways in the Washington area are in fair to poor condition and that 25 percent are in poor or mediocre condition.

"The Surface Transportation Policy Project and the Environmental Working Group used information received through Freedom of Information Act requests to the Federal Highway Administration to compile the report, 'Potholes and Politics.' . . . The study also found that Washington-area drivers spend more than $118,000,000 per year fixing the damage to their cars caused by the District's pothole-ridden urban highways. That's four times what the city's highway department spends fixing the same roads. . . ." (*Washington Post*, September 17, 1997)

"The south Florida cities of Miami and Fort Lauderdale are the most dangerous places in the nation to be a pedestrian, according to a report released last week.

"In fact, vehicle-friendly Sunbelt cities dominate the list of most hazardous cities in the 'Mean Streets' report from the Surface Transportation Policy Project and the Environmental Working Group. Meanwhile, older Eastern cities predominate on the list of safest cities. . . ." (*Washington Post*, April 15, 1997)

"The average New Jersey family could save more than $500 a year in gasoline costs if tighter fuel-efficiency standards were in place, according to a study by environmental groups. . . .

"The report, released on Thursday by the Environmental Working Group and the Surface Transportation Policy Project, based its savings estimates on standards of 45 miles a gallon for cars and 34 miles a gallon for light trucks like sport utilities, mini-vans and pickup trucks. Current standards average 27.5 miles a gallon for cars and 20.7 miles a gallon for light trucks. . . .

"The study said the higher mileage requirements would cut nearly half the amount of gases needed to reduce emissions to 1990 levels between the years 2008 and 2012—a goal that the Clinton Administration plans to take to next month's global warming summit in Japan. . . ." (*New York Times*, November 23, 1997)

Unavailable

## POLITICAL ORIENTATION

# Farm Animal Reform Movement (FARM) (1981)

10101 Ashburton Lane
Bethesda, Maryland 20817
Phone: (301) 530-1737
Fax: (301) 530-5747
Internet: farm@farmusa.org *or* http://www.farmusa.org

| | |
|---|---|
| **PURPOSE** | "To alleviate and eliminate animal abuse and other destructive impacts of animal agriculture on human health, food resources, and environmental integrity." |
| **STAFF** | 7 total—4 professional; 3 support |
| **DIRECTOR** | Alex Hershaft, president and treasurer. Hershaft, founder of the Farm Animal Reform Movement (FARM), was formerly a consultant to the Environmental Protection Agency. Before becoming active in the animal rights movement, Hershaft was involved in the civil liberties and environmental movements, founding public interest organizations in both areas. He attended the University of Connecticut and Iowa State University, where he was awarded a Ph.D. in chemistry. |
| **TAX STATUS** | 501(c)(3) |
| **BUDGET** | 1998—$150,000<br>Proposed 1999—Unavailable |
| **FUNDING SOURCES** | Public contributions, 80 percent; foundation grants, 20 percent |
| **SCOPE** | Members: 12,000<br>Branches/chapters: N/A<br>Affiliates: N/A |
| **PAC** | None |

| | |
|---|---|
| ◆ Advertisements ◆ Awards program ◆ Children's education ◆ Coalition forming ◆ Conferences/seminars ◆ Congressional testimony ◆ Demonstrations ◆ Direct action ◆ Electoral politics ◆ Films/video/ audiotapes ◆ Grassroots organizing ◆ Internet (Web site) ◆ Library/ information clearinghouse (open to public) ◆ Media outreach ◆ Participation in regulatory proceedings (federal) ◆ Research ◆ Training and technical assistance | *METHOD OF OPERATION* |
| ◆ Effect of animal agriculture on world food supplies and on agricultural resources and environmental quality ◆ Effect of animal products on consumer health ◆ Mistreatment of animals in "factory farms" and auction yards | *CURRENT CONCERNS* |
| Brochures, fact sheets, directory of educational materials | *PUBLICATIONS* |
| *The FARM Report* (quarterly) | *NEWSLETTER* |
| None | *CONFERENCES* |
| Alex Hershaft, president and treasurer; Melinda Marks, vice president | *BOARD OF DIRECTORS* |
| Unavailable | *EFFECTIVENESS* |
| Unavailable | *POLITICAL ORIENTATION* |

# Foundation on Economic Trends (1980)

1660 L Street, NW
Suite 216
Washington, D.C. 20036
Phone: (202) 466-2823
Fax: (202) 429-9602

## PURPOSE

"Monitors the development and commercialization of new technologies that are likely to have a destructive effect on our world. Of particular concern are the ethical, environmental, and economic implications of biotechnology."

## STAFF

Unavailable

## DIRECTOR

Jeremy Rifkin, president. Rifkin has been involved in environmental issues and science and technology policy for nearly two decades. He has testified before numerous congressional committees and has been a guest on a variety of television programs. Rifkin holds a B.S. in economics from the Wharton School of Finance and Commerce, University of Pennsylvania, and an M.A. in international affairs from the Fletcher School of Law and Diplomacy, Tufts University.

## TAX STATUS

Tax-exempt organization

## BUDGET

1998—Unavailable
Proposed 1999—Unavailable

## FUNDING SOURCES

Public interest foundations

## SCOPE

Members: N/A
Branches/chapters: N/A
Affiliates: Global Greenhouse Network, Pure Food Campaign, Safe Organic Standards Campaign, Global Days of Action

## PAC

None

| | |
|---|---|
| ◆ Boycott ◆ Coalition forming ◆ Congressional testimony ◆ Education ◆ Grassroots organizing ◆ International activities ◆ Legislative/regulatory monitoring (federal and state) ◆ Litigation ◆ Media outreach ◆ Participation in regulatory proceedings (federal and state) ◆ Research | *METHOD OF OPERATION* |
| ◆ Animal and human cloning ◆ Biotechnology ◆ Bovine growth hormone ◆ Emerging technologies ◆ Genetic research ◆ Organic food standards | *CURRENT CONCERNS* |
| *The Biotech Century: Harnessing the Gene and Remaking the World* <br> *The End of Work: The Decline of the Global Labor Force and the Dawn of the Post-Market Era* | *PUBLICATIONS* |
| None | *NEWSLETTER* |
| None | *CONFERENCES* |
| Unavailable | *BOARD OF DIRECTORS* |
| "Dr. Stuart A. Newman, a professor of cell biology and anatomy at New York Medical College, wanted to do something controversial to evoke public and scientific debate on the morality of genetic engineering. So Dr. Newman and a colleague filed a patent for a process to make 'chimeras,' creatures that are part human, part animal. <br><br> "A resident of Pleasantville, Dr. Newman and his colleague, Jeremy Rifkin, president of the Foundation on Economics Trends in Washington, do not want to make the creatures. In fact, Dr. Newman does not think anyone should be allowed to make them and thinks these kinds of patents should be rejected. But he wants people to talk more about the issues so laws and ethics can be established before science delivers a done deal." (*New York Times*, May 31, 1998) <br><br> "There are few legal obstacles to the cloning of animals or even humans in the U.S., but many ethical questions and commercial disputes are likely to arise if companies start to apply the technology. <br><br> "Bioethicists say groups representing doctors, farmers and churches are likely to object to any attempts to clone human beings and possibly any type of mammal. They expect them to lobby Congress to pass legislation to prohibit or strictly regulate the process. Indeed, the Foundation on Economics Trends said yesterday that it had organized 400 religious and health organizations world-wide to push for new laws banning human cloning." (*Wall Street Journal*, February 25, 1997) | *EFFECTIVENESS* |

"The arrival of the first shipment of genetically engineered soybeans from the United States has triggered a wave of anxious protests and boycott appeals from consumer groups across Germany, threatening one of the most lucrative American exports to Europe.

"The controversy over the new bean, which is endowed with a special gene that protects the crop against a weed-killing chemical, is the latest salvo in a burgeoning billion-dollar trade conflict that rapidly is engulfing the United States and its European allies because of contrasting views about how to harness the wonders of biotechnology. The United States insists that all scientific evidence shows the high-tech beans pose no risk to consumers and should be treated just like ordinary soybeans. Only 2 percent of all American land used in soybean production has been planted with genetically modified seeds.

"Even though the German government and its European Union partners have approved sale of the gene-altered beans and declared them safe, a consumer backlash here has spawned fresh demands—strenuously opposed by the United States—that the new beans be labeled to distinguish them from ordinary ones. . . .

"Even the boycott organizers are surprised by the intensity of support. 'I'm a little amazed by how this has caught fire,' said Jeremy Rifkin, president of the Foundation on Economics Trends, a Washington-based interest group that has called for a boycott of corporations that use engineered soy or corn in their products. 'It shows how people are so worried about these new risks to the environment,' he added.

"Rifkin warned that the gene for herbicide resistance might 'jump' to surrounding weeds, making them resistant as well. 'And we have no idea about the allergenic reaction when you place into plants genetic material that has never before been in the human food chain,' Rifkin said." (*Washington Post*, November 7, 1996)

"Philosophically, the notion that welfare recipients ought to be required to work is an easy sell. Pragmatically, it runs into a small problem: Where will the jobs come from?

". . . Jeremy Rifkin [president of the Foundation on Economic Trends] has been offering a possible answer: the not-for-profit sector.

"Given the trend toward smaller government and the decline of labor-intensive industry, he believes, there's no chance government and private markets can produce enough jobs to take up the slack left by welfare reform. That, he says, will require the creative use of the so-called third sector—the nonprofits.

"It's easy enough to dream up thousands of new jobs. Work requirements for former welfare recipients could mean new jobs in a vastly expanded day-care industry. America's aging population means a growing need for one-to-one care. Neighborhoods need restoring, the environment needs improving, children need mentoring, recreation and after-school supervision—all potential sources of jobs.

"But not of profits. Where will the money for salaries come from?

"Rifkin, who will be broaching some of his ideas this week at the leadership summit of the National League of Cities in Seattle, has an answer for that one, too: Captive taxes. . . .

" 'Look, I know people don't like taxes, but the truth is we're going to pay taxes—if not for programs like the one I'm proposing, then for more prisons. Already Californians are fast approaching the time when they will be paying more for prisons than for education. If poor people can't find work, they are going to commit crime. The average cost of imprisonment at the state level is about $30,000 a year. And inmates have no purchasing power, they pay no taxes and they don't become better citizens. It's a bad investment.'...

" 'The first thing we have to do is to change our notions of the importance of this sort of work,' he says. 'Market capital works on the theory that you optimize the well-being of the community by encouraging each individual to pursue his own best interest. True, but that's only half the picture, and pursuing that half is one reason we're in so much trouble now. The other half is that each citizen, by seeking to optimize the good of the community, optimizes his own well-being.' " (*Washington Post*, August 19, 1996)

Unavailable

# POLITICAL ORIENTATION

# Friends of the Earth (1990)

1025 Vermont Avenue, NW
Washington, D.C. 20005
Phone: (202) 783-7400
Fax: (202) 783-0444
Internet:foe@foe.org *or* http://www.foe.org

| | |
|---|---|
| **PURPOSE** | "Dedicated to protecting the planet from environmental degradation; preserving biological, cultural, and ethnic diversity; and empowering citizens to have an influential voice in decisions affecting the quality of their environment—and their lives." |
| **STAFF** | 30 total—25 professional; 2 support; 3 fellows; plus 4 interns per academic semester |
| **DIRECTOR** | Brent Blackwelder, president. Blackwelder was a founder of the Environmental Policy Institute, which merged with Friends of the Earth in 1989. An environmental lobbyist in Washington for over 20 years, he has also served as board chairman of the League of Conservation Voters and American Rivers, Inc. Blackwelder holds an M.A. in mathematics from Yale University and a Ph.D. in philosophy from the University of Maryland. |
| **TAX STATUS** | 501(c)(3) |
| **BUDGET** | 1997—$2.3 million<br>1998—$2.4 million<br>Proposed 1999—$2.2 million |
| **FUNDING SOURCES** | Grants, 67 percent; membership contributions, 26 percent; bequests, 2 percent; other, 4 percent |
| **SCOPE** | Members: 20,000 individuals<br>Branches/chapters: Office in Seattle<br>Affiliate: Friends of the Earth International, a network of 57 international organizations |
| **PAC** | Friends of the Earth Action |

♦ Coalition forming ♦ Conferences/seminars ♦ Demonstrations ♦ Direct action ♦ Grassroots organizing ♦ International activities ♦ Internet (Web site) ♦ Legislative/regulatory monitoring (federal and state) ♦ Lobbying (federal and grassroots) ♦ Media outreach ♦ Participation in regulatory proceedings (federal) ♦ Research ♦ Telecommunications services (databases and mailing lists)

## METHOD OF OPERATION

♦ Biotechnology ♦ Central American environmental policies ♦ Chemical plant safety ♦ Corporate accountability in the environment ♦ Energy policy ♦ Environmental degradation caused by off-road vehicles ♦ Environmental taxes ♦ Federal appropriations to environmental concerns ♦ Global warming ♦ Groundwater and drinking water contamination ♦ International Monetary Fund, World Bank, and Overseas Private Investment Corp. environmental policies ♦ National coal policy ♦ Ozone depletion ♦ Solid and hazardous waste ♦ Sustainable agriculture ♦ Toxic chemical emergency planning

## CURRENT CONCERNS

*The Anatomy of a Deal*
*Citizens' Guide to Environmental Tax Shifting*
*Citizens' Guide to NAFTA's Environmental Commission*
*Cool It*
*Dirty Little Secrets*
*Earth Budget*
*Environmental Education Kit*
*Green Paycheck Employees Handbook*
*Green Scissors*
*License to Loot*
*Lose the Noose*
*Ozone Reality Check*
*Reaping Havoc*
*Road to Ruin*
*The Technical and Economic Feasibility of Replacing Methyl Bromide*
*Trails of Destruction*
*Understanding Household Chemicals*
*Voting as if Your Planet Depended On It*

## PUBLICATIONS

*Close to Home* (quarterly)
*Friends of the Earth* (quarterly)

## NEWSLETTER

Annual conference

## CONFERENCES

♦ Darryl L. Alexander ♦ Ed Begley Jr. ♦ Jayni Chase ♦ Harriett Crosby ♦ Clarence Ditlow ♦ Dan Gabel ♦ Alisa Gravitz ♦ Michael Herz ♦ Ann Hoffman ♦ Marion Hunt-Badiner ♦ Martin Arthur McCrory ♦ Patricia Matthews ♦ Avis Ogilvy Moore ♦ Josephine Murray ♦ Arlie Schardt ♦ Rick Taketa ♦ LynDee Wells ♦ David Zwick

## BOARD OF DIRECTORS

## EFFECTIVENESS

"A diverse, bipartisan coalition—including the Citizens for a Sound Economy, Friends of the Earth, Public Citizen and the Heritage Foundation—joined together yesterday to 'stop the bailout' of electric utilities as the industry moves toward deregulation.

"The 'bailout' the groups oppose is the payment of 'stranded costs,' or investments utilities made in generation and other assets to serve customers in their specific territories. Utilities say those investments will become stranded when power generation is deregulated because their recovery will no longer be guaranteed through electricity bills paid by consumers.

"Utilities and others have estimated that stranded costs could be between $200 billion and $300 billion. But the 'stop the bailout' coalition said bailing out the industry for bad investments 'would constitute one of the largest transfers of wealth in U.S. history.' " (*Wall Street Journal*, August 8, 1997)

## POLITICAL ORIENTATION

"on the left" (*Wall Street Journal*, December 18, 1996)

# The Fund for Animals (1967)

200 West 57th Street
New York, New York 10019
Phone: (212) 246-2096
Fax: (212) 246-2633

1821 Georgia Avenue
Suite 301
Silver Spring, Maryland 20910
Phone: (301) 585-2591
Fax: (301) 585-2595

Internet: fund4animals@fund.org *or* http://www.fund.org

| | |
|---|---|
| "To speak for those who can't." | **PURPOSE** |
| 60 total—56 professional; 4 support; plus 4 interns | **STAFF** |
| Heidi Prescott, national director | **DIRECTOR** |
| 501(c)(3) | **TAX STATUS** |
| 1997—$4.2 million<br>1998—$4.4 million<br>Proposed 1999—$4.6 million | **BUDGET** |
| Bequests, 50 percent; memberships, 25 percent; merchandise, grants, and miscellaneous, 25 percent (receives no government funding) | **FUNDING SOURCES** |
| Members: 100,000 individuals<br>Branches/chapters: Legislative offices in Albany, New York, and San Francisco; paid coordinators in Connecticut, Michigan, Oregon, and Wyoming<br>Affiliates: N/A | **SCOPE** |
| None | **PAC** |

| | |
|---|---|
| *METHOD OF OPERATION* | ◆ Advertisements ◆ Boycotts ◆ Demonstrations ◆ Direct action ◆ Direct animal care ◆ Films/video/audiotapes ◆ Grassroots organizing ◆ Information clearinghouse ◆ Initiative/referendum campaigns ◆ Internet (E-mail alerts, Web site) ◆ Internships ◆ Legislative/regulatory monitoring (federal and state) ◆ Library (open to the public) ◆ Litigation ◆ Lobbying (federal, state, and grassroots) ◆ Local/municipal affairs ◆ Media outreach ◆ Participation in regulatory proceedings (federal and state) ◆ Polling ◆ Product merchandising ◆ Research ◆ Speakers program |

| | |
|---|---|
| *CURRENT CONCERNS* | ◆ Vegetarianism ◆ Combating sport hunting ◆ Dog and cat overpopulation ◆ Protection of wildlife ◆ Yellowstone bison slaughter ◆ Pigeon shoots in Pennsylvania ◆ Endangered Species Act ◆ Ohio Mourning Dove Initiative |

| | |
|---|---|
| *PUBLICATIONS* | *Fund Facts* |

*—Animal Damage Control*
*—The Bloody Business of Fur*
*—The Destruction of Our Nation's Waterfowl*
*—Factory Farming*
*—Living with Bears*
*—Living with Beavers*
*—Living with Deer*
*—An Overview of Killing for Sport*
*—Pet Overpopulation*
*—War on the Environment*
*—White-Tailed Deer: Creatures or Crops?*
*Gunblast: Culture Clash* (video)
*What's Wrong With Hunting?* (video)

Also publishes action alerts, flyers, curriculum units, education comic books, catalogues, and hunting articles

| | |
|---|---|
| *NEWSLETTER* | *Activist Update* (periodic)<br>*Congressional Scorecard* (periodic)<br>*Fund Newsletter* (3 times per year)<br>*News Bulletin* (3 times per year)<br>*Spay/Neuter Legislative Bulletin* (6 times per year) |

| | |
|---|---|
| *CONFERENCES* | None |

| | |
|---|---|
| *BOARD OF DIRECTORS* | Cleveland Amory, president and chairman; Marian Probst, treasurer-secretary<br><br>Other members:<br>◆ Barbara Brack ◆ Del Donati ◆ Michael Kilian ◆ Judith Ney ◆ Edgar Smith ◆ Allison Stern ◆ Kathryn Walker |

"A bill before the [New York] State Legislature that would lower the minimum age for deer hunting with a firearm from 16 to 14 is being promoted by sponsors as a means to encourage more teen-agers to become lifelong hunters, but the measure has drawn criticism from animal rights activists.

"Legislation sponsored by the majority leader in the Assembly, Michael Bragman of suburban Syracuse, would allow 14-year-olds to receive big-game licenses in the state. The bill would require the teen-agers to complete a 10-hour firearm safety program first and be accompanied on their hunting forays by a parent or guardian licensed to hunt in New York. . . .

"The bill has drawn criticism from an antihunting group, the Fund for Animals, which is based in New York City. Its director of campaigns, Mike Markarian, said Mr. Bragman is sponsoring a 'reprehensible' measure designed to bolster the sale of hunting licenses in the state.

" 'The ethical fabric of society is made weaker and more dangerous by encouraging children, who are in the process of learning values, to inflict pain and suffering upon animals,' he said.

"Mr. Markarian also linked hunting to the shootings last month in Jonesboro, Ark., in which two boys, ages 13 and 11, are accused of gunning down four of their schoolmates and a teacher. Both defendants are reported to have been taught to shoot by relatives during hunting trips.

" 'Our young people should be taught values of kindness and compassion, not taught to hide in ambush and shoot unsuspecting victims,' Mr. Markarian said." (*New York Times*, April 5, 1998)

"The Governor of Montana says a new plan by the Federal Government to stop shipping bison to slaughter and instead herd them back into Yellowstone National Park will not work.

"Gov. Marc Racicot's response to the director of the National Park Service and others is the latest chapter in an increasingly rancorous dispute over the largest herd of wild bison in the United States.

"With heavy snowfalls, the animals have left Yellowstone this year in record numbers. More than 750 have been killed, a greater number than in any other year since 1975.

"The Park Service, a branch of the Interior Department whose very symbol is the bison, has shipped 401 bison to slaughterhouses and has shot 6 others. And agents of the State of Montana, as of Friday, have shot or shipped to slaughter more than 350 bison. There are about 2,100 bison left in the Yellowstone herd.

"Park Service officials have blamed Montana for forcing them to slaughter bison. Last week Mr. Racicot blamed the Federal Government for not solving the problem, and asked President Clinton to intervene . . .

"Montana's interest in resolving the dispute grew this week when the Fund for Animals, an animal rights group based in New York City, placed an advertisement in *USA Today*, calling for a boycott of the state by tourists.

"The advertisement said, 'The State of Montana has zero tolerance for buffalo, so we need you to have zero tolerance for Montana.'

"Last week the group also made public some film of wounded and bleeding bison being shipped to a Montana slaughterhouse.

" 'The ranching industry has bullied Yellowstone officials into committing heinous acts of cruelty against the very wildlife they are supposed to protect,' said Andrea Lococo of Jackson, Wyo., Northwest coordinator for the Fund for Animals." (*New York Times*, February 2, 1997)

"Outdoor-sports supporters in Alabama, worried over animal-rights protests, want to protect their industry from any limit on their ability to hunt or fish. If voted in, the 'sportsperson's bill of rights' would guarantee hunters and fishers the type of leeway usually reserved for such weighty matters as free speech.

"Don't laugh. Hunting and fishing is a $3 billion-a-year industry nationwide, and it provides 37,000 jobs in Alabama alone. More than two-thirds of state representatives sponsored the bill proposing the amendment, which garnered the coveted top spot on the ballot and is expected to be approved handily. . . .

"But the Fund for Animals, an animal-rights group based in New York, is fighting mad and lobbying against the proposal because, says one activist, it could set a precedent in other states. Minnesota recently voted down a similar law. 'We believe it's pretty absurd to use a state constitution to protect someone's hobby,' says Michael Markarian, the fund's national campaign director." (*Wall Street Journal*, October 23, 1996)

## POLITICAL ORIENTATION

Unavailable

# Greenpeace USA (1971)

1436 U Street, NW
Washington, D.C. 20009
Phone: (202) 462-1177
Fax: (202) 462-4507
Internet: http://www.greenpeaceusa.org

| | |
|---|---|
| "Is the leading, independent organization that uses peaceful and creative activism to protect the global environment." | **PURPOSE** |
| 65 total | **STAFF** |
| Kristen Engberg, executive director | **DIRECTOR** |
| 501(c)(3) | **TAX STATUS** |
| 1998—$21 million<br>Proposed 1999—Unavailable | **BUDGET** |
| Individual donations, sale of merchandise, foundation grants | **FUNDING SOURCES** |
| Members: 400,000 individuals<br>Branches/chapters: 4 regional offices<br>Affiliates: Greenpeace International, formed in 1971, has branches in 30 countries in Asia, Australia, Europe, the Middle East, New Zealand, North America, South America, and the former Soviet Union and has a membership of approximately 4 million individuals | **SCOPE** |
| None | **PAC** |
| ♦ Coalition forming ♦ Congressional testimony ♦ Direct action (nonviolent) ♦ Grassroots organizing ♦ International treaties and conventions ♦ Internet (Web site) ♦ Legislative/regulatory monitoring (federal) ♦ Litigation ♦ Lobbying (federal) ♦ Media outreach ♦ Photo/video ♦ Research ♦ Training and technical assistance | **METHOD OF OPERATION** |

| | |
|---|---|
| **CURRENT CONCERNS** | ♦ Climate change ♦ Genetic engineering ♦ Nuclear disarmament ♦ Over fishing ♦ Pollution/toxins ♦ Rainforest preservation ♦ Waste reduction |
| **PUBLICATIONS** | Unavailable |
| **NEWSLETTER** | *Greenpeace* magazine (quarterly) |
| **CONFERENCES** | None |
| **BOARD OF DIRECTORS** | Unavailable |
| **EFFECTIVENESS** | "Greenpeace's double-barreled strategy—media-savvy public demonstrations combined with corporate boycott campaigns—has met with some success, most notably in Clayoquot Sound on the west coast of Vancouver Island. Last year, MacMillan Bloedel Ltd., Vancouver, halted logging in the environmentally sensitive area, caving in to endless protests, customer boycotts and tougher government regulations that made its operations in the area uneconomic. |

"While the protests in the woods themselves have been toned down from the frenzied pitch reached in Clayoquot in 1993, the boycott campaigns are as aggressive as ever, and they have garnered some pretty impressive support, particularly in Europe. Several stationery concerns, building-supply retailers and consumer-product manufacturers have stopped buying supplies made from the clear-cutting of old-growth forests in British Columbia.

" 'Increasingly, customers are making ethical decisions which demand wood products that come from responsibly logged operations, and clear-cutting ancient rain forests doesn't qualify as responsible logging,' said Tamara Stark, forests campaigner for Greenpeace Canada." (*Wall Street Journal*, May 18, 1998)

"The oil giant Shell, hoping to close the embarrassing saga of the Brent Spar oil platform, said it wants to cut up the old offshore rig to help make a pier in Norway.

"Shell, part of the Royal Dutch/Shell Group, had first planned an easier and cheaper approach—sinking the Brent Spar in the North Atlantic. But Greenpeace activists boarded the obsolete vessel in April 1995, stirring environmental protests across Europe that eventually forced the company to back down.

"Greenpeace welcomed Shell's latest plan, which will end one of its more successful campaigns against Big Oil. The environmental pressure group called for a total ban on dumping obsolete petroleum equipment at sea, but Shell executives refused during a news conference to go that far." (*Wall Street Journal*, January 30, 1998)

"Sometime this year, Greenpeace is joining forces with Household Bank to introduce a biodegradable credit card made from a polymer vegetable-base plastic rather than PVC. Why? To raise money, in part—each charged purchase will generate a small percentage to be donated to the group—but also to appeal to consumers who worry about pollution produced by the manufacture of ordinary plastic cards. Another benefit touted by Greenpeace: if baby gets hold of the card and teethes on it, it's nontoxic. 'But it's mainly a symbolic usage,' admits Rick Hind, a Greenpeace spokesman who suggests more heroic possibilities. 'As we see it, Greenpeace activists can use the card to buy handcuffs to lock themselves to the front gates of timber companies.' " (*New York Times*, January 25, 1998)

"British Petroleum PLC won the opening round of a legal battle to prevent the environmental group Greenpeace from disrupting BP's oil drilling off the Scottish coast.

"The Edinburgh Court of Session issued a temporary order barring Greenpeace from interfering with BP operations west of the Shetland Islands. The court also froze Greenpeace's United Kingdom bank account while the court decides if Greenpeace owes BP GBP 1.4 million ($2.3 million) in damages for a protest that ended Sunday with the arrests of four Greenpeace activists who had occupied a BP oil rig for a week.

"Greenpeace and its activists have been sued before by companies trying to stop protests. BP's lawsuit is unusual in that it also seeks compensation for a disruption that BP claims cost it more than GBP 100,000 ($160,000) a day.

"By itself, Greenpeace U.K. would be ill-equipped to weather a $2 million judgment, since its total income last year was just $10.2 million, and it has barely $250,000 in the frozen bank account. But Greenpeace U.K. is part of a world-wide group of Greenpeace organizations that brought in $142 million last year." (*Wall Street Journal*, August 20, 1997)

---

"radical" (*Wall Street Journal*, September 16, 1997)

## POLITICAL ORIENTATION

# Humane Society of the United States (1954)

2100 L Street, NW
Washington, D.C. 20037
Phone: (202) 452-1100
Fax: (202) 778-6132
Internet: http://www.hsus.org

**PURPOSE**

"To create a humane and sustainable world for all animals, including people. Through education, advocacy, and empowerment, we seek to forge a lasting and comprehensive change in human consciousness and behavior; to relieve animal suffering; to prevent cruelty, abuse, neglect, and exploitation; and to protect wild animals and their environments."

**STAFF**

203 total—145 professional and 58 support; plus 6 part-time professional and 20 part-time support

**DIRECTOR**

Paul G. Irwin, president. Irwin has served as an officer of The Humane Society of the United States (HSUS) since 1976. An ordained United Methodist Minister, he serves on the boards of several organizations, including the American Bible Society, the Center for Respect of Life and Environment, the National Association for Humane and Environmental Education, the Renewable Resources Center, the Wilhelm Schole, and the World Society for the Protection of Animals. Irwin has master's degrees from Boston University and Colgate Rochester Divinity School and a doctorate from Rio Grande College.

**TAX STATUS**

501(c)(3)

**BUDGET**

1997—$45 million
1998—$47 million
Proposed 1999—$54 million

**FUNDING SOURCES**

Individuals, 90 percent; investments and other, 6 percent; foundation grants, 4 percent

Members: 6.4 million constituents

Branches/chapters: 9 regional offices; through Humane Society International, HSUS maintains offices in Australia, Canada, Europe, and Latin America; through EarthKind, HSUS maintains offices in Asia, Brazil, Romania, and Russia

Affiliates: Asociación Humanitaria de Costa Rica, Center for Respect of Life and Environment, Earth Voice, Humane Society International, International Center for Earth Concerns, National Association for Humane and Environmental Education, Humane Society of the United States Wildlife Land Trust, and WorldWIDE; all are 501(c)(3) organizations

None

♦ Advertisements ♦ Awards program ♦ Coalition forming ♦ Conferences/seminars ♦ Congressional testimony ♦ Congressional voting analysis ♦ Films/video/audiotapes ♦ Grantmaking ♦ Grassroots organizing ♦ Initiative/referendum campaigns ♦ International activities ♦ Internet (electronic bulletin boards, E-mail alerts, Web site) ♦ Legislative/regulatory monitoring (federal and state) ♦ Litigation ♦ Lobbying (federal, state, and grassroots) ♦ Local/municipal affairs ♦ Media outreach ♦ Participation in regulatory proceedings (federal and state) ♦ Polling ♦ Product merchandising ♦ Professional development services ♦ Research ♦ Scholarships ♦ Speakers program ♦ Training

♦ Animal cruelty ♦ Companion animal overpopulation ♦ Control of "nuisance wildlife" ♦ Disaster preparedness/relief for animals ♦ Factory farming ♦ Habitat preservation ♦ Pain and distress in animal research ♦ Threats to marine mammals ♦ Trade in wildlife parts and fur

*Agricide: The Hidden Farm and Food Crisis That Affects Us All*
*Animals in Peril: How "Sustainable Use" Is Wiping Out the World's Wildlife*
*The Boundless Circle: Caring for Creatures and Creation*
*Bucking the Myth Packet* (brochure, video, and instructional materials to "help stamp out the so-called sport of rodeo")
*Greening the Grassroots*
*The Humane Consumer and Producer Guide: Buying and Producing Farm Animal Products for a Humane Sustainable Agriculture*
*ICMA Management Information Service (MIS) Report: Local Animal-Control Management*
*Sharing the Earth Inservice Guide*
*Superpigs and Wondercorn: The Brave New World of Biotechnology . . . and Where It All May Lead*
*Wild Neighbors: The Humane Approach to Living with Wildlife*

Also publishes brochures, posters, bumper stickers, videos, and fact sheets

## NEWSLETTER

*Animal Activist Alert* (quarterly)
*Animal Sheltering* (bimonthly magazine)
*Earth Ethics* (quarterly)
*HSUS News* (quarterly)
*KIND News* (9 times a year)
*KIND Teacher* (annually)
*Shelter Sense* (6 times a year)

## CONFERENCES

Animal Care Expo (annual)
Workshops nationwide on various topics including cruelty investigation, disaster preparedness, and how to organize a humane society

## BOARD OF DIRECTORS

O. J. Ramsey, chairman; David O. Wiebers, vice chairman; Amy Freeman Lee, secretary; Paul G. Irwin, president and chief executive officer; G. Thomas Waite III, treasurer/chief financial officer; Patricia A. Forkan, executive vice president; Roger A. Kindler, vice president/general counsel; Murdaugh Stuart Madden, vice president/senior counsel

Other members:
♦ Peter A. Bender ♦ Donald W. Cashen ♦ Anita W. Coupe ♦ Judi Friedman ♦ Harold H. Gardiner ♦ Alice R. Garey ♦ Denis A. Hayes ♦ Jennifer Leaning ♦ Amy Freeman Lee ♦ Eugene W. Lorenz ♦ Jack W. Lydman ♦ William F. Mancuso ♦ Joan C. Martin-Brown ♦ Jeffrey O. Rose ♦ James D. Ross ♦ Marilyn G. Seyler ♦ Paula R. Smith ♦ John E. Taft ♦ Robert F. Welborn ♦ Marilyn Wilhelm ♦ K. William Wiseman

## EFFECTIVENESS

"Disney officially opens its Animal Kingdom theme park in central Florida today as controversy continues over the deaths of more than a dozen animals.

" 'Right now, there's a problem. And they need to fix it,' says Richard Farinato of the Humane Society, which this week blanketed newspapers with faxes expressing concerns about the 500-acre, $760 million park." (*USA Today*, April 22, 1998)

"With the help of the Humane Society of the United States, the Red Cross published a first aid book for cats and dogs last April. Sold through Red Cross chapters and book stores for about $10—35,000 copies have been purchased so far—the book is designed to be an at-home reference guide for pet emergencies.

"The 100-page manual, which reviews emergency treatment for everything from choking to electrical shock, is also a teaching companion for a three-hour pet first aid workshop run by a handful of Red Cross chapters nationwide." (*Associated Press*, January 26, 1998)

"In research released yesterday, the Humane Society found that almost 30 percent of animal-cruelty incidents also involved violence against people. It's difficult to prove that violence against animals is increasing, because the majority of cases don't result in prosecution or press coverage. The Humane Society's data come from a survey of press reports nationwide." (*Christian Science Monitor*, September 10, 1997)

"Deer overpopulation has become a vexing issue. Currently there are nearly one million deer in New York State, up from roughly 300,000 in 1954. . . .

"Vigorous action is clearly needed. Deer populations in many areas are out of control. Authorities have no choice but reduce the herds. . . .

"Communities have used a variety of methods to cull their herds. The easiest fix in rural areas is to extend the hunting season or the number of deer that can be taken. . . .

"Then there is the option that animal rights activists prefer: an experimental technology called immunocontraception, or birth control for female deer. The doe is injected either by blowdart or after being tranquilized. A few weeks later a booster shot must be given and then re-administered every year.

"At Fire Island National Seashore, deer have been treated since 1993 by the National Park Service and the Humane Society. Two or more years of vaccinations have reduced pregnancies in treated animals by 85 to 90 percent and significantly slowed the rate of growth of the herd." (*New York Times*, July 26, 1997)

---

Unavailable

# POLITICAL ORIENTATION

# In Defense of Animals (1983)

131 Camino Alto
Suite E
Mill Valley, California 94941
Phone: (415) 388-9641
Fax: (415) 388-0388
Internet: ida@idausa.org *or* http://www.idausa.org

| | |
|---|---|
| **PURPOSE** | "To end the abuse and exploitation of animals by defending their rights, welfare, and habitat." |
| **STAFF** | 20 total—16 professional; 4 support; plus 6 part-time; 2 interns; 3 volunteers |
| **DIRECTOR** | Elliot M. Katz, president. Katz founded In Defense of Animals (IDA) in 1983. A graduate of the Cornell University School of Veterinary Medicine, he is a practicing veterinarian and a community outreach coordinator. |
| **TAX STATUS** | 501(c)(3) |
| **BUDGET** | 1997—$1.57 million<br>1998—$1.4 million<br>Proposed 1999—Unavailable |
| **FUNDING SOURCES** | Donations and grants, 85 percent; interest, royalties, and other income, 7 percent; bequests, 6 percent; other, 2 percent |
| **SCOPE** | Members: 75,000 individuals<br>Branches/chapters: N/A<br>Affiliates: N/A |
| **PAC** | None |

| | |
|---|---|
| Advertisements ◆ Awards programs ◆ Boycotts (Boycott Procter & Gamble Campaign) ◆ Coalition forming ◆ Congressional testimony ◆ Demonstrations ◆ Direct action ◆ Films/video/audiotapes ◆ Grantmaking ◆ Grassroots organizing ◆ Internet (E-mail alerts, Web site) ◆ Internships ◆ Legal assistance ◆ Legislative/regulatory monitoring (federal and state) ◆ Litigation ◆ Lobbying (federal) ◆ Local/municipal affairs ◆ Media outreach ◆ Product merchandising ◆ Research ◆ Shareholder resolutions ◆ Speakers program | *METHOD OF OPERATION* |
| ◆ Anti-fur campaign ◆ Anti-pet theft campaign ◆ Campaign to end invasive and cruel animal experimentation ◆ Elevating the status of animals from that of mere property ◆ Eliminating marine mammal captivity ◆ Promoting plant-based diet | *CURRENT CONCERNS* |
| Offers a catalogue of publications on animal rights | *PUBLICATIONS* |
| *In Defense of Animals* (quarterly) | *NEWSLETTER* |
| Unavailable | *CONFERENCES* |
| Elliot M. Katz, president; Alex Hershaft, vice president; Vicky Ho Lynn, treasurer; Betsy Swart, secretary; Kristin von Kreisler, director | *BOARD OF DIRECTORS* |

*EFFECTIVENESS*

". . . [A]nimal rights activists are rallying to urge that the city outlaw any horse-drawn carriage in town. . . .

"City Council went into a closed 'executive session' on Tuesday night to discuss details of the litigation. Before that happened, however, council members heard a plea from the local representative of In Defense of Animals, Mary E. Hoffman. She urged council to outlaw the very horse-drawn carriage business that [Ray] Murphy plans to establish from his Union Street base. . . .

"Hoffman's presentation included a letter from the 7,000-member Mississippi Animal Rescue League. Both organizations cite the danger that the horses face in extreme heat and humidity of the Mississippi Gulf coast." (*Sea Coast Echo,* June 18, 1998)

"An animal-rights group has planned and international day of protest against Procter and Gamble Co. because it tests products on animals.

"In Defense of Animals (IDA), based near San Francisco, said it has planned protests in 90 cities in 13 countries on March 28. It is calling the protest 'Global Day of Action Against P&G.'

"Lauren Sullivan, international campaign director for In Defense of Animals, said the protests would include a 'death march' to Cincinnati's P&G headquarters, the hoisting of anti-P&G facility in England and an exhibit in Japan." (*Alliance,* May 1998)

"More than 100 animal rights activists gathered yesterday to protest the university's [University of California, Berkeley] use on animals in experiments and show their support for Mike Kennedy—the man who has been hanging from the Campanile for three days.

"Organized by the Mill Valley-based In Defense of Animals, yesterday's rally featured UC Berkeley biochemistry Professor Emeritus Joe Nielands, IDA President Elliot Katz and best-selling author Jeffrey Masson, among a host of other animal rights activists. . . .

"Around 1 p.m., the protestors marched through campus chanting slogans such as 'There's no excuse for animals abuse.' The group went on to California Hall where a coffin with bloody animals was placed in front of the building. From there, the protesters went to the Campanile and voiced their support to Kennedy with a megaphone." (*Daily Californian,* April 24, 1998)

## POLITICAL ORIENTATION

Unavailable

# Izaak Walton League of America (1922)

707 Conservation Lane
Gaithersburg, Maryland 20878
Phone: (301) 548-0150
Fax: (301) 548-0146
Internet: general@iwla.org *or* http://www.iwla.org

---

To "ensure that America's natural resource base is protected, managed and used to assure the quality of life in the long run."

**PURPOSE**

---

30 total—25 professional; 5 support; plus 2 part-time

**STAFF**

---

Paul Hansen, executive director. Hansen has worked for the Izaak Walton League of America since 1982, and became its executive director in 1995. He formerly headed the IWLA Midwest Office and served as a consultant to the Canadian government on acid rain and other environmental issues of bilateral concern. Hansen writes frequently on environmental topics and has served on committees with other environmental organizations. He is a graduate of Antioch University and holds a master's degree in natural resources administration.

**DIRECTOR**

---

501(c)(3)

**TAX STATUS**

---

1997—$2.6 million
1998—$3 million
Proposed 1999—Unavailable

**BUDGET**

---

Individuals, 42 percent; foundation grants, 22 percent; corporate donations, 8 percent; government contracts, 6 percent; legal settlement, 7 percent; Internet, 5 percent; sales, 5 percent; rental, 4 percent; other, 1 percent

**FUNDING SOURCES**

---

Members: 40,000 members
Branches/chapters: 330 chapters
Affiliate: Izaak Walton League of America Endowment, Inc. (related organization)

**SCOPE**

---

None

**PAC**

---

| METHOD OF OPERATION | ◆ Advertisements ◆ Awards program ◆ Coalition forming ◆ Conferences/seminars ◆ Congressional testimony ◆ Films/video/audiotapes ◆ Grantmaking ◆ Grassroots organizing ◆ Hotlines ([800] BUGIWLA, [800] IKE-LINE), [888] IKE-HILL) ◆ Internet (E-mail alerts, Web site) ◆ Internships ◆ Legislative/regulatory monitoring (federal and state) ◆ Library/ information clearinghouse (open to public) ◆ Litigation ◆ Lobbying (federal, state, and grassroots) ◆ Media outreach ◆ Mediation ◆ Participation in regulatory proceedings (state) ◆ Product merchandising ◆ Research ◆ Scholarships ◆ Telecommunications services ◆ Television and radio production ◆ Training and technical assistance |
|---|---|
| CURRENT CONCERNS | ◆ Agriculture ◆ Chapter activities on local conservation issues ◆ Clean air and acid rain ◆ Energy efficiency ◆ Environmental Protection Agency and Interior Department budgets and policies ◆ Fish and wildlife management ◆ Outdoor ethics ◆ Parks and wilderness protection ◆ Public land management ◆ Soil conservation and the Farm Bill ◆ Sustainable development ◆ Upper Mississippi River ◆ Wetlands/stream conservation |
| PUBLICATIONS | Unavailable |
| NEWSLETTER | *Conservation Currents* (5 times per year)<br>*League Leader* (5 times per year)<br>*Outdoor America* (quarterly magazine)<br>*SOS News* (twice per year) |
| CONFERENCES | National convention |
| BOARD OF DIRECTORS | Timothy R. Reid, chairman; Stan Adams, vice chair; William West, president; Donald Ferris, vice president; Birtrun Kidwell, secretary; Charles I. Wiles, treasurer<br><br>Other executive board members:<br>◆ Charlotte Brooker ◆ Michael Chenoweth ◆ Chuck Clayton ◆ James Daniels ◆ Dale Kretchman ◆ Thomas Rodd ◆ Tom Stevens ◆ Samuel Mason<br><br>Regional governors:<br>◆ Gordon Peterson ◆ Charlotta Burton ◆ James Madsen ◆ Dean Knight ◆ Carl Keeler ◆ Richard Sommer |
| EFFECTIVENESS | "The Izaak Walton League of America recently released a new report outlining a funding crisis before the U.S. Bureau of Land Management and its potential impact on the agency's programs and projects in 11 western states.<br><br>"The report found that hundreds of projects in the West may be adversely affected unless federal spending for the BLM increases. |

" 'The Bureau of Land Management is in the midst of a funding crisis,' said IWLA Conservation Director Jim Mosher. 'The League's report underscores the potential dimensions of the problem.'. . ." (*Daily Sparks Tribune*, June 26, 1998)

"The state Department of Environmental Quality and the Izaak Walton League signed an agreement yesterday to expand water quality monitoring in the state.

"The agreement establishes the Virginia Save Our Streams program within the Izaak Walton League's Virginia division. Jay Gilliam, the League's state president, said it will put about 250 trained volunteers from the League in the field to augment the DEQ's testing.

"Gilliam said Secretary of Natural Resources John Paul Woodley Jr. and the acting DEQ director, Dennis H. Treacy, both appointed by Gov. James S. Gilmore III (R), have brought a new attitude. Environmentalists had complained that the former secretary of natural resources, Becky Norton Dunlop, favored industry over the environment. She was not reappointed when Gilmore was elected in November to succeed George Allen (R)." (*Washington Post*, April 30, 1998)

"A local hunting group, with state and county officials, is stepping up efforts to catch poachers and illegal hunters in Loudoun County after a hunter's bullet tore through a house in Ashburn last year.

"With the start of bowhunting season yesterday and the firearms hunting season six weeks away, the Loudoun chapter of the Izaak Walton League announced that it has begun posting reward signs at grocery stores, gas stations and around large vacant properties.

"The League, a hunting and fishing group, also has begun distributing hunting pamphlets with safety tips and regulations.

"The orange signs, 250 so far, offer a reward of as much as $100 for information leading to the arrest and conviction of people who are poaching, hunting illegally or killing wildlife that is off-limits to hunters.

"The reward program began in 1990, but League officials said they are trying to increase the program's visibility, particularly in eastern Loudoun where conflicts between homeowners and hunters have been on the rise. . . .

" 'We're stepping up the information campaign,' said Lance Schul, the League's outdoor ethics director. More than $1,000 has been raised for the program, he added. 'We're going to saturate the county with the signs.' " (*Washington Post*, October 5, 1997)

"In the half-century since Luther Carter and Dave Henderson began hunting, much has changed in America. Where woods were once barren of turkeys and deer, those species abound and have become among the most popular for hunters. In places where quail and woodcock once thrived, they have nearly disappeared.

"Migratory ducks were up, down and are up again in population; geese were down, up and now down again. Little stays the same against the volatile backdrop of America's thundering economy, ballooning population, expanding cities and careering social structure. Yet people still like to hunt and still find a way. Can it last?

"Recently the Izaak Walton League of America conducted focus group studies around the nation on hunter attitudes. Their conclusion: The tenuous link between generations that has kept hunting alive since the advent of human society is in danger.

"'If there was a common question about the future of hunting,' said Laury Marshall, who helped compile the results, 'it was about links between mentors and youngsters and the need to establish them in a way that keeps the messages of conservation and ethics most clear.'

"The IWLA study found that hunting is not something taken up cold; someone must show the way. If older hunters lack the time or place or energy to teach, if the young are disinclined to listen and learn, and if hunters in general prove unable to hew to ever higher standards of ethical behavior, in 50 or 100 years hunting in America may very well wither away to nothing.

"Which wouldn't be the end of the world. Just one more simple pleasure lost to the pitiless march of time." (*Washington Post*, January 9, 1996)

# POLITICAL ORIENTATION

Unavailable

# The Keystone Center Science and Public Policy Program (1975)

P. O. Box 8606
Keystone, Colorado 80435
Phone: (970) 468-5822
Fax: (970) 262-0152

1030 15th Street, NW
Suite 300
Washington, D.C. 20005
Phone: (202) 783-0248
Fax: (202) 783-0328

Internet: tkcsppp@keystone.org *or* http://www.keystone.org

| | |
|---|---|
| "To help solve problems by resolving conflicts and facilitating mutual understanding and education among diverse parties. Through the use of neutral, professionally managed processes of dialogue, mediation, and negotiation, the Program enables decision makers from government, the environmental community, industry, and citizen organizations to come together to clarify issues in dispute, explore productive ways of dealing with them, and develop and document consensus recommendations for creative action." | *PURPOSE* |
| 53 total—35 professional; 18 support | *STAFF* |
| Kathy Prosser, president | *DIRECTOR* |
| 501(c)(3) | *TAX STATUS* |
| 1998—$2.7 million<br>Proposed 1999—Unavailable | *BUDGET* |
| "Funding for Keystone dialogues is provided by private foundations, corporations, international donor organizations, and governmental agencies." | *FUNDING SOURCES* |
| Members: N/A<br>Branches/chapters: N/A<br>Affiliates: In addition to SPPP, the Keystone Center comprises the Science School Program and the Keystone Symposia on Molecular and Cellular Biology. | *SCOPE* |

| **PAC** | None |
| --- | --- |

| **METHOD OF OPERATION** | ◆ Facilitation and consulting servers ◆ Mediation ◆ Policy dialogues |
| --- | --- |

| **CURRENT CONCERNS** | ◆ Agriculture, food, and nutrition ◆ Biotechnology and genetic resources ◆ Chemical weapons ◆ Energy ◆ Environmental quality ◆ Health ◆ Natural resources ◆ Science and technology ◆ Sustainable development |
| --- | --- |

**PUBLICATIONS**

*Action Plan For the Provision of Useful Prescription Medicine Information*

*Constable Commission, Final Report Submitted to the Man and the Biosphere Program*

*Department of Defense Commander's Guide to Biodiversity*

*Development of a Long-Range Action Plan for the Provision of Useful Prescription Medicine Information*

*EPA/Food Safety Advisory Committee (Facilitated by The Keystone Center), Meeting Summary Compilation, September–December 1996*

*Final Consensus Report of the National Commission on Superfund*

*The Final Report of The Keystone National Policy Dialogue on Food, Nutrition and Health*

*The Keystone Center Annual Report*

*The Keystone Center Assessment of MRS Public Involvement*

*The Keystone Center National Policy Dialogue on Ecosystem Management*

*Keystone Center Policy Dialogue on a Department of Defense (DoD) Biodiversity Management Strategy*

*Keystone Dialogue on Incentives to Protect Endangered Species on Private Lands*

*The Keystone Environmental, Citizen, State and Local Leadership Initiative for Biotechnology, Issue Report Series, Biotechnology Decisionmaking: Perspectives on Commercialization*

*The Keystone National Policy Dialogue on Agricultural Management Systems and the Environment*

*The Keystone National Policy Dialogue on Establishment of Studies to Optimize Medical Management of HIV Infection*

*Sharing Risk and Reward, Public-Private Collaboration to Eliminate Micronutrient Malnutrition*

*Summit on Environmental Issues Facing the Pork Industry Meeting Summary*

*U.S. Coast Guard Marine Environmental Protection Forum Meeting Summary*

**NEWSLETTER**

*Consensus* (3 times a year)
*Discovery* (once a year)

| | |
|---|---|
| Sponsors policy dialogues on various topics | **_CONFERENCES_** |
| Unavailable | **_BOARD OF DIRECTORS_** |
| Unavailable | **_EFFECTIVENESS_** |
| Unavailable | **_POLITICAL ORIENTATION_** |

# League of Conservation Voters (1970)

1707 L Street, NW
Suite 750
Washington, D.C. 20036
Phone: (202) 785-8683
Fax: (202) 835-0491
Internet: http://www.lcv.org

| | |
|---|---|
| **PURPOSE** | "To hold members of Congress accountable for their environmental votes and to help elect an environment majority to Congress." |
| **STAFF** | 25 total; plus 6 interns |
| **DIRECTOR** | Debra J. Callahan, president. Before becoming president of the League of Conservation Voters (LCV) in 1995, Callahan was executive director of the Brainerd Foundation. From 1992 to 1995, she was grassroots environmental program director of the W. Alton Jones Foundation. Callahan also has worked in many political campaigns, serving as campaign manager for Rep. Howard Wolpe's reelection in 1990, as national field director of Al Gore's presidential campaign in 1987–88, and as field coordinator of the Mondale/Ferraro presidential campaign in 1984. |
| **TAX STATUS** | 501(c)(4) |
| **BUDGET** | 1998—Unavailable<br>Proposed 1999—Unavailable |
| **FUNDING SOURCES** | Individual contributions and membership dues, 100 percent |
| **SCOPE** | Members: Approximately 25,000<br>Branches/chapters: N/A<br>Affiliates: N/A |
| **PAC** | League of Conservation Voters Action Fund |

♦ Advertisements ♦ Awards program ♦ Campaign contributions ♦ Congressional voting analysis ♦ Electoral politics ♦ Grassroots organizing ♦ Internet (databases, E-mail alerts, Web site) ♦ Internships ♦ Legislative/regulatory monitoring (federal) ♦ Media outreach ♦ Polling ♦ Research ♦ Voting records

♦ Conservation and environmental protection ♦ Promotion of a pro-conservation majority in Congress

*100 Day Scorecard* (1995)
*Election Report* (biannually 1970–1994)
*National Environmental Scorecard* (1970–1998)
*Presidential Profiles* (general election years 1972–1996)

*LCV Insider* (quarterly)

Occasional seminars

Mike Hayden, chair; Gene Karpinski and Theodore Roosevelt IV, vice chairs; Debra J. Callahan, president; Gail Harmon, counsel

Other members:
♦ John H. Adams ♦ Darryl Banks ♦ Bunyan Bryant ♦ Wade Greene ♦ Paul W. Hansen ♦ John A. Harris ♦ Denis Hayes ♦ Rampa R. Hormel ♦ Fred Krupp ♦ Winsome Dunn McIntosh ♦ William Meadows ♦ Roger O. Schlickeisen ♦ Debbie Sease ♦ Victor M. Sher ♦ Bruce Smart ♦ Joanne Witty ♦ Ed Zuckerman

"The most dangerous place to be in this election was on an environmental hit list. Sixteen of 19 defeated Republican incumbents—85 percent—were in this category. That compares to an overall incumbent loss rate of only 6 percent.

"One-half to two-thirds (some races are still in doubt) of the League of Conservation Voters' Dirty Dozen and of the Sierra Club's priority opponents lost.

"The vote did not amount to a national referendum on the environment, but in a substantial number of congressional races it was, for the first time, a decisive factor. 'It was an issue that elected,' said pollster Stan Greenberg, 'and even more, one that defeated.'

"In eight of nine races Greenberg surveyed, the environment was one of the two most important reasons voters cited for opposing a candidate, frequently ahead of Medicare. In three of the nine, it was the most important." (*Washington Post*, November 11, 1996)

"Rep. Martini [of NJ] is the only Republican member of the House fresh-man class to win the Sierra Club's endorsement for 1996. 'Bill Martini has the best environmental record of any Republican freshman,' says Daniel J. Weiss, political director of the Sierra Club. 'He was one of the first fresh-man Republicans to buck the trend.'

"So the Sierra Club is hoping to spotlight Mr. Martini as an ally. He can count on favorable publicity, political-action committee contributions, and door-to-door campaigners from the Sierra Club.

"But, in a year when independent expenditures by special-interest groups may well set new records, many of his fellow House Republicans will be getting a completely different kind of attention from environmentalists. They will be hit by a green flood of independent-expenditure spending aimed at defeating them.

"The League of Conservation Voters, the most election-minded of all environmental groups, this week launched a $1.5 million 'Dirty Dozen' campaign to fund radio and televison ads aimed at ousting 12 of Mr. Martini's fellow House members. President Deb Callahan says her group has already raised 'about two-thirds' of the needed amount.

"The Conservation Voters' effort reflects the growing importance of independent-expenditure campaigns, in which special-interest groups fund their own advocacy efforts rather than contribute directly to candidates' own campaigns. Favorable Supreme Court rulings have made it easier than ever for interest groups to wage such independent campaigns." (*Wall Street Journal*, July 19, 1996)

## POLITICAL ORIENTATION

"The League of Conservation Voters compiles information for its annual score card by analyzing selected congressional votes as selected by representatives of 27 environmental and conservation groups.

"The significance of the League's opinions is a subject of debate each time its score card is issued. Last week was no exception.

"Representative Don Young, an Alaska Republican who is chairman of the House Resources Committee, called the League 'a liberal political action committee closely associated with the national Democratic party.'

"Mr. Pallone, who touted his 100 percent grade with a news release, called the League 'a nonpartisan political organization representing many of the nation's major environmental organizations.' " (*New York Times*, February 8, 1998)

"When the League of Conservation Voters, the environmental movement's political arm, issued its scorecard for the past congressional session, it gave a record 135 legislators 'zero' rankings. All but one were Republicans. The League of Conservation Voters hopes to raise and spend nearly $2 million in House and Senate campaigns this fall. 'The environment hadn't been a partisan issue, but the Republican leadership has made it one,' League President Deb Callahan says." (*Wall Street Journal*, March 5, 1996)

"liberal" (*Wall Street Journal*, February 2, 1996)

# National Audubon Society (1905)

700 Broadway
New York, New York 10003
Phone: (212) 979-3000
Fax: (212) 473-6021

1901 Pennsylvania Avenue, NW
Suite 1100
Washington, D.C. 20006
Phone: (202) 861-2242
Fax: (202) 861-4290

Internet: http://www.audubon.org

| | |
|---|---|
| "To conserve and restore natural ecosystems, focusing on birds and other wildlife, for the benefit of humanity and the earth's biological diversity." | *PURPOSE* |
| 300 total | *STAFF* |
| John Flicker, president. Prior to coming to the National Audubon Society in July 1995, Flicker spent six years as Florida state director of The Nature Conservancy. Flicker previously held a number of other positions with The Nature Conservancy, including Great Plains director, chief legal council, executive vice president, and chief operating officer. | *DIRECTOR* |
| 501(c)(3) | *TAX STATUS* |
| 1998—$47.3 million<br>Proposed 1999—Unavailable | *BUDGET* |
| Contributions, 30 percent; membership, 22 percent; earned income from investments, royalties, miscellaneous, 48 percent | *FUNDING SOURCES* |
| Members: 550,000 individuals<br>Branches/chapters: 518 chapters throughout the U.S. and Canada; other chapters in Central and South America; 100 sanctuaries and nature centers<br>Affiliates: N/A | *SCOPE* |
| None | *PAC* |

| | |
|---|---|
| *METHOD OF OPERATION* | ◆ Awards program ◆ Coalition forming ◆ Congressional testimony ◆ Grassroots organizing ◆ Initiative/referendum campaigns ◆ International activities ◆ Internet (Web site) ◆ Legislative/regulatory monitoring (federal and state) ◆ Library/information clearinghouse ◆ Lobbying (federal, state, and grassroots) ◆ Local/municipal affairs ◆ Media outreach ◆ Participation in regulatory proceedings (federal and state) ◆ Product merchandising ◆ Research |
| *CURRENT CONCERNS* | ◆ Agriculture/farm bill ◆ Arctic National Wildlife Refuge ◆ Bird and wildlife habitat protection ◆ Endangered Species Act ◆ Everglades protection ◆ Forest ◆ Marine conservation ◆ Natural resource protection ◆ Natural wildlife refuges ◆ Population planning ◆ Protection of forests ◆ Water and air quality ◆ Wetlands protection |
| *PUBLICATIONS* | Offers many *National Audubon Society Field Guides*, hardcover and softcover books, oversized illustrated books, reference books, and computer software items. |
| *NEWSLETTER* | *Audubon* (monthly magazine) |
| *CONFERENCES* | National convention (biennial) |
| *BOARD OF DIRECTORS* | ◆ Oakes Ames ◆ John B. Beinecke ◆ Charles G. Bragg Jr. ◆ Howard P. Brokaw ◆ Harriet S. Bullitt ◆ Donald A. Carr ◆ Douglas M. Costle ◆ Leslie Dach ◆ Jack Dempsey ◆ David Dominick ◆ Lynn Dolnick ◆ Helen Engle ◆ W. Hardy Eshbaugh ◆ Ted Lee Eubanks ◆ John W. Fitzpatrick ◆ Pat Heindenreich ◆ Marian S. Heiskell ◆ Reid Hughes ◆ Vivian Johnson ◆ Donal C. O'Brien Jr. ◆ Benjamin Olewine IV ◆ David H. Pardoe ◆ Ruth O. Russell ◆ Norman Shapiro ◆ Amy Skilbred ◆ Robert H. Socolow ◆ John L. Whitmire ◆ Bernard Yokel |
| *EFFECTIVENESS* | " 'Long Island is one of the best places on the East Coast for birding,' said Mary Richard, director of the 75-year-old Theodore Roosevelt Sanctuary in Oyster Bay, 'in large part because there are remarkably diverse ecosystems—wetlands, pine barrens, barrier beaches—in a small physical area.'<br><br>"She added: 'The variety of birds is excellent, too—we often get blowovers from Europe and Asia and get to see some species highly unusual to North America right here on Long Island. We've had visitors from all over the U.S., Europe, even as far away as Africa.'<br><br>"The sanctuary, the National Audubon Society's first, has experienced an enormous attendance growth within the last seven years—from 10,000 registered visitors in 1991 to 100,000 in 1997. |

"The kind of interest in bird-watching evidenced by booming registration rates at preserves and sanctuaries like Theodore Roosevelt has spilled over into commercial areas as well, and record birding numbers have been the boon of retailers and eco-tour guides alike.

" 'We offer birding trips all over the world now,' said Ms. Richard. 'We've taken Long Islanders to locations from Cape Cod and Cape May, to Trinidad and Tobago, Mexico and Venezuela.' " (*New York Times*, February 15, 1998)

"In the 1800s, there were sportsmen who thought it was grand to celebrate Christmas by going out in the field and shooting as many birds as possible. This was a holiday tradition called the 'side hunt' (gentlemen chose sides or teams for the competition). The team that shot the most birds and small, furry animals won the hunting honor of the day.

"But by the turn of the century, conservation was starting to be the rage and ornithologist Frank Chapman, who was concerned about the annual slaughter, devised a more peaceful way to enjoy Noel: On Christmas Day, 1900, he and 27 friends counted birds instead of shooting them. Since then, thousands of bird-watchers across the nation have climbed mountains, roamed riverbanks, poked around forests, prowled fields and stomped city pavements (including Washington's) to survey birds each holiday season. Over the last 97 years, volunteers have noted hundreds of millions of birds, contributing to a valuable survey on the early-winter distribution patterns of various species and the health of the environment.

"Throughout the next 2 weeks, local bird-watchers, from novices to veterans, are invited to help continue this tradition in Washington, Maryland and Virginia. Coordinated by the National Audubon Society, about 1,700 teams of volunteers in 'count groups' across the United States, Canada and other parts of the western hemisphere will look for birds in designated areas, each 15 miles in diameter.

"Volunteers will record every bird they see within a one-day period (most birders will start at daybreak and work for several hours). Each group chooses a particular day on which to go out. For example, the local Washington and Triadelphia count groups will venture out this Saturday, while the Sugarloaf count (which covers parts of Montgomery, Frederick and Loudoun counties) will be one of the last local groups to ferret out the flocks on Jan. 4.

"Their data will be turned over to the Audubon Society, which annually publishes the results in a 600-page national report. In the Washington area, the count has revealed, for example, a decline in the American kestrel (a falcon) and the northern bobwhite (a quail) and an increase in the bald eagle population." (*Washington Post*, December 19, 1997)

"A conservationist's dream—the successful reintroduction of gray wolves into Yellowstone National Park and central Idaho two years ago—has suddenly become a conservationist's nightmare.

"Earlier this month, a Federal judge in Wyoming ordered the Government to 'remove' the wolves. If the court's order is carried out, these wolves will be killed—and two leading environmental groups may be partly to blame. . . .

"In January 1995, after a 20-year struggle by conservationists, scientists and citizens' groups, the Government began perhaps the most significant ecological restoration in history: the reintroduction of the wolf to central Idaho and Yellowstone.

"The project has succeeded beyond its supporters' expectations. The killing of livestock, which many ranchers feared would be ruinous, has been minimal. . . .

"But on Dec. 12, Federal District Judge William Downes ordered the Government to remove the reintroduced wolves and their offspring. He based his decision in part on a narrow interpretation of the Endangered Species Act put forward by the National Audubon Society and the Sierra Club Legal Defense Fund (recently renamed Earth Justice Legal Defense Fund).

"No humane 'removal' is possible. Even if Canada took the wolves back, their original territories have been reoccupied, and resident wolves would kill the interlopers. . . .

"In a compromise plan, the Government agreed to downgrade the wolves' status in central Idaho and Yellowstone from 'endangered' to 'threatened.' That gave ranchers the legal right to shoot wolves attacking their stock. In addition, Defenders of Wildlife, a conservation group, agreed to compensate ranchers for any animals they lost. The wolves would easily reproduce at a rate high enough to make up for the few that would be killed.

"The compromise was not enough, however, for the Wyoming Farm Bureau Federation and several other livestock groups. They sued the Government to stop the reintroduction.

"On the other side, most conservationists were astonished when the National Audubon Society, a mainstream environmental group, decided to sue the Government in 1995 for reasons of its own.

"The Audubon Society and the legal defense fund insisted that all they wanted was full 'endangered' status for the two or three native wolves they believed were already living in central Idaho. . . .

"Now, more than two years later, Judge Downes has found the entire reintroduction illegal—basing his decision principally on the argument put forward by these two groups. . . .

"Maybe the livestock groups would have won on their own. But it may also be that the legalistic absolutism of the Audubon Society and the Sierra Club Legal Defense Fund will have helped destroy one of the conservation movement's greatest triumphs." (*New York Times,* December 24, 1997)

---

## POLITICAL ORIENTATION

Unavailable

# National Coalition Against
# the Misuse of Pesticides (1981)

701 E Street, SE
Suite 200
Washington, D.C. 20003
Phone: (202) 543-5450
Fax: (202) 543-4791
Internet: ncamp@ncamp.org *or* http://www.ncamp.org

| | |
|---|---|
| To "educate the public about the hazards of pesticide use and advocate for the use of alternatives." | *PURPOSE* |
| 3 total—3 professional; plus 1 intern | *STAFF* |
| Jay Feldman, national coordinator. Feldman previously was director of health programs for Rural America. An author of many publications and articles, he has been a member of several Environmental Protection Agency (EPA) advisory bodies. Feldman earned his B.A. at Grinnell College and his M.A. in urban and regional planning at Virginia Polytechnic Institute. | *DIRECTOR* |
| 501(c)(3) | *TAX STATUS* |
| 1997—$401,936<br>1998—$466,000<br>Proposed 1999—Unavailable | *BUDGET* |
| Contributions, 62 percent; grant support, 26 percent; membership dues, 4 percent; other sources, including publication sales and interest income, 8 percent | *FUNDING SOURCES* |
| Members: 1,200<br>Branches/chapters: N/A<br>Affiliate: N/A | *SCOPE* |
| None | *PAC* |

| METHOD OF OPERATION | ♦ Coalition forming ♦ Conferences/seminars ♦ Congressional testimony ♦ Grassroots organizing ♦ Internet (E-mail alerts, Web site) ♦ Internships ♦ Legislative/regulatory monitoring (federal and state) ♦ Library/information clearinghouse ♦ Litigation ♦ Media outreach ♦ Participation in regulatory proceedings (federal and state) ♦ Research ♦ Speakers program ♦ Training and technical assistance |

| CURRENT CONCERNS | ♦ Alternatives to pesticides ♦ Human health effects of toxins ♦ Implementation of Food Quality Protection Act ♦ Pesticides ♦ Pest management |

| PUBLICATIONS | *A Failure to Protect*<br>*Getting Pesticides Out of Food*<br>*The Great American Water Debate*<br>*Pesticides Chemical Fact Sheet*<br>*Pesticides and Schools*<br>*Least Toxic Control of Pests*<br>*Model Ordinance Book*<br>*Safety at Home*<br>*State and Local Pesticide Ordinances* (1998 update)<br>*Taking Action to Control Pesticides and Promote Alternatives*<br>*Unnecessary Risks: The Benefit Side of the Pesticides Risk Benefit Equation*<br><br>Also offers information packets, brochures, T-shirts, and bumper stickers |

| NEWSLETTER | *NCAMP's Technical Report* (monthly)<br>*Pesticides and You* (quarterly) |

| CONFERENCES | National Pesticide Forum (annually in March) |

| BOARD OF DIRECTORS | Allen Spalt, president; Ruth Berlin, vice president; Terry Shistar, secretary; Dan Wartenberg, treasurer; Merrill Clark, at-large<br><br>Other members:<br>♦ Laura Caballero ♦ Nancy Chuda ♦ Jim Chuda ♦ Shelley Davis ♦ Lorna Donaldson-McMahon ♦ Jay Feldman ♦ Tessa Hill ♦ Eric Kindberg ♦ Gregg Small ♦ Allen Spalt ♦ Kenuel Okech Ogwaro ♦ John Wargo |

| EFFECTIVENESS | " 'In 1993 the EPA estimated that over two billion pounds of pesticide-active ingredients a year are applied throughout the United States,' says Jay Feldman, director of the National Coalition Against the Misuse of Pesticides, in Washington, D.C. The agriculture industry accounted for 84 percent of this pesticide use. 'Also, manufacturing industries are disposing of hazardous wastes and using them as fertilizer ingredients—spreading them around to farms,' he says. 'So not only is American produce sprayed with a combination of pesticides, much of the fertilizer plowed into the fields is toxic. Produce is often sprayed again on its way to market and once again at the market. |

" 'Because the current research points to and suspects pesticide poisoning as being carcinogenic and hormone-disruptive, the American public is being forced to think about other ways of doing things,' says Jay Feldman. 'Last year, consumers spent $3.5 billion on certified organic produce. Although that only accounts for one percent of our food-production system, it is a start.' " (*Country Living*, March 1998)

"Public elementary schools throughout Maryland soon will be required to inform parents in writing at least a day before they apply pesticides inside school buildings under a law adopted in the final hours of this year's General Assembly session in Annapolis.

"In passing the law, Maryland's lawmakers placed the state at the forefront of a growing national movement aimed at ultimately curbing the use of pesticides, some of which contain toxins linked to a range of health problems, including cancer and birth defects.

"No other state has passed a law forcing schools to notify parents of its pesticide plans, according to the National Coalition Against the Misuse of Pesticides, though San Francisco recently adopted a similar law and banned several pesticides from school buildings.

" 'This represents a critical move to educate and inform parents about potential adverse impacts on the health of their children,' said Jay Feldman, executive director of the Coalition." (*Washington Post*, April 16, 1998)

"An environmental group is advocating the end of using wooden utility poles because they are usually treated with dangerous pesticides and wood preservatives. 'Under, around, in and on every preservative-treated utility pole is a toxic site that poses a real threat to clean air, water and land,' said a report issued today by the National Coalition Against the Misuse of Pesticides.

"Instead of using wooden poles, which are protected against decay by chemicals that are banned for many other uses, the Coalition said utilities should gradually introduce alternatives like steel, concrete and fiberglass or should bury the lines.

"But the Environmental Protection Agency said utility poles and other approved uses of wood preservatives did not present an unacceptable risk. 'We did a very extensive risk assessment on wood preservatives in the mid-80's,' said an agency spokesman, Al Heier. 'And we finally determined that the benefits outweighed the risks.'

"Mr. Heier said wood preservatives, which are also used on decks, railroad ties and other wood, usually leach out fairly quickly and should not pose a serious hazard. But there are restrictions on their uses, like using them inside the home, he said.

"Utility poles account for about 13 percent of the market for wood preservatives used to kill fungus and insects and retard decay, the report said. The chemicals, which include pentachlorophenol, creosote, arsenic and chromium, 'contain some of the most hazardous toxic contaminants on the market,' the report said." (*New York Times*, February 5, 1997)

Unavailable

## POLITICAL ORIENTATION

# National Parks and
# Conservation Association (1919)

1776 Massachusetts Avenue, NW
Suite 200
Washington, D.C. 20036
Phone: (202) 223-6722
Fax: (202) 659-0650
Internet: http://www.npca.org *or* npca@npca.org

| | |
|---|---|
| **PURPOSE** | "To protect and enhance the natural and cultural heritage of America's national park system through research, education and advocacy." |
| **STAFF** | 65 total—55 professional and 10 support; plus 2 part-time professional; 4 interns |
| **DIRECTOR** | Thomas C. Kiernan, president. Prior to joining the National Parks and Conservation Association (NPCA), Kiernan was president of the Audubon Society of New Hampshire. He also has served with the EPA Office of Air and Radiation and the Oregon Department of Environmental Quality. As a co-founder of E3 Ventures, Kiernan worked to bring together oil companies, utilities, and environmentalists to expedite the implementation of the Clean Air Act. He holds an M.B.A. with an emphasis in non-profit management from Stanford University's Graduate School of Business and a B.A. in environmental computer modeling from Dartmouth College. |
| **TAX STATUS** | 501(c)(3) |
| **BUDGET** | Fiscal year ending June 30, 1998—Unavailable<br>Proposed F.Y. 1999—$17.5 million |
| **FUNDING SOURCES** | Membership dues, 50 percent; individuals, 22 percent; special events/projects, 10 percent; foundation grants, 5 percent; publications, 5 percent; other sources, 5 percent; corporate donations, 3 percent |
| **SCOPE** | Members: 400,000 individuals<br>Branches/chapters: 7 regional offices<br>Affiliates: N/A |
| **PAC** | None |

| | |
|---|---|
| ◆ Advertisements ◆ Awards program ◆ Coalition forming ◆ Conferences/seminars ◆ Congressional testimony ◆ Films/video/audiotapes ◆ Grassroots organizing ◆ Internet (E-mail alerts, Web site) ◆ Internships ◆ Legislative/regulatory monitoring (federal and state) ◆ Litigation ◆ Lobbying (federal, state, and grassroots) ◆ Local/municipal affairs ◆ Media outreach ◆ Participation in regulatory proceedings (federal and state) ◆ Polling ◆ Product merchandising ◆ Research | *METHOD OF OPERATION* |
| ◆ Decreased emphasis on research, interpretation, and resource management relating to the National Park System ◆ Funding of National Parks ◆ National Park concessions ◆ National Park designation and expansion | *CURRENT CONCERNS* |
| None | *PUBLICATIONS* |
| *National Parks* (bimonthly magazine)<br>*ParkWatcher* (bimonthly)<br>Also publishes legislative updates | *NEWSLETTER* |
| Annual dinner | *CONFERENCES* |
| G. Robert Kerr, chairman; Glenn E. Haas, William G. Watson, and Robin W. Winks, vice chairmen; Donald Murphy, treasurer; Sadie Gwin Blackburn, secretary<br><br>Other members:<br>◆ Susan H. Babcock ◆ James E. Bostic Jr. ◆ Martin Brown ◆ Virdin C. Brown ◆ Don H. Castleberry ◆ Wallace A. Cole ◆ Milton T. English III ◆ Gretchen Long Glickman ◆ Charles A. Howell III ◆ James S. Hoyte ◆ Dennis Takahashi Kelso ◆ Robert N. Leggett Jr. ◆ Maryon Davies Lewis ◆ Stephen Mather McPherson ◆ Marie W. Ridder ◆ John B. Roberts ◆ Virgil G. Rose ◆ H. William Walter ◆ Roland H. Wauer | *BOARD OF DIRECTORS* |
| "For the second time in four years, a judicial panel in California has rejected a controversial plan to build the world's largest landfill at a remote desert site bordered on three sides by Joshua Tree National Park. . . .<br><br>"A San Diego County Superior Court panel ruled Wednesday that Mine Reclamation Corp., a Palm Desert-based company, had failed to provide convincing evidence that the 2,000-acre dump would not interfere with the nearby park's ecosystem and people's 'wilderness experience.' The park features huge and haunting desert rock formations and stands of rare Joshua Trees. . . .<br><br>"But activists who for more than seven years have been fighting the proposed landfill called the ruling a major victory and predicted the company would have a difficult time convincing any court that the plan was environmentally sound. | *EFFECTIVENESS* |

" 'We've said all along that it is completely inappropriate to build the country's largest landfill literally in the shadow of one of our most pristine national parks,' said Brian Huse, a regional director of the National Parks and Conservation Association, one of several groups that sued Mine Reclamation over the proposal." (*Washington Post*, February 20, 1998)

"The National Trust for Historic Preservation and the National Parks and Conservation Association have offered tentative support for a National Park Service plan that would allow a private developer to operate commercial ventures within the Gettysburg National Military Park.

"But they and others made clear that the plan would come under close scrutiny.

"Last week, the Park Service announced it would allow a consortium led by a Pennsylvania real estate developer to build it a new visitor center and museum at the Civil War battlefield. In exchange, the developer would gain the right to operate a giant-screen movie theater and private shops in the complex.

" 'The fact that the new facilities would be built within the park boundaries should not by itself disqualify the plan from consideration,' said National Trust president Richard Moe.

" 'The question,' Moe said, 'is whether it can be built in such a way so as to not intrude upon but rather to enhance the visitor experience while maintaining the integrity of the battlefield.' " (*Washington Post*, November 10, 1997)

"Earth Day is observed each April as a reminder to us that we live on a fragile planet that needs our care and attention to stay healthy itself, and in turn provide us with a healthful environment in which to live and grow. Every Earth Day since 1990, the National Parks and Conservation Association has organized 'March for Parks,' a national walking event that involves people in all 50 states. The purpose of March for Parks is to encourage support of local, state and national parks. Here in the Washington area we have many beautiful parks such as Rock Creek Park in Washington and Great Falls in Maryland and Virginia. Today would be a great time to enjoy a park with your family—and to try reconnecting with nature." (*Washington Post*, April 22, 1997)

## POLITICAL ORIENTATION

Unavailable

# National Trust for Historic Preservation (1949)

1785 Massachusetts Avenue, NW
Washington, D.C. 20036
Phone: (202) 588-6000
Fax: (202) 588-6299
Internet: http://www.nationaltrust.org

| | |
|---|---|
| "Committed to saving America's diverse historic environments and to preserving and revitalizing the livability of communities nationwide." | *PURPOSE* |
| (Nationwide) 282 total—196 professional; 86 support; plus 45 interns, 4,000 volunteers, 23 part-time, and 225 hourly employees | *STAFF* |
| Richard Moe, president. Before becoming president of the National Trust in 1993, Moe worked in private law practice. Previously he was an assistant to Walter F. Mondale, first in the Senate and later as Vice President Mondale's chief of staff. Moe also has held positions in city and state government and chaired the Minnesota Democratic-Farmer-Labor Party. He is a graduate of Williams College and received his law degree from the University of Minnesota. | *DIRECTOR* |
| 501(c)(3) | *TAX STATUS* |
| 1997—$36.8 million<br>1998—$38.1 million<br>Proposed 1999—Unavailable | *BUDGET* |
| Private sources (including membership dues and contributions, corporation and foundation grants, endowment income and merchandise sales), 82 percent; matching grant from Congress, 9 percent; other federal and state grants, 9 percent | *FUNDING SOURCES* |
| Members: 275,000<br>Branches/chapters: 6 regional offices<br>Affiliates: Owns 19 historic house museums | *SCOPE* |
| None | *PAC* |

| | |
|---|---|
| *METHOD OF OPERATION* | ♦ Advertisements ♦ Awards program ♦ Coalition forming ♦ Conferences/seminars ♦ Congressional testimony ♦ Films/video/audiotapes ♦ Grantmaking ♦ Grassroots organizing ♦ Internet (Web site) ♦ Legal assistance ♦ Legislative/regulatory monitoring (federal and state) ♦ Litigation ♦ Lobbying (federal and state) ♦ Local/municipal affairs ♦ Media outreach ♦ Participation in regulatory proceedings (federal and state) ♦ Public service announcements ♦ Research ♦ Training and technical assistance |
| *CURRENT CONCERNS* | ♦ Building an effective state and local preservation network ♦ Heritage tourism ♦ Preserving and protecting historic sites, buildings, and places ♦ Protecting and revitalizing America's Main Streets ♦ Revitalization of historic urban communities ♦ Rural heritage ♦ Sprawl and its impact on historic communities |
| *PUBLICATIONS* | Publishes information series (historic preservation information booklets) and books |
| *NEWSLETTER* | *Historic Preservation Forum* (quarterly)<br>*Historic Preservation Forum News* (periodic)<br>*Mainstreet News* (monthly)<br>*Preservation* (bimonthly) |
| *CONFERENCES* | Annual National Preservation Conference<br>National Town Meeting on Main Street |
| *BOARD OF DIRECTORS* | Nancy N. Campbell, chair<br><br>Other trustee members:<br>♦ Robert C. Allen ♦ Michael Andrews ♦ John W. Baird ♦ Richard D. Baron ♦ Claire W. Bogaard ♦ Lovida H. Coleman ♦ D. Ronald Daniel ♦ Mary Werner DeNadai ♦ Katherine Dickenson ♦ Susan Guthrie Dunham ♦ Elinor K. Farquhar ♦ Terry Goddard ♦ Tony Goldman ♦ William W. "Peter" Grant ♦ Graham D. Gund ♦ Bradley Hale ♦ William B. Hart Jr. ♦ Dealey Decherd Herndon ♦ Susan L. Howard ♦ Lily Rice Kendall ♦ Karl A. Komatsu ♦ Melvin B. Lane ♦ Stanley A. Lowe ♦ David McCullough ♦ H. Nicholas Muller III ♦ Louise Bryant Potter ♦ Peter van S. Rice ♦ John F. W. Rogers ♦ Vincent J. Scully ♦ Katherine Ann Slick ♦ Kenneth B. Smith ♦ William M. Spencer III ♦ Camille J. Strachan ♦ Suzanne W. Turner ♦ John H. Welborne ♦ W. Richard West ♦ Robert White |
| *EFFECTIVENESS* | "*Preservation*, the only Washington-based magazine to win [a National Magazine] award this year, is the bimonthly publication of the National Trust for Historic Preservation. It was honored as the best magazine with a circulation between 100,000 and 400,000. '*Preservation*'s jumping off point is architecture, but it's also about politics, art, history, places and people,' said the judges. 'Beautiful and full of surprises, it makes us care about what we have, what we've lost, and what we should fight to save.' |

"The National Magazine Awards, presented since 1966 by the American Society of Magazine Editors, are frequently touted as the Oscars of the business, usually by the mags that win them." (*Washington Post*, April 30, 1998)

"Margaret Donoho died believing the suburbia she loathed would never claim Myrtle Grove, her 160-acre farm on Maryland's Eastern Shore.

"She had placed her farm, which had been in her family for eight generations, under a 'conservation easement,' swearing never to build more than a single new house on her land. In exchange, she received a substantial tax benefit and a promise from a venerable nonprofit institution chartered by Congress, the National Trust for Historic Preservation, that it would forever guard against development on her property.

"It seemed a sacred pact, but its force didn't survive another generation: Donoho died in 1989, and her family sold the land to a Washington couple they thought would maintain the property unchanged. Instead, the couple persuaded the National Trust to allow them to create a small residential subdivision—precisely the 'evil' Donoho had sought to forbid.

"Now Donoho's relatives are seeking to force the trust to honor its agreement in a battle that has landed in D.C. Superior Court. The next hearing is set for this morning.

" 'My mother had a terribly strong feeling that Myrtle Grove should go on as it was,' said Sally Griffen, Donoho's daughter. 'All the big places were being cut up. There was kind of a whole way of life that was going. She very much wanted something left of how life had been there, something of how the Eastern Shore had been. . . . She would feel absolutely betrayed by all that's gone on.'

"Trust officials would not comment in detail yesterday, citing the fact that the matter is under litigation. But in a deposition in July, trust President Richard Moe described a letter he signed in 1994 allowing the developers to proceed as 'a serious mistake' and 'not a document I should have ever signed.'

"The trust later withdrew its permission for the subdivision, bringing legal action from the developers. Now, according to Donoho's family, the trust is moving to settle the suit by allowing the developers fewer lots than initially agreed upon, but some lots nonetheless.

"Preservationists say the trust's actions threaten to weaken the public's faith in conservation easements, which have become one of the most favored means of saving open space.

"According to the Land Trust Alliance, a Washington-based association of preservation groups, about 740,000 acres of land nationwide are covered by conservation easements. Maryland alone has about 70,000 acres." (*Washington Post*, March 20, 1998)

"The National Trust for Historic Preservation and the National Parks and Conservation Association have offered tentative support for a National Park Service plan that would allow a private developer to operate commercial ventures within the Gettysburg National Military Park.

"But they and others made clear that the plan would come under close scrutiny.

"Last week, the Park Service announced it would allow a consortium led by a Pennsylvania real estate developer to build it a new visitor center and museum at the Civil War battlefield. In exchange, the developer would gain the right to operate a giant-screen movie theater and private shops in the complex.

" 'The fact that the new facilities would be built within the park boundaries should not by itself disqualify the plan from consideration,' said National Trust president Richard Moe.

" 'The question,' Moe said, 'is whether it can be built in such a way so as to not intrude upon but rather to enhance the visitor experience while maintaining the integrity of the battlefield.' " (*Washington Post*, November 10, 1997)

"Montgomery County officials are close to signing a deal with a nationally recognized nonprofit group that would recommend how to revitalize a key shopping district in downtown Silver Spring.

"The proposal to contract with the National Main Street Center to seek solutions for one of the county's oldest downtowns drew unanimous support from the Silver Spring Steering Committee. The recently appointed group's first vote last week was to recommend that the county go ahead with the proposal. For $15,000, the program will give the county a comprehensive assessment of the district's strengths and weaknesses and provide a plan for revitalization.

"Main Street, a division of the National Trust for Historic Preservation, has worked with more than 1,200 aging downtowns across the nation during the last two decades. The organization would concentrate on the area around Fenton Street Village, taking in the commercial district bounded by Georgia Avenue on the west, Fenton Street on the east, Wayne Avenue on the north and Burlington Street on the south." (*Washington Post*, March 27, 1997)

"Back in the days of gunslingers, the lawless Montana gold-rush towns of Nevada City and Virginia City really needed a cowboy to ride to their rescue. They still need one—preferably one packing a $7 million check instead of a six-shooter. . . .

" 'We're all individualists here, but we're united in wanting to preserve our towns,' says Virginia City Mayor Robert Gabler. 'If they're sold off to collectors, this would really become a ghost town.'

"In a frantic effort to find a buyer, residents enlisted the aid of experts at the National Trust for Historic Preservation, which quickly donated $50,000 to help stabilize the town's most-tottering structures. The National Trust also came up with the idea of approaching Mr. Turner and Ms. Goldberg.

"But a Turner representative said he wasn't interested in the deal, and Ms. Goldberg didn't even bother to answer the Trust's letters, says Barbara Pahl, the National Trust's regional director in Denver. Mr. Turner's spokesman, Russ Miller, wouldn't confirm that the billionaire, who owns 160,000 acres in the state, had been approached to buy the properties. 'Mr. Turner's proclivities for giving aren't usually for historic towns,' Mr. Miller said. Ms. Goldberg's publicist says she doesn't know anything about the towns.

"The National Trust even tried to approach the U.S. National Park Service, hoping the towns could be turned into a site similar to colonial Williamsburg, Va. 'After all, the Park Service has 29 Civil War battlefields, but no frontier mining towns,' Ms. Pahl says. But the federal agency said no, citing funding restrictions, Ms. Pahl says." (*Wall Street Journal*, October 25, 1996)

Unavailable

# POLITICAL ORIENTATION

# National Wildlife Federation (1936)

8925 Leesburg Pike
Vienna, Virginia 22814
Phone: (703) 790-4000
Fax: (703) 442-7332
Internet: http://www.nwf.org

| | |
|---|---|
| **PURPOSE** | "To educate, inspire, and assist individuals and organizations of diverse cultures to conserve wildlife and other natural resources and to protect the earth's environment in order to achieve a peaceful, equitable, and sustainable future." |
| **STAFF** | 421 total—plus 52 part-time; 20 interns; and 120 volunteers |
| **DIRECTOR** | Mark Van Putten, president and chief executive officer. His National Wildlife Federation career began in 1982 when he became founding director of the Great Lakes Natural Resource Center (GLNRC) in Ann Arbor, Michigan. During his tenure at the GLNRC, Van Putten also served as founding director of the nation's largest environmental law clinic, also located in Ann Arbor. He is a magna cum laude graduate of the University of Michigan Law School. |
| **TAX STATUS** | 501(c)(3) |
| **BUDGET** | Fiscal year ending August 31, 1997—$101.9 million<br>F.Y. 1998—Unavailable<br>Proposed F.Y. 1999—Unavailable |
| **FUNDING SOURCES** | Nature education materials, 36 percent; publications, 23 percent; individuals, 17 percent; investments, 13 percent; foundation grants/corporate donations, 6 percent; royalties, 3 percent; other, 2 percent |
| **SCOPE** | Members: More than 4 million members and supporters<br>Branches/chapters: 46 state groups<br>Affiliates: N/A |
| **PAC** | None |

◆ Awards program (National Conservation Achievement Award) ◆ Advertisements ◆ Coalition formation ◆ Conferences/seminars ◆ Congressional/state legislative testimony ◆ Curriculum materials (Animal Tracks Classroom Guide, National Wildlife Week Classroom Kits) ◆ Environmental Hotline: 202-797-6655 ◆ Films/video/audiotapes ◆ Grassroots organizing ◆ Internet (Web site) ◆ Internships ◆ Legislative/regulatory monitoring (federal and state) ◆ Litigation ◆ Media outreach ◆ Telecommunications services (Fax-on-demand: 202-797-6644)

◆ Clean water ◆ Conservation education ◆ Endangered species/biodiversity/habitats ◆ Land stewardship ◆ Public/private lands ◆ Sustainable communities ◆ Water quality ◆ Wetlands

*Conservation Directory* (annual)
*Wildlife Conservation Stamps*

Also publishes special bulletins on environmental issues

*EnviroAction* (monthly)
*International Wildlife* (bimonthly magazine)
*National Wildlife* (bimonthly magazine)
*NatureLink*
*Ranger Rick* (monthly magazine for ages 6–12)
*Your Big Backyard* (monthly publication for preschoolers)

NWF annual meeting (held in March)
Also sponsors workshops, seminars, special events, and "outdoor discovery and recreation" events

Gerald R. Barber, chair; Edward Clark Jr., Becky Scheibelhut and Paula J. Del Guidice, vice chairs

Other members:
◆ Virginia P. Allery ◆ Richard J. Baldes ◆ James Baldock ◆ Charles T. Brown ◆ James L. Carroll ◆ Dan Deeb ◆ Daryl Durham ◆ Judith M. Espinosa ◆ Thomas Gonzalez ◆ Allen W. Guisinger ◆ Mary C. Harris ◆ Tom Martine ◆ Stanley A. Moberly ◆ Steven L. Montgomery ◆ Stephen E. Petron ◆ Bryan Pritchett ◆ John S. Rainey ◆ Jo Lyn Reeves ◆ Jerome C. Ringo ◆ Harmon Shade ◆ Maxine S. Thomas ◆ Spencer Tomb ◆ Thomas L. Warren

"Two environmental groups have appealed a Dec. 12 ruling by a federal judge who said a controversial federal program to reintroduce wolves to the Rocky Mountain region was illegal.

"Defenders of Wildlife and the National Wildlife Federation filed an appeal on Monday with the 10th Circuit Court of Appeals in Denver and said they were bracing themselves for what could be a long legal battle about reintroducing wolves to Yellowstone National Park and in central Idaho. U.S. District Judge William Downes earlier this month said that under the U.S. Endangered Species Act, the federal government was wrong to have experimentally introduced the wolves three years ago to an area where the animal already was found, siding with the ranchers who brought the case.

"But the judge, expecting an appeal, issued a stay of his own order, delaying the removal of more than 150 reintroduced gray wolves and their offspring. . . .

"Mark Van Putten, president of the National Wildlife Federation, said the judge's decision hinged on the designation of the wolves as 'experimental populations,' which was chosen to give federal managers more flexibility in dealing with the animals.

"Judge Downes said this legal mechanism should not have been used.

" 'We will not let a legal technicality destroy one of conservation's greatest victories,' Van Putten said." (*Washington Post*, December 31, 1997)

"Habitat for Humanity, the nonprofit organization dedicated to building affordable homes for low-income families, is expanding its mission to promote the environment as well.

"The organization late last month signed a partnership agreement with the National Wildlife Federation to encourage construction of more environmentally friendly homes. Among other things, Federation members will teach Habitat volunteers how to build more energy-efficient homes, how to recycle and reuse building materials and how to take better advantage of home sites to create natural backyard habitats.

" 'This definitely gives fuller meaning' to the title of our organization, said Millard Fuller, founder and president of Habitat, a poverty-relief group that Fuller likes to call a 'Christian ministry.' With hundreds of thousands of volunteers, the organization builds about 40 houses per day around the world, making it one of the world's largest home builders.

"Last month the wildlife Federation conducted a three-day training session for Habitat's regional directors. In the future, Habitat and the Federation plan to hold several joint training sessions for volunteers—especially at colleges—to promote healthier homes, ones that conserve water and energy.

" 'Habitat for Humanity has always been interested in the environment,' Fuller said. 'We always felt we wanted to do more than build a bunch of houses. We wanted to create communities into all that God intended.'

" 'A good natural habitat has to be part of the equation of a good human habitat. If there were only people and no other life here on Earth, what a boring, sad world it would be to live in.' " (*Washington Post*, June 14, 1997)

"A coalition of 40 American Indian tribes and the nation's largest conservation group have asked Montana and the National Park Service to stop slaughtering wild bison that leave Yellowstone National Park and instead allow the animals to be used as seed stock to re-establish free-roaming herds throughout the American West.

" 'It's an absolute disgrace the government has assumed the role of executioner,' said Mark Van Putten, president of the National Wildlife Federation, which is working with the InterTribal Bison Cooperative in Rapid City, S.D., to lobby the Government to stop slaughtering bison. . . .

"The National Wildlife Federation and the tribes propose to hold the animals in quarantine. If the bison prove disease free, the group wants them shipped to reservations or other public lands to be used as seed stock for new bison herds and to supplement existing herds. Animals that test positive should still be slaughtered, the group says.

"But Laurence Petersen, the Executive Officer of the Montana Department of Livestock, said his office opposed the plan. 'We do not want an animal from an infected herd in the state of Montana,' for quarantine or other purposes, Mr. Petersen said.

"How to handle wild animals is an especially volatile issue in the West. The state and Federal governments must come to a decision on the bison, and given the politics involved, no one is sure what the rest of the season could bring.

"For the Indian tribes, the bison issue goes deep. 'When they destroyed the buffalo herds,' in the last century, 'they were destroying our culture,' said Mr. DuBray. 'They severed the physical relationship, but the spiritual relationship remains.'

"Tribes around the country raise buffalo for food and spiritual sustenance, he said. When bison are killed, he said, prayers are recited beforehand. The meat is split among tribal members and parts of the animal are used in religious ceremonies. The skulls, for example, are used in a sun dance. 'The skin is pierced and the skulls are tied to the dancer,' Mr. DuBray said, 'who dances until the skull breaks off.' " (*New York Times*, January 21, 1997)

---

"a moderate environmental group" (*Wall Street Journal*, November 4, 1997)

# POLITICAL ORIENTATION

# Natural Resources Defense Council (1970)

40 West 20th Street
New York, New York 10011
Phone: (212) 727-2700
Fax: (212) 727-1773

1250 New York Avenue, NW
Suite 400
Washington, D.C. 20005
Phone: (202) 289-6868
Fax: (202) 289-1060

Internet: nrdcinfo@nrdc.org *or* http://www.nrdc.org

**PURPOSE**

"Dedicated to conserving natural resources and improving the quality of the human environment."

**STAFF**

170 total—125 professional/administrative; 45 support; plus 20 interns and 10 part-time

**DIRECTOR**

John H. Adams, executive director. Adams has directed the NRDC since its founding. A lawyer, he was formerly in corporate practice and served as assistant U.S. attorney in the Southern District of New York. He serves on the boards of many environmental organizations, as well as the President's Council on Sustainable Development. Adams is a graduate of Michigan State University and Duke University School of Law.

**TAX STATUS**

501(c)(3)

**BUDGET**

1997—$26.7 million
1998—Unavailable
Proposed 1999—Unavailable

**FUNDING SOURCES**

Membership, 63 percent; foundations, 20 percent; fees, contracts, and other revenues, 17 percent

**SCOPE**

Members: 400,000 individuals
Branches/chapters: 3 branch offices in Los Angeles, San Francisco, and Washington, D.C.
Affiliates: N/A

**PAC**

None

♦ Coalition forming ♦ Congressional testimony ♦ Grassroots organizing ♦ Initiative/referendum campaigns ♦ International activities ♦ Internet (Web site) ♦ Legal assistance ♦ Legislative/regulatory monitoring (federal and state) ♦ Litigation ♦ Local/municipal affairs ♦ Media outreach ♦ Research

## METHOD OF OPERATION

♦ Clean Air Act ♦ Clean Water Act ♦ Coastal protection ♦ Endangered species ♦ Energy conservation ♦ Fisheries protection ♦ Forestry and public lands management ♦ Nuclear weapons proliferation ♦ Ocean protection ♦ Pesticide reduction ♦ Toxics waste ♦ Urban environmental issues

## CURRENT CONCERNS

The following is a list of sample publications:

*Agricultural Solutions: Improving Water Quality in California Through Water Conservation and Pesticide Reduction*

*Benchmarking Air Emissions of Electric Utility Generators in the United States*

*Contaminated Catch: The Public Health Threat from Toxics in Fish*

*Cool It: Eight Great Ways to Stop Global Warming*

*Energy Innovations: A Prosperous Path to a Clean Environment*

*Exhausted by Diesel: How America's Dependence on Diesel Engines Threatens Our Health*

*Explosive Alliances: Nuclear Weapons Simulation Research at American Universities*

*Fields of Change: A New Crop of American Farmers Finds Alternatives to Pesticides*

*Gathering Storm: Coming Environmental Battles in the 105th Congress*

*The Internet and the Bomb: A Research Guide to Policy and Information About Nuclear Weapons*

*Long Island Sound Municipal Report Cards: Environmental Assessments of 78 Coastal Communities*

*Our Children At Risk: The 5 Worst Environmental Threats to Their Health*

*Putting Children First: Making Pesticide Levels in Food Safer for Infants and Children*

*Reclaiming Our Heritage: What We Need To Do To Preserve America's National Parks*

*Taking Stock: Worldwide Nuclear Weapon Deployments*

*Testing the Waters VII: How Does Your Vacation Beach Rate?*

*Testing the Waters VIII: Has Your Vacation Beach Cleaned Up Its Act?*

*Too Good to Throw Away: Recycling's Proven Record*

*Under the Flight Path: Community Response to Aircraft Noise at Westchester County Airport*

*Wetlands for Clean Water: How Wetlands Protect Rivers, Lakes and Coastal Waters from Pollution*

## PUBLICATIONS

*Amicus Journal* (quarterly)

## NEWSLETTER

## CONFERENCES

Annual member meeting

## BOARD OF DIRECTORS

## EFFECTIVENESS

"Every year hundreds of the 50-foot-long, 40-ton whales travel 5,000 miles from their frigid feeding grounds near Alaska to give birth in the warm, salty waters of this remote lagoon [Laguna San Ignacio, Mexico], which the United Nations lists as a World Heritage Site and Mexico protects as part of an ecological reserve. But the same features that have drawn generations of whales—the water's high salinity, the warmth, the obscurity—are attracting a new potential resident. Mitsubishi Corp., the giant Japanese conglomerate, has proposed building one of the world's largest salt production facilities here in a venture with the Mexican government. . . .

" 'At some point you have to draw a line in the sand and say, This has to be protected,' Joel Reynolds, a staff attorney for the Natural Resources Defense Council, an American environmental group, said during a recent visit to the lagoon. 'We have drawn a line in the sand around Laguna San Ignacio.'. . .

"Opponents are particularly concerned that the Mexican government, which declared Laguna San Ignacio a whale sanctuary and created a massive 'biosphere reserve' to help protect their Baja Peninsula breeding grounds, owns 51 percent of the public-private company that wants to build the saltworks through the Commerce Ministry. Mitsubishi owns the other 49 percent of the company, Exportadora de Sal S.A., known as ESSA.

" 'If the government accepts this project, the concept of a biosphere reserve is nothing—it's meaningless,' said Homero Aridjis, head of the Group of 100, a top Mexican environmental organization that is leading the fight against the saltworks, aided by the Natural Resources Defense Council and the International Fund for Animal Welfare.

"In the end, people on both sides of the dispute agree that there is little scientific data that conclusively shows what impact the proposed salt-works could have on whales. Instead, some activists hope the issue turns on what sort of development is compatible with San Ignacio's designation as a World Heritage Site and its location in the buffer zone of Mexico's El Vizcaino Biosphere Reserve.

" 'This may be appropriate somewhere,' said Robert F. Kennedy Jr., a Natural Resources Defense Council attorney. 'But why put it in an area designated as one of the special spots on earth?' " (*Washington Post*, February 21, 1998)

"When environmental report cards for communities around Long Island Sound were handed out recently, only Westport and Smithtown, L.I., got high marks; both were applauded for doing a 'very good' job of controlling pollution sources.

"The report cards were issued late last month by a coalition of three organizations monitoring the Sound: the Natural Resources Defense Council, Connecticut Fund for the Environment and Save the Sound. Municipalities are rated on policies and programs that affect the estuary's water quality, with coastal communities, including 24 in Connecticut, rated from 'very good' down to 'fair' and 'needs special attention.' " (*New York Times*, February 8, 1998)

"The United States Energy Department is setting a dangerous precedent for academic independence by involving some of the nation's leading universities in nuclear-weapons-related computer research and by pushing classified weapons research programs into the academic arena, according to a report by the Natural Resources Defense Council.

"The report . . . criticizes the Academic Strategic Alliances Program, a $200 million, 10-year project financed by the Energy Department. Last year the program created research centers at five universities in support of the Accelerated Strategic Computing Initiative, or A.S.C.I. . . .

"The Defense Council's report says the nation's program for simulating the testing of nuclear weapons is being aided by university research in related scientific areas that do not directly involve simulating nuclear explosions.

"Energy Department officials rejected the conclusions of the report.

"The report is called 'Explosive Alliances: Nuclear Weapons Simulation Research at American Universities.' Expanding scientific research that is closely related to weapons design at academic centers, the report warned, raises the risk of the proliferation of advanced nuclear weapons technology." (*New York Times*, January 25, 1998)

"The New York-based Natural Resources Defense Council says in a notice of intent to file suit that the airport has violated the federal Clean Water Act over the past three winters by allowing toxic de-icing chemicals to flow from runways into Chesapeake Bay tributaries. . . ." (*Washington Post*, January 9, 1998)

"... [T]here has been concern in recent years about the high lead content of some calcium supplements, particularly for children. Calcium from oyster shells; from dolomite, a natural mineral containing calcium and magnesium; and from bone meal have the highest lead levels, and often information about the lead is not available on the product label.

"The Natural Resources Defense Council and other environmental groups have filed a petition with the Food and Drug Administration to establish federal standards for lead levels in calcium supplements and antacids. In California earlier this year, manufacturers agreed gradually to reduce lead levels in calcium supplements and antacid products during the next two years from 4.0 to 1.5 micrograms of lead per 1,000 milligrams of calcium. (Lead naturally occurs in many food products. A serving of whole milk can contain anywhere from 1.7 to 6.7 micrograms of lead per 1,000 milligrams of calcium.)

"Still, concerns about lead should not keep people from getting calcium, experts said. Consumers Reports on Health noted this month that 'the risk posed by lead in calcium supplements is low and outweighed by the clear benefits of extra calcium in people who need supplements to ward off osteoporosis.' " (*Washington Post*, August 19, 1997)

"Rallying public support for the shark is the focus of an international campaign launched last month by a coalition of aquariums and major environmental groups, including the World Wildlife Fund, National Audubon Society and the Natural Resources Defense Council. Warning that sharks and other large ocean predators are being 'caught and killed faster than they can reproduce,' the Ocean Wildlife Campaign coalition is calling for an international treaty limiting shark harvests, as well as a global ban on 'finning'—the practice of slicing the valuable fins from the shark and then tossing the still-living animal overboard to die.

"... Jack Musick, head of the vertebrate ecology program at the Virginia Institute of Marine Sciences and a leading expert on sharks, worries that a further decline could have consequences that extend far beyond the small universe of people who make a living from these creatures. Sharks in particular, as the 'apex predators' atop the ocean food chain, help preserve the ecological balance in the marine environment, a role they have played for more than 400 million years." (*Washington Post*, August 10, 1997)

"A new study released yesterday ranks the 50 largest electric utility companies in the eastern half of the United States by the amount of pollution they produce for each unit of electricity.

"The study, conducted by the Natural Resources Defense Council (NRDC), Pace University's Center for Environmental Legal Studies and Public Service Electric and Gas Co. of New Jersey, a large utility company, rated utilities based on the amount of different types of pollutants they produce per megawatt hour. The basis for the study was 1995 data provided to the Environmental Protection Agency. The 50 largest electric utility companies in the eastern half of the United States account for 20 percent of nitrogen oxide emissions nationally, 50 percent of emissions of sulfur dioxide and 20 percent of carbon dioxide emissions. . . .

"As Congress and the states move toward deregulation of the electric utility industry—which would replace today's system of regulated monopolies with competition among the utilities for business and residential customers—groups such as the NRDC are raising concerns that firms that pollute more may have an unfair cost advantage." (*Washington Post*, April 25, 1997)

Unavailable

# POLITICAL ORIENTATION

# The Nature Conservancy (1951)

1815 North Lynn Street
Arlington, Virginia 22209
Phone: (703) 841-5300
Fax: (703) 841-1283
Internet: http://www.tnc.org

| | |
|---|---|
| **PURPOSE** | "To preserve plants, animals, and natural communities that represent the diversity of life on Earth by protecting the land and waters they need to survive." |
| **STAFF** | 1,804 total—plus 395 interns/short-term/seasonal |
| **DIRECTOR** | John C. Sawhill, president and chief executive officer. Before joining the Nature Conservancy as president in 1990, Sawhill was a partner in the international management consulting firm of McKinsey & Company. He served as deputy secretary of energy in the Carter administration from 1979 to 1980, president of New York University from 1975 to 1979, head administrator of the first Federal Energy Administration in the Ford administration from 1973 to 1975, and associate director of energy and natural resources in the Nixon administration from 1972 to 1974. Currently Sawhill is chairman of the board of the Whitehead Institute for Biomedical Research at Massachusetts Institute of Technology and the Manville Personal Injury Settlement Trust. He is a member of the President's Council on Sustainable Development, the board of advisors of the Center for Energy and Environmental Policy, a trustee of Princeton University, and a director with Pacific Gas and Electric, Consolidated Edison, RCA, Philip Morris, Crane Corporation, and General American Investors. |
| **TAX STATUS** | 501(c)(3) |
| **BUDGET** | 1997—Unavailable<br>1998—Unavailable<br>Proposed 1999—Unavailable |
| **FUNDING SOURCES** | Individuals, 73 percent; foundations grants, 15 percent; corporate donations, 11 percent; other, 2 percent |
| **SCOPE** | Members: 900,000 individuals; 1,500 corporate associates<br>Branches/chapter: 300 state and program locations<br>Affiliates: N/A |

None

♦ Awards program ♦ Conferences/seminars ♦ Direct action ♦ Films/video/audiotapes ♦ International activities ♦ Internet (Web site) ♦ Land acquisition ♦ Media outreach ♦ Public service announcements ♦ Product merchandising ♦ Research ♦ Training and technical assistance

**METHOD OF OPERATION**

♦ Biodiversity preservation ♦ Campaign for conservation ♦ Last Great Places ♦ Parks in Peril ♦ Rare and endangered species

**CURRENT CONCERNS**

*Hawaii: The Islands of Life*
*Heart of the Land*
*Natural Events Almanac*
*Off the Beaten Path*
*Parks in Peril Source Book*
*Perspectives on Species Imperilment*
*Rare Plant Communities of the Conterminous United States*
*Species Report Card*
*Tallgrass Prairie*

**PUBLICATIONS**

*Biodiversity Network News* (periodic)
*KOA Update* (periodic)
*Natural Assets* (periodic)
*The Nature Conservancy Magazine* (bimonthly)

Plus each chapter has its own newsletter

**NEWSLETTER**

Annual meeting

**CONFERENCES**

Daniel R. Elroymson, chair; John C. Sawhill, president and chief executive officer; Anthony P. Grassi and Wendy J. Paulson, vice chairs; Louesa C. Duemling, secretary; Ward W. Woods, treasurer

Other members:
♦ Richard A. Abdoo ♦ Carter F. Bales ♦ David C. Cole ♦ A.D. Correll Jr. ♦ Ian M. Cumming ♦ Livio D. DeSimone ♦ Carol E. Dinkins ♦ Mary Fleming Finlay ♦ John W. Fitzpatrick ♦ David J. Gutierrez ♦ John W. Hanes Jr. ♦ John S. Hendricks ♦ Kate Ireland ♦ Durk I. Jager ♦ Frances C. James ♦ Glenn Cooper James ♦ Philip J. James ♦ Samuel C. Johnson ♦ Peter M. Kareiva ♦ Barbara A. Lipscomb ♦ Meredith Meiling ♦ Alfredo Novoa Peña ♦ Leigh H. Perkins Jr. ♦ H. Norman Schwarzkopf ♦ John G. Smale ♦ John F. Smith Jr. ♦ Howard Stringer ♦ Cameron M. Vowell ♦ Jeffrey N. Watanabe ♦ John C. Whitehead ♦ Edward O. Wilson ♦ Joy B. Zedler

**BOARD OF DIRECTORS**

# EFFECTIVENESS

"The environmental movement has taken a new turn with the entry of some large conservation organizations into commercial forestry.

"The sandplain ecosystem of coastal Long Island and southeastern New England is among the most unusual on earth. Formed by ice and shaped by wind, rain and fire, grassy sand plain moors are home to dozens of rare plants and animals.

"That is, they used to be.

"Once European settlers arrived, the land was turned to grazing, farming or development. Today, only a few thousand acres of undeveloped sand plain remain, and they have been gradually overrun with alien species, especially the scrubby pitch pines that shade the ground and drive out the native grasses and wildflowers and the insects, mammals and birds they support.

"Now, conservation workers are trying to reclaim this ecosystem by reviving one of the forces that originally shaped it: fire. . . .

"This spring, the Nature Conservancy, working with several other conservation organizations, has conducted 20 'prescribed burns' on Martha's Vineyard, said Joel Carlson, the Conservancy's fire manager in Massachusetts. The burns take place only when wind, temperature, humidity and other weather conditions fit certain limits.

"The idea is to burn a small area at a time, he said, so that the insects, birds and other animals can find habitat nearby until the burned area begins to regrow. 'Fire is an amazingly beneficial process for plants and animals that are adapted, but burning itself is not beneficial to any,' Mr. Carlson said.

"This month, he and his crew finished the season's work at Wasque, a conservation area on the east end of the Vineyard and owned by The Trustees of Reservations, a Massachusetts conservation organization. In the past few years, the Trustees have turned hundreds of acres of pitch-pine forest into broad swaths of grassland moor." (*New York Times*, March 26, 1998)

"More than 20,000 native animal species have been identified in the United States. But once identified, some have disappeared. Of them, 110 have been declared extinct, and 416 others are simply missing, with no one certain whether they still live or not.

" 'The main intent of the grants was to try to re-find' some species that had not been seen in a long time and were feared extinct,' said Bruce Stein, who runs the program for the Nature Conservancy. 'There's a significant number in limbo. People haven't seen them in many years.'

"Scientists mourn the loss of a species, even those as small as a bug or a plant, he said. Each species declared extinct is an unrecoverable resource, a vanished potential that might have held the secret to some knowledge or the cure to some ailment of the world.

" 'If a species is missing and we find them, then we can do something about protecting them,' said John Sawhill, president of the Nature Conservancy. . . .

"... The Nature Conservancy funded searches for 79 missing species in 14 states. Only five species were found: two varieties of land snails in Montana; a freshwater mussel in Tennessee; and in Virginia, Chris Hobson, of the state Department of Conservation and Recreation, led a team that found a quarter-inch water bug called the Virginia Piedmont water boatman." (*Washington Post*, February 8, 1998)

"The Nature Conservancy, based in Arlington, Va., and Vermont Land Trust in Montpelier, Vt., said they have purchased 26,789 acres of timberland in Vermont and upstate New York that they will manage as partners in a commercial demonstration project. The partners said they aim to show that profitable forestry also can protect watersheds and wildlife, while preserving aesthetic and recreation values and supporting jobs for local loggers, sawmills and other wood-based industry.

"The $5.5 million purchase of 23 woodland parcels, equivalent to about 41 square miles, from Atlas Timberland Co. was largely financed by a $5 million grant from the $630 million Freeman Foundation, of Stowe, Vt. The Nature Conservancy, with 828,000 members and 1,500 nature preserves nationwide, is the nation's 20th largest charitable institution and its largest conservation organization, according to John Sawhill, president. The Nature Conservancy and Vermont Land Trust separately hold conservation easements on more than a million acres, which enable them to preserve land from development by enforcing restrictions on its use, including on how it may be logged. But actual ownership of extensive forests for commercial logging is a new venture for both.

" 'We have got to demonstrate that you can earn an economic rate of return on land while also protecting biodiversity,' said Mr. Sawhill. 'It's not only in forestry but also in agriculture, oil drilling and ranching.' He added, 'I really believe that if you don't manage forest holdings for both jobs and the environment, the environment is going to suffer in the long run.'

"The American Forest & Paper Association, the Washington-based trade group for the $200 billion U.S. forest-products industry, welcomed the venture. 'We think it's great,' said John Heissenbuttel, vice president for forestry. 'The key to protecting forestland is to make sure it's profitable to landowners. That's conservation at no cost to the government,' he said.

"Another aim of the project is to answer critics who question the environmental movement's commitment to economic development. 'There's been a lot of rhetoric about sustaining rural economies as well as protecting wild lands,' said Darby Bradley, president of Vermont Land Trust. 'But skeptics say the environmental organizations are pushing only for protection. We want to demonstrate that you can harvest land, create jobs and still protect the environment,' he said. 'To do this on a large scale would really mean something.' " (*Wall Street Journal*, December 31, 1997)

---

"a green group known for its aggressive land deals on behalf of wildlife conservation" (*Wall Street Journal*, September 24, 1996)

"the nation's largest nonprofit environmental group" (*Wall Street Journal*, May 15, 1996)

"avoids the political fray" (*New York Times*, January 1, 1995)

# POLITICAL ORIENTATION

# People for the Ethical Treatment of Animals (1980)

501 Front Street
Norfolk, Virginia 23510
National phone: (757) 622-7382
National fax: (757) 622-0457
Internet: http://www.peta-online.org *or* peta@norfolk.infi.net

## PURPOSE

"To protect animals from exploitation and cruelty and to bring about positive changes in the ways humans regard other species. We seek to expose animal abuse so that it will not be perpetuated or taken for granted. . . . Ultimately, we strive to promote a world in which animals are respected and people are aware of and concerned with how their daily decisions affect the lives of other sentient beings."

## STAFF

90 total—25 professional; 65 support; plus 3 part-time, 12 interns, and 20 volunteers

## DIRECTOR

Ingrid Newkirk, managing director. Before helping found People for the Ethical Treatment of Animals (PETA), Newkirk was a deputy sheriff, a Maryland state law enforcement officer, and chief of Animal Disease Control for the District of Columbia's Commission on Public Health. She has written numerous articles and books and has appeared on many national radio and television programs.

## TAX STATUS

501(c)(3)

## BUDGET

Fiscal year ending July 31, 1998—$11.7 million
Proposed F.Y. 1999—Unavailable

## FUNDING SOURCES

Donations, 92 percent; merchandise sales, 4 percent; interest and dividends, 3 percent; fundraising, 1 percent

## SCOPE

Members: 600,000 individuals

Branch/chapter: Seattle office

Affiliates: PETA Europe, Ltd. (London); Stichting PETA Nederlands (Amsterdam); PETA Deutschland (Stuttgart); Research and Education Foundation (all are nonprofits)

## PAC

## METHOD OF OPERATION

♦ Advertisements ♦ Awards program ♦ Boycotts ♦ Coalition forming ♦ Conferences/seminars ♦ Congressional testimony ♦ Demonstrations ♦ Direct action ♦ Electronic bulletin boards ♦ Films/video/audiotapes ♦ Grassroots organizing ♦ International activities ♦ Internet (electronic bulletin boards, Web site) ♦ Internships ♦ Investigations ♦ Legislative/regulatory monitoring (federal and state) ♦ Library (open to public) ♦ Litigation ♦ Lobbying (grassroots) ♦ Media outreach ♦ Participation in regulatory proceedings (federal) ♦ Performance rating ♦ Product merchandising ♦ Research ♦ Shareholder resolutions ♦ Speakers program ♦ Telecommunications services (Hotline: 301-770-8980) ♦ Training and technical assistance

## CURRENT CONCERNS

♦ Abusive animal laboratories ♦ Animals used for entertainment ♦ Cruelty-free consumer products ♦ Dissection of animals in schools ♦ Factory farming of animals ♦ Hunting and fishing ♦ Product testing on animals ♦ Trapping and ranching of animals for fur ♦ Vegetarianism

## PUBLICATIONS

*The Compassionate Cook*
*Cooking With PETA*
*Cruelty Free Shopping Guide*
*Guide to Compassionate Living*
*PETA Case Reports*
*PETA Fact Sheets*
*Shopping Guide for Caring Consumers*

Also offers T-shirts, petting supplies, videos, and other merchandise

## NEWSLETTER

*GRRR!* (Kids magazine)
*PETA's Animal Times* (quarterly)

## CONFERENCES

Unavailable

## BOARD OF DIRECTORS

Michael Rodman, chairperson/treasurer; Ingrid Newkirk, president; MaryBeth Sweetland, vice president; Jeanne Roush, secretary

## EFFECTIVENESS

"A rundown animal shelter operating in Vega Baja without a use permit is currently the target of a takeover effort by the U.S.-based People for the Ethical Treatment of Animals.

"The shelter is also bringing bad publicity to Puerto Rico.

"PETA's spring issue of *Animal Times* splashed pictures of the shelter's suffering animals over two pages and urged the organization's 600,000 animal lovers worldwide to write to Gov. Rossello and Vega Baja Mayor Luis E. Melendez Cano to protest the conditions.

"PETA's involvement in Puerto Rico is not new. A few years ago, the group took the municipality of Ponce to court in a bid to improve the city-run shelter. And now PETA is working behind the scenes to gain control of the Vega Baja shelter run by a private group headed by former teacher Sara Cordova. . . ." (*San Juan Star*, May 22, 1998)

"The United States Department of Agriculture has fined a New Jersey company $50,000 for violating a Federal law that regulates the care and treatment of laboratory animals. But in a settlement, the company, Huntingdon Life Sciences of East Millstone, N.J., agreed to pay the fine without admitting to the charges. . . .

"Huntingdon conducts animals research for corporations, testing consumer products. It was highly successful, with more than 200 clients, until last year, when one of the largest animal rights groups, People for the Ethical Treatment of Animals, or PETA, secretly investigated the company and publicly released its results. PETA has sent an undercover workers to Huntingdon who found evidence, the group said, that animals used in research were suffering unnecessarily. . . .

"The result was a long battle between PETA and Huntingdon. Huntingdon sued PETA, accusing the group of trying to undermine and destroy its business. Last year, PETA and Huntingdon settled the lawsuit, and both claimed victory. . . .

"When PETA made its public charges against Huntingdon, it gave its information to the Agriculture Department, prompting that agency's investigation. . . ." (*New York Times*, April 16, 1998)

"When Gillette Co. announced in November that it used no animals to test its cosmetics, shaving, dental, and other personal care products or their ingredients, the People for the Ethical Treatment of Animals said it would end its fight with Gillette.

" 'This victory is the culmination of our more than 10-year campaign, which has involved many colorful protests and actions, including the hanging of a banner stating 'Gillette Tortures Animals' outside headquarters,' PETA said in a statement last month. . . .

"The campaign included demonstrations outside the company's corporate headquarters at Prudential Center and at its South Boston plant, as well as calls for boycotts of Gillette products." (*Boston Globe*, February 23, 1997)

"People for the Ethical Treatment of Animals (PETA) recently gained a new ally in its campaign to end the era of fur coats once and for all.

"The large and influential modeling agency Boss Models Worldwide has become the first agency to institute an anti-fur policy. No Boss models will wear any fur in any fashion show or shoot, and if asked, the Boss models working the job have orders to walk off the set.

"PETA has been signing models and celebrities individually to its 'Models of Compassion' contract for years—Tyra Banks, Jenny McCarthy and Brooke Shields are recent signees. But this is the first time an agency has joined its campaign. . . .

"It may sound extreme, but hey, just last month PETA supporters pelted fur-using designer Oscar de la Renta with a pie at a Neiman Marcus fashion show in Dallas. . . ." (*Star Ledger*, November 24, 1996)

"PETA goes beyond humane organizations that believe animals should not be treated poorly. PETA believes animals have their own rights and should not be exploited in any way: not eaten, worn or experimented on." (*Virginian-Pilot*, March 15, 1998)

"They are presumably lefty, but there are Republicans and antiabortion activists among them." (*Washington Post*, May 28, 1995)

# Pesticide Action Network (PANNA)
# North America Regional Center (1984)

49 Powell Street
Suite 500
San Francisco, California 94102
Phone: (415) 981-1771
Fax: (415) 981-1991
Internet: panna@panna.org *or* http://www.panna.org/panna/

**PURPOSE**

"To support worldwide opposition to hazardous pesticides and advocate democratically controlled, socially just, least toxic alternatives."

**STAFF**

15 total—10 program/campaign; 5 administrative; plus 2 full-time volunteers; 1 intern

**DIRECTOR**

Monica Moore, program director. Moore became the founding director of Pesticide Action Network North America Regional Center (PANNA) in 1984. Moore has served on the boards of Environment Liaison Centre International, the Pesticide Education Center, the California Interfaith Committee for Corporate Responsibility, Biotechnology Action Council, and as an advisor to the Environmental Project on Central America and the Rainforest Action Network. She earned a B.S. in environmental science policy at the University of California–Berkeley.

Stephen Scholl-Buckwald, managing director. Since 1997 he has been responsible for coordinating PANNA's administration, finances, and development. He serves as treasurer of the Institute for Food and Development Policy and Earth Share of California and on the executive committee of the California Coalition for Pesticide Use Reduction. He holds a Ph.D. in history from Indiana University.

**TAX STATUS**

501(c)(3)

**BUDGET**

1997—$1.16 million
1998—Unavailable
Proposed 1999—Unavailable

**FUNDING SOURCES**

Grants, 73 percent; fees, contracts, and other, 11 percent; donations, 10 percent; contributions, 6 percent

Members: N/A

Branches/chapters: PANNA is one of five regional centers (with Africa, Asia/Pacific, Europe, and Latin America) of PAN Regional Centers, an international coalition of more than 400 independent, autonomous citizen organizations working for pesticide reform in more than 60 countries.

Affiliates: More than 100, primarily 501(c)(3) organizations, in North America, and more than 400 worldwide

None

♦ Advertisements ♦ Coalition forming ♦ Conferences/seminars ♦ Congressional testimony ♦ Information clearinghouse ♦ International activities ♦ Internet (E-mail alerts, Web site) ♦ Legislative/regulatory monitoring (federal and state) ♦ Library (open to public) ♦ Media outreach ♦ Participation in regulatory proceedings (state) ♦ Telecommunications services (databases) ♦ Technical assistance

♦ Campaign to create a worldwide ban of methyl bromide ♦ Environmental justice ♦ Food security ♦ International agreements on pesticide trade ♦ Pesticide use reduction methods and programs ♦ Public education about pesticide hazards and non-toxic alternatives ♦ Public health related to pesticide use

The following is a list of sample publications:

*Alternatives to Methyl Bromide: Excerpts From the U.N. Methyl Bromide Technical Options Committee 1995 Assessment*

*Demise of the Dirty Dozen* (chart)

*Dirty Dozen Fact Sheets*

*The Economists Who Cried Wolf: How CDFA Exaggerated the Costs of a Methyl Bromide Ban*

*Failing Health: Pesticide Use in California Schools*

*Feeding People Without Poisons: Supporting Health Agriculture*

*Financial Incentives and Their Potential to Reduce Pesticide Use in Three Crops: Cotton, Oranges, and Strawberries*

*Funding a Better Ban: Smart Spending on Methyl Bromide Alternatives in Developing Countries*

*Plaguicidas en America Latina: Participacion Ciudadana en Politicas para Reducir Uso de Plaguicidas*

*Redefining Integrated Pest Management: Farmer Empowerment and Pesticide Use*

*Rising Toxic Tide: Pesticide Use in California 1991–1995*

*Global Pesticide Campaigner* (quarterly magazine)
*Pesticide Action Network Update* (online periodical)

| | |
|---|---|
| *CONFERENCES* | Conferences on pesticide reform, in the Bay Area, every 2–3 years<br>Topical workshops as campaigns require |
| *BOARD OF DIRECTORS* | ♦ Rajiv Bhatia ♦ Ignacio Chapela ♦ Michael DiBartolomeis ♦ Jonathan Fox ♦ Arif Gamal ♦ Rob McConnell ♦ Mary O'Brien ♦ Ivette Perfecto ♦ Cruz Phillips ♦ S. Ravi Rajan ♦ Naomi Roht-Arriaza ♦ Peter Rosset ♦ Lori Ann Thrupp |
| *EFFECTIVENESS* | "To his many customers, exterminator Paul Walls Sr. made but one claim about the cola-colored bug spray he peddled from the back of his truck: 'It kills them all,' he'd say in a near whisper, 'and they don't come back.'<br><br>"He was right about that much. In the small towns along Mississippi's southeastern coast, Walls became celebrated for his 'cotton poison,' a mysterious, odd-smelling concoction that obliterated roaches and anything else that slithered or crawled. Only later, after Walls was arrested, did his customers discover that it can kill people, too. Walls's pesticide business was shut down last fall after federal agents—following complaints from competing exterminators—discovered he was illegally using methyl parathion, a neurotoxin so lethal that it is sometimes used in suicides in Europe. But by then, Walls and a business associate, a local preacher named Dock Eatman Jr., had sprayed poison into scores of homes, motel rooms, restaurants and even day-care centers. In the process, officials say, they helped launch what could soon become one of the decade's costliest environmental disasters, with consequences that are only now being fully realized. . . .<br><br>"Some environmental groups, though, say the pesticide should be banned. In San Francisco, the Pesticide Action Network of North America ranks methyl parathion among its 'dirty dozen' of dangerous pesticides. Spokesman Ellen Hickey said the Mississippi case illustrates how easy it can be to circumvent the law and put large numbers of people at risk.<br><br>" 'That something of this scope can happen here, in a country with some of the world's strictest regulations for pesticides, is just frightening,' Hickey said. 'This stuff isn't supposed to be used indoors but it was—and not just once, but many times.'<br><br>"The full human consequences of the misuse may not be known for years, but some in Moss Point said they have already suffered. Barbara Halmi, whose house was treated four times by Paul Walls, became emotional at his trial as she described her husband's bleeding and the rashes and bouts of tunnel vision she experienced after the exterminator's visits. At one point she paused dramatically and thrust a finger in Walls's direction.<br><br>" 'That right there,' she said, 'liked [sic] to killed us all.' " (*Washington Post*, August 18, 1997) |
| *POLITICAL ORIENTATION* | Unavailable |

# Rainforest Action Network (1985)

221 Pine Street
Suite 500
San Francisco, California 94104
Phone: (415) 398-4404
Fax: (415) 398-2732
Internet: rainforst@ran.org *or* http://www.ran.org

"To protect the Earth's rainforests and support the rights of their inhabitants through education, grassroots organizing, and non-violent direct action."

*PURPOSE*

19 total—11 professional; 8 support; plus interns and volunteers

*STAFF*

Randall L. Hayes, director. Before founding Rainforest Action Network (RAN) in 1985, Hayes was involved in documentary filmmaking, producing the award winning film *The Four Corners, A National Sacrifice Area?* He has traveled, lectured, written and demonstrated extensively on tropical rainforests and activism.

*DIRECTOR*

501(c)(3)

*TAX STATUS*

1998—Unavailable
1996—Unavailable

*BUDGET*

Grants, public contributions, membership dues, sales, special events, investments, and other sources

*FUNDING SOURCES*

Members: 30,000
Branches/chapters: N/A
Affiliates: There are over 150 Rainforest Action Groups (RAGs) based in the United States and Europe that are informally associated with the Rainforest Action Network. They receive support materials, but no funding.

*SCOPE*

None

*PAC*

## METHOD OF OPERATION

♦ Advertisements ♦ Boycotts ♦ Coalition forming ♦ Conferences/seminars ♦ Consumer education ♦ Demonstrations ♦ Direct action ♦ Divestment campaign ♦ Environmental education ♦ Grantmaking ♦ Grassroots organizing (letter writing campaigns) ♦ International activities ♦ Internet (Web site) ♦ Library/information clearinghouse ♦ Media outreach ♦ Negotiation ♦ Product merchandising ♦ Research ♦ Selective bans ♦ Youth outreach

## CURRENT CONCERNS

♦ Amazonia ♦ Hawaiian rainforests ♦ Multinational corporations based in the United States and operating in rainforests ♦ Temperate forest protection ♦ U.S. tropical timber imports ♦ Wood conservation

## PUBLICATIONS

*Amazonia: Voices from the Rainforest*
*Cut Waste Not Trees*
*Mitsubishi Campaign Organizer's Manual*
*Southeast Asia Directory*
*Treasures of the Rainforest*
*Wood Users Guide*
*World Rainforest Report*
*World Rainforest Week Organizer's Packet*

Also publishes brochures and fact sheets

## NEWSLETTER

*Rainforest Action Alert* (monthly)
*World Rainforest Report* (quarterly)

## CONFERENCES

Unavailable

## BOARD OF DIRECTORS

♦ Andre Carothers ♦ Gina Collins ♦ Chris Desser ♦ Martha DiSario ♦ Allan Hunt-Badiner ♦ Michael Klein ♦ Scott Price ♦ Mike Roselle ♦ Steve Stevik ♦ Francesca Vietor ♦ David Weir

## EFFECTIVENESS

"What's an environmental group to do, when eight years of boycotts, letter-writing campaigns and such have not stopped the Mitsubishi Corporation of Japan from cutting down old-growth forests?

"Announce a 'landmark settlement' with two Mitsubishi entities that have never, themselves, so much as nicked a tree.

"Yesterday, amidst much hoopla, the Rainforest Action Network, a small but vocal environmental group based in San Francisco, said it would call off its boycott against Mitsubishi Motor Sales of America and Mitsubishi Electric America.

"Why? The two companies, which make automobiles and electronic products, had pledged that by 2002 they would use only papers and cardboards that are derived from rice, corn husks or other non-tree sources. They promised to finance research into forestry practices. And Mitsubishi Motor said it would funnel voluntary contributions from car buyers to groups that plant trees or buy land for preservation." (*New York Times*, February 12, 1998)

"liberal" (*Business Week,* January 30, 1995)

# POLITICAL ORIENTATION

# Resources for the Future (1952)

1616 P Street, NW
Washington, D.C. 20036
Phone: (202) 328-5000
Fax: (202) 939-3460
Internet: info@rff.org *or* http://www.rff.org

| | |
|---|---|
| **PURPOSE** | "To advance research and public education in the development, conservation, and use of natural resources, and in the quality of the environment." |
| **STAFF** | 78 total—68 professional; 10 support; plus 10 part-time and 12 summer interns |
| **DIRECTOR** | Paul Portney, president |
| **TAX STATUS** | 501(c)(3) |
| **BUDGET** | 1998—Unavailable<br>Proposed 1999—Unavailable |
| **FUNDING SOURCES** | Government sources, 33 percent; investments, 33 percent; corporations, foundations, and individuals, 33 percent |
| **SCOPE** | Members: N/A<br>Branches/chapters: N/A<br>Affiliates: N/A |
| **PAC** | None |
| **METHOD OF OPERATION** | ♦ Conferences/seminars ♦ Congressional testimony ♦ Grantmaking ♦ International activities ♦ Internet (Web site) ♦ Library/information clearinghouse ♦ Media outreach ♦ Participation in regulatory proceedings (federal) ♦ Research ♦ Speakers program |

## CURRENT CONCERNS

♦ Electromagnetic fields ♦ Energy and the environment ♦ Environment and development ♦ Environmental equity ♦ Environmental policy in other nations ♦ Forest economics and policy ♦ Law and economics ♦ Pollution control programs ♦ Product use and the environment ♦ Regulation and competitiveness ♦ Risk management and analysis ♦ Space economics ♦ Superfund ♦ Sustainable development ♦ Transportation and the environment ♦ Waste management ♦ Water resources

## PUBLICATIONS

Publishes books, discussion papers, issue briefs, and special reports

## NEWSLETTER

*CRM Newsletter* (periodic)
*Resources* (quarterly)
*RFF Research Digest* (quarterly)

## CONFERENCES

The RFF Council (annual)
The Wednesday Seminar Series

## BOARD OF DIRECTORS

Darius W. Gaskins Jr., chair; Paul R. Portney, president; Edward F. Hand, vice president, finance and administration

Other members:
♦ Catherine G. Abbott ♦ Jodie Allen ♦ John C. Borum ♦ James H.S. Cooper ♦ John M. Deutch ♦ Anthony S. Earl ♦ Robert E. Grady ♦ F. Henry Habicht II ♦ Robert H. Haveman ♦ Thomas C. Jorling ♦ Donald M. Kerr ♦ Thoma Lovejoy ♦ Frank E. Loy ♦ Lawrence Luchini ♦ Jim Maddy ♦ Karl-Goran Maler ♦ Steven W. Percy ♦ Frank L. Mathhews ♦ Mark A. Pisano ♦ Robert M. Solow ♦ Joseph E. Stiglitz ♦ Edward L. Strohbehn Jr. ♦ Linda Taliaferro ♦ Victoria J. Tschinkel ♦ Mason Willrich

## EFFECTIVENESS

"Failure by the Kyoto conferees to agree to reduce greenhouse gas emissions could be disastrous for the world economy, according to one group of participants in a raging debate over what to do about global warming. A coalition of environmentalists, scientists and political leaders argues that failure to take action to reverse the sharp rise in carbon dioxide emission levels will cause dangerous changes in the world's climate, ultimately wiping out major resources—such as the valuable wheat-growing areas of the American Midwest, for example. . . .

"Opponents of controls—led by an alliance of utilities, oil producers, auto manufacturers, labor groups and conservative think tanks—argue that even Clinton's lower targets would drive energy costs up and do severe damage to the U.S. economy. They also say the science of global warming is too imprecise to justify such pain. . . .

"One analysis by Resources for the Future, an independent think tank specializing in energy and environmental issues, forecast that capping U.S. carbon dioxide emissions at 1990 levels could boost the energy costs of an average U.S. household by about 25 percent, including a 30 cents-per-gallon increase in gasoline prices. The average U.S. household spends about $2,571 a year on energy, according to the most recent government figures available.

"The think tank's study concluded that such caps would probably curtail the nation's total economic output as much as 1 percent, and a worst-case outcome would be a decline of 2 percent.

"So meeting Clinton's targets 'wouldn't be disaster, but it would hurt,' said Ray Kopp, a senior fellow at Resources for the Future. 'The goal is doable, but we shouldn't kid ourselves: Reaching it will have a price.'" (*Washington Post,* November 13, 1997)

"Some of the biggest debates on global warming, in fact, are about whether it does much economic harm at all. If you assume it does little harm, then the models will show little economic gain from curtailing carbon emissions. On the other hand, if you assume global warming will become an economic as well as an environmental disaster, then an effective global warming policy pays big dividends.

"For a country such as the United States, the evidence is ambiguous. A warmer climate requires spending more for air conditioning in summer but less for heating in winter. And while warmer temperatures might reduce yields of some crops, such as wheat, they are likely to boost yields of fruits, vegetables and timber. As a result, the Yale School of Forestry and Environmental Studies recently concluded that global warming would likely result in a small economic gain in countries such as the United States.

"But such analyses often overlook the public health gains from reducing energy consumption and the air pollution that accompanies it. Cleaner air results in lower health care costs, fewer sick days and fewer premature deaths. According to Resources for the Future, another Washington think tank, these collateral health benefits may offset as much as one-quarter of the economic costs of reducing carbon emission." (*Washington Post,* June 12, 1997)

## POLITICAL ORIENTATION

"nonpartisan group" (*New York Times,* October 2, 1997)

# Sea Shepherd Conservation Society (1977)

3007 Washington Boulevard
Suite 225
Marina Del Rey, California 90292
Phone: (310) 301-7325
Fax: (310) 574-3161
Internet: seashepherd@aol.com *or* http://www.seashepherd.org

| | |
|---|---|
| "Involved with the investigation and documentation of violations of international laws, regulations, and treaties protecting marine wildlife species. Also involved with the enforcement of these laws when there is no enforcement by national governments or international regulatory organizations due to absence of jurisdiction or lack of political will." | **PURPOSE** |
| 4 total; plus 12 interns; 30 volunteers | **STAFF** |
| Paul Watson, president. Watson began his career at sea in 1968 with the Norwegian merchant marine, leaving to spend two years with the Canadian Coast Guard in the early 1970s. In 1972, he joined with other members of the Sierra Club in founding the Greenpeace Foundation and served as First Officer on all Greenpeace voyages against whaling until 1977. Watson left Greenpeace in 1977 to found the Sea Shepherd Conservation Society. He is a professor of ecology at Pasadena College of Design. | **DIRECTOR** |
| 501(c)(3) | **TAX STATUS** |
| Fiscal year ending April 31, 1998—$700,000<br>Proposed F.Y. 1999—$700,000 | **BUDGET** |
| Individuals, organizations, grants, information tables, and estates | **FUNDING SOURCES** |
| Members: 42,000 worldwide<br>Branches/chapters: Branches in the United Kingdom, Sweden, Germany, Australia, and Canada<br>Affiliates: N/A | **SCOPE** |
| None | **PAC** |

| METHOD OF OPERATION | ♦ Advertisements ♦ Demonstrations ♦ Direct action ♦ Films/video/audiotapes ♦ Grassroots organizing ♦ High-seas campaigns ♦ International activities ♦ Internet (Web site) ♦ Media outreach ♦ Product merchandising ♦ Speakers program ♦ Undercover documentation |
|---|---|
| CURRENT CONCERNS | ♦ Canadian seal hunt ♦ Destruction of the Galápagos ♦ Destructive fishing practices ♦ Illegal worldwide whaling ♦ Seabird and turtle protection |
| PUBLICATIONS | None |
| NEWSLETTER | *Sea Shepherd Log* (quarterly) |
| CONFERENCES | None |
| BOARD OF DIRECTORS | ♦ Lawrence Mortoff ♦ Carroll Vogel ♦ Rosemary Waldron ♦ Paul Watson |
| EFFECTIVENESS | "A few weeks ago, Olav Olavsen fired his harpoon 18 times and bagged 17 minke whales in the Barents Sea. Each one weighed about two tons and yielded a third of that in dark, purplish meat for Norwegians who like to cook it on the grill this time of year. . . .<br><br>"Mr. Olavsen's spirits are high now, not just because he reached his catch limit in only seven days at sea, but also because Norwegian whalers may be on the verge of international acceptance. . . .<br><br>"The reason is that after years of dispute over counting methods, International Whaling Commission scientists said last year that the minke whale population was robust enough to tolerate a limited hunt—unlike the situation for other species of whales that are still considered near extinction.<br><br>"The peak of anti-whaling activity here was in 1994, when the environmental group Greenpeace International sent speedboats to block harpoon gunners and a ship of the California-based Sea Shepherd Conservation Society collided violently with a Norwegian Coast Guard vessel. . . .<br><br>"But the Norwegian Whaling Commissioner, Kaare Bryn, draws the opposite conclusion: 'The anti-whalers have lost the numbers game and have to admit there are a lot of minke whales. Unless they see whales as human beings, they have to accept that whaling is really no worse than cod or herring fishing.'. . . " (*New York Times,* July 23, 1997) |

"[Paul] Watson is through talking to outlaw ocean harvesters. Instead, he confronts them where they do their dirty work and batters them into submission. After an estrangement from Greenpeace, which he co-founded, Watson started the Sea Shepherd Conservation Society in 1977. The society has taken credit for sinking eight whaling ships and for ramming seven whalers and driftnetters. . . .

"Conflict means more news coverage, as Watson proved in 1994 during a standoff between Sea Shepherd's *Whales Forever* and a Norwegian warship over the 300 Minke whales Norway planned to kill for 'scientific research.' Norway's warning shots, depth charges and collision with *Whales Forever* didn't faze him. The footage ended up on international television, shaming the Norwegian government." (*E Magazine,* November/December 1995)

"Two years ago, Captain [Paul] Watson, a Vancouver resident and founder of the Sea Shepherd Conservation Society, was arrested by the RCMP in international waters for interfering with a Spanish fishing vessel off the tail of the Grand Banks. He was charged with three counts of criminal mischief and faces a maximum penalty of life imprisonment.

"Capt. Watson was engage in precisely the same activity as the Canadian government last week when it detained a Spanish fishing trawler and charged Capt. [Enrique Davila] Gonzalez. There was one difference between the actions of Capt. Watson and the Canadian government: Capt. Watson did not resort to gunplay. He couldn't, as the only cannon on board his vessel was loaded with projectiles of pie filling. . . .

"Capt. Watson insists that his actions are sanctioned by UN protocols and are legal. All the same, there is a greater law that he serves, that of protecting the earth's resources for posterity. 'As a conservationist and a radical, I am reviled now, but in 300 years we [the Society] will be considered as good ancestors. I always remember that Louis Riel was hanged by the government of Canada and now he's on a postage stamp.' " (*The Globe and Mail,* March 18, 1995)

Unavailable

## POLITICAL ORIENTATION

# Sierra Club (1892)

85 Second Street
2nd Floor
San Francisco, California
  94105
Phone: (415) 977-5500
Fax: (415) 977-5799

408 C Street, NE
Washington, D.C. 20002
Phone: (202) 547-1141
Fax: (202) 547-6009

Internet: information@sierraclub.org *or* http://www.sierraclub.org

## PURPOSE

"To explore, enjoy, and protect the wild places of the earth; to practice and promote the responsible use of the earth's ecosystems and resources; to educate and enlist humanity to protect and restore the quality of the natural and human environment; and to use all lawful means to carry out these objectives."

## STAFF

Unavailable

## DIRECTOR

Carl Pope, executive director. Before becoming executive director in 1992, Pope held other positions in the Sierra Club, including political director and conservation director. His background also includes service in the Peace Corps. Pope has served on the boards of many organizations, including the California League of Conservation Voters, Public Voice, National Clean Air Coalition, and Zero Population Growth. He is a graduate of Harvard College.

## TAX STATUS

501(c)(4)

## BUDGET

1997—$45 million
1998—$45 million
Proposed 1999—$45 million

## FUNDING SOURCES

Membership, contributions and grants, book sales, advertising, outings, reimbursement, royalties

## SCOPE

Members: 550,000 individuals
Branches/chapters: 65 chapters, including 408 groups; 20 field offices
Affiliates: Sierra Club Foundation, a 501(c)(3) organization

# PAC

## METHOD OF OPERATION

♦ Advertisements ♦ Boycotts ♦ Campaign contributions ♦ Coalition forming ♦ Congressional testimony ♦ Congressional voting analysis ♦ Demonstrations ♦ Electoral politics ♦ Films/video/audiotapes ♦ Grassroots organizing ♦ Initiative/referendum campaigns ♦ International activities ♦ Internet (Web site) ♦ Legal assistance ♦ Legislative/regulatory monitoring (federal and state) ♦ Library/information clearinghouse ♦ Litigation ♦ Lobbying (federal, state, and grassroots) ♦ Local/municipal affairs ♦ Media outreach ♦ Outings Program (national program of more than 350 outings annually; chapters and groups offer more than 8,000 outings annually, including Inner City Outings) ♦ Participation in regulatory proceedings (federal and state) ♦ Polling ♦ Product merchandising ♦ Research ♦ Telecommunications services (Hotline: 202-675-2394)

## CURRENT CONCERNS

♦ Ancient forests ♦ Clean air ♦ Clean water/wetlands ♦ Endangered Species Act ♦ Energy ♦ Global warming ♦ Human rights and the environment ♦ National forest management reform ♦ Permanent protection of public lands ♦ Population stabilization ♦ Public lands protection ♦ Responsible trade

## PUBLICATIONS

The Sierra Club publishes "everything from 'coffee table' pictorials and children's books to well-organized and helpful travel and wilderness trail guides."

## NEWSLETTER

*The Planet* (bimonthly magazine for activists)
*Sierra* (bimonthly magazine)

All chapters and many groups regularly publish newsletters reporting local environmental news and Club events

## CONFERENCES

None

## BOARD OF DIRECTORS

Chuck McGrady, president; Lois Snedden, vice president; Roy Hengerson, treasurer; Susan Homes, secretary; Michael Dorsey, fifth officer

Other members:
♦ Phil Berry ♦ David Brower ♦ J. Robert Cox ♦ Veronica Eady ♦ Anne Ehrlich ♦ Jennifer Ferenstein ♦ Betsy Gaines ♦ Kathy Gregg ♦ Chad Hanson ♦ Michele Perrault ♦ Adam Werbach

## EFFECTIVENESS

"The Sierra Club invited civic leaders, environmentalists and politicians on a bus ride last week through Northern Virginia to highlight the choices the club says have shaped the landscape and given rise to areas in need of help, such as Sterling Park in Loudoun, Fairfax County's Baileys Crossroads area and the Route 1 corridor.

"In these cases, the club argues, the culprit is sprawl. Or in planning parlance, 'dysfunctional human settlement patterns.'

"Other areas fared well with tour guides, who represented the Coalition for Smarter Growth and the Piedmont Environmental Council, in addition to the Sierra Club.

"Reston got a thumbs up on what organizers called the 'Tour de Sprawl' because development is concentrated and there's plenty of green space for residents.

"Ballston and Rosslyn also earned praise for being pedestrian-friendly areas with high population density that are easily accessible by mass transit.

"Loudoun failed. Sterling Park merited a special stop." (*Washington Post*, May 24, 1998)

"Members of one of the nation's leading environmental organizations have voted to maintain neutrality on U.S. immigration policy, turning back a call for reduced immigration as a means of limiting U.S. population growth to preserve natural resources.

"In a referendum that generated intense debate, Sierra Club members voted 60 percent to 40 percent to 'take no position' on immigration levels but to work toward solving 'the root causes of global population problems,' the club announced yesterday at its San Francisco headquarters. The defeated proposal would have committed the club, one of the oldest and largest environmental groups in the United States, to formulating 'a comprehensive population policy' to stabilize the U.S. population through both birth control and a 'reduction in net immigration.'. . .

"The issue had provoked an often nasty debate within the club, with opposing sides accusing each other of racism or demagoguery. The vote was closely watched by supporters and opponents of current immigration levels." (*Washington Post*, April 26, 1998)

"A proposed theme park on the Anacostia River that developers have described as a mini-Epcot Center has triggered another round of intense opposition by local and national environmental groups, forcing the D.C. Council to postpone a vote that could bolster or doom the controversial project.

"The latest dust-up began Friday when Mayor Marion Barry (D) sent emergency legislation to the council approving a 99-year lease between the District and National Children's Island Inc., a nonprofit group the mayor has long supported in its quest to develop a $150 million theme park on two islands in the river. D.C. Council member Charlene Drew Jarvis (D-Ward 4) had scheduled a vote on the bill today. But she pulled the measure off the calendar after objections from the Sierra Club and fellow council members. Jarvis promised to hold a public hearing on the proposal within the next two weeks.

" 'The public will be heard on this,' she said.

"Jim Dougherty, a spokesman for the Sierra Club, called the proposed theme park 'the biggest taxpayer rip-off this city has ever seen.' He noted that one of its primary backers, Carroll R. Harvey, has ties to Barry dating back three decades. . . .

"In opposing the new lease, Fern Shepard, an attorney with the Sierra Club Legal Defense Fund, said yesterday that the document would put the District on record as approving the project without seeing an environmental impact statement.

"Cooke agreed that an environmental impact statement must be written and said the council would have another chance to accept or reject the project once a final development plan is produced." (*Washington Post*, October 7, 1997)

"The Sierra Club began broadcasting a radio advertisement in the Albany area today attacking Senator Alfonse M. D'Amato's environmental voting record as part of a campaign intended to debunk the Republican's election-year attempts to cast himself as pro-environment.

" 'Instead of helping us rid our river of PCB's, a probable cancer-causing chemical, Senator Al D'Amato's made it harder to protect our families,' the narrator on the 30-second spot says, referring to the Hudson. 'Since 1995, he's voted to weaken the enforcement of clean air and water laws and refused to force polluters to tell us what they are dumping into our air and water.'

"Although the advertising campaign is inexpensive and geographically limited, running only in and around the state capital, it could nonetheless be damaging to the three-term Senator because Mr. D'Amato has been promoting his environmental record as part of a broader effort to appeal to moderate suburban voters. For the last two years, he has run television advertisements asserting that he has fought 'to protect New York's environment.'

"The Democrats seeking their party's nomination to run against Mr. D'Amato have also pledged to make Mr. D'Amato's environmental record a campaign issue this fall. Republican officials, speaking on condition of anonymity, denounced the Sierra Club campaign as partisan, but Sierra Club officials denied that charge." (*New York Times*, April 21, 1998)

"John Muir [an early president of Sierra Club] had it figured out all along. He said that if people would go 'into the woods to hear the trees speak for themselves, all difficulties in the way of forest preservation would vanish.'. . .

"Hundred of thousands of outings later, the Sierra Club continues to help people get acquainted with wild places, while at the same time waging well publicized and often intense battles in the national political arena. For instance, over the years the organization has helped establish the National Park Service; create Glacier, Mt. Rainier, Kings Canyon, and Olympic national parks; protect the boundaries of Yosemite National Park; and ensure passage of the federal Wilderness Act.

"But at no time has the Club's importance been more pronounced than during the past 25 years, when anti-preservationist rhetoric has slowly but steadily risen to its current fevered pitch." (*Backpacker*, April 1998)

"Frustrated by attempts to win change through traditional appeals to government, the Sierra Club decided to take its campaign directly to big business. In this case, the business, DuPont Co., was planning to build a $150 million titanium mine near Georgia's beloved Okefenokee National Wildlife Refuge.

"Sierra Club officials, bracing for a nasty fight, called upon their well-honed methods of protesting aggressively and rallying public support—this time, against a corporate target rather than a government one. To their surprise, though, officials at the Wilmington, Del., chemical giant cut short the protest by suspending all work on the mine and agreeing to bring the environmentalists to the negotiating table.

"So, later this month, for the first time on such a scale, DuPont, the Sierra Club and other groups will huddle with a mediator to see if they can find middle ground in the swamp. . . .

"DuPont's response caught the Sierra Club a little off guard. Now that it has been invited to the bargaining table, the group must work on re-defining the way it deals with business—from an us-vs.-them mode to the art of negotiation." (*Wall Street Journal*, June 4, 1997)

## POLITICAL ORIENTATION

"one of the nation's largest and most influential environmental groups" (*New York Times*, April 26, 1998)

"nonpartisan" (*New York Times*, April 21, 1998)

"liberal" (*Washington Post*, February 10, 1994)

# The Wilderness Society (1935)

900 17th Street, NW
Washington, D.C. 20006
Phone: (202) 833-2300
Fax: (202) 429-3958 or (202) 429-8443
Internet: member@tws.org *or* http://www.wilderness.org

| | |
|---|---|
| "Devoted primarily to preserving wilderness and wildlife, protecting America's prime forests, parks, rivers, deserts, and shorelines, and fostering the development of an American land ethic." | *PURPOSE* |
| 100 total | *STAFF* |
| William H. Meadows, president. Before joining The Wilderness Society in 1996, Meadows was director of the Sierra Club's Centennial Campaign. He also served as vice chair of Sierra Club's Tennessee chapter and was on the board of the Tennessee Environmental Council. Meadows has extensive experience in higher education and has been Vanderbilt University's executive director of alumni relations, Sweet Briar College's vice president for college relations, and the district director of the Council for Advancement and Support of Education. He received his B.A. and M.Ed. from Vanderbilt University. | *DIRECTOR* |
| 501(c)(3) | *TAX STATUS* |
| 1998—$12.6 million<br>Proposed 1999—Unavailable | *BUDGET* |
| Membership, 48 percent; individual contributions, 24 percent; grants, 13 percent; bequests, 5 percent; investments, 2 percent; other, 8 percent | *FUNDING SOURCES* |
| Members: 200,000 individuals<br>Branches/chapters: Field offices in Alaska, California, Colorado, Georgia, Idaho, Massachusetts, Minnesota, Montana, and Washington<br>Affiliates: N/A | *SCOPE* |
| None | *PAC* |

## METHOD OF OPERATION

♦ Awards program ♦ Coalition forming ♦ Conferences/seminars ♦ Congressional testimony ♦ Demonstrations ♦ Films/videos/audiotapes ♦ Grassroots organizing ♦ Internet (Web site) ♦ Information clearinghouse ♦ Legislative/regulatory monitoring (federal and state) ♦ Litigation ♦ Lobbying (federal and grassroots) ♦ Media outreach ♦ Polling ♦ Remote sensing ♦ Research

## CURRENT CONCERNS

♦ Arctic National Wildlife Refuge ♦ Colorado plateau ♦ Forest policy reform ♦ Land and Water Conservation Fund ♦ National parks ♦ National wildlife refuges ♦ Northern forest/New England population ♦ Sierra Nevada ♦ Sustainable communities ♦ Southern Appalachians ♦ Utah wilderness

## PUBLICATIONS

*The Alaska Lands Act: A Broken Promise*
*America's Wilderness*
*Becoming a Better Media Resource*
*The Fifteen Most Endangered Wildlands*
*From Dreams to Realities*
*Georgia's Mountain Treasures*
*Keeping it Wild: A Citizen Guide to Wilderness Management*
*Keeping the Grizzly Bear in the American West*
*The Living Landscape*
*Logging National Forests to Create Jobs: An Unworkable Covenant*
*Measuring Change in Rural Communities*
*National Forests: Policies for the Future* (5 volumes)
*The New Challenge: People, Economics, and the Environment in the Yellowstone to Yukon Region*
*New Home on the Range: Economic Realities in the Columbia River Basin*
*North Carolina's Mountain Treasures*
*The Northern Forest Strategies for Sustainability* (3 volumes)
*River Protection and Water Use*
*Saving Our Ancient Forests*
*Sierra Nevada Conservation Directory*
*South Carolina's Mountain Treasures*
*Sustaining Ecosystems, Economies, and a Way of Life in the Northern Forest*
*Tennessee's Mountain Treasures*
*Virginia's Mountain Treasures*
*Wild Lands and Open Skies*
*Yellowstone: The Wealth of Nature*
*Yosemite Transportation Strategy*

The following is a list of videos:

*Ancient Forests: Vanishing Legacy of the Pacific Northwest* (video)
*Arctic National Wildlife Refuge: A Wilderness in Peril* (video)
*Sacred Trust: Preserving America's Wilderness* (video)

## NEWSLETTER

*Wilderness America* (quarterly)
*Wilderness Magazine* (quarterly)

## EFFECTIVENESS

"Mining, timbering and ranching have been a way of life in rural Utah since the days the first Mormon wagons rolled south from Salt Lake City.

"But according to wilderness advocates, generations of development have destroyed much of Utah's scenic backcountry, and now the remainder is threatened by strip mines, oil and gas development and needless road construction to facilitate development.

"The threat of development has now prompted the politically powerful Wilderness Society to join the contentious Utah wilderness debate by issuing a report naming Utah's canyon country as one of America's 15 most endangered wild places.

" 'Turning these red-rock canyons into strip mines and other quick-buck, boon-and-bust projects would be incredibly short-sighted,' said Pamela Eaton, four corners states regional director for the Wilderness Society. . . .

The Wilderness Society has renewed its pitch for legislation designating 5.7 million acres of Bureau of Land Management lands in Utah as wilderness. It also offers its support for the re-inventory being conducted by the Utah Wilderness Coalition that could expand that wilderness total to 9 million to 10 million acres—almost half of the 22 million acres administered by the BLM in Utah." (*Deseret News,* July 7, 1998)

"When the Wilderness Society listed America's 10 Most Endangered Wild Lands last year, it was most concerned with the value of these places as reservoirs of wilderness. These 10 rank at the top because of their natural resources, national significance and immediate threats to their integrity.

"As destinations, they are not just for hard-body adventurers. Ordinary people with a simple love of wild places can enjoy them, too. And that's the best way to see how you feel about these areas: Visit them. . . .

"In a year since the list was issued, there has been a bright spot: The Whitney Estate in New York was threatened by the subdivision of privately owned Adirondack forest; that danger was eliminated when the state bought the land; it is scheduled to open to the public this summer." (*News & Observer Raleigh,* June 14, 1998)

"The Wilderness Society is asserting that net losses in revenue from timber sales in national forest during FY'96 are significantly greater than the US Forest Service has acknowledged.

"A report released today by the DC-based group concludes that commercial logging sales in national forests cost US taxpayers $204 million in FY'96. In 11/97, the USFS reported a first-ever net loss in revenue from timber sales of just $15 million.

". . . The Society's totals are higher than the USFS's because the federal accounting system does not factor in several costs, especially those resulting from payments to counties of their mandated 25% share of all timber sales from national forests within their borders. . . ." (*Greenwire, The Environment News Daily,* January 1, 1998)

"The Wilderness Society is making an assault on rural New England with an unusual tactic: inviting townspeople to sit down and crunch numbers.

"The conservation group's focus is on the Northern Forest, which stretches west from Maine through New Hampshire, Vermont and into New York. Its weapon: workshops that join people in and near the forest to analyze the local economy. The environmentalists hope to gain credibility with people who normally don't like them—those in rural areas like Farmington.

" 'We have to convince those people who live up there that conservation is in their best financial interest,' says Robert Perschel, regional director of the Wilderness Society in Boston. 'People think their jobs are all cutting down trees.'

"This attitude makes life difficult for environmentalists. Large timber and paper companies have dominated the forest's economy for decades and provided generations of jobs. What's more, in places like this small Franklin County town, outsiders are often viewed as people 'from away.'

"To avoid this stereotype, the Wilderness Society last month sent Spencer Phillips, a Washington, D.C., economist, to live in the Northern Forest, in Craftsbury Common, Vt.

"The goal, he says, isn't to prevent all timber harvesting, but to 'have better information available to a broad range of people so they can make better decisions about economic development and land conservation.'

"At the economic workshops, however, Mr. Phillips steers clear of any kind of rhetoric that smacks of green. 'Spencer didn't come up here and say: 'Thou shalt not cut any more trees,' says Donald Alexander, director of the Franklin County Development Office, who attended the Farmington workshop, held in the back room of the Homestead Bakery. . . .

"The Farmington workshop, which lasts a day, is typical. To begin, Mr. Phillips shows the dozen attendees the databases they'll use, such as county demographics from the Census Bureau and local industry data from the Commerce Department.

"Then the group splits up into four teams to analyze the data. Mr. Phillips starts his workshops with population trends, because he has learned that newcomers to economic data find it easier to manipulate big numbers if the statistics involve people rather than dollars.

"He keeps it simple, allowing only worksheets and calculators. About five minutes into the exercise, someone will ask: 'Hey, can't we do this on an Excel spreadsheet?' " Mr. Phillips says.

"The teams calculate population changes from 1980 to 1990 in Franklin County and compare them with Maine and U.S. averages. They find that growth in the county from 1980 to 1990 was much slower than in Maine and the U.S. With this first discovery, the attendees are on their way to seeing for themselves what the Wilderness Society already knew: Their economy is lagging behind those of the state and the country, and dependence on some traditional industries like timber isn't working.

"Later, the teams pick apart the economy by industry. Using income data, Fred Hardy, a dairy farmer and county commissioner, leads the agriculture team. Mr. Hardy calls the Wilderness Society a 'socialist' group that 'doesn't believe in capitalism whatsoever.'

"The county farming figures Mr. Hardy's team crunch are dismal. From 1969 to 1994, gross income from farming fell 39%. 'It didn't surprise me that the incomes in agriculture were so far below everybody else's,' Mr. Hardy says. But it surprised the others, Mr. Phillips says.

"People also didn't realize how growth in agricultural jobs and forest-service employment lagged behind the rest of Maine and the U.S., especially given how timber companies still seem such a large part of daily life in Franklin County. That's one of the messages the Wilderness Society hopes to get across.

" 'Usually there isn't a lockstep relationship between the amount of timber produced and forest-products jobs,' Mr. Phillips says. Just the reverse: More timber-industry growth doesn't necessarily mean more jobs because the companies can produce more with fewer people due to technology improvements, he says.

"After looking at all the numbers, the next step is for each team to explain to the group what it found. The workshop attendees are dispirited, for instance, after coming up with 200% growth in service jobs, well ahead of state and U.S. growth rates. They associate service jobs with low pay and no benefits. That's troublesome for the Wilderness Society, which wants to encourage tourism in the Northern Forest by arguing it will create good-paying jobs. 'There's a myth about hamburger flipping that we have to attack,' says Mr. Perschel.

"On talking about tourism, people tried to come up with ways to make Franklin County more of a place worth visiting for a few days, including connecting various wilderness trails and promoting them as one big loop. Agriculture also came up because the decline of family farms hurts tourism, as does clear-cutting forests, both of which affect the landscape.

"So what has all the number crunching accomplished? Little that is tangible, says Ms. Burd, but it served as 'a steppingstone to building trust.' "
(*Washington Post*, October 1, 1997)

---

"a leading national environmental organization based in Washington"
(*New York Times*, April 22, 1997)

# POLITICAL ORIENTATION

# World Resources Institute (1982)

1709 New York Avenue, NW
7th Floor
Washington, D.C. 20006
Phone: (202) 638-6300
Fax: (202) 638-0036
Internet: http://www.wri.org

## PURPOSE

"Dedicated to helping governments and private organizations of all types cope with environmental, resource, and development challenges of global significance."

## STAFF

120 total

## DIRECTOR

Jonathan Lash, president. Lash has chaired or served on the board of many environmental and natural resources organizations, including the President's Council on Sustainable Development, the National Commission on Superfund, and the Earth Council. He previously directed the environmental law and policy program of the Vermont Law School and held positions in Vermont state government. Lash's background includes work in the Peace Corps, as a federal prosecutor, and as an attorney for the Natural Resources Defense Council.

## TAX STATUS

501(c)(3)

## BUDGET

1998—Unavailable
Proposed 1999—Unavailable

## FUNDING SOURCES

Private foundations, governmental and intergovernmental institutions, corporations, and individuals

## SCOPE

Members: N/A
Branches/chapters: WRI has staff living and working in Japan, the Philippines, and Vietnam
Affiliates: Network of advisors, collaborators, international fellows, and partner institutions in more than 50 countries

## PAC

None

◆ Congressional testimony ◆ International activities ◆ Internet ◆ Legislative/regulatory monitoring (federal) ◆ Library/information clearinghouse (open to public by appointment) ◆ Media outreach ◆ Research

◆ Biological resources and institutions ◆ Climate, energy and pollution ◆ Developing countries ◆ Economics and population ◆ The global commons ◆ Health, population, and development ◆ Linking national needs to global environmental concerns ◆ Natural resource information management ◆ Natural resources management ◆ Resources and environmental information ◆ Sectoral resource policy and planning ◆ Technology and the environment ◆ U.S. policies

*Africa Data Sampler: A Geo-Referenced Database for All African Countries*

*All That Glitters Is Not Gold: Balancing Conservation and Development in Venezuela's Frontier Forests*

*Agricultural Policy and Sustainability: Case Studies from India, Chile, the Philippines and the United States*

*Air Pollution's Toll on Forests and Crops*

*Backs to the Future: U.S. Government Policy Toward Environmentally Critical Technologies*

*Backs to the Wall in Suriname: Forest Policy in a Country in Crisis*

*Balancing Acts: Community-Based Forest Management and National Law in Asia and the Pacific*

*Balancing the Scales: Managing Biodiversity at the Bioregional Level*

*Beyond Compliance: A New Industry View of the Environment*

*Biodiversity Indicators for Policymakers* (out of print)

*Biodiversity Prospecting: Guidelines for Using Genetic and Biochemical Resources Sustainably and Equitably*

*Breaking the Logjam: Obstacles to Forest Policy Reform in Indonesia and the United States*

*Bittersweet Harvests for Global Supermarkets: Challenges in Latin America's Agricultural Export Boom*

*Carbon Counts*

*Car Trouble*

*Choosing Our Future: Visions of A Sustainable World*

*Climate Protection and the National Interest: The Links Among Climate Change, Air Pollution, and Energy Security*

*Climate Protection Policies: Can We Afford to Delay?*

*The Costs of Climate Protection: A Guide for the Perplexed*

*Environmental Effects of Stabilization and Structural Adjustment Programs: The Philippines Case*

*Environmental Indicators: A Systematic Approach to Measuring and Reporting on Environmental Policy Performance in the Context of Sustainable Development*

*Evaluating the Carbon Sequestration Benefits of Sustainable Forestry Projects in Developing Countries*

*Forging International Agreement: The Role of Institutions in Environment and Development*

*Frontiers of Sustainability*

*Global Biodiversity Strategy*

*Going Rate: What It Really Costs to Drive*

*Green Fees: How a Tax Shift Can Work for the Environment and the Economy*

*Green Ledgers: Case Studies in Corporate Environmental Accounting*

*Greenhouse Trap: What We're Doing to the Atmosphere and How We Can Slow Global Warming*

*Gray Pinstripes with Green Ties: MBA Programs Where the Environment Matters*

*Growing Green: Enhancing Environmental and Economic Performance in U.S. Agriculture*

*Has Environmental Protection Really Reduced Productivity Growth?*

*Indigenous Knowledge in Resource Management: Irrigation in Msanzi, Tanzania*

*Introduction to the Global Environment* (video)

*Investing in Biological Diversity*

*Jobs, Competitiveness, and Environmental Regulation: What Are the Real Issues?*

*Keeping Options Alive: The Scientific Basis for the Conservation of Biological Diversity*

*Keys to the Car: Electric and Hydrogen Vehicles for the 21st Century*

*The Last Frontier Forests: Ecosystems and Economies on the Edge*

*Lessons From the Ground Up: African Development that Works*

*Lessons Learned in Global Environmental Governance*

*Measuring Up: Toward a Common Framework for Tracking Corporate Environmental Performance*

*Missing Links: Technology and Environmental Improvement in the Industrializing World*

*National Biodiversity Planning: Guidelines Based on Early Experiences Around the World*

*New Generation of Environmental Leadership: Action for the Environment and the Economy*

*New Roots: Institutionalizing Environmental Mechanisms in Africa*

*Oil as a Finite Resource: When Is Global Production Likely to Peak?*

*Pesticides and the Immune System: The Public Health Risks*

*Pesticides, Rice Productivity, and Farmers' Health*

*Policy Hits the Ground: Participation and Equity in Environmental Policymaking*

*Population Growth, Poverty, and Environmental Stress: Frontier Migration in the Philippines and Costa Rica*

*Preserving Our Global Environment* (video)

*Profit Without Plunder: Reaping Revenue From Guyana's Tropical Forests Without Destroying Them*

*Promoting Environmentally Sound Economic Progress*

*Public Policy and Legislation in Environmental Management: Terracing in Nyarurembo, Uganda*

*Reefs at Risk: A Map-Based Indicator of Threats to the World's Coral Reefs*

*Right Climate for Carbon Taxes: Creating Economic Incentives to Protect the Atmosphere*

*Resource Flows: The Material Basis of Industrial Economies*

*Rethinking Development Assistance for Renewable Electricity*

*"Second India" Revisited: Population, Poverty, and Environmental Stress over Two Decades*

*Surviving the Cut: Sustainable Forest Management in the Humid Tropics*

*Sustainable Enterprise in Latin America: A Case Book*

*Teacher's Guide Basic Units*

*Tiger By the Tail? Reorienting Biodiversity Conservation and Development in Indonesia*

*Toward Common Ground*

*Toxics and Health: The Potential Long-term Effects of Industrial Activity*

*Transforming Technology: An Agenda for Environmentally Sustainable Growth
    in the Twenty-first Century*
*Trees of Life: Saving Tropical Forests and Their Biological Wealth*
*Trends in Biodiversity Investments*
*Water and Arid Lands of the Western United States*
*World Directory of Country Environmental Studies*
*World Resources 1997–98*

---

None

## NEWSLETTER

---

Sponsors by-invitation-only conferences

## CONFERENCES

---

Maurice F. Strong, chairman; John Firor, vice chairman

Other board members:
Manuel Arango ◆ Frances G. Beinecke ◆ Robert O. Blake ◆ Derek Bok ◆
Bert Bolin ◆ Robert N. Burt ◆ David T. Buzzelli ◆ Deb Callahan ◆
Michael R. Deland ◆ Sylvia A. Earle ◆ Jose Maria Figueres ◆ Shinji
Fukukawa ◆ William M. Haney III ◆ Calestous Juma ◆ Yolanda
Kakabadse ◆ Jonathan Lash ◆ Jeffrey T. Leeds ◆ Jane Lubchenco ◆
C. Payne Lucas ◆ William F. Martin ◆ Julia Marton-Lefevre ◆ Matthew
Nimetz ◆ Paulo Nogueira-Neto ◆ Ronald L. Olson ◆ Peter H. Raven ◆
Florence T. Robinson ◆ Roger W. Sant ◆ Stephan Schmidheiny ◆ Bruce
Smart ◆ James Gustave Speth ◆ Meg Taylor ◆ Mostafa K. Tolba ◆
Alvaro Umana Quesada ◆ Victor L. Urquidi ◆ Pieter Winsemius

## BOARD OF DIRECTORS

---

"The first round of grants from Ted Turner's $1 billion gift to the United
Nations will be announced on Wednesday, with nearly three-quarters of
the initial $22 million going to help women, children and victims of war
in poor countries, the president of the fund, Timothy E. Wirth, said today
[May 19, 1998]. . . .

"The grant, announced last year, is the largest gift the United Nations
has ever received from a private source. United Nations agencies and programs compete for the money by submitting proposals. . . .

"In one of only three environmental projects of 22 supported in the first
round of grants, the United Nations Foundation allocated $900,000 for a
joint one-year project of the United Nations Development Program and
the World Resources Institute to help China, the world's second-largest
source of greenhouse gases, consolidate information about policies to reduce carbon dioxide emissions. . . ." (*New York Times*, May 20, 1998)

"Mothers in the United States and other industrialized countries appear
to be giving birth to proportionally fewer sons than they did decades ago,
researchers reported yesterday. . . .

"Other scientists, however, dismissed the connection to pollution as
highly speculative, and the authors themselves acknowledged that more
research is needed to establish such a link.

## EFFECTIVENESS

" 'The reduction of the proportion of males born may be a sentinel health event that some, as yet, unrecognized environmental health hazards are affecting the sex ratio of births, as well as other unexplained defects in male reproduction,' wrote lead author Devra Lee Davis of World Resources Institute. . . .

"Davis has been a leading proponent of a controversial theory that chemicals in the environment dubbed 'endocrine disruptors' may be having widespread effects on human health and reproduction. These chemicals, commonly used in pesticides and other industrial products, mimic in some ways the effects of naturally occurring hormones. In the laboratory, the substances have been shown to affect the sexual development of animals, and some studies have linked them to an increase in human birth defects such as hypospadias, a malformation of the urethra in boys, and cryptorchidism, or undescended testes." (*Washington Post*, April 1, 1998)

"The debate is heating up over the costs of reducing greenhouse gases in the atmosphere. And like everything else involving global warming, the economics are shrouded in a fog of uncertainty. . . .

"To help make some sense of this, the World Resources Institute yesterday issued a study of the studies on the costs of climate protection. Economists Robert Repetto and Duncan Austin reviewed 16 models for predicting the impact of global warming and policies designed to restrain it; they found they could get either very optimistic or pessimistic economic projections by fiddling with eight of the assumptions that underlie the competing economic models. . . .

"When expert opinions differ that widely, the wisest course may be to take a page from competitive figure skating and throw out the high and low scores. For as Repetto and Austin discovered when they took apart the competing computer models, these best-case and worst-case scenarios are often based on shaky assumptions about technology and human nature." (*Washington Post*, June 12, 1997)

"Of all the many issues in the talks . . . on cutting emissions of heat-trapping greenhouse gases, none carries more considerations of ethics and morality than the question of how big a burden the third-world countries should bear—and how soon they should take it up. . . .

"The poorer nations have long occupied the moral high ground. They insist that since the rich countries got rich largely by burning the coal and oil that produce the heat-trapping carbon dioxide, and since they are still responsible for most emissions today, it is only right that the wealthy be the first to take legally binding steps to reduce them. . . .

"President Clinton and the United States Senate, which will vote on any agreement, raise their own fairness issue. They insist that because warming of the atmosphere by greenhouse gases is a global concern, all countries must share in the solution. This is particularly so, they argue, since third-world countries' emissions are expected to surpass those of the rich countries in 20 or 30 years. . . .

"One good sign, the third-world countries say, is that they have already lessened the rates at which their emissions are increasing. A recent study by the World Resources Institute, a Washington-based research organization, found that many key third-world countries have cut or eliminated energy subsidies and as a result are emitting less carbon dioxide than they otherwise would have.

"Cutting the subsidies has raised energy costs and thereby discouraged the burning of coal and oil. The pricing changes were undertaken for economic reasons, not environmental ones, the report said, but the effect on carbon emissions was the same.

" 'It appears,' the study reported, 'that developing countries are already doing a great deal to limit emissions—a fact largely overlooked in the current debate.' " (*New York Times*, November 30, 1997)

Unavailable

# POLITICAL ORIENTATION

# World Wildlife Fund (1948)

1250 24th Street, NW
Washington, D.C. 20037
Phone: (202) 293-4800
Fax: (202) 293-9211

## PURPOSE

"Dedicated to protecting the world's wildlife and wildlands. . . . WWF directs its conservation efforts toward three global goals: protecting endangered spaces, saving endangered species, and addressing global threats."

## STAFF

302 total—242 professional; 60 support

## DIRECTOR

Kathryn S. Fuller, president. Fuller has been with the World Wildlife Fund (WWF) for nine years, first as a consultant, then as director of its TRAFFIC (U.S.A.) office, a wildlife trade monitoring unit. She became president of WWF in 1989. Prior to joining WWF, Fuller worked at the Office of the Legal Counsel at the Department of Justice in 1977. She helped start the Justice Department's wildlife section, becoming head of the section two years later. Fuller earned a J.D. from the University of Texas Law School.

## TAX STATUS

501(c)(3)

## BUDGET

1997—$80 million
1998—$98 million
Proposed 1999—Unavailable

## FUNDING SOURCES

Individuals, 36 percent; government, 35 percent; investments, 6 percent; foundations and corporations, 6 percent; other, 17 percent

## SCOPE

Members: 1.2 million
Branches/chapters: Offices in Ashland, Oregon, and the Everglades, Florida
Affiliates: WWF is affiliated with 29 other WWF organizations around the world

## PAC

None

♦ Congressional testimony ♦ Direct action ♦ Films/video/audiotapes ♦ Grantmaking ♦ International activities ♦ Internet (Web site) ♦ Legislative/regulatory monitoring (federal and state) ♦ Media outreach ♦ Participation in regulatory proceedings (federal) ♦ Product merchandising ♦ Research ♦ Training and technical assistance

♦ Conservation and development ♦ Endangered habitats ♦ Endangered species ♦ International environmental policy ♦ Tropical rain forest destruction ♦ U.S. environmental policy ♦ Wildlife conservation

A Benchmark for Reporting on Chemicals at Industrial Facilities
The Biodiversity Collection: A Review of Biodiversity Resources for Educators
The Biodiversity Debate: Exploring the Issue
"Biodiversity! Exploring the Web of Life" Education Kit
"Biodiversity—From Sea to Shining Sea" Poster Kit
A Conservation Assessment of the Terrestrial Ecoregions of Latin America and the Caribbean
Choosing a Sustainable Future: The Report of the National Commission on the Environment
Conservation on Private Lands: An Owner's Manual
A Dictionary of Environmental Quotations
Environmental Education in the Schools
The Gardener's Guide to Plant Conservation
Generating Income and Conserving Resources: Twenty Lessons from the Field
Going, Going, Almost Gone! Animals in Danger
A Guide to Human Resource Development
A Guide to the Field of Environmental and Natural Resource Economics
Harvesting Wild Species: Implications for Biodiversity Conservation
Identification Guide for Ivory and Ivory Substitutes
International Wildlife Trade: A CITES Sourcebook
The Myth of Wild Africa: Conservation Without Illusion
Our Stolen Future: Are We Threatening Our Fertility, Intelligence and Survival? A Scientific Detective Story
Ozone Diplomacy: New Directions in Safeguarding the Planet
Prescription for Extinction: Endangered Species and Patented Oriental Medicines in Trade
Reducing Reliance on Pesticides in Great Lakes Basin Agriculture
The Right to Know: The Promise of Low-Cost Public Inventories of Toxic Chemicals
The Science of Conservation Planning: Habitat Conservation Under the Endangered Species Act
The Social Life of Small Urban Spaces
Status, Management, and Commercialization of the American Black Bear (Ursus americanus)
Taking Action: An Educator's Guide to Involving Students in Environmental Action Projects
Vanishing Rain Forests Education Kit
Voices from Africa: Local Perspectives on Conservation
Wildlife Trade Education Kit
WOW! A Biodiversity Primer

## NEWSLETTER

*Focus* (bimonthly)
*TRAFFIC (U.S.A.)* (quarterly)

## CONFERENCES

None

## BOARD OF DIRECTORS

Roger W. Sant, board chair; Rodney B. Wagner; executive committee chair; Adrienne B. Mars, secretary; Paul F. Miller Jr., treasurer; Kathryn S. Fuller, president

Other board members:
♦ Nancy Abraham ♦ Joseph F. Cullman III ♦ Jared M. Diamond ♦ Marshall Field ♦ Lynn A. Foster ♦ Wolcott Henry ♦ Millicent M. Johnsen ♦ Thomas H. Kean ♦ Frederick A. Krehbiel ♦ William T. Lake ♦ Melvin B. Lane ♦ Shelly Lazarus ♦ Mora McLean ♦ Scott McVay ♦ Wendell Mottley ♦ John C. Ogden ♦ Gordon Orians ♦ Anne Pattee ♦ Singleton Rankin ♦ William K. Reilly ♦ Alison F. Richard ♦ Gerald E. Rupp ♦ Roque Sevilla ♦ Anne P. Sidamon-Eristoff ♦ George H. Taber ♦ Margaret Taylor ♦ John Terborgh ♦ Russell E. Train ♦ Thomas Tusher ♦ Robert H. Waterman Jr. ♦ Robert N. Wilson ♦ Jaime Augusto Zobel de Ayala II

## EFFECTIVENESS

"To the Inuits of northern Canada, it is the one of the scariest poisons imaginable: an invisible toxin that has infiltrated the cells of arctic creatures from plankton to people and turned ordinary whales into floating hazardous waste dumps.

"To governments in central Africa, it is a chemical safety net, a primary defense against a worsening malaria epidemic that kills 5,000 children each day in countries south of the equator. On Monday, officials from as many as 120 nations will begin to try to reconcile these starkly contrasting views of DDT, the infamous insecticide long banned in the United States but still widely used in many parts of the developing world.

"Armed with new evidence about the pesticide's global spread, negotiators will gather in Montreal to start work on an unprecedented United Nations treaty to phase out DDT and 11 other toxic compounds that have been linked to cancers, birth defects and ecological disruption. . . .

"But environmental groups, citing evidence of long-term ecological damage, are calling for an expedited phaseout of all 12 compounds—along with economic and technical assistance to help developing countries find replacements. The World Wildlife Fund, in a report earlier this year, said persistent organic pollutants pose a particular health threat to whales and dolphins, who typically store large amounts of man-made chemicals in their body fat. The report suggested toxin contamination may have been an indirect cause of several well-publicized die-offs of marine mammals in recent years.

" 'DDT is clearly impacting the environment in some serious ways,' said Cliff Curtis, WWF's global toxics campaign director. 'We see alternatives [to DDT] that already exist and possibilities for other solutions in the near term. All that's required is political will.'

"The 12 chemicals targeted for phaseout were selected because of their wide distribution—most, like DDT, are commonly found in animals around the world—and because of a high potential for damage to health and ecosystems. In addition to DDT and PCBs, the list includes the industrial compound hexachlorobenzene, dioxins and furans, and seven pesticides. All are banned for commercial use in the United States." (*Washington Post*, June 28, 1998)

"Brazil promised today to set aside 62 million acres of Amazon rain forest for conservation, underscoring the Government's renewed commitment to the faltering preservation of the imperiled tropical wilderness.

"The pledge, to be carried out with financial and technical assistance from the World Bank and a conservation group, WWF International, would put 10 percent of the Brazilian Amazon under Government protection, three times as much as is now protected, the partners said.

"The agreement sets in motion a project that will take years to identify the land to be protected, to arrange the financing for the effort and to decide how to manage the forests and enforce the conservation rules. . . .

"The World Bank and the World Wildlife Fund began a campaign last year to put 10 percent of the world's forests in conservation programs by the year 2000. Brazil had previously said it would join the campaign." (*New York Times*, April 30, 1998)

"The familiar long-snouted reptile on a poster at London's Heathrow Airport has some Florida alligator ranchers vexed.

"The poster, produced jointly by the World Wildlife Fund and the U.S. Fish and Wildlife Service and appearing around the world, is part of a campaign to warn consumers against buying goods made from endangered species, such as the African elephant. It also features photos of a leather handbag and its source, which bears more than a passing resemblance to an alligator.

"The World Wildlife Fund, based in Washington, D.C., says it's a case of mistaken identity: The animal may look like the common U.S. alligator, but it is actually the endangered black caiman of South America.

"But ranchers here and in Louisiana plan to ask the group to rethink the poster campaign anyway. As they see it, the posters only add to what they see as an increasing threat to the state's $30 million alligator industry: the widespread—and erroneous—beliefs that alligators are endangered and that alligator products are illegal. They were for many years, but haven't been since 1987. . . .

". . . Back at the World Wildlife Fund, spokeswoman Dana West says the group has no intention of taking down the save-the-caiman posters, which appear in airports and passport offices around the globe. She apologizes for any untoward implications about U.S. alligators. The point, she adds, is to make people think about what they buy.

"If it's really U.S. alligator, go ahead, she says. In fact, her group considers the American reptile's resurgence a game-management success story in which farming has played a role in preserving habitat and reducing poaching.

"Mr. Ashley, the consultant helping the ranchers, recasts the environmental group's message bluntly: 'If you want to save an alligator,' he says, 'you should buy a purse.' " (*Wall Street Journal*, June 19, 1996)

# POLITICAL ORIENTATION

Unavailable

# International Affairs

## Chapter 7

# American Israel Public Affairs Committee (AIPAC) (1954)

440 First Street, NW
Suite 600
Washington, D.C. 20001
Phone: (202) 639-5200
Fax: (202) 347-4889
Internet: http://www.aipac.org

| | |
|---|---|
| An American grassroots lobby that seeks to maintain and improve friendship and goodwill between the United States and Israel. | **PURPOSE** |
| 110 total nationwide | **STAFF** |
| Howard Kohr, executive director | **DIRECTOR** |
| 501(c)(4) | **TAX STATUS** |
| 1998—$14 million<br>Proposed 1999—Unavailable | **BUDGET** |
| Private funding | **FUNDING SOURCES** |
| Members: 55,000<br>Branches/chapters: Offices in 8 states<br>Affiliates: N/A | **SCOPE** |
| None | **PAC** |
| ♦ Grassroots organizing ♦ Lobbying (federal and grassroots) ♦ Research | **METHOD OF OPERATION** |

| | |
|---|---|
| *CURRENT CONCERNS* | ◆ Mideast peace process ◆ Relations between the U.S. and Israel ◆ U.S. arms sales to Arab countries ◆ U.S. financial aid to Israel |
| *PUBLICATIONS* | Publishes brochures, *The AIPAC Papers on U.S.-Israel Relations, The AIPAC Papers on the Mideast Peace Talks,* and issue briefs on topics of current concern |
| *NEWSLETTER* | *Near East Report* |
| *CONFERENCES* | Annual national meeting held in spring (Washington, D.C.)<br>Also holds a number of smaller, regional conferences throughout the year |
| *BOARD OF DIRECTORS* | Unavailable |
| *EFFECTIVENESS* | "Of all the Jewish organizations devoted to channeling that popular opinion into American policy, there is none so influential—or so feared—as the American Israel Public Affairs Committee, known as Aipac.<br><br>"While the group's tactics have sometimes been controversial, and some consider that its quiet power has made it insufficiently sensitive to the concerns of more liberal American Jews, Aipac is a crucial actor. Founded in 1951, soon after Israel was born, Aipac is the only registered lobby for Jewish organizations, dedicated to nurturing and preserving the American-Israeli relationship no matter what the Government in Washington or Jerusalem. . . .<br><br>". . . Aipac, with more than 55,000 members and a budget of $14.2 million, calls itself 'America's Pro-Israel Lobby.' Its influence is legendary, built on grass-roots political organization, timely research and a network of active, articulate members.<br><br>"Aipac is not a registered foreign lobby but an American organization that plays American politics without apology. Thus it is sensitive to suggestions that it is too close to the Israeli Government." (*New York Times,* April 26, 1998)<br><br>"The Supreme Court heard arguments yesterday on whether lobbying groups that contribute to political campaigns must comply with federal rules requiring them to disclose how their money is collected and spent.<br><br>"But the justices appeared preoccupied by threshold legal problems and suggested they are unlikely to use the case involving the American Israel Public Affairs Committee (AIPAC) to decide whether groups that mostly lobby elected officials but also give to candidates must comply with disclosure rules. If the court were to rule on the merits of the case, it could bring new scrutiny to organizations that mostly lobby but also spend some portion of their time trying to influence elections through contributions. . . . |

"The D.C. Circuit Court of Appeals ruled that the pro-Israeli lobbying group should be classified as a political committee and forced to disclose its financial dealings because it spent more than $1,000 a year on campaigns. The appeals court rejected an FEC view that only groups whose 'major purpose' is the election of a candidate be covered. The FEC has said that requiring a group such as AIPAC, whose mission is primarily advocacy, to disclose its financial dealings would violate free speech rights." (*Washington Post,* January 15, 1998)

"When members of Washington's power elite gather tonight at the Hay-Adams Hotel to celebrate their inclusion in *Fortune* magazine's listing of the most powerful interest groups in the nation's capital, there will be no one from the city's celebrated aerospace-defense lobby to join in toasts.

". . . Aside from the omission of the aerospace-defense industry, the *Fortune* list contains few surprises. The selection of the 33-million member American Association of Retired Persons (AARP) as No. 1 came 'to no one's surprise,' the magazine said. No. 2 was the American Israel Public Affairs Committee; No. 3, the AFL-CIO; No. 4, the National Federation of Independent Business; and No. 5, the Association of Trial Lawyers of America.

"The rankings were based on returns from a questionnaire mailed to 2,200 individuals including members of Congress, lobbyists, academics and senior White House staff. A smaller panel had selected the 120 groups." (*Washington Post,* November 20, 1997)

# POLITICAL ORIENTATION

"Last week, House Speaker Newt Gingrich (R-Ga.) accused President Clinton of blackmailing the Israeli government on behalf of Palestinian leader Yasser Arafat. Yesterday he criticized Secretary of State Madeleine K. Albright as 'the agent for the Palestinians.' Today he will help give Israeli Prime Minister Binyamin Netanyahu a rousing welcome on Capitol Hill—and relish his party's effectiveness in transforming its attitude toward the Jewish state in recent years.

"Though Democrats and Republicans alike have attacked the White House for pressuring Netanyahu to turn over an additional 13 percent of the occupied West Bank to Palestinian control, Gingrich's swift and harsh reaction reflects the culmination of more than a decade of work between Republican conservatives and the pro-Israel lobby. The relationship has produced benefits for both sides in policy and fund-raising. . . .

"Amitay and other lobbyists emphasized that Congress has been consistently supportive of Israel, regardless of which party occupied the White House. 'There's nothing new about Republican support for Israel,' said an [American Israel Public Affairs Committee] AIPAC lobbyist who declined to be identified. 'The difference is these conservative members are now in the majority and they're running the House.' " (*Washington Post,* May 14, 1998)

"In a sharply worded speech, House Speaker Newt Gingrich (R-Ga.) charged President Clinton with threatening Israel's security by giving even-handed treatment to different behavior by Israelis and Palestinians.

" 'When the Clinton-Gore administration treats with moral equivalence Palestinian violence and Israeli housing, they undermine Israel's security,' Gingrich told an enthusiastically supportive meeting of the American Israel Public Affairs Committee, or AIPAC, the influential pro-Israel lobbying group. The speaker's remarks, which echo those by Israeli Prime Minister Binyamin Netanyahu, came a day after talks between Clinton and Netanyahu, long a favorite of conservative Republicans, failed to achieve progress in the Middle East peace process. That effort has faltered in a wave of violence since Israel began construction of apartments in the Har Homa section of traditionally Arab East Jerusalem last month." (*Washington Post*, April 9, 1997)

# Amnesty International USA (1961)

322 Eighth Avenue
New York, New York 10001
Phone: (212) 807-8400
Fax: (212) 627-1451

304 Pennsylvania Avenue, SE
Washington, D.C. 20003
Phone: (202) 544-0200
Fax: (202) 546-7142

Internet: http://www.amnesty-usa.org

Works to:
"Free all prisoners of conscience detained anywhere for their beliefs or because of their ethnic origin, sex, colour or language—who have not used or advocated violence.
"Ensure fair and prompt trials for political prisoners.
"Abolish the death penalty, torture and other cruel treatment of prisoners.
"End extrajudicial executions and 'disappearances.' "

**PURPOSE**

Unavailable

**STAFF**

William F. Schulz, executive director. Schulz was appointed executive director of Amnesty International USA in March 1994. An ordained minister, he came to Amnesty after fifteen years with the Unitarian Universalist Association of Congregations, the last eight as president of the Association. He served on the council of the International Association for Religious Freedom from 1985 to 1993 and has served on the board of many organizations, including People for the American Way and the Planned Parenthood Federation of America. He is a graduate of Oberlin College, holds an M.A. in philosophy from the University of Chicago, and received both an M.A. in theology and a D.Min. degree from Meadville/Lombard Theological School.

**DIRECTOR**

501(c)(3)

**TAX STATUS**

1998—Unavailable
Proposed 1999—Unavailable

**BUDGET**

Financed by members and donors

**FUNDING SOURCES**

| | |
|---|---|
| *SCOPE* | Members: 1 million members in more than 150 countries |
| | Branches/chapters: 5 regional offices; 2,000 volunteer groups in communities and on campuses nationwide |
| | Affiliates: N/A |

| | |
|---|---|
| *PAC* | None |

| | |
|---|---|
| *METHOD OF OPERATION* | ♦ Congressional testimony ♦ Demonstrations ♦ Films/video/audiotapes ♦ Grassroots organizing ♦ International activities ♦ Internet (Web site) ♦ Library/information clearinghouse ♦ Lobbying (federal and grassroots) ♦ Media outreach ♦ Research ♦ Speakers program |

| | |
|---|---|
| *CURRENT CONCERNS* | Human rights protection and promotion worldwide including death row criminals, lesbians and gays, refugees, and women |

| | |
|---|---|
| *PUBLICATIONS* | *Abusive Punishment in Japanese Prisons* |
| | *A.I. Policy Manual* |
| | *Amnesty International Handbook* |
| | *Amnesty International Report 1998—Human Rights for All* |
| | *Arming the Torturers* |
| | *Breaking the Silence: Human Rights Violations Based on Sexual Orientation* |
| | *Death Penalty Developments in 1997* |
| | *The Death Penalty in Georgia: Racist, Arbitrary and Unfair* |
| | *The Death Penalty in Texas: Lethal Injustice* |
| | *"Disappearances"—A Black Hole in the Protection of Human Rights* |
| | *Ethnicity and Nationality* |
| | *Fear, Flight and Forcible Exile* |
| | *Glimpse of Hell: Reports on Torture Worldwide* |
| | *The Hidden Violence—"Disappearances" and Killings Continue* |
| | *Human Rights Concerns in the Border Region with Mexico* |
| | *In Search of Safety: The Forcibly Displaced and Human Rights in Africa* |
| | *Nine Years After Tiananmen* |
| | *Nurses and Human Rights* |
| | *Political Violence Spirals* |
| | *Prescription for Change: Health Professionals and the Exposure of Human Rights Violations* |
| | *Refugees: Human Rights Have No Borders* |
| | *Release Prisoners of Conscience Now!* |
| | *Respect My Rights: Refugees Speak Out!* |
| | *Still Crying Out for Justice* |
| | *The Universal Declaration of Human Rights 1948–1988: Human Rights, the United Nations, and Amnesty International* |
| | *Use of Electro-Shock Stun Belts* |
| | *"Who's Living in My House?"* |
| | *Women in Mexico: Overcoming Fear* |

Regularly publishes country reports and other documents on human rights issues around the world; also offers a selection of posters, videos, and calendars.

| | |
|---|---|
| *Amnesty Action* (quarterly)<br>*Amnesty International Newsletter* (monthly) | *NEWSLETTER* |
| General Meeting (annual, in a city where AI USA has a regional office) | *CONFERENCES* |
| "Amnesty International USA has both a Board of Directors whose members are voted into office by the organization's general membership, and a Leadership Council recruited by the Executive Director as an advisory committee." | *BOARD OF DIRECTORS* |
| | *EFFECTIVENESS* |

"Despite some improvements in the way complaints of abuse are handled, people detained by Federal immigration agents along the United States-Mexican border are still often subject to 'cruel, inhuman or degrading treatment,' according to a lengthy report released today by the human-rights group Amnesty International.

"The abuse includes beatings, sexual assault, racially derogatory comments and denial of medical care and food, said the group, which conducted several weeks of research along the border, including interviews with immigrant advocacy groups, immigration officials and people who said they were victims of brutality. . . .

"The report was issued exactly one year after the shooting death of an American teen-ager in Redford, Tex., by a member of a Marine patrol backing up Federal agents in an anti-drug operation. Two grand juries have declined to indict the marine who fired the fatal shot, but many groups that promote immigrants' rights say the killing was an unjustified homicide that should result in criminal charges. And the report today said that a 'thorough, independent investigation' of the incident was still needed. . . .

"The report, 'Human Rights Concerns in the Border Region with Mexico,' was the first major look at the issue by the group, which has chronicled human-rights abuses around the world. It said that all detainees should be informed of their rights, in their native languages, and that they should not be 'discouraged, threatened or prevented from exercising their right to file a complaint.' " (*New York Times*, May 21, 1998)

"Collectively called NGOs, for nongovernmental organizations, these international pressure groups have coalesced to steer the way the world's nations set policies for international law and conduct in the 1990s. The NGOs' potency was most striking in the drive they led to secure an international land mine ban last year, an effort that ran counter to the initial judgment of most powers.

"But they have left their mark elsewhere as well. In regional crises, such as the 1994 genocide in Rwanda or last year's war in the Congo, international relief agencies—not national governments—have played the central role in aiding victims. That pattern is being repeated today in northern Albania, where international aid organizations are leading efforts to assist refugees fleeing the fighting in the Serbian province of Kosovo. . . .

"The most important organizations, Amnesty International and Human Rights Watch, might as well be major countries, measured by the clout they have in laying the intellectual and political groundwork for the kind of permanent court they want—making what they term 'bilateral' calls on foreign ministers around the world, briefing lawyers and jurists and politicians, producing reams of legal documents and deploying teams of experts. They are supplying, free of charge, the demand of smaller, poorer countries who want a negotiating voice here but do not have the resources to support their participation." (*Washington Post*, June 18, 1998)

"Amnesty International renewed its charge that German police systematically have ill-treated foreigners and that much of the alleged abuse is racially motivated.

"The London-based human rights organization, which first criticized German police behavior in 1995, made the claims in a report that examined evidence from German inquiries into allegations of police violence over the last two years." (*Washington Post*, July 4, 1997)

"With chants of 'They say death row, we say hell no,' about 100 protesters outside the Maryland Correctional Adjustment Center in Baltimore spoke out yesterday against the scheduled execution this week of Flint Gregory Hunt for the murder of Baltimore police Officer Vincent J. Adolfo in 1985.

"The protest was organized by such groups as Amnesty International and the Campaign to End the Death Penalty. Others protested the execution on grounds of racism. . . ." (*Washington Post*, June 29, 1997)

"Homosexuals around the world are being killed, tortured and imprisoned, Amnesty International said in a report on gay human rights.

" 'In countries all over the world, men and women are harassed, abducted, imprisoned, tortured and even murdered for their sexual identity,' Amnesty said in the report, called 'Breaking the Silence.' The international pressure group, whose British division put together the report, said gay men and lesbians face prosecution in up to 60 countries for their sexual orientation. . . .

". . . Amnesty called for the decriminalization of homosexuality around the world, citing such countries as Nigeria, Romania and India where it is still illegal." (*Washington Post*, February 26, 1997)

## POLITICAL ORIENTATION

Unavailable

# The Atlantic Council of the United States (1961)

910 17th Street, NW
Suite 1000
Washington, D.C. 20005
Phone: (202) 778-4940
Fax: (202) 463-7241
Internet: info@acus.org *or* http://www.acus.org

| | |
|---|---|
| Committed "to enhancing U.S. initiative and leadership through sound and skillfully administered policies that identify and pursue national interests in a framework of global interdependence, and through the education of future leaders." | ***PURPOSE*** |
| 22 total—11 professional; 11 support; plus 3 part-time professional; 1 part-time support; 100 volunteers; 12–18 interns per semester | ***STAFF*** |
| David C. Acheson, president | ***DIRECTOR*** |
| 1997—$3 million<br>1998—$3 million<br>Proposed 1999—$3 million | ***BUDGET*** |
| Foundation and government grants and corporate gifts | ***FUNDING SOURCES*** |
| Members: 2,000 individuals, including 400 academic associates<br>Branches/Chapters: N/A<br>Affiliate: ACUS is a member of Atlantic Treaty Association, an international group with institutions in each NATO and Partnership for Peace country. | ***SCOPE*** |
| None | ***PAC*** |
| ♦ Conferences/seminars ♦ Educational foundation ♦ Fellowships (Partnership for Peace, Senior Fellows Seminars Series, Senior Fellows Publications Series) ♦ Information clearinghouse ♦ International activities ♦ Internet (Web site) ♦ Internships ♦ Speakers program | ***METHOD OF OPERATION*** |

| | |
|---|---|
| *CURRENT CONCERNS* | ♦ Central Asia ♦ Economic and security affairs ♦ Global future of nuclear energy ♦ NATO enlargement ♦ U.S. foreign policy ♦ U.S.-European Union relations ♦ U.S.-Russian relations |
| *PUBLICATIONS* | *Energy Technology Cooperation for Sustainable Economic Development*<br>*Reversing Relations with Former Adversaries: U.S. Foreign Policy After the Cold War*<br>*Taiwan 2020—Developments in Taiwan to 2020: Implications for Cross Strait Relations and U.S. Policy*<br>*United States and China Relations at a Crossroad*<br>*The United States and Japan: Cooperative Leadership for Peace and Global Prosperity*<br>*U.S. Energy Imperatives for the 1990s*<br><br>Also publishes bulletins, policy papers, and issue briefs |
| *NEWSLETTER* | *Atlantic Council News* (3 times per year) |
| *CONFERENCES* | Sponsors conferences and seminars on various topics throughout the year |
| *BOARD OF DIRECTORS* | The following is a list of executive board members:<br>Brent Scowcroft, chairman; Lucy Wilson Benson, William H. G. FitzGerald, Barbara H. Franklin, Chas. W. Freeman Jr., Roger Kirk, Richard D. Lawson, John D. Macomber, Jack N. Merritt, Stanley R. Resor, Raymond P. Shafer, Peter W. Smith, and Louise Woerner, vice chairs; David C. Acheson, president; William Y. Smith, treasurer; Robert E. Jordan III, secretary |
| *EFFECTIVENESS* | Unavailable |
| *POLITICAL ORIENTATION* | Unavailable |

# Center for Defense Information (1972)

1779 Massachusetts Avenue, NW
Washington, D.C. 20036
Phone: (202) 332-0600
Fax: (202) 462-4559
Toll-free: (800) 234-3334
Internet: info@cdi.org *or* http://www.cdi.org

| | |
|---|---|
| "The Center for Defense Information (CDI) supports an effective defense. It opposes excessive expenditures for weapons and policies that increase the danger of war. CDI believes that strong social, economic, political and military components and a healthy environment contribute equally to the nation's security." | *PURPOSE* |
| 23 total—20 professional; 3 support; plus 2 part-time, 2 volunteers, and 4 interns per trimester | *STAFF* |
| Gene R. La Rocque, founder and president. La Rocque, a retired U.S. Navy rear admiral, served on active duty for 31 years. He spent 16 years at sea in important staff positions and commanded a variety of warships and task forces. La Rocque also served for 7 years in the Pentagon in strategic planning for the Joint Chiefs of Staff and the Chief of Naval Operations. He was the director of the Inter-American Defense College and graduated from the Industrial College of Armed Forces. | *DIRECTOR* |
| 501(c)(3) | *TAX STATUS* |
| 1997—$1.7 million<br>1998—$1.85 million<br>Proposed 1999—$1.85 million | *BUDGET* |
| Individuals, 46 percent; foundation grants, 37 percent; interest and dividends, 13 percent; publications, 4 percent | *FUNDING SOURCES* |
| Members: N/A<br>Branches/chapters: N/A<br>Affiliates: N/A | *SCOPE* |
| None | *PAC* |

| | |
|---|---|
| **METHOD OF OPERATION** | ◆ Conferences/seminars ◆ Congressional testimony ◆ Films/video/audiotapes ◆ International activities ◆ Internet (databases, Electronic bulletin boards, "Russia Weekly" e-mail alert, "Weekly Defense Monitor" e-mail alert, Web site) ◆ Legislative/regulatory monitoring (federal) ◆ Library/information clearinghouse (open to public) ◆ Media outreach ◆ Research ◆ Speakers program ◆ Television and radio production ("America's Defense Monitor" weekly half-hour television program, "Question of the Week" weekly radio commentary) |
| **CURRENT CONCERNS** | ◆ Arms trade ◆ Force structure ◆ International peacekeeping ◆ Military spending ◆ National security strategy ◆ NATO enlargement ◆ Nuclear weapon abolition ◆ U.S./Cuba relations ◆ U.S./Russia relations |
| **PUBLICATIONS** | *Catalog of "America's Defense Monitor" TV Programs* (transcripts and videotapes)<br>*CDI 1997 Military Almanac* (biennial)<br>*Conventional Arms Trade Citation List*<br>*Conventional Arms Transfer Restraint in the 1990s*<br>*United Nations Peacekeeping Citation List* |
| **NEWSLETTER** | *The Defense Monitor* (10 issues per year) |
| **CONFERENCES** | Regularly hosts seminars with visiting military, educational, and other public interest groups |
| **BOARD OF DIRECTORS** | ◆ Doris Z. Bato ◆ Arthur D. Berliss Jr. ◆ Gay Dillingham ◆ Eva Haller ◆ James D. Head ◆ David H. Horowitz ◆ Alan Kay ◆ Gene R. La Rocque ◆ John M. Rockwood ◆ Julie Schecter ◆ Philip A. Straus ◆ Andrew Ungerleider |
| **EFFECTIVENESSS** | "In the wake of last month's tit-for-tat nuclear tests, the military competition between the two rival nations [India and Pakistan] is now focused on development of missiles and other systems to deliver nuclear warheads.<br><br>"Both nations are working to perfect missile technology, but only India has made progress on developing submarines capable of launching those missiles at sea. By the end of this year, India plans to begin construction of a 2,500-ton attack submarine, based on the design of French Rubis-class vessels, that it hopes to complete by 2004, according to Bombay-based science writer Gopi Rethinaraj, who tracks the Indian nuclear program, and Andrew R. Koch, an analyst at the Center for Defense Information in Washington.<br><br>"Rethinaraj and Koch, who reported their findings in the June issue of Jane's *Intelligence Review,* said that if India is successful in building a nuclear-powered submarine, it would become the only nation outside the five established nuclear powers—the United States, China, Britain, France and Russia—to have such a vessel." (*Washington Post,* June 27, 1998) |

"Across the United States, debate over nuclear disarmament fell out of fashion with the end of the cold war. Indeed, at the Helsinki meeting, plans to expand the North Atlantic Treaty Organization may overshadow an American proposal for the United States and Russia to cut their numbers of operational warheads to one-third of today's levels. . . .

"Under the Administration's proposal, operational strategic warheads on both sides would be reduced to levels of 2,000 to 2,500. Currently, Russia has about 7,500 of these bombs, and the United States has about 7,150, according to the Center for Defense Information, a study group in Washington.

"Since 1990, Russia and the United States have cut their total nuclear stockpiles almost in half." (*New York Times*, March 19, 1997)

"Of the many ventures that have stirred Internet uproar, David Johnson's Russia list has been one of the most tempestuous. A smattering of news, essays and commentary, Johnson's List is sent to roughly 1,000 scholars, journalists, policy makers, and Russophiles from Washington to Hong Kong via electronic mail—a practice increasingly endangered by the intricacies of copyright enforcement on Internet material. . . .

"From his perch at a research center in Washington, Mr. Johnson, who has never been to post-Soviet Russia, has played conductor to the most influential and cacophonous exchange of Russian information on the Internet. Since its debut in May, his list's vitriolic spats over NATO expansion or the shiftiness of Russia's presidential pretender, Aleksandr I. Lebed, have deeply irritated some of the world's leading analysts. But they can't stop reading it. . . .

"Until January, Johnson's List also had a World Wide Web site. But after the *American Spectator* magazine complained of copyright infringement, the site was dropped. When asked, Mr. Johnson invokes the copyright doctrine permitting 'fair use' of portions of printed material, assuming publishers will look the other way as long as their material isn't used commercially. Mostly, they do.

"Though in principle copyrighted material can only be reproduced in full by the owner's permission, this is a 'fuzzy area' for Internet use, said John J. Shanahan, a retired vice admiral and the director of the Center for Defense Information, where Mr. Johnson works. Since the infringement scare, however, the center took its umbrella away from the list. Mr. Johnson now runs it from home.

"Despite a new international treaty asserting that copyright does exist in the digital realm, experts still disagree about its application. . . .

"Though he is safe for now, Mr. Johnson is worried the copyright issue could shut him down. But the list is still distributed several times daily, sending dozens of articles to anyone who asks." (*New York Times*, March 17, 1997)

"In what is expected to be one of the last major takeovers in the weapons industry, the Raytheon Company announced . . . that it had agreed to acquire the military businesses of the Hughes Electronics Corporation from the General Motors Corporation for the equivalent of $9.5 billion. . . .

"With today's announcement there have been about $50 billion in mergers involving military contractors in the last four years, nearly $40 billion worth in the last year. There were 15 major military contractors seven years ago. With today's announcement three huge, dominant weapons producers have emerged: the Boeing Company, Lockheed and now Raytheon, each with $20 billion or more in annual revenues. . . .

"The size and strength of the resulting behemoths have put enormous pressure on the remaining companies to consider merging or being forced to the sidelines.

"But the largest policy impact is that it advances the transformation of the weapons manufacturing business, and perhaps the Pentagon itself because the contractors may now be better than the military at designing and conceiving modern weapons systems. . . .

"The outgoing Defense Secretary, William J. Perry, was an ardent supporter of the consolidation of the industry. In fact, the remaining contractors are enjoying a huge surge in profits. But some experts have argued that the changes are not in the national interest.

" 'It's just profits and politics coming to the fore in this business,' said Gene La Rocque, a retired rear admiral and president of the Center for Defense Information. 'You're going to have private industry telling us what kind of ships we ought to produce, what kind of cannons, what kinds of planes. Private companies will be originating most of these ideas. I think that is a very slippery slope.' " (*New York Times,* January 17, 1997)

# POLITICAL ORIENTATION

"The voters haven't exactly taken to the streets on the question of NATO expansion, but the issue seems hot enough to earn a Loop Strange Bedfellows Award for February.

"The conservative Free Congress Foundation, along with other conservative groups, including the Eagle Forum and the American Defense Institute, have teamed up with the likes of the liberal Council for a Livable World Education Fund, the Center for Defense Information and others to oppose expansion and demand full Senate debate on what the groups say is being treated as an 'insider bill.' " (*Washington Post,* March 2, 1998)

"liberal" (*Washington Post,* July 19, 1997)

# Center for Strategic and International Studies (1962)

1800 K Street, NW
Suite 400
Washington, D.C. 20006
Phone: (202) 887-0200
Fax: (202) 775-3199
Internet: info@csis.org *or* http://www.csis.org

"Policy impact is the basic mission of CSIS. Our goal is to inform and shape policy decisions in government and the private sector to meet the increasingly complex and difficult challenges that leaders will confront in the next century."

*PURPOSE*

160 total—80 research specialists; 80 support; plus 15 fellows; 70 interns

*STAFF*

David M. Abshire, president. Since he cofounded the Center for Strategic and International Studies (CSIS) in 1962, Abshire has headed the organization continuously except for two extended periods of government service. He served as assistant secretary of state for congressional relations from 1970 to 1973 and as U.S. ambassador to NATO from 1983 to 1987. Abshire was a member of the President's Task Force on U.S. Government International Broadcasting and is a former chairman of the U.S. Board for International Broadcasting. He is a past member of the President's Foreign Intelligence Advisory Board and the Murphy Commission on the Organization of the Government for the Conduct of Foreign Policy. Abshire received a B.A. from West Point and a Ph.D. from Georgetown University.

*DIRECTOR*

501(c)(3)

*TAX STATUS*

Fiscal year ending September 30, 1998—$17.2 million
Proposed F.Y. 1999—$17.2 million

*BUDGET*

Foundation grants, 28 percent; corporate contributions, 49 percent; endowment, publications, and other income, 14 percent; government contracts, 5 percent; individuals, 4 percent

*FUNDING SOURCES*

## SCOPE

Members: N/A

Branch/chapter: Pacific Forum/CSIS, a Honolulu-based nonprofit policy institute that merged with CSIS in 1981, researches political, economic, and security interests and trends in the Asia-Pacific region

Affiliates: N/A

## PAC

None

## METHOD OF OPERATION

♦ Action commissions ♦ Awards program ♦ Conferences and seminars ♦ Congressional study groups ♦ Congressional testimony ♦ Consultation with and advice to businesses and governments ♦ Distinguished speakers ♦ Educational foundations ♦ International activities ♦ Internet (Web site) ♦ Internships ♦ Library/information clearinghouse (for employees only) ♦ Media outreach ♦ Research ♦ Telecommunications services (mailing lists)

## CURRENT CONCERNS

♦ Arms control and crisis management ♦ Energy and national security ♦ Environmental affairs ♦ Global organized crime ♦ International business and economics ♦ International communications ♦ Maritime studies ♦ National service for disadvantaged youth ♦ New global economy and the States of the Union ♦ Political-military affairs ♦ Regional studies ♦ Retirement finance ♦ Science and technology ♦ Strategic issues of the 1990s ♦ Strengthening of America ♦ Trade and investment ♦ U.S. defense strategy and interests ♦ U.S. financial market reform ♦ U.S. tax system reform

## PUBLICATIONS

*CSIS Policy Papers on the Americas* (periodic)
*CSIS Panel Reports*
*CSIS Reports*
*Significant Issues Series* (monographs)
*Washington Papers Series* (monographs)

Books copublished with scholarly presses

## NEWSLETTER

*CSIS Briefing Notes on Islam, Society, and Politics* (bimonthly)
*CSIS Euro-Focus* (bimonthly)
*CSIS Hong Kong Update* (monthly)
*CSIS Watch* (weekly)
*CSIS Western Hemisphere Election Study* (periodic)
*NEWS@CSIS* (quarterly)
*Post-Soviet Prospects* (bimonthly)
*The Washington Quarterly* (journal)

## CONFERENCES

2020 Committee
Advisory Board
Dallas Roundtable
Global 2000
Houston Roundtable
International Councillors
International Research Council
Northeast Asia Council
Seminars for senior corporate executives
Statesmen's Forum
Strategic Issues of the '90s
U.S. Council on Security Cooperation in the Asia Pacific
Washington Roundtable

## BOARD OF DIRECTORS

## EFFECTIVENESS

"The most recent example of fearlessness (on Social Security reform) comes from the National Commission on Retirement Policy, formed by the Center for Strategic and International Studies." (*Dallas Morning News*, May 20, 1998)

"A bipartisan panel will endorse the creation of individual investment accounts and a rise in the retirement age to 70 as part of a comprehensive Social Security overhaul package.

"The panel's recommendations . . . have been widely anticipated since the board's creation last year, in part because it is led by four House and Senate lawmakers—including GOP Rep. Jim Kolbe of Arizona and Democratic Rep. Charlie Stenholm of Texas—as well as several leading businessmen and policy experts. The recommendations will carry additional weight in Washington because, unlike some previous high-level efforts to overhaul Social Security, they have the unanimous endorsement of the 24-member panel.

" 'We ended up with a middle-of-the-road approach,' said Urban Institute Senior Fellow Rudolph Penner, a member of the commission, which is sponsored by the Center for Strategic and International Studies.

"The group's recommendation would essentially require workers to put 2% of the 12.4% payroll tax paid into Social Security into individual investment accounts, through which they would be permitted to choose among a handful of investment options. Under the current Social Security system, all 12.4% of payroll taxes goes directly into the Social Security trust fund and is invested in government securities.

". . . Although the CSIS plan includes a number of innovative modifications from plans presented earlier, its emphasis on individual accounts mirrors the proposal by Democratic Sen. Bob Kerrey of Nebraska as part of the January 1995 Bipartisan Commission on Entitlement and Tax Reform." (*Wall Street Journal,* May 18, 1998)

"FBI Director Louis J. Freeh warned yesterday that Russian organized crime networks pose a menace to U.S. national security and asserted that there is now greater danger of a nuclear attack by some outlaw group than there was by the Soviet Union during the Cold War. . . .

"The testimony came on the heels of a report on the international threat posed by Russian organized crime issued by Washington's Center for Strategic and International Studies. The study warned that, if left unchecked, crime networks will turn Russia into a 'criminal-syndicalist state'—a nation controlled by a troika of gangsters, corrupt government officials and crooked businessmen who accumulate vast amounts of wealth 'by promoting and exploiting corruption and the vulnerabilities inherent in a society in transition.'

"The two-year study found that Russia's wealth has been 'plundered since the Soviet Union imploded, and tens of billions of dollars have been moved to safe havens in offshore banking centers.'

" 'Russian organized crime constitutes a direct threat to the national security interests of the United States by fostering instability in a nuclear power,' the report said. 'Russian organized crime groups hold the uniquely dangerous opportunity to procure and traffic in nuclear materials.' " (*Washington Post,* October 2, 1997)

"Two years ago, the Center for Strategic and International Studies, a Washington think tank, mustered a panel of 26 academics and retired officers, headed by former defense secretary Dick Cheney, to undertake a sweeping review of professional military education—prompted by the changing needs of a post-Cold War military and various scandals at the service academies. At the time, Annapolis was still reeling from the discovery of a cheating ring, and all the schools had struggled with instances of sexual harassment or hazing.

"Released this spring, the report came out as a ringing defense of the academy system. It contended that the GAO had underestimated the cost of ROTC by counting only the cost of scholarship money and not including the program's administrative costs or the nonmilitary federal and state tax dollars that help fund the civilian colleges that ROTC beneficiaries attend.

"The report also argued that the academies are worth the extra expense because their graduates stay in the service longer and reach higher ranks. Of 100 Naval Academy graduates, 40 typically will stay in long enough to be promoted to lieutenant commander, the fourth step on the Navy's hierarchy of commissioned officers; the Navy would have to start with 140 ROTC graduates, or 153 OCS graduates, to get that many lieutenant commanders. . . .

"In defending the greater cost of the service academies, boosters often end up citing intangibles. The Center for Strategic and International Studies report argues that the glamour and prestige of the institutions helps persuade 'the brightest and most highly sought-after' high school students to enter the military. Plus, the aggressive recruiting programs of the academies have enabled the officer corps to attract more women and minorities." (*Washington Post*, August 12, 1997)

## POLITICAL ORIENTATION

"This latest panel (on Social Security reform), sponsored by the Center for Strategic and International Studies, may have broken the stalemate by embracing middle-of-the-road solutions that could unite the Democratic White House and the GOP-led Congress." (*Atlanta Constitution*, May 21, 1998)

"conservative" (*Washington Post*, January 27, 1998)

"an independent think tank" (*Washington Post*, October 21, 1997)

# Council on Foreign Relations (1921)

The Harold Pratt House
58 East 68th Street
New York, New York 10021
Phone: (212) 734-0400
Fax: (212) 861-1789

1779 Massachusetts Ave, NW
Washington, D.C. 20036
Phone: (202) 518-3414
Fax: (202) 986-2984

Internet: http://www.foreignrelations.org *or*
http://www.foreignaffairs.org

**PURPOSE**

"Dedicated to improving the understanding of U.S. foreign policy and international affairs through the exchange of ideas."

**STAFF**

150 total; plus interns and visiting fellows

**DIRECTOR**

Leslie H. Gelb, president. Prior to his tenure as Council on Foreign Relations's president, Gelb served at the *New York Times* from 1981 to 1993 in a number of editorial positions, from columnist to diplomatic correspondent. He was senior associate for the Carnegie Endowment for International Peace from 1980 to 1981; assistant secretary of state from 1977 to 1979; a fellow at the Brookings Institution and a visiting professor at Georgetown University from 1969 to 1973; director of policy planning and arms control for international security affairs at the Defense Department from 1967 to 1969; and executive assistant to U.S. Senator Jacob K. Javits from 1966 to 1967. Gelb received his bachelor's degree from Tufts University in 1959 and his master's degree in 1961 and his doctorate in 1964 from Harvard University. He is an award-winning author.

**TAX STATUS**

501(c)(3)

**BUDGET**

1997—$17.9 million
1998—Unavailable
Proposed 1999—Unavailable

**FUNDING SOURCES**

Unavailable

**SCOPE**

Members: 3,300 individuals
Branches/chapters: N/A
Affiliate: Pacific Council on International Policy, a 501(c)(3) organization

| | |
|---|---|
| None | *PAC* |
| ♦ Conferences/seminars ♦ International activities ♦ Internet (Web sites) ♦ Library/information clearinghouse ♦ Media projects and video conferencing ♦ Research ♦ Speakers program | *METHOD OF OPERATION* |
| ♦ National security ♦ International economics ♦ Asia | *CURRENT CONCERNS* |
| *Cases and Strategies for Preventive Action*<br>*The City and the World: New York's Global Future*<br>*Continuing the Inquiry: The Council on Foreign Relations from 1921 to 1996*<br>*The Expanding Role of State and Local Governments in U.S. Foreign Affairs*<br>*India, Pakistan, and the United States: Breaking with the Past*<br>*The New Russian Foreign Policy*<br>*Refugees into Citizens: Palestinians and the End of the Arab-Israeli*<br>*The Reluctant Sheriff: The United States after the Cold War*<br>*The Social Safety Net in Postcommunist Europe*<br>*Toward Comprehensive Peace in Southeast Europe*<br>*Trade Strategies for a New Era: Ensuring U.S. Leadership in a Global Economy*<br>*The World and Yugoslavia's War*<br><br>Also publishes transcripts, proceedings, and special reports | *PUBLICATIONS* |
| *Foreign Affairs* (bimonthly journal) | *NEWSLETTER* |
| Numerous conferences and seminars throughout the year | *CONFERENCES* |
| Unavailable | *BOARD OF DIRECTORS* |
| "President Kim Dae Jung of South Korea told New York business leaders yesterday that his country's once-prized economic miracle was nothing but a 'house of cards' and that his people now needed American help to rebuild the economy in a more Western image.<br><br>"Mr. Kim, a former dissident who assumed the country's highest office in February, lashed out at his predecessors for creating an economy characterized by collusion and corruption. Now, he said, South Korea has turned decisively to democracy and it has opened its borders to foreign investment and trade. | *EFFECTIVENESS* |

" 'My greatest purpose in coming here,' he said, 'is to plead with the American Government and businessmen to invest in South Korea, to tell you that we are doing everything we can to open' the economy. He joked with an audience of executives, diplomats and scholars at the Council on Foreign Relations in Manhattan, saying, 'If each of you today could invest just $100 million, that would be a great help.' . . .

"Many of New York's top business leaders turned out to hear the President's remarks, including Sanford I. Weill, chairman of the Travelers Group; Jon S. Corzine, co-chairman of Goldman, Sachs & Company; and Maurice R. Greenberg, chairman of the American International Group.

" 'He said all the right things—very direct, very positive,' said Robert D. Hormats, vice chairman of Goldman Sachs International. 'It will take some time for businesses to respond, but the direction is right on.' " (*New York Times*, June 9, 1998)

"One-fifth of humanity lives on the Indian subcontinent, but until recent months the region hardly showed up on the map of U.S. policymakers.

"Since last year, the Clinton administration, adopting the thrust recommended by a Council on Foreign Relations panel, has sent waves of officials to the subcontinent in an effort to expand U.S. interests beyond such traditional concerns as concentrated poverty and nuclear proliferation. The latest American official to visit the region, U.N. Ambassador Bill Richardson, acknowledged that 'perhaps in the past we have not paid enough attention to this area . . . of growing political, strategic and economic importance to the United States.' . . .

"Last week, a new ballistic missile flared across Pakistani skies in what the government here described as a successful test. With the launch of the Ghauri, whose range is 930 miles, Pakistan for the first time effectively reached missile parity with India.

"Each country now claims the ability to strike every major city in the other country with nuclear warheads, which both have the capacity to produce. . . .

"Last year, a report on India and Pakistan prepared by 28 specialists for the Council on Foreign Relations recommended that the United States should 'significantly expand its bilateral economic, political and military ties with both countries, providing a broad array of incentives for each country to help bring about restraint in the proliferation area.' " (*Washington Post*, April 17, 1998)

"When Texas-based SBC Communications Inc. and Telekom Malaysia Berhad bought a 30 percent stake in Telkom South Africa, the state-owned phone company, the deal was as significant for its dollar value—$1.26 billion—as for the message it sent to the world about African economic viability.

"One of Africa's largest privatization deals, the Telkom acquisition earlier this year sent a loud and clear signal that the country considered a financial gateway to Africa—as well as a continental role model—was indeed open for business. . . . Despite continued economic and political trouble on the continent, as well as structural economic problems that have yet to be solved, sub-Saharan Africa is posting new highs in economic growth rates, more economic reform and more democracy—all of which have caused investors to consider this once marginalized continent a market worthy of their attention and money.

"The trend is still fragile and new, with some of Africa's largest countries—notably the two Congos, Angola, Sudan and Nigeria—still in political turmoil or economic straits, or both. Some analysts say there is not enough evidence to tell whether the new growth rates in Africa are a new beginning or just a blip; many concede that the rates largely reflect the fact that African economies had nowhere to go but up.

"But a task force sponsored by the Council on Foreign Relations urged U.S. policymakers recently to take advantage of what it called 'the most promising period since the onset of African independence 40 years ago.'

"The task force noted that the United States exports more to Africa than to Eastern Europe and the former Soviet republics combined, and that Africa will become increasingly important as a market because more than a third of U.S. economic growth results from exports.

"Africa's new openness to investment and the news of its apparent upturn have attracted heightened attention from U.S. investors, who have crammed the ballrooms and wood-paneled chambers of Washington, New York and some African capitals during a series of investment summits held in recent months, including one this spring that attracted 700 people." (*Washington Post*, August 15, 1997)

"It's hard to overstate how important it is that Washington and Beijing start getting along better. Right now, it's as if all the hot buttons of international relations over the past two decades—arms control, nuclear proliferation, human-rights abuses, territorial ambitions and huge trade deficits—have been wired together in this one tense relationship. There's no simple fix, of course, and simply bowing to Chinese pressure to keep things calm is no answer. But the single most sensible suggestion on how to begin reducing the mutual animosity came last spring, when a Council on Foreign Relations panel suggested that the American president begin holding regular summit meetings with his Chinese counterpart. Such summits helped stabilize U.S.-Soviet relations for two decades. Today, U.S.-Chinese relations are in the same league. The next president should act accordingly." (*Wall Street Journal*, November 6, 1996)

"a nonpartisan, nonprofit think tank" (*Wall Street Journal*, November 26, 1996)

## POLITICAL ORIENTATION

# DataCenter (1977)

1904 Franklin Street
Suite 900
Oakland, California 94612
Phone: (510) 835-4692
Fax: (510) 835-3017
Toll-free: (800) 735-3741
Internet: datacenter@datacenter.org *or*
http://www.igc.org/datacenter

| | |
|---|---|
| **PURPOSE** | "To promote human rights, social and economic justice, and peace by providing information services in support of domestic and international progressive organizing, advocacy, policy development, and educational efforts." |
| **STAFF** | 12 total; plus 5 part-time; 10 volunteers; 3 interns |
| **DIRECTOR** | Fred Goff, executive director. Goff is cofounder of the Data Center. Previously he cofounded and served as president of the North American Congress on Latin America (NACLA). Prior to founding NACLA, Goff worked with the American Friends Service Committee and served as coordinator of the Commission on Free Elections in the Dominican Republic. He received a B.A. in history from Stanford University. |
| **TAX STATUS** | 501(c)(3) |
| **BUDGET** | 1997—$599,933<br>1998—$673,594<br>Proposed 1999—Unavailable |
| **FUNDING SOURCES** | Foundation grants, 57 percent; research services, 15 percent; individuals, 12 percent; publications, 9 percent; special events/projects, 6 percent; other, 1 percent |
| **SCOPE** | Members: 500 individuals; 50 organizations<br>Branches/chapters: N/A<br>Affiliates: N/A |
| **PAC** | None |

| | |
|---|---|
| ◆ Clipping service ◆ Information clearinghouse ◆ Internet (Web sites [http://www.igc.org/culturewatch *or* http://www.igc.org/isla]) ◆ Library (open to the public) ◆ Online searches ◆ Publications ◆ Research ◆ Training and technical assistance | *METHOD OF* *OPERATION* |
| Foreign and domestic economic, political, and social issues | *CURRENT* *CONCERNS* |
| *The Right to Know* (4 volumes) | *PUBLICATIONS* |
| *CultureWatch* (monthly) <br> *Information Services Latin America* (monthly service) <br> *NewsNotes* (6 times per year) | *NEWSLETTER* |
| None | *CONFERENCES* |
| Dan Geiger, chair; Natalia López, vice chair; Amina Hassan, secretary/treasurer; Fred Goff; president <br><br> Other board members: <br> ◆ Judith Barish ◆ Kevin Cartwright ◆ Isao Fujimoto ◆ Susan Goetz ◆ Eric Leenson ◆ Brenda Payton ◆ Harry Strharsky ◆ Peter Wiley | *BOARD OF* *DIRECTORS* |
| Unavailable | *EFFECTIVENESS* |
| Unavailable | *POLITICAL* *ORIENTATION* |

# Federation for American Immigration Reform (FAIR) (1979)

1666 Connecticut Avenue, NW
Suite 400
Washington, D.C. 20009
Phone: (202) 328-7004
Fax: (202) 387-3447
Internet: fair@fairus.org *or* http://www.fairus.org

| | |
|---|---|
| *PURPOSE* | "To end illegal immigration and reduce legal immigration to numbers consistent with the national interest." |
| *STAFF* | 22 total—15 professional; 7 support; plus 3 interns; 2 part-time |
| *DIRECTOR* | Daniel Stein, executive director. Stein joined the Federation for American Immigration Reform (FAIR) in 1982 and has led the organization since 1988. Stein's professional background includes work with the House Select Committee on Narcotics Abuse and Control and the Immigration Reform Law Institute. An attorney, he also has been in private practice. Stein is a graduate of Indiana University and Catholic University of America School of Law. |
| *TAX STATUS* | 501(c)(3) |
| *BUDGET* | 1998—$3.4 million<br>Proposed 1999—$3.6 million |
| *FUNDING SOURCES* | Foundation grants, 60 percent; membership dues, 40 percent |
| *SCOPE* | Members: 70,000 individuals and families<br>Branch: FAIR-California, Los Angeles<br>Affiliates: N/A |
| *PAC* | None |

| | |
|---|---|
| ◆ Advertisements ◆ Conferences/seminars ◆ Congressional testimony ◆ Demonstrations ◆ Grassroots organizing ◆ Immigration Internship Program ◆ International activities ◆ Internet (Databases, electronic bulletin boards, Web site) ◆ Internships ◆ Legislative/regulatory monitoring (federal) ◆ Library/Information Clearinghouse ◆ Litigation ◆ Lobbying (federal, state, and grassroots) ◆ Local/municipal affairs ◆ Media outreach ◆ Polling ◆ Research ◆ Speakers program ◆ Telecommunications services (Hotline: 202-745-2959, mailing lists) | *METHOD OF OPERATION* |
| ◆ Elimination of immigration entitlements for extended family members to end chain of migration ◆ Fraud-resistant worker eligibility documentation ◆ Immigration moratorium for all but essential immigration ◆ Research and public education on the effects of immigration on urban families | *CURRENT CONCERNS* |
| *Crowding out the Future: World Population Growth, U.S. Immigration, and Pressure on Natural Resources*<br>*FAIR Leading Immigration Indicators*<br>*How to Win the Immigration Debate*<br>*The Immigration Dilemma: Avoiding the Tragedy of the Commons*<br>*The Immigration Handbook*<br>*Immigration 2000: The Century of the New American Sweatshop*<br>*A Tale of Ten Cities: Immigration Effects on the Family Environment in American Cities*<br>*Ten Steps to End Illegal Immigration* | *PUBLICATIONS* |
| *FYI* (monthly)<br>*Immigration Report* (monthly) | *NEWSLETTER* |
| Occasional debates, briefings, and conferences | *CONFERENCES* |
| John Tanton, chairman<br><br>Other board members:<br>◆ Nancy Anthony ◆ Sharon Barnes ◆ C. Henry Buhl III ◆ Donald A. Collins ◆ Sarah G. Epstein ◆ Otis Graham Jr. ◆ Janet Harte ◆ Richard D. Lamm ◆ Stephen B. Swensrud ◆ Max Thelen Jr. | *BOARD OF DIRECTORS* |
| "Under a new and sweeping provision of Mexico's citizenship laws, any person born in Mexico or born to a Mexican national who has become a citizen elsewhere may now officially claim dual nationality. The change entitles them to Mexican passports (while keeping their American ones) and broader rights to own property and to work or invest in Mexico, though not to voting rights in Mexican elections. . . .<br>  "There are plenty of critics of dual nationality. | *EFFECTIVENESS* |

" 'I think the scenario describes somebody who is in effect hedging their bets, which I think displays ambivalence about their identification with the United States,' said John L. Martin, special projects director for the Federation for American Immigration Reform, a group based in Washington that favors greater restrictions in immigration. 'I don't think there's any way that that can be seen as healthy for American society.' " (*New York Times,* April 14, 1998)

"When the U.S. Commission on Immigration Reform issued its final report on Tuesday, Dan Stein, executive director of the Federation for American Immigration Reform, stood ready to comment. Responding to a recommendation that the U.S. citizenship oath be modified to strike antiquated words like 'potentate,' Mr. Stein told the Los Angeles Times, 'If the oath of [allegiance] is too hard for the immigrants to understand . . . we're admitting the wrong immigrants.'

"In the debate over immigration policy, no single group has received more attention than FAIR, a Washington-based nonprofit that claims a membership of 70,000. For close to 20 years, in books, monographs, op-eds and thousands of newspaper stories, FAIR has made the case for tighter national borders.

"Founded in 1979 by a Michigan ophthalmologist named John Tanton, FAIR has from its inception been heavily influenced by the now-discredited theories of Thomas Malthus, an 18th-century English clergyman who predicted that the world's food supply would soon fail to keep pace with its rising population. During the 1970s, Dr. Tanton, now FAIR's chairman, did his part to reduce world population by founding a local Planned Parenthood chapter and running the group Zero Population Growth. With the birthrate of native-born Americans declining, however, Dr. Tanton says he soon realized that the key to population control was reducing immigration. Unless America's borders are sealed, Dr. Tanton explained to the *Detroit Free Press* this March, the country will be overrun with people 'defecating and creating garbage and looking for jobs.' To this day, FAIR's 'guiding principles' state that 'the United States should make greater efforts to encourage population control.' " (*Wall Street Journal,* October 2, 1997)

"[Spence] Abraham, an upstart first-termer from Michigan, has committed the sin of becoming chairman of the Senate's immigration subcommittee. This is more dangerous than it sounds. He replaces Alan Simpson, now retired, in what could be the biggest policy shift since Madonna became a mother. Mr. Abraham is courting the wrath of the anti-immigration lobby, which thought it had captured the GOP. . . .

"Enter Mr. Abraham, who wants to restore some Ellis Island perspective to the immigration fight. 'The debate over the last few years has been about what's wrong with immigration,' says this grandson of Lebanese immigrants. 'We shouldn't do anything more about legal immigration until we have a fuller debate on the benefits of immigration.'

"The senator got a taste of the politics of this message, pro and con, when he took it to Silicon Valley last week. At Cypress Semiconductor, he met high-tech entrepreneurs—from Sun Microsystems, 3Com, Cisco—who told him they need immigrants in America to compete around the world. Cypress chief T.J. Rodgers, who said 40% of his top management is foreign born, hailed the senator as 'a hero of freedom.' "

"Outside, however, Mr. Abraham was denounced in a demonstration promoted by the Federation for American Immigration Reform. FAIR's idea of 'reform' is to stop immigration just about cold. Its 90 or so picketers carried such inspirational signs as 'Close the Border,' 'Drug Cartel' and 'Immigrants Smuggle Drugs.'. . ." (*Wall Street Journal*, January 24, 1997)

## POLITICAL ORIENTATION

"In the debate over immigration policy, no single group has received more attention than FAIR, a Washington-based nonprofit that claims a membership of 70,000. For close to 20 years, in books, monographs, op-eds and thousands of newspaper stories, FAIR has made the case for tighter national borders. And while the group's goal seems clear enough—to curtail immigration into the U.S.—its ideology is harder to pin down. FAIR's supporters include both the conservative magazine *National Review* and former Colorado Gov. Richard Lamm, a Democrat; Pat Buchanan as well as Eugene McCarthy. Where does FAIR stand politically? It's hard to say, says Mr. Stein: 'Immigration's weird. It has weird politics.'. . .

"There are reasonable critics of immigration, but Dan Stein is not one of them. Which makes it all the more puzzling that a number of otherwise sober-minded conservatives seem to be making common cause with Mr. Stein and FAIR. . . .

"FAIR itself has made a conscious play for the support of social conservatives, running ads that blame immigration for 'multiculturalism,' 'multilingualism,' 'increasing ethnic tension' and 'middle-class flight.' Mr. Stein claims that many immigrants are left-wing ideologues, making conservatives FAIR's logical allies." (*Wall Street Journal*, October 2, 1997)

# Human Rights Watch (1978)

350 Fifth Avenue
34th Floor
New York, New York 10018
Phone: (212) 290-4700
Fax: (212) 736-1300

1522 K Street, NW
Washington, D.C. 20005
Phone: (202) 371-6592
Fax: (202) 371-0124

Internet: hrwatchnyc@hrw.org *or* hrwatchdc@hrw.org *or*
http://www.hrw.org

**PURPOSE**

"Dedicated to protecting the human rights of people around the world . . . to prevent discrimination, to uphold political freedom, to protect people from inhumane conduct in wartime, and to bring offenders to justice. We investigate and expose human rights violations and hold abusers accountable."

**STAFF**

127 total; plus 20–30 interns

**DIRECTOR**

Kenneth Roth, executive director. Before becoming executive director of Human Rights Watch in 1993, Roth served as its deputy director from 1987 to 1993. He formerly worked as a prosecutor and in private practice as a litigator. Roth writes extensively on human rights issues and is a member of the Council on Foreign Relations. He is a graduate of Brown University and Yale Law School.

**TAX STATUS**

501(c)(3)

**BUDGET**

1998—$14.3 million
Proposed 1999—Unavailable

**FUNDING SOURCES**

Unavailable

**SCOPE**

Members: 7,000 individuals

Branches/chapters: Offices in Brussels, Hong Kong, London, Los Angeles, Moscow, Rio de Janeiro, Saigon, and Tbilisi, Republic of Georgia

Affiliate: Article 19

None

♦ Awards program ♦ Coalition forming ♦ Fellowships ♦ Films/video/ audiotapes ♦ International activities ♦ International film festival ♦ Internet (Web site) ♦ Internships ♦ Legislative/regulatory monitoring (federal and state) ♦ Library/information clearinghouse ♦ Litigation ♦ Media outreach ♦ Research

*METHOD OF OPERATION*

♦ Abolition of landmines ♦ Academic freedom and freedom of expression ♦ Forced trafficking of women and girls ♦ Labor rights and migrant workers ♦ Prison conditions ♦ Use of children as soldiers ♦ War crimes prosecutions in Bosnia and Rwanda ♦ Women's and children's rights

*CURRENT CONCERNS*

The following is a list of sample publications:

*Bearing the Brunt of the Asian Economic Crisis: The Impact of Labor Rights on Migrant Workers in Asia*

*Bosnia and Hercegovina: "A Closed, Dark Place": Past and Present Human Rights Abuses in Foca*

*Bosnia and Hercegovina: Beyond Restraint—Politics and the Policing Agenda of the United Nations International Police Task Force*

*Cambodia: Fair Elections Not Possible*

*Clinton Administration Policy and Human Rights in Africa*

*Justice for All?: An Analysis of the Human Rights Provisions of the 1998 Northern Ireland Peace Agreement*

*Macedonia: Police Violence in Macedonia*

*"Prohibited Persons": Abuse of Undocumented Migrants, Asylum Seeking Refugees in South Africa*

*Public Scandals—Sexual Orientation and Criminal Law in Romania*

*Republic of Uzbekistan—Crackdown in the Farghona Valley: Arbitrary Arrests and Religious Discrimination*

*Russia—Too Little, Too Late: State Response to Violence Against Women*

*Shielded from Justice: Police Brutality and Accountability in the United States*

*Sowing Terror: Articulates Against Civilians in Sierra Leone*

*Tajikistan—Leninabad: Crackdown in the North*

*Zambia: No Model for Democracy: Continuing Human Rights Violations*

Other publications focus on over 100 countries and regions

*PUBLICATIONS*

*Human Rights Watch Update* (two times per year)

*NEWSLETTER*

None

*CONFERENCES*

## BOARD OF DIRECTORS

## EFFECTIVENESS

". . . Over the course of a month, government delegates from around the world will attempt to reach a final agreement on the setting up of an International Criminal Court.

"The ICC would create an independent body, complete with elected judges and prosecutors, entrusted with the task of indicting individuals suspected of genocide, serious war crimes, and crimes against humanity. . . .

"Whenever multilateral bodies go about their work—whether it is the UN or the International Monetary Fund—they inevitably fall victim to the whims of individual nations worried about questions of sovereignty or funding. Nowhere is this tension between sovereignty and multilateralism more evident than in America, not least because Washington consistently finds itself galling to allow its influence as the world's only superpower to be filtered away by international bodies. . . .

"The US, however, is pushing hard to bring the final version of the ICC under the remit of the Security Council, which would review cases before the ICC prosecutors could go ahead. Washington also believes individual states should be given the chance to veto prosecutions it does not want. . . .

"Human Rights Watch (HRW), which is pushing for a fully independent ICC, says: 'If only the Security Council and the states can bring cases before the ICC, the court's docket will reflect the political biases of the world's strongest states." (*South China Morning Post*, June 11, 1998)

"Connecticut Friends of Bosnia, The Greenwich YWCA and Human Rights Watch will present 'Arrest Now: An Evening of Action on Behalf of Bosnian Women.'. . .

" 'Arrest Now' is part of a national campaign by Human Rights Watch and the YWCA of the USA to highlight war crimes against Bosnian Women and the failure of the international community to bring to justice those responsible. . . .

"Pictures of war survivors and those still currently being held captive will be posted to put a human face on the tragedy. One of those 'faces' will be a survivor of Srebrenica, the so-called United Nations 'safe haven,' which was overrun by Serb nationalistic forces in the summer of 1995. . . ." (*Greenwich Time*, May 12, 1998)

"Human Rights Watch (HRW) is among the few agencies that campaign to end gross violations of children's rights. Under its Children's Rights Project, HRW has investigated children's rights violations in Northern Ireland, India, Bulgaria, Sudan, Jamaica and the United States. . . ." (*The People*, April 15–22, 1998)

Unavailable

# *POLITICAL ORIENTATION*

# Institute for International Economics (1981)

11 Dupont Circle, NW
Suite 620
Washington, D.C. 20036
Phone: (202) 328-9000
Fax: (202) 328-5432
Internet: http://www.iie.com

**PURPOSE**

"Devoted solely to analyzing important international economic issues and developing and communicating potential new approaches for dealing with them. The Institute's studies generally look ahead one to three years; they do not address long-term, theoretical problems."

**STAFF**

39 total—23 professional; 16 support

**DIRECTOR**

C. Fred Bergsten, director. Bergsten has been director of the Institute for International Economics (IIE) since its founding. He was previously assistant secretary of the treasury for international affairs, assistant for international economic affairs at the National Security Council, and a senior fellow at the Carnegie Endowment for International Peace, the Brookings Institution, and the Council on Foreign Relations. Bergsten is chairman of the Competitiveness Policy Council and represents the United States in a working group of the Asia-Pacific Economic Cooperation organization. He serves on many public policy councils and boards and is the author of twenty-two books.

**TAX STATUS**

501(c)(3)

**BUDGET**

1998—Unavailable
Proposed 1999—Unavailable

**FUNDING SOURCES**

Unavailable

**SCOPE**

Members: N/A
Branches/chapters: N/A
Affiliates: N/A

None

## METHOD OF OPERATION

♦ Book publishing ♦ Conferences/seminars ♦ Congressional testimony ♦ International activities ♦ Internet (Web site) ♦ Media outreach ♦ Research ♦ Speakers program

## CURRENT CONCERNS

♦ Asia-Pacific Economic Cooperation (APEC) ♦ Asian financial crisis ♦ China in the world economy ♦ European Community ♦ Exchange rates ♦ Foreign direct investment ♦ Free trade ♦ International financial markets ♦ International economic institutions ♦ International macroeconomic and exchange rate policies ♦ Japan in the world economy ♦ Korean unification ♦ Pacific Basin trade ♦ Regional trade agreements ♦ Taxes, trade, and foreign investments ♦ Third World debt ♦ Trade and labor standards ♦ Trade and wage inequality ♦ U.S.-Japanese economic relations ♦ U.S. trade deficit and its global impact ♦ U.S. trade policy and the international trading system ♦ World Trade Organization

## PUBLICATIONS

*African Economic Reform: The External Dimension*
*Agricultural Trade Policy: Completing the Reform*
*America in the World Economy: A Strategy for the 1990s*
*American Trade Politics*
*Asia-Pacific Fusion: Japan's Role in APEC*
*The Case for an International Banking Standard*
*China in the World Economy*
*Competition Policies for the Global Economy*
*Cooperating with Europe's Monetary Union*
*The Crawling Band as an Exchange Rate Regime*
*Crawling Bands: Lessons from Chile, Colombia, and Israel*
*Currencies and Politics in the United States, Germany, and Japan*
*Currency Convertibility in Eastern Europe*
*Does Foreign Exchange Intervention Work?*
*The Dynamics of Korean Economic Development*
*Economic Integration of the Korean Peninsula*
*The Economic Opening of Eastern Europe*
*Economic Policy Coordination: Requiem or Prologue?*
*Economic Sanctions Reconsidered*
*The Economics of Global Warming*
*Estimating Equilibrium Exchange Rates*
*The Exchange Rate System and the IMF: A Modest Agenda*
*Financial Services Liberalization in the WTO*
*Flying High: Liberalizing Civil Aviation in the Asia Pacific*
*Foreign Direct Investment*
*From Soviet Disunion to Eastern Economic Community?*
*Fundamental Tax Reform and Border Tax Adjustments*
*Global Competition Policy*
*Global Corporations and National Governments*
*Global Economic Leadership and the Group of Seven*
*Global Telecom Talks: A Trillion Dollar Deal*
*Greening the GATT: Trade, Environment, and the Future*

*Has Globalization Gone Too Far?*
*Improving Trade Policy Reviews in the World Trade Organization*
*International Debt and the Stability of the World Economy*
*International Debt Reexamined*
*Japan in the World Economy*
*Korea in the World Economy*
*Korea-United States Cooperation in the New World Order*
*The Korea-United States Economic Relationship*
*Latin American Adjustment: How Much Has Happened?*
*Managing Official Export Credits: The Quest for a Global Regime*
*Managing the World Economy: Fifty Years after Bretton Woods*
*Measuring the Costs of Protection in Japan*
*Measuring the Costs of Protection in the United States*
*Measuring the Costs of Visible Protection in Korea*
*NAFTA: An Assessment*
*The National Economic Council: A Work in Progress*
*North American Free Trade: Issues and Recommendations*
*The Political Economy of Korea-United States Cooperation*
*The Political Economy of Policy Reform*
*Predicting External Imbalances for the United States and Japan*
*Private Capital Flows to Emerging Markets after the Mexican Crisis*
*The Progress of Policy Reform in Latin America*
*Reciprocity and Retaliation in U.S. Trade Policy*
*Reconcilable Differences? United States-Japan Economic Conflict*
*Regional Trading Blocs in the World Economic System*
*Restarting Fast Track*
*Reviving the European Union*
*Sizing Up U.S. Export Disincentives*
*Standards and APEC: An Action Agenda*
*Summitry in the Americas: A Progress Report*
*Sustaining the Asia Pacific Miracle: Environmental Protection and Economic Integration*
*The Trading System after the Uruguay Round*
*Trade and Income Distribution*
*Trade and Migration: NAFTA and Agriculture*
*Transatlantic Trade: A Strategic Agenda*
*Unfinished Business: Telecommunications after the Uruguay Round*
*The Uruguay Round: An Assessment*
*Western Hemisphere Economic Integration*
*What Role for Currency Boards*
*Whither APEC? Progress to Date and Agenda for the Future*
*Who's Bashing Whom? Trade Conflict in High-Technology Industries*
*Why Exports Really Matter! and Why Exports Matter More!*
*Working Papers on Asia Pacific Economic Cooperation*
*The World Trading System: Challenges Ahead*
*WTO 2000: Setting the Course for World Trade*

## NEWSLETTER

None

## CONFERENCES

Conferences and study group discussion meetings are held 2–3 times a month by invitation

"India surprised the international community again by conducting two more nuclear tests, and the U.S. made good on its threat to impose stringent economic sanctions on New Delhi. . . .

"As a measure of how tough the penalties would be on India, the Washington-based Institute for International Economics calculates that if other allies join the U.S. in punishing India, the impact on the Indian economy could total as much as $4 billion. That is potentially a big blow to a nation that imports about $36 billion in goods and services each year." (*Wall Street Journal*, May 14, 1998)

"The other shoe may be dropping in Asia. One worry has always been the possibility that the economic crisis would trigger social and political unrest, which could then deepen and prolong the economic crisis. This may now be happening. Indonesia was rocked last week by riots triggered in part by huge increases in gasoline prices; and in South Korea, strikes loom over higher unemployment. These bad omens ought to dispel the impression—common in the United States—that the worst is certainly over.

" 'People in Asia see this as their Great Depression,' says economist Fred Bergsten of the Institute for International Economics in Washington. 'We don't understand that.' Reduced to its essentials, the plight of Asia's ailing economies is simple. Having overborrowed abroad—mostly in dollars—they now need to repay their loans. They have to cut economic growth and imports, which use scarce foreign exchange; and they have to earn more foreign exchange by raising exports. The International Monetary Fund tries to cushion the process with more loans but insists that countries adopt unpopular reforms and embrace economic austerity." (*Washington Post*, May 13, 1998)

"The Commerce Department yesterday tallied the 1997 U.S. trade deficit at $113.75 billion, the highest in nearly a decade—and if that sounds big, just wait until the Asian financial crisis starts to wreak its effects on this year's trade flows. . . .

" 'The loss of exports should be viewed with extra weight, because exports are in our most dynamic sectors, with the most stable jobs and best paying jobs,' said J. David Richardson, an economist at the Institute for International Economics in Washington, who authored a study showing that jobs associated with exports pay an average of 15 percent more than other jobs. 'So we're losing quality as well as quantity.'

"But falling exports and a rising trade gap shouldn't pose a serious threat to U.S. economic prosperity, many economists say. Job losses in, say, a factory producing machinery for sale in Asia can be offset by job gains elsewhere in the U.S. economy, which has continued to generate employment at a robust pace—as Clinton administration officials were at pains to point out yesterday." (*Washington Post*, February 20, 1998)

"The Almighty Dollar is back. With Asian financial markets in turmoil, Europe in an economic funk and the price of just about everything falling around the world, it seems everyone wants to have and hold dollars. . . .

"Morris Goldstein, a senior fellow at the Institute for International Economics, predicts that by making imports cheaper and exports more expensive, the recent run-up in the value of the dollar is almost certain to drive up the U.S. trade deficit—from $180 billion last year to as high as $300 billion in 1998. And if history is any guide, Goldstein says, such a deficit will set the stage for a sharp reversal in a year or two when Asian markets stabilize, economic growth revives in Europe and global investors decide it's safe to return to their own currencies.

"In the real economy, that kind of volatility can translate into economic dislocation as jobs and profits are shifted from one sector of the economy to another as a consequence." (*Washington Post*, January 15, 1998)

"During the past four years, the American economy has enjoyed a robust expansion with low unemployment, greater international competitiveness and modest inflation. Unfortunately, the economy's expansion has failed to reverse two disturbing long-run trends: stagnant or falling real earnings for the majority of workers and increasing income inequality among workers and households. Although average real earnings for non-supervisory production workers increased slightly in 1996 (a trend that is continuing in 1997), they remain far below their postwar peaks of the mid-1970s. In addition, the gap between rich and poor households is much larger than it was 20 years ago.

"Much of the increasing inequality in family incomes has its origins in the marked increase in inequality of labor earnings. According to the Institute for International Economics, during the past two decades the ratio of wages of the top 10 percent of workers to those of the bottom 10 percent rose from about 360 percent to about 525 percent for men and from about 380 percent to about 430 percent for women.

"Behind these yawning gaps are significant increases in wage differentials by education, age and occupation. To make matters worse and even more difficult to explain, so-called within-group inequality—that is, differentials in earnings for workers with the same educational, age and occupational characteristics—also has risen sharply." (*Washington Post*, July 9, 1997)

# POLITICAL ORIENTATION

Unavailable

# Peace Action (1957)

1819 H Street, NW
Suite 420
Washington, D.C. 20006
Phone: (202) 862-9740
Fax: (202) 862-9762
Internet: http://www.webcom.com/peaceact

| | |
|---|---|
| "Committed to organizing a citizen movement in favor of eliminating war and violence as acceptable means of resolving conflict at home and abroad." | *PURPOSE* |
| 14 total—12 professional; 2 support; plus volunteers; 1–3 interns per semester | *STAFF* |
| Gordon Clark, executive director. Before becoming executive director of Peace Action (formerly SANE/FREEZE) in January of 1996, Clark was the executive director of New Jersey Peace Action for five years. | *DIRECTOR* |
| 501(c)(4) | *TAX STATUS* |
| 1998—$900,000<br>Proposed 1999—Unavailable | *BUDGET* |
| Unavailable | *FUNDING SOURCES* |
| Members: 50,000 individuals<br>Branches/chapters: 28 state organizations; 100 local chapters<br>Affiliates: Peace Action Education Fund, a 501(c)(3) organization | *SCOPE* |
| Peace Action Political Action Committee | *PAC* |

| METHOD OF OPERATION | ◆ Advertisements ◆ Awards program ◆ Campaign contributions ◆ Coalition forming ◆ Conferences/seminars ◆ Congressional voting analysis ◆ Demonstrations ◆ Direct action ◆ Electoral politics ◆ Grassroots organizing ◆ International activities ◆ Internet (Web site) ◆ Legislative/regulatory monitoring (federal and state) ◆ Lobbying (federal, state, and grassroots) ◆ Media outreach ◆ Speakers program ◆ Voting records |
|---|---|
| CURRENT CONCERNS | ◆ "Code of Conduct" on U.S. foreign arms sales ◆ Nuclear weapons abolishment ◆ Nuclear weapons: Comprehensive Test Ban Treaty ◆ Reducing U.S. and worldwide military spending |
| PUBLICATIONS | *Congressional Voting Record 1998*<br><br>Also publishes fact sheets and action alerts |
| NEWSLETTER | *Peace Action* (quarterly) |
| CONFERENCES | National Congress (annual) |
| BOARD OF DIRECTORS | ◆ Olivia Abelson ◆ Nathaniel Batchelder ◆ Lois Booth ◆ Les Breeding ◆ Steven Brion-Meisels ◆ Beth Broadway ◆ Bridgette Burge ◆ Acie Byrd ◆ Lynn Cheatum ◆ Brian Corr ◆ Peter J. Davies ◆ Gary Ferdman ◆ Al Fishman ◆ JoAnn Fuller ◆ Phyllis Gilbert ◆ Addison Goodson ◆ Check Johnson ◆ James C. Johnson ◆ Uric Johnson ◆ Lauri Kallio ◆ Brian Keaney ◆ Michael Keller ◆ Pat Kenoyer ◆ Jay Leonhardy ◆ Judy Lerner ◆ Dan Levant ◆ Gloria Lockett ◆ Colby Lowe ◆ Don Macaulay ◆ Rania Masri ◆ Paul McNeil Jr. ◆ Tom Morse ◆ Sonya Ostrom ◆ Rosalie Paul ◆ Clayton Ramey ◆ Nancy Rising ◆ Marianna Rivera ◆ Robert J. Schwartz ◆ Glen Stassen ◆ William Towe ◆ Carole Watson ◆ Cora Weiss |
| EFFECTIVENESS | "Well, times change, years pass and [campaign guru Steve] Rabinowitz, now running his own company, is hired to work for an organization called Fourth Freedom Forum. The forum, along with another group called Peace Action, opposes U.S. policy in Iraq. The forum hired Rabinowitz to work up full-page ads against a possible U.S. airstrike and to advertise in Columbus, Ohio, for protesters to go to the arena where Secretary of State Madeleine K. Albright, Defense Secretary William S. Cohen and national security adviser Samuel R. 'Sandy' Berger appeared to sell the hard line.<br><br>"Rabinowitz insists that while he gave opponents some 'hard-hitting sample questions' to expose the weaknesses in administration policy, 'I had nothing to do with their being heckled. I was mortified when I saw the heckling.' |

"Asked about rumors he got troublemakers into the arena, he said opponents may have gotten in, but the forum and Peace Action advised against heckling. Besides, 'any [person] off the street could get people in the way the White House organized it,' he said." (*Washington Post*, February 25, 1998)

Unavailable

# POLITICAL ORIENTATION

# Physicians for Social Responsibility (1961)

1101 14th Street, NW
Suite 700
Washington, D.C. 20005
Phone: (202) 898-0150
Fax: (202) 898-0172
Internet: http://www.psr.org

**PURPOSE**

"Committed to the elimination of nuclear and other weapons of mass destruction, the achievement of a sustainable environment and the reduction of violence and its causes."

**STAFF**

17 total—12 professional; 5 support; plus 3 interns and 2 contract workers

**DIRECTOR**

Robert K. Musil, executive director. Prior to joining Physicians for Social Responsibility (PSR), Musil was executive director of the Professionals' Coalition for Nuclear Arms Control. He has been a leader in national advocacy organizations since 1971. Musil writes articles, lectures, and produces documentaries for radio and television on military and foreign affairs. A former captain in the U.S. Army, Musil holds degrees from Yale and Northwestern.

**TAX STATUS**

501(c)(3)

**BUDGET**

1998—$2 million
Proposed 1999—$2 million

**FUNDING SOURCES**

Membership dues and individual contributions, 51 percent; foundation grants, 44 percent; other, 5 percent

**SCOPE**

Members: 15,000 health care professionals and concerned citizens
Branches/chapters: 70 chapters
Affiliates: N/A

**PAC**

None

◆ Congressional testimony ◆ Congressional voting analysis ◆ Demonstrations ◆ Direct action ◆ Electoral politics ◆ Grassroots organizing ◆ Internet (Electronic bulletin boards, Web site) ◆ Legislative/regulatory monitoring ◆ Lobbying (federal) ◆ Media outreach ◆ Participation in regulatory proceedings (federal and state)

◆ Environment: air and water quality, pesticides, lead ◆ Nuclear: DOE, nuclear testing, nuclear waste storage ◆ Violence: gun control, violence in society

*Asthma and the Role of Air Pollution*
*Cancer and the Environment*
*Children and Lead*
*Environmental Pollutants & Health*
*Health Research Bulletin: Summer '97*
*Pesticides and Children*
*PSR Monitor: Comprehensive Test Ban Treaty*
*PSR Monitor: CTBT Moves into Senate Debate*
*PSR Monitor on Climate Change*
*PSR Monitor on Persistent Organochlorine Pesticides*
*Putting the Lid on Dioxin*

PSR also publishes fact sheets and brochures

*PSR Reports* (membership newsletter 4 times a year)

National biennial conference and others on ad hoc basis

Robert K. Musil, executive director; Andrew Harris, president; Thomas E. Hobbins, president-elect

Other board members:
◆ Sidney Alexander ◆ Beth Bowen ◆ Ralph J. Cazort ◆ Ted Conna ◆ Eric Dover ◆ Jefferson Dickey ◆ John J. Downes ◆ Cathey Falvo ◆ Paul Fisher ◆ Lee Francis ◆ Howard Frumkin ◆ Arvin Gee ◆ H. Jack Geiger ◆ Robert Gould ◆ Jimmy Hara ◆ Molly Tan Hayden ◆ Ira Helfand ◆ Daniel Kerlinsky ◆ Harry L. Keyserling ◆ Philip Landrigan ◆ Irvin Mauss ◆ Michael McCally ◆ Arthur Milholland ◆ Amelia Randolph ◆ Karin Ringler ◆ David Rush ◆ Abbey Strauss ◆ James Trombold ◆ Peter Wilk

"... [T]hings changed last week, when India detonated five nuclear bombs and its prime minister proclaimed, 'We mean business.' With Pakistan potentially in line to test bombs, too, Americans have been rudely reawakened to the possibility of accidental annihilation.

"This time, though, the fear has a new twist. No longer a face-off between superpowers, the nuclear threat now originates in less familiar countries whose leaders are little-known in the U.S. It makes anxious people feel especially out of control. . . .

"Feeding the anxiety is a paper published last month in the *New England Journal of Medicine* by members of Physicians for Social Responsibility, a disarmament group. The article, widely reported in the mainstream press, depicts a doomsday scenario of accidental nuclear war. 'There's nothing like a real, live nuclear test,' says Robert K. Musil, the group's executive director, to bring into focus what was once abstract.

"Membership in the physicians' disarmament group has declined to 15,000 from 30,000 in 1985. But over the past week, the phones are ringing 'a lot more,' Mr. Musil says." (*Wall Street Journal*, May 20, 1998)

"Russia's deteriorating control of its nuclear weapons is increasing the danger of an accidental or unauthorized attack on the United States, a Nobel Peace Prize-winning group warned today.

"A dozen missiles fired from a Russian nuclear submarine would kill nearly seven million Americans instantly, and millions more would die from radiation, according to a study conducted under the auspices of Physicians for Social Responsibility, which won the Nobel Peace Prize for its work on nuclear weapons in 1985. The study is to be published tomorrow in *The New England Journal of Medicine*." (*New York Times*, April 30, 1998)

---

# POLITICAL ORIENTATION

"liberal" (*Wall Street Journal*, May 20, 1996)

# TransAfrica (1977)

1744 R Street, NW
Washington, D.C. 20009
Phone: (202) 797-2301
Fax: (202) 797-2382
Internet: transforum@igc.org *or* http://www.igc.org/transafrica

| | |
|---|---|
| "To inform and organize popular opinion in the United States to form a more progressive U.S. foreign policy toward Africa and the Caribbean." | *PURPOSE* |
| Unavailable | *STAFF* |
| Randall Robinson, president. Robinson has headed TransAfrica since its founding in 1977 and has served as executive director of TransAfrica Forum since its inception in 1981. Robinson is a cofounder of the Free South Africa Movement and serves on the board of directors of USA for Africa and the Institute for Policy Studies. He is a member of the Council on Foreign Relations. Robinson earned a B.A. at Virginia Union University and a J.D. from Harvard Law School. | *DIRECTOR* |
| 501(c)(4) | *TAX STATUS* |
| 1998—Unavailable<br>Proposed 1999—Unavailable | *BUDGET* |
| Membership dues, annual benefit dinner, direct mail campaign | *FUNDING SOURCES* |
| Members: More than 40,000 supporters<br>Branches/chapters: N/A<br>Affiliate: TransAfrica Forum (research institute) | *SCOPE* |
| None | *PAC* |
| ♦ Boycotts ♦ Coalition forming ♦ Conferences/seminars ♦ Congressional testimony ♦ Congressional voting analysis ♦ Demonstrations ♦ Direct action ♦ Grassroots organizing ♦ Internet (Web site) ♦ Library/information clearinghouse ♦ Lobbying (federal and grassroots) | *METHOD OF OPERATION* |

## CURRENT CONCERNS

♦ Restoration of democracy in Nigeria ♦ U.S. foreign policy vis-à-vis Africa and the Caribbean

## PUBLICATIONS

None

## NEWSLETTER

*TransAfrica Forum Update*

## CONFERENCES

Annual banquet held in June (Washington, D.C.)

## BOARD OF DIRECTORS

William Lucy, chairman; Randall Robinson, president

Other board members:
♦ John Hurst Adams ♦ Willie Baker ♦ William H. Cosby ♦ Earl Graves ♦ Richard Gordon Hatcher ♦ Dorothy Height ♦ Wade Henderson ♦ Quincy Jones ♦ Ernest Lofton ♦ Pearl Robinson ♦ James Turner ♦ Maxine Waters

## EFFECTIVENESS

"The new Africa Growth and Opportunities Act, which has passed the House but not the Senate, purportedly seeks to wean Africa away from development aid by opening up opportunities for economic self-sufficiency. But the trade opportunities it offers, in such areas as textiles, really are quite limited....

"... Randall Robinson of TransAfrica attacked the new bill as an 'African recolonization act,' saying it would encourage American and European businesses to 'grab the assets' of Africa." (*Wall Street Journal*, March 31, 1998)

"The African Growth and Opportunity Act . . . would allow African textile and apparel makers free access to U.S. markets. Supporters see the textile provision as a boost for African businesses, while U.S. textile workers—a large portion of whom are African-Americans—see it as a threat to their jobs....

"... Randall Robinson, president of the Washington advocacy group TransAfrica and one of the continent's most visible U.S. activists, is actively campaigning against the bill, contending that its requirement that African nations adopt economic reforms leaves them beholden to foreign corporations. 'We do not consider it constructive for the United States to demand via statute solely those policies which make it easier for foreign corporations to function unfettered in African countries,' says Mr. Robinson, an African-American." (*Wall Street Journal*, March 11, 1998)

"As the head of a small, modestly funded organization, TransAfrica's Randall Robinson can claim an impressive record of achievement. Founded in 1977 to press the political establishment on matters concerning Africa and the Caribbean, TransAfrica played a decisive role in leading the U.S. to impose sanctions on South Africa. Under Mr. Robinson's leadership TransAfrica was also instrumental in convincing the Clinton administration to abandon its punitive treatment of refugees fleeing from Haiti, then in the grip of the murderous gang that had overthrown the elected president, Jean-Bertrand Aristide." (*Wall Street Journal*, February 9, 1998)

Unavailable

## POLITICAL ORIENTATION

# Union of Concerned Scientists (1969)

2 Brattle Square
Cambridge, Massachusetts 02238
Phone: (617) 547-5552
Fax: (617) 864-9405

1616 P Street, NW
Suite 310
Washington, D.C. 20036
Phone: (202) 332-0900
Fax: (202) 332-0905

Internet: http://www.ucsusa.org

| | |
|---|---|
| **PURPOSE** | "Combines scientific research with citizen advocacy to ensure a clean, healthy environment and safer world." |
| **STAFF** | 57 total—47 professional; 10 support; plus 10 part-time and volunteers |
| **DIRECTOR** | Howard C. Ris, Jr., executive director. Before becoming executive director of the Union of Concerned Scientists (UCS) in 1984, Ris headed UCS's Nuclear Arms Program. He also has worked for the New England River Basins Commission and the Massachusetts Executive Office of Environmental Affairs. |
| **TAX STATUS** | 501(c)(3) |
| **BUDGET** | 1998—$5 million<br>Proposed 1999—Unavailable |
| **FUNDING SOURCES** | Foundations, 49 percent; general support, 18 percent; capital campaign, 17 percent; major donors, 10 percent; other, 6 percent |
| **SCOPE** | Members: 70,000 individuals<br>Branch/chapter: Berkeley, California<br>Affiliates: N/A |
| **PAC** | None |
| **METHOD OF OPERATION** | ♦ Congressional testimony ♦ Films/video/audiotapes ♦ Grassroots organizing ♦ Internet (Web site) ♦ Legislative/regulatory monitoring (federal and state) ♦ Lobbying (federal, state, and grassroots) ♦ Media outreach ♦ Participation in regulatory proceedings (federal and state) ♦ Policy analysis ♦ Research ♦ Speakers program |

◆ Biotechnology ◆ International conflict ◆ Global warming ◆ Nuclear power safety ◆ Renewable, safe, and cost-effective energy technologies ◆ Sustainable agriculture ◆ Transportation policy ◆ Weapons proliferation

*A Small Price to Pay: U.S. Action to Curb Global Warming is Feasible and Affordable*
*The Ecological Risks of Engineered Crops*
*Keeping the Earth: Religious and Scientific Perspectives on the Environment* (video)
*Meeting the Challenges of Population, Environment, and Resources—The Cost of Inaction*
*Money Down the Pipeline: Uncovering the Hidden Subsidies to the Oil Industry*
*Now or Never: Serious New Plans to Save a Natural Pest Control*
*Will North Korea Negotiate Away Its Missles?*
*Zeroing Out Pollution: The Promise of Fuel Cell Vehicles*

Also offers briefing papers, brochures, posters, and videos

*Nucleus* (quarterly)
*Gene Exchange* (quarterly)

Sponsors periodic conferences and workshops, including regional conferences on energy issues

Henry W. Kendall, chair; Kurt Gottfried, vice chair

Other members:
◆ Peter A. Bradford ◆ Sallie Chisholm ◆ Thomas Eisner ◆ James A. Fay
◆ James S. Hoyte ◆ Mario Molina ◆ Adele Simmons ◆ Thomas Stone ◆
Ellyn Weiss ◆ Victor F. Weisskopf

"In a report released today called 'The Good, The Bad and The Ugly,' the Union of Concerned Scientists analyzed 10 nuclear plants from across the country and labeled Maryland's only nuclear plant among the 'bad.' The report alleges problems that posed safety risks to plant workers but not to the general public. . . .

"The Union of Concerned Scientists, a nonprofit group that monitors commercial nuclear plants to identify safety risks, analyzed 10 plants between December 1996 and January 1998. The organization . . . gave good reviews to four plants." (*Washington Post*, June 17, 1998)

"The nuclear tests by India and Pakistan have undermined the agreements and assumptions on which efforts to stop the spread of nuclear weapons have been based for the last 30 years, a range of officials, analysts and diplomats say.

"They say the tests have also helped to all but doom prospects this year for Senate approval of the Comprehensive Test Ban Treaty, which the Clinton Administration has made a high priority. . . .

"Ten prominent members of the Union of Concerned Scientists—including Adm. William Crowe, former Chairman of the Joint Chiefs of Staff; Hans Bethe, the Nobel Prize-winning physicist; and Herbert York, a former founding director of the Livermore National Laboratories—sent letters to the Senate urging action on the treaty now." (*New York Times*, June 3, 1998)

"The Energy Department is funding research and development it hopes will lead to commercial production of . . . biomass ethanol from crops [other than corn]. . . .

"One good prospect, according to Paul Jefferiss, energy program director of the Union of Concerned Scientists, is switch grass. . . .

"The Union of Concerned Scientists is also excited about blends of ethanol and gasoline that are 85 percent alcohol, in contrast to the more widely available 10 percent ethanol blend. But the higher percentage blend, which is better for the environment, requires engine modification, while the 10 percent blend can be used in existing combustion engines." (*Washington Post*, May 6, 1998)

"Northeast Utilities' three big Millstone nuclear reactors . . . are shut because of problems including the overloading of a spent-fuel cooling pool and the harassment of workers who raised safety concerns. . . .

". . . Last week the Union of Concerned Scientists, which initially helped raise many of the safety concerns, charged the [Nuclear Regulatory Commission] staff has a bias toward recommending a restart. In a letter to the commissioners, the lobbying group asserted the staff lacks proper concern for a myriad of nagging technical questions, such as whether cooling pumps would operate during an accident. The letter states,' . . . after a supposedly extensive readiness effort by NU, [the problems are] truly alarming.' The NRC says it will consider the letter." (*Wall Street Journal*, January 26, 1998)

"Exhausted and bitterly divided delegates to the U.N. climate summit reached a historic accord today, agreeing to substantial cuts in emissions of greenhouse gases among industrialized countries but leaving until next year the contentious issue of whether and how the world's poorer nations would participate. . . .

" 'This is a modest but significant step forward in what will be a long-term battle to protect the Earth's climate system,' said Alden Meyer, of the Union of Concerned Scientists. . . . 'The alternative—collapse and gridlock—would have been a disaster.' " (*Washington Post*, December 11, 1997)

## POLITICAL ORIENTATION

"a watchdog group. . . . considered a neutral observer by the [Nuclear Regulatory Commission]" (*Washington Post*, June 17, 1998)

"an independent environmental advocacy group" (*Washington Post*, December 11, 1997)

# The Washington Institute for Near East Policy (1985)

1828 L Street, NW
Suite 1050
Washington, D.C. 20036
Phone: (202) 452-0650
Fax: (202) 223-5364
Internet: http://www.washingtoninstitute.org

"To develop and advance a balanced and realistic understanding of U.S. national interest in the Near East."

**PURPOSE**

20 total; plus 5 part-time

**STAFF**

Robert Satloff, executive director. A member of the Washington Institute for Near East Policy since 1985, Satloff is a frequent writer and commentator on Islamic politics and Palestinian and Jordanian affairs. A professional lecturer at Johns Hopkins' School of Advanced and International Studies, Satloff holds a bachelor's degree from Duke University, a master's degree from Harvard University, and a doctorate from Oxford University.

**DIRECTOR**

501(c)(3)

**TAX STATUS**

1998—Unavailable
Proposed 1996—Unavailable

**BUDGET**

Private donations, publication sales, and foundation grants

**FUNDING SOURCES**

Members: N/A
Branches/chapters: N/A
Affiliates: N/A

**SCOPE**

None

**PAC**

| | |
|---|---|
| *METHOD OF OPERATION* | ♦ Research ♦ Telecommunication services (fax broadcasts: *PeaceWatch* and *PolicyWatch*) |
| *CURRENT CONCERNS* | U.S. interests in the Middle East |
| *PUBLICATIONS* | Publishes audiotapes, conference proceedings, policy papers, and monographs |
| *NEWSLETTER* | None |
| *CONFERENCES* | Annual Wye Policy Conference (fall)<br>Soref Symposium (spring) |
| *BOARD OF DIRECTORS* | Mike Stein, president; Barbi Weinberg, chairman; Charles Adler, Bob Goldman, and Walter P. Stern, vice presidents; Fred Lafer, secretary/treasurer<br><br>Other members of the executive committee:<br>♦ Richard S. Abramson ♦ Richard Borow ♦ Benjamin Breslauer ♦ Maurice Deane ♦ Lenard Goodman ♦ Martin Gross ♦ Roger Hertog ♦ Laurence Phillips ♦ James Schreiber ♦ Fred Schwartz ♦ Bernard S. White |
| *EFFECTIVENESS* | "The White House says [Iraqi dictator Saddam Hussein] has now backed down under pressure and that U.N. inspectors will return to Iraq. . . . The real heat comes a few months from now, when the U.N. inspectors will say they've done all they can. Then France and [Russian foreign minister Yevgeny] Primakov, and the bravehearts in the Arab world, will push to lift sanctions. Having made inspections (and not Saddam) the main issue, the U.S. will be hard put to resist. Granted, none of Mr. Clinton's options were ideal. But if Saddam really threatens 'the safety of the children of the world,' as the president warned this week, this scenario isn't reassuring.<br><br>"Robert Satloff, director of the . . . Washington Institute for Near East Policy, is even more pessimistic: 'While we averted a short-term war, we've almost guaranteed we'll have a far more dangerous military confrontation sometime in the future, at the time of Saddam's choosing, and with fewer resources available to deal with it.' " (*Wall Street Journal*, November 21, 1997)<br><br>"A Saudi fugitive recently deported from Canada to the United States has implicated a senior Iranian intelligence officer in a 1995 conspiracy to attack American targets [at the Khobar Towers apartment complex] in Saudi Arabia, according to sources familiar with the case. |

". . . A recent bipartisan report on U.S. policy in the Middle East endorsed direct action against Iran if the Khobar connection is proven; the action should involve meaningful military targets and 'not pin-prick airstrikes aimed at relatively minor or remote sites,' said the report, issued by the Washington Institute for Near East Policy." (*Washington Post*, June 28, 1997)

"Addressing a congressional panel earlier this year, CIA Director John Deutch called proliferation of biological, chemical and nuclear weapons the main strategic threat facing the U.S. and its allies. The big danger lies in the Mideast, he added, as so-called rogue states such as Iran, Iraq and Libya seek to acquire such weapons. . . .

"Yet amid America's relentless drive to isolate countries it perceives as its enemies, the growing problem with allies is being overlooked. 'How do you deal with friends who have developed nasty capabilities?' asks Michael Eisenstadt, a Mideast military-affairs analyst at the Washington Institute for Near East Policy.

". . . Most Mideastern countries, whether U.S. allies or not, either deny that they maintain unconventional-weapons programs or simply refuse to talk about them. And gathering intelligence about such programs is getting harder. The Washington Institute's Mr. Eisenstadt says biological weapons, though potentially as destructive as nuclear arms, are hard to detect. . . ." (*Wall Street Journal*, September 6, 1996)

"nonpartisan" (*Wall Street Journal*, November 21, 1997)

# POLITICAL
# ORIENTATION

# Zero Population Growth (1968)

1400 16th Street, NW
Suite 320
Washington, D.C. 20036
Phone: (202) 332-2200
Fax: (202) 332-2302
Toll-free: (800) 767-1956
Internet: info@zpg.org *or* http://www.zpg.org

| | |
|---|---|
| **PURPOSE** | "To mobilize broad public support for a sustainable balance of the earth's people, environment and resources, as well as informing the public on matters related to population, environment, the status of women and the quality of life for all people." |
| **STAFF** | 41 total; plus 6–8 volunteers; 4 interns |
| **DIRECTOR** | Peter Houston Kostmayer, executive director. A former U.S. Representative from Pennsylvania, Kostmayer served in Congress from 1977 to 1981 and from 1983 to 1989. Kostmayer also worked as press secretary to a Pennsylvania attorney general and deputy press secretary to a Pennsylvania governor. He graduated with a B.A. from Columbia University. |
| **TAX STATUS** | 501(c)(3) |
| **BUDGET** | 1997—$4.0 million<br>1998—$4.3 million<br>Proposed 1999—Unavailable |
| **FUNDING SOURCES** | Contributions, 52 percent; membership, 27 percent; grants, 18 percent; other, 3 percent |
| **SCOPE** | Members: 60,000 individuals<br>Branches/chapters: 18 chapters<br>Affiliates: N/A |
| **PAC** | None |

◆ Coalition forming ◆ Conferences/seminars ◆ Congressional testimony ◆ Congressional voting analysis ◆ Direct action ◆ Education and outreach ◆ Films/video/audiotapes ◆ Grassroots organizing ◆ Legislative/regulatory monitoring ◆ Lobbying (federal and state) ◆ Media outreach ◆ Participation in regulatory proceedings (federal) ◆ Product merchandising ◆ Research ◆ Speakers program ◆ Voting records

## METHOD OF OPERATION

◆ Abortion ◆ Domestic family planning ◆ Education ◆ Foreign aid assistance ◆ Immigration and population ◆ International development ◆ Population stabilization ◆ Sustainable development ◆ Teen pregnancy

## CURRENT CONCERNS

*The Children's Environmental Index*
*Earth Matters Teaching Kit*
*For Earth's Sake*
*Guide to Congress*
*Multiplying People, Dividing Resources*
*Planning the Ideal Family*
*The Population Explosion*
*Pro-Choice Action Kit*
*USA by Numbers*
*World Population* (video)

Publishes other teaching materials and fact sheets on specific issues

## PUBLICATIONS

*Campus Organizers Newsletter* (quarterly)
*The Global Citizen* (quarterly)
*The Teacher's Pet Term Paper* (quarterly)
*Population Planet* (6 times per year)
*The ZPG Reporter* (bimonthly)

## NEWSLETTER

Capitol Hill Days (annual, Washington, D.C., and Sacramento, California)
Leadership Institute (annual)
Teaching/training workshops (year-round)
ZPG Earth Day (annual week of events)

## CONFERENCES

◆ Joe Bailey ◆ Catherine Cameron ◆ Dianne Dillon-Ridgley ◆ Jule Hallerdin ◆ Mike Hanauer ◆ Marilyn Hempel ◆ Madeledine Hervey ◆ Judy Jacobsen ◆ Jane Johnson ◆ Elise Jones ◆ Eugene Kutscher ◆ John Lazarus ◆ Edwin Leach II ◆ Martha Monroe ◆ Rosamond Reed Wulsin ◆ Judith Schultz ◆ Ellie Smeal ◆ Scott Vance

## BOARD OF DIRECTORS

"A nationwide survey last year by the advocacy group Zero Population Growth ranked Newark as the third-worst place in the country to raise children (after Detroit and Gary, Ind.)." (*Washington Post*, January 3, 1998)

"For 30 years, one notion has shaped much of modern social thought: that the human species is reproducing itself uncontrollably, and ominously. . . .

## EFFECTIVENESS

"... A 1992 documentary on Ted Turner's CNN described the impending global chaos 'as the planet's population grows exponentially,' and just a few days ago, Turner and his wife, Jane Fonda, were honored at a gala for Zero Population Growth, which preaches the mantra of out-of-control overpopulation." (*New York Times Magazine*, November 23, 1997)

"Washington and Baltimore both ranked among the 10 least healthful cities for children in a quality-of-life study published last month by Zero Population Growth, a Washington-based organization that advocates population control through family planning." (*Washington Post*, September 23, 1997)

## POLITICAL ORIENTATION

Unavailable

# Media/
# Technology
## Chapter 8

# Accuracy in Media, Inc. (1969)

4455 Connecticut Avenue, NW
Suite 330
Washington, D.C. 20008
Phone: (202) 364-4401
Fax: (202) 364-4098
Internet: http://www.aim.org

| | |
|---|---|
| "To provide a watchdog of the news by promoting accuracy and fairness in reporting on critical issues facing America." | **PURPOSE** |
| 16 total—10 professional; 6 support; plus 2 interns | **STAFF** |
| Reed J. Irvine, chairman of the board. Irvine founded Accuracy in Media (AIM) in 1969. He served as an adviser in the international finance division of the board of governors of the Federal Reserve System until he retired in 1977 to devote full time to AIM. He holds degrees from the University of Utah and Oxford University. | **DIRECTOR** |
| 501(c)(3) | **TAX STATUS** |
| 1998—$1.3 million<br>Proposed 1999—Unavailable | **BUDGET** |
| Membership dues, 60 percent; corporate and foundation contributions, 30 percent; other, 10 percent | **FUNDING SOURCES** |
| Members: 13,000 individuals<br>Branches/chapters: N/A<br>Affiliates: N/A | **SCOPE** |
| None | **PAC** |
| ◆ Advertisements ◆ Attendance at media trade association conventions ◆ Conferences/seminars ◆ Films/video/audiotapes ◆ Internet (E-mail alerts) ◆ Media outreach ◆ Speakers program ◆ Television and radio production | **METHOD OF OPERATION** |

| | |
|---|---|
| **CURRENT CONCERNS** | News reporting of activities of governmental officials |
| **PUBLICATIONS** | Produces special reports, weekly newspaper column, and daily radio broadcast |
| **NEWSLETTER** | *AIM Report* (bimonthly) |
| **CONFERENCES** | Yearly conferences that focus on media bias |
| **BOARD OF DIRECTORS** | ♦ Paul Busiek ♦ Beverly Danielson ♦ Joan Heuter ♦ Charles A. Moser ♦ John Uhlmann |
| **EFFECTIVENESS** | Unavailable |
| **POLITICAL ORIENTATION** | "conservative" (*Washington Post*, January 28, 1998)<br><br>"conservative watchdog group" (*Washington Post*, July 4, 1995) |

# Center for Democracy and Technology (1994)

1634 I Street, NW
Suite 1100
Washington, D.C. 20006
Phone: (202) 637-9800
Fax: (202) 637-0968
Internet: info@cdt.org *or* http://www.cdt.org

Dedicated to advocating "for democratic values and consitutional liberties in the digital age. The Center engages in a range of activities and debates that will affect the future of free expression and privacy on global communcations networks. . . . CDT seeks practical solutions to problems and is dedicated to building broad consensus among all parties interested in the future of the Internet and other new communications media."

**PURPOSE**

10 total—7 professionals; 3 support; plus 2 interns

**STAFF**

Jerry Berman, executive director. Berman founded the Center for Democracy and Technology (CDT) in 1994. Prior to founding CDT, he was a director of the Electronic Frontier Foundation. Berman also served as the chief legislative counsel for the ACLU; he also founded and directed ACLU's Projects on Privacy and Information Technology. Currently he serves as the chair of the Advisory Committee to the Congressional Internet Caucus. Berman received his B.A., M.A., and L.L.B. from the University of California–Berkeley.

**DIRECTOR**

501(c)(3)

**TAX STATUS**

1997—$950,000
1998—$1.2 million
Proposed 1999—$1.3 million

**BUDGET**

Corporate donations, 80 percent; foundation grants, 20 percent

**FUNDING SOURCES**

Members: N/A
Branches/chapters: N/A
Affiliates: N/A

**SCOPE**

| | |
|---|---|
| **PAC** | None |
| **METHOD OF OPERATION** | ◆ Coalition forming ◆ Conferences/seminars ◆ Congressional testimony ◆ Congressional voting analysis ◆ Direct action ◆ Educational foundation ◆ Demonstrations ◆ Grassroots organizing ◆ Information clearinghouse ◆ International activities ◆ Internet (databases, E-mail alerts, Web site) ◆ Internships ◆ Legislative/regulatory monitoring (federal) ◆ Litigation ◆ Lobbying (federal and grassroots) ◆ Media outreach ◆ Participation in regulatory proceedings (federal) ◆ Research ◆ Scholarships ◆ Voting records |
| **CURRENT CONCERNS** | ◆ Access to the Internet ◆ Electronic surveillance and cryptography ◆ Free expression on the Internet ◆ Information privacy ◆ Online democracy |
| **PUBLICATIONS** | *Communications Privacy in the Digital Age*<br>*Privacy and Health Information Systems: A Guide to Protecting Patient Confidentiality*<br>*Report to the Federal Trade Commission of the Ad-Hoc Working Group on Unsolicited Commercial E-mail*<br>*The Risk of Key Recovery, Key Escrow, and Trusted Third Party Encryption* |
| **NEWSLETTER** | *Policy Post* (periodic, online) |
| **CONFERENCES** | None |
| **BOARD OF DIRECTORS** | Morton H. Halperin, chair<br><br>Other board members:<br>◆ Jerry Berman ◆ Toni Cabo ◆ Don Edwards ◆ Carol A. Fukunaga ◆ Michael B. Trister ◆ Tracy Westen |
| **EFFECTIVENESS** | "Hewlett-Packard Co. received U.S. government approval to export a strong encryption technology to customers in five countries, and announced a partnership with International Business Machines Corp. to share data-security technologies.<br><br>"The Palo Alto, Calif., computer maker said it received approval to export a version of its VerSecure technology with an encryption key that is 128 bits in length, a level of data-scrambling complexity that is considered virtually unbreakable. The U.S. Commerce Department approved export of the technology to the United Kingdom, Germany, France, Denmark and Australia. |

"Encryption is closely regulated by many governments because its use inhibits the ability of law enforcement and intelligence-gathering agencies to eavesdrop. The Clinton administration has been pushing to require makers of computer technology to build in a kind of back-door decoding method, under which trusted organizations would keep copies of encryption keys for potential recovery later by authorized agencies.

"H-P's technology, first proposed in 1996, must be activated for renewable one-year periods by designated agencies in each country. Users aren't required to use a key recovery system now, but foreign governments could do so in the future as users apply to renew the encryption capability. A spokeswoman for the U.S. Department of Commerce said the export approval for H-P is 'consistent with our policy to encourage adoption of key recovery world-wide.'

"Doug McGowan, director of H-P's VerSecure division, termed export approval of the technology a 'breakthrough.' But critics of Clinton administration policy, such as the Washington-based Center for Democracy & Technology, oppose the H-P technology because it reduces users' control over encryption. 'They are building into their products key recovery that can be turned on or off not by the user but by government,' said Jack Dempsey, senior staff counsel with the group." (*Wall Street Journal*, March 2, 1998)

"The First Amendment went digital yesterday.

"In a 7-2 decision, the Supreme Court struck down the Communications Decency Act, a law that made it a crime to make 'indecent' or 'patently offensive' material available to minors over the fast-growing Internet and other computer networks. The court ruled that constitutional free speech protections apply just as much to online systems as they do to books and newspapers." Finding that the law was overly vague and would infringe on the speech rights of adults in the name of protecting children, Justice John Paul Stevens wrote that 'our cases provide no basis for qualifying the level of First Amendment scrutiny that should be applied to this medium.' The law, he wrote, 'threatens to torch a large segment of the Internet community.'

"Civil libertarians and businesses hoping to profit from the Internet were elated by the strongly worded decision. Jerry Berman of the Center for Democracy and Technology, a high-tech policy group that helped assemble the coalition of business and civil liberties groups opposing the law, called the decision 'the Bill of Rights for the 21st Century.' " (*Washington Post*, June 27, 1997)

Unavailable

# POLITICAL ORIENTATION

# Center for Media and Public Affairs (1985)

2100 L Street, NW
Suite 300
Washington, D.C. 20037
Phone: (202) 223-2942
Fax: (202) 872-4014
Internet: http://www.cmpa.com

| | |
|---|---|
| **PURPOSE** | "To analyze scientifically how news and entertainment media treat social and political issues." |
| **STAFF** | 17 total—12 professional; 5 support; plus 3 interns |
| **DIRECTOR** | S. Robert Lichter, president. In addition to his work with the Center for Media and Public Affairs (CMPA), Lichter teaches media and politics at Georgetown University. Previously, he taught political science at Princeton and George Washington University, was a senior research fellow at Columbia University, and a postdoctoral fellow in politics and psychology at Yale University. Lichter holds a Ph.D. in government from Harvard University and a B.A. from the University of Minnesota. |
| **TAX STATUS** | 501(c)(3) |
| **BUDGET** | 1998—Unavailable<br>Proposed 1999—Unavailable |
| **FUNDING SOURCES** | Unavailable |
| **SCOPE** | Members: N/A<br>Branches/chapters: N/A<br>Affiliates: N/A |
| **PAC** | None |

| | |
|---|---|
| ♦ Media monitoring ♦ Research | *METHOD OF OPERATION* |
| ♦ Environmental messages in popular culture ♦ Election coverage ♦ Media balance ♦ Violence on television | *CURRENT CONCERNS* |

*PUBLICATIONS*

*Good Intentions Make Bad News: Why Americans Hate Campaign Journalism*
*Looking for J.R.: Media Coverage of the Oil and Energy Crisis*
*Media Coverage of the Catholic Church*
*The Media Elite*
*Prime Time: How TV Portrays American Culture*
*The Video Campaign: Network Coverage of the 1988 Primaries*
*Video Villains*
*Watching America: What Television Tells Us About Our Lives*
*What the People Want From the Press*
*When Should the Watchdogs Bark? Media Coverage of the Clinton Scandals*

Also offers monographs, *Political News Watch, Election Watch,* and back issues of *Media Monitor*

| | |
|---|---|
| *Media Monitor* (bimonthly) | *NEWSLETTER* |
| None | *CONFERENCES* |
| Unavailable | *BOARD OF DIRECTORS* |

*EFFECTIVENESS*

"Mainstream television this season is flaunting the most vulgar and explicit sex, language and behavior that it has ever sent into American homes. And as sometimes happens with the spoiled child, the tactic works: attention is being paid.

" 'I'd say there's been a quantum leap downward this year in terms of adolescent, vulgar language and attempts to treat sexuality in shocking terms,' said Robert Lichter, director of the Center for Media and Public Affairs.... 'People used to complain that television was aimed at the mind of a 12-year-old. Now it seems aimed at the hormones of a 14-year-old.'...

" 'I don't think parents have given up caring, but they've almost given up fighting,' Mr. Lichter said. 'Popular culture is so ubiquitous it's almost impossible to combat. It's like the weather, everyone complains about it but no one does anything.' " (*New York Times,* April 6, 1998)

"In perhaps the most comprehensive study of local news shows ever, a survey of health issues on television by the Kaiser Family Foundation and the Washington-based Center for Media and Public Affairs shows that the five most common story topics are crime (20 percent), weather (11), accidents and disasters (9), human interest and health stories (both 7 percent)." (*Washington Post*, March 12, 1998)

"Since 1993, the content of network news appears to have shifted. According to the Center for Media and Public Affairs, a nonprofit media research group, coverage of foreign news dropped while coverage of crime and popular culture rose. From 1993 through 1996, one in seven stories was about crime.

" 'In the past, mainstream news has been pulled into crime reporting by tabloid competition,' said Robert Lichter, the political scientist who runs the center, citing the coverage of the Simpson, Andrew Cunanan and Jon-Benet Ramsey cases. Now, he said, the same is true of sex.

"Mr. Lichter found that the evening news shows of the three major networks did more stories about the White House scandal in the first week than they did about Diana in the first week after her death, and more than the combined first week's coverage of all other scandals involving Mr. Clinton." (*New York Times*, February 1, 1998)

"According to the Center for Media and Public Affairs, nearly two-thirds of the [tabloid television] programs' reports on self-destructive behavior (such as gambling and drug and alcohol abuse) included criticism or negative judgments. Nearly six in 10 crime stories also included such rebukes. But fewer than one in five stories on sexual behavior included any critical remarks." (*Washington Post*, December 22, 1997)

"Research from the Center for Media and Public Affairs . . . found that actual coverage of 'Washington' news—defined as news relating to the White House, government agencies, Congress and the military—has held steady since 1990." (*Wall Street Journal*, August 13, 1997)

# POLITICAL ORIENTATION

"a nonpartisan research group" (*New York Times*, April 6, 1998)

"A new study by the Center for Media and Public Affairs reveals the three big network evening news programs 'have provided relatively balanced coverage of the latest allegations regarding President Clinton.'. . ." (*Washington Post*, February 24, 1998)

"a nonpartisan media-studies organization" (*Washington Post*, October 3, 1997)

# Center for Media Education (1991)

1511 K Street, NW
Suite 518
Washington, D.C. 20005
Phone: (202) 628-2620
Fax: (202) 628-2554
Internet: cme@cme.org *or* http://www.cme.org/cme

| | |
|---|---|
| "To promote the democratic use of the electronic media. CME works to lower barriers to access to telecommunications systems and to improve the quality of the electronic media on behalf of children, families, nonprofit groups, and the general public." | *PURPOSE* |
| 8 total—5 professional; 3 support; plus 1 part-time; 3 interns | *STAFF* |
| Kathryn Montgomery, president. Before cofounding the Center for Media Education (CME) in 1991, Montgomery was a professor of film and television at the University of California–Los Angeles. She has consulted with many nonprofit organizations on media issues and was a fellow of the Woodrow Wilson International Center for Scholars. | *DIRECTOR* |
| 501(c)(3) | *TAX STATUS* |
| 1998—$1 million<br>Proposed 1999—$1.5 million | *BUDGET* |
| Foundation grants, 95 percent; publications, 5 percent | *FUNDING SOURCES* |
| Members: N/A<br>Branches/chapters: N/A<br>Affiliates: Telecommunications Policy Roundtable, Children's Media Policy Network | *SCOPE* |
| None | *PAC* |

| | |
|---|---|
| **METHOD OF OPERATION** | ♦ Coalition forming ♦ Conferences ♦ Films/video/audiotapes ♦ Grass-roots organizing ♦ Internet (Web site) ♦ Internships ♦ Legislative/regulatory monitoring (federal) ♦ Media outreach ♦ Participation in federal regulatory proceedings ♦ Research |
| **CURRENT CONCERNS** | ♦ Educating the nonprofit community about evolving telecommunications technologies and related policy ♦ Establishing guidelines and policy principles for the collection and tracking of information from children on the global information infrastructure and interactive media ♦ Improving programming for children ♦ Promoting a public interest information superhighway ♦ Urging the FCC to strengthen compliance with the Children's Television Act of 1990 ♦ Working with state and local organizations to conduct parent education |
| **PUBLICATIONS** | *Alcohol & Tobacco on the Web*<br>*Choices for Children: A Community Action Kit*<br>*Connecting Children to the Future*<br>*Economic Concentration and Diversity in the Broadcast Media: Public Policy and Empirical Evidence*<br>*The Impact of the Children's Television Act on the Broadcast Market*<br>*The Information Superhighway and the Reinvention of Television*<br>*It's the Law: The Children's Television Act of 1990* (video)<br>*Parent's Guide to Kids' TV*<br>*Web of Deception*<br>*When Pulling the Plug Isn't Enough—A Parent's Guide to Kids' TV* |
| **NEWSLETTER** | *InfoActive Kids* (quarterly) |
| **CONFERENCES** | None |
| **BOARD OF DIRECTORS** | Kathryn Montgomery, president; Jeffrey Chester, secretary-treasurer<br><br>Other board members:<br>♦ Michael Brody ♦ Monroe Price ♦ Wilhelmina Reuben-Cooke ♦ Sally Steenland ♦ Alice Trillin ♦ Lawrence Wallack ♦ Ellen Wartella |
| **EFFECTIVENESS** | "[T]he Teletubbies, British imports appearing on PBS, are breaking ground again, this time in a way that alarms some children's advocates. The merchandising schemes have begun, spawning talk about 'filling the 1-to-2-year-old niche' in the market, and causing concern about nurturing a consumer mentality in children not yet able to speak properly. |

" 'A child that young doesn't say, 'Buy me that,' but in the store she will grab for something,' said Dr. Kathryn Montgomery, president of the Center for Media Education and a respected researcher on media and children. 'And parents want to please their children. Marketing like this helps encourage that first 'Buy me that' exchange between a parent and a child before the kid even knows how to say 'Buy me that.'

"Dr. Montgomery and others also worry that Public Broadcasting Service programmers might be influenced in choosing programs by considerations of how much money PBS could make from toys and other products tied to the program. With public television's chronic financial need, such windfalls could be tempting enough to sway judgments about a program's suitability, critics warn—a notion that PBS rejects." (*New York Times*, April 20, 1998)

"As millions of kids go on-line, marketers are in hot pursuit. Eager to reach an enthusiastic audience more open to pitches than the typical adult buried in junk mail, companies often entertain tykes on-line with games and contests. But to play, these sites frequently require children to fill out questionnaires about themselves and their families and friends—valuable data to be sorted and stored in marketing databases. . . .

" 'Children will unknowingly or innocently give up information about themselves which can be used and sold to others,' says Kathryn Montgomery, president of the Center for Media Education, a Washington, D.C., group that plans to recommend regulatory measures to the FTC to thwart on-line violation of children's privacy. 'There are no rules to prevent marketers from doing that.'

"Even when companies have disclaimers, such as advising children to ask for their parents' permission, such statements are 'ineffective' and aimed simply at giving the illusion of restraint, Mrs. Montgomery contends. 'Most kids I know wouldn't ask their parents,' she says.

"The center is asking marketers to adhere to guidelines that prohibit deceptive data-collection practices and require full disclosure and parental consent in writing until technologies are available to allow parents to provide certifiable authorization. Parents must also be able to prevent further use of their children's information." (*Wall Street Journal*, June 9, 1997)

"The alcohol industry is using the Internet to pitch more than 35 brands of beer and liquor to underage youth, and cigarette companies appear ready to do the same, the Center for Media Education contends.

"The public-interest group released a study saying that 14 liquor companies and 10 major breweries have set up Web sites to promote their products with 'a heady blend of humor, hip language, interactive games and contests.'. . .

"Several antismoking and health groups joined the Center for Media Education in urging government regulators to investigate on-line marketing of alcohol and tobacco. For their part, industry officials denied targeting underage drinkers or smokers, saying their sites are designed to appeal to consumers of legal age. . . .

"The survey found more than 50 smoking-related Web sites that seemed to promote a 'smoking-is-cool culture,' but it didn't detect any overt signs of cigarette advertising in the U.S. Some tobacco companies, however, have launched advertising sites in Germany and elsewhere." (*Wall Street Journal*, March 7, 1997)

## POLITICAL ORIENTATION

Unavailable

# Electronic Frontier Foundation (1990)

1550 Bryant
Suite 725
San Francisco, California 94103
Phone: (415) 436-9333
Fax: (415) 436-9993
Internet: askeff@eff.org *or* http://www.eff.org

| | |
|---|---|
| "Fosters awareness of civil liberties issues arising from the advancements in new computer-based communications media and supports litigation to preserve, protect, and extend First Amendment rights in computing and telecommunications technology." | *PURPOSE* |
| 10 total | *STAFF* |
| Barry Steinhardt, executive director | *DIRECTOR* |
| 501(c)(3) | *TAX STATUS* |
| 1998—Unavailable<br>Proposed 1999—Unavailable | *BUDGET* |
| Unavailable | *FUNDING SOURCES* |
| Members: 2,800<br>Branches/chapters: N/A<br>Affiliates: N/A | *SCOPE* |
| None | *PAC* |
| ♦ Awards program ♦ Coalition forming ♦ Educational programs ♦ Internet (Web site) ♦ Legislative/regulatory monitoring (federal) ♦ Litigation ♦ Speakers program ♦ Telecommunications services (databases) | *METHOD OF OPERATION* |

## CURRENT CONCERNS

♦ Assimilation of new technologies by society ♦ Effects of computing and telecommunications ♦ Ensuring that privacy and security of online communications are preserved ♦ Protecting First Amendment rights in computing and telecommunications

## PUBLICATIONS

*Cracking DES: Secrets of Encryption Research, Wire Tap Politics, and Chip Design*

*Protecting Yourself Online: The Definitive Resource for Safety, Freedom, and Privacy in Cyberspace*

## NEWSLETTER

*Effector Online* (biweekly)

## CONFERENCES

Sponsors conferences periodically

## BOARD OF DIRECTORS

♦ John Perry Barlow ♦ Esther Dyson ♦ David Farber ♦ Lori Fena ♦ John Gilmore ♦ Giles McNamee ♦ Allen Morgan ♦ Tim O'Reilly ♦ Roel Pieper ♦ Louise Velazquez ♦ George Vradenburg III

## EFFECTIVENESS

"The $30 million defamation suit, filed [against cyber-reporter Matt Drudge] in August by presidential adviser Sidney Blumenthal, provides the latest evidence of the twisted loyalties and personal animus that dominate Washington's scandal-obsessed culture. Mr. Drudge has been all but abandoned by media types who typically support reporters fighting political figures, even though his case could help define what constitutes libel on the Internet. . . .

"Even some people at the Electronic Frontier Foundation . . . were reluctant to come out strongly behind Mr. Drudge. Michael Godwin, a lawyer for the foundation, says he had to convince co-workers the case was worth backing. 'A lot of them took the very, in my view, reactive position that Drudge is just getting what he deserves,' Mr. Godwin says." (*Wall Street Journal*, March 11, 1998)

"One of the most striking paradoxes of Internet culture is that children are the most computer literate among us, but their vulnerability to on-line predators prevents their being able to enjoy or explore freely what is likely to be the defining medium of their lives. . . .

"Thomas Morgan, a longtime on-line executive . . . has devised a solution he calls the Safe Playgrounds Initiative. He has been discussing it privately for several months with various organizations, including the Electronic Frontier Foundation, a civil liberties group, and the Children's Advertising Review Unit of the Better Business Bureau. . . .

"Beleaguered executives . . . predict that enacting an initiative like Safe Playgrounds will be difficult, but [they are] also adamant that an industrywide, mandatory solution is 'the only way to solve the problem on the scale that's required.'

"Lori Fena, the chairman of the Electronic Frontier Foundation, agreed. 'No one wants to pay to babyproof the Net, but everybody is willing to support creating child-safe areas like playgrounds in the real world,' she said. 'This initiative is the most sane thing I've seen yet—socially, legally and economically. If the goal is to go after predatory behavior by adults, then let's go for it.' " (*New York Times*, February 16, 1998)

"The global computer network known as the Internet . . . has become a new battleground for refighting the wars that shape our culture: society's attitudes toward sex and obscenity, libel, search and seizure, patent and copyright law, gambling, personal privacy and more. . . .

"It should not be surprising that the conflicts sparked by the Internet haven't been resolved yet . . . Mike Godwin, staff counsel for the Electronic Frontier Foundation, a California-based high-tech civil liberties group, [said]: 'We're going to have to fight this fight every day until we die. You don't get a break.' For Godwin, all of these fights over the Internet come down to one factor: what he calls 'fear of the future.' People, he argues, think the online medium is 'going to change things—and they're right. But they think they won't be able to cope, and they're wrong. If there's any lesson from American life, it's that we're resilient. We're adaptable.' " (*Washington Post*, February 15, 1998)

"The ailing on-line service Prodigy Inc. is expected to launch an Internet service in China today in a joint venture with a state-controlled company, becoming the first government-approved foreign Internet provider in a country that closely controls access to the global computer network. . . .

" 'As they march in here, I hope they understand they're undertaking more than a business opportunity,' said Lori Fena, executive director of the Electronic Frontier Foundation, a high-tech civil liberties group in San Francisco. 'The numbers and upside might be huge, but the impact to individuals and the choices they make as a corporation are going to be under scrutiny,' she said, noting that censorship and potential privacy violations introduce 'a moral imperative to encourage use of the technology in the most responsible way.' " (*Wall Street Journal*, April 29, 1997)

"A vocal proponent of on-line speech rights." (*Wall Street Journal*, March 11, 1998)

"As chairman of the Electronic Frontier Foundation, [Esther Dyson] morphs from libertarian to capitalist and back again, fretting about civil liberties on the Web such as privacy, freedom of expression and access to public information." (*Washington Post*, November 3, 1997)

## POLITICAL ORIENTATION

# Electronic Privacy Information Center (1994)

666 Pennsylvania Ave., SE, #301
Washington, DC 20003
Phone: (202) 544-9240
Fax: (202) 547-5482
Internet: http://www.epic.org

**PURPOSE**

"To focus public attention on emerging civil liberties issues and to protect privacy, the First Amendment, and constitutional values."

**STAFF**

4 total—3 professional; 1 support; plus 2 part-time; 2 interns; 1 volunteer

**DIRECTOR**

Marc Rotenberg, executive director. Rotenberg served on the Senate Judiciary Committee from 1981–1988. A member of *Newsweek's 50 People Who Matter Most on the Internet*, he is an adjunct professor at Georgetown University Law School. Rotenberg received his A.B. degree from Harvard University in 1982 and his J. D. degree from Stanford University in 1987.

**TAX STATUS**

501(c)(3)

**BUDGET**

1998—$400,000
Proposed 1999—$500,000

**FUNDING SOURCES**

Foundation grants, 50 percent; individual contributions, 25 percent; corporate donations, 10 percent; publications, 5 percent; conferences, 5 percent; litigation, 5 percent

**SCOPE**

Members: 6,700 subscribers to EPIC newsletter, *EPIC Alert*
Branches/Chapters: N/A
Affiliate: Fund for Constitutional Government, a 501(c)(3) organization

**PAC**

None

◆ Coalition forming ◆ Conferences/seminars ◆ Congressional testimony ◆ Direct action ◆ Grassroots organizing ◆ Information clearinghouse ◆ International activities ◆ Internet (databases, electronic bulletin board, E-mail alerts, Web site) ◆ Internships ◆ Legislative/regulatory monitoring (federal and state) ◆ Litigation ◆ Media outreach ◆ Participation in federal regulatory proceedings ◆ Performance ratings (companies, products, etc.) ◆ Research

## *METHOD OF OPERATION*

◆ Encryption freedom ◆ Free speech on the Internet ◆ International cyber rights ◆ Privacy protection

## *CURRENT CONCERNS*

*Cryptography and Liberty: An International Survey*
*Electronic Privacy Papers*
*Surfer Beware: Personal Privacy and the Internet*
*Technology and Privacy*

## *PUBLICATIONS*

*EPIC Alert* (biweekly)
*International Privacy Bulletin* (quarterly)

## *NEWSLETTER*

EPIC Cryptography and Privacy Conference (annual)
Computers, Freedom, and Privacy (1999)

## *CONFERENCES*

◆ Phil Agre ◆ John Anderson ◆ D. James Bidzos ◆ Christine Borgman ◆ James Boyle ◆ David Burnham ◆ Vint Cerf ◆ David Chaum ◆ Richard Claude ◆ Simon Davies ◆ Whitfield Diffie ◆ David Flaherty ◆ Oscar Gandy ◆ Deborah Hurley ◆ Judy Krug ◆ Gary Marx ◆ Denise M. Nagel ◆ Peter G. Neumann ◆ Eli Noam ◆ Bruce Schneier ◆ Barbara Simons ◆ Robert Ellis Smith ◆ Frank Tuerkheimer ◆ Willis Ware

## *BOARD OF DIRECTORS*

"If life has become a little more difficult for the cyberspies at the National Security Agency, part of the reason may be Marc Rotenberg. Rotenberg led the campaign against the Clipper encryption scheme last year and continues to battle Big Brother and Big Business in cyberspace. Formerly with Computer Professionals for Social Responsibility, Rotenberg now directs the Electronic Privacy Information Center, and he is often on the front lines of emerging civil-liberties issues." (*Newsweek*, January 1, 1996)

## *EFFECTIVENESS*

Unavailable

## *POLITICAL ORIENTATION*

# Fairness & Accuracy in Reporting (FAIR) (1986)

130 West 25th Street
New York, New York 10001
Phone: (212) 633-6700
Fax: (212) 727-7668
Internet: http://www.fair.org

**PURPOSE**

"To invigorate the First Amendment by advocating for greater media pluralism and the inclusion of public interest voices in national debates."

**STAFF**

11 total—10 professional; 1 support; plus 5 interns

**DIRECTOR**

Jeff Cohen, executive director. Prior to founding Fairness & Accuracy in Reporting (FAIR) in 1986, Cohen worked in Los Angeles as a publicist for public interest groups, a freelance journalist, and a lawyer for the American Civil Liberties Union Foundation of Southern California. He has discussed media issues on numerous national television and radio programs, lectured at many colleges, and written for dozens of leading newspapers. Cohen studied at the University of Michigan and earned his law degree at Peoples College of Law in Los Angeles.

**TAX STATUS**

501(c)(3)

**BUDGET**

1998—$780,000
Proposed 1999—Unavailable

**FUNDING SOURCES**

Memberships, subscriptions, and sales, 60 percent; foundation grants, 40 percent

**SCOPE**

Members/subscribers: 19,000
Branches/chapters: N/A
Affiliates: 10 organizations

**PAC**

None

| | |
|---|---|
| ◆ Conferences/seminars ◆ Films/video/audiotapes ◆ Internet (Web site) ◆ Library/information clearinghouse ◆ Media outreach ◆ Research ◆ Speakers program ◆ Syndicated radio show | *METHOD OF OPERATION* |
| ◆ Corporate takeover of public television ◆ Exclusion of progressive and public interest voices from television news and public affairs ◆ Hate and disinformation on radio talk shows ◆ Media mergers ◆ Press-state cronyism | *CURRENT CONCERNS* |
| *Are You On the Nightline Guest List?*<br>*Examining the "Liberal Media" Claim: Journalists' Views on Politics, Economic Policy, and Media Coverage*<br>*The FAIR Reader: Press and Politics in the 1990s*<br>*Public Television "Prime Time": A Study of Public Affairs Programming and Political Diversity*<br>*The Way Things Aren't: Rush Limbaugh's Reign of Error*<br>*Wizards of Media Oz: Behind the Curtain of Mainstream News* | *PUBLICATIONS* |
| *Extra! Magazine* (6 times a year)<br>*Extra! Update* (6 times a year) | *NEWSLETTER* |
| "The Media and the New World disOrder"<br>"The Media and Women: Does Feminism Get Fair Treatment?" | *CONFERENCES* |
| ◆ Donna Edwards ◆ Karl Grossman ◆ William Hoynes ◆ Norman Solomon ◆ Linda Valentino | *BOARD OF DIRECTORS* |

*EFFECTIVENESS*

"In separate research, professors from Vassar and Johns Hopkins sharply attack Channel One, the 12-minute television program seen daily by an estimated eight million public school students in the United States, as an advertising vehicle loaded with superficial, biased and sometimes hurtful programming.

" 'It's real function is not journalistic but commercial,' Mark Crispin Miller, a professor of media studies at Johns Hopkins University, said in a paper entitled 'How to Be Stupid: The Teachings of Channel One.'

" 'It is meant primarily to get us ready for the ads,' he writes. 'It must keep itself from saying anything too powerful or even interesting, must never cut too deep or raise any really troubling questions, because it cannot ever be permitted to detract in any way from the commercials.'

"Working independently, Professor Miller and a Vassar College sociologist, William Hoynes, did two studies coordinated by the Fairness and Accuracy in Reporting, a liberal media watchdog group based in New York City. They analyzed videotapes of 36 shows distributed in 1995 and 1996. These programs, they said, contained a total of 91 news stories and 177 on-camera sources." (*New York Times*, January 22, 1997) "liberal" (*Wall Street Journal*, October 16, 1997)

"Naderite media hazing group" (*Wall Street Journal*, March 12, 1996)

# Media Access Project (1971)

1707 L Street, NW
Washington, D.C. 20036
Phone: (202) 232-4300
Fax: (202) 466-7656
Internet: http://www.mediaaccess.org

| | |
|---|---|
| "To expand the public's First Amendment rights to speak and to be heard." | **PURPOSE** |
| 4 total—3 professional; 1 support; plus 2 interns | **STAFF** |
| GiGi B. Sohn, executive director | **DIRECTOR** |
| 501(c)(3) | **TAX STATUS** |
| 1998—$250,000<br>Proposed 1999—$275,000 | **BUDGET** |
| Grants, 100 percent | **FUNDING SOURCES** |
| Members: N/A<br>Branches/chapters: N/A<br>Affiliates: N/A | **SCOPE** |
| None | **PAC** |
| ♦ Congressional testimony ♦ Internet (Web site) ♦ Legal assistance ♦ Litigation ♦ Participation in regulatory proceedings (federal) | **METHOD OF OPERATION** |
| Telecommunications and mass media | **CURRENT CONCERNS** |

## PUBLICATIONS

None

## NEWSLETTER

None

## CONFERENCES

None

## BOARD OF DIRECTORS

◆ Peggy Charren ◆ Henry Geller ◆ Kristin Booth Glenn ◆ Albert H. Kramer ◆ Jorge Schement ◆ Andrew Jay Schwartzman

## EFFECTIVENESS

"On May 14, a panel of Federal judges in Manhattan will consider whether WRNN, which broadcasts from Overlook Mountain in Woodstock, N.Y., can force Time Warner Cable of New York and Cablevision Systems Corporation to carry its signal into 1.9 million homes in New York City and Long Island.

"At issue is whether WRNN should be regarded as a 'local' broadcast station in the New York City market under the 'must-carry' law that Congress imposed on cable operators in 1992 to protect local broadcasters. . . .

"Andrew Jay Schwartzman is president of the Media Access Project, a public interest law firm and strong supporter of must-carry. Yet he thinks WRNN's appeal to get into New York City and Long Island is misguided and will shortchange the local viewers and local advertisers that the Kingston station is licensed to serve.

" 'We want must-carry to help small stations care about their own community, not to serve the richer community down the road,' Mr. Schwartzman said. 'We don't want to see must-carry used to create superstations that are going to have their attention everywhere except the community where they are licensed. . . .' " (*New York Times*, April 26, 1998)

"In a decision that could have a far-reaching impact on broadcasters and on the future of affirmative action, a Federal appeals court here today voided a Government requirement that radio and television stations seek minority job applicants. . . .

"If upheld by the Supreme Court, the decision would virtually end a 30-year-old program that some of its supporters say has helped bring diversity to the broadcast industry. . . .

" 'The broadcasting industry has been much more effective in hiring and promoting minorities than the print media, which is the only comparable industry,' said Andrew J. Schwartzman, president of the Media Access Project. . . . 'The main reason for that has been this program.' " (*New York Times*, April 15, 1998)

"A federal appeals court overturned requirements that radio and television broadcasters hire racial minorities, in a setback for efforts by the Federal Communications Commission to bring more diversity to the nation's airwaves. . . .

" 'It means that the steady progress of minorities in broadcast employment may lessen,' said Andrew Schwartzman, president of the Washington-based Media Access Project, a nonprofit public-interest law firm. 'Most troublesome is the narrow, crimped understanding of what the FCC's diversity objectives are.' " (*Wall Street Journal*, April 15, 1998)

"The University of the District of Columbia's popular all-jazz radio station has been sold for $13 million to C-SPAN, which stepped in at the last minute to buy WDCU-FM after a religious broadcaster backed out of the deal, C-SPAN officials said yesterday. . . .

". . . Andy Schwartzman, executive director of the Media Access Project, a public interest law firm that has fought to save WDCU's jazz format, said he is [not happy] with C-SPAN's purchase of the station. 'This is not a satisfactory resolution,' he said." (*Washington Post*, August 14, 1997)

"The Federal Communications Commission recently issued station owners a second license to transmit digital signals while requiring them to return their existing analog-signal licenses by 2006. But broadcasters could have that deadline extended, perhaps indefinitely, under a provision adopted by the House Commerce Committee. . . .

"Critics say the measure would slow down the nation's transition to digital TV and reduce the amount of money the government would collect by auctioning the analog licenses. Also, said Gigi Sohn of the Media Access Project, a Washington consumer group, 'if broadcasters get to hold on to both blocks of spectrum, nobody else can have it, which means no [new] competition.' " (*Wall Street Journal*, June 13, 1997)

Unavailable

# POLITICAL ORIENTATION

# Media Research Center (1987)

113 South West Street
Alexandria, Virginia 22314
Phone: (703) 683-9733
Fax: (703) 683-9736
Internet: http://www.mediaresearch.org

| | |
|---|---|
| **PURPOSE** | "To promote political balance to the media, and to bring responsibility to television programming." |
| **STAFF** | 35 total; plus 2 interns |
| **DIRECTOR** | L. Brent Bozell III, chairman. Prior to founding the Media Research Center (MRC), he was executive director of the National Conservative Foundation and chairman and president of the National Conservative Political Action Committee. Bozell also has served on the board of governors of the Council for National Policy. He graduated from the University of Dallas. |
| **TAX STATUS** | 501(c)(3) |
| **BUDGET** | 1998—$4.8 million<br>Proposed 1999—Unavailable |
| **FUNDING SOURCES** | Individuals, 35 percent; membership/subscriptions, 26 percent; foundations, 21 percent; corporations, 15 percent; royalties, interest, and investments, 3 percent |
| **SCOPE** | Members: 10,000<br>Branches/chapters: None<br>Affiliates: Free Enterprise and Media Institute (FEMI), Alexandria, Virginia; Parents Television Council (PTC), Los Angeles, California |
| **PAC** | None |
| **METHOD OF OPERATION** | ♦ Internet (Web site, *CyberAlerts*) ♦ Media outreach ♦ Research ♦ Special programs (Conservative Experts, Economic Experts Forum, Montgomery Internship Program) |

♦ Business and free enterprise ♦ Hollywood ♦ Media and politics

*And That's the Way It Isn't*
*Conservative Experts Guide*
*How to Identify, Expose and Correct Liberal Media Bias*
*MRC Press Picks* (formerly *National Press Directory for Conservatives*)
*National Press Directory for Conservatives*
*Out of Focus: Network Television and the American Economy*
*Parents' Guide to Prime Time Television* (annual)
*Pattern of Deception: The Media's Role in the Clinton Presidency*
*Press Picks: Recommended Media Professionals*
*The Revolving Door: The Connection Between the Media and Politics*
*Team Clinton: The Starting Line-Up of the Pro-Clinton Press Corps*

Also publishes special reports, monographs, and Internet products

*Convention Watch*
*Flash*
*MediaNomics* (monthly)
*Media Reality Check*
*MediaWatch* (monthly)
*Notable Quotables* (monthly)
*TV, etc.*

None

L. Brent Bozell III, chairman

Other board members:
♦ William A. Rusher ♦ Harold Clark Simmons ♦ Leon J. Weil ♦ Curtin
Winsor Jr.

"Convinced that the Clinton White House is awash in scandals that national television networks have ignored, L. Brent Bozell 3d, chairman of Media Research Center . . . this week opened his own news operation on the Net.

"Mr. Bozell said that his Conservative News Service (www.conservativenews.org) would report news that he says is not touched by traditional television news outlets.

"The press release announcing the formation of the news service said it 'will fill the growing news void left by the establishment media in their chase for the sensational.' " (*New York Times*, June 18, 1998)

"Brent Bozell, the conservative media critic . . . is launching the Conservative Communications Center, an ambitious venture that will include original reporting, marketing, training and an information clearinghouse on the Internet. . . .

"The Web site (www.mrc.org) will recycle news from the mainstream press, 'debunk popular liberal myths' and provide files and experts for journalists—plus links to Rush Limbaugh and other conservative radio hosts. It will also include stories by the group's own reporters. . . .

". . . Spurred by its own difficulty in finding a marketing director, Bozell's group plans to help set up training schools to develop a new generation of marketing and PR experts for the conservative movement.

". . . He is also creating a job bank and a paid internship program." (*Washington Post*, June 15, 1998)

"Anybody who watches crime and courtroom dramas on the tube won't be shocked to learn that a study of prime-time programming over the past three broadcast years by the Media Research Center reveals 'a deep, passionate and pervasive bias' against businessmen, portraying them as criminals and murderers more often than career criminals. . . .

"The study . . . was conducted by the . . . MRC during the first week of each month in 1995, and during the first week of each of the four sweeps months in 1996–97. A total of 864 dramas, sitcoms and made-for-TV movies on ABC, CBS, NBC and Fox were monitored in 17 weeks over the 26 months. . . ." (*Washington Post*, June 17, 1997)

"Coverage of religious events was up last year on major network news programs but overall, religion gets little air time, according to a study released yesterday by the Media Research Center. . . .

"The center, a conservative organization that has monitored TV and news coverage for the past four years, said that over that period, only 1.3 percent of the reports on evening news shows, 955 stories, were devoted to religion. And on the morning shows, just 0.8 percent of the reports contained religion news. . . ." (*Washington Post*, March 25, 1997)

"Two prominent media watchdogs, Consumer Alert and the Media Research Center, released a joint report after the [1996] election analyzing the political content of 13 popular women's magazines over a 12 month period. They found that publications like *Working Woman*, *Glamour* and *Redbook* routinely 'scare women to death' by overstating risks, and they push hard for protective government programs. (In one year, the 13 magazines gave 115 positive portrayals of government activism compared to 18 articles that were critical.) The report calls women's magazines 'a liberal pipeline to Soccer Moms.' " (*Washington Post*, January 5, 1997)

## POLITICAL ORIENTATION

"conservative watchdog group" (*New York Times*, June 18, 1998)

"conservative think tank" (*Wall Street Journal*, June 20, 1997)

"conservative" (*Washington Post*, June 17, 1997)

"The central character of a network sitcom is going to announce that she's gay. . . . The sitcom, as nearly everyone knows, is 'Ellen.' . . .

". . . Many groups are critical of ABC's decision [to air the show]. In a full-page ad in the trade paper *Variety*, the politically conservative Media Research Center implores ABC, now owned by the Walt Disney Co., to re-think what the ad calls 'this slap in the face to America's families.'

". . . The ad says the move amounts to 'a blatant attempt by Disney, ABC and "Ellen" to promote homosexuality to America's families.' " (*Washington Post*, April 27, 1997)

# National Coalition on Television Violence (1980)

5132 Newport Avenue
Bethesda, Maryland 20816
Phone: (301) 986-0362
Fax: (301) 656-7031
Internet: http://www.nctvv.org

| | |
|---|---|
| **PURPOSE** | "To study reports done by the broadcast and cable industries and to monitor violence in media." |
| **STAFF** | 10 part-time volunteers |
| **DIRECTOR** | Mary Ann Banta, acting president/vice president. Banta serves voluntarily as Washington representative for the National Coalition on Television Violence (NCTV) and is a member of NCTV's board of directors. She is a retired educator. |
| **TAX STATUS** | 501(c)(3) |
| **BUDGET** | 1998—$20,000<br>Proposed 1999—$20,000 |
| **FUNDING SOURCES** | Private donations |
| **SCOPE** | Members: N/A<br>Branches/chapters: Offices in Detroit and Boston<br>Affiliates: N/A |
| **PAC** | None |
| **METHOD OF OPERATION** | ♦ Congressional testimony ♦ Legislative/regulatory monitoring (federal) ♦ Participation in regulatory proceedings (federal) ♦ Resource referral service ♦ Speakers program |

| | |
|---|---|
| • Effects of media violence • Electronic blocking on all media children can access • Levels of violence on broadcast and cable television • Teaching critical viewing skills | *CURRENT CONCERNS* |
| None | *PUBLICATIONS* |
| None | *NEWSLETTER* |
| None | *CONFERENCES* |
| Mary Ann Banta, acting president/vice president; Marilyn Droz, vice president<br><br>Other members:<br>• Kay McGinnis Ritter • Louisa C. Stigol | *BOARD OF DIRECTORS* |
| Unavailable | *EFFECTIVENESS* |
| Unavailable | *POLITICAL ORIENTATION* |

# Political/
Governmental
Process

Chapter 9

# Advocacy Institute (1985)

1707 L Street, NW
Suite 400
Washington, D.C. 20036
Phone: (202) 659-8475
Fax: (202) 659-8484
Internet: info@advocacy.org *or* http://www.advocacy.org

| | |
|---|---|
| Dedicated "to strengthening the capacity of social and economic justice advocates to influence and change public policy." | ***PURPOSE*** |
| 21 total—15 professional; 6 support; plus 2–6 interns | ***STAFF*** |
| David Cohen, Michael Pertschuk, and Kathleen D. Sheekey, codirectors. Cohen was formerly chief lobbyist and president of Common Cause. He founded and served as president of the Professionals' Coalition for Nuclear Arms Control. Pertschuk was formerly chairman of the Federal Trade Commission and chief counsel to the Senate Commerce Committee. Sheekey was formerly director of congressional relations at the Federal Trade Commission and legislative director at Common Cause. | ***DIRECTOR*** |
| 501(c)(3) | ***TAX STATUS*** |
| Fiscal year ending September 30, 1998—$2.3 million<br>Proposed F.Y. 1999—Unavailable | ***BUDGET*** |
| Foundation grants, 57 percent; contracts, 33 percent; individual contributions, 4 percent; other, 6 percent | ***FUNDING SOURCES*** |
| Members: N/A<br>Branches/chapters: N/A<br>Affiliates: N/A | ***SCOPE*** |
| None | ***PAC*** |

| | |
|---|---|
| *METHOD OF OPERATIONS* | ♦ Coalition forming ♦ Conferences/seminars ♦ Electronic networking (SCARCNet, "a computerized network designed for communication among tobacco control advocates") ♦ Information clearinghouse ♦ International activities ♦ Internet (Web site) ♦ Internships ♦ Media outreach ♦ Research ♦ Strategic counseling ♦ Training and technical assistance |
| *CURRENT CONCERNS* | ♦ Economic justice issues (domestic and global) ♦ Promoting public interest advocacy in a democratic society ♦ Social justice issues (domestic and global) ♦ Tobacco Control Project |
| *PUBLICATIONS* | *Annual Report*<br>*By Hook and by Crook—Stealth Lobbying: Tactics and Counter-Strategies*<br>*Giant Killers*<br>*Leadership for a Living Democracy*<br>*Media Advocacy and Public Health: Power for Prevention*<br>*Telling Your Story: A Guide to Preparing Advocacy Case Studies*<br><br>Also publishes *Tobacco Action Alerts* |
| *NEWSLETTER* | None |
| *CONFERENCES* | Sponsors workshops, seminars, and intensive training in advocacy skills and strategies |
| *BOARD OF DIRECTORS* | David Cohen, Michael Pertschuk, and Kathleen D. Sheekey, codirectors<br><br>Other board members:<br>♦ Patricia Bauman ♦ Helene G. Brown ♦ John Brown Childs ♦ Garrick C. Francis ♦ Peter Kovler ♦ Terry Lierman ♦ Xuan Nguyen-Sutter ♦ Richard Paisner ♦ Sofia Quintero ♦ Donna Red Wing ♦ Linda Tarr-Whelan ♦ Makani N. Themba ♦ Karen Watson ♦ Arthur White ♦ Kenneth Young |
| *EFFECTIVENESS* | "In full-page ads in national newspapers last week, Big Tobacco warned that proposed antismoking legislation 'would put us out of business.'. . .<br><br>"Mark C. Ellenberg, a Washington bankruptcy lawyer and adjunct professor at Georgetown University Law Center, warns that a company puts itself into play by filing for reorganization. 'Creditors can force a sale to a serious buyer at a fair price,' he says in a report just released by the Advocacy Institute, a nonprofit Washington policy center. That happened in 1989 to A.H. Robins, which was bought by American Home Products Corp. when it emerged from bankruptcy reorganization." (*Wall Street Journal*, April 17, 1998)<br><br>"An increasingly bitter rift between two factions of the nation's public health groups over the proposed national tobacco settlement could be moving toward resolution—and a united and harder stance against cigarette-makers. . . . |

"Michael Pertschuk, co-director of the Advocacy Institute and an adviser to public health groups, said that the balance of power at the time the June 1997 deal was announced has shifted because of new revelations about the industry, including new evidence that cigarette-makers targeted minors. And that has reopened liability issues. 'The parties had really gotten closer,' Pertschuk said, 'but they were yelling at other and not talking to each other until [former surgeon general C. Everett Koop] came along.' " (*Washington Post*, January 22, 1998)

"In last month's proposed tobacco settlement, cigarette manufacturers apparently got what they coveted most: immunity from punitive damages. And while anti-tobacco groups are now at each other's throats over whether they exacted a sufficient price in return, everyone agrees that the potential for sky-high punitive damage awards in individual injury suits immensely strengthened their bargaining power. 'It's the lever that brought the tobacco industry to the table,' said Michael Pertschuk, a former chairman of the Federal Trade Commission who now heads the Advocacy Institute in Washington. . . ." (*New York Times*, July 10, 1997)

"The $368 billion in damages to be exacted from the tobacco industry if the settlement announced last week is ultimately approved has already been sold as punishment that fits the crime. But that is not the way economists are likely to interpret it: since tobacco consumption by adults is not particularly sensitive to price, the industry should be able to pass nearly all of the $368 billion on to their customers. . . .

"Still, Michael Pertschuk, a former chairman of the Federal Trade Commission who now heads the Advocacy Institute . . . views the settlement in pragmatic terms. A deal now, even on terms favorable to the industry, he argues, is better than a harsher deal years down the road. The combination of higher cigarette prices, tighter rules on marketing and direct financial incentives to end recruitment of new smokers should have an enormous positive impact on public health." (*New York Times*, June 26, 1997)

"[Cigarette company Philip Morris's] marketers have been huddling for the past year to prepare the introduction of the company's own recording label. . . . The company plans an ambitious series of CDs in pop, rhythm and blues, country and other genres, all showcasing undiscovered women artists. . . .

". . . Public-health advocates criticize the motives of Philip Morris executives. 'They gain a good product association but also buy loyalty and allies in a culturally influential field,' says Michael Pertschuk, former chairman of the Federal Trade Commission and co-director of the . . . Advocacy Institute. By linking cigarettes to rock musicians, he says, 'they are trying to make a product attractive to the very person who is the role model of the younger kids.' " (*Wall Street Journal*, January 15, 1997)

---

"A nonprofit organization with close ties to the anti-smoking movement."
(*New York Times*, June 26, 1997)
"Liberal." (*Wall Street Journal*, November 10, 1994)

## POLITICAL ORIENTATION

# American Conservative Union (1964)

1007 Cameron Street
Alexandria, Virginia 22314
Phone: (703) 836-8602
Fax: (703) 836-8606
Internet: http//www.conservative.org

| | |
|---|---|
| **PURPOSE** | "To engage in lobbying, public education and related activities to advance conservative political ideas and principles." |
| **STAFF** | 5 total—3 professional; 2 support; plus approximately 10 interns |
| **DIRECTOR** | Thomas R. Katina, executive director. Katina also serves as director of the Conservative Political Action Committee (CPAC). Prior to assuming his current role as executive director of the American Conservative Union (ACU), he served as the ACU field operations director from 1994–1997. Earlier, he was project manager of Citizens Against Rationing Health. Katina holds a B.S. degree from Auburn University. |
| **TAX STATUS** | 501(c)(4) |
| **BUDGET** | 1998—Unavailable<br>Proposed 1999—Unavailable |
| **FUNDING SOURCES** | Membership and donations from individuals, 97 percent; foundation grants, 2 percent; corporate donations, 1 percent |
| **SCOPE** | Members: 1 million<br>Branches/chapters: N/A<br>Affiliate: ACU Foundation, a 501(c)(3) organization |
| **PAC** | American Conservative Union Political Action Committee |

◆ Advertisements ◆ Campaign contributions ◆ Coalition forming ◆ Congressional testimony ◆ Congressional voting analysis ◆ Films/video/audiotapes ◆ Grassroots organizing ◆ Internet (databases, e-mail alerts, Web site) ◆ Internships ◆ Legislative/regulatory monitoring (federal) ◆ Lobbying (federal) ◆ Media outreach ◆ Voting records

## METHOD OF OPERATION

◆ Abolishing the IRS ◆ Tax code termination

## CURRENT CONCERNS

*Annual Rating of Congress*

## PUBLICATIONS

*Battleline* (quarterly)

## NEWSLETTER

Conservative Political Action Committee Conference (annual, Washington, D.C.)

## CONFERENCES

David A. Keene, chairman; Thomas S. Winter, first vice chairman; Leroy Corey, second vice chairman; Jameson Campaigne Jr., secretary; Donald J. Devine, treasurer; Thomas R. Katina, executive director

## BOARD OF DIRECTORS

Other members:
◆ Jeffrey Bell ◆ Charles Black ◆ Morton Blackwell ◆ Beau Boulter ◆ Floyd Brown ◆ Muriel Coleman ◆ M. Stanton Evans ◆ Alan Gottlieb ◆ Louis Guerra ◆ Paul Hart ◆ Jesse Helms ◆ Duncan Hunter ◆ James V. Lacy ◆ Wayne LaPierre ◆ Michael R. Long ◆ Serphin Maltese ◆ Joseph A. Morris ◆ Grover G. Norquist ◆ James Arthur Pope ◆ Ralph Reed Jr. ◆ Allen Roth ◆ Marc E. Rotterman ◆ Craig Shirley ◆ Lewis K. Uhler

"According to an annual voting scorecard compiled by the American Conservative Union (ACU), both the Senate and the House shifted to the left of the political spectrum in 1997. The House, however, saw a moderating trend, where Republicans voted less conservatively and the Democrats less liberally. The Senate, the ACU survey said, showed both parties becoming more liberal." (*Washington Post*, April 8, 1998)

## EFFECTIVENESS

"It was at [the Conservative Political Action Committee Conference] four years ago that Paula Corbin Jones held her sensational news conference to charge that Clinton, when he was governor of Arkansas, propositioned her in a Little Rock hotel room in 1991. . . .

"Yesterday, American Conservative Union Chairman David Keene, who organizes CPAC every year, took pains to distance himself from Jones, saying he had nothing to do with her fateful announcement. 'The reason people try to surface their agendas at this convention is not because I am here but because you all [in the news media] are here,' he said.

"Keene pooh-poohed Hillary Clinton's claim of a right-wing cabal.

" 'All of politics is a conspiracy,' he said. 'Every campaign is a conspiracy. They want an enemy, because in politics you need an enemy. . . . She has slipped into the fever swamp, and has developed a case of paranoia second to none.' " (*Washington Post*, January 30, 1998)

"While you were sleeping, your humble servant repaired to his favorite chair with a stack of reports covering financial contributions to [Republican Rep. Charles H. Taylor of North Carolina] in 1994, 1995 and in the first part of 1997. It should come as no surprise that campaign contributions to a politician who scores 100 percent with the American Conservative Union would run along fairly predictable ideological and interest-group lines. There were plenty of PAC (political action committee) contributions from groups such as the Conservative Campaign Fund, North Carolina Right to Life Inc. and the National Rifle Association Political Victory Fund, and from banks, oil, tobacco, lumber and textile interests." (*Washington Post*, September 20, 1997)

## POLITICAL ORIENTATION

"a conservative ratings group" (*Washington Post*, April 8, 1998)

"David Keene, chairman of the American Conservative Union, which sponsors the [Conservative Political Action Committee Conference], said that this group tended to attract economic conservatives more than social conservatives and that Republicans were smart to heed Mr. Gingrich's early advice to avoid discussing the President's sex life." (*New York Times*, January 30, 1998)

"For the first time in decades, the Republicans' powerful wing of cultural and religious conservatives has charged into the China debate, arguing that Beijing should be denied renewal of most-favored-nation trade status in June because they deem its policies on human rights, abortion and religious persecution morally offensive. . . .

"That stand pits the cultural conservatives, many of them blue-collar voters, directly against its Wall Street wing as well as the libertarians, who consistently favor free trade. Open commerce with China is good 'because of what it does to China to break the stranglehold of the state,' argues David Keene, chairman of the American Conservative Union." (*Wall Street Journal*, April 14, 1997)

# American Legislative Exchange Council (1973)

910 17th Street, NW
Fifth Floor
Washington, D.C. 20006
Phone: (202) 466-3800
Fax: (202) 466-3801
Internet: http://www.alec.org

| | |
|---|---|
| "To develop dynamic partnerships between state legislators and the private sector in order to advance a public policy agenda based on the Jeffersonian principles of free markets, limited government, individual liberty and traditional family values. . . . To help members create effective, innovative public policies which promote free enterprise, spur economic growth, encourage individual responsibility and independence, and enhance the nation's competitiveness in the global marketplace." | *PURPOSE* |
| 29 total—28 professional; 1 support; plus 10 interns | *STAFF* |
| Duane Parde, executive director. Prior to serving as executive director, Parde was American Legislative Exchange Council's (ALEC's) chief of staff. From 1992 to 1995, he served as the director of state affairs for the Council for Affordable Health Insurance. Prior to that, he was ALEC's director of state legislation and research and served as a legislative research assistant in the Kansas attorney general's office. Parde graduated from the University of Kansas. | *DIRECTOR* |
| 501(c)(3) | *TAX STATUS* |
| 1998—$5 million<br>Proposed 1999—$6 million | *BUDGET* |
| Corporate contributions, 55 percent; foundation grants, 30 percent; conferences, membership, and other, 15 percent | *FUNDING SOURCES* |
| Members: 2,900 state legislators (from all 50 states, Puerto Rico, and Guam); 554 corporations and foundations<br>Branches/chapters: N/A<br>Affiliates: N/A | *SCOPE* |

| | |
|---|---|
| **PAC** | None |
| **METHOD OF OPERATION** | ♦ Conferences/seminars ♦ Internet (Web site) ♦ Legislative/regulatory monitoring (state) ♦ Library/information clearinghouse ♦ Local/municipal affairs ♦ Media outreach ♦ Research ♦ Speakers program ♦ State model legislation |
| **CURRENT CONCERNS** | ♦ Bail reform ♦ Balanced Budget Amendment ♦ Capital gains tax ♦ Clean air strategies ♦ Clean water strategies ♦ Cost-benefit analysis of environmental regulations ♦ Curriculum reform ♦ Education finance ♦ Enterprise zones ♦ Free market health care ♦ Insurance fraud ♦ International competitiveness ♦ Interstate banking ♦ Job training ♦ Joint and several liability ♦ Labor market reform ♦ Low-income housing ♦ Medicaid reform ♦ Prison privatization ♦ Privatization of public housing ♦ Product liability ♦ Punitive damages ♦ Rent control ♦ Restoration of state authority ♦ School vouchers ♦ Striker replacement ♦ Taxes and regulations imposed on businesses ♦ Telecommunications regulation ♦ Tourism ♦ Trade, tariffs, and quotas ♦ Transportation issues ♦ Truth in sentencing ♦ Tort reform ♦ Unfunded and underfunded mandates ♦ Victims' rights ♦ Welfare reform ♦ Workers' compensation |
| **PUBLICATIONS** | *Breaking the Chain: From Dependency to Opportunity*<br>*The Crisis in America's State Budgets*<br>*Environmental Partners*<br>*Evidence of a Failed System: A Study of Pretrial Release Agencies in California*<br>*Expanding Transit Service through Regulatory Mechanisms*<br>*Keeping the Promise: A Comprehensive Health Care Plan for the States*<br>*Legislative Issue Briefs*<br>*People, Markets, and Government: How Economic Policy Creates Wealth and Poverty*<br>*Public-Private Partnerships in Transportation Infrastructure*<br>*Report Card on American Education*<br>*Report Card on Crime and Punishment*<br>*The Sourcebook of American State Legislation*<br>*Sovereignty of the People and Devolution: An Agenda for the Restoration of the Tenth Amendment*<br><br>Also publishes issue papers and *ALEC Forum* on a wide range of topics |
| **NEWSLETTER** | *FYI* (biweekly)<br>*Issue Analysis* (periodic)<br>*The State Factor* (periodic) |
| **CONFERENCES/ SEMINARS** | ALEC annual meeting<br>States and Nation Summit |

## BOARD OF DIRECTORS

"By combining their legal forces, the 50 state attorneys general are reviving liberal government activism in a supposedly conservative era.

"They were the first to wound not-so-Big Tobacco, making it possible for President Clinton and Congress to devour the $516 billion carcass. Now they've joined the assault on Microsoft, going even further in their antitrust suit than the Clinton Justice Department. . . .

" 'We're very, very concerned about this trend,' says Duane Parde, executive director of the American Legislative Exchange Council (ALEC), a group of some 3,000 state legislators. 'We're concerned about the way states are ganging up to raise a lot of money.'. . .

". . . Mr. Parde . . . says his group is drafting a proposal to require state-legislative approval for all big contracts an attorney general negotiates, including any with trial lawyers." (*Wall Street Journal*, May 22, 1998)

"In 1995 House Republicans passed a budget that included $245 billion in tax cuts, eliminated four Cabinet-level agencies and dramatically revamped Medicare. The package signed Tuesday has $95 billion in net tax reductions over five years and actually complicates the tax code with a myriad of targeted breaks for specific industries and groups. . . .

"Mike Flynn, an economic analyst at the . . . American Legislative Exchange Council, said Washington's tax-cutting effort is puny. 'Ninety billion dollars sounds like a lot, but the government will spend over $8 trillion in that time period,' he said. 'The states passed $12 billion in tax cuts in the last three years.' " (*Washington Post*, August 13, 1997)

"Through the 1980s and 1990s total government spending as a share of GDP grew dramatically to 34%; almost all that growth was in higher state and county taxation. Voters now are recognizing the long-time fiscal model of raising taxes continually to 'pay for' more government programs has turned out to be a disaster for the states. They're turning now to the [pro–tax cut] policies of a Christie Whitman or John Engler. . . .

"As we've noted before, some of this change at the state level is due to the work of the American Legislative Exchange Council, founded in 1973 to emphasize economic growth as a primary political goal and now inspiriting conservative state legislators to enact policies in their home states that will make that happen." (*Wall Street Journal*, September 18, 1995)

## EFFECTIVENESS

"right-leaning" (*Washington Post*, August 13, 1997)

## POLITICAL ORIENTATION

# Americans for Democratic Action, Inc. (1947)

1625 K Street, NW
Suite 210
Washington, D.C. 20006
Phone: (202) 785-5980
Fax: (202) 785-5969
Internet: adaction@ix.netcom.com *or* http://www.adaction.org

**PURPOSE**

"Dedicated to individual liberty and economic and social justice at home and abroad."

**STAFF**

7 total—4 professional; 3 support; plus interns

**DIRECTOR**

Amy F. Isaacs, national director. Prior to rejoining Americans for Democratic Action (ADA) in 1989, Isaacs was a senior communications coordinator with Planned Parenthood Federation of America. She previously served as a fundraising and volunteer coordinator for the Bob Edgar for U.S. Senate Committee. Her previous experience with ADA, spanning seventeen years, included serving as deputy national director from 1980–1986.

**TAX STATUS**

501(c)(4)

**BUDGET**

1998—$1 million
Proposed 1999—$1 million

**FUNDING SOURCES**

Membership, 75 percent; large contributions, including unions, 25 percent

**SCOPE**

Members: 65,000
Branches/chapters: 20 chapters
Affiliate: ADA Educational Fund, a 501(c)(3) organization

**PAC**

ADA Political Action Committee

| | |
|---|---|
| ◆ Campaign contributions ◆ Coalition forming ◆ Conferences/seminars ◆ Internet (Web site) ◆ Legislative and political education ◆ Legislative/ regulatory monitoring (federal and state) ◆ Publications | *METHOD OF OPERATION* |
| ◆ Domestic policy ◆ Economic policy ◆ Environmental policy ◆ Foreign policy ◆ Military policy | *CURRENT CONCERNS* |
| *ADA Voting Record* (annual)<br>Also publishes special reports and policy briefs | *PUBLICATIONS* |
| *ADA Today* (quarterly)<br>*ADAction News and Notes* (weekly when Congress is in session) | *NEWSLETTER* |
| Annual convention (every June)<br>Sponsors other conferences on selected issues | *CONFERENCES* |
| Jim Jontz, president; William Markus, national executive committee chair; Amy Isaacs, national director<br><br>The complete board list is unavailable | *BOARD OF DIRECTORS* |
| "You have no doubt heard someone say something along these lines: 'I invested a lot in that guy, and look where I am now.' Or: 'What's the pay-off?' People are in the market for almost everything: new jobs, new relationships, new ideas, new sports to play and new novels to read. | *EFFECTIVENESS* |

"If you're looking for evidence of the triumph of capitalism, just watch your language. Think of how many different kinds of capital we talk about besides the kind raised on Wall Street. There's moral capital and intellectual capital. . . . Ann Lewis, former national director of . . . Americans for Democratic Action, once spoke about how liberals tried to toughen up their language by embracing hard-headed commerce terms: 'We used to talk about immunizing little children against disease. Now we call it investing in human capital.' (For the record, Ms. Lewis, now White House communications director, thinks the pendulum is swinging back.)" (*Washington Post*, May 17, 1998)

"[Independent counsel Ken Starr's] demand for records of Monica Lewinsky's book purchases brought howls of protest yesterday from the publishing industry, booksellers and free speech groups. They argued that Starr had corrupted privacy and the First Amendment by asking Kramerbooks in Dupont Circle to cough up Lewinsky's transactions.

"Amy Isaacs, national director of Americans for Democratic Action, called the subpoena 'an outrageous act, deeply insidious to First Amendment freedoms . . . [and] smacks of some of the worst abuses under a totalitarian regime.' " (*Washington Post*, March 26, 1998)

# POLITICAL ORIENTATION

"liberal" (*Washington Post*, June 17, 1998)

"[Sen. Paul Wellstone of Minnesota] . . . came as close as custom permits to declaring his [presidential] candidacy last week at a breakfast of Americans for Democratic Action (ADA) . . . founded 51 years ago by another Minnesotan, Hubert H. Humphrey. . . .

"It was a small crowd—perhaps 60 people, some young activists in their local communities and some who might have attended the 1947 convention when Humphrey formed the ADA as a vehicle for the noncommunist left to fight for civil rights and combat Henry Wallace and his soft-on-the-Soviets friends.

"They talked about how they had supported yet another Minnesotan, former senator Eugene McCarthy, in his challenge to President Lyndon Johnson in 1968 and how their former president, the late Allard Lowenstein, had organized the dump-Johnson movement." (*Washington Post*, June 17, 1998)

# Arab American Institute (1985)

918 16th Street, NW
Suite 601
Washington, D.C. 20006
Phone: (202) 429-9210
Fax: (202) 429-9214
Internet: http://www.aaiusa.org

| | |
|---|---|
| "Serves as a clearinghouse for bipartisan political activity, including voter mobilization and education, and a national resource for government, academe and the media on the policy concerns of Arab Americans and U.S.-Middle East relations." | *PURPOSE* |
| 13 total—8 professional; 5 support; plus 2 interns and 2 part-time field organizers | *STAFF* |
| James J. Zogby, president. A cofounder and chairman of the Palestine Human Rights Campaign in the late 1970s, he later cofounded and served as president of Save Lebanon, Inc. In 1984, Zogby was vice chair and deputy campaign manager for fundraising of the Jesse Jackson for President Campaign. In 1993, he was asked by Vice President Gore to lead Builders for Peace, an American private-sector committee to promote investment in the West Bank and Gaza. Zogby was appointed to the Democratic National Committee in 1994. A lecturer and scholar on Middle East issues, he appears frequently on television and radio and writes a weekly column on U.S. politics for the major newspapers of the Arab world. Zogby received his doctorate from Temple University's department of religion. | *DIRECTOR* |
| 501(c)(4) | *TAX STATUS* |
| 1998—$650,000<br>Proposed 1999—$650,000 | *BUDGET* |
| Individual contributions, 75 percent; conferences and meetings, 10 percent; grants, 10 percent; publications, 5 percent | *FUNDING SOURCES* |
| Members: 10,000 individuals<br>Branches/chapters: 12 regional councils—Illinois, Michigan, Mid-Atlantic, Midwest, National Capital Area, New England, Ohio, Pacific Northwest, Pennsylvania, Southeast, South Central, and Southwest<br>Affiliate: Arab American Leadership Council | *SCOPE* |

| **PAC** | None |

| **METHOD OF OPERATION** | ◆ Coalition forming ◆ Conferences/seminars ◆ Congressional testimony ◆ Congressional voting analysis ◆ Direct action ◆ Electoral politics (Arab American Democratic and Republican Clubs, Arab American Leadership Council) ◆ Grassroots organizing ◆ Initiative/referendum campaigns ◆ International activities ◆ Internet (Web site) ◆ Library/information clearinghouse ◆ Lobbying (state and grassroots) ◆ Local/municipal affairs ◆ Media outreach ◆ Polling ◆ Research ◆ Speakers program ◆ Telecommunications services (databases, mailing lists) ◆ Training and technical assistance ◆ Voter registration ◆ Voting records |

| **CURRENT CONCERNS** | ◆ Arab American civil/political rights ◆ Arab American electoral participation ◆ Demographics and Census 2000 ◆ Ethnic/race relations in urban centers ◆ Immigration reform ◆ Middle East peace process |

| **PUBLICATIONS** | *The 105th Congress and Middle East Peace*<br>*1994 Voter Guides for Key States*<br>*American Voters and Mideast Peace*<br>*Arab Americans Today: A Demographic Profile of the Arab American Community*<br>*Arab Americans: Making a Difference* (brochure)<br>*Election Preview: Races to Watch in 1994 and 1996 Presidential Hopefuls*<br>*The Emerging Majority: American Voters and Palestinian Rights in the 1990s*<br>*Empowerment*<br>*The Financing of U.S. Congressional Elections by Pro-Israel PACs*<br>*Life, Liberty and the Pursuit of Happiness: A Three-Decade Journey in the Occupied Territories*<br>*New Thinking for Israeli-Palestinian Peace*<br>*A Plan That Works Well: A Political Blueprint for Arab Americans*<br>*Preserving America's Freedoms: the Omnibus Counterterrorism Act of 1995 vs. the Bill of Rights*<br>*Profiles on the Middle East Position of the 1992 Presidential Candidates*<br>*Roster of Arab Americans in Public Service and Political Life*<br>*Statements of Major Churches and Religious Institutions on the Question of Jerusalem*<br>*Surveillance and Defamation* |

| **NEWSLETTER** | *ISSUES* (quarterly newsletter about Arab American political work) |

| **CONFERENCES** | National Leadership Conference (annual)<br>Statewide Leadership Meetings |

| **BOARD OF DIRECTORS** | ◆ Jean R. AbiNader ◆ George R. Salem ◆ Helen Hatab Samhan ◆ James J. Zogby ◆ John Zogby |

"So far, backing for Bill Lann Lee, the Los Angeles lawyer who is fighting an uphill battle to become the Justice Department's top civil rights enforcement official, has come from a variety of groups. But the idea of the nomination's making strange bedfellows reached a new level today.

"Abraham H. Foxman, the national director of the Anti-Defamation League of B'nai B'rith, and James J. Zogby, president of the Arab American Institute, today sent a jointly signed letter to a member of the Senate Judiciary Committee in support of Mr. Lee. . . .

"The letter represents one of the few times that Mr. Zogby's group has taken the same position with one of the country's largest Jewish organizations. In the past the two organizations have bitterly disagreed, generally over United States policy in the Middle East." (*New York Times*, November 13, 1997)

"When James Zogby introduced President Clinton as the keynote speaker at a dinner hosted by the Arab American Institute Thursday night, American officials quipped later that he had really made it in terms of whom he got to attend the dinner. 'You are really big,' ribbed one distinguished guest. . . ." (*Washington Post*, May 13, 1998)

"American support for Israel has brought charges of double standards and hypocrisy from many Arabs and Arab-Americans. . . .

" 'The perception of an American double standard has undercut U.S. credibility and that of the Arab governments who are allied to the United States,' said James J. Zogby, president of the Arab American Institute in Washington. 'The ordinary Arab on the street is both angry and alienated, and that is every bit as significant a factor in the political equation as any of the military components.'. . .

". . . Mr. Zogby [notes that] Washington has often used its veto in the Security Council to block many resolutions that criticize Israel or that demand its withdrawal from specific territory.

"After the gulf war, he said, there was an understanding with Arab allies that Washington would press hard for a resolution of the Arab-Israeli conflict.

" 'Seven years later, the process is hugely disappointing and asymmetrical,' Mr. Zogby said. 'The Arabs get threats and force, and Israel gets compassion and aid.' " (*New York Times*, February 21, 1998)

# EFFECTIVENESS

# POLITICAL ORIENTATION

# Business-Industry Political Action Committee (1963)

888 16th Street, NW
Suite 305
Washington, D.C. 20006
Phone: (202) 833-1880
Fax: (202) 833-2338
Internet: http://www.bipac.org

**PURPOSE**

"To elect candidates to Congress who strongly support policies that will strengthen the free-enterprise system, create jobs, and promote economic growth and opportunity."

**STAFF**

10 total—8 professional; 2 support; plus periodic interns

**DIRECTOR**

Charles S. Mack, president and chief executive officer. Mack has worked as a corporate public affairs executive, association president, and management consultant.

**TAX STATUS**

BIPAC consists of two components: Action Fund is a Political Action Committee and the Business Institute for Political Analysis is a for-profit organization.

**BUDGET**

1998—$1.5 million
Proposed 1999—Unavailable

**FUNDING SOURCES**

Supported by the business community through contributions, meeting registration fees, and honoraria

**SCOPE**

Members: "Action Fund is supported by individuals and business-related PACs; the Business Institute for Political Analysis is funded by corporations and trade associations"
Branches/chapters: N/A
Affiliates: N/A

**PAC**

BIPAC's Action Fund is a political action committee

| | |
|---|---|
| ♦ Conferences/seminars ♦ Congressional voting analysis ♦ Electoral politics ♦ Internet (Web site) ♦ PAC contributions ♦ Research ♦ Speakers program ♦ Voting records<br><br>*Note:* The Business Institute for Political Analysis researches candidates, major Congressional issues, PAC operations, campaign finance, and other legislative and regulatory matters affecting the political/electoral process. BIPAC then disseminates this information through regular briefings, seminars, publications, and its Web site. | *METHOD OF*<br>*OPERATION* |

| | |
|---|---|
| Reelection of a pro-business Congress | *CURRENT*<br>*CONCERNS* |

| | |
|---|---|
| *Voting Records* (annual) | *PUBLICATIONS* |

| | |
|---|---|
| *BIPAC Action Report* (quarterly)<br>*Election In Sight* (monthly) | *NEWSLETTER* |

| | |
|---|---|
| Conference (annual)<br>National briefings (periodic)<br>Special workshops (monthly)<br>Washington briefings (monthly) | *CONFERENCE* |

| | |
|---|---|
| ♦ William F. Allyn ♦ Jan Witold Baran ♦ Timothy Barnard ♦ Michail E. Baroody ♦ Gordon T. Beaham III ♦ Bruce D. Benson ♦ Linden Blue ♦ Donald T. Bollinger ♦ Betty H. Bowers ♦ David A. Brandon ♦ Aldo M. Caccamo ♦ Peter R. Carney ♦ John Castellani ♦ C.L. Clemente ♦ Ken W. Cole ♦ James E. Coles ♦ Allan D. Cors ♦ Donald A. Danner ♦ John Dendahl ♦ Richard M. Devos Jr. ♦ Ralph R. DiSibio ♦ Kenneth L. Fisher ♦ Harry S. Flemming ♦ W. Heywood Fralin ♦ Stephen E. Frank ♦ Owsley B. Frazier ♦ Elmer B. Harris ♦ Derek C. Hathaway ♦ Donald E. Hatley ♦ Robert L. Healy ♦ William F. Hecht ♦ Mark V. Heitz ♦ Michael J. Hennessey ♦ Isabel N. Jasinowski ♦ R. Bruce Josten ♦ Ardon B. Judd Jr. ♦ Christopher M. Kinsey ♦ Jere M. Lawrence ♦ William G. Little ♦ Pierce J. Lonergan ♦ Charles S. Mack ♦ Donald R. Margo ♦ James E. Marley ♦ Samuel L. Maury ♦ Mary E. McAuliffe ♦ Norman P. McClelland ♦ John Noble McConnell Jr. ♦ Robert M. McGee ♦ Donald E. Meiners ♦ John M. Mutz ♦ Ralph J. Nagel ♦ J. Larry Nichols ♦ David S. Osterhout ♦ Conrad A. Plimpton ♦ Lisa A. Rickard ♦ John R. Riedman ♦ Chris A. Robbins ♦ Daryl D. Smith ♦ Sherwood H. Smith Jr. ♦ Ted L. Snider Jr. ♦ Steve R. Spencer ♦ Ira N. Stone ♦ Thomas J. Tauke ♦ W. Dennis Thomas ♦ Terence H. Thorn ♦ William B. Trent Jr. ♦ Diemer True ♦ Henry B. Wehrle Jr. ♦ Gerald Whitburn ♦ David B. Whitehurst ♦ Earle C. Williams ♦ Michael B. Yanney ♦ Dean A. Yannucci | *BOARD OF*<br>*DIRECTORS* |

## EFFECTIVENESS

"Things get stranger and stranger around here.... It's getting hard to figure out where anybody stands.

"Consider an issue of paramount importance to the business world: approving new U.S. financing for the International Monetary Fund. With an Asian financial crisis staring it in the face, big business, more than anything, wants Congress to calm global nerves by approving the funding....

"Yet in the unfolding IMF debate, business is finding love in all the wrong places. House Democratic leader Richard Gephardt—supposedly the populist, protectionist tool of labor unions—is solidly, publicly in favor of approving America's multibillion-dollar commitment to the IMF.

"Meanwhile, his Republican counterpart in the House, Dick Armey, GOP presidential aspirant Steve Forbes and some other Republican luminaries ... are holding their noses over IMF funding.

" 'We can't figure out where a lot of the Republicans are on a lot of these issues,' says Charles Mack, president of the Business-Industry Political Action Committee.

"Specifically, BIPAC studied four recent issues—three involving international trade—and found that 40 House members took what business considered the 'wrong' position on all of them. Stunningly, 23 of the 40 are Republicans...." (*Wall Street Journal*, March 11, 1998)

"If you liked the campaign-finance tricks that have been on display [in 1997], just wait. You're likely to see even more next year, with some new twists thrown in for added fun.

"This is the bizarre irony of the campaign fund-raising 'scandals' of 1997. The end result is that nothing will have changed going into congressional elections next year, except maybe that the appetite for cash raised in new and innovative ways has increased....

"Charles Mack, president of the Business-Industry Political Action Committee, summarizes the situation with candor and brevity. Writing in his organization's latest newsletter, he forecasts that, barring some new Supreme Court decision changing the legal landscape, 'issue ads targeting candidates and independent expenditures will continue to grow without limit in future elections, as will candidates' own spending.' " (*Wall Street Journal*, December 3, 1997)

"Big Labor has roused a napping giant. Alarmed by the AFL-CIO's decision to spend $35 million trying to sway voters during this year's elections, business lobbying groups are readying a massive counterpunch....

"In a separate but related project, the Business Industry Political Action Committee is drafting a 'political participation manual.' It will lay out the various election laws and how groups can legally influence elections, says Bernadette Budde, the committee's senior vice president.

" 'I've been doing this for 25 years,' she says, 'and there is greater unity than there ever has been before.' " (*Wall Street Journal*, May 10, 1996)

## POLITICAL ORIENTATION

"... BIPAC ranks all Members on how closely they went along with the business lobby's priorities. While these columns often disagree with the agenda of individual companies or industries, BIPAC's vote rankings are instructive because they include a variety of broad fiscal (tax and spend), tort reform and regulatory issues. BIPAC typically stays away from social and cultural votes...." (*Wall Street Journal*, October 17, 1996)

# Center for Public Integrity (1989)

910 17th Street, NW
17th Floor
Washington, D.C. 20006
Phone: (202) 783-3900
Fax: (202) 783-3906
Internet: contact@publicintegrity.org *or*
http://www.publicintegrity.org

| | |
|---|---|
| "To provide the American people with the findings of our investigations and analyses of public-service, government-accountability, and ethics-related issues. The result of [the Center's] efforts will . . . be a better-informed citizenry." | ***PURPOSE*** |
| 24 total—23 professional; 1 support; plus 1 part-time professional; 6–10 interns | ***STAFF*** |
| Charles Lewis, executive director. Prior to founding the Center for Public Integrity, Lewis worked from 1977 to 1988 as an investigative reporter and producer for network television news at ABC and CBS. He writes articles and books on a range of issues. Lewis also serves on the board of the Fund for Investigative Journalism. A graduate of the University of Delaware, he hold a masters degree from the Johns Hopkins University School of Advanced International Studies in Washington. | ***DIRECTOR*** |
| 501(c)(3) | ***TAX STATUS*** |
| 1997—$1.4 million<br>1998—$1.8 million<br>Proposed 1999—$2 million | ***BUDGET*** |
| Foundations, 85 percent; consulting, 4 percent; book advances, 4 percent; individuals, 2 percent; membership dues, 2 percent; publications, 1 percent; other, 2 percent | ***FUNDING SOURCES*** |
| Members: 2,000<br>Branches/chapters: N/A<br>Affiliates: N/A | ***SCOPE*** |
| None | ***PAC*** |

| METHOD OF OPERATION | ◆ Awards program ◆ Conferences/seminars ◆ Congressional testimony ◆ Congressional voting analysis ◆ International activities ◆ Internet (databases, Web site) ◆ Internships ◆ Media outreach ◆ Research |
| --- | --- |
| CURRENT CONCERNS | ◆ Airline safety ◆ Enforcement of the Illinois Governmental Ethics Act ◆ Food safety ◆ Government regulation of toxic chemicals ◆ Investigative journalism ◆ NAFTA ◆ Reform of campaign funds/expenditures ◆ Superfund ◆ U.S. economic embargo of Cuba |
| PUBLICATIONS | *America's Frontline Trade Officials*<br>*Beyond the Hill: A Directory of Congress from 1984 to 1993—Where Have All the Members Gone?*<br>*Biohazard*<br>*The Buying of the President*<br>*Buying the American Mind*<br>*Fat Cat Hotel*<br>*Place Your Bets: The Gambling Industry and the 1996 Presidential Election*<br>*Saving for a Rainy Day*<br>*Silence of the Laws*<br>*Toxic Deception: How the Chemical Industry Manipulates Science, Bends the Law, and Endangers Your Health*<br>*Toxic Temptation*<br>*Under Fire*<br><br>Also publishes reports and studies on a wide range of topics |
| NEWSLETTER | *The Public I* (8–12 issues per year) |
| CONFERENCES | Annual Conference for International Consortium of Investigative Journalists |
| BOARD OF DIRECTORS | ◆ Josie Goytisolo ◆ Bill Hogan ◆ Charles Lewis ◆ Susan Loewenberg ◆ Charles Piller ◆ Allen Pusey ◆ Ben Sherwood ◆ Marianne Szegedy-Maszak ◆ Paula Walker ◆ Isabel Wilkerson |
| EFFECTIVENESS | "When Charles Lewis of the Center for Public Integrity began to study Fannie Mae's political influence, he was not prepared for the angst his probing questions would prompt on Capitol Hill. 'We had folks who would only meet us in strange places' such as parking garages, Lewis said. 'No one wanted to talk on the record.'... |

"Lewis is well-known for exposing political influence in Washington. The center, of which he is the founder and executive director, was the first to disclose that the Clinton White House was allowing political donors to stay in the Lincoln Bedroom. But Lewis said the center, an investigative think tank specializing in ethics-related issues, is not likely to publish a report on the Fannie Mae study any time soon, because it has not been able to prove what it suspects about Fannie Mae: that many of its hiring and charitable decisions are made to exert maximum political influence.

"Still, Lewis is not alone in his assessment of Fannie Mae's ability to influence the government. . . ." (*CQ Weekly*, June 13, 1998)

"With a full-time staff of 24 and a $2 million annual budget, the center [Center for Public Integrity] has carved out a prominent niche in Washington's watchdog subculture.

"The MacArthur Foundation cited the center for producing 'high quality, high impact, public service journalism, releasing more than 30 influential investigative reports on issues related . . . to government accountability and public and private sector ethics.' " (*Washington Post*, June 2, 1998)

"Who broke the wonderful tale of the White House as a bed-and-breakfast stopover for fat-cat campaign contributors?

"Not the national newspapers.

"Who exposed the monied interests behind the campaigns to pass the NAFTA bill and defeat the Clinton universal health care plan?

"Not the national news magazines.

"Who produced 'The Buying of the President,' a seminal study of the special interests behind the presidential candidates of the 1990s?

"Not the television networks. . . .

"All of these stories were the product of the Center for Public Integrity." (*Washington Post*, October 20, 1997)

". . . Last August, the Center for Public Integrity revealed that more than 75 Democratic donors and fund-raisers had spent the night in the Lincoln Bedroom. . . .

"The Center for Public Integrity report, 'Fat Cat Hotel,' listed such Lincoln Bedroom guests as former MCA chairman Lew Wasserman, who had donated $450,000 to Clinton and the Democrats, along with such celebrities as Barbra Streisand and Tom Hanks. The report received inside-the-paper coverage in *The Post, Los Angeles Times, Washington Times, Baltimore Sun* and *Chicago Tribune*, among others.

"And the story quickly faded in the face of vociferous denials. DNC spokeswoman Amy Weiss Tobe told the center that the allegations had 'become an urban myth, like the alligators in the sewers of New York.'

"Last summer, *Forbes* magazine carried a short item saying that donors could buy a night in the Lincoln Bedroom for $130,000. David Brinkley picked it up in his commentary on ABC's 'This Week.' " (*Washington Post*, March 10, 1997)

# POLITICAL ORIENTATION

"nonpartisan" (*Washington Post*, June 2, 1998, and *Wall Street Journal*, December 15, 1997)

"liberal" (*Wall Street Journal*, October 29, 1996)

# Center for Responsive Politics (1983)

1320 19th Street, NW
Suite 620
Washington, D.C. 20036
Phone: (202) 857-0044
Fax: (202) 857-7809
Internet: info@crp.org *or* http://www.crp.org

| | |
|---|---|
| "To study Congress, particularly the role money plays in its elections and actions. The Center conducts computer-based research on campaign-finance issues. Its work is aimed at creating a more involved citizenry and a more responsive Congress." | *PURPOSE* |
| 15 total; plus interns | *STAFF* |
| Larry Makinson, executive director. Makinson has worked for the Center for Responsive Politics since 1988. He first began tracking patterns in political contributions in 1985, when he was a reporter for the *Anchorage Daily News*. Makinson has since written 10 books and numerous reports on the subject. He graduated from Harvard University with a master's degree in public administration. | *DIRECTOR* |
| 501(c)(3) | *TAX STATUS* |
| 1998—$1.2 million<br>Proposed 1999—$1.2 million | *BUDGET* |
| Foundation grants, 100 percent | *FUNDING SOURCES* |
| Members: N/A<br>Branches/chapters: N/A<br>Affiliates: N/A | *SCOPE* |
| None | *PAC* |

| | |
|---|---|
| *METHOD OF OPERATION* | ◆ Advertisements ◆ Conferences/seminars ◆ Congressional testimony ◆ Congressional voting analysis ◆ Films/video/audiotapes ◆ Internet (electronic bulletin boards, Web site) ◆ Legislative/regulatory monitoring (federal) ◆ Library/information clearinghouse (open to public) ◆ Media outreach ◆ Participation in regulatory proceedings (federal) ◆ Research ◆ Speakers program ◆ Telecommunications services (databases) ◆ Training and technical assistance |
| *CURRENT CONCERNS* | ◆ Campaign finance (federal and state) ◆ Congressional ethics ◆ Congressional structure and operations ◆ Effect of political money on public policy ◆ State campaign finance disclosure |
| *PUBLICATIONS* | *10 Myths About Money in Politics* <br> *1995–1996 Big Picture* <br> *At the Starting Gate . . .* <br> *A Bag of Tricks* <br> *The Best Defense* <br> *A Brief History of Money in Politics* <br> *Beyond the Limits* <br> *Cashing In* <br> *Digital Democracy* <br> *Global Connections* <br> *High-Tech Influence* <br> *In-State Vs. Out-of-State* <br> *Loral Contributions Under Fire* <br> *Money and Politics Survey* <br> *Money in Politics Reform* <br> *Plugging in the Public* <br> *Political Union* <br> *The Politics of Sugar* <br> *Power to the People?* <br> *Speaking Freely* <br> *Tribes Deal Themselves In* <br> *The Wealth Primary* <br> *Who's in the Lobby?* <br> *Who's Paying?* <br> *Why Do Donors Give?* |
| *NEWSLETTER* | *Capital Eye* (bimonthly) |
| *CONFERENCES* | Two series of conferences: one designed for invited journalists, the other designed for issue activists |
| *BOARD OF DIRECTORS* | Paul S. Hoff, chair; Thomas R. Asher, treasurer; Martha Angle, secretary <br><br> Other board members: ◆ Sonia Jarvis ◆ Charles McC Mathias ◆ Ellen S. Miller ◆ John G. Murphy ◆ Whitney North Seymour Jr. ◆ David Stern ◆ Robert A. Weinberger |

"As of June 1, airlines and their political action committees had contributed $2.2 million to congressional candidates and party organizations in the current election cycle, according to the Center for Responsive Politics, a nonprofit group ... that researches the influence of money in politics." (*Wall Street Journal*, June 19, 1998)

"Last week the nonprofit Center for Responsive Politics (www.crp.org) in the District unveiled [a campaign finance Web site offering] detailed profiles of every House and Senate candidate in the race for the primaries and the general election in November. The group promises it will be updated monthly through the post-election period.

" 'Voters are not the only constituents that candidates listen to,' said CRP Executive Director Larry Makinson. 'There is a phantom constituency out there—the cash constituents. Voters need to know who these people are.'

"Visitors to the site can look at spending and fund-raising for 1998 congressional races, compare the candidates in each district, and get breakdowns and rankings of the candidates' contributors by geography and interest group.

"The CRP enriches the FEC data with its own extensive research in identifying individuals, political action committees and their business and ideological interests. The charts and tables make it easy to see who's supporting each candidate with cash. . . ." (*Washington Post*, June 15, 1998)

"In recent years, money flowing from Hollywood to Washington has become more evenly distributed between the two parties. The Center for Responsive Politics said Hollywood's political action committees donated $1.54 million to Republican candidates and $1.04 million to Democrats in campaigns in 1995 and 1996. That marked the first time Republicans received more than Democrats. . . ." (*New York Times*, June 14, 1998)

"[Democratic senator Tom Daschle] hosted a fund-raising breakfast for a dozen lobbyists here last May that included three from the tobacco industry . . . who wrote personal checks totaling $2,000. Daschle collected another $2,000 in tobacco money later in the year from executives at Philip Morris and [U.S. Tobacco Co.].

"[Daschle's political director] said the checks were 'accepted in error.' But the money was returned only last month—nearly a year after some of it was collected—after the Center for Responsive Politics produced a chart detailing members' tobacco receipts." (*Washington Post*, May 8, 1998)

"In the landscape of political Washington, congressional staffers who become lobbyists are as common as dirt. So are lobbyists who raise campaign money for incumbents well-positioned to serve their interests. . . . But [Republican representative Bud] Shuster and [former Shuster chief of staff Ann] Eppard have few peers when it comes to working the current campaign finance system. They have so intertwined their official, professional, political and personal lives that it is often hard to discern one kind of activity from another. . . .

"Kent Cooper, head of the Center for Responsive Politics, which tracks campaign money, says [the Shuster-Eppard partnership] is 'the most blatant example' of questionable ties between members of Congress and lobbyists who prosper while raising money for a former boss. 'He mixes official and campaign activities to such an extent that the fairness of his official actions is immediately called into question.' " (*Washington Post*, April 5, 1998)

"Lobbying has grown into a $1.2 billion-a-year Washington industry. A joint Associated Press-Center for Responsive Politics survey, one of the first to compile data from all lobbying reports filed with Congress, showed that interest groups are spending $100 million a month to pressure the federal government on issues from tobacco industry liability to nude sunbathing. . . .

"The list of Washington's top 30 lobbyists in terms of spending produced few surprises. 'They're all companies we're familiar with,' said Allen Shuldiner, a researcher with the . . . Center for Responsive Politics, which compiled the list for the AP." (*Washington Post*, March 12, 1998)

"A recent study by the Center for Responsive Politics showed that computer hardware, software and services companies and their employees contributed $7.3 million to campaigns during the 1996 election cycle—up from $4.8 million four years earlier." (*Wall Street Journal*, March 4, 1998)

"One telling statistic, compiled by the Center for Responsive Politics, underscores the corrupt system of influence-peddling practiced shamelessly by both parties. In the last election $27.8 million of soft money was raised by Democrats and Republicans in voter-rich California. In New York, the financial capital of the world, $32.6 million was raised. But these fund-raising havens captured only the bronze and silver; the gold-medal venue for sleazy fund-raising, at almost $40 million, went to Washington, D.C." (*Wall Street Journal*, May 15, 1997)

## POLITICAL ORIENTATION

"congressional watchdog" (*Washington Post*, April 5, 1998)

"nonpartisan" (*Washington Post*, March 12, 1998)

# Citizens' Research Foundation (1958)

University of Southern California
3716 South Hope Street
Los Angeles, California 90007
Phone: (213) 743-2303
Fax: (213) 743-2110
Internet: citires@mizar.usc.edu *or* http://www.usc.edu/dept/crf

| | |
|---|---|
| "To study the role of money in the political process; serves as a nonpartisan observer and interpreter of trends in political finance and election reform." | **PURPOSE** |
| 2 total; plus 3 part-time | **STAFF** |
| Herbert E. Alexander, director. A professor of political science at the University of Southern California (USC), Alexander received his Ph.D. in political science from Yale University. He also has taught at Princeton University, the University of Pennsylvania, and Yale University. | **DIRECTOR** |
| 501(c)(3) | **TAX STATUS** |
| 1997—$280,000<br>1998—$188,470<br>Proposed 1999—Unavailable | **BUDGET** |
| Corporations, 28 percent; conferences and seminars, 24 percent; individuals, 19 percent; foundations, 19 percent; other, 10 percent | **FUNDING SOURCES** |
| Members: N/A<br>Branches/chapters: N/A<br>Affiliate: CRF has been affiliated with the University of Southern California since 1978 | **SCOPE** |
| None | **PAC** |

## METHOD OF OPERATION

♦ Conferences/seminars ♦ Educational foundation ♦ Electoral politics ♦ Information clearinghouse ♦ Internet (databases, electronic bulletin boards, Web site) ♦ Local/municipal affairs ♦ Media outreach ♦ Publications ♦ Research

## CURRENT CONCERNS

♦ Election finance reform ♦ Role of money in political process

## PUBLICATIONS

*Financing the 1996 Election*
*New Realities, New Thinking: Report of Task Force on Campaign Finance Reform*

## NEWSLETTER

*Political Moneyline* (periodic)

## CONFERENCES

Sponsors occasional conferences in Washington, D.C., and Los Angeles

## BOARD OF DIRECTORS

Ned W. Bandler, chairman; William B. May, vice chairman; Robert M. Glen, treasurer; Fred J. Martin, assistant treasurer; Vigo G. Nielsen Jr., secretary; Herbert E. Alexander, director and assistant secretary; Gloria N. Cornette, assistant director

Other members:
♦ Jan W. Baran ♦ Nancy R. Barbour ♦ William E. Frenzel ♦ Samuel A. Hartwell ♦ Ruth J. Hinerfeld ♦ Gordon L. Hough ♦ Margaret M. McCallister ♦ Stewart R. Mott ♦ Ross Clayton Mulford ♦ Nancy M. Neuman ♦ John F. Ostronic ♦ Maria C. Pellegrini ♦ Manning J. Post ♦ John A. Schutz ♦ Jeffrey A. Schwartz ♦ Thomas J. Schwarz ♦ Philip S. Smith ♦ Allan B. Swift ♦ Sander Vanocur

## EFFECTIVENESS

"Supporters of New Jersey's public financing system say they are . . . concerned that there are no state laws or rules barring a special interest group or a business owner from running a television advertising campaign to influence the electorate.

" 'It is the same problem that is being faced at the national level, with respect to soft money and issue advertising,' said Herbert E. Alexander, director of the Citizens Research Foundation at the University of Southern California, which studies campaign finance. 'What it says is that politics knows no boundaries. The question is what can you do about it.'

"He added, 'That is an extremely difficult area to legislate because you are involved in questions of free speech.' " (*New York Times*, October 11, 1997)

"In a practice that placed some of its most cherished donors in violation of Federal election laws, the Democratic National Committee took at least $2 million in contributions restricted to generic use by the party and spent it directly on the re-election campaign of President Clinton and other candidates, Federal election records show. . . .

" . . . By shifting contributions from soft-money accounts into hard ones, the Democratic Party shoved many contributors over their hard-money limits, according to a computer analysis of campaign records conducted for *The New York Times.*

"Herbert E. Alexander, a political science professor at the University of Southern California, said the decision to put portions of donations into hard-money accounts without informing donors 'reflects a total break-down of trust between the contributor and the party.'

" 'If the donors feel put upon, as they will in this situation, then obvi-ously some of them will not be willing to give in the future,' said Profes-sor Alexander, who is also the director of the Citizens Research Founda-tion, [which] studies campaign finance." (*New York Times*, September 10, 1997)

"Although campaign finance reform has historically fared well on state ballots, it has not held up so well in the courts. Herbert Alexander, direc-tor of the Citizens' Research Foundation at the University of Southern California, said that voters approved 77 percent of campaign finance re-form initiatives on the ballots between 1972 and 1994, but that a 'signifi-cant number were found unconstitutional' when the contribution limits were in the $100 to $300 range or were limited to residents of the state.

"Several judges have ruled that contribution limits deny citizens their right to exercise their First Amendment guarantees of free speech. 'As long as the courts continue to equate free speech with money, those of us with no money have no speech,' Edwards said." (*Washington Post*, November 7, 1996)

"nonpartisan" (*New York Times*, September 10, 1997)

*POLITICAL ORIENTATION*

# Common Cause (1970)

1250 Connecticut Avenue, NW
6th Floor
Washington, D.C. 20036
Phone: (202) 833-1200
Fax: (202) 659-3716
Internet: http://www.commoncause.org

| | |
|---|---|
| **PURPOSE** | "A citizen's lobby dedicated to increasing government accountability and improving government performance." |
| **STAFF** | 100 total; plus 100 interns and volunteers |
| **DIRECTOR** | Ann McBride, president and chief executive officer. McBride first worked for Common Cause in 1972 as a volunteer working on the Equal Rights Amendment. She joined the Common Cause staff in 1973 and served as a lobbyist, legislative director, vice president for program operations, and senior vice president before becoming president in 1995. McBride is a graduate of American University and was a fellow at the Kennedy School's Institute of Politics at Harvard University. |
| **TAX STATUS** | 501(c)(4) |
| **BUDGET** | 1998—$10.3 million<br>Proposed 1999—Unavailable |
| **FUNDING SOURCES** | Membership contributions, 60 percent; membership dues, 38 percent; other income, 2 percent<br><br>Membership dues and contributions of $100 or less "provide approximately 84 percent of all Common Cause income," and "less than 1 percent is received from contributions over $1,000." Common Cause does not accept government or foundation grants; it also does not accept corporate or labor union contributions of more than $100 in a calendar year. |
| **SCOPE** | Members: 250,000<br>Branches/chapters: 47 state chapters<br>Affiliates: N/A |
| **PAC** | None |

## METHOD OF OPERATION

♦ Advertisements ♦ Awards program ♦ Coalition forming ♦ Computerized listing of Federal Election Commission records ♦ Conferences/seminars ♦ Congressional testimony ♦ Congressional voting analysis ♦ Demonstrations ♦ Grassroots organizing ♦ Initiative/referendum campaigns ♦ Internet (e-mail alerts, Web site) ♦ Legislative/regulatory monitoring (federal and state) ♦ Litigation ♦ Lobbying (federal, state, and grassroots) ♦ Local/municipal affairs ♦ Media outreach ♦ Research ♦ Shareholder resolutions ♦ Voting records

## CURRENT CONCERNS

♦ Campaign finance reform ♦ Civil and equal rights for all citizens ♦ Government accountability and ethics ♦ Lobby reform

## PUBLICATIONS

21 Wealthy Soft Money Donors Gave $100,000 Or More Each to RNC in April; April Was RNC's Biggest Soft Money Month Since 1994 Election

95 Percent of Incumbents Win Reelection in 1996, Aided by Dramatic Fundraising Advantage Over Challengers, According to Common Cause

Business As Usual—Only Worse: Common Cause Study Reveals Top Soft Money Donors during First Six Months of 1997

Carrying a Big Stick: How Big Timber Triumphs in Washington

Channeling Influence: The Broadcast Lobby and the $70-Billion Free Ride

Concrete Victories: The Transportation Lobby Is Riding High

Consumer Credit Industry Pushing For Substantially Changed Bankruptcy Laws, Gave $58 Million in Political Contributions Since 1987

Democratic and Republican Congressional Campaign Committees Raised a Record $63 Million in Soft Money During the '96 Elections, According to Common Cause Analysis of Largest Givers to the Committees

Drilling for Bargains: Big Oil Fights to Protect Special Royalty Deal & Gives $35.2 Million in Political Donations

Fuel's Gold: ADM'S Million-Dollar Soft Money Donations Help the Ethanol Tax Break Survive

Gambling Industry Continues to Give Heavily to Both Republicans And Democrats Amidst Growing Controversy

Gambling Interests Tripled Their Soft Money Giving in 1996; Heaviest Giving Came During Debate Over Gambling Commission

Local & Long Distance Telephone Companies Give Record Soft Money During Final Months of Telecommunications Overhaul; AT&T & MCI Give Huge Contributions at Key Points During Conference

National Parties Raise $115 Million in Soft Money During First Eighteen Months of 1998 Election Cycle, Common Cause Study Finds; Republicans Raise $70 Million, Lead Soft Money Arms Race

National Parties Raise Record $34 Million in Soft Money During First Half of '97; Republicans Outraise Democrats by More Than 2-to-1

National Parties Raise Record $67 Million in Soft Money During '97; Double Soft Fundraising Since '93

National Parties Raise Record $90 Million in Soft Money During First Fifteen Months of 1998 Election Cycle; $23 Million Raised During First Three Months of 1998 Alone

National Republican Senatorial Committee Doubles Soft Money Intake Under Senator McConnell in First Six Months of 1997

*New Kids On the Auction Block: Freshman House Members Raise $24 Million in 1995 With 40 Percent of Receipts Coming From PACs; Enter '96 Election Year With Huge War Chests, Common Cause Finds*

*NRA Gave $3.3 Million in PAC Support During the Past Decade to Representatives Who Voted to Repeal Assault Weapons Ban; Common Cause Releases Member-By-Member Breakdown of NRA Giving*

*"Party Favors": An Analysis of More Than $67 Million in Soft Money Given to Democratic and Republican National Party Committees in 1997*

*"Pocketbook Politics": How Special-Interest Money Hurts the American Consumer*

*"Private Party": "Team 100" Soft Money Donors Qualify for Closed-Door GOP Meeting; Common Cause Releases List of Elite Republican Donors*

*"Smoke & Mirrors" Tobacco Industry Political Giving Hits Record $4 Million in Off-Election Year '95; Industry Tops $20 Million in Pac & Soft Money During Past Decade Return on Investment: The Hidden Story of Soft Money, Corporate Welfare and the 1997 Budget & Tax Deal*

*Senator McConnell's Coalition of Campaign Reform Opponents Gave $243 Million in Political Contributions During Decade; Soft Money Contributions from These Anti-Reformers Tripled in '96*

*Senator Mitch McConnell & National Republican Senatorial Committee Raise Nearly $11 Million in Soft Money in 1997*

*Tobacco Interests, Philip Morris Set New Soft Money Records; Industry Contributed Nearly $2 Million in First Six Months of 1996*

*Tobacco Money Continues Its Death Grip On Washington Industry's Biggest PAC & Soft Money Beneficiaries in the Senate Kill Tobacco Legislation*

*Tobacco Political Giving Hits Record $9.9 Million in '96 Elections, Decade Total Tops $25 Million, Common Cause Study Finds; Industry Looking to Congress for Favorable Treatment*

*Tobacco Political Giving Tops $4 Million in 1997; Total Giving Since 1987 Reaches Nearly $30 Million, Common Cause Study Finds*

*Under the Influence: Congress Backs Down to Big Booze*

*Why Is NABPAC Out to Kill Campaign Finance Reform? Business Pacs Tied to NABPAC Gave More Than $100 Million to Current Members of Congress Since '85; Stand to Lose Valuable Legislative Access & Influence If True Reform Is Enacted*

"Common Cause also regularly publishes updates of campaign fundraising activities of congressional candidates and the soft money fundraising done by both political parties."

---

## NEWSLETTER

*In Common* (periodic)

---

## CONFERENCES

National Governing Board meetings (three times a year in Washington, D.C.)

Edward S. Cabot, chairman

## BOARD OF DIRECTORS

## EFFECTIVENESS

"The House voted last night to rewrite the nation's bankruptcy laws, approving a plan that would make it harder for cash-strapped individuals to wipe out their debts. . . .

"The House bill was hailed by the consumer credit industry, which lobbied hard for its passage. Banks, consumer finance companies and credit card issuers made about $6.7 million in campaign contributions in the past year—twice what the tobacco industry contributed to lawmakers, according to Common Cause, a nonprofit consumer watchdog group. . . .

"The importance of the bill to the consumer credit industry was evident in the amount of money they spent in the latest election cycle, said Common Cause. Republican lawmakers received more than 63 percent of the total $6.7 million, according to Common Cause's figures.

" 'The fact that Congress is rushing to judgment on the issue while experts and analysts say they should use caution and move slowly, shows you the impact money has on the debate,' said Ann McBride, president of Common Cause. 'It's ironic that at the same time they are rushing this through, they are dragging their feet on campaign finance that would end soft money.' " (*Washington Post*, June 11, 1998)

"Agribusiness giant Archer Daniels Midland Co. (ADM), the single largest beneficiary of a controversial federal ethanol tax subsidy, contributed more than $3 million in unregulated 'soft money' to Republican and Democratic national party committees during the past 10 years, according to a study by Common Cause. . . .

"The Common Cause report contended that the tax break—a perennial target of budget hawks and 'pork busters'—escaped its latest brush with death largely on the bountiful political giving by ADM, the nation's largest ethanol producer. . . .

" 'ADM has methodically, over the years, used big money to ingratiate themselves and protect the ethanol subsidy,' said Common Cause president Ann McBride." (*Washington Post*, June 11, 1998)

"The same political class that is now sucking $516 billion from Big Tobacco is already scanning the horizon for its next rich business target. 'Big Booze' is being nominated. . . .

"Or so we infer from the latest work by Common Cause . . . It has just published 'Under the Influence: Congress Backs Down to Big Booze,' which is not exactly a paean to Clydesdales tromping through snow. . . .

"... Common Cause President Ann McBride avers, with her usual restraint, that 'By caving in to the alcohol lobby, Congress is guilty of a DUI—deciding under the influence—the influence of more than $26 million in campaign contributions.' " (*Wall Street Journal*, April 22, 1998)

"The Senate deadlocked again on overhauling campaign-finance laws, an impasse that could force reformers to change tactics and seek incremental changes over time. . . .

"Common Cause President Ann McBride, a leading reform advocate, denounced the outcome as a 'disaster for our democracy' but said she is now prepared to consider scaled-back changes to build the case for broader ones later." (*Wall Street Journal*, February 27, 1998)

"The two chief opponents of efforts to overhaul campaign finance laws in the Senate, Trent Lott and Mitch McConnell, will preside over what is expected to be the most lucrative Senate fund-raising dinner ever. . . .

"Volunteers from the public interest group Common Cause and other campaign finance overhaul advocates plan to protest outside the dinner. 'This dinner shows why Senators Lott and McConnell are filibustering [the McCain-Feingold bill, which would outlaw so-called soft money],' said Ann McBride, the president of Common Cause. 'They want to defend the soft money system.' At the protest, Common Cause will have one million petitions signed by supporters of the McCain-Feingold legislation." (*New York Times*, November 5, 1997)

"Common Cause and Campaign for America, another group lobbying to change the campaign finance system, are launching a $50,000 radio advertising effort aimed at encouraging Republican senators in four states to support the McCain-Feingold campaign finance legislation.

"The 60-second radio spots name individual senators and accuse them of standing in the way of changing the current system, which allows unlimited 'soft money' donations to political parties from corporations, labor unions and individuals. . . ." (*Washington Post*, October 16, 1997)

"Common Cause Virginia has rapped 17 candidates for the General Assembly for failing to meet the spirit of the state's campaign finance disclosure laws, including 15 incumbents who the citizens' lobby said left 'too many Virginians in the dark.'

"The . . . group reviewed July campaign filing reports required by state law for all state candidates and double-checked those who performed the worst in September. The intent was to see whether candidates clearly stated the name, address, occupation and economic interest of individual, corporate and political committee donors as required by law. . . .

"The report was intended to guide future candidates, not punish active ones, said Julie Holt Williams, executive director of Common Cause. Williams said disclosure is especially crucial in Virginia, which does not limit how much individuals or groups can contribute and relies on public scrutiny to deter corruption." (*Washington Post*, October 2, 1997)

"It was the Big Chill in Boston for campaign reform. The two authors, Sen. John McCain (R-Ariz.) and Russell Feingold (D-Wis.) . . . exhorted a gathering of scarcely 100 shiverers to show Washington that outside the Beltway they care about cleansing our sick political fund-raising system. . . .

"... The sponsoring organization, Common Cause, is mounting a drive for 1,776,000 signatures for reform by the Fourth of July. Common Cause president Ann McBride said the group didn't try to raise a crowd, even though nothing would better make her point that the country is secretly seething over congressional inaction. 'These are not rallies,' she explained, 'they are press events.' " (*Washington Post*, March 27, 1997)

## POLITICAL ORIENTATION

"Walks point for the liberal/public health/Naderite/trial lawyer political combine" (*Wall Street Journal*, April 22, 1998)

"campaign finance lobbying group" (*Washington Post*, October 21, 1997)

"nonpartisan" (*Washington Post*, October 2, 1997)

# Concord Coalition (1992)

1019 19th Street, NW
Suite 810
Washington, D.C. 20036
Phone: (202) 467-6222
Fax: (202) 467-6333
Internet: concord@concordcoalition.org *or*
http://www.concordcoalition.org

| | |
|---|---|
| **PURPOSE** | "To eliminate federal budget deficits and ensure [that] Social Security, Medicare, and Medicaid are secure for all generations." |
| **STAFF** | 25 total—23 professional; 2 support; plus 1 part-time, 2 interns; 1,250 volunteers nationwide |
| **DIRECTOR** | Martha Phillips, executive director. Phillips was formerly a key staffer for three committees in the U.S. House of Representatives: Budget, Ways and Means, and the House Republican Policy Committee. She is a graduate of the University of Maryland and holds an M.A. degree from Columbia University. |
| **TAX STATUS** | 501(c)(3) |
| **BUDGET** | 1997—$2.16 million<br>1998—$2.3 million<br>Proposed 1999—$2.4 million |
| **FUNDING SOURCES** | Individual contributions, 55 percent; publications, 20 percent; special events/projects, 10 percent; foundation grants, 8 percent; corporate donations, 7 percent |
| **SCOPE** | Members: 200,000 members<br>Branches/chapters: Chapters in all 50 states<br>Affiliate: Concord Coalition Citizens' Council, a 501(c)(4) organization |
| **PAC** | None |

| | |
|---|---|
| ◆ Advertisements ◆ Coalition forming ◆ Conferences/seminars ◆ Congressional testimony ◆ Congressional voting analysis ◆ Films/video/audiotapes ◆ Grassroots organizing ◆ Internet (e-mail alerts, Web site) ◆ Internships ◆ Lobbying (grassroots) ◆ Media outreach ◆ Polling ◆ Research ◆ Speakers program | *METHOD OF OPERATION* |

| | |
|---|---|
| ◆ Creating a sound economy for future generations ◆ Eliminating federal budget deficits ◆ Reforming Social Security, Medicaid, and Medicare to make these programs sustainable | *CURRENT CONCERNS* |

| | |
|---|---|
| *105th Congress Legislative Scorecard—First Session*<br>*Facing Facts Fax Alerts*<br>*Financing Retirement Security for an Aging America: Background Information About Population Change, Social Security and Medicare*<br>*Saving Social Security: A Framework for Reform*<br>*Ten Questions Voters Should Ask Their Candidates*<br>*The Surplus Mirage* (text of full-page advertisement in *The New York Times*)<br>*Will America Grow Up Before It Grows Old?*<br>*The Zero Deficit Plan* | *PUBLICATIONS* |

| | |
|---|---|
| *The Concord Courier* (quarterly) | *NEWSLETTER* |

| | |
|---|---|
| National Policy Forum (annually in Washington, D.C.) | *CONFERENCES* |

| | |
|---|---|
| Warren B. Rudman and Sam Nunn, cochairmen; Peter G. Peterson, president; Lloyd N. Cutler, secretary-treasurer; Eugene M. Freedman, finance chairman; Harvey M. Meyerhoff, budget chairman; Timothy J. Penny, policy chairman<br><br>Other members (vice chairs):<br>◆ Paul A. Allaire ◆ Roger E. Brinner ◆ James E. Burke ◆ Maria Cantwell ◆ John C. Danforth ◆ Stephen Friedman ◆ Hanna Holborn Gray ◆ William H. Gray III ◆ J. Alex McMillan ◆ Joseph M. Segel ◆ Nicola Tsongas ◆ John G. Turner ◆ Paul A. Volcker ◆ John P. White ◆ Daniel Yankelovich | *BOARD OF DIRECTORS* |

| | |
|---|---|
| "With President Clinton holding his first town hall meeting on Social Security here on Tuesday, many people in Kansas City and its sprawling suburbs have found themselves grappling with [the issue]. . . .<br>    "At Mr. Clinton's request, the town hall meeting is being organized by the A.A.R.P. and the Concord Coalition, [which was] founded by two former United States Senators, Paul E. Tsongas of Massachusetts and Warren B. Rudman of New Hampshire. The two groups are in charge of deciding who will attend the four-hour session and who will have the opportunity to ask questions or make comments." (*New York Times*, April 7, 1998) | *EFFECTIVENESS* |

"We don't expect much today from Mr. Clinton's Social Security confab in Kansas City. At White House request, the made-for-empathy-event is co-sponsored by two forces of the status quo, the Concord Coalition and the American Association of Retired Persons. They've long been the Dumb and Dumber of Social Security reform, with Concord always proposing to cut benefits and AARP insisting on higher taxes. . . ." (*Wall Street Journal*, April 7, 1998)

"Clinton aides have been smart in asking two private groups, the American Association of Retired Persons (AARP) and the Concord Coalition, to take responsibility for organizing the four regional forums that will precede a White House conference on Social Security the president plans to hold next December. The hope is that enough agreement will have emerged by then to make it possible to pass a long-term fix in the 1999 session of Congress. The AARP, the largest organization of seniors, and the Concord Coalition, the most influential lobby for fiscal discipline, can conduct the honest debate that is needed." (*Washington Post*, February 1, 1998)

---

## POLITICAL ORIENTATION

"bipartisan" (*Washington Post*, April 23, 1998)

"a non-partisan fiscal watchdog group" (*New York Times*, February 3, 1998)

"a bipartisan group that lobbies for a balanced budget" (*New York Times*, January 19, 1998)

# Congressional Management Foundation (1977)

513 Capitol Court, NE
Suite 300
Washington, D.C. 20002
Phone: (202) 546-0100
Fax: (202) 547-0936
Internet: http://www.cmfweb.org

---

"To work internally with Member offices, committees, and the leadership to foster improved management practices and systems within Congress."

*PURPOSE*

---

7 total—6 professional; 1 support; plus 2 interns

*STAFF*

---

Richard Shapiro, executive director. Shapiro joined the Congressional Management Foundation (CMF) in 1988 as program director and became executive director in 1990. Prior to joining the CMF, he held several senior staff positions in Congress. Shapiro also worked as a management consultant for Coopers & Lybrand and the state of Arizona. He holds a master's degree in public administration from Princeton University's Woodrow Wilson School of Public and International Affairs.

*DIRECTOR*

---

501(c)(3)

*TAX STATUS*

---

1998—$500,000
Proposed 1999—Unavailable

*BUDGET*

---

Contributions (including corporate, foundation, and association grants), 75 percent; consulting, 15 percent; publications and other income, 10 percent

*FUNDING SOURCES*

---

Members: N/A
Branches/chapters: N/A
Affiliates: N/A

*SCOPE*

---

None

*PAC*

---

| | |
|---|---|
| *METHOD OF OPERATION* | ◆ Group facilitation ◆ Films/video/audiotapes ◆ Internet (Web site) ◆ Leadership management training ◆ Management consulting ◆ Publication of books and reports ◆ Seminars/workshops ◆ Survey research |
| *CURRENT CONCERNS* | ◆ Better use of technology in Congress ◆ Congressional ethics ◆ Employment trends of congressional staff ◆ Management training of top congressional staff ◆ Orientation of freshman members of Congress ◆ Strategic planning for congressional offices |
| *PUBLICATIONS* | *1997 U.S. Senate Employment Practices: A Study of Staff Salary, Tenure, Demographics and Benefits* (biennial)<br>*1998 U.S. House of Representatives Employment Practices: A Study of Staff Salary, Tenure, Demographics and Benefits* (biennial)<br>*A Congressional Intern Handbook*<br>*Frontline Management: A Guide for Congressional District/State Offices*<br>*Setting Course: A Congressional Management Guide* (biennial)<br>*Working in Congress: The Staff Perspective* |
| *NEWSLETTER* | None |
| *CONFERENCES* | "Conducting Staff Evaluations"<br>"Improving Staff Writing"<br>"Improving the D.C./District Office Relationship"<br>"Evaluating Office Performance"<br>"Management Fundamentals for Chief of Staff"<br>"Managing Ethics for Administrative Assistants"<br>"Negotiations and Conflict Management"<br>"Orientation for Freshman Staff"<br>"Streamlining Your Mail System"<br>"Stress Management in the Congressional Environment"<br>"Time/Paper Management"<br>"Teambuilding for Congressional Offices" |
| *BOARD OF DIRECTORS* | ◆ Ira Chaleff ◆ Kelly Johnston ◆ Gary Serota ◆ Diane Thompson |
| *EFFECTIVENESS* | "It's no secret that many of the staffers who do the nitty-gritty work in Congress these days are young and inexperienced. One big reason lies in the tremendous staff turnover. According to surveys, a whopping percentage of congressional aides want to quickly exit the Hill. And even those who decide to stay are switching jobs much faster than before. . . . |

"All of this turnover—both in specific jobs within Congress and in departures from Congress—means that congressional offices have less experience and know-how, says Rick Shapiro, the CMF's executive director. 'The Chicago Bulls win basketball titles not just because Michael Jordan is the best basketball player in the world, or that Scottie Pippen's also an allstar,' said Shapiro, 'but [because] they've had, for a number of years, a bunch of players who worked well together and figured out how to be an effective team.'

"If Congress wants to be more effective, Shapiro contends, it needs to begin to search for ways to retain valuable staffers. Freshman Rep. Ciro Rodriguez, D-Texas, agreed. He cited the 'terrible' hours and low pay that many staffers endure, adding: "There is a need to keep good people for a good duration." (*National Journal*, August 22, 1998)

"Personnel in senators' offices in the Washington area earn only two-thirds as much as executive branch workers here, a gap that has grown dramatically during the 1990s, according to a study released today by the Congressional Management Foundation. . . .

" 'The [pay] gap is increasing, while the trend is toward shorter service,' said Rick Shapiro, executive director of the foundation. . . .

"The . . . Congressional Management Foundation, which studies congressional institutional trends, found that female Senate staff members earn 88 percent as much as men, a significantly higher percentage than in the national economy, where women earn 67 percent as much as men. . . .

"The study analyzed more than 2,000 workers in senators' personal offices in Washington and in the states. . . ." (*Washington Post*, December 8, 1997)

"After grueling campaigns, the 73 House and 15 Senate freshman elected a week ago probably want nothing more than to relax, catch up with family and friends, and sleep. But a newly published handbook for incoming members of Congress warns them not to waste a minute of these next two months if they want to have a successful first term.

"The book, 'Setting Course,' was written by the Congressional Management Foundation (CMF), a nonprofit, nonpartisan group that advocates 'good government through good management.' This is the sixth edition of the manual, which walks members though the steps necessary to set up an office, hire staff and, most importantly, create a 'strategic plan' for the first term." (*CQ Monitor*, November 12, 1996)

"House and Senate offices are embarking on major changes in their operations in an attempt to head off huge overtime costs stemming from the Accountability Act, according to a new study by the Congressional Management Foundation.

"Offices on both sides of the Hill are budgeting very little money to pay new overtime costs and instead are selecting 'strategies that could fundamentally change the way they operate,' concludes the study on how some in Congress are complying with requirements of the Fair Labor Standards Act.

"The survey of 167 House Members' offices and 55 Senators' offices found that most said they intend to enforce shorter hours, more carefully monitor and stagger work schedules, trim office workloads, work to increase efficiency, and allow for less staff 'downtime,' to deal with overtime issues." (*Roll Call*, March 4, 1996)

## POLITICAL ORIENTATION

"nonpartisan" (*Washington Post*, December 8, 1997)

# Council for Excellence in Government
(1983)

1301 K Street, NW, 450 West
Washington, D.C. 20005
Phone: (202) 728-0418
Fax: (202) 728-0422
Internet: http://www.excelgov.org

To promote "results-oriented leadership and management and to raise public understanding and confidence in government." | **PURPOSE**

22 total—20 professional; 2 support; plus 5 interns | **STAFF**

Patricia G. McGinnis, president and chief executive officer. Prior to joining the Council for Excellence in Government (CEG) in 1994, McGinnis was cofounder and principal of the public affairs consulting firm of Winner/Wagner & Francis (formerly the FMR Group) in Washington, D.C. Previously, she worked for the Office of Management and Budget in the Carter Administration, the Senate Budget Committee, and the Commerce and Health and Human Services departments. McGinnis has served on numerous committees and boards including the executive council of Harvard University's Kennedy School of Government and the associate council of George Washington University's School of Business and Public Management. She currently serves as a director of Primark Corp. McGinnis received a B.A. in political science from the University of Virginia's Mary Washington College and an M.P.A. from Harvard University's Kennedy School of Government. | **DIRECTOR**

501(c)(3) | **TAX STATUS**

1997—$2.5 million
1998—$3.7 million
Proposed 1999—Unavailable | **BUDGET**

Foundation grants, 45 percent; government contracts, 25 percent; membership dues, 15 percent; conferences, 10 percent; corporate donations, 5 percent | **FUNDING SOURCES**

Members: 700 private sector executives who formerly served as government officials
Branches/chapters: N/A
Affiliates: N/A | **SCOPE**

| | |
|---|---|
| *PAC* | None |
| *METHOD OF OPERATION* | ♦ Alliances with corporate, foundation, and academic partners ♦ Benchmarking techniques ♦ Conferences/seminars ♦ Fellowships ♦ Internet (Web site) ♦ Internships ♦ Institutional partnerships with government agencies ♦ Media outreach ♦ Performance ratings ♦ Public opinion surveys ♦ Publications ♦ Speakers program ♦ Training and technical assistance |
| *CURRENT CONCERNS* | ♦ Assisting government agencies in restructuring and management ♦ Assisting government career executives in their leadership ♦ Promoting federal systems reform ♦ Public confidence in government ♦ Public-sector innovation ♦ Public understanding of government ♦ Quality of federal political appointments |
| *PUBLICATIONS* | *Accounting for Change*<br>*Directory of Principals* (membership)<br>*Ethical Principles for Public Servants*<br>*Prune Book* (5 volumes)<br>*A Survivors Guide for Government Executives* |
| *NEWSLETTER* | *E-News* (bimonthly) |
| *CONFERENCES* | Leaders Speak Out forums for governmental leaders<br>Whitehead forums<br>Sponsors various CEG fellows events |
| *BOARD OF DIRECTORS* | John D. Macomber, chair; Suzanne H. Woolsey, vice chair; Joseph K. Kasputys, treasurer; Robert H. Craft, secretary; Patricia McGinnis, president and chief executive officer<br><br>Other members:<br>♦ Dennis W. Bakke ♦ Michael S. Berman ♦ Martha O. Blaxall ♦ Letitia Chambers ♦ William Clinger Jr. ♦ Lovida H. Coleman Jr. ♦ Christopher T. Cross ♦ Richard G. Darman ♦ William H. Donaldson ♦ Mickey Edwards ♦ J. Michael Farren ♦ Leslie C. Francis ♦ Thomas P. Glynn ♦ Patrick W. Gross ♦ Edwin L. Harper ♦ Gail Harrison ♦ Fruzsina Harsanyi ♦ Gwendolyn S. King ♦ Mel Levine ♦ Robert J. Libertore ♦ Kenneth Lipper ♦ Rodney McCowan ♦ Harry C. McPherson Jr. ♦ Dana G. Mead ♦ Constance Berry Newman ♦ Philip A. Odeen ♦ Franklin D. Raines ♦ Elliot L. Richardson ♦ Nancy Risque Rohrbach ♦ Isabel Sawhill ♦ Leonard D. Schaeffer ♦ Susan C. Schwab ♦ John P. White ♦ John C. Whitehead ♦ A. Thomas Young |

"How many of you have heard that the Internal Revenue Service had some bad apples who harassed and hounded taxpayers, violating their privacy and maybe even their constitutional rights? Now, how many of you have heard that the IRS recently received an award for coming up with Telefile, a way of filing your tax return by touch-tone phone, a program so successful that after only two years in operation, one in five taxpayers is using it? Oh, by the way, the average time taken is 10 minutes, the processing cost to the government is 85 cents per return. . . .

"That is a point that has been hammered home at a couple of recent events in Washington sponsored by the private Council for Excellence in Government, the Ford Foundation and Harvard's John F. Kennedy School of Government.

"Those three have been giving the innovations awards for creative solutions in local, state and federal government for 11 years. This year, realizing that the success stories clearly have not slowed the rising tide of public cynicism about politics and government, they enlisted a few dozen other organizations—ranging from the AFL-CIO and Alcoa to the United Negro College Fund and the YWCA—in a 'Partnership for Trust in Government' to spread the word about such public-sector successes." (*Washington Post*, November 23, 1997)

"Young Americans 'have a personal thirst for public service' and want to make a difference in the lives of individuals, but they give the government a mixed grade on whether it helps them attain the American Dream, according to a recent survey.

"The poll was commissioned by the 'Partnership for Trust in Government,' a new coalition of 22 organizations that includes the Girl Scouts of America, Tenneco Inc., the AFL-CIO, the United Negro College Fund, *Good Housekeeping* magazine, IBM and the Discovery Channel. The partnership members were brought together by the Ford Foundation and the Council for Excellence in Government. The partners hope to counter popular government-bashing in politics and the news media by drawing attention to the government's accomplishments and important work. . . .

"The results of the partnership, of course, won't be known for some time. But the poll released Wednesday by the Partnership for Trust served as a handy reminder of how much Washington has changed since the era when John F. Kennedy summoned young Americans to ask what they could do for their country." (*Washington Post*, November 21, 1997)

"About 170 presidential appointees, nominees and agency chiefs of staff will gather at the State Department Saturday for a day-long retreat and orientation session aimed at preparing them for President Clinton's second term.

"The political appointees will attend sessions on how to work effectively with Congress and the media, on 'getting results in the public interest' and on 'stewardship of the public trust,' said Patricia G. McGinnis, president of the nonpartisan Council for Excellence in Government, primary sponsor of the retreat. The idea for the meeting grew out of the council's research last year on the appointments process, McGinnis said. 'We identified the lack of orientation and preparation for presidential appointees as a gap that ought to be filled,' she said.

"In subsequent talks with the White House, officials supported the idea of a 'leadership conference' and joined in the planning for the retreat, McGinnis said. . . .

" 'It's probably the first time such a large group of top appointees has gotten together to focus on leadership and management in this intense way,' McGinnis said." (*Washington Post,* May 30, 1997)

"After years of poll data stressing what's wrong with government, a new survey finds Americans optimistic that government could be more effective and work better for them.

"But while there is some improvement in the public's trust in government, only one in five poll respondents expressed confidence in the federal government, and the national government continues to enjoy less confidence than its state and local counterparts. The nonprofit, nonpartisan Council for Excellence in Government sponsored the survey of 1,003 adults, conducted by the research firms of Peter D. Hart and Robert M. Teeter. Hart and Teeter conducted a similar survey for the council in March 1995.

" 'We are returning to a more traditional American view of government,' Teeter said at a Friday briefing on the poll results. 'People think they don't hate government and they don't love government. They think it is an important institution in the country. They think it has some important things it should do, and what they want is good government, better leadership, less politics, better management, better expenditure of their money.'. . ." (*Washington Post,* March 24, 1997)

# POLITICAL ORIENTATION

"nonprofit, nonpartisan" (*Washington Post,* March 24, 1997)

# Council of State Governments (1933)

2760 Research Park Drive
P.O. Box 11910
Lexington, Kentucky 40578
Phone: (606) 244-8000
Fax: (606) 244-8001

444 North Capitol Street, NW
Suite 401
Washington, D.C. 20001
Phone: (202) 624-5460
Fax: (202) 624-5452

Internet: info@csg.org *or* http://www.csg.org

"To foster excellence in all facets of state government."

**PURPOSE**

155 total

**STAFF**

Daniel M. Sprague, executive director. Appointed executive director of the Council of State Governments (CSG) in 1989, Sprague previously was director of the Western Legislative Conference, CSG's western office, and president of WESTRENDS, a CSG project. Prior to joining CSG in 1980, he worked with county and federal organizations and with the Peace Corps in South America. Sprague holds a master's degree in public policy from the University of California–Berkeley and a doctorate in public administration from the University of Southern California.

**DIRECTOR**

501(c)(3)

**TAX STATUS**

1998—$16 million
Proposed 1999—$16 million

**BUDGET**

State dues, grants and contracts, conferences, publications

**FUNDING SOURCES**

Members: 50 states; 6 U.S. territories and commonwealths
Branches/chapters: Regional offices in San Francisco; Atlanta; Lombard, Illinois; and New York City

**SCOPE**

Affiliates: 20 affiliated organizations, including National Association of State Facilities Administrators, National Association of State Personnel Executives, National Association of State Telecommunications Directors, National Association of State Treasurers, National Emergency Management Association, National Association of State Election Directors, American Probation and Parole Association, National Conference of Lieutenant Governors, Eastern Regional Conference, Midwestern Governors' Conference, Midwestern Legislative Conference, Southern Governors' Association, Southern Legislative Conference, and Western Legislative Conference

## PAC

None

## METHOD OF OPERATION

♦ Awards program (Innovations, Guardian of Federalism) ♦ Conferences/seminars ♦ Films/video/audiotapes ♦ International activities ♦ Internet (Web site) ♦ Library/information clearinghouse ♦ Research ♦ Surveys

## CURRENT CONCERNS

♦ Criminal justice ♦ Economic development ♦ Education ♦ Environment/natural resources ♦ Federal/state relations ♦ Health care ♦ Health insurance ♦ Political realignment ♦ Public-private cooperation ♦ State and regional innovations ♦ State trends ♦ Transportation

## PUBLICATIONS

1998–99 The Book of the States (also available on cd-rom)
1998 CSG State Directories (also available on cd-rom)
Directory I— Elective Officials
Directory II— Legislative Leadership, Committees and Staff
Directory III— Administrative Officials
State Trends
Spectrum: The Journal of State Government
Solutions

## NEWSLETTER

State Government News (monthly magazine)

## CONFERENCES

Annual Meeting and State Leadership Forum (December)
Annual Regional Conference held in each of CSG's four regions

## BOARD OF DIRECTORS

"The executive committee includes state officials from all three branches of state government such as governors, lieutenant governors, attorneys general, chief justices, secretaries of state, and state auditors, comptrollers, treasurers, and state legislators."

Officers:
Charlie Williams, chair; Pedro Rosselló, president; Kenneth McClintock, chair-elect; Tommy Thompson, president-elect; Tom Ryder III, vice chair

"State aid accounts for just 7 percent of school funding [in New Hampshire], or a little less than $90 million annually; the national average is about 48 percent, according to a report by the Council of State Governments. . . ." (*Washington Post*, January 10, 1998)

"A survey by the Council on State Governments published this month indicated that 20 governors called for tax cuts in their State of the State addresses last winter, and $4 billion in cuts already have passed, not including Maryland's 10 percent income tax cut signed into law by Gov. Parris N. Glendening (D) on Tuesday.

" 'These tax cuts are widespread. . . . In our analysis, every eastern state governor proposed a tax cut,' said Elaine Stuart, managing editor of *State Government News*. 'It's just a conservative sort of tone states have taken in recent years. They are not thinking of big projects to spend money on.' " (*Washington Post*, April 10, 1997)

"Florida is among only 18 states that say they plan to increase business-development incentives over the next five years, according to a recent survey by the Council of State Governments, a nonprofit research group based in Lexington, Ky. The survey's results show that a majority of states have reached the limit on how much they are willing to pay to attract new business. . . .

"The council's [Drew] Leatherby says the analysis isn't meant to take sides about the wisdom of increasing incentives, merely to list prominent arguments for and against the strategy. 'I'm not sure there's enough evidence out there to determine whether they're good or bad,' he says. 'Of course, there's an argument that the money would be better spent on infrastructure such as schools that enhance the state's image.' " (*Wall Street Journal*, April 2, 1997)

"More states are rethinking their economic-development strategies, as incentives dangled before corporations reach crippling levels. Last week, in a survey by the Council of State Governments, 32 economic-development officials said that they expect the number of business-incentive programs they offer to stabilize or decline over the next five years. . . ." (*Wall Street Journal*, March 31, 1997)

"Today . . . the U.S. Supreme Court will hear arguments on whether IOLTA [interest on lawyers' trust accounts] unconstitutionally expropriates clients' property to fund the social goals of America's legal establishment.

". . . For liberals, IOLTA is a dream come true. It takes the interest generated by private property and uses it to underwrite litigation and other social causes without the inconvenience of seeking the approval of the private parties whose property creates the interest-producing fund. . . .

"The defenders of IOLTA before the Supreme Court include a who's who of the legal and political establishment: the American Bar Association, the Council of State Governments, the National League of Cities, the National Association of Counties, the U.S. Council of Mayors, more than 80 state bar associations, the American Association of Retired Persons, the Conference of State Chief Justices, and the Clinton Justice Department. . . ." (*Wall Street Journal,* January 13, 1998)

"a bipartisan group of state legislators" (*Wall Street Journal,* August 4, 1997)

# Empower America (1993)

1776 Eye Street, NW
Suite 890
Washington, D.C. 20006
Phone: (202) 452-8200
Fax: (202) 833-0388
Internet: http://www.empower.org

| | |
|---|---|
| "To promote progressive conservative public policies at both the state and national level, based on the principles of economic growth, international leadership, and cultural renewal." | **PURPOSE** |
| 26 total | **STAFF** |
| Christian Pinkston, executive director | **DIRECTOR** |
| 501(c)(4) | **TAX STATUS** |
| 1998—Unavailable<br>Proposed 1999—Unavailable | **BUDGET** |
| Individual contributions; "accepts no government funds" | **FUNDING SOURCES** |
| Members: 165,000 individuals<br>Branches/chapters: N/A<br>Affiliates: N/A | **SCOPE** |
| None | **PAC** |
| ◆ Advertisements ◆ Conferences/seminars ◆ Films/video/audiotapes ◆ Grassroots organizing ◆ Internet (Web site) ◆ Internships ◆ Legislative/regulatory monitoring (federal, state, and grassroots) ◆ Media outreach ◆ Speakers program ◆ Telecommunications services (EA FAX/Mail program) ◆ Training and technical assistance | **METHOD OF OPERATION** |

## CURRENT CONCERNS

♦ Education reform ♦ National security ♦ Tax reform ♦ Technology issues

## PUBLICATIONS

Publishes issue briefs, policy papers, and transcripts of lectures and lectures

## NEWSLETTER

None

## CONFERENCES

Candidate schools (for federal, state, and local candidates)
Leadership Council Forums
Congress Freshman Orientation (with Heritage Foundation)
Regional conferences

## BOARD OF DIRECTORS

Theodore J. Forstmann, founding chairman; Thomas W. Weisel, chairman; Nicholas C. Forstmann, vice chairman; Josette Shiner, president; Lamar Alexander, William J. Bennett, Jack Kemp, Jeane J. Kirkpatrick, and Vin Weber, codirectors; Christian Pinkston, executive director

Other board members:
♦ Joseph A. Cannon ♦ Jamie B. Coulter ♦ Steve Forbes ♦ Newt Gingrich ♦ E. Floyd Kvamme ♦ Trent Lott ♦ Michael Novak ♦ Dennis Prager ♦ Julian H. Robertson Jr. ♦ Donald H. Rumsfeld ♦ Judy Shelton ♦ John Skeen ♦ Ward W. Woods

## EFFECTIVENESS

"Several companies and trade associations critical of Microsoft Corp.'s business practices said yesterday that they have banded together to mount an aggressive lobbying campaign against the software giant. The group will encourage federal and state regulators to pursue a broader antitrust case against Microsoft. . . .

"With the filing of a lengthy and potentially enervating antitrust case at stake, each side has been seeking out well-known Washington lobbyists to present their arguments to regulators and legislators. . . .

"Among the lobbyists Microsoft has hired are Grover Norquist, who runs a group called Americans for Tax Reform; Vin Weber, a director of . . . Empower America; and former Rep. Tom Downey (D-N.Y.), a close ally of the Clinton administration." (*Washington Post*, April 21, 1998)

"The virtuous William Bennett and Sen. Joe Lieberman (D-Conn.) had to sift through a lot of smut to pick just the right corporation to receive the first Silver Sewer award for coarsening the culture. But Seagram Co. and company CEO Edgar Bronfman Jr. edged out the competition by distributing shock rocker Marilyn Manson's music and freak booker Jerry Springer's talk show. . . .

"Bennett, who heads Empower America, and Lieberman have a loose partnership they call the 'revolt of the revolted.' Manson is 'in-your-face nihilistic stuff, mixing themes of violence and Satanism, and a lot of kids take it in,' says Bennett. Springer, a former Cincinnati mayor, 'degrades human personality. I am not for censorship and pulling the plug, but I am for holding them accountable.' " (*Washington Post*, March 20, 1998)

"Using a stack of glossy charts and blown-up photographs, and packing in three appearances before three Republican groups in the space of a morning, [New York Mayor Rudolph W.] Giuliani drew a graphic contrast between the condition of the city now and its state under a Democratic administration. . . .

"Two of the events were organized by the Republican National Committee and one by Empower America, the conservative group organized by Jack F. Kemp, the former Congressman from Buffalo. . . ." (*New York Times*, March 13, 1998)

"William F. Weld's public spat with Sen. Jesse Helms (R-N.C.) is spilling over into at least one conservative think tank in town as two of its most outspoken members take opposing sides in the ambassadorial battle.

"Jack Kemp, Robert J. Dole's vice presidential running mate last year, is promoting Weld for ambassador to Mexico. But his colleague at Empower America, William J. Bennett, thinks the libertarian Weld is simply using the contretemps for self-promotion. 'This is a guy who lost an election, was bored with his job and is looking for something else to do,' Bennett said of Weld and his failed Senate bid last year. Helms, chairman of the Senate Foreign Relations Committee, is refusing to hold a hearing on Weld's nomination. As recently as Monday evening, he told CBS News a hearing was 'an exercise in futility.' " (*Washington Post*, August 6, 1997)

"The Republican Revolution was still young in 1995, when a new fundraising list called 'Adamant Conservatives' came on the market here.

"In the small world of professional political fund raising, it was something of a sensation, promising the addresses of thousands of proven donors concerned about a balanced budget, lower taxes and welfare reform. Like-minded groups, including the Heritage Foundation, Empower America, Citizens for a Sound Economy and Citizens Against Government Waste snapped it up for their own prospecting. . . ." (*Wall Street Journal*, January 27, 1997)

"[Lamar Alexander] remains a co-director along with [Jack] Kemp at Empower America . . . the former education secretary will focus on how to improve schools, a glaring weakness for recent GOP candidates." (*Wall Street Journal*, January 23, 1997)

---

"conservative advocacy group" (*New York Times*, June 21, 1998)

"conservative think tank" (*Washington Post*, April 21, 1998)

"high-octane GOP think tank" (*Wall Street Journal*, January 23, 1997)

## POLITICAL ORIENTATION

"In the past two months, perhaps no trio of Republicans has shared the spotlight with Bob Dole as much as Jack F. Kemp, William J. Bennett, and Lamar Alexander.

"All three are influencing Mr. Dole's presidential campaign in different ways, yet they have something in common: All have been waiting in the wings as co-directors of Empower America, the Washington think tank that promotes 'progressive conservative policies based on principles of economic growth, international leadership, and cultural renewal.'

"Empower America was founded in 1993 by Mr. Kemp, who is now Mr. Dole's running mate, and Mr. Bennett, the former secretary of education and White House 'drug czar,' along with former United Nations Ambassador Jeane J. Kirkpatrick and former Minnesota Rep. Vin Weber.

"The organization has not earned the scholarly reputation of more established conservative think tanks such as the Heritage Foundation and the American Enterprise Institute.

"But the Washington-based outfit has provided funding, staffing, and organization to help Messrs. Kemp, Bennett, and Alexander refine their policy ideas—including school choice and the devolution of federal education programs—and expand their political bases after departing from public office." (*Education Week,* September 18, 1996)

# The League of Women Voters of the United States (1920)

1730 M Street, NW
10th Floor
Washington, D.C. 20036
Phone: (202) 429-1965
Fax: (202) 429-0854
Internet: http://www.lwv.org/~lwvus/

| | |
|---|---|
| "Encourages the informed and active participation of citizens in government and influences public policy through education and advocacy." | *PURPOSE* |
| 51 total—30 professional; 21 support; plus 3 interns | *STAFF* |
| Jane Gruenebaum, executive director. Prior to her appointment as executive director of the League of Women Voters, Gruenebaum was deputy director of the Center for Public Policy Education at the Brookings Institution. | *DIRECTOR* |
| 501(c)(4) | *TAX STATUS* |
| Fiscal year ending June 30, 1998—Unavailable<br>Proposed F.Y. 1999—$2.62 million | *BUDGET* |
| Member payments, 48 percent; direct mail contributions, 32 percent; nationally recruited members, 8 percent; investment income, 5 percent; other, 7 percent | *FUNDING SOURCES* |
| Members: 150,000 individual members and supporters<br>Branches/chapters: 50 state leagues and leagues in Washington, D.C., Hong Kong, and the Virgin Islands; 1,100 local leagues<br>Affiliate: The League of Women Voters Education Fund (LWVEF), a 501(c)(3) organization | *SCOPE* |
| None | *PAC* |

## METHOD OF OPERATION

♦ Advertisements ♦ Awards program ♦ Coalition forming ♦ Conferences/seminars ♦ Congressional testimony ♦ Electoral politics ♦ Films/video/audiotapes ♦ Grassroots organizing ♦ Initiative/referendum campaigns ♦ Internet (Web site) ♦ Legislative/regulatory monitoring (federal and state) ♦ Litigation ♦ Lobbying (federal, state, and grassroots) ♦ Media outreach ♦ Participation in regulatory proceedings (federal) ♦ Polling ♦ Research ♦ Television and radio production ♦ Training and technical assistance ♦ Voter registration

## CURRENT CONCERNS

♦ Campaign finance reform ♦ Children's welfare ♦ Environmental issues ♦ Gun control ♦ Health care ♦ Voter registration and participation

## PUBLICATIONS

*10 Steps to a Successful Registration Drive*
*Campaign Watch*
*CARE Package: Tools for Citizen Action on Health Care*
*Expanding School-Age Child Care: A Community Action Guide*
*Fighting Hunger: A Guide for Development of Community Action Projects*
*Focus on the Voter: Lessons from the 1992 Election*
*The Garbage Primer*
*Getting the Most Out of Debates* (English and Spanish)
*Impact on Congress: A Grassroots Lobbying Handbook for Local League Activists*
*Impact on Issues*
*The National Voter Examines Health Care Reform*
*The Nuclear Waste Primer*
*The Plastic Waste Primer*
*Protect Your Groundwater: Educating for Action*
*Public Policy on Reproductive Choice: A Community Action Guide*
*Reaching for the American Dream: Economic Policy for the Future*
*Recycling Is More Than Collections*
*Seeds of Tomorrow: Issues in Agricultural Research and Technology*
*Talking Trash: A Citizen Education Guide for Community Leaders and Activists*
*Tell It to Washington*
*Understanding Economic Policy: A Citizen's Handbook*
*Voicing Your Choice: A Guide to Citizen Participation in Health Reform*
*Your Waste Prevention Tool Kit*

Also offers posters, pins, tote bags, and coffee mugs

## NEWSLETTER

*The National Voter* (quarterly magazine)

## CONFERENCES

National convention

## BOARD OF DIRECTORS

## EFFECTIVENESS

"Alexandria City Council member David G. Speck's proposal to ban political campaign signs in the city didn't go anywhere, but he hasn't given
up yet.

"Now, Speck (D) would like to explore the possibility of limiting the
bouquets of red, white and blue signs to certain intersections. Some people already are opposed to that idea, too. . . .

"Speck's [original] proposal sparked months of discussion among the
city's League of Women Voters and the Democratic and Republican committees—which all opposed the proposed ban. . . .

"League co-president Ginny Hines said Speck's new proposal is 'certainly worth looking at.' She said the League is more interested in cutting
the amount of time signs can be placed in public right of ways. And she
said the League, along with Democratic and GOP representatives, has
agreed to institute a joint training program for candidates regarding the
city's regulations governing campaign signs." (*Washington Post*, May 21,
1998)

"Campaign finance reform may be dead on the Federal level, but the
League of Women Voters of Westchester County is determined to resur-
rect it at the county level.

"The league has made it its No. 1 legislative priority for this year, saying it believes 'the methods of financing political campaigns should insure the public's right to know, combat corruption and undue influence,
enable candidates to compete more equitably for public office and allow
maximum citizen participation in the political process.'

"The league is advocating computerized campaign contribution
records, public financing of some elections in return for spending caps,
controls on so-called soft-money contributions and the establishment of a
Campaign Finance Board to enforce the measures.

"The league's 'Government Reform Package,' a list of proposals it will
be lobbying for, presented recently to the county's Board of Legislators,
also named the following as priorities for action: property tax reassess-
ment . . . budget reform . . . redistricting. . . .

"The league supports recommendations made last year by the Singer
Commission, a nonpartisan group. The commission called for establishment of the Campaign Finance Board, better disclosure of where contributions come from, voluntary caps on spending in county executive and
legislative races, in return for public money to finance the races, and debates, among other things. . . ." (*New York Times*, April 12, 1998)

"House Speaker Newt Gingrich (R-Ga.) promised yesterday to schedule a
House vote on campaign finance legislation by 'sometime in March' but
did not say what it will include or whether votes will be allowed on rival
plans. . . .

"... His announcement drew withering criticism from the League of Women Voters, which has been lobbying for a strong campaign finance bill. 'The speaker's pledge to consider campaign finance reform is so broad and vague as to be meaningless,' said league president Becky Cain. 'This was a renewed commitment to mumbo jumbo—a commitment to complicated, ritualistic activity intended to obscure and confuse.' " (*Washington Post*, November 14, 1997)

"Republicans yesterday rebuffed Democrats' attempts to broaden the scope of the House committee investigating campaign finance abuses or curtail the powers of committee Chairman Dan Burton (R-Ind.) to issue subpoenas. . . .

"League of Women Voters President Becky Cain denounced the outcome as a 'travesty. . . . The Senate is conducting a broad investigation and the House is headed toward a partisan sideshow. Today we saw the kind of political games that disgust the American people.' " (*Washington Post*, April 11, 1997)

# POLITICAL ORIENTATION

Unavailable

# National Conference of State Legislatures (1975)

1560 Broadway
Suite 700
Denver, Colorado 80202
Phone: (303) 830-2200
Fax: (303) 863-8003

444 North Capitol Street, NW
Suite 515
Washington, D.C. 20001
Phone: (202) 624-5400
Fax: (202) 737-1069

Internet: http://www.ncsl.org

---

"To improve the quality and effectiveness of state legislatures; to foster interstate communication and cooperation; and to assure state legislatures a strong cohesive voice in the federal system."

**PURPOSE**

---

150 total

**STAFF**

---

William T. Pound, executive director. Pound became executive director of the National Conference of State Legislatures (NCSL) in 1987. He has been with NCSL since 1975, serving most of that period as director of state services and director of the Denver office. Before joining NCSL, Pound served on the faculties of Colorado State University, the University of Denver, and the University of Colorado.

**DIRECTOR**

---

170(c)(1)

**TAX STATUS**

---

1998—$13.10 million
Proposed 1999—$13.10 million

**BUDGET**

---

State dues, 50 percent; publications and meetings, 25 percent; grants and contracts, 25 percent

**FUNDING SOURCES**

---

Members: 50 states, the District of Columbia, and all U.S. territories
Branches/chapters: N/A
Affiliate: NCSL Foundation for State Legislatures, a 501(c)(3) organization

**SCOPE**

---

None

**PAC**

## METHOD OF OPERATION

♦ Conferences/seminars ♦ Congressional testimony ♦ Electronic databases (Federal Fund Information for States, a computerized service providing detailed information and projections on about 90 percent of the federal funds going to each state; LEGISNET, abstracts of thousands of legislative research reports, public policy documents, journal articles, 50-state surveys and statistical data in spreadsheet format, research reports, and research currently under way; NCSLnet, electronic service center for NCSL products and information and a gateway to the Internet) ♦ Films/video/audiotapes ♦ Internet (Web site) ♦ Legislative/regulatory monitoring (federal and state) ♦ Library/information clearinghouse ♦ Research ♦ Teleconferences ♦ Training and technical assistance

## CURRENT CONCERNS

♦ Budget crisis for state governments ♦ Education ♦ Energy ♦ Federalism ♦ Health planning ♦ Natural resources ♦ Reallocation of federal program monies to states ♦ Redistricting

## PUBLICATIONS

The following is a list of sample publications:

*1996 State Legislative Summary on Children, Youth and Family Issues*
*Creative Solutions for Funding the Arts*
*The Electric Industry in the Balance*
*Experts Analyze State Budgets and Taxes*
*A Guide to Legislative Information Technology*
*HIV/AIDS Facts to Consider: 1996*
*How To Be an Effective Legislator*
*Lead Poisoning Prevention*
*Medicaid Made Simple*
*NCSL Publishes a New Transportation Report Series*
*Playing the Stadium Game*
*Principles of a Sound State School Finance System*
*Protocol: A Handbook*
*Readable Reports on the Rapidly Changing Utility Marketplace*
*State Fiscal Outlook for 1996*
*States and Tribes: Finding a Connection Among Nations*

## NEWSLETTER

*Federal Update* (bimonthly)
*The Fiscal Letter* (bimonthly)
*LegisBriefs* (48 times a year)
*State-Federal Issue Briefs* (12–25 times a year)
*State Legislative Reports* (12–25 times a year)
*State Legislatures* (magazine; 10 times a year)

## CONFERENCES

Assembly on Federal Issues
Assembly on State Issues
Leadership Institute
Legislative Staff Management Institute
Symposium for New Leaders
Sponsors meetings for legislators and staff

Dan Blue, president; Paul Mannweiler, president elect; Jim Costa, vice president; Richard Finan, immediate past president; Tom Tedcastle, staff chair; John Phelps, staff vice chair; Anne C. Walker, immediate past staff chair

Other executive committee members:
♦ Norma Anderson ♦ John Andreason ♦ Neil Bryant ♦ Spencer Cogg ♦ Steve Cohen ♦ Susan Crosby ♦ Lori Daniels ♦ Marilyn Goldwater ♦ Harold Halverson ♦ Wally Horn ♦ Doug Kristensen ♦ Joseph Kyrillos Jr. ♦ Audrey Langworth ♦ Willie Logan Jr. ♦ John Maitland Jr. ♦ Eugene McGill ♦ Angela Monson ♦ Michael Olguin ♦ John Pennington ♦ Jack Regan ♦ Jody Richards ♦ Peggy Rosenzweig ♦ Stephen Saland ♦ Allyson Schwartz ♦ Rob Smith ♦ Helen Thomson ♦ Maggie Tinsman ♦ Jerry Ward ♦ Kathleen Wojcik

# BOARD OF DIRECTORS

# EFFECTIVENESS

"In Virginia, Republican James S. Gilmore III captured the governorship last year with a three-word slogan: 'No Car Tax.' While his antitax efforts have run into some legislative resistance, lawmakers in several other states have taken notice of Virginia's experience and are considering rolling back similar taxes, says a report by Scott Mackey and Mandy Rafool of the National Conference of State Legislatures in Denver.

"The full report is available on the group's Web site (www.ncsl.org)." (*Wall Street Journal*, March 11, 1998)

"Federal tax changes are adopted automatically in some states, but specific legislative action is required in many others. As a result, new federal tax breaks—including the exemption on up to $500,000 of home-sale gains and the Roth IRA—may not be available for many people when figuring their state income taxes. . . .

"To date, only California and Oregon have taken action to adopt provisions in last year's sweeping changes in the U.S. tax code, according to the National Conference of State Legislatures. That means taxpayers in 17 states and the District of Columbia may be caught in a kind of legislative limbo when trying to figure out their state and local income taxes. . . ." (*Wall Street Journal*, February 27, 1998)

"In the aftermath of Congress's rejection of President Clinton's proposed overhaul of the health care system four years ago, state politicians have been seizing upon consumers' and doctors' complaints of abuses under managed care. . . .

"Molly Stauffer, a senior policy analyst for the National Conference of State Legislatures, said that 17 states enacted comprehensive consumer rights laws last year, and she predicted that at least six more would this year. Ms. Riley said most of the provisions states were enacting were high on the agendas of specialist physicians.

"She said more than half of the provisions let women choose obstetrician-gynecologists as personal physicians, bypassing primary care doctors who act as gatekeepers under managed care plans, and mandate hospital stays, typically of at least two days, for childbirth. Many also require plans to make quicker referrals to specialists and to let patients appeal rejections of care to outside arbitrators." (*New York Times*, February 16, 1998)

"State lawmakers gathered [in Scottsdale, Ariz.] from around the country . . . to talk about one of the hottest topics in health care: how to make it easier for patients to sue their managed care plans. . . .

". . . The session [was] sponsored by the National Conference of State Legislatures. . . ." (*Wall Street Journal*, January 12, 1998)

"A survey by the Denver-based National Conference of State Legislatures found that a total of 30 states began this year with revenue running ahead of budgeted expectations (in California, they have been about $1 billion above forecasts), with 19 states indicating that elementary and secondary school spending would be their top priority. . . .

" 'California lagged [behind] everybody else coming out of the recession,' said Arturo Perez, a policy specialist in the fiscal affairs program at the conference of legislatures. 'States are definitely now on the upside of the economic cycle, and that is what you'd expect with low inflation and the stock market humming the way it is.' " (*New York Times*, January 10, 1998)

"With the economy refusing to cool, with most states sitting on sizable surpluses and with gubernatorial and legislative elections scheduled in a majority of states, tax-cut fever is once again sweeping the land as legislatures prepare to open their 1998 sessions. . . .

" 'I think there will be somewhat larger tax cuts in 1998 than in 1997 because, after all, this revenue growth has sustained itself longer than anyone expected,' said Ronald K. Snell, director of the economic and fiscal division of the National Conference of State Legislatures. 'My guess is that they would exceed 1997 just based on the number of states in which governors and legislative leadership are talking about them.' . . .

"In the 1997 fiscal year, which ended June 30 in most states, 44 states had surpluses totaling $14.7 billion, said Arturo Perez, an analyst for the National Conference of State Legislatures. Since then, the good news has only continued. A report issued this week by Mr. Perez concludes that 29 states predict that revenue collections for 1998 will exceed expectations, while spending in nearly all states has remained on target." (*New York Times*, January 4, 1998)

"With welfare rolls down, many states are taking advantage of federal welfare aid to cut their own spending and use the funds to help pay for tax cuts and other popular projects. The falling rolls have given the states a windfall of $3 billion to $4 billion, says Jack Tweedie, welfare analyst for the National Conference of State Legislatures. And they are free to spend about $2 billion of that in areas unrelated to poverty if they wish. . . .

"According to a new study by the National Conference of State Legislatures, 20 of the 44 states surveyed are spending 80% or less of the amount they previously spent on welfare. The federal welfare law, enacted last year, allows states to reduce their own spending, or 'maintenance of effort,' to 75% or 80% of past levels, depending on caseload reductions. Only five are spending at or above prior totals." (*Wall Street Journal*, November 14, 1997)

"Lawmakers in many states are negotiating budgets that include substantial increases in education spending in response to a strong economy, widespread concern about the quality of public schools and, in some cases, court decisions requiring new systems of school financing.

"With these increases, states will likely shoulder a larger share of overall education financing, while local districts will bear a smaller share. . . .

" 'Overall, I think it's a good thing for states to carry more of the burden, both for equity reasons and because it's appropriate for the states to be out in front as we move to more emphasis on standards and assessment,' said Terry Whitney, a senior policy specialist with the National Conference of State Legislatures." (*New York Times*, March 16, 1998)

"nonpartisan" (*New York Times*, November 12, 1994)

# National Governors' Association (1908)

444 North Capitol Street, NW
Suite 267
Washington, D.C. 20001
Phone: (202) 624-5300
Fax: (202) 624-5313
Internet: http://www.nga.org

| | |
|---|---|
| **PURPOSE** | "To help shape and implement national policy and solve state problems." |
| **STAFF** | 80 total; plus interns |
| **DIRECTOR** | Raymond C. Scheppach Jr., executive director. Before joining the National Governors' Association (NGA) in 1983, Scheppach held several positions at the Congressional Budget Office, including deputy director. He also has worked for the Standard Oil Company of Ohio and a consulting firm. An author on economics issues, Scheppach holds a Ph.D. from the University of Connecticut. |
| **TAX STATUS** | 501(c)(3) |
| **BUDGET** | 1998—$11 million<br>Proposed 1999—Unavailable |
| **FUNDING SOURCES** | Federal grants and contracts, 34 percent; state dues, 33 percent; foundation grants, 15 percent; corporate contributions, 6 percent; publications, 1 percent; other, 11 percent |
| **SCOPE** | Members: 55 individuals (governors of the 50 states, Puerto Rico, the Northern Mariana Islands, the Virgin Islands, Guam, and American Samoa)<br>Branches/chapters: N/A<br>Affiliates: Council of Governors Policy Advisors; Federal Funds Information for States; NGA Center for Best Practices; National Association of State Budget Officers; State Services Organization (all are nonprofit) |
| **PAC** | None |

♦ Conferences/seminars ♦ Congressional testimony ♦ Congressional voting analysis ♦ Demonstrations ♦ Direct action ♦ Grantmaking ♦ Legislative/regulatory monitoring (federal and state) ♦ Library/information clearinghouse ♦ Lobbying (federal and state) ♦ Media outreach ♦ Research ♦ Training/technical assistance

## METHOD OF OPERATION

♦ Crime and public safety ♦ Economic development ♦ Education ♦ Environment ♦ Federalism ♦ Health care ♦ Transportation ♦ Welfare ♦ Workforce development

## CURRENT CONCERNS

*Directory of Governors of the American States, Commonwealths, and Territories* (annual)
*Fiscal Survey of the States* (semiannual)
*Governors' Staff Directory* (semiannual)

Also publishes issue briefs and policy papers

## PUBLICATIONS

*Governors' Bulletin* (biweekly)

## NEWSLETTER

Annual meeting
Winter meeting

## CONFERENCES

Thomas R. Carper (Del.), chairman Michael O. Leavitt (Utah), vice chairman

Other executive committee members:
♦ David M. Beasley (S.C.) ♦ Mel Carnahan (Mo.) ♦ Howard Dean (Vt.) ♦ John Engler (Mich.) ♦ Frank Keating (Okla.) ♦ Bob Miller (Nv.) ♦ Paul E. Patton (Ky.) ♦ Tommy G. Thompson (Wis.) ♦ George V. Voinovich (Ohio)

## BOARD OF DIRECTORS

"Hoping to throw cold water on the frenzy to tax the Internet, the House today passed a bill that would bar state and local governments from imposing new Internet taxes for three years. . . .

"For months, the National Governors' Association has opposed the measure, saying it would infringe on the right of state and local governments to levy taxes. The opposition stemmed mainly from the possibility of taxing goods sold on the Internet." (*New York Times*, June 24, 1998)

"Government health policy makers are leaning toward requiring state Medicaid programs to cover Viagra, the popular new impotence drug, but a final decision won't be made until next week, federal officials said. . . .

## EFFECTIVENESS

"The National Governors' Association, citing cost concerns, wrote to Health and Human Services Secretary Donna Shalala earlier this week asking that states be permitted to decide whether to cover Viagra. In the letter, Govs. Lawton Chiles of Florida and Michael Leavitt of Utah said covering Viagra through Medicaid could cost the states and the federal governments more than $100 million a year." (*Wall Street Journal*, May 29, 1998)

"Republican leaders of Congress, looking for ways to help pay for a highway bill that exceeds budget limits, want to cut Medicaid, food stamps and social service programs, but they have encountered vehement objections from governors of both parties. . . .

"The National Governors' Association today declared its 'strong, unalterable opposition to any reductions in the Federal Government's commitment' to Medicaid and the food stamp program. . . .

"[The association] said the cuts would hamper states' ability to enroll children in Medicaid, inspect nursing homes, investigate health care fraud and perform other tasks mandated by the Federal Medicaid law." (*New York Times*, May 12, 1998)

"For the past 20 years, legislative proposals to change the way federal agencies propose and make rules have cratered with resounding thuds. . . .

"Sens. Fred D. Thompson (R-Tenn.) and Carl M. Levin (D-Mich.) thought their compromise bill to 'reform' many aspects of the federal system just might sidestep such a fate. . . .

"The bill has the support of the Business Roundtable, whose members are Fortune 500 companies, the National Governors' Association, and other business groups. Experts in the economics of regulation applauded Thompson and Levin for attempting to bring some rational analysis to rulemaking. . . ." (*Washington Post*, March 20, 1998)

"The nation's governors yesterday agreed to support a three-year ban on special Internet commerce taxes in exchange for a promise by Congress to consider requiring electronic merchants to collect sales taxes after the moratorium.

"The National Governors Association had opposed bipartisan legislation in the House and Senate to enact an Internet tax moratorium, saying the freeze could deprive state and local governments of crucial tax revenue as electronic commerce becomes more popular. . . .

"The governors want to require Internet and mail-order merchants to collect sales taxes even if they do not have a physical presence in the state to which the goods are shipped. . . .

"[They also] want . . . a uniform national system of sales tax rules for electronic commerce and uniform rates for each state. . . ." (*Washington Post*, March 20, 1998)

"Senate leaders from both parties struck a deal yesterday to increase highway spending to $173 billion over the next six years, a more than 40 percent jump over previous years.

"The deal, which was made under pressure from state governors, industry lobbyists and other senators, clears the way for passage of a new highway bill by the full Senate this month and enhances the prospects for a compromise with the House. . . .

"The National Governors Association and other state and local officials have urged Congress to act swiftly on new legislation before a looming May 1 deadline, warning that 42,100 jobs could be lost for every $1 billion of road contracts canceled because of congressional delays. . . ." (*Washington Post*, March 3, 1998)

"It is hardly news that, outside of the White House, Republicans now dominate government in the United States. Democrats are in the minority in the House, the Senate and the governorships. . . .

"The gap is greatest in the governorships, with Republicans controlling 32 of them to the Democrats' 17, along with independent Angus King of Maine. What was brought home during the meeting of the National Governors' Association (NGA) in Washington last weekend is that the difference is not just one of numbers but of quality. . . . Watching a dozen of the Democrats participate in a group news conference during the NGA meeting, a veteran of the Clinton White House whispered to me, 'It's remarkable how few of them can even speak.'. . ." (*Washington Post*, February 25, 1998)

"Governors, predicting dwindling prospects for a national tobacco settlement, plan to redouble their efforts to negotiate individual settlements with cigarette manufacturers.

"At the National Governors' Association meeting, the talk was of the urgent need to negotiate directly with the tobacco industry. A downbeat briefing by two senators on the prospects for passage of a national settlement 'certainly encouraged us to get settlements done,' said Republican Gov. Paul Cellucci of Massachusetts.

"If Congress is able to pass a national settlement, Mr. Cellucci and other governors say they intend to lobby lawmakers and the White House for protection of the states' share of any tobacco money. 'The federal government sat on the sidelines and is now trying to tell the states how the money should be spent,' said Pennsylvania Gov. Tom Ridge, a Republican. 'We don't think that's acceptable.' " (*Wall Street Journal*, February 24, 1998)

"[President Clinton] arrived late at a White House meeting with the National Governors Association (NGA) membership. . . . But he said some things that the governors welcomed. According to participants, he promised to help them lobby Congress to pass pending highway legislation in time for funds to be available to the states for the spring construction season. He also was quoted as saying he has no objections to increasing the payout from the federal highway trust fund as long as the spending caps in last year's budget agreement are not broken. . . .

"He said he would ask Congress to extend to all 50 states a 12-state pilot program that waives most federal regulations on existing aid to elementary and secondary schools in return for states setting high academic standards and testing students' performance. . . .

"Many of the 32 Republican governors and some Democrats have complained that the national tests would duplicate what states already are doing. And there is some discomfort among the GOP executives about the overlap between their state agendas and the program Clinton is pushing in Washington. . . ." (*Washington Post*, February 24, 1998)

"Some years, the annual National Governors' Association dinner at the White House is a chance for presidential hopefuls to size up the digs and see if they might want to move in.

"Last night's dinner, though—at what is typically a good, midterm time for governors to float balloons about running for the Oval Office—was permeated by the possibility of a military strike on Iraq. It was the silent 51st governor at the president's table. Also not helping matters was the topic of this year's conference, which focused on: transportation and infrastructure. . . . Perhaps if the nation weren't teetering on the brink of war, this might have captured the president's undivided attention." (*Washington Post*, February 23, 1998)

## POLITICAL ORIENTATION

"Governor Fob James of Alabama has announced he is leaving the [National Governors Association] because it 'is just another liberal lobbying group' that produces 'streams of generic policy papers that nobody gets to read.'

"He wishes the NGA well in representing the interests of states, but says he can't justify spending $100,900 in taxpayer money to belong. By year's end he could be joined by up to six other governors who may decide that if they want to keep in touch with fellow governors they can just pick up the phone.

"The NGA was founded at the height of the Progressive Era in 1908. Its founders wanted to centralize administrative power in Washington in exchange for grants to the states. It has seldom strayed from its roots, and frequently lobbies against federal tax cuts and for entitlement spending. The NGA chairmanship rotates every year between a Democratic and Republican governor, so no one is in charge long enough to change the organization. The real power is in the hands of a liberal staff, which is largely made up of former Congressional aides. . . .

"Many feel the NGA does some good work, but that it doesn't deserve to have two-thirds of its $13.2 million annual budget funded by taxpayers. . . .

"Governor Fife Symington of Arizona is 'leaning against' paying his state's annual $81,000 in dues, and will make a final decision on withdrawing this month. He told us that he's found the NGA bureaucracy to be 'disconnected from the real world.' Even on issues where there is no liberal bias there is a tendency 'to blend 50 viewpoints into a Cuisinart and end up with mush.'

"For its part, the NGA says its reports and recommendations must naturally represent a 'consensus' of the views of all 50 governors. Raymond Scheppach, its executive director, claims that 'we've shifted our policies somewhat' toward issues favored by the 32 Republican governors and 'we're much more unified now than we've been in a long time.'. . ." (*Wall Street Journal*, June 16, 1997)

"bipartisan" (*New York Times*, April 28, 1995)

# National League of Cities (1924)

1301 Pennsylvania Avenue, NW
Washington, D.C. 20004
Phone: (202) 626-3000
Fax: (202) 626-3043
Internet: http://www.nlc.org

| | |
|---|---|
| "Dedicated to advancing the public interest, building democracy and community, and improving the quality of life by strengthening the capacity of local governance and advocating the interests of local communities." | *PURPOSE* |
| 90 total | *STAFF* |
| Donald J. Borut, executive director. Borut has been executive director of the National League of Cities (NLC) since 1990. He has been involved in urban affairs and public service for thirty years at the local and national levels. For seven years, Borut held a variety of management posts in the city of Ann Arbor, Michigan. In 1971 he joined the staff of the International City Management Association, where he became deputy executive director in 1984. Borut is a graduate of Oberlin College and received an M.P.A. from the University of Michigan. | *DIRECTOR* |
| 501(c)(3) | *TAX STATUS* |
| 1998—Unavailable<br>Proposed 1999—Unavailable | *BUDGET* |
| Dues, 45 percent; conferences, 30 percent; other, 25 percent | *FUNDING SOURCES* |
| Members: 1,500 cities; 49 state municipal leagues<br>Branches/chapters: N/A<br>Affiliates: N/A | *SCOPE* |
| None | *PAC* |

| | |
|---|---|
| *METHOD OF OPERATION* | ◆ Advertisements ◆ Awards program (Innovation Awards, Howland Awards, Community Policing Awards, Cultural Diversity Awards) ◆ Coalition forming ◆ Conferences/seminars ◆ Congressional testimony ◆ Congressional voting analysis ◆ Films/video/audiotapes ◆ International activities ◆ Internet (databases, electronic bulletin boards, Web site) ◆ Legal assistance ◆ Legislative/regulatory monitoring (federal) ◆ Library/information clearinghouse ◆ Litigation ◆ Lobbying (federal and grassroots) ◆ Local/municipal affairs ◆ Media outreach ◆ Participation in regulatory proceedings (federal) ◆ Research ◆ Telecommunications services (mailing lists) ◆ Training and technical assistance |
| *CURRENT CONCERNS* | ◆ Building strong communities ◆ Ensuring the municipals' role in the federal restructuring of electric utilities ◆ Keeping federal budget balanced ◆ Preserving municipal authority ◆ Preserving transportation systems |
| *PUBLICATIONS* | More than 100 titles on topics of interest to cities |
| *NEWSLETTER* | *Nation's Cities Weekly* (50 times a year) |
| *CONFERENCES* | Congress of Cities (annual convention)<br>Congressional City Conference (annual)<br>Leadership Summit<br>Information Technology Conference |
| *BOARD OF DIRECTORS* | Brian J. O'Neill, president; Clarence Anthony, first vice president; Bob Knight, second vice president<br><br>Other members:<br>◆ Floyd Adams Jr. ◆ Arnie Adamsen ◆ E.H. Alexander ◆ John B. Andrews ◆ Dennis W. Archer ◆ Sharon Sayles Belton ◆ George D. Blackwood Jr. ◆ Thomas G. Bredeweg ◆ George A. Brown Jr. ◆ Susan J. Cave ◆ Mary Clark ◆ Frank Clinton ◆ Hal Daub ◆ John DeStefano Jr. ◆ Sue Donaldson ◆ Thomas Duane ◆ Jerry Dunn ◆ Howard E. Duvall Jr. ◆ Gene Feldman ◆ William F. Fulginiti ◆ John A. Garner Jr. ◆ Neil G. Giuliano ◆ Thomas J. Grady ◆ Victor Hernandez ◆ Patsy Jo Hilliard ◆ Glenda E. Hood ◆ Sharpe James ◆ Gregory Lashutka ◆ Patricia Lockwood ◆ Jack Lynch ◆ Linda A. Morton ◆ Joe Murdy ◆ Jenny Oropeza ◆ Mary C. Poss ◆ Cathy Reynolds ◆ Sedalia Sanders ◆ Marjorie B. Schramm ◆ Mark Schwartz ◆ Eric B. Smith ◆ Harry Smith ◆ Daniel M. Speer ◆ Connie Sprynczynatyk ◆ Louisa M. Strayhorn ◆ Tommy Swaim ◆ Jack L. Valencia Jr. |

"Groups including the National Governors' Association and the U.S. Conference of Mayors dropped their opposition to the House [Internet-tax bill] yesterday after winning several changes. Local officials feared the Internet Tax Freedom Act, as originally crafted, would devastate state and local revenues.

"National League of Cities President Brian O'Neill said the groups were concerned that electronic commerce was done 'in a manner that protects our Main Street merchants and prevents erosion of state and local tax bases.' " (*Wall Street Journal,* March 20, 1998)

"In Prince George's County, [Md.,] where tax increment financing [in which government pledges a portion of the anticipated increase in tax revenue from a new development as repayment for bonds used in financing the project] was first used in the early 1980s, officials noted later that the program can have some disadvantages. According to a National League of Cities study devoted to the financing of infrastructure, officials in Prince George's County cautioned that there may be a public perception that TIF districts get public improvements that other areas of a community don't receive.

"The study further showed that developers in a TIF district may feel that funds generated from new projects are 'their' money." (*Washington Post,* January 12, 1998)

"The municipal-bond market's latest controversy features alleged document-shredding, inquiries by two federal agencies, anxiety at numerous city halls around the country, plus hundreds of millions of dollars the federal Treasury could have gotten but didn't. . . .

"The problems trace back to the early 1990s, when declining interest rates prompted municipalities to hire investment banks to refinance their debt in so-called advance refundings. The government says some investment banks slapped excessive markups [known as yield burning] on bonds used in the refundings, pocketing profits that should have gone to the Treasury. . . .

"The National League of Cities [says] that states and cities are bit players in this drama, incapable of understanding, much less conspiring in, yield burning. The league is leaning on members of Congress to win some relief. 'Washington is trying to get us to pay for something that we're not responsible for,' says Mark Schwartz, the league's president, who estimates that once all the states and cities settle up with the IRS, the bill could hit $1 billion. The league thinks investigators should go after Wall Street." (*Wall Street Journal,* August 26, 1997)

"Congressional budget negotiators are on the verge of awarding the politically powerful TV broadcast industry expanded rights to the public airwaves, an action likely to force the U.S. Treasury to forgo some $5 billion in anticipated revenues.

". . . Fire, police and ambulance agencies . . . say the proposal would prevent them from using the channels to upgrade vital communications networks. . . .

"... The National League of Cities estimates that while cash-strapped public safety agencies now control about 50 percent of the frequencies they require to communicate properly, they will be down to about 10 percent by the year 2010. . . .

" 'These frequencies are desperately needed,' said Randy Arndt, a National League of Cities spokesman. 'This is a bold power grab by broadcasters that torpedoes a vital need for public safety all over the country. This isn't pie in the sky. This is an issue, potentially, of life and death.' "
(*Washington Post*, July 20, 1997)

"Two-thirds of the nation's cities say they are better able to meet their financial needs this year than last, and cities generally are increasing their year-end reserves, the National League of Cities reported.

"In its annual survey of city fiscal conditions, the group found more than half of all cities boosted actual levels of capital spending and speeded up operating spending from last year. At the same time, the number of cities taking actions to raise revenue was the lowest in a decade." (*Wall Street Journal*, July 8, 1997)

"The Neighborhood Partnership awards program [sponsored by the National League of Cities and the Food Marketing Institute] is designed to encourage and recognize collaborative initiatives by supermarket companies and local governments in underserved areas. The aim, of course, is to help revitalize communities through public-private partnerships." (*Wall Street Journal*, February 20, 1997)

# POLITICAL ORIENTATION

"Today . . . the U.S. Supreme Court will hear arguments on whether IOLTA [interest on lawyers' trust accounts] unconstitutionally expropriates clients' property to fund the social goals of America's legal establishment.

". . . For liberals, IOLTA is a dream come true. It takes the interest generated by private property and uses it to underwrite litigation and other social causes without the inconvenience of seeking the approval of the private parties whose property creates the interest-producing fund. . . .

"The defenders of IOLTA before the Supreme Court include a who's who of the legal and political establishment: the American Bar Association, the Council of State Governments, the National League of Cities, the National Association of Counties, the U.S. Council of Mayors, more than 80 state bar associations, the American Association of Retired Persons, the Conference of State Chief Justices, and the Clinton Justice Department. . . ." (*Wall Street Journal*, January 13, 1998)

# National Women's Political Caucus
## (1971)

1211 Connecticut Avenue, NW
Suite 425
Washington, D.C. 20036
Phone: (202) 785-1100
Fax: (202) 785-3605
Internet: mailnwpc@aol.com *or* http://www.nwpc.org

| | |
|---|---|
| "Dedicated to increasing the number of women in elected and appointed office at all levels of government, regardless of party affiliation." | **PURPOSE** |
| 7 total | **STAFF** |
| Anita Perez Ferguson, president and chief executive officer | **DIRECTOR** |
| 501(c)(4) | **TAX STATUS** |
| 1997—$983,200<br>1998—$760,500<br>Proposed 1999—Unavailable | **BUDGET** |
| Membership dues, 40 percent; special events, 23 percent; direct mail solicitations, 20 percent; preconvention, 10 percent; other, 7 percent | **FUNDING SOURCES** |
| Members: 35,000<br>Branches/chapters: 300 state and local caucuses<br>Affiliate: NWPC Leadership Development, Education, and Research Fund, a 501(c)(3) organization | **SCOPE** |
| NWPC Campaign Support Committee<br>NWPC Victory Fund | **PAC** |

## METHOD OF OPERATION

◆ Awards program ◆ Campaign contributions ◆ Campaign skills training ◆ Coalition forming ◆ Conferences/seminars ◆ Congressional testimony ◆ Congressional voting analysis ◆ Electoral politics ◆ Grassroots organizing ◆ Internet (Web site) ◆ Lobbying (federal, state, and grassroots) ◆ Media outreach ◆ Polling ◆ Research ◆ Telecommunications services (Hotline: 800-729-NWPC) ◆ Technical assistance

## CURRENT CONCERNS

Number of women elected and appointed to public office

## PUBLICATIONS

*Campaigning to Win: A Workbook for Women in Politics*
*Changing the Face of American Politics* (video)
*Don't Miss That Appointment*
*Facing the Religious Right: A Guide for Women Candidates and State and Local NWPC Chapters*
*Factsheet on Women's Political Progress*
*Grassroots Organizing: How to Start a Local Chapter of the National Women's Political Caucus*
*How to Change the World: A Women's Guide to Grassroots Lobbying*
*Moving More Women Into Public Office: A Three-Step Recruitment Guide for State and Local Caucus Leaders*
*National Directory of Women Elected Officials*
*Perception and Reality: A Study Comparing the Success of Men and Women Candidates*
*Why Don't More Women Run?*
*Women Voters and the Gender Gap*

## NEWSLETTER

*Women's Political Times* (quarterly)

## CONFERENCES

Biennial convention
Young Women's Campaign Training (biennial)

## BOARD OF DIRECTORS

Anita Perez Ferguson, president and chief executive officer; Cathy Allen, Pat Deal, Kate Gooderham, Shaloma Shawmut-Lessner, Irene Radcliff, and Hazel Thomas, vice presidents; Nancy Zamora, treasurer; Shirley Marvin, secretary

Other advisory board members:
♦ Erla Alexander ♦ Polly Baca ♦ Patricia Bailey ♦ Marjorie Benton ♦
Yvonne Brathwaite Burke ♦ Liz Carpenter ♦ Shirley Chisholm ♦
Johnnetta B. Cole ♦ Mary Dent Crisp ♦ Marian Wright Edelman ♦
Linda Ellerbee ♦ Myrlie Evers-Williams ♦ Frances T. Farenthold ♦ Betty
Friedan ♦ Elisabeth Griffith ♦ Elinor Guggenheimer ♦ Dorothy Height
♦ Elizabeth Holtzman ♦ Mildred Jeffrey ♦ Gloria Johnson ♦ Coretta
Scott King ♦ Kate Rand Lloyd ♦ Doris Meissner ♦ Tanya Melich ♦ Joyce
Miller ♦ Iris Mitgang ♦ Irene Natividad ♦ Eleanor Holmes Norton ♦
Ann Richards ♦ Sharon Percy Rockefeller ♦ Sharon Rodine ♦ Audrey
Rowe ♦ Jill Ruckelshaus ♦ Patricia Saiki ♦ Claudine Schneider ♦ Mary
Stanley ♦ Gloria Steinem ♦ Marlo Thomas ♦ Victoria Toensing ♦ C.
Delores Tucker ♦ Carmen Delgado Votaw ♦ Kathy Wilson ♦ Harriet
Woods

---

Unavailable

## *EFFECTIVENESS*

---

Unavailable

## *POLITICAL ORIENTATION*

# OMB Watch (1983)

1742 Connecticut Ave., NW
Washington, DC 20009
Phone: (202) 234-8494
Fax: (202) 234-8584
Internet: http://www.ombwatch.org/ombwatch.html

| | |
|---|---|
| **PURPOSE** | "To increase public participation in government and public access to government information." |
| **STAFF** | 14 total—11 professional; 3 support |
| **DIRECTOR** | Gary D. Bass, executive director |
| **TAX STATUS** | 501(c)(3) |
| **BUDGET** | Fiscal year ending June 30, 1998—$850,000<br>F.Y. 1999—Unavailable |
| **FUNDING SOURCES** | Foundation grants, 75 percent; publications, 5 percent; membership dues, 5 percent; individuals, 1 percent; other, 14 percent |
| **SCOPE** | Members: Nearly 1,000 individuals and community groups<br>Branches/chapters: N/A<br>Affiliates: N/A |
| **PAC** | None |
| **METHOD OF OPERATION** | ◆ Awards program ◆ Coalition forming ◆ Conferences/seminars ◆ Congressional testimony ◆ Grassroots organizing ◆ Internet (electronic bulletin, e-mail alerts, Web site) ◆ Legislative/regulatory monitoring (federal) ◆ Lobbying (federal and grassroots) ◆ Media outreach ◆ Participation in regulatory proceedings (federal) ◆ Research ◆ Technical assistance ◆ Training |

| | |
|---|---|
| ◆ Environment ◆ Federal budget ◆ Government Results and Performance Act ◆ Information policy and technology ◆ Public access ◆ Regulation | *CURRENT CONCERNS* |
| *So You Want To Make A Difference* | *PUBLICATIONS* |
| *OMB Watcher* (bimonthly)<br>*Government Information Insider* (quarterly) | *NEWSLETTER* |
| Unavailable | *CONFERENCES* |
| ◆ Nancy Amidei ◆ Gary Bass ◆ Richard Healey ◆ Kristine Jacobs ◆ Bob Lawrence ◆ Mark Lloyd ◆ Charles Loveless ◆ J. Michail McCloskey ◆ David C. Rice ◆ Mark Rosenman ◆ Margaret Seminario ◆ Barbara Warden | *BOARD OF DIRECTORS* |
| | *EFFECTIVENESS* |

"The government's compliance with a 1996 law making electronic records subject to the Freedom of Information Act has been 'overwhelmingly inadequate,' according to a survey by OMB Watch.

"The independent watchdog group also said the Office of Management and Budget, assigned by statute to provide guidance to federal agencies on implementing the law, has done so little to help that many of them have turned to the Justice Department for advice. The report, issued last week, faulted Congress for failing to provide the funding the agencies need to comply with the new rules.

"Under the Electronic Freedom of Information Act (EFOIA), signed by President Clinton more than 18 months ago, federal agencies must treat electronically created information, such as databases and e-mail, as 'records' that can be sought under FOIA just as paper documents have been for the last 32 years. . . .

"The study said some of OMB's advice was misleading and reflected 'a pattern of apathy toward public access to government information.' As a result, many agencies have taken their cues from the Justice Department, which has provided 'a quality example of an EFOIA electronic reading room' and other helpful materials.

"Despite all the shortcomings, the report praised several agencies, such as the Defense Department and the Federal Communications Commission, for making research easy. It praised others, such as the Small Business Administration and the National Science Foundation, for providing forms on their Web sites so that FOIA requests can be submitted online." (*Washington Post*, April 26, 1998)

"Internet sites operated by federal agencies routinely collect data about visitors without saying how the information will be used, a practice that clashes with the Clinton administration's call for safeguarding privacy on the global computer network, according to a study released yesterday [August 27, 1997].

"Thirty-one of 70 government sites in the survey retrieved details, including names, ages and work histories, from the public. But only 11 of the sites provided statements about how the information was collected and used, according to the report by OMB Watch, a private research group based in the District. Although the study did not uncover any abuses of the information, it concluded that at least four agencies probably violated provisions of the Privacy Act of 1974, which restricts how federal agencies gather and use personal records, said Ari Schwartz, an information issues specialist at OMB Watch.

" 'What we found is that the new medium has blurred the lines created by the Privacy Act of 1974 and subsequent laws,' Schwartz said. 'We feel that guidance clarifying the application of these laws to the Internet would ease tensions of both agencies who are reluctant to supply new information over the Web and users who are concerned about their privacy.'. . ." (*Washington Post*, August 28, 1997)

## POLITICAL ORIENTATION

Unavailable

# Project Vote Smart/Center for National Independence in Politics (1988)

129 NW Fourth Street
Suite 204
Corvallis, Oregon 97330
Phone: (541) 754-2746
Fax: (541) 754-2747
Internet: commments@vote-smart.org *or*
http://www.vote-smart.org

| | |
|---|---|
| "To give all citizens free, instant access to abundant factual information about candidates and elected officials, from a nonpartisan source." | *PURPOSE* |
| 25 total; plus 200 interns and 200 volunteers | *STAFF* |
| Richard Kimball, executive director. Before joining Project Vote Smart, Kimball worked as an educator. | *DIRECTOR* |
| 501(c)(3) | *TAX STATUS* |
| 1998—$1.5 million<br>Proposed 1999—Unavailable | *BUDGET* |
| Individual memberships, 60 percent; foundation grants, 40 percent | *FUNDING SOURCES* |
| Members: 43,000 individuals<br>Branches/chapters: Satellite offices in Boston and Tucson<br>Affiliates: N/A | *SCOPE* |
| None | *PAC* |
| ♦ Internet (databases, Web site) ♦ Library/information clearinghouse (open to public) ♦ Media outreach ♦ Research ♦ Telecommunications services (Hotline: 800-622-SMART) ♦ Voting records | *METHOD OF OPERATION* |

## CURRENT CONCERNS

Giving all citizens free access to relevant factual information about more than 13,000 candidates and elected officials at the federal and state levels

## PUBLICATIONS

*The Reporter's Sourcebook*
*U.S. Government: Owner's Manual*
*Vote Smart Web Yellow Pages* (online)
*Voter's Self-Defense Manual*

## NEWSLETTER

None

## CONFERENCES

None

## BOARD OF DIRECTORS

Richard Kimball, president

Other members:
♦ Adelaide Elm ♦ Bill Frenzel ♦ Sonia Jarvis ♦ Peggy Lampl ♦ Jim Leach ♦ William Proxmire ♦ Claudine Schneider

## EFFECTIVENESS

Unavailable

## POLITICAL ORIENTATION

"nonpartisan" (*New York Times*, November 6, 1994)

# Public Citizen, Inc. (1971)

1600 20th Street, NW
Washington, D.C. 20009
Phone: (202) 588-1000
Fax: (202) 588-7799
Internet: http://www.citizen.org

| | |
|---|---|
| "To fight for government and corporate accountability, consumer rights in the marketplace, safe products, a healthy environment, fair trade, and clean and safe energy sources through lobbying, research, public outreach, and litigation." | *PURPOSE* |
| 75 total | *STAFF* |
| Joan B. Claybrook, president. Claybrook became president of Public Citizen, Inc., in 1982. She was administrator of the National Highway Traffic Safety Administration from 1977 to 1981. Claybrook, who began her association with Ralph Nader projects in 1970, founded Public Citizen's Congress Watch in 1973 and served as its director until 1977. Claybrook has written numerous articles and frequently testifies before congressional committees. She earned a law degree from Georgetown University Law Center. | *DIRECTOR* |
| 501(c)(4)—Public Citizen, Inc.<br>501(c)(3)—Public Citizen Foundation, Inc. | *TAX STATUS* |
| Fiscal year ending September 30, 1997—$9.2 million<br>F.Y. 1998—$9.1 million<br>Proposed F.Y. 1999—Unavailable | *BUDGET* |
| Membership dues, contributions, foundation grants, and sales of publications. Public Citizen does not accept government or corporate contributions. | *FUNDING SOURCES* |
| Members: More than 100,000 supporters<br>Branches/chapters: Public Citizen, Texas in Austin, Texas<br>Affiliate: Public Citizen Foundation, Inc., a 501(c)(3) organization<br>*Note:* Public Citizen, Inc., founded by Ralph Nader in 1971, is an umbrella organization for six projects: Buyers Up, Congress Watch, Critical Mass Energy Project, the Health Research Group, Litigation Group, and Global Trade Watch. | *SCOPE* |

| | |
|---|---|
| *PAC* | None |
| *METHOD OF OPERATION* | ◆ Coalition formation ◆ Conferences/seminars ◆ Congressional testimony ◆ Direct mail ◆ Grassroots organizing ◆ Internet (Web site) ◆ Legislative/regulatory monitoring (federal and state) ◆ Library/information clearinghouse ◆ Litigation ◆ Lobbying (federal) ◆ Media outreach ◆ Participation in regulatory proceedings (federal) ◆ Research |
| *CURRENT CONCERNS* | ◆ Auto safety ◆ Campaign finance reform ◆ Citizen empowerment ◆ Clean and safe energy sources ◆ Consumer rights in the marketplace ◆ Corporate and government accountability ◆ Drug and food safety ◆ Environment ◆ Fair trade policies ◆ Freedom of information and open government ◆ Health care delivery ◆ Healthful environment and workplace ◆ Insurance reform ◆ Nuclear safety ◆ Occupational health ◆ Pesticide regulatory reform ◆ Product liability ◆ Regulatory reform ◆ Safe products |
| *PUBLICATIONS* | *The Green Buyer's Car Guide*<br>*NAFTA's Broken Promises* (a series)<br>*Questionable Doctors*<br>*Representing Yourself*<br>*Women's Health Alert*<br>*Worst Pills Best Pills*<br><br>Also publishes other publications and reports |
| *NEWSLETTER* | *Health Letter*<br>*Public Citizen News*<br>*Worst Pills Best Pills News* |
| *CONFERENCES* | Periodic conferences |
| *BOARD OF DIRECTORS* | Public Citizen, Inc.:<br>◆ Joan Claybrook ◆ Paul W. Gikas ◆ Howard Metzenbaum ◆ Joseph Page ◆ Adolph L. Reed Jr.<br><br>Public Citizen Foundation:<br>◆ Joan Abrahamson ◆ Joan Claybrook ◆ Joseph W. Cotchett ◆ Morris S. Dees Jr. ◆ Robert C. Fellmeth ◆ Jim Hightower ◆ Anthony Mazzocchi |
| *EFFECTIVENESS* | "As the National Archives and Records Administration tries to come up with a workable plan for preserving electronic records produced by the Federal government, a Federal judge ruled last week that the archives administration cannot continue its policy of allowing Government agencies to delete E-mail messages and computer files as long as they print and save paper copies. . . . |

"Public Citizen—an advocacy group representing historians, researchers and journalists—sued in 1996 to stop the practice. It argued that vital information could be lost in the transition from computer to paper files, such as the electronic fingerprints that show who handled each document at each stage." (*New York Times*, April 16, 1998)

"[Dick Thornburgh, attorney general under Presidents Reagan and Bush] was pleasantly surprised recently when [he found himself] nodding in agreement with Ralph Nader's Public Citizen. . . .

". . . Nader and Public Citizen slammed the lead trial lawyer in the celebrated flight attendants' second-hand smoke case. The proposed $349 million settlement—$300 million to establish a medical research foundation on the effects of second-hand smoke and $49 million for lawyers' fees—contained not a penny for the flight attendants who allegedly suffered health damage from working in smoky plane cabins. Public Citizen termed the attorney's fees 'gargantuan.' " (*Washington Post*, April 1, 1998)

"The D.C. financial control board told Congress yesterday that the city's elected officials, and not the board itself, should decide whether to impose a ceiling on damages in medical malpractice cases. . . .

"Frank Clemente, director of Public Citizens' Congress Watch, said the control board's decision was the right one.

" 'The control board hit two home runs for consumers: one that protects our rights to democratic self-determination, and the other that will help protect us from from being injured or killed by negligent doctors or hospitals and HMOs,' Clemente said." (*Washington Post*, March 18, 1998)

"American and foreign auto makers asked Federal regulators late last month to abandon the American side-impact standard for a new standard being introduced in Europe, where cars are much smaller than in the United States. . . .

"But two of the most influential nonprofit safety groups, Public Citizen and the Center for Auto Safety, have decided to oppose the auto makers, arguing that both standards are inadequate because neither is designed to simulate what happens when cars are hit in the side by light trucks. . . .

" 'The current standards do not adequately test for both the weight and the size of light trucks,' said Joan Claybrook, who was the nation's top traffic safety regulator under President Jimmy Carter and is now the president of Public Citizen. 'It is not a realistic test with nearly 50 percent of the vehicles sold now being these bigger, heavier vehicles.' " (*New York Times*, January 17, 1998)

"The tobacco industry, gearing up to do battle over a proposed national settlement with opponents, spent $15.8 million employing 186 different lobbyists to press its views on tobacco-related issues in the first half of this year, according to a study by Public Citizen. . . .

"Public Citizen, which opposes the $368.5 billion tobacco deal, said the companies and industry lobbying organizations used 37 in-house representatives and 149 outside lawyers and lobbyists in that period—'unleashing more than one lobbyist for every three members of Congress.' Much of the money, more than $9.4 million, was spent on the outside lobbyists, Public Citizen found by culling through lobby fee disclosures filed in Congress. . . .

"According to Public Citizen, the lobbyists themselves are also major political donors. This year, the tobacco lobbyists gave more than $345,000 to candidates, political parties and political action committees at their own firms, according to Public Citizen's inspection of the most recent campaign finance reports available." (*Washington Post*, December 20, 1997)

## POLITICAL ORIENTATION

"an advocacy group founded by Ralph Nader" (*New York Times*, April 9, 1998)

"liberal advocacy group" (*Washington Post*, February 24, 1997)

# U.S. Term Limits (1992)

1125 15th St., NW
Suite 501
Washington, D.C. 20005
Phone: (202) 463-3200
Fax: (202) 463-3210
Internet: ustl1@ibm.net *or* http://www.termlimits.org

---

"Restoring citizen control of government through the enactment of national, state and local level term limits."

*PURPOSE*

---

11 total—8 professional; 3 support; plus 4 interns

*STAFF*

---

Paul Jacob, executive director. Before joining U.S. Term Limits, Jacob ran initiative campaigns and grassroots mobilization efforts for other organizations, including Citizens for Congressional Reform and Public Action Incorporated. He writes opinion pieces for periodicals on the issue of term limits.

*DIRECTOR*

---

501(c)(3)

*TAX STATUS*

---

1997—$2.5 million
1998—$3.8 million
Proposed 1999—$4 million

*BUDGET*

---

Individuals, 100 percent

*FUNDING SOURCES*

---

Members: 174,000 individuals
Branches/chapters: 44 independent state term limits organizations
Affiliates: U.S. Term Limits Foundation, a 501(c)(3) organization

*SCOPE*

---

None

*PAC*

---

| | |
|---|---|
| *METHOD OF OPERATIONS* | ◆ Advertisements ◆ Coalition forming ◆ Congressional testimony ◆ Congressional voting analysis ◆ Direct action ◆ Grassroots organizing ◆ Initiative/referendum campaigns ◆ Internet (Web site) ◆ Internships ◆ Legal assistance ◆ Litigation ◆ Lobbying (federal, state, grassroots) ◆ Media outreach ◆ Polling ◆ Research ◆ Speakers program ◆ Telecommunications services (mailing lists) |
| *CURRENT CONCERNS* | Congressional, state, and local term limits on elected officials |
| *PUBLICATIONS* | *The Constitutional Case for Term Limits*<br>*Outlook Series Research Papers* |
| *NEWSLETTER* | *No Uncertain Terms* (10 times a year)<br>*Legal Limit* (quarterly) |
| *CONFERENCES* | State Leadership Conferences (annually in Washington, D.C.)<br>Term Limits Forums (2 times per year) |
| *BOARD OF DIRECTORS* | ◆ Peter Ackerman ◆ Travis Anderson ◆ Steven Baer ◆ Terence Considine ◆ Edward Crane ◆ Cora Fields ◆ J.G. "Mike" Ford ◆ M. Blair Hull ◆ Sally Reed Impastato ◆ Paul Jacob ◆ Michael Keiser ◆ Ken Langone ◆ Ronald S. Lauder ◆ Bill Long ◆ Rob Mosbacher Jr. ◆ Paul Raynault ◆ Howard S. Rich ◆ Joseph Stillwell ◆ Bill Wilson |
| *EFFECTIVENESS* | "In 1994, George Nethercutt sent Speaker Thomas S. Foley back to the bleachers after 30 years in Congress by telling voters he would never become one of them: a Washington insider intoxicated by politics and power. To insure purity of purpose, he said he would serve no more than six years in the House of Representatives. . . .<br><br>"But as Mr. Nethercutt, a Republican, gets ready to run this year for what is expected to be his final term in office, he seems to be backpedaling faster than a unicyclist on a steep slope. . . .<br><br>"The organization, U.S. Term Limits, which closely tracks incumbents, spent \$300,000 on advertising in 1994 in support of Mr. Nethercutt because of his pledge to limit his term in office to six years.<br><br>"Mr. Nethercutt's apparent hedging on that pledge is profoundly upsetting to Paul Jacob, the director of U.S. Term Limits.<br><br>" 'He made the pledge repeatedly during the campaign,' Mr. Jacob said. 'Now he decides that maybe it's not such a great idea because it's standing in the way of his career and all the perks and privileges.'. . .<br><br>'It's not a very complex issue,' Mr. Jacob said. 'He made a promise. He ought to keep it.' " (*New York Times*, February 22, 1998) |

"... After the Supreme Court ruled two years ago that states could not impose term limits on members of Congress, nor could Congress do so by statute, a group called U.S Term Limits suggested a new approach to force a constitutional amendment. It backed voter initiatives in nine states that directed elected representatives at the state and federal levels to support a specific term-limits formula. The proposals also contained what came to be known as 'scarlet letter' provisions, since they mandated that lawmakers who failed to heed the directive have the label 'Disregarded Voter Instruction on Term Limits' marked next to their names on subsequent ballots. In fact, this strategy backfired when the constitutional amendment came to the House floor earlier this month. Most of the members from the nine states that had passed the initiatives felt bound to vote only for their own state's version of the text, and no other. . . . This disarray resulted in 11 votes on different versions of the proposal and contributed to the defeat. . . ." (*Washington Post*, February 25, 1997)

"The movement to impose term limits on members of Congress suffered a devastating defeat tonight [Febuary 13, 1997], with a proposed constitutional amendment not only failing in the House but receiving fewer votes than it did two years ago. . . .

"The final vote came after a day of debating 11 variations of the amendment, an exercise that demonstrated the factional divisions that supporters said hurt their cause.

"Representative Bill McCollum, Republican of Florida, said limits were necessary because too much power was vested in the hands of a few, most members got re-elected and 'careerism does affect too many members of Congress.' . . .

"Mr. McCollum, who has led the forces seeking a 12-year term limit since he arrived in the House in 1981, lamented the 'internecine warfare' that hobbled supporters today. In particular, he blamed an organization known as U.S. Term Limits, which supported the other referendums and denounced as sellouts supporters of 12-year limits in the House. The group has run a television advertisement in which Mr. McCollum's face morphs into that of Fidel Castro, hardly a popular figure in Mr. McCollum's Orlando district. . . ." (*New York Times*, February 13, 1997)

"the most militant of the term-limit groups" (*New York Times*, March 31, 1995)

# POLITICAL ORIENTATION

# United States Conference of Mayors (1932)

1620 Eye Street, NW
Washington, D.C. 20006
Phone: (202) 293-7330
Fax: (202) 293-2352
Internet: http://www.usmayors.org

| | |
|---|---|
| **PURPOSE** | "To provide a policy development and legislative action force in federal-city relationships to ensure that federal policy meets urban needs, and to assist in the capacity building of mayors and their cities." |
| **STAFF** | 50 total—36 professional; 14 support; plus interns |
| **DIRECTOR** | J. Thomas Cochran, executive director. Before becoming executive director in 1987, Cochran was deputy executive director and chief lobbyist of the United States Conference of Mayors. Previously he worked for the president's Office of Economic Opportunity, where he was director of congressional relations for the Job Corps. Cochran holds undergraduate and law degrees from the University of Georgia. |
| **TAX STATUS** | 501(c)(3) |
| **BUDGET** | 1998—Unavailable<br>Proposed 1999—Unavailable |
| **FUNDING SOURCES** | Unavailable |
| **SCOPE** | Members: Mayors of cities with populations of 30,000 or more<br>Branches/chapters: N/A<br>Affiliates: Allied Membership Program; Capital City Mayor Caucus; Employment and Training Council; Municipal Waste Management Association; National Conference of Democratic Mayors; National Public Employer Labor Relations Association; Public Policy Board; Republican Mayors and Local Officials; U.S. Conference of City Human Services Officers; U.S. Conference of Mayors Urban Water Council; Women Mayors' Group |

None

---

♦ Awards program (America's Best Managed Cities, The City Livability Awards Program, Michael A. diNunzio National Recycling Award, The Prevention of Impaired Driving Awards Program) ♦ Coalition forming ♦ Conferences/seminars ♦ Congressional testimony ♦ Grantmaking ♦ Grassroots organizing ♦ International activities ♦ Internet (Web site) ♦ Legislative/regulatory monitoring (federal) ♦ Lobbying (federal) ♦ Local/municipal affairs ♦ Participation in regulatory proceedings (federal) ♦ Research ♦ Task forces ♦ Training and technical assistance ♦ Telecommunications services

*METHOD OF OPERATION*

---

♦ AIDS/HIV ♦ Business/government relations ♦ Brownfields ♦ Census ♦ Drug Control ♦ Education and public schools ♦ Electric utility deregulation ♦ Hunger and homelessness ♦ Recycling ♦ Tourism ♦ Welfare-to-work

*CURRENT CONCERNS*

---

*Best Practices of City Governments, Volume I*
*Best Practices of City Governments, Volume II*
*Choosing A Drug Testing Laboratory* (video)
*City Human Service Officials of America's Principal Cities*
*Clean Your Files Day: Guidelines for Promoting Recycling at Work*
*Directory of Mayors' Employment and Training Administrators*
*Drug and Alcohol Abuse in the Workplace*
*The Federal Budget and the Cities*
*Fiscal and Human Impacts of Potential Congressional Budget Cuts on Local Economies, A 145-City Survey*
*Guide to Recycled Office and Business Paper Containing 20% Post-Consumer Fiber*
*HIV and Other STD's: How Do They Fit Together*
*HIV Prevention Community Planning Profiles: Assessing Year One*
*HOME: Investment Partnerships Program*
*Impact of Brownfields on U.S. Cities: A 39-City Survey*
*Introduction to Pollution Prevention and Local Government: Fact Sheet and Resource List*
*Lessons Learned From USCM Needs Assessment Grants*
*Local Health Departments and Violence Prevention for Youth*
*Local Officials and Affordable Housing: Profiles in Leadership* (video)
*The Mayors of America's Principal Cities*
*Municipal Employee Benefits Survey*
*Overview of New Legislation and Policies for Municipal Solid Waste Reduction and Recycling*
*Preventing Pollution in Our Cities and Counties: A Compendium of Case Studies*
*Public Employer Privacy: A Legal and Practical Guide to Issues Affecting the Workplace*
*Recycling At Work: Building Managers' Guidelines Book*
*Resolutions: Policy Adopted at Each Annual Conference of Mayors*

*PUBLICATIONS*

---

*School-To-Work Systems: A Look at the Development of Partnerships Between
    Education and Employment and Training in America's Language, Culture,
    and Access to Health Care: Three Program Profiles*
*Sexual Harassment Prevention Training Game*
*STD/HIV Demonstration Programs: Five Case Studies*
*Successes in Office Recycling: Examples of Model Recycling Programs*
*Task Force on HUD and the Cities: 1995 and Beyond, Recommendations*
*Winning Arbitration*

## NEWSLETTER

*HIV/AIDS Information Exchange* (periodic)
*U.S. Mayor* (24 times a year)

## CONFERENCES

Annual Conference of Mayors
Annual winter meeting
Sponsors other conferences and seminars on various topics

## BOARD OF DIRECTORS

Deedee Corradini, president; Wellington E. Webb, vice president; H. Brent Coles, chairman, advisory board; J. Thomas Cochran; executive director

Trustees:
♦ Dennis W. Archer ♦ Charles Box ♦ H. Brent Coles ♦ Nancy M. Graham ♦ Sharpe James ♦ Mike Johanns ♦ Patricia J. McManus ♦ Thomas M. Menino ♦ Marc H. Morial ♦ Rita Mullins ♦ Meyera E. Oberndorf ♦ James Perron ♦ M. Susan Savage ♦ David W. Smith

## EFFECTIVENESS

"A study of American cities by the Clinton Administration says the strong national economy has left most of them in their best financial shape in decades.

"But the report, 'The State of the Cities 1998,' also finds that urban centers are still suffering from chronic problems afflicting the poor—unemployment, inadequate housing and substandard education—that could grow worse over the next five years as hundreds of thousands of city residents move off welfare.

"To help those people, as well as the low-income wage earners against whom they will be competing for jobs, the Administration has asked Congress to approve an array of new or expanded programs for the 1999 fiscal year, in what the White House calls 'the most wide-ranging budget for cities in more than a decade. . . .'

"Citing a recent study of 74 urban areas by the Conference of Mayors, the Administration's report says that within five years, employers are likely to find at least two applicants for the same low-paying job. Some cities, like Cleveland, Newark and Providence, are projecting 10 or more." (*New York Times*, June 19, 1998)

"Two prominent groups of mayors today criticized a decision by the Housing Department's chief investigator to examine public housing programs of three cities led by black mayors.

"At its annual meeting in New Orleans, the National Conference of Black Mayors passed a resolution calling on the department's inspector general, Susan Gaffney, to justify her selection of Baltimore, New Orleans and San Francisco as cities for investigation.

"The resolution called on President Clinton, who appointed Ms. Gaffney five years ago, to investigate 'the targeting of cities' led by blacks.

"Also, Tom Cochran, executive director of the United States Conference of Mayors, called Ms. Gaffney's selections 'absolutely astonishing' and said his group would send letters of complaint to Congress and Housing Secretary Andrew M. Cuomo.

"Ms. Gaffney picked the cities as part of a Congressional program, the Urban Fraud Initiative, that was created last year by a House housing subcommittee.

"Ms. Gaffney has denied that race was a factor in her choices but has declined to comment further." (*New York Times*, April 18, 1998)

"The scene outside was pure Denver: a March blizzard. But inside City Hall, Mayor Wellington E. Webb was talking about Africa—human rights, trade expansion, and debt relief.

" 'African-Americans should have the same sense of allegiance, of support, for working with African countries as Irish-Americans have for working with Ireland,' Mr. Webb, Denver's first black Mayor, said as he prepared to join President Clinton and an entourage of about 600 politicians and business leaders for an 11-day, 6-country tour of Africa. . . .

"This grass-roots pressure can be seen here in the heartland, in Denver. Africa ties have become a priority under Mayor Webb, who is the chairman of Africa committees for the United States Conference of Mayors and the National Conference of Black Mayors.

"Last June, a few days before the summit meeting of the world's leading industrialized countries here, Mr. Webb was host to African Ambassadors and black leaders for a 'Town Hall Meeting on Africa.' The event helped prod the visiting leaders to issue a statement on promoting economic development in Africa. . . .

"In Washington in January, he led a daylong 'Africa Summit' attended by 225 mayors, 3 Cabinet members and 4 African Ambassadors. The session opened the winter meeting of the United States Conference of Mayors, a rare foray into foreign affairs for an organization devoted to municipal issues.

" 'America should redefine its relationship with Africa,' Mayor Webb said at the meeting. 'It's time we placed Africa at the top of our foreign policy agenda.'

"In response, Samuel R. Berger, President Clinton's national security adviser, promised the mayors, 'The time has come to place Africa on America's front burner.'. . .

"Pressure by the Conference of Mayors contributed to a House of Representatives vote last week to pass a trade and investment liberalization bill for Africa, the African Growth and Opportunity Act. The bill, which has strong Republican support, is expected to go before the Senate later this year." (*New York Times*, March 22, 1998)

"The Washington region's gross product—the value of all goods and services produced—ranked sixth among the nation's metropolitan regions in 1997, according to a study released by the National Association of Counties and the U.S. Conference of Mayors.

"The gross product for the Washington region was $166 billion, a statistic that, along with those for other metropolitan areas, shows the importance of metropolitan economies, the groups said.

"There can be no doubt that this nation's city-county regions are the engines powering the remarkable economic growth of this nation,' said Paul Helmke, president of the mayors' group.

"The combined gross product of the 10 largest U.S. metropolitan areas would rank fourth among world economies at $1.9 trillion, according to the study.

"The gross product of the Washington region, which includes the District, Maryland, Virginia and West Virginia, ranked above the gross national products of Singapore, Thailand and Saudi Arabia." (*Washington Post*, March 21, 1998)

"Three Texas mortgage lenders have agreed to make nearly $1.4 billion available to low-income and minority home buyers over the next three years in a settlement of housing discrimination complaints.

"The settlement is the largest ever negotiated in a case involving charges of lending discrimination, far surpassing a $1 million settlement in 1996 against a North Carolina bank, according to the Department of Housing and Urban Development.

"Beyond its size, the settlement comes as housing officials are cracking down on lenders who make it harder for minority and low-income families, many of them urban residents, to buy homes. In a recent study, the United States Conference of Mayors found that while more Americans than ever owned their own homes, the rate of ownership in urban areas lagged far behind the suburban rate.

"Federal housing officials predicted that as a result of the Texas settlement as many as 20,000 families would be able to secure mortgages over the next three years.

" 'Discrimination is inherent in the system at this point,' Housing Secretary Andrew M. Cuomo said today. 'This has been going on for 30 years, and in many cases, it's almost subconscious with assumptions about what neighborhoods you should live in, who has good credit, who does not and what neighborhoods are bad risks. These assumptions have become institutionalized, and the disparity is unarguable.'

"The message of the Texas agreement, Mr. Cuomo said, is: 'If you discriminate, we will file a complaint.' " (*New York Times*, March 10, 1998)

# POLITICAL ORIENTATION

"bipartisan" (*Washington Post*, January 26, 1995)

# Women's Campaign Fund (1974)

734 15th Street, NW
Suite 500
Washington, D.C. 20005
Phone: (202) 393-8164
Fax: (202) 393-0649
Internet: http://www.womenconnect.com/wcf

| | |
|---|---|
| "Devoted to helping pro-choice women candidates of both parties achieve elected office." | **PURPOSE** |
| 4 total; plus interns | **STAFF** |
| Charly Carter, managing director | **DIRECTOR** |
| Political action committee | **TAX STATUS** |
| 1998—$1.5 million<br>Proposed 1999—$1.5 million | **BUDGET** |
| Individuals, 80 percent; corporations, 20 percent | **FUNDING SOURCES** |
| Members: 30,000 donors<br>Branches/chapters: N/A<br>Affiliate: Women's Campaign Research Fund, a 501(c)(3) organization | **SCOPE** |
| The Women's Campaign Fund is a political action committee | **PAC** |
| ◆ Campaign contributions ◆ Conferences/seminars ◆ Electoral politics ◆ Media outreach ◆ Research ◆ Training and technical assistance | **METHOD OF OPERATION** |

## CURRENT CONCERNS

Election of qualified, pro-choice women to all levels of public office

## PUBLICATIONS

Informational brochures

## NEWSLETTER

*Winning Choice* (quarterly)

## CONFERENCES

None

## BOARD OF DIRECTORS

Terese Colling and Ruth L. Powers; cochairs

Other board members:
♦ Renee Berger ♦ Dorritt Bern ♦ Maureen Bunyan ♦ R. Nancy Clack ♦ Rebecca Wesson Darwin ♦ George A. Dean ♦ Rick Diegel ♦ Nina S. Eshoo ♦ Lisbeth "Libba" Evans ♦ Doreen Frasca ♦ Frederica S. Friedman ♦ Fabianne Gershon ♦ Jeanne Hanson ♦ Deborah Johns ♦ Barbara Krumsiek ♦ Alexandra Lebenthal ♦ Marion Fennelly Levy ♦ Marcia Mac Harg ♦ Eve Maldonado ♦ Lynn Steppacher Martin ♦ Doris Meister ♦ Leslie Miles ♦ Patrick Murphy ♦ Marine S. Pillsbury ♦ Jeri Sedlar ♦ Dee Soder ♦ Elizabeth A. Vale ♦ Anita Volz Wien ♦ Nancy Zirkin

## EFFECTIVENESS

"Remember Marjorie Margolies-Mezvinsky? She was the Democratic House member from Pennsylvania who cast a deciding vote to pass President Clinton's budget package in 1993, then lost her seat in the next election.

"She has announced that she is seeking the Democratic nomination for Pennsylvania lieutenant governor. For the past two years, Margolies-Mezvinsky was executive director of the Women's Campaign Fund, which assists female candidates of both parties who support abortion rights. The fund contributed more than $300,000 for the 1995–96 federal election cycle. Margolies-Mezvinsky said her decision to seek statewide office was influenced by her work with other female candidates during her tenure. She said she considered her bid 'a continuation of the WCF mission,' the Associated Press reported.

"In 1992, the former television reporter became the first Democrat in some 80 years to win her suburban Philadelphia seat. She was narrowly defeated two years later, largely as backlash for her vote to pass Clinton's budget package, which raised taxes on the wealthiest Americans." (*Washington Post*, March 2, 1998)

## POLITICAL ORIENTATION

"a bipartisan organization that supports political candidates who favor abortion rights" (*New York Times*, June 22, 1997)

# Public Interest Law

## Chapter 10

# Alliance for Justice (1979)

2000 P Street, NW
Suite 712
Washington, D.C. 20036
Phone: (202) 822-6070
Fax: (202) 822-6068
Internet: http://www.afj.org

| | |
|---|---|
| "To advance the cause of justice for all Americans, to strengthen the public interest community's ability to influence public policy, and to foster the next generation of advocates." | **PURPOSE** |
| 16 total—14 professional; 2 support; plus 5 interns | **STAFF** |
| Nan Aron, president. Before founding the Alliance for Justice, Aron worked with the National Prison Project of the American Civil Liberties Union and the Equal Employment Opportunity Commission. | **DIRECTOR** |
| 501(c)(3) | **TAX STATUS** |
| 1997—$1.5 million<br>1998—$2 million<br>Proposed 1999—$2.5 million | **BUDGET** |
| Foundations, 61 percent; individuals, Combined Federal Campaign, and annual luncheon, 24 percent; membership dues, 7 percent; other, 8 percent | **FUNDING SOURCES** |
| Members: 48 public interest, legal, and advocacy organizations<br>Branches/chapters: N/A<br>Affiliates: N/A | **SCOPE** |
| None | **PAC** |
| ♦ Coalition forming ♦ Conferences/seminars ♦ Congressional testimony ♦ Films/video/audiotapes ♦ Grassroots organizing ♦ Internet (Web site) ♦ Legislative/regulatory monitoring (federal and state) ♦ Lobbying (federal, state, and grassroots) | **METHOD OF OPERATION** |

## CURRENT CONCERNS

♦ Access to justice ♦ Erosion of civil rights and civil liberties by the Supreme Court ♦ Judicial selection ♦ Promoting the expansion of public interest law

## PUBLICATIONS

*Annual Report of the Judicial Selection Project*
*Being a Player: A Guide to the IRS Lobbying Regulations for Advocacy Charities*
*The Co-Motion Guide to Youth-Led Social Change*
*Directory of Public Interest Law Centers*
*First Monday Video* (video series)
*Justice for Sale: Shortchanging the Public Interest for Private Gain*
*Justice in the Making: A Citizen's Handbook for Choosing Federal Judges*
*Liberty and Justice For All: Public Interest Law in the 1980s and Beyond*
*Myth v. Fact—Foundation Support of Advocacy*
*National Service and Advocacy*

Also publishes several advocacy guides

## NEWSLETTER

*Pipeline* (2 times a year)

## CONFERENCES

Annual luncheon (Washington, D.C.)

## BOARD OF DIRECTORS

James D. Weill, chair; Nan Aron, president; Mark Silbergeld, secretary

Other members:
♦ Bob Bernstein ♦ John Frank ♦ Ronald Goldfarb ♦ Antonia Hernandez ♦ Rita McLennon ♦ Joel Packer ♦ Douglas Parker ♦ Nancy Register ♦ Kathy Rodgers ♦ Estelle Rogers ♦ Leonard Rubenstein ♦ Robert Schwartz ♦ Greg Wetstone ♦ Joan Vermeulen ♦ Verna Williams

## EFFECTIVENESS

"The Senate, perhaps pushed by an unusual scolding from Chief Justice William H. Rehnquist, has confirmed 20 Clinton nominees so far this year, according to a tally by the . . . Alliance for Justice. That compares with two confirmed at this time last year.

"The group notes that, even so, the pace barely kept up with the vacancy rate. In January, there were 86 openings on the federal bench. Now there are 80. And with the shortened work schedule this election year, it's unlikely the number of vacancies will be much lower next Jan. 1." (*Washington Post*, April 27, 1998)

"The Alliance for Justice, a coalition of advocacy groups interested in the federal courts, has turned to the lobby shop of Foreman, Heidepriem & Mager for help in pushing some of President Clinton's stalled judicial nominees through the Senate.

" 'There are just so many vacancies,' said alliance president Nan Aron, who added that the lobbyists will also help 'defend the judiciary from partisan attacks.'

"The alliance, which has a reputation as a liberal group, is not promoting any particular one of the nearly 50 Clinton nominees awaiting approval by the Senate Judiciary Committee, she said. The organization includes such groups as the National Women's Law Center and the Mexican American Legal Defense and Educational Fund." (*Washington Post*, February 19, 1998)

" 'First Monday,' an event sponsored by Washington's Alliance for Justice to promote careers in public interest law, has gone Hollywood.

"The annual event, which marks the opening of the Supreme Court term, takes on the nation's new immigration law at sessions today at Georgetown University Law Center and 170 law schools around the nation.

"Alliance President Nan Aron snagged Academy Award-winning filmmaker Barbara Kopple, an old high school chum, to direct a 30-minute documentary on the plight of two immigrants. Aron, whose real job is keeping tabs on judicial nominations, got to be executive producer.

"The change was refreshing, she said, but 'I'll be back Tuesday yelling at [White House Deputy Chief of Staff] John Podesta about judges.' " (*Washington Post*, October 6, 1997)

"Last week, the Alliance for Justice . . . criticized both the Senate and the White House for failing to fill the growing number of judicial vacancies, which now stands at 93. Nan Aron, president of the Alliance, blamed the Senate for 'obstructionist tactics' and Clinton for 'silently tolerating' them, asserting that together, those actions have created 'gridlock.'

"Aron believes the infighting has reached a new low. The Republican Senate confirmed a record-low number of U.S. district judges last year, and no appellate judges have been confirmed by the Senate since Jan. 2, 1996. That, Aron says, is an indication Republicans 'are engaged in an all-out campaign to shut down not only the process, but . . . to maintain control over the very influential courts of appeal.' " (*Washington Post*, March 17, 1997)

---

"liberal" (*Washington Post*, April 27, 1998)

"a Washington-based coalition of liberal groups" (*Washington Post*, March 17, 1997)

"a consortium of left-leaning organizations" (*Wall Street Journal*, April 3, 1996)

## POLITICAL ORIENTATION

# Atlantic Legal Foundation, Inc. (1977)

205 East 42nd Street
Ninth Floor
New York, New York 10017
Phone: (212) 573-1960
Fax: (212) 573-1959
Internet: atlanticlaw@earthlink.net *or*
http://www.atlanticlegal.org

| | |
|---|---|
| **PURPOSE** | "Advocates the principles of free enterprise, the rights of individuals and limited government . . . to promote and protect good science in the courtroom and to challenge burdensome governmental regulations." |
| **STAFF** | 3 total—2 professional; 1 support; plus 1 intern and 3 part-time support |
| **DIRECTOR** | Edwin L. Lewis, president. Lewis is the former vice president and general counsel of Borg-Warner Security Corporation. He holds a B.A. from Lafayette College and a J.D. from Temple University School of Law. |
| **TAX STATUS** | 501(c)(3) |
| **BUDGET** | 1997—$484,132<br>1998—Unavailable<br>Proposed 1999—Unavailable |
| **FUNDING SOURCES** | Foundation grants, 55 percent; corporations, 35 percent; individuals, 7 percent; special events/projects, 3 percent |
| **SCOPE** | Members: N/A<br>Branch/chapter: Office in Harrisburg, Pennsylvania<br>Affiliates: N/A |
| **PAC** | None |

| | |
|---|---|
| ♦ Awards program (Annual award to a leader in the fight to maintain and strengthen the principles of private enterprise) ♦ Conferences/ seminars ♦ Films/video/audiotapes ♦ Internet (Web site) ♦ Legal assistance ♦ Litigation | *METHOD OF OPERATION* |
| ♦ Admissibility of scientific evidence ♦ Affirmative action ♦ Civil rights ♦ First Amendment rights ♦ Good science in the courtroom ♦ Governmental intrusion in economic, environmental, and energy matters ♦ Limits on punitive damages ♦ Political correctness ♦ Private property rights ♦ Tort reform | *CURRENT CONCERNS* |
| *Atlantic Legal Foundation Video* | *PUBLICATIONS* |
| *Atlantic Legal Foundation Report* (2–3 times a year) | *NEWSLETTER* |
| Sponsors various seminars | *CONFERENCES* |
| Douglas Foster, vice chairman; Edwin L. Lewis, president; Martin S. Kaufman, senior vice president and general counsel; Rosemary Heckard-Heiling, vice president<br><br>Other members:<br>♦ Lillian R. BeVier ♦ William J. Calise Jr. ♦ Hayward D. Fisk ♦ Douglas Foster ♦ George S. Frazza ♦ Stanley H. Fuld ♦ John W. Galiardo ♦ William H. Graham ♦ Stephen J. Harmelin ♦ Ernest B. Hueter ♦ Quentin J. Kennedy ♦ Lawrence J. McCabe ♦ Paul Miller ♦ John W. Priesing ♦ Howard J. Rudge ♦ Dirk R. Soutendijk ♦ Clifford B. Storms ♦ S. Maynard Turk ♦ Gary P. Van Graafeiland ♦ Malcolm Wilson ♦ Charles R. Work ♦ James I. Wyer | *BOARD OF DIRECTORS* |
| Unavailable | *EFFECTIVENESS* |
| Unavailable | *POLITICAL ORIENTATION* |

# Institute for Justice (1991)

1717 Pennsylvania Avenue, NW
Suite 200
Washington, D.C. 20006
Phone: (202) 955-1300
Fax: (202) 955-1329
Internet: general@ij.org *or* http://www.ij.org

| | |
|---|---|
| **PURPOSE** | To "pursue cutting-edge litigation in the courts of law and in the court of public opinion on behalf of individuals whose most basic rights are denied by the State—rights like economic liberty, private property rights, and the right to free speech, not only on paper but also on the Internet." |
| **STAFF** | 12 total—6 professional; 6 support; plus 5 interns |
| **DIRECTOR** | Chip Mellor, president. Mellor, a co-founder of the Institute for Justice, was previously president of the Pacific Research Institute for Public Policy in San Francisco. During the Reagan Administration, Mellor served as deputy general counsel for legislation and regulations in the Energy Department, and from 1979 to 1983, he practiced public interest law with the Mountain States Legal Foundation in Denver, Colorado. Mellor received his law degree from the University of Denver School of Law and his B.S. from Ohio State University. |
| **TAX STATUS** | 501(c)(3) |
| **BUDGET** | 1997—$2.3 million<br>1998—$3 million<br>Proposed 1999—Unavailable |
| **FUNDING SOURCES** | Funded by individuals, foundations, and corporate philanthropy; does not accept government funding |
| **SCOPE** | Members: N/A<br>Branches/chapters: N/A<br>Affiliates: N/A |
| **PAC** | None |

| | |
|---|---|
| ◆ Advertisements ◆ Coalition forming ◆ Conferences/seminars ◆ Congressional testimony ◆ Internet (E-mail alerts, Web site) ◆ Internships ◆ Legal assistance ◆ Litigation ◆ Media outreach ◆ Speakers program ◆ Training | *METHOD OF OPERATION* |
| ◆ Civil rights ◆ Economic liberty ◆ Interracial adoption ◆ Mandatory community service ◆ Private property protection ◆ Reducing the regulatory welfare state ◆ School choice | *CURRENT CONCERNS* |
| *Barriers to Entrepreneurship Studies*<br>*Law Enforcement or Ideological Activism? The Nomination of Bill Lann Lee as Assistant Attorney General for Civil Rights*<br>*Putting the California Civil Rights Initiative in Context*<br>*State of the Supreme Court: The Justices' Records on Civil and Economic Liberties* | *PUBLICATIONS* |
| *Carry the Torch* (periodic)<br>*Clipbook* (quarterly magazine)<br>*Liberty and Law* (bimonthly) | *NEWSLETTER* |
| Law Student Conference (held in August)<br>Lawyers Conference<br>Policy Activists Conference | *CONFERENCES* |
| ◆ Mark Babunovic ◆ Arthur Dantchick ◆ David Kennedy ◆ Robert Levy ◆ James Lintott ◆ Abigail Thernstrom ◆ Gerrit Warmhoudt | *BOARD OF DIRECTORS* |

*EFFECTIVENESS*

"In November 1995, when [Alvaro] Cardona was interviewed for an AAP [Academic Advancement Program] tutorial position, he says the interviewer repeatedly spoke to him about UCLA's 'institutionalized racism' and interrogated him about his views on affirmative action. Cardona told her he had mixed feelings. Last year he told the *Chronicle of Higher Education* that he had said to the AAP interviewer that many black and Latino students 'seem to carry this complex around that higher education is a God-given right, not something you earn.'

"Today he worries that because of affirmative action programs, 'You start doubting yourself.' He says he experienced some racism at UCLA but was 'so elated to be there' that he did not dwell on it.

"During his interview for the AAP position he says he was never asked about his qualifications or experience as a tutor. He says the interviewer worried that he would stress academics 'too much' because half of a tutor's job is to 'validate' students' feelings about institutionalized racism and discrimination. Indeed, a recruitment flier for AAP tutors lists one hiring criterion as 'sensitivity and commitment to underrepresented and low-income students and the goals of affirmative action.' That is, only persons of certain political beliefs are eligible.

"Cardona says he told the AAP interviewer he would try to allay students' fears and help them find assistance if they experienced discrimination, but that he thought his primary job as a tutor would be to help students become coherent writers so they could express whatever they felt about anything. In December 1995 he says he was told that he would not be hired as a tutor because he did not understand discrimination and did not wholeheartedly support affirmative action, but that he should apply again after he had discovered what UCLA is 'really like.'

"Only in America: Aided by libertarian litigators at Washington's Institute for Justice, Cardona is suing UCLA, charging that he was denied a job for the reason that he did not think sufficiently poorly of UCLA. And apparently he was denied the job because he agreed with the University of California's Board of Regents, which in July 1995 had voted to eliminate race and gender preferences in university programs.

"His contention is that employment was unconstitutionally made conditional on his surrender of his First Amendment right to free speech. He is not challenging the legality of racial preferences, which California voters in 1996 proscribed in government programs. He is asserting a right to speak freely about them in settings that do not involve students or interfere with student-teacher relations." (*Washington Post,* March 1, 1998)


". . . the ACLU has competition. Many of the newer, smaller competitors have grown by taking on easily recognizable points of view that give them a more consistent image than the ACLU.

" 'We are what the ACLU should be,' says John Kramer, a spokesman for the Institute for Justice, a right-leaning litigator that has filed lawsuits in favor of deregulation of private vans used to ferry commuters in the New York boroughs of Brooklyn and Queens, and school vouchers for parents who want to send their children to private schools in Minnesota. The ACLU is against the voucher program.

"Founded in 1991, the Institute for Justice says its membership has grown to 3,700 in 1997, and that its operating budget topped $2.5 million last year." (*Wall Street Journal,* February 6, 1998)


"JoAnne Cornwell, an African American intellectual and entrepreneur, is a petite person. So was Napoleon, breaker of nations. And all Cornwell wants to break is the restraint foolish laws put on her entrepreneurship. She is fighting them with the help of friends far away.

"Ali Rasheed, who has the same problem and friends, operates the Braiderie, a hairstyling salon. He, too, just wants the state of California to get out of his hair. Or, more exactly, out of his customers' hair. He, too, has the help of the Institute for Justice, a merry band of libertarian litigators in Washington who fight for economic rights wherever they are menaced. Which means wherever government dispenses domestic protectionism to organized economic factions. Which means everywhere. On the shores of the shining Pacific it has found the kind of case it most relishes, one combining 'outrageous facts and sympathetic clients.'. . .

"Today tens of thousands of women and increasing numbers of men—'hair renegades,' Cornwell calls them—have various styles of braided hair, but few get their braiding done by licensed cosmetologists. Getting licensed costs a ridiculous amount of time and money. The licensing requirements restrict entry into the hairstyling profession and enrich those private interests who provide the nine months of 'training' that costs $5,000 to $7,000. Of the 1,600 hours of training, only 4 percent pertains to health and safety. . . .

"The Institute for Justice argues that regulations that restrict entry into a field violate constitutional guarantees of liberty and equal protection of the laws when they bear no rational relationship to a legitimate government objective. In recent years the Institute's litigators have opened the taxi markets of Denver, Cincinnati and Indianapolis and have emancipated the providers of jitney services in Houston, generally for the benefit of minorities and to the consternation of protected interests.

"Today the Institute is fighting New York's city council, which lives on a short leash jerked by the Transport Workers Union. The council is trying to stamp out private van services used by up to 40,000 of the city's poorer people each day. Imagine. African American van drivers could transport African American customers to African American braiders, if government would just get out of the way." (*Washington Post*, December 13, 1997)

## POLITICAL ORIENTATION

"When Republicans on the Senate Judiciary Committee blocked Bill Lann Lee's nomination to head the Justice Department's Civil Rights division, the man many considered largely responsible was not sitting on the dais debating Lee's views on affirmative action with his committee colleagues. He was in the audience, sitting quietly and watching the drama he'd helped construct unfold just the way he'd hoped. As cofounder and litigation director for the libertarian-leaning Institute for Justice, Clint Bolick says he does not relish his role in such high-profile political battles. He'd rather fight in the courtroom. But he feels compelled to help eliminate racial preference programs any way he can. As a result, Bolick, 39, seems to be everywhere at times: an appearance on 'Nightline'; an op-ed piece in the *Wall Street Journal*; a profile in the *New York Times*. Whenever and wherever the debate over affirmative action flares, Bolick is there representing the right, detailing the perceived problems with race- and sex-based preference programs." (*Los Angeles Daily Journal*, January 5, 1998)

"a libertarian public interest law group" (*Washington Post*, January 4, 1998)

# Landmark Legal Foundation (1976)

3100 Broadway
Suite 515
Kansas City, Missouri 64111
Phone: (816) 931-5559
Fax: (816) 931-1115

457-B Carlisle Drive
Herndon, Virginia 20170
Phone: (703) 689-2370
Fax: (202) 689-2373

Internet: ecchristen@aol.com *(Virgina office)* or
petehutch@sprynet.com *(Kansas City office)* or
http://www.landmarklegal.org

| | |
|---|---|
| **PURPOSE** | "To use the law to advance conservative principles and policies through the judicial system, government, and public forums." |
| **STAFF** | Unavailable |
| **DIRECTOR** | Mark R. Levin, president. Prior to his appointment as resident, Levin served as Landmark's director of legal policy for more than three years. He worked as an attorney in the private sector and as a top advisor and administrator to several members of former President Ronald Reagan's Cabinet. Levin also served as chief of staff to the U.S. attorney general, deputy assistant secretary for elementary and secondary education at the U.S. Education Department, and deputy solicitor of the U.S. Interior Department. He holds a B.A. from Temple University and a J.D. from Temple University School of Law. |
| **TAX STATUS** | 501(c)(3) |
| **BUDGET** | 1998—Unavailable<br>Proposed 1999—Unavailable |
| **FUNDING SOURCES** | "The Foundation accepts no government funding and is supported by tax-deductible contributions from individuals, businesses and foundations." |
| **SCOPE** | Members: N/A<br>Branches/chapters: N/A<br>Affiliates: N/A |

| | |
|---|---|
| None | *PAC* |
| ◆ Congressional testimony ◆ Information clearinghouse ◆ Internet (Web site) ◆ Legal assistance ◆ Litigation ◆ Media outreach ◆ Participation in regulatory proceedings (federal and state) ◆ Speakers program | *METHOD OF OPERATION* |
| ◆ Education reform and school choice ◆ Internal Revenue Service ◆ Public integrity of public officials | *CURRENT CONCERNS* |
| None | *PUBLICATIONS* |
| *Landmark Legal Foundation Newsletter* (online) | *NEWSLETTER* |
| None | *CONFERENCES* |
| Mark R. Levin, president; Richard P. Hutchison; general counsel; Eric C. Christensen, vice president, development and communications | *BOARD OF DIRECTORS* |
| | *EFFECTIVENESS* |

"But now, many conservatives, even some who were at that news conference when Ms. Jones introduced herself to the nation, question whether the Jones matter and the subsequent accusations involving Ms. Lewinsky have snowballed out of control. Pointing to Mr. Clinton's robust poll ratings, these conservatives worry that the public attention has been as much on the tactics of the President's critics as on Mr. Clinton's own conduct.

" 'Like most things in Washington, it's a double-edged sword,' said William W. Pascoe 3d, political director of the American Conservative Union. 'It's been bad for conservatives because the Paula Jones case makes us look like snooping busybodies who have nothing better to do than to root through trash cans. On the other hand, it's good because we've learned new things about Clinton's propensity to lie and cover up.'

"Craig Shirley, a conservative public relations consultant who helped organize the conservative conference in 1994, said the Jones case had not dramatically affected people's perceptions of Mr. Clinton, but had served to harden the battle lines of anti-Clinton partisans. . . . [S]everal conservatives said the Jones case had exacerbated tensions within Republican ranks. Some conservatives accuse their peers of letting down the cause by being too bashful about speaking out about the President's moral conduct.

" 'In some strange way, it's actually increased the gap between state and local conservatives and their leadership,' said Gary Bauer, president of the Family Research Council. 'In the grass roots, they are shaking their heads in wonderment that there are not more people willing to say the obvious: that if the President of the United States is treating women this way, that alone should call into question the continuation of his Presidency.'

"Mark Levin, who is the president of the Landmark Legal Foundation, put it this way: 'If this has been such a windfall for conservatives, why were most conservatives slow to embrace Jones? And if it's such a windfall for Republicans, why to this day have so few Republican officials spoken out about this case?' " (*New York Times*, March 15, 1998)

"More recently, there have been charges that IRS audits of certain 501(c)3 nonprofit organizations have been politically motivated. Joseph Farah, a former editor of the *Sacramento Union*, says the Western Journalism Center that he runs is being audited after it was the only news outlet mentioned in a White House 'action plan' on how to deal with administration scandals. In a meeting, the Center's accountant questioned why IRS examiners wanted documents 'related to the selection of Christopher Ruddy as an investigative reporter and how the topic [of Whitewater] was selected.' According to Mr. Farah, IRS Field Agent Thomas Cederquist said, 'Look, this is a political case, and it's going to be decided at the national level.' The IRS denies it has any political motives behind its audit decisions.

"Nonetheless, the Landmark Legal Foundation this week announced it will monitor complaints about IRS audits. It points to published reports that the National Rifle Association, the Heritage Foundation and other conservative groups are also the targets of IRS investigations. The conservative American Center for Law and Justice has gone further and sued the IRS. It contends the agency singled out a conservative New York church and revoked its tax-exempt status because it engaged in politics by taking out a 1992 newspaper ad that criticized Bill Clinton. Center attorneys claim Methodist and Episcopal churches frequently raise money for liberal candidates, but are never sanctioned.

"There are also concerns about the privacy of IRS records. Last Sunday, Rep. Charles Rangel, the ranking Democrat on the House Ways and Means committee, announced on 'Face the Nation' that he had 'been in touch with the IRS' and that it was conducting 'an ongoing investigation' of charitable groups associated with Speaker Newt Gingrich. Rep. Bob Barr, a former federal prosecutor, has fired off a letter to Attorney General Janet Reno. 'Taking Rep. Rangel at his word, he has violated section 6103 of the Internal Revenue Code, which prohibits the disclosure of confidential tax information, and is a felony.' Presumably the IRS made it clear to Mr. Rangel how important it is that such information be kept confidential." (*Wall Street Journal*, January 9, 1997)

## POLITICAL ORIENTATION

"a righty group" (*Wall Street Journal*, June 18, 1998)

"conservative" (*Wall Street Journal*, August 22, 1997)

# Mountain States Legal Foundation
## (1977)

707 17th Street
Suite 3030
Denver, Colorado 80202-3408
Phone: (303) 292-2021
Fax: (303) 292-1980
Internet: http://www.mslf.net

"To provide an effective voice for the rights of private property ownership and freedom of enterprise in the development of law by the courts,
administrative agencies and elsewhere."

*PURPOSE*

16 total—11 professional; 5 support; plus 2 interns and 2 part-time
professionals

*STAFF*

William Perry Pendley, president and chief legal officer. Pendley previously served as an attorney to former senator Clifford P. Hansen (R-Wyo.)
and as an attorney to the House Interior and Insular Affairs Committee.
He was deputy assistant secretary, acting assistant secretary for energy
and minerals, and first director of the Minerals Management Service
at the Interior Department. Pendley also was a partner in a Washington,
D.C., law firm specializing in western and natural resources issues. He received a B.A. and an M.A. in political science from George Washington
University and a J.D. from the University of Wyoming College of Law.

*DIRECTOR*

501(c)(3)

*TAX STATUS*

1997—$952,135
1998—$1.03 million
Proposed 1999—$1.1 million

*BUDGET*

Corporate donations, 53 percent; individuals, 28 percent; foundation
grants, 19 percent

*FUNDING
SOURCES*

Members: 6,800 individuals and 2,727 organizations
Branches/chapters: N/A
Affiliates: N/A

*SCOPE*

| | |
|---|---|
| **PAC** | None |
| **METHOD OF OPERATION** | ◆ Congressional testimony ◆ Grassroots organizing ◆ Internet (Web site) ◆ Internships ◆ Legal assistance ◆ Litigation ◆ Media outreach ◆ Speakers program |
| **CURRENT CONCERNS** | ◆ Elimination of racial preferences ◆ Endangered Species Act ◆ Property rights ◆ Toxics ◆ Wetlands ◆ Wise use of natural resources |
| **PUBLICATIONS** | *It Takes A Hero*<br>*War on the West: Government Tyranny on America's Great Frontier* |
| **NEWSLETTER** | *The Litigator* (quarterly) |
| **CONFERENCES** | None |
| **BOARD OF DIRECTORS** | ◆ George A. Alcorn ◆ Bill B. Armstrong Jr. ◆ Tim Babcock ◆ Steven K. Bosley ◆ Peter A. Botting ◆ Scott A. Crozier ◆ John H. Dendahl ◆ Gerald M. Freeman ◆ Ronald Graves ◆ Thomas M. Hauptman ◆ Dallas P. Horton ◆ Jerry D. Jordan ◆ John F. Kane ◆ David L. McClure ◆ James McClure ◆ Roger Bill Mitchell ◆ Gary L. Nordloh ◆ David B. Rovig ◆ Jerry Sheffels ◆ Conley P. Smith ◆ Robert W. Strahman ◆ Don Thorson ◆ Diemer True ◆ Paul T. von Gontard ◆ R. Bruce Whiting ◆ George Yates |
| **EFFECTIVENESS** | "... Taxpayers have footed the bills for nearly $438,000 in outside legal help, $10,000 for private investigators and up to $350 an hour for the services of a Cambridge economist—all to fight the 6-year-old case filed by Concrete Works of Colorado Inc. The lawsuit challenges the city's 15-year-old affirmative-action policy, which sets participation goals on city contracts for women and minority contractors. . . .<br><br>"The legal group representing Concrete Works also says the city is throwing away tax dollars.<br><br>" 'Their case is a loser,' said William Perry Pendley, president of Mountain States Legal Foundation. 'All Denver has to do is lift its head from its lawyers and $300 experts and look at the legal landscape—every city that's tried to defend this kind of policy has lost, big time.'..." (*Denver and The West*, July 5, 1998) |

"Two years after the U.S. Supreme Court gave Randy Pech hope that racial preferences for government contracts would be abolished, the U.S. District Court for Colorado has dealt him an ironic but bitter surprise. Judge John Kane has declared Mr. Pech, a white man who was a central figure in the Supreme Court's landmark case *Adarand Constructors Inc. v. Pena*, eligible for the preference program he had sought to dismantle.

"All Mr. Pech had to do, Judge Kane told him late last month, is to apply to the state of Colorado for certification as a disadvantaged business enterprise. At that point he'll presumably receive the preferences previously restricted to racial minorities. Meanwhile, Judge Kane left Colorado's racial spoils system for highway contractors intact.

"Mr. Pech says he will apply for disadvantaged status, but this is not the ending he had hoped for when he began his quixotic battle with the U.S. Department of Transportation back in 1989. . . .

"Mr. Pech, Adarand's owner, originally challenged a federal Department of Transportation program that awarded bonuses to prime contractors who hired minority subcontractors. Adarand had submitted the low bid for a guardrail portion of a highway project in Colorado, but because of the bonus program, a Hispanic-owned firm won the contract instead. In the litigation that followed, the Supreme Court said such race-based preferences, even when adopted by Congress, must meet the strictest constitutional test: They can only be used to remedy proven past discrimination, and must be narrowly tailored to that goal. . . .

"William Perry Pendley of Mountain States Legal Foundation, which has represented Adarand from the outset, points out that the Department of Transportation has defeated every previous attempt by a state to alter the terms of its highway preference program. Now the department is in a bind. It cannot order Colorado to revert to the old requirements without, in effect, flouting a federal court ruling. But it can hardly concede Colorado's independence without also conceding the independence of the other 12 states controlled by its Central Federal Lands Highway Division." (*Wall Street Journal*, August 13, 1997)

---

"conservative" (*Denver and The West*, July 5, 1998)

## POLITICAL ORIENTATION

# National Legal Center
# for the Public Interest (1975)

1000 16th Street, NW
Suite 500
Washington, D.C. 20036
Phone: (202) 296-1683
Fax: (202) 293-2118
Internet: http://www.nlcpi.org

**PURPOSE**

"To foster knowledge about law and the administration of justice in a society committed to the rights of individuals, free enterprise, private ownership of property, balanced use of private and public resources, limited government, and a fair and efficient judiciary."

**STAFF**

4 total—3 professional; 1 support; plus 1 part-time

**DIRECTOR**

Ernest B. Hueter, president. Hueter formerly was chairman and chief executive officer of Interstate Brands Corporation in Kansas City.

**TAX STATUS**

501(c)(3)

**BUDGET**

1998—$1 million
Proposed 1999—$1 million

**FUNDING SOURCES**

Private sources, 60 percent; foundation grants, 21 percent; conferences and special projects, 10 percent; individuals, 3 percent; interest and other, 6 percent

**SCOPE**

Members: N/A
Branches/chapters: N/A
Affiliates: N/A

**PAC**

None

**METHOD OF OPERATION**

♦ Distinguished Fellow and Resident Scholar chairs ♦ Educational forums: conferences/seminars/lectures/press briefings ♦ Educational publications: research/legislative/regulatory monitoring ♦ Internship program

♦ Alternative dispute resolution ♦ Antitrust litigation ♦ Civil rights ♦ Corporate governance ♦ Employer/employee relations ♦ Environmental protection ♦ Ethics in the courts ♦ Labor law ♦ Private enforcement of public policy ♦ Property rights ♦ Public institutional investors ♦ Science in litigation ♦ State judicial process ♦ Tort reform

The following is a list of sample publications:

*Abolition of Diversity Jurisdiction: An Idea Whose Time Has Come?*

*American Enterprise, the Law, and the Commercial Use of Space*

*Antitrust Contribution and Claim Reduction: An Objective Assessment*

*A Better Way of Doing Business: A Proactive Approach to the Scientific Controversy*

*Civil Rights and the Disabled: The Legislative Twilight Zone*

*Commercial Speech and the First Amendment*

*Constitutional Challenges to Punitive Damages*

*Corporate Criminal Liability: Is It Time for a New Look?*

*Employers' Rights and Responsibilities*

*Employment and Labor Law: Perspectives on Reform*

*Ergonomics: OSHA's Strange Campaign to Run American Business*

*Ethics in the Courts: Policing Behavior in the Federal Judiciary*

*Ethics, Politics and the Independent Counsel: Executive Power, Executive Vice 1789–1989*

*Federal Product Liability Law—It Should Be Enacted Now!*

*Institutional Investors, Social Investing, and Corporate Governance*

*Judicial Selection: Merit, Ideology, and Politics*

*Lawyers' Desk Book on White-Collar Crime*

*Litigating Against the Government: Leveling the Playing Field*

*Natural Resource Damages: A Legal, Economic, and Policy Analysis*

*Permanent Striker Replacements Should Not Be Banned*

*Pernicious Ideas and Costly Consequences: The Intellectual Roots of the Tort Crisis*

*Private Property and National Security: Foreign Economic Sanctions and the Constitution*

*Racial Preferences in Government Contracting*

*Reading Between the Lines of the Dunlop Commission Report*

*Regulatory Takings: Restoring Private Property Rights*

*Restoring the Presidency: Reconsidering the Twenty-Second Amendment*

*Rethinking Superfund: It Costs Too Much, It's Unfair, It Must Be Fixed*

*Securities Class Actions: Abuses and Remedies*

*Securities Regulation and the New Law*

*Sentence First, Verdict Afterwards: The Crisis of Mass Torts*

*State Judiciaries and Impartiality: Judging the Judges*

*Statehood for the District of Columbia: Is It Constitutional? Is It Wise? Is It Necessary?*

*Taxation and the Price of Civilization: An Essay on Federal Tax Reform*

*Three Years of the Americans With Disabilities Act: Lessons for Employers*

*Understanding the Kyoto Protocol*

*Union Plans to Amend the Labor Laws*

| | |
|---|---|
| **NEWSLETTER** | *Judicial/Legislative Watch Report* (monthly)<br>*National Legal Center News* (semiannually) |
| **CONFERENCES** | The Gauer Distinguished Lecture in Law and Public Policy (presents and disseminates an original work by a national or world leader on an important legal, constitutional, or public policy issue of the day)<br>General Counsel Briefing (members of the Cabinet, senior officials of the executive branch, heads of regulatory agencies, and members of the federal judiciary brief senior executives on their agendas and objectives)<br>The Supreme Court Press Briefing (assists journalists in their coverage of the Court and is held annually prior to the opening of each new term) |
| **BOARD OF DIRECTORS** | William H. Webster, chairman; Dean R. Kleckner and Raymond P. Shafer, vice chairmen; Ernest B. Hueter, president; George C. Landrith III, vice president/general counsel/assistance treasurer; Irene A. Jacoby, senior vice president, administration/assistant secretary<br><br>Other board members:<br>♦ Joan D. Aikens ♦ Griffin B. Bell ♦ David L. Boren ♦ K. David Boyer Jr. ♦ Rodney H. Brady ♦ Dick Cheney ♦ Joseph Coors ♦ David Davenport ♦ Arnaud de Borchgrave ♦ Livio D. DeSimone ♦ Willard W. Garvey ♦ Vincent A. Gierer Jr. ♦ Glen A. Holden ♦ P.X. Kelley ♦ Howard H. Leach ♦ Charles T. Manatt ♦ Robert J. Muth ♦ Dwight D. Opperman ♦ Michael D. Parker ♦ Shirley D. Peterson ♦ Enrique J. Sosa ♦ N. David Thompson ♦ Caspar W. Weinberger ♦ Walter E. Williams ♦ James I. Wyer |
| **EFFECTIVENESS** | Unavailable |
| **POLITICAL ORIENTATION** | Unavailable |

# Pacific Legal Foundation (1973)

2151 River Plaza Drive
Suite 305
Sacramento, California 95833
Phone: (916) 641-8888
Fax: (916) 920-3444
Internet: plf@jps.net *or* http://www.pacificlegal.org

"Seeks to represent the economic, social, and environmental interests of the public before judicial and regulatory decision makers. The Pacific Legal Foundation defends competitive free enterprise, a strong economy, private property rights, freedom from excessive government regulation, balance in pursuing environmental goals, and productive and fiscally sound government."

*PURPOSE*

49 total

*STAFF*

Robert K. Best, president and chief executive officer. Best previously served as chief of the environmental and land use sections and as deputy director of the Pacific Legal Foundation (PLF). He has held several positions in California state government, most recently as director of the department of transportation under Gov. George Deukmejian. His background includes military service and private legal practice. Best also serves as an adjunct professor at the University of the Pacific's McGeorge School of Law and is a faculty associate with the Lincoln Institute of Land Policy in Cambridge, Massachusetts.

*DIRECTOR*

501(c)(3)

*TAX STATUS*

1998—Unavailable
Proposed 1999—Unavailable

*BUDGET*

Foundations, 42 percent; individuals and small businesses, 32 percent; corporations and associations, 26 percent

*FUNDING
SOURCES*

Members: N/A
Branches/chapters: Anchorage; Bellevue, Washington; Honolulu; Portland, Oregon; and Stewart, Florida
Affiliates: N/A

*SCOPE*

| | |
|---|---|
| *PAC* | None |
| *METHOD OF OPERATION* | ♦ College of Public Interest Law (postgraduate fellowships) ♦ Conferences/seminars ♦ Congressional testimony ♦ Legal assistance ♦ Legislative/regulatory monitoring (federal and state) ♦ Library/information clearinghouse ♦ Litigation ♦ Media outreach ♦ Mediation ♦ Participation in regulatory proceedings (federal) ♦ Research ♦ Speakers program ♦ Training and technical assistance |
| *CURRENT CONCERNS* | ♦ Discrimination ♦ Education reform ♦ Environmental regulation ♦ Government regulation ♦ Judicial responsibility ♦ Land use ♦ Limited government ♦ Private property rights ♦ Rent control ♦ Taxpayer rights ♦ Tort reform ♦ Victims' rights |
| *PUBLICATIONS* | Publishes monographs |
| *NEWSLETTER* | *Action Reports* (weekly) <br> *At Issue* (monthly) <br> *Guide Post* (quarterly) |
| *CONFERENCES* | Sponsors or cosponsors 5–6 annual conferences on such topics as land use, rent control, wetlands, and endangered species |
| *BOARD OF DIRECTORS* | Ronald E. Van Burkirk, chairman; Robert E. McCarthy and Ben J. Gantt Jr., vice chairmen; April Morris, secretary/treasurer; Robert K. Best, president and chief executive officer; Anthony T. Caso, assistant secretary/treasurer and general counsel <br><br> Other trustee members: <br> ♦ Robin P. Arkley ♦ James J. Busby ♦ James L. Cloud ♦ Greg Evans ♦ Thomas A. May ♦ John L. Schwabe ♦ Michael T. Thomas ♦ Ronald E. Van Buskirk ♦ Brooks Walker Jr. |
| *EFFECTIVENESS* | "On Dec. 30, the Pacific Legal Foundation filed a petition with the court on behalf of Yvette Farmer, asking the justices to review her claim of discrimination against the University of Nevada. . . . <br><br> "The university wanted to fill a vacancy in its sociology department, and its search committee narrowed the field to three finalists, including Ms. Farmer and the person who was ultimately hired, Johnson Makoba, a black immigrant from Uganda. The university concedes that Mr. Makoba's race 'was a key factor in his hiring.' |

"The university's affirmative action plan also had a 'minority bonus policy,' which the Nevada Supreme Court described as an 'unwritten amendment' that allowed a department to hire an additional faculty member following the initial placement of a minority candidate. As a result of the minority bonus policy, the sociology department hired Ms. Farmer a year later. She started, however, with a salary $7,000 less than Mr. Makoba's, a gap that has since widened to $10,838. . . .

"Ms. Farmer challenged both the hiring and pay decisions as discriminatory and she alleged both race and sex discrimination for each. The university's defense was breathtakingly direct. Its response to the claims of sex discrimination was to insist cheerfully that it was motivated only by race. It then argued that the racial discrimination in hiring was justified by its desire for diversity and to correct the existing racial imbalance on its faculty. As to the pay disparity, it was simply responding to the market reality that black academics are more in demand these days than whites.

"The university's response to Yvette Farmer's petition to the Supreme Court is due on Feb. 5[, 1998]. . . ." (*Wall Street Journal*, January 19, 1998)

"conservative" (*New York Times*, March 13, 1998)

# POLITICAL ORIENTATION

# Rutherford Institute (1982)

P.O. Box 7482
Charlottesville, Virginia 22906
Phone: (804) 978-3888
Fax: (804) 978-1789
Internet: tristaff@rutherford.org *or* http://www.rutherford.org

| | |
|---|---|
| *PURPOSE* | "Exists to stand for those who cannot stand for themselves, speak for those whose voices cannot be heard, fight for those who do not have the strength to fight for what has been taken from them." |
| *STAFF* | 50 total |
| *DIRECTOR* | John W. Whitehead, president and founder |
| *TAX STATUS* | 501(c)(3) |
| *BUDGET* | 1998—$52 million<br>1999—Unavailable |
| *FUNDING SOURCES* | Primarily individual donations |
| *SCOPE* | Members: N/A<br>Branches/chapters: Offices in Bolivia, United Kingdom, and Hungary; student chapters on law school campuses<br>Affiliates: N/A |
| *PAC* | None |
| *METHOD OF OPERATION* | ♦ Conferences/seminars ♦ Educational programs (independent study, legal clinics, and work study) ♦ Externships ♦ Films/videos/audiotapes ♦ International affairs ♦ Internet (Web site) ♦ Internships ♦ Legal assistance and services ♦ Legislative/regulatory monitoring (federal) ♦ Litigation ♦ Media outreach ♦ Public service campaigns ♦ Research ♦ Speakers program |

♦ Civil liberties ♦ Free speech ♦ Human rights ♦ International religious persecution ♦ Parents' rights ♦ Religious freedom ♦ Separation of church and state ♦ Sexual harrassment

*Arresting Abortion*
*The End of Man*
*Freedom of Religious Expression*
*Home Education: Rights and Reasons*
*Parents' Rights*
*The Rights of Religious Persons in Public Education*
*The Second American Revolution*

Also publishes videos and audiotapes, booklets, pamphlets, and other resources

*ACTION Newsletter* (monthly)
*Litigation Report* (monthly)

Annual conference

Unavailable

"Facing the prospect of a severe budget shortfall, the Virginia-based law center representing Paula Jones has sent out an emotional fund-raising letter describing its financial situation as 'grim' and pleading with donors to send in generous donations. . . .

"Rutherford Institute officials say a sharp drop in donations over the last several months has forced them to lay off seven of the center's 60 employees, close down its Washington office and dip into a reserve fund to finance its operations. . . .

"Many supporters were angered by the institute's decision to take on such a politically charged case, the letter explains, and as a result stopped giving to the group altogether.

"But Whitehead's problems started when he took the Jones case last October. . . .

"He budgeted around $200,000 to cover costs but the legal bills alone came to twice that amount. Whitehead hoped publicity from the case would make up the gap, but instead the opposite happened." (*Washington Post*, August 7, 1998)

"Members of Paula Corbin Jones's legal team were quick to say they would probably appeal today's court ruling dismissing their case, but it was apparent that they were mostly drenched in disappointment and shock.

" 'It's very hard to take it in, very frustrating' said John W. Whitehead, the president of the Rutherford Institute, the organization in Char- lottesville, Va., that has been paying Ms. Jones's legal costs. 'Is this judge saying that a man can expose himself to a woman, ask for oral sex and put his hand up her crotch and all the while she is saying no, that a woman would have no recourse in such a situation?'

"Mr. Whitehead said he and Ms. Jones's other lawyers all had believed that Judge Susan Webber Wright would allow the trial, scheduled to begin on May 27 in Federal District Court in Arkansas, to go forward. 'We were prepared that perhaps she might dismiss part of the case, but not this,' he said. . . .

"Mr. Whitehead, whose Christian-oriented organization usually subsi- dizes cases with a religious aspect, said he saw the Jones case as a new di- mension in human rights. 'We believe this woman should have her day in court,' he said, noting that Judge Wright's ruling will be appealed.

"For Mr. Whitehead and Ms. Jones's other lawyers, this was the second major defeat at the hands of Judge Wright. In an earlier ruling that was exquisitely frustrating, Judge Wright ruled that Ms. Jones's lawyers could not use any evidence about Monica S. Lewinsky, the former White House intern." (*New York Times*, April 2, 1998)

"The legal and financial energy behind Paula Corbin Jones and her sexual misconduct suit against President Clinton is generated these days from a drab two-story office building alongside a strip mall just north of Char- lottesville, Va.

"The building is home to the Rutherford Institute, a kind of evangelical Christian civil liberties union, whose founder and leader, John W. White- head, chose to take on the Jones case.

"In so doing, Mr. Whitehead seized upon a striking way to raise the profile of his organization, which had existed on a diet of far less cele- brated cases involving religious freedoms. Rutherford, for example, rep- resented student athletes prohibited by school authorities from praying at the end of a game and contended with liberal groups opposed to erecting a nativity scene on a town square. . . .

"But with the sudden entry of the institute into the field of sexual ha- rassment by way of the Jones case, Mr. Whitehead has been subjected to questions about his motives.

"Did he get involved because it is a signal opportunity to wreak havoc with Mr. Clinton's reputation? Is he carrying the Paula Jones banner to weaken a President whose agenda is so at odds with the anti-homosexual and conservative religious views of his core supporters and compatriots in the religious right?

"Mr. Whitehead insists that he did not seek the case to harass the Pres- ident and that he has no political agenda. 'Oh, gosh, no,' he said. . . .

"Mr. Whitehead said he viewed the Jones case as an opportunity to move into a new area of human rights: sexual harassment.

" 'I never saw this in terms of a political agenda,' he said." (*New York Times*, January 18, 1998)

"Feistiest of all [Christian litigation organizations] may be the Rutherford Institute, based in Charlottesville, Va., which also produces the radio pro- gram 'Freedom Under Fire.' The group recently sued the Maryland De- partment of Motor Vehicles for recalling specialty license plates featuring Confederate symbols—and won." (*New York Times Magazine*, March 23, 1997)

"Religious groups and businesses rejoice over a SBA loan policy change. The U.S. Small Business Administration says it has overturned a policy that prevented religion-oriented, for-profit businesses from obtaining loans guaranteed by the agency. . . .

"Previously, the SBA had been prohibited, by statute, from guaranteeing loans to so-called opinion molders. The rule was enacted to prevent the federal government from becoming the owner of, say, a newspaper or radio station if such a business defaulted on an SBA-backed loan. The rule applied to all businesses engaged in the shaping of ideas, including gift shops and schools.

"But some business owners and groups such as the Rutherford Institute and the American Center for Law and Justice, another legal group, argued that for-profit businesses that merely sell or manufacture religious and inspirational goods, rather than actively promote certain beliefs, should be able to obtain government-guaranteed loans.

"The SBA agreed. In March, the agency began accepting loan applications from qualified businesses with religious components." (*Wall Street Journal*, May 21, 1996)

"When a Catholic priest, the Rev. Tim Mockaitis, heard confession last month in a county prison in Eugene from a 20-year-old suspect linked to three killings, he assumed that the session would be private.

"But it was not. Lane County prison authorities surreptitiously taped every word Father Mockaitis and the suspect, Conan Wayne Hale, said as they sat on opposite sides of a plastic partition on April 22, speaking over telephones. The county's District Attorney, Doug Harcleroad, has acquired the tape via court order and may decide to use it in the prosecution of Mr. Hale. He faces burglary and theft charges related to the shooting deaths of three teen-agers in the woods in Springfield, near Eugene, in December. . . .

"The Catholic League for Religious and Civil Rights, an association of lay Catholics based in New York, has called for a Federal investigation of the taping. The Rutherford Institute, a center based in Virginia that defends religious liberties, is getting ready to fight a legal battle to keep the tape from being used in court against Mr. Hale. And Dave Fidanque, executive director of the Oregon chapter of the American Civil Liberties Union, has spoken out. Eugene's daily paper, *The Register-Guard*, quoted him as asking, 'Is there no zone of privacy that we as citizens have from the government?' " (*New York Times*, May 13, 1996)

"a conservative legal center" (*New York Times*, April 6, 1998)

"In 1982, he [Donovan Campbell Jr., the lead attorney for Paula Corbin Jones] heard a tape of a speech by John W. Whitehead, a lawyer who spoke about establishing the Rutherford Institute, which would function as a kind of religious, conservative version of the civil liberties union. He recalled that he was immediately struck by the idea that Mr. Whitehead's concept could satisfy his yearning to combine his religious feeling with the law and he sent off a long letter.

## POLITICAL ORIENTATION

"Mr. Whitehead telephoned and quickly recruited Mr. Campbell, and the two have since become close friends. It has been through the Rutherford Institute, which is based in Charlottesville, Va., that Mr. Campbell has found most of his religious-oriented cases." (*New York Times*, March 1, 1998)

"The organization has a Libertarian streak. . . ." (*Washington Blade*, February 27, 1998)

# Southern Poverty Law Center (1971)

400 Washington Avenue
Montgomery, Alabama 36104
Phone: (334) 264-0286
Fax: (334) 264-0629
Internet: http://www.splcenter.com

| | |
|---|---|
| "To advance the legal rights of victims of injustice through public education and litigation." | **PURPOSE** |
| 60 total—22 professional; 38 support; plus 4 part-time professional; 6 part-time support; 1 volunteer | **STAFF** |
| Edward Ashworth, director of operations. Ashworth began his work with the Southern Poverty Law Center in 1977 as a member of its board of directors. He was named executive director in 1992, then director of operations in 1996. He is the founder and managing partner of Rainbow Exploration Corporation and former president of Ashworth Petroleum Company. Ashworth received a bachelor of fine arts degree from Birmingham-Southern College in 1972 and a juris doctor degree from the University of Alabama in 1976. | **DIRECTOR** |
| 501(c)(3) | **TAX STATUS** |
| Fiscal year ending July 31, 1997—$10.3 million<br>Fiscal year ending October 30, 1998—$11.94 million<br>Proposed F.Y. 1999—Unavailable | **BUDGET** |
| Individuals, 94 percent; sales of educational material and investment income, 4 percent; foundation grants, 2 percent | **FUNDING SOURCES** |
| Members: 450,000 (mostly individuals)<br>Branches/chapters: N/A<br>Affiliate: Klanwatch | **SCOPE** |
| None | **PAC** |

| METHOD OF OPERATION | ◆ Educational services ◆ Films/video/audiotapes ◆ Internet (Web site) ◆ Legal assistance ◆ Litigation ◆ Research ◆ Speakers program |

| CURRENT CONCERNS | ◆ Civil rights abuses ◆ Education ◆ Hate groups ◆ Legal assistance ◆ Violence in schools |

| PUBLICATIONS | The following is a list of sample publications:
*False Patriots*
*Hate Violence and White Supremacy: A Decade Review 1980–1990*
*Intelligence Report*
*The Klan: A Legacy of Hate in America* (film)
*The Ku Klux Klan: A History of Racism and Violence*
*One World* (poster set)
*The Shadow of Hate: A History of Intolerance in America* (video and text kit)
*SPLC Report* (reports the center's activities)
*Ten Ways to Fight Hate*
*Terror in Our Neighborhoods*
*A Time for Justice* (video)
*Us and Them* |

| NEWSLETTER | *Intelligence Report* (bimonthly)
*Teaching Tolerance* (free magazine published twice a year) |

| CONFERENCES | Annual meeting |

| BOARD OF DIRECTORS | Joseph J. Levin Jr., president; JoAnn Chancellor, secretary; Edward Ashworth, treasurer

Other board members:
◆ Patricia Clark ◆ Frances M. Green ◆ Rufus Huffman ◆ Howard Mandell ◆ James McElroy |

| EFFECTIVENESS | "People in the New York metropolitan area tend to think of Ku Klux Klan, skinhead or neo-Nazi groups as being from somewhere else. But analysts who keep track of the hate-group movement nationally say New York, Connecticut and New Jersey are home to an unexpected number of the groups.
" 'The general impression is that these groups are a Southern phenomenon, but that hasn't been true for years,' said Joseph Roy Sr., the intelligence project director for the Southern Poverty Law Center, which follows the groups. 'Technology and the mobility of society,' he said, have given these groups a better chance to spread. 'You find them everywhere.' |

"A report issued this month by the center, which is based in Montgomery, Ala., found 474 active hate groups nationwide in 1997, an increase of about 20 percent from the year before. . . .

"One of the New York area groups identified by the Southern Poverty Law Center serves as an example. In Levittown, on Long Island, a group of teen-agers, calling themselves the Center Lane Skins, drew police attention last summer for harassing Asian residents and spray-painting swastikas and graffiti that read 'White Power' and 'K.K.K.' A police investigation showed that the teen-agers thought of themselves as a loosely organized neo-Nazi skinhead group, said Anthony Rocco, the Levittown precinct commander. By this winter, Officer Rocco said, the group seemed to have dispersed." (*New York Times*, March 22, 1998)

"U.S. Attorney G. Douglas Jones, announcing the arrest warrant in Birmingham, said federal authorities have posted a $100,000 reward for information leading to the capture and conviction of the suspect, 31-year-old Eric Robert Rudolph. Rudolph's gray pickup, they said, was spotted driving away from the New Woman All Women center about five minutes after the Jan. 29 explosion that killed Robert 'Sandy' Sanderson, a moonlighting police officer who was standing guard. The blast also took out the left eye of Emily Lyons, a nurse who was reporting for work. . . .

"In announcing the $100,000 reward for Rudolph's capture, FBI agent Joseph R. Lewis also pointed out that anyone harboring the fugitive could be prosecuted as well. 'It's too early to know if [the bomber] acted alone,' added James Cavanaugh, chief of the federal Bureau of Alcohol, Tobacco and Firearms in Birmingham.

"Cavanaugh also said it is 'an open question' whether there is a link between the clinic bombing in Birmingham and bombings in Atlanta that damaged an abortion clinic on Jan. 16, 1997, and a lesbian nightclub four days later.

"One possible connection is a loose-knit extremist group known as the Army of God, which claimed responsibility for the Atlanta blasts and sent a letter Wednesday to Murphy's weekly newspaper, *The Cherokee Scout*, saying, 'Be advised: The Army of God is more than one.'. . .

"The Southern Poverty Law Center, which tracks extremist groups from its headquarters in Montgomery, Ala., said Rudolph is a disciple of the late Nord Davis, founder of Northpoint Tactical Teams, an anti-government clan based in the mountains here. Rudolph also has gravitated to the 'Christian Identity' movement, which is organized around various 'churches' and pastors who generally promote anti-Semitic, anti-black, anti-government thinking, according to investigators." (*Washington Post*, February 15, 1998)

"Civic leaders were outraged, of course, when they learned that an aggressive new branch of the Ku Klux Klan had made plans to rally in Annapolis today.

"But how should they respond? The answer wasn't so simple. In planning meetings last month, city officials acknowledged that the counter-demonstrations that typically have greeted KKK marches across the country often degenerate into ugly confrontations, or even violence. Yet many Annapolis residents felt they could not simply turn a blind eye to the Klan's presence, as many law enforcement officials had urged.

"So in the style of a growing number of communities, Annapolis today will host a multiracial 'Unity Rally.' Intended as a peaceful and upbeat event, it will convene a block from the planned Klan rally. There, organizers hope they can focus attention away from—rather than toward—the white supremacist cause. . . .

"It will be Annapolis's second major Klan demonstration in four years. Days before the 1994 statewide elections, 35 members of a Frederick-based Klan organization held a recruiting rally on State House grounds. Though more than 10 times that number of anti-Klan protesters arrived to shout them down, the day passed largely without incident. . . .

"The American Knights of the Ku Klux Klan are considered 'the fastest-growing and most heavily recruiting' Klan organization in the country, said Mark Potok, spokesman for the Southern Poverty Law Center in Montgomery, Ala., which tracks hate-group activity nationwide. Formed in 1995 in Butler, Ind., the American Knights have 17 chapters, he said." (*Washington Post*, February 7, 1998)

"The recent attention to the Tuskegee [syphilis study] outrage is welcome—and will be useful if it contributes to more African Americans getting the medical help they need. But regaining their trust is no simple matter, because the syphilis study is only part of the story. By way of example, consider some of the experiments that have involved black women. In 1939, seven years after the Tuskegee experiment began, the Birth Control Federation of America (the successor to the American Birth Control League) planned a 'Negro Project' directed at the 'mass of Negroes, particularly in the South,' because it considered that segment of the population 'least fit, and least able to rear children properly.'. . .

"The population targeted in this campaign did not come to the public's attention until July 1973, when a black couple, Mr. and Mrs. Lonnie Relf, complained to the Southern Poverty Law Center that two of their daughters—Mary Alice, 12 years old, and Minnie Lee, 14—had been surgically sterilized without their knowledge or consent. These adolescents had first been injected regularly with an experimental drug called Depo-Provera, to prevent conception. When federal authorities learned that this drug had been linked with cancer in laboratory animals, they ordered the injections be discontinued. With the drug no longer available, the authorities in Montgomery, Ala., ordered the sterilization procedure. Katie Relf, age 17, a sister of the sterilized girls and a welfare recipient, escaped this surgery only because she physically resisted.

"The Southern Poverty Law Center filed suit on behalf of the Relf sisters. During the course of the trial, Mrs. Relf, who was unable to read, revealed that she had 'consented' to the operation by putting her 'X' on a document. Since the content of the document was not discussed with her, she had assumed it simply authorized continued use of the Depo-Provera injections, not the surgical sterilization of her daughters.

"Shortly after this scandal was reported in the media, other cases came to light." (*Washington Post*, May 29, 1997)

# POLITICAL ORIENTATION

Unavailable

# Trial Lawyers for Public Justice (1982)

1717 Massachusetts Ave., NW
Suite 800
Washington, D.C. 20036
Phone: (202) 797-8600
Fax: (202) 232-7209
Internet: http://www.tlpj.org

| | |
|---|---|
| "Uses the skills and approaches of plaintiffs' trail lawyers to advance the public interest. It utilizes tort and trial litigation as an effective instrument of social change and to vindicate individual rights." | **PURPOSE** |
| 18 total (including the TJPJ Foundation)—12 professional; 6 support; plus 1 part-time support; 1 intern | **STAFF** |
| Arthur H. Bryant, executive director. Bryant, who has been executive director of Trail Lawyers for Public Justice (TLPJ) since 1987, joined the organization as a staff attorney. He previously clerked for a U.S. district court judge and worked for a Philadelphia law firm. Bryant is a graduate of Harvard Law School. | **DIRECTOR** |
| "Professional corporation with bylaws requiring all revenues be used for public interest litigation." | **TAX STATUS** |
| 1998—$1.6 million (includes TLPJ Foundation)<br>Proposed 1999—$2.0 million (includes TLPJ Foundation) | **BUDGET** |
| Membership, foundations, and legal fees | **FUNDING SOURCES** |
| Members: 1,500 attorneys and other individuals<br>Branches/chapters: N/A<br>Affiliate: Trial Lawyers for Public Justice is a project of the Trial Lawyers for Public Justice Foundation, a 501(c)(3) organization | **SCOPE** |
| None | **PAC** |

## METHOD OF OPERATION

♦ Awards program (Trial Lawyer of the Year Award) ♦ Conferences/ seminars ♦ Information clearinghouse (Class Action Abuse Prevention Project, Federal Preemption Project, Federal Rules Project, Lead Paint Litigation Clearinghouse, Project ACCESS) ♦ Internet (Web site) ♦ Internships ♦ Legal assistance ♦ Litigation ♦ Research ♦ Scholarships ♦ Training and technical assistance (Environmental Enforcement Project)

## CURRENT CONCERNS

♦ Auto safety and airbag litigation ♦ Civil rights and civil liberties ♦ Class action abuse ♦ Consumer safety ♦ Discrimination ♦ Electromagnetic radiation ♦ Environmental protection ♦ Equal rights for female intercollegiate athletes ♦ Federal preemption ♦ Lead paint ♦ Pesticides ♦ Product safety ♦ Protective orders and court secrecy ♦ Toxic torts

## PUBLICATIONS

*In the News* (annual)
*Membership Directory* (annual)
*Trial Lawyers Doing Public Justice* (annual)

## NEWSLETTER

*Public Justice* (quarterly)

## CONFERENCES

Public Interest Coalition Conferences

## BOARD OF DIRECTORS

"Through a Board of Directors elected by its members, the TLPJ Foundation controls the operation of TLPJ."

The TLPJ Foundation board of directors' officers:
Joseph A. Power Jr., president; Nicole Sceitheis, president-elect; Susan Vogel Saladoff, vice president; Paul L. Stritmatter, treasurer; Larry Trattler, secretary; Monica M. Jimenez, William A. Trine, Fred Baron, George W. Shadoan, executive committee members

Other board members:
♦ James H. Ackerman ♦ Roberta E. Ashkin ♦ James Bartimus ♦ Ray Boucher ♦ Alan R. Brayton ♦ James Browne ♦ Isaac K. Byrd ♦ Robert E. Cartwright Jr. ♦ Michael V. Ciresi ♦ Joan B. Claybrook ♦ Gerri Colton ♦ Roxanne Barton Conlin ♦ Tracey Conwell ♦ Maron Cowles ♦ Harry Deitzler ♦ Thomas Dempsey ♦ Abraham Fuchsberg ♦ Jeffrey M. Goldberg ♦ Robert Habush ♦ Richard Hailey ♦ Gerald Holtz ♦ Rosalind Fuchsberg Kaufman ♦ Frederick T. Kuykendall III ♦ Stanley Marks ♦ Randy McClanahan ♦ Joseph J. McKernan ♦ Richard H. Middleton Jr. ♦ Richard Miller ♦ Mark Mueller ♦ Jack Olender ♦ Robert Palmer ♦ Peter Perlman ♦ Chrisopher M. Placitella ♦ Kieron Quinn ♦ Tony Roisman ♦ William A. Rossbach ♦ Federico Sayre ♦ Leonard Schroeter ♦ Gerson H. Smoger ♦ Theodore Spearman ♦ James Sturdevant ♦ Mona Lisa Wallace ♦ Simon Walton ♦ David H. Weinstein ♦ Harvey Weitz ♦ Perry Weitz ♦ Martha Wivell ♦ Stephen Zetterberg

"Brown University agreed to settle a Federal lawsuit today that requires it to keep roughly the same percentage of women on intercollegiate teams as in its student body. It also guarantees more money for four women's sports for three years.

"The settlement, which ends a six-year legal battle that reached the Supreme Court, must still get final approval from a Federal judge, a university spokesman and the plaintiffs' lawyers said.

"The lawsuit was brought after the Division I school tried to eliminate its women's volleyball and gymnastics teams in 1991.

"Trial Lawyers for Public Justice, a law firm in Washington, sued on behalf of Brown's female athletes, accusing the university of failing to comply with Title IX of the Education Amendments of 1972, which prohibits sexual discrimination at schools that receive Federal money.

"The Supreme Court's decision last year let stand a ruling against Brown. The agreement, given preliminary approval today by Judge Ernest C. Torres of Federal District Court, would require Brown to insure that the percentage of athletes who are women is no more than 3.5 percentage points lower than the percentage of women enrolled. If Brown eliminates or downgrades women's teams, or improves men's sports without doing the same for women, it would be required to keep its sports participation rate within 2.25 percent of enrollment." (*New York Times*, June 24, 1998)

"For years, the NCAA had a nearly invincible legal record. But that has changed—and so may the look of major college athletics, especially if last week's $67 million judgment against the organization is followed by further losses in cases pending in federal courts around the nation.

"Last week, a federal jury in Kansas City, Kan., ordered the NCAA to pay $67 million in damages to about 1,900 college assistant coaches for unlawfully capping their salaries in violation of antitrust law. The NCAA has appealed, but that case, while potentially burdensome for an organization with a $265 million budget this year, may be the least of its legal concerns. One of the NCAA's primary reasons for existence—providing member schools with a way to make rules designed to keep any school from gaining a competitive advantage—is under challenge. . . .

" 'A lot of these cases have to do with vindicating a person's right to be free from discrimination whether it's based on race, gender, disability or national origin,' said Adele Kimmel of the Washington-based Trial Lawyers for Public Justice, an organization that has represented plaintiffs in a variety of cases against the NCAA and/or its member schools.'. . . I think finally people realize the NCAA is not invincible and should be held accountable for [its] wrongdoing just like any other entity.'. . .

"Said Kimmel of the Trial Lawyers for Public Justice, which is representing the plaintiffs in the freshman-eligibility-rules case: 'I don't think we're talking [entirely] about financial interests but a matter of principle.'

"College athletic directors around the country are sensing that. Within the past two years, Justice Department officials have told the NCAA that the rules governing an athlete's ability to receive an athletic scholarship and play or practice as a freshman do not comply with the Americans With Disabilities Act because students with learning disabilities are unfairly impacted.

"Last month, the new NCAA Division I Board of Directors passed a rule that, for the first time, will allow Division I athletes who receive full scholarships to work part time during the school year. But the rule caps those earnings at $2,000 a year." (*Washington Post,* March 12, 1998)

"Lawyers on both sides of a controversial proposal to settle class-action claims against the mortgage-finance unit of BankAmerica Corp. have reversed course and agreed to a new deal that gives plaintiffs more cash than their lawyers.

"Under a previous agreement, which had the tentative approval of a federal judge in Hattiesburg, Miss., plaintiffs' lawyers would have gotten $5.4 million in legal fees, while the bank's customers would have gotten $4.7 million at most.

"The proposed settlement had drawn fire from Trial Lawyers for Public Justice, a Washington-based public interest law firm, which filed a motion objecting to the deal. Arthur H. Bryant, the firm's executive director, said yesterday that lawyers on both sides had told him that the new settlement would give bank customers $7.4 million and plaintiffs' lawyers only $1.9 million.

"At a hearing on Wednesday in Hattiesburg, U.S. District Judge Charles Pickering announced that the two sides had reached a new deal, but the judge didn't say what the terms were. The new settlement hasn't been committed to paper yet and still requires Judge Pickering's final approval, Mr. Bryant said. . . .

"The suit in Mississippi was brought last year on behalf of people across the country who financed their mobile and prefabricated homes through San Diego-based BankAmerica Housing Services, formerly Security Pacific Housing Services Inc.

"Under its lending agreements, the company was allowed to step in and buy insurance for borrowers who fell behind on their insurance payments. The company then would add the cost of the insurance to the borrowers' monthly mortgage payments. The suit alleges, among other things, that BankAmerica charged excessive amounts for these so-called forced-place policies. . . .

"Class-action settlements have been criticized around the country for generating huge fees for plaintiffs' lawyers and settlements that work out to relatively small payments for individual consumers." (*Wall Street Journal,* April 18, 1997)

"A public interest law group filed suit against the NCAA yesterday, saying the organization discriminates against blacks because it uses standardized test scores to decide whether athletes can compete and receive athletic scholarships as freshmen. Meanwhile, the NCAA unveiled study results showing that the rules being challenged in the suit are contributing to increasing graduation rates for black athletes.

"Under NCAA rules, high school seniors scoring less than 820 out of 1,600 on the Scholastic Assessment Test or 66 out of 120 on the American College Test cannot compete as freshmen and lose a season of eligibility, regardless of their academic achievements. All but a small number of those students also are ineligible for athletic scholarships or to practice with their teams as freshmen. The rules, commonly known as Proposition 48, were adopted by the NCAA member schools in 1983, took effect in 1986 and subsequently have been toughened.

"In a class-action lawsuit filed in U.S. District Court in Philadelphia, Trial Lawyers for Public Justice said the Proposition 48 rules violate the Civil Rights Act of 1964 because black athletes are disproportionately affected by them. The suit seeks an injunction that would prevent the NCAA from enforcing Proposition 48, citing NCAA research about athletes who entered college during the three years prior to Proposition 48's implementation. According to that data, 47 percent of the black athletes in those three classes who graduated would have been declared ineligible as freshmen while 8 percent of the white athletes would have been declared ineligible. . . .

"NCAA officials reacted to the lawsuit by saying that the Proposition 48 standards protect students from exploitation and that freshman eligibility standards based only on grade-point average are 'problematic because of the possibility of grade inflation and fraud due to a student's athletic status,' NCAA spokeswoman Kathryn Reith said in a statement." (*Washington Post*, January 9, 1997)

Unavailable

# POLITICAL
# ORIENTATION

# Washington Legal Foundation (1976)

2009 Massachusetts Avenue, NW
Washington, D.C. 20036
Phone: (202) 588-0302
Fax: (202) 588-0386
Internet: http://www.wlf.org

| | |
|---|---|
| **PURPOSE** | "Defending and promoting the principles of free enterprise and individual rights through an effective combination of precedent-setting litigation; publishing in six formats; and extensive communications and educational outreach." |
| **STAFF** | 15 total—9 professional; 6 support; plus 4 part-time professional; 2 interns |
| **DIRECTOR** | Daniel J. Popeo, chairman and general counsel. Before founding the Washington Legal Foundation (WLF), Popeo was a federal trial attorney for the Interior Department. Formerly he was on the staff of the U.S. attorney general and on the White House legal staff under presidents Nixon and Ford. |
| **TAX STATUS** | 501(c)(3) |
| **BUDGET** | 1997—$3.2 million<br>1998—$3.5 million<br>Proposed 1999—$3.5 million |
| **FUNDING SOURCES** | Unavailable |
| **SCOPE** | Members: N/A<br>Branches/chapters: N/A<br>Affiliates: N/A |
| **PAC** | None |
| **METHOD OF OPERATION** | ◆ Advertisements ◆ Educational foundation ◆ Internet (Web site) ◆ Internships ◆ Litigation ◆ Media outreach ◆ Participation in regulatory proceedings (federal and state) ◆ Research ◆ Speakers program |

◆ Civil Communications program ◆ Environmental Protection Agency reform ◆ Food and Drug Administration reform ◆ Tort reform

*Contemporary Legal Notes*
*Counsel's Advisory*
*Legal Opinion Letter*

Also publishes monographs and working papers

*Legal Backgrounder* (weekly)

Media Press Briefings (monthly)

Dick Thornburgh, chairman; Frank J. Fahrenkopf Jr., Ernest Gellhorn, Richard K. Willard, chairmen emeritus

Other legal advisory board members:
◆ George Allen ◆ Joseph A. Artabane ◆ Haley Barbour ◆ Randy E. Barnett ◆ Thomas Hale Boggs Jr. ◆ Gary B. Born ◆ Susan G. Branden ◆ George M. Burditt ◆ James H. Burnley IV ◆ Arnold Burns ◆ Tom Campbell ◆ Alan F. Coffee Jr. ◆ Joseph E. diGenova ◆ William A. Donohue ◆ Richard Duesenberg ◆ J. Terry Emerson ◆ Kirk Fordice ◆ Kent Frizzell ◆ Albert Gidari ◆ Lino A. Graglia ◆ Thomas J. Graves ◆ William F. Harvey ◆ Richard A. Hauser ◆ Maurice J. Holland ◆ Clarence T. Kipps Jr. ◆ Philip A. Lacovara ◆ H.J. "Tex" Lezar ◆ Susan W. Liebeler ◆ Roger J. Marzulla ◆ Arvin Maskin ◆ Michael W. McConnell ◆ John Norton Moore ◆ Glen D. Nager ◆ Gale A. Norton ◆ Barbara K. Olson ◆ Theodore B. Olson ◆ W. Hugh O'Riordan ◆ Robert D. Paul ◆ Stephen B. Presser ◆ George L. Priest ◆ William H. Pryor Jr. ◆ Charles F. "Rick" Rule ◆ Peter J. Rusthoven ◆ Hal Stratton ◆ Robert S. Strauss ◆ Larry D. Thompson ◆ Steven J. Twist ◆ Dennis C. Vacco ◆ Warren R. Wise ◆ Wayne Withers

"The Washington Legal Foundation . . . had sued the Texas Supreme Court and the Texas IOLTA program, contending the IOLTA program violated Fifth Amendment rights by taking client property without just compensation. . . . In the Phillips decision, a 5–4 majority of the Supreme Court held that interest earned on client funds held in IOLTA accounts is the 'private property' of the client for Takings Clause purposes." (*National Law Journal*, June 29, 1998)

"WLF [The Washington Legal Foundation] has also engaged in several targeted public education campaigns by placing public service educational announcements in the national editions of newspapers. . . . They focus the public's attention on such critical issues as the FDA's negative impact on health care, the EPA's refusal to comply with its own laws, and the damage junk science does to the legal system. WLF litigates at every level of the judicial system, from local courts to the United States Supreme Court. In the last year, WLF has scored many impressive court victories." (*Metropolitan Corporate Counsel*, May 1997)

"Senate Judiciary Committee Chairman Orrin Hatch, a WLF ally since 1977, recently summarized it well: "WLF has become a highly respected and influential voice in the nation's capitol and around the country. It is at the forefront of the public interest law movement promoting America's free enterprise system." (*Metropolitan Corporate Counsel*, May 1997)

## POLITICAL ORIENTATION

"a pro-business public interest legal organization" (*National Law Journal*, June 29, 1998)

"conservative" (*Washington Post*, January 30, 1998)

"WLF initiates cases and publishes legal studies in several formats. Everything is done from an adamantly anti-regulatory, free-market perspective . . . promoters of business civil liberties . . . central to the practice of law in the public arena." (*National Law Journal*, August 26, 1996)

# Religious

## Chapter 11

# American Jewish Committee (1906)

Jacob Blaustein Building
165 East 56th Street
New York, New York 10022
Phone: (212) 751-4000
Fax: (212) 838-2120

1156 15th Street, NW
12th Floor
Washington, D.C. 20005
Phone: (202) 785-4200
Fax: (202) 785-4115

Internet: http://www.ajc.org

| | |
|---|---|
| "To safeguard the welfare and security of Jews in the United States, in Israel, and throughout the world; to strengthen the basic principles of pluralism around the world as the best defense against anti-Semitism and other forms of bigotry; to enhance the quality of American Jewish life by helping to insure Jewish continuity and deepen ties between American and Israeli Jews." | ***PURPOSE*** |
| 214 total—124 professional; 90 support; plus 6 part-time professionals; 14 part-time support; 3 interns | ***STAFF*** |
| David A. Harris, executive director. Harris joined the American Jewish Committee (AJC) in 1979 as a special assistant in the office of the executive vice president. He left AJC to join the National Conference of Soviet Jewry as director of its Washington office. He returned to AJC in 1984 as deputy director of international relations. Harris also has served as AJC's Washington representative. Harris has written more than one hundred articles on East-West relations and the Middle East. An alumnus of the University of Pennsylvania, he did his graduate work in international relations at the London School of Economics. | ***DIRECTOR*** |
| 501(c)(3) | ***TAX STATUS*** |
| Fiscal year ending June 30, 1997—$17.05 million<br>F.Y. 1998—$19.8 million<br>Proposed F.Y. 1999—$22 million | ***BUDGET*** |
| Corporate donations, 40 percent; individuals, 40 percent; special events/projects, 9 percent; membership dues, 6 percent; foundation grants, 5 percent | ***FUNDING SOURCES*** |

| | |
|---|---|
| **SCOPE** | Members: 70,000 members and supporters |
| | Branches/chapters: 32 regional offices across the United States; Israel/ Middle East office; London office |
| | Affiliate: Institute for Human Relations, a 501 (c)(3) organization |
| **PAC** | None |
| **METHOD OF OPERATION** | ◆ Advertisements ◆ Awards program (Akiba Award, American Liberties Medallion, Community Human Relations Awards, Distinguished Service Award, Herbert H. Lehman Human Relations Award, Institute of Human Relations Award, Learned Hand Award, Mass Media Award, National Distinguished Leadership Award) ◆ Coalition forming ◆ Conferences/ seminars ◆ Congressional testimony ◆ Diplomatic outreach ◆ Exchange programs ◆ Grassroots organizing ◆ Information clearinghouse ◆ Initiative/referendum campaigns ◆ International activities ◆ Internet (Web site) ◆ Legislative/regulatory monitoring (federal and state) ◆ Library/ information clearinghouse ◆ Litigation ◆ Local/municipal affairs ◆ Media outreach ◆ Research |
| **CURRENT CONCERNS** | ◆ Combating bigotry and extremism ◆ Democracy ◆ Human rights ◆ Israeli security ◆ Jewish identity and continuity ◆ Jewish security ◆ Pluralism and positive intergroup relations |
| **PUBLICATIONS** | *American Jewish Year Book* (annually) |
| | *AJC in the Courts* |
| | *Annual Survey of American Jewish Opinion* |
| | *Antisemitism World Report 1997* |
| | *The Condition of Jewish Peoplehood* |
| | *The Jewish Dimension in German American Relations* |
| | *Justice Delayed: Three Years After the AMIA Bombing* |
| | *Litigation Report* |
| | *The McVeigh Trial* |
| | *One-Sided: The Ongoing Campaign Against Israel in the United Nations* |
| | *Post Zionism: The Challenge to Israel* |
| | *Religion and Politics* |
| | *The Restitution of Jewish Property in Central and Eastern Europe* |
| | *A Statement of the Jewish Future: Text and Responses* |
| | *A Symposium on Pluralism and Public Policy* |
| | *Switzerland, Swiss Banks, and the Second World War: The Story Behind the Story* |
| | *Understanding Jewish History: Texts and Commentaries* |
| **NEWSLETTER** | *CommonQuest* (quarterly) |

Conference on Catholic/Jewish Educational Enrichment
Conference on Chinese Arms and Technology Transfers to Iran
India and Israel at 50: A Celebration of Two Democracies
The Jewish Dimension in German-American Relations
National Convention and International Leadership Conference
Policy and Advocacy Conference

Bruce M. Ramer, president; Jack Lapin, chair, national board of
governors; E. Robert Goodkind, chair, national council; Morris W. Offit,
chair, board of trustees; Ronald Weiner, treasurer; Jane Silverman,
secretary; Michael Gould and Lawrence J. Ramer, associate chairs; David
A. Harris, executive director; Martin S. Kaplan, Stephen Kurzman,
Nicholar D.J. Lane, Mont Levy, commission chairs

Other officers:
♦ Dottie Bennett ♦ Jarris L. Kempner Jr. ♦ Eleanor Lazarus ♦ Herbert
Mines ♦ Harold Tanner

"A recent 50th birthday party for Israel here was a hybrid: part love-in for
Israel, part exercise in coalition building and part political rally for Vice
President Al Gore, a man who aspires to be the next U.S. president.

"Intermittently inserting flawless Hebrew, Gore quoted biblical scripture, poet Chaim Nachman Rialik and Hebrew prayers, praising Israel as
a 'story of redemption and freedom for all oppressed people everywhere.'

"For the organizers, the American Jewish Committee and the American
Israel Public Affairs Committee, the fact that representatives of the black,
Latino and Asian American communities—as well as elected state and
local officials—turned out was testament enough to the event's success."
(JTA, March 27, 1998)

"Some startling revelations have emerged about American Jews and the
way we view the Middle East, following last week's publication of parts
of the new American Jewish Committee survey. First, the statistics prove
fascination with Jewish opinion has reached an all-time high, at least
among poll-takers. No fewer than four major surveys of American Jews
have now been released since the Hebrew year 5758 began last September. This breaks the previous record of three polls in a six-month period,
set in 5752. . . ." (New York Jewish Week, March 27, 1998)

"The American Jewish Committee's visit to Germany was a big news item
on February 9, 1998 when Chancellor Helmut Kohl, in a note of greetings
sent from Bonn, underscored the importance of the Jewish Community's
presence in the German capital in fostering contacts between the citizens
of Germany and the U.S. as well as the nations of Eastern Europe. Speaking at the opening ceremonies in Berlin, Foreign Minister Klaus Kinkel
similarly called attention to the 'bridge-building functions' the American-
Jewish Committee's Berlin office, its first office in Europe . . . will perform . . . and will also add 'another important strand to the close bonds
between the Federal Republic of Germany and the state and people of
Israel." (Turkish Times, March 1, 1998)

"In a path-breaking deal intended to redress wrongs of both the Nazi era and the Cold War, the German government said Monday that it will create a $110-million reparations fund for Jewish survivors of the Holocaust who live in countries of the former Eastern Bloc. . . .

"Until recently, a budget-conscious Bonn has insisted that since Germany had already paid more than $55 billion to Holocaust survivors, it would pay no more compensation to the individuals. Instead, Germany said it wanted to move on, atoning for Nazi violence in Eastern Europe by helping to restore democracy there and by financing charitable projects such as kindergartens and community centers.

"Bonn dropped this policy in August and then faced an aggressive publicity campaign mounted on behalf of the impoverished East European Jews by the American Jewish Committee, which took out large newspaper advertisements, criticizing Germany's payment of 'victims pensions' to former SS volunteers while the East European Holocaust victims got not a pfennig. The committee also petitioned U.S. senators to lobby German Chancellor Helmut Kohl. . . ." (*Los Angeles Times*, January 13, 1998)

## POLITICAL ORIENTATION

"non-partisan" (*The Independent*, April 19, 1998)

# American Jewish Congress (1918)

15 East 84th Street
New York, New York 10028
Phone: (212) 879-4500
Fax: (212) 249-3672

2027 Massachusetts Avenue, NW
Washington, D.C. 20036
Phone: (202) 332-4001
Fax: (202) 387-3434

Internet: http://www.ajcongress.org

| | |
|---|---|
| "To ensure the creative survival of the Jewish people, deeply cognizant of the Jewish responsibility to participate fully in public life, inspired by Jewish teachings and values, informed by liberal principles, dedicated to an activist and independent role, and committed to making its decisions through democratic processes. . . ." | **PURPOSE** |
| 100 total; plus interns and part-time personnel | **STAFF** |
| Phil Baum, executive director | **DIRECTOR** |
| 501(c)(3) | **TAX STATUS** |
| 1998—$5 million<br>Proposed 1999—$5 million | **BUDGET** |
| Private individuals and Jewish federations | **FUNDING SOURCES** |
| Members: 45,000<br>Branches/chapters: 11 regional offices; office in Jerusalem<br>Affiliates: N/A | **SCOPE** |
| None | **PAC** |

| | |
|---|---|
| *METHOD OF OPERATION* | ♦ Advertisements ♦ Coalition forming ♦ Conferences/seminars ♦ Congressional testimony ♦ Congressional voting analysis ♦ Direct action ♦ Grassroots organizing ♦ Internet (databases, electronic bulletin boards, Web site) ♦ Legal assistance ♦ Legislative/regulatory monitoring (federal and state) ♦ Litigation ♦ Lobbying (federal, state, and grassroots) ♦ Local/municipal affairs ♦ Media outreach ♦ Research ♦ Speakers program ♦ Telecommunications services (mailing lists) |
| *CURRENT CONCERNS* | ♦ Combating terrorism (domestic and international) ♦ Jewish identity and continuity ♦ Middle East peace process ♦ Threats to separation of church and state |
| *PUBLICATIONS* | Publishes analyses of current issues |
| *NEWSLETTER* | *Congress Monthly* (6 times a year)<br>*Judaism* (quarterly)<br>*Radical Islamic Fundamentalism Update* (6 times a year) |
| *CONFERENCES* | Biennial convention<br>Annual conference of U.S. mayors in Jerusalem |
| *BOARD OF DIRECTORS* | Norman Redlich, chair; Fred Blum, Morton Bunis, Barbara Cullen, and Flora Perskie, vice chairs; Jack Rosen, president; Leona Chanin, Alvin Gray, Ira Hechler, John Heffer, Marvin M. Sirota, Alvin Slifka, Susan Jaffe Tane, and Michael Winderbaum, senior vice presidents; Bea Disman and Barry N. Winograd, co-treasurers; Barbara S. Starr, secretary; Susan Myers, corresponding secretary |
| *EFFECTIVENESS* | "In the most significant legal decision yet on the growing use of school vouchers, the Wisconsin Supreme Court ruled yesterday that the City of Milwaukee could spend taxpayer money to send pupils to parochial or other religious schools.<br><br>"Voting 4 to 2 to overturn a lower-court ruling, the state's high court said the Milwaukee Parental Choice Program did not violate Wisconsin's existing ban on spending state money for religious seminaries or the First Amendment's separation of church and state. The court said the program 'has a secular purpose' and 'will not have the primary effect of advancing religion.'...<br><br>"Civil libertarians, upset at what they considered a radical departure in court interpretation of the First Amendment, and teachers' unions, lamenting the ruling as a blow to public schools, vowed an appeal to the United States Supreme Court. Some legal scholars said the decision could form the basis of a test case for the Supreme Court on the extent to which government can support parental choice in using public money to buy a religious school education. |

"The Wisconsin court said United States Supreme Court decisions made clear that the Constitution was not 'violated every time money previously in the possession of a state is conveyed to a religious institution.'

"Quoting a 1971 United States Supreme Court ruling, the Wisconsin court said, 'The simplistic argument that every form of financial aid to church-sponsored activity violates the Religion Clauses was rejected long ago.'. . .

"Voucher programs are sprouting up around the country because of discontent with the public school systems, especially in urban areas that serve the poor. In such areas, the main alternative to public schools are those run by churches, and experts said that the Wisconsin decision, if repeated elsewhere, could remove the biggest obstacle to such plans. . . .

"Phil Baum, executive director of the American Jewish Congress, who was upset by the ruling, said he foresaw 'a possible landmark U.S. Supreme Court decision.' Mr. Baum said the High Court would soon be confronted with a fundamental choice: 'to preserve the principle that the Constitution imposes stringent and special restrictions on Government financing of religion—a policy which has allowed religion and religious liberty to flourish—or to embark on an uncharted course, and put at risk the religious liberty Americans enjoy.' " (*New York Times*, June 11, 1998)

"The Palestinian leader Yasir Arafat arrived here today for his own talks on Thursday with President Clinton, who is taking a much more aggressive role in the effort to break the Middle East stalemate. Rather than simply mediating, as he did last year, Mr. Clinton has begun presenting American proposals. But after the Netanyahu talks here, the Americans and Israelis have failed to agree on the overall size of the Israeli withdrawal and the number of phases, the officials said.

"Mr. Netanyahu and Mr. Arafat are likely to meet in the next two weeks, probably in Europe, at a session mediated by Secretary of State Madeleine K. Albright, the officials said, though they cautioned that nothing was settled.

"In an interview today and at a later news conference, Mr. Netanyahu said: 'I think we made some progress. There is more work to be done. It will probably be done in the next two weeks.'. . .

"In the interview today, Mr. Netanyahu said he and Mr. Clinton had 'cleared the air' over mutual charges of snubs and disrespect, which included the Prime Minister's meeting, as soon as he arrived in Washington on Monday, with Christian fundamentalists like the Rev. Jerry Falwell, who are strong political opponents of the President.

" 'We went to great pains to remove any vestiges of what the President called the "debris" of personal antagonism,' Mr. Netanyahu said. 'He distanced himself from some of these things, and Clinton went beyond that to try to re-establish a personal rapport again. My response was one word: "Sure" '

"Today a key American Jewish organization criticized the Prime Minister for his efforts to reach out to the Christian right. Phil Baum, executive director of the American Jewish Congress, said: 'The Prime Minister is a man of undoubted political skills. Nevertheless these meetings, with these people, at this time, under these circumstances, were a mistake.' "
(*New York Times*, January 22, 1998)

"The Anti-Defamation League and the American Jewish Congress will not take part in D.C. Mayor Marion Barry's 'Day of Dialogue' because they oppose the Nation of Islam's participation in what has been billed as a day of racial healing, officials of the groups said yesterday.

"Guila Franklin, executive director of the American Jewish Congress, had attended the mayor's organizational meeting, held last month at One Judiciary Square, and had agreed to serve on a planning committee for the Jan. 15 event. When she found out that Abdul Arif Muhammad of the Nation of Islam also was on the planning committee, Franklin said, her organization was 'forced to conclude we could not participate in this event with deep regret.'. . .

"Karen Kalish, president and founder of Operation Understanding, which works to improve African American-Jewish relations, said the event appears imperiled, not only because of the harsh words and harsh feelings that have been displayed since it was announced but also because of poor planning. . . . Franklin said the American Jewish Congress runs its own programs aimed at improving African American and Jewish relations and would participate in Barry's program but for the presence of the Nation of Islam.

" 'We welcome the opportunity to dialogue with groups that have respect for all people of other religions,' Franklin said. 'This was just not the type of dialogue we felt comfortable participating in.' " (*Washington Post*, January 7, 1997)

---

# POLITICAL ORIENTATION

Unavailable

# Anti-Defamation League (1913)

823 United Nations Plaza
New York, New York 10017
Phone: (212) 885-7700
Fax: (212) 867-0779

1100 Connecticut Avenue, NW
Suite 1020
Washington, D.C. 20036
Phone: (202) 452-8320
Fax: (202) 296-2371

Internet: http://www.adl.org

---

"To stop the defamation of the Jewish people and to secure justice and fair treatment for all citizens alike."

*PURPOSE*

---

400 total—200 professional; 200 support

*STAFF*

---

Abraham H. Foxman, national director. Foxman joined the Anti-Defamation League (ADL) in 1965 as assistant director of the law department. In 1968 he became head of ADL's Middle Eastern affairs. He held that post until 1973, when he became director of national leadership. Foxman was named associate national director in 1978 and national director in 1987. He earned a B.A. from City College of City University of New York and a J.D. from New York University School of Law. Foxman did graduate work in advanced Judaic studies at the Jewish Theological Seminary and in international economics at the New School for Social Research. He writes books and articles on domestic issues, foreign affairs, and the Holocaust. He also is a member of the United States Holocaust Memorial Council.

*DIRECTOR*

---

501(c)(3)

*TAX STATUS*

---

Fiscal year ending June 30, 1997—$43 million
F.Y. 1998—$45 million
Proposed F.Y. 1999—$46 million

*BUDGET*

---

Private contributions

*FUNDING SOURCES*

## SCOPE

Members: N/A

Branches/chapters: 28 U.S. satellite offices; international offices in Israel and Vienna

Affiliates: Anti-Defamation League Foundation; Leon and Marilyn Klinghoffer Memorial Foundation of the Anti-Defamation League; Braun Holocaust Institute; Jewish Foundation for Christian Rescuers/ADL; Hidden Child Foundation/ADL; William and Naomi Gorowitz Institute on Terrorism and Extremism; ADL: A World of Difference Institute

## PAC

None

## METHOD OF OPERATION

♦ Advertisements ♦ Awards program (Courage to Care Award, Distinguished Statesman Award, Hubert H. Humphrey First Amendment Freedoms Prize, Joseph Prize for Human Rights, Klinghoffer Award) ♦ Coalition forming ♦ Conferences/seminars ♦ Congressional testimony ♦ Curriculum development ♦ Exhibits ♦ Films/videos ♦ International activities ♦ Internet (Web site) ♦ Internships ♦ Legislative/regulatory monitoring (federal and state) ♦ Library/information clearinghouse ♦ Litigation ♦ Media outreach ♦ Monitoring of extremist groups ♦ Polling ♦ Research ♦ Speakers program ♦ Training and technical assistance (A Campus of Difference, A Workplace of Difference, A World of Difference, A Community of Difference)

## CURRENT CONCERNS

♦ Anti-Semitism ♦ Arab-Israeli relations ♦ Civil liberties ♦ Discrimination ♦ Extremism ♦ Hate crimes ♦ Hate in cyberspace ♦ Holocaust education ♦ Interfaith relations ♦ Israel ♦ Separation of church and state ♦ Terrorism

## PUBLICATIONS

The following is a list of sample publications:

*Annual Audit of Anti-Semitic Incidents*

*Anti-Semitism in America*

*Armed and Dangerous: Militias Take Aim at the Federal Government*

*Beyond the Bombing: The Militia Menace Grows*

*Beyond the White House Lawn: Current Perspectives on the Arab-Israeli Peace Process*

*Campus Kit: Countering Anti-Semitism, Racism and Extremist Propaganda*

*Confronting Anti-Semitism—Guidelines for Jewish Parents*

*Danger: Extremism—The Major Vehicles and Voices on America's Far-Right Fringe*

*Extremist Groups in the United States*

*Hate Groups in America: A Record of Bigotry and Violence*

*High-Tech Hate: Extremist Use of the Internet*

*Hitler's Apologists: The Anti-Semitic Propaganda of Holocaust "Revisionism"*

*The Israel Record*

*Jew Hatred as History*

*The Prejudice Book*

*Religion in the Public Schools: Guidelines for a Growing and Changing Phenomenon*

*The Religious Right: The Assault on Tolerance and Pluralism in America*
*The Skinhead International: A Worldwide Survey of Neo Nazi Skinheads*
*Toward Final Status: Pending Issues in Israeli-Palestinian Negotiations*
*Vigilante Justice Militias and "Common Law Court" Wage War Against the Government*

Also publishes videos, posters, and educational materials

---

*ADL On the Frontline* (6 times per year)
*Dimensions* (2 times per year)
*The Hidden Child Newspaper* (periodic)
*Interfaith Connections* (periodic)
*Law Enforcement Bulletin* (2 times per year)
*Terrorism Update* (4 times per year)

Also publishes regional newsletters

## NEWSLETTER

---

National Commission (annual)
Washington Leadership Conference (annual)

## CONFERENCES

---

Officers of the National Commission:
Howard P. Berkowitz, national chair; Abraham H. Foxman, national director; Peter T. Willner, associate national director; Meyer Eisenberg, Thomas C. Homburger, Judith Krupp, Lester Pollack, Alvin J. Rockoff, Robert G. Sugarman, vice chairs

Officers of the National Executive Committee:
Glen A. Tobias, chair; George E. Moss, vice chair; Robert H. Naftaly, treasurer; Murray Koppelman, assistant treasurer; Barbara B. Balser, secretary; I. Barry Mehler, assistant secretary

## BOARD OF DIRECTORS

---

"With the National Rifle Association's multi-billion dollar push last week for national acceptance, featuring Moses-turned-NRA president Charlton Heston, Jews across the country are sparring over what the real Moses would have said about gun ownership. . . .

" 'There is a consistent strain in Jewish history: that we have been safe and secure under democracy. The protection for us as a community has been strongest when democratic institutions are in place, and so we want to keep guns out of the hands of people who wish to overthrow those very institutions,' argues David Friedman, director of the Washington/Maryland regional office of the Anti-Defamation League." (*Long Island Jewish World,* June 12, 1998)

"The Anti-Defamation League has hailed the defeat of the Istook amendment as a significant and important victory for religious liberty.

" 'Americans of all faith can breathe a sigh of relief now that this unprecedented, unnecessary and divisive constitutional amendment has been defeated,' said Shai Goldstein, executive director of the ADL's New Jersey Region. 'Rep. Istook's amendment would have taken us back to the days when our public schools forced a single religion on students of myriad faiths and when our government sent the message that it valued one religion over all others.' " (*MetroWest Jewish News,* June 11, 1998)

## EFFECTIVENESS

"Boys and Girls Clubs of America (B&GCA) and the Anti-Defamation League (ADL) announce they have joined forces to introduce a multifaceted diversity program designed to reduce bigotry and prejudice. Based upon ADL's highly successful *A World of Difference* program, which has been used in public, private and parochial school systems around the country for more than 12 years, the new ADL and B&GCA initiative will be pilot-tested in some 50 Boys and Girls Clubs over the next two years and then rolled out nationally by the year 2000. In April, First Lady Hillary Rodham Clinton visited the Madison Square Boys & Girls Club in New York to participate in the first pilot session of this new initiative." (*Pure News USA,* June 1998)

"Located at the junction where the countries of East meet West, the ADL office base in Vienna, Austria, serves two functions for those Jews left in Eastern Europe. It acts as the ears for those Jews suffering from anti-Semitism and serves as their voice, said the office's director, [Marta S. Halpert]. . . .

" 'The Slovak government tried to tell the children in the school that the Holocaust was not so bad in Slovakia,' she [Halpert] said.

"Once she heard what the government-bought textbooks said, Halpert went into action. At a press conference where the Slovakian Prime Minister spoke, Halpert brought up the problem of the false history books. Since Slovakian officials need to impress Western Europe with a sense of democracy, the question forced him to promise to take the book off the shelves." (*Jewish Voice,* April 1998)

"Anti-Jewish activity has declined to its lowest level since 1989, the Anti-Defamation League said Wednesday in its annual report. . . .

"The latest worry for the ADL, though, is the Internet, where the number of hate sites has more than doubled since 1996, the group said.

" 'With the stroke of a mouse, they can send the same message to millions, whereas before they had to mimeograph it,' said David Lehrer, director of the League's Pacific Southwest region.

" 'The Internet is a hot issue, and a serious, growing problem,' [William] Rothchild [director of ADL's Palm Beach County Regional Office] said. 'What the ADL has done in the short term is to create its own web page: www.adl.org. Through that page, we offer up articles and respond to the anti-Semitic web pages, which we monitor 24 hours a day.' " (*Boca Raton News,* March 12, 1998)

"The Anti-Defamation League—a civil rights organization founded in 1913 to oppose anti-Semitism, bigotry, and hate crimes—is frequently called in to mediate disputes, such as the case of a major retailer who rescinded a job offer to an observant Jew after the new employee told company officials he couldn't work on the Sabbath. The ADL crafted an agreement, and the person got the job.

"In another case, an employee harassed by co-workers who put anti-Semitic messages and cartoons on his desk called for help. The ADL contacted the New York City Human Rights Commission, which ordered the company to pay a monetary settlement and fire the co-workers responsible for the harassment. Under federal anti-discrimination laws, employers are required to maintain a work environment free of harassment, intimidation, and insult." (*Los Angeles Times*, January 24, 1998)

Unavailable

# *POLITICAL ORIENTATION*

# Christian Coalition (1989)

1801 Sara Drive
Suite L
Chesapeake, Virginia 23320
Phone: (804) 424-2630
Fax: (804) 424-9068

227 Massachusetts Avenue, NE
Suite 1001
Washington, D.C. 20002
Phone: (202) 547-3600
Fax: (202) 543-2978

Internet: http://www.cc.org

| | |
|---|---|
| **PURPOSE** | "To educate and mobilize people of faith on issues that impact families." |
| **STAFF** | 65 total—15 professional; 50 support; plus 20 part-time, 5–10 interns annually, and thousands of volunteers |
| **DIRECTOR** | Randy Tate, executive director. Tate served as a Washington state representative from 1989–1995 and in the U.S. House of Representatives from 1995–1997 before taking his current position with the Christian Coalition. He received an A.A. from Tacoma Community College in 1986 and a B.A. from Western Washington University in 1990. |
| **TAX STATUS** | 501(c)(4) |
| **BUDGET** | 1997—$17 million<br>1998—$20 million<br>Proposed 1999—Unavailable |
| **FUNDING SOURCES** | Individuals, 95 percent; other, 5 percent |
| **SCOPE** | Members: 2 million individuals<br>Branches/chapters: More than 1,000 state chapters<br>Affiliate: 49 state affiliates |
| **PAC** | None |

◆ Advertisements ◆ Awards program ◆ Coalition forming ◆ Conferences/seminars ◆ Congressional testimony ◆ Congressional voting analysis ◆ Direct action ◆ Films/video/audiotapes ◆ Grassroots organizing ◆ Initiative/referendum campaigns ◆ Internet (databases, electronic bulletin boards, E-mail alerts, Web site) ◆ Internships ◆ Legislative/regulatory monitoring (federal and state) ◆ Lobbying (federal, state, and grassroots) ◆ Media outreach ◆ Participation in regulatory proceedings (federal and state) ◆ Prayer ◆ Product merchandising ◆ Professional development services ◆ Research ◆ Speakers program ◆ Telecommunications services (fax-on-demand: 757-424-9068, mailing lists) ◆ Training and technical assistance ◆ Television and radio production (monthly satellite broadcast to 250 downlink centers nationwide) ◆ Voter registration ◆ Voting records

## METHOD OF OPERATION

◆ Choice in education ◆ Family tax relief ◆ Protecting the unborn ◆ Religious freedom ◆ Voter education and mobilization

## CURRENT CONCERNS

*Christian Coalition Congressional Scorecard* (semiannually)
*Contract with the American Family*

Also publishes voter guides

## PUBLICATIONS

*Action Alert* (weekly)
*Christian Coalition Insider* (bimonthly)
*Religious Rights Watch* (monthly)

## NEWSLETTER

Road to Victory (annual convention in Washington, D.C.)
Grassroots Activist Training Seminars (weekly)

## CONFERENCES

M.G. "Pat" Robertson, chairman; Donald Hodel, president; Randy Tate, executive director; Richard Weinhold, secretary; Kenneth Hill, chief operating officer

Other members:
◆ Roberta Combs ◆ Billy McCormack ◆ Ralph Reed Jr.

## BOARD OF DIRECTORS

"The factory in Chesapeake is the headquarters of the Christian Coalition; and the factory boss is Randy Tate, a breezy 32-year-old who spins a pen in the air when he clinches an argument. As executive director of the Christian Coalition, Mr. Tate has a big role in deciding which political issues its 2 million supporters should care about. Then he puts the phone banks and envelope-stuffing machinery to work. Then his former colleagues [in Congress] pay attention. . . .

## EFFECTIVENESS

"Besides pressuring Congress, Mr. Tate has increased the Christian Coalition's membership. He has also stepped up efforts to organize and train those members. In February he announced a scheme to create activist cells in 100,000 churches by 2000. He promised to distribute 45 million voter guides this year, a record for a mid-term election. On the eve of the polls, Coalition supporters will get a phone call with a taped message from Mr. Tate; the next day many will be driven to the voting booths by Coalition activists. This could well decide the outcome of the extremely close contest between the parties for the control of the House. Prosperity is likely to depress turnout among mainstream folk, so activists will be decisive.

"All of which calls into question the conventional wisdom of the past year that the Coalition's influence is declining." (*The Economist*, July 11, 1998)

"The Christian Coalition, headed by former presidential candidate Pat Robertson and a pair of politically well-known co-[directors], former Rep. Randy Tate, R-Wash., and Donald Hodel, a former Reagan administration Cabinet member, is seen as a group that works within the system.

"One business lobbyist and former staffer said Tate 'really understands as a former member that you can't take a hard line all the time. Randy Tate has first-hand experience that if you're too conservative for your district, you lose. He brings a sense of realism to the table." (*National Journal's Congress Daily*, July 7, 1998)

## POLITICAL ORIENTATION

"But the success of gambling has also engendered an anti-gambling movement in parts of the country that could be problematic for politicians with strong ties to social and religious conservatives. . . .

"Anti-gambling fervor does not approach abortion or prayer in public schools as a cause that excites the passions of religious conservatives, but it is attracting attention from some of their prominent Republican leaders. Gambling's most vocal critics include Gary Bauer, head of the Family Research Council, who is thinking about running for president, and James C. Dobson, president of Focus on the Family, who not only is an increasingly important player in GOP politics but also a Republican-appointed member of a national commission that is studying the impact of the growth of gambling.

" 'There is definitely an anti-gambling movement' said Charles H. Cunningham, director of national operations for the Christian Coalition. 'It is not organized at all levels or in all states, but there is a movement out there. . . . It's heating up in certain states where the politicians have not gotten the message.'. . ." (*Washington Post*, July 12, 1998)

"[Randy] Tate views his Christian Coalition as a workhorse of the religious right, one willing to 'go out and send postcards, run the radio ads, send the mail, signs the petitions and do our part.' " (*Gannett News Service*, June 25, 1998)

"The [Christian] Coalition [is] the largest group of religious conservatives in the nation." (*New York Times*, June 12, 1997)

# Focus on the Family (1977)

8605 Explorer Drive
Colorado Springs, Colorado 80920
Phone: (719) 531-3400
Fax: (719) 548-4525
Internet: http://www.family.org

| | |
|---|---|
| "To cooperate with the Holy Spirit in disseminating the Gospel of Jesus Christ to as many people as possible, and, specifically, to accomplish that objective by helping to preserve traditional values and the institution of the family." | **PURPOSE** |
| 1,400 total—1,250 regular; 150 temporary; plus 1,100 volunteers per year | **STAFF** |
| James C. Dobson, chairman and president. Before founding Focus on the Family, Dobson was associate professor of pediatrics at the University of Southern California School of Medicine and served on the attending staff of Childrens Hospital of Los Angeles. He has served on many government panels covering such issues as juvenile justice and delinquency prevention, tax reform, pornography, teen pregnancy prevention, and child and family welfare. Dobson is the author of many books and is heard on internationally syndicated radio programs. He earned a Ph.D. at the University of Southern California. | **DIRECTOR** |
| 501(c)(3) | **TAX STATUS** |
| 1997—$112 million<br>1998—$116 million<br>Proposed 1999—$116 million | **BUDGET** |
| Donations, 90 percent; sales, 10 percent | **FUNDING SOURCES** |
| Members: 5 million on mailing list; 2.4 million active<br>Branches/chapters: N/A<br>Affiliates: Family Research Council, a 501(c)(3) organization based in Washington, D.C.; 39 independent 501(c)(3) state family policy councils | **SCOPE** |
| None | **PAC** |

## METHOD OF OPERATION

♦ Advertisements ♦ Awards program ♦ Boycotts ♦ Coalition forming ♦ Conferences/seminars ♦ Congressional testimony ♦ Congressional voting analysis ♦ Films/video/audiotapes ♦ Grassroots organizing ♦ Information clearinghouse ♦ Initiative/referendum campaigns ♦ International activities ♦ Internet (Web site) ♦ Internships ♦ Library services for members only ♦ Media outreach ♦ Product merchandising ♦ Research ♦ Scholarships

## CURRENT CONCERNS

♦ Permanence of marriage ♦ Preeminence of evangelism ♦ Relationship of Church, family and government ♦ Pro-life issues ♦ Sanctity of human life ♦ Value of children

## PUBLICATIONS

Produces films, videos, and radio and television programs

## NEWSLETTER

*Breakaway* (monthly magazine)
*Brio* (monthly magazine)
*Citizen Action Alert* (weekly fax letter)
*Citizen* (monthly magazine)
*Clubhouse* (monthly magazine)
*Clubhouse, Jr.* (monthly magazine)
*Family News From Dr. James Dobson* (monthly)
*Focus on the Family* (monthly magazine)
*Heartlink* (monthly)
*Pastor's Family* (monthly magazine)
*Physician* (monthly magazine)
*Plugged In* (monthly)
*Single Parent Family* (monthly magazine)
*Teacher In Focus*

## CONFERENCES

Inspirational seminars for pastors
Professional/inspirational conferences for attorneys and physicians
Training seminars for public policy involvement

## BOARD OF DIRECTORS

James C. Dobson, chairman and president; Ted Engstrom, vice chairman; Bobb Biehl, treasurer; Lee Eaton, secretary

Other members:
♦ Patrick P. Caruana ♦ Shirley M. Dobson ♦ Robert E. Hamby ♦ Kay Coles James ♦ Elsa D. Prince ♦ Michael F. Roberts ♦ Adrian Rogers ♦ Anthony Wauterlek

"His [Dr. James C. Dobson's] radio and TV broadcasts are heard or seen by 28 million people a week. A core audience of 4 million listens to his *Focus on the Family* radio show every day. That gives him a greater reach than either Jerry Falwell or Pat Robertson at the height of their appeal. Dobson's most popular books have sold more than 16 million copies, and his other tracts and pamphlets have sold millions more. His organization, Focus on the Family, has a budget five times the size of the Christian Coalition's and gets so much mail, it has its own zip code. His mailing list of over two million is one of the most potent organizing religious tools in the world. . . .

"Most of the Focus operation, which receives up to 12,000 letters, calls and E-mails every day, is occupied with 'constituent service.' In one pile of counseling requests at a random Focus cubicle, a long-distance trucker asks how to keep his family together when he is always gone; a woman deals with a miscarriage; a divorced man asks if it OK to remarry. Prototype responses, drawn from Dobson's vast output of advice, guide counselors. All incoming letters are stored by computer, so the next time these people write, the dialog will pick up where it left off. Focus does not just answer mail, it maintains relationships. Some hard cases are referred to licensed counselors. Some people are offered temporary financial help. They deal with one or two suicide threats a week.

"Dobson's reach grows each day. A recent meeting of the Focus 'cabinet'—Dobson plus his senior executives—there were reports on the translation of Focus broadcasts into Zulu. On how three Central and South American countries were putting Focus abstinence material into their public schools. On how *Adventures in Odyssey* is now one of the top five radio programs in Zimbabwe. On how 500 state-owned radio stations in China are about to begin the Focus broadcast." (*U.S. News & World Report*, May 4, 1998)

"The boycott against the Walt Disney Co.—one of the most audacious cultural crusades yet taken on by the nation's Christian conservatives—broadened considerably yesterday when James Dobson's Focus on the Family urged its 4 million contributors to stop buying anything that carries the Disney name.

"The Southern Baptist Convention, the Catholic League, the American Family Association, and now Dobson's group—the influential radio, print and video empire based in Colorado Springs—have embarked on a mission to persuade American parents to deny their children Winnie the Pooh, 'The Lion King,' Mickey Mouse and all of the contemporary icons of the globe's foremost purveyor of children's entertainment. No one, not even the most outraged Disney critics, is confident the boycott will wreck the company's bottom line or transform the company's behavior. . . .

"No, this boycott is about something far bigger than even Mickey. It's about God, contemporary life and the shape of American culture. It is, in the words of political scientist Benjamin Barber, about 'Jihad vs. McWorld,' the battle between fundamentalist faith and global corporations that are growing more powerful than many nations." (*Washington Post*, August 28, 1997)

# POLITICAL ORIENTATION

"But the success of gambling has also engendered an anti-gambling movement in parts of the country that could be problematic for politicians with strong ties to social and religious conservatives. . . .

"Anti-gambling fervor does not approach abortion or prayer in public schools as a cause that excites the passions of religious conservatives, but it is attracting attention from some of their prominent Republican leaders. Gambling's most vocal critics include Gary Bauer, head of the Family Research Council, who is thinking about running for president, and James C. Dobson, president of Focus on the Family, who not only is an increasingly important player in GOP politics but also a Republican-appointed member of a national commission that is studying the impact of the growth of gambling." (*Washington Post*, July 12, 1998)

"[Dr. James C. Dobson] . . . is the central figure in conservative Christianity." (*U.S. News & World Report*, May 4, 1998)

# The Interfaith Alliance (1994)

1012 14th Street, NW
Suite 700
Washington, D.C. 20005
Phone: (202) 639-6370
Fax: (202) 639-6375
Internet: http://www.tialliance.org

---

"Through shared religious principles of responsibility for ourselves and each other, common good for the community, and the dignity of all human beings, the Interfaith Alliance is building a grassroots, mainstream movement based on active and informed civic participation."

**PURPOSE**

---

9 total—8 professional; 1 support; plus 2 part-time professionals; 2 volunteers; 3 interns

**STAFF**

---

Rev. Dr. C. Welton Gaddy, executive director. Gaddy has more than thirty years of experience as a national and community activist, pastor, and writer. His books include *Faith and Politics: What's a Christian to Do?* and *Coming Home: For Those Who Dream of a New Church.* He has served on the boards of the Alliance of Baptists and Americans United for the Separation of Church and State. He has a master of theology and a doctorate of philosophy from Southern Baptist Theological Seminary. Before joining the staff of The Interfaith Alliance, he served as pastor of Northminster (Baptist) Church in Monroe, Louisiana.

**DIRECTOR**

---

501(c)(4)

**TAX STATUS**

---

1997—$1.2 million
1998—$1.5 million
Proposed 1999—$1.8 million

**BUDGET**

---

Membership dues, 94 percent; individuals, 4 percent; corporate donations, 2 percent

**FUNDING SOURCES**

---

Members: 80,000 individuals
Branches/chapters: 100 chapters
Affiliates: N/A

**SCOPE**

---

| | |
|---|---|
| *PAC* | None |
| *METHOD OF OPERATION* | ◆ Coalition forming ◆ Congressional voting analysis ◆ Grassroots organizing ◆ Internet (E-mail alerts, Web site) ◆ Internships ◆ Legislative/regulatory monitoring (federal and state) ◆ Lobbying (grassroots) ◆ Media outreach ◆ Research ◆ Voter registration |
| *CURRENT CONCERNS* | ◆ Civil rights ◆ Poverty ◆ Promoting the positive role of religion in society ◆ Public education ◆ Religious freedom |
| *PUBLICATIONS* | None |
| *NEWSLETTER* | *The Light* (quarterly) |
| *CONFERENCES* | Annual Chapter Conference (Spring in Washington, D.C.) |
| *BOARD OF DIRECTORS* | J. Philip Wogaman, president; Denise T. Davidoff, Frederick Calhoun James, and David J. Gelfand, vice presidents at large; Leonard B. Jackson, secretary; David Currie, treasurer<br><br>Other members:<br>◆ Amos Brown ◆ Joan Brown Campbell ◆ Maher H. Hathout ◆ Arthur Hertzberg ◆ Robert H. Meneilly ◆ Jack Moline ◆ Albert M. Pennybacker ◆ Diane M. Porter ◆ Meg A. Riley ◆ A. Knighton Stanley ◆ John M. Swomley ◆ Gardner C. Taylor ◆ Foy Valentine ◆ Herbert D. Valentine |
| *EFFECTIVENESS* | "Walter Cronkite is coming out of the ideological closet. The former CBS anchor has unleashed a full-throated attack on the Christian Coalition as a 'genuinely radical movement known as the religious right wing.'<br><br>"He has signed a fund-raising letter for the Interfaith Alliance, a religiously based group that claims 40,000 members in 36 states. Cronkite's letter calls the Christian Coalition 'lavishly funded' with 'harsh right-wing views' and a 'militant ideology . . . one that encourages deep hostility toward those who disagree with its agenda.' The letter underscores Cronkite's decision to use the credibility he accumulated over five decades in the news business to bolster a fund-raising appeal that, like most such appeals, is penned in hyperbolic language.<br><br>" 'I'm obviously dropping my impartiality here,' Cronkite said in an interview this week. 'This is a subject I could not handle if I was going back on the air. I do not believe I'm in any way compromising my journalistic role.' |

"Keith Appell, a spokesman for the Christian Coalition, said: 'We raise and distribute $750,000 for burned-out African American churches, and we get attacked by liberals. Go figure. We're trying to hold a meaningful dialogue based on mutual respect, and activities like this really don't help the process.'

"Cronkite has taken on the role of public advocate before. He became a leading spokesman last year for an advocacy group pushing for free air time for presidential candidates. That, however, was an organization with bipartisan backing.

"Cronkite says he became strongly interested in the religious right after interviewing Ralph Reed, the coalition's executive director, for a Discovery Channel report a couple of years ago.

"In the letter, Cronkite urges recipients to say 'no' to Reed and coalition founder Pat Robertson. 'I work very hard at being a Christian,' he writes. 'And certainly, the Christian Coalition does not speak for me.' " (*Washington Post*, March 7, 1997)

---

"a group of ministers formed as an alternative to the Christian Coalition" (*Washington Post*, March 9, 1997)

## POLITICAL ORIENTATION

# Interfaith Center on Corporate Responsibility (1971)

475 Riverside Drive
Room 550
New York, New York 10115
Phone: (212) 870-2295
Fax: (212) 870-2023

**PURPOSE**

"To address issues of corporate social responsibility with our resources, particularly our investments . . . [and] to work ecumenically for justice in and through economic structures and for stewardship of the earth and its resources."

**STAFF**

10 total—7 professional; 3 support

**DIRECTOR**

Timothy Smith, executive director. Smith is a graduate of the University of Toronto and holds an M. Div. degree from Union Theological Seminary in New York.

**TAX STATUS**

501(c)(3)

**BUDGET**

1998—$930,000
Proposed 1999—Unavailable

**FUNDING SOURCES**

Institutional memberships, 55 percent; foundation and individual contributions, 20 percent; special events, 15 percent; publications sales, 10 percent

**SCOPE**

Members: 250 Roman Catholic orders and dioceses and 25 Protestant and Jewish agencies and denominations; ICCR members hold $90 billion in their various investment portfolios
Branches/chapters: N/A
Affiliate: ICCR is "related to the National Council of Churches"

**PAC**

None

| | |
|---|---|
| ◆ Alternative investments ◆ Coalition forming ◆ Congressional testimony ◆ Dialogue with companies ◆ Divestment of stocks and bonds ◆ Legislative/regulatory monitoring ◆ Library/information clearinghouse ◆ Litigation ◆ Mediation ◆ Prayer vigils ◆ Preparation of Securities and Exchange Commission briefs ◆ Public hearings and investigations ◆ Research ◆ Selective purchasing ◆ Shareholder resolutions (coordinates members' shareholder resolutions, but does not itself own stock and therefore does not act in its own name) ◆ Solicitation of votes by institutional investors ◆ Working with business on task forces related to specific issues | *METHOD OF OPERATION* |
| ◆ Alternative investments ◆ Bank community reinvestment responsibilities ◆ CERES Principles on the Environment ◆ Chemical and biological warfare ◆ Conservation ◆ Environmental issues ◆ Equal employment opportunity ◆ Human rights and bank lending ◆ Infant formula abuse ◆ International debt ◆ Investment in Burma ◆ Investment in Northern Ireland ◆ Landmines ◆ Maquiladoras ◆ Minority economic development ◆ Nuclear arms race ◆ Pharmaceutical sales overseas ◆ Sales to repressive countries ◆ South Africa ◆ Space warfare ◆ Standards of global conduct for companies ◆ Sweatshops ◆ Tobacco ◆ Toxic wastes | *CURRENT CONCERNS* |
| *The Conscientious Investors Guide to Socially-Responsible Mutual and Money Market Funds and Investment Services*<br>*Corporate Responsibility Challenges, Spring 1998*<br>*Guide to Church Alternative Investment Funds*<br>*Proxy Resolution Book 1998* | *PUBLICATIONS* |
| *Alternative Investment Newspackets* (quarterly)<br>*Corporate Examiner* (10 times a year)<br>*Corporate Examiner Briefs* (four-page paper on corporate responsibility issues included in the *Corporate Examiner*)<br>*Subscriber Service for Institutions* (bimonthly) | *NEWSLETTER* |
| None | *CONFERENCES* |
| Connie Tohomine, chairperson; Frunh Coleman, vice chairperson; Carol Wester, treasurer<br><br>Each ICCR member agency may name up to four representatives to the ICCR governing board. ICCR's twelve-member executive committee is composed of representatives from member groups and the three officers of the governing board. | *BOARD OF DIRECTORS* |

## EFFECTIVENESS

" 'Nobody doesn't like Sara Lee' has long been one of the catchiest lines in advertising. That is because hardly anyone knew the maker of cheesecake and bagels also sold tobacco. . . ."

"Yesterday [April 7, 1998], Sara Lee Corp. announced plans to sell its cut-tobacco unit—a highly profitable and, until recently, highly invisible business. . . .

"But it wasn't until the American Medical Association released a list of tobacco companies in 1996 that most investors and antitobacco activists realized Sara Lee was in the business of cut tobacco, the kind used in roll-your-own smokes. . . .

". . . [W]hat brought attention to roll-your-own tobacco was its appearance in the movie 'Pulp Fiction.' Sara Lee's Drum brand was featured prominently, fueling a cult of young users. Then Drum ads began to appear in various alternative publications, including New York's *Village Voice*. . . .

"Ads like this one made Sara Lee a target of antitobacco activists. The Interfaith Center on Corporate Responsibility appeared at Sara Lee's annual shareholder meetings in 1996 and 1997 to ask the company to get out of tobacco. Sara Lee recommended against voting for the group's 1997 resolution, but Michael Crosby, the center's program coordinator, said he found Sara Lee almost 'embarrassed' at owning a tobacco company." (*Wall Street Journal*, April 8, 1998)

"The SEC in late September recommended a package of rule changes containing provisions intended to allow shareholders access to the proxy process without unnecessarily burdening companies with irrelevant proposals. The reaction? Neither side is happy.

"Investor groups representing churches, unions and public employees, along with a philanthropic foundation, say the proposal would unfairly prevent them from bringing to the attention of management and other shareholders important social issues relevant to companies. . . .

" 'We are very concerned that these new rules will be a crippling blow to shareholder advocates,' said Timothy Smith of the Interfaith Center on Corporate Responsibility, which represents 275 religious organizations with $80 billion to invest." (*Washington Post*, October 28, 1997)

"Pension funds, endowments and social-issue groups have united to oppose the Securities and Exchange Commission's effort to revamp rules governing how shareholders can raise management issues at company annual meetings.

"The SEC proposed the changes in September to balance activists' ability to present resolutions and companies' prerogative to limit the scope and number of shareholder proposals. But the coalition, led by the Social Investment Forum, maintains the proposal would further restrict shareholder rights. . . .

". . . 'The SEC proposal is a crippling blow to shareholder advocacy,' said Tim Smith, executive director of the Interfaith Center on Corporate Responsibility." (*Wall Street Journal*, October 23, 1997)

"In this sprawling town [Ciudad Juárez, Mexico] of electronics and auto-parts plants across the border from El Paso, General Motors Corp. is helping thousands of its workers buy their first homes, complete with indoor plumbing and electricity.

"By the end of 1999, GM, now the largest private employer in Mexico, aims to help build 7,000 homes for its workers to ease the country's stubborn housing shortage.

"But what began as an effort at good corporate citizenship seems to have drawn more controversy than praise. Rather than holding GM's housing program up as an example, corporate-ethics advocates have instead criticized the auto maker for not raising its wages in Mexico.

"Like many companies, GM pays its Mexican workers a tiny fraction of what its U.S. workers receive. The Interfaith Center on Corporate Responsibility, a coalition of religious shareholders, complains the program is still unaffordable to most workers and benefits too few." *(Wall Street Journal,* June 20, 1997)

"Minnesota Mining & Manufacturing's outdoor advertising unit 3M Media has agreed to eliminate tobacco advertising from its billboards by the end of 1998. . . . 3M Media, which was responding to a petition by the Interfaith Center on Corporate Responsibility, said its decision was due to the 'public perception of tobacco' as well as the fact that 3M is a major player in the health-care industry." *(Wall Street Journal,* May 3, 1996)

Unavailable

## POLITICAL ORIENTATION

# National Conference of Catholic Bishops/United States Catholic Conference (1966)

3211 Fourth Street, NE
Washington, D.C. 20017
Phone: (202) 541-3000
Fax: (202) 541-3129
http://www.nccbuscc.org

| | |
|---|---|
| **PURPOSE** | The National Conference of Catholic Bishops (NCCB) and the United States Catholic Conference (USCC) are organizations of the American Catholic hierarchy. "The NCCB and USCC are separate organizations—the NCCB focuses on internal concerns of the Church, and the USCC carries forward the Church's work in society." |
| **STAFF** | 400 total |
| **DIRECTOR** | Monsignor Dennis Schnurr, general secretary. A priest of the Diocese of Sioux City, Schnurr studied at Gregorian University, Rome. He also earned a doctorate in canon law at Catholic University of America. |
| **TAX STATUS** | 501(c)(3) |
| **BUDGET** | 1998—$20 million<br>Proposed 1999—Approximately $20 million |
| **FUNDING SOURCES** | Dioceses of the United States on a per capita basis |
| **SCOPE** | Members: 385 active and retired U.S. Catholic bishops<br>Branches/chapters: N/A<br>Affiliates: N/A |
| **PAC** | None |

## METHOD OF OPERATION

♦ Awards programs ♦ Congressional testimony ♦ Educational and cate-chetical ministry ♦ Films/video/audiotapes ♦ Grantmaking ♦ Grassroots organizing ♦ International activities ♦ Internet (Web site) ♦ Legisla-tive/regulatory monitoring (federal) ♦ Library/information clearing-house ♦ Litigation ♦ Lobbying (federal) ♦ Media outreach ♦ Movie and television reviews ♦ Participation in regulatory proceedings (federal) ♦ Pastoral letters ♦ Refugee resettlement ♦ Television and radio production ♦ Voluntary relief services

## CURRENT CONCERNS

♦ Agriculture ♦ Capital punishment ♦ Catholic doctrine, worship, evan-gelization, and religious education ♦ Disabled persons ♦ Economic justice ♦ Elderly ♦ Energy ♦ Health ♦ Hispanics ♦ Human rights ♦ Immigration reform ♦ Poverty ♦ Prolife support ♦ Women in society and in the Church ♦ Workers' rights

## PUBLICATIONS

The following is a sample list of publications:
*The American Catholic Heritage*
*Catechism of the Catholic Church*
*Constitution on the Church*
*The Complete Parallel Bible*
*Doctrinal Responsibilities*
*Directory for the Application of Principles and Norms on Ecumenism*
*Directory for the Life and Ministry of Priests*
*Educating for Christian Maturity*
*Formation and Development for Catholic School Teachers* (3 volumes)
*Go and Make Disciples*
*The Gospel on Campus*
*The Harvest of Justice is Sown in Peace*
*Holy Bible: NRSV Catholic Edition*
*In Support of Catholic Elementary and Secondary Schools*
*In the Service of Life*
*Lectionary for Masses with Children*
*Letter to Families From Pope John Paul II*
*A Manual for Bishops*
*On Catholic Universities*
*On Life and Love: A Guide to Catholic Teaching on Marriage and Family*
*Program of Priestly Formation* (4th edition)
*Renewing the Face of the Earth: A Resource for Parishes*
*The Rite of Confirmation*
*Santo Domingo Conclusions*
*Stewardship: A Disciple's Response*
*The Teaching Ministry of the Diocesan Bishop*
*To Be A Christian Steward*
*Value and Virtue*
*Young Adult Ministry Resources*

Also offers video and audiotapes

| | |
|---|---|
| *NEWSLETTER* | Publishes numerous newsletters sent by various departments to their church constituents |
| *CONFERENCES* | Annual Assembly (in November, Washington, D.C.) |
| *BOARD OF DIRECTORS* | Administration Board composed of 50 bishops throughout the United States |
| *EFFECTIVENESS* | "Attorney General Janet Reno decided yesterday that the Justice Department will not use federal drug-control laws to punish physicians who help their dying patients commit suicide under a fledgling Oregon law. |

"Attorney General Janet Reno decided yesterday that the Justice Department will not use federal drug-control laws to punish physicians who help their dying patients commit suicide under a fledgling Oregon law.

"The decision means that Oregon doctors no longer risk having the government revoke their ability to write prescriptions if they prescribe lethal doses to terminally ill people under the state's assisted-suicide law, the only one of its kind in the nation. Reno's action effectively overrules the federal Drug Enforcement Administration (DEA), which had concluded last year that Oregon physicians who helped their patients die were flouting the nation's Controlled Substances Act. . . .

"Richard Doerflinger, associate director for policy development for the National Conference of Catholic Bishops' Secretariat for Pro-Life Activities, said Reno's decision was an 'enormous contradiction' to the Clinton administration's recent move to use the same drug laws to block the legalized use of marijuana for medical purposes in California.

" 'My fear is this ruling will have the effect of encouraging many more doctors to assist suicides in Oregon,' Doerflinger said." (*Washington Post*, June 6, 1998)

"With the stock market roaring to new highs, more mutual-fund companies are offering what they call 'socially responsible' investments.

"It's . . . a mutual-fund style with a strong political element, usually one tailored to people whose politics can be broadly described as 'liberal' or 'progressive.' Defense contractors, gambling companies and alcohol producers are out. Companies that stress racial and gender diversity and other such causes are in.

"Peter Kinder, president of Kinder, Lydenberg, Domini & Co., an investment-management company specializing in socially responsible portfolios, is unabashed about what motivates the average investor looking to put some money into these funds. 'There's an undeniable political element to socially responsible investing,' Mr. Kinder says.

"If there's one framework to follow for social investing, Mr. Kinder says, it's a report that came out of a 1992 National Conference of Catholic Bishops called 'Socially Responsible Investment Guidelines.' The report frowns on investing in companies that profit off the usual activities considered to be vices by the social investing crowd. Mr. Kinder wrote in a recent article on the matter that the guidelines provide the 'finest, [most] concise statement on social investing so far written.' " (*Wall Street Journal*, February 12, 1998)

"An ad hoc committee of the National Conference of Catholic Bishops is studying whether to recommend bringing back meatless Fridays for the faithful. The first mention of the idea, at the bishops' meeting in Washington this fall, aroused two common reactions: Conservatives applauded; liberals hooted.

"Neither was particularly pretty. Many well-meaning Catholics lament the loss of observances and rituals, rules and regulations—at least those backed by the threat of hell fire. On radio talk shows and at coffee shops, people worked themselves up into misty-eyed nostalgia over the good old days of discipline and fear, when many Catholics spent more time making sure they did not chew the communion wafer than contemplating God's presence in the sacrament.

"On the other side, many a liberal Catholic called the bishops' idea laughable. 'This is the sort of thing that makes us look foolish,' one told me. Others thought there were more important jobs at hand than reviving dead customs: feeding the poor, freeing the captives, ordaining women. Other critics favor practices and observances that embody faith, such as the sacraments, so long as these are based in scripture and early Christian history. 'The ritual we need has nothing to do with asceticism,' said John Dwyer, a church historian and theologian at St. Bernard's Institute of Rochester, N.Y. After all, Jesus did ridicule fasting and criticized most religious law.

"Actually, there was a third reaction. The bishops were baffled that this highly preliminary proposal drew so much attention. While some of it came in the form of gag lines from comedians, most of the publicity merely indicated our fascination with religious ritual in an age that has relatively little." (*Washington Post*, December 7, 1997)

---

"The National Right to Life Committee and Senator John McCain are usually allies, joined in their opposition to abortion. But in an odd twist in the battle over campaign financing that shows how important the current system is to interest groups, the committee has been challenging the Senator, even belittling any Presidential ambitions he holds.

"Mr. McCain, the leading Senate Republican sponsor of finance overhaul legislation, has taken the campaign against him and his bill so seriously that he has appealed to the nation's Roman Catholic bishops to argue that a Catholic can be both an opponent of abortion and an advocate of legislation to overhaul campaign finance laws.

"The committee, which has also run advertisements criticizing other members of Congress, has replied to the bishops in an open letter of its own. . . .

"While each side now says it has drawn some individual support, the National Conference of Catholic Bishops has not taken a stand on campaign finance overhaul and does not plan to, said a spokeswoman, Sister Mary Ann Walsh.

" 'We're more likely to take positions on issues such as welfare reform and health care, more related to people's needs than to the electoral process,' she added." (*New York Times*, March 26, 1998)

## POLITICAL ORIENTATION

# National Council of the Churches of Christ in the U.S.A. (1950)

475 Riverside Drive
New York, New York 10115
Phone: (212) 870-2227
Fax: (212) 870-2030

110 Maryland Avenue, NE
Washington, D.C. 20002
Phone: (202) 544-2350
Fax: (202) 543-1297

Internet: news@NCCCUSA.org *or* http://www.nccusa.org

## PURPOSE

"To be a community through which churches can make visible their unity given in Christ and can work together responsibly in witness and service."

## STAFF

350 total

## DIRECTOR

The Reverend Dr. Joan B. Campbell, general secretary. Ordained in 1980, Campbell has standing as a minister both in the Christian Church (Disciples of Christ) and the American Baptist Churches in the U.S.A. Prior to her election as general secretary of the National Council of Churches (NCC), she served as executive director of the U.S. Office of the World Council of Churches (1985–1991) and assistant general secretary of the NCC with responsibility for its Commission on Regional and Local Ecumenism (1979–1985). From 1973 to 1979 Campbell was associate director of the Greater Cleveland Interchurch Council, serving concurrently as pastor of the Euclid Baptist Church from 1977 to 1979. From 1971 to 1973, she served as executive director of the Council for Action in Public Education, a program of the former United Presbyterian Synod of Ohio in Columbus. Campbell also worked for the Catholic Diocese of Cleveland, where she headed a social action organization, Action for a Change, as well as for the Welfare Action Coalition and Community United Headstart, also in Cleveland, and for the Action Training Network of Ohio.

## TAX STATUS

501(c)(3)

## BUDGET

1997—$56 million
1998—Unavailable
Proposed 1999—Unavailable

Public and community appeals, 41 percent; member contributions, 20 percent; refugee resettlement contracts with the U.S. government and federal disaster relief funds, 15 percent; individuals and corporations, 11 percent; sales, royalties, and other income, 10 percent; U.S. government contract for AmeriCorps program, 4 percent

FUNDING SOURCES

Members: NCC is "comprised of 34 Protestant, Orthodox, and Anglican member denominations whose combined membership is more than 52 million. The council is a community of national religious bodies, not a church and not an association of individuals. . . ."

Branches/chapters: Offices in Baltimore, Maryland; Elkhart, Indiana; and Miami; 25 Church World Service/CROP offices across the United States; several regional representatives overseas

Affiliates: N/A

NCC Programs are carried out by two units coordinated through a General Secretariat: Church World Service and Witness and National Ministries.

SCOPE

None

PAC

♦ Advertisements ♦ Coalition forming ♦ Conferences/seminars ♦ Congressional testimony ♦ Films/video/audiotapes ♦ International activities ♦ Internet (Web site) ♦ Legal assistance ♦ Legislative/regulatory monitoring (federal) ♦ Litigation (*amicus* briefs) ♦ Media outreach ♦ Mediation ♦ Research ♦ Shareholder resolutions ♦ Television and radio production ♦ Training and technical assistance

METHOD OF OPERATION

♦ Bible translation and utilization ♦ Children ♦ Christian unity ♦ Environmental racism ♦ Families ♦ Interfaith relations ♦ International development (works in more than 70 countries) ♦ Nuclear weapons/Peace with Justice ♦ Poverty ♦ Racial justice and reconciliation ♦ Refugee resettlement ♦ Relief aid to disaster victims ♦ Religious liberty ♦ Theological dialogue ♦ Urban concerns ♦ Violence in media and society ♦ Welfare reform ♦ Women's issues ♦ World hunger

CURRENT CONCERNS

*Yearbook of American and Canadian Churches* (annual)

Also publishes books, pamphlets, videos, and other resources

PUBLICATIONS

*CORLETTER* (for local and regional ecumenists 5 times a year)
*Ecu-Link* (4 times a year)

NEWSLETTER

## CONFERENCES

General Assembly (annual)

Sponsors frequent issue consultations dealing with specific issues such as families, refugee resettlement, theological dialogue, racism, and economic development

## BOARD OF DIRECTORS

NCC officers:

Joan Brown Campbell, general secretary; Craig Barry Anderson, president; Melvin B. Talbert, immediate past president; Andrew Young, president-elect; Khajag Barsamian, Sylvia M. Faulk, Elenora Giddings Ivory, and Will L. Herzfeld, vice presidents; Cecil Bishop, secretary; Margaret J. Thomas, treasurer

## EFFECTIVENESS

"An American church delegation left for Baghdad today with $100,000 worth of medicine and surgical supplies to help the Iraqi people.

" 'The main purpose of our mission is to bring humanitarian aid to ease the suffering of the people of Iraq,' said the Rev. Rodney Page of New York.

"He said his group would 'express our Christian compassion and solidarity for the churches and the people of Iraq at Easter time.'

"Mr. Page heads a seven-member delegation that will visit members of the Chaldean Christian minority in Iraq.

"The group represents the National Council of the Churches of Christ in the U.S.A. The council has donated $3 million worth of medicine to Iraqis since 1990, the delegation said." (*New York Times*, April 9, 1998)

"... Paul Gorman, executive director of the New York-based National Religious Partnership for the Environment, said the religious community's Earth consciousness goes beyond the campaigns and lobbying of secular environmentalists.

" 'We are not the environmental movement at prayer. We are not the shock troops for the Green Party,' said Gorman, whose group includes the U.S. Catholic Conference, the National Council of Churches, the Evangelical Environmental Network and the Coalition on the Environment and Jewish Life.

" 'What's really happening here,' he said, 'is that the "crisis of creation," or environmental problem, is calling us to rediscover some of the most fundamental teachings of every major faith tradition.'

"There are numerous examples of the growing interest by religious groups in the Earth's physical woes. Seminaries are adding courses on the environment and eco-justice and installing energy-saving devices in buildings. When they met last month at the Religious Action Center of Reform Judaism in Washington, Jewish rabbis put the environment on their agenda for the first time. The National Council of Churches recently mailed its congregations 72,000 information packets on environmental health. And Roman Catholic bishops in Oregon, Idaho, Washington state, Montana and Canada have teamed up for a three-year 'theological reflection' on the Columbia River watershed." (*Washington Post*, February 3, 1998)

"Pope John Paul II will soon add his voice to a growing chorus calling for an end to the United States' economic embargo against Cuba. But the debate that he will be joining is an old one, and opinions in the White House and Congress are deeply entrenched.

"After arriving in Cuba on Wednesday, the Pope is expected to denounce the 37-year-old embargo, as he has denounced embargoes in the past. When he does, he will join what one ardently anti-Castro member of Congress, Representative Ileana Ros-Lehtinen, a Florida Republican, calls an 'unholy alliance': 600 business groups and 140 religious and human-rights organizations asking the Clinton Administration to ease up on the sanctions.

"The embargo's opponents—strange bedfellows including the U.S. Chamber of Commerce, the National Council of Churches, the National Association of Manufacturers and the American Friends Services Committee—say the embargo has starved the Cuban people of food and ideas, but failed to change President Fidel Castro.

" 'Economic embargoes don't work, period,' said John Howard, director of international policy and programs at the Chamber of Commerce. 'We believe the best way to open up the Cuban regime is to open it up to the American system.'

"They hope that the papal visit may compel American political leaders to think again about isolating Cuba." (*New York Times*, January 21, 1998)

"A federal task force set up last year to deal with church burnings said yesterday that almost 200 suspects have been arrested, more than 75 percent of them since the task force's creation, but that the evidence thus far does not support fears of a national conspiracy.

"In a report to President Clinton commemorating the National Church Arson Task Force's first anniversary, Treasury and Justice Department officials said they have opened 429 investigations of arsons, bombings and attempted bombings at houses of worship dating back to Jan. 1, 1995. Almost four out of 10 (37.8 percent) of those attacks were at predominantly black churches and more than three-quarters of the black churches were in the South. While 'the arsons at African American churches raised significant fears about an increase in racially motivated crimes,' the task force said, the attacks, 'at both African American and other houses of worship, were motivated by a wide array of factors, including not only blatant racism or religious hatred, but also financial profit, burglary and personal revenge.'. . .

"Officials of the National Council of Churches (NCC), which brought national attention to the issue, commended members of the task force 'for the thoroughness and scope of their investigation and for the speed of their response when we called for assistance.'

"The task force includes officials from the Department of Housing and Urban Development, whose job is to help the council and other groups with rebuilding efforts, and Federal Emergency Management Agency officials, whose assignment is to promote local and state prevention programs.

" 'The report says that there are mixed motivations, from people being mad at God to being mad at their neighbors, and I think that is unfortunately true,' said the Rev. Joan Brown Campbell, NCC general secretary. She said the council has helped rebuild 90 churches, mostly black churches in the South 'where we feel there is racial motivation,' and it is assessing the needs of 60 others." (*Washington Post*, June 9, 1997)

## POLITICAL ORIENTATION

"liberal" (*Washington Post*, October 18, 1997)

"mainstream" (*Washington Post*, September 30, 1997)

# Traditional Values Coalition (1981)

100 South Anaheim Boulevard
Suite 350
Anaheim, California 92805
Phone: (714) 520-0300
Fax: (714) 520-9602

139 C Street, SE
Washington, D.C. 20003
Phone: (202) 547-8570
Fax: (202) 546-6403

Internet: http://www.traditionalvalues.org

| | |
|---|---|
| "To fight the increasing attacks on our Judeo-Christian heritage." | *PURPOSE* |
| Unavailable | *STAFF* |
| Louis Sheldon, chairman. An ordained minister, Sheldon founded the Traditional Values Coalition in 1981. | *DIRECTOR* |
| 501(c)(4) | *TAX STATUS* |
| 1998—Unavailable<br>Proposed 1999—Unavailable | *BUDGET* |
| Membership dues, donations, publications | *FUNDING SOURCES* |
| Members: 36,000 churches<br>Branches/chapters: N/A<br>Affiliate: Traditional Values Coalition Education and Legal Institute | *SCOPE* |
| None | *PAC* |
| ♦ Conferences/seminars ♦ Films/video/audiotapes ♦ Grassroots organizing ♦ Initiative/referendum campaigns ♦ Internet (Web site) ♦ Legal assistance ♦ Legislative/regulatory monitoring (federal and state) ♦ Media outreach ♦ Voter registration ♦ Voting records | *METHOD OF OPERATION* |

| | |
|---|---|
| *CURRENT CONCERNS* | ♦ Abortion ♦ AIDS and sex education ♦ Euthanasia ♦ Homosexuality ♦ National Endowment for the Arts funding ♦ Parental rights ♦ Religion in public school curriculum ♦ Taxes |
| *PUBLICATIONS* | *Beginning Again*<br>*The Big Lie: A Wall of Separation Between Church and State?*<br>*Gay Rights/Special Rights: Inside the Homosexual Agenda*<br>*SHAPE: Stop Homosexual Advocacy in Public Education*<br>*Traditional Values Coalition's Congressional Directory* |
| *NEWSLETTER* | *Traditional Values Report* (bimonthly)<br>*TVC Talking Points* (addresses specific issues) |
| *CONFERENCES* | National conference held annually (Washington, D.C.)<br>Several regional conferences throughout the year |
| *BOARD OF DIRECTORS* | Unavailable |
| *EFFECTIVENESS* | "... Which brings us to the case of James C. Hormel, whose nomination as ambassador to Luxembourg was overwhelmingly endorsed by the Senate Foreign Relations Committee last November. But it is languishing as Senate Majority Leader Trent Lott, pandering to the religious right, refuses to let it come to a vote in the full Senate. The Christian right engages in all manners of distortion to disguise the reason they oppose the wealthy San Francisco investor: He is openly gay....<br><br>"But the real significance of the confirmation struggle is what it says about the religious right, its clout with the Republican Party and why the intolerance that has become its hallmark turns off many Americans....<br><br>"Even many conservatives worry about the religious right. In a brilliant analysis of the GOP coalition's woes, conservative journalist Christopher Caldwell, in the current *Atlantic Monthly*, writes: 'Conservative Christians are to the Republican Party what blacks were to the Democrats in the 1970s: its most loyal troops, the source of its most talented activists, its moral code. For that reason, they are also the main source of radicalization and overreach.'<br><br>"Overreaching and outright fabrication are ubiquitous in the ugly fight against Mr. Hormel. The religious right insists the issue is not that he's gay but that he has publicly supported and financed an offensive gay lifestyle. The particulars include funding the James Hormel Gay and Lesbian Library in San Francisco, which critics say includes material on pedophilia and incest, not to mention that it's right next to the library's teen center; providing funding for a documentary for school teachers entitled 'It's Elementary,' which critics say promotes homosexuality; and Mr. Hormel's alleged anti-Catholicism, important because Luxembourg is a Catholic country. |

"Andrea Sheldon, executive director of the Traditional Values Coalition, which represents 32,000 conservative Christian churches around the country, spent two full days at the Hormel Gay and Lesbian Library in San Francisco and says she was 'shocked' at some of the material there. But Ms. Sheldon refuses to say whether she believes that homosexuals generally should be barred from diplomatic service. And she ignores the fact that while Mr. Hormel provided funding, he had nothing to do with choosing the library's contents." (*Wall Street Journal*, May 21, 1998)

"A broad coalition of religious groups that united four years ago to pass the Religious Freedom Restoration Act reacted bitterly yesterday to the high court's decision to strike down the law and predicted a dire future without its protection.

"They said they now envision a nation in which prison inmates are prohibited from praying in Arabic, Sikh Little League players are required to remove their turbans, evangelical students are obliged to attend classes on evolution, and churches are forbidden by zoning laws from remodeling or running soup kitchens. 'Every church and synagogue, every religious person in America is going to be hurt by this decision. They just don't realize it yet,' said Oliver Thomas, counsel on religious liberty for the National Council of Churches. 'It'll first start happening to minority faiths, but remember, Catholics are minorities in lots of states, and evangelicals are minorities in lots of places.'. . .

"Congress passed the religious freedom law by a near-unanimous vote. Traditional adversaries like Americans United for Separation of Church and State and the . . . Traditional Values Coalition had united behind its guiding principle that government should not inhibit believers from practicing their faith unless it can prove there were 'compelling' reasons for doing so." (*Washington Post*, June 26, 1997)

"conservative" (*Washington Post*, June 26, 1997)

## POLITICAL ORIENTATION

# Think Tanks
## Chapter 12

# Alexis de Tocqueville Institution (1987)

1611 North Kent Street
Suite 901
Arlington, Virginia 22209
Phone: (703) 351-4969
Fax: (703) 351-0900
Internet: http://www.adti.net

| | |
|---|---|
| "To study, promote and extend the principles of classical liberalism: political equality, civil liberty and economic freedom." | **PURPOSE** |
| Unavailable | **STAFF** |
| Gregory Fossedal, chairman | **DIRECTOR** |
| 501(c)(3) | **TAX STATUS** |
| 1998—Unavailable<br>Proposed 1999—Unavailable | **BUDGET** |
| Corporations, foundations, individuals | **FUNDING SOURCES** |
| Members: N/A<br>Branches/chapters: N/A<br>Affiliates: N/A | **SCOPE** |
| None | **PAC** |
| ♦ Congressional testimony ♦ Internet (Web site) ♦ Legislative/regulatory monitoring (federal) ♦ Media outreach ♦ Research ♦ Special projects (African Development Project, American Immigration Institute, Center on Regulation and Economic Growth, Committee for the Common Defense, IMF Assessment Project, Value Added Tax Project) | **METHOD OF OPERATION** |

| | |
|---|---|
| *CURRENT CONCERNS* | ◆ Africa ◆ China ◆ Cuba ◆ Defense ◆ Education reform ◆ Immigration ◆ International Monetary Fund ◆ Regulation ◆ Taxes and economic growth ◆ Telecommunications |
| *PUBLICATIONS* | The Institute publishes issue briefs; affiliates publish articles and opinion pieces in major periodicals |
| *NEWSLETTER* | None |
| *CONFERENCES* | None |
| *BOARD OF DIRECTORS* | Unavailable |
| *EFFECTIVENESS* | "And you thought turkey day was over. |

"Not at the Alexis de Tocqueville Institution, which is about to release for public consumption 'The Dirty Dozen: The Twelve Worst Regulations in America,' its annual rant about federal regulations. The institution . . . argues that the power of regulatory agencies should be restrained.

"Rather than have the policy wonks carve up the regulators, this year the institution rounded up 'celebrity' critics of regulation, most of them Republican. A governor or two, state officials and members of Congress were persuaded to pick a turkey.

"And they did.

"California Gov. Pete Wilson (R) has a gripe with the Environmental Protection Agency for frustrating a volunteer effort to clean up an abandoned mine in his state. His complaint is that good Samaritanism has been discouraged by rules that make volunteers involved in a cleanup liable for meeting federal standards. . . .

"If this isn't enough, there are [eleven] other examples of what the regulatory critics view as good intentions gone awry, or the federal government going overboard.

" 'We asked people to write about areas where they have expertise,' said Merrick Carey, president of the institution, named for the 19th-century French observer of the American scene who predicted that democratic socialism, with its far-reaching regulations, would create a 'nanny state.' " (*Washington Post*, November 28, 1997)

"In a summer poll taken by the Tocqueville Institution, mayors from 13 cities with populations of 200,000 or more, and significant numbers of immigrants, were asked if they would stop schooling the children of undocumented aliens, given a choice. Absolutely not, came responses from 12 cities ranging from Stockton, Calif., to El Paso, Miami and New York.

"Asked to describe the general impact of immigration, 10 of the 13 chose answers ranging from 'positive' to 'very positive.' 'In response to an open-ended question seeking recommendations for federal immigration policy actions,' study author Phil Peters summed up, 'none of the respondents called for a reduction in legal immigration.'

"Why not?

"Five of the mayors surveyed felt that immigrants had an 'unfavorable' effect on the poverty level of their city, as opposed to a neutral or positive one. But eight were confident that the flow of immigrants had a favorable effect on the rate of new business starts. Six of the pollees—Stockton and Fremont, Calif., Jersey City, N.J., San Francisco and Hialeah, Fla., among them—said immigrants had a 'positive' or 'very positive' effect on job creation. On crime rates, four felt immigrants increased them; the other nine either did not respond or felt immigrants had a neutral or positive effect." (*Wall Street Journal*, September 17, 1996)

---

"conservative" (*Washington Post*, February 13, 1998)

"a think tank that promotes free markets, democracy and civil liberty" (*Washington Post*, November 28, 1997)

"libertarian" (*Wall Street Journal*, March 12, 1996)

# POLITICAL ORIENTATION

# American Enterprise Institute for Public Policy Research (1943)

1150 17th Street, NW
Washington, D.C. 20036
Phone: (202) 862-5800
Fax: (202) 862-7177
Internet: info@aei.org *or* http://www.aei.org

**PURPOSE**

"To preserve the foundations of a free society—limited government, competitive private enterprise, vital cultural and political institutions, and a vigilant defense—through rigorous inquiry, debate, and writing."

**STAFF**

120 total—50 scholars and directors; 70 research associates, staff assistants, supervisors, and editors; plus 140 interns a year and 15 part-time

**DIRECTOR**

Christopher C. DeMuth, president. DeMuth has been president of the American Enterprise Institute (AEI) since 1986. He formerly was publisher of *Regulation* magazine and managing director of a law and economics consulting firm. From 1981 to 1984 he was administrator for information and regulatory affairs in the Office of Management and Budget and executive director of the Presidential Task Force on Regulatory Relief. DeMuth also has been in private practice and a lecturer at the Kennedy School of Government. He earned his A.B. from Harvard College and his J.D. from Chicago Law School.

**TAX STATUS**

501(c)(3)

**BUDGET**

1997—$18 million
1998—$18.5 million
Proposed 1999—Unavailable

**FUNDING SOURCES**

Foundation grants, 41 percent; corporations, 41 percent; individuals, 10 percent; conferences, sales, and other revenues, 8 percent

**SCOPE**

Members: N/A
Branches/chapters: N/A
Affiliates: N/A

**PAC**

None

♦ Conferences/seminars ♦ Congressional testimony ♦ International activities ♦ Internet (Web site) ♦ Library/information clearinghouse ♦ Media outreach ♦ Research ♦ Speakers program

## METHOD OF OPERATION

*Economic Policy Studies:* ♦ Financial markets ♦ Fiscal and monetary policy ♦ Health policy ♦ International trade and finance ♦ Regulation ♦ Telecommunications policy
*Foreign and Defense Policy Studies:* ♦ Area studies ♦ Asian studies ♦ Defense and arms control ♦ U.S. foreign policy
*Social and Political Studies:* ♦ Education, culture, and religion ♦ Legal and constitutional ♦ Political ♦ Social and individual responsibility

## CURRENT CONCERNS

*Agricultural Policy Reform in the United States*
*Agricultural Trade Policy: Letting Markets Work*
*American Trade Policy: A Tragedy in the Making*
*The Antitrust Laws*
*Assessing the Environmental Impact of Farm Policies*
*Attitudes Toward the Environment: Twenty-five Years after Earth Day*
*Choice and Efficiency in Food Safety Policy*
*CIA Estimates of Soviet Military Expenditures: Errors and Waste*
*The Corporation and the Constitution*
*The Dangerous Drift to Preferential Trade Agreements*
*Deregulating Freight Transportation*
*Distributional Analysis of Tax Policy*
*The Economics of Crop Insurance and Disaster Aid*
*The Effects of Credit Policies on U.S. Agriculture*
*The Fiscal Revolution in America: Hoover to Clinton*
*The Foreign Investment Debate: Opening Markets Abroad or Closing Markets at Home?*
*The Germans: Portrait of a New Nation*
*Health Care Choices: Private Contracts as Instruments of Health Reform*
*Industrial Policy and Semiconductors: Missing the Target*
*Making Science Pay: The Economics of Agricultural R&D Policy*
*The Neoconservative Imagination: Essays in Honor of Irving Kristol*
*The New Illustrated Guide to the American Economy* (2nd edition)
*On the Other Hand . . . Essays on Economics, Economists, and Politics*
*Reforming Agricultural Commodity Policy*
*Transmission Pricing and Stranded Costs in the Electric Power Industry*
*The Tyranny of Numbers: Mismeasurement and Misrule*
*The Vaccines for Children Program: A Critique*

## PUBLICATIONS

*AEI Newsletter* (monthly)
*The American Enterprise* (bimonthly)
*Economic Outlook* (monthly)
*Latin American Outlook* (monthly)
*On the Issues* (biweekly)

## NEWSLETTER

## CONFERENCES

AEI World Forum (annual three-day meeting, June, in Beaver Creek, Colorado)

Amgen Forum (occasional series)

Annual policy conference (two-day conference, December)

Bradley Lecture Series (monthly)

Election Watch (monthly series during national election years)

New Members Seminar (in Williamsburg, Virginia, before each new Congress convenes)

Other occasional seminars, debates, roundtables, and conferences

## BOARD OF DIRECTORS

## EFFECTIVENESS

"If your retirement hopes are linked to the bull market, the June issues of two magazines could leave you a bit bewildered: they offer nearly opposite assessments of the market's future.

"In *Bloomberg Personal*, David Hackett Fischer, a professor of history at Brandeis University and an expert on economic cycles, describes what he calls serious structural imbalances in the American economy and hints at a big bust for stocks.

"He cites historically high price-to-earnings ratios, driven by pension, mutual fund and foreign investments; falling per-share earnings even as stock prices rise; a growing trade deficit; excess capacity and shrinking demand; concentration of economic control in a small number of large companies; low productivity growth, and the chasm in wealth distribution, which he says is wider than at any period in the nation's history except the late 1920's.

" 'The evidence suggests that it is time to think about the direction of change in our economy,' Professor Fischer writes. 'Our future may be very different from the recent past.'

"But in *Mutual Funds* magazine, Barbara Mlotek Whelehan cites scholars from the American Enterprise Institute, a conservative research group, who make some eyebrow-raising comments about the market. Because of probable future earnings and interest rates, they say, the market is undervalued by a factor of 4 to 1; were that imbalance corrected, according to such thinking, the Dow could be near 35,000. She also reports a forecast by Don Wolanchuk, the superbull publisher of *The Wolanchuk Report*, that the Dow will hit 16,000 this year. And then there's Glenn Neely of the Elliott Wave Institute, who foresees annual market gains of 50 to 100 percent in the next two years." (*New York Times*, May 17, 1998)

"The Justice Department wants to insure that Microsoft is curbed from using its Windows monopoly unfairly both to maintain that monopoly and to gain an unfair advantage in the emerging markets of Internet commerce and software.

"Specifically, the Government wants to protect competition in the market for Internet browsers, the software required to view World Wide Web sites. It also wants to restrict Microsoft's freedom to use its control of the computer desktop—the main Windows screen that personal computer users see—to steer consumers toward Internet shopping and entertainment sites owned by Microsoft or its favored business partners. . . .

"To encourage browser competition, the Government could order that Microsoft unbundle its browser from Windows, enabling PC makers to load Netscape's Navigator browser, if they choose. But Microsoft charges nothing extra for the browser, so there is no incentive for PC makers to take the unbundled version of Windows.

"To insure competition, though, the Government must go further, according to Robert H. Bork, a former Federal judge who is a fellow at the American Enterprise Institute. One step, he says, would be to insist that Microsoft load another browser, like Netscape's Navigator, on Windows along with Explorer in a 'must carry' order.

" 'Any remedy that does not let the consumer make the ultimate choice will not be effective because of Microsoft's enormous power, often coercive power, in the computer industry,' said Mr. Bork, who is also a consultant to Netscape." (*New York Times*, May 15, 1998)


"Two years ago Social Security privatization probably had no more support in Washington than the legalization of marijuana. Today, the notion is being entertained by such heavyweights as Daniel Patrick Moynihan, the senior Democrat on the Senate Finance Committee. Privatization has become a very real possibility in part because big budget surpluses are apparently available to help pay for the transition.

" 'Something labeled 'partial privatization' is bound to be included in any broad-based Social Security reform,' predicted Sylvester Schieber, an economist at Watson Wyatt Worldwide, a pension consulting company, and a member of the Government's Advisory Council on the system. . . . For some conservative intellectuals—namely Carolyn Weaver of the American Enterprise Institute and Jose Pinera at the Cato Institute—privatization is a matter of cutting Washington down to size. As long as the Government stands ready to play nanny, workers will have little incentive to plan for their own retirement. And as long as pension income amounts to a gift from Government, political coalitions will work to keep the checks rolling in.

"This is surely the oldest and most principled argument for privatization. Though legislators talk the libertarian talk, few really walk the walk. The libertarian stance does, however, offer a high-minded rationale for policies based on other considerations." (*New York Times*, April 9, 1998)

"conservative" (*Washington Post*, May 18, 1997)

*POLITICAL*
*ORIENTATION*

# The Brookings Institution (1916)

1775 Massachusetts Avenue, NW
Washington, D.C. 20036
Phone: (202) 797-6000
Fax: (202) 797-6004
Internet: http://www.brook.edu

| | |
|---|---|
| **PURPOSE** | "Seeks to improve the performance of American institutions, the effectiveness of government programs, and the quality of U.S. public policies." |
| **STAFF** | Unavailable |
| **DIRECTOR** | Michael H. Armacost, president. Before joining Brookings, Armacost was director of the Aspen Strategy Group, worked as an international consultant, and taught as a visiting professor at Stanford University's Asia/Pacific Research Center. He also has served as U.S. ambassador to Japan, as under secretary of state for political affairs, and as U.S. ambassador to the Philippines. Armacost holds degrees from Carleton College and Columbia University. |
| **TAX STATUS** | 501(c)(3) |
| **BUDGET** | 1998—Unavailable<br>Proposed 1999—Unavailable |
| **FUNDING SOURCES** | Foundations, corporations, and individuals, 38 percent; endowment, 30 percent; Center for Public Policy revenue, 18 percent; other, 15 percent |
| **SCOPE** | Members: N/A<br>Branches/chapters: N/A<br>Affiliate: N/A |
| **PAC** | None |

♦ Advertisements ♦ Conferences/seminars (offered through the Center for Public Policy Education and the Government Affairs Institute) ♦ Congressional testimony ♦ Congressional voting analysis ♦ International activities ♦ Internet (Web site) ♦ Legislative/regulatory monitoring (federal and state) ♦ Library/information clearinghouse ♦ Media outreach ♦ Research ♦ Speakers program

## METHOD OF OPERATION

♦ Arms control ♦ Balanced budget amendment ♦ Campaigns and elections ♦ Conflict resolution ♦ Congressional reform ♦ Corporate governance ♦ Crime ♦ Defense spending ♦ Europe ♦ Economic transformation of Russia ♦ Education reform ♦ Environmental sustainability ♦ Federal tax policy ♦ Federalism and devolution ♦ Global economic integration ♦ Government downsizing ♦ Health care ♦ Housing ♦ Income distribution ♦ International trade ♦ Latin America ♦ Middle East ♦ National security ♦ Northeast Asia ♦ Politics and the media ♦ Productivity ♦ Regulatory policy ♦ Telecommunications reform ♦ Urban social policy ♦ U.S.-China relations ♦ U.S. living standards ♦ Welfare reform

## CURRENT CONCERNS

The following is a list of sample publications:

*After the Reinvention*
*The Automobile, Its Enemies, and the Politics of Mobility*
*A Blueprint for Deep Cuts and De-Alerting of Nuclear Weapons*
*The Bureaucratic Entrepreneur*
*The Black-White Test Score Gap*
*Between Ballots & Bullets*
*Beyond Tradeoffs*
*Brookings Papers on Education Policy: 1999*
*Building a Better Tax System*
*Cambodia Reborn?*
*China's Unfinished Economic Revolution*
*The Controversial Pivot*
*Does the Bell Curve Ring True?*
*Driving Forces*
*An Egypt-U.S. Free Trade Agreement*
*Fixing Urban Schools*
*Framing the Social Security Debate*
*From New Federalism to Devolution*
*How to Be Effective in Any Unruly Organization*
*Is Japan Really Changing Its Ways?*
*Japan Reorients: The Quest for Wealth and Security in East Asia*
*Letting Liberalization Lead*
*The Little Book of Campaign Etiquette*
*Market Reforms and Equitable Growth in Latin America*
*The Nuclear Turning Point*
*Opening Windows*
*Post-Conflict Elections in Liberia*
*Private Markets for Public Goods*
*The Promise and Peril of Environmental Justice*
*Regulatory Reform and the Japanese Economy*
*Setting National Priorities: 1999*
*Spinning Wheels: The Politics of Urban School Reform*

## PUBLICATIONS

*Toward an End to Hunger in America*
*Transatlantic Tensions*
*The Transition to Democracy and Development*
*Urban Problems and Community Development*
*The U.S. Congress and North America*
*Values, Politics, and Economics*
*Voting for Peace*

## NEWSLETTER

*The Brookings Newsletter* (quarterly)
*Brookings Papers on Economic Activity* (semiannual journal)
*The Brookings Review* (quarterly magazine)
*Microeconomics* (annual journal)

## CONFERENCES

Briefings and team presentations
Executive forums
Sabbaticals
Teleconferences

## BOARD OF DIRECTORS

James A. Johnson, chairman; Michael H. Armacost, president

Other members:
♦ Elizabeth E. Bailey ♦ Zöe Baird ♦ Alan M. Dachs ♦ Kenneth W. Dam ♦ D. Ronald Daniel ♦ Robert A. Day ♦ Bart Friedman ♦ Stephen Friedman ♦ Henry Louis Gates Jr. ♦ Teresa Heinz ♦ Samuel Hellman ♦ Robert A. Helman ♦ Ann Dibble Jordan ♦ Thomas G. Labrecque ♦ Jessica Tuchman Mathews ♦ David O. Maxwell ♦ Maconda Brown O'Connor ♦ Steven L. Rattner ♦ Judith S. Rodin ♦ Warren B. Rudman ♦ Michael P. Schulhof ♦ Joan Spero ♦ Vincent J. Trosino ♦ Stephen M. Wolf ♦ John D. Zeglis

## EFFECTIVENESS

"Back when Japan looked like an unstoppable economic juggernaut, some American critics were so threatened by Tokyo's rising influence that they urged scrapping the cooperative alliance forged during the Cold War era for a confrontational, get-tough policy of 'containing Japan.'

"Now, with the world's second-largest economy wallowing in recession and its political leaders seemingly oblivious to global demands that they do more to bolster growth, a respected member of the Washington policy establishment is making waves on both sides of the Pacific by advocating an alternative approach. Call it 'disdaining Japan.' In the current issue of *Foreign Affairs* magazine, Brookings Institution scholar Edward J. Lincoln, an adviser to Walter Mondale when he was U.S. ambassador to Tokyo and one of America's best-known experts on the Japanese economy, urges that U.S. officials demonstrate their frustration with Japan's timid economic policies by giving counterparts in Tokyo the cold shoulder—not just on economic matters, but in their dealings on diplomatic and security issues as well.

" 'It is time for the United States to send less-than-subtle signals in other areas of its relationship with Japan,' Lincoln argues. 'The bilateral relationship includes broad consultative arrangements, within which American officials could simply stop consulting. Through canceled meetings, unreturned telephone calls and a lack of advance notice of American policy moves, the United States can send the message that it no longer regards Japan as a global partner.'

"Lincoln's article has touched a raw nerve in Tokyo, where Japan's business and government leaders have grown increasingly worried that the United States is drifting away from their economically moribund and politically fractured nation—even as it cultivates a stronger and more extended relationship with China. . . .

"At Japan's embassy in Washington, Lincoln's essay has officials in an uproar. The article 'displays a rush to judgment and fails to appreciate any of the economic and political constraints in Japan,' fumed a senior Japanese diplomat, who spoke on condition he not be named. 'The idea that the U.S. might break off consultations with Japan is irrational and appalling. . . . Quite the reverse is needed.'. . .

"In his essay, Lincoln laments that, for all the talk about Japan's contribution as an important global partner, Tokyo has shirked its responsibility to help poorer neighbors cope with the financial crisis in Asia. 'Rather than absorbing more imports,' he predicts, 'Japan will shift its burden through more exports to the United States. . . . Tokyo is quite willing to let the United States underwrite the Asian recovery.'

"Lincoln also twits Japanese leaders for their unwillingness to play a constructive role in Washington's latest face-off with Iraq, 'articulating only the request that any military action be postponed until after the Nagano Winter Olympics.'

"Few U.S. experts take issue with Lincoln's grim description of Japan's recent foreign policy record. Japan likely will be subjected to more criticism this month when Hashimoto joins leaders from the other Group of Seven industrial nations in Birmingham, England, for their annual economic summit. . . .

"In the article, Lincoln acknowledges that giving Japan the brush-off 'may seem like a heavy-handed way to treat the world's second-largest economy.' But, he argues, 'it may be the only way to move Japan off a path that is destructive for us all.' " (*Washington Post*, May 2, 1998)


"To be truly hip these days, a fan must be versed in sociology, pharmacology, labor-management issues and the ins and outs of the criminal statutes. It's conceivable that a university could compile a curriculum and offer a Ph.D. in the subject. It would be no surprise to learn that one already is doing so.

"To the above list, economics also belongs, but the applications of that discipline to the erstwhile world of fun and games have become so numerous that they would require a separate course of study, or, maybe, several. Suffice it to say that capital-B Bucks have come to mean far more in sports than a basketball team in Milwaukee.

"If more proof of that proposition were needed, it arrived with a thud the other day with the publication, by the Washington-based Brookings Institution, of a 525-page tome titled 'Sports, Jobs & Taxes: The Economic Impact of Sports Teams and Stadiums.' Edited by the economists Roger G. Noll of Stanford University and Andrew Zimbalist of Smith College, it's an analysis of the rationale for, and engines behind, the process through which professional sports teams have pried billions of dollars out of U.S. taxpayers to finance the fields of their dreams.

"The book is 'must' reading for people living in or around any city still targeted for the stadium-building boom of the present decade, which is to say any city that hasn't already been squeezed for a new facility or two. It contains ammunition aplenty to counter the sports monopolists' claims that the costly playpens they seek—often at the gunpoint of a threatened franchise move—are of direct benefit to many besides themselves and their players. . . .

"Whatever its mysteries, the volume leaves no doubt about its conclusion. 'In every case, the authors [of the 15 self-contained chapters] find that the local economic impact of sports teams and facilities is far smaller than proponents allege; in some cases it is negative,' Messrs. Noll and Zimbalist state in their introduction." (*Wall Street Journal*, December 19, 1997)

"A controversial new paper suggesting that a little bit of inflation may be good for the economy has people talking at the Federal Reserve.

"The Brookings Institution paper, which says the economy wouldn't function efficiently at zero inflation, adds fuel to a debate both inside and outside the Fed over whether policy makers should drive inflation even lower than it is now. The paper suggests the economic and social costs of getting to zero inflation, or 'price stability,' would be far higher than most economists believe. . . .

"The paper challenges mainstream economic assumptions about wages and inflation, including some recent Fed staff research, and makes a case against pending legislation that would force the Fed to make price stability its only goal. The bill-introduced by Sen. Connie Mack (R., Fla.) and endorsed by most key Republicans, including Robert Dole—amends the Humphrey-Hawkins Act, a law requiring the Fed to pursue both stable prices and high employment. . . .

"Many economists now believe the painful costs of going to zero inflation—in higher unemployment and slower growth—would be temporary while the benefits would be permanent. Harvard University economist Martin Feldstein, in a recent paper, says reaching zero inflation 'would cause a perpetual welfare gain equal to about 1% of GDP a year,' a huge growth dividend.

"But the Brookings paper rejects that conclusion. 'We found that the economy doesn't work properly with zero inflation, if productivity growth is also low' as it is now, says George Perry, another of its authors. 'If you get there on purpose, or stumble there as they did in Japan, you create serious inefficiencies in the labor market.' He says these distortions raise unemployment and lower output permanently, not just during a transition period as other economists suggest.

"The labor-market distortions of zero inflation—which the authors identified in complex economic models—have to do with the need for companies to be able to cut wages from time to time as their fortunes rise and fall. In periods of moderate inflation, they can do so by keeping nominal wages steady, allowing inflation to push down real wages. With zero inflation, some firms instead would be forced to cut employment, since they couldn't cut workers' pay to hold down costs. The authors say this effect would permanently add at least one percentage point to the unemployment rate and could cut annual growth by a similar amount.

"Alan Greenspan, the Fed chairman, hasn't formally endorsed the price-stability legislation sponsored by Sen. Mack, but he's embraced the broad goal of the bill. Other Fed officials have spoken both for and against it.

"The Brookings research backs liberal economists who say a little inflation helps grease economic growth. Deputy Treasury Secretary Larry Summers, before joining the Clinton administration, called moderate inflation a 'social lubricant.' " (*Wall Street Journal*, April 13, 1996)

## POLITICAL ORIENTATION

"liberal" (*Washington Post*, April 27, 1998)

"that grandest of democracy-promoting think tanks" (*Washington Post*, April 16, 1998)

"The Brookings Institution often goes unlabeled but is frequently [labeled] 'liberal' and sometimes 'mainstream.' " (*Washington Post*, February 16, 1997)

# Capital Research Center (1984)

1513 16th Street
Washington, D.C. 20036
Phone: (202) 483-6900
Fax: (202) 483-6990
Internet: http://www.capitalresearch.org

| | |
|---|---|
| **PURPOSE** | "To study critical issues in philanthropy with a special focus on public interest and advocacy groups, the funding sources that sustain them, and their combined impact on public policy and society." |
| **STAFF** | 12 total—10 professional; 2 support; plus 1–3 interns |
| **DIRECTOR** | Terrence Scanlon, president. Before becoming president of the Capital Research Center (CRC) in 1994, Scanlon was vice president for corporate relations at the Heritage Foundation. Scanlon also has held positions in the Consumer Product Safety Commission, the Commerce Department, and the Small Business Administration. He was a White House aide under presidents Kennedy and Johnson. |
| **TAX STATUS** | 501(c)(3) |
| **BUDGET** | 1997—$1.5 million<br>1998—Unavailable<br>Proposed 1999—Unavailable |
| **FUNDING SOURCES** | Foundations, 78 percent; individuals, 15 percent; corporations, 6 percent; sales and other, 1 percent |
| **SCOPE** | Members: N/A<br>Branches/chapters: N/A<br>Affiliates: N/A |
| **PAC** | None |

| | |
|---|---|
| ◆ Advertisements ◆ Congressional testimony ◆ Internet (Web site) ◆ Legislative/regulatory monitoring (federal) ◆ Library/information clearinghouse ◆ Media outreach ◆ Performance ratings ◆ Research ◆ Shareholder resolutions | *METHOD OF OPERATION* |
| ◆ Advocacy group activities ◆ Charity in America ◆ Standards in philanthropy ◆ Trends in corporate and foundation giving | *CURRENT CONCERNS* |
| *The Age Lobby: Mortgaging America's Future*<br>*Animal Rights: The Inhumane Crusade*<br>*The Campaign for Human Development: Christian Charity or Political Activism?*<br>*Classical Education: Towards the Revival of American Schooling*<br>*Environmentalism at the Crossroads: Green Activism in America*<br>*Global Greens: Inside the International Environmental Establishment*<br>*The Great Philanthropists and the Problem of "Donor Intent"*<br>*Guide to Nonprofit Advocacy and Policy Groups*<br>*Loving Your Neighbor: A Principled Guide to Personal Charity*<br>*Patterns of Corporate Philanthropy* (annual)<br>*Philanthropically Correct: The Story of the Council on Foundations*<br>*The Rise of the Nanny State: How Consumer Advocates Try to Run Our Lives*<br>*Should Foundations Live Forever? The Question of Perpetuity* | *PUBLICATIONS* |
| *Alternatives in Philanthropy* (monthly)<br>*Foundation Watch* (monthly)<br>*Labor Watch* (monthly)<br>*Organization Trends* (monthly)<br>*Philanthropy, Culture and Society* (monthly) | *NEWSLETTER* |
| None | *CONFERENCES* |
| Terrence Scanlon, chairman<br><br>Other members:<br>◆ Beverly Danielson ◆ Constance C. Larcher ◆ Edwin Meese III ◆ Daniel J. Popeo ◆ Barbara Van Andel-Gaby ◆ Marion G. Wells | *BOARD OF DIRECTORS* |
| "Big publicly held companies are bridling at proposed Federal legislation that would require them to disclose how much money they give individual charities, warning that such a law would have a chilling effect on corporate philanthropy.<br><br>"In letters to the Securities and Exchange Commission, which is studying the potential effect of the bill, dozens of companies and many not-for-profit organizations say that such a requirement would add costs and invite pressure from special interest groups and shareholders, both of which would result in less giving. | *EFFECTIVENESS* |

"Disclosure 'would dangerously expose corporate philanthropy to a broad range of special-interest groups, which could be expected to descend like locusts on such an opportunity to pursue their singularly focused agendas in this new arena,' Federated Department Stores wrote in a typical letter.

"Representative Paul E. Gillmor, Republican of Ohio, introduced the bill a year ago, but only in recent months has the request for comments from the S.E.C. drawn dozens of new letters, most of them critical of the bill. Representative Gillmor said that shareholders had a right to know how managers were distributing corporate assets and that disclosure would discourage managers from making hard-to-justify donations to pet charities. He added that his interest in the subject stemmed from many years of investing his own money and serving on the boards of several private companies, and that he had noticed a tendency on the part of some other companies' management to ignore shareholders. . . .

"Whether companies should disclose their donations is part of a broad and long-running debate about the role of corporations in society. . . .

"The Capital Research Center . . . has for years studied data disclosed by companies about their charitable giving. It concluded after analyzing data gathered from 142 large companies that they gave three-and-a-half times as much to what it termed 'liberal and left-of-Center advocacy groups' as to 'right-of-Center and pro-free market groups.' The Center's latest findings were detailed in its 1996 book 'Patterns of Corporate Philanthropy,' the subtitle of which is 'Funding Enemies, Forsaking Friends.' " (*New York Times*, April 3, 1998)

"Finally, a federal program that works—that's the way anti-tobacco activists describe an unconventional three-year-old project that claims to have reduced cigarette smoking by 10 percent in the 17 states where it operates.

"The program's success suggests it is preventing hundreds of thousands of premature deaths from smoking, federal officials say. They say the program has cost tobacco companies sales of 800 million packs of cigarettes, worth hundreds of millions of dollars. So it's only natural that the tobacco industry and its allies attack the program, called the American Stop Smoking Intervention Study (ASSIST). The industry has used lawsuits and public records laws to divert health workers' energies, say anti-smoking crusaders. Some Republicans in Congress have said they want to derail the project, run by the National Cancer Institute (NCI), because they believe it is improper. . . .

"The $25 million-a-year ASSIST program, which operates at the local level in the 17 states, including Virginia, aims to make smoking an expensive hassle by advocating smoke-free buildings, curbs on tobacco sales to youth and—strikingly, in this anti-tax era—higher excise taxes on cigarettes.

"But ASSIST's critics in Congress, in the tobacco industry and at conservative foundations say the program violates the law by using federal funds to lobby state legislatures and municipalities. . . .

"Tobacco industry officials also commend the research of another ASSIST critic—the Washington-based Capital Research Center, a conservative group that, according to published reports, is partly funded by Philip Morris. (Neither the company nor the Center would comment on the Center's financing.) The Center has published essays saying ASSIST 'diverts millions of dollars to advocacy group politics' and calling the American Cancer Society a 'left-of-Center' group that cares little about sick people." (*Washington Post,* April 19, 1997)

---

## POLITICAL ORIENTATION

". . . tries to discourage corporations from giving charitable donations to nonprofits that support liberal or anti-business policies" (*Washington Post,* July 2, 1997)

"a conservative philanthropy monitoring group" (*Wall Street Journal,* May 28, 1996)

# Cato Institute (1977)

1000 Massachusetts Avenue, NW
Washington, D.C. 20001
Phone: (202) 842-0200
Fax: (202) 842-3490
Internet: cato@cato.org *or* http://www.cato.org

| | |
|---|---|
| **PURPOSE** | "To increase the understanding of public policies based on the principles of limited government, free markets, individual liberty, and peace." |
| **STAFF** | 69 total—31 professional; 38 support; plus 6–12 interns per semester |
| **DIRECTOR** | Edward H. Crane, president. Crane has been president of the Cato Institute since its founding. He also has worked as a chartered financial analyst for two national investment firms. |
| **TAX STATUS** | 501(c)(3) |
| **BUDGET** | 1998—$10.8 million<br>1999—Unavailable |
| **FUNDING SOURCES** | Individuals, 64 percent; foundations, 16 percent; corporations, 14 percent; other, 6 percent |
| **SCOPE** | Members: 10,000 sponsors (individuals, corporations, and foundations)<br>Branches/chapters: N/A<br>Affiliates: N/A |
| **PAC** | None |
| **METHOD OF OPERATION** | ♦ Advertisements ♦ Conferences/seminars ♦ Congressional testimony ♦ International activities ♦ Internet (electronic bulletin boards, Web site) ♦ Library/information clearinghouse ♦ Media outreach ♦ Research ♦ Speakers program ♦ Telecommunications services (mailing lists) ♦ TV and radio production |

◆ Corporate welfare ◆ Defense spending ◆ Deregulation ◆ Educational reform ◆ Environmental reform ◆ Health care reform ◆ Income tax abolition ◆ NATO ◆ Privatization ◆ Social Security reform ◆ Term limits ◆ Welfare reform

**CURRENT CONCERNS**

**PUBLICATIONS**

*The Affirmative Action Fraud: Can We Restore the American Civil Rights Vision?*
*Are We Running Out of Water?*
*Beyond NATO: Staying Out of Europe's War*
*A Brilliant Oxford Scholar Takes a Look at Environmentalism*
*The Captive Press: Foreign Policy Crises and the First Amendment*
*The Cato Handbook for Congress*
*Cato Letters* (series)
*Cato Papers* (series)
*Climate of Fear: Why Shouldn't We Worry about Global Warming*
*Delusions of Grandeur: The United Nations and Global Intervention*
*Economic Freedom of the World 1997*
*Educational Freedom in Eastern Europe*
*Energy: Ending the Never-Ending Crisis*
*The Future of Money in the Information Age*
*Is Generosity a Virtue?*
*Libertarianism: A Primer*
*The Libertarian Reader*
*Money and Markets in the Americas: New Challenges for Hemispheric Integration*
*NATO Enlargement: Illusions and Reality*
*Patient Power: The Free-Enterprise Alternative to Clinton's Health Plan*
*Policy Analysis* (12–15 times a year)
*Renaissance: The Rebirth of Liberty in the Heart of Europe*
*The Revolution in Development Economics*
*School Choice: Why You Need It—How You Get It*
*Science Without Sense: The Risky Business of Public Health Research*
*Simple Rules for a Complex World*
*Spooking the Public Out of House and Home*
*The State of Humanity*
*TripWire: Korea and U.S. Foreign Policy in a Changing World*
*The Ultimate Resource 2*
*Why Schools Fail*
*Why Welfare Can't Be Reformed*

**NEWSLETTER**

*Cato Audio Series* (monthly)
*Cato Journal* (3 times a year)
*Cato Policy Report* (bimonthly)
*Regulation* (quarterly)

**CONFERENCES**

Book Forums (bimonthly)
Monetary Conference (annual)
Policy Forums (weekly)
Regulatory Conference (annual)

## BOARD OF DIRECTORS

## EFFECTIVENESS

"Two years ago Social Security privatization probably had no more support in Washington than the legalization of marijuana. Today, the notion is being entertained by such heavyweights as Daniel Patrick Moynihan, the senior Democrat on the Senate Finance Committee. Privatization has become a very real possibility in part because big budget surpluses are apparently available to help pay for the transition.

" 'Something labeled 'partial privatization' is bound to be included in any broad-based Social Security reform,' predicted Sylvester Schieber, an economist at Watson Wyatt Worldwide, a pension consulting company, and a member of the Government's Advisory Council on the system. . . .

"For some conservative intellectuals—namely Carolyn Weaver of the American Enterprise Institute and Jose Pinera at the Cato Institute—privatization is a matter of cutting Washington down to size. As long as the Government stands ready to play nanny, workers will have little incentive to plan for their own retirement. And as long as pension income amounts to a gift from Government, political coalitions will work to keep the checks rolling in.

"This is surely the oldest and most principled argument for privatization. Though legislators talk the libertarian talk, few really walk the walk. The libertarian stance does, however, offer a high-minded rationale for policies based on other considerations." (*New York Times*, April 9, 1998)

"They are smart, provocative, opinionated, and won't win any points for diplomacy. But you've got to give them this: Libertarians are never boring.

"Exhibit A: last night's dinner to celebrate the 20th anniversary of the libertarian think tank, the Cato Institute. Perhaps this week was not the ideal time to criticize FDR, but that didn't stop Ed Crane, Cato founder and president. 'I think Franklin Roosevelt was a lousy president,' he said. 'What he did—which is to impose this great nanny state on America—was a great mistake.'

"Big government is bad, small government is good.

"After two decades of advocating a balanced budget and welfare reform, Cato is now the hot policy shop, respected for not compromising its core beliefs even when they get in the way of practical politics. Mainstream politicians and pundits—even Hollywood actors—quote its unorthodox mix of free-market economics and individual social rights. 'I'm a libertarian,' said Kurt Russell, who traveled to the dinner to see the Institute firsthand. 'It's fun to be in a room of people who think like you do—as opposed to a room that doesn't. I think a lot of people are libertarians and are afraid to admit it—or don't know it.'

"Last night's eclectic guest list of 2,000 people at the Washington Hilton included past and future presidential candidate Steve Forbes, Federal Reserve Board Chairman Alan Greenspan, writer William F. Buckley Jr., House Majority Leader Dick Armey, ABC correspondent John Stossel, columnist Nat Hentoff and author Nathaniel Branden.

" 'Two thousand people meeting in Washington in support of Cato is a revolution,' said Grover Norquist, president of Americans for Tax Reform. 'Ten years ago, you couldn't find 200 people. I think there is the sense we are the future. This is where history is moving.'

"Stossel said, 'I have no official political affiliation, but I sure seem to be agreeing with them on a lot of things.'

"So do millions of Americans, said Forbes. 'Even though Cato's is located in Washington, they've never fallen for the notion that this is the center of the universe,' he said. . . .

"One could hardly tell last night that the Institute has managed to irritate just about everyone in Washington at some point, even House Speaker Newt Gingrich and the 73 congressional freshmen who brought Cato into national headlines in 1994. . . .

"All this is too much for most politicians, but Cato is prospering." (*New York Times*, May 2, 1997)

---

"libertarian" (*New York Times*, April 21, 1998)

"Holiday Greetings in Washington lobby for more than good cheer. . . .

". . . A Cato Institute card has Santa checking a list that asks for 'Free Enterprise' and 'Peace,' in that order." (*Wall Street Journal*, December 19, 1997)

". . . The Cato Institute, named for the ancient Roman who fought for the Republic against the imperial vision of Julius Caesar, has traditionally been placed on the policy spectrum between the conservative Heritage Foundation and the liberal Brookings Institution. It is nonpartisan like the American Enterprise Institute, but more radical.

"Founded in San Francisco in 1977, the institute was moved to Washington in 1981, despite Crane's disdain for the capital. 'When your ideas are somewhat out of the mainstream—as they were when we moved here—it's important for people to see you face to face,' he said.

"As for those ideas, Cato has proposed dismantling eight Cabinet departments: Commerce, Education, Energy, Labor, Agriculture, Interior, Transportation and Veterans Affairs. Cato economists also want to cut spending across the board, including defense, replace the income tax with a national sales tax, reform Social Security and legalize the sale of drugs to adults." (*Washington Post*, May 2, 1997)

"a pro-market think tank" (*Washington Post*, April 4, 1997)

## POLITICAL ORIENTATION

# Center for National Policy (1981)

1 Massachusetts Avenue, NW
Suite 333
Washington, D.C. 20001
Phone: (202) 682-1800
Fax: (202) 682-1818
Internet: cnp@access.digex.net *or*
http://www.access.digex.net/~cnp/index.html

| | |
|---|---|
| **PURPOSE** | "To advance the public policy process and determine how government can best serve American interests both at home and abroad." |
| **STAFF** | 12 total—9 professional; 3 support; plus 4 part-time professionals; 4 interns |
| **DIRECTOR** | Maureen S. Steinbruner, president. Steinbruner has been with the Center for National Policy (CNP) since its founding, and was previously its policy director and executive vice president. Prior to joining CNP, she served in the U.S. Health, Education and Welfare Department and held positions in state government in Connecticut and Massachusetts. Steinbruner is a graduate of Stanford University and the Harvard University's John F. Kennedy School of Government. |
| **TAX STATUS** | 501(c)(3) |
| **BUDGET** | 1997—$1.28 million<br>1998—Unavailable<br>Proposed 1999—Unavailable |
| **FUNDING SOURCES** | Corporate donations, 40 percent; individuals, 20 percent; government contracts, 15 percent; membership dues, 10 percent; foundation grants, 10 percent; publications, 5 percent |
| **SCOPE** | Members: 400<br>Branches/chapters: N/A<br>Affiliates: N/A |
| **PAC** | None |

| | |
|---|---|
| ♦ Awards program ♦ Conferences/seminars ♦ Congressional testimony ♦ Focus groups ♦ International activities ♦ Internet (Web site) ♦ Internships ♦ Library/information clearinghouse ♦ Media outreach ♦ Policy analysis ♦ Polling ♦ Promoting debate on public policy issues ♦ Research ♦ Speakers program | **METHOD OF OPERATION** |

| | |
|---|---|
| ♦ Domestic and foreign policy ♦ Political process ♦ U.S. economy (wage issues) ♦ Urban policy | **CURRENT CONCERNS** |

| | |
|---|---|
| *CNP Transcripts* (ongoing series)<br>*Common Ground in a Changing World: An American Perspective*<br>*Diagnosing Voter Discontent: Politics, Identity, and the Search for Common Ground*<br>*In Brief* (series of issue papers linking population pressures and U.S. foreign policy interests)<br>*Job Quality Index* (quarterly review of the economy's changing job mix and compensation)<br>*Life in the City: A Status Report on the Revival of Urban Communities in America*<br>*Policywires* (series of issue papers on domestic economic issues) | **PUBLICATIONS** |

| | |
|---|---|
| Center for National Policy (semiannual) | **NEWSLETTER** |

| | |
|---|---|
| Newsmaker breakfasts, lunches, and squaretable debates (monthly) | **CONFERENCES** |

| | |
|---|---|
| Michael D. Barnes, chair; Joyce A. Ladner, vice chair; Maureen S. Steinbruner, president; Ronald M. Ansin, treasurer; Ralph B. Everett, secretary; James L. Tanner Jr., counsel | **BOARD OF DIRECTORS** |

Other members:
♦ John Brademas ♦ Genevieve S. Brooks ♦ Robert J. Brooks ♦ Jack W. Buechner ♦ Kathy Bushkin ♦ John F. Cooke ♦ James H. DeGraffenreidt Jr. ♦ Douglas H. Dority ♦ Carol Tucker Foreman ♦ John Freidenrich ♦ Morton Funger ♦ Allen S. Gartner ♦ Delon Hampton ♦ Ruth R. Harkin ♦ Benjamin W. Heineman Jr. ♦ Henry Y. Hwang ♦ Lester S. Hyman ♦ Charles S. Kim ♦ Peter S. Knight ♦ Peter B. Kovler ♦ Kathleen M. Linehan ♦ Terence R. McAuliffe ♦ Toby Moffett ♦ Sara S. Morgan ♦ Kirk O'Donnell ♦ Andrea S. Panaritis ♦ Howard G. Paster ♦ Robert M. Rubin ♦ Deborah M. Sale ♦ Jonathan B. Sallet ♦ J. Anthony Smith ♦ Vincent R. Sombrotto ♦ Donald M. Stewart ♦ Terrence D. Straub ♦ Eugene F. Swanzey ♦ Maurice Tempelsman ♦ Cyrus R. Vance ♦ Adam Yarmolinsky

## EFFECTIVENESS

"The Center for National Policy (CNP) in Washington reports in a study that jobs without health and pension benefits continue to increase; whereas, the percentage of jobs with high social benefits is reduced, slowing down the increase in total compensation. With the transition of the American economy into a high-tech, third-sector economy, the divided wage structure is more and more pronounced, says NCP Director [of Domestic Policy Programs] Michael Calabrese. . . ." (*Zeitung*, February 11, 1998)

"Ticking off the highlights of her first year as secretary of state, Madeleine Albright pointed Tuesday to the substantive and the personal, from prodding NATO to admit new members to being named one of the 25 most intriguing individuals, alongside a cloned sheep. . . .

"In a speech to the Center for National Policy, the think tank she presided over from 1989–92, Albright denounced the action [blocked payment of U.S. debt to the United Nations] as 'legislative blackmail' that made it harder for the administration to mount a united front against Iraq." (*USA Today*, January 14, 1998)

"According to the Center for National Policy, a Washington study group, the latest available statistics show the number of community development corporations has grown from 200 or more in 1970 to more than 2,000.

"In the South Bronx alone, more than $1 billion worth of housing has been built or renovated.

" 'Charlotte Street was a pioneer, a leading edge of this phenomenon,' said Maureen S. Steinbruner, the Center for National Policy's president." (*Los Angeles Times*, December 11, 1997)

"Bans on affirmative action in California and Texas are producing the most concerted efforts since the landmark Bakke ruling in 1978 to develop alternative approaches that will maintain diversity in higher education without using race as a factor.

"In Texas, for example, the Legislature is considering two measures— one that will admit the top 10 percent of graduates from all state high schools, another that will use a combination of rankings of high school seniors and consideration of economic disadvantage to maintain racial and ethnic diversity.

"Because nearly all high schools in the state are dominated by a single race—black, white, or Hispanic—using a percentage of graduates of all high schools would allow the relative segregation to foster diversity in higher education. Some form of the legislation is considered likely to pass, and Dan Morales, the Texas Attorney General, said he considered the legislation constitutional and consistent with court directives banning the use of race in admissions.

"Experts disagree heatedly on whether accounting for economic disadvantage or coming up with innovative admissions plans can substitute for race. But evidence is mounting that the bans on affirmative action in Texas and California, and under consideration elsewhere, will sharply cut the number of minority students at prestigious undergraduate and professional schools. . . .

"[A] recent analysis of trends at the University of California by Jerome Karabel, a sociologist at the University of California at Berkeley, concludes: 'Colorblind policies are likely to lead to a substantial resegregation of American higher education.'

"The main alternative being discussed is affirmative action based on class and criteria other than race.

" 'Using race per se is no longer sustainable from a moral, political or legal perspective, so we need to look to alternatives,' said Richard Kahlenberg, a fellow at the Center for National Policy who wrote 'The Remedy: Class, Race and Affirmative Action' (Basic Books, 1996).

" 'If you come up with a definition of class that is comprehensive and looks at a variety of factors, you can come up with a system that is fair and provides racial diversity.' " (*New York Times*, April 23, 1997)

"a favorite Democratic think tank" (*Washington Post*, July 14, 1997)

## POLITICAL ORIENTATION

# Center for Policy Alternatives (1975)

1875 Connecticut Avenue, NW
Suite 710
Washington, D.C. 20009
Phone: (202) 387-6030 *or* (800) 935-0699
Fax: (202) 986-2539
Internet: info@cfpa.org *or* http://www.cfpa.org

| | |
|---|---|
| **PURPOSE** | "Engages a new generation of leaders across the states to envision and realize progressive solutions for America's future." |
| **STAFF** | 27 total—22 professional; 5 support |
| **DIRECTOR** | Linda Tarr-Whelan, president and chief executive officer. Tarr-Whelan formerly was director of government relations for the National Education Association, deputy assistant to the president during the Carter Administration, administrative director of the New York State Labor Department, president of the Center for Women in Government, and public policy director for the American Federation of State, County, and Municipal Employees. She currently serves as deputy assistant to the president for Women's Concerns and as the U.S. ambassador to the United Nations Commission on the Status of Women. Tarr-Whelan holds a B.S.N. from Johns Hopkins University and an M.S. from the University of Maryland. |
| **TAX STATUS** | 501(c)(3) |
| **BUDGET** | 1997—$3.1 million<br>1998—$3.8 million<br>Proposed 1999—Unavailable |
| **FUNDING SOURCES** | Private sources, 97 percent; public sources, 2 percent; earned income, 1 percent |
| **SCOPE** | Members: 6,000 state elected officials and activists<br>Branches/chapters: N/A<br>Affiliate: Flemming Fellows Leadership Institute |
| **PAC** | None |

| | |
|---|---|
| ♦ Coalition forming ♦ Conferences/seminars ♦ Internet (Web site) ♦ Leadership development ♦ Legislative/regulatory monitoring (state) ♦ Participation in regulatory proceedings (state) ♦ Research ♦ Training and technical assistance for developing model legislation | *METHOD OF OPERATION* |
| ♦ Citizen participation ♦ Community development ♦ Economic development ♦ Election law reform ♦ Employment policy ♦ Environmental awareness ♦ Family and work ♦ Financial deregulation ♦ Government reform ♦ Health care ♦ Housing ♦ Impact of NAFTA and GATT on states ♦ Investment of employment pension funds ♦ Leadership development ♦ Reproductive rights ♦ Resource conservation ♦ Rural development ♦ Source reduction/waste prevention ♦ Sustainable development ♦ Tax reform ♦ Telecommunications ♦ Trade issues ♦ Unemployment and underemployment ♦ Voter registration ♦ Women's economic issues | *CURRENT CONCERNS* |
| The following is a list of sample publications:<br>*1998 Southeast Community Policy and Leadership Forum Policy Briefing Book*<br>*America's Economic Agenda: Women's Voices for Solutions*<br>*Approaches to Managed Care: A Health Care Briefing Book*<br>*Community Health Workers: A Leadership Brief on Preventive Health Programs*<br>*Financing the Future: Innovations in Child Care Financing*<br>*Integrated Health Systems: A Health Care Briefing Book*<br>*Purchasing Power in the Health Care Market: A Health Care Briefing Book*<br>*Resource Blueprint for California Land Recycling*<br>*The Sale and Conversion of Not-for-Profit Hospitals*<br>*State Report on Citizen Participation* (biannual)<br>*Technology and the Schools: Preparing the Workforce for the 21st Century*<br>*Women's Voices for the Economy '96* | *PUBLICATIONS* |
| *Alternatives* (monthly) | *NEWSLETTER* |
| Periodic seminars and forums | *CONFERENCES* |
| Barbara Davis Blum, chair; Rodney Ellis, vice chair; Linda Tarr-Whelan, president; Ann Beaudry, secretary; Maxine Champion, treasurer<br><br>Other board members:<br>♦ Veronica Biggins ♦ Donna Callejon ♦ Jane Campbell ♦ G. Spencer Coggs ♦ Pat Derian ♦ Ramona Edelin ♦ Doug Fraser ♦ Jack D. Gordon ♦ Spencer Hathaway ♦ William Lucy ♦ Julianne Malveaux ♦ Susan McLane ♦ Norman Y. Mineta ♦ Kenneth C. Montague Jr. ♦ Marylouise Oates ♦ Miles Rapport ♦ Antonio Riley ♦ Steve Protulis ♦ David Ramage ♦ Allyson Schwartz ♦ Juan Sepulveda ♦ Peter Shapiro ♦ Irving Stolberg ♦ John Sweeney ♦ Mary Elizabeth Teasley | *BOARD OF DIRECTORS* |

# EFFECTIVENESS

"Linda Tarr-Whelan, president of the Center for Policy Alternatives, says the women's movement should be looking to state legislatures as well as Congress for action. The center, whose Women's Voices polling project has identified issues that galvanize women to vote, has helped female legislators develop models of legislation that can be passed in states.

" 'The national policy in our country no longer just changes at the federal level,' says Tarr-Whelan. 'The momentum often starts in the states, where there are plenty of women leaders and they want to lead on behalf of other women.' The states, she points out, led the effort to stop insurance companies from limiting hospital stays of new mothers and infants to 24 hours.

"Most recently, legislators in California, Illinois, Georgia, New Mexico and Washington state introduced bills to stop insurance companies from discriminating against victims of domestic violence by denying them coverage or setting premiums based on a victim's increased risk.

"A total of 2 million to 4 million women a year are targets of violence by intimate partners, according to the U.S. Department of Health and Human Services. One survey found that eight of the 16 largest insurers in the country weighed domestic violence in deciding whether to issue insurance and how much to charge for it.

"Tarr-Whelan says other hot issues for women involve work and family conflicts and economic self-sufficiency, such as retirement security. . . . She believes health care issues and coverage are big worries for women that the movement needs to address.

"She says female legislators are energized by this new style of working together, addressing issues 'not just one state at a time, but as a wave across the states.'

"For the women's movement to remain relevant, it has to push issues relevant to women's lives, and it has to continue to give women reasons for electing women who will stand up for their concerns. This is happening with increasing frequency in the states, and it is giving women incentive to stay engaged in the political process." (*Washington Post*, February 5, 1997)

"Six months after the United Nations Fourth World Conference on Women, held in Beijing, we celebrate International Women's Day today with a look at several efforts to 'Bring Beijing Home.' Such is the mantra of some 50,000 conference delegates who are dedicating themselves and their organizations to making the vision of empowerment for women and girls a global reality.

"The new world order in this case is one in which women share leadership with men in their societies' political, social and economic institutions. It is one grounded on the fundamental premise that women's rights are human rights. The Platform for Action, which 189 nations have pledged to implement, states: 'Only a new era of international cooperation among Governments and peoples based on a spirit of partnership, an equitable, international social and economic environment, and a radical transformation of the relationship between women and men to one of full and equal partnership will enable the world to meet the challenges of the twenty-first century.' The Center for Policy Alternatives has just released a report on the Beijing conference, highlighting the major issues that were covered, the actions that were recommended in the platform, and some specific examples of what already is being done in various American communities. . . .

"The center has published a book titled 'Women's Rights Are Human Rights' available from the CPA, and it has joined with the National Education Association to produce a video called 'Cornerstone for the Future,' which will be available through the NEA. Both book and video are geared to help teachers inform their students about the conference, about the conditions of women around the world and about the global commitment to improving them. Hillary Rodham Clinton, who led the U.S. delegation to Beijing, is featured in the video, and she is scheduled to introduce it today at Luther Jackson Middle School in Fairfax County and to lead a discussion with the school's eighth-graders.

" 'The video and the book share one goal, which is to get the word out on the platform and to engage American girls and women in working together to make the world a better place in the next century,' says Linda Tarr-Whelan, president and chief executive of the CPA and a nongovernmental representative to the conference. 'The video is primarily designed to get a discussion going at the intermediate school level about what potential there is for women's leadership and what holds girls back.

" 'The most compelling thing to me about the Beijing experience was a new vision of women and girls as leaders. . . . Going into Beijing, everybody had a theory of something they wanted to correct, about women as victims who needed more services or as beneficiaries of some kind of program to help us out.'

" '. . . Each of the sections [of the report] ranging from health to sustainable development have some very practical ideas of what you can do in the workplace or in your town or your family. . . . It's a guide for every American woman who is interested in how to bring this new sense of leadership home in their own life.' " (*Washington Post*, March 8, 1996)

## POLITICAL ORIENTATION

"As we were heading into a week that promised nothing more uplifting than Linda Tripp at the federal courthouse, the pleasant surprise was provided by five Flemming fellows—young state legislators miraculously uncynical about politics and remarkably committed to advancing their communities. . . .

". . . [The program] brings together about 30 legislators each year, usually first- or second-termers, for three weekends of training aimed at making them more effective leaders.

"It's run by the 21-year-old Center for Policy Alternatives whose president, Linda Tarr-Whelan, was well ahead of the game in seeing that the states were becoming the new arena for domestic legislation and recognizing that liberals needed to lift their sights beyond Washington. The center is unabashedly progressive, but nonpartisan, and Wes Watkins, who runs the Flemming program, has made the Republican legislators—who number about one-quarter of the group—comfortable." (*Washington Post*, July 1, 1998)

# Economic Policy Institute (1986)

1660 L Street, NW
Suite 1200
Washington, D.C. 20036
Phone: (202) 775-8810
Fax: (202) 775-0819
Internet: epi@epinet.org *or* http://www.epinet.org

| | |
|---|---|
| **PURPOSE** | "To broaden the public debate about strategies to achieve a prosperous and fair economy." |
| **STAFF** | 32 total—25 professional; 7 support; plus 1 intern; 2 part-time; 2 visiting scholars |
| **DIRECTOR** | Jeff Faux, president. Prior to becoming president of the Economic Policy Institute, Faux was codirector of the National Center for Economic Alternatives. Previously he was an economist with the U.S. Office of Economic Opportunity and the State, Commerce, and Labor departments. Faux has been a small-businessman, a part-time farmer, and a member of a municipal planning board in Maine. He has written books and articles that have appeared in many anthologies, magazines, and newspapers. Faux was educated at Queens College, George Washington University, and Harvard University. |
| **TAX STATUS** | 501(c)(3) |
| **BUDGET** | 1998—Unavailable<br>Proposed 1999—Unavailable |
| **FUNDING SOURCES** | Foundation grants, unions, corporations and business organizations, individuals, publications, and other income |
| **SCOPE** | Members: N/A<br>Branches/chapters: N/A<br>Affiliates: N/A |
| **PAC** | None |

♦ Conferences/seminars ♦ Congressional testimony ♦ Congressional voting analysis ♦ Electoral politics ♦ Internet (Web site) ♦ Library/information clearinghouse ♦ Media outreach ♦ Research ♦ Speakers program

♦ Globalization of economies ♦ Government and the economy ♦ Labor market problems ♦ Living standards ♦ Politics of public opinion ♦ Productivity ♦ Rural and urban policies ♦ Sustainable economics ♦ Trade and fiscal policies ♦ Trends in wages, incomes, and prices ♦ Work organization

*America's Inheritance: More Than Just Debt*
*The Bottom Line on the Balanced Budget Amendment: The Cost to Each State, The Case for Public Investment*
*Clearing the Air: The Impact of Air Quality Regulations on Jobs*
*Cost and Quality Matters: Workplace Innovations in the Health Care Industry*
*The Decade of Declining Federal Aid*
*EPI Issue Briefs* (various topics)
*Financial Market Constraints and Business Strategy in the U.S.*
*Getting Prices Right: The Debate Over the Consumer Price Index*
*The Impact of Employer Oppositions on Union Certification Win Rates*
*Impact of Health and Safety Committees on OSHA Enforcement Patterns*
*Jobs and the Environment: The Myth of the National Trade-Off*
*The Macroeconomics of Saving, Finance, and Investment*
*Managing Work and Family: Nonstandard Work Arrangements Among Managers and Professionals*
*Paying for Health Care: Affordability and Equity*
*The Political Arithmetic of the NAFTA Vote*
*The Privatization of Public Service: Lessons From Case Studies*
*The Prosperity Gap: A Chartbook of American Living Standards*
*The Role of Labor Market Institutions in Employee Training: Comparing the United States and Germany*
*Restoring Broadly Shared Prosperity: A Conference Volume*
*Small Business, Job Creation, and Wages*
*The State of Working America, 1998–99*
*Up From Deficit Reduction*
*Where's the Money Going? Changes in the Level and Composition of Education Spending, 1991–96*
*Who Wins With a Higher Minimum Wage?*

*The EPI Journal* (quarterly)

Sponsors conferences, seminars, and press briefings on an ongoing basis

## EFFECTIVENESS

"Close to 7 million Americans are scheduled to get a raise today when the federally mandated minimum wage rises to $5.15 an hour. Across the United States, many fast food workers, retail clerks, gas station attendants and others will be earning 40 cents an hour more when they report to work as the second phase of the increase goes into effect. It was raised to $4.75 from $4.25 last Oct. 1.

"Most of the 6.8 million workers affected are women who work in the service sector, according to a report to be issued Tuesday by the Economic Policy Institute, a Washington-based think tank.

"The institute's study found that in 18 states more than 10 percent of the work force will be affected by the increase, which primarily benefits low-income families.

"To critics who warn that increasing the minimum wage could spark a new round of price increases and inflation, institute analyst Jared Bernstein said: 'It's a mistake to think that any increase in wages is inflationary and there is substantial room for non-inflationary wage growth, particularly at the bottom end of the scale.'

"The Federal Reserve, determined to keep a lid on inflation, has held interest rates steady since last March. But it has closely monitored price and wage increases as the economy has expanded at a steady pace. Many analysts believe the Fed may raise interest rates before the end of the year if signs of higher prices appear." (*Washington Post*, September 1, 1997)

"Just a year after winning a 90-cent increase in the nation's hourly minimum wage, Sen. Edward M. Kennedy (D-Mass.) served notice yesterday that he will seek another increase aimed at raising the wage floor by $2.10 to $7.25 over the next five years.

"In a Senate floor speech, Kennedy said the proposal, which is likely to encounter stiff Republican opposition, would restore the inflation-adjusted purchasing power of the minimum wage to its pre-1980s level by 2002. The 1996 bill, which Kennedy pushed through over the opposition of many GOP leaders, increased the minimum wage from $4.25 to $4.75 an hour on Oct. 1, with another increase of 40 cents scheduled to take effect Sept. 1.

"To bolster his case for another round of increases, Kennedy cited an analysis issued yesterday by the liberal Economic Policy Institute, which concluded that last October's increase raised earnings for low-income working families without jeopardizing jobs, contrary to critics' arguments that it would cost jobs.

"The institute found that the increase raised wages for 4 million workers, two-thirds of whom were adults. Despite warnings from critics, the institute said, the increase did not primarily benefit teenagers in part-time, after-school jobs or lead employers to eliminate jobs held by entry-level workers. The biggest beneficiaries were black and Hispanic teenagers, it found.

" 'Employment does not go down because the minimum wage goes up,' Kennedy concluded. 'The overall conditions of the economy determine the levels of employment for all sectors of the work force.' " (*Washington Post*, July 12, 1997)

"The economy may be as good as it gets, but that's not good enough for the folks in both political parties.

"For liberal Democrats, what stands out following month after month of good news on unemployment, inflation, interest rates and stock prices are the stubbornly stagnant wages of the least-skilled workers and, in turn, a growing gap between the incomes of the richest and poorest Americans.

" 'The economy is, on the numbers, better than it's been in 25 or 30 years, and there's no doubt about that,' says House Democratic Leader Richard Gephardt of Missouri. 'Having said that, there are many places, mainly among the low-middle class, people in the middle, and people trying to get in the middle . . . who are not feeling the benefits yet of the productivity they have helped produce.'

"Conservative Republicans, meanwhile, allow that the economy has thrived on President Clinton's watch. But they contend it could be humming even more if taxes were slashed, particularly on investors' capital gains from the sale of stocks and other assets. . . .

"Whatever reservations the public may share with the politicians, 'Americans' attitudes toward today's economy are as bullish as the economic statistics themselves,' say Peter Hart and Robert Teeter, who conducted the Journal/NBC poll. The latest survey questions yielded the most positive responses in the poll's eight-year history, they note.

"Nearly two-thirds of respondents rated the economy a six or more on a scale of one to 10. Three out of five said they are better off today than they were four years ago. 'Satisfaction with the economy cuts across race, income and education level,' Messrs. Hart and Teeter say. More Americans are optimistic about the future: A 53% to 42% majority expects its children's generation to be better off, while the opposite view drew a similar majority just 18 months ago.

"The public attitude is hardly a surprise given the drumbeat of good economic news. At 4.8%, unemployment is at a 24-year low, and consumer confidence is at a 28-year high. Inflation is just 2.2%, and for the first time since 1952, producer prices actually have declined for five months running. Interest rates remain low, and record numbers of Americans own homes. The stock market hits records routinely. The federal budget deficit, as a percentage of the economy's total goods and services, is at its lowest level since 1974.

" 'I'm not surprised if people are feeling a little better,' says Jeff Faux of the Economic Policy Institute. . . . 'But this is not the 1950s,' he adds. 'Growth is not being distributed the way it used to be.' After declining for years, wages for less-skilled workers are at best keeping ahead of inflation now. 'Workers have just begun to share, just a bit, in the prosperity their front-office bosses have enjoyed,' says Rep. David Obey, a leading liberal Democrat from Wisconsin." (*Wall Street Journal*, June 27, 1997)

## POLITICAL ORIENTATION

"pro-labor" (*Washington Post*, November 18, 1997)

"a liberal Democratic think tank" (*Wall Street Journal*, June 27, 1997)

# Ethics and Public Policy Center (1976)

1015 15th Street, NW
Suite 900
Washington, D.C. 20005
Phone: (202) 682-1200
Fax: (202) 408-0682
Internet: ethics@eppc.org *or* http://www.eppc.org

---

"To clarify and to reinforce the bond between the Judeo-Christian moral tradition and the public debate over domestic and foreign policy issues."

*PURPOSE*

---

23 total—12 professional; 11 support

*STAFF*

---

Elliott Abrams, president. Abrams was appointed president of the Ethics and Public Policy Center (EPPC) in 1996. Prior to his becoming president, Abrams was a senior fellow at the Hudson Institute from 1990 to 1996. He also has served as the assistant secretary of state for international organizations affairs, as the assistant secretary of state for human rights and humanitarian affairs, and as the assistant secretary of state for Inter-American affairs. Currently Abrams is a member of the Council on Foreign Relations and chairman of the Francisco Marroquin Foundation and the Nicaraguan Resistance Educational Foundation. He received a bachelor's degree from Harvard College in 1969, an masters of international relations from the London School of Economics in 1970, and a doctorate of law from Harvard Law School in 1973.

*DIRECTOR*

---

501(c)(3)

*TAX STATUS*

---

1997—$1.7 million
1998—Unavailable
Proposed 1999—Unavailable

*BUDGET*

---

Foundations, 64 percent; investments, 19 percent; corporations, 12 percent; individuals, 1 percent; other, 5 percent

*FUNDING SOURCES*

---

Members: N/A
Branches/chapters: N/A
Affiliates: N/A

*SCOPE*

---

| | |
|---|---|
| *PAC* | None |
| *METHOD OF OPERATIONS* | ♦ Conferences/seminars ♦ Congressional testimony ♦ International activities ♦ Internet (Web site) ♦ Media outreach ♦ Political commentary ♦ Research ♦ Speakers program |
| *CURRENT CONCERNS* | ♦ Abortion ♦ American citizenship and identity ♦ Catholic social doctrine ♦ Euthanasia ♦ Jewish culture and politics ♦ Judicial activism ♦ Just war after the Cold war ♦ Marriage and society ♦ Medical science and society ♦ Neuroscience and the human spirit ♦ Religion in public schools ♦ Religious right in American public life ♦ U.S. international human rights policy, with focus on religious freedom |
| *PUBLICATIONS* | *The 9 Lives of Population Control*<br>*Benchmarks: Great Constitutional Controversies in the Supreme Court*<br>*Building the Free Society: Democracy, Capitalism, and Catholic Social Teaching*<br>*Caesar's Coin Revisited: Christians and the Limits of Government*<br>*Changing Witness: Catholic Bishops and Public Policy, 1917–1994*<br>*Close Calls: Intervention, Terrorism, Missile Defense, and 'Just War' Today*<br>*Creation at Risk?*<br>*Disciples and Democracy: Religious Conservatives and the Future of American Politics*<br>*Ending Affirmative Action: The Case for Colorblind Justice*<br>*Faith or Fear: How Jews Can Survive in a Christian America*<br>*The Final Revolution: The Resistance Church and the Collapse of Communism*<br>*Honor Among Nations: Intangible Interests and Foreign Policy*<br>*Idealism Without Illusions: U.S. Foreign Policy in the 1990s*<br>*Last Rights? Assisted Suicide and Euthanasia Debated*<br>*A Preserving Grace: Protestants, Catholics, and Natural Law*<br>*The Price of Prophecy: Orthodox Churches on Peace, Freedom, and Security*<br>*Reinventing the American People: Unity and Diversity Today*<br>*Religious Liberty in the Supreme Court: The Cases that Define the Debate over Church and State*<br>*Soul of the World: Notes on the Future of Public*<br>*American Character* (quarterly; domestic issues commentary)<br>*American Purpose* (quarterly; foreign policy commentary)<br>*Center Newsletter* (quarterly) |
| *CONFERENCES* | Sponsors various lectures, seminars, and conferences on various issues including political attitudes, God and science, bioethics, media and religion, and welfare and religion |

## EFFECTIVENESS

"The Rev. J. Bryan Hehir, a Jesuit priest and veteran of the Washington policy wars who now teaches at the Harvard Divinity School, had it just right at a forum this week on the vexing issue of how to address China's persecution of its Christian citizens.

"Challenging the advocates who have moved the issue of religious freedom into American political consciousness in just a few years, Hehir said the situation in China should be treated in an activist manner but not as a crusade and should be set in the context of American consideration of other human rights violations and of other foreign-policy purposes, too. In short, make a place at the table but don't upset the table. For his realism and balance, he was energetically attacked by Robert Kagan of the Carnegie Endowment for International Peace. Kagan made an unapologetic pitch for single-issue politics, declaring that it was for governments, not advocates, to do the policy blending on Christians in China. Let the advocates advocate, he said.

"This is where we are in Washington these days on a foreign-policy issue of uncommon emotional as well as political saliency. The old human rights regulars are on the defensive, accused in so many words of going stale and selling out. Their new accusers have embraced the Chinese religious freedom issue with a passion.

"With a special passion. While the old liberals fret that religious freedom as a general human rights issue takes Americans onto bumpy constitutional and historical terrain, the conservatives see the specific China human rights issue as the cutting edge of an American China policy intended to contain a likely emerging Chinese threat.

"Says Elliott Abrams, whose Ethics and Public Policy Center organized this week's Washington forum: 'We should have learned from our victory in the Cold War that the assertion of American ideals is essential to the advancement of our security interests.' The reason is simple, Abrams went on, citing Kagan: 'China's political system is a strategic problem for the United States.' " (*Washington Post*, January 9, 1998)

". . . This year, the overlap of Christmas and the eight-day Hanukah celebration has turned an already stressful season into an ecumenical challenge for many Washington area households. In ways large and small, tangible and symbolic, these interfaith families are for the first time in five years trying to accommodate the ancient and closely held customs of Jewish and Christian faiths simultaneously. . . .

"How best to do that has become a hotly debated point, particularly among conservative Jews who fear that intermarriage between Jews and Christians undermines the strength of a historically persecuted religion. National surveys show that one of every two Jews marries outside the faith, and that only 28 percent of those couples raise their children Jewish.

" 'If you are trying to raise a child to be a Jew, then you have to create a sense of Jewish identity,' said Elliott Abrams, president of the Ethics and Public Policy Center in Washington and a former assistant secretary of state. 'You really weaken that sense of identity if you celebrate two religions.'

"For Jews, Abrams said, picking one religion to celebrate is particularly important this year, with Christmas arriving during Hanukah. The last time the holidays coincided was 1992, and they will coincide again in 2000.

" 'What we're talking about here is not celebrating a holiday, but practicing Judaism or practicing Christianity,' Abrams said. 'You are not practicing Judaism if you celebrate Christmas.' " (*Washington Post*, December 24, 1997)

## POLITICAL ORIENTATION

"conservative" (*Washington Post*, February 19, 1997)

# Free Congress Foundation (1977)

717 Second Street, NE
Washington, D.C. 20002
Phone: (202) 546-3000
Fax: (202) 543-8425
Internet: http://www.freecongress.org

| | |
|---|---|
| "Dedicated to conservative governance, traditional values and institutional reform." | **PURPOSE** |
| 25–30 total | **STAFF** |
| Paul M. Weyrich, president. Prior to founding the Free Congress Foundation, Weyrich also founded the American Legislative Exchange Council in 1973 and was the founding president of the Heritage Foundation from 1973–1974. Currently, he serves as the national chairman of the Coalition for America, the national chairman of the Free Congress PAC, and a board member of the Krieble Institute of Russia. A writer, public policy specialist, and political activist, Weyrich has worked extensively in broadcast and print media as well as public policy. | **DIRECTOR** |
| 501(c)(3) | **TAX STATUS** |
| 1998—Unavailable<br>Proposed 1999—Unavailable | **BUDGET** |
| Unavailable | **FUNDING SOURCES** |
| Members: N/A<br>Branches/chapters: N/A<br>Affiliates: America's Voice (formerly the National Empowerment Television network), the Coalition for America, and the Krieble Institute of Russia | **SCOPE** |
| Free Congress Political Action Committee | **PAC** |

| **METHOD OF OPERATION** | ◆ Conferences/seminars ◆ Grassroots organizing ◆ Internet (Web site) ◆ Media outreach ◆ Research ◆ Television and radio production ◆ Training and technical assistance |
|---|---|
| **CURRENT CONCERNS** | Research divisions: ◆ Center for Conservative Governance ◆ Center for Cultural Conservatism ◆ Center for Law and Democracy ◆ Center for Technology Policy ◆ Center for Judicial Selection Monitoring Project |
| **PUBLICATIONS** | *American Investigator* (special reports series)<br>*Cultural Conservatism: Theory and Practice*<br>*Cultural Conservatism: Toward a New National Agenda*<br>*Does the First Amendment Violate Itself?*<br>*Gridlock in Government: How To Break the Stagnation of America*<br>*The Judges War*<br>*Law and Economics and Civil Justice*<br>*Ninth Justice: The Fight for Bork*<br><br>Also publishes special reports, monographs, essays, and policy briefs |
| **NEWSLETTER** | *Constitutional Liberties Weekly Update* (weekly)<br>*Essays on Our Times* (periodic)<br>*Judicial Selection Monitor* (monthly)<br>*Policy Insights* (periodic)<br>*Weyrich Insider* (monthly) |
| **CONFERENCES** | Unavailable |
| **BOARD OF DIRECTORS** | Jeffrey H. Coors, chairman; Ralph M. Hall, secretary; E. Ralph Hostetter, treasurer<br><br>Other board members:<br>◆ William L. Armstrong ◆ William G. Batchelder ◆ Howard H. Callaway ◆ Michael P. Farris ◆ Terry J. Kohler ◆ Elizabeth Lurie ◆ R. Daniel McMichael ◆ Charles A. Moser ◆ Kathleen Teague Rothschild ◆ Paul M. Weyrich |
| **EFFECTIVENESS** | "In Washington, two conservative advocacy groups are airing ads encouraging women to call a toll-free number 'if you believe you have been a victim of sexual harassment by the president.' The $260,000 campaign has been mounted by the Free Congress Foundation, headed by conservative activist Paul Weyrich, and the National Center for Public Policy Research.<br><br>"Brad Keena of Free Congress said the line has received 'thousands' of calls but no 'authentic' complaint against Clinton. He said the purpose was to demonstrate that the definition of sexual harassment is 'too broad' and that the military should not allow personnel to make anonymous complaints to a hot line. |

" 'We're not set up to be a front for Paula Jones,' said Amy Ridenour, president of the public policy center. The goal, she said, was 'to spur a national conversation about sexual harassment.'

"The ads have aired on CNN's Washington outlet and on WTOP radio, Ridenour said, but have been rejected as inappropriate by Fox News Channel and MSNBC and are pending a decision on national distribution by CNN. 'It wasn't anything we wanted to be associated with,' said Fox senior vice president Paul Rittenberg.

"Some of those who have called the hot line, Ridenour acknowledged, offer allegations 'so extreme they can't possibly be true—for instance, the president calls them every hour all night long to harass them.'

"James Carville, the president's adviser, dismissed the ads as 'typical right-wing garbage,' saying: 'This whole Paula Jones thing is rooted in partisanship and money-ship.'

"The ads focus on what Ridenour describes as the condescending reaction to Jones's charges. 'When a working-class woman accused the president of sexual harassment, the clock was turned back,' they say. 'The president's men immediately unleashed a brutal, unsubstantiated attack to discredit the morals and ethics of the woman bringing the charge.' "
(*Washington Post,* November 13, 1997)

"Conservative activist Paul Weyrich, an increasingly divisive figure on the right, has been ousted by NET, the television network he founded three years ago.

"Weyrich, who recently has lambasted such Republicans as House Speaker Newt Gingrich (R-Ga.) and Senate Majority Leader Trent Lott (R-Miss.), said in a statement that he had been 'asked to resign' by the conservative network's board as its president and lead commentator. Weyrich continues to head the Free Congress Foundation, a conservative advocacy group that retains a financial stake in NET, and will remain on the network's board. Sources close to the network say some directors had grown upset with Weyrich's harsh attacks on GOP leaders and with an unflattering cover story on him last month in the *New Republic.* Weyrich, who hosts four NET programs, has accused Sen. Orrin G. Hatch (R-Utah), for example, of having 'psychological problems,' and said after Lott endorsed a chemical weapons treaty: 'I can't have friends who sell out their country.'

" 'He's become a marginal and ineffective figure,' said one Republican strategist. 'With Weyrich, it's either my way or the highway. There's no disagreeing with him. It's all dogma.' This person said that NET, originally called National Empowerment Television, provided the 'glitz and glamour' for Free Congress and that Weyrich's departure 'will diminish his allure.' Weyrich did not return calls yesterday.

"The battle at NET comes as Weyrich is involved in another controversy: Free Congress has gotten into a spat with three Republican senators over its effort to raise $1.4 million to defeat some of President Clinton's judicial nominees.

"For those who give at least $10,000, the fund-raising appeal promises 'periodic private briefings and intimate dinners' with leading conservatives and 'elected public figures closely involved with the judicial confirmation process.'

"But three of the four GOP senators used in a videotaped appeal said this week that while they support the group's aims, they did not authorize the use of their comments for fund-raising purposes.

"Both NET and the judicial campaign involve Weyrich trademarks, an aggressive mix of money, television and conservative advocacy. But NET has by far been his most ambitious project." (*Washington Post*, November 8, 1997)

## POLITICAL ORIENTATION

"conservative" (*Washington Post*, November 6, 1997)

# The Heritage Foundation (1973)

214 Massachusetts Avenue, NE
Washington, D.C. 20002
Phone: (202) 546-4400
Fax: (202) 546-0904
Internet: http://www.heritage.org

---

"To formulate and promote conservative public policies based on the principles of free enterprises, limited government, individual freedom, traditional American values, and a strong national defense."

**PURPOSE**

---

Unavailable

**STAFF**

---

Edwin J. Feulner Jr., president. Feulner has served as president of the Heritage Foundation since 1977. He also serves as vice chairman of the National Commission on Economic Growth and Tax Reform. He is past chairman of both the U.S. Advisory Commission on Public Diplomacy and the Intercollegiate Studies Institute. Feulner previously was executive director of the House Republican Study Committee and an administrative assistant to Rep. Philip M. Crane (R-Ill.). He received a B.S. from Regis College in Denver, an M.B.A. from the Wharton School, and a Ph.D. from the University of Edinburgh.

**DIRECTOR**

---

501(c)(3)

**TAX STATUS**

---

1997—$25 million
1998—Unavailable
Proposed 1999—Unavailable

**BUDGET**

---

Individuals, 47 percent; foundation grants, 21 percent; investment income, 24 percent; publications, 4 percent; corporate donations, 4 percent

**FUNDING SOURCES**

---

Members: More than 200,000
Branch/chapter: Office in Moscow
Affiliates: N/A

**SCOPE**

---

None

**PAC**

---

| | |
|---|---|
| *METHOD OF OPERATION* | ♦ Coalition forming ♦ Conferences/seminars ♦ Congressional testimony ♦ Electronic bulletin boards ♦ Films/video/audiotapes ♦ International activities ♦ Internet (Web site) ♦ Internships ♦ Legislative/regulatory monitoring (federal) ♦ Library/information clearinghouse ♦ Media outreach ♦ Product merchandising ♦ Professional development services ♦ Research ♦ Speakers program |
| *CURRENT CONCERNS* | ♦ Asia ♦ Budget and tax policies ♦ Deregulation ♦ Education reform ♦ Entitlements (including Medicare and Social Security) ♦ Federalism ♦ Foreign aid ♦ Health care ♦ Missile defenses ♦ National security budget ♦ Post–Cold War strategy ♦ Russia ♦ Telecommunications reform ♦ Trade ♦ United Nations peacekeeping ♦ Welfare reform |
| *PUBLICATIONS* | The following is a list of sample publications: *105th Congress Congressional Directory* *1998 Index of Economic Freedom* *Balancing America's Budget: Ending the Era of Big Government* *Between Diplomacy and Deterrence: Strategies for U.S. Relations with China* *Congress and Civil Society: How Legislators Can Champion Civic Renewal in Their Districts* *Courage* (video and lecture booklet) *The Guide to Public Policy Experts* (1997–1998 edition) *Issues '98* *Making America Safer: What Citizens and Their State and Local Officials Can Do to Combat Crime* *Mandate for Leadership IV: Turning Ideas Into Actions* *The March of Freedom: Modern Classics in Conservative Thought* *The Power of Ideas: The Heritage Foundation at 25 Years* *Restoring American Leadership: A U.S. Foreign and Defense Policy Blueprint* *School Choice Programs: What's Happening in the States* (1998 edition) *U.S. and Asia Statistical Handbook* (1997–1998 edition) *Why America Needs a Tax Cut*<br><br>Also publishes policy papers |
| *NEWSLETTER* | *Heritage Members News* (bimonthly) *Heritage Today* (bimonthly) *Policy Review* (bimonthly magazine) *Reforming Congress* (monthly) |
| *CONFERENCES* | Third Generation discussion group (monthly gathering of young conservatives) Variety of lectures, conferences, seminars, and roundtables |

## BOARD OF DIRECTORS

## EFFECTIVENESS

"As the nation begins debating how to shore up Social Security for the aging baby-boom generation, advocates of fundamentally changing the system are honing their argument to a single theme: that as an investment Social Security is a bad deal. . . .

"Younger people, especially, will get a bad deal relative to people born longer ago, the critics said. And some demographic groups, including black men, who have lower life expectancy than the general population, will lose money on Social Security, the advocates add.

"The results, they said, are particularly striking when the system's pay-off is compared with the much higher rates of return available in the stock and bond markets. Allowing part of Social Security taxes to be invested in such areas would allow even low-income workers to accumulate significant wealth in their working lives, the critics contend. . . .

"Proponents of a more market-oriented approach received fresh ammunition this year from a study by the Heritage Foundation, a . . . group that favors changing the system. The study said, 'The Social Security system's rate of return for most Americans will be vastly inferior to what they could expect from placing their payroll taxes in even the most conservative private investments.' . . .

"The Heritage study illustrates the central argument of those who are calling for a more market-oriented system. A couple with children in which both partners are 30 and both earn $26,000 a year would pay, along with their employers, $320,000 in Social Security taxes by the time they retire and would receive $450,000 in retirement benefits before dying, an inflation-adjusted annual return of 1.23 percent, the study said.

"By contrast, the stock market generated average annual returns of 7.56 percent from 1926 to 1996, after accounting for inflation, according to Ibbotson Associates, a research concern. Allowing the couple to invest its Social Security taxes in a mutual fund with a 5 percent rate of return would more than double, to $975,000, the money available for their retirement, the study said." (*New York Times*, March 2, 1998)

"It's not just that Social Security is headed for bankruptcy when the baby boomers retire. It is. But the solvency problem can be fixed without fundamentally changing the system. Raise the retirement age, lower cost-of-living adjustments, tax more benefits, give the payroll tax a nudge, and it's done. Rather, the growing pressure to renovate the retirement program is rooted in the general public's increasing financial sophistication. In the past two decades, many Americans have found out what it's like to have some control over their retirement savings. They have watched their money in IRAs and 401(k)s grow with the market. They know about rates of return. And when they look at Social Security with newly trained eyes, they see a bum deal.

"A new study, scheduled for release by the conservative Heritage Foundation today, will further those misgivings. It calculates expected rates of return from Social Security for a variety of demographic and ethnic groups. And it comes up with some surprising and disturbing findings.

"The overarching conclusion is that the rates are declining. The program is a good deal for today's retirees. Folks born before 1935 can, on average, expect to get back all the money paid into the system on their behalf in payroll taxes, plus inflation, plus an annual rate of return of about 5%.

"But for today's 30-year-old couple-two wage earners with two children and an average income—the system promises a return of just 1.2%. If the same payroll taxes were put in a conservative IRA investment, say, a mutual fund that is half Treasury bills and half blue-chip stocks—the return would be closer to 5%. That's the difference between a retirement kitty of less than $500,000 in today's dollars and nearly $1 million. . . .

"GOP Rep. Mark Sanford, an advocate of Social Security overhaul, has used preliminary Heritage data when speaking to black audiences in his South Carolina district. 'People can't believe there is that kind of unfairness in the system,' he says. 'Black audiences are horrified.'. . .

"All this talk about rates of return makes the system's defenders nervous. In part, they fear people will stop supporting it if they see how income is shifted from the affluent to the poor. The term 'Social Security' has a certain magic in public discourse; the word 'welfare' does not." (*Wall Street Journal*, January 12, 1998)

"A diverse, bipartisan coalition—including the Citizens for a Sound Economy, Friends of the Earth, Public Citizen and the Heritage Foundation—joined together yesterday to 'stop the bailout' of electric utilities as the industry moves toward deregulation.

"The 'bailout' the groups oppose is the payment of 'stranded costs,' or investments utilities made in generation and other assets to serve customers in their specific territories. Utilities say those investments will become stranded when power generation is deregulated because their recovery will no longer be guaranteed through electricity bills paid by consumers.

"Utilities and others have estimated that stranded costs could be between $200 billion and $300 billion. But the 'stop the bailout' coalition said bailing out the industry for bad investments 'would constitute one of the largest transfers of wealth in U.S. history.' " (*Wall Street Journal*, August 8, 1997)

## POLITICAL ORIENTATION

"a body that has guided Republican thinking from Ronald Reagan to Newt Gingrich" (*New York Times*, May 10, 1998)

"conservative" (*New York Times*, March 2, 1998)

# Hoover Institution on War, Revolution and Peace (1919)

Stanford University
Stanford, California 94305
Phone: (650) 723-1754
Fax: (650) 723-1687
Internet: http://www-hoover.stanford.edu

| | |
|---|---|
| "To recall the voice of experience against the making of war, and by the study of these records and their publication to recall man's endeavors to make and preserve peace and to sustain for America the safeguards of the American way of life." | *PURPOSE* |
| 250 total (including resident scholars and support staff) | *STAFF* |
| John Raisian, director. Raisian joined the Hoover Institution in 1986 and was appointed director in 1989. He also holds an appointment as a senior fellow at the Hoover Institution. Raisian was a consultant to the Rand Corporation from 1974 to 1975, after which he was a visiting professor of economics at the University of Washington from 1975 to 1976. From 1976 to 1980, he was an assistant professor of economics at the University of Houston. Raisian worked for the U.S. Labor Department for six years. He was president of Unicon Research Corporation, an economic consulting firm in Los Angeles, before joining the Hoover Institution. Raisian is the author of numerous articles on the economics of labor markets. He received a B.A. in economics and mathematics from Ohio University and a Ph.D. in economics from the University of California at Los Angeles. | *DIRECTOR* |
| 501(c)(3) | *TAX STATUS* |
| Fiscal year ending August 30, 1997—$22 million<br>F.Y. 1998—Unavailable<br>Proposed F.Y. 1999—Unavailable | *BUDGET* |
| Endowment payout, 37 percent; gifts, 37 percent; Stanford University operating funds, 18 percent; royalties, publication sales and miscellaneous, 7 percent; government grants, 1 percent | *FUNDING SOURCES* |
| Members: N/A<br>Branches/chapters: N/A<br>Affiliates: N/A | *SCOPE* |

| | |
|---|---|
| *PAC* | None |
| *METHOD OF OPERATION* | ◆ Conferences/seminars ◆ Congressional testimony ◆ Exhibits ◆ Films/video/audiotapes ◆ Internet (Web site) ◆ International activities ◆ Library/information clearinghouse ◆ Media Fellows Program ◆ Media outreach ◆ National Fellows Program (one-year appointment) ◆ National Security Affairs Program ◆ Research |
| *CURRENT CONCERNS* | ◆ American institutions and economic performance ◆ Continuing evolution of the former Soviet Union ◆ Democracy and free markets ◆ Domestic and international political and economic change ◆ Education reform ◆ Intellectual capital ◆ International rivalries and global cooperation ◆ Welfare reform |
| *PUBLICATIONS* | The following is a list of sample publications:<br>*Breaking the Environmental Policy Gridlock*<br>*Capital for Our Time: The Economic, Legal, and Management Challenges of Intellectual Capitalism*<br>*China and Korea: Dynamic Relations*<br>*Democracy and the Korean Economy*<br>*Facing the Age Wave*<br>*Fixing Russia's Banks: A Proposal for Growth*<br>*Hoover Essays and Essays in Public Policy* (monograph series)<br>*The New Federalism: Can the States Be Trusted?*<br>*North Korea After Kim Il Sung: Continuity or Change?*<br>*Reflections on Europe*<br>*Russia's 1996 Presidential Election: The End of Polarized Politics*<br>*The Wealth of Nations in the Twentieth Century: The Policies and Institutional Determinants of Economic Development*<br>*What's Gone Wrong in America's Classrooms?* |
| *NEWSLETTER* | *The Hoover Newsletter* (quarterly)<br>*Hoover Digest* (quarterly journal) |
| *CONFERENCES* | Capital Formation and Economic Growth<br>Intellectual Capital<br>The New Federalism: Can the States Be Trusted?<br>Facing the Age Wave |
| *BOARD OF DIRECTORS* | Herbert Hoover III, chairman; W. Kurt Hauser, vice chairman<br><br>Other executive committee members:<br>◆ Martin Anderson ◆ Peter B. Bedford ◆ Paul L. Davies Jr. ◆ William C. Edwards ◆ Heather R. Higgins ◆ Andrew Hoover ◆ George H. Hume ◆ Peyton M. Lake ◆ Eff W. Martin ◆ Bowen H. McCoy ◆ Nancy Barry Munger ◆ George F. Russell Jr. ◆ Richard M. Scaife ◆ John R. Stahr ◆ Thaddeus N. Taube |

"If free trade is essential to prosperity, as any respectable economist will tell you, why do free-trade policies seem to be forever under assault? One reason, surely, is that politicians are eager to sacrifice economic logic to the pleadings of special interests and political expediency. Since some well-connected people can profit by denying economic reality, government trade policies continue to be a conspiracy against common sense.

"Melvyn Krauss, a senior fellow at the Hoover Institution, has been arguing for free trade—and against protectionist nonsense—for almost two decades. His first book, 'The New Protectionism' (1978), examined how the inflexibility of welfare-state economies bred new dangers to free trade. His second book, 'Development Without Aid' (1983), showed how free trade is more effective than handouts in helping the Third World. His new book, 'How Nations Grow Rich' (Oxford University Press, 140 pages, $22.50), aims to 'synthesize, extend, and apply the themes and analysis' of his earlier work. And indeed Mr. Krauss demonstrates how events in the past 15 years are confirming his hypotheses.

"Mr. Krauss reminds us that free trade maximizes prosperity by maximizing the incentive for efficient allocation of capital and labor. He notes that such 'reallocation increases income by increasing the average productivity of the nation's stock of productive resources.' Prices are signals, and trade barriers guarantee that government will send the wrong signals to businesses and workers. Every trade barrier undermines the productivity of capital and labor throughout the economy." (*Wall Street Journal*, July 1, 1998)

"The prediction on Wednesday that a one-mile-wide asteroid would pass dangerously close to Earth in the year 2028 sparked bitter debate yesterday about the extent of the danger, but also prompted calls for action to deal with any future menace from space, including the possibility of intercepting it. . . .

"Scientists agreed yesterday that a catastrophic impact by an asteroid or comet at some time in the future is certain, unless measures are taken to head it off. But they disagreed as to what approach to take. Both NASA and the Air Force have programs for tracking near-Earth asteroids, but neither is a major operation. . . .

"Dr. Stephen P. Maran, spokesman of the American Astronomical Society, said he was not aware of any group or government agency that had ever conducted detailed planning for meeting an asteroid threat.

" 'It looks as if it's high time we all started thinking about this problem,' Dr. Maran said.

"Dr. Edward Teller of the Hoover Institution in California, who is sometimes called the 'father of the hydrogen bomb,' has proposed the use of nuclear explosives to divert space objects from collision with Earth. Dr. Chapman said yesterday that nuclear explosives would probably be needed for the job, but other scientists disagreed.

"Yesterday Dr. Teller himself suggested several alternative ways of dealing with asteroid threats.

"Speaking of Asteroid 1997 XF11, he said in an interview that there seemed to be little more than a 1 percent chance it would hit Earth.

" 'But I want to make it clear that if it does hit,' Dr. Teller said, 'it will be a terrible thing for all mankind. I don't know whether conventional explosives or nuclear explosives would be necessary, but the important point is that the sooner we take action the easier it will be to deflect it.

" 'I would like to do something right now: to send a satellite to meet the asteroid in the year 2000, approaching it closely enough to measure and photograph it, and determine its composition. Then, if necessary, the world community working in concert and openly, can find the means of deflecting the threat.'

"One possibility, he said, would be to embed an explosive, 'preferably TNT, but nuclear if necessary,' within the asteroid and then blow a chunk of the object off to one side. The force thus imparted to the main body would deflect it, Dr. Teller said." (*New York Times*, March 13, 1998)

---

## POLITICAL ORIENTATION

"conservative" (*Washington Post*, March 16, 1997)

# Hudson Institute (1961)

Herman Kahn Center
5395 Emerson Way
Indianapolis, Indiana 46226
Phone: (317) 545-1000
Fax: (317) 545-1384

1015 18th Street, NW
Suite 200
Washington, D.C. 20036
Phone: (202) 223-7770
Fax: (202) 223-8537

Internet: http://www.hudson.org

| | |
|---|---|
| "To help shape the future through research designed to anticipate the political, economic, and cultural trends critical to the success of American public policy today and into the 21st Century." | *PURPOSE* |
| 66 total—50 professional; 16 support; plus 5 part-time professional; 5 part-time support; 6–12 interns | *STAFF* |
| Herbert I. London, president. London became president of the Hudson Institute in September 1997. He has been a trustee of the Hudson Institute since 1974 and has been a senior fellow for over thirty years, founding its Center for Education and Employment Policy. The author of many books, he is a tenured professor at New York University. London graduated from Columbia University in 1960 and received his Ph.D. from New York University in 1966. | *DIRECTOR* |
| 501(c)(3) | *TAX STATUS* |
| Fiscal year ending September 30, 1997—$6.9 million<br>F.Y. 1998—$7 million<br>Proposed 1999—$7.1 million | *BUDGET* |
| Foundation grants, 50 percent; corporate donations, 20 percent; individuals, 16 percent; special events/projects, 4 percent; endowment income, 3 percent; government contracts, 1 percent; publications, 1 percent; other, 5 percent | *FUNDING SOURCES* |
| Members: More than 700 individuals, 50 corporations, and 30 foundations<br>Branches/chapters: U.S. offices in Madison, Wisconsin, and Lansing, Michigan; international offices in Brussels and Montreal<br>Affiliates: Hudson Analytics, a for-profit subsidiary | *SCOPE* |
| None | *PAC* |

| | |
|---|---|
| *METHOD OF OPERATION* | ◆ Advertisements ◆ Awards program ◆ Conferences/seminars ◆ Congressional testimony ◆ Information clearinghouse ◆ International activities ◆ Internet (databases, Web site) ◆ Internships ◆ Legislative/regulatory monitoring (federal and state) ◆ Local/municipal affairs ◆ Media outreach ◆ Polling ◆ Research ◆ Speakers program ◆ Technical assistance |
| *CURRENT CONCERNS* | ◆ Agriculture ◆ Education reform ◆ Housing ◆ National security ◆ NATO ◆ Regulation ◆ Religious liberty ◆ Tax and economic policy ◆ Telecommunications ◆ Tort reform ◆ Welfare reform ◆ Workforce issues |
| *PUBLICATIONS* | The following is a list of sample publications: <br> *Charter Schools in Action: What Have We Learned?* <br> *Chinese Divide: Evolving Relations Between Taiwan and Mainland China* <br> *Commonwealth or Empire? Russia, Central Asia, and the Transcaucasus* <br> *Competition and Deregulation in Telecommunications: The Case for a New Paradigm* <br> *The Cost Effectiveness of Home Health Care: A Case Study of Indiana's In-Home/CHOICE Program* <br> *Fathers, Marriage, and Welfare Reform* <br> *The Home Equity Lending Industry* <br> *Heartland Symposium on the Future of the Welfare State* <br> *Is There Life After Big Government? The Potential of Civil Society* <br> *Korea: Pivot of Security in Northeast Asia* <br> *The New Promise of American Life* <br> *The Role of Competition and Regulation in Today's Cable TV Market* <br> *Security and Sacrifice: Isolation, Intervention, and American Foreign Policy* <br> *The State of the American Dream* <br> *Workforce 2020: Work & Workers in the 21st Century* |
| *NEWSLETTER* | *American Outlook* (quarterly magazine) <br> *Global Food Quarterly* (quarterly) <br> *Visions of the Future* (bimonthly) |
| *CONFERENCES* | American Dream Awards Dinner (annually, Indianapolis, Indiana) <br> Annual National Policy Forum <br> Herman Kahn Awards Dinner (periodic) |
| *BOARD OF DIRECTORS* | Walter P. Stern, chairman; Daniel F. Evans Jr., vice chairman <br><br> Other trustees: <br> ◆ Thomas D. Bell Jr. ◆ Jeffrey T. Bergner ◆ Linden S. Blue ◆ Mitchell E. Daniels Jr. ◆ Thomas J. Donohue ◆ Joseph Epstein ◆ Eugene Freedman ◆ Joseph M. Giglio ◆ Frederick W. Hill ◆ Allan B. Hubbard ◆ Roy Innis ◆ Jane Kahn ◆ Paul J. Klaassen ◆ Marie-Josée Kravis ◆ Andre B. Lacy ◆ Herbert I. London ◆ Robert H. McKinney ◆ John M. Mutz ◆ Neil Offen ◆ Steuart L. Pittman ◆ Dan Quayle ◆ Ian M. Rolland ◆ Irving Schatz ◆ Wallace O. Sellers ◆ Roger D. Semerad ◆ Beurt SerVaas ◆ Max Singer ◆ Walter P. Stern ◆ Allan R. Tessler ◆ Jay Van Andel ◆ Edward Wanandi ◆ David R. Williams Jr. |

"Big Tobacco is on the run. While specific provisions of the Federal legislation remain in doubt, there is no question the industry will pay hundreds of billions of dollars to compensate states, individual smokers and their lawyers for the medical costs and premature death of smokers. Nor is there much doubt that the settlements will be financed almost entirely by new cigarette taxes. . . .

"But economists and legal scholars who generally share the public's distaste for cigarette pushers still wonder whether a tax-based fix for tobacco is good public policy. . . .

"Without Federal legislation, Michael Horowitz of the Hudson Institute, a research group, estimates that the private lawyers in the state Medicaid suits stand to reap $1 billion to $3 billion a year, while contingency fees from suits on behalf of individual smokers could run from $2 billion to $12 billion annually. Even with the bill's $8 billion cap on payouts for individual suits, Mr. Horowitz said, the lawyers' total fees could still touch $6.5 billion a year.

"And what is wrong with rewarding the entrepreneurs who spent their own millions to breach the legal defenses of Fortress Tobacco? For one thing, the rewards will be disproportionate to the risk—especially on cases that come after the initial disclosures of the tobacco companies' misdeeds and are built around early settlement precedents. More important from Mr. Horowitz's perspective, failure to cap fees at, say, five times the highest charges paid to cigarette company lawyers, would set back the general cause of legal reform.

" 'Trial lawyers already use their riches to influence legislatures and courts,' he said. 'What will happen when they have billions more to promote their interests?' " (*New York Times,* May 28, 1998)

"To compensate for the nation's aging labor pool, a leading think tank is urging U.S. employers to press for 'enlightened immigration policies' that give preference to people with marketable skills and education. Current policies largely prefer those seeking family reunification or a haven from political persecution.

"In its soon-to-be-released 'Workforce 2020' study, the Indianapolis-based Hudson Institute estimates that the work force growth rate will slow to about 1% a year by 2000 as college-educated baby boomers begin to retire. This will result in growing shortages of highly skilled workers, undermining future growth in the economy. The U.S. will therefore need to increase its supply of skilled workers—partly by attracting more immigrants, the report proposes.

" 'This [recommendation] makes great sense,' says former Secretary of Labor William E. Brock III, who advised researchers involved in the study. 'We need all the skills we can muster.'

"The real issue in the immigration debate isn't whether 'we should either have more immigrants or fewer,' says Alan Reynolds, the institute's director of economic research. 'It's whether or not immigrants can contribute substantially to the economy.' The Hudson report notes that adult immigrants are nearly twice as likely to lack a high-school diploma than are native-born adults. 'We will need to raise the skills levels of immigrant workers,' the study concludes, 'by providing training to those already on our shores, and perhaps by altering our immigration policies to make education and skill level more important criteria.'

"Hudson researchers reject the argument that increased immigration of skilled workers would throw U.S.-born employees out of work. 'It is simply false that immigrants steal jobs from Americans at the higher ends of the job ladder,' says report co-author Carol D'Amico.

"High-technology companies have hired such workers to fill a dearth of qualified applicants, the report notes. Without foreign-born employees, the report adds, 'it might be difficult for America to retain its global lead in information technology.' Immigration now accounts for about half of the labor force's annual increase.

"Foreign-born workers represent about 9.7% of the U.S. labor force, up from 6.4% in 1980. Even as this trend continues, the report predicts, ethnic diversification of the work force will continue 'at a fairly slow pace.' This represents a marked departure from the think tank's earlier study, 'Workforce 2000,' which foresaw increasing rates of racial and gender diversification. That report, published in 1987, helped foster a mini-industry of consultants that advise businesses on diversifying their work forces." (*Wall Street Journal*, April 16, 1997)

## POLITICAL ORIENTATION

"A small group of politically conservative Jews, aligned with evangelical Christian groups on the issue of anti-Christian discrimination around the world, have lodged a complaint against a seemingly improbable target: a 14-minute film shown at the United States Holocaust Museum.

"The film, a sober but wrenching account of the history and consequences of anti-Semitism, describes the role of Christian churches in fomenting sentiment against Jews in Europe.

"Acting out of concerns by their evangelical Christian political allies, the Jewish critics have called the documentary, 'Anti-Semitism,' inaccurate and anti-Christian, and have asked that it be altered. They are led by Michael J. Horowitz, a senior fellow at the Hudson Institute, a conservative research organization, who sent a letter of complaint to the museum last month.

"Museum officials said they would review the film, but they and their board of Christian advisers maintained that it was accurate and not in need of revision.

" 'There was intense anti-Semitism within the Catholic and Protestant communities at a religio-cultural level which helped bring about the Holocaust,' said the chairman of the Holocaust Museum's Church Relations Council, the Rev. John T. Pawlikowski, a professor of social ethics at the Catholic Theological Union in Chicago. 'To pretend otherwise is to distort history.'

"The backdrop for the dispute is a broad political offensive mounted by conservative Jews and the Christian right to establish as a public issue the persecution of Christians abroad, often by Muslim governments, many of which also oppose Israel.

"Miles Lerman, the museum's chairman, said that while the museum took all letters and complaints seriously, the church relations subcommittee, responsible for such issues, had decided that the film was accurate and would not be revised." (*New York Times*, January 20, 1998)

"In a think-tank office just off K Street sits the mastermind of a crusade against foreign regimes that persecute Christians, an issue that is galvanizing evangelical churchgoers across America.

"He is Michael J. Horowitz, a top budget official during the Reagan administration, now a senior fellow at the Hudson Institute—and, as his name suggests, a member of a different religious group from those whose cause he is championing. Why a man who calls himself 'rootedly Jewish' would join forces with the Christian right is a question he gets asked often. 'Jews will call me and say, What are you doing consorting with the enemy?' ' the 59-year-old Horowitz chortles. 'Then I'll get a call from the Jews for Jesus saying, When can we sign you up?' " (*Washington Post*, September 30, 1997)

"conservative"(*Washington Post*, April 18, 1997)

# The Independent Institute (1986)

100 Swan Way
Oakland, California 94621
Phone: (510) 632-1366
Fax: (510) 568-6040
Internet: info@independent.org *or* http://www.independent.org

| | |
|---|---|
| *PURPOSE* | "To produce and widely disseminate comprehensive, nonpoliticized studies of the origins and solutions to critical economic, social, legal, and environmental problems, and conduct numerous conference and media programs based on this work." |
| *STAFF* | 12 total—7 professional; 5 support; plus 134 research fellows; 2 interns |
| *DIRECTOR* | David J. Theroux, founder and president. Theroux formerly was founding president of the Pacific Research Institute for Public Policy. He has also served as vice president and director of academic affairs at the Cato Institute. Theroux holds B.S., A.B., and M.S. degrees from the University of California–Berkeley and an M.B.A. from the University of Chicago. |
| *TAX STATUS* | 501(c)(3) |
| *BUDGET* | 1997—$1.4 million<br>1998—$1.7 million<br>Proposed 1999—$2.1 million |
| *FUNDING SOURCES* | Foundations, 30 percent; business, 23 percent; sales, 21 percent; individuals, 20 percent; other, 6 percent |
| *SCOPE* | Members: 1,200<br>Branch/chapter: N/A<br>Affiliates: N/A |
| *PAC* | None |

## METHOD OF OPERATION

♦ Awards program ♦ College course adoptions ♦ Conferences/seminars ♦ Congressional testimony ♦ Films/video/audiotapes ♦ International activities ♦ Internet (Web site) ♦ Internships ♦ Library/information clearinghouse ♦ Local/municipal affairs ♦ Media outreach ♦ Research ♦ Speakers program ♦ Student fellowships (Olive W. Garvey Fellowships, Sir John M. Templeton Fellowships for the Study of Religion and Liberty) ♦ Telecommunications services

## CURRENT CONCERNS

♦ Agriculture ♦ Antitrust and competition ♦ Banking/finance regulation ♦ Civil liberties ♦ Constitutional law and federalism ♦ Criminal justice ♦ Defense spending and procurement ♦ Drugs ♦ Economic development ♦ Education ♦ Energy ♦ Environment and natural resources ♦ Family and children ♦ Global warming ♦ Government spending ♦ Health care ♦ Immigration ♦ Insurance regulation ♦ International trade ♦ Land use ♦ Legal liability ♦ Privatization ♦ Regulation and deregulation ♦ Taxation ♦ Telecommunications ♦ Transportation ♦ Unemployment and labor ♦ Urban issues ♦ Women's issues

## PUBLICATIONS

*The Academy in Crisis*
*Agriculture and the State*
*Alienation and the Soviet Economy*
*American Health Care*
*Antitrust and Monopoly*
*Arms, Politics, and the Economy*
*Beyond Politics*
*The Capitalist Revolution in Latin America*
*Crime and Justice*
*The Diversity Myth*
*Endangered Species*
*Freedom, Feminism, and the State*
*Hazardous to Our Health? FDA Regulation of Health Care Products*
*Hot Talk, Cold Science: Global Warming's Unfinished Debate*
*The Melting Pot: Immigration Myths and Realities*
*Money and the Nation State*
*Out of Work: Unemployment and Government in Twentieth-Century America*
*Political Ecology: Bureaucratic Myths and Endangered Species*
*Private Prisons*
*Private Rights and Public Illusions*
*Regulation and the Reagan Era*
*Taxing Choice*
*Taxing Energy*
*Taxing Liberty: Predatory Politics and Taxation*
*Technology Innovation, Competition, and Antitrust*
*That Every Man Be Armed*
*To Serve and Protect: Privatization and Community in Criminal Justice*
*Toxic Liability*
*The Voluntary City*
*Writing Off Ideas: Taxation, Philanthropy, and America's Non-Profit Foundations*

Also publishes policy reports, briefings, and studies catalogs

| | |
|---|---|
| **NEWSLETTER** | *The Independent* (quarterly)<br>*The Independent Review: A Journal of Political Economy* (quarterly) |
| **CONFERENCES** | National conferences in Washington, D.C. (roughly 2 per year); independent policy forums in San Francisco (quarterly); conferences around the country (occasional); Summer Seminar in Political Economy (annual, for students) |
| **BOARD OF DIRECTORS** | ♦ Robert L. Erwin ♦ James D. Fair III ♦ John S. Fay ♦ Ellen Hill ♦ Peter A. Howley ♦ Bruce Jacobs ♦ William I. Koch ♦ Willard A. Speakman III ♦ David J. Theroux ♦ Mary L. Garvey Theroux |
| **EFFECTIVENESS** | "Smoking by teen-agers had been declining for years, but that trend has reversed in the 1990's. According to annual surveys by the University of Michigan, the portion of high school seniors who indulge went up to 34 percent last year, from less than 28 percent in 1992.<br>"Part of that increase, Mr. Giglio of the American Cancer Society said, reflects an upward swing in drug and alcohol use, but part of it results from steep price reductions on Marlboros and other heavily advertised cigarettes in 1994. . . .<br>". . . William F. Shughart, who has served as an expert witness for the cigarette industry, said that raising cigarette taxes would reduce teen-age smoking. 'They are more price-sensitive than adults,' said Mr. Shughart, a senior fellow with the Independent Institute. . . . He added, though, that higher taxes could not be justified because the costs to society of smoking were more than covered by existing cigarette taxes." (*New York Times*, April 3, 1997) |
| **POLITICAL ORIENTATION** | "a libertarian research center in Oakland, Calif." (*New York Times*, April 3, 1997)<br><br>"nonpartisan" (*Hospital Formulary*, April 1994) |

# Institute for American Values (1987)

1841 Broadway
Suite 211
New York, New York 10023
Phone: (212) 246-3942
Fax: (212) 541-6665
Internet: iav@worldnet.att.net

| | |
|---|---|
| "To provide research, publication, and public education on major issues of family well-being and civil society." | **PURPOSE** |
| 4 total—2 professional; 2 support; plus 2 part-time professionals; 1 summer intern | **STAFF** |
| David Blankenhorn, president. Prior to founding the Institute for American Values, Blankenhorn worked as a community organizer in Virginia and Massachusetts. In 1994, Blankenhorn also helped to found the National Fatherhood Institute. He served two years as a VISTA volunteer. Blankenhorn has coedited four books of scholarly essays. He graduated from Harvard University in 1977 and received an M.A. from the University of Warwick, Coventry, England, in 1978. | **DIRECTOR** |
| 501(c)(3) | **TAX STATUS** |
| Fiscal year ending February 28, 1998—$540,817<br>Proposed F.Y. 1999—$742,991 | **BUDGET** |
| Foundation grants, 82 percent; individuals, 14 percent; publications, 3 percent; investment income, 1 percent | **FUNDING SOURCES** |
| Members: N/A<br>Branches/chapters: N/A<br>Affiliates: N/A | **SCOPE** |
| None | **PAC** |

| | |
|---|---|
| *METHOD OF OPERATION* | ◆ Conferences/seminars ◆ Congressional testimony ◆ Media outreach ◆ Research ◆ Speaking engagements ◆ Special projects (American Family Panel, The Family in American Culture) |
| *CURRENT CONCERNS* | ◆ Civil society in the United States ◆ The definition of the human person ◆ The family as a social institution |
| *PUBLICATIONS* | *The Abolition of Marriage: How We Destroy Lasting Love*<br>*The Assault on Parenthood: How Our Culture Undermines the Family*<br>*Fatherless America*<br>*Marriage in America: A Report to the Nation*<br>*Promises to Keep: Decline and Renewal of Marriage in America*<br>*Rebuilding the Nest: A New Commitment to the American Family*<br>*Seedbeds of Virtue: Sources of Competence, Character, and Citizenship in American Society* |
| *NEWSLETTER* | *Propositions* (Quarterly) |
| *CONFERENCES* | Seminars and conferences are held throughout the year (attendance is by invitation only) |
| *BOARD OF DIRECTORS* | ◆ Charles Ballard ◆ David Blankenhorn ◆ Don S. Browning ◆ Jean Bethke Elshtain ◆ Sylvia Ann Hewlett ◆ Alphonso Jackson ◆ JoAnn Luehring ◆ Samuel Peabody ◆ J. Douglas Phillips ◆ David Popenoe ◆ Bernard Rapoport ◆ Arthur Rasmussen ◆ Ivan A. Sacks |
| *EFFECTIVENESS* | "... [T]here are warnings that this conference [a White House Conference on Child Care on Oct. 23, 1997] has a hidden agenda: to revive proposals for a massive federal day-care program. 'If what we do is empower government to spend more time with our kids instead of empowering parents to have more private and sectarian [i.e., church-based] options, then we're moving in the wrong direction,' says Gary Bauer, president of the Family Research Council.<br><br>" 'I certainly have qualms,' said David Blankenhorn, president of the Institute for American Values, 'and I know others have qualms, about using recent research on early childhood development to justify new federal child-care programs and regulations.'<br><br>"The research he's talking about found that the amount of stimulation and affection children get in their first three years has a lot to do with how well their brains develop. Many parents know this instinctively, but the scientists helped kick off the new round of concern about infant care." (*Washington Post*, October 10, 1997) |
| *POLITICAL ORIENTATION* | Unavailable |

# Institute for Policy Studies (1963)

1601 Connecticut Avenue, NW
Fifth Floor
Washington, D.C. 20009
Phone: (202) 234-9382
Fax: (202) 387-7915
Internet: irss@apc.org

| | |
|---|---|
| "To serve as an independent center of thought, action, and social invention in the exploration of alternative directions to achieving real security, economic justice, and grassroots political participation of citizens in the life of the nation." | *PURPOSE* |
| 25 total | *STAFF* |
| John Cavanagh, director | *DIRECTOR* |
| 501(c)(3) | *TAX STATUS* |
| 1997—$1.5 million<br>1998—$1.5 million<br>1999—Unavailable | *BUDGET* |
| Foundation grants, individual donations, investment interest, publications and fees; no government funding | *FUNDING SOURCES* |
| Members: 4,200 contributors<br>Branches/chapters: N/A<br>Affiliates: Letelier-Moffitt Memorial Fund for Human Rights; Transnational Institute, Amsterdam | *SCOPE* |
| None | *PAC* |

| | |
|---|---|
| *METHOD OF OPERATION* | ◆ Awards program ◆ Coalition forming ◆ Conferences/seminars ◆ Films/video/audiotapes ◆ International activities ◆ Internship program ◆ Media outreach ◆ Research (reports and books) ◆ Speakers program ◆ Television and radio production ◆ Training and technical assistance (Social Action and Leadership School for Activists; cosponsored with the Fund for New Priorities) |
| *CURRENT CONCERNS* | ◆ Global economy ◆ National security by nonviolent means ◆ Political reform to curb the influence of money on politics ◆ Sustainable communities |
| *PUBLICATIONS* | *Beyond Bretton Woods: Alternatives to the Global Economic Order* <br> *My Dad Was Not Hamlet: Poems by Saul Landau* <br> *Nicaragua: The Price of Intervention* <br> *Paradigms Lost: The Post Cold War Era* <br> *State of the Union* (annual) <br> *Technology for the Common Good* <br> *Towards a Global Village: International Community Development Inititatives* <br> *Trading Freedom: How Free Trade Affects Our Lives, Work and Environment* <br> *Who Pays? Who Profits? The Truth about the American Tax System* |
| *CONFERENCES* | Unavailable |
| *BOARD OF DIRECTORS* | ◆ Ruth Adams ◆ Peter Brown ◆ John Cavanagh ◆ Adrian De Wind ◆ James Early ◆ Ralph Estes ◆ Frances T. Farenthold ◆ Lisa Fuentes ◆ Hal Harvey ◆ Christopher Jencks ◆ Saul Landau ◆ E. Ethelbert Miller ◆ Marcus Raskin ◆ Lewis M. Steel ◆ Katrina vanden Heuvel |
| *EFFECTIVENESS* | "Is the European Union about to slap economic sanctions on the Commonwealth of Massachusetts? It may come to that. . . . <br><br> "This particular story begins on the other side of this interconnected globe, in the beautiful but sad Asian land of Burma. The narco-thug junta of military bullies who misrule that nation may qualify, against stiff competition, as the world's most odious regime. . . . The contrast hasn't gone unnoticed. A grass-roots movement in this country has persuaded a dozen cities, including San Francisco and New York, and one state—Massachusetts—to adopt economic sanctions of their own. . . . <br><br> ". . . While Massachusetts was debating the Burma bill, the United States (in 1994) joined the World Trade Organization, a new Geneva-based body intended to promote fair, universal rules of commerce. As part of the package, Congress signed on to an international code on government procurement, to which most states (but no cities) voluntarily acceded. In so doing, they promised to award contracts based solely on merit, not on extraneous political or cultural factors. |

"Aha! said the European Union last June (joined by Japan a month later): Massachusetts's Burma law is in clear violation. Following WTO procedure, the Europeans requested 'consultations' and may now demand a three-judge panel to hear their case. If it wins, the WTO would demand a change in the Massachusetts law or, as an alternative, economic compensation—perhaps targeted, if possible, at the Bay State. . . .

"But while they're defending the Massachusetts law, administration officials haven't gone so far as to label it defensible. In the long run, some will admit privately, they don't think it would be so bad if states and cities were nudged out of the foreign-policy business. And they point to the advantages U.S. firms gain from an international code on procurement, suggesting it's worth giving up something along the way. To the administration, in fact, and to defenders of the globalizing trade regime in general, the WTO not only can help U.S. multinationals sell more. . . .

"WTO critics on both the left and the right see danger precisely in that drive toward uniformity. They don't want to cede local control on such basic issues, especially when they believe the benefits flow mostly to large corporations.

"For Michael Shuman, a lawyer at the Institute for Policy Studies, the Massachusetts law on Burma is a case in point. The U.S. Constitution may assign foreign-policy powers to Washington, but states and local governments always have nibbled at the edges, he says. 'A large number of voices on foreign policy helps democratize the process,' he says, adding 'creativity and diversity.'

"In truth, the WTO can't force Massachusetts to change its law, nor can it force Washington to make Massachusetts back down, as trade lawyer Alan Wolff points out. The WTO can only hold the United States to what it agreed to and extract a price if our country falls short—exactly as the United States has demanded of many other countries." (*Washington Post*, August 25, 1997)

"The gap between the pay of chief executives and employees widened as the average U.S. worker received a 3 percent raise in wages in 1996, the nonprofit, liberal Institute for Policy Studies said in its fourth annual survey of executive compensation. The study by John Cavanagh, co-director of the institute, and institute fellow Sarah Anderson examined 30 domestic companies that reported layoffs ranging from 2,800 to 48,640 workers. . . .

"According to the study, CEOs at the 30 companies that reported layoffs saw total direct compensation—consisting of salary, bonus and long-term compensation such as stock options—rise 67.3 percent, well above the average increase of 54 percent for executives at the top 365 U.S. companies.

"Most of the increased earnings came in the form of gains from stock options, 'reflecting the continued trend on Wall Street to reward downsizers,' the study asserted.

" 'CEOs should be rewarded for creating good jobs, not destroying them,' said Cavanagh. 'These CEOs claim they have to lay people off to strengthen their businesses, but we are skeptical when all the compensation savings go into the CEO's pocket.' " (*Washington Post*, May 4, 1997)

"liberal" (*Washington Post*, May 4, 1997)

*POLITICAL*
*ORIENTATION*

# Investor Responsibility
# Research Center (1972)

1350 Connecticut Avenue, NW
Suite 700
Washington, D.C. 20036
Phone: (202) 833-0700
Fax: (202) 833-3555
Internet: irrc@aol.com *or* http://www.irrc.org

| | |
|---|---|
| **PURPOSE** | "To conduct impartial research on companies and shareholders worldwide." |
| **STAFF** | 60 total—55 professional; 5 support |
| **DIRECTOR** | Scott A. Fenn, executive director. Fenn joined IRRC in 1978. He served as its treasurer and chief financial officer from 1979 to 1995. He founded IRRC's Environmental Information Service in 1990. |
| **TAX STATUS** | Nonprofit organization (not tax-exempt) |
| **BUDGET** | 1997—$4.8 million<br>1998—$5.2 million<br>Proposed 1999—Unavailable |
| **FUNDING SOURCES** | Subscriptions, 60 percent; royalties, investments, and contracts, 30 percent; foundation grants, 4 percent; publications sales, 3 percent; conferences, 3 percent |
| **SCOPE** | Members: 300 institutional and 200 corporate subscribers<br>Branches/chapters: N/A<br>Affiliates: N/A |
| **PAC** | None |
| **METHOD OF OPERATION** | ♦ Conferences/seminars ♦ Information clearinghouse ♦ Internet (Web site) ♦ Internships ♦ Legislative/regulatory monitoring (federal and state) ♦ Research |

♦ Boards of directors ♦ Environmental policy guidelines ♦ Executive pay
♦ Investment in Southern Africa ♦ Labor rights ♦ Portfolio screening ♦
Proxy voting guidelines ♦ Shareholder resolutions ♦ Shareholder value ♦
Social responsibility ♦ State takeover legislation

## CURRENT CONCERNS

*The Bank Bulletin*
*Business in the Rain Forests: Corporations, Deforestation and Sustainability*
*Corporate Governance Bulletin: Covering Shareholder Issues Worldwide*
*Corporate Social Issues Reporter: Incorporating Investor's Environmental
    Report*
*Director Compensation Practices at S&P 500 Companies*
*Environmetal and Financial Performance: Are They Related?*
*Environmental Reporting and Third Party Statements*
*Equal Opportunity and Disclosure: A Report on U.S. Corporate Practices*
*The Greenhouse Gambit: Business & Investment Responses to Climate Change*
*The Influence of OBRA on Cash and Stock Bonus Plans*
*Investing in Tobacco: Time to Kick the Habit?*
*IRRC Directories of U.S. and International Companies in South Africa*
    (updated monthly)
*Potential Dilution at America's Leading Companies: Total Potential Dilution
    from Stock Plans at S&P 500 Companies*
*The Role of U.S. Corporations in the Development of Southern Africa*
*South Africa: Facts & Figures 1996*
*State Takeover Laws*
*U.S. Companies and Fair Employment in Northern Ireland*

## PUBLICATIONS

*Corporate Governance Bulletin* (bimonthly)
*Corporate Social Issues Reporter*
*Eye on the SEC* (seasonal)
*Global Shareholder* (quarterly)
*Highlights* (weekly)
*Investor's Environmental Report* (bimonthly)
*News for Investors* (monthly)
*Sanctions Update* (monthly)
*South Africa Investor*
*South Africa Reporter* (bimonthly)

## NEWSLETTER

Annual Fall Conference

## CONFERENCES

Rhoda R. Anderson, chair; Gwenn L. Carr, vice chair; Scott A. Fenn,
executive director; Jonathan A. Small, legal counsel

Other board members:
♦ Maryellen F. Andersen ♦ Jerome W. Anderson ♦ Kathleen A. Condon
♦ Jeanmarie C. Grisi ♦ Luther Jones ♦ Nina Lesavoy ♦ Philip R. Lochner
Jr. ♦ Frank P.L. Minard ♦ Allan R. Nelson ♦ Paul M. Neuhauser ♦
Clinton L. Stevenson ♦ David K. Storrs ♦ Edward B. Whitney

## BOARD OF DIRECTORS

# EFFECTIVENESS

"It is the season for annual meetings. So where are all the angry shareholders, imperious directors and bitter proxy fights of seasons past? . . .

"Increasingly . . . shareholder complaints about investment issues are being heard behind the scenes, typically after a letter or call from an influential investor. For good or ill, many of these disputes are being resolved in what amounts to back-room deals, well out of earshot of other investors.

"As a result, the annual meeting, once so suspenseful as management and investors anxiously awaited the results of key proxy votes, is now in danger of becoming a hollow ritual, to the detriment mainly of the small investor. . . .

". . . Shareholder proposals are becoming 'a tool of last resort' for big investors, says the Investor Responsibility Research Center, a group in Washington that advises shareholders on important proxy issues. It has counted 700 shareholder resolutions this year at a sample of roughly 2,000 companies, with very few additional resolutions expected, said Kenneth A. Bertsch, the center's director for corporate governance service. After all the resolutions are submitted for 1998, Mr. Bertsch expects a decline of roughly 10 percent from the 1997 total of 821.

"Fewer resolutions are being voted on because large shareholders are finding it easier to get their way without a fight. Activists like Mr. Kingsley . . . have become more credible with investors like mutual funds, which used to stay on the sidelines but now support them against intransigent managements. In addition, rule changes made in 1992 concerning proxy solicitations made it easier for activists to talk to other investors and win their support. . . .

"All of these quiet negotiations make some observers uneasy because small shareholders are left out of the debate. 'It may stifle public discussion and development of these issues,' argued Mr. Bertsch of the Investor Responsibility Research Center." (*New York Times*, May 28, 1998)

"Over the past three years U.S. trade with Africa has grown by 32.1 percent, tracking the 32.4 percent expansion in total U.S. trade during the same period, the Commerce Department said. But to say the trade is growing is not to say it is large. In 1997, sales to sub-Saharan Africa accounted for less than 1 percent of total U.S. exports, while imports are less than 2 percent of total U.S. imports.

"In South Africa, the continent's most developed economy with a stock market that lists 618 companies, U.S. investment is higher today than it was in the early 1980s before anti-apartheid sanctions were ordered by Congress. According to the Washington-based Investor Responsibility Research Center, which monitors foreign business activity in southern Africa, more than 50 percent of the multinational companies entering South Africa over the last three years have been from the United States.

"Before the disinvestment wave of the mid-1980s, U.S. firms held about $3 billion in assets in South Africa. Today, however, the assets held by 296 U.S. companies total about $9.5 billion and account for about 86,000 jobs in such industries as telecommunications, information technology, food and beverages and motor manufacturing." (*Washington Post*, March 23, 1998)

"Florida officials decided today to divest the state's retirement fund of all tobacco stocks, maintaining that the proliferation of lawsuits against cigarette companies and the growing prospect of tight government regulation made them too risky as investments.

"The state's plan to sell off $825 million of tobacco stocks in the $61 billion Florida Retirement System Trust Fund—one of the nation's 10 largest state pension funds—would represent the nation's largest divestiture of shares in cigarette companies, according to the Investor Responsibility Research Center in Washington, a nonprofit research service. At least a dozen universities have chosen to shed their tobacco holdings in recent years, but only one other state, Maryland, has taken similar action by selling $75 million of tobacco stock in its employee pension fund last year.

"In Florida, the 2-to-1 divestiture vote by the state board that oversees the retirement fund for more than 700,000 current and retired public employees came as at least nine other states, including New York and Texas, have begun to review whether they should sell off their tobacco holdings.

"Public officials are evaluating the financial risk of holding stocks in an industry that has come under increasing legal and political pressure. At the same time, some states have begun to question the wisdom of investing in companies that they are suing because of health care costs associated with smoking." (*New York Times*, May 29, 1997)

---

Unavailable

## POLITICAL ORIENTATION

# Joint Center for Political and Economic Studies (1970)

1090 Vermont Avenue, NW
Suite 1100
Washington, D.C. 20005-4961
Phone: (202) 789-3500
Fax: (202) 789-6390
Internet: jointctr@clarknet.net *or* http://www.jointctr.org

## PURPOSE

"Informs and illuminates the nation's major public policy debates through research, analysis, and information dissemination in order to: improve the socioeconomic status of black Americans; expand their effective participation in the political and public policy arena; and promote communications and relationships across racial and ethnic lines to strengthen the nation's pluralistic society."

## STAFF

46 total—32 professional; 14 support; plus 2 part-time support; 4–6 interns; 4–6 volunteers

## DIRECTOR

Eddie N. Williams, president. Williams has been president of the Joint Center for Political and Economic Studies since 1972. Previously he served as vice president for public affairs and director of the Center for Policy Study at the University of Chicago, director of the Office of Equal Employment Opportunity, and as a foreign service reserve officer at the State Department. He holds a B.S. in journalism from the University of Illinois. Williams is vice chairman of the Black Leadership Forum and serves on many other boards of many corporations and nonprofit organizations.

## TAX STATUS

501(c)(3)

## BUDGET

1997—$5.1 million
1998—$6.1 million
Proposed 1999—$7 million

## FUNDING SOURCES

Foundation grants, 38 percent; government contracts, 19 percent; special events/projects, 17 percent; corporate donations, 13 percent; earned income, 8 percent; individuals, 4 percent; publications, 1 percent

| | |
|---|---|
| Members: N/A<br>Branches/chapters: N/A<br>Affiliates: N/A | *SCOPE* |

| | |
|---|---|
| None | *PAC* |

| | |
|---|---|
| ♦ Coalition forming ♦ Conferences/seminars ♦ Congressional testimony ♦ Congressional voting analysis ♦ Films/video/audiotapes ♦ Grassroots organizing ♦ International activities ♦ Internet (Web site) ♦ Internships ♦ Legislative/regulatory monitoring (federal) ♦ Library/information clearinghouse ♦ Media outreach ♦ Polling ♦ Research ♦ Speakers program ♦ Telecommunications services (databases, mailing lists, Policy Information Network—an interactive information sharing network) ♦ Training and technical assistance | *METHOD OF OPERATION* |

| | |
|---|---|
| ♦ Black economic status ♦ Black voter registration and participation ♦ Business development ♦ Civil rights ♦ Employment ♦ Health policy ♦ International affairs (particularly Africa) ♦ Welfare and poverty | *CURRENT CONCERNS* |

| | |
|---|---|
| *Achieving Equitable Access: Studies of Health Care Issues Affecting Hispanics and African Americans*<br>*Annual Report*<br>*Balancing Act: The Political Role of the Urban School Superintendent*<br>*Black Initiative and Governmental Responsibility*<br>*Blacks and the 1996 Democratic National Convention*<br>*Economic Trends 1980–1992: A Black-White Comparison*<br>*Joint Center National Opinion Poll*<br>*Making Welfare Work: The Principles of Constructive Welfare Reform*<br>*Neglected Voices: What Low-Income Americans Think of Welfare Reform*<br>*Walking With Presidents: Louis Martin and the Rise of Black Political Power*<br>*What Devolution Means to the American Public: Findings From the Joint Center for Political and Economic Studies 1997 National Opinion Poll*<br><br>Also publishes issue briefs and factsheets | *RECENT PUBLICATIONS* |

| | |
|---|---|
| *Focus* (monthly) | *NEWSLETTER* |

| | |
|---|---|
| Annual dinner<br>Also sponsors conferences and forums on various issues | *CONFERENCES* |

## BOARD OF DIRECTORS

## EFFECTIVENESS

"Recent survey data from David Bositis of the Joint Center for Political and Economic Studies, a Washington research organization devoted to black issues, show that African-Americans have a dimmer view by far of public education than whites. A solid majority of whites view their schools as either good or excellent, but only about a third of African-Americans and 40 percent of Latinos are satisfied with their schools.

"Nearly 80 percent of blacks and more than 85 percent of Latinos say the Government spends too little on education, as opposed to about 60 percent of whites. Whites are evenly split on the issue of whether to issue vouchers for use in public, private and parochial schools. But African-Americans and Latinos are overwhelmingly in favor of such a system. Among African-Americans ages 26 to 35, 86.5 percent favor vouchers. In addition, Mr. Bositis's studies show that black support for vouchers jumped by about 19 percent in a single year, from 1996 to 1997. These numbers spell trouble for the Democrats, who have been trying to persuade African-Americans to keep the faith with schools that destroy their children's futures." (*New York Times*, January 4, 1998)

"In black communities from New York to Wisconsin to Arizona, the issue of public school integration has long been settled. To wit: Parents today are much more interested in quality schools than integrated ones. Last year a Wall Street Journal/NBC poll found just 8% of black Americans considered integration a primary concern. Forced integration, and using cross-town busing of school children to achieve it, has lost whatever luke-warm support it may have had.

"Speaking at the convention this week, NAACP President Kweisi Mfume was right on the mark identifying the educational problems of America's black inner-cities: above average dropout and truancy rates, below average test scores and little parental involvement. But the evidence suggests that the search for solutions among increasing numbers of blacks is now centered on such notions as school choice and vouchers.

"Today vouchers enjoy substantial support among blacks, especially those with school-age children. A national poll conducted in June by the Joint Center for Political and Economic Studies found strong approval of the use of school vouchers in public, private or parochial schools (the teachers' subsidy program proposed yesterday by Mr. Clinton is only for public schools and their unionized work force, and as such would eviscerate the nascent voucher movement). More than 57% of blacks—a 19% increase since 1996—and more than 65% of Hispanics voiced support. But, said the survey, 'the most remarkable support for vouchers came from younger blacks,' with 86% of 26- to 35-year-olds and 66% of 18- to 25-year-olds supporting the idea. Support among low-income blacks was a solid 70%.

"When he finished speaking, Mr. Mfume stepped down from the dais and told us his organization opposes vouchers and charter schools. 'Proponents haven't done their homework. They won't work,' the former Congressman from Baltimore said after being shown the Joint Center study." (*Wall Street Journal*, July 18, 1997)

---

"a Washington think tank specializing in issues affecting African Americans" (*Wall Street Journal*, June 25, 1997)

"nonpartisan" (*Washington Post*, April 21, 1997)

"an organization of both Democrats and Republicans" (*Wall Street Journal*, October 9, 1996)

## POLITICAL ORIENTATION

# Manhattan Institute for Policy Research (1977)

52 Vanderbilt Avenue
New York, New York 10017
Phone: (212) 599-7000
Fax: (212) 599-3494
Internet: mi@manhattan-institute.org *or*
http://www.manhattan-institute.org

| | |
|---|---|
| **PURPOSE** | To "develop and encourage public policies at all levels of government, which will allow individuals the greatest scope for achieving their potential, both as participants in a productive economy and as members of a functioning society." |
| **STAFF** | 30 total; plus interns |
| **DIRECTOR** | Lawrence Mone, president |
| **TAX STATUS** | 501(c)(3) |
| **BUDGET** | 1997—$6.3 million<br>1998—Unavailable<br>Proposed 1999—Unavailable |
| **FUNDING SOURCES** | Foundation grants, corporate contributions, individual contributions |
| **SCOPE** | Members: N/A<br>Branches/chapters: N/A<br>Affiliates: N/A |
| **PAC** | None |

| | |
|---|---|
| ◆ Conferences/seminars ◆ Fellowship program ◆ Internet (Web site) ◆ Lecture series ◆ Media outreach ◆ Policy forums ◆ Research ◆ Sponsors debates | *METHOD OF OPERATION* |
| ◆ Civil justice reform ◆ Crime ◆ Education ◆ Environment ◆ Immigration ◆ Racial issues ◆ Social welfare policy ◆ Tax policy ◆ Telecommunications ◆ Urban policy | *CURRENT CONCERNS* |
| None | *PUBLICATIONS* |
| *City Journal* (quarterly magazine) | *NEWSLETTER* |
| Unavailable | *CONFERENCES* |
| Unavailable | *BOARD OF DIRECTORS* |
| | *EFFECTIVENESS* |

"Labeling himself 'a leader, not a panderer,' Mayor Rudolph W. Giuliani insisted this week he will never allow his beloved New York Yankees to skip off to New Jersey or any such hinterland in search of a better stadium. . . .

". . . To keep the Yankees, Giuliani has proclaimed himself the leader of an effort to build a new stadium in Manhattan. So far, however, not much of a crowd is lining up to follow hizzoner's lead. . . .

"To that end, the Republican mayor—who often boasts about trimming city government and cutting the nation's highest city tax burden—proposed that a commercial tax scheduled to be phased out should instead be kept on the books. Giuliani wants to use it to raise $600 million in seed money for a Manhattan stadium, as well as for a new stadium for the Mets in Queens.

"The mayor said the tax would have no effect on the poor, touching 'relatively large to gigantic businesses.' His soak-the-rich approach to stadium finance, however, has fallen on unsympathetic ears in the City Council, which must approve the idea.

"City Council Speaker Peter Vallone, a Democrat running for governor, demands that the plan be approved first by voters in a city-wide referendum. Polls show that four out of five New Yorkers want Yankee Stadium to stay put in the Bronx.

"Moreover, doubters are lining up to discredit a new City Hall projection that a stadium in Manhattan would generate $1 billion a year for the city's economy. A KPMG Peat Marwick study two years ago said the stadium would generate one-tenth of that amount. The study, which was partially paid for by the city, also said that a refurbished stadium in the Bronx would generate nearly as much revenue as a Manhattan stadium, but with less than half the capital investment.

"Such numbers dismay even champions of Giuliani: 'We think he has been just a great mayor, but why should taxpayers of New York be building a stadium for a private entrepreneur?' asks Myron Magnet, editor of *City Journal*, a magazine put out by the Manhattan Institute. . . ." (*Washington Post*, April 25, 1998)

"One of our enduring national illusions is that we can correct every injustice or social imperfection by passing a law. What we don't like we'll just make illegal. The impulse has inspired some disastrous social experiments. Remember Prohibition? But the impulse survives, and it has now brought us employment law: all the laws, regulations and court decisions that tell companies how to hire, fire, promote and supervise their workers. The enterprise exudes good intentions—and absurdities.

"In his new book, 'The Excuse Factory: How Employment Law Is Paralyzing the American Workplace,' Walter Olson of the Manhattan Institute says companies are handcuffed. They can't hire sensibly, because tough job tests or probing questions might violate some anti-discrimination rule (on race, sex, age or disability). They can't fire incompetents for fear of 'wrongful termination' suits. Honest job references are taboo, because any unfavorable comment might trigger a defamation suit. And if they don't police workers, the companies may invite charges of sexual harassment. Gulp. The indictment is grim—a bit too grim. Although the absurdities are genuine, they haven't yet crippled American companies. Employers may have less freedom to fire isolated workers, but they still can engage in mass firings to improve competitiveness. Indeed, these firings (a.k.a. 'downsizings') rose in the 1990s. Companies also cope with the new laws in other ways. One dubious method is to require workers, as a condition of employment, to submit disputes to arbitration." (*Washington Post*, June 26, 1997)

"Several governors were elected in 1994 by pledging to cut taxes and spur economic growth. Some, such as New York's George Pataki, explicitly modeled their plans after Governor Christine Whitman's 30% cut in New Jersey's income tax rates. One conventional argument against tax cuts holds that they're 'fool's gold,' because they will shift costs down to the local level, force cities and counties to raise local taxes and leave taxpayers with no net benefit.

"Well, New Jersey's tax cut is two years old, and the data now in show that the skeptics were wrong. Economic growth is solid, the state taxpayers will save nearly $1 billion between 1994 and 1998, and the tax cut hasn't led to an increase in local property taxes.

"Peter Salins and Timothy Goodspeed, the economics professors who conducted the study for the Manhattan Institute, conclude that over the past decade 'increasing or decreasing income taxes has minimal impact on the rate of growth of property taxes.' There was virtually no real change in property taxes in 1994, the first full year of the Whitman tax cut. A study of 509 New Jersey school districts from 1991 to 1995 found that reductions in state aid were followed by only small increases in property taxes. New Jersey's taxpayers will wind up keeping eight out of every 10 dollars in income tax reductions.

"Messrs. Salins and Goodspeed found that this will happen because local officials are more likely to reduce spending, not increase taxes, when faced with decreasing federal or state aid. It's always easier to spend other people's money, so when state or federal aid is reduced most local officials are reluctant to raise taxes. In New Jersey, Governor Whitman is trying to help them by offering teams of state analysts who can find areas where waste and duplication can be trimmed.

"Tax cutting doesn't mean that local services have to suffer. In New Jersey, school spending in most districts didn't fall as a result of the tax cut. The Garden State still spends an average of $9,000 per year per student—the highest in the country." (*Wall Street Journal*, March 20, 1996)

---

"conservative" (*New York Times*, June 14, 1998)

"The think tank where [New York City Mayor Rudolph] Giuliani gets his ideas." (*Washington Post*, April 25, 1998)

"[One] of the cutting-edge institutions of the GOP revolution." (*Wall Street Journal*, January 31, 1996)

# POLITICAL ORIENTATION

# Pacific Research Institute
# for Public Policy (1979)

755 Sansome Street
Suite 450
San Francisco, California 94111
Phone: (415) 989-0833
Fax: (415) 989-2411

Internet: pripp@pacificresearch.org *or*
http://www.pacificresearch.org

**PURPOSE**

"Promotes the principles of individual freedom and personal responsibility. The Institute believes these principles are best encouraged through policies that emphasize a free economy, private initiative, and limited government."

**STAFF**

20 total—17 professional; 3 support; plus 14 fellows; 3 interns

**DIRECTOR**

Sally C. Pipes, president and chief executive officer. Before becoming president of the Pacific Research Institute (PRI) in 1991, Pipes was assistant director of the Fraser Institute in Vancouver, Canada. She previously worked for the Financial Institutions Commission of British Columbia and was a member of the Vancouver City Planning Commission. Pipes writes a bimonthly column in *Chief Executive Magazine*.

**TAX STATUS**

501(c)(3)

**BUDGET**

1997—$2.2 million
1998—$2.5 million
Proposed 1999—$3 million

**FUNDING SOURCES**

Foundation grants, 75 percent; individual donations, 18 percent; corporate donations, 7 percent

**SCOPE**

Members: N/A
Branches/chapters: Sacramento, California, office
Affiliates: N/A

None

♦ Awards program ♦ Conferences/seminars ♦ Congressional testimony ♦ Educational foundation ♦ Internet (Web site) ♦ Legislative/regulatory monitoring (federal and state) ♦ Library/information clearinghouse ♦ Media outreach ♦ Research ♦ Scholarships ♦ Speakers program

♦ Civil rights ♦ Children's issues ♦ Education ♦ Environmental studies ♦ Health care reform ♦ Legal reform ♦ Privatization ♦ Regulation of the Internet ♦ Urban studies

*Angry Classrooms, Vacant Minds: What's Happened to Our High Schools*
*Continental Water Marketing*
*Cost of Kyoto: Impact of Potential "Greenhouse Gas" Emission Limits on the*
    *People and Economy of California*
*Crisis and Leviathan: Critical Episodes in the Growth of American Government*
*Enterprise of Law*
*Environmental Gore: A Constructive Response to Earth in the Balance*
*Establishing School Choice Including Religious Schools*
*Federal Freedom, Technology and the First Amendment*
*Federal Judge's Desk Reference to Environmental Economics*
*Free Market Environmentalism*
*Grand Theft and Petit Larceny: Property Rights in America*
*The Heated Debate: Greenhouse Predictions Versus Climate Reality*
*How to Start a Charter School*
*Index of Leading Environmental Indicators*
*NAFTA and the Environment*
*Plowing Ground in Washington*
*Privatization and Local Government Essays '94*
*Sovereign Nations or Reservations? An Economic History of American Indians*
*State of the Children*
*Strangers at Our Gate*
*A Ten-Point Agenda for Reforming Education in California*
*Times Change: The Minimum Wage and the New York Times*
*U.S. Encryption Policy: A Free Market Primer*
*Unfinished Business: A Civil Rights Strategy for America's Third Century*
*What Everyone Should Know About Economics and Prosperity*
*What Went Right in the 1980s*
*The Yellowstone Primer: Land and Resource Management in the Greater*
    *Yellowstone Ecosystem*

*Action Alerts* (periodic)
*Capital Ideas* (weekly)
*The Contrarian* (bimonthly)
*Impact* (monthly)
*A Message from the President* (quarterly)

## CONFERENCES

Annual Privatization Dinner
Breakfasts, lunches, receptions, and policy forums

## BOARD OF DIRECTORS

Daniel Oliver, chairman; Roy E. Marden and William E. Oberndorf, vice chairmen; Thomas Magowan, secretary/treasurer; Sally C. Pipes, president and chief executive officer

Other members:
♦ Katherine H. Alden ♦ Frank E. Baxter ♦ Katherine E. Boyd ♦ Robert J. Ernst III ♦ James T. Farrell ♦ James W. Fuller ♦ Daniel L. Gressel ♦ Mark B. Hoffman ♦ Samuel H. Husbands Jr. ♦ David H. Keyston ♦ Howard Leach ♦ Francis A. O'Connell ♦ Richard A. Wallace ♦ Jean R. Wente ♦ F. Christian Wignall

## EFFECTIVENESS

"To increase the cultural diversity of the curriculum, the San Francisco school board is considering a plan to require that at least half the books assigned to every high school student in the district be by authors of color. . . .

"Sally Pipes, president of the conservative Pacific Research Institute in San Francisco, attacked the proposal to redo the reading list as political correctness gone wild.

" 'It's wrong for the board to mandate that children read books by authors of the same ethnic background,' Ms. Pipes said. 'We need to get back to core knowledge. We need to give children the best books possible. They have to go on to college and the work world, and this would destroy their opportunities, and shortchange the children of San Francisco.' " (*New York Times*, March 11, 1998)

"Many Asians still feel a strong sense of their separate ethnic identities, and ethnic clubs still flourish in some cities and colleges. Yet the emerging racial consciousness is giving birth to many pan-Asian clubs, particularly in Queens, lower Manhattan, Los Angeles and San Francisco, where only in the last two decades have Asians of different origins begun to live together.

"Talk of Asian-Americans as a distinct racial group grew out of the civil rights movement. At the University of California at Berkeley and at Los Angeles, students and faculty members sought to unify Japanese- and Chinese-Americans, who had remained divided since immigrating a century ago. But starting in 1965, with the repeal of laws that had sharply restricted immigration from Asia since the 1920's, the number of Americans of Asian descent rose to a critical mass, from one million in 1960 to nine million today. . . .

"Lance T. Izumi, a fellow at Pacific Research Institute in San Francisco who served as a speechwriter to Attorney General Edwin Meese 3d [sic] during the Reagan Administration, said the climate is delaying the integration of Asian-Americans. Although Chinese- and Japanese-Americans were excluded until after World War II, they have assimilated quickly in the last two or three decades, Mr. Izumi said.

"He pointed to the high number of marriages between whites and third- and fourth-generation Japanese- and Chinese-Americans. For Japanese-Americans, about half of all marriages are now interracial.

" 'There are many in my generation, and I include myself, who see more of the commonalities and don't cling on to this idea of Asian-American,' said Mr. Izumi, 37, a third-generation Japanese-American. 'But how many of those third-generation Vietnamese- and Korean-Americans will feel the same as I do now if they had it beaten into their heads that the majority culture is the enemy?'

"Critics like Mr. Izumi say Asian-American advocates, by emphasizing historical wrongs, promote the idea of victimhood, a label that they say rings false when Asian Indians are the most educated ethnic group in the nation, Japanese- and Chinese-Americans earn higher incomes than whites, and two-thirds of all Asian-Americans were born abroad." (*New York Times*, May 30, 1996)

---

"free-market-oriented" (*Wall Street Journal*, October 8, 1997)

"conservative" (*Washington Post*, May 25, 1997)

# POLITICAL
# ORIENTATION

# Political Economy Research Center
(1980)

502 South 19th Avenue
Suite 211
Bozeman, Montana 59715
Phone: (406) 587-9591
Fax: (406) 586-7555
Internet: perc@perc.org *or* http://www.perc.org

## PURPOSE

To promote "a realistic alternative approach to . . . solving environmental and resource allocation problems . . . one characterized by less government and more reliance on private property rights and individual incentives."

## STAFF

15 total—11 professional; 4 support; plus 6 part-time professionals; 10–12 interns per year

## DIRECTOR

Terry L. Anderson, executive director. Anderson also is professor of economics at Montana State University in Bozeman and a senior fellow at the Hoover Institution. He writes books on a range of economic issues and has been a visiting scholar at universities in several countries.

## TAX STATUS

501(c)(3)

## BUDGET

1997—$2.2 million
1998—$2.2 million
1999—Unavailable

## FUNDING SOURCES

Foundation grants, 77 percent; individuals, 13 percent; corporations, 6 percent

## SCOPE

Members: 5,500
Branches/chapters: N/A
Affiliates: N/A

## PAC

None

| | |
|---|---|
| ◆ Awards program ◆ Conferences/seminars ◆ Congressional testimony ◆ Educational foundation ◆ Information clearinghouse ◆ Internet (e-mail alerts, Web site) ◆ Internships ◆ Media outreach ◆ Research ◆ Speakers program | *METHOD OF OPERATION* |

| | |
|---|---|
| ◆ Environmental risk ◆ Free-market environmentalism ◆ Global warming ◆ Hazardous waste ◆ Land use ◆ National and state parks ◆ Privatization ◆ Superfund ◆ Water policy | *CURRENT CONCERNS* |

| | |
|---|---|
| Books written by PERC authors: | *PUBLICATIONS* |

*Continental Water Marketing*
*Doomsday Kids: Scaring Children Green*
*Eco-Sanity: A Common-Sense Guide to Environmentalism*
*Enviro-Capitalists*
*Free Market Environmentalism*
*Multiple Conflicts Over Multiple Uses*
*The Political Economy Forum Series*
*Sovereign Nations or Reservations? An Economic History of American Indians*
*Superfund: Environmental Justice For All?*
*Water Crisis*
*What Everyone Should Know About Economics and Prosperity*

PERC Affiliates also publish articles and opinion pieces in periodicals

| | |
|---|---|
| *Environmental Examiner* (4 times a year) *PERC Reports* (4 times a year) *PERC Policy Series* (4 times a year) *Political Economic Forum* (4 times a year) | *NEWSLETTER* |

| | |
|---|---|
| Academic and teacher workshops Legislative seminars Political Economy Forum (for scholars; annual) Student Summer Seminar (annual) | *CONFERENCES* |

| | |
|---|---|
| ◆ Ryan Amacher ◆ Thomas J. Bray ◆ Dave Cameron ◆ Kim Dennis ◆ William Dunn ◆ Eugene Graf III ◆ Joseph N. Ignat ◆ Byron Lamm ◆ Dwight E. Lee ◆ Adam Meyerson ◆ E. Wayne Nordberg ◆ Jerry Perkins ◆ Leigh Perkins ◆ Marc Pierce ◆ Charles Potter Jr. ◆ Scott W. Rasmussen ◆ Hardy Redd ◆ John Tomlin | *BOARD OF DIRECTORS* |

| | |
|---|---|
| "Dwindling budgets and growing maintenance backlogs are forcing state parks to become entrepreneurs. . . . | *EFFECTIVENESS* |

"... many parks administrators believe they don't have any choice but to pursue profits on their own. Park attendance is up, but overall state-park budgets have fallen by an estimated 22% since 1980, while funds for capital improvements and maintenance have dropped 68%, according to the Political Economy Research Center.... Entrepreneurial fund raising is 'the wave of the future for state parks and someday national parks,' says Donald Leal, the center's senior associate." (*Wall Street Journal*, February 11, 1997)

## POLITICAL ORIENTATION

"a think tank in Bozeman, Mont., devoted to free-market environmentalism" (*Wall Street Journal*, February 11, 1997)

# Progress & Freedom Foundation (1993)

1301 K Street, NW
Suite 650 West
Washington, D.C. 20005
Phone: (202) 289-8928
Fax: (202) 289-6079
Internet: mail@pff.org *or* http://www.pff.org

| | |
|---|---|
| Dedicated "to study the digital revolution and its implications for public policy." | *PURPOSE* |
| 11 total—5 professional; 6 support; plus 3 interns | *STAFF* |
| Jeffrey A. Eisenach, president. Before co-founding the foundation in 1993, Eisenach was executive director of GOPAC, a Republican political action committee. His background includes positions at the Federal Trade Commission and the Office of Management and Budget, public policy consulting, and work as director of research for the presidential campaign of Pete du Pont. Eisenach is a graduate of Claremont McKenna College and holds a Ph.D. from the University of Virginia. He is an author of books, articles, and opinion pieces in periodicals. | *DIRECTOR* |
| 501(c)(3) | *TAX STATUS* |
| Fiscal year ending April 30, 1998—$1.8 million. Proposed F.Y. 1999—$2 million | *BUDGET* |
| Corporate, 90 percent; foundation, 5 percent; other, 5 percent | *FUNDING SOURCES* |
| Members: N/A<br>Branches/chapters: N/A<br>Affiliates: N/A | *SCOPE* |
| None | *PAC* |

| | |
|---|---|
| *METHOD OF OPERATION* | ♦ Coalition forming ♦ Conferences/seminars ♦ Congressional testimony ♦ Fellowships ♦ Films/video/audiotapes ♦ Internet (Web site) ♦ Media outreach ♦ Research ♦ Speakers program |
| *CURRENT CONCERNS* | ♦ Communications ♦ Computer technology ♦ Deregulation of electric utilities ♦ Federal and state governments' use of technology ♦ Federal budget ♦ Federal Communications Commission ♦ Free markets ♦ Individual freedom ♦ Internet ♦ Housing policy ♦ Telecommunications ♦ Welfare reform |
| *PUBLICATIONS* | *The Digital State* (annual)<br><br>Publishes a series of monographs |
| *NEWSLETTER* | *The Progress Report* |
| *CONFERENCES* | Aspen Summit (annual) |
| *BOARD OF DIRECTORS* | ♦ Philip M. Burgess ♦ Jeffrey A. Eisenach ♦ Bryce "Larry" Harlow ♦ George A. "Jay" Keyworth II ♦ R. Mark Lubbers ♦ James C. Miller III ♦ Robert Tollison |
| *EFFECTIVENESS* | "In late 1995, the Progress and Freedom Foundation held a lavish Christmas party at its fancy new digs on K Street. At the time, the 'digital age' think tank founded in 1992 by free-marketeer Jeffrey A. Eisenach was riding high, courtesy of his friend and mentor, House Speaker Newt Gingrich, R-Ga. . . .<br><br>"But over the next two and a half years, those dreams turned into a nightmare that left the foundation barely standing. Its Gingrich links ensnared the PFF in the demoralizing House ethics probe of the speaker and a reportedly continuing Internal Revenue Service audit. The failure of a controversial alliance with conservative provocateuse Arianna Huffington, sources say, weakened the foundation's ability to raise money. Over time, the PFF was forced to share the spotlight on Internet issues with a handful of upstart policy shops. . . .<br><br>". . . The PFF's most serious problem was the ethical cloud surrounding the speaker. This was especially so for Eisenach, who spent hundreds of hours organizing Gingrich's 'Renewing American Civilization' course at a Georgia college. At issue in the Gingrich ethics investigation was whether contributions raised for the course through Gingrich's political and tax-exempt fund-raising arms violated campaign finance laws. Inevitably, Eisenach and the foundation came under intense scrutiny. . . .<br><br>"Over the course of 1996 and early 1997, the PFF's annual income fell 43 percent, from $3.7 million to $2.1 million. . . . |

"With the downsizing, however, came a more focused agenda, and that—combined with the end of the Gingrich investigation—improved the group's finances. . . .

"Some experts agree that a more mature PFF may well accomplish more now than if it were still rolling along on the money and media attention it attracted in the heady days of the Gingrich revolution. 'They're not going to change everything at once,' . . . Kent Lassman [of Citizens for a Sound Economy] says. 'But even though they'll now show up in fewer places, they'll have more impact in those areas' " (*National Journal*, July 22, 1998)

"In the next few months, Marylanders will be able to look up the value of their neighbors' houses, and thousands of professionals will be able to update their state licenses, all through the Internet.

"The new services are part of an ambitious effort by Maryland state government to harness the latest advances in information technology, both to run government more efficiently and to open up more services to the public. The Progress & Freedom Foundation, a think tank in Washington that follows digital technology issues, recently ranked Maryland fifth among all states for technological savvy. 'Every week, another agency is turning around and talking about things that they can do through technology to reach out to citizens and provide more services,' said Major F. Riddick Jr., the governor's chief of staff and point man on technology issues." (*Washington Post*, December 4, 1997)

"The embattled tobacco industry is spending more money than ever to influence the political process, but some of its largess eludes political radar.

"That's because the industry's record $4.1 million in donations to political candidates and parties last year represents but a portion of its contributions—the part that must be disclosed to the public. There's another, largely undisclosed, dimension to the tobacco industry's political giving. Philip Morris Cos. and R.J. Reynolds Tobacco Co., for example, also lavish donations on like-minded think tanks and other groups that share its views—particularly an antipathy toward David Kessler's Food and Drug Administration, which wants to regulate cigarettes.

"These tobacco donations represent a kind of stealth spending that reinforces the industry's direct political contributions. No one knows exactly how much additional money this giving represents because the groups don't have to disclose it. A few groups voluntarily answered queries from *The Wall Street Journal* about their tobacco donations, but most declined to furnish exact numbers. Internal tobacco company documents and tax filings offer a few scraps of additional information. What's clear is that donations to these organizations are considerable and have helped the tobacco industry cultivate influential allies. . . .

"[T]here is Citizens for a Sound Economy, which has spent $2 million in its campaign to overhaul the FDA, arguing that the agency should stick with its 'original mission' of approving new drugs and medical devices. The group received $91,800 from Philip Morris in 1991, according to tobacco company documents that have been made public. (The group refuses to identify donors.)

"Still another group, the Progress and Freedom Foundation, which got contributions last year from both Philip Morris and R.J. Reynolds, wants to drastically reshape the agency, parceling out many duties to private entities. . . .

"The groups, which generally share a conservative philosophy and advocate shrinking the federal government, all say they don't need prodding by the tobacco donations to declare war on federal rules and bureaucracy; it comes naturally." (*Wall Street Journal,* March 25, 1996)

## POLITICAL ORIENTATION

"conservative" (*New York Times,* February 9, 1998)

"a conservative think tank run by Gingrich allies" (*Washington Post,* January 17, 1997)

# Reason Foundation (1978)

3415 South Sepulveda Boulevard
Suite 400
Los Angeles, California 90034
Phone: (310) 391-2245
Fax: (310) 391-4395

1001 Pennsylvania Avenue, NW
Suite 200 South
Washington, D.C. 20004
Phone: (202) 457-8577
Fax: (202) 457-8564

Internet: gpassantino@reason.org *or* http://www.reason.org

To "support the rule of law, private property, and limited government. . . . To preserve and extend those aspects of an open society that protect prosperity and act as a check on encroachments on liberty."

***PURPOSE***

29 total—22 professional; 7 support; plus 2 interns; 2 part-time

***STAFF***

Robert W. Poole Jr., president. Poole has many years of experience as a policy analyst, researcher, and consultant. He worked in aerospace and for several other think tanks before founding the Reason Foundation. He also served as a member of Vice President Dan Quayle's Space Policy Advisory Board. The author or editor of many books and articles, Poole is a graduate of the Massachusetts Institute of Technology.

***DIRECTOR***

501(c)(3)

***TAX STATUS***

1997—$4.9 million
1998—$5.3 million
Proposed 1999—Unavailable

***BUDGET***

Individual contributions, 28 percent; magazine income, 25 percent; foundation grants, 24 percent; corporate contributions, 16 percent; research publications and events, 6 percent; other, 1 percent

***FUNDING SOURCES***

Members: N/A
Branches/chapters: N/A
Affiliates: N/A

***SCOPE***

None

***PAC***

## METHOD OF OPERATIONS

♦ Conferences/seminars ♦ Congressional testimony ♦ Internet (Web site) ♦ Legislative/regulatory monitoring (federal and state) ♦ Local/municipal affairs ♦ Media outreach ♦ Participation in regulatory proceedings (federal and state) ♦ Research ♦ Telecommunications services (hotline: 310-391-6525)

## CURRENT CONCERNS

♦ Devolution ♦ Education (competitive contracting, private practice teaching, school choice) ♦ Environment (deregulation, hazardous waste, risk assessment, solid waste disposal) ♦ Infrastructure (air traffic control, airport management, transportation) ♦ Privatization (competitive government, public/private partnerships, volunteerism) ♦ Social policy (child welfare, welfare reform) ♦ Urban policy (housing, land use, growth)

## PUBLICATIONS

*Alternative Teacher Organizations: Evolution of Professional Associations*
*Bilingual Education: Reading, Writing, and Rhetoric*
*The Case Against Electric Vehicle Mandates in California*
*Class Notes*
*Competitive Government for a Competitive Los Angeles*
*Curb Rights: A Foundation for Free Enterprise in Urban Transit*
*The Counterplan for Transportation in Southern California: Spend Less, Serve More*
*Directory of Private Service Providers*
*Doing More with Less: Competitive Contracting for School-Support Services*
*Free Minds and Free Markets*
*Garbage by the Pound: On the Streets*
*Given the Choice: A Study of the PAVE Program and School Choice in Milwaukee*
*Guidelines for Airport Privatization*
*Health and Social Services in the Post-Welfare State: Are Vouchers the Answer?*
*How to Privatize Orange County's Airports*
*Intergovernmental Contracting for Public Services*
*Looking Beyond ECO: Alternatives to Employer-Based Trip Reductions*
*Making Schools Work: Competitive Contracting for School Services*
*Market-Oriented Planning: Principles and Tools*
*Meeting Space Launch Needs Economically*
*Municipal Wastewater Treatment: Privatization and Compliance*
*On the Frontier of Deregulation: New Zealand Telecommunications and the Problem of Interconnecting Networks*
*Private Prisons: Quality Corrections at a Lower Cost*
*A Plain English Guide to the Science of Climate Change*
*Privatization 1998* (annual)
*Privatizing Milwaukee's Airport*
*Privatizing Public Hospitals*
*Public Authorities and Private Firms as Providers of Public Goods*
*Putting Comparative Risk Assessment Into an Economic Framework*
*Race to the Top: The Innovative Face of State Environmental Management*
*Rescuing Orange County*
*Redesigning the CERCLA Liability: An Analysis of the Issues*
*Regulatory Reform at the Local Level: Regulating for Competition, Opportunity, and Prosperity*

*Restructuring America's Water Industry: Comparing Investor-Owned and Government Water Systems*
*Revitalizing Our Cities: Perspectives from America's New Breed of Mayors*
*Revitalizing State and Local Infrastructure*
*Revolution at the Roots: Making Our Government Smaller, Better, and Closer to Home*
*Rightsizing Government: Lessons from America's Public Sector Innovators*
*School Violence Prevention: Strategies to Keep Schools Safe*
*School Voucher Programs in the United States*
*Shuttle Vans: The Overlooked Transit Alternative*
*Solid Waste Recycling Costs—Issues and Answers*
*Solving the Medicaid Puzzle: Strategies for State Entitlement Reform*
*State Privatization Handbook*
*Teacher, Inc.: A Private-Practice Option for Educators*
*Where the Rubber Meets the Road: Reforming California's Roadway System*

---

*Privatization Watch* (monthly)
*Reason* (monthly magazine)

## NEWSLETTER

---

Frequent presentations and seminars with nonprofit groups, corporations, and governmental organizations

## CONFERENCES

---

♦ Thomas E. Beach ♦ Frank Bond ♦ William A. Dunn ♦ James Glassman ♦ Neal I. Goldman ♦ Borden Gray ♦ Stina Hans ♦ Manuel S. Klausner ♦ David H. Koch ♦ Robert W. Poole Jr. ♦ Al St. Clair ♦ Joel Stern ♦ Harry Teasley Jr. ♦ Walter E. Williams

## BOARD OF DIRECTORS

---

Unavailable

## EFFECTIVENESS

---

"libertarian" (*Washington Post*, February 12, 1997)

## POLITICAL ORIENTATION

# The Rockford Institute (1976)

928 North Main Street
Rockford, Illinois 61103
Phone: (815) 964-5053
Fax: (815) 964-9403
Internet: therockfordinstitute@bossnt.com

**PURPOSE**

"The Institute grounds its work in the promotion of liberty, the defense of natural family, the affirmation of Scriptural Truth, the promotion of self reliance and decentralization in politics and economics, and the celebration of moral and artistic excellence in culture. In the broadest sense, we strive to contribute to the renewal of Christendom in this time and place."

**STAFF**

19 total—9 professional; 10 support

**DIRECTOR**

Thomas J. Fleming, president. Fleming also serves as a member of the board of the League of the South. He was the founding editor of *Southern Partisan*. Fleming also is a former classics professor at the University of Miami of Ohio and former advisor to the U.S. Education Department. He is the co-author of *The Conservative Movement* and author of *The Politics of Human Nature*. Fleming holds a Ph.D. in classics from the University of North Carolina, Chapel Hill.

**TAX STATUS**

501(c)(3)

**BUDGET**

1997—$1.4 million
1998—$1.1 million
Proposed 1999—$1.1 million

**FUNDING SOURCES**

Individuals, 35 percent; publications, 35 percent; foundations/corporations, 20 percent; other, 10 percent

**SCOPE**

Members: N/A
Branches/chapters: N/A
Affiliates: N/A

**PAC**

None

METHOD OF
OPERATION

◆ Awards program (the Ingersoll Prizes, the T.S. Eliot Award for Creative Writing, and the Richard M. Weaver Award for Scholarly Letters) ◆ Coalition forming ◆ Commissioned studies ◆ Conferences/seminars ◆ Congressional testimony ◆ Films/video/audiotapes ◆ International activities ◆ Internet (Electronic bulletin boards) ◆ Library/information clearinghouse ◆ Media outreach ◆ Speakers program ◆ Telecommunications services (mailing lists)

**CURRENT CONCERNS**

◆ Authentic federalism ◆ Classics-based education ◆ Family autonomy ◆ Former Yugoslavia ◆ Home schooling ◆ Immigration ◆ Influence of religion on society ◆ Integrity at the academy ◆ Limited central government ◆ Stewardship of Creation ◆ Strong local government ◆ Subsidiarity ◆ The welfare state

**PUBLICATIONS**

*The Conservative Movement*
*Day Care: Child Psychology and Adult Economics*
*Family Questions*
*The Family Wage*
*From Cottage to Work Station: The Family's Search for Social Harmony in the Industrial Age*
*The Homestead*
*Immigration and the American Identity*
*In Search of a National Morality*
*The Martin Luther King, Jr., Plagiarism Story*
*The Politics of Human Nature*
*The Retreat from Marriage: When Families Fail: The Social Costs*
*The Swedish Experiment in Family Politics*
*Utopia Against the Family*

**NEWSLETTER**

*Chronicles: A Magazine of American Culture* (monthly magazine)
*Main Street Memorandum* (quarterly)

**CONFERENCES**

Family, Culture, and Religious Issues (4–6 a year)

**BOARD OF DIRECTORS**

Norman McClelland, chairman; Mary Kohler, vice chairman

Other members:
◆ William Diehl ◆ George Garrett ◆ David Hartman ◆ James Paul Hunter ◆ Thomas W. Pauken ◆ Thomas Roeser ◆ Sally Wright

## EFFECTIVENESS

"At first sight it looks like one of the countless magazines vying for influence in the New York-Washington media park. But inside the glossy covers of *Chronicles* you find a monthly eruption of defiance and dissent, a collection of incendiary views that are rarely heard in either the liberal or conservative cantons of the establishment. It has 12,000 subscribers, and one of them happens to be Patrick Buchanan. . . .

". . . The magazine is the bulletin board of the purist form of American isolationism. 'We don't call it that, of course, we call it minding our own business,' says [Tom] Fleming [president of the Rockford Institute]." (*Electronic Telegraph*, February 26, 1996)

## POLITICAL ORIENTATION

"An equal enemy of both the Republican and Democratic parties . . . *Chronicles* is the magazine of Right-wing American nationalism." (*Electronic Telegraph*, February 26, 1996)

# The Urban Institute (1968)

2100 M Street, NW
Washington, D.C. 20037
Phone: (202) 833-7200
Fax: (202) 429-0687
Internet: paffairs@ui.urban.org *or* http://www.urban.org

| | |
|---|---|
| "To sharpen thinking about society's problems and efforts to solve them, improve government decisions and their implementation, and increase citizens' awareness about important public choices." | *PURPOSE* |
| 348 total—294 professional; 54 support | *STAFF* |
| William Gorham, president. Before becoming president of the Urban Institute in 1968, Gorham was assistant secretary of the Department of Health, Education, and Welfare and deputy assistant secretary of the Defense Department. | *DIRECTOR* |
| 501(c)(3) | *TAX STATUS* |
| 1997—$55.16 million<br>1998—$46.6 million<br>Proposed 1999—$51.3 million | *BUDGET* |
| Government contracts, 54 percent; foundation grants, 43 percent; investment income, 2 percent; other, 1 percent | *FUNDING SOURCES* |
| Members: N/A<br>Branches/chapters: N/A<br>Affiliates: N/A | *SCOPE* |
| None | *PAC* |

## METHOD OF OPERATIONS

♦ Conferences/seminars ♦ Congressional testimony ♦ Internet (databases, electronic bulletin boards, e-mail alerts, Web site) ♦ Internships ♦ Library/information clearinghouse ♦ Media outreach ♦ Program evaluation ♦ Research ♦ Telecommunications services (fax-on-demand: 202-331-9747, mailing lists) ♦ Training and technical assistance

## CURRENT CONCERNS

Reflected by The Urban Institute's policy centers: ♦ Assessing the New Federalism (cross-center project) ♦ Education ♦ Health policy ♦ Human resources policy ♦ Income and benefits policy ♦ International activities ♦ Metropolitan housing and communities policy ♦ Nonprofits and philanthropy ♦ Population studies ♦ Public finance and housing ♦ State policy

## PUBLICATIONS

*Child Support and Child Well-Being*
*Databook on Nonfatal Injury: Incidence, Costs, and Consequences*
*Entitlements and the Elderly: Protecting Promises, Recognizing Realities*
*The Government We Deserve: Responsive Democracy and Changing Expectations*
*Medicaid Since 1980: Cost, Coverage, and the Shifting Alliance Between the Federal Government and the States*
*Kids Having Kids: Economic Costs and Social Consequences of Teen Pregnancy*
*Older and Wiser: The Economics of Public Pensions*
*Organizing to Count: Change in the Federal Statistical System*
*Poverty Amid Prosperity: Immigration and the Changing Face of Rural California*
*Reality and Research: Social Science and U.S. Urban Policy since 1960*
*Sales Taxation: State and Local Structure and Administration* (Second edition)
*State-Level Databook on Health-Care Access and Financing* (Third edition)
*State Nonprofit Almanac 1997: Profiles of Charitable Organizations*
*The Work Alternative: Welfare Reform and Realities of the Job Market*

## NEWSLETTER

*Briefing Highlights* (periodic)
*Policy Bites* (periodic)
*Sourcebook for Reporters* (annual)

## CONFERENCES

Sponsors 20–25 annually

## BOARD OF DIRECTORS

Richard B. Fisher, chairman; Joel L. Fleishman, vice chairman; Katharine Graham, vice chairman; William Gorham, president

Other trustees:
♦ Joan Toland Bok ♦ Carol Thompson Cole ♦ John M. Deutch ♦ Richard C. Green Jr. ♦ Fernando A. Guerra ♦ Jack Kemp ♦ Robert S. McNamara ♦ Charles L. Mee Jr. ♦ Robert C. Miller ♦ Lucio Noto ♦ Hugh B. Price ♦ Sol Price ♦ Robert M. Solow ♦ Dick Thornburgh ♦ Judy Woodruff

"A study conducted by former Albuquerque mayor David Rusk and the Urban Institute shows what dramatic improvements can result from economic integration. They studied 10 years of test results of 1,100 children from public-housing families in Albuquerque. Poor children in rent-subsidized apartments in middle-class neighborhoods, attending middle-class neighborhood schools, significantly outperformed poor children living in public housing projects and attending schools in poor districts.

"The Albuquerque study measured the effect of improving both school and neighborhood environments simultaneously. The congressional proposal would broaden only school choices, not housing choices. But the D.C. Housing Authority's court-appointed receiver, David Gilmore, is opening up new housing choices for many tenants. For instance, Gilmore is working to reintroduce moderate-income families in replacement developments such as Ellen Wilson Homes. In collaboration with suburban housing authorities, Gilmore also is encouraging more poor D.C. families to use their housing vouchers in suburban locations.

"Collaborative ties with Gilmore's housing choice initiatives might bring many of the poor children participating in Congress's school choice plan the twin benefits of stronger schools and stronger neighborhoods." (*Washngton Post*, August 21, 1997)

"Legal immigrants in New York make more money and pay more taxes the longer they live here, and after 15 years of residence, they earn and pay more than natives. And their children grow up to earn just as much as other Americans, according to a new study of the incomes and taxes of immigrants in the state.

"But even as legal immigrants move into the state's economic mainstream, paying roughly the same proportion of their income in taxes as natives, they also have higher rates of welfare use than natives, the researchers found.

"Demographers at the Urban Institute, a nonprofit research organization in Washington, undertook their study, which will be released today, after Congress voted to reduce welfare benefits to legal immigrants in 1996. The study was financed by several nonprofit groups, including one created by the financier George Soros, an advocate for immigrants.

"The study focuses on the contributions immigrants make to society in earnings and taxes, an approach that has prompted other scholars to criticize the findings for neglecting the costs associated with immigration in welfare, education and criminal justice expenditures.

" 'You want a cost-benefit analysis,' said George J. Borjas, a professor of public policy at Harvard University. 'This is just half the equation. It tells you what they pay, but not what they cost.'

"Jeffrey S. Passel, who conducted the study with Rebecca L. Clark, acknowledged that they examined only one side of the issue, but he said the findings are still crucial to answering the larger questions of whether immigrants, on balance, are good for the country economically, and whether the new restrictive welfare laws will help or hinder them as they try to succeed in the United States." (*New York Times*, April 30, 1998)

"A new study of 1990 U.S. Census data, conducted by the Urban Institute, shows:

"Poverty is highly segregated. Sixty-one percent of poor blacks in the metropolitan area live inside the District; 85 percent of the region's non-black poor live outside the District.

"Black poverty is highly concentrated, while white and Hispanic poverty is highly dispersed. Twenty-six percent of the region's poor blacks live in a high-poverty, inner-city neighborhood, compared with only 2 percent of the non-black poor.

"In the Washington area's high-poverty neighborhoods, all of which are located within the District, almost half the adults lack a high school diploma, compared with only 15 percent for the metropolitan region as a whole. Unemployment is nearly four times greater in these poor neighborhoods than in the metropolitan area, and almost three-quarters of families with children are headed by single women, compared with only one-quarter of families throughout the region. Moreover, as an increasing share of jobs migrate to the suburbs, poor African American communities in the central city are being cut off from access to economic opportunities.

"As relative newcomers to the Washington metropolitan area, poor Hispanics have thus far avoided this kind of concentrated, inner-city poverty. The region's total Hispanic population more than doubled between 1980 and 1990, to 213,000. But only about 5 percent of poor Hispanics live in high-poverty neighborhoods, and only 25 percent of the Hispanic poor live in the District at all." (*Washington Post*, May 18, 1997)

"Now that welfare overhaul is under way across the country, so is something else: an ideologically charged battle of the experts to label the various innovations as successes or failures. Each side—liberal and conservative—fears the other will use early, and perhaps not totally reliable, results of surveys and studies of the impact of welfare reform to push a political agenda. And conservatives, along with other supporters of the law Congress recently passed to allow states to tinker with welfare, worry that they have the most to lose, because of the overwhelming presence of liberal scholars in the field of social science. . . .

"The hopes and fears of both sides are embodied in one of the biggest private social-policy research projects ever undertaken: a five-year, $30-million study of welfare overhaul and other elements of the 'New Federalism.' The kick-off of the study will be announced today by the Washington-based Urban Institute.

"The institute, founded three decades ago to examine the woes of the nation's cities, has assembled a politically balanced project staff and promises to post 'nonpartisan, reliable data' on the Internet for all sides to examine. But memories are still fresh of the institute's prediction last year that the law would toss one million children into poverty, so even some of its top officials fret about how the research will be received in a political culture increasingly driven between opposing ideological camps. . . .

"The massive Urban Institute project aims to take behavioral changes as well as income into account. Teams of researchers have already fanned out into 12 target states to interview state welfare managers about planned changes in eligibility, benefits levels and work requirements. Nearly 50,000 people in those states will be surveyed about their health, employment, income and family status.

"Some supporters of the new welfare law, who didn't welcome the institute's prediction of rising child poverty, have yet to be won over. 'Whatever they produce will be viewed with skepticism,' says Sen. Joseph Lieberman of Connecticut, a leader among centrist 'new Democrats.' " (*Wall Street Journal*, January 30, 1997)

"nonpartisan" (*Washington Post*, February 3, 1997)

*POLITICAL ORIENTATION*

# Worldwatch Institute (1974)

1776 Massachusetts Avenue, NW
Washington, D.C. 20036
Phone: (202) 452-1999
Fax: (202) 296-7365
Internet: worldwatch@worldwatch.org *or*
http://www.worldwatch.org

| | |
|---|---|
| **PURPOSE** | "Dedicated to fostering the evolution of an environmentally sustainable society, one in which human needs are met in ways that do not threaten the health of the natural environment or the prospects of future generations." |
| **STAFF** | 30 total |
| **DIRECTOR** | Lester R. Brown, president. Brown formerly was administrator of the International Agriculture Development Service of the Agriculture Department and senior fellow at the Overseas Development Council. In 1989 he was awarded a $250,000 MacArthur Foundation "genius award." Brown graduated from Rutgers in 1955. He also has earned a graduate degree in agricultural economics from the University of Maryland and a masters in public administration at Harvard. |
| **TAX STATUS** | 501(c)(3) |
| **BUDGET** | 1997—$3.9 million<br>1998—$4 million<br>Proposed 1999—$4.2 million |
| **FUNDING SOURCES** | Foundation grants, 50 percent; sales of publications, 50 percent |
| **SCOPE** | Members: N/A<br>Branches/chapters: N/A<br>Affiliates: N/A |
| **PAC** | None |

| | |
|---|---|
| ◆ Congressional testimony ◆ Internet (Web site) ◆ Media outreach ◆ Press conferences ◆ Product merchandising ◆ Research ◆ Speakers program ◆ Telecommunications services (databases) | *METHOD OF OPERATION* |

| | |
|---|---|
| ◆ Agriculture ◆ Climate change ◆ Community initiatives in problem-solving ◆ Family planning ◆ Economic, political and demographic discontinuities facing the world ◆ Food scarcity ◆ Forestry ◆ Global trends in population growth ◆ "Green" taxes ◆ Human rights and environmental justice ◆ Infectious diseases ◆ Military and the environment ◆ Military security ◆ Oceans ◆ Renewable energy options ◆ Sustainable development ◆ Sustainable industries ◆ Sustaining freshwater ecosystems ◆ Technology ◆ Threat of bio-invasions ◆ Water | *CURRENT CONCERNS* |

| | |
|---|---|
| *Environmental Alert Series:* <br> —*Fighting for Survival: Environmental Decline, Social Conflict, and the New Age of Insecurity* <br> —*Full House: Reassessing the Earth's Population Carrying Capacity* <br> —*How Much is Enough? The Consumer Society and the Future of the Earth* <br> —*Last Oasis: Facing Water Security* <br> —*Life Out of Bounds: Bioinvasions in a Borderless World* <br> —*The Natural Wealth of Nations: Harnessing the Market for the Environment* <br> —*Power Surge: Guide to the Coming Energy Revolution* <br> —*Saving The Planet: How to Shape an Environmentally Sustainable Economy* <br> —*Tough Choices: Facing the Challenge of Food Scarcity* <br> *State of the World* (annually) <br> *Vital Signs: The Trends That are Shaping Our Future* (annually) <br> *Who Will Feed China? Wake-Up Call for a Small Planet* <br> *Worldwatch Database Diskette* (available for IBM and Macintosh) <br> *Worldwatch Papers* (more than 141 papers on the world's resources and their management) <br> *Worldwatch Reader* | *PUBLICATIONS* |

| | |
|---|---|
| *Worldwatch* (bimonthly magazine) | *NEWSLETTER* |

| | |
|---|---|
| None | *CONFERENCE* |

## BOARD OF DIRECTORS

Andrew E. Rice, chairman; Oystein Dahle, vice chairman

Other members:
♦ Lester R. Brown ♦ Carlo M. Cipolla ♦ Edward S. Cornish ♦ Herman Daly ♦ Orville L. Freeman ♦ Lynne Gallagher ♦ Mahbub ul Haq ♦ Hazel Henderson ♦ Abd-El Rahman Khane ♦ Larry Minear ♦ Izaak Van Melle ♦ Wren Wirth

## EFFECTIVENESS

"As thousands of government officials, environmentalists and journalists from Papua New Guinea to Paraguay arrived here today [Nov. 30, 1997] for the U.N. Framework Convention on Climate Change, many Asian countries are preoccupied by bankruptcies, diving stock markets and the disappearing value of their currencies. . . .

"The aim of this month's conference is to forge an agreement that would slow the effects of carbon dioxide and other greenhouse gases that are accumulating in the atmosphere, allowing sunlight through but trapping heat that Earth emits back toward space. Scientists say such global warming eventually could lead to rising sea levels, flooding, droughts and other dangerous changes in world weather.

"A top official with the environmental group Greenpeace International said today that the 'explosive issue of the meeting' is whether developing countries—including such key Asian nations as China, India and Indonesia—should participate in the U.N. effort to curb the emission of greenhouse gases. The United States insists they must. But because some of those countries are in financial chaos, the likelihood that they will agree to potentially pricey measures to reduce carbon-dioxide emissions from factories and cars is even more remote. . . .

" 'There has been a tremendous run-up to this agreement,' said Christopher Flavin, senior vice president of Worldwatch Institute, an environmental research group based in Washington, D.C., who spoke at one of the many environmental discussions held throughout Kyoto today. 'If we don't seize this opportunity and we don't get legally binding targets, it will be a setback of five years.' " (*Washington Post*, December 1, 1997)

"The world's population—now almost 5.8 billion—is growing by 80 million people a year, and to feed them all, grain production will have to increase by 26 million tons annually. Instead, the growth rate of grain harvests, which had expanded steadily for decades, has slowed, prompting the Worldwatch Institute to warn that this trend may usher in an era of scarcity. While not predicting devastating famines, the institute predicts rising prices that would hit people in developing countries the hardest." (*Washington Post*, August 23, 1997)

## POLITICAL ORIENTATION

Unavailable

# Indexes

# Name Index

Aaron, Billye Suber, 112
Aaron, Henry J., 24
Abbott, Catherine G., 471
Abdoo, Richard A., 457
Abelson, Olivia, 538
Abernathy Jr., James W., 350
AbiNader, Jean R., 602
Able Jr., Edward H., 289
Abraham, Nancy, 494
Abrahamson, Dean, 452
Abrahamson, Joan, 670
Abrams, Elliott, 801
Abramson, Richard S., 550
Abshire, David M., 513, 515
Achenbaum, W. Andrew, 135
Acheson, David C., 507, 508
Ackerman, F. Duane, 45
Ackerman, James H., 716
Ackerman, Peter, 674, 786
Adame, Louis, 107
Adams, John H., 429, 450
Adams, John Hurst, 544
Adams, Ruth, 828
Adams, Stan, 422
Adams Jr., Floyd, 658
Adamsen, Arnie, 658
Adamson, Rebecca, 333, 342
Adler, Charles, 550
Adler, Robert S., 274
Adnam, Hamdan bin Hj, 270
Agley, Randolph J., 63
Agne, Joe, 85
Agrama, Olfet, 71
Agre, Phil, 573
Aikens, Joan D., 702
Akhter, Mohammed N., 247, 249
Alberthal Jr., Lester M., 515
Albrecht, Charles, 231
Albright, Adam, 452
Alcorn, George A., 698
Alden, Katherine H., 844
Alderman, Nancy O., 387
Alexander, Darryl L., 405
Alexander, E.H., 658
Alexander, Erla, 663
Alexander, Herbert E., 615, 616
Alexander, Joyce London, 836
Alexander, Lamar, 640
Alexander, Michael B., 157
Alexander, Sidney, 541
Algrant, Roland, 530
Allaire, Paul A., 45, 314, 625
Allan, J. David, 356
Allen, Cathy, 662
Allen, George, 721
Allen, Jodie, 471
Allen, John, 212
Allen, Robert C., 442
Allen, W. Ron, 127

Allen, W.W., 42
Allen, Wayne, 63
Allen Jr., George V., 356
Allenby, Braden, 392
Allery, Virginia P., 447
Alley, Robert S., 78
Allison, Herbert, 314
Allison, Sharon W., 172
Allyn, William F., 605
Alter Jr., Wayne E., 63
Altschul, David E., 168
Amacher, Ryan, 847
Ambrose, Stephen E., 356
Ames, A. Gary, 17
Ames, Edward A., 483
Ames, Oakes, 432
Amidei, Nancy, 665
Amory, Cleveland, 408
Andelson, Arlen H., 244
Andersen, K. Tucker, 786
Andersen, Maryellen F., 831
Anderson, Barbara, 125
Anderson, Betty Lou, 172
Anderson, Craig Barry, 758
Anderson, Jean, 350
Anderson, Jerome W., 831
Anderson, John, 573
Anderson, Lisa, 530
Anderson, Martin, 814
Anderson, Norma, 649
Anderson, R. Gavin S., 329
Anderson, Ralph H., 52
Anderson, Ray, 310
Anderson, Rhoda R., 831
Anderson, Terry L., 846
Anderson, Thomas R., 198
Anderson, Travis, 674
Anderson Jr., Joe M., 63
Andreason, John, 649
Andrews, John B., 658
Andrews, Michael, 442
Andrews, Susan A., 56
Andrews Jr., Albert, 356
Andrews Jr., Ben, 118
Angle, Martha, 612
Anns, Arlene A., 147
Anschutz, Phillip F., 63
Ansin, Ronald M., 789
Anthony, Clarence, 658
Anthony, Nancy, 525
Apfelbaum, William M., 244
Apodaca, Lillian G., 110
Aponte, Mari Carmen, 129
Applewhite, Eleanor S., 112
Arango, Manuel, 333, 489
Aranguren, Ignacio, 42
Arce, Jason, 107
Archer, Dennis W., 658, 678
Archinaco, Frank A., 52

Are, Martha, 125
Arkley, Robin P., 704
Armacost, Michael H., 774, 776
Armstrong, Anne, 515
Armstrong, William L., 806
Armstrong Jr., Bill B., 698
Arnesen, Deborah Arnie, 621
Arnett, Grace-Marie, 803
Arnhold, Henry H., 370
Arnwine, Barbara, 104
Aron, Nan, 685, 686
Aronstein, Michael, 60
Arrington, Kathy, 192
Artabane, Joseph A., 721
Artzt, Edwin L., 772
Asali, Naila, 71
Ash, Roy L., 35
Asher, Thomas R., 612
Ashkin, Roberta E., 716
Ashley, Thomas L., 35
Ashworth, Edward, 711, 712
Askin, Frank, 73
Asner, Edward, 374
Asnes, Norma Ketay, 836
Atkinson, Richard C., 45
Augustine, Norman R., 336
Austin, Dorothy M., 300
Autry, James A., 168
Auzan, Alexander, 270
Avant, Clarence, 112
Averitt, Ophelia, 118
Awde, Halim, 71
Ayer, Donald B., 356
Ayoub, Mouna E., 244
Ayoub, Naim, 71
Ayres, Richard E., 452
Azari, Ann, 265

Baba, Gwen, 96
Babcock, Charles W., 202
Babcock, Susan H., 439
Babcock, Tim, 698
Babunovic, Mark, 691
Baca, James R., 483
Baca, Polly, 663
Bachmann, John W., 63
Baer, Steven, 674
Bagby, Clarence, 140
Bahr, Morton, 168, 798
Bailey, Adrienne Y., 339
Bailey, Barbara, 100
Bailey, Elizabeth E., 776
Bailey, Joe, 553
Bailey, Keith E., 347
Bailey, Patricia, 663
Bailey II, Irving Widmer, 336
Baird, John W., 442
Baird, Zöe, 110, 776
Baker, Brian R., 52

Baker, Dexter F., 52
Baker, Jeanne, 73
Baker, Willie, 544
Bakke, Dennis W., 632
Baldes, Richard J., 447
Baldock, James, 447
Baldwin, Alec, 168
Bales, Carter F., 457
Ball, Carol L., 63
Ballard, Charles, 826
Balser, Barbara B., 735
Balta, Wayne, 392
Bancroft, Anne, 255
Bandler, Ned W., 616
Bandy Jr., William J., 63
Banfield, Emiko, 310
Banks, Darryl, 429
Banks Jr., Fred L., 118
Banta, Mary Ann, 584, 585
Banzhaf, John F., 223, 224
Baran, Jan W., 616
Baran, Jan Witold, 605
Barber, Gerald R., 447
Barbour, Haley, 721
Barbour, Nancy R., 616
Barish, Joseph, 110
Barish, Judith, 523
Barlow, Harriet, 189
Barlow, John Perry, 570
Barnard, Timothy, 605
Barnes, Galen R., 63
Barnes, John L., 231
Barnes, Karen M., 387
Barnes, Michael D., 789
Barnes, Sharon, 525
Barnett, Randy E., 721
Barnett, Robert L., 52
Barney, Shawn M., 157
Baron, Fred, 716
Baron, Richard D., 442
Baroody, Michael, 205
Baroody, Michail E., 605
Barrios, Zulma X., 129
Barron, Thomas A., 483
Barry, John J., 132
Barsamian, Khajag, 758
Bartimus, James, 716
Bartolin, Steve, 17
Barton, Richard S., 63
Bass, Gary, 664, 665
Bastress, Robert, 73
Batchelder, Nathaniel, 538
Batchelder, William G., 806
Batisse, Michel, 370
Bato, Doris Z., 510
Batterson, Robert, 20
Battle, Paul, 212
Batts, Warren L., 52
Bauer, Gary L., 197, 198

Baum, Phil, 729
Baum Jr., Alvin H., 100
Bauman, Patricia, 452, 590
Baumgarten, Jane O'Dell, 237
Bausch, James J., 295
Bavaria, Joan L., 321
Baxter, Frank E., 844
Baxter, Jameson Adkins, 289
Beach, Roger C., 52
Beach, Thomas E., 855
Beaham III, Gordon T., 605
Bean, Terry, 96
Beasley, David M., 653
Beaty, Anita, 125
Beaudry, Ann, 793
Becker, George F., 132, 798
Beckner, Paul, 26
Beckstrom, Rod A., 387
Bedford, Peter B., 814
Beebe, Leo C., 347
Beekman, Philip E., 147
Beem, Marc O., 73
Beene, Betty, 515
Beers, Mark, 135
Begley Jr., Ed, 405
Beinecke, Frances G., 489
Beinecke, John B., 432
Belk, Judy, 342
Bell, Donald R., 45
Bell, Griffin B., 702
Bell, Jeffrey, 593
Bell Jr., Thomas D., 63, 818
Bell-Rose, Stephanie, 157
Belton, Sharon Sayles, 658
Belzberg, Leslie, 140
Benchley, Wendy W., 387
Bender, Donald, 52
Bender, Peter A., 416
Bendheim, Alice, 73
Bendich, Judith, 73
Benecke, Michelle M., 174
Benham, Philip 'Flip', 163
Benkard, James W.B., 387
Bennett, Bruce, 52
Bennett, Dottie, 727
Bennett, Josselyn, 135
Bennett, Roberta, 140
Bennett, William J., 640
Benson, Bruce D., 605
Benson, Lucy Wilson, 508
Benton, Marjorie, 663
Bentsen, Lloyd, 7
Bereano, Phil, 73
Berger, Nini De, 370
Berger, Renee, 682
Berger, Vivian, 73
Bergholz, David, 333
Bergman, Marilyn, 168
Bergner, Jeffrey T., 818
Bergreen, Bernard D., 168
Bergsten, C. Fred, 532
Bergstrom, Charles, 168
Berkowitz, Howard P., 735
Berlin, Ruth, 436
Berliss Jr., Arthur D., 510
Berlyn, Debra, 300, 560
Berman, Jerry, 559
Berman, Michael S., 632
Bern, Dorritt, 682
Berner, Georgia, 52
Bernstein, Bob, 686

Bernstein, Robert L., 530
Berry, Joyce T., 135
Berry, Mary Frances, 112
Berry, Phil, 477
Berthoud, John E., 58, 60
Bertonaschi, Karen 'Bert', 73
Best, Robert K., 703, 704
Betts, Henry, 147
BeVier, Lillian R., 689
Bhatia, Rajiv, 466
Bidzos, D. James, 573
Biehl, Bobb, 742
Bierwirth, John, 361
Biggins, Veronica, 793
Biibe, Diane, 202
Bingham, Sally G., 387
Biondi, Carol Oughton, 89
Birch, Elizabeth, 95, 104
Bird, Michael E., 249
Birenbaum, David, 93
Bishop, Alexandra G., 183
Bishop, Cecil, 758
Bishop, Peggy, 192
Bishop, Richard, 147
Bittker, Boris, 452
Bivens, Bobby, 118
Bjorklund, Christine A., 274
Black, Charles, 593
Black, Robert, 52
Blackburn, Sadie Gwin, 439
Blackwelder, Brent, 404
Blackwell, J. Kenneth, 60
Blackwell, Morton, 593
Blackwood Jr., George D., 658
Blair, William H., 52
Blake, Robert O., 452, 489
Blanchard, Larry, 265
Blanchard, W.H. 'Bill', 202
Blanchard III, James U., 786
Blankenhorn, David, 825, 826
Blankenship, Elmer E., 132
Blaser-Upchurch, Jan, 203
Blaxall, Martha O., 632
Blokker, John, 786
Bloom, Elliot, 286
Bloomberg, Michael R., 63
Bloomfield, Mark A., 6, 7
Blue, Dan, 649
Blue, Linden S., 605, 818
Blue, Ronald, 198
Bluestein, Jeffrey L., 52
Bluestone, Barry, 798
Bluhm, Barbara, 168
Blum, Barbara B., 24
Blum, Barbara Davis, 793
Blum, Fred, 730
Blum, Richard, 483
Blunt, Barbara A., 209
Boardman Jr., Harold F., 52
Boas, Robert B., 202
Bode, Barbara, 350
Boden, Paul, 125
Bogaard, Claire W., 442
Boggs, Timothy, 96
Boggs Jr., Thomas Hale, 721
Bohlen, E.U. Curtis, 361
Bok, Derek, 489
Bok, Joan Toland, 860
Boles, Douglas L., 52
Bolin, Bert, 489
Bollinger, Donald T., 605

Bolton, John R., 772
Bond, Frank, 786, 855
Bond, Julian, 85, 118
Bonderman, David, 483
Bonjean, Charles M., 333
Bonta, Diana M., 249
Boone, Betty Evans, 78
Boone, Eric E., 118
Booth, Edwin, 189
Booth, I. Macallister, 329
Booth, Lois, 538
Boren, Ann Franks, 374
Boren, David L., 702
Borges, Francisco L., 118
Borgman, Christine, 573
Borlaug, Norman E., 241
Born, Gary B., 721
Borokowski, Patricia A., 227
Borow, Richard, 550
Borum, John C., 471
Borut, Donald J., 657
Borwegen, Bill, 265
Bosch, Alan, 300
Bosley, Steven K., 698
Bossidy, Lawrence A., 14
Bostic Jr., James E., 439
Bothwell, Robert O., 349, 350
Botting, Peter A., 698
Boucher, Jim, 189
Boucher, Ray, 716
Boulding, Christie, 310
Boulter, Beau, 593
Bourns, Richard T., 52
Bowen, Beth, 541
Bowers, Betty H., 605
Bowers, Daniel H., 100
Bowers, Dorothy, 392
Bowes, Harry P., 17
Bowlin, John D., 52
Box, Charles, 678
Boyd, Katherine E., 844
Boykins, Ayanna, 118
Boyle, James, 573
Boyle, R. Emmett, 63
Bozell III, L. Brent, 580, 581
Brack, Barbara, 408
Brack, Paulette, 192
Brack Jr., Reginald K., 157
Brademas, John, 789
Braden, Anne, 85
Bradford, Calvin, 212
Bradford, Martina L., 836
Bradford, Peter A., 547
Bradford, William E., 63
Bradford Jr., James W., 52
Brady, James S., 93
Brady, Larry D., 52
Brady, Rodney H., 702
Brady, Sarah, 92
Bragg Jr., Charles G., 432
Brand, Martha C., 356
Brandau, Herman, 227
Branden, Susan G., 721
Brandon, David A., 605
Brandt, Liz Barker, 73
Brann, Alton J., 52
Branson, Jeanne, 96
Brasch, Duane E., 52
Braswell, Tony, 231
Braun, Beatrice S., 237
Braun, Zev, 244

Braveman, Wayne S., 100
Bravo, Ellen, 160
Bray, Thomas J., 847
Brayton, Alan R., 716
Brazier, Arthur M., 189
Breck, Henry, 452
Breckenridge, Franklin E., 118
Bredeweg, Thomas G., 658
Breeding, Les, 538
Brendsel, Leland C., 157
Breslauer, Benjamin, 550
Breslauer, Mary, 96
Brice, Rutherford Jack, 237
Briggs, Richard S., 56
Briglio, John F., 244
Brimigion, Stephen F., 342
Brimmer, Andrew F., 836
Brinner, Roger E., 625
Brion-Meisels, Steven, 538
Bristow, Lonnie, 292
Brittenham, Skip, 370
Broadway, Beth, 538
Brobeck, Stephen, 227, 263, 303
Brock, William E., 7, 515
Brody, Michael, 566
Brokaw, Howard P., 432
Brokaw, Meredith Auld, 370
Brokaw, Thomas C. T., 374
Brooker, Charlotte, 422
Brooks, Bernard E., 274
Brooks, Diana D., 314
Brooks, Genevieve S., 789
Brooks, Glen M., 157
Brooks, Robert J., 789
Brower, David R., 380, 477
Browing, Peter C., 52
Brown, Alma Arrington, 157
Brown, Amos, 746
Brown, Bertram S., 147
Brown, Blair, 168
Brown, Charles T., 447
Brown, David R., 811
Brown, Diane E., 265
Brown, Floyd, 593
Brown, George L., 836
Brown, Harold, 515
Brown, Helene G., 590
Brown, James L., 265
Brown, John H., 314
Brown, Joyce M., 209
Brown, Lester R., 385, 864, 866
Brown, Margaret, 645
Brown, Marie, 645
Brown, Martha, 202
Brown, Martin, 439
Brown, Michael H., 342
Brown, Nick, 93
Brown, Peter, 828
Brown, Reenie, 183
Brown, Virdin C., 439
Brown Jr., George A., 658
Brown Jr., Thomas E., 135
Browne, E. John P., 42
Browne, James, 716
Browning, Don S., 826
Brubaker, Harold J., 597
Brunson, Thelma Scott, 157
Bryant, Arthur H., 715
Bryant, Bunyan, 429
Bryant, Neil, 649
Brzezinski, Zbigniew, 515

Buc, Nancy L., 151
Buchanan, James, 60
Buchanan Jr., John H., 168
Buche, Tom, 96
Budge, Nancy A., 172
Bueche, Wendell F., 52
Buechner, Jack W., 789
Buehler, William F., 52
Buffenbarger, R. Thomas, 132
Buhl, Alice C., 296
Buhl III, C. Henry, 525
Bullitt, Harriet S., 432
Bullock, Ronald D., 52
Bullock Jr., Ellis F., 289
Bumpers, William M., 483
Bunis, Morton, 730
Bunting, W. Clark, 361
Bunyan, Maureen, 682
Burd, Margaret A., 140
Burden, Stuart C., 100
Burditt, George M., 721
Burge, Bridgette, 538
Burgess, Philip M., 16, 17, 850
Burhenne-Guilmin, Francoise, 392
Burke, James E., 625
Burke, Kathleen J., 347
Burke, Yvonne Brathwaite, 663
Burkett, Bob, 168
Burkett, Robert L., 244
Burkholder, Melissa, 265
Burkle, Ronald W., 157
Burnett, Grove T., 374
Burnett, John, 73
Burnham, David, 573
Burnley IV, James H., 721
Burns, Arnold, 721
Burns, Brenda, 597
Burns, M. Anthony, 14
Burns, Scott, 60
Burrell, Cheryl M., 202
Burroughs, Hugh C., 296
Burt, Robert N., 14, 489
Burton, Charlotta, 422
Burton, Richard, 118
Burtt, Mary Ann, 645
Busby, James J., 704
Busch, Barbara, 212
Bush, George, 147
Bushkin, Kathy, 789
Busiek, Paul, 558
Butler, Charles H., 118
Buzzelli, David T., 489
Byrd, Acie, 538
Byrd, Christine, 125
Byrd, Isaac, 73
Byrd, Isaac K., 716
Byrne, Blake, 96
Byrne, John J., 7

Caballero, Laura, 436
Cabo, Toni, 560
Cabot, Edward S., 621
Cabot, Louis W., 370
Caccamo, Aldo M., 605
Cahill, William P., 63
Cain, Becky, 104
Cain, Gordon, 28
Cain, Herman, 205
Cain, Jim, 125
Caine, Virginia A., 249
Caldwell, Kirbyjon, 89

Calise Jr., William J., 689
Callahan, Debra J., 428, 429, 489
Callaway, Howard H., 806
Callejon, Donna, 310, 793
Cameron, Catherine, 553
Cameron, Dave, 847
Cameron, Don, 168
Campaigne Jr., Jameson, 593
Campbell, C. Keith, 237
Campbell, Colin G., 333
Campbell, Jane, 793
Campbell, Joan Brown, 104, 746, 756, 758
Campbell, Nancy N., 442
Campbell, Phyllis J., 289
Campbell, Robert H., 52
Campbell, Tom, 721
Campbell Jr., Calvin A., 52
Campbell Jr., Carroll A., 7
Campoamor, Diana, 333, 342
Canada, Geoffrey, 339
Canales Jr., James E., 289
Canderlaria, Cordelia, 129
Canja, Esther 'Tess', 237
Canno, Jonathan, 244
Cannon, Joseph A., 640, 772
Cantwell, Maria, 625
Capozzi, Louis, 356
Caras, Roger A., 182
Card Jr., Andrew H., 7
Carew, Ruth Harmer, 300
Carey, Michael, 347
Carhart, Wendy H., 183
Carlson, James R., 52
Carlton, Alfreda, 265
Carmichael, William, 530
Carnahan, Mel, 653
Carney, Peter R., 605
Caron, Roger T., 52
Carothers, Andre, 468
Carothers, Leslie, 392
Carpenter, Capt. Thomas T., 175
Carpenter, Liz, 663
Carper, Thomas R., 653
Carr, Donald A., 432
Carr, Gwenn L., 831
Carr, John, 189
Carroll, Candace M., 73
Carroll, James L., 447
Carroll, Philip J., 157, 323
Carroll, Sally G., 118
Carruthers, Garrey, 63
Carswell, Bruce, 347
Carter, Charly, 681
Carter, Larry W., 118
Carter, Leonie, 161
Cartwright, Kevin, 523
Cartwright Jr., Robert E., 716
Caruana, Patrick P., 742
Cashen, Donald W., 416
Caso, Anthony T., 704
Castellani, John, 605
Castillo, Ursulo, 107
Castle Jr., John R., 336
Castleberry, Don H., 439
Castro, Martin R., 110
Castro, Paul S., 350
Cathcart, Kevin M., 99
Catto, Jessica, 387
Catto, Jessica Hobby, 367
Cavanagh, John, 827, 828

Cavanagh, Richard E., 39, 42
Cavanaugh III, William, 63
Cavaney, Red, 7
Cave, John B., 323
Cave, Susan J., 658
Cavill, Ronald W., 135
Cazares, Roger, 129
Cazort, Ralph J., 541
Cecil, Mimi, 387
Cerf, Charlie, 73
Cerf, Vint, 573
Chachkin, Norman J., 112
Chaille, Gregory A., 333
Chaleff, Ira, 628
Challinor, David, 361
Chamberlin, John R., 621
Chambers, Joan L., 274
Chambers, Julius L., 112, 168
Chambers, Letitia, 632
Champion, Maxine, 793
Chan, Pamela, 270
Chancellor, JoAnn, 712
Chandler, J. Harold, 147
Chanin, Leona, 730
Chapa Jr., Amancio J., 129
Chapela, Ignacio, 466
Chapman, Donald E., 135
Chapman, Michael, 140
Charren, Peggy, 578
Chase, Jayni, 405
Chase, JoAnn, 350
Chase, JoAnn K., 126
Chase, Robert, 104
Chase, W. Rowell, 52
Chasen, Jerry Simon, 100
Chasin, Dana, 329
Chaum, David, 573
Chaves, Alex, 110
Chavez-Thompson, Linda, 45
Chavis, Donna, 350
Chavous, Kevin, 93
Cheatum, Lynn, 538
Chellum Jayen, 270
Chen, Nicholas V., 81
Chen, Ronald, 73
Cheney, Dick, 702, 772
Cheng-Khanna, Vivian, 81
Chenoweth, Michael, 422
Chester, Jeffrey, 566
Chew, Denley, 81
Childs, John Brown, 590
Chilton, Kenneth, 20
Chin, Gordon, 189
Chin-Loy, Errol, 231
Chisholm, Sallie, 547
Chisholm, Shirley, 663
Choate, Jerry D., 42, 314
Chopnick, Max, 336
Christensen, Eric C., 695
Christensen Jr., Norman L., 367
Chuda, Jim, 436
Chuda, Nancy, 436
Church, Bethine, 483
Churchill, Kenneth, 52
Cietis, William M., 289
Cincotta, Gale, 211, 212
Ciorciari, Anthony, 52
Cipolla, Carlo M., 866
Ciresi, Michael V., 716
Cizik, Robert, 52
Claassen, Susan, 168

Clack, R. Nancy, 682
Clanton Pinkston, Brandolyn T., 300
Clark, Gordon, 537
Clark, James, 60
Clark, Jerry, 140
Clark, Katt, 125
Clark, Kenneth B., 73
Clark, Mary, 658
Clark, Merrill, 436
Clark, Noelle, 56
Clark, Patricia, 712
Clark Jr., Edward, 447
Clark Jr., Fred D., 265
Clarkson, Lawrence W., 52
Claude, Richard, 573
Clay Jr., Roger A., 189
Claybrook, Joan B., 227, 274, 669, 670, 716
Clayton, Chuck, 422
Clement, Marilyn, 85
Clemente, C.L., 605
Clements Jr., George G., 183
Cleveland, B.L., 132
Cline, Philip E., 63
Clinger Jr., William, 632
Clinton, Frank, 658
Cloud, James L., 704
Clough, G. Wayne, 45
Cochran, J. Thomas, 676, 678
Cody Jr., John T., 63
Coelho, Tony, 147
Coffee Jr., Alan F., 721
Coffelt, Charlotte H., 78
Coffman, Vance D., 63
Cofield, William E., 118
Cogan, Maureen, 89
Cogan, Sarah, 452
Cogg, Spencer, 649
Coggs, G. Spencer, 793
Cohen, David, 589, 590
Cohen, Jeff, 574
Cohen, Sharon, 310
Cohen, Steve, 649
Cohn, Bertram J., 483
Cole, Callie, 125
Cole, Carol Thompson, 860
Cole, David C., 457
Cole, Elbert, 135
Cole, Johnnetta B., 663
Cole, Ken W., 605
Cole, Kenneth, 244
Cole, Wallace A., 439
Coleman, Barbara Bell, 157
Coleman, Carolyn Q., 118
Coleman, Frunh, 749
Coleman, Lewis W., 370
Coleman, Lovida H., 442
Coleman, Muriel, 593
Coleman Jr., Leonard S., 89, 157
Coleman Jr., Lovida H., 632
Coleman Jr., William T., 112
Coles, E. Tyna, 329
Coles, H. Brent, 678
Coles, James E., 605
Collazo, Denise Padin, 189
Colling, Terese, 682
Collins, Arthur D., 52
Collins, Charles M., 157
Collins, Donald A., 525
Collins, Gina, 468

Collins, Richard H., 261
Colouett, Babette, 118
Colton, Gerri, 716
Colton, Marie Watters, 621
Combs, G. Edward, 227
Combs, Roberta, 739
Comer, James P., 836
Comper, F. Anthony, 314
Condit, Madeline K.B., 336
Condon, Kathleen A., 831
Coney, Chloe, 205
Conley, Christopher, 292
Conlin, Roxanne Barton, 716
Conna, Ted, 541
Conners, John, 227
Connor Jr., John, 329
Conran, Jim, 300
Considine, Terence, 674
Conwell, Tracey, 716
Conwill, Kinshasha Holman, 342
Cook, J. Michael, 314
Cook, Ken A., 394
Cooke, John F., 52, 789
Cooley, Arthur P., 387
Cooley, Michael, 135
Cooper, Bonnie Sue, 597
Cooper, James H.S., 471
Cooper, Jim, 35
Coors, Jeffrey H., 52, 806
Coors, Joseph, 702
Coors, Holland, 811
Copeland Jr., James E., 63
Copello, A. Gene, 231
Corbin, Stampp, 96
Corey, Leroy, 593
Cornette, Gloria N., 616
Cornfeld-Urfirer, Leslie, 89
Cornish, Edward S., 866
Cornog, Robert A., 52
Corr, Brian, 538
Corradini, Deedee, 147, 678
Correll Jr., A.D., 457
Correnti, John D., 52
Cors, Allan D., 605
Cortes, Michael, 189
Cortes Jr., Ernesto J., 798
Cosby, William H., 544
Cossé, Steven A., 52
Costa, Jim, 649
Costello, Albert J., 772
Costle, Douglas M., 432
Cotchett, Joseph W., 670
Cothren, Kelvin Lunn, 140
Couch, Jane A., 342
Coughlin, Roger, 212
Coulter, Jamie B., 640
Coupe, Anita W., 416
Cousin, Philip R., 118
Coverson, Ernest, 118
Cowen, Bruce D., 63
Cowles, Maron, 716
Cox, Archibald, 621
Cox, Faye Justice, 645
Cox, J. Robert, 477
Cozier, Ravinia Hayes, 231
Crabtree, Richard D., 227
Craft, Robert H., 632
Craig, Ellen, 300
Crane, Edward H., 674, 784, 786
Crawford, James, 73
Crear, Pete, 265

Crisp, Mary Dent, 663
Critelli, Michael J., 157
Crittenden, Ann, 356
Crittenden, Robert, 282
Cronon, William J., 483
Crosby, Harriett, 405
Crosby, Susan, 649
Cross, Christopher T., 632
Cross, Theodore L., 112
Crow, Harlan, 772
Crowe, Jeffrey C., 63
Crowley, Sheila, 125
Crozier, Scott A., 698
Cruz, Lillian, 129
Cuellar, Hector J., 110
Cullen, Barbara, 730
Cullman, Dorothy, 530
Cullman III, Joseph F., 494
Cumming, Ian M., 457
Cuneo, Dennis C., 52
Curran, James W., 249
Currie, David, 746
Curry Jr., Charles M., 183
Curtis, David, 231
Curtis, Elizabeth H., 333
Cutler, Lloyd N., 625
Cutler, Neal E., 135
Czachorski, Marc S., 52

Dach, Leslie, 432
Dachs, Alan M., 776
Dahlberg, A. William, 63
Dahlberg Jr., C. Frederick, 52
Dahle, Oystein, 866
Daigneault, Michael G., 335, 336
Dalton, Harlon, 73
Dalton, Vernon, 265
Daly, Charles U., 836
Daly, Herman, 866
Dam, Kenneth W., 776
Dampman, Barb, 135
Danforth, John C., 625
Daniel, D. Ronald, 442, 776
Daniel, James H., 118
Daniels, James, 422
Daniels, Lori, 649
Daniels, Ron, 85
Daniels Jr., Mitchell E., 818
Danielson, Beverly, 558, 781
Danmola, Taiwo K., 241
Danner, Donald A., 605
Dantchick, Arthur, 691
Danzeisen, John R., 52
Darby Jr., Roosevelt, 125
Darden, Cal, 157
Darling, Michelle, 347
Darman, Richard G., 632
Dartland, Walter T., 265
Darwin, Rebecca Wesson, 682
Daub, Hal, 658
Dauway, Lois, 85
Davenport, David, 702
David Boyer Jr., K., 702
Davidoff, Denise T., 746
Davidson, James Dale, 60
Davidson, Joan K., 452
Davidson, Sally, 356
Davies, John B., 63
Davies, Peter J., 538
Davies, Simon, 573
Davies Jr., Paul L., 814

Davis, Brenda S., 483
Davis, Don, 140
Davis, Donald W., 52
Davis, Julie, 73
Davis, Robert A., 52
Davis, Shelley, 436
Davis III, Shedrick O., 100
Davis Jr., Thomas R., 172
Dawson, Carol, 261
Day, Robert A., 776
De Armas, Pedro, 100
de Borchgrave, Arnaud, 702
de Ferranti, David, 24
De Stefano, Vincent G., 52
De Wind, Adrian, 828
Deal, Pat, 662
Dean, Earlyn, 52
Dean, George A., 682
Dean, Howard, 653
Dean, John W., 157
Dean, Kathy, 161
Dean, Norman, 321, 392
Deane, Maurice, 550
Deardourff, John, 303
Deardourff, John D., 89
Deavenport Jr., Earnest W., 52
Debro, Ted, 300
Decker, Thomas A., 52
Decrane Jr., Alfred C., 323
Decter, Midge, 811
Dee, Robert F., 52
Deeb, Dan, 447
Dees Jr., Morris S., 670
Deets, Horace B., 104, 234
DeFazio, Jackie, 104
DeGraffenreidt Jr., James H., 789
DeGraw, Bette F., 110
Deitzler, Harry, 716
Del Guidice, Paula J., 447
Deland, Michael R., 147, 489
Dell, Michael S., 63
Dellums, Roscoe, 93
DeMartino, Rita, 129
Dement, Polly, 356
Dempsey, Jack, 432
Dempsey, Thomas, 716
DeMuth, Christopher C., 770, 772
DeNadai, Mary Werner, 442
Dendahl, John H., 605, 698
Denham, Robert E., 42, 452
Denhart, Gun, 310
Dennis, Kim, 847
Dennis, Richard J., 786
Deppe, Cathy, 161
Derian, Pat, 793
Derickson, J. Richard, 52
DeSimone, Livio D., 42, 457, 702
Despres, Gina, 530
Desser, Chris, 468
DeStefano Jr., John, 658
Determan, Sara-Ann, 151
Deutch, John M., 471, 860
Devine, Donald J., 593
DeVos, Richard M., 147
DeVos Jr., Richard M., 52, 605
Dewhurst, David, 28
Dewind, Adrian, 452
DeWind, Adrian W., 530
DeWind, Ellen, 265
Diamond, Irene, 530
Diamond, Jared M., 494

Diaz, William A., 333
DiBartolomeis, Michael, 466
DiCamillo, Gary, 52
DiCenso, Robert E., 52
Dick, Cathleen, 452
Dickenson, Katherine, 442
Dickey, Jefferson, 541
Didier, Calvin W., 78
Diegel, Rick, 682
Diehl, William, 857
Dietsch, Alfred J., 172
Diffie, Whitfield, 573
diGenova, Joseph E., 721
Dillingham, Gay, 510
Dillon, John T., 42
Dillon-Ridgley, Dianne, 553
Dinkins, Carol E., 385, 457
DiSario, Martha, 468
DiSibio, Ralph R., 605
Disman, Bea, 730
Ditlow III, Clarence M., 227, 251, 252, 274, 405
Dittmar Jr., Nelson W., 339
Dixon, Margaret A., 237
Dobson, James, 198, 741, 742
Dobson, Shirley M., 742
Docksai, Ronald, 205
Doggett, Rebecca, 189
Doherty, Diane, 125
Dolnick, Lynn, 432
Domenitz, Janet S., 265, 621
Dominick, David, 432
Donahue, John, 125
Donahue, Maura W., 63
Donald, Joe K., 52
Donaldson, Sue, 658
Donaldson, William H., 632
Donaldson-McMahon, Lorna, 436
Donati, Del, 408
Donnelley, James R., 63
Donohue, Thomas J., 61, 63, 818
Donohue, William A., 721
Donovan, Chuck, 198
Dority, Douglas H., 789
Dorr, Donald W., 63
Dorsey, Michael, 477
Doss, Joe K., 300
Doss, Joe Morris, 621
Dovalina, Rick, 107
Dover, Eric, 541
Dovey, Brian H., 7
Dowell, Duane, 172
Downes, John J., 541
Downs, Bertis, 168
Doyle, Frank P., 323
Doyle, Jack, 321
Doyle, Lee Lee, 172
Drasner, Fred, 183
Drewes, Robert W., 52
Dreyer, John R., 140
Driegert, Robert, 202
Drinan, Robert F., 168
Drinan S.J., Robert J., 621
Driscoll, Dawn-Marie, 319
Droz, Marilyn, 585
Druckenmiller, Fiona, 530
Drury, David J., 7
Duane, Thomas, 658
Duberstein, Kenneth M., 7
Dubrow, Evelyn, 265, 300

Duemling, Louesa C., 457
Duesenberg, Richard, 721
Duff, Patricia, 168
Duffy, Michael T., 96
Dugas, Denise L., 836
Duggan, Stephen P., 452
Duke, Paul, 621
Dukes, Hazel N., 118
Dunham, Susan Guthrie, 442
Dunlap, Jim, 597
Dunn, James M., 78
Dunn, Jerry, 658
Dunn, Mary Lee, 7
Dunn, Robert H., 309, 310
Dunn, Shauna, 231
Dunn, William A., 38, 847, 855
Dunn Jr., H. Stewart, 73
Dunning, Zoe, 175
Dunstan, James M., 52
Durham, Daryl, 447
Durr, Melissa, 645
Duvall Jr., Howard E., 658
Dwyer, Edward J., 52
Dye, H. Michael, 63
Dyson, Esther, 570

Eaddy, Danielle V., 157
Eady, Veronica, 380, 477
Eagle, Michael L., 52
Earl, Anthony S., 471
Earle, Sylvia A., 361, 367, 452, 489
Early, James, 828
Easterling, Barbara J., 132
Eaton, James, 303
Eaton, Lee, 198, 742
Ebert, Thomas A., 52
Echohawk, John E., 350, 385, 452
Echohawk, Lucille A., 342
Edelin, Kenneth C., 112
Edelin, Ramona, 793
Edelman, Ben, 279
Edelman, Marian Wright, 24, 87, 89, 663
Edelman, Peter, 189
Edgerton, Lynne, 392
Edley Jr., Christopher F., 168
Edmo, Lorraine, 350
Edwards, Don, 560
Edwards, Donna, 575
Edwards, Julian, 269
Edwards, Mickey, 632
Edwards, William C., 814
Egan, William M., 319
Ehrlich, Anne, 477
Eichbaum, William M., 321
Eichhorn, Patricia, 202
Eisenach, Jeffrey A., 849, 850
Eisenberg, Meyer, 735
Eisenberg, Pablo, 350
Eisenberg, Susan, 135
Eisenman, William J., 52
Eisman, Paul, 52
Eisner, Jane B., 244
Eisner, Michael D., 370
Eisner, Thomas, 547
El-Sadr, Wafaa, 244
Ellerbee, Linda, 663
Elliman, Christopher J., 387, 483
Elliot, Averell H., 17
Elliott, Robert C., 339
Ellis, Rodney, 793

Elm, Adelaide, 668
Elman, Steven K., 183
Elroymson, Daniel R., 457
Elshtain, Jean Bethke, 826
Emerson, J. Terry, 721
Engberg, Kristen, 411
Engelhardt, Irl F., 52
Engelhardt, Sara L., 296, 337, 339, 342
Engibous, Thomas J., 314
Engle, Helen, 432
Engler, John, 653
English, Glenn, 265, 300
English, John W., 319
English III, Milton T., 439
Engman, Patricia Hanahan, 14
Engstrom, Ted, 742
Epstein, Joseph, 818
Epstein, Sarah G., 525
Erckenbrack, Nancy, 135
Erdman, Sol, 60
Ericson, James, 7
Erikson, Sheldon R., 52
Erlenbusch, Robert, 125
Ernst III, Robert J., 844
Erwin, Robert L., 824
Eshbaugh, W. Hardy, 432
Eshoo, Nina S., 682
Eskelson, Lily, 132
Esman, Marjorie, 73
Espinosa, Judith M., 447
Estes, Milton, 73
Estes, Ralph, 828
Estrada, Ana, 107
Ethridge, Damaris D. W., 370
Eubanks, Ted Lee, 432
Evans, Gorton M., 52
Evans, Greg, 704
Evans, Lisbeth 'Libba', 682
Evans, M. Stanton, 593
Evans, Marilyn, 212
Evans Jr., Daniel F., 818
Everett, Edith, 530
Everett, Edith B., 329
Everett, Ralph B., 789
Everhart, Thomas E., 45
Evers-Williams, Myrlie, 118, 663

Fagan, Joseph, 212
Fahey, Charles J., 135
Fahrenkopf Jr., Frank J., 721
Failor, Edward D., 60
Fair, Janey M., 202
Fair III, James D., 824
Faith, Bill, 125
Faithorn, Lisa, 380
Falcon, Angelo, 350
Falkner, Robert F., 110
Falvo, Cathey, 541
Fanara, Barbara, 192
Fanton, Jonathan, 530
Farber, David, 570
Farenthold, Frances T., 663, 828
Faris, Cheryl, 71
Faris, Jack, 55, 56
Farman, Richard D., 52
Farquhar, Elinor K., 442
Farr, Dagmar, 286
Farrell, Anne V., 296
Farrell, James T., 844
Farren, J. Michael, 632

Farris, Michael P., 806
Faulk, Sylvia M., 758
Faux, Jeff, 796, 798
Fay, James A., 547
Fay, John S., 824
Fay, Toni G., 112
Feder, Judith, 282
Federspiel, Benedicte, 270
Feinberg, Stephen L., 147
Feingold, Ellen, 73
Feingold, Eugene, 73
Feldman, Gene, 658
Feldman, Jay, 435, 436
Feldman, Mark L., 370
Feldman, Ronald, 168
Feldman, Sandra, 45
Feldt, Gloria, 170
Fellmeth, Robert C., 670
Fena, Lori, 570
Fenn, Scott A., 830, 831
Ferdman, Gary, 538
Ferdon, Derre, 621
Ferdon, Elinor J., 157
Ferenstein, Jennifer, 477
Ferguson, Anita Perez, 104, 661, 662
Ferguson II, James E., 74
Ferrari, Giannantio, 52
Ferrari, Loretta, 339
Ferrell, Robert, 125
Ferrer, Luigi, 231
Ferris, Deeohn, 321
Ferris, Donald, 422
Fesperman, John E., 347
Feulner, Edwin J., 811
Feulner Jr., Edwin J., 809
Fiedler, Jeffrey, 265
Field, David J., 483
Field, Marshall, 494
Fielding, Fred F., 336
Fields, Cora, 674
Fienberg, Linda D., 151
Figueres, Jose Maria, 489
Figueroa, Juan A., 350
Finan, Richard, 649
Finberg, Barbara D., 342
Finger, Mary, 300
Fingerhut, Bert, 483
Fink, Matthew P., 7
Finlay, Mary Fleming, 457
Finucane, Matthew, 104
Firman, James P., 134, 135
Firor, John, 489
Firor, John W., 387
Fischer, C. William, 339
Fisher, George M.C., 14, 45, 314
Fisher, John W., 52
Fisher, Kenneth L., 605
Fisher, Paul, 541
Fisher, Richard B., 860
Fisher, Robert J., 452
Fishman, Al, 538
Fisk, Hayward D., 689
Fiske, Joyce S., 74
Fites, Donald V., 14, 52
Fitz-Randolph, Julia, 96
Fitzgerald, Duane D., 319
FitzGerald, William H.G., 508
Fitzpatrick, J. Michael, 52
Fitzpatrick, James, 252
Fitzpatrick, John W., 432, 457

Flaherty, David, 573
Fleishman, Ernest, 292
Fleishman, Joel L., 860
Fleming, Thomas J., 856
Flemming, Harry S., 605
Flicker, John, 431
Flores, Fernando, 129
Flores, Hector, 107
Flowers, Ronald B., 78
Flynn, Michael D., 63
Fodness, Virgil, 265
Fogg, Joseph G., 28
Foley, Timothy, 135
Foord, Deborah C., 296
Forbes, Steve, 60, 640, 772
Ford, David S., 296, 333
Ford, Harrison, 370
Ford, J.G. 'Mike', 674
Ford, Pat, 205
Ford, William D., 52
Ford Jr., William Clay, 370
Fordice, Kirk, 721
Foreman, Carol Tucker, 286, 303, 789
Forkan, Patricia A., 416
Forrest, Carolyn, 300
Forstmann, Nicholas C., 640
Forstmann, Theodore J., 640, 786
Forsyth Jr., William H., 339
Fort, Theola, 125
Fossedal, Gregory, 767
Foster, Clyde, 364
Foster, Douglas, 689
Foster, Lisa, 621
Foster, Lynn A., 494
Foster, Stanley, 93
Foston, Barbara, 645
Fowler, Fred J., 52
Fox, Jane E., 189
Fox, Jean Ann, 274
Fox, Jonathan, 466
Foxman, Abraham H., 733, 735
Fralin, W. Heywood, 605
Francis, F.J., 241
Francis, Garrick C., 590
Francis, Lee, 541
Francis, Leslie C., 632
Frank, John, 686
Frank, Linda, 231
Frank, Stephen E., 605
Franke, William A., 17
Frankel, James, 452
Franklin, Barbara H., 508
Franklin, Jerry F., 483
Franklin, Robert M., 836
Frasca, Doreen, 682
Fraser, Doug, 793
Fraser, Douglas A., 151, 189, 282
Frazier, Mark, 60
Frazier, Owsley B., 605
Frazza, George S., 689
Freedman, Eugene, 818
Freedman, Eugene M., 625
Freedman, Richard S., 356
Freeland, Wendell G., 836
Freeman, Bruce G., 147
Freeman, David, 52
Freeman, Gerald M., 698
Freeman, Lisa D., 100
Freeman, Neal B., 803
Freeman, Orville L., 866

Freeman, William M., 836
Freeman Jr., Chas. W., 508
Freidenrich, John, 789
Fremzel, Bill, 35
French, Mark, 96
French, Paula, 135
French, Theodore R., 63
Frenzel, Bill, 668
Frenzel, Robert, 63
Frenzel, William E., 616
Freundlich, Paul, 279, 321
Friedan, Betty, 663
Friedelson, Bern, 74
Friedman, Bart, 776
Friedman, Donald, 227
Friedman, Frederica S., 682
Friedman, Judi, 416
Friedman, Stephen, 625, 776
Friedman, Tully M., 772
Frizzell, Kent, 721
Frumkin, Howard, 249, 541
Fuchsberg, Abraham, 716
Fudge, Ann M., 42, 314
Fuentes, Humberto, 129
Fuentes, Lisa, 828
Fueri, Bobbie, 172
Fugett, Anthony, 118
Fujimoto, Isao, 523
Fukukawa, Shinji, 489
Fukunaga, Carol A., 560
Fuld, Stanley H., 689
Fulginiti, William F., 658
Fuller, Craig L., 63
Fuller, H. Laurance, 14, 314
Fuller, James W., 844
Fuller, JoAnn, 538
Fuller, Kathryn S., 492, 494
Fung, Margaret, 80, 350
Funger, Morton, 789
Furman, Gloria, 74
Futrell, J. William, 390, 392

Gabel, Caroline, 374
Gabel, Dan, 405
Gaberman, Barry D., 339, 342
Gaddy, C. Welton, 745
Gade, Mary, 392
Gaines, Betsy, 477
Gale, Mary Ellen, 74
Gale, Robert L., 289
Galiardo, John W., 689
Galinsky, Ellen, 47
Gallagher, Lynne, 866
Gallagher, Terence, 326
Gallo, Marcia M., 74
Gallup Jr., George H., 147
Galvin, Christopher B., 772
Galvin, Michael P., 515
Galvin, Robert W., 7
Gamal, Arif, 466
Gambino, Raymond, 241
Gandy, Kim, 143
Gandy, Oscar, 573
Gannon, Robert P., 52
Gantt Jr., Ben J., 704
Garcia, Herlinda, 110
Gardiner, Harold H., 416
Gardner, Frank, 205
Gardner, Stephen, 274
Garey, Alice R., 416
Garland, Carolyn, 189

Garner, Joan P., 100
Garner Jr., John A., 658
Garrett, George, 857
Garrett, John C., 52
Garrity, Morman E., 52
Gartner, Allen S., 789
Garvey, Robert A., 52
Garvey, Willard W., 702
Garza, Alfonso Romo, 370
Gaskins Jr., Darius W., 471
Gates, Jacquelyn B., 319
Gates, Margaret, 350
Gates Jr., Henry Louis, 776
Gaudion, Donald A., 52
Gault, Stanley C., 52
Gauna, Jeanne, 321
Gee, Arvin, 541
Gee, Erayne N., 118
Geiger, Dan, 523
Geiger, H. Jack, 541
Gelb, Leslie H., 518
Gelfand, David J., 746
Geller, Henry, 578
Gellhorn, Ernest, 721
Gendt, Rien van, 333
Gerachty, Diane, 74
Gerard, James, 183
Gerber, Murray A., 52
Gershon, Fabianne, 682
Gerson, David, 772
Getty, Caroline M., 483
Ghee, James E., 118
Gibbs, Lois Marie, 363
Gibson, James O., 24
Gidari, Albert, 721
Gidwitz, Ronald J., 63
Gierer Jr., Vincent A., 702
Giffin, William E., 319
Gifford, Mike, 231
Giglio, Joseph M., 818
Gikas, Paul W., 670
Gilbert, Phyllis, 538
Gile, John, 231
Gilliland, James, 392
Gilmartin, Raymond V., 42, 45, 323, 336
Gilmore, John, 570
Gingrich, Newt, 640
Giuliano, Neil G., 658
Glaske, Paul E., 63
Glasser, Ira, 72, 81
Glasser, Jay H., 249
Glassman, James, 855
Glawe, Michael H., 370
Gleason, Mary Ann, 123
Glen, Robert M., 616
Glendon, Mary Ann, 803
Glenn, Kristin Booth, 578
Glenshaw, Elizabeth, 279
Glickman, Gretchen Long, 387, 439
Glover, Eugene, 132, 300
Glynn, Thomas P., 632
Goddard, Terry, 442
Goetz, Susan, 523
Goff, Fred, 522
Gold, Christina A., 42
Goldberg, Danny, 74
Goldberg, Jeffrey M., 716
Goldberg, Ralph, 74
Golden, Stephen, 361

Goldenberg, Judy, 168
Goldfarb, Ronald, 686
Goldman, Bob, 550
Goldman, Neal I., 855
Goldman, Tony, 442
Goldstein, Frances J., 100
Goldstein, Michael, 329
Goldwater, Marilyn, 649
Golinger, Jon, 265
Golodner, Linda F., 298, 300
Golub, Harvey, 772
Gomez, Kathy, 161
Gomez, Leo, 110
Gonzales, Irma Flores, 129, 189
Gonzalez, Regla, 107
Gonzalez, Thomas, 447
Gonzalez Jr., Joseph E., 52
Gonzalez-Koenig, Mary, 129
Goode, David R., 63
Gooderham, Kate, 662
Goodkind, E. Robert, 727
Goodman, Lenard, 550
Goodson, Addison, 538
Gordon, Edward H., 112
Gordon, Jack D., 793
Gordon, Margaret, 621
Gorham, William, 859, 860
Gorman, Joseph T., 14, 45, 515
Gotsch, Audrey R., 249
Gottfried, Kurt, 547
Gottlieb, Alan, 593
Gottlieb, Daniel M., 63
Gottschall, Bruce, 212
Gould, Jane G., 132
Gould, Michael, 727
Gould, Robert, 541
Goytisolo, Josie, 608
Grade, Jeffery T., 52
Gradison, Willis, 35
Grady, Robert E., 387, 471
Grady, Thomas J., 658
Graf III, Eugene, 847
Graglia, Lino A., 721
Graham, James B., 7
Graham, Jim, 231
Graham, Katharine, 45, 860
Graham, Kathryn G., 100
Graham, Lawrence Otis, 329
Graham, Nancy M., 678
Graham, William H., 689
Graham Jr., Otis, 525
Grandy, Fred, 342
Granoff, Perry, 151
Grant, Paul, 74
Grant, William W. 'Peter', 442
Grassi, Anthony P., 356, 457
Graves, Earl, 544
Graves, Ronald, 698
Graves, Thomas J., 721
Graves, William, 118
Gravitz, Alisa, 278, 279, 321, 405
Gray, Alvin, 730
Gray, Borden, 855
Gray, C. Boyden, 28
Gray, Deecy, 28
Gray, Hanna Holborn, 625
Gray, Kevin A., 74
Gray III, William H., 7, 35, 625
Grayson, Patricia A.M., 112
Green, Frances M., 712
Green, Judson, 370

Green, Winifred, 89
Green Jr., Richard C., 860
Greenberg, David I., 286
Greenberg, Jack, 81, 112, 530
Greenberg, Maurice R., 515
Greenberger, I. Michael, 356
Greenberger, Marcia, 104
Greene, Donald R., 342
Greene, Wade, 429
Greenhill, Robert F., 772
Greenstein, Robert, 22
Greenstreet, Joe, 56
Gregg, Kathy, 477
Gregorian, Vartan, 530
Gresh, Philip M., 361
Gresham Jr., Samuel, 157
Gressel, Daniel L., 844
Greve, Michael, 38
Griffith, Elisabeth, 663
Grisi, Jeanmarie C., 831
Grogan, Hugh, 125
Gross, Martin, 550
Gross, Patrick W., 632
Grossman, Barbara W., 168
Grossman, Jerome H., 347
Grossman, Karl, 575
Grosvenor, Gilbert M., 367
Grow, Mary Lewis, 93
Grow, Robert J., 52
Gruenebaum, Jane, 643
Grusin, Dave, 356
Grzywinski, Ronald, 189
Guenther, Harry, 104, 132
Guerra, Fernando A., 860
Guerra, Louis, 593
Guest, James A., 274
Guggenheimer, Elinor, 663
Guidry, Evangeline, 118
Guisinger, Allen W., 447
Gullander, Werner P., 52
Gund, Graham D., 442
Gunderson, Steve, 96
Gunther, George L. 'Doc', 597
Gunther, Herb Chao, 350
Gupta, Ashok, 321
Gurin, Richard S., 347
Gurule, Al, 110
Gutierrez, David J., 457
Gutierrez, Paul, 110
Gutman, Jeremiah, 74
Guttmacher, Alan E., 172
Guzman, Ana Margarita 'Cha', 110

Haas, Ellen, 303
Haas, Glenn E., 439
Habicht II, F. Henry, 392, 471
Habush, Robert, 716
Hadley, Leonard A., 52
Hagan, J. Michael, 52
Hahn-Baker, David, 452
Hailey, Richard, 716
Hake, Ralph F., 52
Halamandaris, Val, 132
Hale, Bradley, 442
Hall, Elliott S., 836
Hall, Jerry Joseph, 140
Hall, John R., 42
Hall, Ralph M., 806
Hall Jr., James, 74
Hall Jr., Ridgway, 392
Haller, Eva, 510

Hallerdin, Jule, 553
Halperin, Morton H., 560
Halverson, Harold, 649
Halverson, Steven T., 17
Hambly, Larry, 52
Hambrecht, William R., 45
Hamburg, Beatrix Ann, 244
Hamby, Robert E., 742
Hamill, John P., 319
Hamilton, Ann O., 172
Hamilton, Charles H., 333
Hamilton, Everett, 96
Hamilton, Nancy, 96
Hamilton, Wendy J., 212
Hamilton Jr., Charles J., 387
Hamler, Denise, 279
Hammerman, Stephen L., 147
Hampton, Delon, 789
Hampton, Henry E., 89
Hanauer, James D., 52
Hanauer, Mike, 553
Hand, Edward F., 471
Handlan, Raymond L., 342
Hanenkrat, Judy, 85
Hanes, KiKu Hoagland, 367
Hanes Jr., John W., 457
Haney, James S., 52
Haney III, William M., 489
Hannah, Thomas E., 52
Hannay, Roger A., 52
Hans, Stina, 855
Hansen, Darryl D., 202
Hansen, Paul W., 421, 429
Hanson, Chad, 477
Hanson, Jeanne, 682
Haq, Mahbub ul, 866
Hara, Jimmy, 541
Hardymon, James F., 52
Hargarten, Stephen W., 227
Harkin, Ruth R., 52, 789
Harley, John T., 52
Harlow, Bryce 'Larry', 850
Harman, Sidney, 347
Harmelin, Stephen J., 689
Harmon, Clarence, 93
Harmon, Gail, 429
Harper, Edwin L., 632
Harris, Andrew, 541
Harris, David A., 725, 727
Harris, Elmer B., 605
Harris, John A., 429
Harris, Louis, 112
Harris, Mary C., 447
Harrison, Gail, 632
Harsanyi, Fruzsina, 632
Hart, Paul, 593
Hart, Stephanie, 96
Hart Jr., William B., 442
Harte, Janet, 525
Hartman, David, 857
Hartmann, Frank, 93
Hartung, Philip M., 52
Hartwell, Samuel A., 616
Harvey, Hal, 828
Harvey, Thomas, 350
Harvey, William F., 721
Hasenmiller, Steve, 227
Haskell, Paul, 125
Hassan, Amina, 523
Hatch, Francis, 452
Hatch, Whitney, 356

Hatcher, Richard Gordon, 544
Hathaway, Derek C., 52, 605
Hathaway, Michael, 380
Hathaway, Spencer, 793
Hathout, Maher H., 746
Hatley, Donald E., 605
Hauptman, Thomas M., 698
Hauser, Richard A., 721
Hauser, W. Kurt, 814
Haveman, Robert H., 471
Havian, Eric R., 621
Haworth, Howard H., 89
Hayden, Mike, 429
Hayden, Molly Tan, 541
Hayes, Denis, 321, 416, 429
Hayes, Randall L., 467
Hayes, Roger, 212
Hayes Jr., Charles A., 52
Haynes, Ray, 597
Hayward, Thomas B., 336
Hazelwood, Mark, 52
Hazen, Paul, 265
Head, James D., 510
Healey, Richard, 665
Healy, Robert L., 605
Hebe, James L., 63
Hechinger Sr., John, 93
Hechler, Ira, 730
Hecht, William F., 52, 605
Heckard-Heiling, Rosemary, 689
Hedlund, Charles J., 370
Heffer, John, 730
Heidepriem, Nikki, 151
Height, Dorothy I., 89, 104, 544, 663
Heilbroner, Robert, 329
Heindenreich, Pat, 432
Heineman Jr., Benjamin W., 789
Heinz, Teresa, 387, 776
Heiskell, Andrew, 168
Heiskell, Marian S., 432
Heitz, Mark V., 605
Helewicz, Joseph S., 157
Helfand, Ira, 541
Heller, Tom, 265
Hellman, Samuel, 776
Helman, Robert A., 776
Helms, Jesse, 593
Helphand, Lewis A., 296
Hempel, Marilyn, 553
Hemphill, Eileen, 274
Henderson, Hazel, 866
Henderson, James B., 52
Henderson, Wade, 103, 189, 544
Hendricks, John S., 457
Hengerson, Roy, 477
Henkel, Herbert L., 53
Henkin, Alice H., 530
Hennessey, Michael J., 605
Henry, Ted M., 53
Henry, Wolcott, 361, 494
Hensler, David J., 255
Herdery, Edward H., 53
Herman, Susan N., 74
Hernandez, Antonia, 104, 109, 151, 686
Hernandez, Sandra, 244
Hernandez, Victor, 658
Herndon, Dealey Decherd, 442
Hero, Peter, 333
Herr, James S., 56

Herr, Judith 'Judy' N., 168
Herrera Jr., Frank, 110
Herrerra Jr., Pastor, 300
Herrick, John, 303
Herrick, Norton, 168
Hershaft, Alex, 398, 399, 419
Hershey, Edwin M., 183
Hertog, Roger, 550
Hertzberg, Arthur, 746
Hervey, Madeledine, 553
Herz, Michael, 405
Herzfeld, Will L., 758
Hesketh, Darla, 209
Heslin, Mary, 300
Heuter, Joan, 558
Hewes III, William 'Billy', 597
Hewlett, Sylvia Ann, 826
Heyderman, Art J., 74
Heyman, I. Michael, 392
Heyman, Philip, 621
Hiatt, Arnold, 310
Higgins, Heather R., 814
Higgins, Jill Tate, 452
Hightower, Jim, 670
Hill, Bonnie Guiton, 157, 836
Hill, Ellen, 824
Hill, Frederick W., 803, 818
Hill, Jerald L., 241
Hill, Kenneth, 739
Hill, Robert, 205
Hill, Tessa, 436
Hill Jr., Norbert S., 387
Hilleary, William C., 53
Hilliard, Patsy Jo, 658
Hills, Carla A., 515
Hilton Jr., L. Charles, 60
Hinerfeld, Ruth J., 616
Hingson, Ralph, 202
Hinkle, William, 74
Hinman, Alan R., 249
Hixon, Adelaide, 168
Ho Lynn, Vicky, 419
Hobbins, Thomas E., 541
Hobbs, F. Worth, 339, 342
Hochberg, Fred, 96
Hockert, Richard E., 53
Hodel, Donald, 739
Hodgson, Joni, 53
Hodowal, John R., 53
Hoff, Paul S., 612
Hoffman, Ann, 405
Hoffman, Elliot, 310
Hoffman, Mark B., 844
Hoffman, Philip, 597
Hoffman, W. Michael, 317
Hogan, Bill, 608
Hogue, Bobby L., 597
Holayter, Bill, 132
Holbrook, Douglas C., 237
Holden, Glen A., 702
Holland, Maurice J., 721
Holland Jr., Robert, 319
Holman, Scott L., 63
Holmes, Chuck, 96
Holmes, Cynthia S., 78
Holt, Arlene, 300
Holthus, C.G. 'Kelly', 63
Holtz, Gerald, 716
Holtzman, Elizabeth, 663
Homes, Susan, 477
Hood, Glenda E., 658

Hooks, Kevin E., 157
Hoosman Jr., Hubert, 265
Hoover, Andrew, 814
Hoover III, Herbert, 814
Hopkins, Jack, 333
Hopper, Kim, 125
Hopple, Richard V., 356
Hormel, James C., 244
Hormel, Rampa R., 429
Horn, Alan, 452
Horn, Wally, 649
Hornbeck, David W., 89
Horne, Eleanor V., 157
Horne, John R., 53
Horner, Matina S., 323
Horowitz, David H., 510
Horton, Dallas P., 698
Hoser, Albert, 347
Hostetter, E. Ralph, 806
Hotchkiss, Ralf, 227
Hoting, Hilarie, 286
Hough, Gordon L., 616
Howard, Susan L., 442
Howell, William R., 147
Howell III, Charles A., 439
Howlett, C.A., 63
Howley, Peter A., 824
Hoynes, William, 575
Hoyte, James S., 439, 547
Hrabowski, Freeman A., 836
Hrdlicka, Richard F., 53
Hroneo, Steven M., 53
Hsieh, Marina, 74
Hubbard, Allan B., 63, 818
Hubbard, Kenneth D., 17
Hudson, J. Clifford, 63
Hudson, S. Michael, 53
Hudson, William J., 52
Huebler, John, 140
Hueter, Ernest B., 689, 700, 702
Huff Sr., J. Kenneth, 237
Huffman, Rufus, 712
Huggins, George, 172
Hughes, Barbara, 231
Hughes, Charles, 286
Hughes, Colleen C., 249
Hughes, Reid, 432
Hull, Hadlai A., 367
Hull, M. Blair, 674
Hume, George H., 814
Hume, William J., 811
Humphreys, Ethelmae C., 786
Humphries, John, 231
Hunt, Linda K., 74
Hunt, Ray L., 53
Hunt, Vilma, 364
Hunt-Badiner, Allan, 468
Hunt-Badiner, Marion, 405
Hunter, Duncan, 593
Hunter, James Paul, 857
Hunter, Robert C., 63
Hurlbut, Wendell P., 53
Hurley, Charles A., 203
Hurley, Deborah, 573
Husbands Jr., Samuel H., 844
Hussain, Pat, 140
Hussey Jr., Phillip W., 53
Hutchison, Richard P., 695
Hutter, Collie, 53
Hwang, Grace Y., 81
Hwang, Henry Y., 789

Hyacinthe, Hector M., 836
Hyman, Lester S., 789
Hyndman, Cynthia H., 100
Hynes, James E.S., 63

Ignat, Joseph N., 847
Ikard, Jayne Brumley, 836
Impastato, Sally Reed, 674
Ingram, Mark A., 93, 255
Ingram, Robert, 347
Innis, Roy, 818
Irani, Mazin, 71
Iraola, Manuel J., 53
Ireland, Kate, 457
Ireland, Patricia, 104, 142, 143
Irvine, Reed J., 557
Irving, L.J., 140
Irwin, Paul G., 414, 416
Isaacs, Amy, 598, 599
Isaacs, Rebecca, 104
Isbell, Mike, 231
Ishmael Jr., R. Edward, 100
Ivester, M. Douglas, 772
Ivey, Beni, 84
Ivory, Elenora Giddings, 78, 758

Jackson, Alphonso, 826
Jackson, J.L., 53
Jackson, Jerry D., 53, 347
Jackson, Leonard B., 746
Jackson, Sonya, 118
Jackson Fahnbullch, Bridgett, 209
Jacob, John E., 798
Jacob, Paul, 673, 674
Jacobs, Bruce, 824
Jacobs, Kristine, 665
Jacobs, Martin Adam, 224
Jacobsen, Judy, 553
Jacobson, Michael F., 254, 255
Jacoby, Irene A., 702
Jaeger, Arthur, 302
Jager, Durk I., 457
Jagger, Bianca, 168
Jagim, Mary, 227
Jahshan, Khalil E., 121
James, Donna, 125
James, Frances C., 457
James, Frederick Calhoun, 746
James, Glenn Cooper, 457
James, Kay Coles, 742
James, Philip J., 457
James, Sharpe, 658, 678
Jarvis, Sonia, 612, 668
Jasinowski, Isabel N., 605
Jasinowski, Jerry J., 45, 50, 52
Jefferson-Jenkins, Carolyn, 645
Jeffrey, Mildred, 663
Jencks, Christopher, 828
Jenkins, Bill, 249
Jenkins, Robert H., 53
Jensen, Elizabeth ., 274
Jensen, Richard, 172
Jensen, Robert, 63
Jewett, John C., 100
Jimenez, Monica M., 716
Joans, Henry, 326
Johanns, Mike, 678
John, Karlene, 209
Johns, Deborah, 682
Johns, Elizabeth B., 356
Johnsen, Millicent M., 494

Johnson, Chad S., 175
Johnson, Charles S., 53
Johnson, Check, 538
Johnson, Geneva B., 289
Johnson, Genevieve, 132
Johnson, Gloria, 663
Johnson, James A., 776
Johnson, James C., 538
Johnson, Jane, 553
Johnson, Karen, 143
Johnson, Owen H., 597
Johnson, Ron, 231
Johnson, Samuel C., 457
Johnson, Uric, 538
Johnson, Vivian, 432
Johnson, Wendy, 189
Johnston, Gerald E., 53
Johnston, Kelly, 628
Johnston, Lowell Douglass, 151
Johnstone Jr., Rudolph G., 53
Jones, Anna Faith, 333
Jones, Donna M., 597
Jones, Elaine, 104, 111, 112
Jones, Elise, 553
Jones, Frank, 53
Jones, Glenn R., 347
Jones, Hoyle C., 183
Jones, Ingrid Saunders, 333
Jones, James R., 7
Jones, Kathy H., 53
Jones, Luther, 831
Jones, Mary Gardner, 329
Jones, Quincy, 112, 544
Jones, Regina J., 172
Jones, Roberts T., 346, 347
Jontz, Jim, 599
Jordan, Ann Dibble, 314, 776
Jordan, Charles R., 367
Jordan, Jerry D., 698
Jordan, Ruth, 300
Jordan, Vernon E., 112
Jordan III, Robert E., 508
Jordan Jr., Vernon E., 836
Jorling, Thomas C., 471
Josten, R. Bruce, 605
Judd Jr., Ardon B., 605
Juma, Calestous, 489

Ka'Ahumanu, Lani, 140
Kaden, Lewis B., 387
Kahn, Harry, 168
Kahn, Jane, 818
Kakabadse, Yolanda, 489
Kalff, P. Jan, 42
Kallio, Lauri, 538
Kamen, Harry P., 42
Kaminski, Joseph J., 53
Kampelman, Max M., 803
Kampouris, Emmanuel A., 63
Kane, John F., 698
Kang, Young Woo, 147
Kansil, Joli, 224
Kanter, Rosabeth Moss, 798
Kaplan, Martin S., 727
Kaplan, Stuart, 74
Kaplan, Woody, 74
Karas, Barry, 96
Kareiva, Peter M., 457
Karel, Frank, 333
Karp, Roberta, 310
Karpatkin, Rhoda H., 270, 272

Karpinski, Gene, 216, 429
Kashani, Hamid R., 74
Kaskalla, Lela, 127
Kasofsky, Jill, 100
Kasputys, Joseph K., 632
Kass, Stephen L., 530
Katina, Thomas R., 592, 593
Katz, Elliot M., 418, 419
Kaufman, Marina Pinto, 530
Kaufman, Martin S., 689
Kaufman, Rosalind Fuchsberg, 716
Kautz, Richard C., 53
Kautz, Terry S., 53
Kawai, Saburo, 370
Kay, Alan, 510
Kay Combs, Carole, 380
Kean, Hamilton F., 452
Kean, Thomas H., 494
Keane, Bill, 621
Keating, David L., 60
Keating, Frank, 653
Keating-Edh, Barbara, 261
Keaton, Michael Douglas, 356
Keefe, Diane, 279
Keegan, Michael, 168
Keeler, Carl, 422
Keenan, Nancy, 168
Keene, David A., 593
Keilbach, Peter-Hans, 53
Keiser, Michael, 674
Keller, Michael, 538
Kelley, A. Benjamin, 252
Kelley, Bernard J., 53
Kelley, Mary, 56
Kelley, P.X., 702
Kelly, Alan M., 183
Kelly, Edmund F., 63
Kelly, J. Peter, 53
Kelly, James A., 515
Kelly Jr., J. Fredrick, 53
Kelso, Dennis Takahashi, 439
Kemp, Jack, 640, 860
Kemp, John D., 342
Kemp, Maggie, 93
Kempner Jr., Jarris L., 727
Kendall, David E., 112
Kendall, Henry W., 547
Kendall, Lily Rice, 442
Kenna, E. Douglas, 53
Kennard, Donald Ray, 597
Kennedy, David, 691
Kennedy, Quentin J., 689
Kennedy, Victoria Reggie, 93
Kenny, Luella, 364
Kenoyer, Pat, 538
Kent, William H., 370
Kerlinsky, Daniel, 541
Kerr, Donald M., 471
Kerr, G. Robert, 439
Kerr Jr., Robert S., 35
Kersten, William, 231
Kessler, Larry, 231
Kest, Steven, 185
Keyes, James H., 53
Keyserling, Harry L., 541
Keyston, David H., 844
Keyworth II, George A. 'Jay', 850
Khane, Abd-El Rahman, 866
Kidder, C. Robert, 157
Kidwell, Birtrun, 422

Kiely III, W. Leo, 53
Kiernan, Charles E., 157
Kiernan, Thomas C., 438
Kilian, Michael, 408
Kim, Charles S., 789
Kimball, Richard, 667, 668
Kindberg, Eric, 436
Kindler, Roger A., 416
King, Coretta Scott, 663
King, Gwendolyn S., 632
King, Jane, 300
King, Jim, 157
King, Patricia, 151
King, Reatha Clark, 333
King, Sandra, 135
King, Sharon B., 333
King III, Martin Luther, 85
King-Pringle, Marti, 172
Kingfisher, Pame, 364
Kinsey, Christopher M., 605
Kipps Jr., Clarence T., 721
Kirk, Roger, 508
Kirkley-Bey, Marie, 189
Kirkpatrick, Jeane J., 640, 803
Kissinger, Henry A., 515
Klaassen, Paul J., 63, 818
Klatsky, Bruce, 310, 530
Klausner, Manuel S., 855
Kleckner, Dean R., 702
Klein, Arnold, 244
Klein, Michael, 468
Klepner, Jerry, 286
Klinefelter, William J., 265
Klingensmith, Michael J., 244
Klingman, Vern L., 74
Kluge, Patricia, 168
Knight, Bob, 658
Knight, Dean, 422
Knight, Peter S., 789
Knox, John A., 379
Knudsen, Tom, 28
Koch, David H., 786, 855
Koch, William I., 824
Koeberer, John W., 63
Koffel, Martin M., 772
Koh, Harold Hongju, 530
Kohler, Mary, 857
Kohler, Terry J., 806
Kohne, Anne Lore, 270
Kohr, Howard, 501
Kolb, Charles E.M., 322
Komatsu, Karl A., 442
Koob, Charles E., 452
Koppelman, Murray, 735
Korn, Joel, 370
Korpan, Richard, 53
Korsant, Philip, 452
Koski, Robert E., 53
Kostmayer, Peter Houston, 552
Kotchian, Sarah B., 249
Kourpias, George J., 132, 265
Kovler, Peter B., 590, 789
Kovner, Bruce, 772
Krafsur, Howard G. 'Blackie', 168
Kraiem, Ruben, 452
Kramer, Albert H., 578
Kramer, John R., 24
Kramer, Saul, 329
Kranz, Harry, 300
Kravis, Marie-Josée, 314, 818
Krehbiel, Frederick A., 494

Kreisler, Kristin von, 419
Kretchman, Dale, 422
Krim, Mathilde, 244
Kristensen, Doug, 649
Krol, John A., 53, 314
Krowe, Allen J., 7
Krug, Judy, 573
Krughoff, Robert, 265
Krumsiek, Barbara, 682
Krupp, Fred, 342, 386, 429
Krupp, Judith, 735
Kuhlmann, Walter, 374
Kuhn, Thomas R., 63
Kurzman, Stephen, 727
Kutin, Breda, 270
Kutscher, Eugene, 553
Kuttner, Robert, 798
Kuykendall III, Frederick T., 716
Kvamme, E. Floyd, 640
Kyrillos Jr., Joseph, 649

Labrecque, Thomas G., 45, 776
Lackey, Cheryl C., 249
Lackritz, Marc E., 7
Lacovara, Philip A., 721
Lacy, Andre B., 818
Lacy, James V., 593
Ladner, Joyce A., 789
Lafer, Fred, 550
LaHaye, Lee, 192
Lake, Peyton M., 814
Lake, William T., 494
Lamb, Steven G., 53
Lambert, Linda Lloyd, 183
Lamberti, Mrs. Chris, 237
Lambright, Stephen K., 53
Lambrinos, Jorge, 300
Lamm, Byron, 847
Lamm, Richard D., 525
Lampl, Peggy, 668
Landau, Jeremy G., 231
Landau, Saul, 828
Landrigan, Philip, 541
Landrith III, George C., 702
Landuyt, William M., 53
Lane, Melvin B., 442, 494
Lane, Nancy L., 118
Lane, Nicholar D.J., 727
Laney, Scot H., 53
Langford, Judy, 151
Langiotti, Patricia L., 63
Langone, Ken, 674
Langworth, Audrey, 649
Lansing, Sherry, 244
Lapham, Burks, 452
LaPierre, Wayne, 593
LaPierre Jr., Wayne R., 152
Lapin, Jack, 727
Larcher, Constance C., 781
La Rocque, Gene R., 509, 510
Larkin, Jocelyn, 621
Larry, R. Heath, 53
Larsen, Jonathan Z., 452
Lascell, David M., 289
Lash, Jonathan, 486, 489
Lashutka, Gregory, 658
Laskowski, Joan, 74
Latham, Weldon H., 836
Lauder, Ronald S., 674
Laule, William, 53
Lawless, Robert, 53

Lawrence, Bob, 665
Lawrence, David M., 42
Lawrence, Jere M., 605
Lawrence, Joan, 231
Lawrence, William B., 53
Lawson, Richard D., 508
Lawson, Rodger S., 227
Lay, Kenneth L., 7, 772
Layton, Thomas, 350
Lazarus, Eleanor, 727
Lazarus, John, 553
Lazarus, Shelly, 494
Lazzarini, Marilena, 270
Leach, Howard H., 702, 844
Leach, Jim, 668
Leach II, Edwin, 553
Leahy, Sheila A., 296
Leaning, Jennifer, 416
Lear, Norman, 168
Leavitt, Michael O., 17, 653
Lebenthal, Alexandra, 682
LeBoeuf, Denise, 74
Lederer, Peter D., 81
Lederman, Susan S., 621
Lee, Amy Freeman, 416
Lee, Chanwoo, 81
Lee, Dwight E., 847
Leech, Irene, 265
Leeds, Jeffrey T., 489
Leenson, Eric, 523
Leever, Daniel H., 347
Leger de Fernandez, Teresa, 110
Leggett Jr., Robert N., 439
Leher, Linda, 129
Lemmon, D.L., 53
Lentz, James, 205
Leonatti, Jean, 135
Leonhardy, Jay, 538
Lerner, Judy, 538
Lesavoy, Nina, 831
LeSuer, Ken R., 53
Letendre, Gerry, 53
LeVan, A. Carl, 71
Levant, Dan, 538
Levin, Mark R., 694, 695
Levin, Micki, 74
Levin, Thomas A., 17
Levin Jr., Joseph J., 712
Levine, Mel, 632
Levine, Murray, 364
Levinson, Richard A., 227
Levitas, Elliott, 392
Levitt, Marylin B., 89
Levy, Barry S., 249
Levy, Jay A., 244
Levy, Marion Fennelly, 682
Levy, Mont, 727
Levy, Robert, 691
Lewis, Charles, 607, 608
Lewis, Edwin L., 688, 689
Lewis, John, 189
Lewis, Kenneth D., 157
Lewis, M. Calien, 74
Lewis, Marilyn Ware, 772
Lewis, Maryon Davies, 439
Lewis-Rayo, Lynn, 125
Lezar, H.J. 'Tex', 721
Lichter, S. Robert, 562
Lichtman, Judith L., 104, 150, 151
Lichty, Pamela G., 74

Liebeler, Susan W., 721
Liebenow, Larry A., 63
Lierman, Terry, 590
Liggio, Leonard, 38
Likens, Gene E., 387
Likins, Peter, 45
Linares, Guillermo, 129
Lindau, David S., 112
Lindblom, Lance E., 282
Lindsay, Imogene 'Gene', 74
Linehan, Kathleen M., 789
Linen, Jonathan S., 157
Lintott, James, 691
Lione, John G., 237
Lipman, Ira A., 319
Lipp, Hani F., 132
Lipper, Kenneth, 632
Lipscomb, Barbara A., 457
Lipsky, Daniel, 296
Lipton, Patricia, 326
Litchtenberger, H. William, 53
Litman, Roslyn, 74
Little, William G., 63, 605
Litwak, Eleanor, 132
Liu, Clarice, 100
Liu, Donald H., 81
Lizardi, Juan Carlos, 107
Lloyd, Kate Rand, 663
Lloyd, Mark, 665
Lochner Jr., Philip R., 831
Locke, Hubert G., 621
Lockett, Gloria, 538
Lockwood, Patricia, 658
Loewenberg, Susan, 608
Lofton, Ernest, 118, 544
Logan Jr., Willie, 649
London, Herbert I., 817, 818
Lonergan, Pierce J., 605
Long, Bill, 674
Long, Charles E., 53
Long, Michael R., 593
López, Natalia, 523
Lopez, Norma, 350
Lopez, Oscar M., 370
Lorenz, Eugene W., 416
LosSchiavo, Joseph J., 203
Lott, Trent, 640
Lovejoy, Thoma, 471
Loveless, Charles, 665
Lovell Jr., Malcolm R., 347
Lovett, Richard, 157
LoVoi, Annette, 621
Lowe, Colby, 538
Lowe, Stanley A., 442
Lowery, Joseph, 104
Loy, Frank E., 387, 471
Lozano, Monica C., 129
Lozier, John, 125
Lubbers, R. Mark, 850
Lubchenco, Jane, 387, 489
Lucas, C. Payne, 489
Lucas, Donald L., 7
Lucas, Herbert L., 289
Luchini, Lawrence, 471
Lucy, William, 118, 326, 544, 793
Luehring, JoAnn, 826
Lufkin, Dan W., 356
Lum, JoAnn, 81
Luna, Gregory, 110
Lupberger, Edwin A., 63

Luper, Chelle, 118
Lurie, Elizabeth, 806
Luro, Ana Maria, 270
Lydman, Jack W., 416
Lynch, Jack, 658
Lynch, Leon, 104
Lynch Jr., William, 89
Lynette, Eileen, 135
Lynn, Barry W., 77
Lynn, James T., 35
Lyons, Barrie, 192
Lyons, Clinton, 286
Lyons, Henry J., 118
Lyons, Ronald R., 63

Maatman, Gerald, 227
Macaulay, Don, 538
MacDonald, J. Randall, 347
MacGuineas, Maya, 621
MacHarg, Marcia, 682
Mack, Charles S., 604, 605
Mackey, Maureen, 339
MacLeod, William C., 261
Macomber, Caroline, 361
Macomber, John D., 508, 632
Madden, Murdaugh Stuart, 416
Maddy, Jim, 471
Madero, Antonia, 42
Madison, Joseph E., 118
Madonna, Jon C., 42
Madsen, James, 422
Magowan, Thomas, 844
Maguire, John D., 112
Mahoney, Joan, 74
Mahoney, Richard, 20
Mahr, Nancy, 645
Maickel, Roger P., 241
Mailman, Josh, 310, 530
Maisano, Franklin, 183
Maitland Jr., John, 649
Makinson, Larry, 611
Maksoud, Clovis, 71
Maksoud, Hala, 69
Malagreca, Marie, 132
Malcolm, David M., 356
Malcolm, Ellen, 151
Maldonado, Alfonso, 107
Maldonado, Eve, 682
Malek, Frederic V., 7
Maler, Karl-Goran, 471
Malichi, Toby, 63
Malkin, Shelly, 452
Malone, John C., 786
Maltese, Serphin, 593
Malveaux, Julianne, 793, 798
Manatt, Charles T., 702
Mancuso, William F., 416
Mandell, Howard, 712
Mandinach, Gary, 74
Mandl, Alex J., 772
Mannsfeld, Sven-Peter, 53
Mannweiler, Paul, 649
Mansour, Chris, 71
Marano, Cindy, 350
Marcil, William C., 63
Marcum, Candy, 96
Marcus, Daniel, 286
Marden, Bernard A., 370
Marden, Roy E., 844
Margo, Donald R., 605
Mariner, Wendy K., 249

Mark, Reuben, 314
Markley, Rita, 125
Marks, James S., 249
Marks, Melinda, 399
Marks, Stanley, 716
Markus, William, 599
Markusen, Ann, 798
Marley, James E., 605
Marlin, Alice Tepper, 328, 329
Marram, Ellen R., 42
Mars, Adrienne B., 494
Marshall, Ray, 798
Marshall, Raymond C., 110
Marshall, Sir Colin, 42
Marshall III, John E., 342
Marti, Glorin, 125
Martin, Annie B., 118
Martin, Betty Lou, 192
Martin, Conrad, 350
Martin, Eff W., 814
Martin, Fred J., 616
Martin, Lynn Steppacher, 682
Martin, Susan, 361
Martin, William F., 489
Martin-Brown, Joan C., 416
Martine, Tom, 447
Martinez, Arabella, 129
Martinez, Arthur C., 157, 374
Martinez, Herminio, 129
Marton-Lefevre, Julia, 489
Marvin, John, 132
Marvin, Shirley, 662, 663
Marx, Gary, 573
Marzulla, Roger J., 721
Maskin, Arvin, 721
Mason, Carol A., 157
Mason, Russell, 127
Mason, Samuel, 422
Masri, Rania, 71, 538
Masse, Terry, 161
Massie, Robert Kinloch, 320, 321
Mathews, Jessica Tuchman, 776
Mathews, Odonna, 300
Mathhews, Frank L., 471
Mattawa, Khaled, 71
Matthews, Patricia, 405
Mattingly, Kimberly, 198
Mattson, Kellie, 203
Matz, Marshall L., 286
Maury, Samuel L., 13, 14, 605
Mauss, Irvin, 541
Maxwell, David O., 776
Maxwell, Kay, 645
May, Thomas A., 704
May, William B., 616
Maya, Esperanza, 364
Mayer, Kenneth H., 244
Mayer, Rob, 300
Mays, William G., 157
Mazur, Jay, 132, 798
Mazzocchi, Anthony, 670
McAuley, Brian, 347
McAuliffe, Mary E., 605
McAuliffe, Terence R., 789
McBride, Ann, 618, 621
McBride, Kate, 356
McBride, R.G., 53
McC Mathias, Charles, 612
McCabe, Jewell Jackson, 347
McCabe, Lawrence J., 689
McCallister, Margaret M., 616

McCallister-Brock, Roslyn, 118
McCally, Michael, 541
McCarthy, Robert E., 704
McCarty, Mike, 53
McCaw, Craig O., 772
McCaw Jr., John E., 370
McClanahan, Randy, 716
McClelland, Norman, 857
McClelland, Norman P., 605
McClelland, W. Craig, 42
McClintock, Kenneth, 636
McClintock, Richard, 265
McCloskey, J. Michail, 665
McCloskey, Mike, 321
McClure, David L., 698
McClure, James, 698
McConnell, Michael W., 721
McConnell, Rob, 466
McConnell, Robert, 78
McConnell Jr., John Noble, 605
McCormack, Billy, 739
McCowan, Rodney, 632
McCoy, Bowen H., 814
McCrory, Martin Arthur, 405
McCullough, David, 442
McCurry, Dan, 265
McDaniel, Steve, 597
McDaniel, Tom J., 53
McDonald, Timothy, 168
McDougall, Harold, 621
McEldowney, Kenneth, 265
McElroy, James, 712
McEntee, Gerald W., 104, 798
McGeady, Eamonn, 56
McGee, Robert M., 605
McGeever, Elizabeth M., 74
McGeveran, Elizabeth Elliott, 279
McGill, Eugene, 649
McGinn, Richard A., 45
McGinnis, Patricia, 631, 632
McGovern, Cyndy, 74
McGrady, Chuck, 477
McGrath, Judy, 168
McGraw III, Harold, 147
McGray, Sandra, 118
McGregor, Daniel P., 53
McGuire, Andrew, 227
McIntosh, Michael, 452
McIntosh, Winsome Dunn, 374, 429
McIntyre, Robert S., 31
McIntyre Jr., James I., 35
McKay, Mike, 231
McKechnie, Sheila, 270
McKernan, Joseph J., 716
McKernan Jr., John R., 347
McKinnell, Beverly, 645
McKinnell, Henry A., 53, 323
McKinney, Robert H., 818
McKnight, John, 212
McLane, Susan, 793
McLaughlin, Ann D., 314, 367
McLean, Mora, 494
McLennon, Rita, 686
McManus, Patricia J., 678
McManus, Roger E., 359
McMichael, R. Daniel, 806
McMillan, Enolia P., 118
McMillan, J. Alex, 625
McNamara, Robert S., 860
McNamee, Carol H., 203

McNamee, Giles, 570
McNeil, Ronald D., 205
McNeil Jr., Paul, 538
McNeill, Michele V., 244
McPherson, Stephen Mather, 439
McPherson Jr., Harry C., 632
McTier, Charles H., 339
McVay, Scott, 494
Mdallroy, John, 53
Mead, Dana G., 14, 53, 632
Meadows, William H., 429, 481, 483
Measelle, Richard, 347
Medley, Mark A., 53
Mee Jr., Charles L., 860
Meese III, Edwin, 781
Mehler, I. Barry, 735
Meiling, Meredith, 457
Meiners, Donald E., 605
Meiners, Roger, 261
Meissner, Doris, 663, 682
Meléndez, Sara E., 340
Melamed Jr., Bill, 244
Melhelm, Hisham, 71
Melican, James P., 53
Melich, Tanya, 663
Mellor, Chip, 690
Melmed, Matthew E., 286
Mendoza, Charles J., 237
Meneilly, Robert H., 746
Menino, Thomas M., 678
Merrill, Bev, 125
Merritt, Jack N., 508
Merritt, William, 350
Mesinger, Maxine, 244
Metz, Gurdon H., 183
Metzenbaum, Howard, 670
Metzner, Richard, 244
Meyer, Douglas L., 53
Meyer, Katherine A., 252, 374
Meyer, Paulette J., 189
Meyerhoff, Harvey M., 625
Meyers, Michael, 74
Meyerson, Adam, 847
Mfume, Kweisi, 104, 117
Micali, James M., 53
Michaels, David M., 249
Michaels, Jack D., 53
Michelman, Kate, 115
Middendorf II, J. William, 811
Middleton Jr., Richard H., 716
Midkriff, Robert R., 333
Milch, Thomas, 392
Miles, E. Walter, 74
Miles, Leslie, 682
Milholland, Arthur, 541
Milian, Arsenio, 483
Millar, Victor E., 45
Miller, Ann, 237
Miller, Arnie, 168
Miller, Bob, 653
Miller, David A., 53
Miller, Diane D., 292
Miller, E. Ethelbert, 828
Miller, Ellen S., 612
Miller, Fred, 231
Miller, Henry I., 241
Miller, Joyce, 300, 663
Miller, Ken, 364
Miller, Mercedese M., 147
Miller, Paul, 689

Miller, Richard, 716
Miller, Robert C., 860
Miller, Velvet G., 282
Miller III, James C., 28, 850
Miller Jr., Paul F., 494
Millinger, Donald, 100
Minard, Frank P.L., 831
Mindiola Jr., Totcho, 110
Minear, Larry, 866
Mines, Herbert, 727
Mineta, Norman Y., 793
Minnick, Walter C., 483
Minter, Steven A., 339
Misas-Burley, Cheryl, 202
Mitchell, Della, 125
Mitchell, Denise, 189
Mitchell, Edward F., 7
Mitchell, Larry, 300
Mitchell, Larry M., 265
Mitchell, Martha M., 157
Mitchell, Nancy L., 28
Mitchell, Patrice I., 836
Mitchell, Regene, 265
Mitchell, Roger Bill, 698
Mitchell Sackey, Ann, 350
Mitgang, Iris, 663
Mitsch, Ronald A., 53
Mittenthal, Stephen D., 333
Mittermeier, Russell A., 369
Mixon, Kay, 209
Moberly, Stanley A., 447
Moe, Richard, 441
Moffett, Toby, 789
Moffitt, Donald E., 63
Moghissi, A. Alan, 241
Mokhiber, Albert, 71
Molina, Gloria, 110
Molina, Mario, 547
Moline, Jack, 746
Mollner, Carol, 350
Mone, Lawrence, 838
Monroe, Martha, 553
Monson, Angela Z., 282, 649
Montague Jr., Kenneth C., 793
Montgomery, Kathryn, 565, 566
Montgomery, Steven L., 447
Montgomery Jr., George G., 387
Moody, Randall J., 172
Mooney, Harold A., 387
Moore, Avis Ogilvy, 405
Moore, Clyde R., 53
Moore, Gary B., 53
Moore, Gordon E., 370
Moore, James, 392
Moore, James W., 63
Moore, John Norton, 721
Moore, Monica, 464
Moore, Robert, 205
Moore, Thomas G., 38
Moore, W. Henson, 7, 35
Morales, Rolando, 125
More, Robert B., 125
Morgan, Allen, 570
Morgan, Katherine, 380
Morgan, Martha, 74
Morgan, Sara S., 789
Morial, Marc H., 678
Morisky, Lillian, 161
Morris, April, 704
Morris, E.A., 60
Morris, Joseph A., 593

Morris, Rob, 96
Morris, Steven, 279
Morse, Richard L.D., 274
Morse, Tom, 538
Mortoff, Lawrence, 474
Morton, Linda A., 658
Morton, Peter, 452
Mosbacher Jr., Rob, 674
Moser, Charles A., 558, 806
Moskof, Howard, 35
Moss, George E., 735
Moss, Melissa, 151
Mott, Andy, 188
Mott, Stewart R., 616
Mottley, Wendell, 494
Mountcastle, Mary B., 189, 333
Mourany, Adnan, 71
Moya, Rita, 342
Moyer-Angus, Maria, 380
Mueller, Gerd D., 53
Mueller, Mark, 716
Mueller, Robert K., 319
Mujica, Mauro E., 214
Mulford, Ross Clayton, 616
Muller III, H. Nicholas, 442
Mullins, Rita, 678
Mulva, James J., 53
Mulvey, Kathryn, 344
Mulvey, Mary C., 132
Munger, Mark, 172
Munger, Nancy Barry, 814
Munoz, Carolina, 107
Munoz, Diana Olvedo, 209
Murdy, Joe, 658
Murguia, Ramon, 129
Murphy, Donald, 439
Murphy, John G., 612
Murphy, Laura, 104
Murphy, Patrick, 682
Murray, Anne Firth, 342
Murray, Josephine, 405
Murray Jr., Albert R., 168
Murrin, Thomas J., 45
Murthy, Harsha, 81
Murumba, Samuel K., 530
Musgrove, Ruth S., 374
Musil, Robert K., 540, 541
Musser, Robert W., 387
Musser, Tom, 56
Muth, Robert J., 702
Mutz, John M., 605, 818
Myers, Susan, 730
Myers, Thomas G., 227

Nabrit III, James M., 112
Naftaly, Robert H., 735
Nagel, Denise M., 573
Nagel, Ralph J., 605
Nager, Glen D., 721
Naisbitt, John, 17
Nakamura, Wendy C., 74
Narezo, Pedro, 129
Nash, Phil Tajitsu, 81
Nason, Robert E., 53
Nathan, Andrew, 530
Nathan, Richard P., 24
Nathan, Robert R., 300
Nathanson, Jane F., 244
Natividad, Irene, 663
Nava, Arturo, 140
Navarro, Max, 110

Neal, Homer A., 515
Neese, Terry, 261
Negami, Takuya, 370
Nelson, Allan R., 831
Nelson, Barbara J., 17
Nelson, Douglas W., 339
Nelson, Erik G., 53
Nelson, Gaylord, 483
Nelson, Ilene, 74
Nelson, Phoebe, 125
Nelson, Sharon L., 274
Neubauer, Joseph, 314
Neuhaus, Richard John, 803
Neuhauser, Paul M., 831
Neuman, Nancy M., 616
Neumann, Peter G., 573
New, Margaret A., 224
Newall, J. E., 42
Newkirk, Ingrid, 460, 461
Newman, Constance Berry, 632
Newman, Murray H., 172
Newsom, William A., 387
Newton, Charlotte, 300
Ney, Judith, 408
Nguyen-Sutter, Xuan, 590
Nichols, J. Larry, 605
Nichols, Larry, 53
Nichols, Mack G., 53
Nicholson, Will F., 63
Nickel, Albert G., 241
Nielsen Jr., Vigo G., 616
Nieves, Carlos Lopez, 107
Nimetz, Matthew, 489
Nininger, James R., 42
Niskanen, William A., 786
Nitze, Paul H., 387
Noam, Eli, 573
Nobel, Joel J., 274
Noel, Brenda Watkins, 836
Nogueira-Neto, Paulo, 489
Nolan, John S., 7
Nolan, Patricia A., 249
Noland, Mariam C., 333
Noonan, Patrick F., 367
Nordberg, E. Wayne, 847
Nordloh, Gary L., 698
Norquist, Grover G., 10, 593
Norton, Bryan G., 374
Norton, Ed, 621
Norton, Eleanor Holmes, 392,
    663, 798
Norton, Gale A., 721
Notebaert, Richard C., 45
Noto, Lucio, 860
Novak, Michael, 640
Novelli, William D., 291, 292
Noyes, Carol, 452
Nozaki, Roger H., 342
Nugent, Randolph, 244
Nunez, Louis, 350
Nunn, Sam, 515, 625
Nunnallee, Karolyn V., 202, 227
Nylund, Thomas, 231

O, Oscar de la, 231
O'Brien, Mary, 466
O'Brien, William K., 319
O'Brien Jr., Donal C., 432
O'Connell, Francis A., 844
O'Connor, John M.B., 183
O'Connor, Judith, 288

O'Connor, Maconda Brown, 776
O'Donnell, Kirk, 789
O'Grady, Jane, 104
O'Hare, Rolland, 74
O'Leary, Richard E., 63
O'Malley, Shaun F., 336
O'Neil, Jerry A., 339
O'Neill, Brian B., 374
O'Neill, Brian J., 658
O'Neill, Maura, 356
O'Neill, Paul H., 772
O'Reilly, Kathleen, 255
O'Reilly, Tim, 570
O'Riordan, W. Hugh, 721
O'Rourke, J. Tracy, 53
O'Toole, Robert J., 53
Oakes, John B., 452
Oakley, Carolyn, 597
Oates, Marylouise, 96, 793
Obernader Jr., Marne, 35
Oberndorf, Meyera E., 678
Oberndorf, William E., 844
Odeen, Philip A., 632
Odendahl, Terry, 350
Oesterreicher, James E., 147, 157
Offen, Neil, 818
Offit, Morris W., 727
Offner, Ellen, 172
Ogden, John C., 494
Ogden, Jonathan, 157
Oglesby Jr., M.B., 7
Okech Ogwaro, Kenuel, 436
Olender, Jack, 716
Olewine IV, Benjamin, 432
Olguin, Michael, 649
Oliver, Daniel, 844
Ollis Jr., Robert W., 100
Olsen, Kenneth, 17
Olsen, Phil, 198
Olson, Barbara K., 721
Olson, Jane, 530
Olson, Ronald L., 489
Olson, Theodore B., 721
Olyphant, Tatyana D., 183
Onoda, John, 310
Opperman, Dwight D., 702
Ordan, Mark, 255
Orians, Gordon, 494
Oropeza, Jenny, 658
Orr III, James F., 347
Ortega, Katherine D., 314
Ortega Jr., Daniel, 129
Ortiz, Angel Luis, 129
Ortiz, Cecilia, 129
Ortiz, Deborah, 129
Ortiz, Frank, 107
Osburn, C. Dixon, 174
Osmon, Donn R., 63
Osnos, Peter, 530
Osterhout, David S., 605
Ostrom, Sonya, 538
Ostronic, John F., 616
Ottinger, Richard L., 385
Owen, Mary Jane, 147
Owens, Howard, 132
Owens, Phyllis, 161
Owens, Susan, 100
Owens, Wayne, 374

Pace, Norma, 314, 336
Pace, Stanley C., 53

Pacheco, Jose R., 107
Packard, Gordon, 125
Packer, Joel, 686
Padden, David H., 28, 786
Page, Joseph, 670
Paige, Ralph, 85
Paigen, Beverly, 364
Paisner, Richard, 590
Palm, Michael, 96
Palmer, Fred, 17
Palmer, Robert, 716
Panaritis, Andrea S., 789
Pang, Jane K., 237
Pappas, Phillip, 125
Parde, Duane, 595
Pardoe, David H., 432
Parise, Richard, 93
Parkel, James G., 237
Parker, Douglas, 686
Parker, Franklin, 452
Parker, Michael D., 53, 702
Parker, Sharon, 483
Parvensky, John, 125
Pascual, Carlos, 63
Paster, Howard G., 789
Pastor, Verma, 129
Pate, Carmen, 191, 192
Patiño, Douglas X., 339
Patrick, Ruth, 385
Pattee, Anne, 494
Patten, John W., 147, 367
Patton, Paul E., 653
Pauken, Thomas W., 857
Paul, Robert D., 721
Paul, Rosalie, 538
Paulson, Wendy J., 457
Paxton, John W., 53
Payne, D.P., 53
Payne, Greg, 125
Payson, Martin D., 112
Payton, Brenda, 523
Payton, John, 168
Paz, R. Samuel, 74
Peabody, Samuel, 826
Peapples, George A., 53
Peevey, Michael R., 798
Pelaez, Martha, 135
Pelka, Lawrence J., 63
Pellegrini, Maria C., 616
Pelster, Terry C., 374
Peña, Alfredo Novoa, 457
Pendley, William Perry, 697
Penick, George, 296, 333
Penner, Rudolph G., 35
Pennington, John, 649
Penny, Roger P., 53
Penny, Timothy J., 625
Pennybacker, Albert M., 746
Pepper, John E., 515
Peratis, Kathleen, 530
Percival, Robert, 392
Percy, Steven W., 53, 471
Perera, Frederica, 452
Perez, Anna, 836
Perez, Carmen, 161
Perfecto, Ivette, 466
Perkins, Edward J., 836
Perkins, Jerry, 847
Perkins, Joseph S., 237
Perkins, Leigh, 847
Perkins Jr., Leigh H., 457

Perlman, Itzhak, 147
Perlman, Peter, 716
Perrault, Michele, 477
Perron, James, 678
Perry, Carrolle Fair, 333
Perry, F. Noel, 370
Perry, Timothy, 35
Perry, William J., 515
Perskie, Flora, 730
Pertschuk, Michael, 589, 590
Pestillo, Peter J., 53
Peters, Chris, 202
Peterson, Cole, 310
Peterson, Donald K., 53
Peterson, Esther, 300
Peterson, Gordon, 422
Peterson, Peter G., 35, 625
Peterson, Shirley D., 702
Petron, Stephen E., 447
Peulen, Matthew, 132
Pew, Robert C., 147
Pharr, Suzanne, 85
Phelps, John, 649
Phillips, Barbara L., 356
Phillips, Bradley S., 621
Phillips, Cruz, 466
Phillips, David, 379, 380
Phillips, J. Douglas, 826
Phillips, John C., 93, 356
Phillips, Laurence, 550
Phillips, Martha, 624
Phillips, Sue Watlov, 125
Phillips-Taylor, Byrl, 93
Pichler, Joseph A., 314
Pickett, Steward T.A., 374
Pieper, Roel, 570
Pierce, Donald L., 110
Pierce, Marc, 847
Pierpont, Robert, 356
Piers, Matthew J., 110
Pilkington, Alan R., 374
Piller, Charles, 608
Pillsbury, Marine S., 682
Pines, Marion, 24
Pinkerton Jr., W. Stewart, 183
Pinkham, Jaime A., 483
Pinkston, Christian, 639, 640
Pinner Jr., Douglas K., 53
Pipes, Sally C., 842, 844
Pisano, Mark A., 471
Pittman, Steuart L., 818
Placitella, Chrisopher M., 716
Plimpton, Conrad A., 605
Podd, Victor T., 53
Podesta, Anthony T., 168
Poindexter III, Alfred N., 172
Polk, John G., 286
Pollack, Lester, 735
Pollack, Ron, 281
Pollock, Thomas P., 168
Poole Jr., Robert W., 853, 855
Pope, Carl, 476
Pope, James A., 28, 593
Popenoe, David, 826
Popeo, Daniel J., 720, 781
Porter, Diane M., 746
Porter, Michael E., 45
Portney, Paul R., 470, 471
Poser, Susan, 74
Poss, Mary C., 658
Post, Bill, 17

Post, Manning J., 616
Potter, Louise Bryant, 442
Potter Jr., Charles, 847
Pouillon, Nora, 303
Poulard, Othello, 85
Poulson, Judy, 645
Pound, William, 647
Powell, Burnele Venable, 274
Power Jr., Joseph A., 716
Powers, Ann, 392
Powers, Ray, 597
Powers, Ruth L., 682
Prager, Dennis, 640
Prechter, Heinz C., 45
Preiskel, Robert H., 112
Prescott, Heidi, 407
Prescott, John B., 42
Presley, Milton M., 274
Presser, Stephen B., 721
Preston, James E., 314
Preston, Kary D., 241
Price, Hugh B., 104, 156, 157, 860
Price, Monroe, 566
Price, Scott, 468
Price, Sol, 24, 860
Price, Susan C., 172
Price, Timothy F., 347
Price Jr., John R., 53
Priesing, John W., 689
Priest, George L., 721
Prince, Elsa D., 198, 742
Pritchett, Bryan, 447
Pritzker, Nicholas J., 370
Pritzker, Robert, 53
Probst, Marian, 408, 425
Prosser, Kathy, 392
Protulis, Steve, 131, 132, 135, 793
Proxmire, William, 668
Prussia, Leland S., 35
Pryor Jr., William H., 721
Pugh, J. Tyler, 172
Pulliam, H. Ronald, 374
Puriefoy, Wendy D., 296
Purvin, Diane, 209
Pusey, Allen, 608
Putnam, Howard D., 319

Quadracci, Harry, 310
Quayle, Dan, 818
Quevedo, Frank J., 110
Quinlan, Michael R., 314
Quinn, Kieron, 716
Quintero, Sofia, 590

Rabb, Bruce, 530
Rabinowitz, Daniel L., 112
Rabinowitz, Leonard, 244
Radcliff, Irene, 662
Radwin, Jerome J., 243
Rae, Carol A., 63
Raggio, William, 597
Rahn, Richard W., 7
Raimondo, Anthony F., 53
Raines, Franklin D., 632
Rainey, John S., 447
Rainville, Donald D., 53
Raisian, John, 813
Rajan, S. Ravi, 466
Raley, Gordon A., 350
Rall, David P., 387
Ramage Jr., David, 168, 793

Ramer, Bruce M., 727
Ramer, Lawrence J., 727
Ramey, Clayton, 538
Ramsey, O.J., 416
Ramsey, Stephen, 392
Randolph, Amelia, 541
Randolph, C. Carl, 112
Randolph, Korey M., 118
Rands, Tim, 380
Rangel, Irma, 110
Ranieri, Lewis S., 387
Rankin, Singleton, 494
Ranney Jr., George A., 367
Rapoport, Bernard, 798, 826
Rapport, Miles, 793
Raskin, Marcus, 828
Rasmussen, Arthur, 826
Rasmussen, Scott W., 847
Ratcliffe, Richard, 63
Ratliff, Mary, 118
Ratliff, Robert J., 53
Rattner, Steven L., 776
Rauh, John, 621
Rauh Jr., Joseph L., 104
Rauschenberg, Michael S., 100
Rausing, Sigrid, 530
Raven, Peter H., 489
Ravenholt, R. T., 241
Raymont, Wendy Marcus, 621
Raynault, Paul, 674
Raynes, Burt F., 53
Readmond, Ronald W., 7
Redd, Hardy, 847
Redenbaugh, Russell G., 147
Redford, Robert, 452
Redgate, William T., 319
Redlich, Norman, 730
Reed, Donald B., 319
Reed, Nathaniel, 452
Reed, Stephen, 198
Reed Jr., Adolph L., 670
Reed Jr., Ralph, 593, 739
Reed Wulsin, Rosamond, 553
Reese, Mary Ellen, 621
Reese, William S., 342
Reeve, Christopher, 147
Reeves, Jo Lyn, 447
Regan, Jack, 649
Regenstreif, Steve, 132
Register, Nancy, 686
Rehm, Jack D., 7
Reich, Alan A., 146, 147
Reich, Jeffrey P., 147
Reich, Robert B., 798
Reid, Susan Marie, 380
Reid, Timothy R., 422
Reilly, Edward, 129
Reilly, William K., 385, 494
Reinhardt, Richard L., 56
Reis, Jacqueline M., 339
Reischauer, Robert D., 24, 35
Remar, Robert B., 74
Rench, J. Frederic, 811
Resnick, Lynda Rae, 370
Resnick, Myron J., 205
Resor, Stanley R., 508
Resor, Story Clark, 370
Reston, Thomas B., 110
Rethore, Bernard G., 53
Reuben-Cooke, Wilhelmina, 566
Revelle, Eleanor, 645

Reynard, William F., 74
Reynolds, Cathy, 658
Reynoso, Cruz, 452
Rhoads, Dean A., 597
Rhodes, John J., 35
Rhodes, Skip, 333
Rhodes, Thomas L., 811
Rice, Andrew E., 866
Rice, David C., 665
Rice, Florence M., 265
Rice, Linda Johnson, 314
Rice, Peter van S., 442
Rich, Howard S., 674, 786
Rich, Robert L., 53
Richard, Alison F., 494
Richard, John, 258
Richards, Ann, 663
Richards, Cecile, 168
Richards, Gale, 100
Richards, Jody, 649
Richards, R. Barrett, 172
Richards, Thomas E., 347
Richardson, Alan H., 265
Richardson, Elliot L., 632
Richardson, Mrs. Rupert, 118
Richardson, William C., 333
Rickard, Lisa A., 53, 605
Rickard Jr., Norman E., 347
Ridder, Marie W., 439
Ridgway, Rozanne L., 314
Ridings, Dorothy, 331, 333
Riederer, Richard K., 53
Riedman, John R., 605
Rifka, Safa, 71
Rifkin, Jeremy, 400
Riggio, Leonard, 89
Riley, Almeda C., 172
Riley, Antonio, 793
Riley, Judy Bryne, 347
Riley, Meg A., 746
Rimel, Rebecca W., 333
Ringler, James M., 53
Ringler, Karin, 541
Ringo, Jerome C., 447
Ris Jr., Howard C., 546
Rising, Nancy, 538
Ritter, Kay McGinnis, 585
Rivera, Dennis, 89, 132
Rivera, Juan, 205
Rivera, Marianna, 538
Robbins, Chris A., 605
Roberto, Jan, 192
Roberts, Barbara, 96
Roberts, Benson F., 189
Roberts, Cecil E., 132
Roberts, Franklin, 118
Roberts, George R., 772
Roberts, John B., 439
Roberts, Markley, 300
Roberts, Michael F., 742
Roberts, Nanette M., 78
Robertson, M.G. 'Pat', 739
Robertson Jr., Julian H., 640
Robinson, Barbara Paul, 314
Robinson, Cloyd, 60
Robinson, Diane Stevens, 157
Robinson, Florence T., 489
Robinson, Gerald S., 157
Robinson, J. Lawrence, 53
Robinson, John R., 452
Robinson, Kenneth, 265

Robinson, Mark, 231
Robinson, Pearl, 544
Robinson, Randall, 543
Robinson, Turhan E., 74
Robles, Belen B., 107
Rockefeller, Laurance, 452
Rockefeller, Sharon Percy, 663
Rockefeller Jr., Nelson A., 367
Rockoff, Alvin J., 735
Rockwood, John M., 510
Rodd, Thomas, 422
Roddick, Anita, 530
Rodgers, Kathy, 686
Rodin, Judith S., 314, 776
Rodine, Sharon, 663
Rodman, Michael, 461
Roe, Thomas A., 811
Roen, Nancy H., 483
Roeser, Thomas, 857
Rogers, Adrian, 742
Rogers, Estelle, 686
Rogers, James E., 53
Rogers, John F. W., 442
Rogers, Julie L., 339
Rogers, Robert B., 333, 342
Rogers Jr., James E., 7
Rogin, Carole, 53
Rogstad, Barry K., 3, 8
Rohrbach, Nancy Risque, 632
Roht-Arriaza, Naomi, 466
Roisman, Tony, 716
Rolland, Ian M., 818
Rom, Rebecca L., 483
Roman, Kenneth, 147
Romo, John, 172
Ronquillo, Jose R., 110
Roosevelt IV, Theodore, 429, 483
Rose, David S., 168
Rose, Jeffrey O., 416
Rose, Michael T., 147
Rose, Virgil G., 439
Roselle, Mike, 468
Rosen, Jack, 730
Rosen, Rachel, 140
Rosenberg, Sheli, 151
Rosenberg Jr., Claude, 370
Rosenberg Jr., Henry A., 53
Rosenfeld, Arthur H., 329
Rosenfield, Allan, 244
Rosenman, Mark, 665
Rosenthal, John, 93
Rosenthall, John A., 356
Rosenwald Jr., E. John, 147, 387
Rosenzweig, Peggy, 649
Ross, James D., 416
Ross, Worth, 96
Rossbach, William A., 716
Rosselló, Pedro, 637
Rosset, Peter, 466
Roten, Robert W., 63
Rotenberg, Marc, 572
Roth, Allen, 593
Roth, Kenneth, 528
Rothschild, Kathleen Teague, 806
Rotterman, Marc E., 593
Rounds, Don, 300
Roush, Jeanne, 461
Roush, Thomas W., 452
Rovig, David B., 698
Rowe, Audrey, 24, 663
Rowe, John W., 772

Rowe, Phyllis, 265
Roybal, Russell, 140
Royer, Patricia, 300
Ruan III, John R., 63
Rubenfeld, Abby R., 96
Rubenstein, Leonard, 686
Rubin, Alan, 147
Rubin, Robert M., 789
Rucci, Anthony J., 319
Ruckelshaus, Jill, 663
Ruckelshaus, William D., 8
Rucks, Alfred J., 118
Rudge, Howard J., 689
Rudman, Warren B., 625, 776
Rudovsky, David, 74
Ruffin, Benjamin S., 157
Ruhl, Suzi, 364, 392
Rule, Charles F. 'Rick', 721
Rumsfeld, Donald H., 640
Rupp, Gerald E., 494
Rush, David, 541
Rusher, William A., 581
Russell, Christine H., 452
Russell, Jane T., 289
Russell, Leon W., 118
Russell, Margaret, 74
Russell, Ruth O., 432
Russell Jr., George F., 814
Rust Jr., Edward B., 14, 347, 772
Rusthoven, Peter J., 721
Rydell, Charlene, 282
Ryder III, Tom, 636

Saba, George, 71
Sacher, Fred, 205
Sachse, Jeffrey, 96
Sackey, Ann Mitchell, 342
Sacks, Ivan A., 826
Saika, Peggy, 333
Saiki, Patricia, 663
Sailor Jr., Ronald, 118
Saladoff, Susan Vogel, 716
Saland, Stephen, 649
Sale, Chris, 151
Sale, Deborah M., 789
Salem, George R., 602
Sallet, Jonathan B., 789
Saltzman, Murray, 282
Samhan, Helen Hatab, 602
Samuels, William C., 329
Samuels Jr., T. William, 63
Sanchez, Agustin, 107
Sanchez, Elisa Maria, 350
Sanders, Cameron, 361
Sanders, Charles, 132
Sanders, Charles A., 515
Sanders, Gerald, 286
Sanders, Sedalia, 658
Sandmeyer Jr., Ronald P., 53
Sands, Steve, 189
Sanger, Stephen W., 42
Sant, Roger W., 489, 494
Santa Anna, Gloria, 160
Santo Domingo, Julio Mario, 370
Santos, Miriam, 110
Sapan, Joshua, 168
Sapers, Judith T., 112
Saperstein, David, 104, 118, 168
Sarin, Lalit, 53
Sarni, Vincent A., 147
Satloff, Robert, 549

Sauter, W. Gary, 265, 286
Sauvigné, Karen, 81
Savage, M. Susan, 678
Sawhill, Isabel, 457, 632
Sawhill, John C., 456, 515
Sayre, Federico, 716
Scaife, Richard M., 811, 814
Scanlan, John McAllen, 387
Scanlon, Terrence, 780, 781
Sceitheis, Nicole, 716
Schadt, James P., 772
Schaeffer, Leonard D., 632
Schafer, Reba, 135
Schaffer, Nan, 452
Schardt, Arlie, 405
Scheck, Lori, 192
Schecter, Julie, 510
Scheibelhut, Becky, 447
Scheide, William H., 112
Schell, Orville, 530
Schement, Jorge, 578
Scheppach Jr., Raymond C., 652
Scher, Laura, 310
Schiller, Susan, 161
Schlafly, Phyllis, 194, 195
Schlenk, Skip, 135
Schlesinger, James R., 515
Schlickeisen, Roger O., 373, 374, 429
Schmidheiny, Stephan, 489
Schneider, Claudine, 663, 668
Schneider, Pauline A., 151, 836
Schneier, Bruce, 573
Schniderman, Craig, 231
Schnurr, Dennis, 752
Schoenke, Nancy, 93
Scholl-Buckwald, Stephen, 464
Schramm, Marjorie B., 658
Schreiber, James, 550
Schreyer, William A., 515
Schroeder, Steven A., 342
Schroeter, Leonard, 716
Schubert, Richard F., 347
Schuchert, Joseph S., 63
Schulhof, Michael P., 776
Schultz, Judith, 553
Schultz, Otto H., 237
Schultze, Charles, 35
Schulz, William F., 503
Schutz, John A., 616
Schwab, Susan C., 632
Schwabe, John L., 704
Schwartz, Alan D., 244
Schwartz, Allyson, 649, 793
Schwartz, Fred, 550
Schwartz, Jeffrey A., 616
Schwartz, Mark, 658
Schwartz, Robert, 686
Schwartz, Robert J., 538
Schwartzman, Andrew Jay, 578
Schwarz, Frederick, 452
Schwarz, Thomas J., 616
Schwarzkopf, H. Norman, 457
Scofield, Terry, 125
Scott, Judith, 151
Scott, Raymond, 118
Scott, Sue W., 231
Scowcroft, Brent, 336, 508, 515
Scully, John A., 356
Scully, Vincent J., 442
Searcy, Karroll Ann, 202

Searle, Urling I., 183
Sease, Debbie, 429
Sechler, Susan, 24
Secord, William, 183
Sedlar, Jeri, 682
Seffrin, John R., 292, 342
Segal, Phyllis, 93
Segel, Joseph M., 625
Seger, Martha R., 314
Segrest, Mab, 85
Seiberling, John F., 385
Seidenberg, Ivan G., 42, 157
Seidman, Bert, 300
Seidman, L.William, 8
Seifert, Norma, 192
Seligmann, Peter A., 370
Sellers, Wallace O., 818
Semerad, Roger D., 818
Seminario, Margaret, 665
Sepulveda Jr, Juan, 24, 793
Serota, Gary, 628
SerVaas, Beurt, 818
Severyn, Betty J., 237
Sevilla, Roque, 494
Seyler, Marilyn G., 416
Seymour Jr., Whitney North, 612
Shade, Harmon, 447
Shadoan, George W., 716
Shafer, Raymond P., 508
Shafer, Raymond Phillip, 147, 702
Shahan, Rosemary, 265
Shaheen, Gerald L., 63
Shakespeare, Frank, 811
Shallenberger, Mary, 172
Shannon, Michael E., 53
Shapiro, Esther, 300
Shapiro, Norman, 432
Shapiro, Peter, 793
Shapiro, Richard, 627
Sharp, Victoria L., 231
Sharp, William J., 53
Shaw, Theodore M., 112
Shawmut-Lessner, Shaloma, 662
Shea, David, 63
Shearin, Morris L., 118
Shedd, Wilfred G., 53
Sheehan, Dennis W., 63
Sheehan, Jeremiah J., 42
Sheehan, John, 452
Sheehan, John J. 'Jack', 385
Sheekey, Kathleen D., 589, 590
Sheffels, Jerry, 698
Sheft, Wallace, 244
Sheinberg, Sid, 530
Sheinkman, Jack, 45, 329
Sheldon, Karin, 374, 392
Sheldon, Louis, 761
Shelmonson-Bey, Eirther, 125
Shelton, Hilary, 85
Shelton, Judy, 640
Shen, Michael, 81
Shepard, Donald J., 63
Sher, Victor M., 429
Sherwood, Ben, 608
Shields, Carole, 166, 168
Shiffman, Ron, 189
Shiner, Josette, 640
Shipley, Walter V., 14
Shirley, Craig, 593
Shistar, Terry, 436
Shoemate, Charles R., 42

Shore, Herbert, 135
Shorey, Clyde, 168
Shriver, Michael D., 244
Shull, Pat, 135
Shultz, George P., 8
Shute Jr., Benjamin R., 342
Sick, Gary G., 530
Siclari, Rick, 231
Sidamon-Eristoff, Anne P., 494
Siebel Jr., Kenneth F., 370
Sieleman, Maxine, 192
Sievers, Bruce, 333
Sifuentes, Damaris, 107
Silas, C.J., 336
Silber, Norman I., 274
Silbergeld, Mark, 265, 686
Silver, Jonathan, 168
Silverman, Jane, 727
Silverman, Mervyn F., 244
Simmons, Adele, 547
Simmons, Harold Clark, 581
Simms, Margaret C., 836
Simon, Samuel A., 300
Simon, William E., 811
Simoncini, Gregory G., 100
Simons, Barbara, 573
Simpson, Louise A., 118
Singer, Max, 818
Singhaus, Barbara , 172
Sinnott, Faye Harned, 645
Sirota, Marvin M., 730
Sissel, George A., 53
Sive, David, 452
Skeen, John, 640
Skenadore, Donna, 161
Skilbred, Amy, 432
Skilling, Jeffrey K., 53
Sklar, Erik, 310
Skooglund, Carl M., 319
Slattery, James, 35
Slick, Katherine Ann, 442
Slifka, Alvin, 730
Sloan, Katrinka Smith, 265
Slutsky, Lorie A., 289, 339
Smale, John G., 457
Small, Gregg, 436
Small, Jonathan A., 831
Small, Sid, 56
Smaltz, Donald C., 183
Smart, Bruce, 429, 489
Smeal, Ellie, 553
Smith, A.J.C., 63
Smith, Adrian J.R., 53
Smith, Alison, 645
Smith, Andy, 321
Smith, Beth, 329
Smith, Candace N., 157
Smith, Charles H., 135
Smith, Conley P., 698
Smith, Daryl D., 605
Smith, David H., 387
Smith, David R., 292
Smith, David W., 678
Smith, Denny, 261
Smith, Donald R., 135
Smith, Edgar, 408
Smith, Eric B., 658
Smith, Eunice, 195
Smith, Frances, 38
Smith, Frances B., 260, 261
Smith, Frederick W., 786

Smith, Gloria, 231
Smith, Harry, 658
Smith, Hyrum W., 63
Smith, J. Anthony, 789
Smith, Kenneth B., 442
Smith, Larry, 198
Smith, Malcolm, 530
Smith, Patrick L., 483
Smith, Paul M., 175
Smith, Paula R., 416
Smith, Peirce B., 296
Smith, Peter W., 508
Smith, Philip S., 616
Smith, Rita, 208, 209
Smith, Rob, 649
Smith, Robert Ellis, 573
Smith, Shirley L., 202
Smith, Timothy, 748
Smith, Wayne, 202
Smith, William Y., 508
Smith Jr., Fred L., 36, 38
Smith Jr., John F., 14, 314, 457
Smith Jr., Sherwood H., 605
Smith Jr., Turner, 392
Smith Sr., Kenneth B., 237
Smoak Jr., Randolph D., 292
Smoger, Gerson H., 716
Snedden, Lois, 477
Snider Jr., Ted L., 605
Snow, John W., 35, 772
Snowden, Gail, 310
Snyder, Charles E., 265
Snyder, George, 60
Socolow, Robert H., 432
Soder, Dee, 682
Sohn, GiGi B., 577
Solar, J. Michael, 89
Solomon, Norman, 575
Solomon, Peter J., 356
Solow, Robert M., 471, 860
Sombrotto, Vincent R., 789
Some, Mathias, 270
Sommer, Richard, 422
Sonderman, Marie V., 237
Song, Vo Kyung, 270
Sorensen, Christine, 172
Soros, Paul, 168
Sosa, Enrique J., 702
Soutendijk, Dirk R., 689
Spalt, Allen, 436
Speakman III, Willard A., 824
Spearman, Theodore, 716
Spears, Robert M., 53
Speer, Daniel M., 658
Spencer, Alonzo, 364
Spencer, Steve R., 605
Spencer, William I., 367
Spencer III, William M., 442
Speranza, Paul, 63
Spero, Joan, 776
Speth, Gus, 452
Speth, James Gustave, 489
Spitzer, T. Quinn, 347
Spradley, Mark, 135
Sprague, Daniel M., 635
Spratley, William A., 265
Sprynczynatyk, Connie, 658
St. Clair, Al, 855
St. John, Maria Delmar, 209
Staats, Elmer, 35
Stacy, Carey I., 63

Stafford, Ruth, 53
Stahr, John R., 814
Staley, Peter R., 244
Staley, Warren, 53
Stallkamp, Thomas T., 53
Standish, Marion, 286
Stanfield, Judy, 231
Stanley, A. Knighton, 380, 746
Stanley, David M., 60
Stanley, Jennifer, 483
Stanley, Kelly N., 63
Stanley, Mary, 663
Stanton, Domna, 530
Stare, Fredrick J., 241
Stark, Louisa, 125
Stark, Martha E., 100
Starnes, Michael S., 63
Starr, Barbara S., 730
Starrett, Cam, 314
Stassen, Glen, 538
Stata, Ray, 45
Staubach, Roger T., 347
Stauffer, Gordon L., 53
Stavropoulos, William S., 772
Stebbins, James F., 183
Steel, Lewis M., 828
Steele, Mona, 645
Steenland, Sally, 566
Steere Jr., William C., 14, 45
Stein, Daniel, 524
Stein, James, 63
Stein, Mike, 550
Steinbruner, Maureen S., 788, 789
Steinem, Gloria, 663
Steinhardt, Barry, 569
Steketee, Nan, 350
Stella, Frank, 132
Stellmann, Caroline, 300
Stephens, Delena, 125
Stephenson, Richard J., 28
Stephney, William J., 157
Stern, Allison, 408
Stern, Andrew, 326
Stern, David, 612
Stern, Joel, 855
Stern, Joseph, 110
Stern, Walter P., 550, 818
Sternberg, Stephen S., 241
Stevens, Jessica, 96
Stevens, Tom, 422
Stevens Jr., Ernie, 127
Stevenson, Clinton L., 831
Stever, Donald, 392
Stevik, Steve, 468
Stewart, Donald M., 789
Stewart Jr., Jamie B., 63
Stieb, Peter, 63
Stiglitz, Joseph E., 471
Stigol, Louisa C., 585
Stillwell, Joseph, 674
Stith, Charles R., 168
Stochaj, Ricki, 300
Stockman, David A., 35
Stockman, Patti, 192
Stolberg, Irving, 793
Stone, Ira N., 605
Stone, Judith Lee, 226, 227
Stone, Terry, 231
Stool, Thomas, 452, 547
Storms, Clifford B., 689
Storrs, David K., 831

Strachan, Camille J., 442
Strahman, Robert W., 698
Stranahan, Sarah, 350
Strand, Margaret, 392
Straniere, Robert, 597
Stratton, Hal, 721
Straub, Terrence D., 789
Straus, Philip A., 510
Strauss, Abbey, 541
Strauss, Robert S., 8, 35, 721
Straw, Edward M., 63
Strayhorn, Louisa M., 157, 658
Strharsky, Harry, 523
Stringer, Howard, 457
Stritmatter, Paul L., 716
Strohbehn Jr., Edward L., 471
Strong, Maurice F., 489
Strong, Ted, 356
Strossen, Nadine, 73
Strum, Phillippa, 74
Sturdevant, James, 716
Suarez, John M., 78
Sugarman, Robert G., 735
Sullivan, James, 255
Sullivan, Louis W., 224, 336
Sumida, Gerald A., 63
Sun, Andrew I., 110
Susman, Frank, 74
Suter, Albert E., 53
Sutherland, Mimi, 93
Sutherland, Peter D., 42
Swaim, Tommy, 658
Swanson, Eric, 342
Swanson, Jay, 100
Swanzey, Eugene F., 789
Swart, Betsy, 419
Sweat, Joseph, 74
Sweeney, John, 793
Sweetland, MaryBeth, 461
Swenson, Eric P., 361
Swenson, Leland, 265, 300
Swensrud, Stephen B., 525
Swift, Allan B., 616
Swing, William E., 244
Swomley, John M., 74, 746
SyCip, Washington, 42
Sylvan, Louise, 270
Sylvester, Ken, 321
Szegedy-Maszak, Marianne, 608
Szekely, Deborah, 129, 255

Tabaksblat, Morris, 42
Tabankin, Margery, 168
Tabash, Eddie, 78
Tabb, Judy N., 172
Taber, George H., 494
Taft, John E., 416
Tagliabue, Paul, 157
Takanishi, Ruby, 333
Taketa, Rick, 405
Takeuchi, Mitsunobu, 53
Talbert, Melvin B., 758
Taliaferro, Linda, 471
Tanaka, Susan, 35
Tane, Susan Jaffe, 730
Tanner, Harold, 727
Tanner Jr., James L., 789
Tanton, John, 525
Taplin Jr., Frank E., 387
Tarr-Whelan, Linda, 342, 590,
    792, 793

Tate, Randy, 738, 739
Taube, Thaddeus N., 814
Tauke, Thomas J., 605
Taylor, Craig, 212
Taylor, Dixon, 175
Taylor, Elizabeth, 244
Taylor, Gardner C., 746
Taylor, H. LeBaron, 836
Taylor, Herman Art, 342
Taylor, Humphrey, 147
Taylor, James, 452
Taylor, John I., 356
Taylor, Margaret, 494
Taylor, Meg, 489
Taylor, Ralph, 321
Taylor, Robert D., 157
Taylor, William L., 104
Taylor, Wilson H., 772
Taylor III, William A., 53
Teasley, Mary Elizabeth, 793
Teasley Jr., Harry, 855
Tedcastle, Tom, 649
Teel, Lorraine, 231
Teerlink, Richard F., 53
Telles, Cynthia Anne, 151
Tempel, Jean C., 319
Tempelsman, Maurice, 789
Terborgh, John, 494
terHorst, Jerry, 93
Terry Jr., Frederick A., 452
Teslik, Sarah, 325, 326
Tessler, Allan R., 818
Thelen Jr., Max, 525
Thelian, Lorraine, 241
Themba, Makani N., 590
Thernstrom, Abigail, 691
Theroux, David J., 822, 824
Theroux, Mary L. Garvey, 824
Thieneman, Michael, 53
Thomas, C. Stephen, 53
Thomas, Gwen, 74
Thomas, Hazel, 662
Thomas, JoNell, 74
Thomas, Margaret J., 758
Thomas, Marlo, 663
Thomas, Maxine S., 447
Thomas, Michael T., 704
Thomas, Terry, 329
Thomas, W. Dennis, 605
Thomas Jr., Lee B., 329
Thomases, Susan P., 89
Thompson, Craig, 231
Thompson, Diane, 628
Thompson, Larry D., 721
Thompson, N. David, 702
Thompson, Ronald L., 53
Thompson, Tommy, 636
Thompson, Tommy G., 653
Thompson, W. Reid, 147
Thomson, Helen, 649
Thorn, Terence H., 605
Thornburgh, Dick, 721, 860
Thorning, Margo, 7
Thornton Jr., William G., 56
Thorson, Don, 698
Thrupp, Lori Ann, 466
Thurow, Lester, 798
Thursz, Daniel, 135
Tierney, Virginia L., 237
Tigue, Randall D.B., 74

Timken Jr., W.R., 53
Tinsman, Maggie, 649
Tishman, Daniel, 452
Tobias, Andrew, 96
Tobias, Deben, 310
Tobias, Glen A., 735
Todini, Vivian, 100
Toensing, Victoria, 663
Tohbe, Susan, 314
Tohomine, Connie, 749
Tolba, Mostafa K., 489
Toledo, Elizabeth, 143
Toll, Daniel R., 483
Toller, William R., 63
Tollison, Robert, 850
Tomb, Spencer, 447
Tomlin, John, 847
Toney, William, 20
Tooker, Gary L., 45, 314
Topkis, Jay, 112
Torralva-Alonso, Maria Elena, 129
Torres, Arturo G., 129
Torres, Gerald, 392
Torres-Gil, Fernando, 282
Towe, William, 538
Towne, Barbara, 192
Townley, Steve, 231
Train, Russell E., 494
Trattler, Larry, 716
Travis, J. Frank, 53
Treanor, Bill, 350
Tredway, Philip M., 53
Trent Jr., William B., 605
Tribble Jr., Israel, 157
Trillin, Alice, 566
Trine, William A., 716
Trister, Michael B., 560
Trombold, James, 541
Trosino, Vincent J., 776
Trowbridge, Alexander B., 53
Troxell, Richard, 125
Troyer, Thomas A., 89, 452
True, Diemer, 605, 698
Trujillo, Solomon D., 17
Trumka, Richard L., 798
Truog, Greg, 350
Tschinkel, Victoria J., 385, 471
Tsongas, Nicola, 625
Tuchinsky, Joseph S., 265
Tucker, C. Delores, 663
Tuerkheimer, Frank, 573
Tull, Allan W., 237
Tung, Ko-Yung, 81
Turk, S. Maynard, 689
Turner, David C., 227
Turner, Harold E., 63
Turner, James, 544
Turner, John E., 132
Turner, John F., 366, 367
Turner, John G., 625
Turner, Kathleen, 168
Turner, Richard, 96
Turner, Suzanne W., 442
Turnipseed, Tom, 85
Tusher, Thomas, 494
Tuttle, George D., 100
Twist, Steven J., 721
Tyson, Patricia, 300

Udall, Thomas, 392
Uehlein, Joe, 321

Uffner, Michael S., 63
Uher, D.R. 'Tom', 597
Uhler, Lewis K., 593
Uhlmann, John, 558
Umana Quesada, Alvaro, 489
Ungerleider, Andrew, 510
Upchurch, Robert P., 241
Urquidi, Victor L., 489
Usem, Ruth B., 168
Usher, Thomas J., 14

Vacco, Dennis C., 721
Vagley, Robert, 227
Valdez, Robert E., 110
Vale, Elizabeth A., 682
Valencia Jr., Jack L., 658
Valenti, Jack, 147
Valentine, Foy, 746
Valentine, Herbert D., 746
Valentino, Linda, 575
Valles, Jean-Paul, 53
Van Andel, Jay, 811, 818
Van Andel, Steve, 63
Van Andel-Gaby, Barbara, 781, 811
Van Blake, Barbara, 300
van Buren, Ariane, 321
Van Burkirk, Ronald E., 704
Van de Putte, Pete, 56
Van Dongen, Dirk, 28
Van Graafeiland, Gary P., 689
van Lede, Cees J. A., 42
Van Melle, Izaak, 866
Van Putten, Mark, 446
Van Rensselaer, Alex, 60
Van Stekelenburg, Mark, 63
Van Vyven, Dale, 597
Vance, Cyrus R., 789
Vance, Scott, 553
Vancour, Sander, 616
vanden Heuvel, Katrina, 828
Vander Horst, Kathleen P., 836
VanderSloot, Frank L., 63
Vargas, Arturo, 342
Vaughan, Roland H., 63
Vaughn, Gladys Gary, 300
Vedder, Amy, 483
Vedder, Richard, 60
Vega, Matias, 125
Vega, Yvonne Martinez, 129
Vela, Charles E., 129
Velarde, Ray, 107
Velasquez, Carmen, 129
Velazquez, Louise, 129
VeneKlasen, Gordon, 140
Verges, Teresa, 175
Verma, Satya, 135
Vermeulen, Joan, 686
Vernick, Jon S., 252
Vernon, Gerlad B., 53
Verplanck, Joan, 63
Vest, Charles M., 45
Vick, Edward H., 244
Viederman, Stephen, 321
Vietor, Francesca, 468
Vigil, Alfredo, 172
Villano, Clair E., 300
Villarreal, Jose, 129
Villers, Philippe, 282
Vincent, Wayne, 202
Vivian, C.T., 85

Vogel, Carroll, 474
Vogelmann, Hubert, 367
Voinovich, George V., 653
Vokema, Michael A., 53
Volcker, Paul A., 8, 35, 625
Volel-Stech, Frances, 303
von Gontard, Paul T., 698
Votaw, Carmen Delgado, 663
Vowell, Cameron M., 457
Vradenburg III, George, 570

Wagle, N.G., 270
Wagle, Susan, 597
Wagner, David L., 296
Wagner, Rodney B., 494
Wagner, Vallerie D., 100
Wagner III, Frederick W., 183
Wainwright, Arthur D., 53
Wait, Carol Cox, 34, 35
Waite III, G. Thomas, 416
Waldron, Rosemary, 474
Walker, Albert C., 78
Walker, Anne C., 649
Walker, Charles B., 53
Walker, Charles E., 7
Walker, Dorothy, 132
Walker, Douglas W., 483
Walker, John W., 112
Walker, Kathryn, 408
Walker, Kirby, 452
Walker, Lucius, 85
Walker, Paula, 608
Walker Jr., Brooks, 704
Walker-Maddox, Lu Ann, 56
Wallace, Carla F., 140
Wallace, Mona Lisa, 716
Wallace, Richard A., 844
Wallach, Ira D., 168
Wallack, Lawrence, 566
Waller, Jeanne W., 183
Waller, Julian A., 274
Wallerstein, George, 112, 329
Wallinder, Jan L., 249
Wallis, W. Allen, 803
Walter, H. William, 439
Walter, Susan, 53
Walthall, Chet, 53
Walton, Simon, 716
Wanandi, Edward, 818
Wanock, Maurice J., 53
Ward, Jerry, 649
Ward, Jonathan P., 53
Warden, Barbara, 665
Ware, Leland, 74
Ware, Willis, 573
Wargo, John, 436
Warmhoudt, Gerrit, 691
Warren, Melinda, 20
Warren, Robert J., 836
Warren, Thomas L., 447
Wartella, Ellen, 566
Wartenberg, Dan, 436
Wasch, Armand de, 270
Washington, Joan L., 81
Wass, Christopher, 63
Wasserman, Lynne, 93
Watanabe, Jeffrey N., 457
Watanabe, Y. Bill, 350
Waterman Jr., Robert H., 494
Waters, Maxine, 544
Watson, Bonnie, 135

Watson, Carole, 538
Watson, Douglas G., 53
Watson, Joann, 85
Watson, Karen, 590
Watson, Paul, 473, 474
Watson, William G., 439
Wauer, Roland H., 439
Wauterlek, Anthony, 742
Waxse, David, 74
Webb, Wellington E., 678
Weber, Vin, 640
Webster, John W., 78
Webster, William H., 702
Wedekind, Carl, 74
Wegmann, Karen, 110
Wehrle Jr., Henry B., 605
Weidenbaum, Murray, 20, 515
Weil, Leon J., 581
Weill, James D., 686
Weill, Jim, 285
Weinbach, Lawrence A., 314
Weinberg, Barbi, 550
Weinberger, Caspar W., 702
Weinberger, Robert A., 612
Weiner, Ronald, 727
Weinhold, Richard, 739
Weinstein, David H., 716
Weir, David, 468
Weisel, Thomas W., 640
Weisman, Vivian, 74
Weiss, Cora, 538
Weiss, Ellyn, 547
Weiss, Richard T., 261
Weisshaar, Kenneth R., 53
Weisskopf, Victor F., 547
Weitz, Harvey, 716
Weitz, Perry, 716
Weitzen, Jeffrey, 63
Welborn, Robert F., 416
Welborne, John H., 442
Weld, Jacqueline B., 452
Weldon, Virginia V., 19
Wellington, Sheila W., 313, 314
Wells, Ethel R., 224
Wells, Harry K., 53
Wells, LynDee, 405
Wells, Marion G., 781
Wells, Preston A., 811
Wells, Tony, 202
Wenner, Jann, 93
Wente, Jean R., 844
Werbach, Adam, 477
Werk, Doug, 198
Werner, Carol, 384
Wessel, Liz, 279
West, Robert H., 53
West, W. Richard, 442
West, William, 422
West Jr., W. Richard, 387
Westen, Tracy, 560
Westendorp, Dick, 270
Wester, Carol, 749

Wetstone, Gregory, 392, 686
Wewis Jr., William M., 157
Wexler, David, 231
Wexner, Abigail S., 89
Weyrich, Paul M., 805, 806
Wha Hong, Chung, 81
Wharton, Dolores D., 515
Wheelock, Ann Marie, 110
Whelan, Elizabeth M., 239, 241
Whelan, Rosalie, 132
Whitburn, Gerald, 605
White, Arthur, 590
White, Bernard S., 550
White, John P., 625, 632
White, Maureen, 530
White, Robert, 442
White, Robert J., 241
White, William S., 342
Whitehead, Donald, 125
Whitehead, John C., 8, 457, 632, 803
Whitehead, John W., 706
Whitehurst, David B., 605
Whiteing, Jeanne, 374
Whiting, R. Bruce, 698
Whitmire, John L., 432
Whitney, Edward B., 831
Whittlesey, Judith H., 286
Whitwam, David R., 42
Wickersham, Warren G., 296
Wickham, Woodward A., 333
Wicks, Victoria A., 63
Wiebers, David O., 416
Wiederhold, Richard P., 205
Wien, Anita Volz, 682
Wiggenhorn, A. William, 347
Wignall, F. Christian, 844
Wilbert, Herbert S., 135
Wildmon, Donald E., 179
Wiles, Charles I., 422
Wiley, Maya, 530
Wiley, Peter, 523
Wilhelm, Marilyn, 416
Wilk, Peter, 541
Wilke, Harold, 147
Wilkerson, Cynthia, 356
Wilkerson, H. Dean, 201
Wilkerson, Isabel, 608
Wilkes, Brent A., 106, 107
Wilkie Jr., Valleau, 296
Wilkins, Roger, 798
Wilkins, Roger W., 112
Wilkinson, Charles, 483
Wilkinson, Robert, 380
Willard, Richard K., 721
Willhoite, Pam, 209
Williams, Charlie, 132, 636
Williams, Earle C., 605
Williams, Eddie N., 834, 836
Williams, Ella, 310
Williams, Hubert, 227
Williams, Karen Hastie, 112

Williams, Luke G., 53
Williams, Verna, 686
Williams, Walter E., 702, 855
Williams, Walter J., 132
Williams Jr., Bill, 53
Williams Jr., David R., 818
Williamson, R. Glenn, 356
Williamson, Ronald F., 63
Willis, Patricia L., 342
Willner, Peter T., 735
Willrich, Mason, 471
Wilson, Bill, 674
Wilson, Dorothy, 292
Wilson, Edward O., 370, 457
Wilson, Herbert A., 60
Wilson, James Q., 772
Wilson, John H.T., 387
Wilson, Kathy, 663
Wilson, Kirk P., 342
Wilson, Malcolm, 689
Wilson, Robert N., 494
Wilson, Robert W., 387
Wilson, William Julius, 24, 157
Winderbaum, Michael, 730
Wineberg, Don E., 172
Wing, Donna Red, 590
Winkler, Peter, 380
Winks, Robin W., 439
Winograd, Barry N., 730
Winokur Jr., Herbert S., 8
Winsemius, Pieter, 489
Winsor III, Curtin, 60
Winsor Jr., Curtin, 581
Winter, Thomas S., 593
Wirth, Wren W., 387, 866
Wise, Donna W., 385
Wise, Leah, 85
Wise, Warren R., 721
Wiseman, K. William, 416
Withers, Wayne, 721
Witoelar, Erna, 270
Witt, Paul Junger, 387
Witter, William D., 8
Witty, Joanne, 429
Wivell, Martha, 716
Wodder, Rebecca, 355
Woerner, Louise, 508
Wogaman, J. Philip, 746
Wojcik, Kathleen, 649
Wolf, Philip C., 53
Wolf, Rosalie J., 339
Wolf, Stephen M., 776
Womack, Jess, 392
Womack, Richard, 104
Wong, Susan Chong, 81
Woo, Margaret Y.K., 81
Wood, Betty Anderson, 35
Wood, Stephen R., 53
Woodall, Jim, 192
Woodruff, Judy, 860
Woods, Harriet, 663
Woods, Sheryl, 161

Woods, Ward W., 457, 640
Woodson Sr., Robert L., 204, 205
Woodwell, George, 452
Woolsey, R. James, 515
Woolsey, Suzanne H., 632
Work, Charles R., 689
Worley, Kenneth L., 132
Wrenn, Grover, 392
Wright, Patrisha, 104
Wright, Sally, 857
Wright Jr., Joseph R., 35
Wright-Lewis, Carolyn L., 157
Wright-Sirmans, Gail J., 81
Wurster, Charles F., 387
Wurtzel, Alan L., 347
Wyckoff, Peter, 135
Wyer, James I., 689, 702
Wynia, Ann, 621
Wyss, Hansjorg, 483

Yankelovich, Daniel, 625
Yanney, Michael B., 605
Yannucci, Dean A., 605
Yarmolinsky, Adam, 789
Yates, George, 698
Yau, Sam, 347
Yhouse, Paul A., 53
Yochelson, John N., 44
Yokel, Bernard, 432
Yokich, Stephen P., 104, 798
Yost, Larry D., 53
Younan, George, 71
Young, A. Thomas, 632
Young, Andrew, 112, 758
Young, John A., 45
Young, Kenneth, 590
Young, Quentin D., 249
Yzaguirre, Raul, 104, 128, 347

Zacks, Richard, 74
Zambrano, Lorenzo H., 370
Zamora, Nancy, 662
Zamora, Rosie, 333
Zavos, Michele A., 140
Zax, Stanley R., 515
Zeckhauser, Richard, 621
Zedler, Joy B., 457
Zeglis, John D., 776
Zetterberg, Stephen, 716
Zeughauser, Peter D., 110
Zingale, Daniel, 104, 230
Zirkin, Nancy, 682
Zobel de Ayala II, Jaime Augusto, 494
Zogby, James J., 601, 602
Zogby, John, 602
Zorza, Joan, 209
Zuckerman, Ed, 429
Zumwalt Jr., Elmo R., 803
Zurn, Geraldine Day, 168
Zwick, David, 405

# Subject Index

AARP. *See* American Association of Retired Persons (AARP)
AARP Andrus Foundation, 235
ABC Entertainment, 97, 179-181
Abortions, 115-116, 172-173
    anti-abortion groups, 163-165, 195-196
    elections and, 193, 198, 755
    harassment of providers, 143-144, 163-165
    rights, 681-682
Academic Advancement Program, 691-692
Academic Strategic Alliances Program, 453
Accelerated Strategic Computing Initiative, 453
Accountability Act, 629
**Accuracy in Media, Inc., 557-558**
ACLU. *See* American Civil Liberties Union (ACLU)
ACORN. *See* Association of Community Organizations for Reform Now (ACORN)
**Action on Smoking and Health (ASH), 223-225**
ACU. *See* American Conservative Union (ACU)
ADA. *See* Americans for Democratic Action, Inc. (ADA)
*Adarand Constructors Inc. v. Pena*, 699
Adelphi University, 289-290
Adirondack Mountains, 483
*Adventures in Odyssey*, 743
Advertising
    AIDS research, 246
    animal rights, 409-410
    animated characters, 249
    anti-hunger, 287
    anti-regulatory causes, 722
    children and, 570
    civil rights abuses, 76
    Congressional elections, 606
    electronic media use, 567-568
    employment, 42
    environmental records, 479
    Holocaust, 728
    immigration concerns, 527
    insurance, 267
    Internet, 567
    job training program, 196
    manufacturing industries, 53-54
    nonprofits, 342
    nonuse of, 276
    political, 292, 616, 696
    restriction of, 261
    sexual harassment victims, 806-807
    sponsors, 750
    television, 575
    term limits, 674
    tobacco industry, 590-591, 751
Advocacy groups
    Africa, 543-545
    animals, 182-184, 460-463
    Arab Americans, 601-603

Asian Americans, 80-83, 844-845
    auto and highway safety, 226-229
    business, 36-38
    Caribbean areas, 543-545
    children and youth, 87-91
    conservatives, 639-642, 805-808
    consumers, 263-268, 272-276, 298-301, 669-672
    disabled, 146-149
    elderly, 131-133, 134-137, 234-238
    electronic mail, 74
    environment, 363-365, 435-437, 546-548
    families, 150-151
    family planning, 552-554
    First Amendment rights, 574-576, 577-579
    food and nutrition, 254-257, 302-305
    free enterprise, 688-689
    gays and lesbians, 95-98, 99-102, 138-141, 174-176
    government accountability, 669-672
    government participation, 643-646
    gun control, 94
    health care, 254-257, 281-284
    Hispanics, 106-108, 128-130
    historians, 670
    HIV/AIDS, 230-233
    justice, 685-687
    national parks, 438-440
    philanthropy, 780-783
    poverty, 349-351
    public interests, 216-219
    public policy, 30, 589-591
    safety issues, 669-672
    small business, 64
    technology, 559-561
    toxic substance alternatives, 464-466
    women, 150-151, 313-316
    workplace issues, 298-301
**Advocacy Institute, 589-591**
**Advocates for Highway and Auto Safety, 226-229**
Affirmative action, 691-693, 704-705, 790-791
    African Americans, 118-119, 206-207
    attacks on, 105
    media and, 578-579
    policy, 698
AFL-CIO, 501, 606, 633
Africa, 520-521, 543-545, 679, 832
African Growth and Opportunities Act, 544, 679
African Americans
    advancement of, 156-159
    affirmative action, 118-119, 206-207
    African countries and, 679
    birth control, 714
    board members, 130
    church burnings, 759-760
    civil rights, 111-114, 117-120
    college admissions, 112-113
    drug searches, 75

education, 157-158, 836-837
    harassment on the job, 113-114
    home mortgage loans, 187
    Jewish groups and, 732
    as managers, 316
    mayors, 678-679
    mistreatment by police officers, 119-120
    politics, 834-837
    poverty, 862
    public policy, 834-837
    SAT scores, 718
    socioeconomic status, 834-837
    spiritual rally, 144
    Tuskegee Study, 714
    UCLA, 691-692
    wages, 799
Agriculture
    commodities, 312
    conflict resolution, 426
    farm animals, 398-399
    New England, 485
    pesticide use, 435-437
    soybean, 402
    subsidies, 395
Agriculture Department, 287, 462
Aid to Families with Dependent Children, 90, 102
AIDS. *See* HIV/AIDS
**AIDS Action Council, 230-233**
AIPAC. *See* American Israel Public Affairs Committee (AIPAC)
Air pollution, 29, 54, 388, 471-472, 489, 541, 866
Air transportation, 71, 453
Alabama, 410
Alameda County, California, 253
Alaska, 367-368
Alaskan Natives, 126-127
Albany, New York, 479
Alberta, Canada, 18
Alcoa Corporation, 633
Alcohol industry, 621-622
Alexandria, Virginia, 645
**Alexis de Tocqueville Institution, 767-769**
Alley Cat Allies, 375
**Alliance for Justice, 685-687**
AlliedSignal Inc., 8
American Academy of Pediatrics, 249
American Airlines, 130
**American Association of Retired Persons (AARP), 98, 234-238, 501, 625-626, 638, 660**
American Bankers Association, 268
American Bar Association, 638, 660
**American Business Conference, 3-5**
American Business Information Inc., Omaha, Nebraska, 271
American Cancer Society, 233, 294, 783, 824
American Center for Law and Justice, 696, 709
**American Civil Liberties Union (ACLU), 71, 72-76, 78, 168, 692, 709**

American Conservative Union (ACU), 592-594
American Council for Capital Formation, 6-9
American Council on Science and Health, 239-242
American Defense Institute, 512
American Enterprise Institute for Public Policy Research, 90, 207, 642, 770-773, 786, 787
American Express, 268
American Family Association, 179-181, 743
American Forest & Paper Association, 459
American Foundation for AIDS Research (AmFAR), 243-246
American Friends Service Committee, 759
American Heart Association, 132
American Home Products Corporation, 590
American Indians, 112, 126-127, 448-449
American Israel Public Affairs Committee (AIPAC), 238, 499-502, 727
American Jewish Congress, 729-732
American Kennel Club, 184
American Legislative Exchange Council, 595-597
American Medical Association, 294, 750
American Policy Center, 196
American Psychological Association, 184
American Public Health Association, 247-250
American Rivers, 355-358
American Society for the Prevention of Cruelty to Animals (ASPCA), 182-184
American Stop Smoking Intervention Study (ASSIST), 782-783
American-Arab Anti-Discrimination Committee, 69-71
Americans for Democratic Action, Inc. (ADA), 598-600
Americans with Disabilities Act, 717-718
Americans for Tax Reform, 10-12, 219
Americans United for Separation of Church and State, 77-79, 763
Amnesty International USA, 503-506
AMR Corporation, 130
Anacostia River, 478-479
Anheuser-Busch Company, 90, 249
Animal Kingdom, 416
*Animal Times*, 461-462
Animals
  abuse of, 398-399, 414-417, 418-420, 460-463
  cats, 375
  cloning, 401
  disease, 255-256
  emergency treatment of, 416
  ethical treatment of, 460-463
  hormones, 401
  laboratory, 420, 462
  lobbies for, 407-410
  mad cow disease, 255-256, 303-305
  preservation of, 456-459
  product testing on, 419-420, 462
  protection of, 407-410, 414-417
  research, 420, 460-463
  rights of, 182-184, 418-420
  species loss, 458-459
  *See also* marine resources; wildlife
Annapolis, Maryland, 713-714
Anti-Defamation League, 603, 732, 733-737
Antitrust law, 717
Appalachian Mountains, 368
Arab American Institute, 601-603
Arab Americans, 69-71, 121-122, 601-603

Archer Daniels Midland Company, 621
Armed forces. *See* military
Arms control, 542
Arms sales, 510, 538
Army Department, 113-114
Arthritis Foundation, 233
ASH. *See* Action on Smoking and Health (ASH)
Ashland, Wisconsin, 101
Asia
  economic crisis, 3-5, 15, 63, 533, 535-536, 606
  United States and, 810
Asian American Legal Defense and Education Fund, 80-83
Asian Americans, 80-83, 316, 844-845
ASPCA. *See* American Society for the Prevention of Cruelty to Animals (ASPCA)
Association of Community Organizations for Reform Now (ACORN), 185-187
Association of Trial Lawyers of America, 238, 501
AT&T Corporation, 90, 311
Atlanta, Georgia, 190, 713
The Atlantic Council of the United States, 507-508
Atlantic Legal Foundation, Inc., 688-689
*Atlantic Monthly*, 762
Australia, 560-561
Automobile industry, 144-145, 273-274, 319
Automobiles
  air bags, 252
  design defects, 253
  drunk drivers, 201-203, 228
  emissions, 397
  fuel efficiency, 252, 396-397
  insurance, 273
  no car tax, 649
  red-light cameras, 228-229
  safety, 226-229, 251-253, 274-275, 670, 671
  salvage vehicles, 266
  speciality plates, 708
Awards
  Achievement Against the Odds, 205
  Achievement Award (NCOA), 135
  Akiba Award, 726
  American Liberties Medallion, 726
  America's Best Managed Cities, 677
  City Livability Awards Program, 677
  Civil Commitment Award (NCOA), 135
  Community Human Relations Award, 726
  Community Policing Award, 657
  Community Service Award (NCOA), 135
  Corporate Conscience Award, 329
  Courage to Care Award, 734
  Cultural Diversity Award, 658
  Distinguished Achievement Award (NCOA), 135
  Distinguished Service Award, 726
  Distinguished Statesman Award, 734
  Eagle Awards, 195
  FDR International Disability Award, 147
  Fulltime Homemaker Award, 195
  Guardian of Federalism, 636
  Guardian of Small Business Award, 56
  Herbert H. Lehman Human Relations Award, 726
  Howland Award, 658
  Hubert H. Humphrey Civil Rights Award, 103
  Hubert H. Humphrey First Amendment Freedoms Prize, 734

Ingersoll Prizes, 857
Innovation Award, 658
Institute of Human Relations Award, 726
John M. Olin Prize, 20
Joseph Awards, 205
Joseph Prize for Human Rights, 734
Justice In Action Award, 83
Klinghoffer Award, 734
Learned Hand Award, 726
Loop Strange Bedfellows Award, 512
Mass Media Award, 726
Michael A. diNunzio Award, 677
National Conservation Achievement Award, 447
National Distinguished Leadership Award, 726
National Recycling Award, 677
Prevention of Impaired Driving Awards Program, 677
Richard M. Weaver Award for Scholarly Letters, 857
Trial Lawyer of the Year Award, 716
T.S. Eliot Award for Creative Writing, 857

Baja Peninsula, 452-453
Baltimore, Maryland, 364-365, 506, 554, 679
*Baltimore Sun*, 609
Bangladesh, 312, 382
BankAmerica Corp., 718
Bankruptcy, 268
Banks and banking. *See* financial services
Baseball teams, 839-840
Ben & Jerry's Homemade Inc., 311
Bethlehem Steel Corporation, 8
Bettendorf, Iowa, 172-173
Better Business Bureau, Children's Advertising Review Unit, 570
Bible, 168, 181
Bigotry, 84-86, 725-728, 736
Biodiversity, 370, 391, 392, 487-488, 493
  protection of, 431-434
  restoration of, 387, 388
  threats to, 379-383
Biological weapons, 551
Biotechnology, 240, 270, 271, 400-403, 426
BIPAC. *See* Business-Industry Political Action Committee (BIPAC)
Bipartisan Commission on Entitlement and Tax Reform, 516
Birds, 375, 431-434
Birth control, 165, 171-172, 417, 554, 714
Birth Control Federation of America, 714
Blackfoot River, 357
Block grants, 90-91, 196
*Bloomberg Personal*, 772
Blue Cross and Blue Shield Association, 284
Boeing Company, 512
Bolivia, 372
Bond market, 659
Bosnia, 530
Boss Models Worldwide, 462
Boston, Massachusetts, 622-623
Boy Scouts of America, 74, 101
Boycotts and protests
  animal abuse, 419-420
  death penalty, 506
  disabled persons, 148-149
  environmental issues, 480
  gene-altered soybeans, 402
  hotel industries, 120
  immigration reform, 527

logging, 412
Mitsubishi, 144-145, 468-469
oil industries, 412-413
personal care products, 462
redwood forests, 377-378
tobacco industry, 345
tourism, 409-410
U.S. policy in Iraq, 538-539
Walt Disney, 180-181, 743
Boys and Girls Clubs of America, 736
Brazil, 371, 495
Brent Spar oil platform, 412-413
Bristol-Myers Squibb, 371
British Petroleum PLC, 413
Bronx, New York, 790
**The Brookings Institution, 774-779**, 787
Brooklyn, New York, 692
Brown University, 717
Budget
   balanced, 8, 9, 25, 60, 624-626
   deficits, 624-626
   process, 34-36
   programs funding, 422-423
   tax reductions and, 597
Bulgaria, 531
Bureau of Land Management, U.S., 422-423, 483
Burma, 828-829
Business
   CEOs compensation, 829
   civil rights and, 144-145, 720-722
   Congress and, 65
   consumers and, 278-280
   education and, 347-348
   environmental issues, 40, 309-312, 320-321
   ethics and, 317-319
   executive compensation, 290
   government contracts, 65
   investments, 519-520
   loans, 709
   lobbies, 64, 65, 606
   management, 278-280
   marketing via electronic media, 566-567
   minority-owned, 144-145
   policies, 13-15, 19-21, 36-38
   profits, 4-5
   public policy, 55-57
   Republican Party and, 65
   state incentives, 637
   subsidies, 218-219
   takeovers, 511-512
   tax issues, 60
   trade issues, 606
   welfare-to-work, 348
   women-owned, 313-316
   *See also* corporations; small businesses;
      workplace issues
**The Business Roundtable, 13-15**, 64, 654
**Business for Social Responsibility, 309-312**
**Business-Industry Political Action
   Committee (BIPAC), 604-606**

C-SPAN, 579
Cablevision Systems Corporation, 578
California
   affirmative action, 119, 790
   college admissions, 112-113
   hairstyle salon regulations, 692-693
   landfills, 439-440
   spending, 403
   state revenues, 650

taxes, 649
   wages, 57
Campaign for America, 622
Campaign to End the Death Penalty, 506
Canada, 494-495
Candidate Forums, 65
**Capital Research Center, 780-783**
Capital Research and Management
   Company, 280
Capitalism, 599
Caribbean area, 543-545
Carnegie Endowment for International
   Peace, 803
**Catalyst, 313-316**
Catholic Church, 79, 180-181, 709, 752-755
Catholic League for Religious and Civil
   Rights, 709, 743
**Cato Institute, 784-787**
CED. *See* Committee for Economic
   Development (CED)
**Center for Auto Safety, 251-253**, 671
**Center on Budget and Policy Priorities,
   22-25**, 33, 90
**Center for Business Ethics, 317-319**
**Center for Community Change, 188-190**
**Center for Defense Information, 509-512**
**Center for Democracy and Technology, 559-
   561**
**Center for Democratic Renewal, 84-86**
**Center for Health, Environment, and
   Justice, 363-365**
Center Lane Skins, New York, 713
**Center for Marine Conservation, 359-362**
**Center for Media Education, 565-568**
**Center for Media and Public Affairs, 562-564**
**Center for National Independence in
   Politics, 667-668**
**Center for National Policy, 788-791**
**Center for the New West, 16-18**
**Center for Policy Alternatives, 792-795**
**Center for Public Integrity, 607-610**
**Center for Responsive Politics, 611-614**
Center for Science in the Public Interest, 15,
   254-257
**Center for Strategic and International
   Studies (CSIS), 513-517**
Center for the Study of American Business,
   19-21
**Center for Study of Responsive Law, 258-
   259**
**Center to Prevent Handgun Violence, 92-94**
Centers for Disease Control and Prevention,
   232, 245
CERES. *See* Coalition for Environmentally
   Responsible Economies (CERES)
Chambers of commerce, 61-65
Charitable Giving Relief Act, 342
Charities and charitable societies, 136
   disclosures of, 781-783
   electronic media and, 565-568
   IRS audits, 696
   promotion of, 295-297, 331-334, 340-343
   *See also* nonprofit organizations;
      philanthropy
Chattahoochee River, 357
Chemical weapons, 551
Chesapeake Bay, 375, 453
Chicago, Illinois, 42
*Chicago Tribune*, 609
Child Care and Development Block Grant, 90
Child Safety Protection Act, 218

Children and youth
   abortion rights, 116
   abused, 208-210, 714
   African-American, 157-158
   air bags, 252
   calcium supplements, 454
   child labor, 301, 311, 314
   coalitions, 208-210
   costs of, 162
   crime, 204-207
   custody issues, 102
   day care, 48, 49, 88, 90, 826
   drownings, 261
   education, 157-158
   electronic media, 565-568, 570-571
   food and nutrition, 285-287
   gangs, 206
   health care, 89, 240, 248, 282, 291-294, 437,
      541, 554, 654
   homeless, 124
   hunting, 409, 424
   lobbies, 87-91
   marketing to via electronic media, 566-567
   privacy of, 567
   quality of life, 553-554
   reading lists, 844
   rights of, 531
   safety of, 570-571
   school choices, 861
   scouting, 74, 101, 633
   substance abuse, 204-207
   tax credit for, 8-9, 32-33
   teen pregnancy, 171
   television programs, 563
   tobacco use, 234, 249-250, 291-294, 344-345,
      824
   toy risks, 218
   TV programs, 566-567, 575
   violence against, 88
   *See also* families
**Children's Defense Fund, 87-91**
China
   emissions, 489
   human rights violations, 198
   Internet, 571
   religious freedom, 803
   trade, 594
   United States and, 521, 777, 803
Choice Hotels International Inc., 119, 120
**Christian Coalition, 168-169, 192, 738-740**,
   743, 746
Christianity, 820-821, 856-858
*Chronicle of Higher Education*, 691-692
*Chronicles*, 858
Chrysler Corporation, 228
Church of Christ, 756-760
Church and state, 77-79, 730-731, 763
Cincinnati, Ohio, 693
Cirrus Systems Inc., 217-218
Cisco, 526
Citizens Against Government Waste, 12, 641
**Citizens' Research Foundation, 615-617**
**Citizens for a Sound Economy, 26-30**, 54,
   406, 641, 812
**Citizens for Tax Justice, 31-33**
Citizenship, 81, 526
*City Journal*, 840
Civil rights
   abuses, 711-714
   African Americans, 111-114, 117-120,
      718-719

Alaskan Natives, 126-127
American Indians, 126-127
Arab Americans, 601-603
business and, 144-145
discrimination, 69-71, 82, 95-98, 111-114,
    117-120, 128-130, 144-145, 161-162, 528-
    531, 680, 704-705, 736-737
electronic media and, 559-561, 569-571
gays and lesbians, 74, 95-98, 99-102, 105,
    138-141, 174-176
Hispanics, 109-110, 128-130
HIV/AIDS infected, 99-102
Jewish groups, 733-737
law enforcement, 104
legal representation, 690-693
litigation use in, 715-719
lobbies for, 95-98
preservation of, 853-855
promotion of, 103-105, 109-110, 590-600,
    720-722, 767-769, 784-787, 856-858
protection of, 69-71
students, 74-75
Clayoquot Sound, 412
Clean Virginia Waterways, 362
Clean Water Act, 453
Cleveland, Ohio, 677
**Co-op America, 278-280**
Coalition on the Environment, 758
**Coalition for Environmentally Responsible
    Economies (CERES), 320-321**
Coalition for Smarter Growth, 478
Coalition for Voluntary Prayer, 168
Coalition for Working Families PAC, 199
Coalitions
    African Americans, 157-158
    animal rights, 182-184
    budget deficits, 624-626
    children, 208-210
    civil rights, 103-105
    communities, 185-187, 188-190, 657-660
    consumer groups, 274
    electronic mail, 74
    environment, 29, 406
    families, 197-200, 738-740, 741-744
    food and medicine legislation, 64
    homeless, 123-125
    justice access, 685-687
    moral issues, 761-763
    religious groups, 191-193, 745-747
    reproductive health, 173
    women, 208-210
Coast Alliance, 361
Coastal Barriers Resources System, 361
Coca-Cola Company, 311
Colleges. *See* universities and colleges
Colombia, 372
Colorado, 101, 169
Columbia River, 357, 758
Columbia, South Carolina, 86
Columbia/HCA Healthcare Corporation, 345
Commerce Department, 42, 484, 535, 561, 832
**Committee for Economic Development
    (CED), 322-324**
**Committee for a Responsible Federal
    Budget, 34-36**
**Common Cause, 618-623**
Communities
    coalitions, 185-187, 188-190, 657-660
    empowerment of, 211-213
    environmental hazards and, 363-365
    federal policy and, 676-680

lobbies, 211-213
philanthropy in, 349-351
promotion of, 403
public policy, 685-687
Community for Creative Non-Violence, 125
Competition
    electric industries, 28, 29
    Internet browsers, 773
    product testing, 277
    promotion of, 50-54, 770-773
    telephone industry, 267
**Competitive Enterprise Institute, 36-38**, 393
Comprehensive Test Ban Treaty, 547-548
**Concerned Women for America, 191-193**
**Concord Coalition, 624-626**
Concrete Works of Colorado, Inc., 698
**The Conference Board, Inc., 39-43**
Conference of State Chief Justices, 638, 660
Conflict resolution, 425-427, 537-539
Congress
    abortion rights, 116
    African Americans, 679
    ambassador nominations, 641, 762-763
    ATM charges, 218
    auto damage, 266
    balanced budget, 8, 9
    bankruptcy laws, 268
    business and, 65
    campaign finance issues, 611-614, 619-622
    candidates policies, 604-606
    costs, 629
    disclosure requirements, 782
    dolphin protection, 382-383
    domestic violence, 209
    drunk driving standards, 203
    entitlements, 654
    environmental issues, 393, 428-430
    ethics, 612
    family issues, 739-740
    gay and lesbian rights, 97
    government procurement, 828
    highway legislation, 654-655, 656
    IMF funding, 15, 63-64
    Internet tax, 653, 654
    Israel support, 501-502
    job training programs, 195-196
    judicial vacancies, 686-687
    management practices, 627-630
    marine resources, 361
    pay phones, 267
    regulatory reform, 654
    religious freedom, 763
    school choice and, 861
    Social Security privatization, 773
    staff, 628-630
    staffers who become lobbyists, 613
    tax issues, 8, 53-54, 57, 218, 516
    tax-exempt groups, 296
    telecommunications, 275
    term limits, 673-675
    tobacco industry, 225, 250, 293-294, 671-
        672, 819
    trade, 606
    transportation issues, 228
    TV coverage of, 564
    voting records, 56, 429-430, 593, 606
    welfare reform, 862-863
    *See also* government; state government
Congress of National Black Churches, 157-
    158
Congressional Budget Office, 24

**Congressional Management Foundation,
    627-630**
Connecticut, 89, 246, 453, 530
Conservation easements, 443
**The Conservation Fund, 366-368**
**Conservation International, 369-372**
Conservatism, 592-594, 639-642, 694-696,
    805-808
Conservative Communications Center, 582
Conservative News Service, 581
Constitution, United States.
    Bill of Rights, 72-76
    First Amendment rights, 75, 559-561, 569-
        576, 599, 616
    free speech, 164-165
    privacy rights, 74-76, 155, 559-561, 569-571,
        572-573, 599
    religious freedom, 77-79, 166-169, 735, 736,
        763, 803
**Consumer Alert, 260-262**, 582
**Consumer Federation of America, 262-268**,
    274, 275
*Consumer Reports*, 267, 273, 274-275
Consumerism
    advocates for, 263-268, 272-276, 298-301
    auto industry, 252
    bankruptcy, 268
    debt, 266
    education, 260-262
    FDA and, 232-233
    food industry, 271, 302-305
    food labeling, 255
    health care, 282-284, 298-301, 649-650
    international, 269-271
    Internet, 300-301, 773
    lobbies for, 216-219
    needs of, 258-259
    personal data, 270-271
    product testing, 277
    public policy, 260-262, 269-271
    research, 216-219
    rights of, 669-672
    safety issues, 298-301
    water rights, 389
**Consumers International, 269-271**
**Consumers Union of United States, Inc.,**
    266-268, **272-276**
Consumption, 4-5, 471-472
Contract With the American Family, 169
Controlled Substances Act, 754
Conventional weapons, 511
Cooperative Compliance Program, 64
Copyright infringements, 511
Corporations
    accountability of, 344-345
    boards, 130, 316
    campaign donations, 15, 90, 851-852
    CEOs compensation, 829
    communications, 40-41
    community development, 790
    contribution disclosures, 781-783
    environmental issues, 328-330
    ethics and, 317-319
    governance, 318, 831-833
    investments, 325-327
    philanthropy, 42, 331-334
    practices, 40-41
    research, 830-833
    shareholders and, 750, 830-833
    Silver Sewer Award, 640-641
    socially responsible, 748-751

societal issues, 328-330
taxation, 8, 57
women executives, 315
**Council on Competitiveness, 44-46**
**Council on Economic Priorities, 328-330**
**Council for Excellence in Government, 631-634**
**Council on Foreign Relations, 518-521**
**Council on Foundations, 331-334**
**Council of Institutional Investors, 325-327**
Council for Jews with Special Needs Inc., 148
**Council of State Governments, 635-638**, 660
Court of Appeals, United States, 64, 65
Crime and criminals
anti-gay, 140-141
church burnings, 759-760
domestic violence, 208-210
drunk drivers, 201-203, 228
explosives use, 155
handguns, 92-94
hate crimes, 118, 140-141, 712-714
organized, 516
Russia networks, 516
television and, 564, 582
CSIS. *See* Center for Strategic and International Studies (CSIS)
Cuba, 759
Cultural diversity, 844
Cybercasting, 64
Cypress Semiconductor, 526

Dade County, Florida, 74-75
Dairy industry, 303-305
Dallas Area Rapid Transit, 246
**DataCenter, 522-523**
Davenport, Iowa, 172-173
Death penalty, 506
**Defenders of Wildlife, 373-375**, 383, 447-448
Defense. *See* military-defense
Defense Department, 174-176, 665
Democratic National Committee, 617
Democratic Party
campaign finance issues, 614, 617, 621, 645-646
donations to, 15
elderly and, 237
governorships, 655
gun lobby and, 155
IMF funding, 64
Israeli support, 501-502
religious issues, 79
tax policies, 33
the West and, 18
women and, 262
Denmark, 560-561
Denver, Colorado, 693
Deregulation, electric utilities, 28, 812
Digital Partnerships Program, 43
Digital technology, public policy, 849-852
Direct Marketing Association, 74
Disabled persons, 146-149, 236
Discovery Channel, 633
Discrimination. *See* civil rights-discrimination
Disney Network Television, 97
District of Columbia
Anacostia River, 378-379
grants to, 333
gross product, 679-680
medical malpractice, 671
poverty, 862

quality of life, 554
school breakfast program, 286-287
school prayer, 168
District Court, United States, 143-144
Domestic policies, moral issues and, 801-804
Donors Forum of Chicago, 342
Drug abuse. *See* substance abuse
Drug Enforcement Administration, 754

**Eagle Forum,** 192, **194-196**, 512
Earth Day, 440
**Earth First! Journal, 376-378**
**Earth Island Institute, 379-383**
Earth Justice Legal Defense Fund, 434
Eastern Shore, Maryland, 375, 443
Economic growth, 3-5, 50-54, 604-605
Economic issues
Africa, 520-521, 543-545
African Americans, 158-159
analysis of, 532-536
Asian crisis, 3-5, 15, 63, 533, 535-536, 606
cities, 677
citizen participation in, 827-829
Congressional candidates, 604-606
decentralization of, 856-858
elderly, 237
employee benefits, 790
forecasts, 4-5
free enterprise, 36-38, 39-43, 604-606, 697-699, 700-705, 720-722, 784-787, 809-812, 842-845
global warming and, 471-472
globalization, 20, 44-46
Hispanics, 130
immigration, 768-769, 861
index of leading indicators, 42
industries and, 485
inflation, 4-5, 54, 778-779, 798-800
international, 518-520, 532-536
Japan economy, 776-777
metropolitan areas, 679-680
pension plans, 325-327
private enterprise, 19-21
promotion of, 522-523, 767-769, 796-800
property rights, 697-699
protectionism, 815
public attitude toward, 799-800
public policy on, 13-15, 26-30, 322-324, 589-591, 595-597
research, 770-773, 822-824
retirement, 772
savings rates, 324
social problems and, 204-207
sports teams, 777-778
states, 635-638
technology effects and, 400-403
the West, 16-18
women, 160-162
**Economic Policy Institute, 796-800**
Ecosystems, preservation of, 359-362, 456-459, 476-480
Edinburg College, 108
Education
ADA, 717-718
affirmative action, 790-791
African Americans, 157-158, 836-837
AIDS, 232
business ethics, 317-319
children, 157-158
conservative issues, 592-594
consumers, 260-262, 263-268

curriculum, 166-169, 844
discrimination, 111-114
diversity in, 790-791
electronic media, 566
English-only legislation, 104
environmental issues, 379-383, 390-393, 470-472, 476-480
ethics, 335-336
families and, 825-826
financing, 650
first aid treatment of animals, 416
freedom of, 167
gay and lesbian rights, 102
Hispanics, 108
homeless, 123-125
immigrants, 768-769
integration, 836-837
Internet services, 274
job training programs, 195-196
leaders, 507-508
military, 516-517
moral values, 191-193
New Testament, 168
North Carolina, 113
parental rights in, 168-169
pesticide use, 435-437
public housing residents, 861
public schools, 730-731
public service, 722
racial gaps, 119
reform, 640, 641-642
Regents tests, 186-187
religious, 730-731
school breakfast program, 286-287
school prayer, 168, 708
sex, 171
societal issues and, 825-826
state aid, 637
state standards, 655
student spending, 841
taxation, 9, 32, 33
teacher-to-child ratio, 49
textbooks, 181
toxic substances, 464-466
training, 44-46
victims' rights, 711-714
vouchers, 78, 692, 730-731, 836-837
workplace issues, 346-348
*See also* universities and colleges
Education Department, gay and lesbian rights, 101
El Paso, Texas, 768-769
Elderly
advocates for, 131-133, 234-238
elder care, 48
financial services for, 190
lobbies, 234-238, 625-626
promotion of, 134-137
Elections
abortion issue, 198
anti-gay ballot measures, 101
campaign contributions, 15, 98, 343, 430, 500, 594, 606, 611-614, 672, 851-852
campaign finance issues, 216-219, 282, 619-622, 645, 755, 807
candidate information, 667-668
candidate policies, 604-606
environmental issues, 439, 479
influence of church in, 79
legal issues, 606
moral values and, 192

pro-choice candidates, 681-682
reform, 615-617
role of money in, 615-617
term limits, 673-675
voter guides, 740
Electric industries, 28, 406, 454, 455, 812
Electronic Freedom of Information Act, 665
**Electronic Frontier Foundation, 569-571**
Electronic mail, 74, 670-671
Electronic media, 565-568, 665-666, 736
    privacy rights of, 559-561, 569-571, 572-573
    *See also* media
**Electronic Privacy Information Center,
572-573**
Emissions control, 388, 397, 454-455, 471-472,
489, 548
Employment
    advertising, 42
    Africa, 832
    benefits, 790
    broadcast media, 578-579
    child labor, 301, 311, 314
    conditions of, 691-692
    Congress, 628-630
    discrimination, 96-97, 111-114
    equal opportunity, 113
    export-related, 535
    gays and lesbians, 97, 138-141
    growth in, 4-5
    harassment, 113, 737
    Hispanics, 130
    immigrants, 130, 769
    job training programs, 195-196
    jobs creation, 3-5
    labor force, 47-49, 54
    legal issues involved in, 840
    Mexico, 751
    minimum wage, 799
    minorities, 578-579
    school-to-work, 347
    service jobs, 485
    telecommunications industry, 18
    unemployment, 4, 799
    welfare-to-work, 48, 348, 402
    women, 142-145, 150-151, 161-162, 313-316,
    629
Employment Non-Discrimination Act
(ENDA), 97
**Empower America, 639-642**
Endangered species, 297
    awareness of, 495-496
    black caiman, 494-496
    marine ecosystems, 359-362
    preservation of, 373-375
    protection of, 492-496
    sea turtles, 381, 382
    wolves, 373-375, 433-434
Endangered Species Act, 374-375, 434,
447-448
Energy consumption, 471-472
Energy Department, 453, 548
Energy Information Administration, 28
England, 255-256, 560-561
English, as official language, 104, 214-214
**Environmental Defense Fund, 383, 386-389**
**Environmental and Energy Study Institute,
384-385**
Environmental issues, 242
    advocates for, 363-365, 435-437, 546-548
    biodegradable products, 413
    business and, 40

conflict resolution, 426
Congress and, 428-430
consumers and, 278-280
contaminated sites, 392-393
Earth Day, 440
emissions control, 388, 397, 454-455,
    471-472, 489, 548
exterminators, 466
global warming, 27, 397, 471-472, 490-491
hazardous wastes, 363-365
historic, 441-445
housing and, 448
immigration, 478
impact statements, 478-479
international, 369-372, 492-496
landfills, 439-440
marine resources, 359-362
population and, 552-554
promotion of, 309-312, 320-321, 328-330,
    703-705, 842-845, 846-848, 864-866
protection of, 376-378, 390-393, 404-406,
    411-413, 428-430, 431-434, 441-445,
    446-449, 456-459
public policy and, 6-7, 37, 390-393, 394-397,
    486-491, 492-496
quality of, 404-406, 470-472
religion and, 758
research, 216-219, 822-824
resource management, 486-491
rivers protection, 355-358
safety, 669-672
Superfund, 392
sustainable development, 384-385
technology effects on, 400-403
threats to, 379-383
tropical forests, 371-372, 467-469
vehicles, 251-253
*See also* natural resources, conservation of;
    pollution
**Environmental Law Institute, 390-393**
Environmental Protection Agency (EPA)
    air pollution, 54
    clean-up efforts, 768
    electric utilities, 454-455
    endangered rivers, 356-357
    pesticides, 396, 435-437
    reform, 720-722
    regulations, 27-28
    wood preservatives, 437
**Environmental Working Group, 394-397**
Episcopal Church, 345
Ethics
    analysis of, 607-610
    Congress, 612
    environment and, 481-485
    fundraising and, 850-851
    government influence, 609
    greenhouse gases and, 490-491
    hunting, 423-424
    Medicare fraud, 345
    promotion of, 179-181, 317-319, 335-336,
    701
    societal, 309-312
    technology effects on, 400-403
    *See also* moral issues
**Ethics and Public Policy Center, 801-804**
**Ethics Resource Center, 335-336**
Eugene, Oregon, 709
Europe, auto designs, 253
European Union, 402, 828-829
Evangelical Environmental Network, 758

Exportadora de Sal S.A., 452-453
Exxon Corporation, 90

FAA. *See* Federal Aviation Administration
(FAA)
FAIR. *See* Fairness & Accuracy in Reporting
(FAIR); Federation for American
Immigration Reform (FAIR)
Fair Labor Standards Act, 629
Fairfax County, Virginia, 154, 181
**Fairness & Accuracy in Reporting (FAIR),
574-576**
Families
    charitable contributions, 343
    coalitions, 185-587, 197-200, 738-740,
    741-744
    dissolution of, 204-207
    dual-careers, 314-315
    electronic media and, 565-568
    family planning, 554
    government services, 25
    income, 162, 536
    lobbies, 197-200
    moral values, 197-200
    net worth, 24
    parental rights, 168-169
    promotion of, 856-858
    public policy, 47-49, 194-196, 595-597
    relationships in, 144
    research, 825-826
    social programs, 204-207
    taxation, 25, 31-33
    TV and, 583
    values in, 191-193
    women and, 150-151, 161-162
    workplace issues, 150-151
**Families USA Foundation, 281-284**
**Families and Work Institute, 47-49**
Family and Medical Leave Act, 162
Family planning, 171-172
**Family Research Council, 197-200**
Fannie Mae, 311, 608
**Farm Animal Reform Movement (FARM),
398-399**
FDR Memorial Commission, 148-149
Federal Aviation Administration (FAA),
antiterrorism, 71
Federal Communications Commission
(FCC), 266
    cable-subscriptions, 267-268, 275
    digital signals, 579
    Internet in schools, 274
    minority hiring, 578-579, 665
Federal Elections Commission (FEC), 97, 292,
501, 613
Federal Emergency Management Agency, 759
Federal Energy Regulatory Commission
(FERC), 358
Federal Housing Administration (FHA), 213
Federal Reserve, 778-779, 798
Federal Trade Commission (FTC),
unsolicited electronic mail, 74
**Federation for American Immigration
Reform (FAIR), 524-527**
Fidelity Investments, 280, 334
Financial services
    ATMs, 217-218
    campaign finance issues, 621
    consumers and, 264-265
    credit and credit cards, 212-213, 218, 264-
    266, 268, 413, 621

lending practices, 189-190, 212-213, 218
mortgage loans, 187, 212-213, 680, 718
*See also* investments
Fire Island National Seashore, 417
Firearms, 92-94
   domestic abuse and, 209-210
   hunting and, 409
   ownership rights, 152-155
First Chicago NBD, 213
Fiscal policy, 34-36
Fish and fisheries, 357-358
   dolphins, 382-383
   sports person's bill of rights, 410
   tuna, 382-383
   *See also* marine resources
Fish and Wildlife Service, United States, 361,
   378, 495
Flagstar Companies, 82
Flight attendants, 671
Florida
   Animal Kingdom, 416
   business development, 637
   marine resources, 361
   retirement fund, 833
   tobacco industry, 250, 833
**Focus on the Family,** 192, **741-744**
Food and Drug Administration (FDA), 277
   calcium supplements, 454
   food labeling, 255
   mad cow disease, 303-304
   olestra, 256
   reform, 232-233, 721-722, 851-852
   RU-486, 165
Food and nutrition, 240-241, 259
   advocacy groups, 254-257, 302-305
   beef industry, 303-305
   calcium supplements, 454
   children, 88, 285-287
   conflict resolution, 426
   farm animals and, 398-399
   food-borne illnesses, 255-256, 275, 303-305
   genetic engineering and, 271, 400-403
   grain harvests, 866
   hunger and, 285-287
   meatless Fridays, 755
   olestra, 256
   organic, 401, 437
   pesticide use and, 435-437
   public policy, 285-287, 302-305
   research, 285-287, 302-305
   safety, 395-396
   school breakfast program, 286-287
   vegetarianism, 408
**Food Research and Action Center,**
   **285-287**
Food stamp program, 654
*Forbes* magazine, 610
Ford Foundation, 43, 633
Ford Motor Company, 90, 253
*Foreign Affairs,* 776
Foreign relations
   Africa, 543-545
   Arab groups, 121-122
   Caribbean, 543-545
   Christian morals and, 801-804
   improvement of, 774-779
   Iraq, 538-539
   Israel, 499-502
   Middle East, 121-122, 549-551, 601-603
   sanctions, 54, 361, 535, 545, 759
   states' voice in, 829

UN debt, 790
understanding of, 518-521
United States, 507-508
Forest Service, United States, 378, 484
Forests and forestry
   conservation of, 495
   logging, 412, 459, 484
   protection of, 377-378, 459, 468-469, 481-485
   rain forests, 371-372, 467-469, 493, 495
   redwood, 377-378
Fort Lauderdale, Florida, 396
Fort Worth, Texas, 246
*Fortune* magazine, 132, 237
**The Foundation Center, 337-339**
**Foundation on Economic Trends, 400-403**
Foundations, 331-334, 337-339
Fourth Freedom Forum, 538-539
Fox News Channel, 807
France, 560-561
**Free Congress Foundation,** 512, **805-808**
Free enterprise, 700-702
   defense of, 703-705
   improvement of, 39-43
   principles of, 36-38, 720-722, 784-787,
      809-812, 842-845
   rights of, 697-699
   support for, 604-606
Free Willy Keiko Foundation, 381
Freedom of Information Act, 665
Fremont, California, 769
**Friends of the Earth,** 219, **404-406**, 812
Frontier mining towns, 444-445
FTC. *See* Federal Trade Commission (FTC)
**The Fund for Animals, 407-410**

Gambling, 740, 744
GAO. *See* General Accounting Office (GAO)
Garment industry, 81-82, 301
Gauer Distinguished Lecture in Law and
   Public Policy, 702
Gay and lesbian rights
   abuses of, 713
   boy scouts ban, 74
   civil rights, 138-141, 174-176
   health insurance, 165
   human rights, 506
   lobbies, 95-98
   media and, 181, 583
   military issues, 174-176
   support of, 762-763
Gay Men's Health Crisis, 233
General Accounting Office (GAO), 516
General Electric, 357
General Motors Corporation, 253, 311, 319,
   511-512, 751
Genetic engineering, 271, 400-403
Germany, 402, 506, 560-561, 727
Gettysburg National Military Park, 440,
   443-444
Gillette Company, 462
Girl Scouts of America, 633
*Glamour,* 262, 582
Global Business White Papers, 41
Global Environmental Facility, 371
Global warming, 27, 397, 471-472, 490-491
Globalization, 228, 486-491
*Good Housekeeping,* 633
Governance
   conservative, 805-808
   corporations, 831
   District of Columbia, 671

Government
   accountability, 58-60, 607-610, 618-623,
      669-672
   agencies information collection, 665-666
   aid to parochial schools, 79
   citizen control of, 673-675
   citizen participation in, 643-646
   city relationship to, 676-680
   confidence in, 631-634
   conservative issues, 694-696
   contracts, 65, 699
   data on officials, 667-668
   effectiveness of, 774-779, 788-791
   English as official language, 214-215
   fiscally sound, 703-705
   improvement of, 618-623, 859-863
   information access, 664-666
   Internet regulations, 75
   interns, 144, 695-696
   leadership, 631-634
   limited, 36-38, 688-689, 700-702, 770-773,
      784-787, 809-812, 842-845, 846-848,
      853-855
   management, 631-634
   news reporting of, 557-558
   participation in, 664-666
   privatization of services, 351
   procurement, 828
   public perception of, 631-634
   public policies and, 838-841
   reform, 216-219
   sex scandal, 695-696, 707-710
   spending, 22-25, 58-60, 597
   term limits, 673-675
   women in, 661-663
   *See also* Congress; local government; state
      government
Gramm-Rudman-Hollings law, 60
Grants, 331-334, 489
Great Falls, Maryland, 440
Great Plains Economy, 18
Great Universal Stores PLC, Great Britain, 271
Green Pastures, 275
Greenhouse gases, 388, 490-491, 548, 866
Greenpeace International, 474, 866
**Greenpeace USA,** 383, **411-413**
Greenwich YWCA, Connecticut, 530
Guarantee Trust Life Insurance Company, 232
Gun control, 92-94, 154-155, 735
Guyana, 371

Habitat for Humanity, 448
**Handgun Control, Inc./Center to Prevent
   Handgun Violence, 92-94,** 132
Harvard University, John F. Kennedy School
   of Government, 633
Hate groups and crimes, 118, 140-141, 734-735
   anti-Semitism, 736-737
   church burnings, 759-760
   electronic communications, 736
   victims' rights, 711-714
Hattiesburg, Mississippi, 718
Hazardous wastes, 363-365
Head Start, 90
Headwaters Forest, 377, 378
Health care, 793
   advocacy groups, 254-257, 281-284
   air pollution, 472
   assisted suicide, 754
   birth defects, 490
   cancer, 234, 240-241, 357

caregivers, 136-137
children and youth, 89, 240, 248, 282, 291-294, 437, 541, 554, 654
conflict resolution, 426
costs, 136-137, 245-246
elderly, 134-137, 236
environmental risks, 364-365
families, 150-151
food issues, 301-305
food-borne illnesses, 275
forest plant medicines, 371
gays and lesbians, 165, 181
gender equity, 172
HIV/AIDS, 102, 231-233, 245-246, 249
homeless, 123-125
humanitarian aid and, 758
impotency drug, 172, 652-654
insurance, 89, 165, 790
long-term care, 136-137
malpractice, 671
managed care plans, 282-283, 649-650
patient protection, 282-283
pesticide use and, 436
prescription drugs, 136, 245-246
public health, 239-242, 247-250, 275
racial gaps, 119
reform, 248
small businesses, 14-15
TV coverage of, 564
women, 794
*See also* reproductive health; smoking; substance abuse
Health and Human Services Department, 794
Help Endangered Animals-Ridley Turtles, 381
Help Wanted Advertising Index, 42
Hempstead High School, New York, 186-187
**The Heritage Foundation,** 12, 406, 576, 641-642, 696, 787, **809-812**
Hewlett-Packard Company, 560-561
Hialeah, Florida, 769
Hidalgo County, Texas, 108
Hilton Hotels Corporation, 120, 326-327
Hispanics
advocates for, 106-108, 128-130
civil rights, 109-110
college admissions, 112-113
contract awards, 699
discrimination, 128-130
education, 836-837
employment, 82
home-mortgage loans, 187
human rights violations, 505
as managers, 316
poverty, 862
UCLA, 691-692
wages, 799
Historic preservation, 148-149, 440, 441-445
HIV/AIDS, 99-102, 230-233, 243-246, 249
Home Depot, 311
Home Mortgage Disclosure Act, 187
Homelessness, 123-125
Homosexuals. *See* gay and lesbian rights
**Hoover Institution on War, Revolution and Peace, 813-816**
Hotel industry, racial discrimination in, 119-120
Household Bank, 413
Housing
animals and, 184
community development and, 790
discrimination in, 111-114, 680
energy efficient, 448
gays and lesbians, 138-141

homeless, 123-125
homeownership, 189-190, 212-213
insurance, 718
Mexico, 751
mortgage loans, 187, 212-213, 680, 718
new homes, 42
public housing, 678-679
school choice and, 861
Housing and Urban Development Department, 759
Houston, Texas, 79
**Hudson Institute, 817-821**
Hudson River, 356-357, 479
Hughes Electronics Corporation, 511-512
Human cloning, 401
Human rights
gays and lesbians, 506
promotion of, 309-312, 522-523, 803
protection of, 505-508, 528-531, 706-710
**Human Rights Campaign, 95-98**
Human Rights Concerns in the Border Region with Mexico, 505
Human rights violations, 198, 503-506, 528-531, 545
**Human Rights Watch,** 506, **528-531**
**Humane Society of the United States,** 381, **414-417**
Humanitarian aid, 758
Humphrey-Hawkins Act, 778
Hunting and fishing, 408-410
birds, 433
future of, 423-424
game management, 495-496
illegal, 423
safety, 409, 423
Huntingdon Life Sciences, East Millstone, New Jersey, 462
Hydroelectric dams, 358

Idaho, 378, 758
Illinois Facilities Fund, 342
IMF. *See* International Monetary Fund (IMF)
Immigration, 105
Asian, 844
economic impact of, 769, 861
education, 768-769
employment and, 819
Hispanics, 505
law, 687
natural resources and, 478
New York, 861
policies, 819
reform, 524-527
welfare cuts, 287
Immigration and Naturalization Service, 81
**In Defense of Animals, 418-420**
Income
Congressional staff, 629
families, 162
gaps in, 24
increase in, 4-5
trends in, 536
**The Independent Institute, 822-824**
**Independent Sector, 340-343**
India
children's rights, 531
economy, 535
homosexuality, 506
nuclear testing, 510, 520, 535, 547-548
Indianapolis, Indiana, 693
Individual rights, promotion of, 842-845
Indonesia, 382, 535
industrial development, 50-54

**INFACT, 344-345**
Information services, 522-523*
Information superhighway, 566
**Institute for American Values, 825-826**
**Institute for International Economics, 532-536**
**Institute for Justice, 690-693**
**Institute for Policy Studies, 827-829**
*Intelligence Review,* 410
**The Interfaith Alliance, 745-747**
**Interfaith Center on Corporate Responsibility, 748-751**
Internal Revenue Service (IRS)
AMT, 33
audits, 79, 633, 696, 850
political activity and, 79
tax-exempt organizations, 10, 79
International Association of Machinists and Aerospace Workers, 238
International Business Machines Corporation, 560-561, 633
International Communications Association, 266
International Criminal Court, 530
International Forum, 63
International Fund for Animal Welfare, 452
International Labor Organization, 311-312
International Monetary Fund (IMF), 15, 63-64, 535, 606
International Whaling Commission, 474-475
Internet
access bans, 75
advertising on, 567
attitudes toward, 571
browsers, 773
educational use, 274
fraud on, 300-301
free speech and privacy, 559-561, 569-571, 572-573
markets, 773
as news clearinghouse, 582
olestra, 257
pollution offenders, 388
public services and, 851
small businesses and, 64
symbol of, 46
tax on, 653, 654, 659
Internet Fraud Watch, 300-301
Internet Tax Freedom Act, 659
InterTribal Bison Cooperative, 448-449
Intuit Inc., 136
Investment Company of America, 280
Investments
in Africa, 520-521, 679-680, 832
business, 519-520
consumers and, 279-280
corporations, 325-327
electric industries, 406
pension plans, 325-327
retirement and, 811-812, 833
shareholders and, 830-833
Social Security, 515-516
socially-responsible, 329-330, 748-751, 754
in South Korea, 519
tobacco industry, 345
*See also* mutual funds; Social Security
**Investor Responsibility Research Center, 830-833**
IOLTA, 637-638, 660, 721
Iowa City, Iowa, 173
Iraq, 538-539, 550, 758, 777, 790
Ireland, 531

IRS. *See* Internal Revenue Service (IRS)
Isolationism, 858
Israel, 499-502, 551
  birthday celebration, 727
  Germany and, 727
  Palestine and, 731
  security of, 726
  United States and, 603
ITT Corporation, 326-327
**Izaak Walton League of America (IWLA), 421-424**

Jamaica, 531
Japan, 776-777
JCPenney Leadership Institute on School Improvement, 348
Jersey City, New Jersey, 769
**The Jewish Committee, 725-728**
Jewish groups
  African Americans and, 732
  anti-Semitism, 725-728, 734-736, 820
  defamation of, 733-737
  history, 735
  holiday celebrations, 803-804
  Holocaust, 728, 736, 820
  security of, 725-728, 733-737
  survival of, 729-732
  views of, 727
Jewish Life, 758
Job Training Partnership Act, 196
Johnson's List, 511
Johnston County, North Carolina, 113
**Joint Center for Political and Economic Studies, 834-837**
Joshua Tree National Park, 439-440
Judiciary, 686, 694-696, 700-702
Justice, administration of, 111-114, 118-119, 685-687, 700-702
Justice Department, 268, 603, 638, 660, 665, 773

Kaiser Family Foundation, 564
Kaiser Foundation Health Plan of Texas Inc., 284
Kansas, 18
Kansas City, Missouri, 237
Keiko, 381
Kennebec River, 358
Kern River, 357
**The Keystone Center Science and Public Policy Program, 425-427**
KPMG Peat Marwick LLP, 49, 840
Ku Klux Klan, 713-714
Kyoto Protocol, 14, 27, 37, 388, 389

Laguna San Ignacio, Mexico, 452-453
**Lambda Legal Defense and Education Fund, Inc., 99-102**
Land mine ban, 505
Land Trust Alliance, 443
Land use, 366-368, 440, 443-444, 483
**Landmark Legal Foundation, 694-696**
Latinos. *See* Hispanics
Laura and Sarah Sportswear, 82
Law enforcement, 209-210, 235
Leadership
  agenda for, 44-46
  development, 792-795
  government, 631-634
  United States, 507-508
  women, 794-795
**Leadership Conference on Civil Rights, Inc., 103-105**

**League of Conservation Voters, 428-430**
**League of United Latin American Citizens (LULAC), 106-108**
**The League of Women Voters of the United States,** 132, **643-646**
Legal Aid Society, Atlanta, Georgia, 190
Legal issues
  advance refunding, 659
  affirmative action, 697-699, 704-705
  antitrust, 268
  auto safety, 226-229
  campaign financing, 292-293, 755
  class action suits, 716, 718-719
  copyright infringements, 511
  elderly, 236
  electronic media, 570-571, 665-666
  employment, 840
  environment, 386-389, 390-393
  free enterprise, 697-699
  free speech, 691-692
  highway safety, 226-229
  immigration, 687
  interest on trust accounts, 637-638, 660, 721
  international court, 530
  land mines, 508
  lawsuit costs, 707-708
  managed care, 650
  marine resources, 473-475
  medical malpractice, 671
  negotiated contracts, 597
  political advertising, 616
  product liability, 65, 94
  property ownership, 697-699
  protests, 413
  racketeering, 143-144, 164
  representation, 690-693
  research, 822-824
  scientific evidence, 688-689
  second-hand smoke, 671
  tobacco settlement, 249-250, 590-591, 671-672, 819
  tort law, 65, 715-719
  universities and collges, 717-718
  victims' rights, 711-714
  Windows monopoly, 773
  wolves reintroduction, 374-375, 433-434, 447-448
Lesbian and Gay Rights Project, 101
Lesbians. *See* gay and lesbian rights
Liberalism, 767-769
Libya, 551
Life and Family Coalition, 173
Livable Wage Campaign, 57
Livable World Education Fund, 512
Lobbies
  alcoholic beverages, 622
  animals, 407-410
  antitrust, 640
  balanced budget, 624-626
  business, 64-65
  campaign finance issues, 611-614, 618-623, 643-646
  children and youth, 87-91
  churches, 79
  civil rights, 95-98
  communities, 211-213
  Congressional staff and, 613
  conservative issues, 592-594
  consumers, 216-219
  elderly, 132, 234-238, 625-626
  environment, 54, 216-219
  families, 197-200
  firearms, 152-155

gays and lesbians, 95-98
governors, 652-656
marine resources, 359-362
nuclear safety, 548
pro-Israel, 499-502
product liability, 65
religious groups, 179-181
rivers protection, 355-358
small businesses, 8, 9, 55-57
tax issues, 8, 10-12
tobacco industry, 293, 613
Local government, 657-660, 660
  candidate campaign signs, 645
  federal policy and, 677
  term limits, 673-675
Lockheed Corporation, 512
Long Island, New York, 432, 458, 578
Los Angeles, California, 844
Lotus Development Corporation, 311
LULAC. *See* League of United Latin American Citizens (LULAC)

MacArthur Foundation, 609
MacMillan Bloedel Ltd., Vancouver, 412
MADD. *See* Mothers Against Drunk Driving (MADD)
Magic Kingdom, 165
Maine, 484-485
**Manhattan Institute for Policy Research, 838-841**
Manufacturing industries, 50-54
March for Parks, 440
Marine resources, 359-362
  protection of, 473-475
  sharks, 454
  whales, 452-453, 474-475
Marital status
  extra-marital affairs, 144-145
  gays and lesbians, 102
  *See also* sexual harassment
Marriage, 826, 844
Marriott International Inc., 119, 120, 311
Marshals, United States, 82
Martha's Vineyard, Massachusetts, 458
Maryland
  bird watching, 433
  children's health care, 89
  gross product, 679-680
  Internet use, 851
  Motor Vehicles Department, 708
  State Police, 75
  tax revenues, 659
  tobacco industry, 833
Massachusetts, 828-829
Massachusetts Institute of Technology, 46
MasterCard International, 268
Mayors, 676-680
Media
  accuracy of, 557-558, 574-576
  affirmative action and, 578-579
  analysis of, 562-564
  Arab Americans and, 601-603
  Christian conservatives, 743
  *Consumer Reports* and, 273, 274-276
  content, 563-564
  digital TV, 579
  elderly as focus, 235
  employment practices, 578-579
  ethics in, 179-181
  First Amendment rights and, 577-579
  gays and lesbians, 181, 583
  gun control campaign, 154
  politics and, 580-583

quality of, 565-568
violence in, 584-585
whalers, 475
*See also* electronic media; television
**Media Access Project, 577-579**
**Media Research Center,** 262, **580-583**
Mediation, 425-427
Medicaid, 89-91, 137, 624-626, 653-654
Medical care. *See* health care
Medicare, 282, 345, 624-626
MetLife Insurance, 267
Metromail Corporation, Lombard, Illinois, 270-271
**Mexican American Legal Defense and Educational Fund, 109-110,** 687
Mexican Americans. *See* Hispanics
Mexico, 452-453, 505, 641, 751
Miami, Florida, 74-75, 396, 768-769
Microsoft, 597, 773
Microtrace Inc., 155
Middle East, 121-122, 501-502, 550-551, 601-603, 727, 730
Midsize businesses, health care, 14-15
Migratory Bird Project, 375
Military
  contractors, 511-512
  defense, 509-512, 809-812, 827-829
  education, 516-517
  gays and lesbians, 100-102, 138-141
  homosexuality, 174-176
  substance abuse, 203
Milwaukee, Wisconsin, 78, 164, 730
Mine Reclamation Corporation, 439-440
Minorities
  affirmative action, 705
  business owners, 144-145
  contract awards, 699
  discrimination against, 117-120
  employment, 578-579
  military education, 517
  mortgage loans, 680
  *See also specific minority group*
Mississippi Animal Rescue League, 419
Mitsubishi Corporation, 144-145, 452-453, 468-469
Mobil Corporation, 8, 372
Models, anti-fur policy, 462
*Modernizing Government Regulations,* 324
Monsanto Company, 311
Montana, 409-410, 448-449, 758
Montgomery County, Maryland, 119, 347
Moral issues, 191-193
  coalitions, 761-763
  domestic policies and, 801-804
  foreign policy and, 801-804
  promotion of, 809-812, 856-858
  sex scandal, 144, 145, 161, 695-696, 707-710
  *See also* ethics; religion
**Mothers Against Drunk Driving (MADD), 201-203**
**Mountain States Legal Foundation, 697-699**
MSL Sportswear, 82
Municipal government, 658, 659, 677
Music industry, tobacco industry and, 591
Muslims, 71
Mutual funds, 24, 280, 334, 754, 772

NAACP. *See* National Association for the Advancement of Colored People (NAACP)
**NAACP Legal Defense and Educational Fund, Inc., 111-114**

Nation of Islam, 732
**National Abortion and Reproductive Rights Action League, 115-116**
**National Alliance of Business, 346-348**
National Archives and Records Administration, 670-671
**National Association for the Advancement of Colored People (NAACP),** 78, **117-120,** 159
**National Association of Arab Americans (NAAA), Inc., 121-122**
National Association of Child Advocates, 90
National Association of Counties, 660
**National Association of Manufacturers, 50-54,** 64, 759
**National Audubon Society, 431-434,** 454
National Broadcasting Corporation (NBC), 180, 196
National Cancer Institute, 234, 782-783
National Cattlemen's Beef Association, 304
**National Center for Neighborhood Enterprise, 204-207**
**National Center for Nonprofit Boards, 288-290**
National Center for Public Policy Research, 806-807
**National Center for Tobacco-Free Kids, 291-294**
**National Charities Information Bureau, 295-297**
National Children's Island Inc., 478-479
**National Coalition Against Domestic Violence, 208-210**
**National Coalition Against the Misuse of Pesticides, 435-437**
**National Coalition for the Homeless, 123-125**
**National Coalition on Television Violence, 584-585**
National Commission on Restructuring the IRS, 11
National Commission on Retirement Policy, 515
**National Committee for Responsive Philanthropy,** 343, **349-351**
National Conference of Black Mayors, 679
**National Conference of Catholic Bishops/United States Catholic Conference, 752-755**
**National Conference of State Legislatures, 647-651**
**National Congress of American Indians, 126-127**
**National Consumers League, 298-301**
**The National Council on the Aging, 134-137**
National Council of Churches, 148
**National Council of the Churches of Christ in the U.S.A., 756-760**
**National Council of La Raza, 128-130**
**National Council of Senior Citizens (NCSC), 131-133**
**National Federation of Independent Business, 55-57,** 238, 501
**National Gay and Lesbian Task Force, 138-141**
**National Governors' Association, 652-656,** 659
National Green Pages, 279
National Hemophilia Foundation, 233
National Highway Traffic Safety Administration, 228, 252-253, 261
National Institute on Aging, 136

National Institute of Child Health and Development, 49
National Institutes of Health, 371
**National League of Cities,** 638, **657-660**
**National Legal Center for the Public Interest, 700-702**
National Main Street Center, 444
**National Organization on Disability, 146-149**
**National Organization for Women (NOW), 142-145**
National Park Service, 362, 417, 479
National parks
  protection of, 438-440, 479
  *See also names of individual parks;* National Park Service
**National Parks and Conservation Association, 438-440,** 443
**National Partnership for Women and Families, 150-151**
**National People's Action (NPA), 211-213**
National Religious Partnership for the Environment, 758
National Retail Federation, 266
*National Review,* 527
**National Rifle Association,** 12, **152-155,** 594, 696
National Right to Life Committee, 755
National Safety Council, 203
National Science Foundation, 665
National security. *See* foreign relations; military-defense
National Security Agency, 573
National Study of the Changing Workforce, 49
**National Taxpayers Union, 58-60,** 219
**National Training and Information Center (NTIC)/National People's Action (NPA), 211-213**
**National Trust for Historic Preservation,** 440, **441-445**
**National Urban League, 156-159**
**National Wildlife Federation,** 374-375, **446-449**
National Women's Law Center, 687
**National Women's Political Caucus, 662-664**
Nationalism, 858
Nationality, 525-526
NATO. *See* North Atlantic Treaty Organization (NATO)
Natural resources, conservation of
  allocation issues, 846-848
  future of, 864-866
  global management, 486-491
  marine resources, 359-362
  measures to, 366-368
  national parks, 438-440
  preservation of, 450-455
  protection of, 369-372, 373-375, 421-424, 476-480
  research, 470-472
  use of, 470-472
**Natural Resources Defense Council (NRDC),** 29, **450-455**
**The Nature Conservancy, 456-459**
NCSC. *See* National Council of Senior Citizens (NCSC)
Near East, 549-551
Nebraska, 18
Netscape Navigator, 773
Nevada, 705
Nevada City, Montana, 444

*New England Journal of Medicine,* 542
New Hampshire, 484-485
New Jersey
  election law, 616
  endangered species, 297
  HIV/AIDS, 245-246
  Medicaid, 89
  taxes, 840
New Orleans, Louisiana, 679
New Woman All Women, 713
New York
  citizenship drive, 81
  contaminated site cleanup, 393
  deer, 409, 417
  hate groups, 712-713
  HIV/AIDS, 246
  immigrants, 861
  Internet access, 75
  race relations, 82
  Regents, 186-187, 289-290
  taxes, 840
  tobacco industry, 833
New York City
  broadcast coverage, 578
  condition of, 641
  disability award, 148
  education, 768-769
  Housing Authority, 184
  Human Rights Commission, 737
  needle-exchange program, 246
  pro-Asian clubs, 844
*New York Times,* 76, 693
Newark, New Jersey, 553, 677
Newport, California, 381
Nez Perce National Forest, 378
Nigeria, 506
Nike, 311
**9to5, National Association of Working Women, 160-162**
Nobel Peace Prize, 542
Nonprofit organizations
  effectiveness of, 288-290
  tax returns, 12
  *See also* charities and charitable societies;
    philanthropy
North Atlantic Treaty Organization (NATO), 511, 512, 790
North Carolina, 113
North Carolina Right to Life Inc., 594
North Dakota, 18, 29
Northeast Utilities, 548
Northern Forest, 484-485
Northwest Airlines, 261
Norway, Coast Guard, 474
NOW. *See* National Organization for Women (NOW)
NPA. *See* National People's Action (NPA)
Nuclear testing, 535, 542, 547-548
Nuclear weapons, 451, 453, 510-511, 516, 520, 538
  control of, 547-548
  elimination of, 540-542
  inspections in Iraq, 550-551
  proliferation of, 551
  safety risks, 547-548
Nutrition. *See* food and nutrition
*Nutrition Action Healthletter,* 255

Occupational Safety and Health
  Administration, 64
Ocean Wildlife Campaign, 454

Of The People, 169
Ohio, 368
Oil industries, 372, 412-413
Okefenokee National Wildlife Refuge, 480
**OMB Watch, 664-666**
**Operation Rescue National, 163-165**
Operation Understanding, 732
Oregon, 649, 758

**Pacific Legal Foundation, 703-705**
Pacific Lumber Company, 377, 378
**Pacific Research Institute for Public Policy, 842-845**
PACs. *See* political action committees (PACs)
Padre Island National Seashore, 381
Pakistan, 510, 520, 547-548
Palestine, 501, 551, 731
Paralyzed Veterans of America, 148
Parental Choice Program, 730
Partnership for Trust in Government, 633
Patagonia, 311
Patients' Coalition, 233
Peace, 522-523, 784-787, 813-816
**Peace Action, 537-539**
**People for the American Way, 166-169**
**People for the Ethical Treatment of Animals (PETA), 460-463**
Perdue, 275
Peru, 372
**Pesticide Action Network (PANNA) North America Regional Center, 464-466**
Pesticides. *See* toxic substances-pesticides
Pet Food Institute, 184
Pew Charitable Trusts, 136-137
Pharmaceutical industry, 270
Philanthropy
  communities, 349-351
  promotion of, 295-297, 331-333
  research, 780-783
  responsiveness of, 349-351
  technology companies, 42
  *See also* charities and charitable societies
Philip Morris, 280, 783, 851
Philippine Islands, 382
**Physicians for Social Responsibility, 540-542**
Piedmont Environmental Council, 478
PIRG. *See* United States Public Interest Research Group
**Planned Parenthood Federation of America, Inc., 170-173**
Planned Parenthood of Houston, 164
Pluralism, 725-728, 734-735, 834-837
Plus, 217-218
Pocomoke River, 358
Police officers
  domestic abuse and, 209-210
  Germany, 506
  mistreatment by, 119-120, 506
Policy Insiders, 63
Political action committees (PACs)
  business-industry, 604-606
  conservative, 594
  contributions to, 97, 613
  families, 199
  firearms, 152-155
  gays and lesbians, 97
  pro-Israel, 501
  tobacco industry, 672
**Political Economy Research Center, 846-848**
Political freedom, 528-531

Politics
  advertising, 616
  African Americans, 834-837
  campaign-finance issues, 611-614
  candidate information, 667-668
  church and state, 79
  citizen participation in, 827-829
  conservative issues, 593-594
  decentralization in, 856-858
  equality in, 767-769
  family issues, 739-740
  government bashing, 633
  influence peddling, 608-609
  IRS audits, 696
  media and, 580-583
  news analysis of, 562-564
  party donations, 609
  role of money in, 615-617
  tobacco industry influence, 851
  the West, 16-18
  women and, 262, 661-663
  women's magazines and, 582
Pollution
  air, 29, 54, 388, 471-472, 489, 541, 866
  electric utilities, 454-455
  water, 357-358, 360, 388-389, 453
  website notification, 388, 479
Population
  control, 524-527, 552-554
  food issues, 866
  high density, 478
  New England, 484-485
  *See also* immigration
Pornography, 180
Potomac River, 362
Poverty, 186
  advocacy for, 349-351
  African Americans, 862
  children, 86-89
  Hispanics, 128-130, 862
  homeless and, 125
  war on, 25
Presidents, 192, 695-696
  candidates, 600, 642, 656
  sex scandal, 144, 145, 161, 695-696, 707-710, 806-807
Prince George's County, Maryland, 659
Prince William County, Virginia, Internet ban, 75
Prisons and prisoners, 403, 503-506
Privacy Act of 1974, 666
Privacy, right of. *See* Constitution, United States-privacy rights
Private enterprise system, 19-21
Private property, 721, 846-848, 853-855
Privatization, 349-351, 773, 786, 842-845, 853-855
Pro-Life Action League, 164
Procter & Gamble Company, 256-257, 419-420
Prodigy Inc., 571
Product liability, 65, 94
Product testing, 419-420
Productivity, 5, 54
**Progress & Freedom Foundation, 849-852**
**Project Vote Smart/Center for National Independence in Politics, 667-668**
Property rights, 697-699, 700-702, 703-705
Protectionism, 815
Protests. *See* boycotts and protests
Providence, Rhode Island, 677
Public Broadcasting Service, 566-567

**Public Citizen, Inc.,** 217, 219, 252-253, 266, 405, **669-672**, 812
Public interest law, 685-687, 690-693, 715-719, 720-722
Public policy
  advancement of, 788-791
  African Americans and, 834-837
  analysis of, 22-26
  businesses and, 55-57
  citizen participation in, 643-646
  communities and, 685-687
  conflict resolution, 425-527
  conservative, 639-642, 809-812
  consumers, 260-262, 263-268, 269-271
  development of, 595-597, 838-841
  digital technology, 849-852
  economic issues, 13-15, 26-30, 322-324, 589-591, 595-597
  environment, 6-7, 390-393, 394-397, 486-491, 492-496
  families and, 47-49, 194-196, 595-597
  food issues, 285-287, 302-305
  formation of, 513-517
  HIV/AIDS, 243-246
  impact of, 22-26
  philanthropy, 331-334
  promotion of, 3-5
  public interest groups and, 780-783
  quality of, 774-779
  reproductive rights, 170-173
  research, 322-324, 770-773, 834-837
  restructure of, 6-7
  social issues, 589-591
  success of, 817-821
  sustainable development, 384-385
  tobacco industries, 291-294
  understanding of, 785-787
  urban areas, 676-680
**Public Voice for Food and Health Policy, 302-305**
Publishing industry, 599

Quality of life, 421-422, 553-554, 657-660
Queens, New York, 692
Quicken, 136

Race relations, 712-714
  advancement of, 84-86
  African Americans, 75, 86, 111-114, 117-120
  Arab Americans, 69-71, 601-603
  Asian Americans, 80-83
  church burnings, 759-760
  Hispanics, 82, 691-692
  improvement of, 117-120, 731-732, 844-845
  public housing, 679
Racism, UCLA, 691-692
Racketeering law, 143-144, 164
Radio broadcasts, 479, 743
Rain forests, 371-372, 467-469, 493, 495
Rainbow/PUSH Coalition, 144-145
**Rainforest Action Network, 467-469**
Rapid City, South Dakota, 449
Raytheon Company, 511-512
**Reason Foundation, 853-855**
Red Cross, 416
*Redbook*, 262, 582
Redford, Texas, 505
Refugees, 545
Regulatory issues
  anti-regulatory causes, 722

  candidate campaign signs, 645
  challenges to, 688-689
  compliance, 21
  costs of, 10-12, 38
  critics of, 768
  encryption, 561, 573
  environment, 393, 486-491
  hairstyle salons, 692-693
  highways, 226-229
  Internet, 75-76
  public interest in, 703-705
  reform, 29, 50-54, 322-324, 851-852, 853-855
  restructure of, 6-7
  rules proposals, 654
Religion
  accessibility of congregations, 147-148
  biotechnology and, 401
  church burnings, 759-760
  churches and society, 756-760
  corporations and, 750
  environment and, 758
  freedom of, 166-169
  gays and lesbians, 762
  lobbies for, 179-181
  school prayer, 168, 708
  society and, 745-747
  television programs and, 180
  textbooks, 181
  traditional values in, 741-744
  TV coverage, 582
  *See also* Christian Coalition; Jewish groups
Religious Freedom Restoration Act, 763
Religious liberty. *See* Constitution, United States-religious freedom
Religious schools, 78, 730-731
Reproductive health
  abortion clinics, 143-144
  anti-abortion groups, 163-165
  bombings of abortion clinics, 713
  hospital deliveries, 284
  male births, 489-490
  managed care plans, 640-650
  pro-choice, 6811-682
  protection of, 115-116
  provision of, 170-173
Reptiles, 495-496
Republican Leadership Council, 199
Republican National Coalition for Life, 196
Republican National Committee, 641
Republican Party
  abortion issue, 196
  business and, 65
  campaign finance issues, 292, 594, 614, 621, 645-646, 807
  conservative Christians, 762
  donations to, 15
  elderly and, 237
  endorsements, 65
  environmental issues, 430
  governorships, 656
  gun lobby and, 155
  Israeli support, 503-504
  moral values issue, 192-193
  National Convention, 1992, 164
  politics and, 79
  religious issues, 79
  tax policies, 8-9, 33, 53-54
  women and, 262
**Resources for the Future, 470-472**
Restaurant industry, 82
Reston, Virginia, 478

Retirement, 9, 515, 772, 811-812
Richard King Mellon Foundation, 368
Rivers, 355-358, 362, 456-459
R.J. Reynolds Tobacco, 722, 851
Rock Island, Illinois, 172-173
**The Rockford Institute, 856-858**
Rocky Junior, 275
Rocky Mountains, 374-375, 447-448
Romania, 506
Roth IRA, 649
Royal Dutch/Shell Group, 412-413
Rural areas, 459, 483-485
Russia, 511, 542
**Rutherford Institute, 706-710**

Safe Playgrounds Initiative, 570
Safety
  airlines, 71
  airwaves use, 659-660
  automobiles, 226-229, 251-253, 274-275, 670, 671
  children and Internet, 570-571
  children's toys, 218
  drunk driving, 201-203
  firearms, 152-155
  food, 302-305, 395-396
  highways, 252-253, 396
  hunting, 409, 423
  nuclear plants, 547-548
  products, 669-672
  workplace, 64, 298-301
San Francisco, California, 679, 762, 769, 844
Sanctions, 828
  anti-apartheid, 832
  effectiveness of, 54
  India, 535
  South Africa, 545
Sandplain ecosystem, 458
Sara Lee Corporation, 750
Saskatchewan, Canada, 18
Save the Sound, 453
SBC Communications Inc., 520
Scholastic Assessment Test, 718-719
Science and religion, 181
**Sea Shepherd Conservation Society, 473-475**
Seagram Company, 640-641
Securities and Exchange Commission (SEC), 326, 750, 781-782
Senior citizens. *See* elderly
*Seniority*, 133
**Servicemembers Legal Defense Network, 174-176**
Sexual harassment, 144, 145, 161, 695-696, 707-710, 806-807
Sexual orientation. *See* gay and lesbian rights
Shell Corporation, 372
Shetland Islands, 413
**Sierra Club,** 383, 429, 430, **476-480**
Silver Spring, Maryland, 444
60 Plus Association, 133
Slovakia, 736
Small Business Administration, 119, 665, 709
Small businesses
  biodiversity treaty, 393
  health care, 14-15
  lobbies, 8, 9
  policies, 55-57
  regulation compliance, 21
  *See also* business; economic issues
Smithsonian Institution, 372

Smoking, 223-225, 240-241, 655, 819
  anti-smoking legislation, 590-591
  electronic media and, 567-568
  second-hand smoke, 671
  underage, 234, 249-250, 291-294, 344-345, 824
Social issues, 204-207
  Catholic church and, 752-755
  churches role in, 756-760
  consumers and, 278-280
  corporations, 748-751
  ethics and, 317-319
  morals, 179-181
  news analysis of, 562-564
  philanthropy and, 349-351, 780-783
  promotion of, 13-15, 328-330, 522-523, 598-600
  public policy on, 589-591
  research, 822-824, 825-826
  solutions to, 859-863
Social Security, 236-237
  benefits, 11
  privatization of, 773, 786
  reform, 515, 624-626, 811-812
Socially Responsible Investment Guidelines, 754
South Africa, 545
South Carolina, 368
South Dakota, economy, 18
South Korea, 519, 535
Southern Baptist Convention, 180-181, 743
Southern Methodist University, 108
**Southern Poverty Law Center, 711-714**
Southern Regional Council, 119
Southwest Regional Civil Rights Conference, 186
Special interest groups
  campaign-finance issues, 609, 611-614
  contribution disclosures, 781-782
  environment, 430
  governors, 652-656
  most powerful, 501
  political advertising, 616
  tax policies, 8, 9
Sport-utility vehicles, 229, 275
Sports, 777-778
Sri Lanka, 382
Standard of living, 3-5, 44-46, 50-54
Starbucks Coffee Company, 311
State Department, 382, 633
State government
  budgets, 651
  data on officials, 667-668
  entitlements, 90
  governors, 652-656
  legislatures, 647-651
  mayors, 768-769
  negotiated contracts, 597
  parks, 847-848
  policies, 22-25, 652-656
  promotion of, 635-638
  revenue surpluses, 650
  taxation, 597
  term limits, 673-675
  tobacco settlement, 655
  welfare spending, 650
Stewart B. McKinney Act, 124
Stock market, 799
  delisting companies, 326
  future of, 772
  nonprofit holdings, 333-334

rise in, 24
  socially responsible investing, 329-330
Stockton, California, 768-769
Stop Corporate Welfare!, 219
Subsidies, 218-219, 621
Substance abuse, 240
  assisted suicide, 754
  beer advertisements, 249
  children and youth, 204-207
  drug testing, 74-74
  drunk drivers, 201-203, 228
  HIV/AIDS, 245-246
  homeless, 124
  needle-exchange program, 102, 199-200, 246
  *See also* smoking
Sudan, 531
Suicide, 754
Sun Microsystems, 526
Superfund, 392
Supreme Court Press Briefing, 702
Supreme Court, United States
  campaign contributions, 500
  church and state, 731
  contract awards, 698-699
  gays and lesbians, 101
  interest on trust accounts, 637-338, 660
  nominations to, 105
Surface Transportation Policy Project, 396-397
Suriname, 371
Syracuse University, 82

Taggants, 155
Taku River, 357
Tax Foundation, 25
Taxation
  alternative minimum tax, 33
  audits, 10, 633, 696
  automobiles, 649
  capital gains, 8, 9, 32
  captive tax, 402-403
  changes in, 649
  charitable contributions, 342
  child tax credit, 8, 9, 32-33
  cigarettes, 824
  corporate, 8, 57
  costs of, 10-12
  cuts, 53-54, 597
  education, 9
  endangered species donations, 297
  estate, 8, 9, 57
  flat tax, 28, 32
  Indian-operated businesses, 127
  inheritance, 33
  Internet, 653, 654, 659
  investments and, 333-334
  IRAs, 9
  laws, 31-33
  local, 659
  payroll, 516
  property, 840-841
  rates of, 25
  reform, 10-12, 23-24
  restructure of, 6-7
  rights of taxpayers, 58-60
  state, 597, 637, 649-650, 840
  tax increment financing, 659
  tax-exempt organizations, 10
Taxpayer Relief Act of 1997, 32
Technology
  campaign finance issues, 614

communication issues, 559-561, 569-571, 572-573
  cryptography, 560-561, 573
  cybercasting, 64
  data-security, 559-560, 573
  effects of, 400-403
  hate groups and, 712-713
  immigrant workers and, 820
  innovations, 44-46
  missiles, 510
  nuclear weapons and, 453
  public policy, 849-852
Technology companies, philanthropy, 42
Telecommunications, 264-265
  access to, 565-568
  cable subscriptions, 267-268, 275
  civil rights issues, 559-561, 569-571, 572-573
  employment in, 18
  Internet in schools, 274
  *See also* electronic mail; Internet
Telecommunications Act, 275
Telekom Malaysia Berhad, 520
Telephone industry, 264-265
  access charges, 274
  acquisitions, 520-521
  pay phones, 267
Television
  airwaves use, 659-660
  analysis of, 563-564
  Arab-American portrayals, 71
  children and, 563
  ethics of, 179-181
  news shows, 64
  programs, 97, 179-181, 566-567, 575, 580-583
  talk shows, 60
  violence on, 584-585
Telkom South Africa, 520
Tenneco Inc., 633
Terrorism, 71, 155, 730
Texas
  affirmative action, 790
  health care, 284
  mortgage lenders, 680
  Superfund, 392
  Supreme Court, 721
  tobacco industry, 833
  water policy, 388
Texas A&M, 108
Texas Shrimp Association, 381
Thailand, 382
Theme parks, 416, 478-479
Think tanks. *See individual organization by name*
Third World, 490-491, 815
3Com, 526
Tiananmen Square, China, 198
Time Warner Cable, 578
Title IX of Education Amendments, 717
Tobacco industry, 597
  advertising, 590-591, 751
  anti-regulatory causes, 722
  anti-tobacco activities, 750, 782-783
  boycotts of, 344-345
  campaign finance issues, 620-621
  cancer suits, 224-225
  children, 291-294
  lobbies, 293, 613
  musicians and, 591
  politics and, 851-852
  settlement, 249-250, 590-591, 655, 671-672, 819

stock divestiture, 832
stock holdings, 280
Tom's of Maine, 311
Tourism, 371, 409-410
 Alaska, 367
 FDR Memorial, 148-149
 historic sites, 440, 441-445
 Keiko, 382
 New England, 485
Toxic substances, 387
 alternatives to, 464-466
 DDT, 494-495
 de-icing, 453
 herbicides, 271, 402
 misuse of, 435-347
 pesticides, 241, 276, 395-396, 435-437, 451,
  464-466, 494
 pollution prevention, 363-365
 protection from, 405
 rivers, 356-357
Trade, 534, 606, 815
 Africa, 679, 832
 China, 594
 deficit, 535-536
 sanctions, 361
**Traditional Values Coalition, 192, 761-763**
**TransAfrica, 543-545**
Transnational corporations, 344-345
Transport Workers Union, 693
Transportation Department, 699
Transportation issues
 black motorists, 75
 cab drivers, 148
 deregulation of private vans, 692, 693
 drunk driving, 201-203
 highway construction, 698-699
 highway safety, 226-229, 396
 speed limits, 229
 spending, 654-655, 656
 traffic fatalities, 203
Treasury Department, 32-33, 334
**Trial Lawyers for Public Justice, 715-719**
Trustees of Reservations, 458
Tuskegee Study, 714
Tyson Corporation, 275

**Union of Concerned Scientists, 546-548**
United Nations
 Fourth World Conference on Women,
  794-795
 Framework Convention on Climate
  Change, 866
 Security Council, 530, 603
 U.S. debt to, 790
 Working Party 29, 228
United Nations Development Program,
 389
United Nations Foundation, 389
United Negro College Fund, 206, 633
United Parcel Service, 148
United States
 Asia and, 810
 children's rights, 531
 China and, 521, 777, 803
 Israel, 603
 Japan and, 776-777
 leadership, 507-508
 Russia and, 511
 UN debt, 790
**United States Catholic Conference, 752-755,**
 758

**United States Conference of Mayors,** 638,
 660, 659, **676-680**
United States Holocaust Museum, 820
**United States Public Interest Research
 Group, 216-219**
United Way, 343, 350
Universal Fellowship of Metropolitan
 Community Churches, 97
Universities and colleges
 ADA, 717-718
 admissions, 112-113, 206
 affirmative action, 691-692
 African Americans, 112-113, 691-692,
  718-719
 athletes, 718-719
 coaches salaries, 717
 freshman-eligibility rules, 717
 Hispanics, 108, 112-113, 691-692
 military education, 516-517
 SAT scores, 718
 scholarships, 351
 sex discrimination, 716-717
University of California, Berkeley, 112-113,
 420, 791
University of California, Los Angeles,
 112-113, 691-693
University of the District of Columbia, 579
University of Nevada, 704
University of Texas, Austin, 108
University of Texas-Pan American, 108
Urban areas, 442, 444, 676-680
Urban Fraud Initiative, 679
**The Urban Institute,** 33, **859-863**
**U.S. Chamber of Commerce,** 61-65, 293,
 759
**U.S. ENGLISH Foundation, Inc., 214-215**
**U.S. Term Limits, 673-675**
Utah Wilderness Coalition, 483
Utilities industries, 437

Vancouver Island, 412
Vanguard Group, 280
Venezuela, 372
Vermont, 484-485
VerSecure technology, 560-561
Viagra, 172, 653-654
Victims' rights, 201-203, 711-714
Violence
 against children, 88
 against homosexuals, 141
 against women, 208-210
 children and youth, 204-207
 domestic, 208-210, 794
 elimination of, 537-539
 handguns, 92-94, 154
 reduction of, 540-542
 television and, 584-585
Virginia
 bird watching, 433
 campaign finance system, 622
 children's health care, 89
 church and state, 79
 concealed weapons, 154
 Environmental Quality Department, 423
 gross product, 679-680
 lease-purchase agreements, 60
 no car tax, 649
 parental rights, 168-169
Virginia City, Montana, 444
Virginia Save Our Streams, 423
Visa USA, 268

Volunteerism, 340-343, 362
Voting rights, 111-114

W. Alton Jones Foundation, 242
Wages, 790
 gap in, 829
 increase in, 798-800
 Mexico, 751
 minimum, 57
 nonpayment of, 82
Wagner Point, Baltimore, Maryland, 364-365
Wal-Mart Corporation, 311
*Wall Street Journal*, 693, 851
Walt Disney Company, 180, 416, 583, 743
Walt Disney World, 165
War, 537-539, 813-816
Washington, D.C. *See* District of Columbia
**The Washington Institute for Near East
 Policy, 549-551**
**Washington Legal Foundation, 720-722**
*Washington Post*, 91, 249, 609
Washington (state), 154, 758
*Washington Times*, 196, 609
Water
 contaminants of, 357-358
 dams and, 358
 endangered rivers, 357-358
 policy, 388
 pollution, 357-358, 360, 388-389, 453, 479
 protection of, 456-459
 quality, 357-358, 423, 451
 resources, 366-368, 385
Wealth, racial gaps in, 119
Weapons industry, 511-512
Welfare, 186
 children, 90-91
 corporate, 218-219
 cuts in, 287
 entitlements, 90
 reform, 23, 105, 862-863
 state spending, 650
 welfare-to-work, 48, 348, 402
Wellington Farms Free Range, 275
the West, 16-18
West Bank, 501
West Point, 176
West Virginia, 679-680
Westchester County, New York, 645
Western Journalism Center, 696
*Whales Forever*, 475
White House
 leadership conferences, 634
 Lincoln bedroom, 609-610
 media coverage, 581
 TV coverage of, 564
White supremacists, 85
Whitney Estate, New York, 483
Wilderness areas
 Alaska, 367-368
 protection of, 376-378, 481-485, 492-496
 South Carolina, 368
**The Wilderness society, 481-485**
Wildlife, 357, 367-368
 bison, 409-410, 448-449
 preservation of, 373-375, 446-449, 481-485
 protection of, 414-417, 431-434, 456-459,
  492-496
 wolves, 374-375, 433-434, 447-448
 *See also* marine resources
Williamsburg, Virginia, 445
Wilmington, Delaware, 164

Windsor Village Methodist Church, Houston, Texas, 79
Winter Olympics, Nagano, 777
Wisconsin
  anti-gay harassment, 101
  entitlements, 90
  school vouchers, 78
  Supreme Court, 730
Women
  abused, 208-210, 714
  advocates for, 313-316
  athletes, 717
  birth control, 714
  business owners, 144-145
  coalitions, 208-210
  Congressional employment, 629
  contract awards, 698
  discrimination against, 161-162
  economic issues and, 160-162
  employment, 142-145, 150-151, 161-162, 313-316, 629
  empowerment of, 313-316, 794-795
  health care, 794
  Hispanic, 130
  HIV/AIDS, 232, 245-246
  human rights violations, 530
  magazines, 262
  military education, 517
  moral values and, 193
  political content of magazines, 582
  politics and, 262, 661-663

  pro-choice, 681-682
  rights of, 142-145, 171-172, 795
  role of, 144
  sexual harassment of, 144, 145, 161, 695-696, 707-710, 806-807
  UN conference, 794-795
  voting behavior, 794
  wages, 798
  *See also* reproductive health
**Women's Campaign Fund, 681-682**
Women's Legal Defense Fund. *See* National Partnership for Women and Families
*Women's Rights Are Human Rights*, 795
*Women's Voices*, 794
Workforce Investment Partnership Act, 196
*Working Woman*, 262, 582
Workplace issues, 329
  advocates for, 298-301
  African Americans, 120
  child care, 48, 49
  conditions, 311-312
  Congress, 629-630
  consensual sex, 144, 145
  elder care, 48
  ethics, 335-336
  families and, 47-49, 150-151
  frivolous lawsuits, 65
  gays and lesbians, 95-98
  geriatric caregivers, 135-137
  giving programs, 343
  HIV-positive workers, 102

  international, 311-312
  nonpayment of wages, 82
  safety, 64, 298-301, 547-548
  skills enhancement, 346-348
  spouse-relocation, 315
  striking workers, 65
  sweatshops, 81-82, 301
  women and, 161-162, 313-316
  work force 2020, 819
  work-life programs, 49
  workweeks, 4-5
World Bank, 495
World Economic Forum, 15
**World Resources Institute, 486-491**
World Trade Organization (WTO), 361, 828
**World Wildlife Fund, 454, 492-496**
**Worldwatch Institute, 864-866**
Wrangell-St. Elias National Park, 367-368
Wyoming Farm Bureau Federation, 434

Yale University, School of Forestry and Environmental Studies, 472
Yankee Stadium, New York, 839-840
Yellowstone National Park, 374-375, 409-410, 433-434, 447-449
Yosemite National Park, 479
Youth. *See* children and youth
YWCA of the USA, 530, 633

**Zero Population Growth, 526, 552-554**
Zimbabwe, 743